D0417363

# France
# Where to Stay
## 2000

 **Lifestyle Guides**

The directory is compiled by the AA's Hotel and Touring Services
Department and generated from the AA's establishment database

### Picture credits:

Front cover photograph Château de Garrevaques, Garrevaques, Tarn,
Midi-Pyrenées
All other photographs were taken from the AA's picture library
(©AA photo library)
All establishment photos were supplied by the proprietors and managers
of the establishments featured in this guide

### Editorial contributions from:

Nick Channer, David Hancock, Bernadette Hickman and Julia Hynard

French regional maps are based on maps supplied by the French Tourist
Office and reproduced with their kind permission.

Typeset/Reprographics by Avonset, Bath

### Advertisement Sales:

Direct lines:  01256 491546 Dominique Crouzierès

A CIP catalogue record for this book is available from the British Library

### ISBN: 074952328X

Published by AA Publishing, a trading name of Automobile Association
Developments Limited, whose registered office is Norfolk House, Priestley
Road, Basingstoke, Hampshire, RG24 9NY. Registered number 1878835

# Contents

| | |
|---|---|
| Map of French regions | 5 |
| Using the Guide & Useful Information | 6 |
| France at a Glance | 8 |
| Motoring in France & General Information | 10 |
| Booking Accommodation by Letter & Telephone | 16 |
| Useful French Phrases | 18 |
| What's on the Menu? | 21 |
| Spend Spend Spend - Shopping in France | 26 |
| Map of the Paris Périphérique | 28 |
| Eating Out in Paris | 30 |

## Directory of Establishments

| | |
|---|---|
| BRITTANY | 32 |
| NORMANDY | 63 |
| PICARDY | 111 |
| CHAMPAGNE-ARDENNE | 122 |
| NORD/PAS-DE-CALAIS | 130 |
| LORRAINE VOSGES | 144 |
| ALSACE | 154 |
| VAL DE LOIRE | 166 |
| WESTERN LOIRE | 204 |
| PARIS & THE ILE DE FRANCE | 224 |
| BURGUNDY | 256 |
| FRANCHE-COMTÉ | 282 |
| POITOU-CHARENTES | 288 |
| AQUITAINE | 307 |
| LIMOUSIN | 329 |
| AUVERGNE | 336 |
| RHÔNE ALPES | 345 |
| MIDI-PYRÉNÉES | 377 |
| LANGUEDOC-ROUSSILLON | 402 |
| CÔTE D'AZUR | 421 |
| PROVENCE | 432 |
| Index | 466 |

# Regions & *Départements*

In this book France has been divided into 21 regions as numbered and colour-coded on the map opposite. Individual maps of these regions appear at the beginning of each section. The map also shows the départements into which France is divided. Each département has a standard number, as shown on the map and in the key, which for postal purposes replaces its name. These numbers also form part of the registration number of French cars, thus indicating the département in which the car was registered. The départements are listed alphabetically within their regions.

**BRITTANY**
| | |
|---|---|
| Côtes d'Armor | 22 |
| Finistère | 29 |
| Ille-et-Vilaine | 35 |
| Morbihan | 56 |

**NORMANDY**
| | |
|---|---|
| Calvados | 14 |
| Eure | 27 |
| Manche | 50 |
| Orne | 61 |
| Seine-Maritime | 76 |

**NORD/PAS-DE-CALAIS**
| | |
|---|---|
| Nord | 59 |
| Pas-de-Calais | 62 |

**PICARDY**
| | |
|---|---|
| Aisne | 02 |
| Oise | 60 |
| Somme | 80 |

**CHAMPAGNE-ARDENNE**
| | |
|---|---|
| Ardennes | 08 |
| Aube | 10 |
| Haute-Marne | 51 |
| Marne | 52 |

**LORRAINE VOSGES**
| | |
|---|---|
| Meurthe-et-Moselle | 54 |
| Meuse | 55 |
| Moselle | 57 |
| Vosges | 88 |

**ALSACE**
| | |
|---|---|
| Bas-Rhin | 67 |
| Haut-Rhin | 68 |

**WESTERN LOIRE**
| | |
|---|---|
| Loire-Atlantique | 44 |
| Maine-et-Loire | 49 |
| Mayenne | 53 |
| Sarthe | 72 |
| Vendeé | 85 |

**VAL DE LOIRE**
| | |
|---|---|
| Cher | 18 |
| Eure-et-Loir | 28 |
| Indre | 36 |
| Indre-et-Loir | 37 |
| Loir-et-Cher | 41 |
| Loiret | 45 |

**PARIS & ILE DE FRANCE**
| | |
|---|---|
| Essonne | 91 |
| Hauts-de-Seine | 92 |
| Paris | 75 |
| Seine-et-Marne | 77 |
| Seine-St-Denis | 93 |
| Val-de-Marne | 94 |
| Val-d'Oise | 95 |
| Yvelines | 78 |

**BURGUNDY**
| | |
|---|---|
| Côte-d'Or | 21 |
| Nièvre | 58 |
| Saône-et-Loire | 71 |
| Yonne | 89 |

**FRANCHE-COMTE**
| | |
|---|---|
| Doubs | 25 |
| Haute-Saône | 70 |
| Jura | 39 |
| Territoire-de-Belfort | 90 |

**POITOU-CHARENTES**
| | |
|---|---|
| Charente | 16 |
| Charente-Maritime | 17 |
| Deux Sèvres | 79 |
| Vienne | 86 |

**LIMOUSIN**
| | |
|---|---|
| Corrèze | 23 |
| Creuse | 19 |
| Haute-Vienne | 87 |

**AUVERGNE**
| | |
|---|---|
| Allier | 03 |
| Cantal | 15 |
| Haute-Loire | 43 |
| Puy-de-Dôme | 63 |

**RHONE ALPES**
| | |
|---|---|
| Ain | 01 |
| Ardèche | 07 |
| Drôme | 26 |
| Haute-Savoie | 74 |
| Isère | 38 |
| Loire | 42 |
| Rhône | 69 |
| Savoie | 73 |

**AQUITAINE**
| | |
|---|---|
| Dordogne | 24 |
| Gironde | 33 |
| Landes | 40 |
| Lot-et-Garonne | 47 |
| Pyrénées-Atlantiques | 64 |

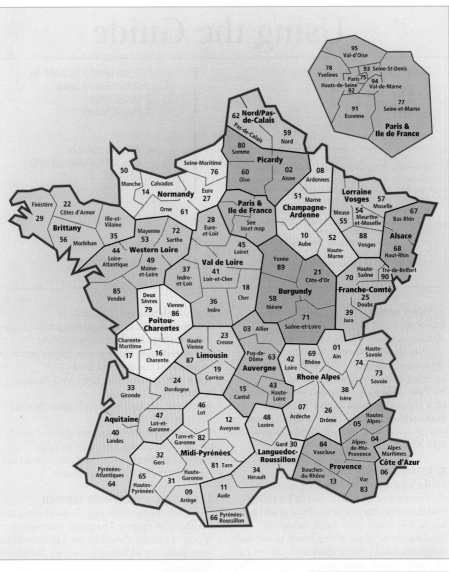

| MIDI-PYRENEES | |
|---|---|
| Ariège | 09 |
| Aveyron | 12 |
| Gers | 32 |
| Haute-Garonne | 31 |
| Hautes-Pyrénées | 65 |
| Lot | 46 |
| Tarn | 81 |
| Tarn-et-Garonne | 82 |

For **CORSICA** please see entry on page 465.

| LANGUEDOC-ROUSSILLON | |
|---|---|
| Aude | 11 |
| Gard | 30 |
| Hérault | 34 |
| Lozère | 48 |
| Pyrénées-Roussillon | 66 |

| PROVENCE | |
|---|---|
| Alpes-de-Haute-Provence | 04 |
| Bouches-du-Rhône | 13 |
| Hautes-Alpes | 05 |
| Var | 83 |
| Vaucluse | 84 |

| COTE D'AZUR | |
|---|---|
| Alpes Maritimes | 06 |

# Using the Guide

| | |
|---|---|
| **ANYTOWN** Département Name | 1) TOWN NAME FOLLOWED BY DEPARTEMENT NAME |
| ★ ★ ★ **Typical Hotel**<br>3 rue General de Gaulle *29270*<br>☎123456789. FAX 12345678 | 2) HOTEL NAME<br>3) PHONE NUMBER |
| (From the motorway, follow signs to the centre of town.)<br>Converted from an ancient priory, the hotel is situated<br>between two abbeys in the centre of Menton.<br>All bedrooms are furnished in traditional rustic style and are<br>charming and comfortable, many containing the priory's<br>original features of wooden beams and stone floors. The<br>restaurant specialises in local seafood and rustic dishes.<br>In wooded area Near motorway | 4) ACCOMMODATION DESCRIPTION AND LOCATION DETAILS |
| 24 rms (8 bth/shr), (7 with balcony). CTV in all bedrooms.<br>Child discount available 10 yrs Last d 21:30. Free parking. | 5) HOTEL FACILITIES |
| ROOMS s260-490FF d300-610FF<br>MEALS Breakfast 50FF dinner fixed price 100-350FF<br>dinner alc 200-300FF | 6) MEALS & ROOMS |
| CARDS ▦ ▦ ▣ Travellers cheques | 7) PAYMENT DETAILS |

## 1. TOWN NAME

Towns are listed in the directory in alphabetical order by region.

After the town name comes the département name. At the back of the book is an index of locations with page numbers. We have provided simple maps at the beginning of each regional section, to give an idea of where in the region a town is, but for driving and precise orientation you will need a large-scale road atlas.

## 2. ESTABLISHMENT NAME

All the establishments listed are approved by the French Tourist Office. Bed & Breakfast establishments do not have offical gradings like hotels. The proprietor's name follows in brackets. Some of the places listed, particularly farmhouses and private residences, do not have an establishment name, just an address, if this is the case, the establishment is referred to as 'B&B'.

Hotels in France use a star rating system, which precedes the establishment name. Hotels in this guide have a star rating given to them by the French Tourist Office; this is very similar, but not identical, to the AA's UK hotel classification scheme. The French Tourist Office description of the star ratings is as follows:

★★★★★ Large luxury hotel offering the highest international standards of accommodation, facilites, services and cuisine

★★★★ Large hotel with spacious accommodation where guests may expect high standards of comfort and food

★★★ Very comfortable hotel with en suite facilities

★★ Good, average hotel with some en suite facilities

★ Plain, comfortable and inexpensive hotel, usually with shared bathroom facilities

Please note that some private châteaux do not subscribe to the star rating scheme.

## 3. ADDRESS & TELEPHONE NUMBER

Please see the notes on page 8 about using the telephone in France. The postal code which appears in italics should be used in front of the town name for address purposes eg 29270 ANYTOWN.

## 4. DESCRIPTION & LOCATION

Descriptions and a summary of the location (e.g. Forest area Near motorway), have been provided by the hotels themselves.

We believe the details to be accurate and we have published them in good faith. Where a hotel has stated that it is 'In town centre' and 'Near Motorway', remember that 'Near Motorway' may refer to the town/village itself, and not to the hotel directly. Similarly, 'In

Forest 'area' may refer to the town or village, not to the grounds of the hotel.

### 4. ACCOMMODATION DETAILS
The first figure shows the number of letting bedrooms, followed by the numbers of rooms that have en suite bath or shower and WC.

### 5. HOTEL FACILITIES
**fmly**    family bedrooms
**CTV/TV**    colour/black & white television in lounge or in bedrooms. Check when booking
**STV**    satellite TV channels at no extra cost, but check details when booking
**Last d**    indicates the latest time at which dinner may be ordered
**Supervised** parking is supervised

### 6. ROOMS & MEALS
Prices are provided by proprietors in good faith and are indications not firm quotations. Proprietors have also informed us of reductions for stays of more than one night, or special break offers. However, you must check when booking. In some establishments children can sleep in the parents' room at no extra cost. Please check when booking.

Details of the style of food and price range are given. If there is a fixed-price menu(s), this is the price range quoted. If the words '& alc' follow, it means an à la carte menu is available and its prices may be much higher. V meals a choice of vegetarian dishes is normally available, but check first.

If the entry is in italics, the establishment has not returned a questionnaire for 2000 and the information is that provided for 1999.

### 7. CREDIT & CHARGE CARDS

    ● MASTERCARD

    ▪ AMERICAN EXPRESS

    ▪ VISA

    ▪ DINERS

      TRAVELLERS CHEQUES

Check the position on credit cards when booking. They may be subject to a surcharge. See the note on payment below.

# Useful Information

### BOOKING
Book as early as possible, particularly for the peak holiday periods from the beginning of June to the end of September, at public holiday weekends and, in some parts of France, during the skiing season. Some establishments ask for a deposit, or even full payment in advance, especially for one-night bookings from chance callers. Not all establishments, however, will take advance bookings for bed and breakfast for overnight or short stays. Some may not make reservations from mid week in high season.

### CANCELLATION
Notify the establishment immediately if you are in any doubt as to whether you can keep your reservation. If your accommodation cannot be re-let you may be liable to pay about two-thirds of the price you would have paid if you had stayed there. A deposit will count towards this payment. Illness is not usually accepted as a release from this contract. You are advised to effect insurance cover, for example, AA Travelsure, against possible cancellation.

### LICENCE TO SELL ALCOHOL
Unless otherwise stated, all establishments listed are licensed.

### PAYMENT
Most establishments will only accept Eurocheques in payment of accounts if notice is given and identification (e.g., a cheque card) produced. Not all take Eurocheques or travellers cheques, even from leading banks and agencies. If credit cards are accepted, the information is shown at the end of the entry.

### PRICES
Throughout all prices are given in French francs and so will fluctuate with the exchange rate.

Prices given usually refer to the cost of a room per night rather than per person per night. Most hotels do not include the cost of breakfast in their room rates, but most B&Bs do. It is always a good idea to check what is included when booking.

An asterisk (*) against prices indicates 1999 prices have been given by the proprietor.

# France at a Glance

## AT-A-GLANCE FACTS AND FIGURES
**Capital:** Paris
**IDD code:** 33.
**Currency:** Franc (Fr1 = 100 centimes).
At the time of going to press £1 = Frs 10.1
**Local time:** GMT + 1 (summer GMT + 2)
**Emergency numbers:** Police 17; Fire 18;
Ambulance - dial number given in callbox, or,
if no number given, the police
**Business hours:**
**Banks:** Mon-Fri 09.00-12.00 & 14.00-16.00;
**Shops:** Mon-Sat 09.00-18.00 (times may vary for
food shops)
**Average daily temperature:**

Paris     Jan 3°C    May 13°C   Sep 15°C
            Mar 6°C    Jul 18°C    Nov 6°C

## TOURIST INFORMATION
**French Tourist Office**
178 Piccadilly, London W1V 0AL Tel: 0891 244123
(premium rate information line; 08.30-21.30
weekdays, 09.00-1700 Saturdays)
**Monaco Government Tourist and**
**Convention Office**
3-18 Chelsea Garden Market Chelsea Harbour
London SW10 0XE
**British Embassy**
75383 Paris, Cedex 08, 35 rue de Faubourg
St-Honoré Tel: 0144513100
**Consular section**
75008 Paris, 16 rue d'Anjou  Tel: 0142663810
There are British Consulates in Bordeaux, Lille, Lyon
and Marseille; there are British Consulates with
Honorary Consuls in Biarritz, Boulogne-sur-Mer,
Calais, Cherbourg, Dunkerque (Dunkirk), Le Havre,
Nantes, Nice, St Malo-Dinard and Toulouse

## USING THE PHONE IN FRANCE
**For all calls inside France** dial 0 before the 9-digit
number eg Paris 01 .. .. .. .., Marseille 04 .. .. .. ..
**To call abroad from France** dial 00 and country
code.
**To call the UK** dial 00 44 followed by the UK
number ignoring the first digit (0).
**For information and directory assistance** dial 12

**To use your mobile phone abroad:**
Contact your service provider before you leave to
arrange international access.

Take your mobile phone handbook with you to ensure
you know how to manually roam onto a foreign
network

## HOW TO GET THERE
Apart from the direct crossing by the Channel Tunnel
(Folkestone-Calais, 35 mins), the following ferry
services are available:

**Short ferry crossings**
Dover to Calais takes between 1 hr 15 mins to 1 hr
30 mins. The Superferry takes 45 mins

**Longer ferry crossings**
Newhaven to Dieppe takes 4 hrs or 2 hrs 15 mins
by Superferry
Portsmouth to Le Havre takes 5 hrs 30 mins (day); 7
hrs 30 mins / 8 hrs (night)
Portsmouth to Caen takes 6 hrs
Portsmouth to Cherbourg takes 5 hrs (day); 7 hrs/8
hrs 15 mins (night)
Portsmouth to St Malo takes 9 hrs (day); 11 hrs 30
mins (night)
Poole to Cherbourg takes 4 hrs 30 mins
Poole to St Malo takes 8 hrs (summer service only)
Plymouth to Roscoff takes 6 hrs
Ramsgate to Dunkirk takes 1 hr 30 mins
Southampton to Cherbourg takes 5-8 hrs

**Fast Hoverspeed services**
Dover to Calais takes 35 mins by Hovercraft/ or 50
mins by Seacat. Folkestone to Boulogne takes 55
mins by Seacat.

**Car sleeper trains**
A daily service operates from Calais to the south of
the country

## FERRY COMPANIES
**Brittany Ferries**
Millbay Docks, Plymouth PL1 3EW Tel: 01752
600698
The Brittany Centre, Wharf Road, Portsmouth
Tel: 0990 360360  Fax: 01705 873237
Caen Tel: 31 96 88 80
Cherbourg Tel: 33 43 43 68
Roscoff Tel: 98 29 28 28
St-Malo Tel: 99 40 64 41

**Holyman Sally Ferries**
Sally Line Ltd, Argyle Centre, York Street, Ramsgate,
Kent CT11 9DS Tel: 0990 595522
Fax: 01843 589329
Dunkirk Tel: 28 21 43 44

**Hoverspeed Fast Ferries**
International Hoverport, Western Docks, Dover,
Kent CT17 9TG Tel: 0990 240241
Fax: 01304 240088
Boulogne Tel: 21 30 27 26
Calais Tel: 21 46 14 14

**P&O European Ferries**
Channel House, Channel View Road, Dover CT17 9TJ
Tel: 0990 980 980  Fax: 01304 223464
Calais Tel: 21 46 04 40
Le Havre Tel: 35 19 78 50
Cherbourg Tel: 33 88 65 70

**SeaFrance**
Eastern Docks, Dover, Kent CT16 1JA
Tel: 01304 212696  Fax: 01304 240033

**Stena Line**
Charter House, Ashford, Kent
Tel: 0990 707070  Fax: 01233 202361
Calais Tel: 21 46 80 00
Cherbourg Tel: 33 20 43 38
Dieppe Tel: 35 06 39 00

## ON THE ROAD

Please see page 10. Remember that during peak
holiday times traffic will be heavy and delays are
likely in some places. During August, most Parisians
leave the city for the coast, so roads leading out of
Paris will be packed. Avoid travelling at weekends,
the beginning/end of school holidays, before/after
public holidays, religious feasts and festival days at
religious centres. Contact local tourist boards for
information on road congestion. See below for dates
to avoid:

**Public Holidays in 2000**

| | |
|---|---|
| New Year's Day | January 1 |
| Easter Sunday | April 23 |
| Easter Monday | April 24 |
| Labour Day | May 1 |
| V.E. Day | May 8 |
| Ascension Day | June 1 |
| Whitsun | May 27-28 |
| Bastille Day | July 14 |
| Assumption Day | August 15 |
| All Saints' Day | November 1 |
| Remembrance Day | November 11 |
| Christmas Day | December 25 |

**French School Holidays for 2000**
(staggered throughout France)

| | |
|---|---|
| Winter half-term | February 3 - March 3 |
| Easter/Spring holiday | April 3 - May 3 |
| Summer | June 30 - September 2 |
| Autumn half-term | October 23 - November 3 |
| Christmas 2000/01 | December 17 - January 3 |

**Garages and service stations**
In France garages are generally open from 08.00 to
18.00 (sometimes with a break at midday, 12.00 to
15.00), Monday to Saturday. On Sunday and public
holidays fuel and service are often unobtainable, and
in some rural areas of France it may be difficult to
get repairs done in August, when many firms close
for the annual holidays. Ask your local dealer for a
list of franchised repairers in Europe before you
leave.
Always ask for an estimate before you have your
repairs done; it can save disputes later. Always
settle any dispute with a garage before you leave;
subsequent negotiations by post are usually lengthy
and unsatisfactory.

## ROAD SIGNS

Although most road signs are the same and
therefore easily identifiable throughout the Continent,
below are explanations of specifically French ones:
**Allumez vos phares** - Switch on your headlights
**Attention travaux** - Road works ahead
**Chaussée déformée** - Uneven road surface
**Fin d'interdiction de stationner** - End of restricted
parking
**Gravillons** - Loose chippings
**Haute tension** - Electrified lines
**Interdit aux piétons** - No pedestrians
**Nids de poules** - Potholes
**Priorité à droite** - Give way to traffic on the right
(see Priority including roundabouts on page 14)
**Passage protégé** - Your right of way
**Rappel** - Means a continuation of the restriction (e.g.
Rappel 50 means remember the speed limit of 50
kph)
**Route barrée** - Road closed

**And finally, remember always when driving
through France, drive on the right and overtake
on the left.**

PRIDE OF LE HAVRE

# Motoring in France

Motoring in France should cause little difficulty to British motorists, but remember to drive on the right-hand side of the road, and take particular care when approaching junctions, traffic lights, roundabouts, etc. Also ensure that you comply with signs showing speed limits.

Ensure that your vehicle is in good order mechanically. We recommend a full service by a franchised dealer. AA members can arrange a thorough check of their car by an experienced AA engineer. There is a fee for this service, and for more information or, if you wish to book an inspection, please telephone 0345 500610.

## ACCIDENTS AND EMERGENCIES

In the event of an accident, you must stop. In the event of injury or damage, you should inform the police, and notify your insurers by letter if possible within 24 hours. If a third party is injured your insurers will advise you, or, if you have a Green Card (see Motor Insurance below), contact the company or bureau given on the back of the card for advice over claims for compensation

## BANKING HOURS

Banks close at midday on the day prior to a national holiday, and all day on Monday if the holiday falls on a Tuesday. Otherwise hours are similar to those in Britain. Most French banks will no longer cash Eurocheques, but if you have a Eurocheque or credit card with a PIN you can withdraw cash from a network of around 15,000 cash dispensers. See also Credit Cards; Fuel/Petrol; Money.

## CHANNEL TUNNEL

Eurotunnel provides a fast, frequent and reliable service between Folkestone and Coquelles/Calais for cars, coaches, motorcycles, campervans and cars with caravans or trailers. Eurotunnel operates 24 hours a day, 365 days a year, with up to four departures an hour at peak times. The journey takes 35 minutes from platform to platform (approximately 45 minutes at night), and just over an hour from the M20 in Kent to the A16 autoroute in France. Tickets can be purchased in advance by calling the Eurotunnel Call Centre on 0990 353535; those booking less than 7 days in advance pick up their tickets at check-in. Eurotunnel also offers the facility for travellers to buy their tickets on arrival at the check-in. Prices are charged per vehicle and not by the number of passengers.

Passengers pass through both UK and French frontier controls before boarding Eurotunnel shuttles. Upon arrival there is no delay and motorists drive straight onto the A16 on the French autoroute network in a matter of minutes.

Eurotunnel's shuttles are spacious, air-conditioned and well-lit. Passengers stay with their vehicles during the short journey but can get out, walk around and use the toilet facilities. The on-board radio station and visual display panels keep passengers informed during the journey.

For further information and details of the latest special offers, call the Eurotunnel Call Centre on 0990 353535 or contact your local travel agent.

The Eurostar passenger service runs direct to Lille and Paris, leaving from Waterloo Station in London and may also be boarded at Ashford in Kent. It links into the 300 km/h TGV network which covers much of France, making many regions more accessible. For bookings call Rail Europe on 0990 300 003.

**NB Check-in time is at least 20 mins before departure. Beyond that time, passengers are not allowed to board the train.**

If using the rest of the SNCF network, the relevant ticket and reservation must be validated before boarding the train by date-stamping (composter) them in one of the orange automatic date-stamping machines. Failure to do so will incur a surcharge.

## CREDIT CARDS

Major credit and charge cards, such as Carte Bleue (Visa/Barclaycard), Diners Club and Eurocard (Mastercard/Access), are widely accepted in France in shops, hotels, restaurants, petrol stations and many hypermarkets for amounts above 80-100FF

(sometimes a higher spend is required, but this should be clearly shown). Motorway tolls may often be paid by credit card. When paying by credit card, check the amount which appears on the receipt. In France no decimal point is shown between francs and centimes.

UK credit cards hold ID information on a magnetic strip and are not always easily read by French card reading machines (French credit cards hold this information on a chip or puce). It is suggested that readers copy the following statement and produce it with their passport for fraud-cautious retailers: *"les cartes internationales ne sont pas des cartes a puce, mais a bande magnetique. Ma carte est valable et je vous serais reconnaissant d'en demander la confirmation aupres de votre banque ou de votre centre de traitement"*.

Do take your bank's and credit card company's 24-hr contact numbers with you. Cash can be withdrawn using UK PIN numbers ATMs displaying the apppropriate symbol

## CUSTOMS AND EXCISE

When you enter the UK from another EU country without having travelled to or through a non-EU country you do not need to go through the red or green channels. Look for the blue channel or blue exit reserved for EU travellers. But please remember that, although the limits on duty and tax paid goods bought within the EU ended on 31 December 1992, EU law establishes guidance levels for tobacco goods and wines and spirits bought elsewhere within the EU. Additionally the importation of certain goods into the UK is prohibited or restricted.

When you enter the UK from a non-EU country or an EU country having travelled to or through a non-EU country, you must go through Customs. If you have more than the customs allowances or any prohibited, restricted or commercial goods, go through the red channel. Only go through the green channel if you are sure that you have "nothing to declare". If you require more information, obtain a copy of Customs Notice 1, available at UK points of entry and exit, or telephone an Excise and Inland Customs Advice Centre (see Customs and Excise in the telephone directory).

## DIESEL

See Fuel/Petrol

## DOCUMENTS

A tourist driving abroad should always carry a current passport, and a full, valid national driving licence, even if an International Driving Permit (IDP) is also held, the vehicle registration document and certificate of motor insurance. (See Motor Insurance below). If you have no registration document, apply to a Vehicle Registration Office (in Northern Ireland a Local Vehicle Licensing Office) for a temporary certificate of registration (V379) to cover the period abroad. Consult the local telephone directory for addresses, or leaflet V100, available from post offices. Apply well in advance of your journey.

The proper International Distinguishing Sign (IDS) should be displayed on the rear of the vehicle and any trailer, and should be of the approved standard design.

If you are carrying skis, ensure that their tips point to the rear. If you have cycle rack, ensure that it does not obscure the number plate or IDS.

## EUROCHEQUES

Most French banks will no longer cash Eurocheques, but they are widely accepted in shops. See also Banking Hours and Money.

## FUEL/PETROL

Motorists will find comparable grades of petrol and familiar brand names along main routes. It is wise to keep the tank topped up, especially in rural areas, and on Sundays and National Holidays when many local service stations may close. Fuel is generally available with 24-hr service on motorways, but on other roads, some service stations may close between 12 noon and 15.00 hours. Do not assume that service stations will accept credit cards. See also Credit Cards or Money. Leaded, unleaded, diesel fuel are all available. Unleaded (sans plomb) and leaded are both available as 'normal' and 'super'. You may also find unleaded 98 octane instead of or as well as 95 octane. It may also be described as 'super plus' or 'premium'. Take care to use the recommended fuel, especially if your car is fitted with a catalytic converter. The octane grade should be the same or higher. Diesel fuel is generally known as diesel or gas oil.

Note: ferry operators and motorail forbid the carriage of fuel in spare cans, though empty cans may be carried.

## LIGHTS

Right-hand drive cars will need headlamp beam converters (available as kits) to divert the beam away from drivers of oncoming left-hand drive vehicles. Dipped headlights should be used in tunnels, irrespective of length and lighting. Police may wait at the end of a tunnel to check vehicles. In fog or mist, two dipped headlights or two fog lights must be switched on. Headlight flashing is used only to signal approach or when overtaking at night. If used at other times, it could be taken as a sign of irritation and lead to misunderstandings. See also Spares.

## MEDICAL TREATMENT

Travellers who normally take certain medicines should ensure they have a sufficient supply as they may be difficult to obtain abroad. Those with certain medical conditions (diabetes, coronary artery diseases) should get a letter from their doctor giving treatment details and obtain a translation. The AA cannot make translations.

Travellers who, for legitimate health reasons, carry drugs or appliances (e.g., a hypodermic syringe), may have difficulty with Customs or other authorities. They should carry translations which describe their special condition and appropriate treatment in the language of the country they intend to visit to present to Customs. Similarly, people with special dietary requirements may find translations helpful in hotels and restaurants.

You are strongly advised to take out adequate insurance before leaving the UK - check whether your homeowner or health insurance policy covers you for travel abroad.

Many European countries have reciprocal agreements for medical treatment which require a certificate of entitlement (E111) is necessary. The E111 can be obtained over the counter of the post office on completion of the forms incorporated in booklet T5. However, the E111 must be stamped and signed by the post office clerk to be valid. Residents of the Republic of Ireland must apply to their Regional Health Board for an E111.

## MONEY

You should carry enough local currency notes for immediate needs and also local currency travellers cheques which can often be used like cash. Sterling travellers cheques can be cashed at banks, and you will need your passport with you. Credit cards are widely accepted, and there are about 15,000 automatic cash dispense machines which you can use to obtain cash. See also Eurocheques.

## MOTORAIL SERVICES

Motorail services carry cars, motorbikes and passengers overnight on the same train from Calais, Lille and Paris to the main holiday areas. Contact the AA, an ABTA travel agent or Rail Europe Travel Centre at 179 Piccadilly, London WIV 0BA on 0171 203 7000

## MOTORING CLUB

The AA is affiliated to the Automobile Club

National (ACN) whose office is at 75009 Paris, 5 rue Auber. Telephone 144515399.

## MOTOR INSURANCE

When driving abroad you must carry your certificate of motor insurance with you at all times. Third-party is the minimum legal requirement in most countries. Before taking your vehicle abroad, contact your insurer or broker to ask for advice. Some insurers will extend your UK or Republic of Ireland motor policy to apply in the countries you intend visiting free of charge; others may charge an additional premium. It is most important to know the level of cover you will actually have, and what documents you will need to prove it.

A Green Card is not essential in France. This document issued by your motor insurer provides internationally recognised proof of insurance. It must be signed on receipt as it will not be accepted without the signature of the insured person. Motorists can obtain expert advice through AA Insurance Services for all types of insurance. Contact AA Insurance Services Ltd, PO Box 2AA Newcastle upon Tyne NE99 2AA. Do also check that you are insured for damage in transit other than when the vehicle is being driven (e.g. on the ferry).

**AA MEMBER BENEFIT:** AA Members with UK Relay entitlement have the free member benefit of 72-hour European Breakdown cover in specified European countries, including France, for an unlimited number of trips up to 72 hours each. However, you must register before each trip by phoning the AA on 0800 731 7072.

## PARKING

As a general rule, park on the right hand side of the road so as not to obstruct traffic or a cycle lane, etc., but better still, park in an authorised place as regulations are stringent, especially in large towns and cities and fines are heavy. In Paris it is absolutely forbidden to stop or park on a red route.

The east-west route includes the left bank of the Seine and the Quai de la Megisserie; the north-south route includes the Avenue du Général Leclerc, part of the Boulevard St Michel, the Rue de Rivoli, the Boulevards Sébastopol, Strasbourg, Barbès and Ornano, the Rue Lafayette and the Avenue Jean Jaurès. Parking is also absolutely forbidden in some parts of the green zone.

## PASSPORTS

Each person must hold, or be named on, a valid passport and should carry it with them at all times. For security, keep a separate note of the number, date and place of issue. If it is lost, report the matter to the police. Full information and application forms are available from main Post Offices or from one of the passport offices in Belfast, Douglas (Isle of Man), Glasgow, Liverpool, London, Newport (Gwent), Peterborough, St Helier (Jersey), St Peter Port (Guernsey). Allow at least 15 working days at peak periods.

## PETROL

See Fuel/Petrol

## POLICE FINES

In France, the police may impose an immediate deposit for a traffic infringement and subsequently may levy a fine which must normally be paid in cash in French francs either to the police or at a post office against a ticket issued by the police. The amount can, for serious offences, exceed the equivalent of £1000. A receipt should be obtained, but motorists should be aware that disputing a fine usually leads to a court appearance with all the extra costs and delays that may entail.

## PRIORITÉ À DROITE

Probably the most unfamiliar aspect of driving in France to British motorists is the rule giving priority to traffic coming from the right - priorité à droite - and unless this priority is varied by signs, it must be strictly observed. In built-up areas (including small villages) you must give way to traffic coming from the right. Also remember that farm vehicles and buses may expect to be given priority. At roundabouts, priority is generally given to vehicles entering the roundabout (the opposite of the rule in Britain). However, at roundabouts bearing the words 'Vous n'avez pas la priorité' or 'Cédez le passage', traffic on the roundabout has the priority.

Outside built up areas, all main roads of any importance have right of way. This is indicated by one of three signs: a red-bordered triangle showing a black cross on a white background with the words 'Passage Protégé' underneath; a red-bordered triangle showing a pointed black upright with horizontal bar on a white background; or a yellow square within a white square with points vertical.

## ROADS

Roads in France are generally very good, but the camber is often severe and edges can be rough. In July and August, especially at weekends, traffic is likely to be very heavy. Special signs are erected to indicate alternative routes and it is usually advantageous to follow them, though they are not guaranteed to save time. A free road map showing marked alternative routes is available from service stations display the 'Bison Futé' poster (a Red Indian chief in full war bonnet). These maps are also available from Syndicats d'Initiative and Information Offices.

## SPARES

Motorists are recommended to carry a set of replacement bulbs. If you are able to replace a faulty bulb when asked to do so by the police, you may still have to pay a fine but you may avoid the cost and inconvenience of a garage call out. Other useful items are windscreen wiper blades, a length of electrical cable and a torch.

Remember when ordering spare parts for dispatch abroad you must be able to identify them clearly - by the manufacturer's part numbers if known. Always quote your engine and vehicle identification number (VIN).

## SPEED LIMITS

**On normal roads - Built up areas:** 50kph (31mph)
**Outside built up areas:** 90kph (55mph).
**Dual Carriageways with central reservation:** 110kph (69mph)
**On motorways:** 130kph (80mph)

Note: minimum speed in the fast lane on a level stretch of motorway in good daytime visibility is 80kph (49mph).

Maximum speed on the Paris Périphérique is 80kph (49mph); on other urban stretches of motorway, 110kph (69mph).

In fog, when visibility is reduced to 50 metres, the speed limit on all roads is 50kph (31mph) and in wet weather speed limits outside built-up areas are reduced to 80kph (49mph), 100kph (62mph) on dual carriageways and 110kph (69mph) on other motoways.

Drivers who have held a licence for less than two years must at all times observe these reduced speed limits.

## TOLL ROADS (PÉAGE)

Tolls are payable on most motorways in France, and over long distances charges can be considerable. Motorists collect a ticket on entering the motorway and pay at the exit. You must have local currency or a credit card. Travellers' cheques and Eurocheques are not accepted. Please note that (for a UK driver) booths are virtually always on the passenger side of the car.

## TRAFFIC LIGHTS

Traffic lights are similar to those in the UK, except that they turn directly from red to green, but from green through amber to red. The intensity of the light is poor, and they could be easily missed, especially those overhead. There is usually only one set by the right-hand side of the road, at some distance before the junction and if you stop too close to the corner, you may not be able to see them change. Watch for 'filter' lights enabling you to turn right and enter the appropriate lane.

## TRAMS

Trams have priority over other vehicles. Never obstruct the passage of a tram. Always give way to passengers boarding and alighting. Trams must be overtaken on the right except in one-way streets.

## WARNING TRIANGLE

If you should break down or be involved in an accident, the use of a warning triangle or hazard warning lights is compulsory. As hazard warning lights may be damaged, we recommend that you carry a warning triangle, which should be placed 30 metres behind the vehicle (100 metres on motorways), about 60 cm from the edge of the road, but not in such a position as to present a danger to oncoming traffic, and be clearly visible from 100 metres, by day and night.

## WEATHER INFORMATION

For weather reports for crossing the Channel and northern France, call 0336 401 361, whilst Continental Roadwatch on 0336 401 904 provides information on traffic conditions to and from ferry ports, ferry news and details of major European events. A worldwide, city-by-city six-day weather forecast is also available on 0336 411 212.

For other weather information for the UK and the Continent (but not road conditions) please contact:
**The Met Office**
**Enquiries Officer, London Road**
**Bracknell, Berkshire RG12 2SZ**
**or telephone 01344 854455 during normal office hours.**

# Booking by Letter

Below is a standard letter whch can be sent out to the place you're planning to stay. Do remember to enclose an International Reply Coupon with your letter. These are available from all post offices. In Briatin, a room with bath/shower automatically includes a WC. In France you have to ask. **Please do not send an SAE with your letter, as English stamps are invalid in France.**

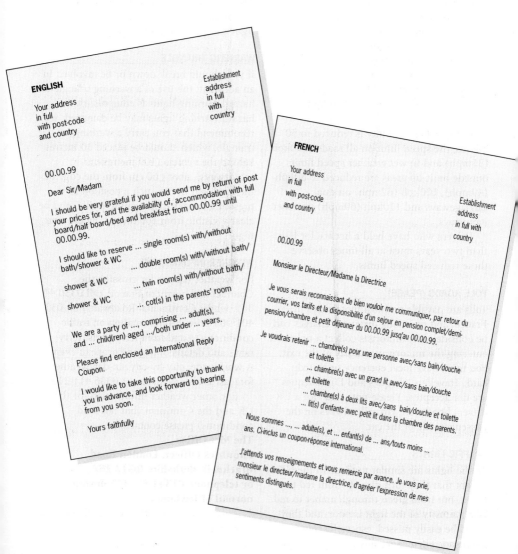

**ENGLISH**

Your address
in full
with post-code
and country

Establishment
address
in full
with
country

00.00.99

Dear Sir/Madam

I should be very grateful if you would send me by return of post your prices for, and the availability of, accommodation with full board/half board/bed and breakfast from 00.00.99 until 00.00.99.

I should like to reserve ... single room(s) with/without bath/shower & WC

... double room(s) with/without bath/shower & WC

... twin room(s) with/without bath/shower & WC

... cot(s) in the parents' room

We are a party of ..., comprising ... adult(s), and ... child(ren) aged .../both under ... years.

Please find enclosed an International Reply Coupon.

I would like to take this opportunity to thank you in advance, and look forward to hearing from you soon.

Yours faithfully

**FRENCH**

Your address
in full
with post-code
and country

Establishment
address
in full with
country

00.00.99

Monsieur le Directeur/Madame la Directrice

Je vous serais reconnaissant de bien vouloir me communiquer, par retour du courrier, vos tarifs et la disponibilité d'un sejour en pension complet/demi-pension/chambre et petit déjeuner du 00.00.99 jusq'au 00.00.99.

Je voudrais retenir ... chambre(s) pour une personne avec/sans bain/douche et toilette

... chambre(s) avec un grand lit avec/sans bain/douche et toilette

... chambre(s) à deux lits avec/sans bain/douche et toilette

... lit(s) d'enfants avec petit lit dans la chambre des parents.

Nous sommes ..., ... adulte(s), et ... enfant(s) de ... ans/touts moins ... ans. Ci-inclus un coupon-réponse international.

J'attends vos renseignements et vous remercie par avance. Je vous prie, monsieur le directeur/madame la directrice, d'agréer l'expression de mes sentiments distingués.

# Booking by Telephone

Remember, even if you make a reservation by telephone, it is always advisable to then write to the establishment confirming your booking arrangements. The French for numbers, days of the week, months and telling the time can be found on pages 19.

| ENGLISH | FRENCH |
|---|---|
| Hello, I'd like to make a reservation please_____ | Bonjour, je voudrais faire une réservation |
| We shall need xx rooms with _____ | Il nous faut xx chambre(s) avec bain/douche et |
| bath/shower and WC for | toilette pour |
| xx nights from (10 July to 13 July): _____ | xx nuits, du (dix juillet jusqu'au treize juillet): |
| xx single rooms _____ | xx chambres pour une personne |
| xx twin-bedded rooms_____ | xx chambres à deux lits |
| xx double rooms _____ | xx chambres à grand lit |
| There are (four) people with a baby and_____ | Nous sommes (quatre) personne(s) accompagnés |
| a child of (10) years | d'un bébé et d'un enfant de (dix) ans |
| Reply a) - I'm sorry, we are fully booked_____ | Reply a) - Je suis désolé, mais l'hôtel est complet |
| Reply b) - Of course; we have rooms available_____ | Reply b) - Bien sûr; nous avons des chambres |
| I'll arrive about midday/4 pm on 10 July_____ | J'arriverai vers midi/seize heures le dix juillet |
| How long will you be staying?_____ | Pour combien de temps voulez-vous rester? |
| For ... nights, please _____ | Pour ... nuits |
| Would you like full board, half-board,_____ | Voulez-vous pension complet, demi pension, ou |
| or bed and breakfast? | chambre avec petit déjeuner? |
| How much does full board/half-board_____ | C'est combien pour pension complet /demi-pension/ |
| /bed and breakfast cost? | chambre avec petit déjeuner? |
| It costs ... francs_____ | ça coute ... franc |
| I'd like full board,/half-board,/bed and _____ | Je voudrais pension complet/demi pension/chambre |
| breakfast please | avec petit déjeuner,  s'il vous plaît |
| a) - Certainly sir/madam; your name, _____ | a) - Bien sûr, monsieur/ madame; votre nom, |
| address and telephone number? | adresse et numéro de téléphone? |
| b) - How many are there in your party? _____ | b) - Vous êtes combien? |
| There are ... of us; ... adult(s) and ... child(ren)_____ | Nous sommes ..., ... adulte(s) et ... enfant(s) |
| How old is/are your child(ren) _____ | Quel age a/ont l'(les) enfant(s)? |
| a) - ...and ... years old _____ | a) - Ils ont  ... ans et ... ans |
| b) - The girl/boy is ... years old _____ | b) - La fille/le garçon a xx ans |
| I'd like a double room and a twin-bedded room_____ | J'aimerais une chambre à grand lit, et une chambre |
| | à deux lits |
| I'm sorry but we only have two doublerooms - _____ | Je suis désolé, mais nous n'avons que deux |
| will that be alright? | chambres à grand lit – ça vous convient? |
| With shower or bath?_____ | Avec douche ou bain? |
| Could you put a cot in the parents' room? _____ | Pouvez-vous mettre un petit lit dans la chambre des |
| | parents? |
| Certainly sir/madam, thank you_____ | Bien sûr monsieur/madame, merci. |

# Useful French Phrases

## GENERAL EXPRESSIONS

Hello_____ Bonjour
Goodbye_____ Au revoir
Good morning_____ Bonjour
Good evening _____ Bonsoir
Good night_____ Bonne nuit
See you later_____ A bientôt
Please/_____ S'il vous plaît/
Thank you          merci
You're welcome ____ Je vous en prie
Yes/no _____ Oui/non
Excuse me _____ Excusez-moi
I'm sorry _____ Pardon
How are you?_____ Comment allez-vous?
I'm fine, thanks_____ Très bien merci
My name is _____ Je m'appelle
Mr/Mrs/Miss _____ Monsieur/Madame/Mademoiselle
I like/don't like ... __ J'aime/je n'aime pas ...
That's fine/OK_____ Ça va/ d'accord
What time_____ A quelle heure
do you open/_____ vous ouvrez/
close?              fermez?

## LANGUAGES AND COUNTRIES

I am English _____ Je suis Anglais(e)
Scottish            Ecossais(e)
Welsh              Gallois(e)
Irish ...            Irlandais(e) ...
Do you speak _____ Parlez-vous
English?            anglais?
I don't speak _____ Je ne parle pas
French             français
I don't _____ Je ne comprends
understand          pas
Could you_____ Pourriez-vous
speak more          parler plus
slowly please?       lentement,
                   s'il vous plaît?

England _____ Angleterre
Ireland_____ Irelande
Scotland _____ Ecosse
Wales_____ Pays de Galles
Germany _____ Allemagne
Italy_____ Italie
Spain _____ Espagne

## NUMBERS

1, 2, 3 _____ un, deux, trois
4, 5, 6 _____ quatre, cinq, six
7, 8, 9, 10 _____ sept, huit, neuf, dix
11, 12, 13 _____ onze, douze, treize
14, 15, 16 _____ quatorze, quinze, seize
17, 18, 19 _____ dix-sept, dix-huit, dix-neuf
20, 21, 22 _____ vingt, vingt-et -un, vingt-deux
30, 40, 50 _____ trente, quarante, cinquante
60, 70, 80 _____ soixante, soixante-dix, quatre-vingt
90, 100, 101 _____ quatre-vingt-dix, cent, cent-et-un
1000, 2000_____ mille, deux mille
1st, 2nd, 3rd_____ premier, deuxième, troisième
4th, 5th, 6th_____ quatrième, cinquième, sixième
7th, 8th, 9th_____ septième, huitième, neuvième
10th, 11th, _____ dixième, onzième, douzième
12th

## TIME

| | |
|---|---|
| What time is it? | Quelle heure est-il? |
| It's one o'clock | Il est une heure |
| Ten past three | Trois heures dix |
| Quarter past four | Quatre heures et quart |
| Half past five | Cinq heures et demi |
| Twenty to six | Six heures moins vingt |
| Quarter to seven | Sept heures moins le quart |
| This morning/evening | Ce matin/soir |
| Now | Maintenant |
| At once | Tout de suite |
| It's late/early | Il est tard/tôt |
| Sorry I'm late | Je suis désolé d'être en retard |
| second, | seconde, |
| minute, hour | minute, heure |
| yesterday, | hier, |
| today, | aujourd'hui, |
| tomorrow | demain |
| midday | midi |
| midnight | minuit |
| day, night | le jour, la nuit |

## DAYS OF THE WEEK

| | |
|---|---|
| Monday | lundi |
| Tuesday | mardi |
| Wednesday | mercredi |
| Thursday | jeudi |
| Friday | vendredi |
| Saturday | samedi |
| Sunday | dimanche |

## MONTHS AND DATES

| | |
|---|---|
| What's the date? | Quelle est la date? |
| It's the first of July / | Nous sommes le premier juillet / le |
| 2nd August | deux août |
| January | janvier |
| February | février |
| March | mars |
| April | avril |
| May, June | mai, juin |
| July | juillet |
| August | août |
| September | septembre |
| October | octobre |
| November | novembre |
| December | décembre |

## SHOPPING

| | |
|---|---|
| How much? | Combien? |
| I'm just looking | Je regarde seulement |
| That's enough, thank you | Ça suffit, merci |
| May I have a bag please? | Puis-je avoir un sac, s'il vous plaît? |
| Have you got...? | Avez vous ... ? |
| I'd like ... | Je voudrai ... |
| Could you show me ... ? | Pouvez-vous me montrer |
| supermarket | supermarché |
| newsagent | tabac |
| newspaper | journal |
| bookshop | librairie |
| writing paper | papier à lettres |
| envelopes | enveloppes |
| a map | une carte |
| (of the area) | (de la région) |
| town plan | plan de la ville |
| a colour/black and white film | une pellicule couleur/noir et blanc |
| tights | un collant |
| a guide book | un guide |
| an umbrella | une parapluie |
| coins | des pièces |
| change | la monnaie |

## CHEMIST — LA PHARMACIE

| | |
|---|---|
| I've got a headache | J'ai mal à la tête |
| stomach ache | mal au ventre |
| I've got a cold | Je suis enrhumé |
| aspirin | de l'aspirine |
| antiseptic | antiseptique |
| cotton wool | du coton |
| disposable nappies | couches en cellulose |
| paper tissues | Kleenex |
| sanitary towels | couches périodiques |
| tampons | tampons périodiques |
| suntan oil | huile solaire |
| toilet paper | papier hygiénique |
| razor blades | lames de rasoir |
| plasters | pansements adhésifs |

| | |
|---|---|
| soap | savon |
| toothpaste | dentifrice |

## POST OFFICE — LA POSTE

| | |
|---|---|
| How much is a stamp for England? | Combien coûte un timbre pour l'Angleterre? |
| Where can I telephone? | Où puis-je téléphoner? |
| letter | lettre |
| postcard | carte postale |
| parcel | paquet |
| post box | boîte aux lettres |
| phone box | cabinet téléphonique |
| tobacconist | bureau de tabac |
| A packet of ... | Un paquet de ... |
| please | s'il vous plaît |
| cigarettes | cigarettes |
| cigars | cigares |
| tobacco | tabac |
| matches | allumettes |
| lighter | briquet |

## FOOD SHOPPING

| | |
|---|---|
| bakery | Boulangerie |
| cake shop | Pâtisserie |
| pastries | pâtisseries |
| bread | pain |
| French stick | baguette |
| cake | gâteau |
| rolls | petits pains |
| butchers/ | boucherie/ |
| delicatessen | charcuterie |
| fishmongers | poissonerie |
| greengrocers | marchand de fruits et legumes |
| one/two | une/deux |
| slice(s) of ... | tranche(s) de ... |
| half a kilo of ... | un demi-kilo de ... |
| a pound (weight) | une livre |
| 250 grams of ... | deux cent cinquante grammes de |
| fresh, raw, | frais, cru |
| cooked | cuit |
| smoked | fumé |

## DIRECTIONS

| | |
|---|---|
| Where is/are ... | Où se trouve/ trouvent ... |
| Turn left / right | Tournez à gauche |

| | |
|---|---|
| won't start | démarre pas |
| has broken _____ down | est en panne |
| I've lost my _____ car key | J'ai perdu ma clef de contact |
| It won't go | Il ne marche pas |
| I have no_____ petrol | Je n'ai plus d'essence |
| to hire a car _____ | louer une voiture |
| the bill?_____ | la facture? |
| broken _____ | cassé |
| engine_____ | le moteur |
| exhaust _____ | l'échappement |
| handbrake _____ | frein à main |
| horn _____ | klaxon |
| ignition _____ | l'allumage |
| puncture _____ | crevaisson |
| tow _____ | remorquer |
| windscreen _____ | pare-brise |

### AT THE STATION _ À LA GARE

[Note: at railway stations, when you have purchased your ticket, you must validate it (i.e. get it date-stamped) in one of the machines you will find on your way to the platform. If you forget to do this, you may incur a fine.]

| | |
|---|---|
| by rail/bus_____ | par train /autobus |
| railway/bus _____ station_____ | gare / gare routière |
| a single to _____ | un billet simple pour |
| a return to _____ | un aller- retour pour |
| When is the_____ next bus/train _____ to ...? | A quelle heure part le prochain autobus/train pour? |
| Is this the _____ train/bus for...? | Est-ce bien le train / le bus pour?... |
| Do I have to _____ change? | Faut-il changer? |
| platform_____ | quai |
| bus stop _____ | arrêt d'autobus |
| entry/exit _____ | entrée/sortie |
| seat _____ | la place |
| Is this seat_____ taken? | Est-ce que cette place est occupée? |
| ticket collector _____ | le contrôleur |
| ticket office_____ | le guichet |
| timetable_____ | horaire |

| | |
|---|---|
| | /à droite |
| Go straight on_____ | Continuez tout droit |
| Take the first _____ left/right | Prenez la première à gauche / droite |

### AT THE HOTEL/B&B

| | |
|---|---|
| I have a _____ booking, my name is ... | J'ai une réservation, je m'appelle |
| What floor is_____ the room on? | À quel étage se trouve la chambre? |
| Is there a lift?_____ | Y a-t-il un ascenseur? |
| Could I see _____ the room? | Pourrais-je voir la chambre? |
| Does the price _____ include ...? | Est-ce que le prix comprend? |
| The key for _____ the room ... please | La clef pour la chambre s'il vous plaît |
| Please call_____ me at ... | Réveillez m'appeler à... |
| Where can _____ I park? | Où puis-je garer la voiture? |
| Are there any _____ letters for me? | Y a-t-il des lettres pour moi? |
| The bill please?_____ | La note, s'il vous plaît? |
| guesthouse_____ | pension |
| inn _____ | auberge |
| single room_____ | chambre à un lit |
| twin bedded _____ room _____ | chambre à deux lits |

| | |
|---|---|
| double room_____ | chambre à grand lit |
| blanket _____ | couverture |
| coat hanger _____ | cintre |
| chambermaid _____ | femme de chambre |
| manager _____ | directeur |
| porter _____ | concierge |
| pillow_____ | oreiller |
| room service _____ | service d'étage |
| sheets_____ | draps |
| towel _____ | serviette de toilette |

### TRAVEL
(See also Directions)

### ON THE ROAD_____ SUR LA ROUTE

| | |
|---|---|
| Fill it up _____ please | Faites le plein, s'il vous plaît |
| (10) litres of _____ 4 star, please | (10) litres de super, s'il vous plaît |
| unleaded_____ | sans plomb |
| diesel_____ | diesel / gas oil |
| LPG_____ | gaz de pétrole liquéfié (GPL) |
| Please check_____ water level | Veuillez vérifier niveau d'eau |
| antifreeze _____ | l'antigel |
| battery _____ | la batterie |
| brake fluid _____ | le liquide des freins |
| oil _____ | huile |
| oil filter_____ | le filtre à huile |
| My car.... _____ | Ma voiture ...ne |

# What's on the Menu?

A holiday in France can be the gastronome's idea of heaven. Each region has a different specialty or drink associated with it, but wherever you are, always look out for the set menu (menu à prix fixé), which will give you the best value for money.

Below is a list of phrases which should be useful when ordering a meal in a restaurant, and the list also includes words for the types of foods and dishes you will come across on the menu. Each section lists some traditional dishes, as well as ordinary menu terms.

## BOOKING AND ARRIVING

| | |
|---|---|
| I'd like to book a _____ table for two at eight o'clock | Je voudrais réserver une table pour deux à huit heures |
| I've booked a table____ | J'ai reservé une table |
| A table for ... please___ | Une table pour ... s'il vous plaît |
| Is this table taken? ____ | Cette table est-elle libre? |
| May we have an _____ ashtray please? | Pouvons-nous avoir un cendrier, s'il vous plaît? |
| Where is the _____ cloakroom? | Où se trouvent les toilettes? |
| bar_____ | bar |
| self service café _____ | libre-service |
| take-away _____ | à emporter |

## Ordering

| | |
|---|---|
| Is there a set menu/___ tourist menu? | Y a-t-il un menu à prix fixe/ menu touristique? |
| Do you serve _____ children's portions? | Servez-vous des portions d'enfant? |
| What is the_____ regional speciality? | Quelle est la spécialité de la région? |
| What is the dish _____ of the day? | Quel est le plat du jour? |
| What do you _____ recommend? | Qu'est-ce que vous recommandez? |
| I'd like ... please_____ | Je voudrais ... s'il vous plaît |
| Do you have ...?_____ | Avez-vous ...? |
| cup, saucer, glass ____ | tasse, soucoupe, verre |
| knife, fork_____ | couteau, fourchette |
| napkin _____ | serviette |
| pepper/salt _____ | poivre/sel |
| plate, dish_____ | assiette, plat |
| spoon_____ | cuillière |

**Problems:**

Where are _____ Où sont nos boissons?
our drinks?
The food is cold_____ Le plat est froid
It is not properly_____ Ce n'est pas bien cuit
cooked

**Paying**

May I have the bill?_____ L'addition s'il vous plaît?
Is service included? ____ Le service, est-il compris?
Do you take credit _____ Acceptez-vous les cartes de
cards/traveller's        crédit/ les chèques de voyage?
cheques?
Thank you, the _____ Merci, c'était très bon
meal was wonderful

## THE MENU

hors d'oeuvres_____ starter
entrée _____ main course
dessert_____ dessert

## CULINARY TERMS

aïoli _____ garlic mayonnaise
aile _____ wing
bien cuit_____ well done
blanc/suprême _____ breast
blanquette_____ stew thickened with double
                        cream, eggs & lemon
au bleu _____ rare meat/trout cooked in fish
                        stock & vinegar
bouilli(e) _____ boiled
Chantilly _____ whipped cream or mayonnaise
                        with same
charcuterie             cooked pork products, from
                        ham to assorted sausages
en chemise _____ food encased in pastry, leaves
                        or crumbs, or jacket potatoes
en coquille _____ food served in a shell or
                        heat-proof dish
coulis _____ liquid purée (fruit/vegetable)
croustades_____ pastry/hollowed-out pieces of
                        bread holding food in sauce
en croute_____ food in pastry & baked
cru, cuit _____ raw, cooked
cuisses de grenouilles _ frogs' legs
daube_____ casserole cooked in an
                        earthenware pot
duxelle_____ mixture of mushrooms & onions
escargot_____ snail
à l'étouffée_____ stewed
estouffade _____ pot-roast with vegetables
faisandé _____ well hung/gamey
farci_____ filled with a savoury stuffing

faux-filet/contre-filet___ sirloin steak
aux fines herbes _____ with herbs
frit(e)_____ fried
au four_____ baked
fumé _____ smoked
fumet _____ highly concentrated meat, fish
                        or vegetable extract
gigot_____ leg of lamb or mutton
grillé(e) _____ grilled
haché_____ minced
herbes de Provence ___ mix of thyme, marjoram,
                        oregano, basil
julienne _____ finely shredded vegetables
jus_____ meat juices, gravy
                        (unthickened), fruit or
                        vegetable juice
à point_____ medium
lard/lardon _____ bacon/fried bacon bits
magret _____ breast fillet of duck
maigre_____ lean
navarin_____ stew of lamb or mutton
nouilles _____ noodles
parmentier _____ any dish incorporating potatoes
rapé(e)_____ grated
rôti(e) _____ roast
rouille _____ hot garlic mayonnaise, often
                        served with fish soup
saignant/bleu _____ rare/very rare
suprême/blanc _____ breast
sur l'os _____ on the bone
tapénade_____ thick Provencal paste made
                        with anchovy fillets, capers,
                        olives, garlic & olive oil
macédoine _____ mix of diced raw or cooked
                        vegetables or fruit
marmite _____ metal or earthenware pot for
                        serving soups

**POISSON/ _____ FISH/SHELLFISH**
**FRUITS DE MER**

anchois_____ anchovies
calmar_____ squid
carpe _____ carp
coquilles St Jacques___ scallops
crabe _____ crab
crevettes _____ shrimps/prawns
écrevisses _____ freshwater crayfish
fruits de mer_____ shellfish
homard _____ lobster
huîtres _____ oysters
langouste _____ rock lobster
langoustines _____ Dublin Bay prawns/scampi
lotte_____ monkfish

loup de mer _____ sea bass
maquereau _____ mackerel
merlan _____ whiting
morue _____ cod
moules _____ mussels
oursin _____ sea urchin
palourdes _____ clams
poulpe _____ octopus
raie _____ skate
sardines _____ sardines
saucisse/saucisson _____ cooked&/or smoked sausage
saumon _____ salmon
sole _____ sole
thon _____ tuna
truite _____ trout
turbot _____ turbot

**Typical dishes:**
Assiettes de fruit _____ mixed platter of seafood &
de mer                     shellfish
Bisque de homard _____ lobster soup
Bouillabaisse _____ Mediterranean fish stew served
                        with rouille (hot mayonnaise
                        which is dropped in small
                        pieces into the soup)
Brandade de morue _____ purée of dried, salt cod with
                           olive oil, milk, garlic & lemon
Matelote _____ freshwater fish & eel stew
Moules marinières _____ mussels in a white wine sauce
Quenelles de brochet _____ classic dish of pike rissoles
Salade Niçoise _____ tuna salad, from Provence
Sole Véronique _____ sole garnished with grapes

**VIANDE _____ MEAT**
agneau _____ lamb
andouille _____ smoky flavoured sausage of
                  chitterlings & tripe, served cold
andouillette _____ thinner version of an andouille,
                     served hot with mustard
animelles _____ bulls' testicles
bifteck _____ steak
boeuf _____ beef
boudin blanc _____ white sausage made with a
                     variety of meats
boudin noir _____ black sausage made with
                    pigs' blood
Châteaubriand _____ thick fillet steak
cervelles _____ brains
cervelas _____ form of saveloy sausage
cheval _____ horse
cochon de lait _____ suckling pig
côtelette _____ chop, cutlet
crépinette _____ small, flat sausage

escalope _____ escalope
foie _____ liver
jambon _____ ham
mouton _____ mutton
porc _____ pork
poulet _____ chicken
ris de veau/d'agneau _____ calves'/lambs' sweetbreads
rognons _____ kidneys
rognons blancs _____ calves' testicles
tripes _____ tripe
veau _____ veal

**Typical dishes:**
Assiette Anglaise _____ plate of assorted cold meats,
                          including beef, ham & tongue
Assiette de _____ plate of assorted sliced
charcuterie          saucissons
Boeuf Bourguignon _____ rich beef stew made with red
                          wine, mushrooms & onions
Carbonnade de boeuf _____ beef & beer stew
Carré d'agneau _____ loin of lamb, cooked with herbs
Cassoulet _____ robust casserole made with
                   haricot beans, smoked & fresh
                   pork
Fromage de tête _____ brawn
Gigot _____ leg of lamb or mutton
Jambon persillé _____ Burgundian speciality of jellied
                        ham & parsley
Navarin _____ lamb or mutton stew
Potée auvergnate _____ salt pork & vegetable stew
                         from Auvergne & Languedoc
Tripes à la mode _____ traditional Norman dish of tripe,
de Caen                   with onions & carrots

**GIBIER _____ GAME**
caille _____ quail
chevreuil _____ roe deer (venison)
daim _____ fallow deer (venison)
faisan _____ pheasant
faisandé _____ well hung, gamey
lapereau _____ young rabbit
lapin _____ rabbit
lièvre _____ hare
magret _____ breast fillet of duck
marcassin _____ young wild boar
perdreau _____ partridge
sanglier _____ wild boar

**Typical dishes:**
Civet _____ red wine stew of game
               classically thickened with the
               blood of the animal e.g.
civet de lièvre _____ (jugged hare)

Gigue _____ haunch of venison or other
game animal

## VOLAILLE _____ POULTRY
aile _____ wing
blanc/suprême _____ breast
caille _____ quail
dinde/dindonneau _____ turkey
canard/caneton _____ duck
lapin _____ rabbit
oie _____ goose
poulet_____ chicken
poussin_____ spring chicken

**Typical dishes:**
Canard à l'orange _____ duck in orange sauce
Caneton à la _____ pink-fleshed duck
Rouennais
Confit de canard/d'oie_ wings or legs of duck or goose,
preserved in their own fat
Coq au vin _____ chicken in red wine, onions,
bacon & mushrooms
Foie gras_____ goose liver, often made into a
very rich pâté

## OEUFS _____ EGGS
brouillés _____ scrambled
en cocotte/sur le plat _ baked
à la coque_____ boiled
frites_____ fried
mollet_____ soft-boiled
pochés _____ poached
soufflé _____ soufflé

**Typical dishes:**
Croque monsieur_____ sandwich of ham & cheese,
dipped in egg & fried
Oeufs à la _____ egg mayonnaise
mayonnaise
Omelette aux _____ savoury omelette
fines herbes
Pipérade_____ scrambled eggs prepared with
peppers & tomatoes
Quiche Lorraine _____ open tart filled with a rich egg
custard filling with bacon &
onion

## LÉGUMES/_____ VEGETABLES/
## GARNITURES SIDE DISHES
ail _____ garlic
carotte _____ carrot
cep/cèpe_____ edible brown mushroom
champignon_____ mushroom

chanterelle _____ edible yellow mushroom
choucroûte_____ sauerkraut
concombre_____ cucumber
fonds d'artichauts_____ artichoke hearts
frites _____ chips
grisette _____ edible wild mushroom
haricot_____ haricot bean
haricot vert _____ green bean
huile_____ oil
laitue_____ lettuce
oignon _____ onion
pâtes _____ pasta
petit pois_____ peas
poivre_____ pepper
pomme de terre_____ potato
riz _____ rice
tomate_____ tomato
truffes _____ truffles
vinaigre_____ vinegar

**Typical dishes:**
Aïoli _____ garlic mayonnaise
Cousinat_____ chestnut, cream & fruit stew
Crudités _____ selection of prepared, raw
vegetables served with dips
Galettes _____ buckwheat pancakes
Mojettes_____ kidney beans in butter or cream
Pissaladière_____ onion, anchovy and olive pizza
Potage julienne _____ vegetable soup
Ratatouille_____ tomato, aubergine, onion &
pepper stew
Salade verte _____ green salad
Salade panachée_____ mixed salad
Vichyssoise _____ creamy leek & potato soup
Vinaigrette _____ French dressing

## FRUITS ET NOIX_____ FRUIT & NUTS
abricot_____ apricot
ananas_____ pineapple
banane _____ banana
cassis _____ blackcurrant
cerise _____ cherry
citron _____ lemon
figue _____ fig
fraises/fraises_____ strawberries/wild strawberries
des bois
framboise _____ raspberry
marron _____ chestnut
melon Charentais _____ canteloupe melon with sweet,
orange flesh
mirabelle _____ small yellow plum
myrtilles _____ blueberries/bilberries
noisette_____ hazelnut

| | |
|---|---|
| noix | walnut |
| orange | orange |
| pêche | peach |
| pomme | apple |
| pamplemousse | grapefruit |
| prune | plum |
| raisin/raisin sec | grape/raisin |
| reine claude | greengage |
| pastèque | water melon |

## DESSERT — DESSERT

| | |
|---|---|
| beignets | fritters |
| clafouti | cherries baked in creamy batter |
| Chantilly | whipped cream |
| crème anglaise | custard |
| crème patissière | confectioner's custard |
| crème épaisse | thick or double cream |
| crêpes | pancakes |
| crème caramel | egg custard |
| fromage blanc | cream cheese |
| gâteau | cake |
| glâce | ice cream |
| îles flottantes | custard sauce with 'floating' spoonfuls of poached meringue |
| pâte | general term for pastry including pasta |
| pâte brisée | short-crust pastry |
| pâte d'amandes | marzipan |
| pâte feuilletée | puff pastry |
| macédoine/salade de fruits | fruit salad |
| sorbet | sorbet |
| tarte (aux fraises) | (strawberry) tart |
| tarte tatin | French-style apple tart |

## BOISSONS — DRINKS

| | |
|---|---|
| bière | beer |
| café décaffiné | decaffeinated coffee |
| café Liègeoise | iced coffee with ice cream & cream |
| café noir/au lait | black/white coffee |
| demi-tasse | small cup of strong coffee |
| digestif | liqueur or brandy taken at the end of a meal |
| eau minérale gazeuse | fizzy mineral water |
| eau minérale non gazeuse | still mineral water |
| frappé | with crushed ice |
| jus de fruit | fruit juice |
| limonade | lemonade |
| orangeade | orangeade |
| thé au lait/avec citron | tea with milk/lemon |
| tisane | herbal infusion or tea |

## WINE

| | |
|---|---|
| pétillant/mousseux | sparkling |
| sec/doux | dry/sweet |
| verre | glass |
| vin rouge/blanc/rosé | red/white/rosé wine |
| bouteille/demi | bottle/half bottle |
| bouteille | |
| pichet/demi pichet | carafe/half carafe |

## SOME TRADITIONAL DRINKS

| | |
|---|---|
| Bénédictine | liqueur made from aromatic herbs by the monks of Fécamp |
| Calvados | apple brandy from Normandy & Brittany |
| Crème de cassis | sweet blackcurrant liqueur |
| Champagne | champagne |
| Cidre | cider |
| Cognac | brandy fom Bordeaux |
| Marc/Vieux Marc | local brandy |
| Pastis | aniseed aperitif |
| Vin de Xérès | sherry |

## FROMAGE — CHEESE

France is justly famous for its many different cheeses. Here are just a few to look out for:

| | |
|---|---|
| Brie | large, creamy flat cheese |
| Brie de Coulommiers | milder, smaller version of Brie |
| Brie de Meaux | said to be the best Brie |
| Brie de Melun | strong, potent Brie with orange-red rind |
| Brillat-Savarin | triple cream cheese (Normandy) |
| Cabichou/Cabécou | small, strong ewes'/goats' cheese |
| Caillebotte | rich, creamy curd cheese in pots |
| Camembert | creamy cheese from Normandy |
| Cantal | hard & yellow (Auvergne) |
| Cendré | small, strong-flavoured cheese matured in wood ash |
| Charolais | cylindrical hard, mature cheese, or soft & creamy if fresh |
| Chateaubriand | triple cream cheese (Normandy) |
| Chèvre | goats' cheese |
| Crottin de Chavignol | small, hard goats' cheese |
| Delices de St Cyr | creamy cheese (Ile-de-France) |
| Epoisses | ripe Burgundian speciality |
| Gruyère | hard cheese with a nutty taste |
| Munster | sharp & aromatic (Alsace) |
| Neufchâtel | slightly salty, sour cream |
| cheese Pont-l'Evêque | hearty cheese with orange rind |
| Reblochon | soft, fruity Alpine cheese |
| Vacherin | rich, creamy/rust-coloured crust |

# Spend, spend, spend.

By Elizabeth Carter

THE BRITISH LOVE AFFAIR with France was sorely tested in the run up to the millennium what with the beef war coming right on top of the apple and lamb spats - all punctuated by the almost obligatory French blockade of Channel ports and major arterial roads. However, with the exchange rate firmly in our favour, the lure of the French way of life remains undiminished, with France proving exceptionally good value both as a holiday destination and as a shopping destination. So much so, British travellers are flooding into France in such numbers that each month record takings are being reported by shops in all major French ports.

Nearly a quarter of all the beer drunk in Britain during the millennium celebrations came from the Calais area. Doom and gloom may have surrounded the abolition of duty free within the European community, but it has just served to focus the minds of the British on the bargains to be had by buying duty-paid goods in France, a situation fuelled by Britain's upwardly mobile duty on alcohol and cigarettes. At the French end of the Channel Tunnel, for example, parking spaces in the immense car park of the Cité Europe shopping mall - as large as 20 football pitches - are frequently hard to come by with row after row of cars bearing yellow British number plates far outnumbering the French.

With wine that sells in French hypermarkets for £3-£4 a bottle costing around £5-£6 in England and beer at half price, it's basic arithmetic to work out the savings. What better way to offset some of the cost of your holiday than by stocking up on wines, beers and cigarettes for the coming year.

As a further incentive to spend, spend spend, the limits on how much can be brought into Britain duty-paid are much higher than the old duty free restrictions of 200 cigarettes and one litre of spirits or two litres of wine. British customs limits for duty-paid goods are:

- **800 cigarettes**
- **10 litres of spirits**
- **90 litres of table wine**
- **20 litres of fortified wine**
- **110 litres of beer**
- **200 cigars**
- **1kg smoking tobacco**

But why stop there. We've all been coming home from France with smelly cheeses and garlicky sausages for years, and the British media fixation on the savings to be had buying washing powder (£4-£5) has raised public awareness in that particular area, but it is the sheer variety of goods in French supermarkets and high-street shops that has tempted the British out of their main stronghold in the booze section. Now, advance parties are reporting that clothes, electrical goods, basic and luxury food items, and household goods are all generally cheaper, even petrol costs less (especially diesel).

The larger French supermarkets sell a wider range of produce than we're used to in Britain. Whereas luxury items such as tins of foie gras, jars of duck confit,

preserved lemons and fish soup, speciality flour for making crêpes, and prime quality charcuterie and cheese require some tracking down in specialist or mail-order shops at home, this is a standard list of produce available to the French shopper, and prices reflect the supermarket setting rather than an upmarket delicatessen. And staples such as butter, meat, vegetables, tinned goods, jams, and biscuits can be seen in a plethora of sorts and varieties, offering greater choice as well as better value.

Chocoholics are advised to head for the chocolate section of the largest supermarket they can find. Picture yourself in the sweet section in your average out-of-town British supermarket and imagine the whole aisle filled with every kind of chocolate bar - white, dark, milk - and with every conceivable filling including liqueurs and brandies such as Poire William and Cognac - and only a handful bearing the name Cadbury. The prices are lower, the quality of chocolate higher. Buy now.

And the most extraordinary things can be cheaper across the Channel. When the French government slashed VAT on building materials such as timber and cement from 20.6% to 5.5%, the rush of little white vans across the Channel was a sight to see, as DIY enthusiasts in southern England quickly caught on.

Garden furniture is worth checking out too. The moulded plastic chairs and sun loungers, as well as sun shades offered for sale in France are no different from those seen in Britain except for the astonishingly low price tags - these obviously offer enormous savings. The best places to buy are the hypermarkets or DIY and garden centres; they all offer good basic ranges during the spring and summer months. In late summer prices of unsold stock are slashed even further.

Also take a look at savings on electrical goods. One of last year's hottest Christmas games consoles, Sega's Dreamcast, retailed in the the Carréfour hypermarket chain at a markedly cheaper price than at home, and the only thing that required changing was the electrical plug. (Alternatively, you can buy a French to British travel plug in the same shop or department.) With a strong pound CDs are noticeably just that little bit cheaper if you can find what you want - French music tastes come into play here and you'll wade through an awful lot of Johnny Halliday.

However, in a case of the more you spend the more you save, it pays dividends to be aware of the options. Be warned, it is vitally important to remember that this is not Supermarket Sweep and not everything is automatically cheaper. French baby shops, for example, offer considerable savings in baby gear in the shape of top-of-the-range push chairs, car seats, cots and baby bike seats, and chic baby clothes such as Petit Bateau are a third cheaper, but disposable nappies and formula milk are more expensive than in Britain. Be aware of prices at home before you spend.

At the time of writing the pound was at an historically favourable rate vis-a-vis the franc; that can obviously change. However, even if the exchange rate were to become less favourable the great disparities in price and value in many of the items discussed above will remain. Why this continues to be so is a mystery, but until this is resolved why not offset the cost of your expensive Channel crossing by a big **spend, spend, spend.**

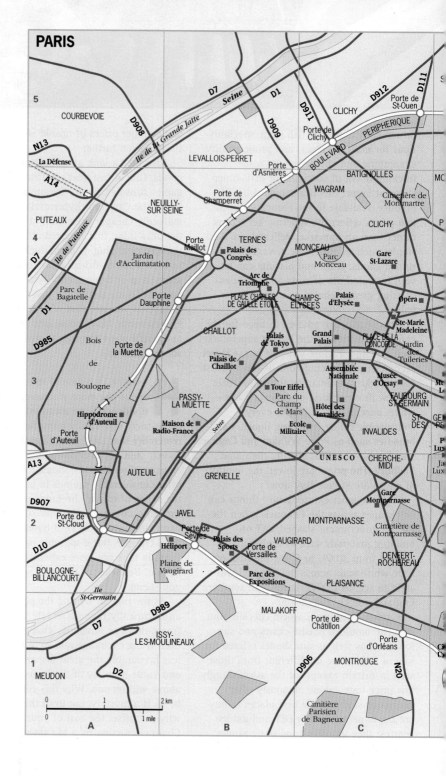

# PARIS

**5**

COURBEVOIE

D7 *Seine* D1

D911 D912 D111

Porte de St-Ouen

CLICHY

D908 *Ile de la Grande Jatte*

D909

PERIPHERIQUE

N13

LEVALLOIS-PERRET

Porte de Clichy

La Défense

Porte d'Asnières

BOULEVARD

BATIGNOLLES

MC

A14

WAGRAM

Porte de Champerret

Cimetière de Montmartre

NEUILLY-SUR SEINE

PUTEAUX

CLICHY

P

*Ile de Puteaux*

D7

**4**

Porte Maillot

TERNES

MONCEAU

Gare St-Lazare

Jardin d'Acclimatation

**Palais des Congrès** ■

Parc Monceau

**Arc de Triomphe**

Parc de Bagatelle

Porte Dauphine

PLACE CHARLES DE GAULLE ETOILE

CHAMPS-ELYSEES

**Palais d'Elysée** ■

**Opéra** ■

D1

CHAILLOT

**Palais de Tokyo** ■

**Grand Palais** ■

PLACE DE LA CONCORDE

**Ste-Marie Madeleine** ■

D985

Bois

Porte de la Muette

**Palais de Chaillot** ■

Jardin des Tuileries

**3**

de

**Assemblée Nationale** ■

**Musée d'Orsay** ■

Mr L

Boulogne

■ **Tour Eiffel**

Parc du Champ de Mars

FAUBOURG ST-GERMAIN

Hippodrome d'Auteuil ■

PASSY-LA MUETTE

**Hôtel des Invalides** ■

ST-DES

GE PE

Porte d'Auteuil

**Maison de Radio-France** ■

*Seine*

Ecole Militaire ■

INVALIDES

P Lu

A13

AUTEUIL

GRENELLE

**UNESCO**

CHERCHE-MIDI

Ja Lux

D907

**Gare Montparnasse** ■

**2**

Porte de St-Cloud

JAVEL

MONTPARNASSE

Cimetière de Montparnasse

D10

Porte de Sèvres

**Palais des Sports** ■

VAUGIRARD

Héliport ■

Porte de Versailles

DENFERT-ROCHEREAU

BOULOGNE-BILLANCOURT

Plaine de Vaugirard

**Parc des Expositions** ■

PLAISANCE

*Ile St-Germain*

D989

MALAKOFF

Porte de Châtillon

D7

Porte d'Orléans

C U

**1**

ISSY-LES-MOULINEAUX

D906

MONTROUGE

N20

MEUDON

D2

Cimetière Parisien de Bagneux

0 ____ 1 ____ 2 km

0 ____ 1 mile

**A**      **B**      **C**

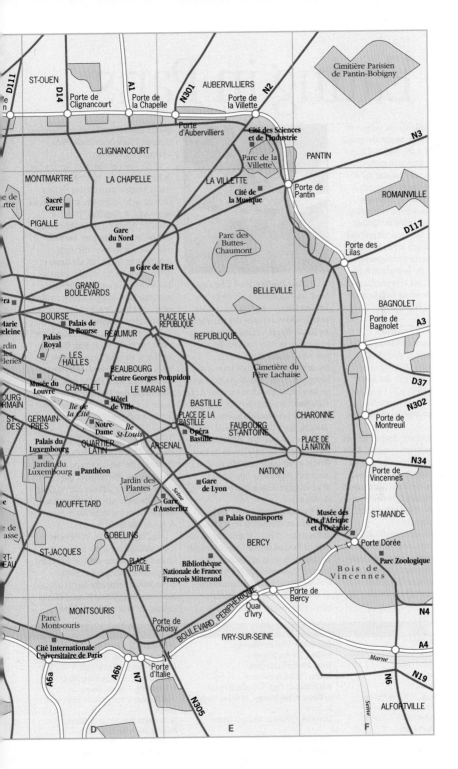

**D111**

ST-OUEN

**D14**

Porte de
Clignancourt

**A1**

Porte de
la Chapelle

**N301**

AUBERVILLIERS

Porte de
la Villette

**N2**

Cimitière Parisien
de Pantin-Bobigny

Porte
d'Aubervilliers

Cité des Sciences
et de l'Industrie

**N3**

CLIGNANCOURT

PANTIN

Parc de la
Villette

MONTMARTRE

LA CHAPELLE

LA VILLETTE

Cité de
la Musique

Porte de
Pantin

ROMAINVILLE

Sacré
Cœur

PIGALLE

Porte des
Lilas

**D117**

Gare
du Nord

Parc des
Buttes-
Chaumont

Gare de l'Est

BELLEVILLE

BAGNOLET

GRAND
BOULEVARDS

Porte de
Bagnolet

**A3**

BOURSE

Palais de
la Bourse

PLACE DE LA
RÉPUBLIQUE

Marie
eleine

Palais
Royal

REAUMUR

REPUBLIQUE

LES
HALLES

BEAUBOURG
Centre Georges Pompidou

Cimetière du
Père Lachaise

**D37**

Musée du
Louvre

CHATELET

LE MARAIS

Hôtel
de Ville

BASTILLE

CHARONNE

**N302**

Île de
la Cité

GERMAIN-
PRES

Notre-
Dame

Île
St-Louis

PLACE DE LA
BASTILLE

FAUBOURG
ST-ANTOINE

Porte de
Montreuil

Palais du
Luxembourg

QUARTIER
LATIN

ARSENAL

Opéra
Bastille

PLACE DE
LA NATION

**N34**

Jardin du
Luxembourg

Panthéon

Jardin des
Plantes

NATION

Porte de
Vincennes

MOUFFETARD

Gare
d'Austerlitz

Gare
de Lyon

Seine

Palais Omnisports

Musée des
Arts d'Afrique
et d'Océanie

ST-MANDE

GOBELINS

BERCY

Porte Dorée

ST-JACQUES

PLACE
D'ITALIE

Bibliothèque
Nationale de France
François Mitterand

Bois de
Vincennes

Parc Zoologique

MONTSOURIS

Porte de
Choisy

BOULEVARD PERIPHERIQUE

Quai
d'Ivry

Porte de
Bercy

**N4**

Parc
Montsouris

IVRY-SUR-SEINE

**A4**

Cité Internationale
Universitaire de Paris

**A6a**

**A6b**

**N7**

Porte
d'Italie

Marne

**N6**

**N19**

**N305**

Seine

ALFORTVILLE

**D**

**E**

**F**

# Eating in Paris

By Clarissa Hyman

Parisiens still take the subject of food seriously, despite the proliferation of *le fast food*. If the city no longer is the beacon of gastronomy it once was, it is only because the rest of the world has caught up, not that Paris has fallen behind. This once unthinkable competition is bringing, in turn, a reinvigoration of classical French cooking and a less narrow and chauvinistic outlook across the board. One welcome recent development, as a result, has been the introduction of menu-cartes, a cross between the traditional fixed-price menu and the more costly full carte. *Bon Appétit!*

## IST ARRONDISSEMENT

As well as the Louvre and Tuileries, the *quartier* includes the elegant Place Vendome, the Palais Royal, Comédie Française, Palais de Justice and Bourse. It is a busy, bustling area with a wealth of restaurants and cafes from which to observe the commercial heartbeat of the city.

The Rue St Honoré is designer heaven with astronomical prices to match. Alain Dutournier's couture-class Gascon cooking is just a platinum credit card throw away at *Le Carre des Feuillants*; superb ingredients underpin full-flavoured but essentially simple dishes that put the 'haute' back into cuisine.

*Goumard-Prunier*, founded in 1872, is still the place for classic fish cuisine, albeit at astronomical prices; don't miss the glorious 1930 toilettes - worth a visit alone. For equally good fish at more realistic prices, try their offshoot restaurant *Gaya* nearby.

At *Chez Pauline*, many a business lunch has concluded satisfactorily over timeless bistro classics such as '*jambon persillé*" and roast Bresse chicken. *Pierre au Palais-Royal*, a bastion of bourgeois cooking has recently had a facelift and now serves a combination of old favourites and French-style risottos and pastas plus cheese from Roger Alléosse, perhaps Paris's best cheesemonger. At *Le Cafe Ruc*, a brasserie popular with theatre-goers, *spécialité de la maison* is 'Madame Ruc's Giant Chocolate Eclair'. British-owned wine bars *Willi's Wine Bar* and *Juvenile's* are known for spectacular wines; stablemate *Macéo*, with a moulded 19th century interior, has sharp-edged cooking and an excellent vegetarian menu.

*Pharamond*, near Les Halles, boasts one of the most beautiful Belle Epoque dining-rooms in Paris. It specialises in traditional Norman cuisine - '*tripes à la mode de Caen*' is served in old-fashioned brass braziers. The market itself may have moved to Rungis, but the memory lives on at *Chez Denise*, an atmospheric bistro where former porters and bon

viveurs alike are served splendid portions of *pot-au-feu* and home-made *crème caramel*, 24 hours a day.

At the Tuileries end of the lengthy Rue de Rivoli, weary feet (as long as they're clad in Jourdan) and a craving for afternoon tea with elegant pâtisseries can both be assuaged at *Angélina*. Their hot chocolate '*Africain*' is irresistible, made with melted chocolate bars. *Verlet*, is cosier but equally venerable; little changed since the 1930s, the aroma of freshly roasted coffee mingles with caddies of fine teas, blended on the spot to your preference. Fashion victims can find salads and a huge choice of waters at the in-store cafe at *Colette*.

Whilst in the area, stop to admire the round country breads at *Max Poilâne* (brother of the more famous Lionel), baked in huge wood-fired ovens, the two hundred varieties of cheese in the tiny *La Maison Du Bon Fromage* and the charcuterie at *Chedeville*. All you need, in fact, for a Tuileries picnic lunch.

## 4TH ARRONDISSEMENT

From the Centre Georges Pompidou to the Marais, the 4th is a vibrant area, trendy yet still old-fashioned, filled with stylish boutiques, galleries and ethnic shops. The other side of the arrondissement is the incomparable Notre Dame, Ile de la Cité and the Ile St Louis.

The Place des Vosges, in the heart of the Marais, has one of the most distingushed and romantic dining-rooms in the city plus one of its greatest cellars. *L'Ambroisie* defines the special occasion restaurant; perfectionist Bernard Pacaud delights the palate with red pepper

## ADDRESSES

**1ST ARRONDISSEMENT**
Le Carré des Feuillants, 14 Rue de Castiglione
Goumard-Prunier, 9 Rue Duphot
Gaya, 17 Rue Duphot
Chez Pauline, 5 Rue Villedo
Pierre au Palais-Royal, 10 Rue de Richelieu
Le Café Ruc, 159 Rue Saint-Honoré
Willi's Wine Bar, 13 Rue des Petits-Champs
Juvenile's, 47 Rue de Richelieu
Macéo, 15 Rue des Petits-Champs
Le Pharamond, 24 Rue de la Grande-Truanderie

Chez Denise, 5 Rue des Prouvaires
Angélina, 226 Rue de Rivoli
Verlet, 256 Rue Saint-Honoré
Colette, 213 Rue Saint-Honoré
Max Poilâne, 42 Place du Marché St-Honoré
La Maison du Bon Fromage, 35 Rue du Marché St-Honoré
Chedeville, 12 Place du Marché St-Honoré

**4TH ARRONDISSEMENT**
L'Ambroisie, 9 Place des Vosges

La Baracane, 38 Rue des Tournelles
Le Temps des Cerises, 31 Rue de la Cerisaie
Patisserie Pottier, 4 Rue de Rivoli
Mariage Frères, 30 rue du Bourg-Tibourg
Jo Goldenberg, 7 Rue des Rosiers
Chez Marianne, 2 Rue des Hospitalières-Saint-Gervais
Sacha Finkelsztajn, 27 Rue des Rosiers
Palais de Fèz, 41 rue du Roi-de-Sicile
Benoit, 20 Rue Saint-Martin
Le Vieux Bistro, 14 Rue Clôitre-Notre-Dame

mousse, crispy roast lamb with rosemary and bitter chocolate tart.

More down to earth, in both price and concept, is *La Baracane*, just a few steps away. One of the best new-wave bistros, the revamped Quercy country cooking includes duck confit and *daube de joue* cooked in well-aged Cahors. Bread is from the famed Paris baker, Poujauran. *Le Temps de Cerises* is an unpretentious zinc-bar bistro, favoured by local workers for steaks, crudités and exemplary egg mayonnaise. Leave room for a pastry from *Pâtisserie Pottier* or start the day with one of their pure-butter croissants. A visit, or rather a pilgrimage, to *Mariage Frères* is a must - one of France's oldest tea importers, the shop-cum-tasting salon offers an astonishing 450 varieties of teas.

Sunday is a good day to visit the lively historic Jewish area centred around the Rue des Rosiers. *Jo Goldenberg's* delidiner is legendary for its stuffed carp and chopped liver, or there's Sephardi-style falafels at *Chez Marianne. Sacha Finkelstajn's* cheesecake rivals the best in New York. At the other end of the arrondissement, near the Hotel de Ville, the family-run *Benoit*, founded in 1912, remains a favourite for their deluxe bistro choice of dishes, from Madame Maigret's favourite, *blanquette de veau*, to impeccable ballotine of duck with foie gras.

*Le Vieux Bistro* defies the rule that restaurants near tourist traps must always be avoided. Close by Notre-Dame, the picturesque bistro has an old-fashioned air and beautifully correct food and service that make it popular with local businessmen and neighbourhood Parisiens. Nearby, *La Charlotte de l'Isle* is a whimsical tea room serving delicious florentines, rich pastries and 36 varieties of tea, including one made with violets. Wednesday afternoons leave the children

at their weekly puppet show, and repair to the *Ferme Saint Aubin*, a fragrant cheese shop where the many seasonal cheeses are aged in the 17th century cellars. Choose one of the legendary 60 flavours of ice-cream at *Berthillon* (wild strawberry sorbet is particularly recommended) - and watch the Seine flow sweetly by.

## 6TH ARRONDISSEMENT

*Les Deux Magots* and *Café Flore* have become tourist shrines but they're still a fine people-watching spot for the bohochic shoppers, students and passing motley that throng the Blvd. St Germain. The Luxembourg Gardens, however, remain a delightful refuge for young mothers, Doisneau lovers and escapees from the unforgiving city traffic, whilst a host of chic little shops are to be discovered around St Suplice and the newly trendy Sèvres/Babylon area.

*Lionel Poilâne* makes the most famous sourdough loaves in France, baked in old wood-burning ovens, and sold all over Paris. Another fine baker, *Gerard Mulot*, sells arguably the best brioche in town. In the Rue de Buci, Rue de Seine, together one of the city's main *Rue Commerçants* or market streets, look out for savoury tarts at *Jean-Pierre Carton*, and goats cheese and fromage frais at the *Hamon Fromagerie*. The *Charcuterie Alsacienne* is a cheery shop selling more sausages than you ever knew existed. In the Rue Dauphine are two other exceptional charcuteries - *Charles* for award-winning boudin blanc, and *Coesnon* for Norman specialities such as boudin noir and andouillettes. Divine chocolates and ice-cream are compulsive buying at *Christian Constant*, one of Paris's most dynamic chocolatiers. The *Marché Volant* on the Blvd Raspail is best on Sundays when it becomes an

organic market.

The picture-postcard Latin Quarter is packed with eating places, but most are poor value for money. One of the best, however, remains *Aux Charpentiers*, a genuine old-style bistro serving daily *plats de jour*. Another safe bet is *Le Bistrot d'Henri*, with a lively, noisy atmosphere, no-frills wooden tables and roast *gigot* and *gratin dauphinois* on the menu. Fish and culture combine at the landmark restaurant, *La Méditerranée*, once frequented by Cocteau, and recently given a new lease of life.

For upbeat, eclectic cooking book a table at *Jacques Cagna*. The 16th century setting contrasts with modern dishes such as Challans duck with citrus zest and red burgundy sauce. Cagna has also opened a mini-chain of mid-priced rôtisseries, including the latest, *L'Espadon Bleu*, a seafood bistro. At his *Rôtisserie d'en Face*, a youthful crowd tucks into roast chicken and saddle of lamb, served with his signature multi-grain bread. *Le Maxence* has fine, updated versions of Northern French dishes, but perhaps the most creative contemporary cooking in the area is the market-fresh menu of François Pasteau at *L'Épi Dupin*.

The 6th has something for everyone - *Café Parisien*, a sassy salad bar, smoke and cell-phone free; *Casa del Habano*, for cigar-puffing, tartare-eating machismo; omelettes *parmentier* at *La Palette*, crowded with gallery-goers and art students; Art Deco and perfect calves liver at the publishers' rendezvous, *Le Petit Zinc*; *La Taverne de Nesle* for artisan French beers......not forgetting, *Alcazar*, a red, white and black 200-seater, that has put the name Conran on the Paris gastronomic map.

La Charlotte de l'Isle, 24 Rue Saint-Louis-en-l'île
La Ferme Saint Aubin, 76 Rue Saint-Louis-en-l'île
Berthillon, 31 Rue Saint-Louis-en-l'île

**6TH ARRONDISSEMENT**
Les Deux Magots, 6 Place Saint-Germain-des-Prés
Café Flore, 172 Blvd Saint-Germain
Lionel Poilâne, 8 Rue du Cherche-Midi
Gerard Mulot, 76 Rue de Seine
Jean-Pierre Carton, 6 rue de Buci
Hamon Fromagerie, 81 Rue de Seine

Charcuterie Alsacienne, 10 Rue de Buci
Charcuterie Charles, 10 Rue Dauphine
Charcuterie Coesnon, 30 Rue Dauphine
Christian Constant, 37 rue d'Assas
Aux Charpentiers, 10 Rue Mabillon
Le Bistrot d'Henri, 16 Rue Princesse
La Méditerranée, 2 Place de l'Odéon
Jacques Cagna, 14 Rue des Grands-Augustins
L'Espadon Bleu, 25 Rue des Grands-Augustins
La Rôtissere d'en Face, 2 Rue Christine
Le Maxence, 9 bis Blv du Montparnasse

L'Épi Dupin, 11 Rue Dupin
Café Parisien, 15 Rue d'Assas
Casa del Habano, 169 Blvd Saint-Germain
La Palette, 43 Rue de Seine
Le Petit Zinc, 11 Rue Saint-Benôit
La Taverne de Nesle, 32 Rue Dauphine
Alcazar, 62 Rue Mazarine

# Brittany

The most westerly point of France, forming a peninsula surrounded on three sides by the Atlantic Ocean, Brittany has a unique character. Its Celtic tradition and Breton language are more akin to those of the Irish, Welsh or Cornish than the French, and are reflected in its folklore and customs. Traditional festivals and local dress are cherished, and festou-noz - evenings of folk dance and music - are held at the drop of a hat. Breton legends, steeped in Celtic mythology, have been handed down from generation to generation and are very much alive today, telling of a land of enchantment inhabited by fantastical creatures.

## ESSENTIAL FACTS

| | |
|---|---|
| DÉPARTEMENTS: | Côtes d'Armor, Finistère, Ille-et-Vilaine, Morbihan |
| PRINCIPAL TOWNS | Rennes, Fougères, St Brieuc, Brest, Quimper, Lorient, Vannes, St Malo |
| PLACES TO VISIT: | The standing stones at Carnac; the castles & fortresses of inland Brittany: Josselin, Vitré, Fourgères & Combourg; the medieval town of Dinan; pilgrimage procession at Carantec on the first Sunday after 15 August. |
| REGIONAL TOURIST OFFICE | 1 Rue Raoul Ponchon, 35069 Rennes Tel 02 99 28 44 30  Fax 02 99 28 44 40 Internet http://www.brittanytourism.com E-mail tourism@region-bretagne.fr |
| LOCAL GASTRONOMIC DELIGHTS | Assiette de fruits de mer, a seafood platter which may include lobster, langoustines, crab, mussels, sea perch, oyster and other seafood. Cotriade, a seafood stew. Coquilles St-Jacques, scallops. Classic homard (lobster) à l'Armoricaine. Far, a local pudding. Galettes, savoury pancakes made with buckwheat flour. Crêpes, sweet pancakes |
| DRINKS | Heady Breton cider, strong local beer, pear cider &lambig, a fiery cider brandy. |
| LOCAL CRAFTS WHAT TO BUY | Breton clothing, such as a striped woollen jumper, yellow sailing jacket, pea jacket or fisherman's smock. Pottery from Quimper and embroidery from Bigoudenoff. Dinan is home to engravers, weavers, glassblowers & woodcarvers. |

## ARRADON Morbihan

### ★ ★ ★ Le Logis de Parc er Gréo
9 rue Mane Guen le Gréo 56610
☎ 297447303 FAX 297448048
(leave N165 at 'Vannes Ouest' and follow signs towards Arradon until you pick up D101 to Moustoir then follow signs to Le Gréo)
Beside the Golf of Morbihan, at the end of a tree-lined drive guests will discover this charming, elegant hotel. The antique furniture, watercolours and model boats create an atmosphere of warmth and refinement.

Near sea  Near beach  Forest area
*Closed 6 Feb-15 Mar*
*12 en suite (bth/shr) (3 fmly)  No smoking in 2 bedrooms  TV in all bedrooms  Direct dial from all bedrooms  Licensed  Full central heating  Open parking available  Child discount available 9yrs  Outdoor swimming pool (heated)  Bicycle rental  Covered terrace  Boat Hire  Languages spoken: English*
ROOMS: s 378-528FF; d 466-666FF
CARDS: ●● ■ ▓ ▣ Travellers cheques

## ARZANO Finistère

### Château de Kerlarec (Prop: Michel Bellin)
*29300*
☎ 298717506 FAX 298717455
(from Quimperle take D22 towards Arzano, then left for Kerlarec.)
Near river  Forest area
*6 en suite (bth/shr) (5 fmly) (5 with balcony)  TV in 2 bedrooms  Full central heating  Open parking available  Supervised  Tennis  Languages spoken: English & Italian*
ROOMS: s 350-420FF; d 380-480FF
CARDS: Travellers cheques

## AUDIERNE Finistère

### ★ ★ Au Roi Gradlon
*29770*
☎ 298700451 FAX 298701473
Near river  Near sea  Near beach  Forest area
*19 en suite (bth/shr) (9 fmly) (7 with balcony)  TV in all bedrooms  STV  Direct dial from all bedrooms  Licensed  Full central heating  Open parking available  Supervised  Child discount available 10yrs  Bicycle rental  Open terrace  Sports Centre close by  Last d 21.00hrs  Languages spoken: English*

contd.

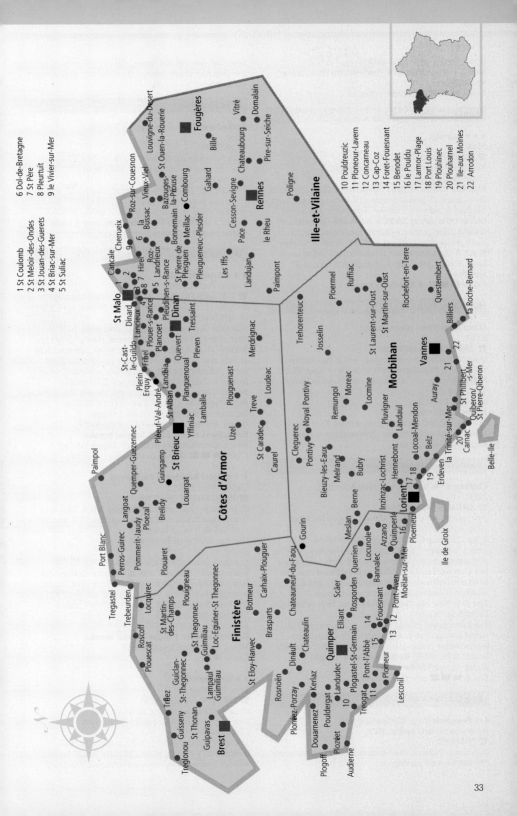

Brest

Finistère

Côtes d'Armor

St Brieuc

St Malo

Dinard

Dinan

Rennes

Ille-et-Vilaine

Fougères

Quimper

Lorient

Vannes

Morbihan

Belle-Ile

Ile de Groix

1 St Coulomb
2 St Meloir-des-Ondes
3 St Jouan-des-Guerets
4 St Briac-sur-Mer
5 St Suliac
6 Dol-de-Bretagne
7 St Père
8 Pleurtuit
9 le Vivier-sur-Mer
10 Pouldreuzic
11 Ploneour-Lavern
12 Concarneau
13 Cap-Coz
14 Foret-Fouesnant
15 Benodet
16 le Pouldu
17 Larmor-Plage
18 Port Louis
19 Plouhinec
20 Plouhamel
21 Ile-aux-Moines
22 Arrodon

33

ROOMS: (room only) d 300-380FF
MEALS: Full breakfast 45FF Lunch 90-250FF&alc Dinner
90-250FF&alc
CARDS: 🔵 ■ ■ 🔲 Travellers cheques

## AURAY Morbihan

### ★ ★ ★ *Fairway*
*56400*
☎ 297568888 FAX 297568828
Near river Near sea Near beach Forest area
*Closed 26 Dec-4 Jan*
*42 en suite (bth/shr) (8 fmly) (42 with balcony) No smoking in*
*21 bedrooms TV in all bedrooms STV Radio in rooms Direct*
*dial from all bedrooms Licensed Night porter Full central*
*heating Open parking available Supervised Child discount*
*available 12yrs Outdoor swimming pool (heated) Golf 9*
*Tennis Sauna Solarium Gym Pool table Boule Jacuzzi/spa*
*Bicycle rental Open terrace Covered terrace Sailing boats*
*Last d 22.00hrs Languages spoken: English, German &*
*Spanish*
CARDS: 🔵 ■ ■ 🔲 Travellers cheques

## BANNALEC Finistère

### *Stang Huel* (Prop: Jaouen Family)
*29380*
☎ 298394396 FAX 298395023
(leave N165 at "Kerandreo-Bannalec" exit in the direction of
Scaer (D4). In Bannalec on traffic circle follow Scaer, 500m
from traffic circle turn left & follow signs "Gites du France-
Stang-Huel")
Near river Forest area
*Jun-Sep & long wknds*
*2 en suite (bth/shr) No smoking on premises TV in all*
*bedrooms Full central heating Open parking available*
*Languages spoken: English*

## BAZOUGES-LA-PÉROUSE Ille-et-Vilaine

### Château de la Ballue (Prop: Alain Schrotter)
*35560*
☎ 299974786 FAX 299974770
(from Rennes or Mont-Saint-Michel follow the N175 then
signposts to the Château)
A fine 17th-century building, near Mont-St-Michel, set in
gardens recreated in period style, offering fine views over the
surrounding countryside. Five large bedrooms, with canopy
bed. Each room has been decorated in a different style. The
wood panelled rooms contain antique furniture and a
collection of contemporary painting and sculpture.
Near river Near lake Near sea Forest area Near motorway
*Closed 6 Jan-14 Feb*
*5 en suite (bth/shr) (5 fmly) No smoking on premises Full*
*central heating Open parking available No children 5yrs*
*Tennis Fishing Riding Languages spoken: English & Italian*
ROOMS: d 750-950FF **Reductions over 1 night**
MEALS: Dinner 190FF✱
CARDS: 🔵 ■ ■ Travellers cheques

## BELLE-ILE-EN-MER Morbihan

### *Les Pougnots* (Prop: Martine Guillouët)
rue de chemin Neuf Saujon *89426*
☎ 297316103
(take boat in Quiberon, reservation needed for cars (telephone
297318001) but not passengers)

Near river Near sea Near beach
*5 en suite (shr) (2 with balcony) Direct dial from all bedrooms*
*Open terrace*

## BELZ Morbihan

### Kercadoret (Prop: Jean-François Rolland)
*56550*
☎ 297554401
(from Auray take D22 towards Belz. Before village take right to
Ninezure. After 0.5 miles take right to the farm)
Near river Near sea Near beach
*5 en suite (shr) (1 fmly) No smoking on premises TV available*
*Full central heating Open parking available Covered parking*
*available Boule Table tennis Languages spoken: English*
ROOMS: s 200FF; d 250FF **Reductions over 1 night**
CARDS: Travellers cheques

## BÉNODET Finistère

### ★ ★ ★ Armoric Hotel
3 rue de Penfoul *29950*
☎ 298570403 FAX 298572128
(from the direction of Quimper towards Bénodet, hotel is first
on right heading towards beach)
Near river Near sea Forest area In town centre
*30 en suite (bth/shr) 10 rooms in annexe (5 fmly) (3 with*
*balcony) TV in all bedrooms Radio in rooms Direct dial from*
*all bedrooms Mini-bar in 7 bedrooms Licensed Lift Night*
*porter Full central heating Open parking available Covered*
*parking available (charged) Supervised Child discount*
*available 12yrs Outdoor swimming pool (heated) Tennis Boule*
*Bicycle rental Open terrace V meals Last d 20.00hrs*
*Languages spoken: English, Danish & German*
ROOMS: (room only) s 395-495FF; d 395-950FF
**Reductions over 1 night Special breaks**
MEALS: Continental breakfast 48FF Dinner 145-240FF
CARDS: 🔵 ■ ■ 🔲 Travellers cheques

### ★ ★ ★ Hotel Residence Eurogreen
Golf de l'Odet *29950*
☎ 298517300 FAX 298517349
(from Quimper take direction of Bénodet D34, in 10km at Le
Drennec take direction of Clohars-Fouesnant D134, then follow
signs Golf de l'Odet or Eurogreen)
Near sea Near beach Forest area
*Closed Oct-Mar*
*43 en suite (bth/shr) (37 fmly) (14 with balcony) TV in all*
*bedrooms STV Direct dial from all bedrooms Licensed Full*
*central heating Open parking available Supervised Outdoor*
*swimming pool (heated) Golf 18 Tennis Sauna Solarium Gym*
*Pool table Boule Mini-golf Bicycle rental Open terrace*
*Languages spoken: English*
ROOMS: (room only) d 390FF
**Reductions over 1 night Special breaks**
MEALS: Continental breakfast 35FF
CARDS: 🔵 ■

### ★ ★ Ker Vennaik
45 av de la Plage *29950*
☎ 298571540 FAX 298572748
(15km S of Quimper towards the sea via D34)
Near river Near sea Near beach In town centre
*Closed Oct-Mar*
*16 en suite (bth/shr) (2 fmly) (5 with balcony) TV in all*
*bedrooms STV Radio in rooms Direct dial from all bedrooms*
*Mini-bar in all bedrooms Room-safe (charged) Full central*

heating Open parking available Covered parking available Supervised Child discount available Pool table Open terrace
Languages spoken: English
ROOMS: (room only) s 250-300FF; d 250-360FF
CARDS: ●● ■ ▆ 🐾 Travellers cheques

★ ★ Le Minaret
Corniche de l'Estuaire 29950
☎ 298570313 FAX 298662372
Near river Near beach In town centre
RS half board only in high season
20 en suite (bth/shr) (6 with balcony) TV in all bedrooms STV Direct dial from all bedrooms Licensed Lift Full central heating Open parking available Open terrace Last d 21.45hrs
Languages spoken: English
ROOMS: (room only) d 285-330FF
MEALS: Full breakfast 45FF Lunch 90-235FF&alc Dinner 90-235FF&alc
CARDS: ●● ▆ Travellers cheques

### BERNÉ Morbihan

Marta (Prop: Isabelle Bregardis)
Marta 56240
☎ 297342858
(20km N of Lorient off D769 exit at Vallée du Scorff, Pont-Calleck)
Near river Near lake Forest area Near motorway
6 en suite (shr) (2 fmly) Full central heating Open parking available Child discount available 3yrs Outdoor swimming pool (heated) Boule Bicycle rental Languages spoken: English
CARDS: Travellers cheques

### BIEUZY-LES-EAUX Morbihan

Lezerhy (Prop: Martine Maignan)
56310
☎ 297277459 FAX 297277459
(from Pontivy take D768 towards Lorient. At Port Arthur turn right onto D1 to St-Nicholas-de-Eaux. Then right after the bridge and follow signs for 'Chambre d'Hôte/Poterie')
Near river Forest area
Closed Nov-Mar
2 en suite (shr) Full central heating Open parking available Child discount available Bicycle rental Languages spoken: N
ROOMS: s 190FF; d 230FF

### BILLÉ Ille-et-Vilaine

Mesauboin (Prop: J Roussel)
35133
☎ 299976157 FAX 299975076
(from Fougères take D179 towards Billé, then right onto D23 towards St-Georges-de-Chesné)
Near river
6 en suite (bth/shr) (4 fmly) Full central heating Open parking available Child discount available 10yrs Boule
ROOMS: s 182FF; d 235FF **Reductions over 1 night**
MEALS: Lunch fr 93FF Dinner fr 86FF✱
CARDS: ●● ▆ Travellers cheques

### BILLIERS Morbihan

★ ★ ★ ★ Domaine de Rochevilaine
Pointe de Pen Lan 56190
☎ 297416161 FAX 297414485
(from Nantes take the E60 in direction of Vannes & exit at Muzillac, then follow signs to Billies & Pen Lau)
Near sea Near beach
38 en suite (bth/shr) (6 fmly) No smoking in 4 bedrooms TV in all bedrooms STV Direct dial from all bedrooms Mini-bar in 12 bedrooms Licensed Lift Night porter Full central heating Open parking available Supervised Child discount available 12yrs Indoor swimming pool (heated) Outdoor swimming pool (heated) Sauna Solarium Gym Mini-golf Jacuzzi/spa Bicycle rental Open terrace Covered terrace Wkly live entertainment Last d 21.30hrs Languages spoken: English
CARDS: ●● ■ ▆ 🐾 Travellers cheques

### BONNEMAIN Ille-et-Vilaine

Colibri (Prop: Colin et Brigitte Adams)
Le Rocher-Cordier 35270
☎ 299734545 FAX 299734545
(follow signposts from village square for half a mile to house up hill on right)
Near river Near lake Forest area
3 en suite (bth/shr) (1 fmly) Radio in rooms Full central heating Open parking available Covered parking available Child discount available Bicycle rental Languages spoken: English & Italian
CARDS: Travellers cheques

Mont Servin (Prop: Mme B M Froud)
35270
☎ 299737062 FAX 299737062
(from St Malo take N137 towards Rennes. Turn left to Miniac Morvan & onto Lanhelin. At x-rds turn left onto D10. 2nd left into Montservin, house 1st left)
Near lake Near sea Near beach Forest area Near motorway
2 rms No smoking on premises Open parking available Child discount available Languages spoken: English

### BOTMEUR Finistère

Kreisker (Prop: M-T Solliec)
29690
☎ 298996302 FAX 298996302
(leave Morlaix/Quimper road D785 and take D42 in the direction of Botmeur, at 'La Croix Cassee' follow signs 'chambre d'hotes' for 2.50kms)
Near river Near lake Forest area
1 en suite (bth) Full central heating Open parking available Child discount available 3yrs Languages spoken: English
ROOMS: d fr 250FF

### BOUSSAC, LA Ille-et-Vilaine

Moulin du Brégan (Prop: Mary-Anne Briand)
35120
☎ 299800529 FAX 299800622
(from A71 (Vierzon-Clermont-Ferrand) exit Montlucon take D916 to Boussac)
Near river Near lake Forest area
4 en suite (bth/shr) Full central heating Child discount available 3yrs Last d 20.00hrs Languages spoken: English German Italian Spanish
CARDS: Travellers cheques

## BRASPARTS Finistère

**Garz Ar Bik** (Prop: Marie Chaussy)
*29190*
☎ 298814714 FAX 298814799
Near river  Near sea  Forest area
*4 en suite (bth/shr)  (2 fmly)  No smoking on premises  Radio in rooms  Full central heating  Open parking available  Covered parking available  Child discount available  TV room  Languages spoken: English*
ROOMS: s 210FF; d 260FF ✱
MEALS: Dinner 90FF✱
CARDS: ■ Travellers cheques

## BRÉLIDY Côtes-D'Armor

★ ★ ★ *Château Hotel de Brélidy*
*22140*
☎ 296956938 FAX 296951803
(from N12 Paris-Brest exit in direction Lannion/Begard on D767 in direction of Treouier, then D15 to Brelidy)
Near river  Near lake  Forest area
*Closed 3 Nov-2 Apr*
*10 en suite (bth/shr)  Some rooms in annexe  (2 fmly)  TV in all bedrooms  Direct dial from all bedrooms  Licensed  Full central heating  Open parking available  Covered parking available  Child discount available 12yrs  Fishing  Pool table  Jacuzzi/spa  Bicycle rental  Open terrace  Last d 21.00hrs  Languages spoken: English*
CARDS: ●● ■ ▓ Travellers cheques

## BREST Finistère

★ ★ ★ *Hotel Mercure*
24 rue de Lyon *29200*
☎ 298805040 FAX 298431747
(Approach via N12 from Rennes or N165 from Nantes)
In town centre
*75 en suite (bth/shr)  (17 fmly)  (16 with balcony)  No smoking in 14 bedrooms  TV in all bedrooms  STV  Radio in rooms  Direct dial from all bedrooms  Mini-bar in 21 bedrooms  Licensed  Lift  Night porter  Full central heating  Child discount available 16yrs  Pool table  Languages spoken: English German Italian & Spanish*
CARDS: ●● ■ ▓ ⊙ Travellers cheques

## BUBRY Morbihan

★ ★ *Auberge de Coet Diquel*
*56310*
☎ 297517070 FAX 297517308
(In town take the road opposite the entrance to the church for 500mtrs)
Near river  Forest area
*Closed Jan*
*20 en suite (bth/shr)  TV in all bedrooms  Radio in rooms  Direct dial from all bedrooms  Licensed  Full central heating  Open parking available  Child discount available 12yrs  Indoor swimming pool (heated)  Tennis  Pool table  Boule  Open terrace  Last d 22.00hrs  Languages spoken: English*
CARDS: ●● ▓ Travellers cheques

## CANCALE Ille-et-Vilaine

★ ★ *Emeraude*
7 Quai Albert Thomas *35260*
☎ 299896176 FAX 299898821
Near sea  In town centre  Near motorway

*16 en suite (bth/shr)  5 rooms in annexe  (2 fmly)  (4 with balcony)  TV in all bedrooms  Licensed  Full central heating  Child discount available  Open terrace  Last d 22.00hrs  Languages spoken: English*
CARDS: ●● ■ ▓ Travellers cheques

**La Gaudichais** (Prop: M & Mme Loisel)
Les Oyats *35260*
☎ 299897361
(from Cancale proceed in direction of St Malo on the D201, 2km before Pointe du Grouin turn right Chambre d'Hote signposted)
Near sea  Near beach
*4 en suite (shr)  (4 fmly)  No smoking on premises  Full central heating  Open parking available  Reading room  Languages spoken: English & German*

**La Ville et Gris** (Prop: Marie Christine Masson)
67 rue des François Libres *35260*
☎ 299896727
(from town centre take D76 towards Dinan/Rennes. Establishment on right)
Near sea  Near beach
*5 en suite (bth/shr)  (3 fmly)  Full central heating*
CARDS: Travellers cheques

## CAP-COZ Finistère

★ ★ *Belle Vue*
30 descente de Belle Vue *29170*
☎ 298560033 FAX 298516085
(between Lorient & Quimper, leave the N165 towards Fouesnant, arriving near Fouesnant, keep driving towards Beg-Meil & turn left at the roundabout)
Near sea  Forest area
*Closed 4 Nov-Feb RS Mar & Oct*
*20 en suite (bth/shr)  (4 fmly)  TV in 10 bedrooms  Direct dial from all bedrooms  Licensed  Full central heating  Open parking available  Child discount available 12yrs  Open terrace  Last d 21.45hrs  Languages spoken: English, German & Italian*
CARDS: ●● ▓ Travellers cheques

## CARHAIX-PLOUGUER Finistère

**Manoir de Prévasy** (Prop: M & Mme Novak)
*29270*
☎ 298932436 FAX 298932436
(take the bypass to the south of Carhaix (RN164) turn between Distri Center and Hotel des Impots in 800m turn right follow signs to Prevasy)
Forest area
*Closed 2 Nov-Etr*
*5 en suite (bth/shr)  (1 fmly)  No smoking in all bedrooms  Full central heating  Open parking available  No children 12yrs  Boule  Bicycle rental  Open terrace  Covered terrace  Languages spoken: English & Spanish*
CARDS: Travellers cheques

## CARNAC Morbihan

**L'Alcyone** (Prop: M & Mme Balsan)
Impasse de Beaumer *56340*
☎ 297527811 FAX 297521302
Near sea
*5 en suite (shr)  TV available  Direct-dial available  Full central heating  Open parking available*

★ ★ ★ ★ **Le Diana**
21 bd de la Plage *56340*
☎ 297520538 FAX 297528791
Near sea  Near beach
*Closed Oct-Etr*
*32 en suite (bth/shr) (6 fmly) (30 with balcony) TV in all*
*bedrooms STV Direct dial from all bedrooms Mini-bar in all*
*bedrooms Room-safe Lift Night porter Full central*
*heating Open parking available Child discount available 5yrs*
*Outdoor swimming pool (heated) Solarium Mini-golf*
*Jacuzzi/spa Bicycle rental Open terrace Last d 22.00hrs*
*Languages spoken: English*
CARDS: ●● ■■ ☲☲ ⑩ JCB Travellers cheques

★ ★ *Ibis Hotel*
Av de l'Atlantique *56343*
☎ 297525354 FAX 297525366
(head towards Carnac/Quiberon then Carnac Beach, hotel near
yacht club)
Near lake  Near sea  Near beach
*119 en suite (shr) (23 fmly) (115 with balcony) No smoking in*
*33 bedrooms TV in all bedrooms STV Direct dial from all*
*bedrooms Licensed Lift Night porter Full central heating*
*Open parking available Child discount available 12yrs Indoor*
*swimming pool (heated) Tennis Riding Sauna Solarium Gym*
*Boule Jacuzzi/spa Bicycle rental Covered terrace Last d*
*22.00hrs Languages spoken: English*
CARDS: ●● ■■ ☲☲ ⑩ Travellers cheques

★ ★ *Tumulus*
31 rue du Tumulus *56340*
☎ 297520821 FAX 297528188
Near sea  Forest area
*Closed Oct-Dec RS Jul & Aug half board only*
*27 rms (16 bth 10 shr) 6 rooms in annexe (5 fmly) (7 with*
*balcony) TV in 12 bedrooms Direct dial from all bedrooms*
*Licensed Full central heating Open parking available Child*
*discount available Outdoor swimming pool (heated) Boule*
*Jacuzzi/spa Bicycle rental Open terrace Volley-Ball V meals*
*Languages spoken: English, Italian & Spanish*
CARDS: ●● ■■ ☲☲ ⑩ Travellers cheques

**CARNAC-PLAGE** Morbihan

★ ★ ★ **Hotel Celtique** (Best Western)
17 av de Kermario *56340*
☎ 297521149 FAX 297527110
Near beach  In town centre
*53 en suite (bth/shr) 3 rooms in annexe (7 fmly) (15 with*
*balcony) No smoking in 9 bedrooms TV in all bedrooms STV*
*Direct dial from all bedrooms Licensed Lift Night porter Full*
*central heating Open parking available (charged) Covered*
*parking available (charged) Child discount available 12yrs*
*Indoor swimming pool (heated) Outdoor swimming pool*
*(heated) Sauna Solarium Pool table Jacuzzi/spa Bicycle rental*
*Open terrace Languages spoken: English, German & Spanish*
ROOMS:  (room only) s 300-415FF; d 295-730FF
CARDS: ●● ■■ ☲☲ ⑩ Travellers cheques

**CAUREL** Côtes-D'Armor

★ ★ *Le Beau Rivage*
*22530*
☎ 296285215 FAX 296260116
(S of town on the Lac de Guerlédan)
Near lake  Near sea  Forest area

8 *en suite (bth) TV in all bedrooms STV Licensed Full central*
*heating Open parking available Open terrace Covered terrace*
*Last d 21.00hrs Languages spoken: English*
CARDS: ●● ■■ ☲☲ Travellers cheques

**CESSON-SEVIGNE** Ille-et-Vilaine

★ ★ ★ *Germinal*
9 cours se la Vilaine *35510*
☎ 299831101 FAX 299834516
Near river  Near lake  Forest area  In town centre  Near
motorway
*(2 fmly) (2 with balcony) TV in 20 bedrooms Direct dial from*
*20 bedrooms Licensed Lift Full central heating Open parking*
*available Fishing Open terrace Covered terrace Last d*
*21.30hrs Languages spoken: English*

**CHÂTEAUBOURG** Ille-et-Vilaine

★ ★ ★ *Ar-Milin*
30 rue de Paris *35220*
☎ 299003091 FAX 299003756
Near river  In town centre  Near motorway
*Closed end Dec-early Jan*
*31 en suite (bth/shr) 20 rooms in annexe (13 with balcony) TV*
*in all bedrooms Licensed Lift Full central heating Open*
*parking available Child discount available Tennis Fishing*
*Boule Bicycle rental Open terrace Last d 21.30hrs Languages*
*spoken: English,German,Spanish*
CARDS: ●● ■■ ☲☲ ⑩ Travellers cheques

**CHÂTEAULIN** Finistère

★ ★ *Au Bon Accueil*
A Port Launay *29150*
☎ 298861577 FAX 298863625
(via express route Quimper/Brest)
Near river  Forest area  Near motorway
*Closed Jan*
*50 rms (45 bth/shr) 17 rooms in annexe (3 fmly) No smoking in*
*3 bedrooms TV in 15 bedrooms Radio in rooms Direct dial*
*from all bedrooms Licensed Lift Full central heating Open*
*parking available Child discount available 12yrs Outdoor*
*swimming pool (heated) Fishing Sauna Mini-golf Open*
*terrace Last d 21.15hrs Languages spoken: English*
CARDS: ●● ☲☲ Travellers cheques

**CHÂTEAUNEUF-DU-FAOU** Finistère

★ ★ *Relais de Cornouaille*
9 rue Paul Serusier *29520*
☎ 298817536 FAX 298818132
Near river  Forest area  In town centre  Near motorway
*30 en suite (bth/shr) (4 fmly) TV in all bedrooms Direct dial*
*from all bedrooms Licensed Lift Full central heating Open*
*parking available Covered parking available (charged) Child*
*discount available V meals Last d 21.00hrs Languages spoken:*
*English*
CARDS: ●● ☲☲ Travellers cheques

**CHERRUEIX** Ille-et-Vilaine

**La Croix Gaillot** (Prop: Michel Taillebois)
*35120*
☎ 299489044
Near sea

*contd.*

*5 en suite (shr) (2 fmly) No smoking on premises Full central heating Open parking available Child discount available Languages spoken: English*
CARDS: ■■ Travellers cheques

## CLÉGUÉREC Morbihan

**Kerantourner** (Prop: A & P Jouan)
*56480*
☎ 297380614
(from Cléguérec, take D18 towards Guémené sur Scorff. After 2kms turn left. Parking on left after 80 metres)
Near river  Near lake  Forest area
*4 en suite (shr) (1 fmly) TV available Full central heating Open parking available Child discount available 10yrs Boule Languages spoken: English & German*
MEALS: Lunch 90-140FF Dinner 90-140FF✱

## COMBOURG Ille-et-Vilaine

★ ★ ★ **Hotel Restaurant du Château**
1 pl Châteaubriant *35270*
☎ 299730038 FAX 299732579
Near river  Near lake  In town centre  Near motorway
*Closed 15 Dec-16 Jan*
*35 en suite (bth/shr) (3 fmly) TV in all bedrooms STV Direct dial from all bedrooms Mini-bar in all bedrooms Licensed Night porter Full central heating Open parking available Covered parking available Supervised Child discount available Boule Open terrace V meals Last d 22.00hrs Languages spoken: English & German*
ROOMS: (room only) d 280-520FF **Special breaks**
MEALS: Full breakfast 48FF Lunch 98-350FF&alc Dinner 98-350FF&alc
CARDS: ●● ■■ ☲ ◐ Travellers cheques

★ ★ **Du Lac**
2 pl Châteaubriand *35270*
☎ 299730565 FAX 299732334
(from St-Malo on N137 exit at Hédé)
Near river  Near lake  Forest area  Near motorway
*Closed Feb*
*28 en suite (bth/shr) 6 rooms in annexe (2 fmly) TV in all bedrooms Direct dial from all bedrooms Licensed Full central heating Open parking available Covered parking available Child discount available 10yrs Pool table Open terrace Billard table V meals Last d 21.30hrs Languages spoken: English & German*
ROOMS: (room only) d 250-380FF **Special breaks**
MEALS: Full breakfast 45FF Lunch 70-200FF Dinner 70-200FF
CARDS: ●● ■■ ☲ ◐ Travellers cheques

## CONCARNEAU Finistère

★ ★ **Des Sables Blancs**
Plage des Sables Blancs *29110*
☎ 298970139 FAX 298506588
Near sea  Forest area  Near motorway
*Closed Oct-4 Jan & 28 Feb-Mar*
*48 rms (44 bth/shr) (9 fmly) (25 with balcony) TV in all bedrooms Direct dial from all bedrooms Licensed Full central heating Child discount available 5yrs Open terrace V meals Last d 21.00hrs Languages spoken: English, German & Spanish*
CARDS: ●● ■■ ☲ ◐ Travellers cheques

## DINAN Côtes-D'Armor

**Moulin de la Fontaine des Eaux** (Prop: M Garside)
Vallée de la Fontaine des Eaux *22100*
☎ 296879209 FAX 296879209
(from Dinan town centre drive past Château towards Port of Dinan. Down hill & turn right before viaduct. Along river through Port, 1st left at blue Chambre d'Hôtes sign. Moulin 100m on right after Youth Hostel)
This eighteenth-century water mill makes an ideal base for a holiday exploring the historic beauty of Brittany. It is situated in the heart of magnificent countryside, with its own gardens and lake and is within easy walking distance of the famous medieval town of Dinan and the port. From here a daily ferry trip can be taken to St Malo and Dinard. Comfortable, modern en-suite facilities are available. Dinners are sometimes available on request. Your British hosts, Marjorie and Harry Garside and their young family welcome couples and families alike.
Near river  Near lake  Forest area  In town centre  Near motorway
*Closed closed in winter at certain times*
*5 en suite (shr) (3 fmly) No smoking on premises Full central heating Open parking available Covered parking available Child discount available 12yrs Languages spoken: English & Welsh*
MEALS: Dinner 90FF✱

**La Rénardais** (Prop: John & Suzanne Robinson)
Le Repos, Plouër-Sur-Rance *22490*
☎ 296868981 FAX 296869922
(From N176, take Plouër exit and turn towards Plouër. Driving along D12, do not enter village, stay on road for 3km and the house is on right hand side.)
This elegant 19th-century, stone-built country house is situated on the outskirts of the village, and was restored by its British owners both to preserve its original charm, and to offer modern-day comforts. Enjoy summer meals on a private terrace set in a lovely floral garden; in winter you have the warmth of full central heating, plus a traditional open fireplace in the spacious lounge. There is a fine watercolour collection for art lovers. The area offers river/countryside walks, excellent restaurants and simple bistros.
Near river  Near lake  Near sea  Near beach  Forest area  Near motorway
*Closed Feb*
*4 en suite (bth/shr) (3 fmly) No smoking on premises Full central heating Open parking available Bicycle rental Open terrace Last d 20.00hrs Languages spoken: English & German*
ROOMS: s 330FF; d 350FF
MEALS: Dinner 99-119FF
CARDS: ●● ☲ Travellers cheques

## DINARD Ille-et-Vilaine

★ ★ **Altair**
18 bld Féart *35800*
☎ 299461358 FAX 299882049
(in Dinard follow signs for 'Plage')
Near sea  Near beach  In town centre
*RS Mon in winter*
*21 en suite (bth/shr) (7 fmly) (2 with balcony) TV in all bedrooms Direct dial from all bedrooms Licensed Full central heating Child discount available Last d 21.30hrs Languages spoken: English*
ROOMS: (room only) s 250-290FF; d 310-490FF

**Reductions over 1 night  Special breaks**
MEALS: Full breakfast 38FF  Continental breakfast 38FF
Lunch 78-250FF&alc  Dinner 95-250FF&alc
CARDS: ● ▆ ▆ ● JCB Travellers cheques

★ ★ *Hotel Amethyste*
pl du Calvaire *35800*
☎ 299466181 FAX 299469691
Near sea  Near beach  In town centre
*20 en suite (shr)  (3 fmly)  (2 with balcony)  TV in all bedrooms*
*STV  Direct dial from all bedrooms  Licensed  Full central*
*heating  Open parking available  Supervised  Bicycle rental*
*Open terrace  Languages spoken: English & Italian*
CARDS: ● ▆ ▆ Travellers cheques

★ ★ **Inter Hotel Balmoral**
26 rue du Ml-Leclerc *35800*
☎ 299461697 FAX 299882048
In the town centre, the hotel is only 200 metres from the beach,
promenade and casino. It has a relaxed atmosphere
throughout and offers traditionally decorated guest rooms
with well equipped private facilities. It has a congenial bar
where guests can enjoy an aperitif, before seeking out one of
the restaurants in the vicinity.

Near sea  Near beach  In town centre  Near motorway
*Closed 15 Nov-15 Dec*
*31 en suite (bth/shr)  (2 fmly)  (22 with balcony)  TV in all*
*bedrooms  Direct dial from all bedrooms  Licensed  Lift  Night*
*porter  Full central heating  Child discount available 8yrs*
*Languages spoken: English,Spanish & German*
CARDS: ● ▆ ▆ ● JCB Travellers cheques

★ ★ ★ *Roche Corneilée*
4 rue Georges Clemenceau *35800*
☎ 299461447 FAX 299464080
Near sea  In town centre  Near motorway
*Closed mid Nov-mid Mar*
*28 en suite (bth/shr)  (3 fmly)  (5 with balcony)  TV in all*
*bedrooms  Direct dial from all bedrooms  Licensed  Lift  Full*
*central heating  Child discount available 12yrs  Last d 21.30hrs*
*Languages spoken: English*
CARDS: ● ▆ ▆ Travellers cheques

★ ★ *La Vallée*
6 av George V *35800*
☎ 299469400 FAX 299882247
(On the western extremity of the town overlooking the sea)
The hotel enjoys a peaceful location by the sea, yet is situated
just seconds away from the centre. It offers rooms with all

modern conveniences and a gourmet restaurant where lobster
and other seafood specialities feature strongly on the menu.
Near sea  Near beach
*RS Tue in low season*
*23 en suite (bth/shr)  (6 fmly)  (6 with balcony)  TV in all*
*bedrooms  Direct dial from all bedrooms  Room-safe  Licensed*
*Lift  Full central heating  Open parking available (charged)*
*Child discount available 8yrs  Bicycle rental  Open terrace*
*Covered terrace  V meals  Last d 21.00hrs  Languages spoken:*
*English, German & Italian*

*La Valée*
ROOMS: (room only) s 300-450FF; d 300-550FF
✱ **Reductions over 1 night**
MEALS: Continental breakfast 40FF  Lunch 120-300FF&alc
Dinner 120-300FF&alc✱
CARDS: ● ▆ Travellers cheques

**DINÉAULT** Finistère

*Rolzac'h* (Prop: Anne-Marie L'Haridon)
*29150*
☎ 298862209
Near river  Forest area
*4 en suite (shr)  No smoking in all bedrooms  TV in 2*
*bedrooms  Full central heating  Open parking available*
*Supervised*

**DOL-DE-BRETAGNE** Ille-et-Vilaine

*Manoir de Launay Blot* (Prop: M Bernard Mabile)
Baguer Morvan *35120*
☎ 299480748
(from Dol-de-Bretagne take N176 to Dinan. At last set of lights
take D119 to Baguer-Morvan. Follow signs for Manoir de
Launay Blot)
Near lake  Forest area
*3 en suite (bth)  No smoking in 1 bedroom  Full central heating*
*Open parking available  Supervised  Fishing  Languages*
*spoken: English*
CARDS: ▆ Travellers cheques

**DOMALAIN** Ille-et-Vilaine

*Les Hairies* (Prop: Mauries Templon)
*05680*
☎ 299763629
Forest area  Near motorway
*2 en suite (shr)  (1 fmly)  (1 with balcony)  No smoking on*
*premises  Full central heating  Open parking available  No*
*children 6yrs* contd.

## DOUARNENEZ Finistère

**Kerleguer** (Prop: Jean Larour)
*29100*
☎ 298923464
(from Douarnenez take D765 towards Audierne for 1km, then 3rd on right and follow 'Chambre d'Hôte' signs for 500mtrs)
Near sea  Near beach
*2 en suite (bth/shr)  Full central heating  Open parking available*

**Manoir de Kervent** (Prop: Marie-Paule Lefloch)
Pouldavid *29100*
☎ 298920490 FAX 296920490
Near sea  Near beach  Forest area
*(1 fmly)  Full central heating  Open parking available  Child discount available 5yrs*
CARDS: Travellers cheques

## ELLIANT Finistère

**Ferme de Quelennec** (Prop: M & Mme Le Berre)
Quelennec *29370*
☎ 298591043
(on D15 between Coray and Quimper)
Near river  Forest area
*4 en suite (bth/shr)  No smoking on premises  TV available  Full central heating  Open parking available  Child discount available*
CARDS: Travellers cheques

## ERDEVEN Morbihan

★★ **Auberge du Sous Bois**
rte de Pont Lorois *56410*
☎ 297556610 FAX 297556882
(Access via N165 to Auray, D768 to Plouharnel, then D781 to Erdeven)
This is a typical Breton hotel situated in a park with pine trees, where the proprietor and his family offer their visitors a warm welcome. The rooms are equipped with modern amenities and provide a high standard of comfort. The menu comprises traditional dishes combined with fresh seafood specialities.

Near sea  Near beach  Forest area
*Closed Oct-Mar*
*21 en suite (bth/shr)  TV in all bedrooms  STV  Direct dial from all bedrooms  Licensed  Full central heating  Open parking available  Child discount available 10yrs  Open terrace  Last d 21.00hrs  Languages spoken: English*

ROOMS: (room only) d 180-380FF
**Reductions over 1 night**
MEALS: Full breakfast 45FF  Lunch 84-192FF&alc  Dinner 84-192FF&alc
CARDS: ●● ■■ ▄▄ ⑩ Travellers cheques

★★ **Des Voyageurs**
14 rue de l'Océan *56410*
☎ 297556447 FAX 297556424
Near sea  Near beach  Forest area  In town centre  Near motorway
*Closed Oct-Mar*
*20 rms (1 fmly)  (4 with balcony)  TV in all bedrooms  Licensed  Open parking available  Child discount available  V meals  Last d 21.00hrs  Languages spoken: English*
CARDS: ●● ▄▄ Travellers cheques

## ERQUY Côtes-D'Armor

★★★ **Les Ruaux Les Bruyères** (Prop: M & Mme Dutemple)
*22430*
☎ 296723159 FAX 296720468
Quiet and comfort await you in this typical Breton home, which has a kitchen and dining room at guests' disposal. There is also a gite, with half-board available for four persons. There are plenty of restaurants nearby. Erquy has a pretty fishing harbour and is within 15 kilometres of the Fort La Latte. The beaches are of fine sand.
Near sea  Near beach
*6 en suite (shr)  (2 fmly)  (1 with balcony)  No smoking on premises  Full central heating  Open parking available  Child discount available 18yrs  Boule  Bicycle rental*
ROOMS: s 250FF; d 330FF
MEALS: Lunch 110-180FF  Dinner 110-180FF
CARDS: ●● ■■ ▄▄ Eurocard Travellers cheques

## FORÊT-FOUESNANT, LA Finistère

★★ **Aux Cerisiers**
3 rue des Cersiers *29940*
☎ 298569724
*16 en suite (shr)  TV available  STV  Licensed  Full central heating  Open parking available  Supervised  Child discount available  Golf  Open terrace  Last d 21.30hrs  Languages spoken: English*
CARDS: ●● ▄▄

★★ **Hotel de l'Espérance**
6 rue Charles-de-Gaulle *29940*
☎ 298569658 FAX 298514225
(from Quimper take D783 towards Concarneau)
Near sea  Near beach  Forest area  In town centre  Near motorway
*Closed Oct-Mar*
*27 rms (24 bth/shr)  18 rooms in annexe  (9 fmly)  (2 with balcony)  TV in all bedrooms  Direct dial from all bedrooms  Licensed  Full central heating  Open parking available  Child discount available 12yrs  Open terrace  Last d 21.00hrs  Languages spoken: English & German*
ROOMS: (room only) s 176-288FF; d 220-360FF
**Reductions over 1 night**
MEALS: Continental breakfast 36FF  Lunch 95-250FF&alc  Dinner 95-250FF&alc
CARDS: ●● ▄▄ Travellers cheques

**★ ★ ★ ★ Manoir du Stang**
*29940*
☎ 298569737 FAX 298569737
(from N165 take Concarneau/Fouesnant exit and follow D783
to hotel on private drive)
Near lake  Near sea  Near beach  Forest area
*24 en suite (bth/shr)  Direct dial from all bedrooms  Licensed*
*Lift  Full central heating  Open parking available  Child discount*
*available 10yrs  Golf 18  Tennis  Open terrace  Covered terrace*
*Last d 20.30hrs*
ROOMS: (room only) s 490-570FF; d 580-960FF
**Reductions over 1 night**
MEALS: Continental breakfast 50FF  Dinner 180-190FF
CARDS: Travellers cheques

**★ ★ De la Pointe de Mousterlin**
108 route de la Pointe, de Mousterlin *29170*
☎ 298560412 FAX 298566102
(from Quimper enter Fouesnant and turn right after the cinema)
This comfortable family hotel is tucked away amidst rocks with
a beautiful beach either side and has fine views of the small
fishing harbour. All the bedrooms have en suite facilities,
whilst a number of larger rooms also have balconies. The
restaurant serves local fresh fish produce as well as shellfish.
The comfortable lounge invites guests for a game of bridge or
chess, whilst a large choice of leisure facilities is available for

the more energetic.
Near sea  Near beach
*Closed 30 Sep-mid Oct*
*47 en suite (bth/shr)  20 rooms in annexe  (40 fmly)  (30 with*
*balcony)  TV in all bedrooms  Direct dial from all bedrooms*
*Licensed  Lift  Full central heating  Open parking available*
*Child discount available  Tennis  Sauna  Gym  Boule  Jacuzzi/spa*
*Bicycle rental  Open terrace  V meals  Last d 22.00hrs*
*Languages spoken: English & German*
ROOMS: (room only) s 286-400FF; d 300-490FF
MEALS: Continental breakfast 45FF  Lunch 85-200FF  Dinner
95-200FF
CARDS: 💳 💳 💳 Travellers cheques

**Bed & Breakfast** (Prop: M & Mme Juban)
5 chemin du Patis *35300*
☎ 299990052
Near river  Forest area
*Closed Dec-Feb*
*4 rms (2 bth/shr)  No smoking on premises  Full central heating*
*Open parking available  Supervised*

**Le Manoir St-Michel**
La Carquois *22240*
☎ 296414887 FAX 296414155
Near lake  Near sea  Near beach
*Closed 4 Nov-Mar*
*5 en suite (bth/shr)  (1 fmly)  TV in all bedrooms  Full central*
*heating  Open parking available  Child discount available  Fishing*
*Riding  Boule  Bicycle rental  Languages spoken: English*

**Le Relais de Frehél** (Prop: Myriam Fournel)
Plevenon *22240*
☎ 296414302 FAX 296413009
(from A11 to Rennes/St Malo N137 St Malo/Matignon then
onto D16 for Cap Fréhel)
Restored old farm close to bird reserve and the Fort la Latte. In
an attractive area where the many activities include fishing,
hiking, golf and riding.

Near sea  Near beach  Forest area
*Closed Nov-Mar*
*5 en suite (bth/shr)  (3 fmly)  No smoking on premises  Full*
*central heating  Open parking available  Child discount*
*available  Tennis  Table tennis  Languages spoken: English*
ROOMS: d 300FF
CARDS: 💳 💳

**Les Viviers** (Prop: Mr Dugueperoux)
*35490*
☎ 299395019 FAX 299395019
(from Rennes take N175 north, through St Aubin and turn
right to Gahard)
Near river  Forest area  Near motorway
*4 en suite (bth/shr)  (2 fmly)  TV in 1 bedroom  Full central*
*heating  Open parking available  Child discount available  10*
*Languages spoken: N*
ROOMS: s fr 180FF; d 200-255FF
MEALS: Dinner 65-95FF
CARDS: 💳 Travellers cheques

**Moulin de Kerlaviou** (Prop: Mme Therese Cornily)
*29410*
☎ 298796057
Near river  Forest area  Near motorway
*Closed Etr-Oct*
*2 en suite (bth/shr)  No smoking on premises  Full central*
*heating  Open parking available  Supervised  Fishing*    *contd.*

### GUIMILIAU Finistère

**Croas Avel** (Prop: Christine Croguennec)
*29400*
☎ 298687072
*3 en suite (bth/shr) No smoking on premises TV available Full central heating Open parking available*

### GUIPAVAS Finistère

**La Chataigneraie Keraveloc** (Prop: Michelle Morvan)
*29490*
☎ 298415268 FAX 298414840
(from Guipavas take D712 towards Brest for 3.5km, then left at traffic lights towards Keraveloc and follow signs)
The house stands on high ground amidst its own pleasant gardens, that boast panoramic sea views. Nearby are the 'Vallon du Stangalard' and its botanic gardens. Oceanopolis Marine Centre and the harbour are only 2km away.

Near sea Near beach Forest area
*4 en suite (bth/shr) (1 fmly) No smoking on premises TV in all bedrooms Full central heating Open parking available Covered parking available Child discount available 6yrs Indoor swimming pool (heated) Boule Games room Garden barbecue Library Languages spoken: English & Spanish*
ROOMS: s 240FF; d 280FF **Reductions over 1 night**
CARDS: Travellers cheques

### GUISSENY Finistère

**Keraloret** (Prop: M Pierre Le Gall)
*29880*
☎ 298256037 FAX 298256988
(from Roscoff take D10 (right off D58) towards Brest. At Goulven take D10 to Plouguerneau to milestone 37)
An old granite farmhouse with tasteful antique furnishings, comfortable bedrooms and well equipped public areas.
Near river Near lake Near sea Near beach
*6 en suite (bth/shr) (3 fmly) No smoking in 2 bedrooms TV in 1 bedroom Full central heating Open parking available Covered parking available Supervised Child discount available 12yrs Games room Volleyball V meals Last d 21.00hrs Languages spoken: English, German & Spanish*
ROOMS: s fr 235FF; d 285FF
MEALS: Dinner 100FF
CARDS: 💳 💳 Travellers cheques

### HENNEBONT Morbihan

★ ★ ★ ★ **Château de Locguénolé**
rte de Port-Louis *56700*
☎ 297762904 FAX 297768235
Near river Near sea Near beach Forest area
*Closed 4 Jan-5 Feb*
*22 en suite (bth) 10 rooms in annexe (5 fmly) TV in all bedrooms STV Direct dial from all bedrooms Mini-bar in all bedrooms Room-safe Licensed Full central heating Open parking available Child discount available 12yrs Outdoor swimming pool (heated) Tennis Fishing Sauna Solarium Bicycle rental Open terrace V meals Last d 21.30hrs Languages spoken: English, German & Italian*
CARDS: 💳 💳 💳 💳 Travellers cheques

### HIREL Ille-et-Vilaine

**La Maison de Quokelunde** (Prop: M Jean Paul Raux)
41 rue Bord-de-Mer *35120*
☎ 299488012 FAX 299488012
Four of the rooms in La Maison de Quokelunde look directly out onto the bay of Mont St Michel. Communal living room for breakfast. Picnic tables outside. Special offers out of season, discounts for children.

Near sea
*5 en suite (shr) (4 fmly) No smoking in 4 bedrooms TV in all bedrooms Full central heating Open parking available Child discount available*
ROOMS: s 200FF; d 250-300FF
CARDS: Travellers cheques

### IFFS, LES Ille-et-Vilaine

**Château de Montmuran** (Prop: Herne de la Villeon)
*35630*
☎ 299458888 FAX 299458490
(autoroute Rennes-St Malo exit Tinteniac/Becherel then follow signs)
Forest area Near motorway
*Closed Nov-Apr*
*2 en suite (bth/shr) Full central heating Open parking available Languages spoken: English*

### ILE-AUX-MOINES Morbihan

**Le San Francisco**
Le Port *56780*
☎ 297263152 FAX 297263559
(N165 Nantes/Brest, exit Vannes-Ouest take direction Ile aux Moines)

Near lake  Near sea  Near beach  Forest area
*Closed 4 Dec-24 Mar*
*8 en suite (bth/shr) (1 fmly) (1 with balcony) TV in all*
*bedrooms  Direct dial from all bedrooms  Licensed  Child*
*discount available 10yrs  Open terrace  Last d 20.30hrs*
*Languages spoken: English & German*
CARDS: 💳 💳 💳 💳 Travellers cheques

---

### ILE-DE-GROIX Morbihan

**Les Cornorans** (Prop: Jacques & Catherine Hardy)
rue du Chalutier les Deux Ange *56590*
☎ 297865767
Near sea
*3 en suite (shr) (1 fmly)  No smoking on premises  Full central*
*heating  Open parking available  Supervised*

**La Grek** (Prop: Pascale Le Touze)
3 pl du Leurhé *56590*
☎ 297868985 FAX 297865828
(regular passenger/vehicle ferry service to the island. La Grek
situated 150mtrs from St-Tudy church)
Charming old restored house, furnished with antiques. It is set
on Groix Island in Southern Brittany, and guests may enjoy the
pleasures of solitude; sea breeze, fresh air and a sense of
escape. Take advantage of these pleasures from the garden or
stroll around the island. Breton continental breakfast served.
Free for children under six years.
Near sea  Near beach
*4 en suite (bth/shr) (2 fmly)  No smoking on premises  Full*
*central heating  Open parking available  Child discount*
*available 6yrs  Boule  Bicycle rental  Badminton  Table tennis*
*Languages spoken: English*
ROOMS: s 270FF; d 300FF

---

### INZINZAC-LOCHRIST Morbihan

**Tymat-Penquesten** (Prop: Catherine Spence)
*56650*
☎ 297368926 FAX 297368926
(from Lochrist towards Penquesten establishment 3.5kms on
left)
Near river  Forest area
*4 en suite (bth)  No smoking on premises  Full central heating*
*Open parking available  Supervised  Languages spoken: English*
CARDS: Travellers cheques

---

### JOSSELIN Morbihan

**Bed & Breakfast** (Prop: M & Mme Jean & Marie Guyot)
Butte St-Laurent *56120*
☎ 297222209 FAX 297339010
(half a mile from the town centre. Signposted)
Near river  Forest area  Near motorway
*Closed 21 Sep-Mar*
*4 en suite (bth/shr) (1 fmly)  No smoking on premises  Full*
*central heating  Open parking available  Covered parking*
*available  Child discount available 15yrs*

**Bed & Breakfast** (Prop: Mr & Mrs A Braidley)
13 rue St Jacques *56120*
☎ 297739317 FAX 297739317
(from N24 Rennes/Ploermel, pass Ploermel & take 2nd sign for
Josselin off autoroute, at junction turn left, towards rdbt at
rdbt take 2nd turning towards town centre follow main road
for approx 0.5 miles B&B on right)

Near river  Near lake  Near sea  Near beach  Forest area  In
town centre  Near motorway
*Closed Oct-Jan*
*4 en suite (shr) (2 fmly)  Open parking available  Child discount*
*available 14yrs  Languages spoken: English*
ROOMS: s 150FF; d 220FF  **Special breaks**
MEALS: Dinner 100FF
CARDS: Travellers cheques

**La Carrière** (Prop: M et Mme Bignon)
8 rue de la Carrière *56120*
☎ 297222262 FAX 297222262
(just over midway between Rennes and Lorient off the N24)
Near river  Forest area  In town centre  Near motorway
*7 rms (6 bth/shr)  Full central heating  Open parking available*
*Languages spoken: English & German*
CARDS: 💳 💳 Travellers cheques

---

### KERLAZ Finistère

**Bed & Breakfast** (Prop: M & Mme H Gonidec)
Lanevry *29100*
☎ 298921912 FAX 298921912
Near river  Near sea  Forest area
*Full central heating  Open parking available  Covered parking*
*available  Supervised*
CARDS: Travellers cheques

---

### LAMBALLE Côtes-D'Armor

**★ ★ Alizes**
La Ville es Lan *22400*
☎ 296311637 FAX 296312389
Near lake  Near motorway
*Closed 24 Dec-8 Jan*
*72 rms (3 fmly) (16 with balcony)  TV in all bedrooms  Direct*
*dial from all bedrooms  Mini-bar in all bedrooms  Licensed*
*Night porter  Full central heating  Open parking available*
*Tennis  Pool table  Open terrace  Covered terrace  V meals  Last*
*d 21.45hrs  Languages spoken: English,Portuguese & Spanish*
CARDS: 💳 💳 💳 Travellers cheques

**★ ★ ★ D'Angleterre**
29 bd Jobert M Toublanc *22400*
☎ 296310016 FAX 296319154
In town centre
*20 rms (19 bth/shr)  TV in all bedrooms  Radio in rooms  Direct*
*dial from all bedrooms  Mini-bar in all bedrooms  Licensed  Lift*
*Night porter  Full central heating  Covered parking available*
*(charged)  Supervised  Child discount available 8yrs  Bicycle*
*rental  Open terrace  V meals  Last d 21.30hrs  Languages*
*spoken: English*
MEALS: Continental breakfast 40FF  Lunch 80-240FF&alc
Dinner 99-240FF&alc
CARDS: JCB

---

### LAMPAUL-GUIMILIAU Finistère

**★ ★ Hotel de L'Enclos**
rte de St-Jacques *29400*
☎ 298687708 FAX 298686106
(leave N12 at Landivisau exit, turn right at 1st roundabout &
left at 2nd roundabout)
Near river  Forest area  Near motorway
*36 en suite (bth)  TV in all bedrooms  Direct dial from all*
*bedrooms  Licensed  Open parking available  Child discount*

*contd.*

available 12yrs  Open terrace  V meals  Last d 21.30hrs
Languages spoken: English
CARDS: ●● ■■ ▨▨ ◎ Travellers cheques

**Pen Ar Yed** (Prop: Claude Gaschet)
*29400*
☎ 298686105
Near river  Forest area  Near motorway
Closed mid Oct-mid Nov
2 en suite (shr)  Full central heating  Open parking available
Supervised  Languages spoken: English
CARDS: Travellers cheques

## LANCIEUX Côtes-D'Armor

**Les Hortensias** (Prop: Cosson)
40 rue du Moulin *22770*
☎ 296863115
(between Ploubalay and Lancieux)
Near sea  Near beach  Forest area
4 en suite (shr)  (2 fmly)  No smoking on premises  Full central
heating  Open parking available  Languages spoken: English
CARDS: Travellers cheques

## LANDAUL Morbihan

**Bed & Breakfast** (Prop: Mme Odile Plunian)
27 rue de Kermabergal *56690*
☎ 297246110
Near river  Near sea  Forest area  Near motorway
Closed mid Sep-Etr
3 en suite (bth/shr)  No smoking on premises  Full central
heating  Open parking available  Child discount available

## LANDÉBIA Côtes-D'Armor

**Le Pont a l'Ane** (Prop: Nichole Robert)
*22130*
☎ 296844752
(Rennes-Dinan-Plancoet)
Near river  Forest area
Closed Dec-Feb
5 en suite (shr)  No smoking on premises  Full central heating
Open parking available  Languages spoken: English

## LANDUDEC Finistère

**Château du Guilguiffin** (Prop: Philippe Davy)
*29710*
☎ 298915211 FAX 298915252
(in Quimper follow direction to Audierne on D784, approx
16km from Quimper & 3km before arriving in the village of
Landudec, turn left & follow the sign for chateau entrance)
Near river  Near sea  Near beach  Forest area  Near motorway
Apr-15 Nov
6 en suite (bth/shr)  (2 with balcony)  TV in 2 bedrooms  Full
central heating  Open parking available  Languages spoken:
English & German
ROOMS: d 650-800FF ✱
CARDS: ●● ■■ ▨▨ ◎ Travellers cheques

## LANDUJAN Ille-et-Vilaine

**Château-de-Leauville**
*35360*
☎ 299072114 FAX 299072180
Near sea  Forest area  Near motorway

Closed 16 Oct-Mar open Etr
8 en suite (bth/shr)  (4 fmly)  Radio in rooms  Full central
heating  Open parking available  No children 6yrs  Child
discount available 12yrs  Outdoor swimming pool (heated)
Open terrace  Languages spoken: English
CARDS: ●● ▨▨ Travellers cheques

## LANGOAT Côtes-D'Armor

**Bed & Breakfast** (Prop: Marie Francoise Bouget)
9 rue du Fort Castel *22450*
☎ 296913212
(from Guingamp take D8 towards La Roche-Derrien, then D6
towards Langoat. In Langoat centre follow Bégard road and
take 1st left)

In an ideal situation between Perros-Guirec and Paimpol on
the Côte de Granit, with comfortable accommodation and a
large garden.
Near river  Near sea  Near beach
1 rms (1 fmly)  No smoking on premises  Full central heating
Open parking available
ROOMS: d 300FF

## LARMOR-PLAGE Morbihan

**Les Camelias** (Prop: Paulette Allamo)
9 rue des Roseaux *56520*
☎ 297655067
(exit N165 signposted Lorient Larmor Plage and in town centre
take direction for Kerpape Lomener for 100mtrs, house by
traffic lights)
Near sea  Near beach
5 en suite (shr)  No smoking on premises  Full central heating
CARDS: Travellers cheques

## LESCONIL Finistère

★ ★ **Atlantic**
11 rue Jean Jaurès *29740*
☎ 298878106 FAX 298878804
(Approach via Quimper. Hotel close to Port de Pêche)
Near sea  Forest area  In town centre
Closed 30 Sep-1 Apr
24 en suite (bth/shr)  (2 fmly)  TV in all bedrooms  Direct dial
from all bedrooms  Licensed  Full central heating  Air
conditioning in bedrooms  Open parking available  Supervised
Child discount available 10yrs  Riding  Boule  Bicycle rental
Open terrace  Covered terrace  ping pong  Last d 21.00hrs
Languages spoken: English
CARDS: ●● ■■ ▨▨ Travellers cheques

## LOC-EGUINER-ST-THÉGONNEC Finistère

**Ty Dreux** (Prop: Anne Martin)
*29410*
☎ 298780821
Near river Forest area
*2 en suite (bth/shr) No smoking on premises TV available Full central heating Open parking available Supervised*

## LOCMINÉ Morbihan

★ ★ **L'Argoat**
pl Anne de Bretagne *56500*
☎ 297600102 FAX 297442055
Forest area In town centre
*Closed 15 Dec-15 Jan*
*TV available Licensed Full central heating Open parking available Covered parking available Supervised Child discount available V meals Last d 21.00hrs Languages spoken: English & Spanish*
CARDS: 💳 Travellers cheques

## LOCOAL-MENDON Morbihan

**Kervihern** (Prop: Gabriel Maho)
*56550*
☎ 297246409
Near river Near sea
*6 en suite (shr) (1 fmly) Full central heating Open parking available Child discount available 14yrs Languages spoken: English*
ROOMS: d 240-260FF ✱
MEALS: Dinner 85FF✱
CARDS: Travellers cheques

## LOCQUIREC Finistère

**Bed & Breakfast** (Prop: Comte/Comtesse Hubert Germiny)
11 rue de Kerael *29241*
☎ 298674711 FAX 298674711
(approach via D84. Signposted in Locquirec)
This property is owned by the Count and Countess Hubert Le Bègue de Germiny and is situated on the edge of a protected village. Elegant décor, with antique furniture. Comfortable and spacious rooms. Pretty garden with view of the sea and the coast. Excellent breakfasts and dinners by arrangement.
Near river Near sea Near beach
*Closed 15 Oct-14 Apr*
*4 rms (3 bth/shr) (1 fmly) No smoking on premises Full central heating Open parking available No children 1yr Child discount available Boule TV room Table tennis Languages spoken: English, Italian, German & Spanish*
ROOMS: s fr 350FF; d fr 400FF **Reductions over 1 night**
CARDS: Travellers cheques

## LOCUNOLÉ Finistère

**La Biquerie** (Prop: C Guimard)
*29310*
☎ 298713226 FAX 298714120
Near river Near lake Near sea Near beach Forest area Near motorway
*6 en suite (shr) Open parking available Languages spoken: English*

## LOUARGAT Côtes-D'Armor

★ ★ **Hotel le Manoir du Cleuziou**
St-Eloi *22540*
☎ 296431490 FAX 296435259
(14 km W of Guingamp via N12, exit at Louargat from the church in the village follow signs)
A 15th century manor house, beautiful buildings full of character with carved stone fireplaces, lovely doors and tapesteries. All the small bedrooms are comfortable. Good food is served in the dining room and there is an interesting bar in the old cellars.
Near river Near sea Near beach Forest area Near motorway
*Closed Jan-Mar*
*22 en suite (bth/shr) (3 fmly) TV available STV Licensed Full central heating Open parking available Supervised Child discount available 12yrs Outdoor swimming pool (heated) Tennis Boule Mini-golf Open terrace V meals Last d 21.30hrs Languages spoken: English & German*
ROOMS: (room only) d 420FF
MEALS: Continental breakfast 40FF Lunch 160-260FF&alc Dinner 160-260FF&alc
CARDS: 💳 💳 💳

## LOUDÉAC Côtes-D'Armor

★ ★ **Des Voyageurs**
10 rue de Cadélac *22600*
☎ 296280047 FAX 296282230
(SW of town centre)
Near lake Forest area In town centre
*28 en suite (bth/shr) (2 fmly) (12 with balcony) TV in all bedrooms STV Direct dial from all bedrooms Mini-bar in 4 bedrooms Licensed Lift Full central heating Covered parking available Supervised Child discount available 12yrs Bicycle rental V meals Last d 21.30hrs Languages spoken: English & German*
CARDS: 💳 💳 💳 💳 Travellers cheques

## LOUVIGNÉ-DU-DÉSERT Ille-et-Vilaine

**La Basse Grezilière** (Prop: M & Mme R K Tubbs)
St-Georges-de-Reintembault *35420*
☎ 299971019
(St-James is on the D998 & is equidistant from Avranches & Fougères. St-Georges de Reintembault is well signposted from St-James off the D30, approx 6kms)
17th-century stone farmhouse, which has been beautifully restored, retaining its original oak beams, open fireplace and bread oven. Two double bedrooms are on offer, sharing a large bathroom/WC. Guests are completely separate from their English hosts. Situated just over a mile from the Normandy/Brittany border surrounded by fields and orchards. Many restaurants in close proximity.
Near river Near lake Near sea Near beach Forest area Near motorway
*2 rms No smoking on premises Full central heating Open parking available Supervised No children 5yrs Languages spoken: English*
ROOMS: d fr 250FF

## MEILLAC Ille-et-Vilaine

**Bed & Breakfast** (Prop: Nelly & Christian Dragon)
La Ville Guimon *35270*
☎ 299731717
Forest area
*Closed Nov-Feb*
*2 en suite (shr) Full central heating Open parking available*

## MELRAND Morbihan

**Bed & Breakfast** (Prop: M & Mme Chauvel)
Quenetevec *56310*
☎ 297277282 FAX 297277282
(5km from Melrand, 10km from Pontivy)
Near river Forest area
*Closed Jan-Feb & 8 days Oct*
*4 en suite (bth/shr) (1 fmly) TV in 1 bedroom Full central heating Open parking available Child discount available Outdoor swimming pool (heated) Table tennis Volleyball*

## MERDRIGNAC Côtes-D'Armor

**Manoir de la Peignie** (Prop: François Rogis Marie)
rue du Mené *22230*
☎ 296284286 FAX 296674229
Near river Near lake Forest area In town centre
*5 en suite (bth/shr) (2 fmly) No smoking in 3 bedrooms TV available Radio in rooms Full central heating Open parking available Covered parking available*

## MESLAN Morbihan

**Bed & Breakfast** (Prop: Mme Jambou)
Roscalet *56320*
☎ 297342413 FAX 297342413
(from D769 towards Morlaix, take exit for Meslan on D6, then left towards 'Les Roches du Diable' for 4km)
Near river Forest area
*Closed Nov-Mar*
*5 en suite (shr) No smoking on premises Full central heating Open parking available Covered parking available Supervised Boule Languages spoken: English*
Rooms: s 230FF; d 260FF ✱

## MOËLAN-SUR-MER Finistère

**Trenogoat** (Prop: M & Mme Williams)
*29350*
☎ 298396282 FAX 298397809
(from centre of Moëlan-sur-Mer, take D24 signposted Clohars/Carnoët/Lorient and at roundabout turn right. After 50mtrs turn left signposted Merrien-le-Port. Follow road for 2.5kms)
An English family-run, restored Breton farmhouse situated two minutes from the sea in the midst of unspoilt countryside. En suite bedrooms, dining room, large comfortable sitting room, games room, laundry. Two and half acres of grounds, including orchard, farmyard with small animals, barbecue, boules. Generous breakfasts.
Near river Near sea Near beach Forest area
*Closed mid Oct-Etr*
*6 en suite (shr) (1 fmly) No smoking in all bedrooms Licensed Full central heating Open parking available Supervised Boule Open terrace Billiard table Languages spoken: English*
Rooms: s 220FF; d 270FF
Cards: ●● ▆▆

## MORÉAC Morbihan

**Kerivin** (Prop: M & Mme Le Sergent)
*56500*
☎ 297601888 & 683031845
Forest area Near motorway
*4 en suite (shr) No smoking in 2 bedrooms Full central heating Open parking available*
Rooms: s 175FF; d 240FF

## NOYAL PONTIVY Morbihan

**Pennerest** (Prop: P Roberts)
*56920*
☎ 297383576 FAX 297382380
(on arrival in Pontivy follow direction to Vannes/Josselin, fork left on D764 to Josselin, after 4km there is crossroads take the next turn on right 'Pennerest')
A friendly welcome awaits guests at this attractively decorated, inexpensive accommodation. There are three acres of grounds, with lawns, orchard and garden furniture, amenities include a swimming pool, table tennis and games room. Weekly barbecue is organised for approx 40 people.
Near river Near lake Forest area Near motorway
*2 en suite (shr) (1 fmly) Full central heating Open parking available No children 5yrs Outdoor swimming pool Tennis Boule Croquet Badminton Table tennis Languages spoken: English*

## PACÉ Ille-et-Vilaine

**Manoir de Méhault** (Prop: Herve Barre)
*35740*
☎ 299606288
(6km from Rennes in direction St Brieuc. In Pacé continue towards L'Hermitage for 2km)
This restored 17th-century manor near Rennes, is surrounded by a park of trees and flowers. Guests may use the barbecue in the garden. Golf, riding, tennis, swimming, lakes and forests nearby. 35 minutes from St Malo.
Near river Forest area Near motorway
*Closed Nov-Mar*
*5 rms (4 bth/shr) (2 fmly) Full central heating Open parking available Supervised Languages spoken: English*

## PAIMPOL Côtes-D'Armor

★ ★ ★ *Le Barbu*
Pointe de l'Arcouest *22620*
☎ 296558698 FAX 296557387
Near sea Near beach
*20 en suite (bth/shr) (6 fmly) No smoking in 2 bedrooms TV in all bedrooms Direct dial from all bedrooms Licensed Full central heating Open parking available Covered parking available Supervised Child discount available 8yrs Outdoor swimming pool (heated) Sauna Solarium Gym Bicycle rental Open terrace Covered terrace Last d 21.00hrs Languages spoken: English*
Cards: ●● ▆▆ ▆▆ Travellers cheques

**Bed & Breakfast** (Prop: Jeanette le Goaster)
Ferme de Kerloury *22500*
☎ 296228523
(From Paimpol in direction of Lèzardrieux 1km after Leclerc supermarket then right then 3rd on left to village)
Renovated farm with attractive flower filled porch. The large lawned garden has a pond and a barbecue.

Near river  Near sea  Near beach
*4 rms (1 shr) (1 fmly) No smoking on premises  Open parking available  Languages spoken: English*

**★ ★ ★ Répaire de Kerroch**
29 quai Morand *22500*
☎ 296205013 FAX 296220746
(from St Briac, take 1st turn to Paimpol by coastal route or 2nd turn straight into town)
Near sea  Near beach  In town centre  Near motorway
*13 en suite (bth/shr) (1 fmly) (2 with balcony)  TV in all bedrooms  Direct dial from all bedrooms  Mini-bar in all bedrooms  Licensed  Lift  Full central heating  Child discount available 12yrs  Open terrace  V meals  Last d 21.30hrs  Languages spoken: English & Spanish*
CARDS: ● 🔲 Travellers cheques

**PAIMPONT** Ille-et-Vilaine

**★ ★ Relais de Broceliande**
5 rue des Forges *35380*
☎ 299078107 FAX 299078108
Near river  Near lake  Forest area
*23 rms  15 rooms in annexe  (6 fmly)  TV in all bedrooms  Licensed  Full central heating  Open parking available  Supervised  Child discount available 10yrs  Tennis  Fishing  Boule  Bicycle rental  Open terrace  Covered terrace  Casino  V meals  Last d 21.00hrs  Languages spoken: English & German*
CARDS: ● ■ 🔲 ⃝ Travellers cheques

**PERROS-GUIREC** Côtes-D'Armor

**★ ★ Hermitage Hotel**
20 rue le Montréer *22700*
☎ 296232122 FAX 296911656
Located in the centre of town and surrounded by a large garden,this hotel offers guests a relaxing stay in a warm and friendly atmosphere. The guest rooms are equipped with every modern convenience and provide a good level of comfort. The restaurant, open only in the evening, serves a range of dishes to suit most tastes.

Near sea  Near beach  In town centre
*Closed Oct-Apr*
*25 en suite (bth/shr) (2 fmly)  TV in all bedrooms  STV  Direct dial from all bedrooms  Licensed  Full central heating  Open parking available  Child discount available 10yrs  Open terrace  Last d 20.30hrs  Languages spoken: English*
ROOMS: (room only) s 230-250FF; d 285-320FF
**Reductions over 1 night**
MEALS: Continental breakfast 34FF  Dinner 98-120FF
CARDS: ● ■ 🔲 Travellers cheques

**PIRÉ-SUR-SEICHE** Ille-et-Vilaine

**Les Épinays** (Prop: M & Mme Colleu)
*35150*
☎ 299000116
Near river  Near motorway
*4 en suite (shr) (1 fmly)  No smoking on premises  TV available  Full central heating  Open parking available  Supervised  Languages spoken: English*

**PLANCOËT** Côtes-D'Armor

**La Pastourelle** (Prop: E Lede)
St-Lormel *22130*
☎ 296840377 FAX 296840377
Near river
*6 en suite (bth/shr) (1 fmly) (5 with balcony)  Full central heating  Child discount available 9yrs  Boule  Open terrace  Languages spoken: English*
CARDS: ■ Travellers cheques

**PLANGUENOUAL** Côtes-D'Armor

**★ ★ ★ Domaine du Val**
*22400*
☎ 296327540 FAX 296327150
Near river  Near sea  Forest area
*53 en suite (bth)  19 rooms in annexe  (6 fmly) (1 with balcony)  TV in all bedrooms  Direct dial from all bedrooms  Licensed  Night porter  Full central heating  Open parking available  Child discount available 12yrs  Indoor swimming pool (heated)  Tennis  Fishing  Squash  Sauna  Solarium  Gym  Boule  Jacuzzi/spa  Open terrace  Covered terrace  V meals  Languages spoken: English*
CARDS: ● 🔲 Travellers cheques

**PLÉNEUF-VAL-ANDRÉ** Côtes-D'Armor

**Hotel de la Mer**
63 r Amiral Charner *22370*
☎ 296722044 FAX 296728572
Near sea  Near beach
*Closed 5 Jan-15 Feb & 15 Nov-20 Dec*
*21 en suite (bth/shr)  8 rooms in annexe  (10 fmly) (6 with balcony)  TV in all bedrooms  Direct dial from all bedrooms  Licensed  Open parking available  Last d 21.30hrs*
ROOMS: (room only) d 210-300FF ✳
MEALS: Continental breakfast 32FF  Lunch 77-260FF  Dinner 77-260FF
CARDS: ● ■ 🔲 Travellers cheques

**PLÉRIN** Côtes-D'Armor

**★ ★ Chêne Vert**
rte de St-Laurent-de-la-Mer *22190*
☎ 296798020 FAX 296798021
(From the RN 12 exit rte de St-Laurent-de-la-Mer)
Near sea  Near beach  Forest area  Near motorway
*70 en suite (bth/shr)  16 rooms in annexe  (10 fmly)  No smoking in 10 bedrooms  TV in all bedrooms  STV  Radio in rooms  Direct dial from all bedrooms  Mini-bar in 13 bedrooms  Licensed  Full central heating  Open parking available  Child discount available 12yrs  Squash  Boule  Open terrace  Sqaush courts  Last d 22.00hrs  Languages spoken: English, German, Italian & Spanish*
CARDS: ● ■ 🔲 ⃝ Travellers cheques

### PLEUDIHEN-SUR-RANCE Côtes-D'Armor

**La Cour aux Meuniers** (Prop: Mme Therese Tartar-Hue)
6 rue des Camèlias *22690*
☎ 296833423 FAX 296832051
(on dual carriageway between St-Malo & Rennes, take the
Châteauneuf/Pleudihen exit (D74), then follow directions for
Pleudihen. Chambre d'hôte is behind church towards the
'Mairie')
Located on the Rance estuary, between Dinan and St Malo, this
traditional stone-built house in the village centre has
bedrooms with panoramic views of the fields and river. Tailor-
made breakfasts on offer in the typically Breton living room.
Near river  In town centre
*4 rms (1 bth 2 shr) (1 fmly) Radio in rooms*
*Full central heating Open parking available Child discount*
*available 5yrs Tennis nearby Table tennis Languages spoken:*
*English*
ROOMS: d 230-250FF **Reductions over 1 night**

**Le Vau Nogues** (Prop: Simone Mousson)
*22690*
☎ 296832294 FAX 296832294
Near river  Near sea  Forest area  Near motorway
*3 en suite (shr) (2 fmly) No smoking on premises Full central*
*heating Open parking available Supervised Child discount*
*available Last d 18.00hrs Languages spoken: English &*
*German*
CARDS: Travellers cheques

### PLEUGUENEUC-PLESDER Ille-et-Vilaine

**★ ★ ★ Château de la Motte-Beaumanoir**
La Motte-Beaumanoir *35720*
☎ 299694601 FAX 299694249
Near lake  Forest area  Near motorway
*6 en suite (bth) (2 fmly) Licensed Full central heating Open*
*parking available Supervised Child discount available 3yrs*
*Outdoor swimming pool (heated) Tennis Fishing Solarium*
*Bicycle rental Open terrace Languages spoken: English*
CARDS: ●● ■ ▓ Travellers cheques

### PLEURTUIT Ille-et-Vilaine

**★ ★ ★ Manoir de la Rance**
Château de Jourvente
☎ 299885376 FAX 299886303
(From Dinard or St Malo, head towards Richardais on the
D114 and take the second road on the left)
Near river  Near lake  Near sea  Near beach  Forest area
Closed 13 Nov-19 Mar
*10 en suite (bth/shr) 3 rooms in annexe (2 fmly) (1 with*
*balcony) TV in all bedrooms Licensed Full central heating*
*Open parking available Fishing Open terrace Languages*
*spoken: English & German*
CARDS: ●● ▓ Travellers cheques

### PLÉVEN Côtes-D'Armor

**★ ★ ★ Manoir du Vaumadeuc**
*22130*
☎ 296844617 FAX 296844016
(From Plancoet take the D768 towards Lamballe for 2km, Then
go left onto the D28 for about 7km to the village of Pleven. Go
through the village and you will see the Manoir Du Vaumadeuc)
A magnificent location in the heart of Penthièvre, is the setting

for this 15th-century building which will delight guests with its
authenticity and the warm welcome of the owners. The manor,
which has been in the same family for 200 years, has award-
winning formal French gardens.
Near river  Near lake  Forest area

**Manoir du Vaumadeuc**
Closed Nov-Etr
*13 en suite (bth/shr) 2 rooms in annexe (4 fmly) Direct dial*
*from all bedrooms Licensed Full central heating Open parking*
*available Child discount available 5yrs Fishing Open terrace*
*Last d 21.00hrs Languages spoken: English & Spanish*
ROOMS: (room only) s 590-1100FF; d 590-1100FF
**✱ Reductions over 1 night Special breaks**
MEALS: Continental breakfast 50FF  Dinner 195FF&alc✱
CARDS: ●● ■ ▓ ⑤ Travellers cheques

### PLOEMEUR Morbihan

**Le Petit Hanvot** (Prop: M Georges Mestric)
*56270*
☎ 297862234
(from Vannes to Quimper road exit Ploemeur Airport)
*3 en suite (shr) Full central heating Open parking available*
*Child discount available*

### PLOËRMEL Morbihan

**★ ★ ★ Golf Hotel du Roi Arthur**
Le Lac au Duc *56800*
☎ 297736464 FAX 297736450
(follow direction of Le Lac au Duc from Rennes or Vannes
roads)
Near lake  Near beach  Forest area
*46 en suite (bth/shr) (41 fmly) TV in all bedrooms STV Direct*
*dial from all bedrooms Licensed Lift Night porter Full central*
*heating Open parking available Supervised Indoor swimming*
*pool (heated) Golf 9 Fishing Riding Sauna Solarium Gym*
*Boule Jacuzzi/spa Bicycle rental Open terrace Last d 21.30hrs*
*Languages spoken: English, German & Spanish*
CARDS: ●● ■ ▓ ⑤ Travellers cheques

### PLOËZAL Côtes-D'Armor

**Ferme de Kerléo** (Prop: M & Mme Jean Louis Hervé)
*22260*
☎ 296956578 FAX 296951463
Near river  Forest area
*4 rms (2 shr) No smoking on premises Full central heating*
*Open parking available Supervised Child discount available*
*12yrs*
CARDS: Travellers cheques

## PLOGASTEL-ST-GERMAIN Finistère

**Kerguérnou** (Prop: M & Mme le Henaff)
*29710*
☎ 98545630
*6 en suite (bth/shr) Full central heating Open parking available*

## PLOGOFF Finistère

★ ★ **Ker Moor**
Plague de Loch-Pointe du Raz *29770*
☎ 298706206 FAX 298703269
Near sea
*16 rms (8 bth 4 shr) (2 fmly) No smoking in 1 bedroom TV in
all bedrooms Licensed Full central heating Open parking
available Boule Bicycle rental Open terrace Last d 21.30hrs
Languages spoken: English & Spanish*
CARDS: ● ■ Travellers cheques

**Ferme de Kerguidy Izella** (Prop: Jean Noel Le Bars)
*29770*
☎ 298703560
(exit Quimper Sud road in the direction Audierne Points du
Raz take D765 then D784)
Forest area
*6 en suite (shr) (1 fmly) TV available Full central heating Open
parking available Child discount available 7yrs*

## PLOMEUR Finistère

**Keraluic** (Prop: Irene et Luis Gomez-Centurion)
*29120*
☎ 298821022 FAX 298821022
(20km S from Quimper, D785 from Pont-l'Abbé to St Jean
Trolimon. Signposted.)
Irene and Luis welcome you to their old, restored Breton farm,
situated in the heart of the region, in the countryside and just
6km from the sea, near many tourist sites. The rooms are
located in a separate thatched cottage. Dinner by reservation.
Small camping area also available.
Near sea Near beach Forest area
*5 en suite (bth/shr) (2 with balcony) No smoking in 3 bedrooms
Full central heating Open parking available Child discount
available 3yrs Boule Bicycle rental Table tennis Volleyball
Languages spoken: English, German & Spanish*
ROOMS: d 340-380FF
MEALS: Dinner 110FF
CARDS: Travellers cheques

## PLONÉOUR-LAVERN Finistère

★ ★ **De La Mairie**
3 rue Jules Ferry *29720*
☎ 298876134 FAX 298877704
*18 rms (1 fmly) TV in all bedrooms Licensed Full central
heating Open parking available Child discount available Boule
Bicycle rental Open terrace V meals Last d 21.00hrs*
CARDS: ● ■ Travellers cheques

★ ★ **Manoir de Kerhuel**
Kerhuel *29720*
☎ 298826057 FAX 298826179
(towards Quimper exit Plonéour)
Near river Near lake Near sea Near beach Forest area
*Closed 4 Jan-Mid Mar*
*26 en suite (bth/shr) 3 rooms in annexe (6 fmly) (1 with
balcony) TV in all bedrooms Direct dial from all bedrooms*

*Licensed Full central heating Open parking available
Supervised Child discount available 12yrs Outdoor swimming
pool (heated) Sauna Gym Pool table Jacuzzi/spa Open terrace
V meals Last d 21.30hrs Languages spoken: English,German*
CARDS: ● ■ ■ ▣ Travellers cheques

## PLONÉVEZ-PORZAY Finistère

**Bed & Breakfast** (Prop: Claude Revel)
Crec'h Levern, St-Anne-le-Palud *29550*
☎ 298925098 FAX 298925098
(from Quimper direction to Plonevez-Porzay the St Anne-la-
Palud, 2nd street on left marked with blue sign)
Near beach
*Closed mid Nov-Etr*
*3 rms (1 bth 1 shr) No smoking in 2 bedrooms TV in 2
bedrooms Full central heating Open parking available Child
discount available 10yrs Bicycle rental V meals*
CARDS: Travellers cheques

## PLOUARET Côtes-D'Armor

**Le Presbytère** (Prop: Nicole de Morchoven)
Trégrom *22420*
☎ 296479415
(from the N12 exit at Louargat for Tregrom)
This old presbytery is in the centre of a small, peaceful village.
Built in the 17th century, the place is enclosed by high walls

bedecked with violets and roses. Ideal spot from which to
explore Western Brittany.
Near river Forest area
*3 en suite (bth/shr) No smoking on premises Full central
heating Open parking available Languages spoken: English*
ROOMS: s 280FF; d 300FF
MEALS: Dinner 125FF

## PLOUËR-SUR-RANCE Côtes-D'Armor

★ ★ **Manoir de Rigourdaine**
rte de Langrolay *22490*
☎ 296868996 FAX 296869246
(from St Malo, take dual-carriageway towards Rennes (N137),
after 15km follow the road signposted Dinan/St Brieuc (N176).
Leave the dual-carriageway, after the bridge on the Rance, take
Plouër exit. Take the road to Langrolay, then follow sign)
A charming stone-built, historic house with beams and open
fireplace. Set in extensive grounds with views of the Breton
estuary.
Near river Near sea Near beach Forest area
*Closed mid Nov-Mar*
*19 en suite (bth/shr) (6 fmly) TV in all bedrooms Direct dial*
*contd.*

49

**Manoir de Rigourdaine**
from all bedrooms Licensed Full central heating Open parking
available Supervised Fishing Pool table Boule Open terrace
Languages spoken: English & German
ROOMS: (room only) s 330-380FF; d 380-450FF
CARDS: ⬤ ▬ ☲ Travellers cheques

## PLOUESCAT Finistère

### ★ ★ La Caravelle
20 rue du Calvaire 29430
☎ 298696175 FAX 298619261
(from ferry terminal follow D769 then D10 to Plouescat)
Hotel la Caravelle is located in the small seaside village of
Plouescat, and, at only 15 minutes from the ferry terminal in
Roscoff, it is a good venue for an overnight stop. Bedrooms are
furnished in a simple fashion and provide good levels of
comfort, while the restaurant offers a high standard of home-
cooked dishes including seafood specialities.
Near sea Near beach Near motorway

17 en suite (bth/shr) (1 fmly) TV in all bedrooms Radio in
rooms Direct dial from all bedrooms Licensed Full central
heating Child discount available 13yrs Boule Bicycle rental V
meals Last d 21.00hrs Languages spoken: English & German
ROOMS: (room only) s 220FF; d 280-300FF
**Reductions over 1 night**
MEALS: Continental breakfast 35FF Lunch 70-200FF&alc
Dinner 70-200FF&alc
CARDS: ⬤ ▬ ☲ ⒹTravellers cheques

**Pen-Kéar** (Prop: Marie & Raymond Le Duff)
29430
☎ 298696287 FAX 298696733
(situated between Plouescat and the sea)
Near sea Near beach
2 en suite (bth/shr) TV in all bedrooms Radio in rooms Full

central heating Open parking available Supervised Bicycle
rental
ROOMS: s 320FF; d 380FF ✱
CARDS: Travellers cheques

## PLOUGUENAST Côtes-D'Armor

**Garmorin** (Prop: Bernard & Madeleine Lucas)
22150
☎ 296287061 FAX 296268500
Near river
4 rms (3 shr) (1 fmly) Full central heating Open parking
available

**St-Theo** (Prop: Eliane Collet)
22150
☎ 296287001
Near river Near lake Forest area
3 rms (2 bth/shr) No smoking on premises Full central heating
Open parking available Supervised

## PLOUHARNEL Morbihan

### ★ ★ Hostellerie les Ajoncs D'Or
Kerbachique 56340
☎ 297523202 FAX 297524036
(from Auray take D768 to Plouharnel, then road to Carnac)
This friendly inn is set amidst leafy parkland in the heart of
Brittany. Situated only a few minutes away from fine, sandy
beaches, it is a good base for excursions to Quiberon, the Gulf
of Morbihan, and other points of interest. The cuisine consists
of regional dishes, prepared with fresh farm and sea produce.
Near sea Near beach Forest area

Closed 3 Nov-15 Mar
17 rms (2 bth 14 shr) (4 fmly) TV in all bedrooms STV Direct
dial from 16 bedrooms Full central heating Open
parking available Supervised Child discount available 2yrs
Boule Open terrace V meals Last d 21.00hrs Languages
spoken: English
ROOMS: (room only) s 320FF; d 350-480FF
MEALS: Continental breakfast 40FF Dinner 110-150FF
CARDS: ⬤ ☲ Travellers cheques

## PLOUHINEC Morbihan

### ★ ★ Hotel de Kerlon
56680
☎ 297367703 FAX 297858114
(leave N165 at Hennebont & take D194 in direction of
Carnac/Quiberon, then onto D9)

A warm welcome awaits guets from the friendly proprietors at this charming hotel. Situated in a beautiful area of peaceful countryside, only five kilometres from the beach, the hotel is surrounded by extensive gardens with a play area. Breakfast is continental style, and good value local dishes are prepared in the rustic dining room. Half-board only available in July and August.
Near sea  Near beach  Forest area

**Hotel de Kerlon**
*Closed 16 Nov-14 Mar*
*16 rms (15 bth/shr) (1 fmly) TV in all bedrooms Direct dial from all bedrooms Licensed Full central heating Open parking available Supervised Child discount available 12yrs Open terrace Last d 21.00hrs Languages spoken: English*
ROOMS: (room only) s 260-290FF; d 290-320FF
MEALS: Continental breakfast 40FF Lunch fr 110FF Dinner 82-160FF
CARDS: ● ■ ▤ Travellers cheques

**PLOUIGNEAU** Finistère

**Manoir de Lanleya** (Prop: André Marrec)
*29610*
☎ 298799415
(from N12 (Paris-Brest) turn off at Plouigneau and head for Lanmeur, following signs for 'Manoir de Lanleya')
Near river  Near sea  Forest area
*5 en suite (shr) No smoking on premises Full central heating Open parking available Languages spoken: English*

**PLOZEVET** Finistère

**Kerongard Divisquin** (Prop: M & Mme Trepos)
*29710*
☎ 298543109
Near sea
*3 en suite (shr) No smoking on premises Full central heating Boule*

**PLUVIGNER** Morbihan

**Chaumière de Kerréo** (Prop: M Gerard Greves)
*56330*
☎ 297509048 FAX 297509069
(from N24, leave motorway in Baud, head towards Auray, then leaving Baud, turn right to Landevant, after 10km turn right again following signs for Chambre d'Hôtes)
Forest area
*5 en suite (bth/shr) Full central heating Open parking available Child discount available 7yrs Languages spoken: English*
CARDS: Travellers cheques

**Kerdavid-Duchentil** (Prop: M & Mme Collet)
*56330*
☎ 297560059
Near river  Near lake  Near sea  Forest area
*5 en suite (bth/shr) Radio in rooms Open parking available*

**Kermec** (Prop: Noemi Lorgeoux)
*56330*
☎ 297249297
(motorway Rennes-Lorient, exit at Baud, follow the direction to Auray and at Pluvigner, towards Ste-Anne-d'Auray, Kermec is a hamlet on the right, halfway between Pluvigner and Ste-Anne.)

A tastefully renovated, stone-built property, located in the hamlet of Kermec. There is also a large garden and barbecue. The sea is within 20 kilometres.
Near river  Forest area
*4 en suite (bth/shr) TV in 2 bedrooms Full central heating Open parking available Languages spoken: English*
ROOMS: d fr 260FF ✱ **Reductions over 1 night**
CARDS: Travellers cheques

**POLIGNÉ** Ille-et-Vilaine

**Château du Bois Glaume**
*35320*
☎ 299438305 FAX 299437940
Near river  Near lake  Forest area  Near motorway
*4 en suite (bth/shr) (2 fmly) (1 with balcony) TV in 2 bedrooms Radio in rooms Mini-bar in 2 bedrooms Full central heating Open parking available Supervised Child discount available 12yrs Fishing Last d 18.30hrs Languages spoken: Spanish*
CARDS: Eurocheques Travellers cheques

**POMMERIT-JAUDY** Côtes-D'Armor

**Château de Kermézen** (Prop: Comte and Comtesse de Kermel)
*22450*
☎ 296913575 FAX 296913575
(take motorway N12 as far as Guingamp, then follow signs to Tréguier, (on D8), continue for 23km, at traffic lights in Pomerit, turn left- Kermézen is 2km further on)
Near river  Near sea  Near beach  Forest area
*5 en suite (bth/shr) (2 fmly) Full central heating Open parking available  Child discount available 12yrs Fishing Riding Boule Open terrace Languages spoken: English*
ROOMS: s 450-520FF; d 480-550FF
CARDS: ■ Travellers cheques

**Quillevez Vraz** (Prop: Georges Beauverger)
*22450*
☎ 296913574
*Closed Oct-Etr*
*3 en suite (bth) No smoking on premises Full central heating*
*Open parking available*

**Kermentec** (Prop: Alain Larour)
*29930*
☎ 298060760
(from the centre of the village take direction of
Quimper/Rosporden D24 then right turn for La Chapelle de
Tremalo in 200m house on the right)
*Near river Forest area In town centre*
*3 en suite (shr) (1 fmly) Full central heating Open parking*
*available Languages spoken: English*
ROOMS: d 250FF ✱
CARDS: Travellers cheques

★ ★ ★ **Roz-Aven**
11 quai Théodore Botrel *29930*
☎ 298061306 FAX 298060389
*Near river Near sea Near beach Forest area*
*Near motorway*
*Closed 16 Dec-14 Feb*
*25 en suite (bth/shr) 8 rooms in annexe (3 fmly) TV in all*
*bedrooms Mini-bar in 3 bedrooms Licensed Full central*
*heating Open parking available Child discount available 12yrs*
*Pool table Open terrace Languages spoken: English &*
*German*
CARDS: ●● ▆▆ Travellers cheques

**La Bretonnière Bel Air** (Prop: Adele Miloux)
*56300*
☎ 297396248 FAX 297396248
(3km from Pontivy towards Guingamp, 3km from Neulliac)
Adèle Miloux welcomes you to her home, situated in the heart
of Brittany. Garden with boules and childrens games, leading
into a huge park. The Guerlédan Lake is only 15 kilometres
away. Many sporting activities available.
*Near river Near lake Forest area*

*4 en suite (bth/shr) (1 fmly) (1 with balcony) No smoking on*
*premises TV in all bedrooms Full central heating Open*
*parking available Boule Languages spoken: English*
ROOMS: d fr 230FF ✱

★ ★ **Château Hotel de Kernuz**
rte de Penmarc'h *29120*
☎ 298870159 FAX 298660236
*Near sea Near beach Forest area*
*Closed Oct-Mar*
*24 en suite (bth/shr) 7 rooms in annexe (8 fmly) (1 with*
*balcony) Licensed Full central heating Open parking available*
*Child discount available 10yrs Outdoor swimming pool Tennis*
*Pool table Bicycle rental Open terrace Last d 21.30hrs*
*Languages spoken: English & Spanish*
CARDS: ●● ▆▆ ▆▆ Travellers cheques

★ ★ **D'Auvergne**
22 pl Gambetta *29120*
☎ 298870047 FAX 298823378
*Near river In town centre Near motorway*
*27 en suite (bth/shr) TV in all bedrooms STV Licensed Full*
*central heating Child discount available 12yrs Bicycle rental*
*Languages spoken: English*
CARDS: ▆▆ ▆▆ Travellers cheques

★ ★ **Grand Hotel**
bd de la Mer *22710*
☎ 296926652 FAX 296928157
The hotel occupies a fine location on the Brittany coast and
offers beautiful views across the sea. The cheerful interior and
informal atmosphere create a feeling of well being in this
attractive hotel. The restaurant offers a range of well prepared
dishes, and the gardens and play area provide a carefree place
for children to enjoy themselves.
*Near sea Near beach*
*Closed Nov-mid Mar RS Half board obligatory Jul-Aug*
*29 rms (22 bth 9 shr) (4 fmly) Direct dial from all bedrooms*
*Licensed Full central heating Open parking available Child*
*discount available 10yrs Tennis Pool table Boule Open terrace*
*Table Tennis V meals Last d 22.00hrs Languages spoken: English*
MEALS: Continental breakfast 30FF Lunch 80-190FF Dinner
80-190FF
CARDS: ●● ▆▆ Travellers cheques

★ ★ **Du Commerce**
1 pl du Marché *56290*
☎ 297824605 FAX 297821102
*Near sea Near beach In town centre Near motorway*

36 rms (14 bth 17 shr) 11 rooms in annexe (2 fmly) TV in all bedrooms Direct dial from all bedrooms Licensed Full central heating Child discount available 8yrs Open terrace V meals Last d 21.30hrs Languages spoken: English
CARDS: ● ⬛ Travellers cheques

### POULDERGAT Finistère

**Listi Vras** (Prop: Louis et Angele Kervares)
29100
☎ 298524800
3 en suite (shr) (3 fmly) Full central heating Open parking available Supervised
CARDS: Travellers cheques

### POULDREUZIC Finistère

★ ★ ★ **Ker Ansquer**
Lababan 29710
☎ 298544183 FAX 495543224
Near sea Near beach
Closed Nov-Apr
16 en suite (bth/shr) 10 rooms in annexe (2 fmly) TV in all bedrooms Direct dial from all bedrooms Mini-bar in all bedrooms Licensed Full central heating Open parking available Supervised Child discount available Pool table Boule Open terrace Last d 21.00hrs Languages spoken: English
CARDS: ● ⬛

### POULDU, LE Finistère

★ ★ ★ **Armen**
rte du Port, Le Pouldu 29360
☎ 298399044 FAX 298399869
(from N165 exit Quimperle, take D49 to Le Pouldu)
Near river Near sea Near beach Forest area
Closed end Sep-end Apr
38 en suite (bth/shr) (3 fmly) (9 with balcony) TV in 32 bedrooms Direct dial from all bedrooms Licensed Lift Full central heating Open parking available Covered parking available Child discount available 12yrs Open terrace Last d 21.00hrs Languages spoken: English
CARDS: ● ⬛ ⬛ Travellers cheques

### QUEMPER-GUÉZENNEC Côtes-D'Armor

**Kergocq** (Prop: Marie Claire Thomas)
22260
☎ 296956272 296956398
(from Guimgamp head towards Treguier-Pontrieux. At St-Clet continue towards Paimpol for 3km then bear right following signs for Kergoc on left)
2 en suite (bth/shr) No smoking on premises Full central heating Open parking available Covered parking available

### QUERRIEN Finistère

**Kerfaro** (Prop: Yves Le Gallic)
29310
☎ 298713002 & 685179643 FAX 298713002
(from Quimperlé take D790 towards Le Faouët for 9km, then left to Querrien and follow signs towards Mellac and take 1st left. Last house in lane)
Forest area
2 en suite (shr) No smoking on premises TV in all bedrooms Full central heating Open parking available Supervised Child discount available Fishing

ROOMS: s fr 200FF; d fr 230FF ✱
CARDS: ⬛ Travellers cheques

### QUESTEMBERT Morbihan

★ ★ ★ **Bretagne**
13 rue St-Michel 56230
☎ 297261112 FAX 297261237
(leave N24 at Ploermel in direction of Vannes, then N166 to Questembert)
Near river Near lake Forest area In town centre Near motorway
Closed 5-30 Jan
9 en suite (bth/shr) 9 rooms in annexe (1 fmly) (3 with balcony) No smoking in 4 bedrooms TV in all bedrooms Direct dial from all bedrooms Mini-bar in all bedrooms Licensed Full central heating Air conditioning in bedrooms Open parking available Supervised Child discount available 12yrs Indoor swimming pool (heated) Golf Tennis Fishing Riding Solarium Gym Bicycle rental Open terrace Covered terrace V meals Last d 22.00hrs Languages spoken: English & Spanish
CARDS: ● ⬛ ⬛

### QUÉVERT Côtes-D'Armor

**Le Chêne Pichard** (Prop: M & Mme Boullier)
22100
☎ 296850921
(from Dinan take the N176 in the direction of St Brieuc establishment in 2km on the right)
4 rms (1 bth 2 shr) (1 with balcony) TV available Full central heating Open parking available

### QUIMPER Finistère

★ ★ **Hotel Mascotte**
6 rue Théodore le Hars 29000
☎ 298533737 FAX 298903151
Near river In town centre Near motorway
63 en suite (bth/shr) (2 fmly) No smoking in 6 bedrooms TV in all bedrooms STV Radio in rooms Direct dial from all bedrooms Licensed Lift Night porter Full central heating Child discount available 12yrs V meals Last d 22.00hrs Languages spoken: English
CARDS: ● ⬛ ⬛ ⬛ Travellers cheques

### REMUNGOL Morbihan

**La Villeneuve** (Prop: Jean an Solanges Le Texier)
Le Texier, La Villeneuve 56500
☎ 297609835
Forest area
4 en suite (bth/shr) (1 fmly) Full central heating Child discount available

### RENNES Ille-et-Vilaine

★ ★ ★ **Hotel Lecoq-Gadby**
156 rue d'Antrain 35000
☎ 299380555 FAX 299385340
(from the centre of town, head in the direction of Mont St Michel to find rue d'Antrain St, hotel by Thabor Park)
In town centre Near motorway
11 en suite (bth/shr) (4 fmly) (3 with balcony) TV in all bedrooms Direct dial from all bedrooms Mini-bar in all bedrooms Licensed Lift Night porter Full central heating Open parking available Child discount available 14yrs

*contd.*

*Solarium Open terrace Covered terrace Last d 21.30hrs
Languages spoken: English & Spanish*
CARDS: ● ▬ ▣ 🔘 Travellers cheques

### RHEU, LE Ille-et-Vilaine

**Domaine de la Freslonniere** (Prop: Mme C D'Alincourt)
*35650*
☎ 299148409 FAX 299149498
(4km from Rennes. Take N24 Lorient road until 'Le Rheu
Nordelles Est' exit, then right towards town centre)
Guest rooms, cottages and fully-furnished apartments, either
in or near the Château de la Freslonnière, a 17th-century
building set in the heart of a wooded parkland near an 18-hole
golf course and a lake. Three kilometres from town centre.
*Near lake Forest area
2 en suite (bth/shr) (1 fmly) TV available Full central heating
Open parking available Child discount available 12yrs Outdoor
swimming pool (heated) Golf 18 Tennis Fishing Boule Mini-
golf Table tennis Languages spoken: English & Spanish*
ROOMS: d 380-460FF ✱
MEALS: Dinner 67-200FF✱
CARDS: ● ▣ Travellers cheques

### ROCHE-BERNARD, LA Morbihan

**★★ Auberge des Deux Magots**
pl du Bouffay *56130*
☎ 299906075 FAX 299908787
*Near river Near sea Near beach In town centre Near
motorway
Closed 20 Dec-20 Jan
36 rms (14 bth/shr) (4 fmly) TV in 15 bedrooms STV Licensed
Full central heating Languages spoken: English*
CARDS: ● ▣ Travellers cheques

**★★★ Domaine de Bodeuc**
Nivillac *56130*
☎ 299908963 FAX 299909032
*Near river Near sea Forest area
8 en suite (bth/shr) TV in all bedrooms Direct dial from all
bedrooms Licensed Lift Full central heating Open parking
available Child discount available Outdoor swimming pool
(heated) Pool table Boule Last d 21.00hrs Languages spoken:
English*
CARDS: ● ▬ ▣ 🔘 Travellers cheques

**★★★ L'Auberge Bretonne**
2 pl Duguesclin *56130*
☎ 299906028 FAX 299908500
*Near river Near sea In town centre Near motorway
Closed mid Nov-early Dec & early Jan-end Jan
10 en suite (bth/shr) (3 fmly) TV in all bedrooms Licensed Lift
Full central heating Open parking available (charged) Covered
parking available (charged) Supervised Open terrace V meals
Last d 21.00hrs Languages spoken: English*
CARDS: ● ▬ ▣

### ROCHEFORT-EN-TERRE Morbihan

**Château de Talhouet**
*56220*
☎ 297433472 FAX 297433504
*Near river Forest area
8 en suite (bth/shr) Full central heating Open parking available
Pool table Open terrace V meals Languages spoken: English*
CARDS: ▬ ▣

### ROSCOFF Finistère

**★★★ Hotel Brittany**
blvd St Barbe, BP47 *29681*
☎ 298697078 FAX 298611329
(From the Motorway,take the Morlaix exit in the direction of
Roscoff. Arriving at Roscoff take the Car Ferry direction. The
Hotel is on the left 200 metres after the traffic lights. It is the
nearest hotel to the ferries terminal)
*Near sea Near beach
Closed Nov-mid Mar
25 en suite (bth/shr) (3 fmly) (6 with balcony) TV in all
bedrooms STV Direct dial from all bedrooms Licensed Lift
Night porter Full central heating Open parking available
Supervised Child discount available 10yrs Indoor swimming
pool (heated) Sauna Solarium Jacuzzi/spa Open terrace V
meals Languages spoken: English,German & Italian*
CARDS: ● ▬ ▣ Travellers cheques

### ROSNOËN Finistère

**Ferme Auberge du Seillou** (Prop: M Herve le Pape)
*29590*
☎ 298819221 FAX 298810714
(on the N165 Brest/Quimper exit Le Faou take D791 direction
Crozon for 6km signposted)
*Near river Near sea Near beach Forest area Near motorway
6 en suite (bth/shr) (2 fmly) Full central heating Open parking
available Child discount available Last d 21.00hrs Languages
spoken: English*
CARDS: ● ▬ ▣

### ROSPORDEN Finistère

**Kerantou** (Prop: M Bernard)
*29140*
☎ 298592779
(in Rosporden head towards Scaër; after the level-crossing
take 2nd road on right)
Rooms available in an old farm close to the proprietor's house,
including one family room. Kitchen area and living room
available to guests. Babysitting by arrangement. Barbecue in
the garden. The beach is fifteen minutes away.
*Near river Near lake Forest area
6 en suite (bth/shr) (1 fmly) Full central heating Open parking
available Covered parking available Child discount available
Table tennis Languages spoken: English*
ROOMS: s fr 200FF; d fr 240FF
CARDS: ▬

### ROZ-LANDRIEUX Ille-et-Vilaine

**Manoir de la Méttrie** (Prop: Mr Claude Jourdan)
*35120*
☎ 299482921
*Near sea Near beach Forest area Near motorway
5 en suite (shr) (2 fmly) No smoking on premises Full central
heating Open parking available Child discount available 10yrs
V meals Last d 21.00hrs*
CARDS: ▬ Travellers cheques

### ROZ-SUR-COUESNON Ille-et-Vilaine

**Bed & Breakfast** (Prop: Helene Gillet)
Le Val St-Révert *35610*
☎ 299802785
*Near sea Near beach Near motorway*

5 en suite (bth/shr) (1 fmly) (3 with balcony) No smoking on premises TV in 4 bedrooms Full central heating Open parking available Child discount available
CARDS: Travellers cheques

**La Bergerie** (Prop: M Jacky Piel)
*35610*
☎ 299802968 FAX 299802968
(follow D797 coast road to La Poultiére then right)
Near lake Near sea
5 en suite (bth/shr) (4 fmly) Full central heating Open parking available Covered parking available Fishing Boule Languages spoken: English
ROOMS: s 210-250FF; d 230-280FF ✻
CARDS: Travellers cheques

**RUFFIAC** Morbihan

**Ferme de Rangera** (Prop: Germaine and Gilbert Couedelo)
*56140*
☎ 297937218
5 en suite (shr) (1 fmly) No smoking on premises Full central heating Open parking available Child discount available 10yrs

**ST-ALBAN** Côtes-D'Armor

**Ferme de Malido** (Prop: M Legrand)
*22400*
☎ 296329474 FAX 296329267
Near motorway
6 en suite (shr) (2 fmly) (1 with balcony) Full central heating Open parking available Bicycle rental Languages spoken: English
ROOMS: d 220-260FF ✻
CARDS: ▄ Travellers cheques

**ST-BRIAC-SUR-MER** Ille-et-Vilaine

**The Laurel Tree** (Prop: Oliver & Helen Martin)
41 blvd de la Houle *35800*
☎ 299880193
Near sea Near beach
5 en suite (shr) (3 fmly) No smoking on premises TV in 4 bedrooms Full central heating Open parking available Child discount available 4yrs Languages spoken: English & German
CARDS: Travellers cheques

**Manoir de la Duchée** (Prop: M S F Stenou)
*35800*
☎ 299880002
Near river Near sea Near beach Forest area
Closed Jan & Feb
5 en suite (bth/shr) (1 fmly) (1 with balcony) TV available Full central heating Open parking available
CARDS: Travellers cheques

**ST-CARADEC** Côtes-D'Armor

**Ferme de L'Hilvern** (Prop: Collette Nagat)
*22600*
☎ 680203411 FAX 296250266
(N164 between Rennes and Brest to St Caradec, on leaving village, first turning on right)
Near river Near lake Near sea Near beach Forest area Near motorway

6 en suite (bth/shr) (1 fmly) No smoking on premises TV in 3 bedrooms Full central heating Open parking available Covered parking available Tennis Boule Table tennis, Children's Billiards Languages spoken: English German & Spanish
ROOMS: s 160-180FF; d 220-250FF
**Reductions over 1 night**
CARDS: Travellers cheques

**ST-CAST-LE-GUILDO** Côtes-D'Armor

★ ★ ★ **Les Arcades**
*22380*
☎ 296418050 FAX 296417734
Near sea Near beach In town centre
Closed 16 Sep-Mar
32 en suite (bth/shr) (18 with balcony) TV in all bedrooms STV Direct dial from all bedrooms Licensed Lift Child discount available Open terrace Covered terrace Last d 23.00hrs Languages spoken: English & Spanish
CARDS: ●● ▄▄ ▨▨ ⑤ Travellers cheques

**Château du Val d'Arguenon** (Prop: M & Mme de La Blanchardière)
Notre-Dame du Guildo *22380*
☎ 296410703 FAX 296410267
(25km west of St-Malo in the direction St-Cast)
Near river Near sea Near beach Forest area
Closed Oct-Mar
6 en suite (bth/shr) Full central heating Open parking available Tennis Languages spoken: English

★ ★ **Des Dunes**
*22380*
☎ 296418031 FAX 296418534
Near sea Near beach In town centre
Closed early Nov-mid Mar
29 rms (20 bth 7 shr) (2 fmly) (8 with balcony) TV in all bedrooms Direct dial from all bedrooms Full central heating Open parking available Child discount available 7yrs Tennis Last d 21.30hrs Languages spoken: English
CARDS: ●● ▨▨ Travellers cheques

★ ★ **Les Mielles**
*22380*
☎ 296418095 FAX 296417734
Near sea In town centre
Closed 16 Sep-Mar
19 en suite (bth/shr) 5 rooms in annexe (5 fmly) (2 with balcony) TV in all bedrooms STV Direct dial from all bedrooms Licensed Child discount available Open terrace Covered terrace Last d 22.30hrs Languages spoken: English & Spanish
CARDS: ●● ▄▄ ▨▨ ⑤ Travellers cheques

**Villa Griselidis** (Prop: Rita Ragot)
rue des Hauts de Plume *22380*
☎ 296419522
(on left side of the 'Mairie' town hall, take the 'rue Tourneuf' which links with the 'rue de la Fosserolle' and on the right side is 'rue des Hauts de Plume')
Near sea Near beach
2 en suite (shr) Full central heating Open parking available No children Bicycle rental Languages spoken: English
ROOMS: d fr 290FF
CARDS: Travellers cheques

## ST-COULOMB Ille-et-Vilaine

**La Ville Jaquin** (Prop: Mme Dominque Lesne)
*35350*
☎ 299890562
Near sea  Near beach
*3 en suite (shr)  (2 fmly)  Open parking available  Supervised
Child discount available  Languages spoken: English & Spanish*

## ST-ÉLOY-HANVEC Finistère

**Kerivoal** (Prop: Mme N le Lann)
*29460*
☎ 298258614 FAX 298258614
(from N12 exit Landivisiau head towards Sizun for 5km then
right towards St-Eloy and follow signposts)
Near river  Forest area
*2 en suite (shr)  No smoking on premises  Full central heating
Open parking available  Child discount available 10yrs  Bicycle
rental  Languages spoken: English & Italian*

## ST-JOUAN-DES-GUÉRETS Ille-et-Vilaine

★ ★ ★ **Malouinière des Longchamps**
Les Longchamps *35430*
☎ 299827400 FAX 299827414
Near river  Near sea  Near beach  Forest area  Near motorway
*Closed 15 Nov-1 Apr*
*9 en suite (shr)  4 rooms in annexe  (4 fmly)  TV in all bedrooms
STV  Direct dial from all bedrooms  Licensed  Full central
heating  Open parking available  Covered parking available
Child discount available 10yrs  Outdoor swimming pool (heated)
Tennis  Pool table  Boule  Mini-golf  Bicycle rental  Open terrace
Languages spoken: English & German*
ROOMS: (room only)  s 350-580FF;  d 390-780FF  ✱
**Reductions over 1 night**
CARDS: ●● ■■ ■■ Travellers cheques

**Manoir de Blanche-Roche** (Prop: M Pilorget)
*35430*
☎ 299824747
Near motorway
*Closed 16 Nov-Dec*
*5 en suite (bth/shr)  (1 fmly)  Open parking available  Boule
Languages spoken: English*

## ST-LAURENT-SUR-OUST Morbihan

**Evas** (Prop: Jean & Madeleine Gru)
*56140*
☎ 297750262
Near river  Forest area
*1 en suite (bth)  TV in all bedrooms  Full central heating*

## ST-MALO Ille-et-Vilaine

★ ★ ★ **Hotel Antinea**
55 Chaussée de Sillon *35400*
☎ 299561075 FAX 299562211
Near sea  Near beach
*25 en suite (bth/shr)  (2 fmly)  (6 with balcony)  TV in all
bedrooms  STV  Direct dial from all bedrooms  Mini-bar in all
bedrooms  Licensed  Lift  Full central heating  Open parking
available (charged)  Child discount available 12yrs  Open
terrace  Languages spoken: English*
CARDS: ●● ■■ ■■ ⑨ Travellers cheques

★ ★ ★ **L'Ascott**
35 rue du Chapitre *35400*
☎ 299818993 FAX 299817740
Near sea  Near beach  Forest area  In town centre  Near
motorway
*10 en suite (bth/shr)  (2 fmly)  (1 with balcony)  TV in all
bedrooms  Direct dial from all bedrooms  Licensed  Night
porter  Full central heating  Open parking available  Solarium
Covered terrace  Languages spoken: English*
CARDS: ●● ■■ Travellers cheques

★ ★ ★ **Elizabeth Hotel**
2 rue des Cordiers *35400*
☎ 299562498 FAX 299563924
(from Paris take A10 to Rennes and onto St Malo, hotel within
the fortress walls)
Near river  Near sea  Near beach  In town centre
*17 en suite (bth/shr)  7 rooms in annexe  (5 fmly)  TV in all
bedrooms  STV  Radio in rooms  Direct dial from all bedrooms
Licensed  Lift  Night porter  Full central heating  Covered
parking available (charged)  Supervised  Child discount
available 12yrs  Languages spoken:
English,Spanish,German,Japanese & Italian*
CARDS: ●● ■■ ■■ ⑨ JCB Travellers cheques

★ ★ **Hotel France & Châteaubriand**
B P 77 *35412*
☎ 299566652 FAX 299401004
Near sea  Near beach  In town centre
*78 en suite (bth/shr)  41 rooms in annexe  (10 fmly)  TV in all
bedrooms  STV  Direct dial from all bedrooms  Licensed
Lift  Night porter  Full central heating  Open parking
available (charged)  Covered parking available (charged)
Supervised  Bicycle rental  Open terrace  V meals  Last d
22.00hrs  Languages spoken: English, German, Italian &
Spanish*
ROOMS: (incl. dinner & full-board)  s 365-423FF;  d 450-
560FF
CARDS: ●● ■■ ■■ ⑨ JCB Travellers cheques

**La Goelettrie** (Prop: M Henri Trevilly)
*35400*
☎ 299819264
Near sea
*5 en suite (shr)  (1 fmly)  Full central heating  Open parking
available  Child discount available*

★ ★ ★ **Grand Hotel des Thermes**
100 blvd Hebert *35400*
☎ 299407575 FAX 290407600
Near sea  Near beach  In town centre
*Closed Jan*
*185 en suite (bth/shr)  28 rooms in annexe  (24 fmly)  (20 with
balcony)  TV in all bedrooms  STV  Direct dial from all
bedrooms  Mini-bar in 166 bedrooms  Room-safe  Licensed  Lift
Night porter  Full central heating  Open parking available
Covered parking available (charged)  Supervised  Child
discount available 12yrs  Indoor swimming pool (heated)  Sauna
Solarium  Gym  Pool table  Jacuzzi/spa  Bicycle rental  Open
terrace  Covered terrace  Last d 21.30hrs  Languages spoken:
English, German & Italian*
ROOMS: (room only)  s 280-1490FF;  d 485-1730FF
**Reductions over 1 night**
MEALS: Full breakfast 85FF  Continental breakfast 85FF
Lunch 150-350FF&alc  Dinner 150-350FF&alc
CARDS: ●● ■■ ■■ ⑨ Travellers cheques

**★ ★ ★ Hotel Albatros**
8 pl Duguesclin *35400*
☎ 299404711 FAX 299561049
Near sea  Near beach  In town centre
*22 en suite (bth/shr) (3 fmly) (3 with balcony)  No smoking in 6 bedrooms  TV in all bedrooms  STV  Direct dial from all bedrooms  Licensed  Lift  Full central heating  Open parking available  Supervised  Child discount available 10yrs  Sauna  Solarium  Gym  Jacuzzi/spa  Bicycle rental  Languages spoken: English & German*
CARDS: ●● ■■ ⅠⅠ Travellers cheques

**★ ★ ★ Hotel Central** (Best Western)
6 Grande Rue *35400*
☎ 299408770 FAX 299404757
Town centre
Near river  Near sea  Near beach  In town centre
*46 en suite (bth/shr) (2 fmly)  Direct dial from all bedrooms  STV  Direct dial from all bedrooms  Mini-bar in all bedrooms  Room-safe  Licensed  Lift  Night porter  Full central heating  Open parking available (charged)  Covered parking available (charged)  Supervised  Child discount available 12yrs  V meals  Last d 22.00hrs  Languages spoken: English,German & Italian*
ROOMS: d 450-680FF
CARDS: ●● ■■ ⅠⅠ ⑤ JCB Travellers cheques

**★ ★ Ibis**
58 Chaussée du Sillon *35400*
☎ 299405777 FAX 299405778
Near sea  Near beach  In town centre  Near motorway
*60 en suite (bth/shr)  No smoking in 18 bedrooms  TV in all bedrooms  STV  Direct dial from all bedrooms  Licensed  Lift  Night porter  Full central heating  Open parking available (charged)  Covered parking available (charged)  Supervised  Child discount available 12yrs  Languages spoken: English German Italian & Spanish*
ROOMS: (room only) s 235-485FF; d 235-560FF
CARDS: ●● ■■ ⅠⅠ ⑤ Travellers cheques

**★ ★ Inter Hotel Ligne Bleue**
138 bd des Talards *35400*
☎ 299820510 FAX 299817910
Near sea  In town centre
*Closed mid Nov-mid Mar*
*60 en suite (bth/shr) (3 fmly)  TV available  Direct dial from all bedrooms  Licensed  Lift  Full central heating  Open parking available  Covered parking available (charged)  Child discount available 12yrs  Last d 21.30hrs  Languages spoken: English & German*
CARDS: ●● ■■ ⅠⅠ ⑤ Travellers cheques

**★ ★ Hotel Mascotte**
76 Chaussée du Sillon *35400*
☎ 299403636 FAX 299401878
Near sea  Near beach
*88 rms (14 fmly) (3 with balcony)  No smoking in 8 bedrooms  TV in all bedrooms  Radio in rooms  Direct dial from all bedrooms  Licensed  Lift  Night porter  Full central heating  Covered parking available (charged)  Pool table  Open terrace*

**★ ★ ★ Valmarin**
7 rue Jean XXIII *35400*
☎ 299819476 FAX 299813003
(go to old city (intra muros) and follow walls from outside, pass bridges of ferry terminal and turn right at second roundabout)
Near sea  Near beach  In town centre

*Closed 16 Nov-24 Dec & 7 Jan-part Feb*
*12 en suite (bth/shr) (3 fmly)  TV in all bedrooms  Radio in rooms  Direct dial from all bedrooms  Mini-bar in all bedrooms  Licensed  Full central heating  Open parking available  Supervised  Open terrace  Languages spoken: English,German & Italian*
CARDS: ●● ■■ ⅠⅠ Travellers cheques

**Ville Auray** (Prop: Josette Feret)
*35400*
☎ 299816437 FAX 299822327
(travel towards St Malo centre, over rdbts, at last rdbt, travel towards St Michel, take 2nd road on left after campsite, house is along road)
Near sea  Near beach  Forest area
*4 en suite (bth/shr) (1 fmly)  TV in all bedrooms  Full central heating  Open parking available  Covered parking available  Table tennis, Baby foot, Billiards  Languages spoken: English & Spanish*
CARDS: Travellers cheques

**★ ★ ★ Villefromoy**
7 bd Hebert *35400*
☎ 299409220 FAX 299567949
Near sea  Near beach
*Closed 16 Nov-14 Mar*
*21 en suite (bth) (3 fmly) (6 with balcony)  No smoking in 1 bedroom  TV in 22 bedrooms  STV  Radio in rooms  Direct dial from 22 bedrooms  Mini-bar in 2 bedrooms  Licensed  Lift  Night porter  Full central heating  Open parking available  Supervised  Open terrace  Ping pong  Languages spoken: English German & Spanish*
CARDS: ●● ■■ ⅠⅠ ⑤ Travellers cheques

**ST-MARTIN-DES-CHAMPS** Finistère

**Kereliza** (Prop: N Abiven-Gueguen)
*29600*
☎ 298882718
(from St-Martin-des-Champs (nr Morlaix) take D58 towards Roscoff. After second roundabout take St-Seve road, chambre d'hôte signed)
Near motorway
*6 en suite (bth/shr)  Full central heating  Open parking available  Languages spoken: English*
ROOMS: s fr 160FF; d fr 230FF ✱
CARDS: ■ Travellers cheques

**ST-MARTIN-SUR-OUST** Morbihan

**Le Château de Castellan** (Prop: P et M Cosse)
*56200*
☎ 299945169 FAX 299915741
Near river  Forest area
*7 rms (5 bth/shr) (2 fmly)  No smoking on premises  Radio in rooms  Full central heating  Open parking available  Child discount available 10yrs  V meals  Languages spoken: English*
CARDS: ●● ■■ ⅠⅠ ⑤ Travellers cheques

**ST-MÉLOIR-DES-ONDES** Ille-et-Vilaine

**Les Croix Gibouins** (Prop: Denise Basle)
*35350*
☎ 299821197 FAX 299821197
Near sea  Near beach
*2 en suite (bth/shr) (1 fmly)  Full central heating  Open parking available  Supervised  Child discount available 2yrs  Languages spoken: English*                                        *contd.*

**Langa Van** (Prop: M Loic Collin)
*35350*
☎ 299892292
Near sea Near motorway
*Closed 30 Sep-Mar*
*5 en suite (shr) (3 fmly) Full central heating Open parking*
*available Child discount available 10 yrs Open terrace Last d*
*19.30hrs Languages spoken: English*
CARDS: ■ Travellers cheques

**★ ★ ★ Tirel & Guerin**
Gare de la Gouesnière *35350*
☎ 299891046
(from St Malo head for Rennes, then off the double
carriageway towards La Govesniere. First rdbt turn left
towards Cancale D76, 600m down road on the left.)
Near sea Near beach
*15 Jan - 20 Dec*
*63 en suite (bth/shr) (5 fmly) (23 with balcony) TV in all*
*bedrooms STV Direct dial from all bedrooms Mini-bar in 12*
*bedrooms Licensed Night porter Full central heating Open*
*parking available Covered parking available (charged)*
*Supervised Child discount available 10yrs Indoor swimming*
*pool (heated) Tennis Sauna Solarium Gym Jacuzzi/spa Open*
*terrace Last d 21.30hrs Languages spoken: English & German*
CARDS: ●● ■■ ≡≡ ⑩ Travellers cheques

**ST-OUEN-LA-ROUËRIE** Ille-et-Vilaine

**La Morissais** (Prop: Francois Legros)
*35460*
☎ 299983880
Near river Forest area Near motorway
*4 en suite (shr) (2 fmly) No smoking on premises Full central*
*heating Open parking available Supervised Child discount*
*available 4yrs*

**ST-PÈRE-MARC-EN-POULET** Ille-et-Vilaine

**La Ville Hermessan** (Prop: Marcel Lebihan)
*35430*
☎ 299582202 FAX 299582202
(from St-Malo take D4 in direction of Gouesnière)
Near sea Forest area
*Closed 16 Nov-14 Mar*
*4 en suite (shr) (2 fmly) No smoking on premises Full central*
*heating Open parking available Child discount available 12yrs*
*Boule Bicycle rental Pitching green Languages spoken: English*
ROOMS: s 210-230FF; d 240-270FF
CARDS: ■■

**ST-PHILIBERT-SUR-MER** Morbihan

**Cuzon du Rest**
Lann Kermane, 13 rue des Peupliers *56470*
☎ 297550375 FAX 297300279
Near river Near sea Near beach
*2 en suite (bth/shr) No smoking on premises Full central*
*heating Open parking available Languages spoken: English*
ROOMS: s fr 350FF; d fr 450FF
CARDS: Travellers cheques

**ST-PIERRE-DE-PLESGUEN** Ille-et-Vilaine

**Le Clos du Rouvre** (Prop: M & Mme Harrison)
*35720*
☎ 299737272
(follow the N137 from St-Malo to St-Pierre-de-Plesguen, then
take D794 for 1km in direction of Combourg take left turn
signposted Lanhelin Clos de Rouve is 2km on the left)
Near river Near lake Near sea Forest area Near motorway
*6 en suite (bth/shr) (2 fmly) Full central heating Open parking*
*available Child discount available Boule Last d 11.00hrs*
*Languages spoken: English*
CARDS: Travellers cheques

**Le Petit Moulin du Rouvre** (Prop: Mme Annie Michel-
Quebriac)
*35720*
☎ 299738584 FAX 299737106
(situated between Rennes and St Malo, St Pierre de Plesguen is
on N137, from here take D10 in the direction Lanhelin)
Near river Forest area
*4 en suite (bth/shr) (2 fmly) No smoking on premises TV in all*
*bedrooms Full central heating Open parking available No*
*children 5yrs Child discount available Fishing*
ROOMS: d fr 380FF
CARDS: ●● ≡≡ Travellers cheques

**Le Pont Ricoul**
*35720*
☎ 299739265 FAX 299739417
(leave N137 at village of St Pierre de Plesguen, at church take
D10 to Lanhelin for 1.8km and follow signs for
establishment)
Near lake Forest area Near motorway
*2 en suite (shr) (2 fmly) Full central heating Open parking*
*available Covered parking available Child discount available*
*Fishing Bicycle rental Languages spoken: English*
MEALS: Dinner 80FF
CARDS: Travellers cheques

**ST-PIERRE-QUIBERON** Morbihan

**★ ★ ★ De La Plage**
BP 6 *56510*
☎ 297309210 FAX 297309961
Near sea Near beach In town centre
*Closed Oct-Mar*
*46 en suite (bth/shr) (4 fmly) (28 with balcony) TV in all*
*bedrooms STV Direct dial from all bedrooms Licensed Lift Full*
*central heating Open parking available Supervised Child*
*discount available 7yrs Solarium Open terrace Terrace with sea*
*view Last d 20.45hrs Languages spoken: English & German*
ROOMS: (room only) d 250-620FF
MEALS: Full breakfast 47FF Lunch 72-160FF&alc Dinner
72-160FF&alc
CARDS: ●● ■■ ≡≡ ⑩ Travellers cheques

**★ ★ Hotel St Pierre**
34 rte de Quiberon *56510*
☎ 297502690 FAX 297503798
Near lake Near sea Forest area Near motorway
*Closed Nov-Mar*
*30 en suite (bth/shr) (5 fmly) No smoking in 5 bedrooms TV*
*available STV Licensed Full central heating Open parking*
*available Supervised Child discount available Tennis Boule*
*Bicycle rental Open terrace V meals Languages spoken:*
*English & German*
CARDS: ●● ■■ ≡≡ ⑩ Travellers cheques

## ST-SULIAC Ille-et-Vilaine

**Les Mouettes** (Prop: Isabelle Rouvrais)
*35430*
☎ 299583041 FAX 299583941
(3km from Chateauneuf off the St Malo/Rennes road)
Near river Near sea Near beach Forest area
*5 en suite (bth/shr) Full central heating Languages spoken: English*
CARDS: ▨ Travellers cheques

## ST-THÉGONNEC Finistère

★ ★ ★ *Auberge St-Thégonnec*
6 pl de la Mairie *29222*
☎ 298796118 FAX 298627110
Forest area In town centre Near motorway
*19 en suite (bth/shr) (2 fmly) (3 with balcony) TV in all bedrooms Licensed Night porter Full central heating Open parking available Supervised Child discount available 10yrs Open terrace V meals Last d 21.00hrs Languages spoken: English & German*
CARDS: ● ■ ▨ ◎ Travellers cheques

**AR Prespital Koz** (Prop: Mme Christine Prigent)
18 rue Lividic *29140*
☎ 298794562 FAX 298794847
(take main Morlaix-Brest for 10km. At St-Thégonnec exit take D118 for 800mtrs, then 3rd right, then left into Rue Lividic)

A 250 year old former village presbytery in pleasant grounds. Bedrooms are well decorated, spacious and comfortable and a variety of jams and marmalades, made on the premises, are available with breakfast.
Near river Near motorway
*6 en suite (bth/shr) No smoking on premises Full central heating Open parking available Last d 20.00hrs Languages spoken: English*
CARDS: Travellers cheques

## ST-THONAN Finistère

**Bed & Breakfast** (Prop: Marie Jo Edern)
*29800*
☎ 298202699 FAX 298202713
Forest area Near motorway
*3 en suite (shr) (1 fmly) TV available Full central heating Open parking available*
CARDS: Travellers cheques

## SCAER Finistère

**Kerloai** (Prop: M & Mme Penn)
*29390*
☎ 298594260
(from Scaer take D50 towards Quimper turn left Cafe Ty Ru, Kerloal on left fork)
Near river
*4 en suite (shr) Open parking available Languages spoken: English & German*

## TRÉBEURDEN Côtes-D'Armor

★ ★ ★ *Ti Al Lannec*
allée de Mézo Guen *22560*
☎ 296150101 FAX 296236214
Near sea Forest area Near motorway
*Closed mid Nov-mid Mar*
*29 en suite (bth/shr) (7 fmly) (14 with balcony) TV in all bedrooms STV Direct dial from all bedrooms Licensed Lift Full central heating Open parking available Child discount available 14yrs Sauna Solarium Gym Pool table Jacuzzi/spa Open terrace Covered terrace V meals Last d 21.30hrs Languages spoken: English & German*
CARDS: ● ■ ▨ ◎ Travellers cheques

## TRÉFLEZ Finistère

**Pen Ar Roz** (Prop: Yvette Roue)
*29430*
☎ 298614284
Near sea In town centre
*2 en suite (bth/shr) No smoking on premises Full central heating Open parking available*
CARDS: Travellers cheques

## TRÉGASTEL Côtes-D'Armor

★ ★ *Beau Séjour*
*22730*
☎ 296238802 FAX 296234973
Near sea Near beach
*Closed 15 Nov-15 Feb*
*16 en suite (bth/shr) (6 fmly) (2 with balcony) TV in all bedrooms STV Direct dial from all bedrooms Licensed Full central heating Open parking available Child discount available Open terrace V meals Last d 21.30hrs Languages spoken: English & German*
MEALS: Full breakfast 40FF Lunch 94-120FF&alc Dinner 94-120FF&alc
CARDS: ● ■ ▨ ◎ Travellers cheques

★ ★ ★ *Belle-Vue*
rue des Calculots *22730*
☎ 296238818 FAX 296238991
Near sea Near beach
*Closed Oct-Etr*
*31 en suite (bth/shr) (1 fmly) (4 with balcony) TV in 20 bedrooms Direct dial from all bedrooms Licensed Night porter Full central heating Open parking available Supervised Child discount available 6yrs Boule V meals Last d 21.15hrs Languages spoken: English & Italian*
CARDS: ● ■ ▨ ◎ Travellers cheques

**TRÉGLONOU** Finistère

**Keredern** (Prop: Viviane Le Gall)
29870
☎ 298040260
Near river Near sea Forest area
3 en suite (bth/shr) No smoking on premises TV available Full
central heating Open parking available Supervised Child
discount available 4yrs Languages spoken: English &
German
CARDS: Travellers cheques

**Manoir de Trouzilit** (Prop: M. Stephan)
29870
☎ 298040120 FAX 298041714
Near river Near sea Near beach Forest area Near motorway
5 en suite (bth) Full central heating Open parking available
Tennis Fishing Riding Mini-golf Languages spoken: English &
German
CARDS: ●● ▄▄ Travellers cheques

**TRÉHORENTEUC** Morbihan

**Belle-Vue** (Prop: Mme Jagoudel)
56430
☎ 297930280
Near river Near lake Forest area Near motorway
2 en suite (shr) No smoking on premises Full central heating
Open parking available Supervised Child available
2yrs Languages spoken: English

**TRÉOGAT** Finistère

**Keramoine** (Prop: M & Mme Faou)
29720
☎ 298876398
Near river Near lake Near sea
2 en suite (shr) (1 fmly) No smoking on premises Full central
heating
CARDS: Travellers cheques

**TRESSAINT** Côtes-D'Armor

**La Ville Améline** (Prop: Huguette Lemarchand)
22100
☎ 296393369
Near river Forest area
4 en suite (bth/shr) (3 fmly) No smoking on premises Full
central heating Open parking available Covered parking
available Child discount available 10yrs
CARDS: Travellers cheques

**TRÉVÉ** Côtes-D'Armor

**Ferme Sejour** (Prop: Paulette et Jean Donnio)
22600
☎ 296254453
Near lake
4 en suite (bth/shr) Full central heating Open parking available
Child discount available 8yrs Bicycle rental Table tennis
Barbecue Languages spoken: English
CARDS: Travellers cheques

**La Ville aux Véneurs** (Prop: Marie Chauvel)
22600
☎ 296250202
Near river Forest area

2 en suite (bth/shr) No smoking on premises Full central
heating Open parking available Supervised Child discount
available 10yrs

**TRINITÉ-SUR-MER, LA** Morbihan

★ ★ **Aux Algues Brunes**
Le Bourg-St-Philbert 56470
☎ 297550878 FAX 297551859
Near river Near sea
20 rms (2 fmly) (14 with balcony) TV available Licensed Open
parking available Supervised Child discount available 12yrs
Open terrace Languages spoken: English & Italian

★ ★ **Le Rouzic**
17 cours des Quais 56470
☎ 297557206 FAX 297558225
(from N165 take D28, then D781, then D186 to La Trinité-sur-
Mer)
Near sea Near beach In town centre Near motorway
Closed 3-14 Jan and 16 Nov-14 Dec
32 en suite (bth/shr) (4 with balcony) TV in all bedrooms
Direct dial from all bedrooms Licensed Lift Full central
heating Last d 21.00hrs
CARDS: ●● ■■ ▄▄ ⑩ Travellers cheques

**La Maison du Latz** (Prop: Le Rouzic)
Le Latz 56470
☎ 297558091 FAX 297301410
Near river Forest area
4 en suite (bth) No smoking on premises TV in 1 bedroom Full
central heating Open parking available Supervised Fishing
Open terrace
CARDS: Travellers cheques

**UZEL** Côtes-D'Armor

**Bizoin** (Prop: Marie Cadoret)
22460
☎ 296288124 FAX 296262842
Near river Forest area
4 en suite (shr) (2 fmly) Full central heating Open parking
available Child discount available 12 yrs
CARDS: Travellers cheques

**VANNES** Morbihan

★ ★ **Hotel Mascotte**
av Jean Monnet 56000
☎ 297475960 FAX 297470754
(follow directions for town centre, in front of Palais des Arts et
des Congres)
In town centre
65 en suite (bth/shr) (2 fmly) No smoking in 6 bedrooms TV in
all bedrooms STV Radio in rooms Direct dial from all
bedrooms Licensed Lift Night porter Full central heating
Open parking available Covered parking available (charged)
Child discount available 12yrs Pool table Last d 22.00hrs
Languages spoken: English, German, Italian & Spanish
ROOMS: (room only) s 355-415FF; d 445-505FF
CARDS: ●● ■■ ▄▄ ⑩

★ ★ ★ **Manche Océan**
31 rue du Lieut Col Maury 56000
☎ 297472646 FAX 297473086
(in the centre of Vannes. From Le Port, follow the walls
(ramparts) and then head towards Pontiny, Lorient.)

Near sea  Near beach  In town centre
*41 en suite (bth/shr)  (5 fmly)  (6 with balcony)  TV in all
bedrooms  Direct dial from all bedrooms  Mini-bar in all
bedrooms  Lift  Night porter  Full central heating  Open parking
available (charged)  Covered parking available (charged)
Supervised  Child discount available 12yrs  Languages spoken:
English*
CARDS: ●● ■■ ▄▄ ◨ Travellers cheques

## VIEUX-VIEL Ille-et-Vilaine

**Le Vieux Presbytère** (Prop: Madeline Stracquadanio)
*35610*
☎ 299486529 FAX 299486529
Near river  Near lake  Forest area
*5 rms (3 shr)  (3 fmly)  No smoking on premises  Full central
heating  Open parking available  Covered parking available
Supervised  Child discount available 12yrs  Boule  V meals
Languages spoken: English*

## VITRE Ille-et-Vilaine

★★ **Hotel Perceval**
Aire d'Erbrée *35500*
☎ 299494999 FAX 299493022
(From Paris motorway toll booth continue towards Rennes and
take exit 'Aire d'Erbrée after 5kms from Vitre towards
Laval.7kms on right 'Erbree' and follow signs)
Forest area  Near motorway
*46 en suite (bth/shr)  (2 fmly)  TV in all bedrooms  STV  Direct
dial from all bedrooms  Night porter  Full central heating  Open
parking available  Pool table  Open terrace  V meals  Last d
21.30hrs  Languages spoken: English*
CARDS: ●● ■■ ▄▄ ◨ Travellers cheques

## VIVIER-SUR-MER, LE Ille-et-Vilaine

★★ **Hotel Le Bretagne**
6 Rond Point du Centre *35960*
☎ 299489174 FAX 299488110
Near sea  Near beach  Forest area  In town centre  Near
motorway
*Closed 30 Nov-15 Feb*
*16 en suite (bth/shr)  10 rooms in annexe  (3 fmly)  TV in all
bedrooms  Direct dial from all bedrooms  Licensed  Full central
heating  Open parking available  Child discount available 12yrs
Sauna  Solarium  Bicycle rental  V meals  Last d 20.45hrs
Languages spoken: English*
CARDS: ●● ■■ ▄▄ ◨

## YFFINIAC Côtes-D'Armor

**Le Grenier** (Prop: Marie-Reine Loquin)
rte de Plédran *22120*
☎ 296726455 FAX 296726874
(in town centre, head towards Pledran)
Near sea  Near beach  Forest area
*3 en suite (bth/shr)  (1 fmly)  No smoking on premises  Full
central heating  Open parking available  Supervised  Child
discount available  Boule  Bicycle rental  Languages spoken:
English German & Spanish*
CARDS: ■ Travellers cheques

# Normandy

Normandy is a 'land of milk and honey', with a pleasant climate, beautiful scenery, and lovely half-timbered buildings. Much of the region's economy is derived from the rich harvests of both land and sea, and its fine produce features in a generous cuisine with plenty of cream-laden sauces. Just a hop over the Channel, Normandy is close enough for a weekend break and full of interest for a longer visit. Stretching from the majestic Mont-Saint-Michel in the west, almost to Paris, it covers a vast area, including seaside resorts, historical buildings, beautiful gardens, the regional capital Rouen (immortalised by Flaubert in Madame Bovary), and the D-Day beaches forever associated with the liberation of France.

## ESSENTIAL FACTS

| | |
|---|---|
| DÉPARTEMENTS: | Calvados, Eure, Manche, Orne, Seine-Maritime |
| PRINCIPAL TOWNS | Bayeux, Caen, Alençon, Rouen, Le Havre, Cherbourg, Lisieux, Dieppe, Evreux |
| PLACES TO VISIT: | The famous Bayeux Tapestry; The D-Day beaches, The Memorial, A Museum for Peace at Caen; Château Gaillard, Monet's Garden at Giverny, Mont-St-Michel |
| REGIONAL TOURIST OFFICE | 14 Rue Charles Corbeau, 27000 Evreux Tel 02 32 33 79 00  Fax 02 32 31 19 04 |
| LOCAL GASTRONOMIC DELIGHTS | Chicken or pork with apples, cream and cider. Cheeses: Pont l'Evêque, Livarot, Camembert. Duck à la Rouennaise (a pink fleshed duck); tripes à la mode de Caen (traditional dish featuring tripe); marmite Dieppoise, a local fish stew. Apples and cream are the star ingredients of desserts, particularly the famous Normandy apple tart. |
| DRINKS | Calvados: apple-flavoured brandy. Cider: doux (sweet), bouché (sparkling), sec (dry). Poire: pear cider. Pommeau: apple liqueur. Benedictine, liqueur made from the aromatic herbs of the Pays de Ceux. |
| LOCAL CRAFTS WHAT TO BUY | Lace: Alençon & Bayeux. Copperware & pewter: Villedieu-les-Poleles. Stone-carving: Avrancles & Mortain. Textiles: Louviers. Linen: Orbec. |

## ACQUEVILLE Manche

**La Belangerie** (Prop: M & Mme Geoffroy)
*50440*
☎ 233945949
A 16th-century manor house, recently renovated. The dining area has an unusual chimney breast which has been recognised by the Department of Fine Arts. The bedrooms are on the first floor and all have beamed ceilings. Meals are mainly prepared from local farm products, including beef, pork, lamb chicken and fish.
Near river  Near lake  Near sea  Near beach  Near motorway
*3 rms (1 bth)  (1 fmly)  Radio in rooms  Full central heating  Open parking available  Child discount available 6yrs  TV room  V meals  Last d 20.30hrs  Languages spoken: English*
ROOMS:  d fr 230FF  ✱
MEALS:  Dinner fr 85FF✱

## ACQUIGNY Eure

**Bed & Breakfast** (Prop: C & M Heullant)
Quartier St-Mauxé *27400*
☎ 232502010
(off N154, 15km from Evreux, 5km from Louviers)
Near river  Near lake  Near motorway
*3 en suite (bth/shr)  (1 fmly)  Open parking available  Child discount available  Languages spoken: English*
CARDS: Travellers cheques

## AIGLE, L' Orne

**★ ★ ★ Hotel du Dauphin** (Best Western)
pl de la Halle *63100*
☎ 233841800 FAX 233340928
Near river  Near lake  Forest area  In town centre  Near motorway
*30 rms (28 bth)  (6 fmly)  TV in all bedrooms  STV  Direct dial from all bedrooms  Mini-bar in all bedrooms  Licensed  Night porter  Full central heating  Open parking available  Supervised  Open terrace  Last d 22.00hrs  Languages spoken: English*
ROOMS:  (room only) d 359-523FF
MEALS:  Continental breakfast 45FF  Lunch 170-280FF&alc  Dinner 170-280FF&alc
CARDS: 💳 💳 💳 💳 Travellers cheques

## ALENÇON Orne

**★ ★ Le Grand St-Michel**
7 rue du Temple *61000*
☎ 233260477 FAX 233267182
Forest area  In town centre  Near motorway
*Closed Jul, 2 wks in Feb & 2 wks in Nov*
*13 en suite (bth/shr)  (3 fmly)  TV in all bedrooms  Direct dial from all bedrooms  Licensed  Full central heating  Air conditioning in bedrooms  Open parking available  Covered parking available (charged)  Supervised  Child discount available 10yrs  V meals  Last d 22.00hrs  Languages spoken: English, German, Italian & Spanish*
CARDS: 💳 💳 💳 💳 Travellers cheques

**★ ★ De L'Industrie**
22 pl Général-de-Gaulle *61000*
☎ 233271930 FAX 233284956
In town centre  Near motorway

*contd.*

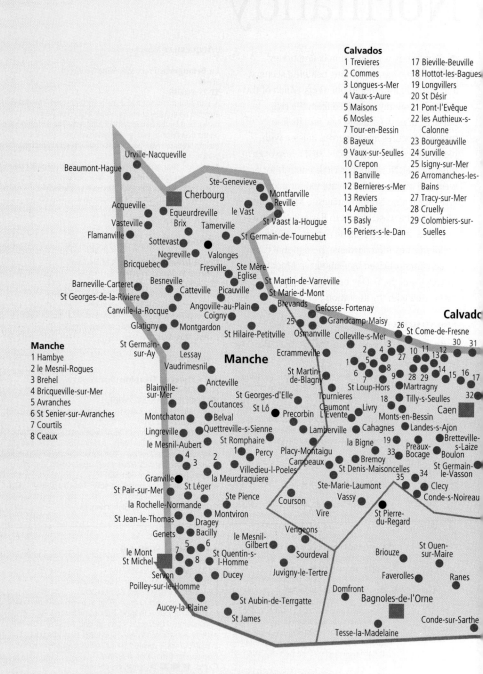

**Calvados**

1 Trevieres
2 Commes
3 Longues-s-Mer
4 Vaux-s-Aure
5 Maisons
6 Mosles
7 Tour-en-Bessin
8 Bayeux
9 Vaux-sur-Seulles
10 Crepon
11 Banville
12 Bernieres-s-Mer
13 Reviers
14 Amblie
15 Basly
16 Periers-s-le-Dan
17 Bieville-Beuville
18 Hottot-les-Bagues
19 Longvillers
20 St Désir
21 Pont-l'Evêque
22 les Authieux-s-Calonne
23 Bourgeauville
24 Surville
25 Isigny-sur-Mer
26 Arromanches-les-Bains
27 Tracy-sur-Mer
28 Cruelly
29 Colombiers-sur-Suelles

**Manche**

1 Hambye
2 le Mesnil-Rogues
3 Brehel
4 Bricqueville-sur-Mer
5 Avranches
6 St Senier-sur-Avranches
7 Courtils
8 Ceaux

Towns marked with a black symbol are places of interest or points of reference
Those marked with a red symbol have gazetteer entries

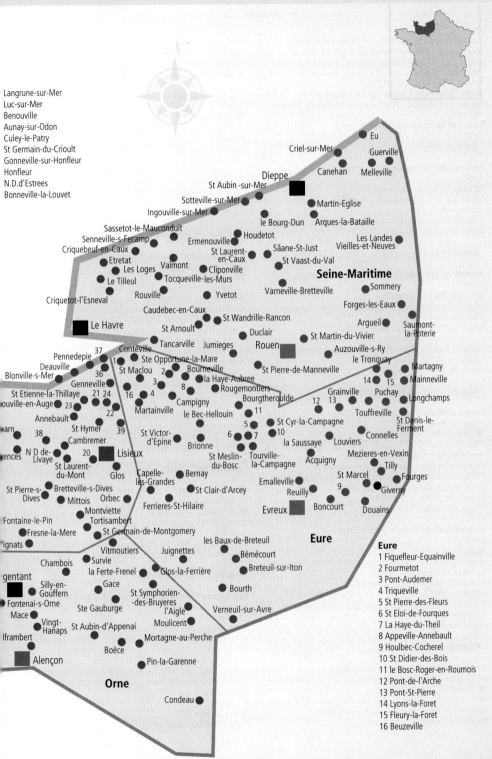

Langrune-sur-Mer
Luc-sur-Mer
Benouville
Aunay-sur-Odon
Culey-le-Patry
St Germain-du-Crioult
Gonneville-sur-Honfleur
Honfleur
N.D.d'Estrees
Bonneville-la-Louvet

Eu
Criel-sur-Mer
Guerville
Canehan  Melleville
Dieppe
St Aubin -sur-Mer
Martin-Eglise
Sotteville-sur-Mer
Ingouville-sur-Mer
le Bourg-Dun  Arques-la-Bataille
Sassetot-le-Mauconduit
Houdetot  Les Landes
Senneville-s-Fecamp  Ermenouville  Vieilles-et-Neuves
Criquebeuf-en-Caux  St Laurent-  Sâane-St-Just
en-Caux
Etretat  Valmont  Cliponville  St Vaast-du-Val  Seine-Maritime
Les Loges
Le Tilleul  Tocqueville-les-Murs  Sommery
Rouville  Yvetot  Varneville-Bretteville
Criquetot-l'Esneval
Caudebec-en-Caux  Forges-les-Eaux
St Wandrille-Rancon
Le Havre  Argueil  Saumont-
St Arnoult  Duclair  la-Poterie
Tancarville  Jumieges  St Martin-du-Vivier
37  Contèville  Rouen  Auzouville-s-Ry
Pennedepie  Ste Opportune-la-Mare  le Tronquay
Deauville  36  St Maclou  2  Bourneville  St Pierre-de-Manneville  Martagny
Blonville-s-Mer  3  la-Haye-Aubree  14  15  Mainneville
Genneville  8  Rougemontiers  Grainville  Puchay
St Etienne-la-Thillaye  21 24  16  4  Bourgtheroulde  Longchamps
ouville-en-Auge  23  Campigny  12  13  St Denis-le-
Annebault  22  Martainville  le Bec-Hellouin  11  Touffreville  Ferment
arn  St Hymer  39  St Victor-  5  St Cyr-la-Campagne  Connelles
38  Cambremer  d'Epine  6  7  10  la Saussaye  Louviers  Mezieres-en-Vexin
ences  N D de-  20  Brionne  Tourville-  Acquigny  Tilly
Livaye  Lisieux  St Meslin-  la-Campagne  St Marcel  Fourges
St Laurent-  du-Bosc  Emalleville  9  Giverny
du-Mont  Glos  Bernay  Reuilly  Douains
St Pierre-s-  Bretteville-s-Dives  Capelle-  St Clair-d'Arcey  Evreux  Boncourt
Dives  Mittois  Orbec  les-Grandes  Ferrieres-St-Hilaire
Montviette  Eure
Fontaine-le-Pin  Tortisambert
Fresne-la-Mere  St Germain-de-Montgomery  les Baux-de-Breteuil  Eure
ignats  Vitmoutiers  Juignettes  Bémécourt  1 Fiquefleur-Equainville
Chambois  Survie  Glos-la-Ferrière  Breteuil-sur-Iton  2 Fourmetot
gentant  la Ferte-Frenel  3 Pont-Audemer
Silly-en-  Gace  Bourth  4 Triqueville
Gouffern  St Symphorien-  5 St Pierre-des-Fleurs
Fontenai-s-Orne  des-Bruyeres  Verneuil-sur-Avre  6 St Eloi-de-Fourques
Mace  Ste Gauburge  l'Aigle  7 La Haye-du-Theil
Vingt-  Moulicent  8 Appeville-Annebault
Iframbert  Hanaps  St Aubin-d'Appenai  9 Houlbec-Cocherel
Mortagne-au-Perche  10 St Didier-des-Bois
Boëce  11 le Bosc-Roger-en-Roumois
Alençon  Pin-la-Garenne  12 Pont-de-l'Arche
13 Pont-St-Pierre
Orne  14 Lyons-la-Foret
Condeau  15 Fleury-la-Foret
16 Beuzeville

7 en suite (shr) TV in all bedrooms Direct dial from all bedrooms Licensed Full central heating Child discount available 12yrs Last d 21.30hrs Languages spoken: English, German & Spanish
ROOMS: s 180-200FF; d 220-250FF
**Reductions over 1 night Special breaks**
MEALS: Full breakfast 25FF Lunch 70-160FF&alc Dinner 70-160FF&alc
CARDS: ●● ▩▩ Travellers cheques

### AMBLIE Calvados

**Hameau de Pierrepont** (Prop: Elaine Ringoot Fiquet)
14480
☎ 231801004 FAX 231081759
(from Caen Memorial take D22 to Pierrepont, approx 12km)
Near river Forest area
2 en suite (shr) Full central heating Open parking available
CARDS: Travellers cheques

### ANCTEVILLE Manche

**Manoir de la Foulerie** (Prop: Michel & Sylvie Enouf)
50200
☎ 233452764 FAX 233457369
(from Coutances take D2 towards Lessay. Follow signs for Ancteville on the right)
Near river Near lake Near sea Near beach
5 en suite (bth/shr) (3 fmly) TV in all bedrooms Open parking available Tennis Riding Boule Mini-golf Bicycle rental Languages spoken: English & German
CARDS: ▩▩ Travellers cheques

### ANGOVILLE-AU-PLAIN Manche

**Ferme d'Allain** (Prop: Jeanne Flambard)
12 rue de l'Eglise 50480
☎ 233421130
(from Cherbourg take N13 south, on through Valognes. Angoville-au-Plain is on left off D913)
Near river Near sea Near beach Near motorway
2 en suite (shr) (1 fmly) No smoking in all bedrooms Full central heating Open parking available
ROOMS: s fr 180FF; d 200-220FF
MEALS: Dinner fr 90FF✱

**La Guidonnerie** (Prop: M & Mme Leonard)
50480
☎ 233423351
(from N13 at St Come du Mont take D913 towards Utah Beach, turn right for Angoville-au-Plain)
Near sea Forest area Near motorway
Closed Oct-mid Mar
2 en suite (bth) Full central heating Open parking available
Languages spoken: English
CARDS: Travellers cheques

### ANNEBAULT Calvados

**Bed & Breakfast** (Prop: M & Mme Leroy)
rte de Rouen, La Basse Cour 14430
☎ 231648086 FAX 231648086
(from A13 exit at la Haie-Tondue. Take N175 towards Caen for 4kms. 3rd house after crossroads in Annebault)
Forest area Near motorway

4 rms (3 bth/shr) (2 fmly) Radio in rooms Full central heating Open parking available
ROOMS: s 190FF; d 220FF
**✱ Reductions over 1 night Special breaks**

★★ **Le Cardinal**
14430
☎ 231648196 FAX 231646465
Near lake Near sea Near beach In town centre Near motorway
Closed mid Jan-Feb
7 rms (6 shr) TV in all bedrooms STV Direct dial from all bedrooms Licensed Full central heating Air conditioning in bedrooms Open parking available Child discount available 12yrs Boule Open terrace Last d 21.00hrs Languages spoken: English
CARDS: ●● ▩▩ ▩▩

### APPEVILLE-ANNEBAULT Eure

**Les Aubepines** (Prop: Mr & Mrs Closson-Maze)
aux Chauffourniers 27290
☎ 232561425 FAX 232561425
(A13 exit26, take direction Pont Audemer, at Medine rdbt take D89. Evreux to Appeville-Annebault at 2.5kms, Les Marettes just after on the left signed "chambre d'hôte")
This charming restored old cottage has bedrooms of character with many modern facilities. Galleried reception rooms are another feature of this attractive property which is surrounded by pretty gardens in quiet typical Normandy countryside.
Near river Near lake Forest area Near motorway
Closed Oct-Mar
4 en suite (bth/shr) (1 fmly) (1 with balcony) No smoking on premises Open parking available Covered parking available Child discount available 12yrs Tennis Fishing Riding Bicycle rental V meals Languages spoken: English & Spanish
ROOMS: d 250-270FF
MEALS: Dinner 110FF
CARDS: Travellers cheques

### ARGENCES Calvados

**Bed & Breakfast** (Prop: M & Mme G & A Jautee)
28 rue Maréchal-Joffre 14370
☎ 231236482 & 0685262987
(south east of Caen off N13)
Near river
3 rms (2 bth) (1 fmly) No smoking on premises TV available Full central heating Open parking available

### ARGUEIL Seine-Maritime

**Les Quatre Oiseaux** (Prop: Jeanette & Keith Mills)
St-Lucien 76780
☎ 235905195
(from Dieppe take D915 to Forges-les-Eaux. In market square turn right onto D921 to Argueil, then onto Nolleval. Turn right to St Lucien)
Forest area Near motorway
4 rms (1 fmly) No smoking in all bedrooms Full central heating Open parking available Boule Last d 11.00hrs Languages spoken: English
ROOMS: s 165FF; d 215FF
MEALS: Dinner 85FF
CARDS: Travellers cheques

## ARQUES-LA-BATAILLE Seine-Maritime

**Villa del Kantara** (Prop: Daniele Lasgouses)
2 rue de la Petite Chaussée *76800*
☎ 235855885
Near river  Near lake  Near sea  Forest area  Near motorway
*3 en suite (bth)  No smoking on premises  TV in all bedrooms
Radio in rooms  Full central heating  Open parking available
Child discount available  Languages spoken: English*

## ARROMANCHES-LES-BAINS Calvados

**★ ★ D'Arromanches**
2 rue du Colonel René Michel *14117*
☎ 231223626 FAX 231222329
(access from Caen via N13)
This small hotel has undergone extensive renovation over the
years, with the emphasis being on the bathrooms and the
decoration of the bedrooms, and it now offers comfortable
accommodation. The owner takes pride in his cooking and the
lady of the house is a charming host.

Near sea  Near beach  In town centre
*Closed Jan
9 en suite (bth/shr)  (2 fmly)  TV in all bedrooms  STV  Direct
dial from all bedrooms  Licensed  Full central heating  Open
parking available  Supervised  Child discount available 10yrs
Open terrace  Last d 21.00hrs  Languages spoken: English*
ROOMS: (room only) d 310FF
MEALS: Continental breakfast 40FF  Lunch 88-180FF  Dinner
88-180FF
CARDS: ●● ■■ Travellers cheques

**★ ★ De La Marine**
2 quai La Marine *14117*
☎ 231223419 FAX 231229880
Near sea  Near beach
*Closed 15 Nov-15 Feb
30 rms (26 bth/shr)  (2 fmly)  TV in all bedrooms  Radio in rooms
Direct dial from all bedrooms  Mini-bar in all bedrooms
Licensed  Full central heating  Open parking available
Supervised  Child discount available 8yrs  Fishing  Bicycle rental
Open terrace  V meals  Last d 21.30hrs  Languages spoken:
English*
CARDS: ■■ ■■ Travellers cheques

## AUCEY-LA-PLAINE Manche

**La Provostière** (Prop: René & Maryconne Feuvrier)
*50170*
☎ 233603367 FAX 233603700
Forest area

*2 en suite (shr)  No smoking on premises  TV available  Full
central heating  Open parking available  Child discount
available  Languages spoken: English*
CARDS: ■■

## AUNAY-SUR-ODON Calvados

**★ ★ De la Place**
rue du 12 Juin *14260*
☎ 231776073 FAX 231779007
Near river  Near lake  Forest area  In town centre  Near
motorway
*19 rms (13 bth)  (1 fmly)  (1 with balcony)  TV available  Licensed
Full central heating  Open parking available  Covered parking
available  Supervised  Child discount available 10yrs  Boule
Open terrace  Covered terrace  V meals  Last d 21.00hrs
Languages spoken: English*
CARDS: ●● ■■ ■■ Travellers cheques

## AUTHIEUX-SUR-CALONNE, LES Calvados

**Bed & Breakfast** (Prop: M & Mme Leroux)
rte de Blangy-le-Château *14130*
☎ 231646728 FAX 231646728
(from N175 (Caen-Rouen) take D534 towards Cormeilles for
1.5km, then D140 for 1.5km towards Blangy-le-Château)
Near river  Near lake  Near sea  Forest area
*5 rms (1 bth 2 shr)  No smoking on premises  Radio in rooms
Full central heating  Open parking available  Child discount
available 10yrs*

## AUZOUVILLE-SUR-RY Seine-Maritime

**Gentilhommière** (Prop: Paul & Ginette Cousin)
*76766*
☎ 235234074
Near river  Forest area  Near motorway
*2 en suite (bth/shr)  TV available  Full central heating  Open
parking available  Supervised  Child discount available 12yrs  V
meals*
CARDS: ■■

## AVRANCHES Manche

**★ ★ Abrincates**
37 bd du Luxembourg *50300*
☎ 233586664 FAX 233584011
(A84, exit Avranches Center. S of Avranches on N175, close to
Mt St Michel)
In town centre  Near motorway
*Closed 21 Dec-9 Jan RS Sun evening Oct-May
29 en suite (bth/shr)  (4 fmly)  (27 with balcony)  TV in all
bedrooms  STV  Direct dial from all bedrooms  Licensed  Lift
Full central heating  Open parking available  Supervised  Child
discount available 12yrs  Boule  Bicycle rental  Open terrace
Last d 22.00hrs  Languages spoken: English*
ROOMS: (room only) s 280-330FF; d 298-380FF
**Reductions over 1 night**
MEALS: Continental breakfast 38FF  Lunch 75-150FF&alc
Dinner 75-150FF&alc
CARDS: ●● ■■ JCB Travellers cheques

**★ ★ Du Jardin des Plantes**
10 pl Carnot *50300*
☎ 233580368 FAX 233600172
Near sea  In town centre  Near motorway
*26 rms (22 bth/shr)  (9 fmly)  (3 with balcony)  TV in all*

*contd.*

bedrooms Licensed Night porter Full central heating Open parking available Supervised Open terrace V meals Last d 21.30hrs Languages spoken: English
CARDS: ● ▥ JCB Travellers cheques

## BACILLY Manche

**Le Grand Moulin Lecomte** (Prop: Alan Harvey)
*50530*
☎ 233709208
(from channel ports follow signs for Mont St Michel and Avranches, before reaching Avranches take D41 into village of Bacilly then D231 in the direction of Genêts)

A restored 18th-century farmhouse, with English owners, where two rooms on the ground floor have private entrances and a further three rooms are on the first floor. There is a large dining room with original Norman, granite fireplace and a lounge with TV English and French channels available. Situated just three kilometres from Genêts which faces Mont St Michel in an area of beautiful sandy beaches.
Near river Near sea Near beach
*5 en suite (bth/shr) (3 fmly) Full central heating Open parking available Covered parking available Languages spoken: English, German & Welsh*
CARDS: Travellers cheques

## BAGNOLES-DE-L'ORNE Orne

### ★ ★ Beaumont
26 bd Lémeunier de la Raillère *61140*
☎ 233379177 FAX 233389061
This charming turn-of-the-century building is peacefully situated in a flower-filled park just five minutes from the town centre. It has cosy lounges, an attractive conservatory, congenial bar, and delightful garden. The bedrooms are well equipped, and meals are served in the romantic atmosphere of the candlelit restaurant.
Near river Near lake Forest area
*RS Restaurant closed Nov-Mar*
*40 rms (35 bth/shr) 17 rooms in annexe (1 fmly) (2 with balcony) TV in all bedrooms STV Direct dial from all bedrooms Licensed Night porter Full central heating Open parking available Supervised Child discount available 12yrs Open terrace Last d 21.30hrs Languages spoken: English*
ROOMS: (room only) s 315-330FF; d 315-375FF
**Reductions over 1 night**
MEALS: Continental breakfast 35FF Lunch 98-290FF&alc Dinner 98-290FF&alc
CARDS: ● ▥ ▤ ⑩ JCB & Eurocard Travellers cheques

### ★ ★ ★ Bois Joli
av Philippe-du-Rozier *61140*
☎ 233379277 FAX 233370756
This Anglo-Norman, timbered villa dates back to 1870 and is set in a 3,000 square-metre park near a lake. The restaurant and wine cellar have earned a reputation in the area for both their first-class cuisine and comprehensive wine list. The bedrooms, some with balconies, offer a good standard of comfort, and in addition, there is a fitness room, sauna, Turkish bath and solarium.
Near river Near lake Forest area In town centre
*Closed 4 Jan-9 Feb*

*20 en suite (bth/shr) (2 with balcony) TV in all bedrooms Direct dial from all bedrooms Licensed Lift Full central heating Open parking available Supervised Child discount available 12yrs Bicycle rental Open terrace Last d 22.00hrs Languages spoken: English & German*
ROOMS: (room only) d 345-585FF
**Reductions over 1 night**
MEALS: Continental breakfast 45FF Lunch 95-245FF&alc Dinner 95-245FF&alc
CARDS: ● ▥ ▤ ⑩ Travellers cheques

### ★ ★ ★ Lutetia
bd Paul Chalvet *61140*
☎ 233379477 FAX 233300987
Near lake Forest area In town centre
*Closed mid Oct-early April*
*34 rms (30 bth/shr) 14 rooms in annexe TV in all bedrooms Direct dial from all bedrooms Licensed Lift Full central heating Open parking available Supervised Child discount available Boule Covered terrace V meals Last d 21.00hrs Languages spoken: English,German & Italian*
CARDS: ● ▥ ▤ ⑩ Travellers cheques

### ★ ★ ★ *Manoir du Lys*
La Croix Gauthier, rte de Juvigny *61140*
☎ 233378069 FAX 233300580
(in direction of Juvigny-sous-Andaines pass golf course on right)
Near lake Forest area
*Closed 4 Jan-14 Feb RS Nov-3 Jan & 15 Feb-Etr*
*24 en suite (bth/shr) (3 fmly) (7 with balcony) TV in all bedrooms STV Direct dial from all bedrooms Mini-bar in all bedrooms Licensed Lift Full central heating Open parking available Covered parking available (charged) Child discount available 10yrs Indoor swimming pool (heated) Outdoor swimming pool (heated) Tennis Fishing Solarium Boule Bicycle rental Open terrace V meals Last d 21.30hrs Languages spoken: English & Spanish*
CARDS: ● ▥ ▤ ⑩ Travellers cheques

**★ ★ De Normandie**
2 av du Dr Paul Lémuet *61140*
☎ 233308016 FAX 233370619
Near lake Forest area In town centre
*Closed 6 Nov-Mar*
*22 rms (5 bth 13 shr) (3 fmly) (2 with balcony) TV in all*
*bedrooms Direct dial from all bedrooms Licensed Lift Full*
*central heating Open parking available Covered parking*
*available Supervised Child discount available 5yrs Bicycle*
*rental Open terrace V meals Languages spoken: English*
CARDS: ●● ■ ▦ ◉ Travellers cheques

**★ ★ Nouvel Hotel**
8 av Albert Christophle, Tessi-la-Madeleine *61140*
☎ 233307500 FAX 233307513
(Near the church and the castle, 400mtrs from the thermal
baths)
Near river Near lake Forest area In town centre
*Closed Nov-Mar*
*30 en suite (bth/shr) (1 fmly) (2 with balcony) TV in all*
*bedrooms Direct dial from all bedrooms Room-safe Licensed*
*Lift Night porter Full central heating Open parking available*
*Supervised Child discount available 10yrs Boule Open terrace*
*Wkly live entertainment V meals Last d 21.00hrs Languages*
*spoken: English*
MEALS: Continental breakfast 38FF Lunch 90-170FF Dinner
90-170FF
CARDS: ●● ▦

**BANVILLE** Calvados

**Ferme le Petit Val** (Prop: Gerard Lesage)
24 r du Camp Romain *14480*
☎ 231379218 FAX 231379218
Near river Near sea Forest area
*5 en suite (bth/shr) (1 fmly) Full central heating Open parking*
*available Covered parking available Supervised Child discount*
*available 7yrs V meals Last d 17.00hrs Languages spoken:*
*English & Spanish*
CARDS: Travellers cheques

**BARNEVILLE-CARTERET** Manche

**Bed & Breakfast** (Prop: M G Lebourgeois)
5 rue du Pic-Mallet *50270*
☎ 233049022 FAX 233045461
(centre of Barneville-Carteret, near the church)
Near sea Near beach In town centre Near motorway
*Closed 12 Nov-Etr*
*3 en suite (bth/shr) (2 fmly) Full central heating Open parking*
*available Child discount available Bicycle rental*
ROOMS: s 210FF; d 240FF **✱ Reductions over 1 night**
CARDS: Travellers cheques

**★ ★ Les Isles**
*50270*
☎ 233049076 FAX 233945383
(Approach from Cherbourg via D904)
Near sea Near beach
*Closed 16 Nov-Jan*
*32 rms (30 bth) (3 fmly) (7 with balcony) TV in all bedrooms*
*Direct dial from all bedrooms Licensed Full central heating*
*Open parking available Child discount available Solarium*
*Bicycle rental Open terrace Water skiing, Cycling Last d*
*21.30hrs Languages spoken: English*
CARDS: ●● ■ ▦ Travellers cheques

**BASLY** Calvados

**Bed & Breakfast** (Prop: C Desperques)
14 rte de Douvres *14610*
☎ 231809415
Near sea Forest area
*6 rms (1 shr) (1 fmly) TV available Full central heating Open*
*parking available*
CARDS: Travellers cheques

**BAUX-DE-BRETEUIL, LES** Eure

**La Bourganière** (Prop: Mme M Noël)
*27160*
☎ 232306818 FAX 232301993
(from Breteuil take D833)
Old farm-style house run by welcoming hostess, Marie Noël.
Living/dining room is traditionally furnished, with original
wooden beams. Two spacious rooms, one of which is a family
room. Reductions offered for children under eight years.
Forest area
*2 en suite (bth/shr) (1 fmly) (1 with balcony) Full central*
*heating Open parking available Child discount available 10yrs*
*Last d 8.30pm*
ROOMS: s 200FF; d 250FF ✱
MEALS: Dinner fr 90FF✱

**BAYEUX** Calvados

**★ ★ De Brunville**
9 rue Génas Duhomme *14400*
☎ 231211800 FAX 231517089
In town centre
*38 en suite (bth/shr) 5 rooms in annexe (2 fmly) (1 with*
*balcony) TV in all bedrooms STV Direct dial from all*
*bedrooms Licensed Lift Full central heating Open parking*
*available Open terrace Covered terrace Last d 22.00hrs*
*Languages spoken: English*
CARDS: ●● ■ ▦ Travellers cheques

**★ ★ ★ Château de Bellefontaine**
49 rue de Bellefontaine *14400*
☎ 231220010 FAX 231221909
Near river Forest area Near motorway
*15 en suite (bth/shr) (3 fmly) No smoking in 1 bedroom TV in all*
*bedrooms Direct dial from all bedrooms Mini-bar in all*
*bedrooms Licensed Lift Night porter Full central heating Open*
*parking available Supervised Child discount available 10yrs*
*Tennis Bicycle rental Open terrace Languages spoken: English*
ROOMS: (room only) s 450-550FF; d 550-750FF
CARDS: ●● ■ ▦ ◉ Travellers cheques

**★ ★ ★ Hotel Churchill**
14-16 rue St-Jean *14404*
☎ 231213180 FAX 231214166
(Situated in the town center near the Tapestry and the
Cathedral.)
Situated in the old quarter of the town, Monsieur and Madame
Selmi welcome their visitors into a warm, informal
atmosphere. The guest rooms are individually styled and offer
a high standard of comfort; and the cuisine incorporates
quality home cooking and regional specialities.
Near river Forest area In town centre Near motorway
*Closed Dec-17 Feb*
*32 en suite (bth/shr) (6 fmly) TV in all bedrooms STV Direct*
*dial from all bedrooms Mini-bar in 5 bedrooms Full central*
*heating V meals Languages spoken: English* contd.

**Hotel Churchill**
ROOMS: (room only) s fr 320FF; d 360-540FF
**Reductions over 1 night**
CARDS: 💳 💳 💳 Travellers cheques

★ ★ ★ **Grand Hotel du Luxembourg** (Best Western)
25 rue des Bouches *14400*
☎ 231920004 FAX 231925426
Near sea Forest area In town centre Near motorway
*22 en suite (bth/shr) 5 rooms in annexe (1 fmly) (1 with balcony) TV in all bedrooms STV Radio in rooms Direct dial from all bedrooms Mini-bar in all bedrooms Lift Full central heating Open parking available Covered parking available Child discount available 12yrs Last d 21.30hrs Languages spoken: English*
CARDS: 💳 💳 💳 Travellers cheques

★ ★ ★ **Lion d'Or**
71 rue St-Jean *14400*
☎ 231920690 FAX 231221564
(from A13 follow directions to SNCF station. Then at station take 1st right, then straight ahead following arrows)

The Hotel Lion d'Or is a former coaching inn dating back to the 17th century, that offers tastefully furnished guest rooms offering a high standard of accommodation, a cosy bar-lounge with an open fireplace and a peaceful flower-filled courtyard. The menu features traditional, skilfully prepared dishes, served by friendly, attentive staff.
Near river In town centre
*Closed 20 Dec-20 Jan*
*25 en suite (bth/shr) (8 fmly) TV in all bedrooms STV Direct dial from all bedrooms Mini-bar in all bedrooms Licensed Night porter Full central heating Open parking available Covered parking available Supervised Child discount available 12yrs Open terrace Bar & Lecture Room V meals Last d 21.30hrs Languages spoken: English*
ROOMS: (room only) s 450-505FF; d 450-630FF
**Reductions over 1 night**

70

MEALS: Continental breakfast 65FF Lunch 100-230FF&alc Dinner 150-230FF&alc
CARDS: 💳 💳 💳 💳 Travellers cheques

**Manoir du Carel** (Prop: M et Mme Aumond)
Maisons *14400*
☎ 231223700 FAX 231215700
(leave N13 onto D6 in direction of Port-de-Bessin, after 4.5km turn left, manor 1km on right)
Near beach Forest area Near motorway
*4 en suite (bth/shr) TV in all bedrooms Full central heating Open parking available Covered parking available Tennis Riding Languages spoken: English & German*
CARDS: 💳 💳

★ ★ ★ **Novotel Bayeux**
117 St-Patrice *14400*
☎ 231921611 FAX 231218876
(situated on the route from Caen to Cherbourg, close to town centre and railway station)
Near motorway
*77 en suite (bth/shr) (25 fmly) No smoking in 30 bedrooms TV in all bedrooms Radio in rooms Direct dial from all bedrooms Mini-bar in all bedrooms Licensed Lift Night porter Full central heating Air conditioning in bedrooms Open parking available Child discount available 16yrs Outdoor swimming pool Pool table Open terrace Covered terrace V meals Last d 22.30hrs Languages spoken: English*
CARDS: 💳 💳 💳 💳 Travellers cheques

**River Cottage** (Prop: Soria Pirot)
3 Impasse Moulin de la Rivière *14400*
☎ 231923123 FAX 231923123
(from Cherbourg follow signs for Arromanches. Pass Champion supermarket on right and campsite on left, take next left. From Caen 1st right after lights to Arromanches)
An old renovated cottage where the en suite bedrooms are decorated in English style with matching duvet and curtains and Edwardian furniture. The garden extends to the river.
Near river Near sea Near beach Forest area
*3 en suite (shr) No smoking on premises Full central heating Open parking available Fishing Languages spoken: English*
ROOMS: d 250FF
MEALS: Dinner 65FF
CARDS: Travellers cheques

**BEAUMONT-HAGUE** Manche

**Le Closet** (Prop: M & Mme Dalmont)
2 allée des Jardins *50440*
☎ 233527246
(in the town take Vauville road. Le Closet is situated 150mtrs from the church)
Near sea Near beach
*3 en suite (shr) (2 fmly) No smoking on premises Full central heating Open parking available Languages spoken: English*
ROOMS: s 155FF; d 200-220FF
CARDS: 💳 Travellers cheques

**BEC-HELLOUIN, LE** Eure

★ ★ ★ **Auberge de l'Abbaye**
*27800*
☎ 232448602 FAX 232463223
Near river Forest area In town centre Near motorway
*10 en suite (bth/shr) (1 fmly) No smoking in 1 bedroom Direct dial from all bedrooms Mini-bar in all bedrooms Licensed Full*

central heating Open parking available Covered parking available Supervised Child discount available Boule Bicycle rental Open terrace V meals Last d 22.00hrs Languages spoken: English
CARDS: ●● ▦ ▩ Travellers cheques

### BELVAL Manche

**La Guerandiere** (Prop: Paul & Lesley Trout)
*50210*
☎ 233452103 FAX 233452103
(From Coutances follow D972 towards St Lo for 6km, turn right onto the D276 towards Beval Bourg for 3km, house on right, signposted)

A beautiful Norman stonehouse has been patiently renovated by a young English couple, in a peaceful rural spot within easy reach of Coutances. The bedrooms are country cottage style with pine furniture and pastel colour schemes. The guests have their own lounge with a beautiful open fire. A welcoming homely atmosphere.
Near river Near sea Forest area
*Closed Nov-Feb*
*4 rms (3 shr) (3 fmly) No smoking on premises Full central heating Open parking available Covered parking available Child discount available 5yrs Boule Languages spoken: English*
ROOMS: s 155FF; d 225FF *
MEALS: Dinner 90FF

### BÉMÉCOURT Eure

**Le Vieux Château** (Prop: Maryvonne Lallemand-Legras)
*27160*
☎ 232299047
(from Breteuil take D141 towards Rugles, through forest. At Bémécourt turn left 300m after traffic lights)
Built on the site of a fortified castle, this half-timbered manor house is flanked by two 15th-century towers and encircled by a moat. The garden is a haven of peace. Breakfast can be described as 'more of a brunch', with homemade bread and jams.
Forest area Near motorway
*Closed 16-31 Dec*
*3 rms Full central heating Open parking available No children 8yrs Child discount available 12yrs Fishing Riding Boule Bicycle rental Open terrace Languages spoken: English & German*
ROOMS: s 300FF; d 450FF **Reductions over 1 night**
MEALS: Dinner fr 100FF*
CARDS: Travellers cheques

### BÉNOUVILLE Calvados

★ ★ ★ *Glycine*
11 pl du Commando *14970*
☎ 231446194 FAX 231436730
Near river Near sea Near motorway
*25 en suite (bth/shr) (8 fmly) TV in all bedrooms STV Direct dial from all bedrooms Mini-bar in all bedrooms Licensed Full central heating Open parking available Supervised Open terrace Last d 21.45hrs Languages spoken: English*
CARDS: ●● ▩

### BERNAY Eure

★ ★ **Le Lion d'Or**
48 rue du Général-de-Gaulle *27300*
☎ 232431206 FAX 232466058
(in the town centre near the Tourist Office)

This 150-year-old former coaching inn is set in the heart of the town of Bernay and offers its visitors quality Normandy cuisine and traditional hospitality. Built in the distinct architecture of the region and featuring an interior courtyard, it offers comfortable bedrooms with private facilities and an informal restaurant which serves a large choice of local produce.
Near river Forest area In town centre Near motorway
*26 en suite (bth/shr) (8 fmly) (1 with balcony) No smoking in 6 bedrooms TV in all bedrooms STV Direct dial from all bedrooms Licensed Lift Full central heating Open parking available Supervised Child discount available 12yrs Open terrace V meals Last d 21.30hrs Languages spoken: English*
ROOMS: (room only) s 170-250FF; d 230-300FF
**Reductions over 1 night**
MEALS: Continental breakfast 35FF Dinner 107-165FF
CARDS: ●● ▦ ▩ ⚫ Travellers cheques

### BERNIÈRES-SUR-MER Calvados

***Bed & Breakfast*** (Prop: M Michel Lambard)
31 rue Montauban, "La Louveraie" *14990*
☎ 231965312 FAX 231965312
Near sea In town centre
*1 en suite (shr) TV available Radio in rooms Full central heating Open parking available Boule Mini-golf Bicycle rental Languages spoken: English & Spanish*

contd.

## BESNEVILLE Manche

**Hotel Danois** (Prop: Michel Lamy)
*50390*
☎ 233416263
Forest area
*Closed Oct-14 Apr*
*2 rms  Open parking available*

## BEUZEVILLE Eure

### ★ ★ Cochon d'Or et Petit Castel
pl du Général-de-Gaulle *27210*
☎ 232577046 FAX 232422570
Whether situated on the garden or village side, the bedrooms in this establishment ensure peaceful accommodation. Tastefully decorated, they offer modern amenities and are suitable for both business and leisure travellers. The elegant restaurant serves imaginative dishes.
In town centre

*Closed 15 Dec-15 Jan*
*20 rms (17 bth 1 shr)  16 rooms in annexe  (3 fmly)  TV in 16 bedrooms  Direct dial from all bedrooms  Licensed  Full central heating  Open parking available  V meals  Last d 21.00hrs*
*Languages spoken: English*
ROOMS: (room only) d 205-340FF
MEALS: Continental breakfast 38FF  Lunch 82-245FF&alc  Dinner 82-245FF&alc
CARDS: ● ■ Travellers cheques

### ★ ★ De la Poste
60 rue Constant Fouché *27210*
☎ 232577104 FAX 232421101

(on N175 between Caen and Rouen)
This old coaching inn was built in 1844, and features cheerfully

decorated bedrooms with good modern amenities and a classic French-style restaurant, offering a well balanced choice of dishes served by attentive staff. A golf course and mini-golf can be found within driving distance of the hotel.
Forest area  In town centre  Near motorway
*Closed mid Nov-mid Mar*
*14 en suite (bth/shr)  (2 fmly)  (3 with balcony)  TV in 12 bedrooms  Direct dial from all bedrooms  Licensed  Full central heating  Open parking available  Covered parking available (charged)  Supervised  Child discount available 12yrs  Open terrace  V meals  Last d 21.00hrs  Languages spoken: English*
MEALS: Continental breakfast 40FF  Lunch 79-195FF&alc  Dinner 99-195FF&alc✱
CARDS: ● ■ ▥ ▣ JCB

## BIÉVILLE-BEUVILLE Calvados

**Bed & Breakfast** (Prop: J M & A Bartassot)
4 rue Haute *14112*
☎ 231443499 FAX 231439415
Near motorway
*5 en suite (shr)  Full central heating  Open parking available  Child discount available*

**Le Londel** (Prop: Jean-Claude & Danielle Bruand)
*14112*
☎ 231445174 FAX 231445174
Near sea  Near motorway
*3 en suite (bth/shr)  Full central heating  Open parking available  Covered parking available  Child discount available*
CARDS: Travellers cheques

**La Petite Londe** (Prop: Françoise Lance)
*14112*
☎ 231445203 FAX 231445203
(leave the Northern peripheric at exit no. 5: Côte de Nacre D7, 3km further at La Bijude turn right in direction of Le Londel, 700m further at first farm on right take gravel lane)
Near motorway
*2 en suite (bth/shr)  (2 fmly)  TV in 1 bedroom  Full central heating  Open parking available  Languages spoken: English*
CARDS: Travellers cheques

## BIGNE, LA Calvados

**Le Quettevillière** (Prop: Andre & Elizabeth Bamford)
*14260*
☎ 231774594 FAX 231775927
Near river  Near lake  Forest area  Near motorway
*7 en suite (bth/shr)  (5 fmly)  (2 with balcony)  No smoking in 3 bedrooms  Radio in rooms  Full central heating  Open parking available  Child discount available  V meals  Languages spoken: English*

## BLAINVILLE-SUR-MER Manche

**Bed & Breakfast** (Prop: M Jean Bouton)
Villa "Alice", 21 rte de la Louverie *50560*
☎ 233472839 & 145223923 FAX 233472839 & 145223923
(from Coutances take D44 to Tourville and Coutainville, then D651 to Blainville-sur-Mer)
Near sea  Near beach
*15 May-Sep*
*3 rms  Full central heating  Open parking available  No children 6yrs  Child discount available 10yrs  Languages spoken: English, German & Spanish*

ROOMS: s fr 180FF; d fr 200FF ✻
CARDS: Travellers cheques

## BLONVILLE-SUR-MER Calvados

### ★ ★ L'Epi d'Or
23 av Michel d'Ornano *14910*
☎ 231879048 FAX 231870898
(access via Deauville heading towards Blonville & Villers)
Near sea  Near beach  In town centre
*40 en suite (bth/shr)  (6 fmly)  (16 with balcony)  TV in 30
bedrooms  Direct dial from all bedrooms  Mini-bar in 4
bedrooms  Licensed  Lift  Full central heating  Open parking
available  Child discount available 10yrs  Open terrace  Covered
terrace  V meals  Last d 22.00hrs  Languages spoken: English &
Spanish*
ROOMS: (room only) s 280-350FF; d 300-400FF
**Reductions over 1 night**
MEALS: Full breakfast 40FF  Lunch 100-360FF&alc  Dinner
100-360FF&alc
CARDS: ●● ■ ☲ ☑ Travellers cheques

## BOËCÉ Orne

### La Fosse
*61560*
☎ 233254179
Forest area  Near motorway
*3 en suite (bth/shr)  (1 fmly)  No smoking on premises  Full
central heating  Open parking available  Child discount
available  Outdoor swimming pool (heated)  Last d 20.00hrs
Languages spoken: English*

## BONCOURT Eure

### Les Ormes (Prop: Mme Beghini)
5 rue Divette *27120*
☎ 232369244 & 232367301 FAX 232263911
(take D534 to Boncourt from N13 between Pacy-sur-
Eure/d'Evreux)
Forest area  Near motorway
*5 en suite (bth/shr)  No smoking in all bedrooms  TV available
Open parking available  Open terrace  Languages spoken:
English*

## BONNEVILLE-LA-LOUVET Calvados

### La Ferme des Tostes
rte de Blangy *14130*
☎ 231643774 FAX 231649547
(A25 exit Pont-l'Évêque in direction of Caen then N175 take
D534 towards Cormeilles for 1.5km towards Blagny-le-Château)

In the heart of the Pays d'Auge, not far from Trouville and
Deauville. This half timbered farmhouse has been completely
restored.
*5 en suite (bth/shr)  (2 fmly)  (1 with balcony)  No smoking in 3
bedrooms  Full central heating  Open parking available
Covered parking available  Child discount available 2yrs
Languages spoken: English*
ROOMS: s 230FF; d 270FF
MEALS: Dinner 95FF

## BOSC-ROGER-EN-ROUMOIS, LE Eure

### Bed & Breakfast (Prop: Nicole & Pierre Fontaine)
1034 ch du Bas-Boscherville, La Queue Bourguignon
*27670*
☎ 235877516 FAX 235877516
(from Bourgtheroulde take D313 towards Elbeuf. 500m after
Lampes Berger follow sign for 'Chambres d'Hôte 1ère à
droite'. Establishment in 1km.)
Near river  Near lake  Forest area  Near motorway
*4 rms (3 shr)  No smoking on premises  Radio in rooms  Full
central heating  Open parking available  Child discount
available 2yrs  Boule  Last d 12.00hrs  Languages spoken:
English*
ROOMS: s 160-170FF; d 200-220FF ✻
MEALS: Dinner 90-100FF✻
CARDS: ■ Travellers cheques

## BOULON Calvados

### Bed & Breakfast (Prop: Mme Duchemin)
789 rue de la République *14220*
☎ 231392386
(from Caen take D562 in the direction of Flers/Thury-Harcourt.
Take left turn for Boulon)
Mme Duchemin welcomes you to her home in Boulon, where
two comfortable rooms are on offer. Your hostess makes every
effort to ensure that you enjoy your stay in this undiscovered
part of France. Garden for the use of guests.
Forest area
*2 en suite (bth/shr)  (2 fmly)  No smoking on premises  Full
central heating  Open parking available  Languages spoken:
English*
ROOMS: s 170-180FF; d 220-240FF

## BOURG-DUN Seine-Maritime

### La Pommerie
rte d'Englesqueville *76740*
☎ 235835892 FAX 235042123
*No smoking on premises  Full central heating*
ROOMS: (room only) d 300FF ✻
MEALS: Dinner fr 95FF✻

## BOURGEAUVILLE Calvados

### La Belle Epine (Prop: M et Mme Clouet)
*14430*
☎ 231652726
(Leave A13 at Pont l'Eveque in direction of Annebault to Caen.
At Annebault take direction of Cabourg & 1st left after
Annebault towards Bourgeauville, then 1st right & Le Belle
Epine on left)
Near sea  Near beach  Forest area
*4 en suite (shr)  (3 fmly)  No smoking on premises  Open
parking available  Riding  Boule  Languages spoken: English*
CARDS: Travellers cheques

## BOURGTHEROULDE Eure

**Château de Boscherville** (Prop: Mme du Plouy)
*27520*
☎ 235876212 & 235876141 FAX 235876212
(from A13 Paris to Caen exit Maison Brulée in direction of
Bourgtheroulde. On 3rd roundabout, take D80 towards La
Haye du Theil, after 2kms turn left, chateau on right)
Mme Henry du Plouy welcomes you to her eighteenth century
chateau in a park, offering peace and tranquillity in this
comfortable and attractive residence. Local specialities of
Normandy directly from the farm are offered.
Forest area
*5 en suite (bth/shr) (1 fmly) Full central heating Open parking
available Child discount available 5yrs Riding Boule Bicycle
rental Bridge tables Languages spoken: English*
ROOMS: s fr 220FF; d fr 270FF ✱
CARDS: Travellers cheques

## BOURNEVILLE Eure

**La Grange** (Prop: C & J Brown)
rte d'Aizier *27500*
☎ 232571143
(from A13 Paris to Caen exit 26 westbound then D89 Bourneville.
From Le Havre A131 (Le Havre-Paris) exit Bourneville)
Near river Forest area Near motorway
*Closed 20 Dec-Feb*
*2 en suite (shr) No smoking on premises Full central heating
Open parking available Languages spoken: English*
ROOMS: d 240FF **Reductions over 1 night**

## BOURTH Eure

**Bed & Breakfast** (Prop: M & G Brugger)
21 av de Kronstorf *27580*
☎ 232327029
(from Verneuil-sur-Avre take N26 in the direction of l'Aigle
after 6km turn right to Bourth)
Near river Forest area In town centre Near motorway
*4 en suite (bth/shr) (2 with balcony) Full central heating Open
parking available Child discount available 18yrs TV room
Languages spoken: English*
CARDS: Travellers cheques

## BRÉHAL Manche

★ ★ *De La Gare*
1 pl Commandant Codart *50290*
☎ 23361611 FAX 233611802
(approach via D971 (Granville-Coutances) exit Bréhal)
Near sea In town centre
*9 rms (8 bth/shr) (2 fmly) TV in all bedrooms Direct dial from
all bedrooms Licensed Night porter Full central heating Open
parking available Covered parking available Supervised Child
discount available 10yrs Open terrace V meals Last d 21.30hrs
Languages spoken: English*
CARDS: ●● ■■ ▄▄ Travellers cheques

## BRÉMOY Calvados

**Carrefour des Fosses** (Prop: Jacqueline et Gilbert
Lalleman)
*14260*
☎ 231778322
*2 en suite (shr) No smoking on premises Full central heating
Open parking available Table tennis*

## BRETEUIL-SUR-ITON Eure

**Bed & Breakfast** (Prop: P & R Mieuset)
79 rue J-Girard *27160*
☎ 232297047 FAX 232297047
Near river Forest area In town centre
*1 en suite (shr) Full central heating Open parking available
Covered parking available Supervised*

## BRETTEVILLE-SUR-DIVES Calvados

**Le Pressoir de Glatigny**
*14170*
☎ 231206893
*3 rms (1 bth 1 shr) No smoking on premises Full central
heating Open parking available Child discount available 8yrs
Table tennis*
CARDS: Travellers cheques

## BRETTEVILLE-SUR-LAIZE Calvados

**Château des Riffets** (Prop: Anne-Marie & Alain Cantel)
*14680*
☎ 231235321 FAX 231237514
(from Caen take N158 towards Falaise/Alençon to La Jalousie
then D23 towards Bretteville, then right onto D235 towards
Caillouet)
Forest area
*4 en suite (bth/shr) (2 fmly) (1 with balcony) Licensed Full
central heating Open parking available Supervised Child
discount available 13yrs Outdoor swimming pool (heated)
Open terrace Last d 17.00hrs Languages spoken: English &
German*
ROOMS: (room only) d 550FF
MEALS: Dinner fr 240FF
CARDS: Travellers cheques

## BRÉVANDS Manche

**La Capitainerie** (Prop: Jaqueline Feron)
*50500*
☎ 233423309
Near river Near sea Near motorway
*2 rms Full central heating Open parking available Supervised
Barbecue*
CARDS: Travellers cheques

## BRICQUEBEC Manche

**La Butte** (Prop: Mme D Mesnil)
14 rue de Bricqueville *50260*
☎ 233523313
*3 en suite (bth/shr) TV in all bedrooms Full central heating
Open parking available*

## BRICQUEVILLE-SUR-MER Manche

**Les Brules** (Prop: Mr Eugene-Jean Labous)
Bricqueville-sur-Mer *50290*
☎ 233510124
(Just off the D971 (Cherbourg to Mont St Michel), at
Bricqueville-sur-Mer junction 2km N of Bréhal turn eastward
into rte de Mont Rabec (D98) follow signs to the Brûlés 1km)
One and a half hours from Cherbourg and 3 miles from the
sea, this 18th-century farmhouse, set in three-quarters of an
acre of grounds, offers a warm welcome and comfortable
accommodation.

***Les Brules***
*2 rms No smoking on premises Full central heating Open parking available No children 7 yrs Languages spoken: English*
ROOMS: (room only) s 120FF; d 170FF **Special breaks**

### BRIONNE Eure

**Le Coeur de Lion** (Prop: P & H Baker)
14 bd de la République *27800*
☎ 232434035 FAX 232469531
(from Brionne follow directions for 'Base de Loisirs' this will bring you to blvd de la République 150 yds turn right into 'Impass du Lac'-ignore no entry sign)
This large detached house, with enclosed garden terrace and stream, is just five minutes walk from the historic town of Brionne in the Risle Valley. Situated next to a lake, with leisure area. Market twice weekly at Brionne.
Near river Near lake Forest area Near motorway
*Closed end Nov-14 Jan*
*5 en suite (shr) (2 fmly) Full central heating Open parking available Tennis Riding Boule Mini-golf Bicycle rental Languages spoken: English*
ROOMS: s 215FF; d 265FF *
CARDS: ⬤⬤ 💳 Travellers cheques

**★ ★ ★ *Le Logis de Brionne***
1 pl St-Denis *27800*
☎ 232448173 FAX 232451092
Near river Near lake Near sea Near beach Forest area Near motorway
*12 en suite (bth/shr) (3 fmly) TV in all bedrooms Direct dial from all bedrooms Mini-bar in all bedrooms Licensed Full central heating Open parking available Covered parking available Supervised Open terrace V meals Last d 21.15hrs Languages spoken: English & Spanish*
CARDS: ⬤⬤ ■ 💳 Travellers cheques

### BRIOUZE Orne

**Bed & Breakfast** (Prop: M & Mme Pierrot)
rte de Bellou *61220*
☎ 233660798
(from Argentan take D924 towards Flers. At the church in Briouze take D21 to Bellou)
*Closed Aug*
*1 en suite (shr) Full central heating Open parking available Table tennis*
ROOMS: s 170FF; d 200FF
CARDS: Travellers cheques

### BRIX Manche

**Château Mont Eqinguet** (Prop: M Berridge)
*50700*
☎ 233419631 FAX 233419877
(from Cherbourg take N13 towards Valognes. After 11kms turn right onto D119 for Ruffosses (not Brix), cross motorway & follow blue and white signs to the château approx 2kms)
An informal 18th-century château guest house. where English hosts, Mark and Fiona Berridge, hope their guest will enjoy the peaceful rural surroundings as much as they do. There is plenty of faded splendour and friendly atmosphere. A golf course is five kilometres away, superb beaches some 30 kilometres distant and many good restaurants close by. Riding and bicycle hire on site.
*Closed 3 Jan-1 Mar & 22 Jul-2 Sep*
*4 rms (2 bth) (1 fmly) (1 with balcony) Open parking available Child discount available 14yrs Languages spoken: English*
ROOMS: s 140-160FF; d 220-280FF
**✱ Reductions over 1 night**
CARDS: Travellers cheques

### CAEN Calvados

**★ Hotel Bernières**
50 rue de Bernières *14000*
☎ 231860126 FAX 231865176
(In town centre follow signs 'Château', then the one-way system around the castle to take 4th street on left shortly after St-Pierre church)

Situated in the heart of Caen, the hotel offers well furnished bedrooms, most with private facilities. Guests are made to feel at home by the proprietors who offer a friendly and attentive service.
In town centre
*17 rms (3 bth 13 shr) (2 fmly) (3 with balcony) TV in all bedrooms Direct dial from all bedrooms Licensed Night porter Full central heating Languages spoken: English*
ROOMS: (room only) s 200-220FF; d 220-240FF
**Reductions over 1 night**
CARDS: ⬤⬤ ■ 💳 🔲 Travellers cheques

**★ ★ *Climat de France***
av Montgomery, Quartier du Memorial *14000*
☎ 231443636 FAX 231956262
(from the Périphérique Nord take direction towards Cherbourg & towards the Mémorial de Caen exit6 Courseulles, turn right for le Mémorial)
*72 en suite (bth) (3 fmly) No smoking in 21 bedrooms TV in all bedrooms Radio in rooms Direct dial from all bedrooms*
*contd.*

Licensed  Full central heating  Open parking available
Supervised  Pool table  Open terrace  Covered terrace  Last d
20.00hrs  Languages spoken: English, German & Spanish
CARDS: ● ■ ■ ⑩ Travellers cheques

★ ★ ★ **Dauphin** (Best Western)
29 rue Gémare *14000*
☎ 231862226 FAX 231863514
Forest area
22 en suite (bth/shr)  7 rooms in annexe  TV in all bedrooms
Direct dial from all bedrooms  Mini-bar in 11 bedrooms
Licensed  Full central heating  Open parking available  Child
discount available  Last d 21.30hrs  Languages spoken: English
CARDS: ● ■ ■ ⑩ Travellers cheques

### CAHAGNES Calvados

**Bed & Breakfast** (Prop: M & Mme Joseph Guilbert)
Benneville *14240*
☎ 231775805 FAX 231773784
(7km from Villers-Bocage and 4km from Cahagnes)
Near river  Near lake  Forest area  Near motorway
5 en suite (bth/shr)  2 rooms in annexe  (3 fmly)  No smoking on
premises  Open parking available  Child discount available
Boule  Open terrace  Table tennis, Volley ball  Languages
spoken: English
CARDS: Travellers cheques

### CAMBREMER Calvados

**Bed & Breakfast** (Prop: M & Mme Bernard)
Le Clos de St-Laurent, St-Laurent-du-Mont *14340*
☎ 231634704 FAX 231634692
(on the D50 between Lisieux and Carrefour Saint-Jean)
This charming, 19th-century style house with garden and park
enjoys pleasant views over the Dive Valley. Explore the cider
road or the springs of St Laurent. Thirty-five minutes to the
American landing beaches. Enjoy meals cooked by the
proprietor, with regional dishes a speciality.
Forest area  Near motorway
4 en suite (bth/shr)  (2 fmly)  No smoking on premises  TV
available  Radio in rooms  Full central heating  Open parking
available  Child discount available 5yrs
ROOMS: s fr 250FF;  d fr 300FF  ✱ **Reductions over 1 night**
MEALS: Dinner fr 100FF✱

★ ★ ★ **Château les Bruyères**
rte du Cadran *14340*
☎ 231637830 FAX 231637838
(A13 exit29 La Haietondue in direction of Falaise, take N13 in
direction of Caen & village La Boissiere on right)
Near sea  Near beach  Forest area
Closed Jan-Mar
13 en suite (bth/shr)  TV in all bedrooms  STV  Direct dial from
all bedrooms  Mini-bar in 10 bedrooms  Licensed  Night porter
Full central heating  Open parking available  Child discount
available 10yrs  Outdoor swimming pool (heated)  Tennis  Open
terrace  Covered terrace  Last d 20.00hrs  Languages spoken:
English & German
CARDS: ● ■ ■ ⑩

### CAMPEAUX Calvados

**Le Champ Touillon**
*14350*
☎ 231686686
Near lake  Forest area  Near motorway

5 en suite (shr)  (4 fmly)  Full central heating  Open parking
available  Child discount available  V meals  Languages spoken:
English
CARDS: ■

### CAMPIGNY Eure

**Le Clos Mahiet** (Prop: Alain Vauquelin)
*27500*
☎ 232411320
Forest area
Closed 22 Dec-3 Jan
3 en suite (shr)  Full central heating  Open parking available
Child discount available 10yrs
CARDS: Travellers cheques

### CANEHAN Seine-Maritime

**Les Terres du Thil** (Prop: M et Mme William Blangez)
rue de Laiterie *76260*
☎ 235867256 FAX 235867256
Near river  Near lake  Near sea  Near beach  Forest area  Near
motorway
6 rms (4 bth/shr)  (1 fmly)  (2 with balcony)  TV available  Full
central heating  Open parking available

### CANVILLE-LA-ROCQUE Manche

**La Rue** (Prop: Gisele Frugier)
*50580*
☎ 233530306
1 en suite (shr)  No smoking in all bedrooms  Full central
heating  Open parking available

### CAPELLE-LES-GRANDS Eure

**Val Perrier** (Prop: P et M Beaudry)
*27270*
☎ 232447633 FAX 232430315
(from Bernay take Orbec D131, from Broglie take N138 then
follow arrows to establishment)

A large house situated in the heart of the peaceful Normandy
countryside, surrounded by fields with a pleasant garden to
relax in. The bedrooms are large and comfortable, each with a
kitchen and lounge. Guests can enjoy meals that include many
well-known Normandy specialities. A garden lounge has been
added, containing tourist information.
Near river  Forest area  Near motorway
2 en suite (shr)  (1 fmly)  (1 with balcony)  No smoking on
premises  Full central heating  Open parking available  Covered
parking available  Supervised  Child discount available 12yrs

Bicycle rental Table tennis Exercise equipment Last d 20.00hrs
Languages spoken: English
ROOMS: s 170FF; d 220-250FF
MEALS: Dinner 90-110FF

### CATTEVILLE Manche

**Le Haul** (Prop: Gerard Langlois)
*50390*
☎ 233416469 FAX 233416469
(on the D900 St-Sauveur-le-Vicomte/La Haye-du-Puits, take
D215)
Near river Near sea Near beach Forest area
*5 en suite (bth/shr) (1 fmly) Full central heating Open parking
available Covered parking available Child discount available
5yrs Fishing Bicycle rental Table tennis, Games room V meals*
ROOMS: s fr 180FF; d 220-2800FF
MEALS: Dinner fr 90FF
CARDS: Travellers cheques

### CAUDEBEC-EN-CAUX Seine-Maritime

**Bed & Breakfast** (Prop: Christiane Villamaux)
68 rue République *76490*
☎ 235961015 FAX 235967525
(in village in front of the tourist office take the direction of
Yvetot D131, chambres d'hôtes 500m on the right)

This house is only 500 metres from the Seine, the forest, the
restaurants and the shops along the Route of the Abbeys.
There is a large garden and you are assured of a warm
welcome and this establishment is ideally situated as a
stopover from the ferries to the South of France, or as a base
for visiting Normandy with Jumièges and St-Wandrille only
3km away.
Near river Forest area
*4 en suite (shr) (2 fmly) No smoking on premises Full central
heating Open parking available Languages spoken: English*
ROOMS: s 225FF; d 265FF
MEALS: Dinner fr 260FF✱

**Normotel**
18 quai Guilbaud *76490*
☎ 235962011 FAX 235565440
Near river Forest area In town centre Near motorway
*31 en suite (bth/shr) (6 fmly) (24 with balcony) TV in all
bedrooms STV Direct dial from all bedrooms Licensed Lift
Full central heating Open parking available (charged) Covered
parking available (charged) Supervised Child discount
available 12yrs Bicycle rental Open terrace V meals Last d
21.00hrs Languages spoken: English*
CARDS: ■ ▣ ◉ Travellers cheques

### CAUMONT-L'ÉVENTÉ Calvados

**Bed & Breakfast** (Prop: Mr & Mrs A Bamford)
19 rue Thiers *14240*
☎ 231774785 FAX 231775927
(from Caen take N175 (A84) towards Mont-St-Michel/
Avranches, then take D54 to Cahagnes and Caumont-l'Eventé.
Or from Caen take D9 direct.)

Andrew and Elizabeth Bamford welcome you to their home
and garden. Swimming pool, table-tennis, boules and tennis.
Near lake Forest area Near motorway
*5 en suite (bth/shr) (3 fmly) (3 with balcony) No smoking in 3
bedrooms Full central heating Open parking available
Covered parking available Child discount available 14yrs
Outdoor swimming pool (heated) Tennis Boule Mini-golf
Bicycle rental Open terrace Table tennis Snooker Languages
spoken: English*
MEALS: Dinner fr 120FF
CARDS: ◉● ■■ ▣ ◉ Travellers cheques

### CEAUX Manche

★ ★ *Le Relais du Mont*
*50220*
☎ 233709255 FAX 233709457
Near sea Forest area Near motorway
*30 en suite (bth/shr) (14 fmly) TV in all bedrooms Licensed
Full central heating Open parking available Supervised Child
discount available 12yrs Boule Jacuzzi/spa Open terrace V
meals Last d 21.30hrs Languages spoken: English, German &
Italian*
CARDS: ◉● ■■ ▣ Travellers cheques

### CHAMBOIS Orne

**Le Château** (Prop: Mme Clapeau)
rte de Vimoutiers *61160*
☎ 233367134
This recently restored building, in the heart of the village
of Chambois, is situated in the middle of a wooded park
and in the shadow of a 12th century keep. A warm
welcome awaits you and bedrooms are comfortable and
quiet. Fishing, swimming, riding and walks all available
locally.
Near river Near lake Forest area In town centre Near
motorway

*contd.*

**Le Chateau**
5 en suite (bth/shr) (2 fmly) TV available  Full central heating
Open parking available  Child discount available  Boule  Table
tennis  Languages spoken: English
ROOMS: s 250FF; d 290FF ✱
CARDS: Travellers cheques

### CHATRES Seine-Maritime

**Le Portail Bleu** (Prop: Pierre Laurent)
2 rte de Fontenay 77610
☎ 164258494 FAX 164258494
(From A4 exit on D231 to Villeneuve le Comte, then right on
D96 through Neufmoutiers to Châtres. House is in village
centre to left of church)

Big blue porch doors are a feature of this establishment hence
the name. The doors shelter an old farmhouse which has been
attractively furnished and includes two comfortable rooms for
guests.
Near lake  Forest area  Near motorway
4 en suite (shr) (3 fmly) TV in all bedrooms  Full central heating
Open parking available  Child discount available 6yrs  Open
terrace  Table tennis  Languages spoken: English
ROOMS: s 260FF; d 290FF **Reductions over 1 night**
MEALS: Dinner 110FF
CARDS: Travellers cheques

### CHERBOURG Manche

**★ ★ La Régence**
42 Quai de Caligny 50100
☎ 233430516 FAX 233439837
Near sea  In town centre
21 rms (18 bth/shr) (2 fmly) TV in all bedrooms  Direct dial
from all bedrooms  Full central heating  Open parking available

(charged)  Supervised  Child discount available  Last d 22.00hrs
Languages spoken: English
CARDS: ●● ■■ ⌷⌷ Travellers cheques

### CLÉCY Calvados

**La Loterie** (Prop: R Aubry)
14570
☎ 231697438
(leave Clécy for Pont-le-Vey, continue south of river on D133
for 1m. House is on left with Gite sign)
Near river  Forest area
3 en suite (bth/shr)  Full central heating  Open parking available
Child discount available

**★ ★ ★ Hostellerie du Moulin du Vey**
Le Vey 14570
☎ 231697108 FAX 231691414
(S of Caen, on the D133 which connects D562/N158)
Near river  Forest area
25 en suite (bth/shr) 2 rooms in annexe (2 fmly) (3 with
balcony) TV in all bedrooms  Direct dial from all bedrooms
Licensed  Full central heating  Open parking available
Supervised  Child discount available 10yrs  Fishing  Boule  Open
terrace  Last d 21.00hrs  Languages spoken: English & Spanish
MEALS: Continental breakfast 56FF  Lunch 138-380FF
Dinner 138-380FF&alc✱
CARDS: ●● ■ ⌷⌷ ⌷⌷ Travellers cheques

**★ ★ Au Site Normand**
1 rue des Châtelets 14570
☎ 231697105 FAX 231694851
(centre of village)
Near river  Forest area
RS 24-31 Dec (restaurant closed evenings)
18 en suite (bth/shr) (1 fmly) (4 with balcony) TV in all
bedrooms  Direct dial from all bedrooms  Licensed  Full central
heating  Open parking available  Child discount available 10yrs
Solarium  Gym  Open terrace  V meals  Languages spoken:
English
CARDS: ●● ⌷⌷ ⌷⌷ Travellers cheques

### CLIPONVILLE Seine-Maritime

**Hameau de Rucquemare** (Prop: Beatrice & J-Pierre
Levêque)
76640
☎ 235967221 FAX 235967221
(from Yvetot take D131 towards Héricourtthen D5 towards
Hautot-le-Vatois. On entering town turn left before the church
for 2km then right before the château and take 2nd entrance
on left)
4 en suite (shr) (3 fmly) TV in 1 bedroom  Full central heating
Open parking available  Languages spoken: English

### COIGNY Manche

**Château de Coigny** (Prop: Odette Ionckheere)
50250
☎ 233421079
(from Carentan take D903 towards Barneville-Carteret for
10.5kms. Then right on D223 towards Coigny. The château is
1st entrance on left)
Closed Nov-Etr
2 en suite (bth/shr) No smoking on premises  Full central
heating  Open parking available  Supervised  No children 3yrs
Child discount available 12yrs

### COLLEVILLE-SUR-MER Calvados

**Ferme du Clos Tassin** (Prop: Daniel Picquenard)
*14710*
☎ 231224151 FAX 231222946
(on D514 coastal road, drive through Arromanches & Port-en-Bessin on D514 through village of Ste-Honorine-des-Pertes & then just before Colleville & immediately after Camping du Robinson, look on right for sign Le Clos Tassin)

A relaxing atmosphere, in comfortable rooms is on offer at this working farm, where milk is produced alongside cider, Pommeau and Calvados. Breakfast is served at the family table. Numerous walks available.
Near sea  Near beach
*5 rms (3 bth 1 shr)  (1 fmly)  No smoking on premises  TV in 3 bedrooms  Full central heating  Open parking available  Boule  Bicycle rental  Free use of two bicycles*
ROOMS: s 160FF; d 170-190FF
CARDS: ●● ■■ ▅▅ Travellers cheques

### COLOMBIERS-SUR-SEULLES Calvados

★ ★ *Château du Baffy*
Le Bourg *14480*
☎ 231080457 FAX 231080829
Near river  Forest area
*Closed Jan-Feb*
*35 en suite (bth/shr)  Some rooms in annexe  (2 fmly)  TV in 5 bedrooms  Licensed  Full central heating  Open parking available  Child discount available  Tennis  Fishing  Riding  Gym  Boule  Bicycle rental  Open terrace  Last d 21.30hrs  Languages spoken: English*
CARDS: ●● ■■ ▅▅ ◨ Travellers chéques

### COMMES Calvados

*Bed & Breakfast* (Prop: M & L Cairon)
Quartier de l'Église *14520*
☎ 231217108
(approach via N13, then D6 towards Port-en-Bessin and D100 to Commes)
Near sea
*4 en suite (bth/shr)  Full central heating  Open parking available*

### CONDEAU Orne

★ ★ ★ *Moulin de Villeray*
*61110*
☎ 233733022 FAX 233733828
(from A11 Nogent-le-Rotrou then D918 to Condé-sur-Huisne)
Near river  Forest area

*25 en suite (bth/shr)  8 rooms in annexe  (4 fmly)  (1 with balcony)  No smoking in 5 bedrooms  TV in all bedrooms  Direct dial from all bedrooms  Mini-bar in all bedrooms  Licensed  Full central heating  Open parking available  Covered parking available (charged)  Outdoor swimming pool (heated)  Fishing  Riding  Bicycle rental  Open terrace  V meals  Last d 22.00hrs  Languages spoken: English*
CARDS: ●● ▅▅

### CONDÉ-SUR-NOIREAU Calvados

★ ★ **Du Cerf**
18 rue du Chêne *14110*
☎ 231694055 FAX 231697829
(from ferry at Ouistreham/Caen in direction Flers/Laval)
Near river  In town centre
*Closed All Saints school holiday RS Sun evening*
*9 en suite (bth/shr)  (2 fmly)  TV in all bedrooms  Direct dial from all bedrooms  Licensed  Full central heating  Open parking available  Child discount available 12yrs  Open terrace  V meals  Last d 21.15hrs  Languages spoken: English*
ROOMS: (room only)  d 204-240FF
**Reductions over 1 night**
MEALS: Continental breakfast 32FF  Lunch 67-175FF  Dinner 67-175FF
CARDS: ●● ■■ ▅▅ Travellers cheques

### CONDÉ-SUR-SARTHE Orne

*Le Clos des Roses* (Prop: M et Mme P Pellegrini)
10 rue de la Jardinière *61250*
☎ 233277068
(travelling in the direction of Rennes/St Malo exit at Alencon on D112 and proceed to Boissiere take the r du Chateau d'Eau on the left turn right Conde-sur-Sarthe)
Near river  Near motorway
*3 en suite (bth/shr)  No smoking on premises  Radio in rooms  Full central heating  Open parking available*

### CONNELLES Eure

★ ★ ★ ★ *Moulin de Connelles*
40 rte d'Amfreville-sur-les-, Monts *27430*
☎ 232595333 FAX 232592183
(A13 exit Louviers direction of Pont de L'Arche then St Pierre du Vauvray, Ande, Herqueviue to Connelles)
Near river  Near lake  Forest area  Near motorway
*13 en suite (bth/shr)  (6 fmly)  (4 with balcony)  TV in all bedrooms  STV  Direct dial from all bedrooms  Mini-bar in all bedrooms  Licensed  Full central heating  Open parking available  Supervised  Child discount available 12yrs  Outdoor swimming pool (heated)  Tennis  Fishing  Solarium  Boule  Bicycle rental  Open terrace  Languages spoken: English & Spanish*
CARDS: ●● ■■ ▅▅ ◨ Travellers cheques

### CONTEVILLE Eure

*Ferme du Pressoir*
Le Clos Potier *27210*
☎ 232576079
Forest area
*No smoking on premises  Full central heating  Open parking available  Bicycle rental*

*contd.*

**COURSON** Calvados

**La Brandonnière** (Prop: Maurice Perrard)
*14380*
☎ 231688571
(100mtrs from church on left in direction of Sept Freres)
*Closed Nov-27 Mar*
*2 en suite (bth) Open parking available Child discount available*

**COURTILS** Manche

★ ★ ★ **Manoir de la Roche Torin**
La Roche Torin *50220*
☎ 233709655 FAX 233483520
Near river
*Closed 16 Nov-14 Feb ex Xmas & New Year*
*13 en suite (bth/shr) Some rooms in annexe (1 fmly) TV in all*
*bedrooms Direct dial from all bedrooms Mini-bar in 3*
*bedrooms Licensed Full central heating Open parking*
*available Child discount available 12yrs Boule Bicycle rental*
*Open terrace Covered terrace Last d 21.00hrs Languages*
*spoken: English & German*
CARDS: ●● ■ ■■ ⑩ Travellers cheques

**COUTANCES** Manche

★ ★ **Cositel Coutances**
rte de Coutainville, BP 231 *50200*
☎ 233075164 FAX 233070623
(on the D44)
Forest area
*55 en suite (bth/shr) (7 fmly) TV in all bedrooms STV Direct*
*dial from all bedrooms Mini-bar in all bedrooms Licensed*
*Night porter Full central heating Open parking available*
*Covered parking available (charged) Supervised Child*
*discount available 14yrs Mini-golf Open terrace Covered*
*terrace V meals Last d 22.30hrs Languages spoken: English &*
*German*
ROOMS: (room only) d 298-350FF
MEALS: Full breakfast 45FF Lunch 118-190FF&alc Dinner
118-190FF&alc
CARDS: ●● ■ ■■ ⑩ Travellers cheques

**CRÉPON** Calvados

**Le Haras de Crépon** (Prop: Pascale Landeau)
Le Clos Mondeville *14480*
☎ 231213737 FAX 231211212
(coming from Caen in the direction of Cherbourg, exit D158B
signed Creully then Brécy-St-Gabriel to Arromanches. At
Villiers Le Sec passing the church, continue for 2 kms)
This restored 16th-century manor house is situated close to the
Second World War landing beaches. The bedrooms are quiet
and offer outstanding comfort and tasteful decoration. Race
horses are bred on the estate.
Near river Near sea Near beach
*5 en suite (bth/shr) (1 fmly) Full central heating Open parking*
*available Child discount available 11yrs Fishing Boule Bicycle*
*rental Table tennis Languages spoken: English & Spanish*
ROOMS: d 390-550FF
MEALS: Full breakfast 35FF Dinner 150FF✱
CARDS: ●● ■■

**Manoir de Crépon** (Prop: Anne-Marie Poisson)
rte d'Arromanches *14480*
☎ 231222127 FAX 231228880
(exit A13 at Creully and take D22 and then D65 in direction of

Arromanches. On reaching Crépon, house is on left in
direction of Ver-sur-Mer as you leave village)
The first-floor guest rooms are large, with views over the park
and rear garden. All are furnished in the style of the manor
and some have stone fireplaces. Peaceful walks in the park.
Continental breakfast served. The beach is within four
kilometres.
*RS winter*
*5 en suite (bth/shr) (2 fmly) TV in 2 bedrooms Full central*
*heating Open parking available Child discount available 15yrs*
*Bicycle rental Languages spoken: English*
ROOMS: s 330FF; d 400FF **Special breaks**
CARDS: ●● ■■ Y

**CREULLY** Calvados

★ ★ **Ferme de la Ranconnière**
rte d'Arromanches *14480*
☎ 231222173 FAX 231229839
This ancient farmhouse dates back to the 18th-century and is
classified as a historic monument. The bedrooms are furnished
with period pieces and have en suite facilities. The cuisine
incorporates high quality ingredients using seasonal produce.
Near sea
*34 en suite (bth/shr) 10 rooms in annexe (5 fmly) TV in all*
*bedrooms Direct dial from all bedrooms Licensed Full central*
*heating Open parking available Child discount available*
*Fishing Last d 21.30hrs Languages spoken: English-Dutch-*
*German*
ROOMS: (room only) d 295-680FF
MEALS: Full breakfast 50FF Lunch 98-280FF&alc Dinner
98-280FF&alc
CARDS: ●● ■ ■■ ⑩ Travellers cheques

**CRIEL-SUR-MER** Seine-Maritime

★ ★ **Hostellerie de la Veille Ferme**
23 rue de la Mer-Mesnil Val *76910*
☎ 235867218 FAX 235861264
Near sea
*Closed Jan*
*22 rooms in annexe (3 fmly) TV in 33 bedrooms Direct dial*
*from 33 bedrooms Licensed Full central heating Open parking*
*available Child discount available 9yrs Open terrace Last d*
*20.30hrs Languages spoken: English*
CARDS: ●● ■ ■■ ⑩

**CRIQUEBEUF-EN-CAUX** Seine-Maritime

**Ferme Auberge de la Cote** (Prop: Michel Basille)
190 Le Bout de la Ville *76111*
☎ 235280132 FAX 235280132
(from Le Havre take D489 to Fécamp, then D940. Turn right
onto D211 towards Yport)
Near sea Near beach
*2 en suite (shr) (1 fmly) Full central heating Open parking*
*available Child discount available 12yrs*
ROOMS: s fr 130FF; d fr 245FF ✱
MEALS: Lunch 115-170FF Dinner 115-170FF
CARDS: ●● ■ ■■

**CRIQUETOT-L'ESNEVAL** Seine-Maritime

**Bed & Breakfast** (Prop: G et D Paumelle)
30 rte de Gonneville *76280*
☎ 235272847
Near sea Near beach Forest area

*Closed Nov-Mar*
*5 rms (3 bth) (3 fmly) No smoking on premises Full central heating Open parking available Supervised*

### CULEY-LE-PATRY Calvados

***Bed & Breakfast*** (Prop: Mme C Ballanger)
allée des Chânes *14220*
☎ 231796000
*Near river Forest area*
*3 rms (2 shr) (1 with balcony) No smoking on premises Radio in rooms Full central heating Open parking available Child discount available 2yrs Languages spoken: English*

### DEAUVILLE Calvados

★ ★ ★ ★ ***Hotel du Golf***
Mont Canisy, St-Arnoult *14800*
☎ 231142400 FAX 231142401
(A13 Paris/Caen exit Deaiville and take direction of `Hippodrome`)
*Near river Near sea Near beach Forest area Near motorway*
*Closed 3 Nov-28 Dec & 9 Feb-20 Mar*
*178 en suite (bth/shr) (66 fmly) (3 with balcony) No smoking in 12 bedrooms TV in all bedrooms STV Radio in rooms Direct dial from all bedrooms Mini-bar in all bedrooms Licensed Lift Night porter Full central heating Open parking available Child discount available 12yrs Outdoor swimming pool (heated) Golf 27 Tennis Sauna Solarium Gym Boule Bicycle rental Open terrace Covered terrace V meals Last d 22.30hrs Languages spoken: English, German, Italian & Spanish*
CARDS: ●● ■■ ☲☲ ◑ JCB

★ ★ ★ ★ ***Hotel Royal***
bd Cornuche *14800*
☎ 231986633 FAX 231986634
(From A13 exit 'Deauville/Trouville' follow signs for 'Deauville' and 'Plage')
*Near sea Near beach In town centre Near motorway*
*Closed early Nov-Mar*
*245 en suite (bth/shr) (8 fmly) (50 with balcony) TV in all bedrooms STV Radio in rooms Direct dial from all bedrooms Mini-bar in all bedrooms Room-safe Licensed Lift Night porter Full central heating Open parking available Outdoor swimming pool (heated) Golf 27 Tennis Sauna Solarium Gym Mini-golf Bicycle rental Open terrace Wkly live entertainment Casino Last d 22.00hrs Languages spoken: English, German & Spanish*
CARDS: ●● ■■ ☲☲ ◑ JCB

★ ★ ★ ★ ***Hotel Normandy***
38 rue Jean Mermoz *14800*
☎ 231986622 FAX 231986623
(from A13 exit 'Deauville/Trouville' follow signs for 'Deauville' and 'Plage')
*Near sea Near beach In town centre*
*291 en suite (bth) TV in all bedrooms STV Radio in rooms Direct dial from all bedrooms Mini-bar in all bedrooms Room-safe Licensed Lift Night porter Full central heating Open parking available (charged) Covered parking available (charged) Supervised Child discount available 12yrs Indoor swimming pool (heated) Golf 27 Tennis Sauna Solarium Gym Pool table Mini-golf Bicycle rental Open terrace Wkly live entertainment Casino Last d 22.00hrs Languages spoken: English, German, Italian & Spanish*

ROOMS: (room only) d 1190-2650FF
**Reductions over 1 night Special breaks**
MEALS: Continental breakfast 130FF Lunch 285-325FF&alc Dinner 285FF&alc
CARDS: ●● ■■ ☲☲ ◑ JCB

★ ★ ★ ***Park Hotel***
81 av de la République *14800*
☎ 231880971 FAX 231879949
*Near sea Near beach In town centre Near motorway*
*15 en suite (bth/shr) (3 fmly) (5 with balcony) TV in all bedrooms Direct dial from all bedrooms Mini-bar in 5 bedrooms Licensed Full central heating Open parking available Child discount available 13yrs Bicycle rental Open terrace Languages spoken: English*
CARDS: ●● ■■ ☲☲ ◑

### DOMFRONT Orne

**La Demeure d'Olwen** (Prop: Sylvia Tailhandier-Jacobson)
1 rue de Godras *61700*
☎ 233371003 FAX 233371003
(follow signs for Centre Ancien on reaching Domfront. House in immediate vicinity of Court of Justice, in front of the Post Office)
*Near river Forest area In town centre*
*3 en suite (shr) (2 fmly) No smoking in 1 bedroom Full central heating Supervised Languages spoken: English & Italian*
ROOMS: d 290FF
CARDS: Travellers cheques

### DOUAINS Eure

★ ★ ★ ★ ***Château de Brécourt***
*27120*
☎ 232524050 FAX 232526965
*Forest area Near motorway*
*31 en suite (bth) (5 fmly) Licensed Full central heating Open parking available Child discount available 12yrs Indoor swimming pool (heated) Tennis Boule Jacuzzi/spa Bicycle rental Open terrace Covered terrace V meals Last d 21.30hrs Languages spoken: German & Spanish*
CARDS: ●● ■■ ☲☲ ◑ Travellers cheques

### DOUVILLE-EN-AUGE Calvados

***Ferme de l'Oraille*** (Prop: Gisele Louis Haulet)
chemin de Deraine *14430*
☎ 231792549
*Near sea Forest area Near motorway*
*3 en suite (shr) No smoking on premises Full central heating Open parking available*

### DRAGEY Manche

**Belleville** (Prop: O et F Brasme)
L'Église, rte de St Marc *50530*
☎ 233489396 FAX 233485975
(approach via D911 from Avranches towards Vains, then Genêts and Dragey and follow signs to house surrounded by white fences)
*Near sea Near beach*
*2 en suite (bth) No smoking on premises Full central heating Open parking available Languages spoken: English*
ROOMS: s 300FF; d 340FF

### DUCEY Manche

**★★ Auberge de la Sélune**
2 rue St-Germain *50220*
☎ 233485362 FAX 233489030
Near river Forest area Near motorway
*3 rooms in annexe (1 fmly) Licensed Full central heating Open parking available Child discount available Fishing Open terrace Last d 20.30hrs Languages spoken: English & Spanish*
CARDS: ●● ■ ▆▆ ⑨

### DUCLAIR Seine-Maritime

**Bed & Breakfast** (Prop: M & Mme B Lemercier)
282 chemin du Panorama *76480*
☎ 235376884
(From place Hôtel-de-Ville in Duclair take rue J-Ferry towards Maromme for 150mtrs and then next right)
Your hosts welcome you to their house which offers panoramic views over the Seine. Nearby, lakes are open all year round for fishing enthusiasts. There is tennis within one kilometre, and golf and canoeing just eight kilometres away. Bikes available. Several restaurants to choose from in the town of Duclair.
Near river Near lake Forest area Near motorway
*5 en suite (bth/shr) No smoking on premises Full central heating Open parking available Cycling*
ROOMS: s 200FF; d 260-280FF ✱ **Special breaks**
CARDS: ■ Travellers cheques

### ECRAMMEVILLE Calvados

**Ferme de l'Abbaye** (Prop: A Fauvel)
*14710*
☎ 231225232 FAX 231224725
(from Bayeaux take N13 west. After 14kms take D30 to Ecrammeville. Farm is near church)

In the 15th century this farmhouse was a monks' dormitory, and still looks out onto the abbey church which is floodlit at night. Situated in a peaceful area, close to the landing beaches of WWII, the house has a fine stone staircase and stone columns, a large fireplace, and exposed beams. Trotting horses and cattle are bred, and cider is made on the farm. Madame Fauvel, a grandmother of nine, has plenty of time for her guests. All rooms have independent access. Dinner is available at a fixed price.
Near river Near sea Near beach
*5 en suite (bth/shr) (2 fmly) No smoking on premises Full central heating Child discount available 9yrs V meals*
ROOMS: s 200FF; d 240FF ✱ **Reductions over 1 night**
MEALS: Dinner 90FF✱

### ÉMALLEVILLE Eure

**Château d'Émalleville** (Prop: M & Mme C Thieblot)
17 rue de l'Église *27930*
☎ 232340187 FAX 232343027
(from Louviers, south of Rouen, take D155 towards Evreux. Through Le Boulay Morin & 500m after leaving village turn left to Emalleville. Château on right in village)
Near river Forest area
*5 en suite (bth/shr) (2 fmly) No smoking in 1 bedroom Full central heating Open parking available Covered parking available Tennis*
CARDS: ●● ■ ▆▆ ⑨ Travellers cheques

### EQUEURDREVILLE Manche

**★★ Climat de France**
200 rue de la Paix *50120*
☎ 233934294 Cen Res 64460123 FAX 233934554
Near sea
*42 en suite (bth) TV in all bedrooms Radio in rooms Direct dial from all bedrooms Licensed Full central heating Open parking available V meals Languages spoken: English*
CARDS: ●● ▆▆

### ERMENOUVILLE Seine-Maritime

**Château de Mesnil-Geoffroy** (Prop: Docteur et Madame Kayali)
*76740*
☎ 235571277 FAX 235571024
(leave A13 at exit 25 to Yvetot. In Yvetot take direction for St-Valery-en-Caux. 1 mile after Ste-Colombe, to the right the château is signed as an historic monument)
Near sea Near beach
*6 en suite (bth/shr) Full central heating Open parking available Supervised Boule Bicycle rental Open terrace Last d 20.00hrs*
CARDS: ●● ▆▆ Travellers cheques

### ÉTRETAT Seine-Maritime

**★★★ Donjon**
Chemin de St-Clair *76790*
☎ 235270823 FAX 235299224
Near sea Near beach
*10 en suite (bth/shr) (4 fmly) (1 with balcony) TV in all bedrooms Mini-bar in all bedrooms Full central heating Open parking available Child discount available 10yrs Outdoor swimming pool Jacuzzi/spa Open terrace Last d 22.30hrs Languages spoken: English*
CARDS: ●● ■ ▆▆ ⑨ Travellers cheques

**Villa St-Sauveur** (Prop: Yanick & Anne-Marie)
Chemin d'Anilaville *76790*
☎ 235271216
The house, dating from the end of the last century, is situated in the middle of a large garden surrounded by walls, six or seven minutes from the centre of Etretat by foot. Beaches, tennis, golf, sailing club, riding centre and many walks are within close proximity.
Near sea Near beach Forest area
*3 rms (1 shr) No smoking on premises Full central heating Open parking available Supervised Child discount available 10yrs Languages spoken: English & Italian*
ROOMS: d 260-330FF ✱ **Reductions over 1 night**

## EU Seine-Maritime

**Manoir de Beaumont** (Prop: Catherine Demarquet)
76260
☎ 235509191
(from D49 on entering Eu, turn left in the direction of the
Forest of Eu and Beaumont - 2kms)
Near river  Near sea  Near beach  Forest area
*3 en suite (shr)  (2 fmly)  No smoking in 1 bedroom  TV in all
bedrooms  Full central heating  Open parking available
Supervised  Child discount available 2yrs  Bicycle rental
Languages spoken: English*
ROOMS: s 200FF; d 270FF  **Special breaks**
CARDS: Travellers cheques

## ÉVREUX Eure

**★ ★ France**
29 rue St-Thomas *27000*
☎ 232390925 & 117 986 0386 (UK booking) FAX 232383856
(follow signs 'Centre Ville' then hotels are signposted)
This traditional hotel occupies a tranquil location in the centre
of Evreux, and offers its clientele pleasant bedrooms with
private amenities and outstanding cuisine, incorporating
classic dishes with a contemporary touch, augmented by an
interesting wine list.
Near river  In town centre
*RS restaurant closed Sun evening & Mon
16 en suite (bth/shr)  (2 fmly)  TV in all bedrooms  Direct dial
from all bedrooms  Licensed  Full central heating  Open parking
available  Covered parking available  Child discount available
12yrs  Bicycle rental  V meals  Last d 22.00hrs  Languages
spoken: English, Spanish & German*
ROOMS: (room only) s 255-275FF; d 300-345FF
**Reductions over 1 night  Special breaks: Golf and
gastronomic fixed price breaks**
MEALS: Full breakfast 40FF  Lunch 150-215FF&alc  Dinner
150-215FF&alc
CARDS: ●● ■ ■■ ■ Travellers cheques

## FAVEROLLES Orne

**Le Mont Roti** (Prop: Bernard Fortin)
61600
☎ 233373472
(from Argentan take D924 to Fromentel then left onto D19
towards La Ferté-Macé. Farm on right just before the entrance
to Faverolles)
All the rooms are set apart from the main residence, which is a
farm where peace and quiet reign. Breakfasts served - you'll
love the home-made jam. Evening meal with hosts by request.
Half-price rooms for children. Fishing, swimming, tennis and
golf within easy access.
Near river  Near lake  Forest area
*2 en suite (shr)  No smoking on premises  Full central heating
Open parking available  Child discount available  Boule
Languages spoken: English*
ROOMS: s 160FF; d 200FF
MEALS: Dinner 80FF✱

## FERRIÈRES-ST-HILAIRE Eure

**La Fosse Nardière** (Prop: Madeline Drouin)
27270
☎ 232432667 FAX 231323116
Near river  Forest area  Near motorway

*4 rms (2 bth/shr)  (1 fmly)  (1 with balcony)  Full central heating
Open parking available  No children  Last d 19.00hrs*

## FERTÉ-FRÊNEL, LA Orne

**Le Château** (Prop: M & Mme Sodechaff)
61550
☎ 233242323 FAX 233245019
Near river  Forest area  Near motorway
*18 rms (12 bth)  (3 fmly)  TV in all bedrooms  Full central
heating  Open parking available  Supervised  Child discount
available 12yrs  Fishing  Languages spoken: English German &
Spanish*
CARDS: ●● ■ ■■ ■

## FIQUEFLEUR-ÉQUAINVILLE Eure

**Bed & Breakfast** (Prop: M & Mme J Delanney)
27210
☎ 232576646
Forest area
*2 en suite (bth/shr)  (1 fmly)  Full central heating  Open parking
available*

## FLAMANVILLE Manche

**Hameau Cavelier** (Prop: Nicole Travers)
50340
☎ 233524283
Near sea  Near beach  Forest area
*2 en suite (shr)  No smoking on premises  Full central heating*

## FLEURY-LA-FORÊT Eure

**Château de Fleury** (Prop: Kristina Boulanger)
☎ 232496391 FAX 232494639
(Between Rouen & Paris take N31 at La Feuille follow direction
of Fleury-la-Forêt; from N14 at Écouis follow direction Lyons-
la-Forêt and then Fleury-la-Forêt)
In the heart of the Forest your host will be your guide to the
local history. A lovely property where guests will enjoy
relaxation and a high level of hospitality
Forest area
*2 en suite (bth)  No smoking on premises  Full central heating
Child discount available 10yrs  Bicycle rental  Languages
spoken: English & Finnish*
ROOMS: d 500FF

## FONTAINE-LE-PIN Calvados

**Laize** (Prop: Tim & Carolyn Knowlman)
Laize *14190*
☎ 231902362 FAX 231902362
(From Caen take N158 Falaise road, continue approx 12km &
then exit at Granville-Langamerie. Follow the D239 to St
Germain-le-Vasson, pass through village and in 1km bear right
signed Bray-en-Cinglais. House on right after 1km with fir-.
lined drive)
Near river  Forest area
*Closed Nov-Feb
2 en suite (shr)  No smoking on premises  Full central heating
Child discount available  Fishing  Languages spoken: English*
CARDS: Travellers cheques

### FONTENAI-SUR-ORNE Orne

**★ ★ Le Faisan Doré**
*61200*
☎ 233671811 FAX 233358215
(on road to Flers, 3km from Argentan)
Forest area
*14 en suite (bth/shr) (2 fmly) (1 with balcony) No smoking in 2 bedrooms TV in all bedrooms Direct dial from all bedrooms Licensed Full central heating Open parking available Supervised Child discount available 10yrs Pool table Open terrace V meals Last d 22.00hrs Languages spoken: English & German*
CARDS: ●● ■■ ▨▨ Travellers cheques

### FORGES-LES-EAUX Seine-Maritime

**La Bellière** (Prop: Rebecca Hooper)
*76400*
☎ 235908570
(take A28 from Calais exit Forges-les-Eaux, from Forges take D915 for Gournay-en-Bray, after 5km La Bellière is signposted to the left)
The accomodation is on a farm in an attractively converted stable, with a split-level oak floor and antique furniture. As well as the usual farm animals there is a large stable and horse-riding is offered. Beautiful views over the Normandy countryside.
Near river Near lake Forest area Near motorway
*2 en suite (bth/shr) (1 fmly) Full central heating Open parking available Child discount available Indoor swimming pool (heated) Outdoor swimming pool (heated) Tennis Riding Bicycle rental Bird watching clay piggeon shooting Last d 19.00hrs Languages spoken: English German & Spanish*
ROOMS: s 200-300FF; d 300-400FF
**✳ Reductions over 1 night**
MEALS: Dinner 100FF✳
CARDS: Travellers cheques

### FOURGES Eure

**Bed & Breakfast** (Prop: M & Mme P Stekelorum)
24 rue du Moulin *27630*
☎ 232521251 FAX 232521312
(close to the Claude Monet Museum and Garden at Giverny)

Country lovers will appreciate the Fourges area and the hospitality of the owners. Many leisure opportunities are available within easy distance: golf, riding, fishing, gliding, windsurfing, tennis, a swimming pool and leisure centre. There are also plenty of restaurants nearby.

Near river Forest area
*3 en suite (shr) No smoking on premises Full central heating Open parking available*
ROOMS: s fr 190FF; d 230-250FF

### FOURMETOT Eure

**L'Aufragère** (Prop: N Dussartre)
La Croisée *27500*
☎ 232569192 FAX 232577534
(from Pont Audemer take the direction towards Le Havre on N182 and fork right towards Fourmetot on D139. In town turn right before the church and house is 1km on your left through 2 brick pillars)
Forest area
*5 en suite (bth/shr) (2 fmly) No smoking in all bedrooms Licensed Full central heating Open parking available Covered parking available Riding Boule Open terrace Last d 19.30hrs Languages spoken: English*
CARDS: Travellers cheques

### FRESNÉ-LA-MÈRE Calvados

**La Vieille Ferme** (Prop: M & Mme Bass)
Le Bourg *14700*
☎ 231903498 FAX 231903498
(from Falaise take route to Trun and after 6kms turn to the left immediately after the automatic barrier at Fresné-La-Mère. After 500mtrs turn right by the side of the bakery)
Near river Near lake Near sea Near beach Forest area Near motorway
*4 en suite (bth/shr) (1 fmly) No smoking in all bedrooms Full central heating Open parking available Supervised Child discount available 12yrs Enclosed children's play area Last d 10.00hrs Languages spoken: English*
ROOMS: s 250FF; d 250-275FF
MEALS: Dinner 100FF

### FRESVILLE Manche

**Grainville** (Prop: B Brecy)
*50310*
☎ 233411049 FAX 233210757
Near river Near lake Near sea Near beach In town centre Near motorway
*3 en suite (bth/shr) (2 fmly) Full central heating Open parking available Supervised Languages spoken: English & Spanish*
CARDS: Travellers cheques

### GACÉ Orne

**★ ★ Hostellerie les Champs**
rte d'Alençon-Rouen, RN 138 *61230*
☎ 233390905 FAX 233368126
Surrounded by the lush scenery of the Normandy countryside this manor house dates back to the mid 1800s. It offers a peaceful stay in the elegant interior of an ancient mansion. Bedrooms are tastefully furnished and feature modern facilities, and the restaurant serves a wide range of superb dishes.
Near river Forest area Near motorway
*14 en suite (bth/shr) (3 fmly) Direct dial from all bedrooms Licensed Full central heating Open parking available Covered parking available Supervised Outdoor swimming pool Tennis Open terrace Last d 21.30hrs Languages spoken: English*

**Hostellerie Les Champs**
ROOMS: (room only) s 190-335FF; d 230-380FF
MEALS: Continental breakfast 50FF Lunch 95-230FF Dinner
130-230FF
CARDS: ●● 💳 Travellers cheques

### GÉFOSSE-FONTENAY Calvados

**L'Hermerel** (Prop: Francois & Agnes Le Marie)
*14230*
☎ 231226412 FAX 231226412
(On N13, leave Osmanville towards Grandcamp-Maisy. 4km
after village of Osmanville turn left towards Géfosse-Fontenay.
Follow signs "L'Hermerel, 2nd lane on right)
Near sea Near beach
*Closed 15 Dec-15 Jan RS Oct-Apr*
*4 en suite (shr) (2 fmly) No smoking on premises Full central
heating Open parking available Languages spoken: English*
ROOMS: s fr 250FF; d fr 300FF **Reductions over 1 night**
CARDS: Travellers cheques

### GENÊTS Manche

**Le Moulin** (Prop: M L Daniel)
*50530*
☎ 233708378
(from Avranches take the coast road "Église de Genêts", pass
Vains and entering the town, take second turning on right)
Near river Near lake Near sea Near beach
*4 en suite (shr) No smoking on premises Full central heating
Open parking available Supervised Child discount available
12yrs Languages spoken: English*
CARDS: Travellers cheques

### GENNEVILLE Calvados

**Bed & Breakfast** (Prop: M & Mme Crenn)
Le Bourg *14600*
☎ 231987563
(signposted from the church square)
Bernadette and Daniel Crenn welcome guests to their
establishment situated in a small village six kilometres from
Honfleur. Five comfortable rooms are available. This typical
Norman half-timbered house dates back to the 18th and 19th
centuries. Breakfast served in the attractive dining room. Gite
accommodation also available in the grounds.
*5 en suite (shr) (2 fmly) Full central heating Open parking
available*
ROOMS: s 160FF; d 230FF
CARDS: ▬

### GLATIGNY Manche

**Le Manoir** (Prop: M Duvernois)
*50250*
☎ 233070833 FAX 233479680
(from La Haye-du-Puits head towards Barnville-Carteret. At
Bolleville turn left towards Glatigny and follow signs for 'Le
Manoir')
Near river Near sea Near beach Forest area
*4 en suite (bth/shr) (1 fmly) Full central heating Open parking
available*

### GLOS Calvados

**La Haute-Follie** (Prop: Mme Roue)
*14100*
☎ 231627128
Forest area
*4 rms Full central heating Open parking available*

### GLOS-LA-FERRIÈRE Orne

**Haras-du-Boîle** (Prop: Catherine Dussaut)
*61550*
☎ 233348759 FAX 233240326
(in l'Aile take direction of Lisieux and after 10km come to
village. Farm at end of village on right)
Forest area Near motorway
*5 en suite (bth/shr) TV available Full central heating Open
parking available Supervised Child discount available Outdoor
swimming pool Tennis Riding Languages spoken: English*
CARDS: Travellers cheques

### GONNEVILLE-SUR-HONFLEUR Calvados

**La Ferme de Beauchamp** (Prop: Daniel Andre Michel)
*14600*
☎ 231891993
Near river Near lake
*Closed Xmas & family holidays*
*2 en suite (shr) No smoking on premises TV available Full
central heating Open parking available Covered parking
available*

### GRAINVILLE Eure

**Ferme du Château** (Prop: M Ammeux)
2 r Grand-Mare *27380*
☎ 232490953
Near river Forest area Near motorway
*2 rms (1 fmly) No smoking on premises Full central heating
Open parking available Supervised Child discount available*

### GRANDCAMP-MAISY Calvados

**Ferme du Colombier** (Prop: M Legrand)
*14450*
☎ 231226846 FAX 231221433
Near sea Near beach In town centre
*5 en suite (shr) (1 fmly) Full central heating Open parking
available Supervised Child discount available V meals Last d
21.00hrs Languages spoken: English*
ROOMS: d 230FF ✳
CARDS: Travellers cheques

**Vaumanoir** (Prop: M & Mme Maudelonde)
11 r du chateau-d'Eau *14450*
☎ 231219541 FAX 232172205
Near sea  Near beach  Near motorway
*Closed Oct-May*
*2 en suite (shr)  (1 fmly)  Full central heating  Open parking available  Supervised  Child discount available 8yrs*

### GUERVILLE Seine-Maritime

**Ferme de la Haye** (Prop: Jean and Dominique Mairesse)
*76340*
☎ 322261426
Forest area
*1 en suite (shr)  Full central heating  Open parking available  Child discount available 5yrs  Languages spoken: English & Spanish*

### HAMBYE Manche

**★ ★ Auberge de L'Abbaye**
BP2
☎ 233614219 FAX 233610085
Near river  Forest area  In town centre  Near motorway
*7 rms (1 bth 5 shr)  TV in all bedrooms  STV  Licensed  Full central heating  Open parking available  Supervised  Child discount available  Open terrace  Last d 21.00hrs  Languages spoken: English*
CARDS: ●● ▆▆ Travellers cheques

### HAYE-AUBRÉE, LA Eure

**Bed & Breakfast** (Prop: M & Mme Verhaeghe)
rue du Bois *27350*
☎ 232573109
Forest area
*1 en suite (bth/shr)  Radio in rooms  Full central heating  Open parking available  Supervised  Child discount available*

### HAYE-DU-THEIL, LA Eure

**Domaine de la Coudraye** (Prop: L Demaegdt)
*27370*
☎ 232355207 FAX 232351721
(autoroute de Normandie exit 24 (Maison Brulée) establishment on the D26)
Near river  Forest area  Near motorway
*2 en suite (bth/shr)  Full central heating  Open parking available  Tennis  Languages spoken: English*
CARDS: ●● ▆▆ ▆▆ ▆ Travellers cheques

### HONFLEUR Calvados

**★ ★ ★ Hotel Antares**
La Rivière St-Sauveur *14600*
☎ 231891010 FAX 231895857
(from A13 take the exit 'Honfleur', 15kms before Honfleur take direction 'Caen/Pont-l'Évêque', hotel 100ms on left. From Le Havre, take Normandy Bridge, then follow signs Caen/Pont-l'Évêque)
Near sea  Near beach  Forest area  Near motorway
*Closed 2-26 Jan*
*48 en suite (bth/shr)  (16 fmly)  TV in all bedrooms  STV  Direct dial from all bedrooms  Licensed  Lift  Night porter  Full central heating  Open parking available  Child discount available 11yrs  Indoor swimming pool (heated)  Sauna  Solarium  Gym  Open*

*terrace  Billiards  Last d 21.00hrs  Languages spoken: English & Spanish*
ROOMS:  (room only) s 320-550FF;  d 350-550FF
MEALS:  Lunch 120FF  Dinner 120FF
CARDS: ●● ▆▆ ▆▆ ▆ Travellers cheques

**★ ★ ★ ★ La Chaumière**
rte du Littoral *14600*
☎ 231816320 FAX 231895923
Near sea  Near beach  Forest area
*9 en suite (bth/shr)  (1 fmly)  TV in all bedrooms  STV  Licensed  Full central heating  Open parking available  Supervised  Child discount available  Bicycle rental  Open terrace  V meals  Last d 21.30hrs*
CARDS: ●● ▆▆ ▆▆ Travellers cheques

**★ ★ ★ Écrin**
19 rue Eugène Boudin *14600*
☎ 231144345 FAX 231892441
In town centre
*26 en suite (bth/shr)  (6 fmly)  (1 with balcony)  TV in all bedrooms  STV  Direct dial from all bedrooms  Mini-bar in 22 bedrooms  Licensed  Night porter  Full central heating  Open parking available  Supervised  Sauna  Pool table  Open terrace  Covered terrace  Languages spoken: English & German*
CARDS: ●● ▆▆ ▆▆ ▆ Travellers cheques

**★ ★ ★ ★ Le Ferme Saint-Simeon**
Adolphe Marais *14600*
☎ 231892361 FAX 231894848
Near river  Near sea  Near beach
*34 en suite (bth/shr)  (8 fmly)  (8 with balcony)  TV in all bedrooms  STV  Mini-bar in all bedrooms  Licensed  Lift  Night porter  Full central heating  Open parking available  Supervised  Indoor swimming pool (heated)  Sauna  Solarium  Jacuzzi/spa  Bicycle rental  Open terrace  V meals  Last d 21.30hrs*
CARDS: ●● ▆▆ ▆▆ JCB Travellers cheques

### HOTTOT-LES-BAGUES Calvados

**Le Vallon** (Prop: Cecile Grenier)
*14250*
☎ 231081185 FAX 231081185
(from the west of Caen leave A13, take D9 at Carpiquet towards Caumont-l'Eventé, and on to Hottot-les-Bagues. Follow signs for Le Vallon from village centre)
Forest area
*9 rms (5 shr)  (1 fmly)  No smoking on premises  Full central heating  Open parking available  Covered parking available  Supervised  Fishing  Boule*
CARDS: Travellers cheques

### HOUDETOT Seine-Maritime

**Bed & Breakfast** (Prop: M J F Bocquet)
*76740*
☎ 235790873 FAX 235971921
*3 rms (2 shr)  Full central heating  Open parking available  Supervised*

### HOULBEC-COCHEREL Eure

**★ ★ ★ Ferme de Cocherel**
rte de la Vallée d'Eure *27120*
☎ 232366827 FAX 232262818
(from A13 take exit 16)

The hotel is located in a small village surrounded by unspoilt countryside. Maisonette-style rooms are situated in the garden, and are equipped with modern facilities which offer a good standard of comfort. There is a restaurant, and with Paris and the coast just one hour's drive away, it provides a good base for touring the surrounding region.

**Ferme de Cocherel**
Near river  Forest area  Near motorway
*Closed 3 wks Jan & 2 wks Sep*
*2 en suite (bth/shr) Licensed Full central heating Open parking available Supervised Open terrace Last d 21.00hrs*
ROOMS: (room only) d 600-800FF
MEALS: Continental breakfast 60FF Lunch fr 220FF Dinner fr 220FF
CARDS: ●● ■■ ■■ ⑩ Travellers cheques

**INGOUVILLE-SUR-MER** Seine-Maritime

**Les Hêtres**
rue des Fleurs-le Bourg *76460*
☎ 235570930 FAX 235570931
*4 en suite (bth/shr) TV in all bedrooms Radio in rooms Direct dial from all bedrooms Mini-bar in all bedrooms Licensed Night porter Full central heating Open parking available Covered parking available Boule Jacuzzi/spa Bicycle rental Open terrace Last d 22.00hrs Languages spoken: English*
CARDS: ●● ■■ Travellers cheques

**ISIGNY-SUR-MER** Calvados

**Bed & Breakfast** (Prop: M R le Devin)
7 rue du Docteur Boutrois *14230*
☎ 231211233 FAX 231211875
Near river  In town centre  Near motorway
*1 en suite (bth/shr) TV available Full central heating Open parking available Child discount available*

★★ **De France**
13-15 rue Emile Demagny *14230*
☎ 231220033 FAX 231227919
The hotel has been in the hands of the same family for the last 40 or so years, and a warm welcome and friendly service awaits guests on arrival. The bedrooms are well equipped and of a good size, and the cuisine incorporates a choice of specialities from the region.
Near river  Near lake  Forest area  In town centre  Near motorway
*Closed 15 Nov-15 Feb*
*19 rms (16 bth) 3 rooms in annexe (5 fmly) TV in all bedrooms Direct dial from all bedrooms Licensed Night porter Full central heating Open parking available Supervised Child discount available 12yrs Outdoor swimming pool (heated)*

*Fishing Boule Bicycle rental V meals Languages spoken: English & German*
CARDS: ●● ■■ ■■ Access/ Eurocard Travellers cheques

**La Rivière** (Prop: M & Mme Marie)
St-Germain-du-Pert *14230*
☎ 231227292 FAX 231220163
(from Bayeux take N13 to Carentan, then D113 south. After 1km take D124 towards St-Germain-du-Pert)
Near river  Near sea  Near motorway
*Closed Nov-Mar*
*3 en suite (bth/shr) (1 fmly) Full central heating Open parking available Supervised Child discount available 8yrs Open terrace*
CARDS: Travellers cheques

**JUIGNETTES** Eure

**Ferme Auberge de la Pommeraie** (Prop: M & Mme Vaudron)
*27250*
☎ 233349184
(7km from Rugles in the direction of Lisieux)
Near motorway
*3 en suite (bth/shr) No smoking on premises Full central heating Open parking available Child discount available 10yrs Boule V meals Last d 20.30hrs*
CARDS: Travellers cheques

**JUMIÈGES** Seine-Maritime

**Le Relais de l'Abbaye** (Prop: M Patrick Chatel)
798 rue du Quesney *76480*
☎ 235372498
(25kms from Rouen)
Near lake  Forest area
*4 en suite (shr) Full central heating Open parking available*
ROOMS: s 200FF; d 230FF

**JUVIGNY-LE-TERTRE** Manche

**Bed & Breakfast** (Prop: Marylene Fillatre)
Le Logis *50520*
☎ 233593820 FAX 233593820
(in Jurigny go towards St Hilaire (D55) for 1km, turn left towards 'Le Logis' for less than 1km. The manor-house 'Le Logis' is on the left)
Marylène Fillatre welcomes you to her 17th-century manor farm, offering comfortable accommodation and meals prepared with fine local produce. Two rooms are in the restored "Pigeon House". Breakfast is served in the spacious dining room with exposed stone walls and wooden beams.
*contd.*

Near river  Near lake  Forest area
*3 en suite (shr)  (2 fmly)  Radio in rooms  Full central heating*
*Open parking available  Child discount available 12yrs  Fishing*
*Boule  Bicycle rental  V meals  Last d noon  Languages spoken:*
*English*
ROOMS:  d 220-240FF  **Reductions over 1 night**
MEALS:  Dinner fr 75FF
CARDS: Travellers cheques

### LAMBERVILLE Manche

*Le Château* (Prop: Francoise de Brunville)
*50160*
☎ 233561570 FAX 233563526
Near lake  Forest area
*Closed 16 Dec-14 Feb*
*3 en suite (bth/shr)  (1 fmly)  TV available  Full central heating*
*Open parking available  Child discount available*

### LANDES-SUR-AJON Calvados

*Le Château* (Prop: Therese Vauquelin)
*14310*
☎ 231770888
Near river
*1 en suite (bth/shr)  Full central heating  Open parking available*
*Supervised  Child discount available 10yrs*

### LANDES-VIEILLES-ET-NEUVES, LES Seine-Maritime

**Château des Landes** (Prop: Jacqueline Simon-Lemettre)
*76390*
☎ 235940379 FAX 235940379
(leave N29 between Neufchâtel/Aumale, take D16 in direction
of Caule then St-Beuve, then D7 towards Richemont Les
Landes in 2km)

A pretty brick-built, 19th-century château, close to the Eu
forest, stands in 2.5 acres of tree-lined parkland. The
bedrooms, four large rooms and one suite, have been
individually decorated in pastel colours and are appointed with
family heirlooms. In spring and summer guests may enjoy
eating breakfast on the veranda. Shops and sporting facilities
nearby.
Forest area  Near motorway
*5 en suite (shr)  Full central heating  Open parking available*
*Child discount available 3yrs  Languages spoken: English*
ROOMS:  s 260-300FF; d 300-350FF
MEALS:  Dinner 110FF
CARDS: Travellers cheques

### LANGRUNE-SUR-MER Calvados

**Bed & Breakfast** (Prop: A & A Jeanne)
5 av de la Libération *14830*
☎ 231972449
Near sea
*Closed 12 Nov-7 Apr*
*2 en suite (bth/shr)  (1 fmly)  No smoking on premises  Full*
*central heating  Open parking available  Languages spoken:*
*English*
CARDS: Travellers cheques

### LE BOURG-DUN Seine-Maritime

**La Pommeraie** (Prop: Jean-Pierre Brault)
30 rte d'Englesqueville *76740*
☎ 235835892 FAX 235042123
(from Dieppe take D925 in direction of Fécamp, cross Petit
Appeville then Ouville-la-Rivière at Boueg-Dun turn right after
the post office)

Your hosts welcome you to their century old cottage,
surrounded by a landscape garden.
Near river  Near sea  Near beach
*2 en suite (bth/shr)  No smoking on premises  TV in all*
*bedrooms  Full central heating  Open parking available*
*Languages spoken: English*
ROOMS:  s 260FF; d 300FF  **Special breaks**
MEALS:  Dinner 95FF

### LESSAY Manche

**Bed & Breakfast** (Prop: M & Mme Boulland)
15 r Geslonde *50430*
☎ 233460484
In town centre
*2 en suite (shr)  Full central heating  Open parking available*
*Supervised*

### LINGREVILLE Manche

**Blanche Pré** (Prop: M et Mme Gautier)
Village Hue *50660*
☎ 233079124
Near sea  Near beach
*2 en suite (bth)  (1 fmly)  Full central heating  Open parking*
*available  Languages spoken: English & German*
ROOMS:  d 180FF
CARDS: Travellers cheques

## LISIEUX Calvados

**La Drouetterie** (Prop: Alain Gran)
Marolles *14100*
☎ 231627393
(At Lisieux take N13 towards Paris for 8km, at the x-rds of the May turn right towards Marolles. On entering the village, turn right onto D75 in direction of Courtonne la Meurdrac. The house is on D75B)

In the area of Pays d'Auge, in a nice valley with quiet surroundings. A half-timbered restored house where the attractive bedrooms have exposed beams.
Near river Forest area
*2 en suite (shr) (1 fmly) Full central heating Open parking available Child discount available 2yrs Fishing Riding Minigolf Bicycle rental Languages spoken: English & Spanish*
Rooms: d 250FF

**★ ★ ★ Hotel de la Place**
pl François Mitterand
☎ 231482727 FAX 231482720
(in centre of the town near the cathedral)
Near river Forest area In town centre Near motorway
*15 Mar-Oct*
*35 en suite (bth/shr) (3 fmly) (3 with balcony) TV in all bedrooms Direct dial from all bedrooms Lift Full central heating Open parking available (charged) Covered parking available (charged) Child discount available 12yrs Languages spoken: English & Spanish*
Rooms: (room only) s 280-360FF; d 360-480FF
Cards: ●● ■ ▥

## LIVRY Calvados

**La Suhardière** (Prop: Alain Petitoy)
*14240*
☎ 231775102
Near lake Near sea Forest area
*3 en suite (shr) Full central heating Open parking available Child discount available*

## LOGES, LES Seine-Maritime

**Ferme du Jardinet** (Prop: Beatrice Vasse)
*76790*
☎ 235270407
(from village centre take D74/follow signs for Chambre d'hôte)
Near sea Near beach Forest area
*7 rms (2 shr) (1 fmly) Radio in rooms Full central heating Open parking available*
Rooms: s 200FF; d 230FF ✱

## LONGCHAMPS Eure

**Bed & Breakfast** (Prop: Mme Reine Thibert)
67 rue du Bourgerue *27150*
☎ 232555439
Forest area Near motorway
*4 en suite (shr) Full central heating Open parking available*
Cards: Travellers cheques

## LONGUES-SUR-MER Calvados

**Ferme de la Tourelle** (Prop: Le Carpentier)
Hameau de Fontenailles *14400*
☎ 231217847 FAX 231218484
(from Bayeux take D1043 to Longues-sur-Mer, then D514 to house on right)
Near sea Near beach Forest area
*5 en suite (shr) (3 fmly) Full central heating Open parking available Child discount available Golf*

**Hameau de Fontenailles** (Prop: Jean Chatel)
*14400*
☎ 231217849
Near sea Near beach
*4 rms (3 shr) (2 fmly) Full central heating Open parking available Supervised*
Cards: ●● ■ Travellers cheques

## LONGVILLERS Calvados

**La Nouvelle France** (Prop: Anne-Marie Godey)
*14310*
☎ 231776336
(Autoroute exit 43 Caen/Rennes D6 Aunay-sur-Odon take D216 to Longuillers, 1st house on the left)

Constructed of typical country stone, this old grange is decorated in Normandy style with three rooms available for bed & breakfast in a separate building from the main house. Traditional French breakfast served. Parking at the back of the house, with large shaded lawn.
Forest area
*3 en suite (shr) No smoking on premises Full central heating Open parking available Child discount available 10 yrs Languages spoken: English*
Rooms: d fr 220FF ✱

## LOUVIERS Eure

### ★ ★ ★ Haye Le Comté
4 rte de la Haye-le-Comte *27400*
☎ 232400040 FAX 232250385
(From Paris A13 exit 18 to Louviers, then take D133 towards le Neubourg. Take left turn following signs for La Haye le Comte)

Once two separate buildings, this 16th-century manor house and ancient farm now offer, a spacious interior where contemporary features and traditional furnishings go hand in hand. Surrounded by an extensive park and various leisure pursuits, it provides the ideal base for walking and exploring the surroundings. The menu lists a choice of seasonal dishes and specialities from the Normandy region.
Forest area
16 en suite (bth/shr) (1 fmly) No smoking in all bedrooms TV in all bedrooms STV Direct dial from all bedrooms Licensed Full central heating Open parking available Child discount available Tennis Boule Bicycle rental Open terrace Table tennis croquet V meals Last d 21.00hrs Languages spoken: English
ROOMS: (room only) s 390-550FF; d 390-550FF
**✳ Reductions over 1 night**
**Special breaks: 3 night breaks**
MEALS: Full breakfast 55FF Lunch 100-190FF Dinner 100-190FF
CARDS: ●● ■■ ▦ ⑳ JCB Travellers cheques

## LUC-SUR-MER Calvados

### ★ ★ ★ *Hotel des Thermes et du Casino*
av Guynémer *14530*
☎ 231973237 FAX 231967257
(A13 exit no 5 direction Douvres la Delivrande)
Near sea Near beach In town centre
Closed Nov-Mar
48 en suite (bth/shr) (18 with balcony) TV in all bedrooms STV Direct dial from all bedrooms Licensed Lift Full central heating Open parking available Covered parking available (charged) Supervised Child discount available Indoor swimming pool (heated) Outdoor swimming pool (heated) Sauna Gym Jacuzzi/spa Open terrace Last d 22.00hrs Languages spoken: English & Spanish

## LYONS-LA-FORÊT Eure

### ★ ★ Domaine St-Paul
*27480*
☎ 232496057 FAX 232595605
(off D321 near the swimming pool)

The hotel is situated on the edge of the typical Normandy village of Lyons-La-Forêt and surrounded by the most extensive beech-tree forest in France. It is owned and run by the Lorrain family, who extend a warm welcome to their visitors. Charming guest rooms with modern amenities are offered, as well as classical French cuisine.
Near river Forest area

*Domaine St Paul*

Closed 2 Nov-2 Apr
17 en suite (bth/shr) (1 fmly) Direct dial from all bedrooms Licensed Full central heating Open parking available Supervised Child discount available 10yrs Outdoor swimming pool (heated) Solarium Pool table Boule Bicycle rental Open terrace Covered terrace Table tennis Last d 21.00hrs Languages spoken: English & German
ROOMS: (incl. dinner) s 455-615FF; d 650-800FF
MEALS: Continental breakfast 45FF Lunch 125-210FF Dinner 150-210FF
CARDS: ●● ▦ Travellers cheques

### ★ ★ ★ *Licorne*
27 pl Bensérade *27480*
☎ 232496202 FAX 232498009
Near river Forest area In town centre
Closed 20 Dec-20 Jan RS Sun evening & Mon
19 en suite (bth/shr) 2 rooms in annexe (1 fmly) TV in all bedrooms STV Direct dial from all bedrooms Licensed Full central heating Open parking available Supervised Child discount available Mini-golf Bicycle rental Open terrace V meals Last d 21.30hrs Languages spoken: English & Italian
CARDS: ●● ■■ ▦ ⑳ Travellers cheques

## MACÉ Orne

### ★ ★ Ile de Sées
*61500*
☎ 233279865 FAX 233284122
Near river Forest area
Closed 15 Jan-Feb
16 en suite (bth/shr) (4 fmly) TV in all bedrooms Direct dial from all bedrooms Licensed Full central heating Open parking available Child discount available 2yrs Tennis Open terrace Last d 21.00hrs Languages spoken: English
ROOMS: (room only) s 300FF; d 360FF
MEALS: Full breakfast 35FF Lunch 85-185FF Dinner 113-185FF
CARDS: ●● ▦

### MAINNEVILLE Eure

**Ferme Ste-Genévieve** (Prop: Jean-Claude & Jeannine Marc)
*27150*
☎ 232555126 FAX 232275089
(leave Paris from Porte St-Ouen, on Porte de Clignancourt in direction of Pontoise. Go towards Gisors until Eragny-sur-Epte, turn left just before rail bridge, go along for 13km to Mainneville)
Near river  Forest area
*4 en suite (shr) (3 fmly) No smoking on premises Full central heating Open parking available Baby Foot Table tennis Badminton Languages spoken: English*
ROOMS: s 200FF; d 230FF
CARDS: Travellers cheques

### MAISONS Calvados

**Moulin Gerard** (Prop: Bernard Pierre)
☎ 231214416
(N13 Bayeux direction Port en Besson 5km -D6)
Near river  Near sea
*3 en suite (bth/shr) Full central heating Open parking available Child discount available Golf Tennis Boule Bicycle rental*
ROOMS: s fr 200FF; d fr 250FF

### MARTAGNY Eure

**Ferme des Simons** (Prop: Jacques Laine)
21 r de la Chasse *27150*
☎ 232555722 FAX 232551401
Near river  Forest area
*3 en suite (shr) (1 fmly) Open parking available Child discount available 12yrs Languages spoken: English*

### MARTAINVILLE Eure

**Bed & Breakfast** (Prop: J & O Bouteiller)
*27210*
☎ 232578223
(from A13 (Paris-Caen) exit 28 take D27 Epaignes. At 6Km marker turn right and follow signs)
Forest area  Near motorway
*2 en suite (bth/shr) (1 fmly) No smoking on premises Full central heating Open parking available Child discount available 10yrs*

### MARTIN-ÉGLISE Seine-Maritime

★ ★ **Auberge de Clos Normand**
22 rue Henri IV
☎ 35044034 FAX 35044849
(5km from Dieppe via D1)
*Closed 15 Nov-15 Dec*
*8 en suite (bth/shr) (2 fmly) (5 with balcony) TV in all bedrooms STV Direct dial from all bedrooms Full central heating Open parking available Open terrace V meals Last d 21.00hrs*
CARDS: ●● ■ 💳

### MARTRAGNY Calvados

**Manoir de l'Abbaye** (Prop: M & Y Godfroy)
15 rue de Creully *14740*
☎ 231802595
(from Caen take N13 direction of Cherbourg exit Martragny take direction of Creully)

Near sea  Near beach  Near motorway
*5 rms (4 shr) (2 fmly) TV in 4 bedrooms Full central heating Open parking available Covered parking available Supervised Child disco…: available 10yrs Riding Boule Bicycle rental Languages spoken: English*
ROOMS: s 200-250FF; d 235-280FF
❋ **Reductions over 1 night**
CARDS: Travellers cheques

### MELLEVILLE Seine-Maritime

**La Marette** (Prop: M & Mme Etienne Garconnet)
rte de la Marette *76260*
☎ 235508165 FAX 325508165
(from Rouen take A28, exit at Blangy-sur-Bresle. Then D49 towards Le Tréport. At Gamaches turn left to Guerville then Melleville. Through village and La Marette on right)

Surrounded by gardens, this turn-of-the-century house is situated on the edge of the Forest of Eu. The rooms are spacious, have modern facilities and offer comfortable accommodation. The sitting room overlooks the garden and breakfast is served with delicious home-made jams. In the annexe is a kitchen for guests wishing to prepare their own meals.
Forest area  In town centre  Near motorway
*5 rms (2 bth/shr) (4 fmly) No smoking on premises Full central heating Open parking available Supervised table tennis and swings*
ROOMS: d 200-280FF ❋ **Reductions over 1 night**

### MESNIL-AUBERT, LE Manche

**Ferme de le Peurie** (Prop: Antoinette Davenel)
*50510*
☎ 233519631
Near river  Near sea  Forest area
*3 en suite (shr) No smoking on premises Full central heating Open parking available*

### MESNIL-GILBERT, LE Manche

**La Motte** (Prop: Marcel & Agnes Lemarchant)
*50670*
☎ 233598309 FAX 233694546
(from Brécey take D911 for approx 8km in direction of Mortain Sourdeval)
Deep in the Vallomme countryside, on the banks of the Sec, Agnes and Marcel welcome guests to their farm, where peace and quiet are assured. The old house is exclusively for guests. Five rooms available with use of fireplace and kitchen area. Farm produce served. The area is perfect for those who enjoy walking. *contd.*

Near river Forest area
5 rms (4 shr) (1 fmly) No smoking on premises Full central
heating Open parking available Child discount available 10yrs
Boule Games room
ROOMS: s 170FF; d 200-220FF
CARDS: Travellers cheques

### MESNIL-ROGUES, LE Manche

**La Pinotière** (Prop: Etiennette Legallais)
50450
☎ 233613898
Near river Forest area
4 en suite (bth/shr) (1 fmly) Full central heating Open parking
available Supervised
CARDS: ■ Travellers cheques

### MEURDRAQUIÈRE, LA Manche

**La Butte** (Prop: Marie-Therese)
50510
☎ 233613152
(between Gavray and La Haye-Pesnel on the D7)
Near river Forest area
3 en suite (shr) Full central heating Open parking available

### MÉZIÈRES-EN-VEXIN Eure

**Hameau de Surcy** (Prop: Simone Vard)
29 rue de l'Huis 27510
☎ 232523004 FAX 232522877
(approach via D1 towards Les Andelys, then left to Surcy)
This farmhouse is situated on the Vexin Plateau, and all rooms
face south. The breakfast room is reserved for the use of
guests. Piano available. The Claude Monet Museum is within
close proximity, as is the Château Gaillard.
4 en suite (bth/shr) No smoking on premises Full central
heating Open parking available
ROOMS: s 160-190FF; d 200-250FF ✱

### MITTOIS Calvados

**Le Vieux Château** (Prop: Pierre Pflièger)
14170
☎ 231207394
(off the D4 between St-Pierre-sur-Dives and Boissey)
Forest area
1 en suite (shr) (1 fmly) No smoking on premises TV in all
bedrooms Full central heating Open parking available
Languages spoken: English

### MONTCHATON Manche

**Le Quesnot** (Prop: Andre Palla)
50660
☎ 233450588 FAX 233455249
(from Coutances to Montmartin-sur-Mer, and from Cherbourg
to Le Pont-de-la-Roque, 1200m by D72 to Montchaton)
Near river Near motorway
3 en suite (shr) No smoking on premises Full central heating
Open parking available Open terrace Languages spoken:
English
CARDS: Travellers cheques

### MONTFARVILLE Manche

**Le Manoir** (Prop: Claudette Gabroy)
50760
☎ 233231421
(from Cherbourg to Barfleur on D901 and then D1 towards St-
Waast La Hougue. Take second turning on right after leaving
Barfleur and then first left - chambre d'hôte signposted)
Near sea Near beach
2 en suite (shr) (1 fmly) No smoking on premises Full central
heating Open parking available Supervised No children 6 yrs
CARDS: Travellers cheques

### MONTGARDON Manche

**Le Mont-Scolan** (Prop: Yves Seguineau)
50250
☎ 233461127
4 en suite (shr) (1 fmly) (1 with balcony) No smoking on
premises Full central heating Open parking available
Supervised Child discount available 12yrs V meals Last d
17.00hrs

### MONT-ST-MICHEL, LE Manche

**★ ★ ★ De La Digue**
50116
☎ 233601402 FAX 233603759
Near river
Closed 15 Nov-25 Mar
36 en suite (bth/shr) (5 fmly) (9 with balcony) TV in all
bedrooms STV Direct dial from all bedrooms Licensed Full
central heating Open parking available 10yrs Bicycle rental Open terrace Covered terrace V
meals Last d 21.30hrs Languages spoken: English & German
ROOMS: (room only) s 320-380FF; d 350-460FF
✱ **Reductions over 1 night**
MEALS: Full breakfast 53FF Lunch 92-210FF&alc Dinner
92-210FF&alc
CARDS: ●● ■ ▄▄ ⑤ JCB Travellers cheques

**★ ★ ★ Relais du Roy**
50116
☎ 233601425 FAX 233603769
(approach via Avranches)

The building, with its 14th and 15th-century fireplaces, has
been a family hotel for many generations. Entirely refurbished
in recent years, it now offers pleasant bedrooms with modern
facilities, which have splendid views of Mont-St-Michel and
out to sea. The head chef, Yann Galton, is a very accomplished
cuisinier who has acquired many accolades.

Near river  Forest area
*Closed Dec-22 Mar  RS Half board obligatory in season
27 en suite (bth/shr)  (5 fmly)  (20 with balcony)  TV in all
bedrooms  STV  Direct dial from all bedrooms  Licensed  Night
porter  Full central heating  Open parking available  Open
terrace  V meals  Last d 21.00hrs  Languages spoken: English,
German, Italian & Spanish*
ROOMS: (room only)  d 360-450FF
MEALS: Full breakfast 50FF  Lunch 90-200FF&alc  Dinner
90-200FF&alc
CARDS: ●● ■■ ⅢⅢ Travellers cheques

### ★★★ Terrasses Poulard
Grande Rue *50116*
☎ 233601409 FAX 233603731
(approach via Avranches)
Near beach  Near motorway
*29 en suite (bth/shr)  12 rooms in annexe  (5 fmly)  (4 with
balcony)  TV in all bedrooms  STV  Direct dial from all
bedrooms  Mini-bar in all bedrooms  Licensed  Night porter
Full central heating  Supervised  Child discount available 12yrs
V meals  Last d 22.00hrs  Languages spoken: English & German*
ROOMS: (room only)  d 350-900FF
MEALS: Continental breakfast 40FF  Lunch 75-150FF&alc
Dinner 75-150FF&alc
CARDS: ●● ■■ ⅢⅢ ⑨ Travellers cheques

MONTS-EN-BESSIN Calvados

### La Varinière (Prop: P L Edney)
La Vallée *14310*
☎ 231774473 FAX 23771172
(from Caen take N175 towards Rennes/Mont-St-Michel and
exit D92 Monts-en-Bessin, turn right and straight over
cross-roads, turning right just before the château. House
2nd on left)
Near motorway
*5 en suite (bth/shr)  (32 fmly)  No smoking in all bedrooms  Full
central heating  Open parking available  Supervised  Last d
19.30hrs  Languages spoken: English*
CARDS: Travellers cheques

### MONTVIETTE Calvados

### Le Manoir d'Annique (Prop: Anni & Nick Wiltshire)
La Gravelle *14140*
☎ 231202098 FAX 231207436
(from Livarot take D4 towards St Pierre sur Dives. After 4km,
turn left D273A towards Tortisambert. Annique is 1st house on
right after 2km)
A warm welcome awaits you in this typical 16th-century
manor house of the Pays d'Auge, sympathetically restored and
with an enchanting use of colours to enhance the natural oak
beams. Anni and Nick invite you to join them around their
large dining table for a traditional French style meal using
local produce.
Near river  Near lake  Forest area  In town centre
*7 rms (1 bth 4 shr)  (2 fmly)  No smoking in all bedrooms  Full
central heating  Open parking available  Supervised  Child
discount available 10yrs  Indoor swimming pool (heated)
Outdoor swimming pool  Riding  Boule  Mini-golf  Bicycle rental
Languages spoken: English*
ROOMS: s 220FF; d 285-310FF
MEALS: Dinner fr 125FF
CARDS: Travellers cheques

### MONTVIRON Manche

### La Turinière (Prop: M & Mme Leroy)
*50530*
☎ 233488837
Near river  Forest area  Near motorway
*7 rms (2 shr)  Full central heating  Open parking available  Child
discount available 4yrs  Languages spoken: English*

### MORTAGNE-AU-PERCHE Orne

### ★★ Du Tribunal
4 pl du Palais *61400*
☎ 233250477 FAX 233836083
(on the N12 between Verneuil sur Avre and Alençon)
The building dates back to the 16th century and is situated in
the old centre of Montagne in the heart of the Normandy
forests. When visitors step over the threshold, they are
transported back in time. The interior has a charming
atmosphere, with silk fabrics, fine polished floors, and exposed
beams, and in addition there is a flower-filled, enclosed garden
with a terrace. The bedrooms offer comfortable
accommodation and the restaurant serves splendid dishes to
suit most palates.
Forest area  In town centre

*Closed 21 Dec-6 Jan
14 en suite (bth/shr)  (3 fmly)  (1 with balcony)  TV in all
bedrooms  STV  Direct dial from all bedrooms  Licensed  Full
central heating  Child discount available 10yrs  Open terrace  V
meals  Last d 21.00hrs  Languages spoken: English*
ROOMS: (room only)  d 240-320FF
MEALS: Continental breakfast 40FF  Lunch 90-190FF&alc
Dinner 90-190FF&alc
CARDS: ●● ⅢⅢ Travellers cheques

### MOSLES Calvados

### Quartier d'Argouges (Prop: Anne Marie Lefevre)
*14400*
☎ 231924340
(leaving Bayeaux in the direction of Cherbourg, take D37 in
direction of Ste-Honorine-des-Pertes, house first on right)
Near river  Near sea  Near beach  Forest area  Near motorway
*Closed Nov-Apr
2 en suite (shr)  (1 fmly)  No smoking in all bedrooms  Full
central heating  Open parking available  Supervised  Languages
spoken: English*

contd.

### MOULICENT Orne

**La Grande Noe** (Prop: M & Mme de Longcamp)
*61290*
☎ 233736330 FAX 233836292
(on N12, at the Ste-Anne x-roads between Verneuil and
Mortagne-au-Perche, head S for Longny-au-Perche, then left
for Moulicent. The entry is on the right after 0.5mile)
Set in a beautiful 30 acre park 90 miles from Paris, this château
has belonged to the same family since 1393. The owners will
share their evening meal with you in the warmth of the 18th-
century oak panelled dining room. Reservations are needed.
Forest area

*Closed Dec-Feb RS winter*
*3 en suite (bth/shr) No smoking on premises TV available Full*
*central heating Open parking available Covered parking*
*available Child discount available 2yr Bicycle rental Table*
*tennis, Piano*
ROOMS: s 500-600FF; d 550-650FF
**Reductions over 1 night**
MEALS: Dinner 100-220FF
CARDS: Travellers cheques

### NÉGREVILLE Manche

**La Vignonnerie** (Prop: Cecile & Jules Rose)
*50260*
☎ 233400258
(from Cherbourg N13 exit St-Joseph take D146 towards
Rocheville)
*Near river Near motorway*
*2 en suite (shr) No smoking in all bedrooms Full central*
*heating Open parking available Child discount available*
*2yrs*

### NOTRE-DAME-DE-LIVAYE Calvados

**Les Pommiers de Livaye** (Prop: Lambert-Dutrait)
*14340*
☎ 231630128 FAX 231637363
(N13 between Caen and Lisieux)
*Forest area Near motorway*
*Closed 16 Nov-28 Feb*
*5 en suite (bth/shr) (4 fmly) Licensed Full central heating*
*Open parking available Supervised Child discount available*
*5yrs Boule Bicycle rental Open terrace V meals Last d*
*20.00hrs Languages spoken: English & Dutch*
CARDS: Eurocheques Travellers cheques

### NOTRE-DAME-D'ESTRÉES Calvados

★★ *Au Repos des Chineurs*
Chemin de l'Église *14340*
☎ 231637251 FAX 231636238
Forest area
*10 en suite (bth/shr) (2 fmly) (1 with balcony) Licensed Night*
*porter Full central heating Open parking available Supervised*
*Child discount available Languages spoken: English*
CARDS: ●● ▆▆ Travellers cheques

### ORBEC Calvados

**Le Manoir de l'Engagisté** (Prop: M Dubois)
14 rue de Géolé *14290*
☎ 231325722 FAX 231325558
A recently restored 16th-century manor house, with
comfortable bedrooms and a warm welcome. Breakfast is
served in a gallery of paintings. Hosts Christian and Annick
will be happy to advise you on the best tours and walks in the
area. Table-tennis, billiards and bikes available.
*Near river Forest area In town centre Near motorway*
*5 en suite (bth/shr) (1 fmly) No smoking in 2 bedrooms TV in*
*all bedrooms Full central heating Open parking available*
*Child discount available 8yrs Bicycle rental Table tennis*
*Languages spoken: English & Spanish*
ROOMS: d 400FF ✱

### OSMANVILLE Calvados

**Le Champ Manlay** (Prop: M Guy Manlay)
*14230*
☎ 231220291 FAX 231220291
*Forest area Near motorway*
*Closed mid Sep-Etr*
*2 en suite (shr) (4 fmly) Full central heating Open parking*
*available Supervised Outdoor swimming pool (heated)*
*Languages spoken: English*
CARDS: Travellers cheques

### PENNEDEPIE Calvados

★★ *Romantica*
Chemin du Petit Paris *14600*
☎ 231811400 FAX 231815478
(from Honfleur take D513 towards Trouville, pass through
hamlet of Pennedepie and 1km past junction with D62 turn left
at church, hotel on right)
*Near sea Forest area*
*32 en suite (bth/shr) (2 fmly) (20 with balcony) TV in all*
*bedrooms STV Direct dial from all bedrooms Mini-bar in all*
*bedrooms Full central heating Open parking available*
*Covered parking available Supervised Child discount available*
*Indoor swimming pool (heated) Outdoor swimming pool*
*(heated) Open terrace Last d 22.00hrs Languages spoken:*
*English, German & Italian*
CARDS: ●● ▆▆ ▆▆ ▣

### PERCY Manche

**La Voisinnière** (Prop: Mary Duchemin)
*50140*
☎ 233611847 & 685818175 FAX 233614347
(from Percy take D58 towards Hambye the immediately left on
D98 towards Sourdeval for 1.5km. House signposted on right)
David and Mary-Claude Duchemin welcome you to their
country cottage. So fond are the Duchemins of all things floral,

that they've named the guest bedrooms after the flowers in their garden. Luckily, they speak English so garden-lovers will be able to converse freely with them. Restaurants nearby.
Near river
*5 en suite (shr) (2 fmly) Full central heating Open parking available Child discount available Fishing Languages spoken: English*
ROOMS: s 220-250FF; d 230-260FF ✱

### PÉRIERS-SUR-LE-DAN Calvados

**Le Clos Fleuri du Dan** (Prop: Marie Carmen)
11 rue du Bont-Perdu *14112*
☎ 231441152
Near sea  Near beach  Near motorway
*1 May-30 Sept*
*3 en suite (bth/shr) (1 with balcony) No smoking in all bedrooms Radio in rooms Full central heating Open parking available*

### PICAUVILLE Manche

**Château de l'Isle-Marie** (Prop: Dorothea de La Houssaye)
*50360*
☎ 233213725 FAX 233214222
(close to Ste-Mère-Église and the N13 between Caen and Cherbourg, located on the D67 between Chef-du-Pont and Picauville)
Near river  Near sea  Near beach  Forest area  Near motorway
*Closed Oct-Etr*
*5 rms (4 bth/shr) No smoking on premises Full central heating Open parking available Supervised Tennis Fishing Riding Boule Bicycle rental Tennis Bicycles Languages spoken: English, Dutch & German*
CARDS: Travellers cheques

**Manoir de Founecroup** (Prop: Mr Ben Trumble)
*50360*
☎ 233213663
Near river  Near sea  Forest area  Near motorway
*Closed Dec-Mar*
*(1 fmly) No smoking in 3 bedrooms Full central heating Open parking available Supervised Open terrace Languages spoken: English*
CARDS: Travellers cheques

### PIN-LA-GARENNE Orne

**La Miotère**
*61400*
☎ 233838401
Near river  Forest area  Near motorway
*7 en suite (bth/shr) (7 fmly) Full central heating Open parking available*

### PLACY-MONTAIGU Manche

**Arpents Verts** (Prop: Philip Voisin)
*50160*
☎ 233575376
Forest area  Near motorway
*2 en suite (bth/shr) (1 fmly) (1 with balcony) TV available Open parking available Supervised Languages spoken: English*

### POILLEY-SUR-LE-HOLME Manche

★ ★ ★ **Le Château du Logis** (Prop: M Lambert)
*50220*
☎ 233583590 FAX 233583590
(from A84 (Caen-Rennes) take exit 33 and follow signs for Poilley. Hotel entrance just in front of the church)
Renovated 16th-century building set in a large park which boasts formal gardens and a small lake. Mont St Michel is only 15 kilometres away.
Near river  Forest area  Near motorway
*3 en suite (bth) (1 fmly) No smoking in 2 bedrooms Full central heating Open parking available Child discount available 8yrs Boule Bicycle rental Languages spoken: English & German*
CARDS: Travellers cheques

### PONT-AUDEMER Eure

★ ★ **Auberge Du Vieux Puits (S)**
6 rue Notre-Dame-du-Pré *27500*
☎ 232410148 FAX 232423728
In town centre
*Closed 21 Dec-Jan, and Mon-Tue ex summer months*
*12 rms (11 bth/shr) (2 fmly) In 6 bedrooms Direct dial from all bedrooms Licensed Full central heating Open parking available Supervised Open terrace V meals Last d 21.00hrs Languages spoken: English & Italian*
CARDS: ● ▦ Travellers cheques

★ ★ ★ **Belle Isle Sur Risle**
112 rte de Rouen *27500*
☎ 232569622 FAX 232428896
(from A13 exit 26 in direction Pont-Audemer after 12km take Pont-Audemer North direction for 1km, hotel on left)
Near river  Near sea  Forest area  Near motorway
*Closed 7 Jan-mid Mar*
*19 en suite (bth) (4 fmly) (4 with balcony) No smoking in 4 bedrooms TV in all bedrooms STV Mini-bar in all bedrooms Licensed Night porter Full central heating Open parking available Supervised Child discount available 10yrs Indoor swimming pool (heated) Outdoor swimming pool (heated) Tennis Fishing Riding Sauna Solarium Gym Jacuzzi/spa Bicycle rental Open terrace Canoeing, table tennis Wkly live entertainment V meals Last d 21.30hrs Languages spoken: English & Arabic*
CARDS: ● ▦ ▦ ⑩ Travellers cheques

★ ★ ★ **Les Cloches de Corneville**
rte de Rouen, Corneville-sur-Risle
☎ 32570104 FAX 32571096
(exit 26 of A13 onto N175)
Near river  Forest area  Near motorway
*Closed Feb & Mon lunchtime*
*13 rms (12 bth/shr) (3 fmly) TV in all bedrooms Direct dial from all bedrooms Licensed Full central heating Open parking available Covered parking available Supervised Child discount available Open terrace Covered terrace V meals Last d 21.45hrs Languages spoken: English & German*
CARDS: ● ▦ Travellers cheques

★ ★ ★ **Petit Coq Aux Champs**
Campigny *27500*
☎ 232410419 FAX 232560625
Forest area
*Closed 6-26Jan*
*25 rms (1 fmly) (12 with balcony) TV in all bedrooms STV Direct dial from all bedrooms Licensed Night porter Full*
*contd.*

central heating Open parking available Supervised Child
discount available 12yrs Outdoor swimming pool (heated)
Boule Bicycle rental Open terrace Wkly live entertainment V
meals Last d 21.30hrs Languages spoken: English
CARDS: ●● ■■ ☲ ⑩ Travellers cheques

**La Ricardière** (Prop: Mme Denise Carel)
Tourville *27500*
☎ 232410914 FAX 232425828
(from Pont-Audemer follow D139 towards Lisieux for approx
1.5km. Pass sawmill (Sonorbois) on left and 150mtrs further on
take small private road as far as purple beech tree)
This old house is set at the foot of a hill which looks out over a
park with trees and a trout river. Originally constructed in the
Middle Ages, it was destroyed during the Revolution and was
only rebuilt in the last century.
Near river Forest area
*4 en suite (bth/shr) No smoking on premises Full central
heating Open parking available No children Open terrace
Languages spoken: English*
ROOMS: d 350FF
CARDS: Travellers cheques

**St-Germain-Village** (Prop: Mme Roux)
94 rue Jules-Ferry *27500*
☎ 232412532
Forest area In town centre Near motorway
*3 en suite (bth/shr) (1 fmly) No smoking in 1 bedroom Radio in
rooms Full central heating Open parking available Supervised*
CARDS: Travellers cheques

## PONT-DE-L'ARCHE Eure

★ ★ **Hotel de la Tour**
41 quai Foch *27340*
☎ 235230099 FAX 235234622
(leave A13 exit 20 & continue for 3km)
Near river Near lake Near sea Forest area
*18 en suite (bth/shr) (4 fmly) No smoking on premises TV in all
bedrooms STV Direct dial from all bedrooms Night porter
Full central heating Open parking available Supervised Open
terrace Languages spoken: English & German*
ROOMS: (room only) d 330FF **Reductions over 1 night**
CARDS: ●● ■■ ☲ ⑩

## PONT-L'ÉVÊQUE Calvados

★ ★ *Climat de France*
Centre de Loisirs du Lac-CD 48 *14130*
☎ 231646400 FAX 231641228
(off A13 exit at 'Pont-l'Évêque' in the direction of Caen, at the
gendarmerie turn left in direction of D48 & Coquainvilliers)
Near lake Forest area Near motorway
*56 en suite (bth/shr) (3 fmly) TV in 57 bedrooms Direct dial
from 57 bedrooms Licensed Full central heating Open parking
available Fishing Pool table Open terrace Covered terrace
Pedalos Canoe hire V meals Last d 9.30pm Languages spoken:
English, Dutch, German, Greek & Italian*
CARDS: ●● ☲

★ ★ ★ **Clos Saint Gatien**
St-Gatien des Bois *14130*
☎ 231651608 FAX 231651027
The hotel occupies a peaceful location between the towns of
Deauville, Trouville and Honfleur, next to a forest. It has a
comfortable and informal interior, where the bedrooms are
cheerfully decorated and have private facilities. In addition,

there is an attractive restaurant and a choice of leisure
pursuits.
Near sea Near beach Forest area Near motorway

*Clos Saint Gatien*

*60 en suite (bth/shr) (5 fmly) (5 with balcony) TV in all
bedrooms STV Direct dial from all bedrooms Mini-bar in 50
bedrooms Licensed Lift Night porter Full central heating
Open parking available Child discount available 10yrs Indoor
swimming pool (heated) Outdoor swimming pool (heated)
Tennis Sauna Gym Pool table Boule Jacuzzi/spa Bicycle
rental Open terrace V meals Last d 21.30hrs Languages
spoken: English*
ROOMS: (room only) s 370-680FF; d 370-885FF
**Reductions over 1 night**
MEALS: Continental breakfast 70FF Lunch 100-390FF
Dinner 150-390FF
CARDS: ●● ■■ ☲ ⑩ Travellers cheques

**Manoir du Poirier de Chio** (Prop: Mme Piat)
40 av Libération *14130*
☎ 231641178 FAX 231641178
(in direction of Pont-l'Évêque take the D48 towards "Centre de
Loisirs", front of the "Place du Tribunal". at the end of this road
is the Manoir du Poirier de Chio opposite the horse riding
centre)
Near river Near lake Forest area Near motorway
*4 en suite (bth/shr) (2 fmly) No smoking on premises Full
central heating Open parking available Child discount
available 7yrs Leisure centre within 1km Languages spoken:
English & Spanish*
ROOMS: s 350-450FF; d 350-550FF
**Reductions over 1 night**
MEALS: Dinner 100-150FF

## PONT-ST-PIERRE Eure

★ ★ ★ *Hostellerie La Bonne Marmite*
10 rue Réné Raban *27360*
☎ 232497024 FAX 232481241
Near river Forest area In town centre Near motorway
*9 en suite (bth/shr) (2 with balcony) TV in all bedrooms STV
Direct dial from all bedrooms Mini-bar in all bedrooms
Licensed Full central heating Open parking available
Supervised Child discount available 11yrs Last d 21.15hrs
Languages spoken: English*
CARDS: ●● ■■ ☲ ⑩ Travellers cheques

### PRÉAUX-BOCAGE Calvados

**La Crête aux Oiseaux** (Prop: M Claude Chesnel)
*14210*
☎ 231796352
Near river Forest area
*No smoking on premises Radio in rooms Full central heating Open parking available Languages spoken: English*

### PRÉCORBIN Manche

**Le Manoir** (Prop: Simone Octave Feret)
Le Bourg *50810*
☎ 233561681
Near river Forest area
*5 rms (2 fmly) No smoking on premises Full central heating Open parking available Supervised Child discount available V meals Languages spoken: English & German*

### PUCHAY Eure

**Bed & Breakfast** (Prop: M & Mme Deceunink)
14 rue Gossé *27150*
☎ 232557355 FAX 232521828
(signposted in the village)
Forest area
*2 en suite (bth/shr) No smoking in all bedrooms TV in 1 bedroom Full central heating Open parking available Covered parking available Supervised Bicycle rental*
ROOMS: s fr 210FF; d fr 260FF **Reductions over 1 night**

### QUETTREVILLE-SUR-SIENNE Manche

**La Lande** (Prop: Francoise Martin)
*50660*
☎ 233074829
(from Quettreville-sur-Seine head towards Coutances)
Near river Near sea Near beach Near motorway
*2 en suite (shr) No smoking on premises Full central heating Open parking available*

### RANES Orne

★ ★ **St-Pierre**
*61150*
☎ 233397514 FAX 233354923
(On D909)
Forest area In town centre
*12 en suite (bth/shr) (4 fmly) TV in all bedrooms STV Direct dial from all bedrooms Licensed Full central heating Open parking available Child discount available 12yrs Tennis Fishing Boule Mini-golf Open terrace V meals Last d 21.00hrs*
MEALS: Continental breakfast 40FF Lunch fr 120FF&alc Dinner fr 150FFalc✱
CARDS: ●● ■■ ■■ ⬛ Travellers cheques

### REUILLY Eure

**Ferme de Reuilly** (Prop: Lucien Nuttens)
20 rue de l'Église *27930*
☎ 232347065
Near river Forest area
*5 en suite (bth/shr) Full central heating Open parking available Covered parking available Child discount available Last d 18.00hrs*

### REVIERS Calvados

**Bed & Breakfast** (Prop: L Fras-Julien)
6 rue des Moulins *14470*
☎ 231378562 FAX 231374628
(3km south of Courseulles-sur-Mer)
Near river Near sea Near beach Near motorway
*3 rms (2 bth/shr) (3 fmly) Full central heating Open parking available Boule Languages spoken: English*
CARDS: Travellers cheques

### RÉVILLE Manche

**La Gervaiserie** (Prop: M Travert)
*50760*
☎ 233545464 FAX 233239593
(from Réville take D168)
Near river Near sea Near beach
*2 en suite (bth/shr) Full central heating Open parking available Riding Languages spoken: English*
ROOMS: s fr 225FF; d fr 285FF
CARDS: Travellers cheques

### ROCHELLE-NORMANDE, LA Manche

**La Bellangerie** (Prop: J & M Mesenge)
*50530*
☎ 233609040
Near sea Forest area
*4 rms (3 shr) (2 fmly) Full central heating Open parking available Supervised Child discount available 10yrs*

### ROUEN Seine-Maritime

★ ★ ★ **Hotel de Dieppe** (Best Western)
pl Bernard Tissot *76000*
☎ 235719600 FAX 235896521
(in front of railway station)
The hotel is ideally situated in the heart of this historic city. Founded in 1880, the interior has been gradually transformed and now provides attractive modern surroundings. The bedrooms are all tastefully decorated and well equipped and there is an inviting cocktail bar and grill where breakfast is also taken.
In town centre Near motorway

*41 en suite (bth/shr) (4 fmly) TV in all bedrooms STV Direct dial from all bedrooms Licensed Lift Night porter Full central heating Child discount available 12yrs V meals Last d 22.30hrs Languages spoken: English & German*

*contd.*

ROOMS: (room only) s 455-525FF; d 530-630FF
MEALS: Continental breakfast 50FF Lunch 138-218FF&alc
Dinner 138-218FF&alc
CARDS: ● ■ ■ ● JCB Travellers cheques

### ★ ★ ★ Hotel Frantour
15 rue de la Pie 76000
☎ 235710088 FAX 235707594
In town centre
48 en suite (bth/shr) (3 fmly) (4 with balcony) TV in all
bedrooms STV Direct dial from all bedrooms Mini-bar in all
bedrooms Licensed Lift Night porter Full central heating
Open parking available Covered parking available (charged)
Supervised Child discount available 12yrs Languages spoken:
English, German & Italian
CARDS: ● ■ ■ ● Travellers cheques

### ★ ★ Vidéotel
20 pl de Liéglise, St-Sever 76000
☎ 235628182 FAX 235639362
In town centre
139 en suite (shr) (27 fmly) No smoking in 16 bedrooms TV in
all bedrooms Direct dial from all bedrooms Licensed Lift
Night porter Full central heating Open parking available
Covered parking available Child discount available 12yrs Pool
table V meals Last d 22.00hrs Languages spoken: English
CARDS: ● ■ ■ Travellers cheques

## ROUGEMONTIERS Eure

### Bed & Breakfast (Prop: M & F Letellier)
27350
☎ 232568480 FAX 232568480
(on the N175)
Françoise and Michel welcome you to their house filled with
antique furniture. The lounge is at your disposal with TV,
books and hi-fi. Situated on the edge of the forest of Brotonne,
where you can go riding or visit the various abbeys in the
region. Fishing available within three kilometres.
Forest area Near motorway

2 en suite (bth/shr) (2 fmly) Full central heating Open parking
available Child discount available Languages spoken: English
ROOMS: d 300FF **Reductions over 1 night**
MEALS: Dinner 100FF
CARDS: Travellers cheques

## ROUVILLE Seine-Maritime

### Ferme du Château (Prop: M & Mme Hervieux)
76210
☎ 235311398 FAX 235390077
(D149 for 6km towards Bolbec/Fauville-en-Caux)

Suites are available in this attractive red-brick house of
character, set outside the village and 20 minutes from
Honfleur. The house looks out on to flower beds, and all the
bedrooms are prettily decorated. Dinner is available and the
dining room features an open fireplace.
Forest area Near motorway

**Ferme du Chateau**
3 en suite (shr) No smoking on premises TV in all bedrooms
Full central heating Open parking available Child discount
available 10yrs Open terrace V meals Last d 16.00hrs
ROOMS: s 200-220FF; d 220-250FF
**Reductions over 1 night**
MEALS: Dinner fr 80FF

## SAÂNE-ST-JUST Seine-Maritime

### Bed & Breakfast (Prop: D & J Fauvel)
rte de la Mer 76730
☎ 235832437 FAX 235835126
Near river Forest area
5 en suite (bth/shr) (2 fmly) No smoking on premises Open
parking available
CARDS: Travellers cheques

## ST-ARNOULT Seine-Maritime

### Le Bergerie (Prop: C et L Lefrancois)
rte de la Bergerie 76490
☎ 235567584 & 681545183 FAX 235567584
(from Autoroute de Normandie exit 25 Bourg-Achard follow
D313 to Caudebec-en-Caux. On the Pont de Brotonne then
take D982 towards Lillebonne)
Forest area
4 rms (3 shr) (1 fmly) Full central heating Open parking available
Covered parking available Child discount available 10yrs Bicycle
rental Last d 20.00hrs Languages spoken: English
ROOMS: s 200-250FF; d 230-300FF
MEALS: Lunch 86-145FF Dinner 86-145FF
CARDS: ● ■ Travellers cheques

## ST-AUBIN-D'APPENAI Orne

### Le Gueé-Falot (Prop: M & Mme Flochlay)
61170
☎ 233286812
(from Le Mêle-sur-Sarthe take D4 to Courtomer. 3km after Le
Mêle take on left D214 to Boitron, there are two 'pub's' to drive
by, at 2nd pub turn left, this road leads to farm.)
Near river Near lake Forest area
3 en suite (shr) (2 fmly) No smoking on premises Full central
heating Open parking available Supervised Child discount available 18months Table tennis Languages spoken: English German

ROOMS: s fr 160FF; d fr 220FF ✱
MEALS: Lunch fr 95FF Dinner fr 95FF
CARDS: Travellers cheques

### ST-AUBIN-DE-TERREGATTE Manche

**Ferme de la Patrais** (Prop: Jean Pierre et Helene Carvet)
*50240*
☎ 233484313 FAX 233485903
(take D178 SW from Ducey and turn left at St-Aubin-de-
Terregatte in direction of St-Laurent-de-Terregatte for 2kms)
Near lake
*Closed Feb*
*4 en suite (shr) (2 fmly) No smoking on premises TV available*
*Full central heating Open parking available Supervised*
*Languages spoken: English & German*
CARDS: Travellers cheques

### ST-AUBIN-SUR-MER Seine-Maritime

★★ *Clos-Normand*
Les Pieds dans L'Eau, Digue Guynemer *14750*
☎ 231973047 FAX 231964623
(from A13 exit 5 in direction of Douvres, then Langrune & St
Aubin-sur-Mer)
Near sea Near beach
*Closed 16 Nov-1 Mar RS Jul-Aug*
*31 en suite (bth/shr) (3 fmly) (2 with balcony) No smoking in 1*
*bedroom TV in all bedrooms Direct dial from all bedrooms*
*Licensed Full central heating Open parking available Child*
*discount available 12yrs Golf Open terrace V meals Last d*
*21.30hrs Languages spoken: English & German*
CARDS: ●● ■ ⬛ Travellers cheques

**La Fermette de Ramouville** (Prop: Serge et Gisele Genty)
rte de Quiberville *76740*
☎ 235834705
Near river Near sea Near beach
*5 en suite (bth/shr) (3 fmly) No smoking on premises Full*
*central heating Open parking available Supervised Child*
*discount available*
ROOMS: s 210-250FF; d 260-360FF ✱
CARDS: Travellers cheques

### ST-CLAIR-D'ARCEY Eure

**Domaine du Plessis** (Prop: M Gouffier)
*27300*
☎ 232466000 FAX 232466000
Forest area
*Closed 23 Dec-5 Jan*
*3 en suite (bth/shr) Full central heating Open parking available*
*Languages spoken: English Italian & Spanish*
ROOMS: s 270-310FF; d 300-340FF
CARDS: ⬛

### ST-CÔME-DE-FRESNÉ Calvados

**La Poterie** (Prop: Catherine Le Petit)
5 rte de Bayeux *14960*
☎ 231929578 FAX 231518969
Near sea Near beach Forest area
*TV in 1 bedroom Radio in rooms Full central heating Open*
*parking available Supervised Languages spoken: English*
CARDS: ●● ■ ⬛ 🔲 Travellers cheques

### ST-CYR-LA-CAMPAGNE Eure

**Bed & Breakfast** (Prop: Chambre d'Hôtes Communales)
*27370*
☎ 235819098 FAX 235878086
(access via D86)
Near river Forest area
*4 en suite (bth/shr) No smoking on premises Full central*
*heating Open parking available Covered parking available*
*Child discount available Tennis*
CARDS: Travellers cheques

### ST-DENIS-LE-FERMENT Eure

**Bed & Breakfast** (Prop: M & Mme Bourillon-Vlieghe)
29 rue de St-Paer *27140*
☎ 232552786
(from Gisors take D14bis for 3km then turn right towards St-
Denis-le-Ferment D17)
Near river Near lake Forest area
*4 en suite (shr) No smoking on premises Radio in rooms Full*
*central heating Open parking available*

### ST-DENIS-MAISONCELLES Calvados

**La Valette** (Prop: Alain et Odile Gravey)
*14350*
☎ 231687431
Near river Forest area
*2 rms (1 shr) (3 fmly) Full central heating Open parking*
*available Supervised Languages spoken: English & German*

### ST-DÉSIR Calvados

**La Cour St-Thomas** (Prop: Brigitte Besnehard)
*14100*
☎ 231628746 FAX 231528746
(3km from centre of Lisieux alongside the St-Désir Church.
Take D182 to Leosand & Le Chêne for about 3km, then follow
green "chambre d'hôte" signs - property down lane on right)
Near river
*5 rms (4 bth/shr) 2 rooms in annexe (2 with balcony) No*
*smoking on premises TV in 1 bedroom Full central heating*
*Open parking available Child discount available 10yrs Bicycle*
*rental*
ROOMS: s 250FF; d 300FF **Special breaks**

### ST-DIDIER-DES-BOIS Eure

**Au Vieux Logis** (Prop: Annick Auzoux)
1 pl de l'Église *27370*
☎ 232506093
(approach via D313 between Louviers and Elbeuf. At entrance
to St-Pierre-les-Elbeuf take D60 (not D52) to St-Didier. House
facing the church)
Near river Near lake Forest area
*4 en suite (shr) (2 fmly) Full central heating Open parking*
*available Supervised Languages spoken: English*

### ST-ÉLOI-DE-FOURQUES Eure

**Manoir d'Hermos** (Prop: P et B Noel-Windsor)
*27800*
☎ 232355132 FAX 232355132
(exit A13 at Maison Brulée in the direction of Alençon onto
N138 & 5km after Bourgtheroulde turn left onto D83 then 5km
on right take D92, then 3rd entrance on right)                    *contd.*

Near lake Forest area Near motorway
2 en suite (bth/shr) (1 fmly) Full central heating Open parking
available Supervised Fishing Bicycle rental Languages
spoken: English
ROOMS: s 220-320FF; d 250-350FF ✱
CARDS: Travellers cheques

### ST-ÉTIENNE-LA-THILLAYE Calvados

**Bed & Breakfast** (Prop: M & Mme P Champion)
Chemin de la Barberie 14950
☎ 231652197 FAX 231651831
Near river Near motorway
3 rms (2 bth/shr) (1 fmly) Full central heating Open parking
available Child discount available Outdoor swimming pool
Tennis Fishing Riding
CARDS: Travellers cheques

**Le Friche Saint-Vincent** (Prop: Monique & Guy Baratte)
14950
☎ 231652204 FAX 231651016
(from St-Étienne-la-Thillaye SE to Les Capucins, then on to
Classy and left onto D278 in the direction of Pont-l'Évêque)
Near river Near lake Near sea Near beach Forest area Near
motorway
4 en suite (shr) (3 fmly) (1 with balcony) Full central heating
Open parking available Supervised

### ST-GEORGES-DE-LA-RIVIÈRE Manche

**Manoir de Caillemont** (Prop: Michel et Elaine
Coupechoux)
50270
☎ 233538116 FAX 233532566
(from Barneville-Carteret, take the D903 towards Coutances.
At the cross 'St Georges de la Rivière' turn left towards St-
Maurice-en-Cotentin. The manor house is the first building on
the left.)
Near sea Near beach
RS Oct-Mar
3 en suite (bth/shr) (1 fmly) TV in 1 bedroom Full central
heating Open parking available Outdoor swimming pool
(heated) Billiards Languages spoken: English

### ST-GEORGES-D'ELLE Manche

**Bed & Breakfast** (Prop: Jocelyne Heurtevent)
Le Muthier 50680
☎ 233058147 FAX 233571417
Near river Forest area
4 rms (1 shr) (1 fmly) Full central heating Open parking
available Child discount available 10yrs Boule V meals
CARDS: Travellers cheques

### ST-GERMAIN-DE-MONTGOMERY Calvados

**Le Vaucery** (Prop: M F Catel)
14140
☎ 233390391
(from Vimoutiers or Livarot, take the road to 'St-Germain-de-
Montgommery' and follow the 'Chambre d'hôte/Gite de
France' signs.)
Near lake Forest area
Closed Nov-Mar
3 rms (2 shr) (1 fmly) Open parking available Child discount
available 14yrs Languages spoken: English
CARDS: Travellers cheques

### ST-GERMAIN-DE-TOURNBUT Manche

**Château de la Brisette** (Prop: M de la Hautiere)
50700
☎ 233411178 FAX 233412232
(from Cherbourg take N13 and at Valognes turn left onto D902,
after approx 4m turn right onto D63, 1.5m to St Germain-de-
Tournebut)
This magnificent castle, looking out onto a lake, is surrounded
by woodland. It has been owned by the same family for more
than 200 years. The chapel and outbuildings are particularly
delightful. The bedrooms are decorated in different styles:
Gothic, Empire and Louis XVI. The castle is full of stunning
historical features and furniture. Continental breakfast.
Near lake Forest area
Closed Nov-Apr
3 en suite (bth) No smoking on premises TV in all bedrooms
STV Full central heating Open parking available Covered
parking available Child discount available 4yrs Fishing
ROOMS: d 450-500FF **Special breaks**
CARDS: ●● ▆▆ ⓪

### ST-GERMAIN-DU-CRIOULT Calvados

**★★Auberge Saint-Germain**
14110
☎ 231690810 FAX 231691467
Near motorway
Closed 20 Dec-10 Jan & 1-8 August
9 en suite (bth/shr) 9 rooms in annexe (1 fmly) TV in 6
bedrooms Direct dial from all bedrooms Licensed Full central
heating Open parking available Covered parking available
Child discount available 8yrs Last d 21.00hrs
ROOMS: (room only) s 170-215FF; d 210-230FF
MEALS: Continental breakfast 26FF Lunch 72-155FF&alc
Dinner 72-155FF&alc
CARDS: ●● ▆▆ ▆▆ Travellers cheques

### ST-GERMAIN-LE-VASSON Calvados

**Le Broguette** (Prop: M & Mme Giard)
14190
☎ 231905175
(on N158 between Caen and Falaise, take exit for Grainville.
Through village then take D239 towards St-Germain-le-Vasson
and follow signs 'Chambre d'Hôtes')

In a separate building from the main house on a large farm
restored by the hosts. Golf, riding and tennis in close
proximity. Bikes, table-tennis and billiards on-site.
Near river Forest area Near motorway

*2 en suite (shr) (2 fmly) (2 with balcony) TV in 1 bedroom Full central heating Open parking available Bicycle rental Billiards Pool Table tennis Languages spoken: English*
ROOMS: s 150FF; d 200FF **Reductions over 1 night**

### ST-GERMAIN-SUR-AY Manche

**Bed & Breakfast** (Prop: M & Mme Moisan)
26 rue de l'Anjou *50430*
☎ 233463249
Near sea Near beach Forest area Near motorway
*4 rms (3 bth/shr) (2 fmly) TV available Open parking available Supervised Open terrace*
CARDS: ●● Travellers cheques

### ST-HILAIRE-PETITVILLE Manche

**Ferme de Marigny** (Prop: M & Mme D & R Picquenot)
*50500*
☎ 232420440
Near sea Near beach Near motorway
*4 rms (2 fmly) Full central heating Open parking available*
ROOMS: s fr 160FF; d fr 180FF

### ST-HYMER Calvados

**Le Moulin** (Prop: M et Mme Valle)
*14130*
☎ 231642351 FAX 231643972
(at Deauville, go towards the A13, then take the N117 as far as Pont-L'Évêque. Turn right on to N175 towards Caen. After 'Le Preui de St-Hymen' sign turn left and go down to the watermill - Signposted)
Near river Near lake Near sea Near beach Forest area Near motorway
*5 rms (4 bth/shr) (2 fmly) No smoking on premises TV in 1 bedroom Full central heating Open parking available Supervised All listed activities are nearby. Last d noon*
CARDS: ▩▩▩

### ST-JAMES Manche

**Le Ferme de L'Étang** (Prop: Brigitte Gavard)
"Bouceel", Vergoncey *50240*
☎ 233483468 FAX 233484853
(from Avranches, go towards Rennes. After 12km turn right to Rennes the Mont-St-Michel, just after turn left to Rennes D40, then the D308, turn left, there is a sign just before B&B which is the 2nd house)
Near lake Forest area Near motorway
*5 rms (4 bth/shr) (2 fmly) Full central heating Open parking available Covered parking available Child discount available 12yrs Pool table Boule Billiards Table tennis Last d 19.00hrs Languages spoken: English*
CARDS: Travellers cheques

**La Gautrais** (Prop: Tiffaine)
*50240*
☎ 233483186 FAX 233485817
(A84 exit St-James in direction of Autrain on D12)
Near river
*4 en suite (bth/shr) (2 fmly) (1 with balcony) Radio in rooms Full central heating Open parking available Supervised Child discount available 12yrs Languages spoken: English*

### ST-JEAN-LE-THOMAS Manche

★ ★ **Des Bains**
8 allée Clemenceau *50530*
☎ 233488420 FAX 233486642
(On D911 towards Jullouville)

Located in a 1,000-year-old village on the coastal road between Granville and Avranches, the hotel has been in the hands of the same family for four generations. Its attractive interior is enhanced by pretty flower arrangements which create a warm and friendly atmosphere. Most of the comfortable guest rooms have modern amenities. The restaurant serves an honest cuisine, with choice of well prepared, tasty dishes.
Near sea Near beach Forest area In town centre
*Closed 2 Nov-Mar*
*30 rms (16 bth 11 shr) 6 rooms in annexe (15 fmly) (10 with balcony) Direct dial from all bedrooms Licensed Full central heating Open parking available Supervised Child discount available 6 yrs Outdoor swimming pool (heated) Pool table Boule Open terrace Last d 21.00hrs Languages spoken: English*
ROOMS: (room only) s 176-206FF; d 262-360FF
**Reductions over 1 night**
MEALS: Full breakfast 34FF Lunch 80-179FF&alc Dinner 80-179FF&alc
CARDS: ●● ▬▬ ▭▭ ◑ Travellers cheques

### ST-LAURENT-DU-MONT Calvados

**La Vignerie** (Prop: Marie-France Huet)
*14340*
☎ 231630865 FAX 231630865
(from Lisieux take the N13 to La Boissiere, then onto the D50. Pass the village, after approx 700m, there is a sign for 'La Vignerie', take the small road, the house is 500m along.)
*5 en suite (bth/shr) (4 fmly) (1 with balcony) Full central heating Open parking available Child discount available 4yrs Bicycle rental Languages spoken: English*
CARDS: Travellers cheques

### ST-LAURENT-EN-CAUX Seine-Maritime

**Hameau de Caltot** (Prop: M & Mme Mayeu)
*76560*
☎ 235966526
*2 en suite (bth/shr) Full central heating Open parking available*
CARDS: Travellers cheques

## ST-LÉGER Manche

**Le Clos Serena** (Prop: Jacqueline Miconnet)
Les Landes *50320*
☎ 233906346 FAX 233906346
(From Granville D973 in direction of Avranches in 8km turn left onto D309 pass the village of St Aubin des Préaux & continue on D309 until the first sign St Léger & "chambre d'hôte" sign)
Near sea Forest area
*18 rms (2 bth 3 shr) (2 fmly) No smoking in 1 bedroom Full central heating Open parking available Child discount available 10yrs Languages spoken: English*

## ST-LOUP-HORS Calvados

**Bed & Breakfast** (Prop: M & Mme Jeanette)
Chemin des Marettes *14400*
☎ 231922468
(near 'Bataille Normandy' museum)
Near sea Near beach Forest area In town centre Near motorway
*1 en suite (shr) TV in all bedrooms Radio in rooms Full central heating Open parking available Child discount available 12yrs*
ROOMS: s 170FF; d 200FF
CARDS: Travellers cheques

**Manoir du Pont Rouge** (Prop: Lt Col M J P Chilcott)
*14400*
☎ 231223909 FAX 231219784
(take D572 towards St Lo from the Southern Peripherique of Bayeux. Then 2nd right at chambre d'hote sign continue for approx 1km)
Near river Near sea Near beach Forest area Near motorway
*4 en suite (bth/shr) No smoking on premises Full central heating Open parking available Child discount available 14yrs Indoor swimming pool (heated) Outdoor swimming pool (heated) Tennis Fishing Riding Boule Bicycle rental Table tennis, Table football Languages spoken: English German Italian & Russian*

## ST-MACLOU Eure

**La Brière** (Prop: M Gilbert Aube)
*27210*
☎ 232566335 FAX 232569562
(exit Beuzeville off A13)
Forest area Near motorway
*2 rms (1 shr) Open parking available Supervised Child discount available 10yrs*
CARDS: Travellers cheques

## ST-MARCEL Eure

★ ★ **Climate de France**
17 rue de la Poste *27950*
☎ 232711000 FAX 232212095
(off A13 at Véron exit onto D181)
Near river Forest area Near motorway
*44 en suite (bth/shr) (7 fmly) TV in all bedrooms STV Direct dial from all bedrooms Licensed Full central heating Open parking available Child discount available 12yrs Pool table Open terrace Last d 10pm Languages spoken: English, German*
CARDS: ●● ■■ ▨ ▨ Travellers cheques

## ST-MARTIN-DE-BLAGNY Calvados

**Le Coquerie** (Prop: Genevieve et Alain Pasquet)
*14710*
☎ 231225089
*2 en suite (shr) No smoking on premises Open parking available Child discount available 6yrs Petanque ping-pong volley ball*

## ST-MARTIN-DE-VARREVILLE Manche

**Les Mézières** (Prop: Leone Dessoliers)
*50790*
☎ 233413502
Near sea Near beach
Closed Oct-Mar
*2 en suite (bth/shr) (1 fmly) Full central heating Supervised*

## ST-MARTIN-DU-VIVIER Seine-Maritime

★ ★ ★ **La Bertelière**
*76160*
☎ 235604400 FAX 235615663
Forest area Near motorway
*44 en suite (bth/shr) (4 fmly) TV in all bedrooms STV Direct dial from all bedrooms Mini-bar in all bedrooms Licensed Night porter Full central heating Open parking available Supervised Child discount available 15yrs Pool table Bicycle rental Open terrace Table tennis V meals Last d 22.00hrs Languages spoken: English*
CARDS: ●● ■■ ▨ ▨ Travellers cheques

## ST-MESLIN-DU-BOSC Eure

**Le Bourg** (Prop: Michel Chalumel)
33 rue de l'Église *27370*
☎ 232355453
Forest area
*2 en suite (bth/shr) (1 fmly) TV available Full central heating Open parking available Supervised Languages spoken: English*

## ST-PAIR-SUR-MER Manche

**Bed & Breakfast** (Prop: M & Mme Elie)
152 rue de la Hogue *50380*
☎ 233505842
Forest area In town centre Near motorway
Closed Nov-Apr
*3 rms (1 bth 1 shr) No smoking on premises TV available Full central heating Open parking available Table tennis*

## ST-PIERRE-DE-MANNEVILLE Seine-Maritime

**Bed & Breakfast** (Prop: M & Mme Bernard)
78 rue de Bas *76113*
☎ 235320713
Near river Forest area
*4 en suite (bth/shr) (2 fmly) No smoking on premises Full central heating Open parking available Languages spoken: English*
ROOMS: (room only) d fr 190FF
✱ **Reductions over 1 night**
CARDS: ●● ■■ Travellers cheques

### ST-PIERRE-DES-FLEURS Eure

**Bed & Breakfast** (Prop: Mme Bonvoisin)
35 rue de la Mare St-Pierre *27370*
☎ 235878191
Near river Forest area Near motorway
*3 rms (1 bth/shr) Full central heating Open parking available
Languages spoken: English*

### ST-PIERRE-SUR-DIVES Calvados

**Le Pressoir** (Prop: Annick Duhamel)
Berville *14170*
☎ 231205126 FAX 231200303
Forest area
*4 en suite (bth/shr) (2 fmly) Fishing Open terrace Languages
spoken: English & German*
CARDS: Travellers cheques

### ST-QUENTIN-SUR-LE-HOMME Manche

**Les Vallées** (Prop: Jean Louis Beaucoup)
*50220*
☎ 233606151
Near river Near motorway
*4 en suite (shr) (1 fmly) No smoking on premises Full central
heating Open parking available Child discount available*

### ST-ROMPHAIRE Manche

**Le Mariage** (Prop: Renee Letellier)
*50860*
☎ 233558006
Near motorway
*2 en suite (shr) No smoking in all bedrooms Full central
heating Open parking available*

### ST-SENIER-SOUS-AVRANCHES Manche

**Le Champs du Genêt** (Prop: M & Mme Jouvin)
rte de Mortain *50300*
☎ 233605267 FAX 233605267
(from Avranches follow D5 towards Mortain/Juvigny. After
5km pass Irish Bar on right and take next on left)
A château, set in its own grounds, offering stylish
accommodation with traditional decorations and furniture just
a short distance from Avranches.
Near river Forest area
*4 en suite (bth/shr) Full central heating Open parking available
Riding Languages spoken: English*
ROOMS: d 200-230FF **Special breaks**
CARDS: Travellers cheques

### ST-SYMPHORIEN-DES-BRUYÈRES Orne

**La Fransonniere**
*61300*
☎ 233240458 FAX 233240458
Near lake Forest area Near motorway
*2 en suite (shr) (1 fmly) TV in all bedrooms Full central heating
Open parking available Boule Bicycle rental Table tennis
Languages spoken: English & Italian*
ROOMS: s fr 180FF; d fr 240FF
**Reductions over 1 night**

### ST-VAAST-DU-VAL Seine-Maritime

**Parc du May** (Prop: M & Mme Pascal Vandenbulcke)
Hameau de Glatigny *76890*
☎ 235346191
Near river Forest area Near motorway
*1 en suite (bth/shr) Full central heating Open parking available
Child discount available*

### ST-VAAST-LA-HOUGUE Manche

★ ★ ★ **Granitière**
74 r du Ml-Foch *50550*
☎ 233545899 FAX 233203491
(From Quettehou on D1 enter town and continue straight
ahead into Rue Maréchal Foch)
Near sea In town centre
*Closed mid Dec-mid Mar*
*10 rms (8 bth/shr) (2 fmly) (2 with balcony) TV in 5 bedrooms
Direct dial from all bedrooms Licensed Full central heating
Open parking available Supervised Child discount available
12yrs Bicycle rental Open terrace V meals Last d 21.30hrs
Languages spoken: English*
ROOMS: (room only) d 285-460FF
MEALS: Full breakfast 45FF Dinner fr 250FFalc
CARDS: ●● ■■ ▨ ⑤ Travellers cheques

### ST-VICTOR-D'ÉPINE Eure

**Le Clos St-François** (Prop: M Jacques Canse-Grandhomme)
*27800*
☎ 232459890 FAX 232464309
Near river Near lake Forest area
*1 en suite (shr) TV available Radio in rooms Full central
heating Open parking available No children 10yrs Boule
Languages spoken: English*

### ST-WANDRILLE-RANÇON Seine-Maritime

**Manoir d'Abbeville** (Prop: Mme Sautreuil)
*76490*
☎ 235962089
Near river Forest area
*1 en suite (shr) (4 fmly) Full central heating Open parking
available Child discount available 12yrs*

### STE-GAUBURGE Orne

**La Bussière** (Prop: Mr & Mme Le Brethon)
*61370*
☎ 233340523 FAX 233347147
Near river Forest area Near motorway
*2 en suite (bth/shr) (1 fmly) No smoking on premises Full
central heating Open parking available Child discount
available 12yrs Languages spoken: English & German*
CARDS: Travellers cheques

### STE-GENEVIÈVE Manche

**La Fèvrerie** (Prop: Marie-France Caillet)
*50760*
☎ 233543353
(from Cherbourg take D901 towards Barfleur. After Tocqueville
take D10 and 1st on left) *contd.*

Near sea  Near beach
3 en suite (bth/shr)  Full central heating  Open parking available
CARDS: Travellers cheques

### STE-MARIE-DU-MONT Manche

**Bed & Breakfast** (Prop: M & Mme Nauleau)
pl de l'Église 50480
☎ 233719106 FAX 233719106
(take N13 Cherbourg to Caen road exit onto D913 in the
direction of Ste-Marie-du-Mont)
Near sea  Near beach
2 en suite (bth/shr)  Child discount available 4yrs  Languages
spoken: Engish
CARDS: Travellers cheques

**Bed & Breakfast** (Prop: M S Busquet)
Le Hameau Hubert 50480
☎ 233424349
Near river  Near sea  Near beach  Near motorway
2 en suite (bth)  (2 fmly)  Radio in rooms  Full central heating
Open parking available  Supervised  Languages spoken: English

**La Chaussée** (Prop: Ann & Clifford Longlands)
50480
☎ 233424659 FAX 233424659
(from Ste-Marie-du-Mont go towards Utah Beach, at 2km from
village, go left, down small hill for 2km turn right, 4th farm on
left with white railings and flags)
Ideally situated in the touristic heart of Normandy, this ancient
establishment has comfortable bedrooms with good facilities.
There is a pleasant restaurant which caters for most tastes, and
with a fresh, oceanic climate which attracts visitors from all
parts of the world. Guests enjoy a relaxed atmosphere and it is
the ideal region for walking, cycling and other sporting
pursuits.
Near river  Near sea  Near beach  Forest area  Near motorway
3 en suite (bth/shr)  (1 fmly)  No smoking on premises  STV  Full
central heating  Open parking available  Child discount
available 12yrs  Languages spoken: English
MEALS: Lunch 90FF
CARDS: Travellers cheques

**Reuville** (Prop: M et P Chevallier)
50480
☎ 233715716
(take N13 Cherbourg-Paris, at 40km from Cherbour take exit
signed Sainte-Marie-du-Mont, in town between town hall &
butchers shop, take right fork signed Boutteville(D424),
Renville 2km from x-rds on opposite the chateau)
In the countryside, but close to sandy beaches - Utah Beach is
seven kilometres away. The property has two guests bedrooms
on the ground floor with views into a pleasant garden.
Near sea  Near beach
2 en suite (shr)  Full central heating  Open parking available
Covered parking available  Child discount available 10yrs
Languages spoken: English & Spanish
ROOMS: s fr 180FF; d fr 210FF **Reductions over 1 night
Special breaks**

### STE-MARIE-LAUMONT Calvados

**Le Picard** (Prop: Nelly Guillaumin)
14350
☎ 231684321
Near river  Forest area
Etr-Oct

1 en suite (shr)  Full central heating  Open parking available
Child discount available 2yrs
ROOMS: s 150FF; d 200FF ✱

### STE-MÈRE-ÉGLISE Manche

**Ferme Riou** (Prop: Victor Destres)
50480
☎ 233416340
3 en suite (shr)  Open parking available  Supervised

**La Fière (Le Pont du Merdéret)** (Prop: Chantal et Yves
Poisson)
50480
☎ 233413177
Near river
2 en suite (shr)  Full central heating  Open parking available
Supervised  Child discount available  Languages spoken:
English
CARDS: Travellers cheques

**Musée de la Ferme**
50480
☎ 233413025 FAX 233453474
Near river  Near motorway
Closed Dec
4 en suite (bth/shr)  Open parking available

**Village de Beauvais** (Prop: Emile et Marie Viel)
3 chemin de Beauvais 50480
☎ 233414171 FAX 233414171
Near motorway
3 en suite (bth/shr)  No smoking on premises  Open parking
available  Child discount available 10yrs
ROOMS: s 185FF; d 220FF
CARDS: ■ Travellers cheques

### STE-OPPORTUNE-LA-MARE Eure

**La Vallée** (Prop: Etienne Blondel)
Quai de la Forge 27680
☎ 232421252
Near river  Near lake  Forest area
2 en suite (bth/shr)  No smoking on premises  Supervised  Child
discount available  V meals  Languages spoken: English &
German

### STE-PIENCE Manche

**Manoir de la Porte** (Prop: M Lagadec)
50870
☎ 233681361 FAX 233682954
(from N175 take D39 and at 'Le Parc' follow signs to the manor
on D175)
Near river  Near sea  Forest area  Near motorway
5 rms (2 bth 1 shr)  (5 fmly)  No smoking on premises  TV in 1
bedroom  Radio in rooms  Full central heating  Open parking
available  Child discount available 6yrs  Fishing  Bicycle rental
V meals  Last d 20.00hrs  Languages spoken: English & German

### SASSETOT-LE-MAUCONDUIT Seine-Maritime

★ ★ **Château de Sassetot**
Le Mauconduit 76540
☎ 235280011 FAX 235285000
Near sea  Near beach  Forest area  Near motorway
29 en suite (bth/shr)  TV in all bedrooms  STV  Direct dial from

all bedrooms Mini-bar in all bedrooms Licensed Night porter Full central heating Open parking available Supervised Child discount available 12 yrs Boule Bicycle rental Open terrace V meals Last d 22.00hrs Languages spoken: Anglais, Italian, Espagnol
ROOMS: (room only) d 470-950FF
**Reductions over 1 night**
MEALS: Full breakfast 60FF Lunch 110-230FF&alc Dinner 110-230FF&alc
CARDS: ●● ■■ ☲ ☜ Travellers cheques

**Ferme du Manege** (Prop: M & Mme M Soudry)
Hameau de Criquemauville 76540
☎ 235274564
Forest area Near motorway
4 en suite (shr) (1 with balcony) Full central heating Open parking available

**SAUMONT-LA-POTERIE** Seine-Maritime

**La Ramée**
rue d'Auvergne 76440
☎ 235092017
(from Forges-les-Eaux head towards Gournay-en-Bray on D915 for 7km, then left to Saumont-la-Poterie and follow 'Chambre-d'Hôte' signs)

A restored 19th-century farm on 4 acres of land facing a lake. Rooms are comfortably furnished in rustic style and meals are provided if booked in advance.
Near lake Forest area Near motorway
4 en suite (shr) (2 fmly) No smoking in all bedrooms TV in 2 bedrooms Full central heating Open parking available Fishing Boule Bicycle rental Billards, Croquet, Table tennis Last d 20.30hrs Languages spoken: English
ROOMS: s 220-250FF; d 250-270FF
MEALS: Lunch fr 85FF Dinner fr 85FF

**SAUSSAYE, LA** Eure

**Le Manoir des Saules (S)**
2 pl St-Martin 27370
☎ 235872565 FAX 235874939
Near river Near lake Forest area Near motorway
Closed Nov-Feb
9 en suite (bth/shr) (3 fmly) (1 with balcony) TV in all bedrooms Radio in rooms Direct dial from all bedrooms Licensed Full central heating Open parking available Covered parking available Supervised Bicycle rental Open terrace V meals Last d 21.00hrs Languages spoken: English
CARDS: ●● ■■ ☲ ☜ Travellers cheques

**SENNEVILLE-SUR-FÉCAMP** Seine-Maritime

**Val de la Mer** (Prop: Mme Mireille Lethuillier)
76400
☎ 235284193
Near sea Near beach
Closed holidays & end of year
3 en suite (bth/shr) No smoking on premises Full central heating Open parking available
ROOMS: s 250FF; d 320FF

**SERVON** Manche

**Le Petit Manoir** (Prop: Annick Gedouin)
21 rue de la Pierre-du-Tertre 50170
☎ 233600344 FAX 233601779
(from Mont-St-Michel, take the D225, after 5km on right take D107, Servon is along this road.)
An 18th-century farm just nine kilometres from Mont St Michel. Restaurants, tennis and swimming pool all close by. Riding school five kilometres away.
Near sea Forest area Near motorway
2 en suite (bth) No smoking on premises Full central heating Open parking available Child discount available 2yrs Outdoor swimming pool Bicycle rental Languages spoken: English & Italian
ROOMS: d fr 220FF
CARDS: Travellers cheques

**SILLY-EN-GOUFFERN** Orne

**★ ★ ★ Pavillon De Gouffern (S)**
Le Pavillon 61310
☎ 233366426 FAX 233365381
Near river Forest area
20 en suite (bth) 7 rooms in annexe TV in all bedrooms Direct dial from all bedrooms Licensed Full central heating Open parking available Child discount available 8yrs Tennis Fishing Pool table Boule Bicycle rental Open terrace Last d 21.30hrs
ROOMS: (room only) s 250-350FF; d 350-450FF
**Reductions over 1 night**
CARDS: ●● ■■ ☲ ☜ Travellers cheques

**SOMMERY** Seine-Maritime

**Ferme de Bray** (Prop: Liliana et Patrice Perrier)
76440
☎ 235905727
Near river Near lake Forest area
5 en suite (bth/shr) (2 fmly) Full central heating Open parking available Supervised
CARDS: Travellers cheques

**SOTTEVAST** Manche

**Hameau Ès Adam** (Prop: Francoise Lebarillier)
50260
☎ 233419835
(from Cherbourg N13 South, exit to Brix and the D50 to Sottevast in village, D62 towards Rauville-la-Biget. 2nd right towards Hameau És Adam, then 1st left.)
3 en suite (bth/shr) (2 fmly) Full central heating Open parking available Supervised Child discount available 2yrs Boule Languages spoken: English
CARDS: Travellers cheques

### SOTTEVILLE-SUR-MER Seine-Maritime

**Bed & Breakfast** (Prop: M & Mme Lefebvre)
rue du Bout du Haut *76740*
☎ 235976105
(from Dieppe, take D925 in direction of Fécamp-Le Haire after
the exit for La Chapelle-sur-Dun 1st right)
Near sea Near beach Forest area
*3 en suite (shr) (1 fmly) (1 with balcony) Full central heating
Open parking available Covered parking available Supervised
Child discount available 1yr Farm visits.*
ROOMS: d 220FF
CARDS: Travellers cheques

### SOURDEVAL Manche

★ ★ *Le Temps de Vivre*
12 rue St-Martin *50150*
☎ 233596041 FAX 233598834
Near river Forest area In town centre
*7 rms (6 shr) (1 fmly) (1 with balcony) TV in all bedrooms
Radio in rooms Licensed Full central heating Open parking
available Child discount available 9yrs Open terrace V meals
Last d 21.00hrs*
CARDS: ●● ▅▅ Travellers cheques

### SURVIE Orne

**Les Gains** (Prop: M & Mme Wordsworth)
*61310*
☎ 233360556 FAX 233350365
(from Liseux & Vimoutiers on D579 take Argentan road
through Vimoutier. On leaving Vimoutier take the road signed
Exmes. Follow signs for Exmes on D26. Les Gains signed on
left. Turn right opposite after church between two houses)
*4 en suite (bth/shr) (1 fmly) No smoking on premises Full
central heating Open parking available Child discount
available 12yrs V meals Last d am Languages spoken: English*

### SURVILLE Calvados

**Le Prieuré Boutefol** (Prop: M & Mme B Colin)
rte de Rouen *14130*
☎ 231643970
A timbered manor house dating from the 17th century with a
large garden. All rooms are charmingly decorated with old
French country style furniture.
Near river Near lake Forest area Near motorway

*4 en suite (bth/shr) (1 fmly) No smoking on premises Full
central heating Open parking available Child discount
available 12yrs Languages spoken: English*
ROOMS: s 250-300FF; d 350-450FF

### TAMERVILLE Manche

**Manoir de Belaunay** (Prop: Jacques Allix Desfauteaux)
*50700*
☎ 233401062
(N13 exit Valognes and D902 in direction of Quettchoa.
Bellamey on left)
Set in a manor built between the 15th and 16th centuries on
the ruins of a monastery, the charming and traditional guest
rooms open out onto the park. One room is on the ground
floor, with exposed beams; the other two are on the first floor,
one with a large stone fireplace and the second in Louis XV
style. French breakfast served.
Near sea Forest area Near motorway
*Closed 15 Nov-15 Mar*
*3 en suite (bth/shr) Some rooms in annexe Radio in rooms
Open parking available Covered parking available Supervised
Languages spoken: English*
ROOMS: s 200-270FF; d 250-330FF
CARDS: Travellers cheques

### TANCARVILLE Seine-Maritime

★ ★ ★ *De La Marine*
Au Pied du Pont *76430*
☎ 235397715 FAX 235380330
(On D982 near the river bridge)
Near river
*RS Sun & Mon evening*
*9 en suite (bth/shr) (1 fmly) TV in all bedrooms Direct dial
from all bedrooms Mini-bar in all bedrooms Licensed Full
central heating Open parking available Supervised Child
discount available Bicycle rental Open terrace Last d 21.00hrs
Languages spoken: English*
CARDS: ●● ■■ ▅▅ CB

### TESSÉ-LA-MADELEINE Orne

★ ★ *Residence du Pont Bridge Hotel*
7 pl du Pont, 1 av des Thermes *61140*
☎ 466476003 FAX 466476278
(From Mende take N88 towards Langogne,then take D901 to
Bagnols-les-Bains)
Near river Forest area Near motorway
*Closed 15 Oct-30 Mar*
*26 en suite (bth/shr) (4 fmly) (9 with balcony) TV in all
bedrooms Direct dial from all bedrooms Licensed Lift Full
central heating Open parking available Covered parking
available (charged) Supervised Child discount available 7yrs
Outdoor swimming pool Solarium Open terrace Covered
terrace Last d 21.00hrs Languages spoken: English &
Spanish*
CARDS: ●● ▅▅ Travellers cheques

★ ★ *Hotel de Tessé*
1 av de la Baillée *61140*
☎ 233308007 FAX 233385192
Near river Near lake Forest area
*Closed end Oct-early Apr*
*43 en suite (bth/shr) (2 fmly) (16 with balcony) TV in all
bedrooms Licensed Lift Night porter Full central heating
Open parking available Covered parking available (charged)
Supervised Child discount available 12yrs Last d 21.00hrs
Languages spoken: English & Spanish*
CARDS: ●● ▅▅ ▣ Travellers cheques

### TILLEUL, LE Seine-Maritime

**Bed & Breakfast** (Prop: M & Mme Delahais)
pl General-de-Gaulle *76790*
☎ 235271639
Near sea  Forest area  Near motorway
*6 rms (4 shr)  (2 fmly)  Full central heating  Open parking
available*

### TILLY Eure

**Bed & Breakfast** (Prop: M & Mme Lefebvre)
1 rue Grande *27510*
☎ 232535617 FAX 232529211
Forest area  Near motorway
*2 en suite (bth)  No smoking on premises  TV available  Full central
heating  Open parking available  Covered parking available*
CARDS: Travellers cheques

### TILLY-SUR-SEULLES Calvados

**Bed & Breakfast** (Prop: M & Mme S Brilhault)
7 rue de la Varènde *14250*
☎ 231082573 FAX 231081946
(from Caen: ring road around Caen towards Cherbourg, come
off at Carpiquet / D9 Tilly-sur-Seulles. From Bayeux: D6 to Tilly
sur Seulles)
Near river  Near sea  Forest area
*2 en suite (bth/shr) (2 fmly)  No smoking on premises  Full
central heating  Open parking available  Covered parking
available  Child discount available 12yrs  Languages spoken:
English*
CARDS: Travellers cheques

### TOCQUEVILLE-LES-MURS Seine-Maritime

**Ferme du Rome** (Prop: M Antoine Daubeuf)
*76110*
☎ 235277084
Near river  Near sea  Near beach  Forest area
*2 en suite (shr)  No smoking on premises  Full central heating
Open parking available  Child discount available 10yrs  Bicycle
rental  Last d noon  Languages spoken: English*
ROOMS: d 230FF **Reductions over 1 night**
MEALS: Dinner 80FF
CARDS: Travellers cheques

### TORTISAMBERT Calvados

**La Boursaie** (Prop: Peter et Anja Davies)
*14140*
☎ 231631420 FAX 231631428
(in Livarot take D4 for 500m, then turn right onto D38, the
village is 600m along road, turn left and follow signs.)
Near river  Near sea  Near beach  Forest area
*2 en suite (shr)  No smoking on premises  Full central heating
Open parking available  Supervised  Child discount available
10yrs  Tennis  Fishing  Riding  Bicycle rental  Languages spoken:
English & German*
CARDS: Travellers cheques

### TOUFFRÉVILLE Eure

**Bed & Breakfast** (Prop: Daniel & Therese Herman)
*27440*
☎ 232491737
Near river  Forest area

*1 en suite (shr)  (1 fmly)  Full central heating  Open parking
available  Child discount available 4yrs  Open terrace*

### TOUR-EN-BESSIN Calvados

**La Vignette** (Prop: M & Mme Girard)
rte de Crouay *14400*
☎ 231215283
(from Bayeux N13 towards Cherbourg, through Tour-en-
Bessin, then left towards Route de Crouay for about 1km.
House is on right with cartwheel)
Near river  Near sea  Near beach  Forest area  Near motorway
*3 en suite (shr)  (2 fmly)  No smoking on premises  TV in all
bedrooms  Full central heating  Open parking available
Covered parking available  Supervised  Child discount available
10yrs  Bicycle rental  Stables are 1km away  Languages spoken:
English*
CARDS: Travellers cheques

### TOURNIÈRES Calvados

**Ferme du Marcelet** (Prop: M & Mme Isidor)
*14330*
☎ 231229086 FAX 231229086
(from Bayeux, D5 towards Molay Littry and continue on D15
towards Tournières. On entering Tournières farm on left just
before butchers)
Near river  Near sea  Forest area
*5 en suite (shr)  (3 fmly)  No smoking in 2 bedrooms  Open
parking available  Supervised  Child discount available 2yrs
Languages spoken: English*

### TOURVILLE-LA-CAMPAGNE Eure

**Le Michaumière** (Prop: M Paris)
72 rue des Canadiens *27370*
☎ 232353128
Forest area
*3 en suite (bth/shr)  Full central heating  Open parking available*

### TRACY-SUR-MER Calvados

★ ★ **Victoria**
24 chemin de l'Église, BP5 *14117*
☎ 231223537 FAX 231229338
(from Bayeux take D516 towards Arromanches)

A 19th-century manor house of traditional appearance set in
peaceful green surroundings. Situated seven kilometres from
Bayeux with its famous tapestry, imposing 11th-century
cathedral and museums. The D-Day landing beaches are also
within easy reach. It offers spacious, elegantly furnished
*contd.*

bedrooms with fine views of the park or the flower-filled courtyard.
Near sea  Near beach  Forest area
*Closed Oct-Mar*
*14 en suite (bth/shr) (4 fmly) TV in all bedrooms  Direct dial from all bedrooms  Mini-bar in 1 bedroom  Full central heating  Open parking available  Supervised  Open terrace*
ROOMS: (room only) s fr 300FF; d 350-530FF
**Reductions over 1 night**
MEALS: Continental breakfast 42FF
CARDS: ●● ▆▆ Travellers cheques

### TRÉVIERÉS Calvados

**Château de Colombières** (Prop: Comte Etienne de Maupeou)
*14710*
☎ 231225165 FAX 231922492
(21kms from Bayeux. From Bayeux N13 towards Cherbourg, turn left D29 Trevières then D5 to Colombières. From Cherbourg take N13 to Isigny-sur-Mer turn right onto D5 to Colombières)
A private chateau where guests are welcomed in a personal way. The comfortable rooms are furnished with antiques. The castle, different parts of which date from 14th-18th century, is located in a peaceful and romantic private park close to Bayeux and is surrounded by a moat..
Near river  Near sea  Near beach  Forest area  Near motorway
*Closed Oct-Apr*
*3 en suite (bth/shr)  No smoking on premises  Open parking available  No children 12yrs  Tennis  Fishing  Bicycle rental  Languages spoken: English*
ROOMS: (room only) d 1000FF
CARDS: ▆ Travellers cheques

### TRIQUEVILLE Eure

**La Clé des Champs** (Prop: Mme Michelle Le Pleux)
*27500*
☎ 232413799
(at Pont-Audemer take D87 toward St Germain, straight on to sign Triqueville (C19) - follow signs to hotel)
Near river  Near lake  Near sea  Near beach  Forest area  Near motorway
*2 en suite (shr)  No smoking on premises  Full central heating  Open parking available  Covered parking available  No children 8yrs  Bicycle rental*

**Ferme du Ponctey** (Prop: M. Jaouen)
*27500*
☎ 232421037 FAX 232575453
(from Port Audemer (level crossing/restaurant La Forge) take N175 in direction of St Germain. after 1km turn left onto D87 towards Triqueville and after 3km turn right onto D623. Straight on for 700m)
Near river  Forest area  Near motorway
*2 en suite (bth/shr)  Full central heating  Open parking available  Covered parking available  Child discount available  Boule  Croquet  Table tennis  V meals  Languages spoken: English & German*
CARDS: Travellers cheques

### TROARN Calvados

**Manoir des Tourpes** (Prop: Landon-Cassady)
Bures-sur-Dives *14670*
☎ 231236247 FAX 231238610
Near river  Near sea  Near motorway

*4 en suite (bth/shr) (1 fmly) (1 with balcony)  No smoking on premises  Full central heating  Open parking available  Child discount available 4yrs .  Languages spoken: English*
CARDS: Travellers cheques

### TRONQUAY, LE Eure

**La Grand Fray** (Prop: M Gerard Monnier)
1 rue des Angles *27480*
☎ 232495338
(from Rouen towards Lyons-la-Forêt, then onto Le Tronquay)
Forest area
*1 en suite (shr)  TV available  Full central heating  Open parking available  Bicycle rental  Languages spoken: English*
CARDS: ▆

### URVILLE-NACQUEVILLE Manche

**La Blanche Maison** (Prop: Michael Potel)
874 rue St-Laurent *50460*
☎ 233034879
Near sea  Forest area
*1 en suite (shr)  Full central heating  Open parking available  Covered parking available  Supervised  Languages spoken: English & German*

### VALFRAMBERT Orne

**Haras du Bois Beulant** (Prop: M Siri)
*61250*
☎ 233286233
Forest area  In town centre  Near motorway
*2 en suite (shr)  Full central heating  Open parking available  Supervised  Languages spoken: English, German, Italian & Spanish*

### VALMONT Seine-Maritime

**Le Clos du Vivier** (Prop: Mme Dominique Cachera)
4 chemin du Vivier *76540*
☎ 235299095 FAX 235274449
Near river  Near lake  Near sea  Near beach  Forest area
*3 en suite (bth/shr) (2 fmly)  No smoking on premises  TV in 2 bedrooms  Radio in rooms  Full central heating  Open parking available  Languages spoken: English & Spanish*

### VARNÉVILLE-BRETTEVILLE Seine-Maritime

**Bed & Breakfast** (Prop: M & Mme Auberville)
Les Vernelles *76890*
☎ 235340804
(From A29 exit Dieppe. A151 exit Totes D927,D25,D101=Les Vernelles)

The guest house is an individual cottage situated near the main house in the middle of a wooded area, surrounded by apple trees. Here you will find peace and quiet in the heart of the Normandy countryside. There is a dining room, a small lounge, plus an open fire. The bedrooms feature beams. Breakfast is served at the cottage.
Near motorway
*1 en suite (shr) (1 fmly) TV in all bedrooms Full central heating Open parking available Covered parking available Tennis Riding Bicycle rental Open terrace Languages spoken: English*

## VASSY Calvados

**La Calbrasserie** (Prop: M & Mme de Saint-Leger)
La Calbrasserie *14410*
☎ 231685153
Forest area
*2 en suite (shr) (2 fmly) Radio in rooms Full central heating Open parking available Covered parking available Supervised Child discount available 2yrs Bicycle rental Table Tennis*
CARDS: Travellers cheques

## VAST, LE Manche

**La Dannevillerie** (Prop: Francoise & Benoit Passenaud)
*50630*
☎ 233445045
(from motorway exit Quetteham, head towards Barfleur, then then right on D26 and continue 4km to house on right)
Near river Near sea Forest area
*3 en suite (shr) (3 fmly) No smoking on premises TV available Full central heating Open parking available Child discount available -2 Free Languages spoken: English*
ROOMS: s fr 180FF; d 210-240FF

## VASTEVILLE Manche

**Le Manoir** (Prop: M Hubert Damourette)
*50440*
☎ 233527608 FAX 233935988
Near sea Forest area
*2 en suite (bth/shr) Full central heating Open parking available Child discount available Bicycle rental*
ROOMS: s fr 150FF; d fr 200FF ✱
CARDS: Travellers cheques

## VAUDRIMESNIL Manche

**La Rochelle** (Prop: Alain & Olga Berthou)
*50490*
☎ 233467495
Near sea Forest area
*2 en suite (shr) No smoking on premises Full central heating Open parking available Supervised Table tennis*

## VAUX-SUR-AURE Calvados

**Hammeau du Quesnay** (Prop: M Louis Roulland)
*14400*
☎ 231921126
Near river Near motorway
*1 en suite (bth) Radio in rooms Open parking available*
CARDS: ●● ■ Travellers cheques

## VAUX-SUR-SEULLES Calvados

**Ferme du Clos Mayas** (Prop: Marie-Helene Bastard)
*14400*
☎ 231223271 FAX 231223350
Near river Near sea Near motorway
*4 en suite (bth/shr) (1 fmly) Full central heating Open parking available Child discount available*
CARDS: Travellers cheques

## VENGEONS Manche

**Le Val** (Prop: Jeanne Desdoits)
*50150*
☎ 233596416 FAX 233693699
(from town centre take D32 to Mortain, then D977 towards Sourdeval)
Near lake Near motorway
*4 rms (1 bth 1 shr) (1 fmly) No smoking on premises Full central heating Open parking available Covered parking available Supervised Child discount available Boule Bicycle rental Languages spoken: English*
ROOMS: s 140FF; d 185FF
MEALS: Dinner 70FF
CARDS: ■ Travellers cheques

## VERNEUIL-SUR-AVRE Eure

★ ★ ★ **Hostellerie du Clos**
98 rue de la Ferté Vidame *27130*
☎ 232322181 FAX 232322136
(from Paris take A12 towards Dreux, then N12 Verneuil. From N12 turn right at 1st traffic lights)
Near river Forest area Near motorway
*Closed 16 Dec-19 Jan*
*10 en suite (bth/shr) 3 rooms in annexe (3 fmly) TV in all bedrooms STV Direct dial from all bedrooms Licensed Full central heating Air conditioning in bedrooms Open parking available Supervised Child discount available 8yrs Tennis Sauna Jacuzzi/spa Bicycle rental Open terrace Covered terrace V meals Last d 21.00hrs Languages spoken: English, German, Portuguese & Spanish*
ROOMS: (room only) s 800FF; d 850FF
MEALS: Full breakfast 90FF Lunch 195-375FF&alc Dinner 195-375FF&alc
CARDS: ●● ■■ ══ ⑩ JCB Travellers cheques

★ ★ **Moulin de Balisne**
RN12, Balisne *27130*
☎ 232320348 FAX 232601122
This 18th-century mill is located in extensive landscaped gardens with rivers and lakes. The interior is adorned with assorted knick-knacks which create a homely, personal atmosphere. Inventive cuisine is served in the restaurant, prepared with only the finest fresh produce and including a whole range of house specialities. The bedrooms are full of character, and are equipped with good modern amenities.
Near river Near lake Forest area Near motorway
*12 en suite (bth/shr) (2 fmly) TV in all bedrooms Direct dial from all bedrooms Mini-bar in all bedrooms Licensed Full central heating Open parking available Child discount available 10yrs Tennis Fishing Boule Bicycle rental Open terrace Canoeing Table tennis V meals Last d 21.30hrs Languages spoken: English*

contd.

**Moulin De Balisne**
ROOMS: (room only) d 400-450FF
**Reductions over 1 night Special breaks**
MEALS: Full breakfast 50FF Lunch 165-275FF&alc Dinner 165-275FF&alc
CARDS: ●● ■ ■■ ● Travellers cheques

### VIGNATS Calvados

**Bed & Breakfast** (Prop: M & Mme Brunton)
La rue d'Avé *14700*
☎ 231408323 FAX 231408323
Forest area
*2 rms No smoking on premises Full central heating Open parking available Supervised Child discount available 12yrs Languages spoken: English & Spanish*
CARDS: Travellers cheques

### VILLEDIEU-LES-POÊLES Manche

★ ★ **Le Fruitier**
pl des Costils *50800*
☎ 233905100 FAX 233905101
Near river Forest area In town centre Near motorway
Closed 23 Dec-5 Jan
*48 en suite (bth/shr) (10 fmly) TV in all bedrooms STV Direct dial from all bedrooms Licensed Lift Full central heating Open parking available Covered parking available (charged) Supervised Pool table V meals Last d 21.30hrs Languages spoken: Englsih*
CARDS: ●● ■■ Travellers cheques

### VIMOUTIERS Orne

★ ★ **L'Escale du Vitou**
rte d'Argentan *61120*
☎ 233391204 FAX 233361334
(On D916 between Vimoutiers and Argentan)
Near river Near beach Forest area

*17 en suite (bth/shr) 18 rooms in annexe TV in all bedrooms Radio in rooms Direct dial from all bedrooms Licensed Full central heating Open parking available Outdoor swimming pool Tennis Fishing Riding Boule Mini-golf Last d 22.45hrs Languages spoken: English*
CARDS: ●● ■■

### VINGT-HANAPS Orne

**Les Quatre Saisons** (Prop: M Claude Ivaldi)
Les Chauvières *61250*
☎ 233288292
Near lake Forest area Near motorway
*4 en suite (bth/shr) (4 fmly) (2 with balcony) TV available Full central heating Open parking available Supervised V meals Languages spoken: English*

### VIRE Calvados

★ ★ **Hotel de France**
4 rue d'Aignaux *14500*
☎ 231680035 FAX 231682265
In town centre Near motorway
*50 en suite (bth/shr) TV in all bedrooms Direct dial from all bedrooms Licensed Lift Night porter Full central heating Open parking available Covered parking available (charged) Child discount available 8yrs V meals Last d 22.00hrs Languages spoken: English*
CARDS: ●● ■ ■■ Travellers cheques

### YVETOT Seine-Maritime

**Auberge du Val au Cesne**
*76190*
☎ 235566306 FAX 235569278
(3km SW of Yvetot via D5)
Forest area Near motorway
*5 en suite (bth/shr) (3 fmly) (5 with balcony) TV in all bedrooms Direct dial from all bedrooms Licensed Night porter Full central heating Open parking available Supervised Bicycle rental Open terrace Last d 21.00hrs Languages spoken: English*
ROOMS: (room only) d 480FF
MEALS: Full breakfast 50FF Lunch 150FF&alc Dinner 150FF&alc
CARDS: ●● ■ ■■

# Picardy

The countryside of Picardy features fertile plains, green river valleys and sparsely populated villages. The region is mainly agricultural, growing wheat, sugar-beet and plants used in textile manufacture. The north prospered during the Middle Ages and the profits were poured into the magnificent cathedrals and Gothic architecture, which are unsurpassed in the rest of France. Leave the motorways behind and drive through a landscape which have seen almost endless fighting through the ages, the worst being in this century. Despite much upheaval, the region's patois, traditions and beliefs have survived.

## ESSENTIAL FACTS

| | |
|---|---|
| DÉPARTEMENTS: | Aisne, Oise, Somme |
| PRINCIPAL TOWNS | Amiens, Beauvais, Abbeville, Noyon, Laon, Compàgne, St Quentin, Soissons, Château-Thierry. |
| PLACES TO VISIT: | Cathedrals : Amiens, Beauvais & Laon. Les Hortillonnages, floating market-gardens which can only be reached by small boats. Grottes de Naours, ancient underground town. Samara, leisure park, exhibition centre, archaeological trail & botanical garden. Baie de la Somme steam train (rides last 1-3 hrs). Chantilly: Living Museum of the Horse, Castle, Condé museum, Park. War museum at Péronne (Historial de la Grande Guerre). |
| REGIONAL TOURIST OFFICE | 3 rue Vincent Auriol, 80011 Amiens Tel: 03 22 22 33 66  Fax: 03 22 97 92 96 |
| LOCAL GASTRONOMIC DELIGHTS | Duck paté. Pré-salé, lamb with a distinctive taste from salt-marsh grazing. Sauterelles, shrimps. Marquenterre mussels, eels, sole & shellfish. Ficelle picarde, rolled pancake with ham & mushrooms with a creamy sauce. Flamiche aux poireaux, creamy leek tart. Cheeses: Maroilles, Rollot, Dauphin. Gâteau Battu, traditional dessert |
| DRINKS | Cider, ales, berry-based spirits, champagne, mineral water from many regional 'sources'. |
| LOCAL CRAFTS WHAT TO BUY | Chantilly & Sinceny: pottery, porcelain, ceramics. Beauchamps le Vieuc: handmade furniture. Ercuis: jewellery. |

## ABBEVILLE Somme

### ★ ★ ★ Best Western Hotel de France
19 pl du Pilori *80100*
☎ 322240042 FAX 322242615
(From Boulogne or Paris take A16 exit Abbeville-Centre-Ville, from Rouen take A28)

Picardie Maritime, nature's paradise with a preserved ecology, a notable stop on the road to the South of France. In the heart of Abbeville, in this privileged environment, the hotel offers the best of tradition, comfort and welcome
Near sea  Near beach  In town centre  Near motorway
*69 en suite (bth/shr)  (13 fmly)  No smoking in 1 bedroom  TV in all bedrooms  STV  Direct dial from all bedrooms  Mini-bar in all bedrooms  Licensed  Lift  Night porter  Full central heating  Open parking available (charged)  Covered parking available (charged)  Supervised  Pool table  Bicycle rental  V meals  Last d 22.30hrs  Languages spoken: English German Hebrew Portuguese & Spanish*
ROOMS: (room only) s 225-380FF;  d 340-460FF
**Special breaks**
MEALS: Lunch 70-98FF&alc  Dinner 70-98FF&alc
CARDS: 💳 🏧 💳 Travellers cheques

### *La Maison Carrée-Bonance* (Prop: J et M Maillard)
Port-Le-Grand *80132*
☎ 322241197 FAX 322316377
(A16 exit N23 Abbeville Centre/Rouen in the direction of St Valery-le-Crotoy at Port-le-grand turn right, 2km on right)
Near sea  Near beach  Forest area
*Closed Nov-Oct*
*6 en suite (bth/shr)  Full central heating  Open parking available  Supervised  Child discount available 2yrs  Outdoor swimming pool (heated)  Languages spoken: English & German*
CARDS: 💳 Travellers cheques

## AGNETZ Oise

### ★ ★ Le Clermotel
60 Rue des Buttes, Zone Hotelière *60600*
☎ 344500990 FAX 344501300
(take Agnetz exit from A1 in the direction of Creil Puis Amiens Hotel on N31 on L'Axe Reims to Rouen in the Zone Hotelière)
Near river  Forest area  Near motorway
*37 en suite (bth/shr)  (4 fmly)  No smoking in 2 bedrooms  TV in all bedrooms  Direct dial from all bedrooms  Licensed  Full central heating  Open parking available  Child discount*
*contd.*

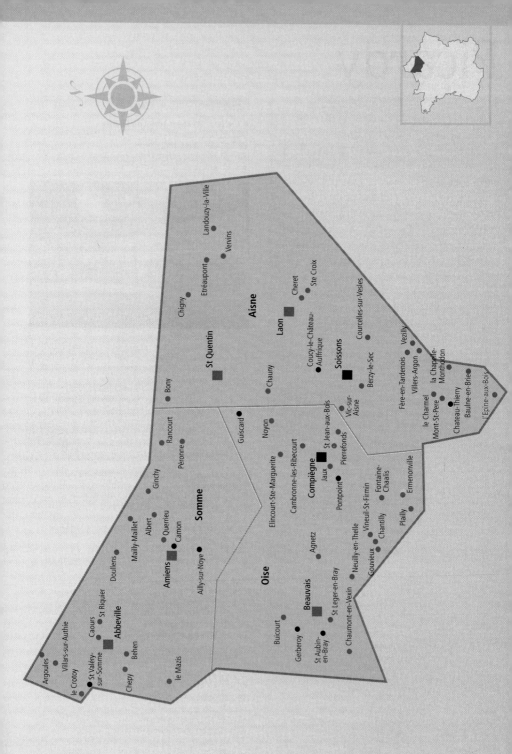

Landouzy-la-Ville
Vervins
Etréaupont
Ste Croix
Cheret
Chigny
**Aisne**
Courcelles-sur-Vesles
Vézilly
**Laon**
St Quentin
Coucy-le-Château-
Auffrique
**Soissons**
Fère-en-Tardenois
la Chapelle-
Monthodon
Bony
Chauny
Berzy-le-Sec
Villers-Argon
le Charmel
Baulne-en-Brie
Mont-St-Père
Chateau-Thierry
Rancourt
Guiscard
Vic-sur-
Aisne
Épine-aux-Bois
Péronne
Noyon
St Jean-aux-Bois
Ginchy
Elincourt-Ste-Marguerite
Cambronne-les-Ribecourt
Pierrefonds
**Somme**
Jaux
**Compiègne**
Albert
Querrieu
Mailly-Maillet
Camon
Pontpoint
Vineuil-St-Firmin
Fontaine-
Chaalis
Ermenonville
Doullens
Amiens
Ailly-sur-Noye
Agnetz
Neuilly-en-Thelle
Gouvieux
Chantilly
Plailly
**Oise**
St Riquier
Caours
Abbeville
Buicourt
Beauvais
St Leger-en-Bray
Chaumont-en-Vexin
Villars-sur-Authie
Behen
Gerberoy
St Aubin-
en-Bray
Argoules
St Valéry-
sur-Somme
le Crotoy
Chepy
le Mazis
112

available 10yrs Tennis Boule Bicycle rental Open terrace Table tennis, volleyball V meals Last d 22.00hrs Languages spoken: English & German
ROOMS: (room only) s fr 290FF; d fr 320FF
**Reductions over 1 night Special breaks**
MEALS: Full breakfast 39FF Lunch 95-155FF&alc Dinner 95-151FF&alc
CARDS: ●● ■■ ☲ ▣ Travellers cheques

**ALBERT** Somme

### ★★ Hotel de la Basilique
3-5 rue Gambetta 80300
☎ 322750471 FAX 322751047
(A1/A2 exit Albert then D938 or A16 to Amiens then D929)
Family-run hotel in the heart of the Great War's battlefields, close to the Basilica and Sommme 1916 Musuem. Country side specialities and home made creations are served in the restaurant

In town centre Near motorway
Closed 13 Aug-3 Sep & 23 Dec-7 Jan
10 en suite (bth/shr) (2 fmly) (3 with balcony) TV in all bedrooms Direct dial from all bedrooms Licensed Full central heating Child discount available 10yrs Last d 20.30hrs Languages spoken: English & Spanish
ROOMS: (room only) s 240FF; d 290-330FF
MEALS: Continental breakfast 35FF Lunch 68-200FF&alc Dinner 68-200FF&alc
CARDS: ●● ☲ Travellers cheques

**AMIENS** Somme

### ★★★ Grand Hotel de l'Univers (Best Western)
2 rue de Noyon 80000
☎ 322915251 FAX 322928166
(from A1 take exit Amiens and head for town centre hotel in front of station)
In town centre Near motorway
41 rms (25 bth 15 shr) TV in all bedrooms STV Direct dial from all bedrooms Mini-bar in all bedrooms Licensed Lift Night porter Full central heating Child discount available 12yrs Languages spoken: English Italian & Spanish
CARDS: ●● ■■ ☲ ▣ Travellers cheques

### ★★ Vidéotel
rue le Greco, Zac Vallée St-Iadre 80085
☎ 322520404 FAX 322449495
(From A16 exit 'Amiens Nord', take Amiens-Arras road and follow signs for 'Amiens Centre' and 'Centre Commercial Continent')
Near motorway

---

44 en suite (bth/shr) (26 fmly) No smoking in 8 bedrooms TV in all bedrooms Direct dial from all bedrooms Licensed Full central heating Open parking available Supervised Child discount available 12yrs Open terrace V meals Last d 22.00hrs Languages spoken: English & German
CARDS: ●● ■■ ☲ ▣ Travellers cheques

**ARGOULES** Somme

### Abbaye de Valloires
80120
☎ 322296233 FAX 322296224
Near river Forest area
Full central heating Open parking available Languages spoken: English
CARDS: ■■ ☲ Travellers cheques

### ★★★ Auberge le Gros Tilleul
pl du Château 80120
☎ 322299100 FAX 322239164
(from Calais or Boulogne take N1 or A16 in the direction Montreuil/Mer-Abbeville to Nampont-St-Martin turn left in direction Argoules)

The Beugé family welcomes you warmly to their auberge, nestling in the village of Argoules amid the quiet beauty of the Authie valley. It is full of country charm, with small but pretty beamed bedrooms and a rustic dining room in which to enjoy the traditional country cooking.
Near river Forest area Near motorway
RS Monday
16 en suite (bth/shr) (3 fmly) No smoking on premises TV in all bedrooms STV Direct dial from all bedrooms Mini-bar in all bedrooms Licensed Full central heating Open parking available (charged) Supervised Child discount available 10yrs Outdoor swimming pool (heated) Solarium Boule Bicycle rental Open terrace Covered terrace Putting green Table tennis V meals Last d 21.00hrs Languages spoken: English & Spanish
MEALS: Continental breakfast 45FF Lunch 70-190FF&alc Dinner 70-190FF&alc✻
CARDS: ●● ■■ ☲ ▣ Travellers cheques

**BAULNE-EN-BRIE** Aisne

### ★★ Auberge de l'Omois
Grande rue 02330
☎ 323820813 FAX 323826988
Near river Forest area Near motorway
7 en suite (bth/shr) Licensed Night porter Full central heating Open parking available Supervised Child discount available
contd.

Tennis Fishing Riding Boule Bicycle rental Open terrace
Wkly live entertainment V meals Last d 22.00hrs Languages
spoken: English
CARDS: 💳 🏧 💳 💳 Travellers cheques

## BEAUVAIS Oise

**★ ★ Hostellerie St-Vincent**
rue de Clermont 60000
☎ 344054999 FAX 344055294
48 en suite (bth/shr) (2 fmly) No smoking in 10 bedrooms TV
in all bedrooms Direct dial from all bedrooms Licensed Night
porter Full central heating Open parking available Child
discount available 10yrs Jacuzzi/spa Open terrace V meals
Last d 22.00hrs Languages spoken: English
CARDS: 💳 🏧 💳 Travellers cheques

## BEHEN Somme

**Château des Alleux** (Prop: Réne-François de Fontanges)
Les Alleux 80870
☎ 322316488 FAX 322316488
(from Abbeville take A28 towards Rouen, exit at Monts-
Caubert, at the stop turn right, then at Les Croisettes turn right
& follow signs 'Les Alleux'. Do not follow signs for Behen)
Near sea Near beach Forest area Near motorway
4 en suite (bth/shr) TV available Full central heating Open
parking available Child discount available Languages spoken:
English
MEALS: Dinner 130FF✱

## BERZY-LE-SEC Aisne

**Ferme Lechelle** (Prop: Mme N Maurice)
02200
☎ 323748329 FAX 323748247
Forest area Near motorway
5 rms (1 bth 1 shr) (1 fmly) No smoking on premises TV in 1
bedroom Full central heating Open parking available Covered
parking available Child discount available 6yrs Boule Open
terrace V meals Languages spoken: English
CARDS: Travellers cheques

## BONY Aisne

**Ferme-Auberge du Vieux Puits** (Prop: M & Mme
Gyselinck)
5 rue de l'Abbaye 02420
☎ 323662233 FAX 323662527
(25km from Cambrai in the direction of St Quentin)
Near motorway
6 en suite (bth/shr) (2 fmly) TV in 5 bedrooms STV Full central
heating Open parking available Child discount available 8yrs
Outdoor swimming pool (heated) Boule Table tennis Last d
21.00hrs
CARDS: 💳 💳

## BUICOURT Oise

**Bed & Breakfast** (Prop: M & Mme Verhoeven)
3 rue de la Mare 60380
☎ 344823115
(from Songeons take D143 towards Gournay-en-Bray. Guest
house is in then centre of Buicourt)
Eddy and Jacqueline Verhoeven welcome you to their home in
the countryside, surrounded by forests, flowers and

tranquillity. There is a choice of restaurants in nearby Gerbury,
just two kilometres away.
Forest area In town centre
2 en suite (bth/shr) Full central heating Open parking available
Child discount available
ROOMS: s fr 180FF; d fr 250FF **Reductions over 1 night**

## CAMBRONNE-LES-RIBECOURT Oise

**Farm Hotel Bellerive** (Prop: Pauline Brunger)
492 rue de Bellerive 60170
☎ 344750213 FAX 344761034
(from North : A1 junct 12 follow direction Noyon then
Compiègne N32 then D66. From South : A1 junct 10 towards
Noyon on N32, then D66)

Situated in an old farm alongside the canal and close to the
Forest of Compègne. Disneyland and the Champagne area are
within an easy drive and the farm is approximately 2 hours
from Calais and 1 hour from Paris.
Near river Near lake Forest area
5 en suite (bth/shr) No smoking in all bedrooms Full central
heating Open parking available Child discount available 10yrs
Fishing Bicycle rental V meals Last d 9pm Languages spoken:
English
ROOMS: s 190FF; d 275FF
**Reductions over 1 night Special breaks**
MEALS: Lunch 90FF Dinner 90FF✱
CARDS: Travellers cheques

## CAOURS Somme

**La Rivierette** (Prop: M & Mme de Lamarliere)
2 rue de la Ferme 80132
☎ 322247749 FAX 322247697
(from Calais, take A16 exit 22 towards Abbeville/St-Riquier.
Take St-Riquier road up hill, then left to Caours and follow
signposts to 'Chambre-d'Hôte' in village)

Marc and Hélène (a former English teacher), and their young children have six rooms to offer to guests. Each room has its own entrance. The bed & breakfast is situated on the banks of the Rivièrette. A super restaurant is open nearby but guests may also cook for themselves in the kitchen provided.
*Near river Forest area Near motorway*
*6 en suite (bth/shr) 1 rooms in annexe (5 fmly) TV in 1 bedroom Full central heating Open parking available Covered parking available Indoor swimming pool (heated) Fishing Bicycle rental Open terrace Table tennis Croquet Basketball Languages spoken: English & German*
ROOMS: s fr 250FF; d 350FF ✱
CARDS: Travellers cheques

## CHANTILLY Oise

**Bed & Breakfast** (Prop: Mrs S Lokmer)
30c Rue Victor Hugo
☎ 344576391 FAX 344576391
(from Paris by A1 exit Survillers/St Witz)
Near lake Forest area Near motorway
*1 en suite (shr) No smoking on premises TV in all bedrooms Full central heating Open parking available Covered parking available Languages spoken: English*
ROOMS: s 290FF; d 370FF

★ ★ ★ **Hotel du Parc** (Best Western)
36 av Maréchal Joffe 60500
☎ 344582000 FAX 344573110
(From A1(Paris to Lille)exit 8 (Senlis), follow signs for Chantilly, approx 10kms)
Forest area In town centre Near motorway
*58 en suite (bth/shr) (4 fmly) (12 with balcony) No smoking in 25 bedrooms TV in 52 bedrooms STV Direct dial from 52 bedrooms Licensed Lift Night porter Full central heating Open parking available (charged) Covered parking available (charged) Supervised Child discount available 12yrs Bicycle rental Open terrace Wkly live entertainment Languages spoken: English, German & Portuguese*
CARDS: ●● ■■ ⚏ ⓪ Travellers cheques

## CHAPELLE-MONTHODON, LA Aisne

*Bed & Breakfast* (Prop: M & Mme Christian Douard)
Hameau de Chezy 02330
☎ 323824766 FAX 323727296
Forest area
*(1 fmly) No smoking on premises Child discount available 12yrs Languages spoken: English*
CARDS: Travellers cheques

## CHARMEL, LE Aisne

**Bed & Breakfast** (Prop: M & Mme Gaston Assailly)
6 rue du Moulin 02850
☎ 323703127 FAX 323701508
(A4, exit at Château-Thierry, then take D34 towards Dormans. Follow road through Jaulgonne and onto Le Charmel)
This house is located in a quiet village near the Champagne tourist route. A modern home, set in a large, well-manicured garden, full of fruit trees and flowers. There are four spacious and comfortable double rooms. Guests are invited to dine with their hosts, the Assailly family. Meals are served in the dining room or on the patio.
*Near river Near lake Near beach Forest area Near motorway*
*4 en suite (bth/shr) (1 with balcony) No smoking on premises*

*TV in all bedrooms STV Full central heating Open parking available Child discount available Bicycle rental*
ROOMS: s 280FF; d 300FF **Special breaks**
MEALS: Dinner fr 80FF

## CHAUMONT-EN-VEXIN Oise

★ ★ **La Grange de St-Nicolas**
17 rue de la République 60240
☎ 344491100 FAX 344499997
Near river Forest area In town centre Near motorway
*RS 20 Dec-5 Jan*
*14 en suite (bth/shr) (8 fmly) TV in all bedrooms STV Direct dial from 11 bedrooms Mini-bar in 6 bedrooms Full central heating Open parking available Supervised Child discount available 16yrs V meals Last d 21.30hrs Languages spoken: English*
CARDS: ●● ■■ ⚏ ⓪ Travellers cheques

## CHAUNY Aisne

★ ★ ★ **La Toque Blanche**
24 av Victor Hugo 02300
☎ 323399898 FAX 323523279
In town centre
*Closed 1-12 Jan, 15-23 Feb & 2-24 Aug*
*6 en suite (bth/shr) No smoking in 2 bedrooms TV in all bedrooms Direct dial from all bedrooms Mini-bar in all bedrooms Licensed Full central heating Open parking available Tennis Last d 21.00hrs Languages spoken: English*
CARDS: ●● ⚏ Travellers cheques

## CHEPY Somme

★ ★ **Auberge Picarde**
pl de la Gare 80210
☎ 322262078 FAX 322263334
Near motorway
*Closed 26 Dec-5 Jan*
*25 en suite (bth/shr) (3 fmly) TV in all bedrooms Direct dial from all bedrooms Licensed Full central heating Open parking available Sauna Pool table Open terrace V meals Last d 21.00hrs*
ROOMS: (room only) s 240-360FF; d 265-385FF ✱
MEALS: Full breakfast 35FF Lunch 90-205FF&alc Dinner 90-205FF&alc✱
CARDS: ●● ■■ ⚏ Travellers cheques

## CHÉRÊT Aisne

*Le Clos* (Prop: Michel Monnot)
02860
☎ 323248064
Near lake Forest area
*Closed 15 Oct-15 May*
*5 rms (3 bth/shr) (1 fmly) Full central heating Open parking available Child discount available Languages spoken: English*
CARDS: Travellers cheques

## CHIGNY Aisne

**Melle Piette** (Prop: Françoise & Bernadette Piette)
6 et 7 pl des Maronniers 02120
☎ 323602204
(from St-Quentin take N29 through Guise towards la Capelle. Right for Chigny)

*contd.*

115

### Melle Piette
Your hosts welcome you to their 18th-century home, which is surrounded by a flower garden. Evening meals including wine are available on request. A very relaxing time will be enjoyed here.
Near river  Near lake  Forest area  Near motorway
*7 rms (2 bth/shr) (2 fmly) Full central heating  Open parking available  Covered parking available  Supervised  Child discount available  Boule  V meals  Last d 20.00hrs*
ROOMS: s 190FF; d 250-270FF **Reductions over 1 night**
MEALS: Dinner 95FF
CARDS: ■ Travellers cheques

#### COURCELLES-SUR-VESLES Aisne

★ ★ ★ ★ *Château de Courcelles*
*02220*
☎ 323741353 FAX 323740641
Forest area
*18 en suite (bth/shr) 6 rooms in annexe (1 with balcony) TV in all bedrooms STV Direct dial from all bedrooms Licensed Full central heating  Open parking available  Supervised  Outdoor swimming pool (heated) Tennis  Fishing  Sauna  Bicycle rental Open terrace  Covered terrace  3 jogging circuits V meals Last d 21.30hrs  Languages spoken: English*
CARDS: ●● ■ ☲ ⑩ Travellers cheques

#### CROTOY, LE Somme

**Villa "La Mouclade"** (Prop: M et Mme C Weyl)
Quai Jules Noiret, plage Promenades *80550*
☎ 322270944 FAX 322278829
(from Calais to Abbeville, D40 to Le Crotoy, in town go right towards "La Plage" along rue Desjardins, Victor Pelletier, Gourlain, Victor Petit; house on sea right)
Near sea  Near beach  Near motorway
*5 en suite (bth) (1 with balcony) TV in all bedrooms Full central heating  Languages spoken: English German & Italian*

#### DOULLENS Somme

**Château de Remaisnil**
*80600*
☎ 322770747 FAX 322774123
(from Doullens take D925 in direction of Auxi-le-Château. At Risquetout take D938 keeping same direction, at village of Mezerolles turn right in direction of Remaisnil & after 1km look for tree-lined avenue on left)
Guests are welcomed into this elegant home, built in 1760 and previously owned by Laura Ashley. Rare 18th-century tapestries and furniture, and glittering sconces and

chandeliers highlight the unique period mouldings. The hotel offers comfort, tranquillity, gastronomy and leisure in a country house atmosphere in the heart of historic Picardy. Forest area

#### Chateau de Remaisnil
*Closed 15 Feb-1 Mar*
*19 en suite (bth/shr) 9 rooms in annexe  No smoking in all bedrooms  TV in all bedrooms  Direct dial from all bedrooms Mini-bar in all bedrooms  Licensed  Night porter  Full central heating  Open parking available  Covered parking available  Supervised  Child discount available 12yrs  Outdoor swimming pool (heated) Tennis  Pool table  Boule  Open terrace  Last d 21.00hrs  Languages spoken: English*
ROOMS: (room only) s 800-1050FF; d 800-1750FF
MEALS: Continental breakfast 95FF  Dinner 385FF
CARDS: ●● ■ ☲ ⑩

#### ÉLINCOURT-STE-MARGUERITE Oise

★ ★ ★ ★ *Château de Bellinglise*
rte de Lassigny *60157*
☎ 344960033 FAX 344960300
(A1 exit 11, D82 to Ressons sur Matz, then D15)
Near river  Near lake  Forest area
*35 en suite (bth) 11 rooms in annexe (1 fmly) (4 with balcony) TV in 46 bedrooms  Direct dial from 46 bedrooms  Mini-bar in 46 bedrooms  Licensed  Lift  Night porter  Full central heating  Open parking available  Child discount available 12yrs  Tennis  Fishing  Pool table  Boule  Bicycle rental  Open terrace  Table tennis, Volley ball  Last d 22.15hrs  Languages spoken: English, German & Spanish*
CARDS: ●● ■ ☲ ⑩ Travellers cheques

#### ÉPINE-AUX-BOIS, L' Aisne

**Les Patrus** (Prop: Mary-Ann Royal)
*02540*
☎ 323698585 FAX 323699849
Near river  Forest area
*6 en suite (bth/shr) (2 fmly) Full central heating  Open parking available  Child discount available  Languages spoken: English & German*
CARDS: ☲

#### ERMENONVILLE Oise

★ ★ *Hotel de la Croix d'Or*
2 rue Prince *60950*
☎ 344540004 FAX 344540544
Near river  Near lake  Forest area  In town centre  Near motorway
*Closed late Dec-late Jan*

*8 en suite (bth/shr) (1 fmly) TV in all bedrooms Licensed Full central heating Open parking available No children Last d 21.00hrs Languages spoken: English*
CARDS: ● ■ Travellers cheques

## ÉTRÉAUPONT Aisne

**★ ★ Le Clos du Montvinage**
8 rue Albert Ledent *02580*
☎ 323974018 & 323979110 FAX 323974892
(5m N of Vervius via N2)
This delightful hotel, created from a late 19th-century mansion, is in the heart of the Thierache region close to the Belgian border.
Near river Near motorway
*Closed 1 wk Feb, 1 wk Aug*
*20 en suite (bth/shr) TV in all bedrooms STV Direct dial from all bedrooms Mini-bar in 18 bedrooms Licensed Night porter Full central heating Open parking available Supervised Child discount available 12yrs Tennis Pool table Boule Bicycle rental V meals Last d 21.15hrs Languages spoken: English*
ROOMS: (room only) s 298-425FF; d 355-475FF
**Reductions over 1 night Special breaks**
MEALS: Continental breakfast 50FF Lunch 95-225FF&alc Dinner 95-225FF&alc
CARDS: ● ■ ■ ● JCB Travellers cheques

## FÈRE-EN-TARDENOIS Aisne

**★ ★ ★ ★ Château de Fére**
rte de Fismes *02130*
☎ 323822113 FAX 323823781
Near lake Forest area
*Closed mid Jan-mid Feb*
*25 rms (24 bth) (6 fmly) TV in all bedrooms Mini-bar in all bedrooms Licensed Night porter Full central heating Open parking available Supervised Outdoor swimming pool (heated) Tennis Boule Bicycle rental Open terrace Last d 21.30hrs Languages spoken: English*
CARDS: ● ■ ■ ● Travellers cheques

**La Porte de Fère** (Prop: Martine Desruelle)
13 rue du Château
☎ 323823039
(Access via autoroute A4 exit Château-Thierry or St-Quentin)

An 18th-century house providing an authentic atmosphere and pleasant, comfortable accommodation.
Near lake Forest area Near motorway
*Closed Dec-Mar*

*4 en suite (bth/shr) (1 fmly) No smoking on premises Full central heating Open parking available Supervised Child discount available 10 yrs Outdoor swimming pool Tennis Bicycle rental Languages spoken: English & Spanish*

## FONTAINE-CHAALIS Oise

**★ ★ Auberge de Fontaine**
22 Grande rue *60300*
☎ 344542022 FAX 344602538
(A1 exit8 at Senlis onto N330 to Ermenonville, then D330 to Nanteuil le Haudouin)
Near river Forest area
*Closed 4-24 Jan*
*8 en suite (bth/shr) (1 fmly) TV in all bedrooms Direct dial from all bedrooms Licensed Full central heating Child discount available 12yrs Open terrace V meals Last d 21.45hrs Languages spoken: English*
ROOMS: (room only) s 275-305FF; d 275-335FF
MEALS: Continental breakfast 40FF Lunch 98-255FF&alc Dinner 135-255FF&alc
CARDS: ● ■ ■ ●

## GINCHY Somme

**L'Hermitage** (Prop: M et Mme Samain)
1 Grand Rue *80360*
☎ 322850224 FAX 322851160
(exit A1 no14 in dircetion of Péronne & Le Translou on right, pass the village of Les Bouefs to Ginchy)
Forest area Near motorway
*Closed Nov-Apr*
*4 en suite (shr) (1 fmly) No smoking on premises Full central heating Open parking available Covered parking available Child discount available Boule Bicycle rental*
MEALS: Dinner 80-100FF✱

## GOUVIEUX Oise

**★ ★ ★ Château de la Tour**
ch de la Chaussée *60270*
☎ 344570739 FAX 344573197
Forest area
*41 en suite (bth/shr) (2 fmly) TV in all bedrooms STV Licensed Night porter Open parking available Child discount available 12yrs Outdoor swimming pool (heated) Tennis Pool table Bicycle rental Open terrace Last d 21.30hrs Languages spoken: English & German*
CARDS: ● ■ ■ ● Travellers cheques

## JAUX Oise

**La Gaxottière** (Prop: Francoise Gaxotte)
363 rue du Champ du Mont, Varanval
☎ 344832241 FAX 344832241
((A1 exit no.10 in direction of Compiègne after 4km turn right towards Jaux, Varanval on right)
Renovated farmhouse with two bedrooms, both rooms have exposed beams, fireplace and antique furnishings. Hidden behind high walls is a lovely quiet garden with a terrace in front of the bedrooms.
Forest area Near motorway
*2 en suite (bth/shr) Full central heating Open parking available*
ROOMS: d 300FF ✱ **Reductions over 1 night**

## LANDOUZY-LA-VILLE Aisne

**Bed & Breakfast** (Prop: M Jean Tirtiaux)
*02140*
☎ 323984344 FAX 323984499
Near river  Near lake  Forest area  Near motorway
*3 en suite (bth/shr)  TV in all bedrooms  Full central heating
Open parking available  Supervised*
CARDS: Travellers cheques

## LAON Aisne

**★ ★ ★ Hotel de la Bannière de France**
11 rue Franklin Roosevelt *02000*
☎ 323232144 FAX 323233156
(A26 exit 13 follow signs to Ville Haute, hotel clearly signed)
In town centre
*Closed 23 Dec-23 Jan & 1 May*
*18 rms (17 bth/shr)  (6 fmly)  TV in all bedrooms  STV  Direct
dial from all bedrooms  Licensed  Full central heating  Open
parking available (charged)  Covered parking available
(charged)  Supervised  Child discount available 12yrs  V meals
Last d 21.30hrs  Languages spoken: English, German & Spanish*
ROOMS: (room only) s 255-315FF; d 315-380FF
**Reductions over 1 night**
MEALS: Continental breakfast 42FF  Lunch 95-315FF&alc
Dinner 95-315FF&alc
CARDS: ●● ■ ■ ●JCB Travellers cheques

**★ ★ Hostellerie St-Vincent**
av Charles-de-Gaulle
☎ 323234243 FAX 323792255
(from town centre head towards 'Zone Industrielle')
Near motorway
*Closed 3 weeks Xmas*
*47 en suite (bth/shr)  (2 fmly)  TV in all bedrooms  Direct-dial
available  Night porter  Full central heating  Open parking
available  V meals  Last d 21.30hrs  Languages spoken: English*
CARDS: ●● ■ ■

## MAILLY-MAILLET Somme

**Les Bieffes** (Prop: M Harle d'Hermonville)
27 rue Pierre Lefebvre *80560*
☎ 322762144 FAX 322762144
(A1 exit Albert, Mailly-Maillet is on the D919)
Near river  Forest area
*3 en suite (bth/shr)  No smoking on premises  TV in all
bedrooms  Full central heating  Open parking available  Child
discount available 10yrs  Languages spoken: English*
CARDS: Travellers cheques

## MAZIS, LE Somme

**Bed & Breakfast** (Prop: Onder Delinden)
*80430*
☎ 322259010 322259088 FAX 322257604
Near river  Forest area
*4 en suite (shr)  Full central heating  Open parking available
Languages spoken: Dutch*

## MONT-ST-PÈRE Aisne

**Bed & Breakfast** (Prop: M & Mme Comyn)
7 bis rue Fontaine Ste-Foy *02400*
☎ 323702879 FAX 323703644
(from A4 exit 20 (Château-Thierry) take D3 via Brasles and

Gland to Mont-St-Pèrethen D4 towards Epieds for 100mtrs
then right)
Near river  Forest area  Near motorway
*Closed 15 Dec-15 Feb*
*2 en suite (bth/shr)  Open parking available  Supervised
Covered terrace  Languages spoken: English*
CARDS: ●● ■ ■

## NEUILLY-EN-THELLE Oise

**Les Relais du Thelle**
16 Hameau Belle *60530*
☎ 344267112 FAX 344749129
(leave Beauvais in direction of Paris N1 at Ste Genevieve turn
left in direction Neuilly en Thelle, through Neuilly turn right
for le Belle)
Forest area  Near motorway
*4 en suite (shr)  Full central heating  Open parking available
Riding*

## NOYON Oise

**★ ★ Le Cèdre**
8 rue de l'Evêché *60400*
☎ 344442324 FAX 344095379
(A1 exit 12 & A26 exit 12)
Forest area  In town centre  Near motorway
*34 en suite (bth/shr)  (1 fmly)  TV in all bedrooms  STV  Direct
dial from all bedrooms  Licensed  Night porter  Full central
heating  Open parking available  Supervised  Child discount
available 5yrs  Bicycle rental  Open terrace  Billiards  V meals
Last d 21.30hrs  Languages spoken: English*
CARDS: ●● ■ ■ Travellers cheques

## PÉRONNE Somme

**Château d'Omiécourt** (Prop: M et Mme de Thezy)
rte de Chaulnes *80320*
☎ 322830175 FAX 322832183
(A1 onto N73 take direction of St Quentin into Villers
Carbonnel turn right in direction of Roye. After 10km arrive at
Omiecourt)
The château is in a large landscaped mature park and has been
restored in its original style. Each room has oak floors, marble
fireplace and a comfortable bathroom. A warm and friendly
welcome is assured by all the family. Meals are prepared by
Mme de Thizy using traditional recipes.
Forest area  Near motorway
*Closed 24 Dec-1 Jan*
*3 en suite (bth/shr)  (4 fmly)  No smoking on premises  Full
central heating  Open parking available  Child discount
available 7yrs  Riding  Table tennis  Last d 14.00hrs  Languages
spoken: English*
ROOMS: s 280FF; d 330FF
**Reductions over 1 night  Special breaks**
MEALS: Dinner 80-130FF✱

**★ ★ Hostellerie des Remparts**
21 rue Beaubois *80200*
☎ 322840122 FAX 322843196
(A1/A2 exit Maurepas & take direction of Péronne,
approx 5km)
Tucked away in the ramparts of the old town, the hotel
provides comfortable, en suite bedrooms. An excellent
restaurant offers both fixed price and à la carte menu.
Near lake  In town centre  Near motorway
*16 en suite (bth/shr)  (4 fmly)  TV in all bedrooms  STV  Direct*

dial from all bedrooms Licensed Night porter Full central heating Open parking available Covered parking available (charged) Supervised Child discount available 12yrs Fishing Riding Bicycle rental Open terrace V meals Last d 21.30hrs Languages spoken: English

### Hostellerie des Remparts
ROOMS: (room only) s 220-350FF; d 280-450FF
**Reductions over 1 night Special breaks: fishing/sport**
MEALS: Continental breakfast 35FF Lunch 90-350FF&alc Dinner 95-350FF&alc
CARDS: ●● ■■ ▄▄ ⑨ Travellers cheques

---

### PIERREFONDS Oise

★ ★ **Hotel des Etrangers**
10 rue Baudon *60350*
☎ 344428018 FAX 344428674
An attractive inn with a friendly atmosphere, close to the medieval castle of Pierrefonds.
Near river Near lake Forest area In town centre Near motorway 16 rms (10 bth/shr) TV in 5 bedrooms Direct dial from 15 bedrooms Licensed Full central heating Open parking available Covered parking available Supervised Child discount available 5yrs Open terrace V meals Last d 21.30hrs Languages spoken: English, German & Italian
CARDS: ●● ■■ ▄▄ ⑨ Travellers cheques

---

### PLAILLY Oise

★ ★ *Auberge du Petit Cheval d'Or*
rue de Paris *60128*
☎ 344543633 FAX 344543802
(leave A1 exit 7/Survilliers in direction of Ermenonville)
Forest area Near motorway
27 rms (25 bth/shr) (6 fmly) (1 with balcony) TV in all bedrooms Direct dial from all bedrooms Mini-bar in 12 bedrooms Licensed Lift Full central heating Open parking available Child discount available 12yrs Boule Bicycle rental Open terrace Last d 22.00hrs Languages spoken: English
CARDS: ●● ■■ ▄▄ ⑨ Travellers cheques

---

### QUERRIEU Somme

*Château de Querrieu* (Prop: Yves D'Alcantara)
11 rue du Bois Galhaut *80115*
☎ 322401555 322401342 FAX 322401753
(8km from Amiens on the D929)
Near river Near lake Forest area
5 en suite (bth/shr) (1 fmly) TV available Full central heating Open parking available Covered parking available Supervised Child discount available Languages spoken: English

---

### RANCOURT Somme

★ ★ *Prièure*
RN 17 *80360*
☎ 322850443 FAX 322850669
Near motorway
27 en suite (bth/shr) (6 fmly) No smoking in 2 bedrooms TV in all bedrooms STV Direct dial from all bedrooms Mini-bar in all bedrooms Licensed Night porter Full central heating Open parking available Supervised Child discount available 12yrs Tennis Pool table Boule V meals Last d 22.00hrs Languages spoken: English, German & Italian
CARDS: ●● ■■ ▄▄ Travellers cheques

---

### ST-JEAN-AUX-BOIS Oise

★ ★ ★ **Auberge a la Bonne Idée**
3 rue des Meuniers
☎ 99 344428409 FAX 344428045
(take D332 through Forest of Compiègne turn towards St-Jean-aux-Bois and continue for 1km)
Forest area
24 rms (23 bth/shr) 9 rooms in annexe (3 fmly) TV in all bedrooms STV Direct dial from all bedrooms Full central heating Open parking available Child discount available Boule Bicycle rental Open terrace Covered terrace V meals Last d 21.30hrs Languages spoken: English & Spanish
ROOMS: (room only) d 280-480FF
**Reductions over 1 night Special breaks**
CARDS: ●● ■■ ▄▄

---

### ST-LÉGER-EN-BRAY Oise

*Domaine du Colombier* (Prop: M Menard)
1 Grande rue *60155*
☎ 344476716 FAX 344477263
(from Rouen take main route to N31 turn left at Rainvillers in direction of St Léger-en-Bray)
Near river Near lake Forest area Near motorway
3 en suite (shr) Full central heating Open parking available Child discount available 12yrs Fishing Languages spoken: English

---

### ST-QUENTIN Aisne

★ ★ ★ **Hotel des Canonniers**
15 rue des Canonniers *02100*
☎ 323628787 FAX 323628786
(from A26 or A1 follow signs 'Centre Ville')
Situated in a quiet street, and just a few steps away from the town centre, this former private residence dates back to the 18th century. Bought in 1990 and renovated throughout by the present owners, it has the atmosphere of a private house with the added convenience of attentive service. Elegant lounges are decorated with fine period furniture and rich fabrics. There are splendid suites, and bedrooms with ancient exposed beams, which are mostly situated in the old attic. In addition, there is a small shaded park for relaxation.
In town centre Near motorway
Closed 2nd & 3rd weeks Aug
9 en suite (bth/shr) (4 fmly) (1 with balcony) TV in all bedrooms STV Direct dial from all bedrooms Mini-bar in all bedrooms Night porter Full central heating Open parking available Supervised Pool table Open terrace Languages spoken: English & German                                   *contd.*

ROOMS: (room only) s 280-450FF; d 280-650FF
**Reductions over 1 night**
MEALS: Continental breakfast 45FF
CARDS: ●● ■■ ☲ ◍

**★ ★ ★ Le Grand Hotel**
6 rue Dachery *02100*
☎ 323626977 FAX 323625352
In town centre
*24 en suite (bth/shr) (2 fmly) TV in all bedrooms STV Radio in rooms Direct dial from all bedrooms Mini-bar in all bedrooms Licensed Lift Night porter Full central heating Open parking available Supervised Child discount available 10yrs V meals Last d 22.00hrs Languages spoken: English, German, Italian & Spanish*
CARDS: ●● ■■ ☲ ◍ Travellers cheques

**★ ★ Hotel Ibis**
14 pl de la Basilique *02100*
☎ 323674040 FAX 323626936
(in the town centre in front of the Basilique)
Forest area In town centre Near motorway
*49 en suite (bth/shr) (3 fmly) No smoking in 10 bedrooms TV in all bedrooms STV Direct dial from all bedrooms Licensed Lift Night porter Full central heating Child discount available 12yrs V meals Last d 22.00hrs Languages spoken: English & Spanish*
CARDS: ●● ■■ ☲ ◍ Travellers cheques

**★ ★ Hotel de la Paix et Albert 1er**
3 pl du 8-Octobre *02100*
☎ 323627762 FAX 323625352
Near river Near lake Forest area In town centre Near motorway
*52 en suite (bth/shr) (4 fmly) TV in all bedrooms STV Direct dial from all bedrooms Mini-bar in all bedrooms Licensed Lift Night porter Full central heating Open parking available Covered parking available Supervised Child discount available 12yrs V meals Last d 0.45hrs Languages spoken: English & Spanish*
CARDS: ●● ■■ ☲ ◍ Travellers cheques

**ST-RIQUIER** Somme

**★ ★ ★ Jean de Bruges**
18 pl de l'Église, BP 4 *80135*
☎ 322283030 FAX 322280069
(from A16 Calais/Paris motorway exit Abbeville Est and take D925 in the direction Saint-Riquier for 6km)

Dating from the 15th Century, white stone walls inside and out and ideally situated between Calais and Paris, the former abbot

house is sober and restful on the eye. Modern art and surprisingly comfortable Lloyd loom furniture both harmoniously enhance the style of the hotel. Try the glass roofed summer-house styled dining room for dinner, before retiring to the classically white bedroom to contemplate the eternal.
Near river Near lake Near sea Near beach Forest area In town centre Near motorway
*Closed Jan RS services unavalible Sunday Eve*
*9 en suite (bth/shr) (3 fmly) No smoking in 1 bedroom TV in all bedrooms STV Direct dial from all bedrooms Mini-bar in all bedrooms Licensed Lift Night porter Full central heating Open parking available Covered parking available (charged) Supervised Tennis Covered terrace Afternoon tea lounge V meals Last d 21.00hrs Languages spoken: English, Dutch & German*
ROOMS: (room only) s 450-550FF; d 550-1000FF
CARDS: ●● ■■ ☲ JCB Travellers cheques

**STE-CROIX** Aisne

**La Besace** (Prop: Jean Lecat)
21 rue Haute *02820*
☎ 323224874 FAX 323224874
(off N44 Laon-Reims road)
Five guests rooms available in a pretty village 15 kilometres from Laon. Meals available by reservation. Table-tennis, volley ball and bikes available on site.
Near lake Forest area Near motorway
*RS Oct-Mar, by reservation*
*5 en suite (bth/shr) (1 fmly) No smoking in 4 bedrooms Full central heating Open parking available Covered parking available Supervised Child discount available 10yrs Boule Bicycle rental V meals Last d 21.00hrs*
ROOMS: s 250FF
MEALS: Dinner 90FF
CARDS: ■■ Travellers cheques

**VERVINS** Aisne

**★ ★ ★ Tour Du Roy**
45 rue Général Leclerc *02140*
☎ 323980011 FAX 323980072
(from Calais take A26. Exit at J13 (Laon) and take N2 to Vervins. From Paris take N2, through Soissons, Laon to Vervins)
This handsome manor house was the historic setting for the announcement of Henry IV's ascencion to the throne, and in later years has welcomed many eminent heads of state. Stained-glass windows and hand-painted bathrooms are just a few of the attractive features. Fully renovated, the bedrooms have fine views of the terraces, park and landscaped square, and are equipped with modern facilities. The menu offers of a choice of skilfully executed dishes by chef Annie Desvignes, which are served in the elegant restaurant.
Near lake Forest area In town centre Near motorway
*22 en suite (bth/shr) 3 rooms in annexe (5 fmly) (5 with balcony) No smoking in 5 bedrooms TV in all bedrooms STV Direct dial from all bedrooms Mini-bar in 18 bedrooms Room-safe Licensed Full central heating Open parking available Supervised Child discount available 12yrs Open terrace V meals Last d 21.30hrs Languages spoken: English*
ROOMS: (room only) s 350-800FF; d 500-1000FF
**Reductions over 1 night Special breaks: St Valentine/Easter/Christmas/4 day breaks**
MEALS: Full breakfast 80FF Lunch 180-350FF&alc Dinner 180-350FF&alc
CARDS: ●● ■■ ☲ ◍ Travellers cheques

## VÉZILLY Aisne

**Bed & Breakfast** (Prop: M & Mme Noel)
6 rte de Fisnes *02130*
☎ 323692411 FAX 323692411
(access from Reims via A4 exit 21 (Dormans). Head towards
Fismes and Vézilly is second village, 4km from A4)
Forest area  Near motorway
*Closed Jan*
*2 en suite (bth/shr)  (1 fmly)  TV in 1 bedroom  Full central
heating  Open parking available  Covered parking available
Supervised  Boule  Open terrace  Table tennis*
CARDS: Travellers cheques

## VIC-SUR-AISNE Aisne

**Domaine des Jeanne** (Prop: M & Mme Martner)
r Dubarle *02290*
☎ 323555733 FAX 323555733
(approach via N31. In Vic-sur-Aisne, turn right opposite town
hall, then right again)
Constructed in 1611, this house was once the property of
Napoleon's finance minister and sits in a 2.5 hectare park
which leads down to the river. All the bedrooms open out onto
the park and guests may use the swimming pool and tennis
court. The house is sometimes used for conferences and social
gatherings. Shops nearby.
Near river  Forest area  In town centre  Near motorway
*5 en suite (shr)  (3 fmly)  TV in all bedrooms  Radio in rooms
Full central heating  Open parking available  Child discount
available 8yrs  Outdoor swimming pool (heated)  Tennis  Fishing
Boule  Mini-golf  Bicycle rental  Open terrace  Table tennis  Last
d 20.00hrs  Languages spoken: English*
ROOMS: s 340FF; d 380FF  **Special breaks**
MEALS: Dinner 100FF
CARDS: 💳 💳 Travellers cheques

**L'Orchidée** (Prop: M & Mme Henry)
2 bis av de la Gare *02290*
☎ 323553276 FAX 323559398
(from A1, exit for Compiègne and onto Vic-sur-Aisne)
Near river  Forest area  In town centre
*5 en suite (shr)  (2 fmly)  Full central heating  Open parking
available  Supervised  Child discount available 12 yrs  Barbecue
Languages spoken: English, German & Spanish*
CARDS: Travellers cheques

## VILLERS-AGRON Aisne

**Ferme du Château** (Prop: Xavier et Christine Ferry)
*02130*
☎ 323716067 FAX 323693654
(on A4 between Paris and Reims, take exit 21 then take second
right towards Villers Agron)
Set in its own grounds, on the route between Paris and Reims,
this charming 15th-century manor house is set on a farm in a
pretty village on the borders of Champagne and Picardy.
Guests are given a warm welcome and advice on local areas of
interest. Ideal for golfers.

***Ferme du Château***
Near river  Near lake  Forest area  Near motorway
*4 en suite (shr)  (1 fmly)  No smoking on premises  TV in all
bedrooms  Full central heating  Open parking available
Covered parking available  Child discount available 10 yrs
Tennis  Fishing  Bicycle rental  Last d 18.00hrs  Languages
spoken: English & German*
ROOMS: s fr 330FF; d 360-430FF  **Reductions over 1
night  Special breaks: (7 nights for price of 6)**
MEALS: Dinner 80-180FF
CARDS: Travellers cheques

## VILLERS-SUR-AUTHIE Somme

**La Bergerie** (Prop: M et Mme P Singer de Wazières)
*80120*
☎ 322292174 FAX 322293958
(approach via A16 Boulogne-Paris exit 24)
Guests receive a warm welcome at this traditional 19th century
farmhouse situated in pleasant parkland.
Near river  Near sea  Near beach  Forest area  Near motorway
*2 en suite (bth/shr)  No smoking on premises  Full central
heating  Open parking available  Bicycle rental  Languages
spoken: English*

## VINEUIL-ST-FIRMIN Oise

★ ★ ★ ★ **Golf Hotel Blue-Green**
rte d'Apremont *60500*
☎ 344584777 FAX 344585011
(A1 exit Chantilly, follow signs until you arrive at Château de
Chantilly)
Forest area  Near motorway
*102 en suite (bth/shr)  (20 with balcony)  TV in all bedrooms
STV Direct dial from all bedrooms  Mini-bar in all bedrooms
Licensed  Lift  Night porter  Full central heating  Air
conditioning in bedrooms  Open parking available  Child
discount available 12yrs  Outdoor swimming pool (heated)  Golf
18  Tennis  Pool table  Boule  Bicycle rental  Covered terrace
Archery  Table tennis  Volleyball  Last d 22.00hrs  Languages
spoken: English*
MEALS: Continental breakfast 100FF  Lunch 135-225FF&alc
Dinner 225FF&alc
CARDS: 💳 💳 💳 💳

# Champagne-Ardenne

Just three hours from Calais and a little over an hour from Paris, the region of Champagne-Ardenne has much to offer. Stretching from the Belgian frontier to the source of the Seine, the scenery is among the most varied in France. Here, you can escape into a world of sprawling Ardennes forests and wooded river valleys or gain a sense of perspective in the wide open spaces of the grain-growing plains. The region is actively promoted as a tourist destination and no visit is complete without calling at one of the many vineyards, where you can see at first hand how the famous sparkling wine is produced.

## ESSENTIAL FACTS

| | |
|---|---|
| DÉPARTEMENTS: | Ardennes, Aube, Haute-Marne, Marne |
| PRINCIPAL TOWNS | Troyes, Charleville-Mézières, Reims, Chaumont, Châlons-en-Champagne, Langres |
| PLACES TO VISIT: | Europe's largest fortified castle at Sedan; Centre des Métiers d'Art at Givet, housing contemporary art exhibitions; Parc de Vision at Belval is home to wild boar, deer & bears. |
| REGIONAL TOURIST OFFICE | 15, Avenue du Général Leclerc, B.P. 319 51013 Châlons-en-Champagne. Tel: 03 26 21 85 80 or 03 24 53 94 20 |
| LOCAL GASTRONOMIC DELIGHTS | Boudin blanc from Rethel, a delicious white sausage which can be grilled, boiled or served uncooked .Smoked hams & pâtés. Bayenne, a dish made from potatoes cooked in their own juice with slices of onions. Wild boar. Pied de cochon, pigs' feet cooked to a secret recipe in Ste-Ménehould. Croquignolles, pink biscuits from Reims. Cheeses: Grand Condé, Chaource, Remparts, Langres & the strong Rocroi. |
| DRINKS | Champagne, made by famous houses & many small producers. Still wines of the Coteaux Champenois or the Haute-Marne where wine making has been revived with great enthusiasm. The rosé wine from Les Riceys was a favourite of Louis XIV. |
| LOCAL CRAFTS WHAT TO BUY | Fayl-Billot: wickerwork & basketry. Nogent: artistic cutlery, superb knives, professional tools & luxury items |

## AIX-EN-OTHE Aube

### ★ ★ ★ *Auberge de la Scierie*
La Vove *10160*
☎ 325467126 FAX 325466569
(From Troyes A5 exit20 (Torvilliers) then N60 in direction of Sens, then D374 in direction 0f Aix-en-Othe & Tonnerre. From Paris A5 exit19 (Vulaines) then N60 in direction of Troyes, then D374)
Near river  Forest area
*Closed mid Oct-mid Apr Mon evening & Tues*
*14 en suite (bth/shr)  TV in all bedrooms  Direct dial from all bedrooms  Licensed  Full central heating  Open parking available  No children 12yrs  Outdoor swimming pool (heated)  Open terrace  Covered terrace  Last d 21.30hrs  Languages spoken: English German & Spanish*
CARDS: 💳 ▨ ▨ 🄳 Travellers cheques

## ARSONVAL Aube

### ★ ★ *Hostellerie de la Chaumière*
Sur N19 *10200*
☎ 325279102 FAX 325279026
(6km W of Bar-sur-Aube on N19 in the direction of Paris)
The owner and his English wife offer a warm welcome to their hotel. A stone country house once the home of a general of the empire era. In the grounds the coach house has been cleverly converted into modern bedrooms with views of the river.

Near river  Near lake  Forest area  Near motorway
*Closed 15 Feb-15 Mar*
*11 en suite (bth/shr)  9 rooms in annexe  (3 fmly)  TV in all bedrooms  Direct dial from all bedrooms  Licensed  Full central heating  Open parking available  Supervised  Child discount available 12yrs  Boule  Bicycle rental  Open terrace  V meals  Last d 21.00hrs  Languages spoken: English & Spanish*
ROOMS: (room only) s 300FF;  d 320-335FF
✱ **Special breaks**
MEALS: Continental breakfast 50FF  Lunch 100-300FF&alc  Dinner 100-300FF&alc✱
CARDS: 💳 ▨ ▨ Travellers cheques

## BANNAY Marne

### *Ferme de Bannay* (Prop: M & Mme Curfs)
*51270*
☎ 326528049 FAX 326594778
(from Èpernay, D951 towards Sézanne, at Baye, just before church turn right onto D343. At Bannay turn right, farm is before small bridge)
contd.

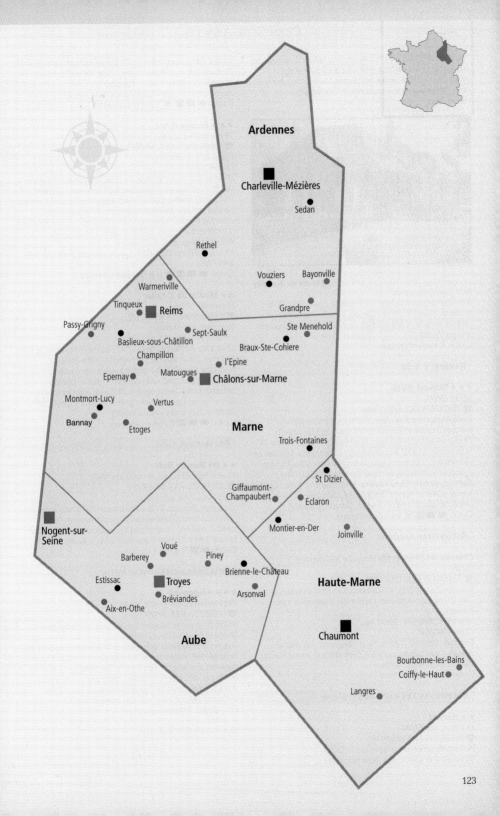

Ardennes

Charleville-Mézières

Sedan

Rethel

Vouziers

Bayonville

Warmeriville

Tinqueux

Reims

Grandpre

Passy-Grigny

Sept-Saulx

Ste Menehold

Baslieux-sous-Châtillon

Braux-Ste-Cohiere

Champillon

l'Epine

Epernay

Matougues

Châlons-sur-Marne

Montmort-Lucy

Vertus

Bannay

Etoges

Marne

Trois-Fontaines

St Dizier

Giffaumont-
Champaubert

Eclaron

Nogent-sur-
Seine

Montier-en-Der

Joinville

Voué

Barberey

Piney

Estissac

Brienne-le-Château

Troyes

Haute-Marne

Bréviandes

Arsonval

Aix-en-Othe

Chaumont

Aube

Bourbonne-les-Bains

Coiffy-le-Haut

Langres

The Curf family is happy to welcome you to Brie Champenoise, and to share their evening meal, where specialities could include guinea-fowl served with apples and cabbage, hot beef, farm cheeses and home-made jam. Relaxation is the order of the day here.

**Ferme de Bannay**
Near river Forest area
*4 en suite (bth/shr) (3 fmly) No smoking on premises TV in 1 bedroom Licensed Air conditioning in bedrooms Open parking available Child discount available V meals Languages spoken: English*
CARDS: Travellers cheques

**BARBEREY** Aube

★★★ **Novotel RN19**
RN 19 *10600*
☎ 325717474 FAX 325717450
(from A5 exit 20 follow 'Aéroport' signs, or from A26 exit 31 towards Troyes and Provins then follow signs for airport)
*83 en suite (bth/shr) (40 fmly) No smoking in 18 bedrooms TV in all bedrooms STV Direct dial from all bedrooms Mini-bar in all bedrooms Licensed Night porter Full central heating Air conditioning in bedrooms Open parking available Child discount available 16yrs Outdoor swimming pool Boule Open terrace Covered terrace Table tennis, Badminton, Karting V meals Languages spoken: English, German & Spanish*
CARDS: ●● ■■ ■■ ⑩ Travellers cheques

**BAYONVILLE** Ardennes

**Château de Landreville** (Prop: De Meixmoron)
*08240*
☎ 324300439 FAX 324300439
(from Reims take D980 to Mazagran,then D947 to Buzancy. Take D12 to Bayonville,then Landreville. Signposted from Buzancy)
Near river Near lake Forest area
*Closed Dec-Mar*
*4 en suite (bth/shr) (3 fmly) TV in 1 bedroom Full central heating Open parking available Child discount available 5yrs Languages spoken: English*
CARDS: Travellers cheques

**BOURBONNE-LES-BAINS** Haute-Marne

★★ **Hérard**
29 Grand Rue *52400*
☎ 325901333 FAX 325887767
(A31 exit Bourbonne-les-Bains & take D417)
Forest area In town centre Near motorway

*38 rms (18 bth/shr) (3 fmly) STV Direct dial from all bedrooms Licensed Lift Full central heating Child discount available 10yrs Tennis Bicycle rental Open terrace Covered terrace V meals Last d 21.00hrs Languages spoken: English*
CARDS: ●● ■■ ■■ ⑩ Travellers cheques

★★★ **Jeanne d'Arc**
12 rue Amiral *52400*
☎ 325904600 FAX 325887871
Forest area In town centre
*Closed 31 Oct-15 Mar*
*29 en suite (bth/shr) (2 fmly) TV in all bedrooms STV Direct dial from all bedrooms Mini-bar in 10 bedrooms Licensed Lift Full central heating Open parking available (charged) Covered parking available (charged) Supervised Child discount available Outdoor swimming pool Solarium Open terrace Last d 20.30hrs Languages spoken: English*
ROOMS: (room only) d 270-650FF
MEALS: Full breakfast 45FF Lunch 100-180FF Dinner 100-180FF&alc
CARDS: ●● ■■ ■■ ⑩ JCB Travellers cheques

★★ **Moulin de L'Achat**
Enfonvelle *52400*
☎ 325900954 FAX 325902182
Near river Forest area
*Closed 2 Nov-Etr*
*13 en suite (bth/shr) (2 fmly) (2 with balcony) No smoking in 1 bedroom Direct dial from all bedrooms Mini-bar in all bedrooms Licensed Full central heating Open parking available Supervised Child discount available Outdoor swimming pool Tennis Fishing Riding Sauna Gym Boule Bicycle rental Open terrace Covered terrace V meals Last d 22.30hrs Languages spoken: English*
CARDS: ●● ■■ ■■ Travellers cheques

**BRÉVIANDES** Aube

★★ **Du Pan De Bois**
35 av Général Leclerc, rte de Dijon *10450*
☎ 325750231 FAX 325496784
Forest area Near motorway
*31 en suite (bth/shr) TV in all bedrooms STV Radio in rooms Direct dial from all bedrooms Full central heating Open parking available Covered parking available (charged) Open terrace Last d 22.00hrs Languages spoken: English*
CARDS: ●● ■■ Travellers cheques

**CHÂLONS-EN-CHAMPAGNE** Marne

★★★ **Angleterre**
19 pl Monseigneur Tissier *51000*
☎ 326682151 FAX 326705167
(In the town centre between the church of Notre-Dame-en-Vaux and the Hôtel de la Préfecture)
Due to the impeccable management of the hosts Elisabeth and Jacky Michel, visitors to the Hotel Angleterre will look back on their stay as a delightful experience. The hotel features pretty bedrooms with well-co-ordinated decor and soft furnishings, and a private lounge for functions and social events. The restaurant has earned a first-class reputation in the Champagne-Ardenne region.
In town centre
*Closed Xmas & 14 Jul-5 Aug*

### Hotel D'Angleterre

*18 en suite (bth/shr) (2 fmly) TV in all bedrooms STV Direct dial from all bedrooms Mini-bar in all bedrooms Licensed Full central heating Air conditioning in bedrooms Open parking available Covered parking available (charged) Open terrace V meals Last d 21.30hrs Languages spoken: English & German*
CARDS: ●● ■■ ⅢⅢ ⅢⅢ Travellers cheques

### ★ ★ ★ Le Rénard
24 pl de la République *51000*
☎ 326680378 FAX 326645007
Near river Near lake In town centre Near motorway
*35 en suite (bth/shr) (4 fmly) No smoking in 12 bedrooms TV in all bedrooms STV Mini-bar in all bedrooms Licensed Full central heating Open parking available Supervised Child discount available 10yrs V meals Languages spoken: English & Spanish*
CARDS: ●● ■■ ⅢⅢ Travellers cheques

CHAMPILLON Marne

### ★ ★ ★ ★ Royal Champagne
Bellevue *51160*
☎ 326528711 FAX 326528969
Forest area Near motorway
*TV in 30 bedrooms STV Radio in rooms Direct dial from 30 bedrooms Mini-bar in 30 bedrooms Licensed Night porter Full central heating Open parking available Covered parking available Child discount available Tennis Solarium Bicycle rental Last d 21.30hrs Languages spoken: English & German*
CARDS: ●● ■■ ⅢⅢ ⅢⅢ Travellers cheques

**COIFFY-LE-HAUT** Haute-Marne

### Ferme du Granges du Vol-Adrien (Prop: M et Mme Pelletier)
*52400*
☎ 325900676
(exit A31 Montigny-le-Roi in direction Bourbonne-les-Bains)
Near river Forest area Near motorway
*5 en suite (bth/shr) Full central heating Open parking available Child discount available Bicycle rental*

**ECLARON** Haute-Marne

### ★ ★ Hotellerie du Moulin
rue du Moulin *52290*
☎ 325041776 FAX 325556701
This old wooden mill is situated on the banks of a river in lush green surroundings. The establishment offers its visitors a warm and friendly atmosphere and good traditional cuisine. Visitors can be assured of a good night's sleep in the spacious guest accommodation, where the only sound to be heard is the murmur of the river. In addition the hotel is close the Lac du Der-Chantecoq, the largest artificial lake in Europe.
Near river Near lake Near beach Forest area
*Closed 3 wks Jan & 2 wks Sep*
*5 en suite (bth/shr) (2 fmly) TV in all bedrooms Direct dial from all bedrooms Licensed Full central heating Open parking available Open terrace V meals Last d 21.00hrs Languages spoken: English, German & Spanish*
ROOMS: (room only) d 280-300FF
**Reductions over 1 night**
MEALS: Continental breakfast 35FF Lunch 85-165FF&alc Dinner 85-165FF&alc
CARDS: ●● ⅢⅢ Travellers cheques

**ÉPERNAY** Marne

### ★ ★ Climat de France
rue de Lorraine *51200*
☎ 326541739 FAX 326518878
(near village centre)
Near river Forest area In town centre Near motorway
*33 en suite (bth/shr) TV in all bedrooms Radio in rooms Direct dial from all bedrooms Licensed Full central heating Open parking available Open terrace Covered terrace Last d 10pm Languages spoken: English*
CARDS: ●● ⅢⅢ

**ÉPINE, L'** Marne

### ★ ★ ★ Aux Armes de Champagne
pl de la Basilique *51460*
☎ 326693030 FAX 326669231
(on N3, Metz-Verdun)
*Closed early Jan-mid Feb RS Nov-Mar (closed Sun evening & Monday)*
*21 en suite (bth/shr) 16 rooms in annexe (3 fmly) TV in 37 bedrooms Direct dial from 37 bedrooms Mini-bar in 37 bedrooms Licensed Full central heating Open parking available Child discount available 12yrs Tennis Mini-golf V meals Last d 21.00hrs Languages spoken: English*
ROOMS: (room only) d 550-850FF ✱
MEALS: Full breakfast 70FF Lunch 240-525FF Dinner 240-525FF
CARDS: ●● ■■ ⅢⅢ ⅢⅢ Travellers cheques

**ESTISSAC** Aube

### Moulin d'Eguebaude (Prop: Edouard Mesley)
*10190*
☎ 325404218 FAX 325404092
(in Estissac take rue Pierre-Brossolette and continue to the end)
Built in 1255 and set in a flower-filled garden beside a clear running river, this guest house is part of an old flour mill which has been superbly renovated. Restaurant available, which seats 80 people, or guests are invited to eat with their hosts. Specialities include trout and salmon (both fresh and smoked).
Near river Near lake Forest area Near motorway
*5 en suite (bth/shr) (1 fmly) No smoking on premises TV in all bedrooms Full central heating Open parking available Supervised Child discount available 4yrs Fishing Sauna V meals Last d 16.00hrs Languages spoken: English, German & Spanish*
ROOMS: s 280-320FF; d 320-360FF
✱ **Reductions over 1 night**
MEALS: Lunch 108-169FF Dinner 108-169FF✱
CARDS: Travellers cheques

contd.

## ÉTOGES Marne

**★ ★ ★ Château d'Etoges**
par Montmort-Lucy 51270
☎ 326593008 FAX 326593557
(from Paris take A4 and exit La Ferté-sous-Jouarre and take
direction of Châlons-sur-Marne to Etoges, or exit for Epernay
cross the village and take direction of Sézanne, to Etoges)
Near river Near lake Forest area Near motorway
*20 en suite (bth/shr) (3 fmly) TV available Direct dial from all
bedrooms Licensed Full central heating Open parking
available Supervised Child discount available 10yrs Fishing
Pool table Bicycle rental Open terrace Boating Croquet Last d
21.30hrs Languages spoken: English & German*
CARDS: ●● ■■ ☲ ⑩ Travellers cheques

## GIFFAUMONT-CHAMPAUBERT Marne

**★ ★ Le Cheval Blanc**
rue du Lac 51290
☎ 326726265 FAX 326739697
Near river Near lake Forest area Near motorway
*16 rms (8 bth 6 shr) TV in all bedrooms Direct dial from all
bedrooms Licensed Full central heating Open parking
available Supervised Child discount available 12yrs Open
terrace Last d 21.30hrs Languages Spoken: English, German &
Spanish*
CARDS: ●● ■■ ☲ Travellers cheques

## GRANDPRÉ Ardennes

**Ferme d'Argonne** (Prop: Mme Dominique Arnould)
rue de Montflix 08250
☎ 324305287 FAX 324305287
(near Vouziers in the south of Ardenne in the direction of
Verdun, at the beginning of the village the third house on the
left)
Near river Near lake Forest area
*5 rms (4 bth) (3 fmly) (4 with balcony) No smoking on
premises TV in 1 bedroom Full central heating Open parking
available Covered parking available Child discount available
8yrs Fishing V meals Last d 19.00hrs*
ROOMS: s 160FF; d 220FF
MEALS: Dinner 70FF✱
CARDS: Travellers cheques

## JOINVILLE Haute-Marne

**★ ★ Poste**
pl de la Grêve 52300
☎ 325941263 FAX 325943623
Near river In town centre Near motorway
Closed 10-31 Jan
*10 en suite (bth/shr) (3 fmly) TV in all bedrooms Direct dial
from all bedrooms Licensed Full central heating Open parking
available Covered parking available (charged) Supervised
Child discount available 11yrs Boule Open terrace Last d
21.30hrs Languages spoken: English*
ROOMS: (room only) d 220-280FF
MEALS: Full breakfast 28FF Lunch 80-220FF&alc Dinner
80-220FF
CARDS: ●● ■■ ☲ ⑩ Travellers cheques

## LANGRES Haute-Marne

**★ ★ Le Cheval Blanc**
4 rue de l'Estres 52200
☎ 325870700 FAX 325872313
In town centre Near motorway
Closed 8-17 Feb
*22 en suite (bth/shr) 11 rooms in annexe (6 fmly) TV in all
bedrooms STV Direct dial from all bedrooms Mini-bar in 11
bedrooms Licensed Full central heating Open parking
available (charged) Covered parking available (charged)
Supervised Open terrace V meals Last d 21.30hrs Languages
spoken: English & Spanish*
ROOMS: (room only) s 300-320FF; d 320-400FF
MEALS: Full breakfast 48FF Lunch 95-125FF&alc Dinner
135-350FF&alc
CARDS: ●● ■■ ☲ Travellers cheques

**★ ★ Auberge des Voiliers**
1 rue des Voiliers, Lac de La Liez 52200
☎ 325870574 FAX 325872422
(follow signs to Lac de Liez. Hotel is on lake shore)
The Auberge des Voiliers stands on the shores of Lac de la
Liez, the largest lake in the region, and offers a stunning view
of the lake and the fortified city. For those guests who want to
relax and take in the sun, the beach is just a few steps away
from the hotel, whilst a large choice of leisure pursuits is
available for the more energetic. The bedrooms are
comfortable with good amenities, and the restaurant serves a
wide range of fresh fish delicacies and regional dishes.

Near lake Near beach Forest area
Closed 31 Jan-14 Mar
*8 en suite (bth/shr) 3 rooms in annexe (1 fmly) (4 with balcony)
TV in all bedrooms STV Direct dial from all bedrooms
Licensed Full central heating Open parking available Child
discount available 10yrs Open terrace V meals Last d 21.00hrs
Languages spoken: English & German*
ROOMS: (room only) d 300-350FF **Special breaks**
MEALS: Full breakfast 38FF Lunch fr 80FF&alc Dinner fr
100FF&alc
CARDS: ●● ☲ Maestro Travellers cheques

## MATOUGUES Marne

**La Grosse Haie** (Prop: Jacques & Nicole Songy)
chemin de St-Pierre 51510
☎ 326709712 FAX 326701242
(A26 exit St-Gibrien onto N27 after toll on to D3 in direction of
Epernay)
*3 en suite (bth/shr) No smoking on premises Full central
heating Open parking available Child discount available 10yrs*

*Bicycle rental Last d 18.00hrs Languages spoken: English &
German*
ROOMS: s 200FF; d 265FF
MEALS: Dinner 105FF

### NOGENT-SUR-SEINE Aube

★ ★ **Le Beau Rivage**
20 rue Villiers aux Choux *10400*
☎ 325398422 FAX 325391832
(on N19 between Provins and Troyes)
Near river
*Closed 3 wks Feb*
*7 en suite (bth/shr) TV in all bedrooms STV Direct dial from all
bedrooms Licensed Full central heating Open terrace Last d
21.00hrs Languages spoken: English*
ROOMS: (room only) s 250-260FF; d 280-290FF
MEALS: Continental breakfast 35FF Lunch 100-205FF&alc
Dinner 100-205FF&alc
CARDS: ● ● ▨ Travellers cheques

### PASSY-GRIGNY Marne

**Le Temple** (Prop: Michel and Chantal Le Varlet)
*51700*
☎ 326529001 FAX 326521886
(from A4 towards Paris exit 21 (Dormans) take N980 and turn
right. After 1km take small road with trees and continue
400mtrs)
A working farm in the heart of the country. Close by are the
Champagne vineyards of Reims and Epernay. Dinner is not
taken with your hosts.
Forest area Near motorway
*9 rms (4 shr) Full central heating Open parking available
Supervised Child discount available -2 yrs Languages spoken:
English*
ROOMS: s fr 280FF; d fr 300FF
MEALS: Dinner 135-150FF
CARDS: Travellers cheques

### PINEY Aube

★ ★ **Le Tadorne**
3 pl de la Halle *10220*
☎ 325463035 FAX 325463649
The hotel is housed in a half-timbered 18th-century building
which is typical of the region. All the bedrooms are
individually appointed and all are equipped with modern
amenities and quality furnishings - some have exposed beams
and timbered walls. The restaurant serves regional cuisine,
and house specialities include home-made foie gras and mille-
feuille de St Jacques à la ciboulette.

Near river Near lake Forest area In town centre Near
motorway
*Closed 1-15 Feb*
*20 rms (17 bth/shr) 5 rooms in annexe (6 fmly) TV in all
bedrooms STV Licensed Night porter Full central heating
Open parking available Supervised Child discount available
3yrs Outdoor swimming pool (heated) Pool table Boule Mini-
golf Bicycle rental Open terrace V meals Last d 22.00hrs
Languages spoken: English & German*
ROOMS: (room only) s 160-345FF; d 250-315FF
**Special breaks**
MEALS: Full breakfast 40FF Lunch 100-250FF&alc Dinner
88-245FF
CARDS: ● ● ▨ Travellers cheques

### REIMS Marne

★ ★ ★ ★ *Boyer Les Crayeres*
64 bd Henri Vasnier *51100*
☎ 326828080 FAX 326826552
(From A4 take exit Reims St-Remi, then head towards
Luxembourg & Charleville. Turn right at rdbt towards Reims
Prunay)
Forest area Near motorway
*Closed 23 Dec-13 Jan*
*19 en suite (bth/shr) 3 rooms in annexe (2 with balcony) TV in
all bedrooms STV Radio in rooms Direct dial from all
bedrooms Mini-bar in all bedrooms Licensed Lift Night porter
Full central heating Air conditioning in bedrooms Open
parking available Covered parking available (charged)
Supervised Tennis Boule Open terrace V meals Last d
22.30hrs Languages spoken: English ,German & Italian*
CARDS: ● ● ▨ ▣ Travellers cheques

★ ★ ★ *Hotel Holiday Inn Garden Court*
46 rue Buirette *51100*
☎ 326475600 FAX 326474575
In town centre Near motorway
*82 en suite (bth/shr) (5 fmly) (16 with balcony) No smoking in
40 bedrooms TV in all bedrooms STV Radio in rooms Direct
dial from all bedrooms Mini-bar in all bedrooms Licensed Lift
Night porter Full central heating Air conditioning in bedrooms
Covered parking available (charged) Child discount available
Open terrace Last d 22.00hrs Languages spoken: English &
German*
CARDS: ● ● ▨ ▣ Travellers cheques

★ ★ ★ *Hotel de la Paix* (Best Western)
9 rue Buirette *51100*
☎ 326400408 FAX 326477504
In town centre
*106 en suite (bth/shr) (15 fmly) No smoking in 4 bedrooms TV
in all bedrooms STV Direct dial from all bedrooms Mini-bar in
all bedrooms Licensed Lift Night porter Full central heating
Air conditioning in bedrooms Open parking available (charged)
Covered parking available (charged) Supervised Child
discount available 12yrs Outdoor swimming pool Open terrace
V meals Languages spoken: English, German, Italian &
Spanish*
CARDS: ● ● ▨ ▣ JCB Travellers cheques

★ ★ ★ **New Hotel Europe**
29 rue Buirette *51100*
☎ 326473939 FAX 326401437
(From A4 exit 'Reims Centre' follow signs for 'Hôtels
Buirette'and New Hotel Europe.)
In town centre Near motorway *contd.*

**New Hotel Europe**
54 en suite (bth/shr) (16 fmly) (3 with balcony) No smoking in 10 bedrooms TV in all bedrooms STV Radio in rooms Direct dial from all bedrooms Mini-bar in all bedrooms Room-safe (charged) Licensed Lift Night porter Full central heating Air conditioning in bedrooms Open parking available (charged) Supervised Child discount available 12yrs Open terrace Languages spoken: English & German
ROOMS: (room only) s 395-430FF; d 430-495FF
CARDS: ●● ■■ ☲☲ ⑨ JCB Travellers cheques

★ ★ ★ **Quality Hotel**
37 bd Paul Doumer 51100
☎ 326400108 FAX 326403413
Near lake In town centre Near motorway
79 en suite (bth/shr) (4 fmly) (1 with balcony) No smoking in 12 bedrooms TV in all bedrooms STV Direct dial from all bedrooms Mini-bar in all bedrooms Licensed Lift Night porter Full central heating Air conditioning in bedrooms Open parking available (charged) Covered parking available (charged) Child discount available 12yrs Open terrace Last d 22.00hrs Languages spoken: English
CARDS: ●● ■■ ☲☲ ⑨ Travellers cheques

★ ★ **Reflets Bleus**
12 rue Gabriel Voisin 51100
☎ 326825979 FAX 326825392
Near motorway
41 rms (4 fmly) No smoking in 2 bedrooms TV in all bedrooms Radio in rooms Direct dial from all bedrooms Mini-bar in all bedrooms Licensed Night porter Full central heating Open parking available Supervised Child discount available 12yrs Open terrace V meals Last d 21.45hrs Languages spoken: English & German
CARDS: ●● ■■ ☲☲ ⑨ Travellers cheques

★ ★ **Du Cheval Rouge**
1 rue Chanzy 51800
☎ 326608104 FAX 326609311
Near river Forest area In town centre Near motorway
Closed 20 Nov-11 Dec
20 en suite (bth/shr) (1 fmly) TV in all bedrooms STV Radio in rooms Direct dial from all bedrooms Licensed Full central heating V meals Last d 22.00hrs Languages spoken: English & Spanish
ROOMS: (room only) s 240-270FF; d 260-270FF
MEALS: Continental breakfast 35FF Lunch 92-280FF&alc Dinner 92-280FF&alc
CARDS: ●● ■■ ☲☲ ⑨ Travellers cheques

★ ★ ★ **Cheval Blanc**
rue du Moulin 51400
☎ 326039027 FAX 326039709
(from Reims-A4-exit 'Cormontreuil' towards Chalons-sur-Marne-N44-exit Les Petites Loges/Sept Saulx. From Troyes-A26-exit Laveuve/Metz towards Reims-N44-exit les Petites Loges/Sept Saulx.)
Near river Forest area Near motorway
Closed 23 Jan-20 Feb
25 en suite (bth/shr) 4 rooms in annexe (1 fmly) (11 with balcony) TV in all bedrooms Direct dial from all bedrooms Mini-bar in all bedrooms Licensed Full central heating Open parking available Covered parking available Supervised Child discount available 10yrs Tennis Fishing Mini-golf Bicycle rental Open terrace V meals Last d 21.30hrs Languages spoken: English, German & Spanish
CARDS: ●● ■■ ☲☲ ⑨ Travellers cheques

★ ★ ★ **Assiette Champenoise**
40 av P V Couturier 51430
☎ 326846464 FAX 326041569
(Access via A4/A26 exit22)
In town centre Near motorway
62 en suite (bth/shr) TV in all bedrooms STV Direct dial from all bedrooms Mini-bar in all bedrooms Room-safe Licensed Lift Night porter Full central heating Open parking available Supervised Child discount available 12yrs Indoor swimming pool (heated) Sauna Open terrace V meals Last d 22.00hrs Languages spoken: English, German & Italian
CARDS: ●● ■■ ☲☲ ⑨ Travellers cheques

★ ★ ★ **Novotel Reims Tinqueux**
rte de Soissons BP 12 51431
☎ 326081161 FAX 326087205
(From A4/A26 take exit Reims-Tinqueux)
Near motorway
127 en suite (bth/shr) (50 fmly) No smoking in 42 bedrooms TV in all bedrooms STV Radio in rooms Direct dial from all bedrooms Mini-bar in all bedrooms Licensed Night porter Full central heating Air conditioning in bedrooms Open parking available Supervised Child discount available 16yrs Outdoor swimming pool (heated) Open terrace V meals Last d 24.00hrs Languages spoken: English & German
CARDS: ●● ■■ ☲☲ ⑨

★ ★ ★ **Royal Hotel**
22 bld Carnot 10000
☎ 325731999 FAX 325734785
(leave A26 in direction of Troyes centre, then follow signs "gare SNCF" or "Office of Tourisme", hotel close to the boulevard overlooking public gardens)
In town centre
Closed 20 Dec-12 Jan
37 en suite (bth/shr) (3 fmly) (7 with balcony) TV in all bedrooms STV Radio in rooms Direct dial from all bedrooms Licensed Lift Night porter Full central heating Child discount available 12yrs Pool table V meals Last d 21.30hrs Languages spoken: English, Dutch & German
MEALS: Full breakfast 50FF Continental breakfast 50FF Lunch 125-165FF&alc Dinner 125-165FF&alc
CARDS: ●● ■■ ☲☲ ⑨

### VERTUS Marne

**★ ★ Le Thibault IV**
2 pl de la République *51130*
☎ 326520124 FAX 326526800
(off A26)
Forest area
*Closed 12-29 Feb*
*17 en suite (bth/shr) (4 fmly) TV in all bedrooms Direct dial*
*from all bedrooms Licensed Full central heating Child*
*discount available V meals Last d 21.30hrs Languages spoken:*
*English & German*
ROOMS: (room only) s fr 270FF; d fr 299FF
**Special breaks**
MEALS: Continental breakfast 40FF Lunch 100-195FF&alc
Dinner 100-195FF&alc
CARDS: ●● ▆ Travellers cheques

### VOUÉ Aube

**★ ★ ★ Le Marais**
39 rte Imperiale *10150*
☎ 325375533 FAX 325375329
(approach via A26 exit 30/31)
Near river Near lake Near motorway
*20 en suite (bth/shr) (2 fmly) TV in all bedrooms Direct dial*
*from all bedrooms Night porter Full central heating Open*
*parking available Child discount available 2yrs Outdoor*
*swimming pool Pool table Open terrace Last d 21.00hrs*
*Languages spoken: English & German*
ROOMS: (room only) s fr 270FF; d fr 320FF **✽ Reductions**
**over 1 night Special breaks: 3 night breaks**
MEALS: Full breakfast 45FF Lunch 100-160FF
Dinner 100-160FF✽
CARDS: ●● ▆ Travellers cheques

### VOUZIERS Ardennes

**Le Pied des Monts**
Grivy-Loisy *08400*
☎ 324719238 FAX 324719621
Near river Near lake Forest area
*6 en suite (bth/shr) (4 fmly) TV in 5 bedrooms Full central*
*heating Open parking available Child discount available 10yrs*
*Last d 20.00hrs*
ROOMS: d 265-365FF **✽ Special breaks**
MEALS: Continental breakfast 25FF Lunch 95-160FF
Dinner 95-160FF✽
CARDS: ●● ▆

### WARMERIVILLE Marne

**★ ★ Auberge du Val des Bois**
3 rue du 8 Mai 1945 *51110*
☎ 326033209 FAX 326033784
(NE of Reims on the RN51)
Near river Forest area Near motorway
*21 en suite (bth/shr) TV in 19 bedrooms Direct dial from all*
*bedrooms Mini-bar in 2 bedrooms Licensed Full central*
*heating Open parking available (charged) Covered parking*
*available (charged) Supervised Child discount available 5yrs*
*Open terrace V meals Last d 21.00hrs Languages spoken:*
*German*
CARDS: ●● ▆

---

### EVENTS & FESTIVALS:

| | |
|---|---|
| Jan | Joinville Winter Festival |
| Mar | Poucy La Nuit de la Chouette; Tintamars (March Madness) - music & comedy in numerous villages in southern Haute-Marne; |
| Apr | Sedan Arts Festival & Craft Market; |
| May | Revin Bread Festival; Troyes Champagne Fair; |
| Jun | Sedan Medieval Fair; Reims Folklore Festival Celebration of St Joan; Trois-Fontaines Horse & Carriage Festival; Châlons-Sur-Marne Furies Festival (street theatre & circus artists); Launois sur- Vence Art & Creative Crafts Festival; |
| Jul | Aube Wine Festival; Baslieux-sur-Châtillon Champagne Festival; Langres Festival (Sats & Suns); Vendresse Light & Sound Show at Cassina Castle; |
| Aug | Estissac Local Food Fair; Aube Wine Festival; Langres Halbardiers' Round - spectators mix with the cast & become actors for an evening (Fris & Sats); |
| Sep | Brienne-le-Château Choucroute Festival; Montier-en Der,Thursdays at The Stud (Haras) - horses & carriages in ceremonial dress at 3pm; Brienne-le Château Sauerkraut Fair; Charleville-Mézières World Puppet Theatre Festival |
| Oct | Sedan Model Collectors Fair; Reims Marathon; Montier-en-Der Thursdays at The Stud (Haras) - |

horses & carriages in ceremonial dress at 3pm; Reims Marathon; Troyes Nights of Champagne (voice festival)

| | |
|---|---|
| Nov | Montier-en-Der, Thursdays at The Stud Farm - horses & carriages in ceremonial dress at 3pm |
| Dec | Braux-Ste-Cohière Shepherds' Christmas -traditiona gathering of shepherds in the Castle on Christmas Eve, with music followed by midnight mass. |

### Discovering 2000 Years of History

With the remains of numerous fortifications acting as monuments to the past, the ravages of war still cast a dark shadow over Champagne-Ardenne. It is hard to imagine it now, but by the end of the First World War, the city of Reims, where the Kings of France were crowned in the magnificent cathedral, had been reduced to little more than a heap of rubble, and the castle at Sedan, constructed between the 11th and 16th centuries, has witnessed numerous bloody conflicts over the years. The Fortifications Route, one of several signposted tourist routes in the Ardennes, brings 2000 years of history and bloodshed to life, providing a unique insight into how this corner of France has defended itself against attack down the centuries.

# Nord/Pas de Calais

The gateway to France, Nord-Pas de Calais is often overlooked by the tourist, but it has much to offer. The Opal Coast, an unspoilt coastline with vast sandy beaches, stretches from the Belgian border right down to Berck-sur-Mer. Characteristic bell towers and carillons represent periods of the region's often turbulent history, and there are museums, attractions, fortified towns and five regional nature parks. This is a land of old customs and warm hospitality, where barely a week passes without the celebration of a fête, fair, festival, procession or parade.

## ESSENTIAL FACTS

| | |
|---|---|
| DÉPARTEMENTS: | Nord, Pas-de-Calais |
| PRINCIPAL TOWNS | Calais, Lille, Arras, Bourlogne-sur-Mer, Cambrai, Dunkirk (Dunkerque), Valenciennes |
| PLACES TO VISIT: | Boulogne-sur-Mer: Nausicaà (National Sea World Centre), Chateau des Comtes de Boulogne. La Coupole (history of war & rockets), Helfaut. Historical Mining Centre, Lewarde. Palais de Beaux Arts, Lille |
| REGIONAL TOURIST OFFICE | 6 Place Mendès-France, 59800 Lille Tel 33 320 14 57 75  Fax 33 320 14 57 58 |
| LOCAL GASTRONOMIC DELIGHTS | Carbonade flamande, beef cooked in beer. Pot'je vleish, cold meat brawn. Anguille vert, eel with herbs. Soupe de poissons, fish soup. Tarte aux sucre, brown sugar tart. Gaufres, waffles. Cramique, type of brioche with currants. Betises, mint humbugs. Chuques du Nord, coffee sweets with caramel centre. Babeluttes de Lille, caramels. Cheeses: Maroilles, Vieux Lille, Boulette d'Avesnes, Mont des Cats. |
| DRINKS | Speciality beers: Jenlain, Ch'ti, 3 Monts, Septante-Cinq, Angelus, Choulette, among many. Juniper gin in Houlle, Wambrechies & Loos.  Perlé de Groseille (sparkling redcurrant) |
| LOCAL CRAFTS WHAT TO BUY | Bellignies: glass engraving. Camphin-en-Carambault: puppets. Cassel: wood sculpture. Desvres: pottery & ceramics. Masny: miniature paintings. St-Laurent-Blangy: silk paintings. Valenciennes: lace. |

**AIRE-SUR-LA-LYS** Pas-de-Calais

★ ★ ★ ★ *Hostellerie des 3 Mousquetaires*
Château du Fort de la Rédoute *62120*
☎ 321390111 FAX 321395010
(from Calais A26 exit4, direction of Aire-sur-la-Lys, on N43)
Near river  Near lake  Forest area  Near motorway
Closed 20 Dec-20 Jan
*33 en suite (bth/shr)  3 rooms in annexe  (2 fmly)  (2 with balcony)  TV in all bedrooms  STV  Direct dial from all bedrooms  Licensed  Night porter  Full central heating  Open parking available  Supervised  Child discount available 12yrs  Gym  Boule  Mini-golf  Open terrace  V meals  Last d 21.45hrs  Languages spoken: English*
CARDS: ● ■ ▆ ◉ Travellers cheques

**AMETTES** Pas-de-Calais

**Bed & Breakfast** (Prop: M & Mme Gevas)
2 rue de l'Église *62260*
☎ 321271502
Near river  Near motorway
*3 en suite (shr)  No smoking on premises  TV in 1 bedroom  Full central heating  Open parking available  Supervised  Child discount available 5yrs  Languages spoken: English*
ROOMS: s fr 120FF;  d fr 170FF
**Reductions over 1 night**

**ARDRES** Pas-de-Calais

★ ★ ★ **Le Manoir de Bois-en-Ardres** (Prop: Françoise et Thierry Roger)
1530 rue de St-Quentin *62610*
☎ 321859778 FAX 321364807
(from Calais take N43 towards St Omer.On entering Bois-en-Ardres cross 1st rdbt & turn left at 2nd & continue for 1km)

Françoise and Thierry Roger welcome guests to their recently restored manor house, set in 12.5 acres of parkland 1km from the historical town of Ardres.
Near lake  Forest area  Near motorway
*2 en suite (shr)  (2 fmly)  No smoking on premises  Full central heating  Open parking available  Child discount available 3yrs  Pool table  Boule  Table tennis  Languages spoken: English*
ROOMS: d 330-490FF
CARDS: Travellers cheques

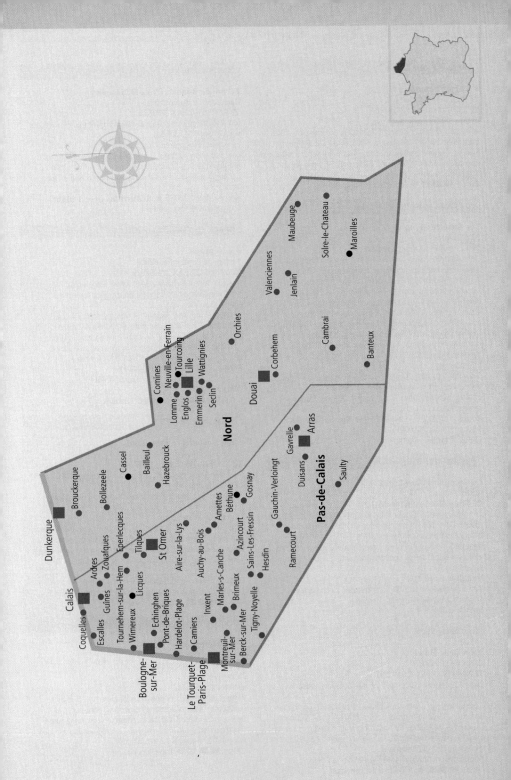

Nord

Pas-de-Calais

Maubeuge
Solre-le-Chateau
Maroilles
Valenciennes
Jenlain
Orchies
Cambrai
Corbehem
Banteux
Douai
Comines
Neuville-en-Ferrain
Tourcoing
Lille
Wattignies
Englos
Emmerin
Seclin
Lomme
Arras
Gavrelle
Duisans
Saulty
Gauchin-Verloingt
Bailleul
Cassel
Hazebrouck
Brouckerque
Bollezeele
Dunkerque
Eperlecques
St Omer
Tilques
Aire-sur-la-Lys
Amettes
Béthune
Gosnay
Ramecourt
Calais
Ardres
Zoutafques
Licques
Auchy-au-Bois
Azincourt
Sains-Les-Fressin
Hesdin
Tournehem-sur-la-Hem
Coquelles
Escalles
Guînes
Wimereux
Echinghen
Pont-de-Briques
Hardelot-Plage
Camiers
Inxent
Marles-s-Canche
Brimeux
Tigny-Noyelle
Berck-sur-Mer
Boulogne-
sur-Mer
Le Tourquet-
Paris-Plage
Montreuil-
sur-Mer

131

## ARRAS Pas-de-Calais

**★★ Trois Luppars**
49 Grand Place *62000*
☎ 321074141 FAX 321242480
In town centre  Near motorway
*42 en suite (bth/shr)  (8 fmly)  TV in all bedrooms  Direct dial from all bedrooms  Mini-bar in 2 bedrooms  Lift  Full central heating  Covered parking available (charged)  Supervised  Child discount available 6yrs  Sauna  Bicycle rental  Table tennis  Languages spoken: English*
CARDS: ●● ■■ ☲ ◨ Travellers cheques

## AUCHY-AU-BOIS Pas-de-Calais

**Les Cohettes** (Prop: Gina Bulot)
28 r de Pernes
☎ 321020947 FAX 321028168
(45 mins from Calais. Take A26 to exit 4, onto D341 towards Arras. Approx 12 minutes after Therouanne is Auchy-au-Bois. At x-rds "Vert Dragon" turn right & follow green & white "chambre d'hôtes" sign, 2nd house after church)
Five guest rooms - in a restored old stone farmhouse, all of which are very comfortable. A quiet place ideal for walkers and children. A large garden has been laid to lawn and there is a garden room with table-tennis, javelot (a local game with javelins) and pétanque. Situated near the church in the village, between Vimy and St Omer, 45 minutes from Calais.
Forest area
*5 en suite (bth/shr)  (2 fmly)  No smoking on premises  Radio in rooms  Full central heating  Open parking available  Child discount available 10yrs  Boule  Last d 17.00hrs  Languages spoken: English & German*
ROOMS: s fr 200FF; d 240-280FF  ✱ **Special breaks**
MEALS: Dinner fr 100FF
CARDS: Travellers cheques

## AZINCOURT Pas-de-Calais

**La Gacogne** (Prop: M-J & P Fenet)
*62310*
☎ 321044561 FAX 321044561
(from A26 S of Calais take D928 towards Abbeville, Hesdin. After Fruges take left turn in Ruisseauville towards Blangy/Tramecourt for Azincourt)
Near the woods of Agincourt and the pretty village of Artois, visitors will find an old converted schoolhouse built from white stones.
Near river  Forest area
*4 en suite (shr)  No smoking on premises  Open parking available  Languages spoken: English*
ROOMS: d 300FF  ✱

## BAILLEUL Nord

**★★★ Belle Hotel**
19 rue de Lille *59270*
☎ 328491900 FAX 328492211
(from A25 take exit 10 in the direction of town centre)
In town centre  Near motorway
*31 en suite (bth)  4 rooms in annexe  (10 fmly)  No smoking in 12 bedrooms  TV in all bedrooms  Direct dial from all bedrooms  Licensed  Night porter  Full central heating  Open parking available  Supervised  Child discount available 11yrs  Languages spoken: English & Portuguese*
ROOMS: (room only) s 415FF; d 490FF
CARDS: ●● ■■ ☲ ◨ JCB Travellers cheques

## BANTEUX Nord

**Ferme de Bonavis** (Prop: M Delcambre)
Carrefour de Bonavis *59266*
☎ 327785508 FAX 327785508
(off N44, 10km from Cambrai, 25km from St Quentin. Access via A26 exit 9 Masnières)
Near river  Forest area  Near motorway
*6 en suite (shr)  (3 fmly)  (1 with balcony)  No smoking on premises  TV in 4 bedrooms  Full central heating  Open parking available  Covered parking available  Boule  Open terrace*
ROOMS: d 250-280FF  ✱ **Reductions over 1 night**
CARDS: Travellers cheques

## BERCK-SUR-MER Pas-de-Calais

**★★ Neptune**
Esplanade Parmentier *62600*
☎ 321092121 FAX 321092929
(Calais A16 exit Berck-sur-Mer, follow plage signs)
Near sea  Near beach  In town centre  Near motorway
*Closed 1st 3 wks Jan*
*63 en suite (bth/shr)  (6 fmly)  (4 with balcony)  TV in all bedrooms  STV  Direct dial from all bedrooms  Licensed  Lift  Night porter  Full central heating  Open parking available (charged)  Child discount available  Open terrace  Last d 22.00hrs  Languages spoken: English & German*
ROOMS: s 210-290FF; d 250-380FF
MEALS: Full breakfast 38FF  Lunch fr 95FF  Dinner fr 95FF
CARDS: ●● ■■ ☲ ◨ Travellers cheques

## BOLLEZEELE Nord

**★★★ Hostellerie Saint-Louis**
47 rue de l'Église *59470*
☎ 328688183 FAX 328680117
(A25 Lille-Dunkerque exit 16 Bergues in direction St Omer for 10km to Bollezeele)
Near sea  Near beach  Forest area  In town centre  Near motorway
*Closed 2-29 Jan*
*28 en suite (bth/shr)  (3 fmly)  TV in all bedrooms  STV  Direct dial from all bedrooms  Licensed  Lift  Full central heating  Open parking available  Pool table  Open terrace  Table tennis  V meals  Last d 21.00hrs  Languages spoken: English & Dutch*
ROOMS: (room only) s 250-300FF; d 320-450FF
MEALS: Continental breakfast 35FF  Dinner 140-280FF
CARDS: ●● ■■ ☲ Travellers cheques

## BOULOGNE-SUR-MER Pas-de-Calais

**★★★ Metropole**
51 rue Thiers *62200*
☎ 321315430 FAX 321304572
In town centre
*Closed 21 Dec-5 Jan*
*25 en suite (bth/shr)  (2 fmly)  (7 with balcony)  TV in all bedrooms  Direct dial from all bedrooms  Mini-bar in all bedrooms  Licensed  Lift  Night porter  Full central heating  Open parking available (charged)  Covered parking available (charged)  Languages spoken: English*
CARDS: ●● ■■ ☲ ◨ Travellers cheques

## BRIMEUX Pas-de-Calais

**Ferme du Saule** (Prop: M et Mme G Trunnet)
20 rue de l'Église *62170*
☎ 321060128 FAX 321814014
(6km from Monreuil-sur-Mer, towards Beaurainville on D349.
In Brimeux, turn left at X-roads. Establishment 300mtrs on
right opposite church)
This establishment is an 18th-century working farm close to a
river. It has well appointed spacious bedrooms and a pleasant
garden which is at the disposal of guests.
Near river  Near lake
*4 en suite (shr)  (3 fmly)  TV in all bedrooms  Full central heating
Open parking available  Covered parking available  Child
discount available 3yrs  Tennis  Fishing  Boule  Table tennis
Languages spoken: English*
ROOMS: s fr 230FF; d fr 275FF

## BROUCKERQUE Nord

**Le Middel-Houck**
6 pl du Village *59630*
☎ 328271346 FAX 328271510
(approach via A16 exit 24b or 25)
Near lake  In town centre  Near motorway
*4 en suite (shr)  TV in all bedrooms  Full central heating  Last d
21.30hrs  Languages spoken: English & German*
ROOMS: (room only) d 220FF **Reductions over 1 night**
MEALS: Continental breakfast 30FF  Lunch 98-228FF&alc
Dinner 98-228FF&alc
CARDS: ●● ■■ ☲ ⑩ Travellers cheques

## CALAIS Pas-de-Calais

**★ ★ ★ George-V**
36 rue Royale *62100*
☎ 321976800 FAX 321973473
(In the NW area of the town between the station and the ferry
terminal)
Near beach  In town centre
*42 en suite (bth/shr)  (3 fmly)  (12 with balcony)  TV in all
bedrooms  STV  Direct dial from all bedrooms  Mini-bar in 16
bedrooms  Licensed  Lift  Night porter  Full central heating
Open parking available  Supervised  Child discount available
12yrs  V meals  Last d 22.00hrs  Languages spoken: English*
ROOMS: (room only) d 330-490FF
**Reductions over 1 night**
MEALS: Full breakfast 47FF  Lunch 95-170FF&alc  Dinner
95-170FF&alc
CARDS: ●● ■■ ☲ ⑩ Travellers cheques

**★ ★ ★ Holiday Inn Garden Court**
6 bd des Allies
☎ 321346969 FAX 321970915
(follow signs for 'Calais Nord' or 'Calais Port')
Near sea  Near beach  In town centre  Near motorway
*65 en suite (bth/shr)  (17 fmly)  No smoking in
30 bedrooms  TV in all bedrooms  STV  Direct dial from all
bedrooms  Mini-bar in all bedrooms  Licensed  Lift  Night porter
Full central heating  Open parking available (charged)  Covered
parking available (charged)  Supervised  Child discount
available 12yrs  Sauna  Fitness room  V meals  Last d 22.30hrs
Languages spoken: English, Dutch & German*
ROOMS: (room only) d 610-630FF
MEALS: Full breakfast 70FF  Lunch fr 45FF&alc  Dinner 90-
150FFalc✱
CARDS: ●● ■■ ☲ ⑩ JCB Travellers cheques

**★ ★ ★ Metropol Hotel**
45 quai de Rhin *62100*
☎ 321975400 FAX 321966970
(from motorway exit 14 head towards town centre. Straight on
at first rdbt, then right at traffic lights and next right)

The Metropol Hotel has been completely renovated and
decorated throughout in English style. It is ideally situated in
the centre of the town and is just a few minutes away from the
shuttle and ferries. It has functional bedrooms with en suite
facilities, a stylish foyer and bar, and a spacious lounge with
high quality furniture. The attractive restaurant features a good
selection of dishes.
Near sea  Near beach  In town centre
Closed 19 Dec-3 Jan
*40 en suite (bth/shr)  (5 fmly)  No smoking in 2 bedrooms  TV in
all bedrooms  STV  Radio in rooms  Direct dial from all
bedrooms  Mini-bar in 10 bedrooms  Licensed  Lift  Night porter
Full central heating  Open parking available  Covered parking
available (charged)  Supervised  Child discount available 12yrs
Languages spoken: English*
ROOMS: (room only) s 200-380FF; d 300-380FF
MEALS: Continental breakfast 48FF✱
CARDS: ●● ■■ ☲ ⑩ Maestro,Electron

**★ ★ ★ Meurice**
5 rue E-Roche *62100*
☎ 321345703 FAX 321341471
Near sea  Near beach  Forest area  In town centre
*39 en suite (bth/shr)  (1 fmly)  No smoking in 2 bedrooms  TV in
all bedrooms  Direct dial from all bedrooms  Licensed  Lift
Night porter  Full central heating  Open parking available
Covered parking available (charged)  Child discount
available 12yrs  V meals  Last d 23.00hrs  Languages spoken:
English*
CARDS: ●● ■■ ☲ ⑩ Travellers cheques

## CAMBRAI Nord

**★ ★ ★ Hotel Beatus**
718 av de Paris *59400*
☎ 327814570 FAX 327780083
(from A26 exit8 Marquion, in Cambrai folow St Quentin - hotel
is just after the hospital - 600 metres from town centre)
In a quiet, shaded location 600mtrs from the town centre. The
bedrooms are comfortably furnished, many of them
overlooking the garden, and a lounge-bar and conference
room are also available.
In town centre  Near motorway
*32 en suite (bth/shr)  (1 fmly)  No smoking in 12 bedrooms  TV
in all bedrooms  STV  Direct dial from all bedrooms  Licensed
Night porter  Full central heating  Open parking available*
contd.

**Hotel Beatus**
Covered parking available (charged) Supervised Bicycle rental
Open terrace Last d 21.15hrs Languages spoken: English
Rooms: s 350FF; d 390FF
Meals: Full breakfast 55FF Dinner 140-140FF&alc
Cards: ●● ■■ ■■ ⑩

**★★★ Château de la Motte Fenélon**
sq du Château 59403
☎ 327836138 FAX 327837161
(N of town centre towards Valenciennes)
Forest area
40 en suite (bth/shr) 8 rooms in annexe (14 fmly) TV in all
bedrooms STV Direct dial from all bedrooms Mini-bar in all
bedrooms Licensed Lift Night porter Full central heating
Open parking available Supervised Child discount available
12yrs Tennis Pool table Open terrace Covered terrace Last d
22.00hrs Languages spoken: English & German
Cards: ●● ■■ ■■ ⑩ Travellers cheques

**La Chope** (Prop: M & Mme Roussel)
17 rue des Docks 59400
☎ 327813678 FAX 327839760
Near river Near lake Forest area In town centre Near
motorway
10 en suite (shr) (3 fmly) TV in all bedrooms Direct dial from
all bedrooms Licensed Full central heating Open parking
available Covered parking available Child discount available
12yrs V meals
Cards: ●● ■■ ■■ Travellers cheques

**★★★ Au Mouton Blanc**
33 rue d'Alsace Lorraine 59400
☎ 327813016 FAX 327818354
In town centre
32 en suite (bth/shr) Some rooms in annexe (5 fmly) (4 with
balcony) TV in all bedrooms Direct-dial available Lift Night
porter Full central heating Open parking available Covered
parking available V meals Last d 21.30hrs Languages spoken:
English

**CAMIERS** Pas-de-Calais

**★★ Les Cèdres**
64 rue du Vieux Moulin 62176
☎ 321849454 FAX 321092329
(6km S of Hardelot)
Near sea Forest area Near motorway
Closed 16 Dec-4 Jan RS Sun
29 rms (17 bth 6 shr) (3 fmly) TV in all bedrooms Direct dial
from all bedrooms Mini-bar in 25 bedrooms Licensed Full
central heating Open parking available Supervised Child
discount available Bicycle rental Open terrace V meals Last d

21.00hrs Languages spoken: English, German, Italian & Spanish
Cards: ●● ■■ ■■ ⑩ Travellers cheques

**COQUELLES** Pas-de-Calais

**★★★ Hotel Copthorne**
av Charles de Gaulle 62231
☎ 321466060 FAX 321857676
Near river Near lake
118 en suite (bth/shr) No smoking in 13 bedrooms TV in all
bedrooms STV Direct dial from all bedrooms Mini-bar in 20
bedrooms Licensed Lift Night porter Full central heating
Open parking available Child discount available 12yrs Indoor
swimming pool (heated) Squash Sauna Solarium Gym Pool
table Covered terrace V meals Last d 22.30hrs Languages
spoken: English, Dutch & German
Cards: ●● ■■ ■■ ⑩ Travellers cheques

**★★ Vidéotel**
RN 1 62231
☎ 321368181 FAX 321368787
Near sea Near motorway
43 en suite (bth/shr) (3 fmly) No smoking in 8 bedrooms TV in
all bedrooms STV Direct dial from all bedrooms Licensed Full
central heating Open parking available Supervised Child
discount available 12yrs Open terrace Last d 22.00hrs
Languages spoken: English
Cards: ●● ■■ ■■ ⑩

**CORBEHEM** Pas-de-Calais

**★★★★ Le Manoir de Fourcy**
48 rue de la Gare 62112
☎ 327959100 FAX 327959109
(from Douai take N50 in direction of Arras to Corbehem)
In town centre Near motorway
8 en suite (bth/shr) TV in all bedrooms Direct dial from all
bedrooms Night porter Full central heating Open parking
available Supervised Last d 20.45hrs Languages spoken:
English
Cards: ●● ■■ ■■

**DOUAI** Nord

**★★★★ La Terrasse**
36 Terrasse St-Pierre 59500
☎ 327887004 FAX 327883605
(A1 exit Fresues les Bautaubau in direction Douai)
In town centre Near motorway
26 en suite (bth/shr) TV in all bedrooms STV Direct dial from
all bedrooms Mini-bar in all bedrooms Licensed Night porter
Full central heating Open parking available V meals Last d
22.00hrs Languages spoken: English
Cards: ●● ■■ ■■ ⑩ Travellers cheques

**DUISANS** Pas-de-Calais

**Le Clos Grincourt** (Prop: Annie Senlis)
18 rue du Château 62161
☎ 321486833 FAX 321486833
(first house on left on entering village from direction of Arras
on D56)
Near river Forest area
3 en suite (bth/shr) No smoking on premises Full central
heating Open parking available Covered parking available
Supervised Child discount available
Rooms: s 183FF; d 260FF

### DUNKERQUE Nord

**★ ★ ★ Hotel Borel**
6 rue l'Hermitte *59140*
☎ 328665180 FAX 328593382
Near sea  Near beach  In town centre
*48 en suite (bth/shr)  (6 fmly)  No smoking in 10 bedrooms  TV
in all bedrooms  Direct dial from all bedrooms  Mini-bar in all
bedrooms  Room-safe  Licensed  Lift  Night porter  Full central
heating  Languages spoken: English & German*
CARDS: 💳 💳 💳 💳

**★ ★ ★ Welcome**
37 r Poincare *59140*
☎ 328592070 FAX 328210349
(from motorway A16 or A25 take exit "centre ville", at 3rd set of
traffic lights turn left. At the 4th traffic lights turn right and
first left)
Near sea  Near beach  In town centre  Near motorway
*39 en suite (bth/shr)  (1 fmly)  TV in all bedrooms  STV  Direct
dial from all bedrooms  Licensed  Lift  Night porter  Full central
heating  Covered parking available (charged)  Child discount
available 12yrs  V meals  Last d 22.45hrs  Languages spoken:
English & German*
CARDS: 💳 💳 💳

### ECHINGHEN Pas-de-Calais

*Le Clos d'Ecsh* (Prop: Mme J Boussemaere)
rue de l'Église *62360*
☎ 321911434 FAX 321311505
Near river
*4 en suite (shr)  Languages spoken: English*

### EMMERIN Nord

**★ ★ ★ ★ La Howarderie**
1 rue des Fusilles *59320*
☎ 320103100 FAX 320103109
(from Calais/Dunkerque A25 exit 7, follow in direction of Lens
then Haubourdin & Emmerin. From Paris take A1 exit 19
follow signs for Loos/Haubourdin)
Forest area  Near motorway
*Closed New Year-Etr,Xmas & 15 days Aug*
*8 en suite (bth/shr)  TV in all bedrooms  STV  Direct dial from all
bedrooms  Mini-bar in all bedrooms  Full central heating  Open
parking available  Supervised  Child discount available 12yrs
Languages spoken: English & German*
ROOMS: (room only) s fr 650FF;  d fr 800FF
**Reductions over 1 night**
CARDS: 💳 💳 💳 💳

### ENGLOS Nord

**★ ★ ★ Novotel Lille Englos**
Autoroute Lille Dunkerque - *59320*
☎ 320105858 FAX 320105859
Novotel offer their clients good quality accommodation in
modern, well equipped bedrooms and have refined
restaurants serving good quality cuisine. They have excellent
meeting and conference facilities and some have food and
beverages available 24 hours a day. All their hotels have at
least one bedroom suitable for handicapped guests.
Near motorway
*124 en suite (bth/shr)  (13 fmly)  No smoking in 20 bedrooms
TV in all bedrooms  STV  Radio in rooms  Direct dial from all
bedrooms  Mini-bar in all bedrooms  Licensed  Night porter*

*Full central heating  Open parking available  Supervised  Child
discount available 16yrs  Outdoor swimming pool  Boule
Bicycle rental  Open terrace  Covered terrace  Last d 24.00hrs
Languages spoken: English & German*
CARDS: 💳 💳 💳 💳 Travellers cheques

### ÉPERLECQUES Pas-de-Calais

**Château du Ganspette** (Prop: M & Mme Pauwels)
133 rue du Ganspette *62910*
☎ 321934393 FAX 321957498
Situated in Audomarois in eight hectares of wooded park, this
19th-century castle gives you comfort and relaxation, with
bedrooms opening onto the park. A restaurant and swimming
pool are open from May to September. The castle was
occupied by the Germans during World War II, and is located
close to a former V2 base.

Near river  Forest area  Near motorway
*4 rms (3 shr)  No smoking on premises  Full central heating
Open parking available  Supervised  Outdoor swimming pool
Tennis  Boule  Languages spoken: English*
ROOMS: d 300FF

### ESCALLES Pas-de-Calais

**★ ★ Hotel de L'Escale**
de la Mer *62179*
☎ 321852500 FAX 321354422
(A16 exit 11/12 if coming from Calais, exit 10/11 if coming from
Boulogne)
Near sea  Near beach  Forest area  Near motorway
*11 Feb-17 Dec & 27-31 Dec*
*38 rms (15 bth 15 shr)  23 rooms in annexe  (12 fmly)  TV in 31
bedrooms  STV  Direct dial from all bedrooms  Open parking
available  Child discount available 2 yrs  Boule  Bicycle rental
Open terrace  Covered terrace  V meals  Last d 21.30hrs
Languages spoken: English*
ROOMS: (room only) d 205-340FF
MEALS: Continental breakfast 38FF  Lunch 82-160FF&alc
Dinner 82-160FF&alc
CARDS: 💳 💳

*Le Grand'Maison* (Prop: M & Mme Boutnoy)
Hameau de La Haute Escalles *62179*
☎ 321852775 FAX 321852775
(take A16 from Channel Tunnel and take exit 10/11, passing the
village of Peuplingues, then after 2kms turn into first house on
left)
Near sea  Near beach

*contd.*

6 en suite (bth/shr) (1 fmly) No smoking on premises TV in 3 bedrooms Full central heating Open parking available Supervised Child discount available Boule Bicycle rental
CARDS: Travellers cheques

### GAUCHIN-VERLOINGT Pas-de-Calais

**Le Loubarre** (Prop: M C Vion)
550 rue des Montifaux *62130*
☎ 321030505 FAX 321030505
(at St-Pol-sur-Ternoise take D343 towards Anvin and after 1km turn right following "Chambre d'Hôte" sign before entering village)

A lovely 19th-century manor furnished with antiques and a dining room with an open fireplace. The bedrooms are located in a converted dovecot with original beams. Croix-en-Ternois racing track is two kilometres away. Restaurants within a short distance. You can enjoy country walks which start right outside the front door!
Near river Forest area
(2 fmly) No smoking on premises TV in 2 bedrooms Full central heating Open parking available Covered parking available Supervised Child discount available 5yrs Open terrace Badminton Languages spoken: English,German & Spanish
ROOMS: s 200FF; d 240FF **Reductions over 1 night**

### GAVRELLE Pas-de-Calais

★★ *Manoir*
35 rue Nationale *62580*
☎ 321586858 FAX 321553787
Near lake Forest area Near motorway
*Closed 1-18 Aug*
*20 en suite (bth) (1 fmly) TV in all bedrooms Radio in rooms Direct dial from all bedrooms Licensed Full central heating Open parking available Covered parking available (charged) Supervised Child discount available 10yrs Pool table Boule Open terrace Last d 21.00hrs Languages spoken: English & German*
CARDS: ●● ■■ ■■ Travellers cheques

### GOSNAY Pas-de-Calais

★★★★ *La Chartreuse du Val Saint-Esprit*
1 rue Fouquières *62199*
☎ 321628088 FAX 321624250
(A26 exit 6)
Forest area Near motorway
*56 en suite (bth/shr) 11 rooms in annexe (3 fmly) TV in all bedrooms STV Direct dial from all bedrooms Mini-bar in all bedrooms Licensed Lift Night porter Full central heating*

Open parking available Child discount available 12yrs Tennis Open terrace V meals Last d 21.30hrs Languages spoken: English
CARDS: ●● ■■ ■■ ●● Travellers cheques

### GUÎNES Pas-de-Calais

**Auberge du Colombier**
la Bien Assise *62340*
☎ 321369300 FAX 321367920
*7 en suite (bth/shr) (2 fmly) No smoking in 2 bedrooms TV in all bedrooms Direct dial from all bedrooms Licensed Open parking available Covered parking available Supervised Child discount available Outdoor swimming pool (heated) Tennis Pool table Boule Mini-golf Bicycle rental V meals Last d 21.30hrs Languages spoken: English*
ROOMS: (room only) s fr 230FF; d 240-270FF
**Reductions over 1 night**
CARDS: ●● ■■ Travellers cheques

### HARDELOT-PLAGE Pas-de-Calais

★★★ *Hotel du Parc*
av François-1er *62152*
☎ 321332211 FAX 321832971
(From Calais take A16 to Boulogne then D940 signed Le Touquet. From Paris A1, then A26 exit Boulogne/Mer)
Near lake Near sea Near beach Forest area Near motorway
*Closed 16-31 Dec*
*81 en suite (bth/shr) (81 fmly) (51 with balcony) No smoking in 27 bedrooms TV in all bedrooms STV Radio in rooms Direct dial from all bedrooms Mini-bar in all bedrooms Licensed Lift Night porter Full central heating Open parking available Supervised Child discount available 12yrs Outdoor swimming pool (heated) Golf 18 Tennis Riding Sauna Gym Pool table Boule Bicycle rental Open terrace Covered terrace Childrens play area V meals Last d 22.30hrs Languages spoken: English, German & Spanish*
CARDS: ●● ■■ ■■ ●● Travellers cheques

### HAZEBROUCK Nord

★★ **Auberge de la Forêt**
La Motte au Bois *59190*
☎ 328480878 FAX 328407776
(5km from Hazebrouck, in the direction of Merville)

This rustic inn is situated in the heart of the forest of Nieppe. A warm and friendly atmosphere prevails, the bedrooms are cosy with good amenities, and the restaurant serves a good range of specialities and innovative dishes, complemented by some great wines from the house cellar.

Forest area
*Closed 1-25 Jan*
*12 en suite (bth/shr) TV in all bedrooms Direct dial from all bedrooms Licensed Full central heating Open parking available Open terrace V meals Last d 21.00hrs Languages spoken: English*
ROOMS: (room only) d 250-340FF
MEALS: Continental breakfast 40FF Lunch 140-285FF&alc Dinner 140-285FF&alc
CARDS: ●● ☎ Travellers cheques

**★★ Le Gambrinus**
2 rue Nationale *59190*
☎ 328419879 FAX 328431106
Hotel Le Gambrinus is a 19th-century style building on a small square between the station and the town centre. Totally renovated in recent years, the bedrooms have been decorated in light pastel shades and equipped with modern amenities. Guests can relax in a cosy bar, and there is a choice of restaurants in the vicinity.
*In town centre*
*15 rms (14 shr) TV in 14 bedrooms Direct dial from 14 bedrooms Licensed Full central heating Open parking available*
ROOMS: (room only) d 310FF **Reductions over 1 night**
CARDS: ●● ☎ Travellers cheques

### HESDIN Pas-de-Calais

**★ La Chope**
48 rue d'Arras *62140*
☎ 321868273
Near river Forest area In town centre Near motorway
*Closed Nov*
*7 rms (3 shr) (2 fmly) No smoking on premises Licensed Full central heating Air conditioning in bedrooms Open parking available Child discount available V meals Last d 20.45hrs Languages spoken: English, Dutch & Flemish*
CARDS: ●● ■■ ☎ ⚫ Travellers cheques

**★★ Les Flandries**
22 rue d'Arras *62140*
☎ 321868021 FAX 321862801
Near river Forest area In town centre Near motorway
*Closed 20 Dec-10 Jan & 28 Jun-13 Jul*
*14 en suite (bth/shr) (2 fmly) TV in all bedrooms Direct dial from all bedrooms Licensed Full central heating Open parking available Covered parking available Supervised Child discount available 8yrs V meals Last d 21.00hrs Languages spoken: English*
CARDS: ●● ☎

### HESDIN-L'ABBÉ Pas-de-Calais

**★★★ Château Hotel Cléry**
rue du Château *62360*
☎ 321831983 FAX 321875259
(on A16 take exit 28 Isques. At rdbt follow N1)
A friendly welcome awaits visitors to this charming establishment where cheerful, attentive staff create a warm atmosphere. It features a bar and an elegant lounge where guests can relax in front of the open fireplace. The spacious bedrooms are decorated in soft pastels and offer a high degree of comfort. The cuisine comprises skilfully executed dishes prepared with the finest fresh produce.
Near sea Near beach Forest area Near motorway
*Closed 15 Dec-Jan*

*22 en suite (bth/shr) 11 rooms in annexe (2 fmly) TV in all bedrooms STV Radio in rooms Licensed Night porter Full central heating Open parking available Tennis Boule Bicycle rental Open terrace Table tennis Languages spoken: English*
CARDS: ●● ■■ ☎ ⚫ Travellers cheques

### INXENT Pas-de-Calais

**★★★ Auberge d'Inxent**
318 rue de la Vallée *62170*
☎ 321907119 FAX 321863167
(from Boulogne take N1 towards Montreuil. Take D147 to Bernieulles, to Beussent, then D127 to Inxent)
This typical 18th-century farm-presbytery stands in wooded

surroundings on the banks of a river and features completely renovated bedrooms offering comfortable accommodation. The informal restaurant, with its ancient fireplace, serves a range of regional dishes prepared with fresh market produce.
Near river Near sea Near beach Forest area Near motorway
*Closed Jan RS Tue evening & Wed in high season*
*6 en suite (bth/shr) (2 fmly) Licensed Full central heating Open parking available Covered parking available Child discount available 12yrs Fishing Riding Boule Bicycle rental Open terrace V meals Last d 21.00hrs Languages spoken: English*
ROOMS: (room only) s 255-310FF; d 295-370FF
**Special breaks**
MEALS: Continental breakfast 40FF Lunch 85-225FF&alc Dinner 85-225FF&alc
CARDS: ●● ☎ Travellers cheques

### JENLAIN Nord

***Château d'en Haut*** (Prop: M & Mme Demarcq)
*59144*
☎ 327497180 FAX 327497180
(from A2 exit at junction 22A towards Le Quesnoy)
Forest area Near motorway
*6 en suite (bth/shr) (2 fmly) No smoking on premises TV in 2 bedrooms Full central heating Open parking available Covered parking available Supervised*
CARDS: Travellers cheques

### LILLE Nord

**Bed & Breakfast** (Prop: Mme Jeannine Hulin)
28 rue de Hannetons *59000*
☎ 320534612 FAX 320534612
(S of Lille near Ronchin. From A25 exit Porte de Postes, on the roundabout take Blvd de Strasbourg then Blvd d'Alsace. Turn right into rue Armand Carrel, follow rue du Faubourg de
*contd.*

137

Douai. Turn right rue L Senault then 1st right into rue de Hannetons)
Located in a quiet street near a tube station. The house has a garden, and the cosy rooms, decorated with a personal touch and are furnished with antique pieces.
In town centre  Near motorway
*1 en suite (bth)  Full central heating  No children 3yrs  Child discount available 14yrs  Languages spoken: English*
ROOMS: d 170-235FF  **Reductions over 1 night**

★ ★ ★ ★ *Carlton*
3 rue de Paris *59000*
☎ 320133313 FAX 320514817
(from Eastern Ring Road follow signs 'Centre Ville', then right at 4th set of traffic lights and continue)
In town centre
*60 en suite (bth/shr)  (40 with balcony)  No smoking in 13 bedrooms  TV in all bedrooms  STV  Direct dial from all bedrooms  Mini-bar in all bedrooms  Room-safe  Licensed  Lift  Night porter  Full central heating  Air conditioning in bedrooms  Open parking available (charged)  Covered parking available (charged)  Supervised  Child discount available 12yrs  V meals  Last d 00.30hrs  Languages spoken: English German & Italian*
CARDS: ●● ■■ ☲☲ ⑩ JCB Travellers cheques

★ ★ *Climat de France*
1 rue Christophe-Colomb *59000*
☎ 320552155 FAX 320558749
(follow signs Lille Centre and take exit marked no4 off La Madeleine)
Forest area  In town centre  Near motorway
*61 en suite (shr)  (4 fmly)  No smoking in 15 bedrooms  TV in 60 bedrooms  STV  Direct dial from 60 bedrooms  Licensed  Lift  Night porter  Full central heating  Open parking available  Covered parking available (charged)  Supervised  Child discount available 13yrs  Open terrace  Billiard table  Last d 22.00hrs  Languages spoken: English*
CARDS: ●● ■■ ☲☲ ⑩

★ ★ ★ ★ **Hotel Golden Tulip Alliance Lille**
17 Quai du Wault, Lille Couvent des Minimes *59027*
☎ 320306262 FAX 320429425
(from the motorway follow signs 'Lille Centre' and then Boulevard Louis XIV and Boulevard de la Liberté. Then follow signs for Hotel)

This building dates back to the 17th century, when it was a convent. Its imposing façade conceals the tranquil cloisters which house the hotel, where comfort and space blend harmoniously with the splendid Flemish architecture of the period. Bedrooms are tastefully furnished and offer a high standard of comfort. There is an informal piano-bar, delightful garden and a restaurant serving traditional cuisine.
Near river  Near lake  Forest area  In town centre  Near motorway
*83 en suite (bth/shr)  (8 fmly)  No smoking in 4 bedrooms  TV in all bedrooms  STV  Direct dial from all bedrooms  Mini-bar in all bedrooms  Room-safe  Licensed  Lift  Night porter  Full central heating  Open parking available (charged)  Supervised  Child discount available 12yrs  Wkly live entertainment  Languages spoken: English*
ROOMS: (room only) s 840-1050FF; d 890-1050FF
**Reductions over 1 night  Special breaks:**
**Weekend/Bed-Breakfast & Dinner**
CARDS: ●● ■■ ☲☲ ⑩ Travellers cheques

★ ★ ★ *Grand Hotel Bellevue* (Best Western)
5 rue Jean Roisin *59000*
☎ 320574564 FAX 320400793
In town centre  Near motorway
*61 rms  (4 fmly)  (4 with balcony)  No smoking in 16 bedrooms  TV in all bedrooms  Direct dial from all bedrooms  Mini-bar in all bedrooms  Licensed  Lift  Full central heating  Languages spoken: German & Spanish*
CARDS: ●● ■■ ☲☲ ⑩ Travellers cheques

★ ★ *Ibis Opéra*
21 rue Lépelletier *59000*
☎ 320062195 FAX 320749130
In town centre
*60 en suite (bth/shr)  (4 fmly)  (2 with balcony)  No smoking in 7 bedrooms  TV in 55 bedrooms  Radio in rooms  Lift  Night porter  Full central heating  Child discount available 12yrs  Languages spoken: English, German & Portuguese*
CARDS: ●● ■■ ☲☲ ⑩

**LOMME** Nord

★ ★ *Climat de France*
rue du Grand But *59160*
☎ 320082054 FAX 320082057
(off A25 exit7 onto rocade Nord Ouest no.6 St Philibert-Lomme)
Forest area  Near motorway
*56 en suite (bth/shr)  TV in all bedrooms  Radio in rooms  Direct dial from all bedrooms  Licensed  Lift  Full central heating  Open parking available  Pool table  Open terrace  V meals  Last d 10pm  Languages spoken: English, German & Spanish*
CARDS: ●● ☲☲

**MARLES-SUR-CANCHE** Pas-de-Calais

**Manoir Francis** (Prop: M & Mme Leroy)
1 rue de l'Église *62170*
☎ 321813880 FAX 321813856
(from Calais or Boulogne take A16 to Montreuil-sur-Mer (exit 26), then go towards Neuville and take the D113 to Marles-sur-Canche)
A 17th century manor house, situated in a small village four kilometres from Montreuil-sur-Mer. It features a living room with vaulted ceiling, a courtyard and private lake, and the surroundings are beautiful.
Near river  Forest area
*3 en suite (bth)  (1 fmly)  Full central heating  Open parking available  Languages spoken: English*
ROOMS: s 250FF; d 300FF ✱

## MAUBEUGE Nord

### ★★ Le Grand Hotel
1 Porte de Paris *59600*
☎ 327646316 FAX 327650576
In town centre Near motorway
*31 rms (28 bth/shr) 35 rooms in annexe (7 fmly) TV in all bedrooms STV Direct dial from all bedrooms Mini-bar in all bedrooms Licensed Lift Night porter Full central heating Open parking available Covered parking available (charged) Supervised Child discount available 11yrs Open terrace Wkly live entertainment V meals Last d 22.00hrs Languages spoken: English*
ROOMS: (room only) s 240-420FF; d 260-440FF
**Reductions over 1 night Special breaks: wknds**
MEALS: Continental breakfast 35FF Lunch 80-350FF Dinner 80-350FF
CARDS: ●● ■■ ☲ ⑩ Travellers cheques

## MONTREUIL-SUR-MER Pas-de-Calais

### ★★★ Les Hautes de Montreuil
21-23 rue Pierre Lédent *62170*
☎ 321819592 FAX 321862883
Near river In town centre
*27 en suite (bth/shr) (4 fmly) (4 with balcony) TV in all bedrooms STV Direct dial from all bedrooms Mini-bar in all bedrooms Room-safe Licensed Full central heating Open parking available (charged) Covered parking available (charged) Supervised Child discount available 2yrs Pool table Bicycle rental Open terrace V meals Last d 22.00hrs Languages spoken: English & German*
ROOMS: (room only) d 495-550FF
**✳ Reductions over 1 night**
MEALS: Continental breakfast 70FF Lunch 120-460FF Dinner 120-460FF
CARDS: ●● ■■ ☲ ⑩ Travellers cheques

### ★★★★ Relais et Château de Montreuil
4 Chaussée des Capucins *62170*
☎ 321815304 FAX 321813643
(A16 exit 26 and follow signs for Montreuil, opposite the Roman Citadelle)
In town centre
*Closed 18 Dec-3 Feb*
*14 en suite (bth/shr) 3 rooms in annexe (2 fmly) (1 with balcony) TV in all bedrooms STV Direct dial from all bedrooms Licensed Night porter Full central heating Open parking available (charged) Covered parking available (charged) Supervised Child discount available 12yrs Outdoor swimming pool (heated) Bicycle rental Open terrace Covered terrace Last d 21.30hrs Languages spoken: English, German & Spanish*
ROOMS: (room only) s 860-1200FF; d 910-1200FF
MEALS: Continental breakfast 70FF Lunch 200-400FF&alc Dinner 300-400FF&alc
CARDS: ●● ■■ ☲ ⑩ JCB Travellers cheques

## NEUVILLE-EN-FERRAIN Nord

### ★★★ Acacias
39 rue du Dronckaert *59960*
☎ 320378927 FAX 320463859
Forest area Near motorway
*42 en suite (bth/shr) (2 fmly) No smoking in 5 bedrooms TV in all bedrooms STV Direct dial from all bedrooms Mini-bar in all bedrooms Licensed Lift Night porter Full central heating Open parking available Covered parking available (charged)*

*Supervised Child discount available 16yrs Solarium Boule Open terrace V meals Last d 22.00hrs Languages spoken: English, Dutch, German & Italian*
CARDS: ●● ■■ ☲ ⑩ JCB

## ORCHIES Nord

### ★★★ Manoir
rte de Séclin *59310*
☎ 320646868 FAX 320646869
(near A23 motorway, 500m from intersection of Orchies, exit Orchies towards Seclin)
Forest area Near motorway
*34 en suite (bth/shr) (2 fmly) TV in all bedrooms STV Radio in rooms Direct dial from all bedrooms Mini-bar in all bedrooms Licensed Lift Night porter Full central heating Open parking available Supervised Child discount available Boule Open terrace Last d 22.00hrs Languages spoken: English*
CARDS: ●● ■■ ☲ ⑩ Travellers cheques

## PONT-DE-BRIQUES Pas-de-Calais

### ★★ Hostellerie de La Rivière
17 rue de la gare *62360*
☎ 321322281 FAX 321874548
(from Boulogne, take direction of Montreuil/Le Touquet, hotel close to railway station)
Near river In town centre Near motorway
*Closed 17 Aug-7 Sep*
*8 en suite (bth/shr) TV in 5 bedrooms Direct dial from all bedrooms Licensed Full central heating Open parking available Child discount available 12yrs Open terrace V meals Last d 21.15hrs Languages spoken: English*
CARDS: ●● ■■ ☲ Travellers cheques

## RAMECOURT Pas-de-Calais

### La Ferme du Bois Quesnoy (Prop: M Deleau)
*62130*
☎ 321416660
Forest area
*4 en suite (bth/shr) Radio in rooms Full central heating Open parking available Covered parking available Child discount available Languages spoken: English & German*

## SAINS-LÈS-FRESSIN Pas-de-Calais

### Chantelouve (Prop: Jo & Jacques Rieben)
35 rue Principale *62310*
☎ 321906013
(from Montreuil take N39 towards Hesdin, left onto D928 towards St Omer after Hesdin Forest 2nd left onto D155 to Sains-Les-Fressin; house at PR5 milestone)   *contd.*

A restored old farm, in large grounds with flower garden and woods; the properties history dates back to Henry ll.
Forest area
*4 rms (3 bth/shr) (1 with balcony) No smoking in all bedrooms Full central heating Open parking available Child discount available 3yrs Languages spoken: English*
ROOMS: d 270FF

## ST-OMER Pas-de-Calais

### ★ ★ Au Vivier
22 rue Louis Martel *62500*
☎ 321957600 FAX 321954220
Despite being located in the busy centre of Saint Omer, the hotel features peaceful guest rooms with modern appointments. Entirely renovated throughout, decorated with good quality furnishings and conveniently situated close to the ferry ports, it provides a pleasant setting for an overnight stop. The restaurant has a varied menu where fresh fish, oysters and seafood take pride of place.
Forest area  In town centre  Near motorway
*7 en suite (bth/shr) (3 fmly) TV in all bedrooms Direct dial from all bedrooms Mini-bar in all bedrooms Licensed Full central heating Open terrace V meals Last d 21.30hrs*
ROOMS: (room only) s fr 240FF; d fr 290FF
MEALS: Continental breakfast 35FF Lunch fr 92FF&alc Dinner fr 92FF&alc
CARDS: ● ■ ⬛ ⬤ Travellers cheques

### ★ ★ ★ Bretagne (S)
2 pl du Vainquai *62500*
☎ 321382578 FAX 321935122
One of the most popular hotels in the region, it now features modern guest rooms with up-to-date facilities and two restaurants: Le Gastronomique which serves a refined, classic cuisine, with a half bottle of wine and coffee included in the price.
Near river  Forest area  In town centre

*75 en suite (bth/shr) 12 rooms in annexe TV in all bedrooms Direct dial from all bedrooms Licensed Lift Night porter Full central heating Open parking available Supervised Child discount available 12yrs V meals Last d 22.00hrs Languages spoken: English & German*
ROOMS: (room only) s fr 320FF; d fr 480FF
**Reductions over 1 night  Special breaks**
MEALS: Continental breakfast 45FF Lunch fr 170FF Dinner fr 250FFalc
CARDS: ● ■ ⬛ ⬤ Travellers cheques

### ★ ★ Les Frangins
3 rue Carnot *62500*
☎ 321381247 FAX 321987278
In the heart of the old centre, the hotel offer bedrooms with modern facilities nad restaurant with choice of menu.
Forest area  In town centre  Near motorway

*26 en suite (bth/shr) (1 fmly) (1 with balcony) No smoking in 2 bedrooms TV in all bedrooms Direct dial from all bedrooms Room-safe Licensed Lift Full central heating Covered parking available (charged) Child discount available 4yrs Golf Open terrace V meals Last d 21.30hrs Languages spoken: English*
ROOMS: (room only) s 290FF; d 350FF
**Reductions over 1 night**
CARDS: ● ■ ⬛ ⬤ Travellers cheques

## SAULTY Pas-de-Calais

### Bed & Breakfast (Prop: Françoise & Pierre Dalle)
82 r de la Gare *62158*
☎ 321482476 FAX 321481832
(from Arras take N25 to Saulty. Chambre d'hôte is the first big house on the left)

Magnificent 18th century château set in a lawned park, where guests are treated as friends and can enjoy the quiet, the gardens and the library. Living room available for guests' use. Fifteen minutes from the historic towns of Arras and Doullens, guests will find plenty on offer to visit in this area. Restaurants within six kilometres. Reductions for stays of more than three nights.
Forest area  Near motorway
*Closed Jan*
*5 en suite (bth/shr) (2 fmly) No smoking on premises Full central heating Open parking available Child discount available 5yrs Languages spoken: English*
ROOMS: s fr 190FF; d fr 290FF  **Reductions over 1 night**
CARDS: Travellers cheques

## SECLIN Nord

**★ ★ ★ Auberge Du Forgeron**
17 rue Bourvy *59113*
☎ 320900952 FAX 320327087
*19 rms (16 shr) TV in all bedrooms Direct dial from all bedrooms Licensed Full central heating Air conditioning in bedrooms Open parking available (charged) Supervised Child discount available Open terrace V meals Languages spoken: English, German & Spanish*
CARDS: ●● ■■ ▆▆ Travellers cheques

## SOLRE-LE-CHÂTEAU Nord

**Bed & Breakfast** (Prop: Patrick & Pierrette Mariani)
5 Grand'Place *59740*
☎ 327616530 FAX 327616371
Near lake Forest area In town centre Near motorway
*6 rms (2 bth 2 shr) (2 fmly) Full central heating Open parking available Child discount available 4yrs Languages spoken: English & Italian*

## TIGNY-NOYELLE Pas-de-Calais

**Le Prieure Impasse de L'Église** (Prop: Mr Roger Delbecque)
*62180*
☎ 321860438 FAX 321813995
Near river Near motorway
*5 en suite (bth/shr) (2 fmly) (1 with balcony) TV in all bedrooms Open parking available Supervised Child discount available 5yrs Boule Open terrace Languages spoken: English*
CARDS: ●● ▆▆ Travellers cheques

## TILQUES Pas-de-Calais

**★ ★ ★ ★ Château Tilques**
rue du Château
☎ 321889999 FAX 321383423
(leave A26 at exit 3 and follow N42 towards St-Omer. At next roundabout take 3rd exit N43 towards Calais to Tilques. In village turn right and follow 'Château' signs)
Near river Forest area
*54 rms (53 bth/shr) 24 rooms in annexe (27 fmly) (12 with balcony) No smoking in 29 bedrooms TV in 53 bedrooms STV Direct dial from 53 bedrooms Night porter Full central heating Open parking available Supervised Child discount available 14yrs Tennis Boule Mini-golf Bicycle rental Open terrace Covered terrace V meals Last d 21.30hrs Languages spoken: English, Arabic, German & Spanish*
CARDS: ●● ■■ ▆▆ ◉ Travellers cheques

## TOUQUET-PARIS-PLAGE, LE Pas-de-Calais

**★ ★ ★ Manoir Hotel - Golf du Touquet**
av du Golf
☎ 321062828 FAX 321062829
(from A16 follow signs for Étaples, then Le Touquet. In Le Touquet turn left at 3rd traffic lights. Le Manoir is on right half a mile further on facing Le Touquet Golf Club)
In a beautiful wooded location, this former manor hopuse has been tastefully converted into an hotel. Ideal for a restful stay or for a golfing holiday.
Forest area
*Closed 28 Dec-27 Jan*

**Manoir Hotel – Golf Du Touquet**
*42 en suite (bth/shr) (2 fmly) TV in all bedrooms STV Direct dial from all bedrooms Mini-bar in 24 bedrooms Night porter Full central heating Open parking available Supervised Child discount available 12yrs Outdoor swimming pool (heated) Golf Tennis Pool table Bicycle rental Open terrace Last d 21.30hrs Languages spoken: English*
ROOMS: s 635-685FF; d 870-970FF
MEALS: Continental breakfast 65FF Lunch 150FF&alc Dinner 150FF&alc
CARDS: ●● ■■ ▆▆ ◉ Travellers cheques

**★ ★ Red Fox**
Angle rue St-Jean/rue de Metz *62520*
☎ 321052758 FAX 321052756
(In town follow signs to 'Centre Ville'. From Boulevard Da Loz turn left into Rue St-Jean)
Near sea Near beach Forest area In town centre Near motorway
*48 en suite (bth/shr) (3 fmly) No smoking in 10 bedrooms TV in all bedrooms STV Direct dial from all bedrooms Licensed Lift Night porter Open parking available (charged) Covered parking available (charged) Child discount available 12yrs Languages spoken: English*
CARDS: ●● ■■ ▆▆ ◉ Travellers cheques

**★ ★ Résidence Hippotel**
av de l'Hippodrome *62520*
☎ 321050711 FAX 321054488
(from Channel ports take A16 to Etaples then follow signs for Le Touquet, hotel is signed from the main road leading to Le Touquet)

In peaceful woodlands, a short walk from the town centre and beach, the hotel offers spacious rooms ideal for couples and families, supervised by an English manageress. The restaurant overlooks the park and racecourse.
Near sea Near beach Forest area Near motorway       *contd.*

141

72 en suite (bth/shr) (72 fmly) (72 with balcony) TV in 50 bedrooms Licensed Night porter Full central heating Open parking available Child discount available 12yrs Riding Pool table Open terrace pin ball, video games, table football Last d 21.00hrs Languages spoken: English
ROOMS: (room only) s 290-380FF; d 290-400FF
MEALS: Continental breakfast 35FF Lunch 64-89FF Dinner 64-89FF
CARDS: ●● ■■ ☲☲ Travellers cheques

**★ ★ ★ ★ Westminster Hotel**
av du Verger 62520
☎ 321054848 FAX 321054545
Near sea Near beach Forest area In town centre Near motorway
115 en suite (bth/shr) TV in all bedrooms STV Radio in rooms Direct dial from all bedrooms Mini-bar in all bedrooms Licensed Lift Night porter Full central heating Open parking available Covered parking available (charged) Indoor swimming pool (heated) Riding Sauna Pool table Jacuzzi/spa Bicycle rental Open terrace Last d 21.30hrs Languages spoken: English
ROOMS: (room only) s 630-2300FF; d 730-2300FF
**Reductions over 1 night**
MEALS: Full breakfast 95FF Dinner 250-380FF&alc
CARDS: ●● ■■ ☲☲ ⑨ Travellers cheques

**TOURNEHEM-SUR-LA-HEM Pas-de-Calais**

**★ ★ Bal Parc Hotel**
500 rue de Vieux Chateau 62890
☎ 321356590 FAX 321351857
(A26 exit 2 or N43 then D218 or D217)
Near river Near lake Near sea Near beach Forest area Near motorway
26 en suite (bth/shr) TV in all bedrooms Direct dial from all bedrooms Licensed Night porter Full central heating Air conditioning in bedrooms Open parking available Tennis Mini-golf Volleyball court Last d 22.00hrs Languages spoken: English
ROOMS: (room only) s 170-205FF; d 205-250FF
MEALS: Full breakfast 25FF Lunch 85-130FFalc Dinner 85-150FFalc
CARDS: ●● ■■ ☲☲ ⑨ Travellers cheques

**VALENCIENNES Nord**

**★ ★ ★ ★ Auberge Du Bon Fermier**
64 rue de Famars 59300
☎ 37466825 FAX 327337501
(town centre)

Discover the secrets of regional cuisine in an authentic 17th-century setting. Dating back to 1560, and becoming an inn in 1840 this building is now classified as an historic monument. Painstakingly restored by its owners, Auberge du Bon Fermier is full of atmosphere, with oak floors and beams, and sparkling copper and pewterware. Bedrooms are stylish, with modern comforts tastefully incorporated. In the restaurant, there is old-fashioned cooking over a wood fire, and meat and game cooked on a spit.
In town centre
16 en suite (bth/shr) TV in all bedrooms STV Direct dial from all bedrooms Mini-bar in all bedrooms Licensed Night porter Full central heating Open parking available (charged) Covered parking available (charged) Supervised V meals Last d 22.30hrs Languages spoken: English & German
ROOMS: (room only) s 500-650FF; d 570-750FF
MEALS: Full breakfast 65FF Continental breakfast 45FF Lunch 128-295FFalc Dinner 128-295FFalc
CARDS: ●● ■■ ☲☲ ⑨

**WATTIGNIES Nord**

**Le Bot** (Prop: Chantal Le Bot)
59 rue Faidherbe 59139
☎ 320602451
(from A1 exit 19 on D549 to Wattignies. At Pharmacy bear left to village centre, house on left just before the church on right)
Forest area In town centre Near motorway
3 en suite (bth/shr) TV in all bedrooms Full central heating Open parking available Child discount available 14yrs Bicycle rental V meals Last d 15.00hrs Languages spoken: English & Spanish
ROOMS: s fr 195FF; d fr 260FF
MEALS: Dinner fr 100FF
CARDS: Travellers cheques

**WIMEREUX Pas-de-Calais**

**★ ★ Centre**
78 rue Carnot 62930
☎ 321324108 FAX 321338248
(From Calais via A16 exit 'Wimereux Nord' follow signs for 'Centre Ville')
Near sea Near beach Forest area In town centre Near motorway
25 en suite (bth/shr) (5 fmly) TV in all bedrooms Direct dial from all bedrooms Licensed Full central heating Open parking available (charged) Covered parking available (charged) Supervised Child discount available 3yrs Open terrace Last d 21.30hrs Languages spoken: English
ROOMS: (room only) s 245FF; d 325FF
MEALS: Full breakfast 35FF Lunch 105-175FF&alc Dinner 105-175FF&alc
CARDS: ●● ■■ ☲☲ Travellers cheques

**ZOUAFQUES Pas-de-Calais**

**La Ferme de Wolphus** (Prop: Jean-Jacques Behaghel)
39 route national 62890
☎ 321356161 FAX 321356161
(A26 exit2 after paytoll take 1st right then 2nd left in direction of Calais for th N43, the property is 1.5km on the left)

**La Ferme de Wolphus**

A farmhouse outside the village offering comfortable
accommodation with modern furnishings. The property is well
situated for the many tourist interests of this area and close to
Channel crossing points.

Near lake  Forest area

*3 rms (1 shr) (1 fmly)  No smoking on premises  Full central
heating  Open parking available  Fishing  Boule  Languages
spoken: English & Spanish*

ROOMS: s 160-180FF;  d 210-230FF

## EVENTS & FESTIVALS

**Feb**  Motorcycle race across the sand dunes, Le Touquet;
Dunkirk Carnival

**Mar**  Kite Flying Festival, Berck-sur-Mer; Paris-Roubaix
Cycle Race; Regional Fortified Towns Open Day

**Apr**  Cassel Carnival with the 'giants' Reuze Papa &
Reuze Maman

**May**  Boulogne-sur-Mer Music Festival; Tourcoing
'Franche Foire' Medieval Games Festival

**Jun**  Maroille Antiques Street Market; Douai 'Gayant'
Summer Festival with the town's 'giants'; Lille
Summer Festival; Samer Strawberry Fair

**Jul**  Boulogne-sur-Mer Napoleonic Celebrations; Côte
d'Opale Music Festival; Hardelot Music Festival;
Bray Dunes International Folklore Festival

**Aug**  Benediction of the Sea in many coastal towns & vi
lages; Les Quesnoy 'Bimberlot' Festival with
'giants'; Le Touquet International Music Festival;
Montreuil sur-Mer Son et Lumière; Wissant 'Flobart'
Festival (flobart is a small fisherman's boat);
Wimereux Mussels Festival

**Sep**  Lille 'Braderie'; Wattrelos 'Berlouffes' Festival;
Regional Nature Parks Fairs; Arleux Garlic Fair;
Bethune Charity Fair

**Oct**  Comines 'Louches' Fête; Mont de Cats Saint Hubert
Festival; Tourcoing Jazz Festival

**Dec**  Licques Turkey Fair; Boulogne-sur-Mer 'Guenels'
Lantern Festival

## The remembrance Tour

In the First World War thousands of men met their death in
the Artois hills, where many horrific battles were fought
between the Allied Forces and the Germans. Canadian
conifers now grow in the enormous craters left by the shells
and mines, but the trenches and restored underground
shelters can still be seen. The Circuit du Souvenir
(Remembrance Tour), enabling visitors to pay homage to the
thousands of French, British, Canadian and German soldiers
who died in action, begins at La Targette cemetries, where
the Torch of Peace burns constantly. The route continues to
the Mont Saint-Eloi Abbey, from where a narrow road leads
to Lorette Hill. By the white basilica and the Tour-Lantern lie
the remains of some 35,000 soldiers. The European Peace
Centre in Souchez offers a historic account of the Artois,
particularly the tragic upheaval of the First World War.

## The Vimy Memorial

The 80-metre high monument of white Adriatic Limestone
pays tribute to soldiers who lost their lives on Vimy Ridge in
the First World War. For three years the Allied Forces tried
to capture this ridge, which had become a stronghold of the
German defence. In April 1917 four divisions of Canadian
troops took the ridge in a battle lasting three days, which left
more than 10,000 soldiers dead, 3,600 of them Canadian. The
Canadian sculptor and architect Seymour Allward spent 11
years working on the Vimy Memorial, which depicts Peace
and Justice, standing atop two enormous pillars. At the foot
of the monument a young soldier passes the flame of hope to
his comrade in arms, and a woman weeps for her lost
husband.

## The Audomarois Marshlands

The Audomarois Marshlands are a protected nature reserve
set in a maze of rivers and watergangs (small canals). Visitors
can cruise at a leisurely speed in bacoves (small punt-like
boats), passing coots, herons and crested grebes, as well as
cauliflower and cabbage fields, for this is also a market
garden region. As there are no roads, everyone who lives
and works in these marshes travels by bacove, even the
postman!

# Lorraine Vosges

Lorraine is situated at the junction of all the major cross-European routes and has been subject to invasion since Roman times, which in turn has influenced the region's art, architecture, heritage and history. The landscape is rich in variety and a place of remarkable natural beauty, from gently rolling hills to rugged peaks, vast forests, miles of waterways, lakes, flower-decked villages and a verdant countryside. Lorraine is the only region of France to offer three Regional Natural Parks; these all are well signposted with tourist information, way-marked paths, picnic areas and splendid views. Spa towns, winter and summer sports are among many other reasons for visiting Lorraine Vosges.

## ESSENTIAL FACTS

| | |
|---|---|
| DÉPARTEMENTS: | Moselle, Meuse, Meurthe-en-Moselle, Vosges |
| PRINCIPAL TOWNS | Bar-Le-Duc, Briey, Metz, Nancy, Epinal, Verdun |
| PLACES TO VISIT: | The Vosges vineyards. Château de la Varenne. Haironville. Nancy Museum. La Hallière Folk Museum, Celles-sur-Plaine. Funfair Museum, Conflans-en-Jarnisy. Lorraine Farming Centre, an everyday living museum, Lucey.; Village Folk Museum, Ville-sur-Yron; |
| REGIONAL TOURIST OFFICE | 1 place Gabriel Hocquard, BP 81004, 57036 Metz Tel: 03 87 37 02 16  Fax: 03 87 37 02 19 Internet: www.cr-lorraine.fr E-mail: crt@cr-lorraine.fr |
| LOCAL GASTRONOMIC DELIGHTS | Rabbit in Mirabelle jelly.Quiche Lorraine. Carp with Glasswort. Frogs' legs pie. Choux puff buns with Mirabelle plums. Walnut & Vosges honey cake. Cheeses: Géromé, pavé du Saulnois, Munster & goats' cheese. Côtes de Meuse truffles. Chocolates: Nancy, Longwy, Verdun. |
| DRINKS | White wines: Riesling, Muscat, Sylvaner, Tokay. Beer: Tourtel Brewery. Mineral water: Vittel, Contrexéville |
| LOCAL CRAFTS WHAT TO BUY | Glassware: Baccarat, Daum, Hartzviller, Portieux, Meisenthal, St-Louis, Vannes-le-Châtel. Pottery & enamelware: Longwy, Lunéville, St-Clement. Faience: Niderviller. The Vosges : wickerwork, clogs, weaving, stone & wood carving |

144

## ABRESCHVILLER Moselle

### ★ ★ Cigognes
74 rue Jordy 57560
☎ 387037009 FAX 387097906
(A4 then Phalsbourg N4 and D44 to Abreschviller)
This family hotel, part of the Minotel group, is situated near the Donon Forest. The guest rooms have a terrace that overlooks the garden where on fine days breakfast and dinner may be taken. Several fixed price menus are offered, and carte with specialities from Alsace and Lorraine.
Near river  Forest area
*29 rms (14 bth 13 shr) (1 fmly) (10 with balcony) TV in 24 bedrooms STV Direct dial from all bedrooms Licensed Full central heating Open parking available Covered parking available Child discount available 10yrs Indoor swimming pool (heated) Sauna Bicycle rental Open terrace Last d 21.00hrs Languages spoken: English & German*
ROOMS: (room only) s 150-270FF; d 150-340FF
MEALS: Continental breakfast 37FF Lunch 72-200FF&alc Dinner 72-200FF&alc
CARDS: ●● ■■ ■■ ⑨ Travellers cheques

## ANCEMONT Meuse

### Château de Labessière (Prop: M & Mme Eichenauer)
55320
☎ 329857021 FAX 329876160
(from A4 exit Verdun Voie Sacrée, then in direction of Bon le Duc until Lemmes, left to Senoncourt & Ancemont)
Small, 18th-century château near Verdun. The bedrooms are traditionally furnished and there is a Louis XV lounge with fireplace available to guests. The quality of the welcome is second to none and guests are assured of delicious home-made meals in the beautiful Louis XVI dining room. A small garden containing a swimming pool can be enjoyed by guests. Covered parking is available. Tandem bikes can be hired. Full breakfast available.
Near river  Near lake  Forest area  In town centre  Near motorway
*4 en suite (bth/shr) (1 fmly) TV available Full central heating Covered parking available Child discount available 12yrs Outdoor swimming pool Tandem bikes for hire Languages spoken: English & German*
CARDS: ■■

## ARRY Moselle

### Les Fougeres (Prop: Francois Mangin)
25 Grande Rue 57680
☎ 387528297 FAX 387528297
(off N57)
Near river  Near lake  Forest area  Near motorway
*3 en suite (bth/shr) Radio in rooms Full central heating Open parking available Child discount available 12yrs Languages spoken: English*
CARDS: Travellers cheques

## AUTREVILLE Vosges

### ★ ★ Le Relais Rose
88300
☎ 383520498 383528237 FAX 383520603
Forest area  Near motorway

*contd.*

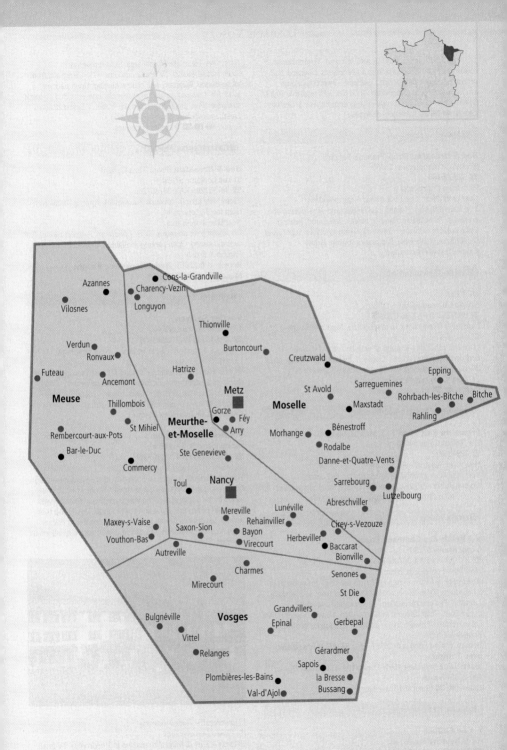

17 rms (13 bth/shr) (5 fmly) (6 with balcony) No smoking in 2
bedrooms STV Direct dial from all bedrooms Licensed Full
central heating Open parking available Covered parking
available (charged) Supervised Child discount available 10yrs
Open terrace V meals Languages spoken: English & German
CARDS: 🐾 ■■ 🎫 Travellers cheques

### AZANNES Meuse

**Bed & Breakfast** (Prop: Francois Fazzari)
9 route de Mangiennes 55150
☎ 329856188
(8km from Damvillers)
Near river Near lake Forest area Near motorway
3 en suite (bth/shr) (1 fmly) (1 with balcony) No smoking on
premises TV available Radio in rooms Full central heating
Open parking available Covered parking available Supervised
Child discount available Languages spoken: Italian
CARDS: Travellers cheques

### BAYON Meurthe-et-Moselle

**De l'Est**
6 pl du Château 54290
☎ 383725368 FAX 383725906
Near river Forest area In town centre Near motorway
Closed 16-31 Oct
16 rms (5 bth 2 shr) (2 fmly) (2 with balcony) TV in all
bedrooms Radio in rooms Licensed Full central heating Child
discount available Fishing Bicycle rental V meals Last d
21.00hrs Languages spoken: English
CARDS: 🐾 🎫 Travellers cheques

### BIONVILLE Meurthe-et-Moselle

**Ferme du P'tit** (Prop: M & Mme Hoblingre)
Les Noires Colas 54540
☎ 329411217
Near river Near lake Forest area
3 en suite (shr) (1 fmly) (2 with balcony) Full central heating
Open parking available Supervised Child discount available
12yrs Last d 20.00hrs Languages spoken: English

### BITCHE Moselle

★ ★ **Relais des Châteaux Forts**
6 quai Branly 57230
☎ 387961414 FAX 387960736          .
Near lake Forest area Near motorway
30 en suite (bth/shr) (5 fmly) (15 with balcony) No smoking in
2 bedrooms TV in all bedrooms Direct dial from all bedrooms
Licensed Full central heating Open parking available
Supervised Child discount available 10yrs Sauna Bicycle rental
Open terrace V meals Last d 21.30hrs Languages spoken:
English & German
ROOMS: (room only) s fr 265FF; d fr 365FF **Reductions
over 1 night**
MEALS: Full breakfast 45FF Lunch 100-200FF&alc Dinner
100-200FF&alc★
CARDS: 🐾 🎫 Eurocard Travellers cheques

### BULGNÉVILLE Vosges

★ ★ **Le Colibri**
rte de Neufchâteau 88140
☎ 329091570 FAX 329092140
(A31 exit 9 (Dijon/Nancy)

Near river Near lake Forest area Near motorway
20 en suite (bth/shr) TV in all bedrooms STV Direct dial from
all bedrooms Licensed Full central heating Open parking
available Covered parking available Supervised Child discount
available 10yrs Boule Open terrace V meals Last d 22.00hrs
Languages spoken: English & German
CARDS: 🐾 ■■ 🎫 Travellers cheques

### BURTONCOURT Moselle

**Bed & Breakfast** (Prop: Alina Cahen)
51 rue Lorraine 57220
☎ 387357265 FAX 387357265
(from Metz take D3 towards Bouzonville. Approx 20kms turn
right for Burtoncourt)
Near lake Forest area
No smoking on premises TV in 1 bedroom Radio in rooms Full
central heating Open parking available Languages spoken:
English & Polish
ROOMS: d fr 250FF **Reductions over 1 night**
MEALS: Dinner 75-100FF★

### BUSSANG Vosges

★ ★ **Des Sources**
12 rte des Sources 88540
☎ 329615194 FAX 329616061
Near lake Forest area In town centre Near motorway
Closed 10 Oct-5 Apr
40 rms 10 rooms in annexe (6 fmly) (11 with balcony) Direct
dial from all bedrooms Licensed Full central heating Child
discount available Solarium Open terrace V meals Last d 21.00hrs
Languages spoken: English,Portuguese,Spanish
CARDS: 🎫 🐾 Travellers cheques

★ ★ **Hotel du Tremplin**
rue du 3 ème R.T.A. 88540
☎ 329615030 FAX 329615089
(between Epinal and Mulhouse on N66)
This comfortable family-run hotel provides a pleasant setting
for an overnight stop or a longer break. Set in a picturesque
valley in the upper part of the Vosges region, it features well
equipped bedrooms, a bar and cosy lounge. The dining room
with its impressive fireplace serves a wide choice of dishes
from Alsace-Lorraine as well as some imaginative creations by
the chef.

In town centre Near motorway
RS Closed Sun evenings
18 rms (13 shr) (6 fmly) No smoking in 2 bedrooms TV in all
bedrooms STV Direct dial from all bedrooms Licensed Full
central heating Open parking available Covered parking

available (charged) Supervised Child discount available 8yrs V meals Last d 21.00hrs Languages spoken: English & German
ROOMS: (room only) s 160-230FF; d 180-270FF
**Reductions over 1 night**
MEALS: Continental breakfast 36FF Lunch 80-300FF&alc Dinner 80-300FF&alc
CARDS: ●● ■■ ▥▥ ◲ Travellers cheques

### CHARENCY-VEZIN Meurthe-et-Moselle

**L'An 12** (Prop: Viviane Jakircevic)
1 Grand Rue *54260*
☎ 382266626 FAX 382266626
(near N43 between Montmédy and Longuyon)
Nineteenth-century building with guest rooms situated on one floor. Each room has its own kitchen and living room, with stone fireplaces. Oak doors and beams all lend character, and there is a large garden. It is situated in the centre of a small village, which sits on the borders of Belgium and Luxembourg.
Near river Near lake Forest area Near motorway
*5 rms (1 bth 2 shr) (2 fmly) No smoking on premises TV in 4 bedrooms STV Radio in rooms Full central heating Open parking available Child discount available Open terrace Languages spoken: English & German*
ROOMS: s 200FF; d 250FF
MEALS: Dinner 70FF

### CHARMES Vosges

★★ **Dancourt**
6 pl de Hôtel-de-Ville *88130*
☎ 329388080 FAX 329380915
(from Voie Rapide 57 take exit 'Charmes/Mirecourt' and follow signs for town centre)
Near river Forest area In town centre Near motorway
Closed 15 Dec-15 Jan
*15 en suite (bth/shr) (4 fmly) TV in all bedrooms Radio in rooms Direct dial from all bedrooms Licensed Full central heating Open parking available Covered parking available (charged) Supervised Child discount available 2yrs Boule Bicycle rental Open terrace V meals Last d 21.30hrs Languages spoken: English & German*
CARDS: ●● ■■ ▥▥ Travellers cheques

### CIREY-SUR-VEZOUZE Meurthe-et-Moselle

**Bed & Breakfast** (Prop: Monique Bouvery)
18 rue du Val *54480*
☎ 383425838 FAX 383425150
Near river Forest area
*5 en suite (bth/shr) Full central heating Open parking available Child discount available Last d 18.00hrs Languages spoken: English*

### DANNE-ET-QUATRE-VENTS Moselle

★★ **Notre-Dame-de-Bonne-Fontaine**
*57370*
☎ 387243433 FAX 387242464
(exit A4 for Phalsbourg and take direction of Strasbourg to Danne et 4 Vents)
Forest area Near motorway
Closed 10-30 Jan
*34 en suite (bth/shr) (3 fmly) (19 with balcony) TV in all bedrooms Direct dial from all bedrooms Licensed Lift Full central heating Open parking available Child discount*

available 12yrs Indoor swimming pool (heated) Sauna Open terrace Covered terrace Last d 20.50hrs Languages spoken: English & German
ROOMS: (room only) s 265-320FF; d 320-450FF
**Reductions over 1 night**
MEALS: Full breakfast 45FF Lunch 87-270FF&alc Dinner 87-270FF&alc
CARDS: ●● ■■ ▥▥ ◲ JCB Travellers cheques

### ÉPINAL Vosges

★★★ **Hotel La Fayette** (Best Western)
Parc Economique, "Le Saut-le-Cerf" *88000*
☎ 329811515 FAX 329310708
Near motorway
*48 en suite (bth/shr) (3 with balcony) No smoking in 9 bedrooms TV in all bedrooms STV Radio in rooms Direct dial from all bedrooms Mini-bar in all bedrooms Licensed Night porter Full central heating Air conditioning in bedrooms Open parking available Covered parking available (charged) Supervised Child discount available 12yrs Indoor swimming pool (heated) Tennis Sauna Jacuzzi/spa Open terrace Last d 21.30hrs Languages spoken: English & German*
ROOMS: (room only) d 470-600FF **Special breaks**
CARDS: ●● ■■ ▥▥ ◲ Travellers cheques

### EPPING Moselle

**Bed & Breakfast** (Prop: M & Mme R Faber)
34a rue de Rimling *57720*
☎ 387967612
(from A4 exit south of Saarbrücken and take N61 to Sarreguemines. From there take N62 towards Bitche. Turn left onto D34 to Epping)
Near river Near lake Near beach Forest area
*2 en suite (shr) (2 fmly) No smoking on premises TV in 1 bedroom STV Radio in rooms Full central heating Open parking available Covered parking available Child discount available 5yrs Languages spoken: German*
ROOMS: d 190FF ✱

### FÉY Moselle

★★ **Les Tuilleries**
rte de Curry *57420*
☎ 387520303 FAX 387528424
(close to Metz, from Metz/Nacy highway take exit 29, hotel in 150mtrs, next to highway)
Forest area Near motorway
*41 en suite (bth/shr) (2 fmly) No smoking in 2 bedrooms TV in all bedrooms Direct dial from all bedrooms Licensed Night porter Open parking available Child discount available 12yrs Sauna Boule Bicycle rental Open terrace Last d 22.00hrs Languages spoken: English, German & Italian*
CARDS: ●● ■■ ▥▥ ◲ Travellers cheques

### FUTEAU Meuse

★★ **Orée du Boise**
*55120*
☎ 329882841 FAX 329882452
Forest area Near motorway
Closed Jan
*7 en suite (bth/shr) TV in all bedrooms Licensed Full central heating Open parking available Child discount available Open terrace Last d 21.30hrs Languages spoken: English*

contd.

## GÉRARDMER Vosges

**★★ Auberge de Martimprey**
26 Col de Martimpré 88400
☎ 329630684 FAX 329630685
(4km from Gérardmer, D8 in direction St Die)
Near lake Near beach Forest area
*11 rms (10 bth/shr) (3 fmly) (2 with balcony) TV in 6 bedrooms Licensed Full central heating Open parking available Child discount available 15yrs Pool table Open terrace Last d 21.30hrs Languages spoken: English & German*
CARDS: ▨ ◑ Travellers cheques

**★★★ Hostellerie des Bas-Rupts et son Chalet**
rte de la Bresse 88400
☎ 329630925 FAX 329630040
(3km from Gérardmer in direction la Bresse D486)
Near lake Forest area
*31 en suite (bth/shr) 13 rooms in annexe (1 fmly) (25 with balcony) TV in all bedrooms STV Direct dial from all bedrooms Mini-bar in 25 bedrooms Licensed Full central heating Open parking available Covered parking available (charged) Supervised Child discount available Outdoor swimming pool (heated) Tennis Bicycle rental Open terrace V meals Last d 21.30hrs Languages spoken: English & German*
CARDS: ▨ ▩ ▦ Travellers cheques

**★★★ Le Grand Hotel**
17-19 Charles-de-Gaulle, pl du Tilleul 88400
☎ 329630631 FAX 329634681
Near lake In town centre
*62 en suite (bth/shr) (18 fmly) (9 with balcony) No smoking in 12 bedrooms TV in all bedrooms STV Direct dial from all bedrooms Licensed Lift Night porter Full central heating Open parking available Covered parking available (charged) Supervised Child discount available 12yrs Outdoor swimming pool (heated) Sauna Pool table Open terrace Last d 21.30hrs Languages spoken: English & German*
CARDS: ▨ ▩ ▦ ◑ Travellers cheques

**★★★ Du Parc**
12-14 av de la Ville de Vichy 88400
☎ 329633243 FAX 329631703
(From Remiremont keep to the side of the lake. Hotel in first turning on right near the Casino)
The hotel occupies an attractive location and offers views over the park and lake. The interior is decorated with fine pastel shades and good quality furniture, whilst the bedrooms with their pine-clad walls provide comfortable accommodation.
Near lake Forest area In town centre Near motorway
*Closed mid Oct-mid Dec & mid Mar-mid Apr*

*30 en suite (bth/shr) 14 rooms in annexe (2 fmly) (4 with balcony) TV in all bedrooms Radio in rooms Direct dial from all bedrooms Full central heating Open parking available Covered parking available (charged) Child discount available 10yrs Outdoor swimming pool (heated) Open terrace Last d 21.00hrs Languages spoken: English & German*
ROOMS: (room only) d 300-360FF
MEALS: Full breakfast 45FF Lunch 120-260FF&alc Dinner 120-260FF&alc
CARDS: ▨ ▩ ▦ Travellers cheques

## GERBEPAL Vosges

**Bed & Breakfast**
17 rte de Gérardmer 88430
☎ 329507385
(10km from Gérardmer towards St-Die)
A restored 17th-century building in a pleasant rural setting between Gérardmer and St-Die.
Near river Near lake Forest area
*4 en suite (bth/shr) (2 fmly) Full central heating Open parking available Languages spoken: English & Sweedish*
ROOMS: s 200FF; d 260FF
MEALS: Dinner 50-80FF

## GRANDVILLERS Vosges

**★★★ Hotel du Commerce et de l'Europe**
88600
☎ 329657117 FAX 329658523
(on N420, 5km from Bruyères)
Near river Near lake Forest area
*20 en suite (bth/shr) 5 rooms in annexe (3 fmly) (11 with balcony) TV in all bedrooms STV Direct dial from all bedrooms Mini-bar in 4 bedrooms Licensed Full central heating Open parking available Covered parking available (charged) Child discount available 12yrs Tennis Fishing Riding Gym Pool table Boule Bicycle rental Open terrace V meals Last d 21.15hrs Languages spoken: English, German & Spanish*
CARDS: ▨ ▩ ▦ Travellers cheques

## HATRIZE Meurthe-et-Moselle

**La Trembloisière** (Prop: M Arizzi)
54800
☎ 382331430 FAX 382201555
(from A4 exit Jarny and take N103)
Near river Near lake Forest area Near motorway
*5 en suite (bth/shr) No smoking on premises Radio in rooms Full central heating Open parking available Languages spoken: English*
CARDS: Travellers cheques

## HERBEVILLER Meurthe-et-Moselle

**Bed & Breakfast** (Prop: M & Mme Bregeard)
7 rue Nationale 54450
☎ 383722473
(from Nancy or Lunéville take the direction of Strasbourg)
Near river Forest area Near motorway
*2 en suite (bth/shr) (1 fmly) Full central heating Open parking available Child discount available 12yrs Last d 20.00hrs*
ROOMS: s fr 180FF; d fr 250FF ✱
MEALS: Dinner fr 90FF
CARDS: Travellers cheques

## LONGUYON Meurthe-et-Moselle

**★ ★ Lorraine**
pl de la Gare *54260*
☎ 382265007 FAX 382392609
Near river Forest area In town centre Near motorway
*Closed 3 wks in Jan*
*14 en suite (bth/shr) (3 fmly) TV in all bedrooms STV Direct
dial from all bedrooms Licensed Full central heating Covered
parking available (charged) Supervised Open terrace Covered
terrace Last d 21.30hrs Languages spoken: English & German*
ROOMS: s 260FF; d 330FF ✱ **Special breaks:
(gastronomic weekends)**
MEALS: Full breakfast 40FF Lunch 120-380FF Dinner 120-
380FF
CARDS: ●● ■■ ☲☲ ⑩ JCB Travellers cheques

## LUNÉVILLE Meurthe-et-Moselle

**Bed & Breakfast** (Prop: M Jacques Durin)
37 rue Francois Richard *54300*
☎ 383737526
(exit Nancy to Strasbourg motorway exit Luneville-Chateau
after 10km take direction of Luneville onto N4 until Luneville
continue to rdbt in direction of Chateau Salin)
Near sea Forest area
*2 en suite (shr) (1 fmly) (2 with balcony) TV in 1 bedroom Full
central heating Open parking available Child discount
available Outdoor swimming pool*

**★ ★ ★ Hotel Oasis**
3 av Voltaire *54300*
☎ 383735285 FAX 383730228
Near river Near lake Forest area Near motorway
*Closed 20 Dec-5 Jan*
*32 en suite (bth/shr) (3 fmly) (3 with balcony) No smoking in 3
bedrooms TV in all bedrooms Radio in rooms Direct dial from
all bedrooms Lift Full central heating Open parking available
Supervised Indoor swimming pool (heated) Outdoor
swimming pool (heated) Pool table Bicycle rental Open
terrace Languages spoken: English & Spanish*
CARDS: ●● ■■ ☲☲ ⑩ Travellers cheques

**★ ★ ★ Hotel des Pages**
5 quai des Petits Bosquets *54300*
☎ 383741142 FAX 383734663
Near river Forest area In town centre
*30 en suite (bth/shr) TV in all bedrooms Direct dial from all
bedrooms Licensed Lift Night porter Full central heating Air
conditioning in bedrooms Open parking available Child
discount available 12yrs Bicycle rental Covered terrace Last d
22.30hrs Languages spoken: English*
CARDS: ●● ■■ ☲☲ Travellers cheques

## LUTZELBOURG Moselle

**★ ★ Hotel Au Lion Bleu**
176 rue Koeberle *57820*
☎ 387253188 FAX 387254298
(A4 exit Phalsbourg after toll take 3rd exit at rdbt in 600 metres
turn right at Esso Station, continue for 4km through the village
hotel is in front of the post-office)
Family-run hotel off the Paris to Strasbourg motorway. Local
and traditonal cuisine is a feature at the hotel, Charilais beef is
a house speciality. The hotel is very convenient for overnight
stops or excursions to Alsacienne wine-cellars, château's,
museums and several other places of interest.

*Hotel au Lion Bleu*

Near river Forest area
*Closed 22 Dec-15 Mar*
*26 rms (4 bth 14 shr) (5 fmly) Direct dial from all bedrooms
Licensed Full central heating Open parking available Covered
parking available Supervised Child discount available 5yrs V
meals Last d 09.30hrs Languages spoken: English German &
Spanish*
MEALS: Full breakfast 58FF Continental breakfast 30FF
Lunch 85-185FF&alc Dinner 85-185FF&alc✱
CARDS: ●● ■■ ☲☲ Travellers cheques

## MAXEY-SUR-VAISE Meuse

**Bed & Breakfast** (Prop: Daniella Cardot)
*55140*
☎ 329908519 FAX 329908288
(in centre of village)
Near river Forest area Near motorway
*2 en suite (shr) Full central heating Open parking available
Indoor swimming pool Languages spoken: English &
German*
CARDS: Travellers cheques

## MEREVILLE Meurthe-et-Moselle

**★ ★ ★ Maison Carrée**
12 rue du Bac *54850*
☎ 383470923 FAX 383475075
(A330 exit6, D331 to Mereville)
Near river Near lake Forest area Near motorway
*23 en suite (bth/shr) (4 fmly) (10 with balcony) TV in all
bedrooms STV Radio in rooms Direct dial from all bedrooms
Mini-bar in all bedrooms Licensed Full central heating Open
parking available Covered parking available (charged)
Supervised Child discount available 12yrs Outdoor swimming
pool (heated) Tennis Boule Bicycle rental Open terrace
Covered terrace Table tennis Last d 21.30hrs Languages
spoken: English & German*
ROOMS: (room only) s 310-360FF; d 360-440FF
**Reductions over 1 night Special breaks**
MEALS: Full breakfast 46FF Lunch 138-245FF&alc Dinner
138-245FF&alc
CARDS: ●● ☲☲ Travellers cheques

## METZ Moselle

**★ ★ Grand Hotel de Metz**
3 rue des Clercs *57000*
☎ 387361633 FAX 387741704
Near river In town centre Near motorway
*62 en suite (bth) (10 fmly) No smoking in 2 bedrooms TV in all
bedrooms STV Direct dial from all bedrooms Lift* contd.

*Night porter Full central heating Open parking available (charged) Covered parking available (charged) Child discount available Languages spoken: English, German & Italian*
CARDS: ● ■ ☲ ⑩ Travellers cheques

### ★ ★ ★ Novotel Metz Centre
Ctre St-Jacques, pl des Paraiges *57000*
☎ 387373839 FAX 387361000
*Near river Forest area In town centre Near motorway 120 en suite (bth) (15 fmly) No smoking in 26 bedrooms TV in all bedrooms STV Radio in rooms Direct dial from all bedrooms Mini-bar in all bedrooms Licensed Lift Night porter Full central heating Air conditioning in bedrooms Open parking available (charged) Covered parking available (charged) Supervised Child discount available 16yrs Outdoor swimming pool Bicycle rental Open terrace Languages spoken: English, Spanish & German*
ROOMS: (room only) s 550FF; d 590FF
CARDS: ● ■ ☲ ⑩ Travellers cheques

### ★ ★ ★ Hotel Royal Concorde Bleu Marine
23 av Foch *57000*
☎ 387668111 FAX 387561316
*Near lake In town centre Near motorway 62 en suite (bth/shr) No smoking in 18 bedrooms TV in all bedrooms STV Radio in rooms Direct dial from all bedrooms Mini-bar in all bedrooms Licensed Lift Night porter Full central heating No children Child discount available 16yrs Sauna V meals Last d 23.00hrs Languages spoken: English German & Spanish*
CARDS: ● ■ ☲ ⑩ Travellers cheques

### ★ ★ ★ Hotel du Théâtre
Port St-Marcel, 3 rue du Pont St-Marcel *57000*
☎ 387311010 FAX 387300466
The hotel stands on the banks of the River Moselle in the historic heart of Metz and provides the ideal base from which to discover this 3,000-year-old city. The bedrooms are spacious and well equipped with luxury, en suite facilities. The restaurant is housed in a 17th-century building and offers a wide choice of regional dishes, served by attentive staff wearing traditional Lorraine costume.

*Near river Near lake In town centre Near motorway 36 en suite (bth/shr) (5 fmly) No smoking in 3 bedrooms TV in all bedrooms STV Direct dial from all bedrooms Mini-bar in all bedrooms Licensed Lift Night porter Full central heating Open parking available Covered parking available Child discount available 10yrs Outdoor swimming pool Fishing Sauna Solarium Gym Pool table Jacuzzi/spa Bicycle rental Open terrace V meals Last d 23.00hrs Languages spoken: English, German, Italian & Spanish*

ROOMS: (room only) s 395-550FF; d 490-990FF
**Reductions over 1 night Special breaks**
MEALS: Continental breakfast 55FF Lunch 98-168FF&alc Dinner 98-168FF&alc
CARDS: ● ■ ☲ ⑩ Travellers cheques

### MIRECOURT Vosges

### ★ ★ Le Luth
av de Chamiec *88500*
☎ 329271212 FAX 329372344
*Forest area Near motorway 29 en suite (bth/shr) 17 rooms in annexe (8 fmly) (7 with balcony) TV in all bedrooms Licensed Full central heating Open parking available Child discount available Bicycle rental Open terrace V meals Last d 21.15hrs*
CARDS: ● ■ ☲ Travellers cheques

### MORHANGE Moselle

### La Musardière Lidrezing (Prop: M & Mme Mathis)
Lidrezing *57340*
☎ 387861405 FAX 387864016
(from Ham-sur-Nied take D999 to Morhange, then 10km towards Dieuze. Follow signs)
*Near lake Forest area Closed Nov-Mar 3 en suite (bth/shr) (1 fmly) No smoking on premises TV in all bedrooms Radio in rooms Full central heating Open parking available Covered parking available Child discount available 8yrs Fishing Boule V meals Last d 15.00hrs Languages spoken: English & German*
ROOMS: s 250FF; d 310FF
MEALS: Dinner 120-160FF
CARDS: ● ☲

### NANCY Meurthe-et-Moselle

### ★ ★ Albert 1er - Astoria
3 rue de l'Armée Patton *54000*
☎ 383403124 FAX 383284778
(in town centre)
*In town centre Near motorway 83 en suite (bth/shr) No smoking in 17 bedrooms TV in all bedrooms Direct dial from all bedrooms Licensed Lift Night porter Full central heating Open parking available (charged) Covered parking available (charged) Child discount available 12yrs Pool table Open terrace Languages spoken: English & German*
CARDS: ● ■ ☲ ⑩ JCB Travellers cheques

### ★ ★ ★ La Résidence
30 blvd Jean Jaurés *54000*
☎ 383403356 FAX 383901628
In town centre
*22 en suite (bth/shr) (5 with balcony) No smoking in 4 bedrooms TV in all bedrooms Direct dial from all bedrooms Licensed Lift Full central heating Child discount available 10yrs Languages spoken: English & German*
CARDS: ● ■ ☲ ⑩ JCB

### RAHLING Moselle

### Bed & Breakfast (Prop: M & Mme Bach)
2 r du Vieux Moulin *57410*
☎ 387098685
*Forest area Near motorway*

*3 en suite (shr) (1 fmly) No smoking on premises TV available Radio in rooms Full central heating Open parking available Languages spoken: English & German*

### REHAINVILLER Meurthe-et-Moselle

**★ ★ ★ ★ Château d'Adomenil**
*54300*
☎ 383740481 FAX 383742178
Near river Forest area
*12 en suite (bth/shr) 9 rooms in annexe (1 fmly) (1 with balcony) TV in all bedrooms STV Mini-bar in all bedrooms Licensed Full central heating Air conditioning in bedrooms Open parking available Supervised Child discount available Outdoor swimming pool (heated) Fishing Bicycle rental Open terrace Last d 21.30hrs Languages spoken: English*
CARDS: 💳 ■ ☰ 💳 Travellers cheques

### RELANGES Vosges

**Chateau de Lichécourt** (Prop: Elisabeth Labat)
*88260*
☎ 329093530 0660693530 FAX 329098534
A 17th century house offering two suites, one with a canopied bed and a child's bed; the other on the first floor, with a mezzanine floor. Continental breakfast. Bikes are available and there are walks in the forest.
Near river Near lake Forest area Near motorway
*2 en suite (bth/shr) No smoking in 1 bedroom TV in all bedrooms Full central heating Open parking available Fishing Languages spoken: English & Spanish*
ROOMS: (incl. full-board) d fr 600FF
**✱ Reductions over 1 night Special breaks**
MEALS: Lunch fr 100FF Dinner fr 100FF

### REMBERCOURT-AUX-POTS Meuse

**Bed & Breakfast** (Prop: Marie-Christine Oury)
24 rue des Cordeliers *55250*
☎ 387606810 & 329706263 FAX 387607173
(from motorway exit Verdun head towards Chaumont/Aire)
Near river Forest area
*1 en suite (bth) No smoking on premises Radio in rooms Full central heating Open parking available Child discount available*

### RODALBE Moselle

**Bed & Breakfast** (Prop: Robert Schmitt)
26 r Principale *57340*
☎ 387015670 387015665 FAX 387015019
Near lake Forest area
*5 en suite (bth/shr) (1 fmly) TV available Full central heating Open parking available Child discount available Languages spoken: German*
CARDS: ☰ Travellers cheques

### ROHRBACH-LÈS-BITCHE Moselle

**Bed & Breakfast** (Prop: Marlyse & Rene Neu)
40 r des Verges *57410*
☎ 387027123
Near river Forest area Near motorway
*3 en suite (shr) (1 fmly) (2 with balcony) No smoking in all bedrooms TV available Radio in rooms Full central heating Open parking available Child discount available Table tennis Barbecue Languages spoken: English & German*
CARDS: Travellers cheques

### RONVAUX Meuse

**Le Logis des Côtes** (Prop: Mme Marie José Wurtz)
4 rue Basse *55160*
☎ 329873221
(A4 exit 32 towards Fresnes-en-Woevre D908, then direction Verdun D903 after Manheulles take D24 for Ronvaux)
Situated in a small country village at the foot of the Côtes de Meuse, near to Verdun. Communal rustic living room with fireplace. Fixed-price dinner, including wine. Garden games and bikes available.
Near river Near lake Near sea Forest area Near motorway
Closed Nov-Mar
*2 en suite (bth/shr) (1 fmly) (1 with balcony) No smoking on premises Full central heating Open parking available Covered parking available Child discount available 8yrs Bicycle rental Last d 6pm Languages spoken: English & German*
ROOMS: s 190FF; d 240FF **Special breaks: 10% off if stay is longer than 3 nights**
MEALS: Dinner 95FF
CARDS: Travellers cheques

### ST-AVOLD Moselle

**★ ★ ★ De L'Europe**
7 rue Altmayer *57500*
☎ 387920033 FAX 387920123
Forest area Near motorway
*34 en suite (bth/shr) (3 fmly) TV available STV Direct dial from all bedrooms Licensed Lift Full central heating Open parking available Covered parking available (charged) Supervised Child discount available 12yrs Open terrace V meals Last d 22.00hrs Languages spoken: English German & Italian*
CARDS: 💳 ■ ☰

**★ ★ ★ Novotel Saint-Avold**
RN 33-Autoroute A4 *57500*
☎ 387922593 FAX 387920247
(from St Avold town take direction of American Cemetery/motorway, from motorway exit St Avold in direction of town)
Forest area Near motorway
*61 en suite (bth/shr) (8 fmly) No smoking in 11 bedrooms TV in all bedrooms STV Radio in rooms Direct dial from all bedrooms Mini-bar in all bedrooms Licensed Night porter Full central heating Air conditioning in bedrooms Open parking available Child discount available 16yrs Outdoor swimming pool Boule Bicycle rental Open terrace Last d 24.00hrs Languages spoken: English, German & Spanish*
ROOMS: (room only) s 475FF; d 525FF
**Special breaks: wknds**
MEALS: Continental breakfast 55FF Lunch 130-180FF&alc Dinner 130-180FF&alc✱
CARDS: 💳 ■ ☰ 💳 Travellers cheques

### ST-MIHIEL Meuse

**★ ★ Le Rive Gauge**
pl de l'Ancienne Gare *55300*
☎ 329891583 FAX 329891535
Near river
*10 en suite (bth/shr) TV in all bedrooms STV Direct dial from all bedrooms Licensed Full central heating Air conditioning in bedrooms Open parking available Child discount available Outdoor swimming pool Pool table Open terrace V meals Languages spoken: English*
CARDS: 💳 ☰ 💳 Travellers cheques

151

## STE-GENEVIÈVE Meurthe-et-Moselle

**Ferme Auberge St Genevieve** (Prop: Marc Gigleux)
4 rte de Bezaumont *54700*
☎ 383822555 FAX 383822555
(A31 enter Nancy et Matz exit 27 (Atton-Nomeny) in direction Nomeny)
Near river  Forest area  Near motorway
*3 en suite (bth/shr)  (1 fmly)  No smoking on premises  TV available  Radio in rooms  Full central heating  Child discount available 10yrs  Last d 20.30hrs  Languages spoken: English & German*
CARDS: Travellers cheques

## SARREBOURG Moselle

★ ★ **Hotel les Cèdres**
Zone Loisirs, chemin d'Imling *57400*
☎ 387035555 FAX 387036633
Near lake  Near motorway
*44 en suite (bth/shr)  (5 fmly)  No smoking in 3 bedrooms  TV in all bedrooms  STV  Direct dial from all bedrooms  Licensed  Lift  Night porter  Full central heating  Open parking available  Supervised  Child discount available  Pool table  Bicycle rental  Open terrace  Covered terrace  Games for children  V meals  Last d 22.00hrs  Languages spoken: English German Italian & Dutch*
CARDS: ●● ■■ ▨ Travellers cheques

## SARREGUEMINES Moselle

★ ★ ★ **Hotel a'Alsace**
10 rue Poincaré *57200*
☎ 387984432 FAX 387983985
Near river  Forest area  In town centre  Near motorway
Closed 24 Dec & Good Fri
*28 en suite (bth/shr)  No smoking in 7 bedrooms  TV in all bedrooms  Direct dial from all bedrooms  Licensed  Lift  Night porter  Full central heating  Open parking available  Supervised  Open terrace  V meals  Last d 22.00hrs  Languages spoken: English, German & Italian*
CARDS: ●● ■■ ▨ ⑩ Travellers cheques

## SAXON-SION Meurthe-et-Moselle

**Les Grands Champs** (Prop: M T Leclerc)
*54330*
☎ 383251033 FAX 383251024
Forest area
*2 en suite (bth/shr)  Full central heating  Open parking available  Covered parking available  Supervised  Child discount available  Languages spoken: English*
ROOMS: s 150FF; d 180FF **Reductions over 1 night**

## SENONES Vosges

★ ★ **Au Bon Gite**
3 pl Vautrin *88210*
☎ 329579246 FAX 329579392
Near river  In town centre
*7 en suite (bth/shr)  TV in all bedrooms  Direct dial from all bedrooms  Mini-bar in all bedrooms  Licensed  Full central heating  Open parking available (charged)  Covered parking available (charged)  Child discount available 14yrs  Jacuzzi/spa  Open terrace  V meals  Last d 21.30hrs  Languages spoken: English*
CARDS: ●● ■■ ▨ Travellers cheques

## THILLOMBOIS Meuse

**Le Clos du Pausa** (Prop: Mme Lise Tanchon)
r du Château
☎ 329750785 FAX 329750072
Near river  Near lake  Forest area
*4 en suite (bth/shr)  (3 fmly)  No smoking on premises  Radio in rooms  Full central heating  Open parking available  Covered parking available  Child discount available 8yrs  Boule  Languages spoken: English*
CARDS: Travellers cheques

## VAL-D'AJOL Vosges

★ ★ ★ **La Résidence**
5 rue des Mousses *88340*
☎ 329306852/329306460 FAX 329665300
(from N57 (between Remiremont and Luxeiul) take D20 at 'Le Val d'Ajol' to hotel.Or from Remiremont take D23 or from Fougerolles take D83/D23)
Forest area
Closed 15 Nov-15 Dec
*55 rms (29 bth 24 shr)  30 rooms in annexe  (23 fmly)  (3 with balcony)  TV in all bedrooms  Direct dial from all bedrooms  Licensed  Full central heating  Open parking available  Child discount available 12yrs  Indoor swimming pool (heated)  Outdoor swimming pool (heated)  Tennis  Fishing  Riding  Bicycle rental  Open terrace  Covered terrace  Games for children  Last d 21.30hrs  Languages spoken: English, German & Spanish*
CARDS: ●● ■■ ▨ ⑩ Travellers cheques

## VERDUN Meuse

★ ★ **Orchidées**
Z I de d'Etain *55100*
☎ 329864646 FAX 329861020
Forest area  Near motorway
Closed 19 Dec-6 Jan
*42 en suite (shr)  (2 fmly)  No smoking in 3 bedrooms  TV in all bedrooms  STV  Direct dial from all bedrooms  Licensed  Full central heating  Open parking available  Outdoor swimming pool  Tennis  Open terrace  Last d 21.30hrs  Languages spoken: English*
CARDS: ●● ■■ ▨ Travellers cheques

## VILOSNES Meuse

★ ★ **Le Vieux Moulin**
3 rue des Petits Ponts *55110*
☎ 329858152 FAX 329858819
Near river  Forest area  Near motorway
Closed Feb/Xmas & New Year
*18 rms  (2 fmly)  TV in all bedrooms  Direct dial from all bedrooms  Full central heating  Open parking available  Covered parking available  Supervised  Child discount available  Bicycle rental  Open terrace  V meals  Languages spoken: English*
CARDS: ●● ■■ ▨ ⑩ Travellers cheques

## VIRECOURT Meurthe-et-Moselle

**Les Marguerites** (Prop: M & F Beyel)
14 rue de la République *54290*
☎ 383725420 FAX 383725420
(1km from Bayon on D112)
At the foot of the Vosges mountains, three spacious rooms are

offered in a renovated country house of character. Small kitchen for guests' use. Communal use of dining room, games area and barbecue. Reductions for stays of more than three nights.
Near river Near lake Forest area Near motorway *3 en suite (shr) (2 fmly) No smoking on premises TV in all bedrooms Full central heating Open parking available Child discount available Languages spoken: Portuguese* ROOMS: s 180FF; d fr 230FF ✱ **Special breaks** CARDS: Travellers cheques

### VITTEL Vosges

#### ★ ★ ★ Angleterre
rue de Charmey *88800*
☎ 329080842 FAX 329080748
(From A31 exit Bulgneville continue through Contrexeville to Vittel)
Forest area In town centre Near motorway
*61 en suite (bth/shr) No smoking in 8 bedrooms TV in all bedrooms STV Direct dial from all bedrooms Licensed Lift Night porter Full central heating Open parking available Child discount available 10yrs Bicycle rental Open terrace V meals Last d 21.30hrs Languages spoken: English, German & Italian* ROOMS: (room only) s 370-460FF; d 480-600FF
**Reductions over 1 night**
CARDS: ●● ■ ☲ ▣ Travellers cheques

#### ★ ★ Bellevue
503 av de Chatillon *88800*
☎ 329080798 FAX 329084189
Forest area ʼʼear moto. way
*Closed 1 Oct-1 May*
*36 en suite (bth/shr) (2 fmly) (4 with balcony) No smoking in 2 bedrooms TV in all bedrooms STV Direct dial from all bedrooms Licensed Full central heating Open parking available Covered parking available Child discount available 14yrs Boule Bicycle rental Open terrace V meals Last d 21.00hrs Languages spoken: English*
CARDS: ●● ■ ☲ ▣ Travellers cheques

### VOUTHON-BAS Meuse

#### Bed & Breakfast (Prop: Simone Robert)
*55130*
☎ 329897400 FAX 329897442
Near river Forest area Near motorway
*2 en suite (shr) TV in all bedrooms Radio in rooms Full central heating Open parking available Covered parking available Supervised*

## EVENTS & FESTIVALS

**Jan** Gérardmer Film Festival;

**Feb** Epinal Paper Boat Festival; Sarreguemines: Carnival, Music Festival ; Fonentay La Joute Book & Paper Fair;

**Mar** Commercy Jazz Festival; Creutzwald Carnival & Pageant; Epinal Classical Music Festival

**Apr** Gérardmer Daffodil Festival; Toul French Wine Festival; Sarrebourg Ancient Music Festival; Nancy Antiques Fair; Nancy International Piano Competition

**May** Azannes Traditional Crafts Festival (Sundays); La Bresse Woodcarving Festival; Domrémy Joan of Arc Festival; Vandoeuvre-lès-Nancy Contemporary Music Festival; Epinal Caricature Festival; Gorze Medieval Fair; Nancy Choral Song Festival; Montmédy City Ramparts Festival; Sarrebourg Ancient Music Festival; Mirecourt Mechanical Music Festival; Vittel Antiques Fair

**Jun** Metz Summer Book Festival; Mirecourt Music Festival; Verdun Sound & Light Show (Jun-Jul); Epinal Street Entertainment Festival; Rodemack: Medieval Festival, Comedy Festival; Meuse Organ Music Festival: Bar-le Duc, Verdun, Bouchon sur Saulx; Lunéville Castle Festival (Suns Jun Sep);Nancy: Old Town Medieval Festival, Theatre Festival. Summer Solstice: bonfires are lit in the main towns & mountain villages.

**Jul** Metz Sound & Light Show, Lac aux Cyngnes (Jul Sep); St-Dié des Vosges:Liberty Week (mid-Jul-traditional entertainment); Flower Festival (last Sun); Contrexéville Traditional Crafts Festival; Maxstadt Threshing Festival; Nancy Music Festival; Vittel Chamber Music Festival; Bitche Sound & Light Show; La Bresse Forest Festival;

**Aug** Montmédy Evening Historical Pageant; Dabo Culture Festival; Nancy Music Festival; Bénéstroff Harvest Festival; Sapois TraditionalFestival; Gérardmer Lake, Fireworks; Madine Lake Festival (concert & fireworks); Jaulny Medieval Festival; Contrexéville Fireworks Display; Cons-la-Grandville Medieval Festival; Metz, Mirabelle Plum Festival; Briey Hot Air Balloon Festival & Fireworks

**Sep** Cons-la-Grandville Music Festival; Vittel International Eventing; Baccarat Lorraine Pâté Festival; Lunéville Pumpkin Festival; Bar-le-Duc Antiques Fair;Pont-a Mousson Music Festival;

**Oct** Epinal Theatrical Farce Festival; Nancy: Jazz Festival, Puppet Festival; Vandoeuvre-lès-Nanc Sledge-Dog Racing; Metz International Fair

**Nov** Lachaussée Fishi Festival; Lindre Basse Grand Fishing Festival; Metz: Sacred Songs Festival, Antiques Fair

**Dec** St Nicholas Festivals in most towns & villages - esp cially St-Nicholas-de-Port, Epinal, Metz & Nancy (torchlight processions, fireworks); Christmas markets: Metz, Nancy, St-Dié

## Art Nouveau
Lorraine has good reason to be proud of the prestigious Nancy School of Art Nouveau, whose driving force was Emile Gallé. Through his enthusiasm and entrepreneurial skill, many eminent glassmakers, cabinetmakers, engravers, sculptors and painters received commissions and so created works of startling and audacious beauty,many of which were inspired by the intricate shapes and patterns of the natural world. Some, like the "Dawn and Dusk" bed featuring exquisite butterfly designs, are now displayed in the Nancy School Museum.

# Alsace

The smallest region in France, neither truely French nor truely German, Alsace has carefully preserved customs, folklore and a regional dialect. This unique position at the crossroads of Europe, makes it an ideal location for major institutions such as the Council of Europe, the European Parliament and the European Court of Human Rights. The legacy of Franco-German influences and conflicts provides historical remains, cultural tradition and generous cuisine. But perhaps the Alsatian heritage is expressed most obviously through its architecture, particularly the distinctive half-timbered houses.

## ESSENTIAL FACTS

| | |
|---|---|
| DÉPARTEMENTS: | Bas-Rhin, Haut-Rhin |
| PRINCIPAL TOWNS | Strasbourg, Colmar, Mulhouse, Haguenau |
| PLACES TO VISIT: | Cathedral & Petit France area of Strasbourg; Krutenau district of Colmar; Castle of Haut-Koenigsbourg; old St Bartélemy mine at Ste-Marie-aux-Mines; Mont Ste-Odile Monastery; Ecomuseum near Guebwiller; Four à Chaux Maginot Line Fortress in Lembrach |
| REGIONAL TOURIST OFFICE | 6 Avenue de la Marseilles BP 219, F 67005 STRASBOURG Tel 03 88 25 01 66  Fax 03 88 52 17 06 Internet http://www.tourisme-alsace.com |
| LOCAL GASTRONOMIC DELIGHTS | Baeckeoffe, a local stew.Sauerkraut & sausages. Fish stew with Riesling wine. Pâté de foie gras with truffles. Flammekueche, thin bread dough topped with cream, onion and bacon. Quetsche plum tart. Kougelhopf, a type of cake |
| DRINKS | Beers: Kronenbourg, Météor, Schutzenberger, Adelscott. Wines: Riesling, Gewurztraminer, Sylvaner, Tokay Pinot Gris, Muscat d'Alsace, 50 Grand Cru wines; Crémant d'Alsace (sparkling white). Eaux-de-Vie: fruit brandies Kirsch (cherry), Mirabelle (plum) or Framboise (raspberry). |
| LOCAL CRAFTS WHAT TO BUY | Betschdorf: salt stoneware pottery. The Vosges Valley: blown glass. Local produce, fruit brandies, pâté de foie gras. |

## AMMERSCHWIHR Haut-Rhin

### ★ ★ À l'Arbre Vert
7 rue des Cigognes 68770
☎ 389471223 FAX 389782721
Forest area  In town centre
*Closed 17-29 Nov & 9 Feb-21 Mar RS high season (half board only)*
*16 en suite (bth/shr)  4 rooms in annexe  (4 fmly)  TV in all bedrooms  Direct dial from all bedrooms  Mini-bar in all bedrooms  Licensed  Full central heating  V meals  Last d 21.15hrs  Languages spoken: English, German & Japanese*
MEALS:  Continental breakfast 38FF  Lunch 80-235FF&alc  Dinner 80-235FF&alc✱
CARDS: 💳 💳 💳 💳 Travellers cheques

## ANDOLSHEIM Haut-Rhin

### ★ ★ *Du Soleil*
1 rue de Colmar 68280
☎ 389714053 FAX 389714036
Forest area  Near motorway
*Closed 26 Jan-5 Mar*
*6 rms (1 shr)  (1 fmly)  (1 with balcony)  TV in 1 bedroom  Licensed  Full central heating  Open parking available  V meals  Last d 21.00hrs  Languages spoken: English & German*
CARDS: 💳 💳 💳 💳 Travellers cheques

## BALDERSHEIM Haut-Rhin

### ★ ★ Au Cheval Blanc
27 rue Principale 68390
☎ 389454544 FAX 389562893
This attractive building is situated in the heart of the village of Baldersheim. It has been in the hands of the same family for more than a 100 years, during which time the art of hospitality has been passed down from father to son. The bedrooms are comfortable and equipped with modern amenities. The menu features first class cuisine and is particularly noted for its specialities from the Alsace; it is complemented by a good selection of French and regional wines.
Forest area  Near motorway

*83 en suite (bth/shr)  30 rooms in annexe  (4 fmly)  (6 with balcony)  No smoking in 6 bedrooms  TV in all bedrooms  STV  Direct dial from all bedrooms  Mini-bar in all bedrooms  Licensed  Lift  Full central heating  Open parking available  Indoor swimming pool (heated)  Sauna  Jacuzzi/spa  Last d 22hrs  Languages spoken: English & German*  contd.

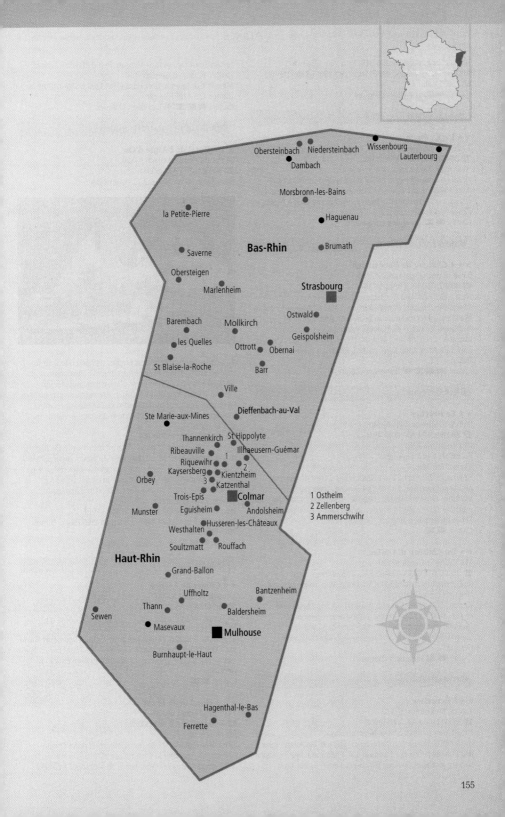

Obersteinbach  Niedersteinbach  Wissenbourg
Dambach  Lauterbourg

Morsbronn-les-Bains

la Petite-Pierre

Haguenau

**Bas-Rhin**

Saverne  Brumath

Obersteigen

Marlenheim

Strasbourg

Ostwald

Barembach  Mollkirch

Geispolsheim

les Quelles  Ottrott  Obernai

St Blaise-la-Roche  Barr

Ville

Dieffenbach-au-Val

Ste Marie-aux-Mines

Thannenkirch  St Hippolyte

Ribeauville  Illhaeusern-Guémar

Riquewihr  1

Kaysersberg  2

Orbey  Kientzheim

3  Katzenthal

Trois-Epis  Colmar

Munster  Eguisheim  Andolsheim

Husseren-les-Châteaux

Westhalten

Soultzmatt  Rouffach

**Haut-Rhin**

Grand-Ballon

Uffholtz  Bantzenheim

Thann  Baldersheim

Sewen  Masevaux  Mulhouse

Burnhaupt-le-Haut

1 Ostheim
2 Zellenberg
3 Ammerschwihr

Hagenthal-le-Bas

Ferrette

ROOMS: (room only) s 250-345FF; d 290-375FF ✱
MEALS: Full breakfast 43FF Lunch 88-250FF&alc Dinner
88-250FF&alc
CARDS: 💳 💳 Travellers cheques

### BANTZENHEIM Haut-Rhin

★ ★ *De La Poste*
1 rue de Bale *68490*
☎ 389833434 FAX 389833435
Near river Forest area Near motorway
*19 rms (15 bth/shr) (4 fmly) TV in all bedrooms Direct dial*
*from all bedrooms Licensed Full central heating Open parking*
*available Child discount available 10yrs Boule Last d 20.30hrs*
*Languages spoken: English & German*
CARDS: 💳 💳 Travellers cheques

### BAREMBACH Bas-Rhin

★ ★ ★ *Château de Barembach*
5 rue Maréchal-de-Lattre *67130*
☎ 388979750 FAX 388471719
Near river Near lake Forest area Near motorway
*15 en suite (bth/shr) (1 with balcony) TV in all bedrooms Radio*
*in rooms Direct dial from all bedrooms Mini-bar in all*
*bedrooms Licensed Full central heating Open parking*
*available Child discount available 12yrs Open terrace V meals*
*Last d 21.30hrs Languages spoken: English, Danish, German &*
*Italian*
CARDS: 💳 💳 💳 💳 Travellers cheques

### BARR Bas-Rhin

★ ★ *Le Brochet*
9 pl de l'Hôtel-de-Ville *67140*
☎ 388089242 FAX 388084815
(Approach via A35)
Forest area In town centre
Closed Nov-Mar
*23 en suite (bth/shr) TV in all bedrooms Direct dial from all*
*bedrooms Licensed Full central heating Open parking*
*available Covered parking available Supervised Child discount*
*available 12yrs Open terrace V meals Last d 22.00hrs*
*Languages spoken: English, German*
CARDS: 💳 💳

★ ★ *Du Château d'Andlau*
113 Vallée St-Ulrich *67140*
☎ 388089678 & 388089403 FAX 388080093
(in Barr, follow road to Mont Ste Odile, 3km from town centre)
Near river Forest area
*23 rms (7 bth 15 shr) (3 with balcony) TV in all bedrooms*
*Direct dial from all bedrooms Mini-bar in 6 bedrooms*
*Licensed Full central heating Open parking available*
*Supervised Open terrace Languages spoken: English &*
*German*
CARDS: 💳 💳 Travellers cheques

### BRUMATH Bas-Rhin

★ ★ *L'Écrevisse*
4 av de Strasbourg *67170*
☎ 385511108 FAX 388518902
Forest area In town centre Near motorway
*21 rms (20 bth/shr) (1 with balcony) TV in 18 bedrooms Direct*
*dial from all bedrooms Licensed Lift Full central heating Open*
*parking available Covered parking available Sauna Gym*

Jacuzzi/spa Open terrace V meals Last d 21.30hrs Languages
spoken: English & German
MEALS: Continental breakfast 40FF Lunch 135-420FF&alc
Dinner 135-420FF&alc✱
CARDS: 💳 💳 💳 💳 Travellers cheques

### BURNHAUPT-LE-HAUT Haut-Rhin

★ ★ ★ *Hotel de l'Aigle d'Or*
24 rue du Pont d'Aspach *68520*
☎ 389831010 FAX 389831033
(from Lyon on A6 take exit 15 towards Belfort)

This contemporary hotel was built in 1993 and offers up-to-
date accommodation in cheerful, attractive surroundings. It
features a day room with a fire-place which provides cosy
seating, a bar, terrace and a garden where guests may want to
stroll and children play. The bedrooms are equipped with
modern amenities and the elegant restaurant serves dishes to
suit all tastes.
Forest area Near motorway
*26 en suite (bth/shr) (2 fmly) TV in all bedrooms STV Radio in*
*rooms Direct dial from all bedrooms Licensed Night porter*
*Full central heating Open parking available Covered parking*
*available Supervised Child discount available 5yrs Boule*
*Bicycle rental Open terrace Last d 21.30hrs Languages*
*spoken: English, German & Italian*
ROOMS: (room only) s 310FF; d 310-410FF
MEALS: Full breakfast 48FF Lunch 68-298FF&alc Dinner
78-298FF&alc
CARDS: 💳 💳 💳 💳 Travellers cheques

### COLMAR Haut-Rhin

★ ★ *Climat de France*
1 rue de la Gare *68000*
☎ 389413480 FAX 389412784
(in village centre)
In town centre
*41 en suite (bth/shr) (4 with balcony) TV in all bedrooms Radio*
*in rooms Direct-dial available Licensed Lift Night porter Full*
*central heating No children Languages spoken: English &*
*German*
CARDS: 💳 💳

★ ★ ★ *Hotel de la Fecht*
1 rue de la Fecht *68000*
☎ 389413408 FAX 389238028
In town centre
*39 en suite (bth/shr) 22 rooms in annexe (1 fmly) (1 with*
*balcony) No smoking in 4 bedrooms TV in all bedrooms Direct*
*dial from all bedrooms Mini-bar in all bedrooms Licensed*

*Night porter Full central heating Open parking available (charged) Covered parking available (charged) Supervised Child discount available 12yrs Sauna Bicycle rental Open terrace V meals Last d 22.00hrs Languages spoken: English & German*
CARDS: ●● ■■ ▆▆ ⑩ Travellers cheques

★ ★ ★ **Grand Hotel Bristol** (Best Western)
7 pl de la Gare *68000*
☎ 389235959 FAX 389239226
(in the city centre facing railway station)
The Hotel Bristol, situated in the gardens and walkways of the Château d'Eau and Champ de Mars, extends a warm welcome to its visitors. The interior is pleasantly furnished, and bedrooms have every modern amenity. Guests can sample specialities from the Alsace prepared with fresh regional ingredients, complemented by a wine-list offering a selection of fine, fruity Alsace wines.
In town centre
*70 en suite (bth/shr) (15 fmly) (19 with balcony) No smoking in 20 bedrooms TV in all bedrooms STV Radio in rooms Direct dial from all bedrooms Mini-bar in all bedrooms Licensed Lift Night porter Full central heating Open parking available Child discount available 12yrs Open terrace Covered terrace V meals Last d 22.00hrs Languages spoken: English & German*
ROOMS: (room only) s 295-420FF; d 520-750FF
**Reductions over 1 night**
**Special breaks: weekend breaks**
MEALS: Full breakfast 59FF Lunch 195-350FF&alc Dinner 195-450FF&alc
CARDS: ●● ■■ ▆▆ ⑩ Travellers cheques

★ ★ ★ ★ **Hostellerie Le Maréchal**
4 pl des Six Montagnes Noires *68000*
☎ 389416032 FAX 389245940
(from A35 exit at Colmar Sud, follow directions for town

centre, then signs for 'Le Maréchal')
The hotel dates back to 1534 and is situated in the most beautiful part of the old town, called Little Venice. Surrounded by half-timbered houses with waterside terraces and gardens, the hotel provides a romantic setting for a memorable stay. Exquisitely furnished guest rooms with spacious en suite facilities offer the highest level of comfort, whilst the cuisine incorporates outstanding dishes, unique in flavour and presentation, executed by some of the most skilled chefs in the whole of France.
Near river In town centre Near motorway
*30 en suite (bth/shr) (1 fmly) No smoking in 4 bedrooms TV in all bedrooms STV Direct dial from all bedrooms Mini-bar in all bedrooms Licensed Lift Night porter Full central heating*

*Air conditioning in bedrooms Open parking available (charged) Sauna Jacuzzi/spa Open terrace Covered terrace V meals Last d 23.00hrs Languages spoken: English & German*
ROOMS: (room only) d 500-1400FF
**Special breaks: two day breaks**
MEALS: Full breakfast 85FF Lunch fr 140FF&alc Dinner 200-430FF&alc
CARDS: ●● ■■ ▆▆ Travellers cheques

★ ★ ★ *Novotel Colmar*
49 rte de Strasbourg *68000*
☎ 389414914 FAX 389412256
Near motorway
*66 rms 36 rooms in annexe (30 fmly) No smoking in 12 bedrooms TV in 170 bedrooms STV Radio in rooms Direct dial from 170 bedrooms Mini-bar in 170 bedrooms Licensed Night porter Full central heating Air conditioning in bedrooms Open parking available Supervised Child discount available 16yrs Outdoor swimming pool Open terrace V meals Last d 24.00hrs Languages spoken: English & German*
CARDS: ■■ ▆▆ ⑩ Travellers cheques

★ ★ ★ **Hotel St-Martin**
38 Grand Rue *68000*
☎ 389241151 FAX 389234778
(in the heart of the historical centre of Colmar, 50 yds from the Old Customs House)

Ideally located in the heart of the old quarter of Colmar, the Hotel Saint Martin was originally a coaching inn and dates back to 1361. All of its magnificent period architecture has been preserved, especially its façade and Renaissance turret at the rear of the building, flanked by a handsome 17th-century spiral staircase. The cosy bedrooms have modern facilities and the hotel is perfectly placed for sightseeing and all the shops and restaurants.
In town centre
*Closed Jan-Feb*
*24 en suite (bth/shr) (4 fmly) (2 with balcony) TV in all bedrooms Direct dial from all bedrooms Mini-bar in all bedrooms Room-safe Lift Night porter Full central heating Air conditioning in bedrooms Child discount available 12yrs Open terrace Languages spoken: English & German*
ROOMS: (room only) s 320-480FF; d 370-750FF
**Reductions over 1 night**
**Special breaks: Christmas breaks**
CARDS: ●● ■■ ▆▆ ⑩ JCB Travellers cheques

### DIEFFENBACH-AU-VAL Bas-Rhin

**La Romance** (Prop: M et Mme Serge Geiger)
17 rue de Neuve-Eglise
☎ 388856709 FAX 388576158
(from Sélestat via Châtenois in direction Villé (D424) to St
Maurice (D697) signs to Dieffenbach on left)
Forest area
*4 en suite (bth/shr) (2 fmly) No smoking on premises Full
central heating Open parking available Boule Languages
spoken: English & German*
ROOMS: d 360-420FF
CARDS: ●● ⚞⚞ Travellers cheques

### EGUISHEIM Haut-Rhin

★★ **Auberge des Comtes**
1 pl Charles-de-Gaulle *68420*
☎ 389411699 FAX 389249710
Forest area In town centre Near motorway
*18 rms (14 bth) (3 with balcony) Licensed Lift Full central
heating Open parking available Supervised Child discount
available 12yrs Open terrace Languages spoken: German*
CARDS: ●● ⚞⚞

★★★ **Hostellerie du Pape**
10 Grande'Rue *68420*
☎ 389414121 FAX 389414131
Forest area In town centre Near motorway
*Closed early Jan-mid Feb*
*33 en suite (bth) (8 fmly) TV in all bedrooms Direct dial from
all bedrooms Mini-bar in all bedrooms Licensed Lift Full
central heating Open parking available Child discount
available 12yrs Open terrace V meals Last d 21.00hrs
Languages spoken: English & German*
CARDS: ●● ■■ ⚞⚞ ⓪ Travellers cheques

### FERRETTE Haut-Rhin

★★ **Collin**
*68480*
☎ 389404072 FAX 389403826
Forest area
*Closed 13 Jan-1 Feb/8 Sep-2 Oct*
*9 en suite (bth/shr) TV in all bedrooms STV Direct dial from all
bedrooms Licensed Full central heating Child discount
available 12yrs Open terrace V meals Last d 21.00hrs
Languages spoken: English & German*
CARDS: ●● ⚞⚞ Travellers cheques

### GEISPOLSHEIM Bas-Rhin

★★★ **Novotel Strasbourg Sud**
rte de Colmar *671118*
☎ 388662156 FAX 388672163
(from Strasbourg or Airport A35 exit 7: Illkirch-Benfeld. From
Colmar A35 Exit 14: Erstein then N83)
Near motorway
*76 en suite (bth) (38 fmly) No smoking in 50 bedrooms TV in
all bedrooms Radio in rooms Direct dial from all bedrooms
Mini-bar in all bedrooms Licensed Night porter Full central
heating Air conditioning in bedrooms Open parking available
Child discount available 16yrs Outdoor swimming pool Golf 18
Mini-golf Bicycle rental Open terrace Covered terrace Table
tennis Volley ball Mini golf Languages spoken: English,
German, Italian & Spanish*
CARDS: ●● ■■ ⚞⚞ ⓪ Travellers cheques

### GRAND-BALLON Haut-Rhin

★★ **Du Grand Ballon**
*68760*
☎ 389487799 FAX 389627808
Near lake Forest area Near motorway
*23 rms (9 shr) (5 fmly) No smoking on premises Licensed Full
central heating Open parking available Supervised Child
discount available 12yrs Open terrace Last d 20.00hrs
Languages spoken: English & German*
MEALS: Full breakfast 40FF Lunch 55-130FFalc
Dinner 55-95FFalc
CARDS: ●● ⚞⚞

### HAGENTHAL-LE-BAS Haut-Rhin

★★★ **Jenny**
84 rue de Hagenheim *68220*
☎ 389685009 FAX 389685864
Near river Forest area Near motorway
*Closed 20 Dec-30 Dec*
*26 en suite (bth/shr) (3 fmly) (21 with balcony) TV in all
bedrooms Radio in rooms Licensed Lift Full central heating
Open parking available Supervised Indoor swimming pool
(heated) Fishing Sauna Solarium Bicycle rental Open terrace
Covered terrace V meals Last d 21.30hrs Languages spoken:
English & German*
CARDS: ●● ■■ ⚞⚞ ⓪ Travellers cheques

### HUSSEREN-LES-CHÂTEAUX Haut-Rhin

★★★ **Husseren les Châteaux**
rue du Schlossberg *68420*
☎ 389492293 FAX 389492484
Near river Forest area
*38 en suite (bth/shr) (9 fmly) (34 with balcony) No smoking in
6 bedrooms TV in all bedrooms Direct dial from all bedrooms
Mini-bar in all bedrooms Licensed Lift Full central heating
Open parking available Child discount available Indoor
swimming pool (heated) Tennis Sauna Solarium Boule Bicycle
rental Open terrace Covered terrace Last d 22.00hrs
Languages spoken: English, German, Danish, Dutch*
CARDS: ●● ■■ ⚞⚞ ⓪

### ILLHAEUSERN-GUÉMAR Haut-Rhin

★★★ **Clairère**
rte de Guemar *68970*
☎ 389718080 FAX 389718622
Forest area Near motorway
*Closed Jan-Feb*
*25 en suite (bth) (8 with balcony) TV in all bedrooms Direct-
dial available Mini-bar in all bedrooms Licensed Lift Open
parking available (charged) Outdoor swimming pool (heated)
Tennis Boule Bicycle rental Languages spoken: English &
German*
CARDS: ●● ⚞⚞ Travellers cheques

### KATZENTHAL Haut-Rhin

★★ **A l'Agneau**
16 Grande Rue *68230*
☎ 389809025 FAX 389275958
(from Ingersheim and Ammerschwihr on the Wine Road)
Forest area Near motorway
*Closed 10 Jan-10 Mar*

*12 en suite (bth/shr) 2 rooms in annexe (1 fmly) (1 with balcony) TV in 6 bedrooms STV Direct dial from all bedrooms Licensed Full central heating Open parking available Supervised Child discount available 12yrs Open terrace Last d 22.00hrs Languages spoken: English & German*
Rooms: (room only) s fr 275FF; d 275-350FF
Meals: Continental breakfast 45FF Lunch 75-210FF&alc
Dinner 95-280FF&alc
Cards: ●● ▒▒ Travellers cheques

### KAYSERSBERG Haut-Rhin

#### ★ ★ ★ Les Remparts
4 rue Flieh *68240*
☎ 389471212 FAX 389473724
Near river Forest area Near motorway
*43 en suite (bth/shr) 15 rooms in annexe (8 fmly) (18 with balcony) No smoking in 2 bedrooms TV in all bedrooms STV Mini-bar in all bedrooms Licensed Lift Full central heating Open parking available Covered parking available (charged) Sauna Pool table Open terrace Languages spoken: English & German*
Cards: ●● ▒▒ ▒▒ Travellers cheques

### KIENTZHEIM Haut-Rhin

#### ★ ★ Hostellerie Schwendi
2 pl Schwendi *68240*
☎ 389473050 FAX 389490449
(E of Kaysersberg)
Forest area
*Closed 24 Dec-16 Mar*
*17 en suite (bth) (2 fmly) TV in all bedrooms Direct dial from all bedrooms Licensed Full central heating Open parking available Open terrace V meals Last d 21.00hrs Languages spoken: English & German*
Cards: ●● ▒▒ ▒▒ Travellers cheques

### MARLENHEIM Bas-Rhin

#### ★ ★ ★ Cerf
30 rue du Général-de-Gaulle *67520*
☎ 388877373 FAX 388876808
(take the motorway at Starsbourg then N4 for Saverne. La Cerf is located 18km W of Strasbourg)
Forest area In town centre Near motorway
*17 rms (8 bth 7 shr) (4 fmly) TV in all bedrooms Direct dial from all bedrooms Mini-bar in 3 bedrooms Licensed Full central heating Open parking available (charged) Child discount available Open terrace V meals Last d 21.30hrs Languages spoken: English & German*
Cards: ●● ▒▒ ▒▒ ⑩ Travellers cheques

### MOLLKIRCH Bas-Rhin

#### Fischhutte (Prop: Schahl)
rte de Grendelbruch *67190*
☎ 388974203 FAX 388975185
(on RD204 between Mollkirch and Grendelbruch)
A modern chalet situated in the Magel Valley. The restaurant offers game, fish and regional specialities.
Near river Forest area
*Closed 2 Feb-14 Mar & 28 Jun-8 Jul*
*17 rms (5 bth 10 shr) (2 fmly) (6 with balcony) TV in all bedrooms STV Full central heating Open parking available Child discount available 10yrs Fishing Boule Bicycle rental V meals Last d 21.00hrs Languages spoken: English & German*

*Fischhutte*

Rooms: (room only) s 220-270FF; d 300-350FF
Meals: Continental breakfast 55FF Lunch 72-280FF Dinner 95-280FF&alc
Cards: ●● ▒▒ ▒▒ Travellers cheques

### MORSBRONN-LES-BAINS Bas-Rhin

#### ★ ★ Ritter Hoft
23 rue Principale *67360*
☎ 388540737 FAX 388093339
Forest area
*17 en suite (bth/shr) Some rooms in annexe (4 with balcony) TV in all bedrooms Direct dial from all bedrooms Licensed Lift Full central heating Air conditioning in bedrooms Open parking available Supervised Child discount available 12yrs Indoor swimming pool (heated) Sauna Boule Jacuzzi/spa Bicycle rental Open terrace V meals Last d 1.30hrs Languages spoken: English & German*
Cards: ●● ▒▒ Travellers cheques

### MUNSTER Haut-Rhin

#### ★ ★ Aux Deux Sapins
49 rue du 9ème Zouaves *68140*
☎ 389773396 FAX 389770390
(on the D417 between Colmar and Gerardmer)
Near river Forest area Near motorway
*Closed 20 Nov-19 Dec*
*25 en suite (bth/shr) 6 rooms in annexe (7 fmly) (3 with balcony) TV in all bedrooms STV Direct dial from all bedrooms Mini-bar in all bedrooms Licensed Lift Full central heating Open parking available Supervised Child discount available 8yrs Boule Bicycle rental Open terrace Last d 21.00hrs Languages spoken: English & German*
Cards: ●● ▒▒ ▒▒ ⑩ Travellers cheques

### NIEDERSTEINBACH Bas-Rhin

#### ★ ★ Cheval Blanc
11 rue Principale *67510*
☎ 388095531 FAX 388095024
Near river Near lake Forest area Near motorway
*Closed Feb also 1 week Jun & Dec*
*26 rms (8 bth 16 shr) 4 rooms in annexe (5 fmly) (3 with balcony) TV in all bedrooms Direct dial from all bedrooms Licensed Full central heating Open parking available Covered parking available Child discount available 13yrs Outdoor swimming pool (heated) Tennis Fishing Boule Bicycle rental Open terrace Childrens play area,table tennis V meals Last d 20.45hrs Languages spoken: English & German*
Cards: ●● ▒▒ Travellers cheques

### OBERNAI Bas-Rhin

**★ ★ Hostellerie la Diligence**
23 pl de la Mairie *67210*
☎ 388955569 FAX 388954246
(A35 exit Obernai onto N422)
Forest area  In town centre  Near motorway
*41 rms (27 bth 13 shr) 15 rooms in annexe (9 fmly) TV in all
bedrooms STV Direct dial from all bedrooms Mini-bar in 15
bedrooms Licensed Lift Full central heating Open parking
available (charged) Supervised Open terrace Languages
spoken: English & German*
CARDS: ● ■ ⬛ Travellers cheques

**★ ★ ★ ★ Hotel le Parc**
169 rte d'Ottrott *67210*
☎ 388955008 FAX 388953729
Forest area
*Closed Dec*
*56 en suite (bth) (5 fmly) (15 with balcony) TV in all bedrooms
STV Direct dial from all bedrooms Licensed Lift Night porter
Full central heating Air conditioning in bedrooms Open
parking available Supervised Child discount available 8yrs
Indoor swimming pool (heated) Outdoor swimming pool
(heated) Riding Sauna Solarium Pool table Boule Jacuzzi/spa
Bicycle rental Open terrace V meals Last d 21.00hrs
Languages spoken: English & German*
CARDS: ● ■ ⬛ Travellers cheques

### OBERSTEIGEN Bas-Rhin

**★ ★ ★ Hostellerie Belle-Vue**
16 rte de Dabo *67710*
☎ 388873239 FAX 388873777
(from A4 (Paris to Strasbourg) exit at Saverne, follow directions
for Wangenbourg/Dabo)
Forest area
*Closed 5 Jan-1 Apr*
*38 en suite (bth/shr) 3 rooms in annexe (1 fmly) (8 with
balcony) TV in all bedrooms Direct dial from all bedrooms
Mini-bar in 7 bedrooms Licensed Lift Full central heating
Open parking available Covered parking available (charged)
Supervised Child discount available 12yrs Indoor swimming
pool (heated) Sauna Solarium Gym Pool table Boule
Jacuzzi/spa Bicycle rental Open terrace Covered terrace Last
d 21.00hrs Languages spoken: English & German*
ROOMS: (room only) s 300-400FF; d 400-500FF
MEALS: Full breakfast 50FF Lunch 90-200FF&alc Dinner
90-200FF&alc
CARDS: ● ■ ⬛ ⬛ JCB Travellers cheques

### OBERSTEINBACH Bas-Rhin

**★ ★ Alsace Villages**
49 rue Principale *67510*
☎ 388095059 FAX 388095356
Near river  Near beach  Forest area
*Closed 12 Nov-10 Dec*
*12 en suite (shr) (4 fmly) (5 with balcony) No smoking in 2
bedrooms TV in all bedrooms Licensed Full central heating
Open parking available Supervised Child discount available
11yrs Riding Boule Bicycle rental Open terrace V meals Last
d 21.00hrs Languages spoken: English & German*
CARDS: ● ⬛ Carte Blanche Travellers cheques

### ★ ★ Hotel Anthon
40 rue Principale
☎ 388095501 FAX 388095052
(approach from Strasbourg via A4, then Lembach and
Niedersteinbach)
Near river  Forest area
*Closed Jan & Tue-Wed*
*9 en suite (bth/shr) Direct dial from all bedrooms Mini-bar in 7
bedrooms Full central heating Open parking available Open
terrace Last d 20.30hrs Languages spoken: English & German*
CARDS: ● ⬛

### ORBEY Haut-Rhin

**★ ★ ★ Hostellerie Motel Au Bois Le Sire**
20 rue Général de Gaulle *68370*
☎ 389712525 FAX 389713075
(from A35 take N415, then D48)
Near river  Forest area  In town centre
*Closed 3 Jan-3 Feb*
*35 en suite (bth/shr) 24 rooms in annexe (3 fmly) (6 with
balcony) TV in all bedrooms STV Direct dial from all
bedrooms Mini-bar in 23 bedrooms Licensed Full central
heating Open parking available Child discount available 10yrs
Indoor swimming pool (heated) Sauna Jacuzzi/spa Open
terrace V meals Last d 21.00hrs Languages spoken: English &
German*
ROOMS: (room only) s 250-340FF; d 285-370FF
**Reductions over 1 night Special breaks**
MEALS: Full breakfast 50FF Lunch 56-300FF&alc Dinner
90-300FF&alc
CARDS: ● ■ ⬛ ⬛ JCB Travellers cheques

**★ ★ ★ Les Bruyères**
35 rue Général de Gaulle *68370*
☎ 389712036 FAX 389713530
(exit Colmar from A35 onto N83, then onto N415. At
Kaysenberg take D48 to Orbey)
Near river  Forest area  In town centre  Near motorway
*Closed 15 Nov-20 Dec & 2 Jan-15 Feb*
*29 en suite (bth/shr) 4 rooms in annexe (11 fmly) (14 with
balcony) TV in all bedrooms STV Direct dial from all bedrooms
Licensed Lift Full central heating Open parking available Child
discount available 12yrs Sauna Boule Open terrace Covered
terrace Games room with Table tennis V meals Last d 20.45hrs
Languages spoken: English German & Italian*
ROOMS: (room only) s 230-300FF; d 230-350FF
**Special breaks**
MEALS: Full breakfast 38FF Lunch 78-165FF&alc Dinner
78-165FF&alc
CARDS: ● ■ ⬛ ⬛ Travellers cheques

### OSTHEIM Haut-Rhin

**★ ★ ★ Au Nid de Gogognes**
2 rte de Colmar *68150*
☎ 389479144 FAX 389479988
(8km N of Colmar on A35 exit Ostheim-Ribeauville)
Near river  Forest area  In town centre  Near motorway
*Closed 15 Feb-26 Mar*
*50 en suite (bth/shr) 12 rooms in annexe (2 fmly) (9 with
balcony) TV in all bedrooms Radio in rooms Direct dial from
all bedrooms Licensed Lift Full central heating Open parking
available Covered parking available Child discount available
Boule Bicycle rental Open terrace Wkly live entertainment
Last d 21.30hrs Languages spoken: English & German*
CARDS: ● ⬛ Travellers cheques

### OSTWALD Bas-Rhin

**★ ★ ★ ★ Château de l'Ile**
4 Quai Heydt *67540*
☎ 388668500 FAX 388668549
(from A35 exit 7 towards Ostwald and follow signs for Château
de l'Ile)
Near river  Forest area  Near motorway
*62 en suite (bth/shr) (1 fmly) (14 with balcony) TV in all
bedrooms STV Radio in rooms Direct dial from all bedrooms
Mini-bar in all bedrooms Licensed Lift Night porter Full
central heating Air conditioning in bedrooms Open parking
available Supervised Child discount available 12yrs Indoor
swimming pool (heated) Fishing Sauna Solarium Gym
Jacuzzi/spa Bicycle rental Open terrace V meals Last d
22.00hrs Languages spoken: English, German, Italian &
Spanish*
CARDS: ● ■ ■ ● JCB Travellers cheques

### OTTROTT Bas-Rhin

**★ ★ ★ ★ Hostellerie des Châteaux**
11 rue des Châteaux *67530*
☎ 388481414 FAX 388959520
Near river  Forest area
*Closed Feb*
*67 en suite (bth/shr) 18 rooms in annexe (5 fmly) (32 with
balcony) TV in all bedrooms Direct dial from all bedrooms
Licensed Lift Full central heating Open parking available
(charged) Supervised Child discount available 5yrs Indoor
swimming pool (heated) Riding Sauna Solarium Gym Pool
table Jacuzzi/spa Bicycle rental Open terrace Fitness studio &
jacuzzi Last d 21.00hrs Languages spoken: English & German*
CARDS: ● ■ ■ ● Travellers cheques

### PETITE-PIERRE, LA Bas-Rhin

**★ ★ Au Lion d'Or**
15 rue Principale *67290*
☎ 388704506 FAX 388704556
Forest area  Near motorway
*Closed 4 Jan-4 Feb & 28 Jun-6 Jul*
*40 en suite (bth/shr) (2 fmly) (13 with balcony) TV in all
bedrooms STV Direct dial from all bedrooms Licensed Lift
Full central heating Open parking available Supervised Child
discount available 12yrs Indoor swimming pool (heated) Tennis
Sauna Jacuzzi/spa Bicycle rental Open terrace V meals Last d
21.00hrs Languages spoken: English & German*
ROOMS: (room only) s 270-300FF; d 390-450FF
**Special breaks**
MEALS: Full breakfast 50FF Lunch 120-250FF&alc Dinner
120-250FF&alc
CARDS: ● ■ ■ Travellers cheques

**★ ★ ★ Clairière**
63 rte d'Ingwiller *67290*
☎ 388717500 FAX 388704105
Forest area
*50 en suite (bth/shr) (20 fmly) (36 with balcony) TV in all
bedrooms STV Direct dial from all bedrooms Mini-bar in all
bedrooms Licensed Lift Full central heating Open parking
available Indoor swimming pool (heated) Sauna Solarium Pool
table Boule Jacuzzi/spa Open terrace V meals Last d 21.30hrs
Languages spoken: English, Dutch & German*
CARDS: ● ■ ■ ● Travellers cheques

**★ ★ Auberge d'Imsthal**
rte Forestière sur D 178 *67290*
☎ 388014900 FAX 388704026
Near river  Forest area
*23 rms (20 bth/shr) (3 fmly) (4 with balcony) TV in all
bedrooms STV Direct dial from all bedrooms Licensed Lift
Full central heating Open parking available Child discount
available Fishing Sauna Solarium Pool table Mini-golf
Jacuzzi/spa Open terrace V meals Last d 21.00hrs Languages
spoken: English & German*
CARDS: ● ■ ■ ● Travellers cheques

### QUELLES, LES Bas-Rhin

**★ ★ Neuhauser**
*67130*
☎ 388970681 FAX 388971429
Forest area
*17 rms (5 shr) 6 rooms in annexe (3 fmly) TV in all bedrooms
STV Licensed Full central heating Open parking available
Child discount available 10yrs Outdoor swimming pool (heated)
Tennis Jacuzzi/spa Bicycle rental Open terrace Last d 20.45hrs
Languages spoken: English*
CARDS: ● ■ Travellers cheques

### RIBEAUVILLÉ Haut-Rhin

**★ ★ Au Cheval Blanc**
122 Grande Rue *68150*
☎ 389736138 FAX 389733703
Forest area  In town centre  Near motorway
*25 rms (20 shr) (6 fmly) Licensed Full central heating*

**★ ★ De La Tour**
1 rue de la Mairie *68150*
☎ 389737273 FAX 389733874
(off N83)
In town centre
*Closed Jan-mid Mar*
*35 en suite (bth/shr) (8 fmly) TV in all bedrooms STV Direct
dial from all bedrooms Licensed Lift Full central heating Open
parking available (charged) Covered parking available
(charged) Tennis Sauna Solarium Jacuzzi/spa Bicycle rental
Open terrace Table tennis Languages spoken: English &
German*
CARDS: ● ■ ■ ● Travellers cheques

### RIQUEWIHR Haut-Rhin

**★ ★ Du Cerf**
5 rue Général-de-Gaulle *68340*
☎ 389479218 FAX 389490458
In town centre
*15 en suite (bth/shr) 2 rooms in annexe (1 fmly) (2 with
balcony) TV in all bedrooms Licensed Full central heating
Open terrace Last d 21.15hrs Languages spoken: English &
German*
CARDS: ● ■ Travellers cheques

### ROUFFACH Haut-Rhin

**★ ★ ★ ★ Château d'Isenbourg** (Relais et Châteaux)
*68250*
☎ 389785850 FAX 389785370
(from Colmar take N83 towards Belfort, exit at Rouffach Nord.
At first traffic lights turn right, then second right. Château on
right after crossroads) *contd.*

Forest area  Near motorway
*Closed mid Jan-mid Mar*
*40 en suite (bth/shr)  8 rooms in annexe  (1 fmly)  (2 with
balcony)  TV in all bedrooms  Direct dial from all bedrooms
Mini-bar in all bedrooms  Licensed  Lift  Night porter  Full
central heating  Open parking available  Supervised  Child
discount available 12yrs  Indoor swimming pool (heated)
Outdoor swimming pool (heated)  Tennis  Sauna  Gym  Boule
Jacuzzi/spa  Bicycle rental  Open terrace  Covered terrace
Massage, Musical eve's in low season  V meals  Last d 21.15hrs
Languages spoken: English, Dutch, German, Italian & Spanish*
ROOMS: (room only) s 900-1600FF; d 900-2100FF
**Special breaks**
MEALS: Continental breakfast 90FF  Lunch 280-700FF&alc
Dinner 280-700FF&alc
CARDS: ● ■ ■ ◍ JCB Travellers cheques

### ST-BLAISE-LA-ROCHE Bas-Rhin

★ ★ **Auberge de la Bruche**
rue Principale 67420
☎ 388976868 FAX 388472222
Forest area  Near motorway
*Closed 23 Dec-23 Jan*
*13 en suite (bth/shr)  2 rooms in annexe  (2 fmly)  TV in all
bedrooms  Direct dial from all bedrooms  Licensed  Full central
heating  Open parking available  Covered parking available
(charged)  Supervised  Child discount available 8yrs  Indoor
swimming pool (heated)  Outdoor swimming pool (heated)
Sauna  Boule  Open terrace  Last d 20.45hrs  Languages spoken:
English*
ROOMS: (room only) d 280-330FF
MEALS: Continental breakfast 45FF  Lunch 130-172FF&alc
Dinner 130-172FF&alc
CARDS: ● ■ Travellers cheques

### ST-HIPPOLYTE Haut-Rhin

★ ★ ★ **Hostellerie Munsch Aux Ducs de Lorraine**
68590
☎ 389730009 FAX 389730546
(From A35 (Mulhouse-Strasbourg) take exit 12 to St-Hippolyte)
*15 Feb-24 Nov, and 10 Dec-10 Jan*
*42 en suite (bth/shr)  (9 fmly)  (32 with balcony)  TV in all
bedrooms  Radio in rooms  Direct dial from all bedrooms  Mini-
bar in 1 bedroom  Licensed  Lift  Full central heating  Open
parking available  Covered parking available (charged)  Child
discount available 12yrs  Tennis  Bicycle rental  Open terrace
Last d 21.30hrs  Languages spoken: English & German*
CARDS: ● ■ Travellers cheques

### SAVERNE Bas-Rhin

★ ★ **Chez Jean Winstub S'Rosestube**
3 rue de la Gare 67700
☎ 388911019 FAX 388912745
Near river  Forest area  In town centre  Near motorway
*25 en suite (bth/shr)  (6 fmly)  (4 with balcony)  TV in all
bedrooms  STV  Radio in rooms  Direct dial from all bedrooms
Room-safe  Licensed  Lift  Full central heating  Covered parking
available (charged)  Supervised  Child discount available  Sauna
Solarium  Bicycle rental  Open terrace  Covered terrace  V
meals  Last d 21.15hrs  Languages spoken: English &
German*
CARDS: ● ■ ■ ◍

### SEWEN Haut-Rhin

★ ★ **Des Vosges**
38 Grande rue 68290
☎ 389820043 FAX 389820833
Near river  Near lake  Forest area
*Closed 1-27Dec approx*
*17 rms (8 bth 7 shr)  (3 fmly)  (6 with balcony)  TV in all
bedrooms  Direct dial from all bedrooms  Licensed  Full central
heating  Open parking available  Covered parking available
(charged)  Child discount available 15yrs  Bicycle rental  Open
terrace  Covered terrace  V meals  Last d 20.30hrs  Languages
spoken: German*
CARDS: ● ■ Travellers cheques

### SOULTZMATT Haut-Rhin

★ ★ **Klein**
44 rue de la Vallée 68570
☎ 389470010 FAX 389476503
(off N83 between Rouffach & Guebwiller)
*11 rms (1 bth 5 shr)  TV in 4 bedrooms  Direct dial from 4
bedrooms  Licensed  Full central heating  Open parking
available  Supervised  Open terrace  V meals  Languages
spoken: English, German & Spanish*
CARDS: ● ■ ■ ◍ Travellers cheques

### STRASBOURG Bas-Rhin

★ ★ ★ **Baumann**
16 pl Cathédrale 67000
☎ 388324214 FAX 388230392
In town centre
*9 en suite (bth/shr)  (3 fmly)  TV in all bedrooms  STV  Radio in
rooms  Direct dial from all bedrooms  Mini-bar in all bedrooms
Licensed  Lift  Night porter  Full central heating  Air
conditioning in bedrooms  Child discount available 10yrs  Golf
Tennis  Squash  Riding  Gym  Pool table  Bicycle rental  Open
terrace  V meals  Last d 23.30hrs  Languages spoken: English,
German & Italian*
CARDS: ● ■ ■ ◍ Travellers cheques

★ ★ ★ **Comfort Hotel Plaza**
10 pl de la Gare 67000
☎ 388151717 FAX 388151715
(opposite the railway station)
In town centre
*78 en suite (bth/shr)  (12 fmly)  No smoking in 14 bedrooms  TV
in all bedrooms  STV  Direct dial from all bedrooms  Mini-bar in
all bedrooms  Licensed  Lift  Night porter  Full central heating
Child discount available 12yrs  Open terrace  V meals  Last d
23.00hrs  Languages spoken: English & German*
CARDS: ● ■ ■ ◍ Travellers cheques

★ ★ ★ **Hotel du Dragon**
2 rue de l'Ecarlate
☎ 388357980 FAX 388257895
(from motorway exit follow 'Centre Ville' signs. Access via
Quai St-Nicolas or Quai Charles Frey)
A tastefully converted 17th-century house in a quiet location
just south of the River Ill.
Near river  In town centre

### Hotel du Dragon
*32 en suite (bth/shr) (3 fmly) No smoking in 4 bedrooms TV in all bedrooms STV Direct dial from all bedrooms Lift Night porter Full central heating Open terrace Languages spoken: English, Germany, Portuguese & Spain*
ROOMS: (room only) s 430-655FF; d 495-705FF
CARDS: ●● ■■ ⬛ ⬛ Travellers cheques

### ★★★ Grand Hotel Concorde
12 pl de la Gare *67000*
☎ 388528484 FAX 388528400
(opposite the railway station)
Near river Forest area In town centre Near motorway
*83 en suite (bth/shr) (39 with balcony) No smoking in 10 bedrooms TV in all bedrooms STV Direct dial from all bedrooms Mini-bar in all bedrooms Licensed Lift Night porter Full central heating Child discount available 12yrs Bicycle rental Open terrace Languages spoken: English & German*
CARDS: ●● ■■ ⬛ ⬛ Travellers cheques

### ★★★ Hotel Cathedrale
12 pl de la Cathédrale *67061*
☎ 388221212 FAX 388232800
(from A4 or A35 take exit 4 'Place de l'Étoile' and follow signs for town centre and cathedral)
In town centre Near motorway
*47 en suite (bth/shr) 5 rooms in annexe No smoking in 2 bedrooms TV in 52 bedrooms STV Radio in rooms Direct dial from 52 bedrooms Mini-bar in 52 bedrooms Room-safe Licensed Lift Night porter Full central heating Air conditioning in bedrooms Covered parking available (charged) Supervised Child discount available 12yrs Languages spoken: English & German*
ROOMS: d 350-800FF
CARDS: ●● ■■ ⬛ ⬛ JCB Travellers cheques

### ★★★ Maison Rouge
4 r des Frances-Bourgeois *67000*
☎ 388320860 FAX 388224373
(from Paris, Ex51, toward city centre. From Basel/Kehl, Ex2, toward Place des Halles, parking Kléber Place)
In town centre
*142 en suite (bth/shr) (8 fmly) (90 with balcony) TV in all bedrooms STV Radio in rooms Direct dial from all bedrooms Mini-bar in all bedrooms Room-safe Licensed Lift Night porter Full central heating Open parking available (charged) Supervised Child discount available 12 yrs Languages spoken: English, German & Italian*
CARDS: ●● ■■ ⬛ ⬛ Travellers cheques

### ★★★ Rohan
17 rue du Maroquin *67000*
☎ 388328511 FAX 388756537
(on right of cathedral)
A small, peaceful hotel situated next to the cathedral in the historic town centre. The bedrooms are furnished in varied styles, alternating between rustic and Louis XV, and are equipped with every modern convenience. Porters are on hand to carry guests' luggage from the surrounding parking places to the hotel, which is located in a pedestrianised area.
In town centre

*36 en suite (bth/shr) (4 fmly) No smoking on premises TV in all bedrooms STV Radio in rooms Direct dial from all bedrooms Mini-bar in all bedrooms Room-safe Licensed Lift Night porter Full central heating Air conditioning in bedrooms Child discount available Languages spoken: English & German*
ROOMS: (room only) s 410-700FF; d 695-795FF
MEALS: Continental breakfast 55FF
CARDS: ●● ■■ ⬛ ⬛ JCB Travellers cheques

### ★★★★ Sofitel
4 pl St-Pierre-le-Jeune *67000*
☎ 388362626 FAX 388371370
Near river In town centre Near motorway
*158 en suite (bth/shr) (15 with balcony) TV in all bedrooms STV Radio in rooms Direct dial from all bedrooms Mini-bar in all bedrooms Licensed Lift Night porter Full central heating Air conditioning in bedrooms Open parking available (charged) Covered parking available (charged) Open terrace V meals Languages spoken: English, German & Italian*
CARDS: ●● ■■ ⬛ ⬛ Travellers cheques

### ★★ Tour Service Hotel
18 rue de la Tour-Koenigshoffe *67000*
☎ 388294141 FAX 388295770
In town centre Near motorway
*38 en suite (bth/shr) 10 rooms in annexe (7 fmly) TV in all bedrooms STV Licensed Full central heating Open parking available Child discount available 12yrs Open terrace V meals Last d 22.00hrs Languages spoken: English, German & Italian*
CARDS: ●● ⬛ Travellers cheques

### ★★ YG Hotel
14 rue Jean Monnet *67201*
☎ 388778560 FAX 388778533
(access via A351, exit 4)
Near motorway
*67 en suite (bth/shr) (4 fmly) (3 with balcony) TV in all bedrooms STV Direct dial from all bedrooms Licensed Night*
contd.

porter *Full central heating Open parking available Supervised Child discount available 12yrs Outdoor swimming pool Tennis Pool table Boule Open terrace V meals Last d 22.00hrs Languages spoken: English, German & Italian* CARDS: ●● ⅢⅢ Travellers cheques

## THANNENKIRCH Haut-Rhin

★ ★ *Auberge la Meuniére*
30 rue Ste Anne *68590*
☎ 389731047 FAX 389731231
(on the Colmar to Strasbourg road N83 take 2nd exit for Bergheim then signed to Thannenkirch)
*Forest area* In town centre
*Closed 21 Dec-24 Mar*
*19 en suite (bth/shr) 4 rooms in annexe (9 fmly) (12 with balcony) TV in all bedrooms Direct dial from all bedrooms Licensed Lift Full central heating Open parking available Child discount available 12yrs Sauna Gym Pool table Jacuzzi/spa Bicycle rental Open terrace Covered terrace Children's play area V meals Last d 21.00hrs Languages spoken: English, German, Italian & Spanish* CARDS: ●● ■■ ⅢⅢ Travellers cheques

## THANN Haut-Rhin

★ ★ ★ *Du Parc*
23 rue Kléber *68800*
☎ 389373747 FAX 389375623
*Forest area* Near motorway
*20 en suite (bth/shr) (3 fmly) (1 with balcony) No smoking in 5 bedrooms TV in all bedrooms STV Direct dial from all bedrooms Mini-bar in all bedrooms Room-safe Licensed Full central heating Open parking available Supervised Child discount available 13yrs Outdoor swimming pool (heated) Tennis Riding Bicycle rental Open terrace V meals Last d 21.30hrs Languages spoken: English, German, Italian & Portuguese* CARDS: ●● ■■ ⅢⅢ ⑨ Travellers cheques

## TROIS-ÉPIS Haut-Rhin

★ ★ *Villa Rosa*
*68410*
☎ 389498119 FAX 389789045
*Forest area*
*Closed 12 Feb-1 Apr*
*10 en suite (bth/shr) (4 fmly) (4 with balcony) No smoking in all bedrooms Direct dial from all bedrooms Licensed Full central heating Child discount available 15yrs Outdoor swimming pool (heated) Sauna Jacuzzi/spa Bicycle rental Open terrace Last d 20.30hrs Languages spoken: English & German* CARDS: ●● ⅢⅢ Travellers cheques

## UFFHOLTZ Haut-Rhin

★ ★ *Frantz*
41 rue de Soultz *68700*
☎ 389755452 FAX 389757051
(from N83 exit at Cernay and take D431 (Route des Cretes), then right onto D5)
*Forest area* In town centre  Near motorway
*45 rms (12 bth 11 shr) 8 rooms in annexe (1 with balcony) TV in 40 bedrooms Direct dial from all bedrooms Licensed Full central heating Open parking available Child discount available Boule Bicycle rental Open terrace V meals Last d 21.30hrs Languages spoken: English & German* CARDS: ●● ■■ ⅢⅢ ⑨ Travellers cheques

## VILLE Bas-Rhin

**La Maison Fleurie** (Prop: Mme Doris Engel-Geiger)
19 rte de Neuve Église, Dieffenbach-au-Val *67220*
☎ 388856048 FAX 388856048
*Forest area*
*(1 fmly) No smoking on premises Full central heating Open parking available Child discount available Childs play area Languages spoken: English & German*
ROOMS: s 250FF; d 265-285FF

## WESTHALTEN Haut-Rhin

★ ★ ★ *Auberge du Cheval Blanc*
20 rue de Rouffach *68250*
☎ 389470116 FAX 389476440
(access via Rouffach on N83)
*Forest area*
*Closed 21 Feb-16 Mar & 3-14 Jul*
*12 en suite (bth/shr) (2 fmly) (4 with balcony) TV in all bedrooms Direct dial from all bedrooms Mini-bar in all bedrooms Room-safe Licensed Full central heating Air conditioning in bedrooms Open parking available Child discount available 12yrs Open terrace Last d 21.00hrs Languages spoken: English & German*
ROOMS: (room only) s 580-670FF; d 440-510FF
MEALS: Full breakfast 55FF Lunch 190-450FF&alc Dinner 180-450FF&alc
CARDS: ●● ⅢⅢ

## ZELLENBERG Haut-Rhin

★ ★ *Au Riesling*
5 rte du Vin *68340*
☎ 389478585 FAX 389479208
*Forest area*
*Closed Jan-10 Feb*
*36 en suite (bth/shr) (6 with balcony) Direct dial from all bedrooms Licensed Lift Open parking available Covered parking available Child discount available 10yrs Open terrace V meals Last d 21.00hrs Languages spoken: German*

# Val de Loire

S et in the historic heart of France and possessing a rich mosaic of landscapes, the vast and beautiful region of the Loire Valley quite simply has it all. Follow tranquil country lanes through meandering river valleys lined with vineyards, charming medieval villages and a wealth of magical châteaux such as impressive Chenonceau, fairytale Château d'Ussé and magnificent Villandry with Renaissance formal gardens. Historic towns and cities abound, most notably Chartres with an awesome Gothic cathedral, or famous Orléans, the former royal city and capital of France, associated with Joan of Arc, and elegant Tours, a lively provincial capital renowned for art and architecture.

## ESSENTIAL FACTS

| | |
|---|---|
| DÉPARTEMENTS: | Eure-et-Loire, Loiret, Loir-et-Cher, Indre, Indre-et-Loire, Cher |
| PRINCIPAL TOWNS | Chartres, Orléans, Blois, Tours, Bourges, Châteauroux |
| PLACES TO VISIT: | The Renaissance châteaux of the Loire - there are over 150 in the area so it pays to be selective - Amboise, Beauregard, Blois, Chambord, Cheverny, Chenonceau and Villesavin. Sologne, a region of wild forest and heath broken by streams and lakes. The city of Chartres and the magnificent Cathedral of Notre-Dame. |
| REGIONAL TOURIST OFFICE | 9 rue St-Pierre-Lentin, 45041 Orléans Tel: 38 54 95 42 |
| LOCAL GASTRONOMIC DELIGHTS | Fresh fish - brochet (pike), carpe (carp), saumon (salmon) - cooked with sorrel or butter, vinegar and shallot sauce. Pork with prunes (a speciality of Tours). Asparagus. Mushrooms. Rillettes, cold potted pork. Tarte Tatin, caramelized upside-down apple pie. |
| DRINKS | There are many distinctive wines of the Loire region, dry whites and reds from Touraine, the richer reds from Bourgueil or the flinty-tasting white from Sancerre. |
| LOCAL CRAFTS WHAT TO BUY | Many of the local crafts are of the edible variety: goats' cheese from Berry; spicy partridge & duck pâté from Chartres; cotignac, a delicately coloured quince jelly from Orléans. |

## AIX-D'ANGILLON, LES Cher

**La Chaume** (Prop: Odile & Yves Proffit)
Rians
☎ 248644158 FAX 248642971
(from Bourges follow Auxerre to La Charité take D955 to les Aix-d'Angillon. 2nd right (rte Ste Solange). Follow signs 'Chambres d'hôtes'. 4kms)
Odile and Yves Proffit are happy to welcome you to their guest house. Located twenty kilometres from Bourges and thirty kilometres from the wine-producing town of Sancerre. Guest rooms enjoy their own access, independent of the rest of the house. Dinner by reservation only.
Near river Forest area Near motorway
*Closed Xmas*
*3 en suite (shr) No smoking on premises Full central heating Open parking available Covered parking available Fishing Bicycle rental Languages spoken: English*
ROOMS: s 190FF; d 240FF **Reductions over 1 night**
MEALS:
CARDS: Travellers cheques

## AMBOISE Indre-et-Loire

**Bed & Breakfast** (Prop: Mme Lucette Jolivard)
2 clos de la Gabilière *37400*
☎ 247572190
(off D751)
Near river Forest area
*Closed 11 Jan-14 May*
*6 en suite (bth/shr) (1 fmly) No smoking on premises TV available STV Full central heating Open parking available Languages spoken: English*
CARDS: Travellers cheques

**★ ★ ★ Bellevue**
12 quai Charles Guinot *37400*
☎ 247570226 FAX 247305123
Near river Forest area In town centre Near motorway
*32 en suite (bth/shr) (4 fmly) (4 with balcony) TV in all bedrooms STV Direct dial from all bedrooms Licensed Lift Full central heating Pool table Open terrace Languages spoken: English*
CARDS: ●● ▆▆ Travellers cheques

**★ ★ La Brèche**
26 rue Jules Ferry *37400*
☎ 247570079 FAX 247576549
(on right side of river, take street from train station)
Near river Forest area Near motorway
*RS high season (half board only)*
*12 rms (11 bth/shr) (5 fmly) (1 with balcony) TV in 10 bedrooms Direct dial from all bedrooms Licensed Full central heating Open parking available Covered parking available Child discount available 10yrs Boule Bicycle rental Open terrace V meals Last d 21.30hrs Languages spoken: English*
CARDS: ●● ▆▆ Travellers cheques

**Château de la Barre** (Prop: M & Mme Marliere)
Mosnes *37530*
☎ 247573340 FAX 247573340
(8km from Amboise in the direction of Blois via D751)
Overlooking the River Loire, between Blois and Amboise, the Château de la Barre offers a friendly atmosphere with en suite
*contd.*

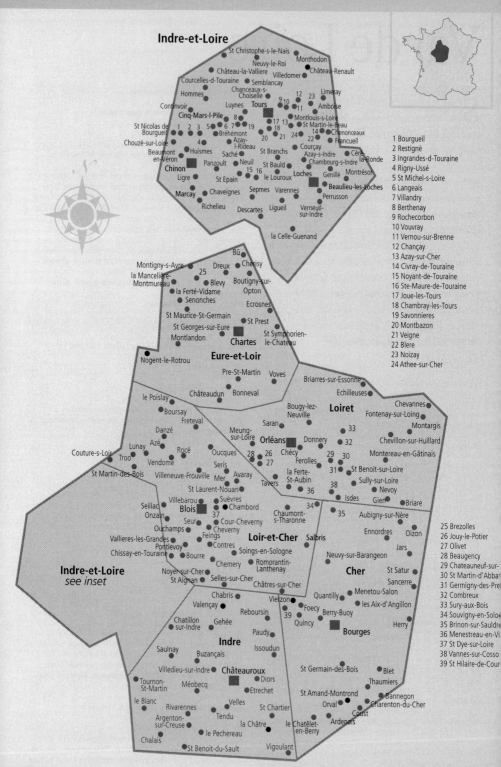

# Indre-et-Loire

St Christophe-s-le-Nais
Neuvy-le-Roi     Monthodon
Château-la-Valliere   Villedomer   Château-Renault
Courcelles-d-Touraine   Semblancay
Hommes          Chanceaux-s-      12  23   Limeray
                Choiselle     9 10
Continvoir      Luynes        Tours        11    Amboise
Cinq-Mars-l-Pile    8                    17  13    Montlouis-s-Loire
St Nicolas de    1  2  3  5   6  7  19   18        St Martin-le-Beau
Bourgueil         Bréhémont            20  21  24  14    Chenonceaux
Chouzé-sur-Loire   Azay-       4                22    Francueil
Beaumont         l-Rideau   Huismes              Courçay   Cère-
en-Véron                    Saché       St Branchs   Azay-s-Indre   la-Ronde
Chinon           Panzoult   Neuil       St Bauld   Chambourg-s-Indre
Ligre            15  16              le Louroux  Loches   Genillé   Montrésor
        St Epain              Sepmes   Varennes         Beaulieu-les-Loches
Marcay   Chaveignes                            Perrusson
        Richelieu    Descartes   Ligueil   Verneuil-
                                    sur-Indre
                    la-Celle-Guenand

Bû
Montigny-s-Ayre           Dreux   Chérisy
la Mancelière-      25
Montmureau              Blevy   Boutigny-sur-
        la Ferté-Vidame        Opton
        Senonches          Ecrosnes
    St Maurice-St-Germain
    St Georges-sur-Eure      St Prest
    Montlandon              St Symphorien-
                Chartres    le-Chateau
        Nogent-le-Rotrou

## Eure-et-Loir

            Pre-St-Martin    Voves      Briarres-sur-Essonne
    le Poislay   Châteaudun   Bonneval    Echilleuses
        Boursay                          Chevannes
        Freteval        Bougy-lez-   Loiret   Fontenay-sur-Loing
        Danzé              Neuville                Montargis
    Lunay   Azé        Meung-   Saran     33
Couture-s-Loir   Rocé    sur-Loire   Orléans   Donnery   32   Chevillon-sur-Huillard
    Troo   Vendome        Oucques  28  26  Chécy          Montereau-en-Gâtinais
St Martin-des-Bois      Seris     27    Ferolles   29  30
        Villeneuve-Frouville  Mer  Avaray        31   St Benoit-sur-Loire
                St Laurent-Nouan   Tavers  la-Ferte-  38   Sully-sur-Loire
        Villebarou   Suèvres            St-Aubin        Nevoy
    Seillac          Chambord      36   Isdes   Gien   Briare
    Onzain   Blois   37          34   35   Aubigny-sur-Nère
            Seur   Cour-Cheverny   Chaumont-
    Ouchamps       Cheverny      s-Tharonne    Ennordres   Oizon
    Vallieres-les-Grandes  Feings              Jars
        Pontlevoy   Contres   Loir-et-Cher   Salbris
    Chissay-en-Touraine   Bourre          Neuvy-sur-Barangeon   Cher
                Chemery   Soings-en-Sologne              St Satur
    Noyer-sur-Cher      Romorantin-               Sancerre
Indre-et-Loire   St Aignan   Selles-sur-Cher   Lanthenay
see inset          Châtres-sur-Cher     Menetou-Salon
        Chabris   Vierzon   Quantilly   les Aix-d'Angillon
    Valençay            Foecy
            Reboursin   39   Berry-Buoy   Herry
    Chatillon   Gehée      Quincy
    sur-Indre        Paudy        Bourges
            Issoudun
        Buzançais
    Saulnay        Indre
    Villedieu-sur-Indre   Châteauroux   St Germain-des-Bois   Blet
Tournon-      Méobecq   Diors              Thaumiers
St-Martin              Etrechet   St Amand-Montrond   Bannegon
le Blanc      Velles                Orval   Coust   Charenton-du-Cher
    Rivarennes   Tendu   St Chartier   le Chatêlet-   Ardenais
    Argenton-        la Châtre   en-Berry
    sur-Creuse   le Pechereau
Chalais                      Vigoulant
        St Benoit-du-Sault

1 Bourgueil
2 Restigné
3 Ingrandes-d-Touraine
4 Rigny-Ussé
5 St Michel-s-Loire
6 Langeais
7 Villandry
8 Berthenay
9 Rochecorbon
10 Vouvray
11 Vernou-sur-Brenne
12 Chançay
13 Azay-sur-Cher
14 Civray-de-Touraine
15 Noyant-de-Touraine
16 Ste-Maure-de-Touraine
17 Joue-les-Tours
18 Chambray-les-Tours
19 Savonnieres
20 Montbazon
21 Veigne
22 Blere
23 Noizay
24 Athee-sur-Cher

25 Brezolles
26 Jouy-le-Potier
27 Olivet
28 Beaugency
29 Chateauneuf-sur-
30 St Martin-d'Abba
31 Germigny-des-Pre
32 Combreux
33 Sury-aux-Bois
34 Souvigny-en-Solo
35 Brinon-sur-Sauldre
36 Menestreau-en-Vi
37 St Dye-sur-Loire
38 Vannes-sur-Cosso
39 St Hilaire-de-Cour

bedrooms, authentic regional cooking and a pleasant terraced garden.
Near river  Forest area

**Chateau de la Barre**
*5 en suite (bth/shr) (2 fmly) No smoking on premises Full central heating Open parking available Child discount available 10yrs Last d 21.00hrs Languages spoken: English*
ROOMS: s 215-315FF; d 320-400FF
MEALS: Dinner 100-150FF
CARDS: 💳 💳 Travellers cheques

**Château des Ormeaux** (Prop: Xavier Merle)
Nazelles *37510*
☎ 247232651 FAX 247231931
(leave A10 Amboise and take direction Amboise turn for St Ouen les Vignes then Poce/Amboise and Nazelles)
Near river  Forest area  Near motorway
*6 en suite (bth/shr) Full central heating Open parking available Supervised No children 12yrs Outdoor swimming pool Fishing Bicycle rental Languages spoken: English German Italian & Spanish*
ROOMS: d 550-650FF ✳
MEALS: Dinner 250FF✳
CARDS: Travellers cheques

★ ★ ★ ★ **Le Choiseul** (Relais et Châteaux)
36 quai Charles Guinot *37400*
☎ 247304545 FAX 247304610
(from Amboise, take A10 to Château-Renault, take D31 and cross bridge, turn right onto D751. From Tours or Blois take N152 to the New Bridge, cross and turn onto D751)

This small, charming, family run establishment dates back to the 18th-century and is near a mature park and Italian-style gardens. Its comfortable bedrooms are attractively furnished - some are in the attic and have sloping ceilings. The restaurant serves a choice of delicious regional dishes. Sporting facilities

include table tennis, tennis and mini-golf are available opposite the hotel.
Near river  Forest area
*Closed 11 Dec-14 Jan*
*32 en suite (bth/shr) (4 fmly) (7 with balcony) TV in all bedrooms STV Direct dial from all bedrooms Mini-bar in all bedrooms Licensed Night porter Full central heating Air conditioning in bedrooms Open parking available Covered parking available Supervised Child discount available 12yrs Outdoor swimming pool (heated) Boule Bicycle rental Open terrace Covered terrace Table tennis V meals Last d 21.00hrs Languages spoken: English, German & Spanish*
ROOMS: (room only) d 650-1450FF **Special breaks**
MEALS: Continental breakfast 90FF Lunch fr 190FF&alc Dinner 290-500FF&alc
CARDS: 💳 💳 💳 JCB Travellers cheques

★ ★ *Le Fleuray*
*37530*
☎ 247560925 FAX 247569397
(From A10 exit 18 take D31 to Autreche, D55 to Dame Marie, then D74 towards Cangey to hotel 2km on left)

This delightful French manor house occupies a peaceful location in unspoilt countryside with the Loire, famous châteaux, vineyards, and the historic towns of Amboise, Tours and Blois nearby. Dating back to 1870, it offers attractively furnished bedrooms, friendly and attentive service from the English owners and a restaurant renowned for its excellent cuisine. In summer guest may relax in the pretty garden whilst in winter there is a welcoming log fire.
Near river  Forest area  Near motorway
*Closed School autumn/winter hols & last wk Feb*
*11 en suite (bth/shr) 2 rooms in annexe (10 fmly) (2 with balcony) Direct dial from all bedrooms Licensed Full central heating Open parking available Covered parking available Supervised Child discount available 11yrs Boule Open terrace Covered terrace V meals Last d 20.00hrs Languages spoken: English, German & Spanish*
ROOMS: s 375FF; d 450-550FF **Reductions over 1 night**
MEALS: Continental breakfast 68FF Dinner 155-265FF&alc
CARDS: 💳 💳 Travellers cheques

★ ★ ★ *Novotel Amboise*
17 rue des Sabionnières *37400*
☎ 247574207 FAX 247304076
(A10 exit 18 in direction Bléré on D31 for 13kms, after mini châteaux park on your right in 500m)
Forest area
*121 en suite (bth/shr) (39 fmly) No smoking in 12 bedrooms TV in all bedrooms STV Direct dial from all bedrooms Mini-bar in 70 bedrooms Licensed Lift Full central heating Air*
*contd.*

conditioning in bedrooms Open parking available Supervised Child discount available 16yrs Outdoor swimming pool Tennis Pool table Mini-golf Bicycle rental Open terrace Languages spoken: English, German, Italian & Spanish
CARDS: ●● ■■ ■■ ■■ Travellers cheques

## ARDENAIS Cher

**La Folie** (Prop: Mme Jacquet)
*18170*
☎ 248961759
(from A71-E11 exit at J8.Take D925 towards Lignières.Take left to Orcenais, then Marcais. In Marcais turn left onto D38 towards Culan. Left to Ardenais.)
Near river Forest area
*Closed Nov-Mar*
2 en suite (bth/shr) (2 fmly) Full central heating Open parking available Child discount available 3yrs Boule Bicycle rental
CARDS: Travellers cheques

**Vilotte** (Prop: Jacques Champenier)
*18170*
☎ 248960496 FAX 248960496
(from the A71 exit St-Amand Montrond, then take D951 to Ardenais, then D38 in the direction of Reigny)
Near river Near lake Forest area
*Closed Jan*
6 rms (5 bth/shr) (1 fmly) No smoking in 3 bedrooms Full central heating Open parking available Child discount available Fishing Boule Bicycle rental 3 hectare gardens Table tennis Languages spoken: English & Spanish

## ARGENTON-SUR-CREUSE Indre

★★ **Hotel de La Gare et du Terminus**
7 rue de la Gare *36200*
☎ 254011081 FAX 254240254
Near river Forest area In town centre
*Closed 4-21 Jan*
14 rms (8 shr) (2 fmly) TV in all bedrooms Licensed Full central heating Open parking available Covered parking available Child discount available 10yrs Open terrace Last d 21.00hrs Languages spoken: English
CARDS: ●● ■■ Travellers cheques

## ATHÉE-SUR-CHER Indre-et-Loire

**Le Pavillon de Vallet** (Prop: Denise et Augustin Chaudiére)
4 rue de l'Aqueduc *37270*
☎ 247506783 FAX 247506831
(turn off N76 to the left, before Bléré and head for Vallet and the banks of the Cher, 22km east of Tours)
Near river Forest area Near motorway
3 en suite (bth) (1 fmly) No smoking in 2 bedrooms TV in all bedrooms Full central heating Open parking available Child discount available 10yrs Fishing Riding Boule V meals Last d 19.00hrs Languages spoken: English
MEALS: Dinner 120FF
CARDS: Travellers cheques

## AUBIGNY-SUR-NÈRE Cher

★★ **Bien Dormir**
12 av Paris *18700*
☎ 248810404
(from centre of town take D940, 150mtrs before Intermarché supermarket)

***Bien Dormir***
A 19th-century house with tasteful decoration. All rooms have tea-making facilities. Breakfast is served at separate tables or in bedrooms if required. There is a large garden with a terrace.
Near river In town centre
6 rms (4 bth/shr) (2 fmly) (1 with balcony) TV in 3 bedrooms Full central heating Open parking available Covered parking available Child discount available Bicycle rental Last d 22.00hrs Languages spoken: English
ROOMS: s 180-270FF; d 300FF **Reductions over 1 night**
MEALS: Lunch fr 65FF Dinner fr 100FF✱
CARDS: ●● ■■

★★ **La Fontaine**
2 av Général Leclerc *18700*
☎ 248580259 FAX 248583680
(from Gien take Bourges/Clermont-Ferrand (greenway) then Lamotte-Bevron by A71 then take Auxerre Way)
Forest area In town centre Near motorway
*Closed 21-31 Dec RS Sun Evenings*
16 en suite (bth/shr) (3 fmly) (1 with balcony) TV in all bedrooms STV Mini-bar in all bedrooms Licensed Full central heating Open parking available Child discount available 12yrs Bicycle rental Open terrace V meals Languages spoken: English & Spanish
CARDS: ●● ■■ ■■ ■■ Travellers cheques

## AVARAY Loir-et-Cher

**Bed & Breakfast** (Prop: Mireille & Didier Sauvage)
2 r de la Place *41500*
☎ 254813322
Near river Forest area Near motorway
2 en suite (shr) Some rooms in annexe Full central heating Open parking available Covered parking available Languages spoken: English
CARDS: Travellers cheques

## AZAY-LE-RIDEAU Indre-et-Loire

**Le Clos Philippa** (Prop: A de Dreziglie)
10,12 r de Pineau *37190*
☎ 247452649
(22km from Tours, take N751 in direction of Chinon, turn off in Azay-le-Rideau)
Near river Forest area In town centre Near motorway
(2 fmly) TV in 1 bedroom Full central heating Open parking available Boule Bicycle rental
CARDS: ●● ■■ ■■ Travellers cheques

**Manoir de la Remonière**
Cheille *37190*
☎ 247452488 FAX 247454569
(from D151 Tours-Chinon take D17 to Azay-le-Rideau and la
Remonière)
Near river Forest area
*6 en suite (bth/shr) (2 fmly) Full central heating Open parking
available Outdoor swimming pool Fishing Boule Open terrace
Languages spoken: English*
CARDS: Travellers cheques

**Le Vaujoint** (Prop: Bertrand Jolit)
Cheille *37190*
☎ 247454889 FAX 247586811
(from centre of Azay-le-Rideau towards Chinon, after 700m
into village La Chapelle St Blaise turn right opposite the
"mairie" turn right in direction of Usse Castle, turn left at Le
Vaujoint sign & follow signs for Chambre d'Hôte)
Rooms available in the outbuildings of this 19th-century family
property, set in a small hamlet four kilometres from Azay-le-
Rideau. This residence is beautifully renovated, with exposed
beams and stone floors. A lounge is reserved for guests, with
TV, fireplace and antique furniture. Large, shady garden with
barbecue and conservatory. Within 20 kilometres you will find
at least a dozen châteaux, golf courses, canoeing, sailing,
tennis and horse-riding centres.
Near river Forest area
*3 en suite (shr) (3 with balcony) Full central heating Open
parking available Languages spoken: English & Italian*
ROOMS: s 250FF; d 280FF
CARDS: Travellers cheques

**AZAY-SUR-CHER** Indre-et-Loire

**La Patouillard** (Prop: Mme Moreau)
*37270*
☎ 247504132 FAX 247504765
*3 en suite (bth/shr) No smoking on premises Full central
heating Open parking available*
CARDS: Travellers cheques

**AZAY-SUR-INDRE** Indre-et-Loire

**Le Prieure** (Prop: Danielle Papot)
*37310*
☎ 247922529
Near river Forest area
*3 rms (2 bth) TV available Radio in rooms Full central heating
Open parking available Supervised Child discount available*
CARDS: Travellers cheques

**AZÉ** Loir-et-Cher

**Bed & Breakfast** (Prop: M & Mme Boulai)
Gorgeat Azé *41100*
☎ 254720416 FAX 254720494
Forest area
*6 en suite (shr) (3 fmly) No smoking on premises Full central
heating Open parking available Supervised Child discount
available 8yrs Languages spoken: English*

**Bed & Breakfast** (Prop: M & Mme Guellier)
Ferme de Crisliane *41100*
☎ 254721409 FAX 254721803
Forest area
*5 en suite (shr) Full central heating Open parking available
Covered parking available Child discount available 11yrs
Outdoor swimming pool Table tennis*

**BANNEGON** Cher

★ ★ ★ **Auberge du Moulin de Chameron**
*18210*
☎ 248618380 FAX 248618492
(from St Amand Montrond D951 in direction Sancoins, then
D76 in direction Bannegan. Inn 2km out of village. From
Bourges N76 in direction Moulins, then D953 to Dun S/Auron,
then D41)
Near river Forest area
*Closed mid Nov-Feb*
*13 en suite (bth/shr) TV in all bedrooms Direct dial from 130
bedrooms Full central heating Open parking available
Outdoor swimming pool (heated) Fishing Bicycle rental
Open terrace V meals Last d 21.00hrs Languages spoken:
English,German & Spanish*
CARDS: 💳 💳 💳

**BEAUGENCY** Loiret

★ ★ ★ **L'Abbaye**
2 quai de l'Abbaye *45190*
☎ 238446735 FAX 238448792
Near river Forest area Near motorway
*18 en suite (bth/shr) (4 fmly) TV in all bedrooms Licensed
Night porter Full central heating Open parking available
Open terrace Close by Last d 22.00hrs Languages spoken:
English*
CARDS: 💳 💳 💳 💳 Travellers cheques

★ ★ ★ **La Tonnellerie**
12 rue des Eaux Bleues *45190*
☎ 238446815 FAX 238441001
(3km from Beaugency towards Blois)

Standing at the gateway to Sologne and in a region with an
abundance of châteaux, the hotel is evocative of past times and
exudes the discreet charm of an old manor house with the
comfort of modern days. All the bedrooms are individually
decorated with tasteful and quality furnishings and there is a
shaded garden where meals are served on fine days. The
restaurant serves the best of local cuisine and a selection of
Loire Valley wines. Numerous leisure pursuits are to be found
nearby.
Near river Forest area Near motorway
*Closed 3 Dec-1 Mar*
*20 en suite (bth/shr) (2 fmly) TV in all bedrooms Direct dial
from all bedrooms Licensed Lift Full central heating Open
parking available Child discount available 12yrs Outdoor
swimming pool (heated) Boule Bicycle rental Open terrace
V meals Last d 22.00hrs Languages spoken: English &
Spanish* *contd.*

169

ROOMS: (room only) s 375-840FF; d 475-1290FF
**Reductions over 1 night**
MEALS: Continental breakfast 75FF  Lunch 145-260FF&alc
Dinner 145-260FF&alc
CARDS: ● ■ ■ Travellers cheques

## BEAULIEU-LÈS-LOCHES Indre-et-Loire

### ★ ★ Hotel de Beaulieu
*37600*
☎ 247916080
(1km from Loches in the direction of Valencay)

This building dates back to the 16th century and is part of the Benedictine abbey of Beaulieu, where a tomb contains the remains of Foulques Nerra, grandfather of England's Henry II. Situated in the medieval town of Loches, this partly renovated residence features a flagstone spiral staircase, exposed beams, and an attractive interior flower garden. All the guests rooms are en suite and have modern facilities.
Near river  Near lake  Forest area  In town centre  Near motorway
*Closed Oct-March*
*9 en suite (shr)  (2 fmly)  Direct dial from all bedrooms  Licensed Boule  Bicycle rental  Open terrace  Last d 21.00hrs  Languages spoken: English*
ROOMS: (room only) d fr 195FF
MEALS: Continental breakfast 28FF  Lunch 70-100FFalc
Dinner 70-100FFalc
CARDS: Travellers cheques

## BEAUMONT-EN-VÉRON Indre-et-Loire

### La Balastière (Prop: Antoinette Degremont)
Grézille *37420*
☎ 247588793 FAX 247588241
Near river  Forest area
*3 en suite (bth/shr)  (2 fmly)  Radio in rooms  Full central heating  Open parking available  Languages spoken: English, German & Spanish*

### Château de Coulaine (Prop: M & Mme Bonnaventure)
*37420*
☎ 247930127
Forest area
*Etr-mid Nov*
*5 en suite (bth/shr)  Full central heating  Open parking available*
CARDS: Travellers cheques

### ★ ★ Manoir de la Giraudière
*37420*
☎ 247584036 FAX 247584606
(From Chinon take road towards Bourgueil for 5km, then turn left towards Savigny-en-Véron. Hotel 1km on right)

A handsome manor, once a private residence, that dates back to the 17th century. It is now a welcoming country hotel surrounded by vineyards, copses and grasslands. It features a 16th-century dovecote, as well as attractively furnished bedrooms and a terrace, where on fine days guests can enjoy a drink or a meal.
Near river  Forest area
*25 en suite (bth/shr)  (10 fmly)  (2 with balcony)  TV in 24 bedrooms  Direct dial from all bedrooms  Licensed  Night porter  Full central heating  Open parking available  Supervised  Child discount available 5yrs  Boule  Bicycle rental  Open terrace  Last d 21.30hrs  Languages spoken: English, Spanish & german*
ROOMS: (room only) d 200-590FF
**Reductions over 1 night**
MEALS: Continental breakfast 38FF  Lunch 120-230FF&alc
Dinner 120-230FF&alc
CARDS: ● ■ ■ ◉ Travellers cheques

## BERRY-BUOY Cher

### L'Ermitage (Prop: Mme de la Farge)
*18500*
☎ 248268746 FAX 248260328
Near river  Near motorway
*5 en suite (bth/shr)  (2 fmly)  TV in all bedrooms  Full central heating  Open parking available  Languages spoken: English, German*
ROOMS: s 190-200FF; d 250-270FF ✱
CARDS: Travellers cheques

## BERTHENAY Indre-et-Loire

### La Grange Aux Moines (Prop: J Millet)
*37510*
☎ 247500691 FAX 247500691
Restored 18th-century farmhouse, situated in a leafy park. There is a private swimming pool and bicycles are available for hire.
Near river  Forest area
*Closed 12 Nov-14 Mar*

**La Grange Aux Maines**
*5 en suite (bth/shr) (2 fmly) Full central heating Open parking available Covered parking available Outdoor swimming pool Bicycle rental*
ROOMS: s fr 290FF; d 340-390FF
CARDS: Travellers cheques

### BLANC, LE Indre

**Les Chezeaux** (Prop: A & A Jubard)
36300
☎ 254373217 254374021
*Near river*
*Closed mid Oct-mid Mar*
*2 en suite (bth/shr) Open parking available Supervised*

### BLÉRÉ Indre-et-Loire

**★ ★ Cheval Blanc**
5 pl Ch Bidault *37150*
☎ 247303014 FAX 247235280
*Near river Forest area In town centre Near motorway*
*Closed early Jan-early Feb*
*12 en suite (bth/shr) TV in all bedrooms STV Direct dial from all bedrooms Mini-bar in all bedrooms Licensed Full central heating Open parking available Covered parking available Supervised Child discount available 8yrs Outdoor swimming pool (heated) Open terrace V meals Last d 21.15hrs Languages spoken: English*
CARDS: 🅰🅱💳 Travellers cheques

**Moulin du Fief Gentil** (Prop: Ann & Roger Mason)
Culoison *37150*
☎ 247303251 FAX 247579572
(from Paris A10 exit18 Château-Renault, then D31 Amboise-Loche, bypassing Amboise, 2km after Pagope-de-Chanteloup left to La Croix-en-Touraine, cross River Cher turn left signed for Luzille, around small park, continue towards Luzille, mill right) Ann and Roger Mason have lovingly restored this 16th century monastic water mill in the heart of the Loire Valley. The mill is ideally situated in the château region with the famous vineyards of Chinon, Montlouis and Vouvray close at hand. The town is within walking distance along the River Cher. Luxurious bedrooms have been tastefully furnished and guests have use of the lounge; a room full of character and designed very much in keeping with the style of the building. Breakfast is served in the dining room which boasts impressive views over the mill stream. Dinner is available by prior arrangement. Ann is very passionate about food and offers a menu which combines the best of international and French flavour making good use of local seasonal produce. Guests can fish in the millpond or simply relax by the water's edge. Further details on website http://perso.wanadoo.fr/fiefgentil.

*Near river Near lake Near motorway*
*4 en suite (bth/shr) No smoking in all bedrooms Full central heating Open parking available No children 12yrs Fishing Boule Bicycle rental Last d 20.00hrs Languages spoken: English*
ROOMS: s 400-450FF; d 450-500FF
**Reductions over 1 night**
MEALS: Dinner 150FF
CARDS: Travellers cheques

### BLET Cher

**Château de Blet**
18350
☎ 248747202 & 248747666
(after the Bourges exit take the N76 towards Moulins, Blet is 35km south-east of Bourges on this road)
*Forest area Near motorway*
*3 en suite (bth/shr) (2 fmly) TV in all bedrooms Full central heating Open parking available Pool table*
CARDS: Travellers cheques

### BLÉVY Eure-et-Loir

**Bed & Breakfast** (Prop: Daguy & Roger Parmentier)
2 rue des Champarts *28170*
☎ 237480121 FAX 237480180
(exit Chartres on A11. In Chartres take D939 towards Verneuil sur Arre. In Maillebois turn right on D20 towards Brevy. In Brevy, towards Laons, leaving village, house first right)
A warm welcome is assured at the 200-year-old home of Daguy and Roger Parmentier. Roger is a retired chef and prepares some delicious meals. Both the comfortable bedrooms are en suite, are nicely furnished and have a TV and a fridge.
*Near river Forest area Near motorway*
*Closed Feb*
*2 en suite (bth/shr) (2 fmly) TV in all bedrooms Radio in rooms Full central heating Open parking available Child discount available 10yrs Languages spoken: English & German*
ROOMS: s 240-290FF; d 270-320FF
MEALS: Dinner fr 110FF

### BLOIS Loir-et-Cher

**★ ★ ★ Holiday Inn Garden Court** (Holiday Inn Gdn Ct)
26 av Maudoury *41000*
☎ 254554488 FAX 254745797
(Opposite Palais de Congris convention centre)
*In town centre Near motorway*
*78 en suite (bth/shr) No smoking in 40 bedrooms TV in all bedrooms Radio in rooms Direct dial from all bedrooms Mini-bar in 40 bedrooms Licensed Lift Night porter Full central heating Open parking available Child discount available 12yrs Bicycle rental Open terrace Last d 22.00hrs Languages spoken: English & German*
CARDS: 🅰🅱💳 Travellers cheques

### BONNEVAL Eure-et-Loir

**★ ★ Hostellerie du Bois Guibert**
Hammeau de Guibert *28800*
☎ 237472233 FAX 237475069
*Near motorway*
*14 en suite (bth/shr) (2 fmly) TV in all bedrooms Licensed Full central heating Open parking available Solarium Boule Bicycle rental Open terrace V meals Last d 21.30hrs Languages spoken: English,German & Spanish*
CARDS: 🅰🅱💳

## BOUGY-LEZ-NEUVILLE Loiret

**Le Climat des Quatre Coins** (Prop: Mme Glotin)
*45170*
☎ 238918089
(leave the D97 north of Orléans and take D297 to Bougy-lez-Neuville)
Quiet and spacious rooms are available on this small horse farm, where guest rooms are in a building separate to the family home. The ground floor overlooks parkland and a kitchen is provided for guests' use, as is a barbecue.
Near lake Forest area
*2 en suite (bth/shr) (1 fmly) TV available Full central heating Open parking available Languages spoken: English & German*
ROOMS: s 160FF; d 220FF ✱

## BOURGES Cher

★ ★ *Climat de France*
Z.A.C du Val d'Auron, Av de Robinson *18000*
☎ 248503278 Cen Res 64460123 FAX 248504598
(off N151)
Near river Near lake Near motorway
*43 en suite (bth/shr) (1 fmly) TV in all bedrooms Direct dial from all bedrooms Licensed Full central heating Open parking available Child discount available 13yrs Open terrace Last d 20.00hrs Languages spoken: English & Dutch*
CARDS: ●● ■■ ■ ⑨ Travellers cheques

## BOURGUEIL Indre-et-Loire

**Château des Réaux** (Prop: Florence Goupil de Bouille)
Chouzé-sur-Loire *37140*
☎ 247951440 FAX 247951834
(from A85 towards Chinon/Bourgueil leave at exit towards Chinon & at traffic lights turn right onto N152 take 1st road on right, Château signed)
Near river Forest area Near motorway
*18 en suite (bth/shr) 5 rooms in annexe (3 fmly) Full central heating Open parking available Child discount available 12yrs Tennis Bicycle rental*
CARDS: ●● ■■ ■ ⑨ Travellers cheques

## BOURRÉ Loir-et-Cher

**Manoir de la Salle** (Prop: Jean Boussard)
69 rte de Vierzon *41400*
☎ 254327354 FAX 254324709
(leave A10 at Blois Sud and proceed to Bourre via D764)
Near river Forest area Near motorway
*5 en suite (bth/shr) TV available Full central heating Open parking available Child discount available Tennis Open terrace Covered terrace Languages spoken: English*
CARDS: ●● ■ ⑨ Travellers cheques

## BOURSAY Loir-et-Cher

**La Madeleinière** (Prop: Colette le Guay)
21 rue des Écoles *41270*
☎ 254809261
(from A11 at Chartres take N10 and turn right for Boursay)
Near river Forest area Near motorway
*3 en suite (shr) (2 fmly) Radio in rooms Full central heating Open parking available Child discount available 10yrs*
CARDS: Travellers cheques

## BOUTIGNY-SUR-OPTON Eure-et-Loir

**Bed & Breakfast** (Prop: Serge & Jeanne-Marie Marechal)
11 rue des Tourelles, La Musse *28410*
☎ 237651874 FAX 237651874
(leave the N12 at the village of Houdan and proceed to La Musse via Boutigny)
Forest area Near motorway
*4 en suite (bth/shr) (2 fmly) No smoking on premises Full central heating Open parking available Child discount available 5yrs Languages spoken: English*

## BRÉHÉMONT Indre-et-Loire

**Les Brunets** (Prop: Angela Smith)
*37130*
☎ 247965581
(situated in the village of Langeais, route D57 to Azay-le-Rideau cross Langeais bridge then take D16 establishment on the right in 2kms)
Near river Near lake Forest area
*3 en suite (shr) (1 fmly) No smoking on premises TV available Full central heating Open parking available Child discount available 8yrs Open terrace V meals Languages spoken: English*
CARDS: Travellers cheques

## BRÉZOLLES Eure-et-Loir

★ ★ *Le Relais*
*28270*
☎ 237482084 FAX 237482846
Near river Forest area
Closed Aug
*25 en suite (bth/shr) (4 fmly) TV in all bedrooms Direct dial from all bedrooms Licensed Full central heating Open parking available Supervised Child discount available 11yrs Boule Bicycle rental Open terrace V meals Last d 21.30hrs Languages spoken: English*
CARDS: ●● ■ ⑨ Travellers cheques

## BRIARE Loiret

★ ★ *Hotel Le Cerf*
22-24 bd Buyser *45250*
☎ 238370080 FAX 238370515
Near river In town centre Near motorway
Closed 21 Dec-4 Jan
*21 en suite (bth/shr) 8 rooms in annexe (4 fmly) (2 with balcony) TV in all bedrooms Licensed Full central heating Open parking available Covered parking available (charged) Supervised Child discount available Boule Bicycle rental Open terrace*
ROOMS: (room only) s 240FF; d 275FF
CARDS: ■ Travellers cheques

**Domaine de la Thiau** (Prop: B Francois-Ducluzeau)
*45250*
☎ 238382092 & 238370417 FAX 238674050
(midway between Gien and Briare on D952, close to nurseries)
This imposing 18th century building is the home of Mme François-Ducluzeau. Set in a large estate by the Loire, the guest accommodation is separate from the family living quarters. Swimming, fishing and cycling all nearby. Shops within four kilometres. Private access to Loire.
Near river Forest area Near motorway

*4 en suite (bth/shr) (2 fmly) No smoking in all bedrooms TV in 3 bedrooms Radio in rooms Full central heating Open parking available Covered parking available Supervised Child discount available 2yrs Tennis Pool table Boule Bicycle rental Open terrace Table tennis,Children's playground Languages spoken: English, German & Spanish*
ROOMS: s 215-230FF; d 250-320FF **Special breaks: 10% reduction for 3 nights**

### BRIARRES-SUR-ESSONNE Loiret

**Moulin de Francorville** (Prop: M Bernard Coulon)
*45390*
☎ 238391359
(from Malesherbes take D25 to Briarres-sur-Essonne, on towards Villereau.Take left turn towards Châtillon.)
Situated on the River Essonne in a peaceful setting, this old mill has two double rooms with en suite facilities, one having an additional single bed. There is a small lounge with TV on the first floor.
*Near river Forest area*
*2 en suite (bth/shr) TV in all bedrooms Full central heating Open parking available Fishing*
ROOMS: s fr 180FF; d fr 230FF **Reductions over 1 night**
CARDS: Travellers cheques

### BRINON-SUR-SAULDRE Cher

★ ★ *La Solognote* (Relais du Silence)
Grande Rue *18410*
☎ 248585029 FAX 248585600
*Near river Forest area*
*Closed mid Feb-mid Mar*
*13 en suite (bth/shr) (2 fmly) TV in all bedrooms Direct dial from all bedrooms Licensed Full central heating Open parking available Child discount available Open terrace Last d 21.00hrs Languages spoken: English*
CARDS: ●● ▥ Travellers cheques

### BU Eure-et-Loir

**Auberge de l'Avloir** (Prop: Christian Borbot)
8 rue St-Antoine *28410*
☎ 237821385 FAX 237821698
(In the middle of the triangle formed by Dreux (12kms), Anet (8kms), and Houdan (7kms))
Christian and Anne-Marie Barbot offer a traditional welcome. They breed horses so why not hire a pony and cart to explore the local countryside? All rooms are on the first floor, with independent access. Evening meals by arrangement.
*Forest area*

*3 en suite (shr) No smoking on premises Full central heating Open parking available Covered parking available Child discount available 10yrs Riding V meals Last d 21.00 hr Languages spoken: English & German*
ROOMS: s fr 170FF; d 220-250FF **Reductions over 1 night Special breaks: 10% for 1/2 board 3 nights+**
MEALS: Continental breakfast 20FF Lunch 62-92FF Dinner 62-92FF
CARDS: ●● ▥

### BUZANÇAIS Indre

**Château du Boisrenault** (Prop: Yves du Manoir)
*36500*
☎ 254840301 FAX 254841057
(A20/E9 Paris/Limoges after Vierzon take exit 11 Levroux then D926 to Buzançais)
This impressive 19th-century château is steeped in history. The mysterious initials 'HB' are engraved on the living room mantelpiece - are they those of Huard du Boisrenault, who built the château for his daughter? Private swimming pool. Acres of woodland and park. 18-hole golf course just eight kilometres away. Tennis court and riding school within easy reach.
*Forest area Near motorway*
*Closed 16 Dec-1 Feb*
*7 en suite (bth/shr) Full central heating Open parking available Child discount available Outdoor swimming pool (heated) Open terrace Covered terrace Library TV Table tennis Languages spoken: English*
ROOMS: d 395-560FF
CARDS: ●● ■■ ▥ Travellers cheques

### CELLE-GUENAND, LA Indre-et-Loire

**Château de la Guénand** (Prop: Jane de l'Aigle)
*37350*
☎ 247949449 (after 19.30hrs)
(from Liguiel follow D50 through Preuilly-sur-Clais to La Celle-Guénand)
*Forest area In town centre*
*7 en suite (bth/shr) Full central heating Open parking available*

### CÉRÉ-LA-RONDE Indre-et-Loire

**Bed & Breakfast** (Prop: Mme Martine Laizé)
Le Petit Biard *37460*
☎ 247595118 FAX 247595118
(from Bloise take D764 to Montrichard and then on towards Loches. After 15km at Castle of Montpoupon keep to D764 for a further 2km then left to Le Petit Biard)     *contd.*

This character residence is in quiet countryside, 15 kilometres south of Chenonceau, in the centre of the Châteaux of the Loire. Four rooms are available, including a family room, furnished with antiques. Living room with fireplace, for guests use. Breakfasts served all morning. Reductions of 10 percent for stays of more than three nights.
Near river  Forest area  Near motorway
*4 en suite (shr)  (1 fmly)  Full central heating  Open parking available  Languages spoken: English*
ROOMS: s 165FF; d 200-230FF **Reductions over 1 night**
CARDS: Travellers cheques

### CHABRIS Indre

**Les Bizeaux** (Prop: Bernadette Planques)
*36210*
☎ 254401451
(Chabris is south of N76 (Tours/Vierzon). On D35 follow signs 'Gites de France')
Les Bizeaux is a small farm in the Loire Valley, within driving distance of many chateaux. The farm is one mile outside the town of Chabris, beside the River Cher. All the bedrooms have pleasant views over the fields and woods in the distance. Breakfast is served on the terrace. English hosts.
Near river  Near sea  Forest area
*3 en suite (shr)  (1 fmly)  Full central heating  Open parking available  Child discount available 10yrs  Languages spoken: English*
ROOMS: s 220FF; d 280FF **Reductions over 1 night**
CARDS: Travellers cheques

★ ★ **De la Plage**
42 rue du Pont *36210*
☎ 254400224 FAX 254400859
(between Tours and Vierzon on the N76, south of Romorantin via D128 to Châteauroux)
Near river  Forest area  In town centre  Near motorway
*Closed end Jun & early Sept & January*
*10 en suite (shr)  TV in all bedrooms  Direct dial from all bedrooms  Licensed  Full central heating  Open parking available  Covered parking available  Child discount available 2yrs  Tennis  Boule  Bicycle rental  Open terrace  V meals  Last d 21.00hrs  Languages spoken: English*
CARDS: ●● ⬛

### CHALAIS Indre

**Le Grand Ajoux** (Prop: A de la Jonquiere-Aymé)
*36370*
☎ 254377292 FAX 254375660
(from A20 take N151 towards Poitiers. At Ciron take D44, then turn right onto D927 towards Bélâbre. Establishment is 5kms before Bélâbre)
Near river  Near lake  Forest area
*Closed Nov-Mar*
*4 en suite (bth/shr)  (2 fmly)  TV in all bedrooms  Open parking available  Child discount available 4yrs  Outdoor swimming pool (heated)  Fishing  Riding  Boule  Bicycle rental  Table tennis  Last d 18.00hrs  Languages spoken: English & Spanish*
CARDS: Travellers cheques

### CHAMBOURG-SUR-INDRE Indre-et-Loire

**Le Petit Marray** (Prop: M Mesure)
*37310*
☎ 247925058 FAX 247925067
(A10 exit 23 in direction Loches/Chateauroux, N143 1.5km after Chambourg turn right)

Near river  Forest area
*4 en suite (bth/shr)  (2 fmly)  TV in all bedrooms  Full central heating  Open parking available  Child discount available 10yrs  Boule  Table tennis  Languages spoken: English*

### CHAMBRAY-LES-TOURS Indre-et-Loire

★ ★ **Ibis Hotel Sud**
10 rue Michael Faraday *37170*
☎ 247282528 FAX 247278426
(A10 exit 23 Chambray/Montbazon)
Near motorway
*80 en suite (bth/shr)  No smoking in 30 bedrooms  TV in all bedrooms  STV  Direct dial from all bedrooms  Licensed  Night porter  Full central heating  Open parking available  Child discount available 12yrs  Open terrace  Covered terrace  V meals  Last d 22.30hrs  Languages spoken: English*
CARDS: ●● ⬛ ⬛ ⬛ Travellers cheques

### CHANÇAY Indre-et-Loire

**Ferme de Launay** (Prop: J-P Schweizer)
*37210*
☎ 247522821 FAX 247522821
(15km NE of Tours via N152, north bank of Loire, direction Amboise. In Vouvray take D46 direction Vernou-sur-Brenne, then Chançay - signs before Chançay)
18th-century farmhouse set in the heart of the Vouvray wine region, between Tours and Amboise. Luxurious, comfortable en suite bedrooms. Large salon with fireplace. Gourmet meals served at the family table. English breakfasts available. Walking, fishing and riding nearby. Bicycle rentals and wine-tastings arranged.
Near river  Forest area  Near motorway
*3 en suite (bth/shr)  No smoking on premises  Open parking available  No children 10yrs  Last d 10.00hrs  Languages spoken: English, German & Italian*
ROOMS: s 350-400FF; d 400-500FF
**Reductions over 1 night**
MEALS: Full breakfast 50FF  Dinner fr 150FF
CARDS: Travellers cheques

### CHANCEAUX-SUR-CHOISILLE Indre-et-Loire

**Le Moulin de la Planche** (Prop: Jacqueline Chauveau)
Langennerie *37390*
☎ 247551196 FAX 247562434
(just north of Tours in the direction of Beaumont la Ronce)
Near river  Forest area
*3 en suite (shr)  (1 fmly)  (2 with balcony)  No smoking in 2 bedrooms  TV in all bedrooms  Full central heating  Open parking available  Child discount available  Fishing  Boule  Bicycle rental  Last d 21.00hrs*
CARDS: ●● ⬛

### CHARENTON-DU-CHER Cher

**La Serre** (Prop: M & Mme Moreau)
Laugère *18210*
☎ 248607582
(from A71 exit St-Amand-Montrond take D951 towards Sancoins)
Near river  Near lake  Forest area  Near motorway
*Closed Oct-Mar*
*3 en suite (bth/shr)  (1 fmly)  (1 with balcony)  Full central heating  Open parking available  Covered parking available  Child discount available 12yrs  Fishing  Riding  Boule  Bicycle*

rental *Open terrace Covered terrace Languages spoken: English*
CARDS: Travellers cheques

## CHARTRES Eure-et-Loir

★ ★ ★ **Grand Monarque** (Best Western)
22 pl des Épars *28005*
☎ 237210072 FAX 237363418
(town centre)
In town centre
*54 en suite (bth/shr) (8 fmly) TV in all bedrooms STV Radio in rooms Direct dial from all bedrooms Mini-bar in all bedrooms Licensed Lift Night porter Full central heating Open parking available (charged) Covered parking available (charged) Child discount available 12yrs Open terrace Last d 22.00hrs Languages spoken: English, German & Spanish*
CARDS: ●● ■■ ■■ ⑩ JCB Travellers cheques

★ ★ **De la Poste**
3 rue Général Koenig *28000*
☎ 237210427 FAX 237364217
(Follow signs for town centre. Hotel Place des Epars)
This pleasant establishment is situated in the city centre, not far from all the shops, restaurants and cafès. It features soundproofed bedrooms with a good level of comfort, and a fine cuisine, augmented by excellent wines from the renowned house cellar.
In town centre Near motorway
*57 rms (55 bth/shr) (3 fmly) No smoking in 7 bedrooms TV in all bedrooms STV Direct dial from all bedrooms Licensed Lift Night porter Full central heating Open parking available (charged) Covered parking available (charged) Supervised Child discount available 10yrs Last d 21.45hrs Languages spoken: English, German & Spanish*
MEALS: Full breakfast 42FF Lunch 84-170FF Dinner 84-170FF✱
CARDS: ●● ■■ ■■ ⑩ Travellers cheques

## CHÂTEAUDUN Eure-et-Loir

**Bed & Breakfast** (Prop: Monique Allezy)
Crépainville, 8 rue de l'Étoile *28200*
☎ 237453744
(from Châteaudun take D955 towards Alençon. After 3kms turn left onto D23 to Crépainville. In village take 3rd road on right)
Near river Forest area
*3 rms (2 shr) No smoking on premises Radio in rooms Full central heating Open parking available Covered parking available Child discount available Boule Table tennis Swing Last d 19.00hrs Languages spoken: English*
CARDS: Travellers cheques

## CHÂTEAU-LA-VALLIÈRE Indre-et-Loire

**Vaujours** (Prop: Gerard & Martine Ribert)
*37330*
☎ 247240855
(on the D959, Le Lude 17km, Tours 33km)
Near river Near lake Forest area Near motorway
*4 en suite (shr) (1 fmly) TV available Open parking available Child discount available 4yrs Outdoor swimming pool Barbecue Languages spoken: English*

## CHÂTEAUNEUF-SUR-LOIRE Loiret

★ ★ **La Capitainerie**
1 Grande Rue *45110*
☎ 238584216 FAX 238584681
Near river Forest area In town centre Near motorway
*14 rms (4 bth 8 shr) (3 fmly) (3 with balcony) TV in 12 bedrooms Radio in rooms Direct dial from all bedrooms Licensed Full central heating Open parking available Supervised Open terrace Last d 21.00hrs Languages spoken: English, German & Spanish*
CARDS: ●● ■■ Travellers cheques

★ ★ **Nouvel Hotel du Loiret**
4 pl Aristife Briand *45110*
☎ 238584228 FAX 235584399
Near river Near beach Forest area In town centre
*Closed 20 Dec-20 Jan*
*16 en suite (bth/shr) (3 fmly) TV in all bedrooms Licensed Night porter Full central heating Open parking available (charged) Covered parking available (charged) Supervised Open terrace Languages spoken: English*
CARDS: ●● ■■ ■■

## CHÂTEAUROUX Indre

★ ★ **Auberge de l'Arc en Ciel**
La Forge de l'Isle *36000*
☎ 254340983 FAX 254344674
(on D943 towards Montluçon)

On the banks of the River Indre and close to the forest of Chênes de Châteauroux, the Auberge Arc en Ciel offers its guests old fashioned service in an informal atmosphere. The bedrooms are comfortable and have good amenities, and guests can relax in the lounge with its rustic furniture, or on the terrace. The restaurant, which is situated opposite the hotel, offers enjoyable meals prepared with only fresh produce.
Near river Forest area Near motorway
*Closed Last week Dec & first week Jan RS Sun & Mon*
*25 rms (8 bth 9 shr) (9 fmly) TV in all bedrooms Direct dial from all bedrooms Licensed Full central heating Open parking available Child discount available 10yrs Boule Open terrace Languages spoken: English*
CARDS: ●● ■■ Travellers cheques

## CHÂTELET-EN-BERRY, LE Cher

***Estiveaux*** (Prop: Mme Faverges)
rte de La Chatre *18170*
☎ 248562264
(off the D951)
Near river Near lake Forest area
*5 rms (3 bth) (4 fmly) (1 with balcony) No smoking in 1
bedroom TV available Full central heating Open parking
available Child discount available*

## CHÂTILLON-SUR-INDRE Indre

### ★ ★ Auberge de la Tour
2 rte du Blanc *36700*
☎ 254387217 FAX 254387485
(approach via N143 & D975)
Near river Near lake Forest area In town centre Near
motorway
*11 rms (1 bth 6 shr) (2 fmly) TV in 6 bedrooms Direct dial from
all bedrooms Licensed Full central heating Open parking
available Covered parking available (charged) Supervised
Child discount available Open terrace Covered terrace V
meals Last d 22.00hrs*
Rooms: (room only) d 170-260FF
Meals: Full breakfast 26FF Lunch 60-220FF&alc Dinner
60-220FF&alc
Cards: ●● ▆ Travellers cheques

## CHÂTRES-SUR-CHER Loir-et-Cher

### Bed & Breakfast (Prop: M & Mme Laclautre)
19 rue Jean Segrétin *41320*
☎ 254981024
(N76 Tours/Vierzon, 20km from Vierzon)
Bedrooms with private access are available at this old market
town house, close to both the Canal and the Cher River.
Sailing, fishing, cycling and walking available on site. Riding,
three kilometres, swimming pool, three kilometres.
Near river Forest area Near motorway
*4 en suite (shr) (2 fmly) Full central heating Open parking
available Child discount available 5yrs Open terrace*
Rooms: s fr 180FF; d fr 210FF **Reductions over 1 night**
Cards: ▆ Travellers cheques

## CHAUMONT-SUR-THARONNE Loir-et-Cher

### La Farge (Prop: De Grangeneuve et Lansier)
*41600*
☎ 254885206/254885022 FAX 254889730
(A71 exit Lamotre Beunon-Chaumont-sur-Tharonne D35 Vouson
to C1 in 4km La Farge turn right to Centre Equestre de la Farge)
Near lake Forest area Near motorway

## CHAVEIGNES Indre-et-Loire

### La Varenne (Prop: Joëlle et Gérard Dru-Sauer)
*37120*
☎ 247582631 FAX 247582747
(from Tours head towards Ste-Maure-de-Touraine, then
Richelieu on D58. 1 mile before Richelieu left on D20 towards
Baslou for 2km to establishment on left 200mtrs after
'Chizeray' sign)
This 17th-century house in the middle of the countryside is
near to the châteaux of the Southern Loire and Futuroscope.
La Varenne is a harmonious dwelling which produces honey,
grows nuts and provides a peaceful holiday setting.

*La Varenne*

Forest area
*3 en suite (bth) (1 with balcony) Full central heating Open
parking available Child discount available Outdoor swimming
pool (heated) Bicycle rental Table tennis Languages spoken:
English & German*
Rooms: d 450-600FF **Reductions over 1 night**

## CHÉCY Loiret

### Les Courtils (Prop: Annie Meunier)
rue de l'Ave *45430*
☎ 238913202
(on N60 Checy exit)
Near river Forest area
*4 en suite (bth/shr) (1 fmly) No smoking on premises Full
central heating Languages spoken: English & German*

### Les Courtils (Prop: Annie Meunier)
14 place Jeanne d'Arc *45430*
☎ 238913202 FAX 238914820
Near river Forest area
*4 en suite (bth/shr) (1 fmly) No smoking in all bedrooms Full
central heating Languages spoken: English*
Rooms: s 230FF; d 300FF

## CHÉMERY Loir-et-Cher

### Château de Chémery (Prop: M & Mme Fontaine)
*41700*
☎ 254718277 FAX 254717134
(on the road from Contres to Selles-sur-Cher, between
Chambord and Valencay.)
Near lake Forest area
*5 rms (4 bth) (2 fmly) (1 with balcony) No smoking on
premises Open parking available Child discount available
14yrs Fishing Boule Bicycle rental Stables 3km away. Last d
21hrs Languages spoken: English*
Rooms: s 300-450FF; d 400-450FF
**✳ Reductions over 1 night Special breaks**
Meals: Lunch 120FF Dinner 120FF
Cards: Travellers cheques

## CHENONCEAUX Indre-et-Loire

### ★ ★ Hostellerie de la Renaudière
24 rue du Docteur Bretonneau *37150*
☎ 247239004 FAX 247239051
Near river Forest area
*15 en suite (bth/shr) 5 rooms in annexe (1 fmly) TV in all
bedrooms Direct dial from all bedrooms Mini-bar in all
bedrooms Licensed Full central heating Open parking
available Supervised Child discount available 8yrs Outdoor*

swimming pool (heated) Sauna Jacuzzi/spa Bicycle rental
Open terrace Covered terrace V meals Last d 21.30hrs
Languages spoken: English
ROOMS: (room only) s 265-345FF; d 290-480FF
**Reductions over 1 night**
MEALS: Continental breakfast 25FF Lunch 99-204FF&alc
Dinner 99-204FF&alc
CARDS: ⬤ ■ ▥ ⑩ Travellers cheques

### ★★ Hostel du Roy
9 rue Bretonneaux 37150
☎ 247239017 FAX 247238981
(A10 exit Blois direction Montrichard and Chenonceaux or exit
Amboise direction Bléré and Chenonceaux)
A family atmosphere pervades this charming hotel which is set
near the Loire Châteaux, in a rural setting. M Goupil, the chef
offers several regional and house specialities accompanied by
Loire wines.
Near river Forest area
37 rms (28 bth/shr) 11 rooms in annexe (2 fmly) TV in 30
bedrooms Direct dial from all bedrooms Licensed Full central
heating Open parking available Supervised Child discount
available Boule Open terrace Covered terrace V meals Last d
21.30hrs Languages spoken: English, German & Spanish
ROOMS: (room only) s 110-240FF; d 130-310FF
**Reductions over 1 night**
MEALS: Continental breakfast 30FF Lunch 68-185FF&alc
Dinner 68-185FF&alc
CARDS: ⬤ ■ ▥ ⑩ JCB Travellers cheques

### CHERISY Eure-et-Loir

### ★★★ Domaine de la Reposee
1 rue du Prieuré 28500
☎ 237438604 FAX 237438351
(from Paris on N12 to Dreux take exit Cherisy. At roundabout,
towards Cherisy centre, continue downhill until church then
right to Fermaincourt)
Near river Forest area Near motorway
7 en suite (bth/shr) TV in all bedrooms STV Direct dial from all
bedrooms Licensed Night porter Full central heating Open
parking available Indoor swimming pool (heated) Tennis
Fishing Riding Sauna Solarium Jacuzzi/spa Open terrace
Languages spoken: English
CARDS: ⬤ ■ ▥

### CHEVANNES Loiret

### Bed & Breakfast (Prop: Oliver Tant)
Le Village 45210
☎ 238909223
Near river Forest area
3 en suite (shr) (3 fmly) No smoking on premises Radio in
rooms Open parking available Child discount available
Languages spoken: English

### CHEVERNY Loir-et-Cher

### Le Clos Bigot
rte le Buchet 41700
☎ 254792638 FAX 254792638
(17km S of Blois off the D765)
Forest area
4 en suite (bth/shr) (2 fmly) No smoking on premises Full
central heating Open parking available No children 10yrs
Child discount available Outdoor swimming pool Languages
spoken: English, Spanish

### Ferme des Saules (Prop: Didier Merlin)
41700
☎ 254792695 FAX 254799754
(from A10 head towards Vierzon and Cheverny. In Cheverny
take D102 towards Contres. Establishment 1.6 miles on right)

Five lovely bedrooms, and table d'hôte prepared by the owner,
make this an appealing place from which to discover the
charms of the Loire Valley.
Forest area
5 en suite (bth/shr) (2 fmly) Full central heating Open parking
available Child discount available Outdoor swimming pool
(heated) Fishing Riding Boule V meals Last d 19.30hrs
Languages spoken: English, Dutch
ROOMS: s 220-300FF; d 295-350FF
MEALS: Dinner fr 120FF
CARDS: Travellers cheques

### CHEVILLON-SUR-HUILLARD Loiret

### Bed & Breakfast (Prop: Gerard Granddenis)
Le Grande Casseau 45700
☎ 238978045
Near river Forest area Near motorway
Closed Nov-Mar
3 rms (1 shr) No smoking on premises Full central heating
Open parking available Languages spoken: English

### CHINON Indre-et-Loire

### ★★★★ Château de Danzay
Danzay 37500
☎ 247584686 FAX 247588435
Near river Forest area
Closed Nov-Apr
10 en suite (bth/shr) TV in all bedrooms Direct dial from all
bedrooms Licensed Full central heating Open parking
available Supervised Child discount available Outdoor
swimming pool Open terrace Last d 21.30hrs Languages
spoken: English & Italian
CARDS: ⬤ ■ ▥ ⑩ Eurocard Travellers cheques

### ★★ Didérot
4 rue Buffon/7 rue Didérot 37500
☎ 247931887 FAX 247933710
(45km south west of Tours, take D751 to place Jeanne d'Arc,
then rue Buffon & the rue Diderot)
The Hotel Diderot is housed in a handsome building dating
back to the 18th century. Peacefully situated close to the old
town and the Place Jeanne D'Arc, the interior features half-
timbered walls, a beautiful staircase and a restaurant with a
15th century fireplace where delicious home-made jams are
*contd.*

**Diderot**

served with breakfast. The bedrooms are individually furnished and equipped with modern facilities.
In town centre
*27 en suite (bth/shr) 4 rooms in annexe (4 fmly) No smoking in 4 bedrooms TV in 10 bedrooms Direct dial from all bedrooms Licensed Night porter Full central heating Open parking available Supervised Child discount available Bicycle rental Open terrace Languages spoken: English & Greek*
ROOMS: (room only) s 260-330FF; d 310-410FF
CARDS: ● ■ ■ ⓓ Travellers cheques

**La Gabelle** (Prop: Vincent Hearne)
Briancon, Cravant-les-Côteaux *37500*
☎ 247932297 FAX 247932297
(take the D8 from Chinon towards L'Ile Bouchard follow the signs 4km from Chinon)
Near river Near beach Forest area Near motorway
*Closed Nov-Etr*
*8 en suite (bth/shr) Open parking available Child discount available 12yrs Tennis Fishing Riding Boule Bicycle rental Riverside terrace Languages spoken: English*
CARDS: ● ■ Travellers cheques

★ ★ ★ **Le Chinon**
Digue St-Jacques *37500*
☎ 247984646 FAX 247983544
Forest area In town centre
*52 en suite (bth/shr) (7 fmly) (52 with balcony) TV in all bedrooms STV Direct dial from all bedrooms Mini-bar in all bedrooms Licensed Lift Full central heating Open parking available Child discount available 12yrs Outdoor swimming pool (heated) Tennis Riding Mini-golf Bicycle rental Open terrace Last d 21.15hrs Languages spoken: English & German*
CARDS: ● ■ ■ ⓓ Travellers cheques

**Moulin de la Voie** (Prop: Mme Cottereau)
Cinais *37500*
☎ 247958290 FAX 247959116
(in Chinon cross bridge over River Vienne towards Saumur. At 1st & 2nd roundabouts follow signs for Saumur. 'Moulin de Ca Voie' 150m on left)
Near river Forest area
*4 en suite (bth/shr) Full central heating Open parking available Supervised Fishing Languages spoken: English & Italian*

**CHISSAY-EN-TOURAINE** Loir-et-Cher

★ ★ ★ **Château de la Menaudière**
*41401*
☎ 254712345 FAX 254713458
(from Blois take direction of Montrichard D764, then D115 to the hotel)

178

**Chateau de la Menaudiere**

Situated in the heart of the Vallée des Rois, surrounded by parklands, this elegant establishment welcomes its guests to a warm, friendly atmosphere. The peaceful bedrooms are beautifully appointed and provide maximum comfort. The dining room offers an innovative selection of well prepared dishes, making good use of high quality produce. Visitors can relax in the congenial bar, or for the more energetic there is the tennis court.
Forest area
*Closed 5 Jan-Feb*
*27 en suite (bth/shr) (1 fmly) TV in all bedrooms STV Radio in rooms Direct dial from all bedrooms Mini-bar in all bedrooms Licensed Full central heating Open parking available Supervised Child discount available 4yrs Outdoor swimming pool (heated) Tennis Boule Bicycle rental Open terrace Last d 21.30hrs Languages spoken: English*
ROOMS: (room only) s 400-500FF; d 600-850FF
MEALS: Continental breakfast 70FF Lunch 120-180FF&alc Dinner 220-320FF&alc
CARDS: ● ■ ■ ⓓ Travellers cheques

**CHOUZE-SUR-LOIRE** Indre-et-Loire

**Montachamps** (Prop: M & Mme Plassais)
*37140*
☎ 247951073
Near river Near sea Forest area
*5 en suite (bth/shr) (1 fmly) No smoking in all bedrooms Full central heating Open parking available Languages spoken: English & Spanish*

**CINQ-MARS-LA-PILE** Indre-et-Loire

**La Meulière** (Prop: Patrick Voisin)
10 rue de la Gare *37130*
☎ 247965363 FAX 247965363
Forest area
*4 en suite (bth/shr) (1 fmly) (1 with balcony) TV in 1 bedroom Full central heating Open parking available Languages spoken: English*

**CIVRAY-DE-TOURAINE** Indre-et-Loire

**Les Cartes** (Prop: M & Mme Pinquet)
*37150*
☎ 247579494 FAX 247578933
(in Amboise on D31, southwards, take D81 towards Civray-de-Touraine for 3kms. Take lane on right, follow signs on right,then left & left again)
Near river Forest area

*2 en suite (bth/shr) TV in all bedrooms Full central heating Open parking available Child discount available Indoor swimming pool (heated) Table tennis Languages spoken: English*
CARDS: Travellers cheques

## COMBREUX Loiret

### ★ ★ L'Auberge de Combreux
34 rte du Gatinais *45530*
☎ 238468989 FAX 238593619
(from Paris A10 exit Orléans Nord-Montargis N60 then exit Châteauneuf and proceed left to Combreux)

In a rural setting on the threshold of the Loire Valley château region, this former post house offers the visitor comfortable, elegantly decorated accommodation and traditional local cuisine. Leisure facilities are available and there is a golf course nearby.
Near river Near lake Forest area Near motorway
*Closed 16 Dec-19 Jan*
*19 en suite (bth/shr) (2 fmly) (3 with balcony) TV in all bedrooms STV Direct dial from all bedrooms Licensed Full central heating Open parking available 12yrs Outdoor swimming pool (heated) Tennis Bicycle rental Covered terrace Last d 21.30hrs Languages spoken: English & German*
ROOMS: (room only) d 325-495FF
MEALS: Continental breakfast 40FF Lunch 110-210FFalc Dinner 110-210FFalc
CARDS: ●● ■■ ▦ Travellers cheques

## CONTINVOIR Indre-et-Loire

**La Butte de l'Épine** (Prop: Michel Bodet)
*37340*
☎ 247966225 FAX 247960736
(from Tours take N152 towards Saumur-Langrais. At St-Patrice take D35 to Bourguiel. Then take D749 to Gizeux & onto Continvoir. In village, turn left, follow signpost)
Built in the style of the 17th century using traditional materials, this distinctive house offers comfortable rooms on the first floor with independent access. Breakfast is served in the large dining room. Set in a peaceful wooded area close to the vineyards of Bourgueil. Restaurants close by.
Near lake Forest area
*3 en suite (shr) No smoking on premises Full central heating Open parking available No children 10yrs Open terrace Covered terrace*
ROOMS: d fr 330FF **Reductions over 1 night**

## CONTRES Loir-et-Cher

**Bed & Breakfast** (Prop: M & Mme Bonnet)
r de Stade *41700*
☎ 254795278
(from Blois take D956 to Contres, then on towards Saint-Aignan. Take 1st right to Oisly on D21. Establishment is last on right, before stadium and after church)
*3 en suite (shr) TV in 2 bedrooms Full central heating Open parking available*

### ★ ★ ★ France
33 rue Pierre Henri Mauger *41700*
☎ 254795014 FAX 254790295
Forest area In town centre
*37 en suite (bth/shr) (18 with balcony) TV in all bedrooms STV Radio in rooms Licensed Full central heating Open parking available Covered parking available (charged) Child discount available 12yrs Outdoor swimming pool (heated) Tennis Sauna Jacuzzi/spa Bicycle rental Open terrace V meals Last d 21.15hrs Languages spoken: English & German*
CARDS: ●● ■■ ▦ Travellers cheques

**La Rabouillère** (Prop: M & Mme Thimonnier)
chemin de Marcon *41700*
☎ 254790514 FAX 254795939
Forest area
*7 en suite (bth) TV in all bedrooms Full central heating Child discount available Languages spoken: English*
CARDS: ●● ▦ Travellers cheques

## COURCAY Indre-et-Loire

**Manoir de Chemalle** (Prop: Anne-Marie-Valiere)
*37310*
☎ 247941048 FAX 247941048
(from Tours take N143 towards Loches. At Comery take D17 to Courcay. After Courcay take 2nd right & Manor is on right)
Near river Forest area
*17 en suite (shr) Full central heating Open parking available V meals Languages spoken: English, German & Italian*

## COURCELLES-DE-TOURAINE Indre-et-Loire

### ★ ★ ★ Château des Sept Tours
Le Vivier des Londes *37330*
☎ 247246975 FAX 247242374
(30km from Tours. Follow signs for Angers/Château la Vallière. Just before entering Château la Vallière, turn left on the rdbt. After 6km the Château is on right)
Near river Near lake Forest area
*46 en suite (bth/shr) 24 rooms in annexe TV in all bedrooms STV Direct dial from all bedrooms Mini-bar in all bedrooms Room-safe Licensed Lift Night porter Full central heating Air conditioning in bedrooms Open parking available Supervised Outdoor swimming pool Golf 18 Bicycle rental Open terrace Languages spoken: English*
ROOMS: (room only) d 690-1090FF
CARDS: ●● ▦ Travellers cheques

**La Grande Galléchère** (Prop: M Jean Marie Gabarre)
3 La Grande Galléchère *37330*
☎ 247249077 FAX 247249077
(exit A10 at Château-Renault or Tours Nord and take direction for Château Lavallière, then D67 direction for Angers)

*contd.*

**La Grande Galléchère**
A an old farmhouse offering comfortable accommodation and fine traditional French cuisine. A good base from which to tour the surrounding Châteaux of the Loire.
Near river  Near lake  Near sea  Near beach  Forest area
*4 en suite (bth)  (2 fmly)  Full central heating  Open parking available  Supervised  Child discount available 12yrs  Boule  Table tennis*
ROOMS: d fr 250FF
✳ **Reductions over 1 night  Special breaks**
MEALS: Dinner 120FF
CARDS: Travellers cheques

### COUR-CHEVERNY Loir-et-Cher

**Le Beguinage** (Prop: Brice et Patricia Deloison)
*41700*
☎ 254792992 FAX 254799459
(exit A10 at Blois and head towards Vierzon D765, Cour-Cheverny)
This house, close to the Château de Cheverny, is set in an extensive landscaped park. River fishing available, as is petanque. Fixed-price dinner menu.
Near river  Forest area
*6 en suite (bth/shr)  (2 fmly)  No smoking on premises  TV in 2 bedrooms  Full central heating  Open parking available  Supervised  Child discount available 4yrs  Fishing  Boule  Last d noon  Languages spoken: English & Spanish*
ROOMS: s 270-320FF;  d 290-360FF  **Reductions over 1 night**
MEALS: Dinner 100FF
CARDS: Travellers cheques

### COUST Cher

**Changy** (Prop: M Maurice Luc)
*18210*
☎ 248635403
Near motorway
*3 en suite (shr)  No smoking on premises  TV available  Full central heating  Open parking available  Supervised  Child discount available 5yrs  Languages spoken: Spanish*

### COUTURE-SUR-LOIR Loir-et-Cher

★★ *Le Grand St-Vincent*
6 rue Pasteur *41800*
☎ 254724202 FAX 254724155
Near river  Near lake  Forest area  In town centre
*7 en suite (shr)  (1 fmly)  TV in all bedrooms  Licensed  Full central heating  Open parking available  Supervised  Child discount available 8yrs  Boule  Bicycle rental  Open terrace  Last d 21.00hrs*
CARDS: ●● ▄▄

### DANZÉ Loir-et-Cher

**La Borde** (Prop: N Kamette)
*41160*
☎ 254806842 FAX 254806368
(on D24 between La Villeaux Clercs and Danze, next to N157 (Orléans-Le Mans))
This family-run guesthouse is situated in a manor overlooking a lovely park. There is a large indoor swimming pool, which can be opened up in fine weather. Tennis facilities are available within two miles and horse-riding within 10 miles. The owner is a former English teacher.
Near river  Forest area  Near motorway
*5 en suite (shr)  (2 fmly)  (2 with balcony)  Full central heating  Open parking available  Supervised  Indoor swimming pool (heated)  Fishing  Languages spoken: English, Spanish & German*
ROOMS: s 180-260FF;  d 240-320FF
✳ **Reductions over 1 night**
CARDS: ■

### DESCARTES Indre-et-Loire

★★ *Moderne*
15 rue Déscartes *37160*
☎ 247597211 FAX 247924490
(Approach from St-Maure via N10)
Near river  Forest area  In town centre  Near motorway
*Closed 21 Dec-4 Jan*
*11 en suite (bth)  (3 fmly)  TV in all bedrooms  Direct dial from all bedrooms  Licensed  Full central heating  Open parking available  Child discount available 12yrs  Open terrace  V meals  Last d 21.30hrs  Languages spoken: English, Dutch & German*
CARDS: ●● ▄▄ Carte Bleue Travellers cheques

**Villouette** (Prop: M & Mme Delaunay)
*37160*
☎ 247598007
Near river  Forest area
*3 rms  (2 with balcony)  Full central heating  Open parking available  Covered parking available  Supervised  Child discount available  V meals*
CARDS: Travellers cheques

### DIORS Indre

**Le Parc** (Prop: Astrid Gaignault)
*36130*
☎ 254260443 FAX 254261332
Forest area
*6 rms  (3 bth)  Full central heating  Open parking available  Child discount available*

### DONNERY Loiret

**Cornella** (Prop: Jacques Avril)
27 rue de Vennecy *45450*
☎ 238592674 FAX 238592674
(take rue A Bolland to the right of the church and Mayor's office and after 600mtrs r du Vennecy is on right)
Near river  Near lake  Forest area
*2 en suite (bth/shr)  TV in 1 bedroom  Full central heating  Open parking available  Child discount available 10yrs  Last d 18.00hrs  Languages spoken: English*

**La Poterie** (Prop: M & Mme D & M C Charles)
*45450*
☎ 238592003 FAX 238570447
(from A10 exit at Orléans Nord & take N60 towards
Châteauneuf. Take left to Fay-aux-Loges. With church on your
right take 1st left and take D709 to Donnery. Farm 2.5kms on
right)
Quietly situated on a working farm that grows cereal products,
just outside the village. Meals available by arrangement,
served at the family table. Simple, traditional French food.
Your hosts have booklets available for guests, giving details of
places of interest in the region. Walk along the canal, visit
Orleans, Orleans Forest or the Loire River. Golf one kilometre
away.
Near river  Forest area  Near motorway
*3 en suite (shr)  No smoking on premises  Open parking
available  Languages spoken: English*
ROOMS: s 190FF; d 245FF
MEALS: Dinner 90FF
CARDS: Travellers cheques

### DREUX Eure-et-Loir

★ ★ **Vidéotel Dreux**
8 pl Misirard *28100*
☎ 237426410 FAX 237461911
In town centre
*41 en suite (shr)  (9 fmly)  No smoking in 8 bedrooms  TV in all
bedrooms  Direct dial from all bedrooms  Licensed  Lift  Night
porter  Full central heating  Open parking available (charged)
Child discount available 12yrs  V meals  Last d 22.00hrs
Languages spoken: English*
CARDS: ● ■ ▥ ⑩

### ÉCHILLEUSES Loiret

**Bed & Breakfast** (Prop: Mme F Hyais)
3 Cour du Château *45390*
☎ 238336016
(autoroute du Sud A6 exit at Ury and take direction for La
Chapelle-la-Reine, Puiseaux and Bellegarde)
Near motorway
*Closed 15 Nov-15 Dec
2 en suite (shr)  (1 fmly)  Open parking available  Supervised
Bicycle rental  Last d 18.00hrs*

### ÉCROSNES Eure-et-Loir

**Château de Jonvilliers** (Prop: M & Mme Thompson)
17 rue d'Epernon, Hameau de Jonvilliers *28320*
☎ 237314126 FAX 237315674
(from A1 exit at junct 1(Ablis) & take N10 towards Rombouillet.
Take left onto D176 & at Orphin take D32 to Ecrosnes. In
Ecrosnes take 2nd right towards Jonvilliers)
Near river  Forest area  Near motorway
*Closed Nov-Feb
5 en suite (shr)  (1 fmly)  No smoking on premises  TV available
Full central heating  Open parking available  Supervised
Languages spoken: English*
CARDS: Travellers cheques

### ENNORDRES Cher

**Moulin Laurent** (Prop: Lahalle Daniel)
Le Gué de la Pierre *18380*
☎ 248580470 FAX 248584545
Near river  Near lake  Forest area

*3 rms (2 bth/shr)  (2 fmly)  No smoking on premises  TV
available  Full central heating  Open parking available  No
children 4yrs  Child discount available 8yrs*

### ÉTRECHET Indre

**Manoir en Berry** (Prop: Mme N Lyster)
Les Ménas *36120*
☎ 254226385 FAX 254226385
(A20 exit 12 at Châteauroux follow signs for Montluçon-la-
Châtre onto D67, between N20 & D943, Les Ménas signposted)
Near river  Near lake  Near beach  Forest area  Near motorway
*5 en suite (bth/shr)  (2 fmly)  (3 with balcony)  No smoking on
premises  Full central heating  Open parking
available  Child discount available 11yrs  Fishing  Riding  Bicycle
rental  Open terrace  Last d 21.00hrs  Languages spoken:
English & Spanish*
CARDS: ● ■ ▥ Travellers cheques

### FEINGS Loir-et-Cher

**Le Petit Bois Martin** (Prop: M & Mme Papineau)
*41120*
☎ 254202731
Forest area
*Closed 15 Mar-15 Oct
3 en suite (bth/shr)  (2 fmly)  (1 with balcony)  No smoking on
premises  TV available  Full central heating  Open parking
available  Supervised*

### FÉROLLES Loiret

**Bed & Breakfast** (Prop: Mme Susan de Smet)
8 rte de Martroi La Breteche *45150*
☎ 238597953 FAX 238590377
(from Orléans take N460 to Jargeau, then D921 to Ferolles -
Chambres d'Hôtes is signposted)
The proprietor, Susan de Smet, has her own self-imposed B&B
code. The rooms should be clean and comfortable, the host
should be welcoming and available. This guest house certainly
conforms to those criteria. In addition, guests can enjoy a
continental breakfast and meals in the evening (reservations
needed). There is a large garden with fine flowerbeds and
plenty of shady trees.
Near river  Forest area  Near motorway
*3 en suite (shr)  (2 fmly)  No smoking on premises  Full central
heating  Open parking available  Languages spoken: English*
ROOMS: s 180FF; d 230FF
MEALS: Dinner 80FF✱

### FERTÉ-ST-AUBIN, LA Loiret

**Ravenel**
rte de Jouy le Potier *45240*
☎ 238765720
(A71 exit at Orléans and take RN20 towards La Ferté-St-Aubin,
then D18 towards Jouy-le-Poitier for 5km turn right for La
Vielle Forêt)
Forest area  Near motorway
*3 en suite (bth)  (1 fmly)  Full central heating  Open parking
available  Languages spoken: English, German & Spanish*
CARDS: Travellers cheques

### FERTÉ-VIDAME, LA Eure-et-Loir

**Manoir de la Motte** (Prop: Anne Jallot)
*28340*
☎ 237375169 FAX 237375156
(from Verneuil, head towards La Ferté-Vidane, then straight on, then left up hill to manor)
Forest area
*2 en suite (bth) (2 fmly) No smoking on premises Full central heating Open parking available Supervised Child discount available 3yrs Languages spoken: English*
CARDS: Travellers cheques

### FOËCY Cher

**Le Petit Prieure** (Prop: Claude et Chantal Alard)
7 rue l'Église *18500*
☎ 248510176
(from Bourges take N76 to Vignoux/Barengeon, then D60 to Foëcy)
This small, delightful Priory is positioned against a backdrop of forests between the Loire châteaux and the Jacques Coeur Highway. Warm welcome, peace and quiet, and superb breakfast.
Near river Forest area
*3 en suite (bth/shr) (3 fmly) No smoking on premises TV in all bedrooms Full central heating Open parking available Child discount available 14yrs*
ROOMS: s 250FF; d 290-340FF **Reductions over 1 night**

### FONTENAY-SUR-LOING Loiret

★ ★ ★ **Domaine et Golf de Vaugouard**
chemin des Bois *45210*
☎ 238957185 FAX 238957978
(A6 to Lyon exit Dordives, then follow signs to Vangouard from Fontenay-sur-loing)
Near river Near lake Forest area Near motorway
*31 en suite (bth/shr) 9 rooms in annexe (9 fmly) (9 with balcony) TV in 40 bedrooms STV Direct dial from 40 bedrooms Mini-bar in all bedrooms Licensed Night porter Full central heating Open parking available Covered parking available Child discount available 12yrs Outdoor swimming pool (heated) Golf Riding Sauna Gym Boule Open terrace Last d 21.30hrs Languages spoken: English*
CARDS: ■ ■ ■

### FRANCUEIL Indre-et-Loire

**Le Moulin** (Prop: M & Mme Naess)
28 rue du Moulin Neuf *37150*
☎ 247239344 FAX 247239467
(from Bléré take N76 towards Vierzon & Bourges for 7km follow signs to Francueil. Then take D80 in direction of Luzille for 300mtrs).
Roses adorn the length of the garden and fill the air with perfume. Each guest room looks out onto the park, and a large entrance hall, music room and veranda all contribute to an enjoyable stay. A swimming pool is available for guests' use.
Near river Forest area Near motorway
*5 en suite (bth/shr) (2 fmly) TV in 3 bedrooms Full central heating Open parking available Covered parking available Child discount available Outdoor swimming pool Fishing Bicycle rental Languages spoken: English Spanish German & Scandinavian*

ROOMS: s 350-780FF; d 420-850FF
**Reductions over 1 night**
MEALS: Dinner 130FF
CARDS: Travellers cheques

### FRÉTEVAL Loir-et-Cher

★ ★ ★ **Hostellerie de Rocheux**
*41160*
☎ 254232680 FAX 254230414
Near river Forest area Near motorway
*15 en suite (bth) (1 fmly) TV available Mini-bar in all bedrooms Licensed Full central heating Open parking available Child discount available 14yrs Pool table Bicycle rental Open terrace Table Tennis Last d 21.30hrs Languages spoken: English & Italian*
CARDS: ●● ■■ ■■ ⑩

### GEHÉE Indre

**Château de Touchenoire** (Prop: De Clerck)
*36240*
☎ 254408734 FAX 254408734
(on D8 12km from Ecueillé towards Levroux)
Near river Near lake Forest area
*Closed Oct-Apr*
*6 en suite (bth/shr) (2 fmly) No smoking on premises Full central heating Open parking available Supervised Child discount available 5yrs Last d 20.30hrs Languages spoken: English, Dutch & Italian*

### GENILLÉ Indre-et-Loire

**Le Moulin de la Roche** (Prop: Josette & Clive Miéville)
*37460*
☎ 247595658 FAX 247595962
(from A10 exit at Château-Renault-Amboise,left onto A10 to Genille. Mill 1km before Genille)

The mill, dating back to the 15th-century, is surrounded by cool and lush vegetation. From the bedrooms, decorated in colourful fabrics and stencil designs, you can hear the soft and relaxing sounds of the river. All bedrooms have tea and coffee-making facilties. Your hosts are a Franco-British couple.
Near river Near lake Forest area
*Closed 21 Dec-3 Jan*
*4 en suite (bth/shr) (1 fmly) No smoking on premises Full central heating Open parking available Supervised Fishing Table tennis BBQ Languages spoken: English & Spanish*
ROOMS: d 340FF **Reductions over 1 night**

**GERMIGNY-DES-PRÉS** Loiret

**Bed & Breakfast** (Prop: M & Mme Kopp)
28 rte de Chateauneuf *45110*
☎ 238582115 FAX 238582115
(from Chateauneuf-sur-Loire take D952 towards Vien, then D60 to Germigny-des-Prés)
Near river Near lake Forest area
5 en suite (shr) No smoking on premises Full central heating Open parking available Supervised Child discount available 5yrs Table tennis

**GIEN** Loiret

★ ★ ★ **Rivage**
1 quai de Nice *45500*
☎ 238377900 FAX 238381021
(approach via D940 beside the river)
Near river In town centre
19 en suite (bth/shr) TV in all bedrooms STV Direct dial from all bedrooms Licensed Night porter Full central heating Air conditioning in bedrooms Open parking available Supervised V meals Last d 21.30hrs Languages spoken: English & German
MEALS: Lunch 145-205FF&alc Dinner 250-325FF&alc✱
CARDS: ●● ■■ ■■ ⑩ Travellers cheques

**HERRY** Cher

**Bed & Breakfast** (Prop: M Genoud)
10 pl du Champ de Foire *18140*
☎ 248795902
Near river Forest area
3 en suite (shr) (2 fmly) TV available Full central heating Open parking available Languages spoken: English

**HOMMES** Indre-et-Loire

**Le Vieux Château d'Hommes** (Prop: A & H Hardy)
*37340*
☎ 247249513 FAX 247246867
(on D64 towards Giseux)
In the heart of the Loire Valley stands this 15th-century medieval château. The comfortable guest rooms are situated in the authentic tithe barn. Meals are served in the restaurant, which is in the original Knight's Hall. Swimming pool available to guests.
Near river Near lake Forest area
5 en suite (shr) (1 fmly) TV in all bedrooms Full central heating Open parking available Covered parking available Child discount available Outdoor swimming pool Fishing Riding Boule Bicycle rental V meals Last d 21.30hrs Languages spoken: English & Italian
ROOMS: s 420-495FF; d 495-615FF
✱ **Reductions over 1 night**
MEALS: Dinner 150-175FF✱

**HUISMES** Indre-et-Loire

**Le Clos de l'Ormeau** (Prop: Anne et Jean-Marc Bureau)
4 rue du Presbytère *37420*
☎ 247954154 FAX 247954154
(at side of the church pass under arch then 1st left, 2nd house on right)
An attractive house with a great deal of character in the middle of the village presided over by Anne and Jean-Marc who keep a well stocked wine cellar.

Near river Near lake Forest area In town centre
3 rms (2 bth/shr) No smoking on premises Full central heating Open parking available Child discount available 2yrs Outdoor swimming pool Table tennis
ROOMS: s fr 230FF; d 260-300FF **Special breaks**

**La Pilleterie** (Prop: Mme Prunier-Guilletat)
*37420*
☎ 247955807
Near river Forest area
4 en suite (bth/shr) No smoking on premises Full central heating Open parking available

**INGRANDES-DE-TOURAINE** Indre-et-Loire

**Le Clos St-André** (Prop: M Pincon)
*37140*
☎ 247969081 FAX 247969081
(in Ingrandes on the main road from Bourgueil to Langeais D35, look for telephone box turn into street opposite, then right into second street follow signs)

Clos Saint Andre is a small working vineyard on the outskirts of a pretty and very quiet village, offering comfortable quiet accommodation in the 18th-century extension to the 16th-century farmhouse. Ask for details of the 'weekends Gourmands'. Half board is compulsory Apr-Oct. Your hostess offers guests a traditional evening meal, accompanied by the estate Bourgueil wine. You will be joined by your hosts, who both speak excellent English. Children's games, pétanque and table-tennis available.
Near river Near lake Forest area
Closed 16 Nov-14 Mar
6 en suite (bth/shr) (4 fmly) Full central heating Open parking available Child discount available 12yrs Boule Bicycle rental Table tennis Languages spoken: English
ROOMS: s fr 250FF; d 280-330FF
MEALS: Dinner fr 125FF✱
CARDS: ●● ■■ Travellers cheques

**ISDES** Loiret

**Bed & Breakfast** (Prop: Mme Renée Hatte)
30 rue de Clémont *45620*
☎ 238291089
(A71 exit Lamotte/Beuvron in direction Sully-sur-Loire)
A charming house set in a quiet village location with spacious and comfortable rooms available, one of which is a suite with french doors that open onto a vast shaded garden close to the Loire and Orléans.
Near river Near lake Near beach Forest area In town centre Near motorway contd.

*2 en suite (bth) No smoking in 1 bedroom Radio in rooms Full central heating Open parking available Golf Languages spoken: English & Spanish*
ROOMS: d 280-300FF ✳

**Bed & Breakfast** (Prop: Mme Bernard)
4 rte de Clémont *45620*
☎ 238291210 FAX 238291000
(A71 exit 3 Lamotte/Beuvron direction Sully-sur-Loire)

This partially restored manor house offers elegantly decorated rooms, one is in the annexe of the house, charmingly called The Dolls House, and opens directly onto the well stocked walled garden; the others are located in the proprietors' home. On sunny days a delicious breakfast is served outside. Close to the Loire and Orléans.
Near river Near beach Forest area In town centre Near motorway
*3 en suite (bth/shr) No smoking on premises Radio in rooms Full central heating Open parking available Golf Languages spoken: English & Spanish*

### ISSOUDUN Indre

#### ★ ★ ★ *La Cognette*
bd Stalingrad *36100*
☎ 254212183 FAX 254031303
Forest area In town centre Near motorway
*14 en suite (bth/shr) 1 rooms in annexe TV in all bedrooms STV Radio in rooms Direct dial from all bedrooms Mini-bar in all bedrooms Licensed Night porter Full central heating Covered parking available (charged) Child discount available Open terrace V meals Last d 22.00hrs Languages spoken: English & German*
CARDS: ●● ■■ ▥▥ ◨ Travellers cheques

### JARS Cher

**La Brissauderie** (Prop: M Philippe Jay)
*18260*
☎ 248587089 & 248587494 FAX 248587176
Forest area
*1 en suite (shr) Full central heating Open parking available*
ROOMS: d 190-200FF
CARDS: Travellers cheques

### JOUÉ-LES-TOURS Indre-et-Loire

#### ★ ★ Ariane
8 av du Lac *37300*
☎ 247676760 FAX 247673336
(hotel situated near the town centre, easy access by N10 or A10)

***Ariane***
This is a purpose-built establishment which offers modern accommodation with good amenities. It stands on the shores of a lake and features cheerfully decorated bedrooms and attractive public areas. In addition, there is a good choice of leisure opportunities and two restaurants nearby.
Near lake Forest area Near motorway
*Closed Xmas-early Jan*
*31 en suite (bth/shr) (5 fmly) TV in all bedrooms STV Direct dial from all bedrooms Mini-bar in all bedrooms Licensed Night porter Full central heating Open parking available Covered parking available (charged) Child discount available 10yrs Outdoor swimming pool (heated) Bicycle rental Open terrace Languages spoken: English & Spanish*
CARDS: ●● ▥▥ Travellers cheques

#### ★ ★ ★ Château de Beaulieu
67 rue de Beaulieu *37300*
☎ 247532026 FAX 247538420
*19 en suite (bth/shr) 10 rooms in annexe TV in all bedrooms Direct dial from all bedrooms Mini-bar in all bedrooms Licensed Full central heating Air conditioning in bedrooms Open parking available Child discount available Boule Open terrace Last d 21.30hrs Languages spoken: English, German & Spanish*
MEALS: Continental breakfast 60FF Lunch 195-480FF Dinner 195-480FF
CARDS: ●● ■■ ▥▥ ◨ Travellers cheques

### JOUY-LE-POTIER Loiret

**Bed & Breakfast** (Prop: Jacques & Christiane Becchi)
778 rue de Chevenelles *45370*
☎ 238458307
(12km from A71 exit2)

A comfortable home in a pretty wooded area of the Sologne. The hosts make sure that visitors know the best places to visit

in the area; the Châteaux of Chambord, Cheverny and Blois are nearby.
Forest area Near motorway
*2 rms (1 shr) No smoking on premises Radio in rooms Full central heating Open parking available*
ROOMS: s fr 210FF; d fr 260FF
MEALS: Dinner fr 95FF

## LANGEAIS Indre-et-Loire

**Château de Cinq-Mars** (Prop: M & Mme Untersteller)
*37130*
☎ 247964049 FAX 247963660
(from Tours take N152 follow River Loire towards Saumur at Cinq Mars la Pile the chateau is on right, follow signposts)
Near river Near lake Near sea Forest area Near motorway
*Closed Mon & 10-19 Feb & 19-29 Oct*
*3 en suite (bth/shr) (1 fmly) Full central heating Open parking available Child discount available 16yrs Languages spoken: English & German*
CARDS: Travellers cheques

**★ ★ ★ Errard Hosten**
2 rue Gambetta *37130*
☎ 247968212 FAX 247965672
(in city centre)
Near river Forest area In town centre Near motorway
*Closed 15 Feb-15 Mar*
*10 en suite (bth/shr) TV in all bedrooms STV Direct dial from all bedrooms Licensed Full central heating Open parking available (charged) Covered parking available (charged) Child discount available 10yrs Bicycle rental Open terrace Last d 21.30hrs Languages spoken: English*
ROOMS: (room only) s 280FF; d 360FF
MEALS: Continental breakfast 55FF Lunch 145-165FF&alc Dinner 145-165FF&alc
CARDS: ● ■ ■ ⑩ Eurocard & JCB Travellers cheques

## LIGRÉ Indre-et-Loire

**Bed & Breakfast** (Prop: M & Mme Marolleau)
5 rue St-Martin *37500*
☎ 247933753 FAX 247933674
Near river Forest area
*3 en suite (bth/shr) (1 fmly) No smoking on premises Full central heating Open parking available Child discount available Table tennis Languages spoken: English & Spanish*
ROOMS: s 230-240FF; d 240-270FF
**Reductions over 1 night**
CARDS: Travellers cheques

## LIGUEIL Indre-et-Loire

**Moulin de la Touche** (Prop: Michael Rees)
*37240*
☎ 247920684 FAX 247599638
(A10 to St-Maure, D59 to Ligueil, chambre d'hôte is 2km out of Ligueil on the right of the D31 Ligueil to Loches road).
This is an 18th-century watermill, attached to a large, comfortable millers house. Bedrooms are spacious and prettily furnished. The guest lounge and dining room have open fireplaces. The watermill and house are surrounded by 30 acres of private land and two rivers run through the grounds. Minimum stay of 2 nights during the summer. Fishing available on site.
Near river Near lake Forest area
*Closed Xmas*

***Moulin de la Touche***
*5 en suite (shr) (4 fmly) (1 with balcony) No smoking on premises Full central heating Open parking available Outdoor swimming pool Fishing Last d 18.00hrs Languages spoken: English*
ROOMS: s 280-400FF; d 310-450FF
**Reductions over 1 night**
MEALS: Dinner 130FF✱
CARDS: ● ■ Travellers cheques

## LIMERAY Indre-et-Loire

**Les Grillons** (Prop: M & Mme Guichard)
*37530*
☎ 247301176
(approach via N152 (Tours-Blois). Turn off towards Limeray. Establishment near River Cisse)
Near river Near motorway
*Closed 15 Dec-5 Jan*
*5 en suite (bth) (3 fmly) (1 with balcony) TV available Open parking available Child discount available 10yrs Boule Last d 20.00hrs Languages spoken: English & German*
ROOMS: d 260-320FF
MEALS: Lunch 90-140FF Dinner 90-140FF✱
CARDS: ● ■ Travellers cheques

## LOCHES Indre-et-Loire

**★ ★ De France**
6 rue Picois *37600*
☎ 247590032 FAX 247592866
(In the town centre, beside the Medieval City)
Near river Forest area In town centre
*Closed 12 Jan-12 Feb*
*19 rms (18 bth/shr) (2 fmly) (4 with balcony) TV in all bedrooms STV Direct dial from all bedrooms Licensed Full central heating Open parking available (charged) Covered parking available (charged) Supervised Bicycle rental Open terrace V meals Last d 21.15hrs Languages spoken: English*
ROOMS: (room only) s 240-365FF; d 300-370FF
**Reductions over 1 night**
MEALS: Full breakfast 37FF Lunch 97-270FF&alc Dinner 97-270FF&alc
CARDS: ● ■ ⑩ Travellers cheques

**★ ★ ★ George Sand**
39 rue Quintéfol *37600*
☎ 247593974 FAX 247915575
Near river Near lake Forest area In town centre Near motorway

*contd.*

20 en suite (bth/shr) (3 fmly) TV in all bedrooms Direct dial from all bedrooms Licensed Full central heating Child discount available 12yrs Open terrace V meals Last d 21.00hrs Languages spoken: English
CARDS: ●● ▨▨ Travellers cheques

**Les Jolletières** (Prop: Elisabeth Douard)
37600
☎ 247590661 FAX 247590661
(approach via D25 in Indre Valley)
Four bed & breakfast rooms available on this farm in a rural setting between the river and the forest. Meals in the evening by arrangement, residents only, aperitif and wine included. Panoramic view over the Château de Loches.

Near river Near lake Forest area
Closed Jan
4 en suite (bth/shr) (1 fmly) No smoking on premises Full central heating Open parking available Child discount available 10 yrs Bicycle rental ULM Last d 18.00hrs Languages spoken: English
ROOMS: s 210FF; d 240FF **Reductions over 1 night**
MEALS: Dinner 95FF

**Le Moulin** (Prop: Susan Hutton)
St-Jean St-Germain 37600
☎ 247947012 FAX 247947798
(take N143 from Loches direction of Châteauroux, go through Perusson, then left into St-Jean, Moulin last house on left)
Situated on its own private island in the middle of the River Indre, this lovely property features a garden with lawns sloping down to the water's edge. All rooms are well-furnished and meals are made with local produce. Within easy reach of most major chateaux and many vineyards. Private small sandy beach plus 300 metres of private fishing with a small boat available. Not suitable for young children. English hosts.
Near river Near beach Forest area Near motorway
Closed Dec-Feb
6 en suite (bth/shr) (1 fmly) (2 with balcony) No smoking in all bedrooms Full central heating Open parking available No children 8yrs Child discount available Tennis Fishing Riding Boule Bicycle rental Open terrace 2 rowing boats V meals Last d 8.30pm Languages spoken: English
ROOMS: d 300-400FF **✱ Reductions over 1 night**
MEALS: Dinner 150FF✱
CARDS: Travellers cheques

**LOUROUX, LE** Indre-et-Loire

**La Chaumine** (Prop: M & Mme Baudoin)
37240
☎ 247928209
Near river Near lake Forest area
4 rms (2 bth/shr) (2 fmly) TV available Full central heating Open parking available Child discount available Last d 18.30hrs Languages spoken: English & Spanish
CARDS: Travellers cheques

**LUNAY** Loir-et-Cher

**Château de la Vaudourière**
41360
☎ 254721946 FAX 254721946
(from Vendôme, follow signs to Montoire-sur-le-Loir via D5. After 11km follow signs to Lunay, then to château)
Near lake Near beach Forest area
3 en suite (bth/shr) Full central heating Open parking available Covered parking available Indoor swimming pool (heated) Languages spoken: English
ROOMS: d 450-580FF ✱
MEALS: Dinner 100-150FF✱
CARDS: ●● ▨▨ Travellers cheques

**LUYNES** Indre-et-Loire

**★ ★ ★ ★ Domaine de Beauvois**
Le Pont Clouet, rte de Cléré-les-Pins, BP27 37230
☎ 247555011 FAX 247555962
(from A10 at Tours Nord take N10 towards Tours and then take N152 to Luynes)
Near river Near lake Forest area Near motorway
Closed 31 Jan-12 Mar
38 en suite (bth/shr) 2 rooms in annexe (24 fmly) TV in all bedrooms STV Direct dial from all bedrooms Mini-bar in 40 bedrooms Licensed Lift Night porter Full central heating Open parking available Supervised Child discount available 12yrs Outdoor swimming pool (heated) Tennis Fishing Boule Bicycle rental Open terrace boating, hot air ballooning, archery Last d 21.00hrs Languages spoken: English, German & Spanish
CARDS: ●● ▨▨ ▨▨ ▣ JCB Travellers cheques

**Moulin Hodoux** (Prop: Jocelyne Vacher)
37230
☎ 247557627 FAX 247557627
(A10 exit Ste-Radegande, direction of Saumur on N152. 12km after Tours is Luynes centre and D76 for St-Étienne-de-Chigny for 1.25km to Le Pont de Grenouille, then right for 1.25km)
Near river Forest area
4 en suite (shr) (3 fmly) Full central heating Open parking available Child discount available 2 yrs Outdoor swimming pool Fishing Boule Bicycle rental Open terrace Covered terrace Languages spoken: English & German

**MANCELIÈRE-MONTMUREAU, LA** Eure-et-Loir

**La Musardière** (Prop: M & Mme Schaffner)
28270
☎ 237483909 FAX 237483909
(on the D4 8km from Brezolles, 8km from La Ferté-Vidame)
Near river Near lake Forest area
Closed Nov-Mar

*3 en suite (bth/shr) (1 fmly) TV in 1 bedroom Full central heating Open parking available Supervised Child discount available Indoor swimming pool (heated) Outdoor swimming pool (heated) Table tennis Languages spoken: English & German*

## MARÇAY Indre-et-Loire

**★ ★ ★ ★ Château de Marcay**
*37500*
☎ 247930347 FAX 247934533
Forest area
*34 en suite (bth/shr) 7 rooms in annexe (4 fmly) (6 with balcony) TV in all bedrooms STV Direct dial from all bedrooms Licensed Lift Night porter Full central heating Open parking available Supervised Child discount available Outdoor swimming pool (heated) Tennis Boule Bicycle rental Open terrace V meals Last d 21.30hrs Languages spoken: English, German & Spanish*
MEALS: Full breakfast 100FF Lunch 280-450FF&alc Dinner 250-450FF&alc
CARDS: ● ■ ■ ■ Travellers cheques

## MÉNESTREAU-EN-VILLETTE Loiret

**Bed & Breakfast** (Prop: Oliver Cadel)
115 Chemin de Bethleem *45240*
☎ 238769070
(turn of N20 at La Ferte St Aubin in direction Menestreau en Villette)
Forest area
*4 rms (1 bth) (2 fmly) No smoking on premises Full central heating Open parking available Child discount available Languages spoken: English & German*

**Ferme des Foucault** (Prop: Rosemary Beau)
*45240*
☎ 238769441
(6km after Marcilly-en-Villette on the D64 (route to Sennely) turn right at the small sign "Les Foucault", then turn right at mailboxes at the end of road)
Near river Forest area
*RS Nov-Apr*
*No smoking on premises TV in 2 bedrooms Full central heating Open parking available Covered parking available Bicycle rental Languages spoken: English & German*

## MENETOU-SALON Cher

**Bed & Breakfast** (Prop: Mme Marguerite Jouannin)
17 rue Franche *18510*
☎ 248648085
Forest area
*7 rms (4 shr) No smoking on premises Full central heating Open parking available No children*

## MÉOBECQ Indre

**Le Bourg** (Prop: Ceecile Benhamou)
1 rue de Neuillay *36500*
☎ 254394436
Near river Near lake Near sea Forest area Near motorway
*Closed Nov-Mar*
*2 rms Full central heating Open parking available No children Languages spoken: English*

## MER Loir-et-Cher

**Bed & Breakfast** (Prop: Claude & Joelle Mormiche)
Le Clos, 9 rue Dutems *41500*
☎ 254811736 FAX 254817019
(A10, exit 16, Paris-Bordeaux 2km, near church, town centre)
Near river Forest area In town centre Near motorway
*5 en suite (bth/shr) (1 fmly) No smoking on premises Full central heating Open parking available Covered parking available Bicycle rental Billiards Languages spoken: English*
CARDS: ● ■ Eurocard Travellers cheques

## MEUNG-SUR-LOIRE Loiret

**Bed & Breakfast** (Prop: Raymonde Bechu)
30 rte de la Batisière *45130*
☎ 238443438 FAX 238443438
Near river Forest area Near motorway
*4 en suite (bth/shr) (1 fmly) No smoking on premises Full central heating Open parking available Supervised Child discount available Table tennis*

## MONTARGIS Loiret

**★ ★ Climat de France**
1250 av d'Antides-Amilly *45200*
☎ 238982021 FAX 238891916
(off N7, signed Montargis Sud Centre Commercial)
*40 en suite (bth/shr) (4 fmly) TV in 41 bedrooms Direct dial from 41 bedrooms Licensed Full central heating Open parking available Open terrace Covered terrace Last d 10pm Languages spoken: English & French*
CARDS: ● ■

## MONTBAZON Indre-et-Loire

**★ ★ ★ ★ Château d'Artigny**
rte de Monts *37250*
☎ 247343030 FAX 247343039
(highway N10 Paris - Bordeaux, exit 23 towards Montbazon. When there, follow signs Azay-le-Rideau.)
The château is perfectly in keeping with the royal estates surrounding it and reflects, in its classical splendour, the great past of the Touraine region. The public areas feature ornate ceilings and antiques, and the guest accommodation is decorated with quality furnishings that are completely in style with the building. There is a spacious lounge-bar, an elegant restaurant and a 65-acre park with unsurpassed leisure facilities.
Near river Forest area
*Closed 1-7 Jan & 3-31 Dec*　　　　　　　　*contd.*

44 en suite (bth/shr) 13 rooms in annexe (4 fmly) TV in all
bedrooms STV Radio in rooms Direct dial from all bedrooms
Mini-bar in all bedrooms Licensed Lift Night porter Full
central heating Open parking available Child discount
available 10yrs Outdoor swimming pool (heated) Golf Tennis
Fishing Sauna Gym Boule Jacuzzi/spa Bicycle rental Open
terrace Covered terrace Musical evenings,signposted walks V
meals Last d 21.15hrs Languages spoken: English, German &
Spanish
ROOMS: (room only) d 900-1800FF
MEALS: Continental breakfast 90FF Lunch 310-480FF&alc
Dinner 310-480FF&alc
CARDS: ●● ■■ ☰☰ ⅅ JCB Travellers cheques

★ ★ ★ **Domaine de la Tortinière**
Les Guis de Veigni, rte de Ballan-Miri 37250
☎ 247343500 FAX 247659570
(A10 exit 23 follow Montbazon on N10, 2km N 1st set of traffic
lights on left after railway track just outside Montbazon)
Near river Forest area Near motorway
Closed 21 Dec-Feb RS Half board compulsory Jul-Sep
21 en suite (bth/shr) 10 rooms in annexe (9 fmly) (6 with
balcony) TV in all bedrooms STV Direct dial from all
bedrooms Mini-bar in 5 bedrooms Room-safe Licensed Full
central heating Open parking available Supervised Child
discount available 12yrs Outdoor swimming pool (heated)
Tennis Fishing Solarium Boule Bicycle rental Open terrace V
meals Last d 21.15hrs Languages spoken: English, Dutch,
German, Italian & Spanish
ROOMS: (room only) s 530-1150FF; d 530-1450FF
**Special breaks**
MEALS: Full breakfast 85FF Lunch fr 230FF&alc Dinner
295-420FF&alc
CARDS: ●● ☰☰ Travellers cheques

### MONTEREAU-EN-GATINAIS Loiret

**Hostellerie Rurale de Courpale** (Prop: Christiane
Hamelin)
Courpalet 45260
☎ 238877244
(access via N7 Montargis-Paris to Nogent then D41. Or via
Gien and Ouzouer, then D119)

Situated on the edge of the Orléans Forest, this residence is set
in four hectares of grounds and offers pretty, newly decorated
double guest rooms on the ground floor. Independent access
to terrace and swimming pool. Lounge and dining room,
furnished in Louis XIII style, are availabe to guests. Dinner
served by request at a fixed price. Reductions available for
children under 10 years.
Near river Forest area Near motorway

7 rms (2 fmly) (1 with balcony) Full central heating Open
parking available Covered parking available Child discount
available 10yrs Outdoor swimming pool Boule Bicycle rental
Last d 21.00hs
MEALS: Lunch fr 90FF Dinner fr 90FF✱

### MONTHODON Indre-et-Loire

**La Marechalerie** (Prop: Niedbalski)
6 r des Rosiers, Le Sentier 37110
☎ 247296166
(at Château-Renault, head in the direction of Angers for 2km,
turn right onto D54 towards Le Boulay - Le Sentier is 3km after
leaving Le Boulay)

Six rooms are offered in this 18th-century blacksmith's forge,
furnished with original French antiques, which is located close
to the region's châteaux in rural surroundings. The rooms have
a private entrance seperate from the main house. Bike hire,
tackle and games are available from your hosts.
Near river Near lake Forest area
6 en suite (bth/shr) (2 fmly) Open parking available Covered
parking available Child discount available 12yrs Fishing Bicycle
rental Last d 16.00hrs Languages spoken: English & German
ROOMS: s fr 190FF; d fr 210FF
MEALS: Dinner 80FF
CARDS: Travellers cheques

### MONTIGNY-SUR-AVRE Eure-et-Loir

★ ★ *Moulins des Planches*
28270
☎ 37482597 FAX 37483563
Near river Forest area Near motorway
19 en suite (bth/shr) (2 fmly) (1 with balcony) TV in all
bedrooms STV Direct dial from all bedrooms Full central
heating Open parking available Languages spoken: English
CARDS: ●● ☰☰

### MONTILOUIS-SUR-LOIRE Indre-et-Loire

**Le Colombier** (Prop: M A Moreau Recoing)
4 Grande Rue, Husseau 37270
☎ 247508524
(from A10 exit Amboise continue towards Tours for 7km. Pass
a small cross and enter Husseau. 300mtrs further on Le
Colombier is the first house)
Near river Forest area Near motorway
3 en suite (bth/shr) (2 fmly) (2 with balcony) Full central
heating Open parking available Pool table Boule Table tennis
Languages spoken: English & German
CARDS: Travellers cheques

### MONTLANDON Eure-et-Loir

**Bed & Breakfast** (Prop: M & Mme Gallet)
7 rue de la Tour *28240*
☎ 237498106
Forest area  Near motorway
*2 en suite (bth/shr)  No smoking on premises  Full central heating  Open parking available  Supervised  Child discount available 10yrs  Last d 20.00hrs*
CARDS: Travellers cheques

### MONTRÉSOR Indre-et-Loire

**Le Moulin** (Prop: Willems de Laddersous)
8 Impasse de la Mécorique *37460*
☎ 247927461
(17km from Loches and 25km from Valençay, take direction of Chemillé-sur-Indrois & then follow signs to bed & breakfast)
Near river
*4 en suite (bth/shr)  (2 fmly)  Full central heating  Open parking available  Child discount available 12yrs  Fishing  Boule  Languages spoken: English, German & Polish*

### NEUIL Indre-et-Loire

**Les Hautes Mougonnières** (Prop: Jean Mestivier)
*37190*
☎ 247268771
Forest area
*5 en suite (bth/shr)  (2 fmly)  No smoking on premises  Full central heating  Open parking available  Child discount available 10yrs  V meals  Languages spoken: English*
CARDS: ▆ Travellers cheques

### NEUVY-LE-ROI Indre-et-Loire

**Bed & Breakfast** (Prop: Mme Ghislaine de Couesnongle)
20 rue Pilate *37370*
☎ 247244148
(from Tours/La Membrolle N138 towards Le Mans, at Neuillé-Pont-Pierre take D68 to Neuvy-le-Roi; house on road through village, opposite turning to Louestault)
Near lake  Forest area  Near motorway
*2 rms (1 bth/shr)  Full central heating  Open parking available  Bicycle rental  Languages spoken: English*

**Ferme le Château-du-Bois**
*37370*
☎ 247244476 FAX 247248658
Near river  Forest area  Near motorway
*4 en suite (bth/shr)  (2 fmly)  TV available  Open parking available  Child discount available  Fishing  Riding  Boule  Open terrace  V meals  Languages spoken: English & Spanish*

### NEUVY-SUR-BARANGEON Cher

**Le Bas Guilly**
*18330*
☎ 248516446
Near river  Near sea  Forest area  Near motorway
*6 en suite (shr)  No smoking on premises  Full central heating  Open parking available  Covered parking available  Jacuzzi/spa  Languages spoken: English & German*
CARDS: ●● ▆▆ Travellers cheques

### NEVOY Loiret

**Domaine de Ste Barbe** (Prop: Annie Le Lay)
route de Lorris *45500*
☎ 238675953 FAX 238672896
(A6 exit Dordives follow route for Montargis/Bourges/Gien. At rdbt take direction of Gien-Nord to Orléans. Turn right and take D44 to Lorris turn left off this road onto small road signed "chambre d'hôte")
Surrounded by woods and fields, Sainte Barbe is an old house with comfortable guest bedrooms decorated with taste and antiques furnishings. Guests are assured of a warm welcome.
Forest area
*3 en suite (bth/shr)  TV in 1 bedroom  Full central heating  Open parking available  Child discount available 12yrs  Outdoor swimming pool (heated)  Tennis  Fishing  Jacuzzi/spa  Last d 20.30hrs  Languages spoken: English*
ROOMS: s 180-220FF;  d 350FF
MEALS: Dinner 100-150FF

### NOIZAY Indre-et-Loire

**★ ★ ★ ★ Château de Noizay**
rte de Chancay *37120*
☎ 247521101 FAX 247520464
(A10 exit Amboise/Château-Renault, D31 direction Amboise, N152 direction Vouvray/Tours, D78 to Noizay)
Near river  Forest area  Near motorway
*Closed mid Jan-mid Mar*
*14 en suite (bth/shr)  (3 fmly)  TV in all bedrooms  STV  Direct dial from all bedrooms  Mini-bar in all bedrooms  Licensed  Full central heating  Open parking available  Covered parking available  Child discount available 12yrs  Outdoor swimming pool  Tennis  Fishing  Pool table  Boule  Bicycle rental  Open terrace  Covered terrace  Last d 21.45hrs  Languages spoken: English, German & Spanish*
ROOMS: (room only) d 685-1450FF
**Reductions over 1 night**
MEALS: Full breakfast 95FF  Lunch 165-240FF&alc  Dinner 240-370FF&alc
CARDS: ●● ▆▆ ▄▄ ◎ Travellers cheques

### NOYANT-DE-TOURAINE Indre-et-Loire

**Château de Brou**
*37800*
☎ 247658080 FAX 247658292
(A10 exit 25 to Sainte-Maure turn left after 2nd set of lights property 100 metres on right)

All the rooms have views of the park or the Courtineau valley with its troglodyte grottoes. The furnishings and decoration
*contd.*

reflect the colours and character of the regions famous historical personalities.
Near river  Forest area  Near motorway
*Closed Jan-Feb*
*12 en suite (bth/shr)  (2 fmly)  No smoking in 6 bedrooms  TV in all bedrooms  STV  Direct dial from 2 bedrooms  Mini-bar in 2 bedrooms  Room-safe  Full central heating  Air conditioning in bedrooms  Open parking available  Child discount available 10yrs  Fishing  Riding  Boule  Bicycle rental  Open terrace  Languages spoken: English & Spanish*
ROOMS: (room only) d 490-1600FF  **Special breaks**
CARDS: ●● ■■ ☰☰ ⑩

### NOYERS-SUR-CHER Loir-et-Cher

★ ★ ★ **Clos du Cher**
rte de St-Aignan *41440*
☎ 254750003 FAX 254750379
Near river  Forest area  Near motorway
*Closed Jan-mid Feb*
*10 en suite (bth/shr)  (3 fmly)  TV in all bedrooms  STV  Direct dial from all bedrooms  Mini-bar in all bedrooms  Licensed  Full central heating  Open parking available  Child discount available 10yrs  Fishing  Bicycle rental  Open terrace  V meals  Last d 21.30hrs  Languages spoken: English, German, Italian & Spanish*
ROOMS: (room only) d 390-580FF
MEALS: Continental breakfast 60FF  Lunch 140-320FF&alc  Dinner 140-320FF&alc
CARDS: ●● ■■ ☰☰ ⑩ Travellers cheques

### OIZON Cher

★ ★ ★ ★ **Château de la Verrerie**
*18700*
☎ 248815160 FAX 248582125
(from Aubigny-sur-Nère take D89 to Château)
Near river  Near lake  Forest area
*Closed 16 Dec-14 Jan*
*12 en suite (bth/shr)  6 rooms in annexe  (4 fmly)  (1 with balcony)  No smoking in 2 bedrooms  Direct dial from all bedrooms  Licensed  Open parking available  Covered parking available  Supervised  Child discount available 12yrs  Tennis  Fishing  Riding  Pool table  Boule  Bicycle rental  Open terrace  Last d 21.30hrs  Languages spoken: English, German, Italian, Portuguese & Spanish*
CARDS: ●● ■■ ☰☰ Travellers cheques

### OLIVET Loiret

★ ★ ★ **Rivage**
635 rue de la Reine Blanche *45160*
☎ 238660293 FAX 238563111
Near river  Forest area
*17 en suite (bth/shr)  (5 fmly)  (12 with balcony)  TV in all bedrooms  Licensed  Full central heating  Open parking available  Supervised  Child discount available  Tennis  Open terrace  Pedalos  Languages spoken: English*
CARDS: ●● ■■ ☰☰ ⑩

### ONZAIN Loir-et-Cher

★ ★ ★ **Château des Tertres**
11 rte de Monteaux *41150*
☎ 254208388 FAX 254208921
(A10 from Paris exit Blois then 16kms on N152 direction of Tours)

Forest area
*Closed 12 Dec-1 Apr*
*14 en suite (bth/shr)  5 rooms in annexe  Direct dial from all bedrooms  Licensed  Full central heating  Open parking available  Child discount available 10yrs  Bicycle rental  Open terrace  Languages spoken: English & German*
CARDS: ●● ■■ ☰☰ Travellers cheques

### ORLÉANS Loiret

★ ★ **L'Éscale du Port Arthur**
205 rue de l'Église *45160*
☎ 238763036 FAX 238763767
Tucked away in lush vegetation on the banks on the River Loiret, the hotel is surrounded by unspoilt countryside. Completely renovated throughout it now offers tastefully furnished bedrooms with en suite facilities, three dining rooms and a shaded terrace with views of the river. A choice of enjoyable meals is served on the terrace in summer or in front of the open fireplace in winter.
Near river  Forest area

*20 en suite (bth/shr)  (3 fmly)  No smoking in 2 bedrooms  TV in all bedrooms  STV  Direct dial from all bedrooms  Room-safe  Licensed  Full central heating  Open parking available  Child discount available 2yrs  Fishing  Riding  Solarium  Boule  Bicycle rental  Open terrace  Covered terrace  Wkly live entertainment  V meals  Last d 22.0hrs  Languages spoken: English, Italian, Spanish & German*
ROOMS: (room only) s 260-285FF; d 285-340FF
**Reductions over 1 night**
**Special breaks: Gastronomic/Cultural/Sports breaks**
MEALS: Full breakfast 42FF  Lunch 118-196FF&alc  Dinner 118-196FF&alc
CARDS: ●● ■■ ☰☰ ⑩ JCB Travellers cheques

★ ★ ★ **Terminus**
40 rue de la République *45000*
☎ 238532464 FAX 238532418
Forest area  In town centre  Near motorway
*47 en suite (bth/shr)  (3 fmly)  (20 with balcony)  TV in all bedrooms  STV  Direct dial from all bedrooms  Licensed  Lift  Night porter  Full central heating  Languages spoken: English*
CARDS: ●● ■■ ☰☰ ⑩ Travellers cheques

### ORVAL Cher

**La Trolière** (Prop: M Dussert)
*18200*
☎ 248964745
Near river  Forest area  Near motorway

*3 en suite (bth/shr) No smoking on premises Full central heating Open parking available Supervised Child discount available 10yrs Fishing Languages spoken: English*
CARDS: ● Travellers cheques

### OUCHAMPS Loir-et-Cher

**★ ★ ★ Relais des Landes** (Best Western)
Les Montils *41120*
☎ 254444040 FAX 254440389
(take A10 exit Blois-Sud south of the Loire, then in direction of Montrichard & onto D751, then onto D764)
*Forest area*
*Closed end Nov-Feb*
*28 en suite (bth) TV in all bedrooms Radio in rooms Direct dial from 10 bedrooms Mini-bar in 10 bedrooms Licensed Full central heating Open parking available Child discount available 12yrs Bicycle rental Open terrace V meals Last d 21.30hrs Languages spoken: English & German*
CARDS: ● ■ ☲ ⑩ Travellers cheques

### OUCQUES Loir-et-Cher

**★ ★ Commerce**
9 rue de Beaugency *41290*
☎ 254232041 FAX 254230288
The hotel is situated just a few miles outside Paris and offers a contemporary, cheerful interior where individually styled bedrooms are equipped with modern facilities offering a good standard of comfort. The cuisine is of a high standard and consists of well prepared dishes to suit most palates.
*In town centre*
*Closed 16 Dec-14 Jan*

*12 en suite (bth/shr) (2 fmly) TV in all bedrooms Radio in rooms Direct dial from all bedrooms Mini-bar in 3 bedrooms Licensed Full central heating Covered parking available Child discount available Last d 21.00hrs Languages spoken: English*
ROOMS: (room only) s 230-280FF; d 260-310FF
**Reductions over 1 night**
MEALS: Continental breakfast 41FF Lunch 97-275FF&alc Dinner 97-275FF&alc
CARDS: ● ■ ☲

### PANZOULT Indre-et-Loire

**Domaine de Beauséjour** (Prop: Marie Chauveau)
*37220*
☎ 247586464 FAX 247952713
(Panzoult is located 12km east of Chinon, take D21 in the direction of of L'Ile Bouchard through the village, 2km out of town signposted on the right)

*Near river Near lake Forest area*
*5 en suite (bth/shr) (1 fmly) Full central heating Open parking available Outdoor swimming pool Tennis Fishing Riding Mini-golf Bicycle rental Table tennis Languages spoken: English*

### PAUDY Indre

**Château de Dangy** (Prop: G M & Lucie Place)
*36260*
☎ 254494224 FAX 254494299
*Near lake Forest area Near motorway*
*Closed Oct-Mar*
*17 rms (14 bth/shr) (3 fmly) No smoking on premises Night porter Open parking available Child discount available Languages spoken: English*
CARDS: Travellers cheques

### PERRUSSON Indre-et-Loire

**Beausoleil La Madeleine** (Prop: M Mingotaud)
La Madeleine *37600*
☎ 247591003
*Forest area*
*5 en suite (bth/shr) (3 fmly) (2 with balcony) No smoking on premises TV in all bedrooms Full central heating Open parking available Child discount available Boule*

### POISLAY, LE Loir-et-Cher

**Les Coteaux** (Prop: Gaec Coigneau)
*41270*
☎ 254805319 FAX 254801911
*Near river Forest area*
*3 en suite (shr) (1 fmly) Full central heating Open parking available Child discount available 8yrs Boule Bicycle rental Cycling Table tennis Last d 20.00hrs Languages spoken: English*
MEALS: Dinner 85FF✱
CARDS: Travellers cheques

### PONTLEVOY Loir-et-Cher

**Les Bordes** (Prop: Josianne & François Galloux)
*41400*
☎ 254325108 FAX 254326443
*Forest area*
*6 en suite (bth/shr) (2 fmly) No smoking in all bedrooms Full central heating Open parking available Child discount available 10yrs*

### PRÉ-ST-MARTIN Eure-et-Loir

**Le Carcotage Beauceron** (Prop: M & Mme Violette)
8 rue St Martin *28800*
☎ 237472721 FAX 237473809
*4 en suite (shr) (2 fmly) No smoking on premises Full central heating Open parking available Covered parking available Languages spoken: English*

### QUANTILLY Cher

**Château de Champgrand** (Prop: M Alain Gazeali)
*18110*
☎ 248641215 FAX 248244100
(between St-Martin D'Auxigny and Menetou Salon)
*Forest area Near motorway*
*4 en suite (bth/shr) TV available Full central heating Open parking available Languages spoken: English* contd.

### QUINCY Cher

**Domaine du Pressoir** (Prop: M Claude Houssier)
18120
☎ 248513004
Near river  Near lake  Forest area  Near motorway
*Closed Jan & Feb*
*4 en suite (shr)  (3 fmly)  No smoking on premises  Full central heating  Open parking available*

### REBOURSIN Indre

**Le Moulin** (Prop: M Gerard Cheneau)
36150
☎ 254497205 FAX 254497205
(from Vierzon S on N20 to Vatan, then N on D922 towards Garçay)
Near river  Near lake  Forest area  Near motorway
*Closed 10 Sep-May*
*2 en suite (shr)  TV available  Full central heating  Open parking available  Tennis  Fishing  Mini-golf  Languages spoken: English, Spanish & Portuguese*

### RESTIGNÉ Indre-et-Loire

**Château Louy** (Prop: J S Luff)
37140
☎ 247969522
(off the E60 between Saumur and Restigne)
Near river  Near lake  Forest area
*1 en suite (bth/shr)  (1 fmly)  Full central heating  Open parking available  Supervised  Child discount available 14yrs  Bicycle rental  Languages spoken: English*

### RICHELIEU Indre-et-Loire

**L'Escale** (Prop: Marion & Tim Lawrence)
30 rue de la Galère 37120
☎ 247582555 & 0685591629
(A10 from Paris-St-Mauré exit 25 direction Richelieu. After passing Richelieu sign take second left)
Near river  Near lake  Forest area  In town centre  Near motorway
*3 en suite (bth/shr)  (2 fmly)  TV in 1 bedroom  Full central heating  Open parking available  Covered parking available  Child available 2yrs  Outdoor swimming pool (heated)  Tennis  Fishing  Riding  Boule  Bicycle rental  Languages spoken: English*
ROOMS: s fr 270FF;  d fr 310FF
CARDS: Travellers cheques

**La Maison** (Prop: Mme Couvrat-Desvergnes)
6 rue Henri Proust 37120
☎ 247582940 FAX 247582940
(in Richelieu cross Place des Réligieuse and take first left)
Forest area  In town centre
*Closed Oct-Apr*
*4 en suite (bth/shr)  Night porter  Full central heating  Open parking available  Covered parking available  Languages spoken: English & Italian*
ROOMS: s 450FF;  d 500FF ✱
CARDS: Eurocheques

**Les Religieuses** (Prop: Mme Marie Josephe Leplatre)
24 place de Religueuses, /1 rue Jarry 37120
☎ 247581042 FAX 247581042
(A10 exit Ste-Maure onto D760 to Noyant then D757. At the corner of place des Religieuses & rue Jarry)

Forest area  In town centre  Near motorway
*Closed Jan*
*4 en suite (bth/shr)  No smoking on premises  Full central heating  Open parking available*

### RIGNY-USSÉ Indre-et-Loire

**Le Pin** (Prop: M Porousset)
314320
☎ 247955299 FAX 247954321
(A10 exit Chamray-les-Tours direction Chinon)
Near river  Forest area
*4 en suite (bth/shr)  Outdoor swimming pool  Sauna  Pool table  Table tennis*

### RIVARENNES Indre

**Château de la Tour** (Prop: Mme de Clemont Tonnerre)
36800
☎ 254470612 FAX 254470608
(East of Rivarennes beside the River Creuse. Cross bridge and bear left, then left again to château)

Turreted château with comfortably furnished rooms on the edge of the River Indre in a beautiful wooded park. Hundreds of small lakes in the area, which is renowned for hunting and fishing. There are many châteaux, forts, Roman churches and medieval villages to visit in the area.
Near river  Forest area  Near motorway
*10 en suite (bth/shr)  (3 fmly)  TV in 1 bedroom  Full central heating  Open parking available  Covered parking available  Child discount available 12yrs  Tennis  Fishing  Riding  Boule  Mini-golf  Bicycle rental  Covered terrace  V meals  Last d 12.00*
ROOMS: d 600-1200FF ✱
MEALS: Dinner fr 375FF
CARDS: Travellers cheques

### ROCÉ Loir-et-Cher

**La Touche - Rocé** (Prop: Jean Louis Nouvellon)
41100
☎ 254771952 FAX 254770645
(La Touche is situated 6km east of Vendôme, off the D92)
Near river  Near lake  Forest area  Near motorway
*Closed 16 Sep-14 May*
*6 rms (4 shr)  (1 fmly)  Full central heating  Open parking available  Child discount available  Fishing  Bicycle rental  Languages spoken: English*
CARDS: Travellers cheques

## ROCHECORBON Indre-et-Loire

**Château de Montgouverne** (Prop: Christine & Jacques Desvignes)
*37210*
☎ 247528459 FAX 247528461
(from A10 exit Tours Ste-Radegonde, take N521 then N152 direction Vouvray then turn left to St-Georges)

Located in listed parkland, this splendid 18th-century residence is surrounded by Vouvray vineyards and overlooks a lake. Both bedrooms and suites are beautifully furnished, all with en suite facilities and TV. Heated swimming pool, and bicycles are available. Gourmet dinner by reservation.
Near river Forest area
*6 en suite (bth) (2 fmly) TV in all bedrooms Full central heating Open parking available No children 12yrs Outdoor swimming pool (heated) Bicycle rental Open terrace Last d 20.00hrs Languages spoken: English*
ROOMS: s 650-1050FF; d 700-1100FF
MEALS: Dinner 260-360FF
CARDS: ● ■ ■ ● Eurocard Travellers cheques

**Les Hautes Gatinières** (Prop: Jacqueline Gay)
7 chemin de Bois Soleil *37210*
☎ 247528808 FAX 247528590
(A10 exit20 Vouvray & Ste Radegonde, take direction of Vouvray via N152 3km after exit of motorway are traffic lights in Rochecorbon, turn left at traffic lights & follow "chambre d'hôte" sign)
The house is in quiet and pleasant surroundings overlooking the Rochecorbon village. Bedrooms are equipped with antique furniture.
Near river Near motorway
*4 rms (3 bth) (1 fmly) TV in 3 bedrooms Full central heating Open parking available Child discount available 10yrs Bicycle rental Languages spoken: English*
ROOMS: s 260FF; d 295FF **Special breaks**
CARDS: Travellers cheques

## ROMORANTIN-LANTHENAY Loir-et-Cher

### ★ ★ ★ ★ Grand Hotel du Lion d'Or
69 rue Georges Clemenceau *41200*
☎ 254941515 FAX 254882487
(From Paris A10, A71 to the north of Orléans, towards Bourges, exit Slabris and D724)
In town centre
*Closed 17 Feb-20 Mar*
*16 en suite (bth/shr) (4 with balcony) TV in all bedrooms STV Radio in rooms Direct dial from all bedrooms Mini-bar in all bedrooms Room-safe Licensed Lift Full central heating Air*

conditioning in bedrooms Open parking available (charged)
Supervised Open terrace Covered terrace V meals Last d 21.30hrs Languages spoken: English
ROOMS: (room only) s fr 700FF; d 1100-2200FF
MEALS: Full breakfast 110FF Lunch 450-650FF&alc Dinner 450-650FF&alc
CARDS: ● ■ ■ ● Travellers cheques

## SACHÉ Indre-et-Loire

**Les Tilleuls** (Prop: Michelle Piller)
La Sablonnière *37190*
☎ 247268145 FAX 247268400
(coming from Tours, take direction for Chinon and turn off for Saché. In Saché follow signs for La Sablonnière where house is signposted)
Near river Forest area
*Closed Dec-14 Mar*
*4 en suite (shr) No smoking on premises Full central heating Open parking available No children 10yrs Fishing Bicycle rental*

## ST-AIGNAN Loir-et-Cher

### ★ ★ Grand Hotel Saint-Aignan
7-9 quai J-J-Délorme *41110*
☎ 254751804 FAX 254751259
(A10 exit Blois in direction of Vierzon-Châteauroux & continue towards St-Aignan, at St-Aignan after Le Pont Hotel in a 100mtrs on left)
Near river Forest area Near motorway
*21 rms (5 bth 11 shr) (7 fmly) TV in 9 bedrooms Direct dial from all bedrooms Licensed Full central heating Open parking available Covered parking available (charged) Child discount available 12yrs Open terrace V meals Last d 22.00hrs Languages spoken: English & German*
ROOMS: (room only) d 135-360FF
MEALS: Full breakfast 50FF Lunch 90-205FF Dinner 90-205FF
CARDS: ● ■ ■ ● Travellers cheques

## ST-AMAND-MONTROND Cher

**Château de la Commanderie**
a Farges-Allichamps *18200*
☎ 248610419 FAX 248610184
(A71 exit 8 onto D925 after 5km take D92 until Farges-Allichamps)
Near river Forest area
*8 en suite (bth) (1 fmly) (2 with balcony) No smoking in 3 bedrooms Licensed Night porter Full central heating Open parking available Covered parking available Supervised Child discount available Riding Boule Bicycle rental Open terrace Languages spoken: English*
ROOMS: d 800-1200FF **Reductions over 1 night**
MEALS: Lunch 400FF
CARDS: ● ■ ■ Travellers cheques

## ST-BAULD Indre-et-Loire

**Le Moulin de Coudray** (Prop: Sylvie Peria)
*37310*
☎ 247928264 FAX 247928264
(approach via D82 towards Tauxiguy or D58 towards Manthelan)
Near river Near lake Forest area *contd.*

*3 en suite (bth/shr) No smoking on premises Full central heating Open parking available Supervised Child discount available 10yrs Fishing Bicycle rental Last d noon Languages spoken: English*

### ST-BENOÎT-DU-SAULT Indre

**Le Portail** (Prop: Marie France Boyer Barral)
*36170*
☎ 254475720 FAX 254475720
(enter medieval city by the fortified gate in direction of priory and church)
Near river Forest area In town centre Near motorway
*3 en suite (shr) (1 fmly) No smoking on premises TV in 2 bedrooms Full central heating Open parking available Supervised Child discount available 10yrs Languages spoken: English*

### ST-BENOÎT-SUR-LOIRE Loiret

**Bed & Breakfast** (Prop: M & Mme Bouin)
6 chemin de la Borde *45730*
☎ 238257053 FAX 238351006
(approach via D60 or D148)
Near river
*6 en suite (shr) No smoking on premises TV in 1 bedroom Full central heating Open parking available Child discount available 8yrs Boule Bicycle rental Table tennis V meals Languages spoken: English*
ROOMS: d 260-300FF **Reductions over 1 night**
MEALS: Dinner fr 100FF
CARDS: Travellers cheques

### ST-BRANCHS Indre-et-Loire

**La Paqueraie** (Prop: Monique Binet)
*37320*
☎ 247263151 FAX 247263915
(from Paris on the A10 exit Chambray and turn left onto N143 to Cormery, after railway crossing follow sign towards St-Branchs then sign Borne PR3, La Paqueraie is 4th house on the right)
Surrounded by the castles of the Loire valley, 'La Paqueraie' has a garden with 100-year-old oaks and a swimming pool. Meals are based on local produce accompanied by regional wine.
Near river Forest area
*4 en suite (bth/shr) TV in all bedrooms Full central heating Open parking available Child discount available Outdoor swimming pool Fishing Boule V meals Last d 20.00hrs Languages spoken: English & Spanish*
MEALS: Dinner 135FF✱
CARDS: Travellers cheques

### ST-CHARTIER Indre

**★ ★ ★ Château de la Vallée Bleue**
rte de Verneuil *36400*
☎ 254310191 FAX 254310448
Set in a ten-acre park, regional specialities can be enjoyed in the restaurant and meals are taken on the terrace in summer.
Near river Near motorway
*Closed mid Nov-early Mar*
*15 en suite (bth/shr) 3 rooms in annexe (1 fmly) (1 with balcony) TV in all bedrooms Radio in rooms Direct dial from all bedrooms Mini-bar in all bedrooms Licensed Full central heating Open parking available Child discount available 12yrs*

***Château de la Vallée Bleue***
*Outdoor swimming pool Golf Gym Boule Bicycle rental Open terrace Bouldorome, childrens games V meals Last d 21.30hrs Languages spoken: English, German & Spanish*
ROOMS: (room only) d 390-690FF
**Reductions over 1 night**
MEALS: Continental breakfast 55FF Lunch 110-295FF Dinner 150-295FF
CARDS: ●● ▇▇

**Château de Maitres Sonneurs** (Prop: M Peubrier)
*36400*
☎ 254311017
Near river Forest area Near motorway
*Closed 16 Nov-Apr*
*4 en suite (bth/shr) TV in 1 bedroom Open parking available Languages spoken: English*

### ST-CHRISTOPHE-SUR-LE-NAIS Indre-et-Loire

**★ Les Glycines**
5 pl Johan d'Alluyé *37370*
☎ 247293750 FAX 247293754
Near river Forest area In town centre Near motorway
*7 rms (6 bth/shr) TV in all bedrooms Direct dial from all bedrooms Mini-bar in all bedrooms Licensed Full central heating Child discount available 12yrs Last d 21.30hrs Languages spoken: English*
CARDS: ●● ▇▇ Travellers cheques

### ST-DYÉ-SUR-LOIRE Loir-et-Cher

**★ ★ Manoir de Bel Air**
1 rte d'Orleans *41500*
☎ 254816010 FAX 254816534
Near river Forest area Near motorway
*40 en suite (bth) TV in all bedrooms Direct dial from all bedrooms Licensed Night porter Full central heating Open parking available Covered parking available Child discount available 10 yrs Boule Bicycle rental Open terrace V meals Last d 21.30hrs Languages spoken: English*
CARDS: ●● ▇▇ Travellers cheques

### ST-ÉPAIN Indre-et-Loire

**Château de Montgoger** (Prop: Mireille et Paul Thilges-Porte)
*37800*
☎ 247655422 FAX 247658543
(A10 exit 25 Sainte-Maure-de-Touraine and take direction for Noyant-de-Touraine on D760, then Saint-Épain via D21)
Near river Forest area Near motorway
*Closed Nov-Mar*

*4 en suite (bth) (4 with balcony) No smoking on premises TV in all bedrooms STV Full central heating Open parking available Supervised Child discount available 6-12yrs Languages spoken: English & German*
ROOMS: d 500-650FF ✱ **Special breaks**
CARDS: Travellers cheques

### ST-GEORGES-SUR-EURE Eure-et-Loir

**Hameau de Berneuse** (Prop: Mme Marie-Laurence Varriale)
*12 rue Basse 28190*
☎ 237268049
(autoroute Paris/Le Mans, exit Thivars, then in direction Fontenay-sur-Eure, then St-Georges-sur-Eure and Berneuse)
Set in large country garden, this modern house offers well-furnished accommodation, with one room overlooking the terrace. Boules available and bikes for hire. Fishing close by.
*Near river Near lake Forest area Near motorway*
*2 rms (1 bth) No smoking on premises Radio in rooms Full central heating Open parking available Child discount available 5yrs Fishing Boule Languages spoken: English, Italian & Spanish*
ROOMS: s fr 220FF; d fr 250FF
**Special breaks: (3 or more nights, 10% off)**

### ST-GERMAIN-DES-BOIS Cher

**Bannay** (Prop: M & Mme Chambrin)
*18340*
☎ 248253103
(from Bourges N144 to Levet, then D28 towards Dun-sur-Auron, after 2km turn right, house 300mtrs from junction)
*Forest area Near motorway*
*3 en suite (shr) Full central heating Open parking available Child discount available 10yrs*
CARDS: 💷

### ST-HILAIRE-DE-COURT Cher

★ ★ *Château de la Beuvrière*
*45580*
☎ 248751463 FAX 248754762
*Near river Forest area Near motorway*
*Closed 15 Dec-15 Mar*
*15 rms (10 bth) (1 fmly) (3 with balcony) Direct dial from all bedrooms Licensed Full central heating Open parking available Covered parking available Child discount available Outdoor swimming pool (heated) Tennis Fishing Boule Open terrace Last d 21.00hrs Languages spoken: English*
CARDS: 💷 💷 💷 💷 Travellers cheques

### ST-LAURENT-NOUAN Loir-et-Cher

**Bed & Breakfast** (Prop: M & Mme Libeaut)
*41220*
☎ 254872472
*Forest area*
*3 en suite (shr) Open parking available Child discount available*

### ST-MARTIN-D'ABBAT Loiret

**Bed & Breakfast** (Prop: Chantal Pelletier)
*Le Haut des Bordes 45110*
☎ 238582209
(from Orléans take N60 and leave at Châteauneuf/Loire. Stay on D952 in direction of Gien, through St Martin d'Abbat and

go straight on. 2km after railway bridge and turn left in direction of 'les places', after 800mtrs turn left)
*Near river Near lake Forest area*
*1 en suite (bth) No smoking on premises Full central heating Open parking available Fishing Boule Languages spoken: English*
ROOMS: d 260FF

**Bed & Breakfast** (Prop: Francoise Vanaldre)
*La Polonerie, Les Places 45110*
☎ 238582151
(from Orléans, travel towards Montargis on the N60 for 35km. Exit at Châteauneuf-sur-Dome, D952 towards Gien. Through St-Martin d'Abbat, 3km on follow signs on left.)
Farmhouse, built at the beginning of the century, set in two hectares of garden, situated on the edge of the Orléans forest. You are warmly welcomed by Françoise and Thierry Vanalder and your hostess is happy to cook dinner for you. Both rooms are decorated in a charming fashion.
*Near river Forest area Near motorway*
*Closed 16 Feb-15 Mar & 16 Aug-5 Sep*
*2 en suite (shr) No smoking in all bedrooms Full central heating Open parking available Supervised Child discount available Last d 21.00hrs Languages spoken: English, German & Italian*
ROOMS: s fr 200FF; d fr 260FF ✱
MEALS: Dinner 110FF

### ST-MARTIN-DES-BOIS Loir-et-Cher

*Les Pignons* (Prop: Guy & Elisabeth Chevereau)
*41800*
☎ 254725743 FAX 254725739
(from Montoire take road signed 'Tours/Château-Renault', cross River Loir and take next right to Artins. After 2m left towards St Martin and after 0.5m towards Ternay)
*Forest area*
*4 en suite (shr) (2 fmly) Full central heating Open parking available Supervised Child discount available Bicycle rental Volley ball Ponies Languages spoken: English & German*
CARDS: Travellers cheques

### ST-MARTIN-LE-BEAU Indre-et-Loire

*Fombêche* (Prop: M Jean Guestault)
*37270*
☎ 247502552 FAX 247502823
*Near river Near lake Forest area Near motorway*
*6 en suite (bth/shr) Full central heating Open parking available Riding V meals*
CARDS: 💷 💷 Travellers cheques

### ST-MAURICE-ST-GERMAIN Eure-et-Loir

**Le Clos Moussu** (Prop: M et Mme J Thomas)
*28240*
☎ 237370446
(located on the D349, 7kms from La Loupe and 3km from Pontgouin, close to the Châteaux-des-Vaux)
One hour from Paris, in the centre of the ancient forest of Perche on the river Ure. Marie and Joseph Thomas welcome you to their 18th-century house.
*Near river Near lake Forest area*
*3 en suite (bth/shr) (2 fmly) No smoking in 2 bedrooms TV in 2 bedrooms Full central heating Open parking available Covered parking available Child discount available 10yrs Tennis Fishing Boule Table tennis Last d 20.00hrs* contd.

ROOMS: d 250-300FF
**Reductions over 1 night Special breaks**
MEALS: Dinner 75-95FF
CARDS: Travellers cheques

**Les Evesqueries** (Prop: M F Goupil)
*28240*
☎ 237370047
(from Chartres take direction for Le Mans and turn off at Couville in the direction of La Loupe. Farm situated between Pontgoin and La Loupe on left)
Forest area  Near motorway
*2 en suite (bth/shr)  (1 fmly)  TV available  Full central heating  Open parking available  Covered parking available  Boule*
ROOMS: s 180FF; d 200FF

### ST-MICHEL-SUR-LOIRE Indre-et-Loire

**Château de Montbrun** (Prop: Rita van Royen)
Langeais *37130*
☎ 247965713 FAX 247960128
(A10 Paris-Bordeaux exit Tours-Vouvray onto N152 in direction of Saumur at Langeais follow signs)
Near river  Near lake  Forest area  Near motorway
*6 en suite (bth/shr)  (2 fmly)  (1 with balcony)  TV in all bedrooms  Direct dial from all bedrooms  Full central heating  Open parking available  Supervised  Outdoor swimming pool (heated)  Solarium  Boule  Bicycle rental  Open terrace  Languages spoken: English German Dutch*

### ST-NICOLAS-DE-BOURGUEIL Indre-et-Loire

**Manoir du Port Guyet** (Prop: Mme Genevieve Valluet)
*37140*
☎ 247978220
Near river  Near lake  Forest area  Near motorway
*Closed early Nov-Mar*
*3 en suite (bth/shr)  Full central heating  Child discount available  Languages spoken: English & Spanish*
CARDS: Travellers cheques

### ST-PREST Eure-et-Loir

**Bed & Breakfast** (Prop: Jacques & Ginette Ragu)
28 rue de la Pierre Percée *28300*
☎ 237223038
(from D6 enter St-Prest, cross River Eure and turn left onto D134 towards Jouy. House on right)
Modern house in the Eure Valley, located between Chartres and Maintenon. Large bedrooms, living room, open fire, kitchenette. Reservations are required for dinner. Patio available with sun loungers and garden furniture. Only children over 10 please.

Near river  Near lake  Forest area  Near motorway
*1 en suite (shr)  TV in all bedrooms  Full central heating  Open parking available  No children 10yrs  Riding  Boule  Bicycle rental  V meals  Languages spoken: English & German*
ROOMS: s fr 180FF; d fr 220FF  **Special breaks: (10% off)**
MEALS: Lunch fr 70FF  Dinner fr 70FF
CARDS: Travellers cheques

★ ★ ★ **Manoir des Pres du Roy**
allée des Prés du Roy *28300*
☎ 237222727 FAX 237222492
(on D6 N of Chartres)
Near river  Forest area  Near motorway
*18 en suite (bth/shr)  (1 with balcony)  TV in all bedrooms  STV  Direct dial from all bedrooms  Mini-bar in all bedrooms  Licensed  Lift  Night porter  Full central heating  Open parking available  Supervised  Child discount available  12yrs  Tennis  Fishing  Pool table  Bicycle rental  Open terrace  V meals  Last d 21.30hrs  Languages spoken: English, German & Spanish*
CARDS: ●● ■■ ☵ ◉ Travellers cheques

### ST-SATUR Cher

★ ★ **Le Laurier**
29 rue de Commerce *18300*
☎ 248541720 FAX 248540454
(from A6 exit Dordives, then N7 towards Cosne-sur-Loire and Sancerre)
Near river  Forest area  In town centre  Near motorway
*8 rms (5 bth)  (1 fmly)  TV in all bedrooms  Direct dial from all bedrooms  Licensed  Full central heating  Open parking available  Supervised  Open terrace  V meals  Last d 22.00hrs  Languages spoken: English*
CARDS: ●● ☵ Travellers cheques

### ST-SYMPHORIEN-LE-CHÂTEAU Eure-et-Loir

★ ★ ★ ★ **Château Hotel d'Ésclimont** (Relais et Châteaux)
*28700*
☎ 237311515 FAX 237315791
From Paris Sud A6 Lyon-A10 Bordeaux, follow A10 Palaiseau Etampes. After the toll(St.Arnoult en Yvelines)A11 Chartres-Le Mans-exit Autoroute at Ablis-N10 Chartres-after 6km right turn D18 direction St Symphorien (65km total)
Near river  Forest area  Near motorway
*53 en suite (bth/shr)  53 rooms in annexe  No smoking in 10 bedrooms  TV in all bedrooms  Direct dial from all bedrooms  Mini-bar in all bedrooms  Licensed  Lift  Night porter  Full central heating  Open parking available  Supervised  Outdoor swimming pool (heated)  Golf  Tennis  Fishing  Boule  Bicycle rental  Open terrace  V meals  Last d 21.30hrs  Languages spoken: English*
CARDS: ●● ■■ ☵ ◉ JCB Travellers cheques

### STE-MAURE-DE-TOURAINE Indre-et-Loire

★ ★ ★ **Hauts de Ste-Maure**
2-4 av du Général-de-Gaulle *37800*
☎ 247655065 FAX 247656024
Near river  Near lake  Forest area  In town centre  Near motorway
*19 en suite (bth/shr)  (3 fmly)  No smoking in 2 bedrooms  TV in all bedrooms  STV  Direct dial from all bedrooms  Mini-bar in all bedrooms  Licensed  Lift  Night porter  Full central heating  Air conditioning in bedrooms  Open parking available  Covered parking available (charged)  Supervised  Child discount*

*available 10yrs Fishing Bicycle rental Open terrace V meals
Last d 21.30hrs Languages spoken: English & Italian*
CARDS: ●● ■■ ㏄ ㏒ Travellers cheques

### SALBRIS Loir-et-Cher

**★ ★ ★ Domaine de Valaudran**
av de Romorantin *41300*
☎ 254972000 FAX 254971222
*Forest area Near motorway
31 en suite (bth/shr) No smoking in 2 bedrooms TV in all
bedrooms Direct dial from all bedrooms Mini-bar in all
bedrooms Licensed Full central heating Open parking
available Child discount available 5yrs Outdoor swimming
pool (heated) Pool table Boule Bicycle rental Open terrace
Table tennis Last d 21.30hrs Languages spoken: English &
German*
ROOMS: (room only) s 450FF; d 550-650FF
**Reductions over 1 night**
MEALS: Full breakfast 70FF Lunch 98-240FF Dinner 300-350FFalc
CARDS: ●● ■■ ㏄ ㏒ Travellers cheques

**★ ★ ★ Le Parc**
8 av d'Orleans *41300*
☎ 254971853 FAX 254972434
(A71 exit Salbris)
*Near lake Forest area Near motorway
Closed 15 days in winter RS Restaurant closed Sun eve & Mon
Dec-Mar
27 rms (23 bth/shr) (5 with balcony) TV in 24 bedrooms STV
Direct dial from 24 bedrooms Licensed Full central heating
Open parking available Covered parking available (charged)
Supervised Child discount available 12yrs Open terrace Last d
21.00hrs Languages spoken: English*
CARDS: ●● ㏄ Travellers cheques

### SANCERRE Cher

**Bed & Breakfast** (Prop: M & Mme Thibaudat)
31 r Saint-Andre *18300*
☎ 248780004
*Near river Forest area In town centre Near motorway
1 en suite (shr) TV available Full central heating Open parking
available Child discount available*

**Manoir de Vaudrédon** (Prop: M Raymond Cirotte)
*18300*
☎ 248790029
*Forest area Near motorway
5 en suite (bth) TV available Full central heating Open parking
available Child discount available Boule Open terrace*
CARDS: ●● ■■ ㏄ Travellers cheques

### SARAN Loiret

**★ ★ Climate de France**
Par d'Activités d'Ormé-Saran *45770*
☎ 238738080 Cen Res 164460123 FAX 238737878
(off A10 at junction for Orléans Nord then follow signs for
Saran Centre)
*Near lake Forest area Near motorway
44 en suite (bth/shr) (16 fmly) TV in all bedrooms Radio in
rooms Direct dial from all bedrooms Licensed Open parking
available Open terrace Covered terrace Languages spoken:
English, German, Italian & Spanish*
CARDS: ●● ㏄

### SAULNAY Indre

**La Marchandière** (Prop: M & Mme Alain Renoncet)
*36290*
☎ 254384294
(from Saulnay towards Villiers, then 1st right, 1st right and first
left-sign "La Marchandière")
Alain and Jocelyne welcome you to their farm in the quiet of
the countryside of Brennouse. Fully equipped kitchen for the
use of guests. Table-tennis, mountain bikes and billiards on
site.
*Near river Forest area
2 en suite (shr) (1 fmly) (1 with balcony) Full central heating
Open parking available Child discount available Bicycle rental
Languages spoken: English (little)*
ROOMS: (room only) d fr 230FF

### SAVONNIÈRES Indre-et-Loire

**La Martinière**
35 rte de la Martinière *37510*
☎ 247500446 FAX 247501157
(leave Tours on the D7 for approx 10km turn left into the village
follow yellow sign 'Relais de la Martinière', 2km from the
village)
*Closed Oct-Apr
10 rms (6 shr) Open parking available Outdoor swimming pool
Golf Tennis Bicycle rental Languages spoken: English*

**Le Prièure des Granges** (Prop: Eric & Christine Salmon)
15 rue de Fontaines *37510*
☎ 247500026 FAX 247500643
(A10 exit Joué-les-Tours, south of Tours, towards Villandry-Savonnières)
*Near river Forest area
Closed Dec-mid Feb
6 en suite (bth/shr) (1 fmly) (1 with balcony) No smoking on
premises Full central heating Open parking available No
children 6yrs Outdoor swimming pool Tennis Riding Bicycle
rental*

### SEILLAC Loir-et-Cher

**★ ★ Domaine de Seillac**
*41150*
☎ 254207211 FAX 254208288
(from Paris A10, exit Blois towards Angers, take D766, cross
the wood and arrive at Molineuf, turn left towards Seillac.)

The hotel, at the heart of the village, is surrounded by an
extensive park with a lake, with the famous Loire châteaux
nearby. The bedrooms are situated in the main building, but in
*contd.*

addition there are maisonettes with small private terraces are available in the park. The dining rooms serve regional cuisine prepared with fresh local produce, and weather permitting, guests can also eat on the terrace.
Forest area
*4 Jan-20 Dec*
*87 en suite (bth/shr) (70 fmly) (70 with balcony) TV in all bedrooms Direct dial from all bedrooms Licensed Full central heating Open parking available Child discount available 11yrs Outdoor swimming pool (heated) Tennis Fishing Boule Open terrace Covered terrace Table tennis Last d 21.30hrs Languages spoken: English & German*
ROOMS: s 410-600FF; d 480-700FF
MEALS: Lunch 130-180FF&alc Dinner 130-180FF&alc
CARDS: ● ■ ⬛ ⬤ Travellers cheques

### SELLES-SUR-CHER Loir-et-Cher

**Bed & Breakfast** (Prop: M & Mme Lerate)
29 r des Rieux *41130*
☎ 254975135
Near river Forest area
*2 en suite (bth/shr) Full central heating Open parking available Outdoor swimming pool*
ROOMS: (room only) s 250FF; d 300FF
CARDS: ■ Travellers cheques

**Maison de la Rive Gauche** (Prop: Mme Harvey Bacon)
15 r du four *41130*
☎ 254976385
Near river Forest area In town centre Near motorway
*Closed Jan-Feb*
*6 rms (4 bth/shr) (2 fmly) Full central heating Open parking available Child discount available 6yrs Last d 20.30hrs Languages spoken: English & German*
CARDS: Travellers cheques

### SEMBLANCAY Indre-et-Loire

★ ★ **Hostellerie de la Mère Hamard**
pl de l'Église *37360*
☎ 247566204 FAX 247565361
Forest area
*Closed Feb school holidays*
*9 en suite (bth/shr) (2 fmly) TV in all bedrooms Direct dial from all bedrooms Licensed Full central heating Open parking available Supervised Child discount available Tennis Riding Open terrace V meals Last d 21.00hrs Languages spoken: English & German*
CARDS: ● ⬛ Travellers cheques

### SENONCHES Eure-et-Loir

★ ★ **De la Forêt**
pl du Champ de Foire *28250*
☎ 237377850 FAX 237377498
Near lake Forest area
*Closed Feb*
*13 en suite (bth/shr) (1 fmly) TV in all bedrooms STV Licensed Full central heating Open parking available Covered parking available Child discount available 12yrs Open terrace V meals*
CARDS: ● ■ ⬛

### SEPMES Indre-et-Loire

**La Ferme les Berthiers** (Prop: Anne Vergnaud)
*37800*
☎ 247655061
(exit St-Maure-de-Touraine from A10 onto N760 towards Loches, then take D59 towards Liguiel, from D59 the road for Sepmes is on the left)
*7 rms (1 bth 5 shr) (3 fmly) Full central heating Open parking available Child discount available Boule Open terrace Basketball Languages spoken: English*
CARDS: Travellers cheques

### SÉRIS Loir-et-Cher

**Bed & Breakfast** (Prop: Annie & Jean-Yves Peschard)
*41500*
☎ 254810783 FAX 254813988
Bed & breakfast is offered at this working farm, situated in the heart of the countryside, in a small village between Orléans and Blois. Dinner is available and includes local specialities, cheeses and wines. Breakfast includes Mme Peschard's home-made jams. All meals are served at your hosts' table. Facilities include outdoor games, table-tennis and pétanque.

*Closed 1-14 Oct*
*5 en suite (bth/shr) (2 fmly) No smoking on premises TV in 1 bedroom Full central heating Open parking available Child discount available 2yrs Languages spoken: English*
ROOMS: s 230FF; d 280FF **Reductions over 1 night**
MEALS: Dinner fr 95FF

### SEUR Loir-et-Cher

**La Valinière** (Prop: J Pierre D'Elia)
10 rte de Cellettes *41120*
☎ 254440385 FAX 254440385

(From Blois take direction of Limoges/Châteauroux. In 6km turn right arriving in Cellettes then Seur. On arriving in Seur 100 metres on right follow sign "chambre d'hôte") In the heart of the Châteaux of the Loire, a large house with much to interest families, including a room with childrens games. Information available on visiting the surrounding region.
Near river  Forest area
*5 en suite (bth)  (2 fmly)  Full central heating  Open parking available  Child discount available 11yrs  Last d noon  Languages spoken: English*
ROOMS: s fr 230FF; d fr 275FF
**Reductions over 1 night  Special breaks**
MEALS: Dinner fr 95FF
CARDS: Travellers cheques

## SOINGS-EN-SOLOGNE Loir-et-Cher

★ **Les 4 Vents**
rte de Contres *41230*
☎ 254987131 FAX 254987561
(from Blois take D765 towards Romorantin. Turn right to Soings-en-Sologne)
Near lake  Forest area
*12 rms (7 shr)  4 rooms in annexe  (4 fmly)  TV in 7 bedrooms  Direct dial from 7 bedrooms  Licensed  Full central heating  Air conditioning in bedrooms  Open parking available  Covered parking available  Supervised  Child discount available 12yrs  Fishing  Boule  Bicycle rental  Open terrace  Covered terrace  V meals  Last d 21.00hrs  Languages spoken: English*
ROOMS: (room only) d 140-250FF
**Reductions over 1 night  Special breaks**
MEALS: Continental breakfast 30FF  Lunch 65-130FF  Dinner 75-130FF
CARDS: ●● ▆▆ Travellers cheques

## SOUVIGNY-EN-SOLOGNE Loir-et-Cher

★ ★ **Auberge Croix Blanche**
1 rue des Etangs *41600*
☎ 254884008 FAX 254889106
(leave A71, to Lamotte Beuvron and then on to Souvigny-en-Sologne)

In a typical Sologne village this auberge is a resting place well rooted in the soil of its homeland, with a strong family tradition spanning four generations. This half-timbered brick-built resting place offers a warm, welcoming atmosphere, deep in this area of France where they really know how life should be lived. Indulge yourself with a wide range of original, seasonal specialities.
Near lake  Forest area  In town centre

*Closed mid Jan-Feb*
*8 en suite (bth/shr)  8 rooms in annexe  TV in 2 bedrooms  Radio in rooms  Direct dial from all bedrooms  Full central heating  Open parking available  Supervised  Child discount available  Last d 21.00hrs*
MEALS: Continental breakfast 35FF  Lunch 100-235FF  Dinner 100-235FF
CARDS: ●● ▆▆

## SUÈVRES Loir-et-Cher

*Le Moulin de Choiseaux* (Prop: M-F et A Seguin)
8 rue des Choiseaux *41500*
☎ 254878501 FAX 254878644
(A10 exit Mer in direction of Blois. 3km after Mer look out for roadsign "chambres d'hôte", go right in direction of Diziers)
Near river  Forest area
*5 en suite (bth/shr)  (1 fmly)  No smoking on premises  TV in 2 bedrooms  Full central heating  Child discount available  Outdoor swimming pool  Fishing  Bicycle rental  Languages spoken: English*

## SULLY-SUR-LOIRE Loiret

*Bed & Breakfast* (Prop: M & Mme Meunier)
43-45 Ch de la Chevesserie *45600*
☎ 238365488
Near river  Forest area  Near motorway
*2 en suite (bth/shr)  Full central heating  Open parking available  Supervised  Languages spoken: English & Spanish*

## SURY-AUX-BOIS Loiret

★ ★ *Domaine de Chicamour*
Chicamour *45530*
☎ 238558542 FAX 238558043
Forest area  Near motorway
*Closed 16 Nov-14 Mar*
*12 en suite (bth/shr)  Direct dial from all bedrooms  Licensed  Full central heating  Open parking available  Covered parking available  Child discount available 10yrs  Tennis  Riding  Boule  Bicycle rental  Open terrace  Covered terrace  Last d 21.00hrs  Languages spoken: English, Dutch & German*
CARDS: ●● ▆▆ ▆▆ ◉ Travellers cheques

## TAVERS Loiret

*Le Clos de Pont-Pierre* (Prop: Patricia Fournier)
115 r des eaux Bleues *45190*
☎ 238445685 FAX 238445894
(exit A10 at Meung-sur-Loire, N152 at 2km to Beaugency) Situated in Vallee de La Loire's centre, Patricia Fournier welcomes you to this old 18th century farm set in a park of gardens and forest. A large terrace with garden sitting room surrounds the swimming pool. All the comfortable rooms look onto a peaceful view of the park and have their own entrance. Regional dishes can be enjoyed.
Near river  Forest area  Near motorway
*Closed Dec-Feb*
*4 en suite (shr)  (2 fmly)  No smoking on premises  TV in all bedrooms  Full central heating  Open parking available  Outdoor swimming pool  Last d 19.30hrs*
ROOMS: d 290FF
MEALS: Dinner 100FF
CARDS: Travellers cheques

**Les Grattelievres** (Prop: Patrick Terlain)
74 bis r des Eaux Bleues *45190*
☎ 238449258
Near river  Forest area  Near motorway
*2 en suite (shr) (1 fmly) No smoking on premises Full central heating Open parking available Child discount available 7yrs Languages spoken: English*
CARDS: Travellers cheques

### TENDU Indre

**La Chasse** (Prop: M & Mme Mitchell)
Prunget *36200*
☎ 254240776
(leave A20 (N20) at Tendu, take D30 signposted to Chavin. Shortly after the turn behind Tendu Church signposts for La Chasse)
Near river  Near lake  Forest area  Near motorway
*4 rms (1 shr) (1 fmly) No smoking on premises Full central heating Open parking available Supervised Child discount available 12yrs Languages spoken: English*
CARDS: Travellers cheques

### THAUMIERS Cher

**Château de Thaumiers**
*18210*
☎ 248618162 FAX 248618182
Near river  Near lake  Forest area
*10 en suite (bth) (2 fmly) Full central heating Open parking available Outdoor swimming pool (heated) Fishing Boule Open terrace Languages spoken: English*
CARDS: ● ▇ Travellers cheques

### TOURNON-ST-MARTIN Indre

★ ★ **Auberge du Capucin Gourmand**
8 rue Bel Air *36220*
☎ 254376685 FAX 254378754
(from Tours take A10 south. Exit at Châtellerault Nord. Take D725 via la Roche-Posay & Yzeures-sur-Creuse, then D750 to Tournon-St-Martin)

Set in the heart of the Berry countryside and near the National Park de la Brenne, this auberge prides itself on the excellence of its restaurant's cuisine. Comfortable bedrooms and a flower-filled garden ensure your stay will be a pleasant one, but for a truly memorable experience you should try some of the regional specialities on offer in the dining room.
Near river  Near lake  Forest area  Near motorway
*Closed 2wks Oct-2wks Feb*

*7 rms (6 bth/shr) (1 fmly) TV in all bedrooms Direct dial from all bedrooms Licensed Full central heating Open parking available Covered parking available Supervised Child discount available 10yrs Fishing Boule Open terrace V meals Last d 21.00hrs Languages spoken: English*
ROOMS: (room only) d 235-300FF
**Reductions over 1 night**
MEALS: Continental breakfast 40FF Lunch 80-230FF&alc Dinner 80-230FF&alc
CARDS: ● ▇ ▇ ● Eurocard Travellers cheques

### TOURS Indre-et-Loire

★ ★ ★ **Hotel Alliance Trois Rivières**
292 av de Grammount *37200*
☎ 247280080 FAX 247277761
Near river  Near lake  Near motorway
*125 en suite (bth/shr) (6 fmly) (10 with balcony) No smoking in 6 bedrooms TV in all bedrooms Mini-bar in all bedrooms Licensed Lift Night porter Full central heating Open parking available Child discount available 10yrs Outdoor swimming pool Tennis Pool table Open terrace Last d 22.00hrs Languages spoken: English, German & Spanish*
CARDS: ● ▇ ▇ ● Travellers cheques

★ ★ ★ **Holiday Inn Tours City Centre**
15 rue Edward Vaillant *37000*
☎ 247311212 FAX 247385335
In town centre  Near motorway
*105 en suite (bth) (2 fmly) (2 with balcony) No smoking in 11 bedrooms TV in all bedrooms STV Radio in rooms Direct dial from all bedrooms Mini-bar in all bedrooms Licensed Lift Night porter Full central heating Air conditioning in bedrooms Open parking available (charged) Covered parking available (charged) Child discount available 19yrs Sauna Fitness Salon V meals Last d 22.00hrs Languages spoken: English, German & Spanish*
CARDS: ● ▇ ▇ ● Travellers cheques

★ ★ ★ **Jean Bardet**
57 rue Croison *37100*
☎ 247414111 FAX 247516872
(from A10 follow signs for Tours centre. Do not cross River Loire but turn right into Avenue de la Tranchée, then 2nd right, then into Rue Groison )
Near river  Forest area  In town centre
*21 en suite (bth/shr) (5 fmly) (4 with balcony) TV in all bedrooms Radio in rooms Direct dial from all bedrooms Mini-bar in all bedrooms Licensed Night porter Full central heating Air conditioning in bedrooms Open parking available Supervised Child discount available 12yrs Outdoor swimming pool (heated) Open terrace table tennis, petanque V meals Last d 22.00hrs Languages spoken: English, German, Italian & Spanish*
CARDS: ● ▇ ▇ ● JCB Travellers cheques

★ ★ **Moderne**
1-3 rue Victor Laloux *37000*
☎ 247053281 FAX 247057150
In town centre  Near motorway
*23 rms (5 fmly) TV in all bedrooms STV Direct dial from all bedrooms Mini-bar in all bedrooms Licensed Full central heating Last d 21.30hrs Languages spoken: English*
CARDS: ● ▇ ▇ Travellers cheques

**★ ★ ★ Royal Clarine**
65 av de Grammont *37000*
☎ 247647178 FAX 247058462
(follow directions for Tours Centre)
In town centre
*50 en suite (bth) (4 with balcony) TV in all bedrooms STV Direct dial from all bedrooms Licensed Lift Night porter Full central heating Open parking available (charged) Covered parking available (charged) Child discount available 12yrs Languages spoken: English, German, Iranian*
CARDS: ● ■ ▥ ▣ Travellers cheques

### TROO Loir-et-Cher

**Château de la Voûte** (Prop: Veronique & Richard Provenzano)
*41800*
☎ 254725252 FAX 254725252
(from Paris N10 to Vendôme, then D917 to Montoire and Troo. From Blois, take D957 up to Vendôme, then D917 to Montoire and Troo)
An impressive 18th century chateau facing the Loir valley and offering spacious guestrooms tastefully decorated with antique furniture. Breakfast can be served in the rooms or on the terrace. Within walking distance of a good restaurant and the village.
*Near river Forest area*
*5 en suite (bth/shr) Full central heating Open parking available No children 6yrs Languages spoken: English & Spanish*
ROOMS: d 450-580FF **Reductions over 1 night**
CARDS: Travellers cheques

### VALLIÈRES-LES-GRANDES Loir-et-Cher

**La Ferme de la Quantinère** (Prop: Andrée Veys)
*41400*
☎ 254209953 FAX 254209953
(from Vallières-les-Grandes follow D27/28 towards Montrichard. Take 2nd road on left after Château-d'Eau)
*Forest area*
*Closed 3 Dec-Mar*
*5 rms Full central heating Open parking available Supervised Child discount available 5 yrs Outdoor swimming pool (heated) Boule Jacuzzi/spa Bicycle rental Barbecue Jacuzzi*
CARDS: Travellers cheques

### VANNES-SUR-COSSON Loiret

**Bed & Breakfast** (Prop: M & Mme Nicourt)
6 rue de la Croix Ste Madelein *45510*
☎ 238581543
*Near river Forest area In town centre Near motorway*
*4 en suite (bth/shr) Full central heating Open parking available Supervised Child discount available 12yrs Tennis Fishing Boule Mini-golf Bicycle rental Languages spoken: English*

**Domaine Ste-Hélène** (Prop: Mme A Celerier)
rte d'Isdes *45510*
☎ 238580455 FAX 238582838
(from Orléans N60 to Jargean, cross the River Loire, take D951 to Tigy then D83 to Vannes-sur-Cosson towards Isdes. Approx 1.5km aftre Vannes watch for signpost on right for St Hélène)
*Near lake Forest area Near motorway*
*2 en suite (bth/shr) (1 fmly) No smoking on premises TV in 1 bedroom Full central heating Open parking available Covered parking available Outdoor swimming pool (heated) Tennis Fishing Bicycle rental Last d 21.00hrs Languages spoken: English*

### VARENNES Indre-et-Loire

**Crene**
*37600*
☎ 247590429
*3 en suite (bth/shr) (2 fmly) No smoking in all bedrooms Full central heating Open parking available Child discount available 13yrs Last d 20.30hrs*

### VEIGNE Indre-et-Loire

**★ ★ Le Moulin Fleuri**
rte du Ripault *37250*
☎ 247260112 FAX 247340471
(from Tours take N10 south towards Montbazon. Turn right onto D87 towards Monts, then follow signposts)
*Near river Forest area*
*12 rms (8 shr) (5 fmly) TV in all bedrooms Radio in rooms Direct dial from all bedrooms Mini-bar in 10 bedrooms Licensed Full central heating Open parking available Supervised Fishing Open terrace V meals Last d 21.15hrs Languages spoken: English, Italian & Spanish*
CARDS: ● ■ ▥ Travellers cheques

### VELLES Indre

**Manoir de Villedoin** (Prop: M et Mme Limousin)
*36330*
☎ 254251206 FAX 254242829
(approach via A20 exit 15 towards Velles, then on Mosnay road)
*Near river Near lake Forest area*
*Closed Jan*
*5 en suite (bth/shr) (1 fmly) TV in 4 bedrooms Full central heating Open parking available Supervised Child discount available Tennis Fishing Boule*
ROOMS: s 430FF; d 480FF ✱
MEALS: Dinner 150FF✱
CARDS: Travellers cheques

### VENDÔME Loir-et-Cher

**★ ★ ★ Hotel Vendôme**
15 Faubourg Chartrain *41100*
☎ 254770288 FAX 254739071
*Near river Forest area In town centre Near motorway*
*35 en suite (bth/shr) (1 fmly) (3 with balcony) TV in all bedrooms STV Radio in rooms Direct dial from all bedrooms Licensed Lift Full central heating Covered parking available (charged) Last d 21.30hrs Languages spoken: English*
ROOMS: (room only) s 229-349FF; d 289-409FF
**Reductions over 1 night**
MEALS: Full breakfast 48FF Lunch 75-240FF&alc Dinner 75-240FF&alc
CARDS: ● ■ ▥ JCB Travellers cheques

### VERNEUIL-SUR-INDRE Indre-et-Loire

**La Capitainerie** (Prop: Malvina Masselot)
*37600*
☎ 247948815 FAX 247947075
(from Loches stay in lane for Châteauroux until roundabout, look out for Leclerc supermarket. Follow Châteauroux signs, cross Perrusson then turn right towards Verneuil. La Capitainerie 150mtrs before "leaving Verneuil" sign)
Right in the heart of the Loire valley, the owner welcomes guests to her 18th-century property, surrounded by 8 hectares

*contd.*

**La Capitainerie**
of countryside. In the evening your hostess may, by reservation only, introduce guests to the gourmet pleasures of authentic Touraine cooking.
Near river  Forest area
*4 en suite (shr) (1 with balcony) No smoking on premises  Full central heating  Open parking available  Outdoor swimming pool  Last d 14.00hrs  Languages spoken: English*
ROOMS: s 230-290FF; d 290-310FF ✱
MEALS: Dinner 110FF
CARDS: Travellers cheques

**VERNOU-SUR-BRENNE** Indre-et-Loire

**Château de Jallanges** (Prop: Stephane Ferry-Balin)
*372110*
☎ 247520171 FAX 247521118
(from Tours take N152 towards Blois. In Vouvray take D46 to Vernou-sur-Brenne & from there the D76 to Château)
Near river  Forest area
*7 en suite (bth/shr) (2 fmly) No smoking in 4 bedrooms  TV available  Full central heating  Open parking available  Covered parking available  Supervised  Child discount available  Outdoor swimming pool (heated)  Boule  Mini-golf  Bicycle rental  Languages spoken: English & Italian*
CARDS: ● ■ ■ ◑ Travellers cheques

**VIGOULANT** Indre

**Les Ferme des Vacances** (Prop: M & Mme Hyzard)
Les Pouges *36160*
☎ 254306060
Near river  Forest area
*4 en suite (shr) (3 fmly) Open parking available  Child discount available  Boule  Table tennis  Play room  Last d 21.00hrs  Languages spoken: English*
CARDS: ● ■ Travellers cheques

**VILLANDRY** Indre-et-Loire

**Manoir de Foncher** (Prop: Michel et Francoise Salles)
*37510*
☎ 247500240 FAX 247500994
(from Tours D7 to Savonnières, turn right across the bridge then immediately left. House is 3km along on right)
Near river  Forest area
*Closed Oct-Mar*
*2 rms (1 bth/shr) (2 fmly) (2 with balcony) No smoking on premises  Open parking available  Languages spoken: English*
CARDS: Travellers cheques

**VILLEBAROU** Loir-et-Cher

**Bed & Breakfast** (Prop: Agnès & Jacques Masquilier)
8 rte de la chaussée, St-Victor *41000*
☎ 254784024 FAX 254561236
(on D924 towards Châteaudun-Chartres, at lights turn right to Francillon. Alternatively from A10 take D50 towards Villerbon, in 300m turn first left)

Situated in a typical Beauceronne farm, these bedrooms all look out over the grassy courtyard. Your initial welcome and breakfast takes place in the main residence of the proprietors, but guests have use of a kitchen which has a wood oven, currently being restored. A park is adjacent to the property with a games area and a small wood.
Near river  Near lake  Forest area  Near motorway
*RS winter*
*3 en suite (shr) (3 fmly) No smoking on premises  Full central heating  Open parking available  Covered parking available  Child discount available 2yrs  Bicycle rental  Languages spoken: English*
ROOMS: s fr 250FF; d fr 280FF **Reductions over 1 night**
CARDS: ■ Travellers cheques

**VILLEDIEU-SUR-INDRE** Indre

**La Bruère** (Prop: M Stone)
*36320*
☎ 254261717
Near river  Near lake  Forest area  Near motorway
*4 rms (3 shr) (1 fmly) No smoking on premises  Open parking available  Covered parking available  Languages spoken: English*

**VILLEDÔMER** Indre-et-Loire

**La Hémond** (Prop: Gosseaume Gaetan)
*37110*
☎ 247550699 FAX 247550936
(access via A10 and N10)
A warm welcome is offered on this farm in the heart of the Loire. Swings and pétanque area are available in the garden. Evening meal available by reservation.
Near river  Forest area  Near motorway

**La Hemond**
*5 rms (1 bth 2 shr) (3 fmly) Open parking available Covered parking available Fishing Boule Languages spoken: English*
ROOMS: s 60FF ✱ **Reductions over 1 night**
MEALS: Lunch 20FF Dinner 65FF
CARDS: Travellers cheques

### VILLENEUVE-FROUVILLE Loir-et-Cher

**Bed & Breakfast** (Prop: Bernard et Micheline Pohu)
5 pl de l'Église *41290*
☎ 254232206 FAX 254232206
(in Blois take D924 towards Châteaudun-Chartres into village of Villeneuve-Frouville. House near the church)

A pleasant farm within a large courtyard, the home of Bernard and Micheline Pohu. It offers easy access to the châteaux of the Loire. Leisure facilities within 4 kilometres.
Near motorway
*3 en suite (shr) (1 fmly) (2 with balcony) No smoking on premises Full central heating Open parking available Covered parking available Child discount available Languages spoken: English*
CARDS: Travellers cheques

### VOUVRAY Indre-et-Loire

**Le Chêne Morier**
*37210*
☎ 247527883
Forest area Near motorway
*5 rms (3 bth/shr) (1 fmly) TV available Radio in rooms Open parking available Outdoor swimming pool*

### VOVES Eure-et-Loir

★ ★ ★ **Quai Fleuri**
15 rue Texier Gallas *28150*
☎ 237991515 FAX 237991120
(On D17)
Situated in lush, green surroundings between Chartres and Orléans, the hotel is set in a large wooded park and is an ideal place in which to relax and unwind. After a drink in the cosy bar, guests can savour a choice of specialities in the restaurant or Le Guillaume, a private dining room. The bedrooms have modern facilities and there is no shortage of sporting activities at the hotel, whilst the surrounding region offers many places of interest.
Forest area Near motorway
*Closed 21 Dec-4 Jan*

*17 en suite (bth/shr) (2 fmly) No smoking in 2 bedrooms TV in all bedrooms STV Direct dial from all bedrooms Mini-bar in 2 bedrooms Licensed Night porter Full central heating Open parking available Supervised Gym Pool table Boule Bicycle rental Open terrace play room,library,TV lounge Languages spoken: English*
ROOMS: (room only) d 345-440FF
**Reductions over 1 night**
CARDS: ✿ ▦ ▬ Travellers cheques

# Western Loire

Throughout the Middle Ages until the 19th century, Western Loire was the principal trade and travel route in the west of France and accounts for the strategic placement of the great castles and wonderful vineyards scattered along the undulating banks of the Loire. Rich in culture and heritage, the hallmark colours of this colourful region are blue and green, where the landscape of cool, calm rivers, dense woodland and verdant meadows are dotted with red-tiled roofs and white stone walls and edged by the brilliant blue of the sea.

## ESSENTIAL FACTS

| | |
|---|---|
| DÉPARTEMENTS: | Loire-Atlantique, Maine-et-Loire, Mayenne, Sarthe, Vendée |
| PRINCIPAL TOWNS | La Roche-sur-Yonne, Angers, Fontenay-le-Compte, Chateaubriant, Saumur, Le Mans, Laval, Cholet |
| PLACES TO VISIT: | Castles: Apremont, Brissac, Baugé, Bazoges-en-Pareds, Chateaubriant, Clisson, Goulaine, Le Lude, La Motte-Glain, Montgeoffroy, Montmirail, Montreuil-Bellay, Le Plessis-Bourré, Serrant & Tiffauges (Bluebeard's castle). Saumur: Cadre Noir (High School riding), Troglodyte caves, Rochemenier. Puy de Fou medieval theme park. Medieval villages: Guérande, Lassay-les-Châteaux, Vouvant. Olfactorium at Coëx (collection of plants producing perfumes) Fontrevaud Abbey, resting place of the Plantagenets. Roman remains, Jublains. |
| REGIONAL TOURIST OFFICE | 2 rue de la Loire, BP 2171, 44204 Nantes, Tel: 40 48 24 20 Fax: 40 08 07 10 |
| LOCAL GASTRONOMIC DELIGHTS | Charcuterie, terrines, pâtés of game & foie gras. Pike with beurre blanc (butter sauce); Smoked eel. Lobsters, crayfish, oysters. Matelote d'anguille, eels stewed in wine. Citrouillat, pumpkin pie. Cotignac, apple & almond pastry. Petit Lu, butter biscuits from Nantes. Glinottes, fattened corn-fed chickens. |
| DRINKS | Wines: Muscadet, Saumur-Champigny & Saumur Brut, Anjou white & rosé, Coteaux d'Ancenis red & rosé. Cider. |
| LOCAL CRAFTS WHAT TO BUY | Malicorne: fine china. Jupilles: wood crafts. Montreuil-Bellay: silk. Le Fuilet: pottery. Clisson & Cholet: textiles. |

204

## ALLONNES Maine-et-Loire

**Château Le Courbet** (Prop: Mme Canivet-Golfar)
49650
☎ 241528365 FAX 241387934
Near river Near lake Forest area Near motorway
*3 en suite (bth/shr) No smoking on premises Full central heating Open parking available No children 14yrs Languages spoken: English & German*
CARDS: Travellers cheques

**Manoir de Beauséjour** (Prop: Colette Thimoleon)
49650
☎ 241528668 FAX 241388558
Near river Forest area Near motorway
*3 en suite (bth/shr) No smoking on premises Full central heating Open parking available Child discount available 6yrs Outdoor swimming pool (heated) Bicycle rental Pool, Table tennis Languages spoken: English*
CARDS: Travellers cheques

## ANDARD Maine-et-Loire

**Ferme Fruitière de la Pocherie** (Prop: Mme M M Boutreux)
49800
☎ 241767225 FAX 241768441
(at Angers take N23 towards Parc-Expo & Pellovailles-les-Vignes, turn right onto D115 towards Le Plessis-Grammoire cross Le Plessis-Grammoire & turn left at Les Deux-Croix junction, farm on right 600mtrs after junction)
Near river Forest area Near motorway
*2 en suite (shr) (2 fmly) TV in 1 bedroom Full central heating Open parking available Child discount available 12yrs V meals Last d noon*
CARDS: Travellers cheques

## ANGERS Maine-et-Loire

**★ ★ ★ D'Anjou** (BW)
1 bd Maréchal-Foch 49100
☎ 241882482 FAX 241872221
In town centre Near motorway
*53 en suite (bth/shr) (4 fmly) TV in all bedrooms STV Direct dial from all bedrooms Mini-bar in all bedrooms Licensed Lift Night porter Full central heating Open parking available (charged) Covered parking available (charged) Bicycle rental V meals Last d 21.30hrs Languages spoken: English German Italian & Spanish*
ROOMS: (room only) d 390-790FF
MEALS: Continental breakfast 62FF Lunch 150-235FF&alc Dinner 150-235FF&alc
CARDS: ●● ■ ■ ● Travellers cheques

**★ ★ Hotel du Mail**
8 rue des Ursules 49100
☎ 241250525 FAX 241869120
(behind Hotel de Ville in town centre)
A peacefully situated mansion in the heart of Angers, a city famous for its history, arts and festivals and popular for its proximity to the Loire. All bedrooms offer every modern amenity and provide maximum comfort. The hotel caters for commercial and leisure guests alike, and the friendly, efficient staff ensure an enjoyable stay.

*contd.*

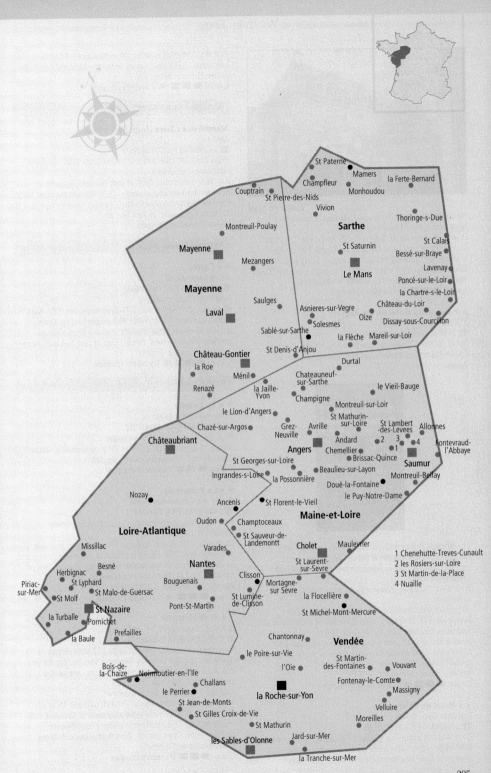

St Paterne
Mamers
la Ferte-Bernard
Champfleur
Monhoudou
Couptrain
St Pierre-des-Nids
Vivion
Thoringe-s-Due

**Sarthe**

Montreuil-Poulay
St Calais
St Saturnin
Bessé-sur-Braye
**Mayenne**
Lavenay
Mezangers
Le Mans
Poncé-sur-le-Loir
la Chartre-s-le-Loir
**Mayenne**
Saulges
Asnieres-sur-Vegre
Château-du-Loir
Laval
Oize
Dissay-sous-Courcillon
Solesmes
Sablé-sur-Sarthe
Mareil-sur-Loir
la Flèche
St Denis-d'Anjou
**Château-Gontier**
Durtal
la Roe
le Vieil-Bauge
Chateauneuf-
Ménil
sur-Sarthe
la Jaille-
Renazé
Yvon
Champigne
Montreuil-sur-Loir
le Lion-d'Angers
St Mathurin-
sur-Loire
St Lambert
Allonnes
Chazé-sur-Argos
-des-Levees
Grez-
Avrille
2   3
4
**Châteaubriant**
Neuville
Andard
1
Fontevraud-
**Angers**
Chemellier
l'Abbaye
St Georges-sur-Loire
Brissac-Quince
**Saumur**
Beaulieu-sur-Layon
Ingrandes-s-Loire
la Possonnière
Montreuil-Bellay
Doué-la-Fontaine
Nozay
le Puy-Notre-Dame
Ancenis
St Florent-le-Vieil
**Maine-et-Loire**
Oudon
Champtoceaux
**Loire-Atlantique**
St Sauveur-de-
Landemontt
Missillac
Varades
Cholet
Mauleyrier
**Nantes**
St Laurent-
Herbignac
Besné
Clisson
sur-Sevre
St Lyphard
Bouguenais
Piriac-
Mortagne-
la Flocellière
sur-Mer
St Molf
Pont-St-Martin
St Lumine-
sur Sevre
la Turballe
de-Clisson
St Michel-Mont-Mercure
**St Nazaire**
Pornichet
Prefailles
la Baule
Chantonnay
**Vendée**
Bois-de-
le Poire-sur-Vie
la-Chaize
Noirmoutier-en-l'Ile
St Martin-
l'Oie
des-Fontaines
Vouvant
Challans
le Perrier
Fontenay-le-Comte
**la Roche-sur-Yon**
Massigny
St Jean-de-Monts
St Gilles Croix-de-Vie
Velluire
St Mathurin
Moreilles
les Sables-d'Olonne
Jard-sur-Mer
la Tranche-sur-Mer

1 Chenehutte-Treves-Cunault
2 les Rosiers-sur-Loire
3 St Martin-de-la-Place
4 Nuaille

**Hotel du Mail**
Near river  Near lake  Near sea  Near beach  Forest area  In town centre  Near motorway
*26 en suite (bth/shr)  (7 fmly)  TV in 27 bedrooms  Direct dial from 27 bedrooms  Mini-bar in 27 bedrooms  Full central heating  Open parking available (charged)  Covered parking available  Supervised  Open terrace  Languages spoken: English*
ROOMS:  (room only)  s 215-260FF;  d 285-335FF
CARDS: 💳 ■ ▩ ⑩ Travellers cheques

★ ★ ★ **Quality Hotel de France**
8 pl de la Gare *49100*
☎ 241884942 FAX 241867670
(leave the Paris/Nantes motorway at Angers, take the direction Cholet-Potiers and follow signs for Château and railway station)

The Hotel de France is an old building dating from 1893. Situated in a lively quarter of the city centre, the fourth generation of the Bouyer family continue the tradition of French hospitality.
Near river  Near lake  Forest area  In town centre  Near motorway
*55 en suite (bth)  No smoking in 3 bedrooms  TV in all bedrooms  STV  Direct dial from all bedrooms  Mini-bar in all bedrooms  Licensed  Lift  Night porter  Full central heating  Air conditioning in bedrooms  Covered parking available (charged)  Supervised  Child discount available 11yrs  V meals  Languages spoken: English & German*
ROOMS:  (room only)  d 400-600FF
CARDS: 💳 ■ ▩ ⑩ JCB Travellers cheques

★ ★ **Hotel de l'Univers**
2 pl de la Gare *49100*
☎ 241884358 FAX 241869728
(from A11 exit at the sign 'Château, Maison du Tourisme' then after traffic lights follow signs 'La Gare' or 'Hotel l'Univers)
Near river  Near lake  In town centre  Near motorway

*45 rms (35 bth/shr)  (6 fmly)  (10 with balcony)  TV in all bedrooms  Direct dial from all bedrooms  Licensed  Lift  Night porter  Full central heating*
CARDS: 💳 ■ ▩ ⑩ Travellers cheques

### ASNIÈRES-SUR-VÈGRE Sarthe

**Manoir des Claies** (Prop: Jean Anneron)
*72430*
☎ 243924050 FAX 243926572
(from Paris A11 then A81 and D22 towards Sable-sur-Sarthe)
Near river  Forest area
*4 en suite (bth/shr)  (2 fmly)  (1 with balcony)  Full central heating  Open parking available  Child discount available 10yrs  Outdoor swimming pool (heated)  Fishing  Open terrace  Last d 22.30hrs  Languages spoken: English*
CARDS: Travellers cheques

### AVRILLÉ Maine-et-Loire

★ ★ **Cavier**
rte de Laval *49240*
☎ 241423045 FAX 241424032
Near river  Near motorway
*43 en suite (bth/shr)  (7 fmly)  TV in all bedrooms  STV  Radio in rooms  Licensed  Night porter  Full central heating  Open parking available  Child discount available 10yrs  Outdoor swimming pool (heated)  Boule  Open terrace  Last d 21.30hrs  Languages spoken: English*
CARDS: 💳 ■ ▩ ⑩ Travellers cheques

### BAULE, LA Loire-Atlantique

★ ★ **Le Lutetia**
13 av des Evens *44500*
☎ 240602581 FAX 240427352
Near sea  Near beach  In town centre
*14 rms (1 fmly)  (6 with balcony)  TV in all bedrooms  Riding  Open terrace  Languages spoken: English*
CARDS: 💳 ■ ▩ Travellers cheques

★ ★ **La Palmeraie**
7 allée des Cormorans *44500*
☎ 240602441 FAX 240427371
Near sea  Near beach  In town centre  Near motorway
*Closed Oct-Feb*
*23 en suite (shr)  (8 with balcony)  No smoking on premises  TV in all bedrooms  STV  Direct dial from all bedrooms  Full central heating  Child discount available 6yrs  Open terrace  Covered terrace  Last d 21.00hrs  Languages spoken: English*
ROOMS:  (room only)  d 320-380FF
CARDS: 💳 ■ ▩ ⑩ Travellers cheques

★ ★ **St-Christophe**
pl Notre Dame *44500*
☎ 240603535 FAX 240601174
(from the first main junction in La Baule follow avenue de Gaulle, passing the Office de Tourisme. Turn right at the end into boulevard de Mer, then right again into avenue des Impairs. 100mtrs)
Near sea  Near beach  In town centre
*33 rms (20 bth 11 shr)  (5 fmly)  (11 with balcony)  TV in all bedrooms  STV  Direct dial from all bedrooms  Licensed  Full central heating  Open parking available  Child discount available 12yrs  Open terrace  Table tennis  Last d 22.00hrs  Languages spoken: English*
CARDS: 💳 ■ ▩ Travellers cheques

## BEAULIEU-SUR-LAYON Maine-et-Loire

**Bed & Breakfast** (Prop: Mme June Friess)
35 rue St Vincent *49750*
☎ 241786082 FAX 241786082
(from Angers follow directio:. of Cholet on the N160. Turn left
at crossroads Beaulieu/Layon, the property is situated in the
centre of the village beside the church)
This house dates back to the early 18th century and was once
known as the Old Post Office Inn of the village. All the rooms
are comfortable and nicely decorated.
Near river  Forest area  Near motorway
*4 en suite (shr)  (1 fmly)  (1 with balcony)  No smoking on
premises  Full central heating  Open parking available  Covered
parking available  Child discount available 12yrs  Languages
spoken: English*
CARDS: Travellers cheques

## BESNÉ Loire-Atlantique

**Les Pierres Blanches** (Prop: Anthony & Denise Debray)
*44160*
☎ 240013251 FAX 240013818
(from main Nantes/St-Nazaire road take exit Prinquiau towards
Besne for 2.5km, then left and follow signs)
Near sea  Near beach  Forest area
*2 en suite (bth/shr)  (1 fmly)  No smoking on premises  TV in all
bedrooms  Full central heating  Open parking available
Supervised*
ROOMS: s 230-250FF;  d 250-270FF  ✱
CARDS: Travellers cheques

## BESSÉ-SUR-BRAYE Sarthe

**Le Moulin de l'Étang** (Prop: Claude & Jacqueline Leger)
La Chapelle-Huon *72310*
☎ 243355486 FAX 243352217
(From A11 exit La Ferté-Bernard/St Calais, La Chapelle-Huon
is 2km before Besse-sur-Braye. Le Moulin de l'Étang signed in
village)
Near river  Near lake  Forest area
*Closed Mar*
*1 en suite (bth/shr)  No smoking on premises  TV in all
bedrooms  Full central heating  Open parking available  No
children 10yrs  Fishing  Boule  Mini-golf  Languages spoken:
English*
CARDS: ●● ■■ Travellers cheques

## BOIS-DE-LA-CHAIZE Vendée

★ ★ ★ *Hotel St-Paul*
Bois de la Chaize
☎ 51390563 FAX 51397398
Near sea  Near beach  Forest area
*Closed 2 Nov-15 March*
*(10 fmly)  (20 with balcony)  TV in 37 bedrooms  Direct dial from
37 bedrooms  Licensed  Full central heating  Open parking
available  Child discount available  Indoor swimming pool
(heated)  Outdoor swimming pool (heated)  Tennis  Last d
22.00hrs  Languages spoken: English*
CARDS: ●● ■■ ■■ Travellers cheques

## BOUGUENAIS Loire-Atlantique

★ ★ ★ *Hotel Océania*
Aéroport de Nautes Atlantique *44340*
☎ 240050566 FAX 240051203
Near motorway
*87 en suite (bth/shr)  (70 fmly)  No smoking in 30 bedrooms  TV
in all bedrooms  STV  Radio in rooms  Direct dial from all
bedrooms  Mini-bar in all bedrooms  Licensed  Lift  Night porter
Full central heating  Air conditioning in bedrooms  Open
parking available  Child discount available 12yrs  Outdoor
swimming pool (heated)  Tennis  Sauna  Gym  Pool table
Covered terrace  Last d 23.30hrs  Languages spoken: English,
German & Spanish*
CARDS: ●● ■■ ■■ ■ Travellers cheques

## BRISSAC-QUINCÉ Maine-et-Loire

**Bed & Breakfast** (Prop: Mme Monique Deforge)
Ste-Anne *49320*
☎ 241912217
(from Angers take D748 towards Poitiers. Exit to Brissac.
House on left, immediately after Domaine Sainte Anne)
Near motorway
*Closed 1 Nov-30 Apr*
*2 en suite (bth/shr)  (1 fmly)  Radio in rooms  Full central
heating  Open parking available  Languages spoken: English*
CARDS: Travellers cheques

## CHALLANS Vendée

★ ★ *Hotel de l'Antiquité*
14 rue Galliéni
☎ 251680284 FAX 251355574
(from Nantes follow Bordeaux signs then towards La Roche-
sur-Yon)
Near sea  Near beach  In town centre  Near motorway

*16 en suite (bth/shr)  TV in all bedrooms  Direct dial from all
bedrooms  Room-safe  Licensed  Full central heating  Open
parking available  Child discount available  Outdoor swimming
pool  Open terrace  Languages spoken: English*
ROOMS: (room only)  d 220-360FF
**Reductions over 1 night**
CARDS: ●● ■■ ■■ ■ Travellers cheques

★ ★ ★ *Château de la Vérie*
rte de St Gilles-Croix-de-Vie *85300*
☎ 251353344 FAX 251351484
(cross Challan until the town hall, then straight on and follow
direction of St Gilles-Crois-De-Vie, establishment on the right
about 2km from town hall)                                 *contd.*

Near river Near sea Near beach Forest area
*23 en suite (bth/shr) 4 rooms in annexe (4 fmly) TV in all
bedrooms STV Direct dial from all bedrooms Mini-bar in all
bedrooms Room-safe Licensed Full central heating Open
parking available Child discount available 10yrs Outdoor
swimming pool Tennis Fishing Bicycle rental Open terrace V
meals Last d 21.30hrs Languages spoken: English*
CARDS: ●● ■■ ☲ ⓪ Travellers cheques

## CHAMPFLEUR Sarthe

**Garencière** (Prop: Denis et Christine Langlais)
*72610*
☎ 33317584
Situated in the heart of the rural countryside, this handsome
18th-century farmhouse has individually furnished bedrooms
with private facilities. Meals are taken at the hosts' table and
are prepared with fresh farm produce. The specialities of the
house are poulet aux cidre, canard au vin and tarte du
camembert.
Forest area
*5 en suite (shr) No smoking on premises Full central heating
Open parking available Covered parking available Indoor
swimming pool (heated) Boule V meals Last d 8.30pm
Languages spoken: English*
MEALS: Dinner fr 100FFalc✱
CARDS: Travellers cheques

## CHAMPIGNÉ Maine-et-Loire

**Château des Briottières**
*49330*
☎ 241420002 FAX 241420155
(4km from the village. Signposted)

This magnificent 18th-century residence, in the hands of the
same family for six generations, is surrounded by 40 hectares
of parkland. Guests receive a warm welcome in the grand
surroundings of this typical French château, and immaculate
service and good old-fashioned hospitality go hand in hand
here. Places of interest nearby are the many châteaux of the
Anjou region, Angers with its famous tapestries, and the
Cointreau distillery.
Near lake Forest area
*14 rms (9 bth/shr) 4 rooms in annexe (2 fmly) (1 with balcony)
No smoking in 1 bedroom TV in 5 bedrooms STV Direct dial
from 10 bedrooms Licensed Full central heating Open parking
available Covered parking available Child discount available
7yrs Outdoor swimming pool (heated) Fishing Pool table
Boule Bicycle rental Open terrace V meals Languages spoken:
English & Spanish*
CARDS: ●● ■■ ☲ Travellers cheques

## CHAMPTOCEAUX Maine-et-Loire

**★★ Champalud**
Promenade du Champalud *49270*
☎ 240835009 FAX 240835381
(from A6 exit 'Ancenis' take Nantes road for 8km then to
Dudon)
Near river In town centre Near motorway
*16 rms (11 bth/shr) (3 fmly) TV in 10 bedrooms Radio in rooms
Direct dial from all bedrooms Licensed Full central heating
Child discount available 10yrs Pool table Bicycle rental
Open terrace Last d 21.30hrs Languages spoken: English*
ROOMS: (room only) s 175-220FF; d 230-260FF
**Reductions over 1 night**
MEALS: Full breakfast 35FF Lunch 65-220FF&alc Dinner
65-220FF&alc
CARDS: ●● ☲ Travellers cheques

## CHANTONNAY Vendée

**Manoir de Ponsay**
St-Mars-des-Pres *85110*
☎ 251469671 FAX 251468007
(From A83 take Chantonnay exit. Take D960 towards
Pouzauges. From Puy Belliard follow signs for hotel)
Near river Near lake Forest area Near motorway
*8 en suite (bth/shr) (1 fmly) TV in all bedrooms Licensed Full
central heating Open parking available Covered parking
available Fishing Open terrace Last d 16.00hrs Languages
spoken: English*
ROOMS: (room only) s 360FF; d 580FF
**Reductions over 1 night**
MEALS: Continental breakfast 50FF Dinner 190FF
CARDS: ■■ ⓪ Travellers cheques

**★★ Moulin Neuf**
*85110*
☎ 251943027 FAX 251945776
The Hotel Moulin Neuf occupies a splendid lakeside position
and is the ideal venue for both the commercial and leisure
traveller. It offers airy, well equipped bedrooms, a lounge and a
congenial bar, or guests can relax on the terrace with fine
views over the lake. The menu features a good choice of fresh
seafood and fish specialities from the lake, complemented by
regional dishes. Sporting facilities include mini-golf, archery,
two tennis courts, sauna and outdoor heated swimming pool.

Near river Near lake Forest area Near motorway
*60 en suite (bth/shr) 22 rooms in annexe (10 fmly) (29 with
balcony) TV in all bedrooms STV Direct dial from all
bedrooms Mini-bar in 3 bedrooms Licensed Full central
heating Open parking available Child discount available 10yrs*

*Indoor swimming pool (heated) Outdoor swimming pool (heated) Tennis Sauna Solarium Pool table Boule Mini-golf Bicycle rental Open terrace Covered terrace V meals Last d 21.00hrs Languages spoken: English*
ROOMS: (room only) s 240-350FF; d 250-400FF
**Reductions over 1 night**
MEALS: Continental breakfast 39FF Lunch 65-180FF&alc Dinner 65-180FF&alc
CARDS: ●● ■■ ☲☲ ⑩ Travellers cheques

### CHARTRE-SUR-LE-LOIR, LA Sarthe

**★ ★ Hotel de France**
20 pl de la République *72340*
☎ 243444016 FAX 243796220
The hotel is located in the centre of the village and has an abundance of flowers adorning its façade and terrace. Its rustic interior features a spacious foyer with cosy armchairs and large windows, a congenial bar and a handsome wooden staircase leading to the bedrooms. All guest rooms have modern facilities.

*Near river Forest area In town centre Near motorway*
*Closed Sun eve & Mon 15 Sep-Jun*
*28 en suite (bth/shr) 12 rooms in annexe (3 fmly) TV in all bedrooms Direct dial from all bedrooms Licensed Full central heating Open parking available Supervised Child discount available 10yrs Fishing Bicycle rental Open terrace V meals Last d 21.30hrs Languages spoken: English*
ROOMS: (room only) s 210-210FF; d 250-310FF
**Special breaks: weekend breaks**
MEALS: Continental breakfast 37FF Lunch 74-210FF&alc Dinner 74-210FF&alc
CARDS: ●● ☲☲ Travellers cheques

### CHÂTEAUBRIANT Loire-Atlantique

**★ ★ ★ Hostellerie de la Ferrière**
rte de Nantes *44110*
☎ 240280028 FAX 240282921
(on D963/D178)
*Forest area Near motorway*
*25 en suite (bth) 14 rooms in annexe (4 fmly) TV in all bedrooms STV Direct dial from all bedrooms Mini-bar in all bedrooms Licensed Full central heating Open parking available Child discount available 12yrs Boule Open terrace V meals Last d 21.00hrs Languages spoken: English*
ROOMS: (room only) d 360-400FF
**✱ Reductions over 1 night**
MEALS: Full breakfast 40FF Continental breakfast 40FF Lunch 85-240FF&alc Dinner 85-240FF&alc✱
CARDS: ●● ■■ ☲☲ ⑩ Travellers cheques

### CHÂTEAU-DU-LOIR Sarthe

**Bed & Breakfast** (Prop: Mme Le Goff)
22 rue de l'Hôtel de Ville *72500*
☎ 243440338
(at Le Mans take N138 towards Tours. In Château-du-Loir, the B & B is on the main square behind the bandstand.)

This house was built in 1850 and is situated in the heart of the of the Loire Valley, and is ideally located for travellers coming from the car-ferries to the South of France. One of the rooms has fine views over the oldest parts of the town. The rooms are comfortable and furnished with antiques.
*Near river Near lake Forest area In town centre Near motorway*
*Closed Oct-Mar*
*4 rms (3 shr) (2 fmly) Full central heating Open parking available Covered parking available Supervised Languages spoken: English*
ROOMS: s 225FF; d 270FF ✱
CARDS: Travellers cheques

### CHÂTEAU-GONTIER Mayenne

**Les Boisards** (Prop: Mme May)
*53200*
☎ 243702738
(N162 (Laval-Angers). 7km south of Château-Gontier turn right towards Molières (C2) at crossroads Menil/Molières, farm is 300m on left)
An 18th-century farmhouse in traditional Mayenne style, with high beamed rooms and metre-thick stone walls, set in extensive gardens and on a working farm with sheep and free-range ducks. Convenient to the N162.
*Near river Forest area Near motorway*
*3 en suite (bth/shr) Full central heating Open parking available Child discount available 14yrs Fishing Boule Chlidrens play area Last d 8pm Languages spoken: English & Spanish*
ROOMS: s 160FF; d 240FF
MEALS: Dinner 85FF
CARDS: Travellers cheques

**Château de Mirvault-Azé** (Prop: Françoise d'Ambrières)
*53200*
☎ 243071082 FAX 243071082
(Mirvault is 1km north of the centre of Château-Gontier, entrance is on the N162 which links Laval/Angers)
*Near river Forest area Near motorway*
*RS Nov-Mar (by reservation)*
*5 rms (2 bth) TV in 2 bedrooms Open parking available Covered parking available Child discount available 5yrs Fishing Open terrace Languages spoken: English*     *contd.*

ROOMS: s 300FF; d 400FF
**Reductions over 1 night Special breaks**
CARDS: Travellers cheques

★ ★ **Hostellerie de Mirwault**
rue du Val de la Mayenne *53200*
☎ 243071317 FAX 243076690
(From S enter town on N162, cross bridge and follow the river
to the right towards Ecluse-de-Mirwault)

This family-run hotel stands on a peaceful stretch of the River
Mayenne just outside the historic town of Château-Gontier,
making it the ideal spot for relaxing or touring the Loire Valley.
It features comfortable bedrooms with good amenities and an
attractive restaurant.
Near river Near motorway
*Closed 23 Dec-14 Jan*
*11 en suite (bth/shr) (2 fmly) (3 with balcony) TV in all
bedrooms STV Direct dial from all bedrooms Mini-bar in all
bedrooms Licensed Full central heating Air conditioning in
bedrooms Open parking available Child discount available
12yrs Golf Fishing Bicycle rental Open terrace Boating V
meals Last d 21.00hrs Languages spoken: English, Spanish &
German*
ROOMS: (room only) s 250-285FF; d 285-320FF
**Reductions over 1 night Special breaks: Fishing,
boating,cycling breaks**
MEALS: Full breakfast 48FF Lunch 82-138FF&alc Dinner
80-200FFalc
CARDS: ● ■ ■ Travellers cheques

**CHÂTEAUNEUF-SUR-SARTHE** Maine-et-Loire

★ ★ **Les Ondines**
Quai de la Sarthe *49330*
☎ 241698438 FAX 241698359
(from A11 exit at Durtal, take D859 to Châteauneuf)
Near river
*24 en suite (bth/shr) (4 fmly) (7 with balcony) TV in 20
bedrooms Direct dial from all bedrooms Licensed Lift Full
central heating Open parking available Supervised Child
discount available 4yrs Fishing Open terrace Covered terrace
Languages spoken: English*
CARDS: ● ■ ■ Travellers cheques

★ **De La Sarthe**
1 rue du Port *49330*
☎ 241698529
(From A11 exit at Durtal, take D859 to Châteauneuf)
Near river In town centre Near motorway
*Closed 6-31 Oct*

*7 rms (2 bth 4 shr) (1 fmly) (1 with balcony) Licensed Full
central heating Open parking available Supervised Child
discount available 10yrs Open terrace V meals Last d 21.15hrs
Languages spoken: English*
CARDS: ● ■ Travellers cheques

**CHAZE-SUR-ARGOS** Maine-et-Loire

**La Chaufournaie** (Prop: Susan & Peter Scarboro)
*49500*
☎ 241614905 FAX 241614905
(ignore signs to Chaze-sur-Argos and travel along the D770,
establishment situated between the villages of Vern D'Anjou
and Angrie)
This 1850's farmhouse standing in 44 acres of land is an ideal
base for exploring this area, renowned for the Chateaux,
waterways and wine. The south facing garden with sun
loungers, giant chess and petanque court is available to guests.
Meals are taken communally, breakfast round the large kitchen
table or in the garden, and there is a lounge/games room with
a snooker table.
Near river Near lake Forest area
*5 en suite (shr) (1 fmly) No smoking in all bedrooms Full
central heating Open parking available Boule Games room
with full size snooker table Casino Last d 16.00hrs Languages
spoken: English*
ROOMS: s 210FF; d 240FF
**Special breaks: Golfing breaks**
MEALS: Dinner 90FF

**CHEMELLIER** Maine-et-Loire

**Bed & Breakfast** (Prop: Eliette Edon)
Maunit *49320*
☎ 241455950 FAX 0241450144
(from D761 south of Angers take D90 on left at Les
Alleuds.Take 6th exit left, Maunit on right)
The peaceful bedrooms are situated on the first floor. This is a
super environment for relaxing and getting away from it all.
Visit the tapestries of the Château at Angers. Meals are served
in the evenings.
Forest area
*3 en suite (shr) (1 fmly) Full central heating Open parking
available Child discount available 10yrs Pool table Table tennis
V meals Last d 21.00hrs*
ROOMS: d fr 260FF **Reductions over 1 night**
MEALS: Dinner 110FF✱

**CHÉNEHUTTE-TRÈVES-CUNAULT** Maine-et-Loire

★ ★ ★ **Hostellerie du Prieuré**
*49350*
☎ 241679014 FAX 241679224
This gracious Renaissance manor house dates back to the 12th
century and occupies a magnificent location surrounded by 65
acres of parkland, with splendid views over the Loire Valley.
The elegant bedrooms are furnished to a high standard and
offer every conceivable amenity. Leisure facilities include a
tennis court, open-air heated swimming pool, mini-golf and
pétanque. Guests can visit to the famous vineyards, the town
of Saumur or L'Abbaye de Fontevraud. The restaurant, with
panoramic views, serves a wide choice of regional specialities
and is complemented the delightful wines of the Loire region.
Near river Forest area
*35 en suite (bth/shr) 15 rooms in annexe (4 fmly) (5 with
balcony) TV in all bedrooms Direct dial from all bedrooms
Mini-bar in all bedrooms Licensed Night porter Full central*

**Hostellerie du Prieure**
heating Open parking available Supervised Child discount
available 12yrs Outdoor swimming pool (heated) Tennis Boule
Mini-golf Bicycle rental Open terrace V meals Last d 22.00hrs
Languages spoken: English, Italian & Spanish
ROOMS: (room only) s 450-1600FF; d 600-1600FF
MEALS: Continental breakfast 60FF Lunch 240-425FF&alc
Dinner 240-425FF&alc
CARDS: ●● ■ ☲ ◎ JCB Travellers cheques

### CHOLET Maine-et-Loire

★★ **Grand Hotel de la Poste**
26 bd Gustave Richard 49300
☎ 241620720 FAX 241585410
(follow station and town centre signs, hotel is in front of Jardin
de Verre theatre)
In town centre
Closed Xmas & New Year
53 en suite (bth/shr) (9 fmly) TV in all bedrooms STV Direct
dial from all bedrooms Licensed Lift Night porter Full central
heating Covered parking available (charged) Open terrace
Covered terrace Last d 21.30hrs Languages spoken: English &
German
CARDS: ●● ■ ☲ ◎

### COUPTRAIN Mayenne

**Bed & Breakfast** (Prop: Mireille et Georges Merten)
34 rue de la Magdeleine 53250
☎ 243038494 FAX 243038494
(in Couptrain turn at 1st left, house on right)
Near river Forest area
2 en suite (shr) TV in 1 bedroom Full central heating Open
parking available Covered parking available Tennis Table
tennis Languages spoken: English & Italian

### DISSAY-SOUS-COURCILLON Sarthe

**La Chataigneraie** (Prop: Mme M Letanneux)
72500
☎ 243794530
(from N138 just south of Dissay, take left turn onto small road
on a bend and follow signs for Chambre d'Hôtes.
Establishment in 1km)
This establishment has been described as 'a fairy tale cottage',
built of mellow old stone, with white shutters, and covered in
green ivy. It is set in the heart of the Loire Valley, in a quiet
location, and the rooms overlook fields of sunflowers or the
large garden. Guests can use a separate entrance. Meals by
prior arrangement. Nearby is a 12th-century chateau. The
proprietors will be happy to help organise your visits to local
places of interest.

Near river Near lake Forest area Near motorway
Apr-Oct
3 rms (1 bth/shr) No smoking on premises Full central heating
Open parking available Supervised Child discount available
Tennis Languages spoken: English & Spanish
ROOMS: s 190FF; d 260FF ✱ **Special breaks**
MEALS: Dinner 80-90FF✱

★★ **Auberge du Val de Loir**
pl Morand 72500
☎ 243440906 FAX 243445640
(N158 from Le Mans to Château-du-Loir then to Dissay sous
Courcillon)
Near river Near lake Forest area Near motorway
10 en suite (bth/shr) 3 rooms in annexe (4 fmly) TV in all
bedrooms Direct dial from all bedrooms Licensed Full central
heating Open parking available Supervised Child discount
available Open terrace Last d 21.00hrs Languages spoken:
English
CARDS: ●● ☲ Travellers cheques

### DURTAL Maine-et-Loire

**Château de Gouis** (Prop: Mme Linossier)
Grande Rue 49430
☎ 241760340 FAX 241760340
(access via A11 exit Durtal)
Near river Forest area Near motorway
Closed Oct
8 rms (6 bth/shr) (4 fmly) (1 with balcony) Radio in rooms
Night porter Full central heating Open parking available
Supervised Child discount available 4yrs Fishing Open terrace

**Château de la Motte** (Prop: Michel Francois)
Baracé 49430
☎ 241769375
(A11 exit at Durtal, take D859 towards Châteauneuf for 2km,
then to the left D68 to Baracé via Huillé)
Near river Near lake Forest area
5 en suite (bth/shr) (1 with balcony) Open parking available
(charged) Child discount available Fishing Boule Languages
spoken: English & Spanish
CARDS: Travellers cheques

### FERTÉ-BERNARD, LA Sarthe

★★ **Climat de France**
43 bd Général-de-Gaulle 72400
☎ 243938470 FAX 243712814
(off A11 exit La Ferté-Bernard in Le Mans direction)
Near river Near lake Near sea Near motorway
50 en suite (bth) (11 fmly) TV in all bedrooms Licensed Full
central heating Open parking available Supervised Open
terrace V meals Last d 10pm Languages spoken: English,
German & Portuguese
CARDS: ●● ☲

### FLÈCHE, LA Sarthe

★★ **Le Vert Galant**
70 Grande Rue 72200
☎ 243940051 FAX 243451124
Near river Near lake Forest area In town centre Near
motorway
9 en suite (bth/shr) (4 fmly) TV in all bedrooms Licensed Full
central heating Open parking available Fishing Open terrace
V meals Last d 21.00hrs Languages spoken: English
CARDS: ●● ☲ Travellers cheques

## FLOCELLIÈRE, LA Vendée

**Château de la Flocellière** (Prop: Erika & Sandrine Vignial)
*85700*
☎ 251572203 FAX 251577521
(from Cholet take N160 towards La Roche. At Les Herbiers take D755 towards Pouzauges.In St Michael-Mont-Mercure take D64 to La Flocellière and follow signs for the Château)
Near lake Forest area
*8 en suite (bth/shr) (1 fmly) TV in 3 bedrooms Full central heating Open parking available Child discount available 12yrs Outdoor swimming pool (heated) Boule Table tennis Billiards Languages spoken: English, German & Italian*
CARDS: Travellers cheques

## FONTENAY-LE-COMTE Vendée

★ ★ **Le Rabelais**
rte de Parthenay *85200*
☎ 251698620 FAX 251698045
(approach via A83 exit 8)
Near river Forest area In town centre Near motorway
*54 en suite (bth/shr) (3 fmly) (15 with balcony) TV in all bedrooms Radio in rooms Direct dial from all bedrooms Licensed Lift Night porter Full central heating Open parking available Covered parking available (charged) Child discount available 12yrs Outdoor swimming pool Boule Bicycle rental Open terrace Table tennis Last d 21.30hrs Languages spoken: English & Spanish*
CARDS: ●● ■ ▥ ▣ Travellers cheques

## FONTEVRAUD-L'ABBAYE Maine-et-Loire

★ ★ **Croix Blanche**
7 pl des Plantagenets *49590*
☎ 241517111 FAX 241381538
(16kms from Saumur A85, D947)
Forest area In town centre Near motorway
Closed 18-26 Nov & 10 Jan-4 Feb
*21 en suite (bth/shr) (2 fmly) TV in 20 bedrooms Direct dial from all bedrooms Mini-bar in 20 bedrooms Licensed Full central heating Open parking available Covered parking available (charged) Child discount available Boule Bicycle rental Open terrace V meals Last d 21.30hrs Languages spoken: English*
CARDS: ●● ■ ▥ Travellers cheques

**Le Domaine de Mestre**
*49590*
☎ 241517587 & 241417232 FAX 241517190
Near river Forest area Near motorway
*12 en suite (bth/shr)*

## GREZ-NEUVILLE Maine-et-Loire

**La Croix d'Étain** (Prop: Auguste Bahuaud)
2 r de l'Ecluse *49220*
☎ 241956849 FAX 241180272
(access via N162 Laval-Angers. In village between the church and the river)
Near river In town centre Near motorway
*4 en suite (bth/shr) Full central heating Open parking available Child discount available 16yrs Languages spoken: English*
CARDS: Travellers cheques

## HERBIGNAC Loire-Atlantique

★ ★ ★ **Château de Coëtcaret** (Prop: M & Mme de la Monneraye)
*44410*
☎ 240914120 FAX 240913746
(from Nantes take N165 direction of Vannes before La Roche-Bernard take D774 direction La Baule at Herbignac take D47 for 4kms Coëtcaret on left)
This small 19th century château is the home of M and Mme de la Monneraye. It is set in 100 hectares, with horse-riding on site. The bedrooms include two family rooms and are welcoming and comfortable. Mme de la Monneraye is a teacher of floral art and her skills are evident throughout the house. Dinner by candlelight is offered at your hosts' table, by prior arrangement. Forest area
*4 en suite (bth/shr) (2 fmly) No smoking on premises Full central heating Open parking available Child discount available 2yrs Riding Pool table Boule Table tennis Languages spoken: English & Spanish*
ROOMS: d 500-650FF
MEALS: Dinner 250FF
CARDS: Travellers cheques

## INGRANDES-SUR-LOIRE Maine-et-Loire

★ ★ **Lion d'Or**
26 rue du Pont *49123*
☎ 241392008 FAX 241392103
(Between Angers and Nantes by the nationale 23, heading towards Ingrandes)
*16 rms (4 bth 6 shr) (2 fmly) (2 with balcony) TV in all bedrooms STV Licensed Full central heating Open parking available Covered parking available Child discount available 2yrs Last d 21.00hrs Languages spoken: English*
CARDS: ●● ■ ▥ Travellers cheques

## JAILLE-YVON, LA Maine-et-Loire

**Château-du-Plessis-Anjou**
*49220*
☎ 241951275 FAX 241951441
Near river Forest area Near motorway
Closed Nov-Mar
*8 en suite (bth/shr) (3 with balcony) Full central heating Open parking available Child discount available Solarium Boule Languages spoken: English & Spanish*
CARDS: ●● ■ ▥ ▣ Travellers cheques

## JARD-SUR-MER Vendée

★ ★ ★ **Hotel du Parc de la Grange**
rte de l'Abbaye *85520*
☎ 251334488 FAX 251334058
Near sea Near beach Forest area
RS Half board obligatory at high season
*48 en suite (bth/shr) (16 fmly) (40 with balcony) TV in all bedrooms STV Radio in rooms Direct dial from all bedrooms Licensed Night porter Full central heating Open parking available Child discount available 12yrs Outdoor swimming pool (heated) Tennis Solarium Pool table Boule Bicycle rental Open terrace Covered terrace Last d 21.00hrs Languages spoken: English & German*
ROOMS: (room only) s 275-420FF; d 320-580FF
MEALS: Full breakfast 40FF Lunch 120-200FF&alc Dinner 120-200FF&alc
CARDS: ●● ■ ▥ ▣ Travellers cheques

## LAVAL Mayenne

**Le Bas du Gast** (Prop: François-Charles Williot)
6 rue de la Halle aux Toiles *53000*
☎ 243492279 FAX 243564471
(on the south bank of the River Mayenne joining the town hall
square - follow signs - the château is close to the cathedral)
A lovely château in private parkland, yet uniquely situated in
the lovely old city of Laval. The building is listed as 17th-18th
century, each room has been carefully retained in its former
magnificence with delicately tinted carved wooden wall
panelling, crested marble fireplaces and furniture of the
period.
In town centre  Near motorway
*Closed Dec-Jan*
*5 en suite (bth/shr) (3 fmly) (5 with balcony) TV in 2 bedrooms*
*Full central heating  Open parking available  Child discount*
*available 10yrs  Boule  Open terrace  Special arrangements for*
*AA guide users  Languages spoken: English*
ROOMS: (room only) d 550-650FF ✳
CARDS: ▅

**★ ★ Climat de France**
bd des Trappistines *53000*
☎ 243028888 Cen Res 64460123 FAX 243028700
(off N157/N171)
Near river  Forest area  Near motorway
*44 en suite (bth/shr) (8 fmly) TV in all bedrooms  Radio in*
*rooms  Direct dial from all bedrooms  Licensed  Open parking*
*available  V meals  Last d 10pm  Languages spoken: English &*
*Italian*
CARDS: ●● ▄▄

## LAVENAY Sarthe

**Les Patis du Vergas** (Prop: M et Mme J Deage)
*72310*
☎ 243352818 FAX 243353818
(from A11 exit La Ferté-Bernard towards St-Calais)
Ideal for those who wish to relax in a peaceful park close to
nature. For anglers there is a 1.2-hectare pond, storage for
fishing equipment and a fridge for keeping the fish fresh.
Walking in the nearby Vallee du Loire is popular.
Near river  Near lake  Forest area
*Closed 4 Nov-Feb*
*5 en suite (shr) TV in 1 bedroom  Full central heating  Open*
*parking available  Child discount available 10yrs  Fishing  Boule*
*Bicycle rental  Croquet  Table tennis  Sauna  Volley ball  Last d*
*7pm  Languages spoken: English*
ROOMS: s 250FF; d 270FF ✳ **Reductions over 1 night**
MEALS: Dinner fr 90FF✳
CARDS: Travellers cheques

## LION-D'ANGERS, LE Maine-et-Loire

**Le Petit Carqueron** (Prop: M & Mme Carcaillet)
*49220*
☎ 241856265
(from Le Lion D'Angers take D770 in approx 1.5km Le Petit
Carqueron)
Forest area
*Closed Nov-29 Mar*
*4 rms (1 fmly) (2 with balcony) Open parking available*
*Outdoor swimming pool  Fishing  Riding  Open terrace*
*Languages spoken: English*

## MANS, LE Sarthe

**★ ★ Vidéotel**
av Paul Courboulay *72000*
☎ 243244724 FAX 243245841
Near river  In town centre
*91 en suite (shr) (17 fmly) No smoking in 12 bedrooms  TV in*
*all bedrooms  Direct dial from all bedrooms  Mini-bar in all*
*bedrooms  Licensed  Lift  Night porter  Full central heating*
*Open parking available  Covered parking available (charged)*
*Supervised  Child discount available 12yrs  Pool table  V meals*
*Last d 22.00hrs  Languages spoken: English*
CARDS: ●● ▅ ▄▄ ⑩ JCB Travellers cheques

## MAREIL-SUR-LOIR Sarthe

**Le Logis de Semur**
*72200*
☎ 243454684 FAX 243454684
(8km NE of the Flèch along N23 towards Le Mans, at
Clermont-Créans take D13 towrads Mareil-sur-Loir. The farm
is 1km from the village - signposted)
The owners of this 14th-century farmhouse are artists, a talent
that is evident in the profusion of colours. Situated one
kilometre from the village in the heart of the countryside. Each
of the cosy rooms has its own terraced area. Art and cookery
classes are available.
Near river  Forest area
*6 rms (5 bth/shr) (1 with balcony) No smoking in 1 bedroom*
*Full central heating  Open parking available  Covered parking*
*available  Child discount available 3yrs  Fishing  Riding  Boule*
*Bicycle rental  Languages spoken: English*
ROOMS: s fr 313FF; d fr 320FF
✳ **Reductions over 1 night**

## MASSIGNY Vendée

**Bed & Breakfast** (Prop: Marie-Françoise Neau)
*85770*
☎ 251523032 FAX 251523032
(from A83 exit at Fontenay-le-Comte onto D938 head SW
towards La Rochelle for 6km then right at small sign for
Massigny)
Light and airy rooms are available at this establishment, plus a
large sitting room with television and video tapes about the
Vendée. In the garden is a barbecue and picnic area.
Near river  Forest area
*4 rms (2 shr) No smoking on premises  Full central heating*
*Open parking available  Child discount available  Outdoor*
*swimming pool  Languages spoken: English*
ROOMS: s 220FF; d 250FF

## MAULEVRIER Maine-et-Loire

**★ ★ Château Colbert**
*49360*
☎ 241555133 FAX 241550902
Near river  Near lake  Forest area  In town centre  Near
motorway
*26 en suite (bth/shr) (5 fmly) TV in all bedrooms  Direct dial*
*from all bedrooms  Mini-bar in all bedrooms  Licensed  Lift  Full*
*central heating  Open parking available  Supervised  Child*
*discount available 12yrs  Fishing  Boule  Open terrace  V meals*
*Last d 21.00hrs  Languages spoken: English*

*contd.*

213

ROOMS: (room only) d 300-600FF
**Reductions over 1 night**
MEALS: Full breakfast 45FF Lunch 110-205FF Dinner 110-205FF
CARDS: ● ▭ ▣ Travellers cheques

## MAYENNE Mayenne

**★ ★ ★ Grand Hotel**
2 rue Ambroise-de-Loré *53100*
☎ 243009600 FAX 243006920
This charming hotel on the banks of the river offers a genuine welcome and has a friendly atmosphere throughout. The restaurant serves traditional cuisine with a regional flavour and the lounge bar has a wide variety of wines and spirits.

Near river In town centre Near motorway
*28 rms (26 bth/shr) (4 fmly) TV in all bedrooms STV Direct dial from all bedrooms Licensed Full central heating Open parking available Covered parking available Supervised Child discount available 10yrs Bicycle rental Open terrace V meals Last d 21.30hrs Languages spoken: English*
ROOMS: (room only) s 265-350FF; d 306-420FF
✻ **Reductions over 1 night**
MEALS: Continental breakfast 40FF Lunch 78-215FF&alc Dinner 78-215FF&alc✻
CARDS: ● ▥ ▤ Travellers cheques

## MÉZANGERS Mayenne

**Le Cruchet** (Prop: Léopold Nay)
*53600*
☎ 243906555
(from Laval N157 towards Le Mans at Soulge-sur-Ouette D20 left to Evron then D7 towards Mayenne, in Mézangers signposted)
Near lake Forest area
*2 en suite (bth/shr) (1 fmly) Full central heating Open parking available Supervised Languages spoken: English*
CARDS: ▥ Travellers cheques

## MISSILLAC Loire-Atlantique

**La Ferme de Morican** (Prop: Oliver & Brigitte Cojean)
Morican *44780*
☎ 240883882 FAX 240883882
(from Missillac D2 to St-Gildas-des-Bois, in Perny turn left. From Redion way to Portchâteau, in St-Gildas-des-Bois D2 to Missillac, in Perny turn right)
Near lake Forest area
*5 en suite (bth/shr) (2 fmly) Full central heating Open parking available Fishing Riding Languages spoken: English & Spanish*

ROOMS: s 210-240FF; d 250-280FF
MEALS: Dinner 95-140FF✻
CARDS: Travellers cheques

**★ ★ ★ ★ Hotel de la Bretèsche**
*44780*
☎ 251768696 FAX 240669947
The hotel stands on the shores of the lake with views over the water and of the castle. Surrounded by a magnificent forest, once the royal hunting grounds, it is an ideal place for business travellers and holidaymakers alike. The bedrooms are furnished with co-ordinated fabrics and offer restful accommodation. There is a cosy lounge and a congenial bar in which to relax before sampling regional dishes in the restaurant.
Near river Near lake Forest area Near motorway

*Closed Jan-Feb*
*29 en suite (bth/shr) (29 fmly) TV in all bedrooms STV Radio in rooms Direct dial from all bedrooms Mini-bar in 21 bedrooms Licensed Lift Full central heating Open parking available Covered parking available (charged) Supervised Child discount available 12yrs Outdoor swimming pool (heated) Golf Tennis Pool table Bicycle rental Open terrace V meals Last d 21.00hrs Languages spoken: English, German, Italian, Portuguese & Spanish*
ROOMS: (room only) s 450-580FF; d 750-1050FF
MEALS: Continental breakfast 80FF Lunch 160-420FF&alc Dinner 195-420FF&alc
CARDS: ● ▥ ▤ ▣ Travellers cheques

## MONHOUDOU Sarthe

**Château de Monhoudou** (Prop: Michel de Monhoudou)
*72260*
☎ 243974005 FAX 243331158
(from Paris: exit La Ferté-Bernard onto D2, after St Cosme-en-Vairais go left towards Moncé & Monhoudou: from Alençon: N138 towards Le Mans to Le Hutte then D310, drive 10km & turn right, at Courgains head towards Monhoudou)
Forest area
*4 en suite (bth/shr) (4 fmly) Licensed Full central heating Open parking available Supervised Child discount available 12yrs Fishing Bicycle rental Last d 19.00hrs Languages spoken: English*

## MONTREUIL-BELLAY Maine-et-Loire

**Démeure des Petits Augustins** (Prop: M & Mme Guezenec)
pl des Augustins *49260*
☎ 241523388 FAX 241523388
(take D147 S from Saumur towards Poitiers for 16km. In Montreuil-Bellay, Place des Augustins is parallel to, and on the left of 'Rue Nationale'- near the church 'Église des Grands Augustins Soie Vivante'- and chapelle 'des Petits Augustins')
Near river Forest area In town centre Near motorway
*Closed Dec-Feb*
*3 en suite (bth/shr) (1 fmly) Open parking available Languages spoken: English*
Rooms: s 220FF; d 320FF ✱
Cards: ●● ⬛ Travellers cheques

★ ★ **Splendid Hotel**
139 rue du Dr Gaudrez *49260*
☎ 241531000 FAX 241524517
(15km from Saumur in direction Poitier)
Near river Forest area In town centre
*60 en suite (bth/shr) Some rooms in annexe (8 fmly) TV in all bedrooms Radio in rooms Direct dial from all bedrooms Licensed Lift Full central heating Open parking available Supervised Child discount available 10yrs Indoor swimming pool (heated) Outdoor swimming pool (heated) Fishing Sauna Pool table Jacuzzi/spa Bicycle rental Open terrace V meals Last d 22.00hrs Languages spoken: English*
Meals: Full breakfast 50FF Lunch 85-225FF&alc Dinner 85-225FF&alc✱
Cards: ●● ⬛ Travellers cheques

## MONTREUIL-POULAY Mayenne

**Le Vieux Presbytère** (Prop: Legras-Wood)
*53640*
☎ 243008632 FAX 243008142
(between Mayenne, N12 Paris-Rennes, and Lassay-les-Châteaux (D34); at church, turn onto D160 Montreuil-Poulay to Chantrigné. Presbytère half a mile from village)
Near river Near lake Forest area Near motorway
*2 en suite (bth/shr) Radio in rooms Full central heating Open parking available Covered parking available Supervised No children 8yrs Open terrace Languages spoken: English, German, Spanish & Russian*

## MONTREUIL-SUR-LOIR Maine-et-Loire

**Château de Montreuil** (Prop: M Bailliou)
*49140*
☎ 241762103
(leave A11 "Océane" at Seiches-sur-le-Loir. In Seiches cross N23 and take D74 towards Montreuil. Château on the right on leaving the village)
This château was constructed in the middle of the 19th century by the Angevin architect, Hodé, following the neo-gothic Troubadour style. In a beautiful location overlooking the Loire Valley, in a large wooded park with direct access to the river. One floor is exclusively for guests.
Near river Forest area Near motorway
*Closed 16 Nov-14 Mar*
*5 rms (2 bth 2 shr) (2 fmly) Open parking available Child discount available 10yrs Open terrace Boating Last d noon*
Rooms: s 250-330FF; d 300-380FF **Special breaks**
Meals: Dinner fr 135FF
Cards: Travellers cheques

## MOREILLES Vendée

**Le Château**
*85450*
☎ 251561756 FAX 251563030
(A83 Nantes-Bordeaux take exit 7 Ste Hermine then N137 towards Rochelle and in 12km the Château is at end of village)
Near motorway
*8 en suite (bth/shr) 2 rooms in annexe (3 fmly) Direct dial from all bedrooms Licensed Full central heating Open parking available Covered parking available Supervised Child discount available 12yrs Outdoor swimming pool Boule Bicycle rental Covered terrace V meals Last d 21.00hrs*
Cards: Travellers cheques

## MORTAGNE-SUR-SÈVRE Vendée

★ ★ **Hotel de France & Restaurant La Taverne**
(Minotel)
4 pl du Dr Pichat *85290*
☎ 251650337 FAX 251672783
(at intersection N160/N149)
Near river Near lake Near motorway
*Closed 28 Jul-9 Aug RS Half board obligatory Jun-15 Sep*
*25 rms (23 bth/shr) (3 fmly) (10 with balcony) TV in all bedrooms STV Direct dial from all bedrooms Mini-bar in all bedrooms Licensed Lift Full central heating Open parking available Covered parking available (charged) Supervised Child discount available 10yrs Indoor swimming pool (heated) Fishing Riding Boule Bicycle rental Open terrace V meals Last d 21.30hrs Languages spoken: English & German*
Cards: ●● ⬛⬛ ⬛ Ⓓ Travellers cheques

## NANTES Loire-Atlantique

★ ★ ★ **Hotel Le Jules Verne** (Best Western)
3 rue du Couédic *44000*
☎ 240357450 FAX 240200935
In town centre
*65 en suite (bth) TV in all bedrooms Direct dial from all bedrooms Lift Full central heating Air conditioning in bedrooms Child discount available 12yrs Languages spoken: English, German, Spanish & Russian*
Cards: ●● ⬛⬛ ⬛ Ⓓ Travellers cheques

★ ★ ★ **Novotel Nantes**
Cité des Congrés, 3 rue de Valmy *44000*
☎ 251820000 FAX 251820740
Near river In town centre
*105 en suite (bth/shr) (28 fmly) No smoking in 28 bedrooms TV in all bedrooms STV Radio in rooms Direct dial from all bedrooms Mini-bar in all bedrooms Licensed Lift Night porter Full central heating Air conditioning in bedrooms Open parking available Covered parking available (charged) Supervised Child discount available 16yrs Open terrace Last d 24.00hrs Languages spoken: English, German & Spanish*
Cards: ●● ⬛⬛ ⬛ Ⓓ Travellers cheques

## NOIRMOUTIER-EN-L'ILE Vendée

★ ★ ★ **Genéral d'Elbée**
pl d'Armes *85330*
☎ 251391029 FAX 251390823
(on the small harbour)
Near sea Forest area In town centre
*Closed Oct-Mar* *contd.*

215

26 en suite (bth/shr) (7 fmly) (4 with balcony) No smoking in 7 bedrooms Direct dial from all bedrooms Licensed Full central heating Child discount available 10yrs Outdoor swimming pool Bicycle rental Open terrace Languages spoken: English, German & Spanish
CARDS: 💳 🔲 🔲 🔲

### ★ ★ ★ Prateaux
Bois de la Chaize, 8 allée du Tambourin 85330
☎ 251391252 FAX 251394628
(close to the Plage des Dames)
Near sea Near beach Forest area
Closed mid Nov-mid Feb
22 rms (21 bth/shr) (3 fmly) (2 with balcony) No smoking in 7 bedrooms TV in all bedrooms STV Direct dial from all bedrooms Room-safe Full central heating Open parking available Child discount available Open terrace Last d 20.30hrs Languages spoken: English & German
ROOMS: (room only) s 380-730FF; d 450-820FF
MEALS: Continental breakfast 55FF Lunch 132-298FF&alc Dinner 132-298FF&alc
CARDS: 💳 🔲 🔲 🔲 Travellers cheques

### NUAILLÉ Maine-et-Loire

### ★ ★ Relais des Biches Baumotel
pl de l'Église 49340
☎ 241623899 FAX 241629624
Forest area
13 en suite (bth/shr) (2 fmly) TV in all bedrooms Radio in rooms Direct dial from all bedrooms Mini-bar in all bedrooms Licensed Night porter Full central heating Open parking available Covered parking available (charged) Supervised Child discount available Outdoor swimming pool Boule Bicycle rental Open terrace Last d 22.00hrs
CARDS: 💳 🔲 🔲 🔲 Travellers cheques

### OIE, L' Vendée

### La Gauvrière (Prop: M et Mme Sherwin)
85140
☎ 251661305 FAX 251661305
(A83 south from Nantes towards Bordeaux, leave at exit 5 Les Essarts. Turn left onto N160 in 5km turn right at Les 4 Chemins de L'Oie x-rds onto N137. Pass through the village L'Oie & turn right into a country lane at the top of the 2nd hillock)
Delightful 18th-century Vendée farmhouse with large garden set in rolling countryside. Large comfortable rooms with views of the garden. Close to a natural lake and convenient for Nantes and the Western Loire.
Near river Near lake Forest area Near motorway
Closed Nov-week before Etr
6 en suite (shr) (3 fmly) No smoking on premises Open parking available Covered parking available Outdoor swimming pool Fishing Riding Boule Mini-golf Bicycle rental Languages spoken: English Chinese & Spanish
ROOMS: d 250-300FF ✱
MEALS: Dinner fr 95FF✱

### OIZÉ Sarthe

### Château de Montaupin (Prop: Alain & Nicole David)
72330
☎ 243878170 FAX 243872625
Located in a small country village, Nicole and Alain welcome you to their 17th-century property. Guests may dine with the family. Private swimming pool, fishing.

***Château de Montaupin***
Near river Near lake Forest area Near motorway
8 rms (3 bth 3 shr) (3 fmly) TV in 4 bedrooms Full central heating Open parking available Child discount available 10yrs Outdoor swimming pool (heated) Fishing Last d 20.00hrs Languages spoken: English
ROOMS: s 230-260FF; d 280-320FF
MEALS: Dinner fr 110FF
CARDS: 💳 🔲 Travellers cheques

### OUDON Loire-Atlantique

### ★ ★ Du Port
10 rue du Port 44521
☎ 240836858 FAX 240866979
Near river Forest area In town centre Near motorway
6 en suite (bth/shr) (3 fmly) TV in all bedrooms STV Radio in rooms Mini-bar in all bedrooms Licensed Night porter Full central heating Air conditioning in bedrooms Open parking available Supervised Child discount available 7yrs Outdoor swimming pool Fishing Riding Gym Pool table Mini-golf Bicycle rental Open terrace Covered terrace V meals Last d 22.30hrs Languages spoken: English
CARDS: 💳 🔲 🔲 🔲 Travellers cheques

### PIRIAC-SUR-MER Loire-Atlantique

### ★ ★ De La Poste
25 rue de la Plage 44420
☎ 240235090 FAX 240236896
Near sea In town centre
Closed 12 Nov-Mar
15 rms (5 bth 5 shr) (1 with balcony) TV in 5 bedrooms Direct dial from all bedrooms Licensed Open terrace Languages spoken: English
CARDS: 💳 🔲 🔲 Travellers cheques

### POIRE-SUR-VIE Vendée

### ★ ★ Du Centre
pl du Marché 85170
☎ 251318120 FAX 251318821
In town centre
27 rms (24 bth/shr) TV in all bedrooms Direct dial from all bedrooms Mini-bar in all bedrooms Licensed Full central heating Outdoor swimming pool Open terrace Last d 21.00hrs Languages spoken: English
CARDS: 💳 🔲 🔲 Travellers cheques

## PONCÉ-SUR-LE-LOIR Sarthe

**Château de La Volonière** (Prop: Mme B Becquelin)
72340
☎ 243796816 FAX 243796818
(from Paris on A11 exit La Ferté-Bernard to St Calais and then in direction of La Charte-sur-Loir to Poncé)
Near river Near lake Forest area In town centre
*Closed Dec-Feb*
*6 rms (5 bth/shr) (1 fmly) Radio in rooms Full central heating Open parking available Child discount available 12yrs*

## PONT-ST-MARTIN Loire-Atlantique

★★★★ **Château du Plessis-Atlantique**
44860
☎ 240268172 FAX 240327667
Near river Near lake
*4 rms (3 bth/shr) Mini-bar in 2 bedrooms Licensed Night porter Full central heating Open parking available Covered parking available Supervised Child discount available 12yrs Boule Bicycle rental Open terrace Covered terrace Games for children V meals Last d 2100hrs Languages spoken: English*
CARDS: ●● ■ ■ ■

## PORNICHET Loire-Atlantique

★★ **Le Regent**
150 bd des Océanides 44380
☎ 240610568 FAX 240612553
Near sea Near beach
*15 en suite (bth/shr) (3 fmly) (8 with balcony) TV in all bedrooms Direct dial from all bedrooms Licensed Full central heating Open parking available Supervised Child discount available 5yrs Solarium Open terrace Covered terrace Languages spoken: German, Spanish*
ROOMS: (room only) s 255-360FF; d 275-460FF **Special breaks**
CARDS: ●● ■■ ■ Travellers cheques

## POSSONNIÈRE, LA Maine-et-Loire

**La Rousselière** (Prop: Mme J Charpentier)
49170
☎ 241391321 FAX 241391321
(at Angers take N20 towards Nantes, in St Georges-sur-Loire turn left on D961 towards Challonnes for 3km; just before railway bridge turn left on D111 towards La Possonnière, continue for 1.5km & turn left)
Near river
*Closed mid Nov-mid Dec*
*6 en suite (bth/shr) (6 fmly) (1 with balcony) TV in 3 bedrooms Full central heating Open parking available Child discount available 10yrs Outdoor swimming pool Fishing Boule Bicycle rental Trampoline, Table tennis Languages spoken: English*

## PREFAILLES Loire-Atlantique

★★ **La Flottille**
Pointe St-Gildas 44770
☎ 240216118 FAX 240645172
Near sea Near beach
*26 en suite (bth/shr) (2 fmly) (18 with balcony) TV in all bedrooms STV Direct dial from all bedrooms Mini-bar in all bedrooms Licensed Full central heating Open parking available Indoor swimming pool (heated) Fishing Sauna*

*Solarium Pool table Boule Jacuzzi/spa Bicycle rental Open terrace V meals Languages spoken: English & German*
CARDS: ●● ■ ■ ■ Travellers cheques

## PUY-NOTRE-DAME, LE Maine-et-Loire

**Le Moulin de Couché** (Prop: Jean François Berville)
49260
☎ 241388711 FAX 241388699
(from Montreuil-Bellay take D938 towards Thouars. After 3km take D158 to Passay, continue towards Sanziers, cross the River Thouet then turn left)
Near river Near lake Near sea Forest area
*9 en suite (bth/shr) (3 fmly) No smoking in all bedrooms TV in 6 bedrooms Open parking available Supervised Child discount available Fishing Boule V meals Last d 22.00hrs Languages spoken: English*
CARDS: ●● ■ ■ Travellers cheques

## RENAZÉ Mayenne

**Le Petit Bois Gleu** (Prop: M Goodman)
53800
☎ 243068386 FAX 243068386
Susan Goodchild and Paul Goodman welcome you to their old farmhouse, nestling in an unspoilt corner of the Loire. A paradise for painters, birdwatchers and ramblers. Fresh, local, home-grown produce prepared and served by Paul, either in the vaulted dining room or under the shade of the trees. Your hostess is an artist and offers special painting holidays to budding artists.
Near river Near lake Near sea Forest area Near motorway
*5 en suite (shr) (1 fmly) No smoking on premises Open parking available Child discount available 10yrs Outdoor swimming pool (heated) Boule Open terrace Painting courses V meals Last d 21.00hrs Languages spoken: English*
ROOMS: s fr 250FF; d fr 300FF **Special breaks**
MEALS: Dinner fr 85FF
CARDS: Travellers cheques

## ROË, LA Mayenne

**Château Le Boulay** (Prop: G Mitchell)
53350
☎ 243065104 FAX 243065104
(On D25 between Le Guerche de Bretagne and Craon)
Small 19th-century château in six acres of grounds, on the edge of the village. All bedrooms have pleasing aspects with those at the rear enjoying open views of the surrounding Mayenne countryside. Most rooms have French and English period furniture.
Near lake Forest area
*5 en suite (bth/shr) (1 fmly) (1 with balcony) No smoking on premises Full central heating Open parking available Languages spoken: English*
ROOMS: s 275-400FF; d 275-450FF

## ROSIERS-SUR-LOIRE, LES Maine-et-Loire

★★★ **Jeanne de Laval et Ducs d'Anjou**
54 rue Nationale 49350
☎ 241518017 FAX 241380418
(From Angers take D952)
A charming small hotel with a pleasant garden. Some bedrooms are located in an old manor 300 metres from the main building, along the Loire valley. The restaurant offers specialities of the region. *contd.*

Near river In town centre Near motorway
*Closed end Nov-end Dec RS Mon (out of season)*
*10 en suite (bth/shr) 7 rooms in annexe (3 fmly) TV in all*
*bedrooms Direct dial from all bedrooms Mini-bar in all*
*bedrooms Licensed Full central heating Open parking*
*available Supervised Child discount available 10yrs Open*
*terrace V meals Last d 21.30hrs Languages spoken: English*
ROOMS: (room only) s 300-350FF; d 350-550FF ✱
MEALS: Full breakfast 60FF Lunch 180-400FF&alc Dinner
180-400FF&alc
CARDS: ●● ■■ ━━ Travellers cheques

### SABLES-D'OLONNE, LES Vendée

**★ ★ Admiral's Hotel**
pl Jean David Nau Port Olonna *85100*
☎ 251214141 FAX 251327123
Near sea Forest area
*Closed 25 Dec-2 Jan*
*32 en suite (bth/shr) (7 fmly) (32 with balcony) TV in all*
*bedrooms Direct dial from all bedrooms Mini-bar in all*
*bedrooms Lift Full central heating Open parking available*
*Child discount available 10yrs Open terrace Covered terrace*
CARDS: ●● ■■ ▨▨ ◉ Travellers cheques

**★ ★ *Les Hirondelles***
44 rue des Corderies *85100*
☎ 251951050 FAX 251323101
Near sea In town centre
*Closed Sep-30 Mar*
*65 en suite (shr) 38 rooms in annexe (2 fmly) (21 with balcony)*
*TV in all bedrooms Direct dial from all bedrooms Licensed Lift*
*Full central heating Open parking available (charged) Covered*
*parking available (charged) Child discount available 6yrs*
*Bicycle rental Open terrace Last d 21.00hrs Languages*
*spoken: English*
CARDS: ●● ■■ ━━ Travellers cheques

**★ ★ *Le Calme des Pins***
43 av Aristide-Briand *85100*
☎ 251210318 FAX 251215985
Near lake Near sea Near beach Forest area In town centre
*Closed Etr-Sep*
*46 en suite (bth/shr) (7 fmly) (15 with balcony) TV in all*
*bedrooms STV Direct dial from all bedrooms Licensed Lift*
*Full central heating Open parking available (charged) Bicycle*
*rental Open terrace Wkly live entertainment Languages*
*spoken: English & German*
CARDS: ●● ━━ Travellers cheques

### ST-CALAIS Sarthe

**Le Boulay** (Prop: Mme Guillon)
Conflans sur Anille *72120*
☎ 243350741
(D98 towards Semur and 3kms after Conflans-sur-Anille
passing the church, take left turning 20mtrs after cross-roads)
Forest area Near motorway
*Closed 16 Nov-Mar*
*2 en suite (bth/shr) No smoking on premises Full central*
*heating Open parking available Bicycle rental Languages*
*spoken: English & Spanish*
ROOMS: d 350FF ✱ **Reductions over 1 night Special**
**breaks**

### ST-DENIS-D'ANJOU Mayenne

**Le Logis du Ray** (Prop: M & Mme Lefebure)
*53290*
☎ 243706410 FAX 243706553
(at 9km SW de Sable-sur-Sarthe take D309 then D27 in
direction of Angers)
Near lake
*Closed Jan*
*3 en suite (shr) (2 fmly) No smoking on premises TV available*
*Full central heating Open parking available Child discount*
*available 12yrs Bicycle rental Last d prev day Languages*
*spoken: English*
CARDS: ●● ━━ Travellers cheques

### ST-GEORGES-SUR-LOIRE Maine-et-Loire

**Prieure de L'Épinay** (Prop: Mme Genevieve Gaultier)
*49170*
☎ 241391444 FAX 241391444
(from St Georges-sur-Loire take N23 for 1 km in direction of
Nantes then turn left for Prieure-de-l'Épinay)
Situated in charming countryside, with the Loire, vineyards
and the châteaux all nearby. The historical character of the old
priory, the comfort of the large rooms and the home made
food all combine to make a relaxing stay.
Near river
*Closed Nov-Mar*
*3 en suite (bth/shr) (3 fmly) TV in all bedrooms STV Full*
*central heating Open parking available Covered parking*
*available Child discount available 4 yrs Outdoor swimming*
*pool Fishing Bicycle rental Last d 19.00hrs Languages spoken:*
*English*
MEALS: Dinner 140FF
CARDS: Travellers cheques

### ST-GILLES-CROIX-DE-VIE Vendée

**★ ★ Le Lion d'Or**
84 rue de Calvaire *85800*
☎ 251555039 FAX 251552284
(access from La Roche-sur-Yon via D948 and D6)
Near river Near sea In town centre
*52 rms (50 bth/shr) (20 fmly) (25 with balcony) TV in all*
*bedrooms STV Direct dial from all bedrooms Licensed Full*
*central heating Open parking available Covered parking*
*available (charged) Child discount available 12yrs Indoor*
*swimming pool (heated) Pool table Open terrace Covered*
*terrace Games for children Last d 21hrs Languages spoken:*
*English*
ROOMS: (room only) s 145-398FF; d 165-398FF
MEALS: Continental breakfast 38FF Lunch 76-180FF&alc
Dinner 76-180FF&alc✱
CARDS: ●● ■■ ━━ Travellers cheques

### ST-JEAN-DE-MONTS Vendée

**★ ★ *La Chaumière***
103 av d'Orouët *85160*
☎ 251586744 FAX 251589812
(6km from town centre via D38 towards Sables-d'Olonne)
Near sea Forest area
*Closed Oct-Mar*
*37 en suite (bth/shr) (8 fmly) (20 with balcony) TV in all*
*bedrooms Radio in rooms Direct dial from all bedrooms Mini-*
*bar in 10 bedrooms Licensed Night porter Full central heating*
*Open parking available Covered parking available Supervised*

Child discount available 10yrs  Indoor swimming pool (heated)
Outdoor swimming pool (heated)  Tennis  Sauna  Boule  Bicycle
rental  Open terrace  Last d 21.00hrs  Languages spoken:
English
CARDS: 💳 💳 💳 💳 Travellers cheques

### ★ ★ La Chaumière
Lieu dit Orouet 85160
☎ 251586744 FAX 251589812
The Boucher family will give you a discreet and friendly
welcome at their inn, renowned for its surroundings, close to
the woods and sea. The comfortable bedrooms are sound-
proofed and most have balconies. Chef de cuisine, Nicholas
Boucher, prepares a varied menu of traditional regional dishes
using local produce and seafood.
Near sea  Near beach  Forest area

Closed Oct-Mar
37 en suite (bth/shr)  (8 fmly)  (20 with balcony)  TV in 19
bedrooms  Direct dial from all bedrooms  Mini-bar in 10
bedrooms  Licensed  Night porter  Full central heating  Open
parking available  Covered parking available  Supervised  Child
discount available  Indoor swimming pool (heated)  Outdoor
swimming pool  Tennis  Sauna  Boule  Bicycle rental  Open
terrace  V meals  Last d 21.00hrs  Languages spoken: English
ROOMS: d 270-450FF
MEALS: Continental breakfast 40FF  Lunch 88-250FF&alc
Dinner 99-250FF&alc
CARDS: 💳 💳 💳 💳 Travellers cheques

### ST-LAMBERT-DES-LEVEES Maine-et-Loire

*La Croix de la Voulte* (Prop: Jean Pierre & Helga Minder)
rte de Boumois 49400
☎ 241384666 FAX 241384666
(from the train station of Saumur follow the D229 in direction
of St Lambert-des-Levées. After leaving village continue on
D229 for 1500m - property signed)
Near river
Closed 2 Oct-Apr
4 en suite (bth/shr)  Open parking available  Outdoor swimming
pool  Languages spoken: English & German
CARDS: Travellers cheques

### ST-LAURENT-SUR-SÈVRE Vendée

### ★ ★ ★ Baumotel et la Chaumière
La Trique-15 Rte de Poitiers 85290
☎ 251678081 FAX 251678287
(10 km from Cholet on the D752)
Near river  Near lake  Forest area  Near motorway
Closed 1 wk in Feb & Dec

20 en suite (bth/shr)  (2 fmly)  (18 with balcony)  TV in all
bedrooms  Direct dial from all bedrooms  Mini-bar in all
bedrooms  Licensed  Full central heating  Open parking
available  Child discount available 12yrs  Outdoor swimming
pool  Open terrace  Covered terrace  Park  Last d 21.30hrs
Languages spoken: English
ROOMS: (room only) s 290-490FF; d 390-590FF
**Reductions over 1 night  Special breaks**
MEALS: Continental breakfast 50FF  Lunch 99-300FF&alc
Dinner 140-300FF&alc
CARDS: 💳 💳 💳 💳 Travellers cheques

### ST-LUMINE-DE-CLISSON Loire-Atlantique

*Le Tremblay* (Prop: Mme Jacqueline Bossis)
44190
☎ 240547111
Set in a wine-growing region, this modern solar-powered
house has two guest rooms with independent access. There is
a quiet garden, full of flowers, to relax in. French breakfast is
served and dinner can be eaten with the hosts by
arrangement. Nearby you will find canoeing and kayaking.
Near river  Forest area
2 en suite (shr)  Full central heating  Open parking available
Child discount available 2yrs  Outdoor swimming pool
Languages spoken: English
ROOMS: s 165FF; d 200-220FF
MEALS: Dinner 75-85FF

### ST-LYPHARD Loire-Atlantique

*Le Pavillon de la Brierie* (Prop: Mme Anny Hulcoq)
23 rue des Aubrépines 44410
☎ 240914471 FAX 240913468
Near river  Near lake
4 en suite (bth/shr)  No smoking on premises  TV available  Full
central heating  Supervised

### ST-MALO-DE-GUERSAC Loire-Atlantique

**25 Errand Ty Gwenn** (Prop: M & Mme Collard/Lecarrer)
44550
☎ 240911504
(from St Nazaire to Nantes road take D50 Montoir de Bretagne)
Near river
Apr-Oct
4 en suite (shr)  No smoking on premises  TV in all bedrooms
Full central heating  Open parking available  Child discount
available 2yrs
ROOMS: d fr 300FF
CARDS: Travellers cheques

### ST-MARTIN-DE-LA-PLACE Maine-et-Loire

### ★ ★ Auberge du Cheval Blanc
2 rue des Mariniers 49160
☎ 241384296 FAX 241384262
Near river  Near motorway
Closed 5 Jan-5 Feb
12 en suite (bth/shr)  (6 fmly)  TV in all bedrooms  Direct dial
from all bedrooms  Licensed  Full central heating  Open parking
available  Covered parking available  Supervised  Child discount
available 10yrs  Boule  Open terrace  Last d 21.30hrs
Languages spoken: English
CARDS: 💳 💳 Travellers cheques

### ST-MARTIN-DES-FONTAINES Vendée

**Roselyne Garreau** (Prop: Mme Porcher)
*85570*
☎ 251001262 FAX 251877974
(turn right off the N148 just north of Fontenay-le-Comte, take D30/D99 or D14 all these roads lead to St Martin-des Fontaines)
Near river Forest area Near motorway
*5 en suite (shr) No smoking on premises Covered parking available Child discount available 5yrs Outdoor swimming pool (heated) Tennis Fishing Riding Mini-golf Bicycle rental Languages spoken: English*
ROOMS: s 250-300FF
✱ **Reductions over 1 night Special breaks**
CARDS: Travellers cheques

### ST-MATHURIN Vendée

**Château de la Millière**
*85150*
☎ 251227329 FAX 251227329
Near lake Near sea Forest area
*Closed Oct-Apr*
*5 en suite (bth/shr) (1 fmly) Full central heating Open parking available*
CARDS: ▨

### ST-MATHURIN-SUR-LOIRE Maine-et-Loire

**La Bouquetterie** (Prop: Mme C Pinier)
118 rue du Roi René *49250*
☎ 241570200 FAX 241573190
(from Angers, take D952 W along Loire for 20km. About 1km before centre of St Mathurin-sur-Loire house on left) Claudine Pinier looks forward to welcoming guests to her home, built in the 19th century. The well lit rooms are spacious and overlook the garden and the Loire. Two new rooms, with kitchenette and independent entrance, have been created in converted outbuildings, and are decorated in a rustic style. There is a summer house in garden, with games for the children.
Near river Forest area
*6 en suite (shr) (3 fmly) No smoking in 3 bedrooms Full central heating Open parking available Child discount available 7-15yrs Fishing Riding Bicycle rental Languages spoken: English*
ROOMS: s 215-275FF; d 300-350FF
✱ **Reductions over 1 night Special breaks**
MEALS: Dinner 125FF
CARDS: ▨ ▨ Travellers cheques

### ST-MOLF Loire-Atlantique

**Kervenel** (Prop: J Brasselet)
*44350*
☎ 240425038
Near sea Near beach Forest area
*Closed Apr-Oct*
*6 rms (3 shr) No smoking on premises Full central heating Open parking available Supervised Child discount available 3yrs Languages spoken: English & German*
CARDS: Travellers cheques

### ST-NAZAIRE Loire-Atlantique

★ ★ ★ **Hotel Aquilon Arcantis (S)**
Rond-Point Océanis, 2 rue Michel Ange *44600*
☎ 240535020 FAX 240531560
(St-Nazaire Ouest - Zone Oceanis)
Near lake Near sea Near beach Forest area Near motorway
*72 en suite (bth/shr) (4 fmly) (7 with balcony) No smoking in 24 bedrooms TV in all bedrooms STV Direct dial from all bedrooms Licensed Lift Night porter Full central heating Open parking available Covered parking available (charged) Supervised Child discount available 12yrs Outdoor swimming pool Pool table Boule Bicycle rental Open terrace Covered terrace Last d 23.30hrs Languages spoken: English, German & Spanish*
ROOMS: (room only) s 340-605FF; d 380-750FF
**Reductions over 1 night Special breaks**
MEALS: Full breakfast 50FF Lunch 69-245FF Dinner 69-245FF✱
CARDS: ▨ ▨ ▨ ▨ JCB Travellers cheques

### ST-PATERNE Sarthe

**Château de St-Paterne**
*72610*
☎ 233275471 FAX 233291671
Forest area Near motorway
*7 en suite (bth/shr) (3 with balcony) TV in all bedrooms Licensed Full central heating Supervised Child discount available 10yrs Last d 21.30hrs Languages spoken: English & Spanish*
CARDS: ▨ ▨ ▨ Travellers cheques

### ST-PIERRE-DES-NIDS Mayenne

★ ★ ★ **Du Dauphin**
*53370*
☎ 243035212 FAX 243035549
Forest area In town centre
*9 rms (1 fmly) TV in all bedrooms Radio in rooms Direct dial from all bedrooms Licensed Full central heating Open parking available Supervised Open terrace V meals Last d 21.00hrs Languages spoken: English & German*
CARDS: ▨ ▨ Travellers cheques

### ST-SATURNIN Sarthe

★ ★ **Climat de France**
rte d'Alençon *72650*
☎ 243253121 FAX 243253379
(from A11 take exit 'sortie Nord' then in direction of Alençon for hotel on left)
Forest area Near motorway
*50 en suite (bth) (2 fmly) TV in all bedrooms Radio in rooms Direct dial from all bedrooms Licensed Full central heating Open parking available Pool table Open terrace Covered terrace Last d 10pm Languages spoken: English & Spanish*
CARDS: ▨ ▨

### ST-SAUVEUR-DE-LANDEMONT Maine-et-Loire

★ ★ ★ **Château de la Colaissière**
Claude Cohen *49270*
☎ 240987504 FAX 240987415
Near river Near lake Forest area Near motorway
*Closed early Jan-early Feb*
*16 en suite (bth/shr) (6 fmly) (2 with balcony) No smoking in 1*

*bedroom TV in all bedrooms STV Radio in rooms Mini-bar in all bedrooms Licensed Night porter Full central heating Open parking available Child discount available 14yrs Outdoor swimming pool (heated) Fishing Boule Open terrace V meals Languages spoken: English, German, Italian & Spanish* CARDS: ● ▣ Travellers cheques

### SAULGES Mayenne

**★ ★ ★ L'Ermitage**
*53340*
☎ 243905228 FAX 243905661
(Take A81 between Laval & Le Mans, ex2 at Vaiges, L onto D24, L after 2km, D554 to Saulges, hotel in village)
Near river Forest area
*Closed Feb*
*36 en suite (bth/shr) (4 fmly) TV in all bedrooms STV Direct dial from all bedrooms Mini-bar in all bedrooms Room-safe Licensed Full central heating Open parking available Covered parking available (charged) Supervised Child discount available 12yrs Indoor swimming pool (heated) Outdoor swimming pool (heated) Golf 9 Sauna Solarium Gym Pool table Boule Mini-golf Jacuzzi/spa Bicycle rental Open terrace Covered terrace Last d 21.00hrs Languages spoken: English, German* CARDS: ● ▣ ▣ Travellers cheques

### SAUMUR Maine-et-Loire

**★ ★ ★ Anne d'Anjou**
32-33 quai Mayaud *49400*
☎ 241673030 FAX 241675100
(autoroute 85)
A beautiful 18th-century building situated between the River Loire and the château, with a charming interior courtyard and comfortable, well equipped bedrooms, some decorated in period style.

Near river In town centre
*45 rms (5 fmly) (1 with balcony) TV in all bedrooms Direct dial from all bedrooms Mini-bar in 20 bedrooms Licensed Lift Night porter Full central heating Open parking available (charged) Supervised Child discount available 10yrs Languages spoken: English* ROOMS: (room only) s fr 290FF; d 440-590FF CARDS: ● ▣ ▣ Travellers cheques

**La Bouère Salée** (Prop: E Bastid)
rue Grange Couronne, St-Lambert des Levées *49400*
☎ 241673885 & 241511252 FAX 241511252
(from A85 head into Saumur centre, do not cross the Loire, at

the Renault garage, turn right, the rue Grange Couronne is the first right and the house entrance is the first gate on the right)
Near river Forest area Near motorway
*4 en suite (bth/shr) (1 fmly) (1 with balcony) TV in 1 bedroom Full central heating Open parking available Child discount available 10yrs Languages spoken: English* ROOMS: s 200-250FF; d 250-370FF CARDS: Travellers cheques

**★ ★ Central**
23 rue Daillé *49400*
☎ 241510578 FAX 241678235
In town centre Near motorway
*27 en suite (bth/shr) (2 fmly) (5 with balcony) No smoking in 10 bedrooms TV in all bedrooms STV Direct dial from all bedrooms Licensed Full central heating Open parking available (charged) Covered parking available (charged) Supervised Bicycle rental Languages spoken: English* CARDS: ● ▣ ▣ Travellers cheques

**Château de Beaulieu** (Prop: Andra Michaut)
rte de Montsoreau *49400*
☎ 249676951 FAX 249676364
(in Saumur, head towards Chinon (D947), house is next to the caves 'Gratien and Meyer', on the border of the Loire)
Near river Forest area Near motorway
*Closed Dec & Jan*
*7 en suite (bth/shr) (2 fmly) Full central heating Open parking available Child discount available 4yrs Outdoor swimming pool (heated) Languages spoken: English & German* CARDS: ● ▣ Travellers cheques

**★ ★ Clos des Benedictins**
4 rue des Lilas *49400*
☎ 241672848 FAX 241671371
(at Saumur take direction for St Hilaire/St Florent, then follow arrows to École Nationale d'Equitaion and/or Aérodrome)
Near river Forest area
*Closed 15 Nov-31 Jan RS Half board obligatory 15 May-15 Sep*
*35 en suite (bth/shr) (10 fmly) (6 with balcony) TV in all bedrooms STV Direct dial from all bedrooms Licensed Full central heating Open parking available Supervised Child discount available 12yrs Outdoor swimming pool Pool table Open terrace V meals Last d 21.15hrs Languages spoken: English* ROOMS: (room only) s 300-500FF; d 300-600FF
**Reductions over 1 night Special breaks**
MEALS: Continental breakfast 60FF Lunch 130-199FF&alc Dinner 199900FF&alc
CARDS: ● ▣ ▣ JCB Travellers cheques

**★ ★ ★ Loire Hotel**
rue du Vieux Port *49400*
☎ 241672242 FAX 241678880
Near river In town centre Near motorway
*44 en suite (bth) (2 fmly) (4 with balcony) TV in all bedrooms Direct dial from all bedrooms Mini-bar in all bedrooms Licensed Lift Full central heating Open parking available Covered parking available (charged) Supervised Child discount available 12yrs Open terrace Last d 21.30hrs Languages spoken: English & German* ROOMS: (room only) s 370-540FF; d 470-590FF
**Reductions over 1 night**
MEALS: Continental breakfast 48FF Lunch 115-210FF&alc Dinner 115-210FF&alc
CARDS: ● ▣ ▣ JCB Travellers cheques

**★★ Hotel du Roi René**
94 av du Gl-de-Gaulle
☎ 241674530 FAX 241677459
(on N138 beside the River Loire)
Near river In town centre
*Closed 15 Nov-15 Dec*
*39 en suite (bth/shr) (4 fmly) TV in all bedrooms STV Direct*
*dial from all bedrooms Lift Night porter Full central heating*
*Covered parking available (charged) Supervised V meals*
*Languages spoken: English*
CARDS: 💳 💳 💳

---

**SOLESMES** Sarthe

---

**★★★ Grand Hotel**
16 pl Dom-Guéranger *72300*
☎ 243954510 FAX 243952226
(from A11 exit at Sable)
This hotel offes a comfortable interior with attractive, fully
equipped bedrooms and pleasant public areas. The chef,
inspired by seasonal produce, creates a wide variety of
excellent dishes. For guests who wish to take a little exercise
there is the Club Forme. In addition, there is an art gallery and
four specially equipped meeting rooms.
Near river Forest area

*34 en suite (bth) 2 rooms in annexe (6 fmly) (26 with balcony)*
*TV in all bedrooms STV Direct dial from all bedrooms Mini-*
*bar in all bedrooms Licensed Lift Full central heating Open*
*parking available Child discount available 12yrs Sauna*
*Solarium Jacuzzi/spa Bicycle rental Open terrace Last d*
*21.30hrs Languages spoken: English*
ROOMS: (room only) d 450-550FF
**Reductions over 1 night**
MEALS: Continental breakfast 55FF Lunch 140-220FF&alc
Dinner 140-220FF&alc
CARDS: 💳 💳 💳 💳 Travellers cheques

---

**THORIGNÉ-SUR-DUE** Sarthe

---

**★★ Saint Jacques**
pl du Monument *72160*
☎ 243899550 FAX 243765842
(S of Connerré on D302)
Near river Forest area Near motorway
*15 en suite (bth/shr) (2 fmly) TV in all bedrooms STV Direct*
*dial from all bedrooms Licensed Full central heating Open*
*parking available Covered parking available Supervised Child*
*discount available 7yrs Sauna Boule Bicycle rental Open*
*terrace Last d 21.00hrs Languages spoken: English*
CARDS: 💳 💳 💳 💳 Travellers cheques

---

**TRANCHE-SUR-MER, LA** Vendée

---

**★★ De l'Océan**
49 rue Anatole France *85360*
☎ 251303009 FAX 251277010
Near sea Near beach Forest area In town centre
*Closed mid Oct-mid Mar*
*47 rms (5 bth 40 shr) (4 fmly) (3 with balcony) TV in all*
*bedrooms Licensed Full central heating Open parking*
*available Child discount available Last d 22.00hrs Languages*
*spoken: English & German*
CARDS: 💳 💳

---

**TURBALLE, LA** Loire-Atlantique

---

**Ker Kayenne**
744 Bd de Lauvergnac *44420*
☎ 240627430 FAX 240628338
Near sea Near beach Forest area
*Closed 16 Nov-14 Mar*
*8 en suite (shr) (2 fmly) Full central heating Open parking*
*available Outdoor swimming pool (heated)*

---

**VARADES** Loire-Atlantique

---

**Chambres d'Hôte au Palais Briau**
La Madeleine
☎ 240834500 FAX 240834930
(Between Nantes & Angers on N23 take Varades direction
35km after Angers. Turn left at rdbt in direction of Le Ferté, Le
Palais Briau then straight on for 2km. Property well
signposted)
Near river Near lake Forest area Near motorway
*Closed mid Dec-Feb*
*4 en suite (bth/shr) Night porter Full central heating Open*
*parking available Fishing Riding Boule Bicycle rental Open*
*terrace Languages spoken: English*

---

**VELLUIRE** Vendée

---

**★★ Auberge de la Rivière**
*85770*
☎ 251523215 FAX 251523742
(take N11 east of La Rochelle, then N137. Just north of Marans
take D938 towards Fontenay. Approx 15kms turn left for
Velluire)
Near river Near motorway
*Closed Jan-Feb*
*11 en suite (bth) 9 rooms in annexe (1 fmly) TV in 6 bedrooms*
*Direct dial from all bedrooms Licensed Full central heating*
*Open parking available Child discount available 2yrs Open*
*terrace Last d 21.15hrs*
ROOMS: (room only) d 400-490FF
MEALS: Continental breakfast 65FF Lunch 200-240FF&alc
Dinner 200-240FF&alc
CARDS: 💳 💳 Travellers cheques

---

**VIEIL-BAUGÉ, LE** Maine-et-Loire

---

**La Chalopinière** (Prop: M & Mme Kitchen)
*49150*
☎ 241890438 FAX 241890438
(from Le Mans follow road for Saumur, pass through La Flèche
to Baugé, at traffic lights on Baugé by-pass turn right to Vieil
Baugé, through village approx 2km from church)
Forest area

*3 en suite (bth/shr) (3 fmly) Full central heating Open parking available Child discount available 12yrs Outdoor swimming pool Tennis Riding Bicycle rental Table tennis Last d 1800hrs Languages spoken: English*
CARDS: Travellers cheques

## VIVOIN Sarthe

### ★★ Hotel du Chemin de Fer
pl de la Gare *72170*
☎ 243970005 FAX 243335217
(From N138 take D26 in direction of Mamers)
Near river  Near motorway
*9 Nov-15 Feb & 2 Mar-15 Oct*

*15 en suite (bth/shr) (2 fmly) (1 with balcony) TV in all bedrooms Direct dial from all bedrooms Licensed Night porter Full central heating Open parking available Covered parking available Child discount available 12yrs Boule Open terrace Last d 21.00hrs Languages spoken: English*
ROOMS: (incl. full-board) d 290-390FF
MEALS: Continental breakfast 33FF  Lunch 89-250FF&alc  Dinner 89-250FF&alc
CARDS: ●● ■■ ▆▆ ⑩ Travellers cheques

## VOUVANT Vendée

### ★★ Auberge de Maitre Pannetier
pl du Corps-de-Garde *85120*
☎ 251008012 FAX 251878937
Near river  Forest area  In town centre
*7 en suite (bth/shr) TV in all bedrooms Direct dial from all bedrooms Licensed Full central heating Open terrace V meals Last d 21.00hrs Languages spoken: English*
ROOMS: (room only) d 200-250FF
CARDS: ●● Travellers cheques

# Paris & Ile de France

With its bustling pavement cafes, elegant shop fronts and beautiful gardens, Paris has an air of unmistakable quality. Among the city's most distinguished landmarks are the Arc de Triomphe, stranded like a huge tiered wedding cake in the Champs Elysées, the distincitve white cupolas of the breathtaking Sacré Coeur Basilica and the 900-year-old Notre Dame Cathedral. But no trip to the French capital is complete without a visit to the world famous Eiffel Tower, which can be seen soaring above the city from countless vantage points. Whether you are enjoying a boat trip on the Seine or taking a leisurely stroll in the Tuileries Gardens, exploring Paris reveals something new and unexpected at every turn.

## ESSENTIAL FACTS

| | |
|---|---|
| DÉPARTEMENTS: | Paris, Essonne, Hauts de Seine, Seine-et-Marne, Seine-St -Denis, Val-d'Oise, Val-de-Marne, Yvelines |
| PRINCIPAL TOWNS | Paris, Mantes-la-Jolie, Pontoise, Creil, St Denis, Meaux, Melun, St-Germain |
| PLACES TO VISIT: | The magnificent château of Versailles; the royal château at Fontainebleau where the visitor can take a unique journey through the heart of French history, from Louis IX (St Louis) to Napoleon III. Paris, with its shops, museums and art galleries, offers a bewildering choice of attractions. |
| REGIONAL TOURIST OFFICE | 26 av de l'Opéra, 75001 Paris. Tel: 42 60 28 62 |
| LOCAL GASTRONOMIC DELIGHTS | Dishes à la Parisienne decribe savoury recipes typical of Parisian cuisine: soup à la Parisienne: soup of potatoes, leeks, milk & chervil; fish Parisian-style is served with mayonnaise, artichoke hearts & hard-boiled eggs. Paris-Brest is a ring-shaped eclair filled with praline cream. Meaux mustard is made with crushed mustard seed. Cheeses: Brie from Meaux or Melu, Coulommiers, Boursault, Fontainebleau |
| LOCAL CRAFTS WHAT TO BUY | For shopaholics, the Galeries Lafayette in Paris is described as the Louvre of department stores. Local crafts include items made of wood, silver, brass, porcelain, lace & tapestry. |

★ ★ ★ *Hotel de France*
2 pl du Marché, BP14 *91670*
☎ 169951130 FAX 164953959
(from N20 exit Angerville, from A10 exit Allainville or Allaines)
In town centre  Near motorway
*17 en suite (bth/shr)  (4 fmly)  TV in all bedrooms  Direct dial from all bedrooms  Licensed  Lift  Full central heating  Open parking available  Child discount available  Pool table  Open terrace  Last d 21.30hrs*
CARDS: ●● ■■ ■■ Travellers cheques

**Bed & Breakfast** (Prop: Mme Denise Woehrle)
44 r du Chef de Ville *77440*
☎ 164355122 FAX 164354295
(from Meaux take N3 to Chalons-sur-Marne via Trilport, turn left to Armentiéres through village. pass church, house is one before last on right)
This house is conveniently situated only thirty kilometres from Roissy Airport and EuroDisney Paris. A warm and personal welcome is offered. Continental breakfasts are large and served with jam made by your hosts. Well situated in the countryside with attractive garden and views.
Near river  Forest area
*Closed Nov-Feb*
*4 en suite (bth/shr)  (2 with balcony)  No smoking on premises  Full central heating  Open parking available  Open terrace  Languages spoken: English*
ROOMS: s 180FF; d 280-340FF

★ ★ *Les Relais Bleus d'Aulnay*
rue Léonard de Vinci *93600*
☎ 248669946 Cen Res 164460616 FAX 2486699216
Near motorway
*117 en suite (bth/shr)  (2 fmly)  TV in all bedrooms  STV  Direct dial from all bedrooms  Night porter  Full central heating  Open parking available  Supervised  Child discount available 12yrs  Pool table  Open terrace  Languages spoken: English, Italian & Spanish*
CARDS: ●● ■■ ■■ ◨ Travellers cheques

★ ★ ★ *Hotel-Village la Désirade*
Le Petit Cosquet *56360*
☎ 297317070 FAX 297318963
Near sea
*Closed early Jan-mid Feb*
*24 en suite (bth/shr)  TV in all bedrooms  STV  Direct dial from all bedrooms  Licensed  Full central heating  Open parking available  Child discount available  Outdoor swimming pool (heated)  Bicycle rental  Open terrace  V meals  Last d 21.30hrs  Languages spoken: English,Spanish*
CARDS: ●● ■■ ■■ ◨ Travellers cheques

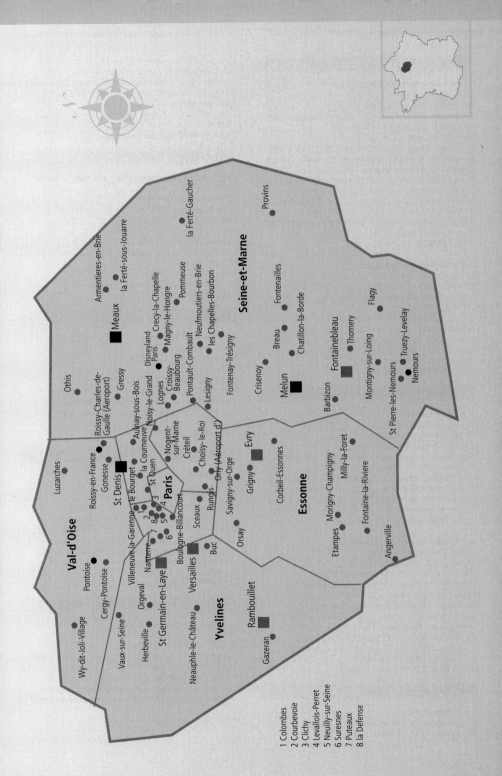

Provins

la Ferté-Gaucher

Armentières-en-Brie

la Ferté-sous-Jouarre

**Seine-et-Marne**

Pommeuse

Crecy-la-Chapelle

Magny-le-Hongre

Neufmoutiers-en-Brie

les Chapelles-Bourbon

Fontenailles

Meaux

Disneyland
Paris

Croissy-
Beaubourg

Pontault-Combault

Fontenay-Trésigny

Breau

Chatillon-la-Borde

Flagy

Thomery

Truezy-Levelay

Othis

Roissy-Charles-de-
Gaulle (Aeroport)

Gressy

Crisenoy

Fontainebleau

Montigny-sur-Loing

Nemours

Aulnay-sous-Bois

Melun

Barbizon

St Pierre-les-Nemours

Luzarches

Roissy-en-France

Gonesse

la Courneuve

St Ouen

Nogent-
sur-Marne

Créteil

Choisy-le-Roi

Orly (Aéroport d')

Evry

Grigny

Morigny-Champigny

Milly-la-Foret

**Val-d'Oise**

St Denis

le Bourget

**Paris**

Corbeil-Essonnes

**Essonne**

Fontaine-la-Riviere

Pontoise

Villeneuve-la-Garenne

Boulogne-Billancourt

Sceaux

Rungis

Savigny-sur-Orge

Orsay

Etampes

Angerville

Cergy-Pontoise

Nanterre

St Germain-en-Laye

Versailles

Buc

Wy-dit-Joli-Village

Herbeville

Orgeval

**Yvelines**

Vaux-sur-Seine

Neauphle-le-Château

Rambouillet

Gazeran

1 Colombes
2 Courbevoie
3 Clichy
4 Levallois-Perret
5 Neuilly-sur-Seine
6 Suresnes
7 Puteaux
8 la Defense

225

## BARBIZON Seine-et-Marne

**★ ★ ★ ★ Hotellerie du Bas-Breau** (Relais et Châteaux)
22 rue Grande *77630*
☎ 160664005 FAX 160692289
(A6 between Paris and Lyon exit for Fontainebleau and follow directions to Barbizon)
Forest area
*20 en suite (bth/shr) TV in all bedrooms STV Direct dial from all bedrooms Mini-bar in all bedrooms Room-safe Licensed Night porter Full central heating Air conditioning in bedrooms Open parking available Covered parking available Supervised Outdoor swimming pool (heated) Tennis Bicycle rental Open terrace Last d 21.30hrs Languages spoken: English & Italian*
Rooms: (room only) s fr 950FF; d 950-1600FF
Meals: Continental breakfast 150FF Lunch fr 365FF&alc Dinner fr 400FF&alc
Cards: ●● ■■ ☲☲ ◙ Travellers cheques

**★ ★ ★ Hostellerie La Clé d'Or**
73 Grande rue *77630*
☎ 160664096 FAX 160664271
(A6 direction of Lyon exit Fontainbleau)
Forest area Near motorway
*17 en suite (bth/shr) TV in all bedrooms Direct dial from all bedrooms Mini-bar in all bedrooms Licensed Full central heating Open parking available Supervised Bicycle rental Open terrace Covered terrace Last d 21.30hrs Languages spoken: English German & Spanish*
Cards: ●● ■■ ☲☲ ◙ Travellers cheques

## BOULOGNE-BILLANCOURT Hauts-de-Seine

**★ ★ Excelsior**
12 r de la Ferme *92100*
☎ 146210808 FAX 146217615
(Close to Metro station Billancourt)
Near river Forest area In town centre Near motorway
*52 en suite (bth/shr) TV in all bedrooms STV Direct dial from all bedrooms Licensed Lift Night porter Full central heating Open parking available (charged) Covered parking available (charged) Child discount available Languages spoken: English German & Arabic*
Cards: ●● ■■ ☲☲ ◙ Travellers cheques

**★ ★ Jardins de Paris Boulogne**
210 bis bd Jean Jaurès *92100*
☎ 146214525 FAX 146216110
(From Paris Porte de St Cloud, take the direction Chartres/Bordeaux via N10. Stay right, do not take the tunnel. At Place Marcel Sembat take left towards Clamart, Meudon. The Hotel is 100m on right after a traffic light.)
Forest area In town centre
*49 en suite (bth/shr) (8 fmly) TV in all bedrooms STV Direct dial from all bedrooms Lift Night porter Full central heating Child discount available 12yrs Languages spoken: English*
Rooms: s 405-550FF; d 465-580FF
Cards: ●● ■■ ☲☲ ◙ Travellers cheques

## BOURGET, LE Seine-St-Denis

**★ ★ ★ Bleu Marine**
Aéroport Bourget, ZAA Bat 412 *93550*
☎ 149341038 FAX 149341035
(exit A1 at Le Bourget Airport & Zone d'Aviation d'Affaires, hotel off N17)
Near motorway

*86 en suite (bth/shr) (4 fmly) No smoking in 43 bedrooms TV in all bedrooms STV Radio in rooms Direct dial from all bedrooms Mini-bar in all bedrooms Room-safe Licensed Lift Night porter Air conditioning in bedrooms Open parking available Supervised Child discount available 12yrs Sauna Gym Open terrace V meals Languages spoken: English, German, Italian & Spanish*
Cards: ●● ■■ ☲☲ ◙ Travellers cheques

## BREAU Seine-et-Marne

**Ferme Relais du Couvent** (Prop: M & Mme Le Grand)
*77720*
☎ 164387515 FAX 164387575
(leave A5 at exit 16, Chatillon La Borde, turn right in direction of Nangis then left to Breau)
Near river Forest area Near motorway
*9 en suite (shr) (4 fmly) TV in 4 bedrooms Open parking available Child discount available 10yrs Tennis Boule Open terrace V meals*
Rooms: s 230FF; d 260FF
Meals: Lunch fr 85FF Dinner fr 85FF
Cards: ●● ■■ ☲☲ ◙ Travellers cheques

## BUC Yvelines

**★ ★ Climat de France**
rue Loius Pasteur *78530*
☎ 139564811 FAX 139568154
(from A86 take D938)
Forest area Near motorway
*44 en suite (bth) TV in all bedrooms Direct dial from all bedrooms Licensed Full central heating Open parking available Open terrace Covered terrace Languages spoken: English*
Cards: ●● ☲☲

## CERGY-PONTOISE Val-D'Oise

**★ ★ Vidéotel**
3 av des Trois Fontaines *95300*
☎ 130309393 FAX 130388520
Forest area In town centre
*133 en suite (shr) (16 fmly) No smoking in 12 bedrooms TV in all bedrooms Direct dial from all bedrooms Mini-bar in all bedrooms Licensed Lift Night porter Full central heating Open parking available Supervised Child discount available 12yrs Pool table Open terrace V meals Last d 22.00hrs Languages spoken: English*
Cards: ●● ■■ ☲☲ ◙ JCB

## CHAPELLES-BOURBON, LES Seine-et-Marne

**Le Manoir de Beaumarchais**
*77610*
☎ 164071108 FAX 164071448
(A4 exit13 onto D231 in direction of Provins, at Villeneuve le Comte join D96 in direction of Tournan after Neufmoutiers take 1st small road on left signed Beaumanchais at 1m on left)
This manor is classified as an historic monument. Stylishly furnished and decorated, the house is surrounded by thirty acres of parkland.
Forest area

**Le Manoir de Beaumarchais**
*1 en suite (bth/shr) TV in all bedrooms Open parking available Covered parking available Fishing Languages spoken: English*
ROOMS: d 750FF

### CHÂTILLON-LA-BORDE Seine-et-Marne

**Labordière** (Prop: Yves Guerif)
16 Grande rue la Borde *77820*
☎ 160666054
(A5 to Châtillon-la-Borde, Honeur-de-la-Borde in 3km)
Forest area
*3 rms (2 shr) Full central heating Open parking available Child discount available 12yrs Languages spoken: English*
CARDS: Travellers cheques

### CHOISY-LE-ROI Val-de-Marne

**★ ★ Climat de France**
rue du Docteur Roux *94600*
☎ 146824343 FAX 145732191
Near river Near lake In town centre Near motorway
*58 en suite (bth) TV in all bedrooms STV Direct dial from all bedrooms Licensed Lift Night porter Full central heating Open parking available Supervised Open terrace Languages spoken: English, German & Spanish*
CARDS: ● ■ ■ ⑩

### CLICHY Hauts-de-Seine

**★ ★ ★ Hotel de l'Europe**
52 blvd du Général Leclerc *92110*
☎ 147371310 FAX 140871106
In town centre
*71 en suite (bth/shr) 28 rooms in annexe (5 fmly) No smoking in 5 bedrooms TV in all bedrooms STV Direct dial from all bedrooms Licensed Lift Night porter Full central heating Covered parking available (charged) Child discount available 12yrs Bicycle rental Languages spoken: English, German, Italian & Portuguese*
ROOMS: (room only) s 410-510FF; d 460-560FF ✴
CARDS: ● ■ ■ ⑩ Travellers cheques

**★ ★ Hotel Savoy**
20 rue Villeneuve
☎ 147371701 FAX 142705517
*45 en suite (bth/shr) TV in all bedrooms STV Direct dial from all bedrooms Licensed Lift Night porter Full central heating Open parking available (charged) Supervised Child discount available 5yrs Languages spoken: English*
CARDS: ● ■ ■ ⑩ JCB

### COLOMBES Hauts-de-Seine

**★ ★ Climat de France**
1 rue Albert Camus *92700*
☎ 147803230 FAX 147816054
(just off A86 at junct with N309)
Near motorway
*58 en suite (bth) (8 fmly) TV available Radio in rooms Direct dial from all bedrooms Licensed Lift Full central heating Open parking available Languages spoken: English*
CARDS: ● ■

### CORBEIL-ESSONNES Essonne

**★ ★ Aux Armes de France**
1 bd Jean Jaurès *91100*
☎ 164962404 FAX 160880400
Near river In town centre
*11 en suite (shr) (7 fmly) TV in all bedrooms Direct dial from all bedrooms Licensed Full central heating Open parking available Supervised Child discount available Last d 22.00hrs Languages spoken: English, French, Italian & Spanish*
CARDS: ● ■ ■ ⑩

### COURBEVOIE Hauts-de-Seine

**★ ★ Hotel la Régence**
69 av Gambetta *92400*
☎ 147880698 FAX 147894827
*22 en suite (bth/shr) TV in all bedrooms STV Direct dial from all bedrooms Lift Open parking available*
CARDS: ■

### COURNEUVE, LA Seine-St-Denis

**★ ★ ★ Climat de France**
104 av Jean-Mermoz *93120*
☎ 148383333 FAX 148385884
(off A1, next to the Regional Park of La Courneuve)
Forest area Near motorway
*72 en suite (bth/shr) (10 fmly) No smoking in 4 bedrooms TV in all bedrooms STV Radio in rooms Direct dial from all bedrooms Licensed Lift Night porter Full central heating Open parking available Supervised Child discount available 12yrs Bicycle rental Open terrace Last d 22.00hrs Languages spoken: English, German & Spanish*
CARDS: ● ■ ■

### CRÉCY-LA-CHAPELLE Seine-et-Marne

**Bed & Breakfast** (Prop: Jocelyne Laubier)
34 rue Ch-Dullin, Hameau de Férolles *77580*
☎ 164638998 FAX 164638998
(A4 exit Crécy-la-Chapelle)
Near river Forest area
*1 en suite (shr) No smoking on premises TV in all bedrooms Full central heating Open parking available Bicycle rental Languages spoken: English*
ROOMS: d 280FF

### CRÉTEIL Val-de-Marne

**★ ★ Climat de France**
rue de Archives *94000*
☎ 149800800 FAX 149801599
(leave A4/A86 for centre of Créteil)
Near lake Forest area In town centre Near motorway *contd.*

*51 en suite (bth/shr) No smoking in 10 bedrooms TV in all bedrooms Radio in rooms Direct dial from all bedrooms Licensed Lift Full central heating Open parking available V meals Last d 20.00hrs Languages spoken: English*
CARDS: 💳 ▦ ▩ 🅓 Travellers cheques

### CRISENOY Seine-et-Marne

**Ferme de Vert Saint Père** (Prop: Philippe & Jeanne Mauban)
*77390*
☎ 164388351 FAX 164388352
(A5 to Troyes, 1st exit after toll (15) St-Germain-Laxis. Take N36 to the right, then 1st right to Crisenoy at the entrance to Crisenoy 1st right (Stade,Tennis) straight ahead to Vert-St-Père after tennis court)

A 17th-century stone farmhouse set in wide open fields, one hour from Paris by car. One family room with a double and single bed and a family suite with four beds and kitchenette are on offer. There is a good restaurant in the village within walking distance.
Near motorway
*Closed Xmas week*
*2 en suite (shr) (1 fmly) TV in 1 bedroom Full central heating Open parking available Child discount available 5yrs Languages spoken: English & Spanish*
ROOMS: (room only) d 290FF **Reductions over 1 night**
CARDS: Travellers cheques

### CROISSY-BEAUBOURG Seine-et-Marne

**Bed & Breakfast** (Prop: C et J-L Pasquier)
allée de Clotomont *77183*
☎ 160064450 FAX 160050345
Near lake Forest area Near motorway
*(1 fmly) No smoking on premises Full central heating Open parking available Boule Mini-golf Languages spoken: English*

### DÉFENSE, LA Hauts-de-Seine

**★ ★ ★ Novotel Paris la Défense**
Pont de Neuilly-Défense 1, 2 Boulevard de Neuilly *92081*
☎ 141452323 FAX 141452324
(from the ring road exit Défense 1)
Near river Forest area Near motorway
*280 en suite (bth/shr) (66 fmly) No smoking in 120 bedrooms TV in all bedrooms STV Radio in rooms Direct dial from all bedrooms Mini-bar in all bedrooms Licensed Lift Night porter Full central heating Air conditioning in bedrooms Open parking available (charged) Covered parking available*

*(charged) Supervised Child discount available 16yrs Last d 24.00hrs Languages spoken: English, German, Italian & Spanish*
CARDS: 💳 ▦ ▩ 🅓 Travellers cheques

### ÉTAMPES Essonne

**★ ★ Climat de France**
av de Coquérive, rte de Corbeil *91150*
☎ 160800472 FAX 160800477
Near lake In town centre Near motorway
*44 en suite (bth) TV in all bedrooms Radio in rooms Direct dial from all bedrooms Licensed Full central heating Open parking available Open terrace Last d 10pm Languages spoken: English, German & Spanish*
CARDS: 💳 ▩

### ÉVRY Essonne

**★ ★ ★ Hotel Mercure Evry Centre**
52 bd de Coquibus *91000*
☎ 169473000 FAX 169473010
Forest area In town centre Near motorway
*114 en suite (bth/shr) (27 fmly) No smoking in 14 bedrooms TV in all bedrooms STV Radio in rooms Direct dial from all bedrooms Mini-bar in all bedrooms Licensed Lift Night porter Full central heating Open parking available (charged) Covered parking available (charged) Child discount available 14yrs Pool table Open terrace Last d 22.30hrs Languages spoken: English*
CARDS: 💳 ▦ ▩ 🅓 Travellers cheques

### FERTÉ-GAUCHER, LA Seine-et-Marne

**★ ★ Du Bois Frais**
32 av des Allies *77320*
☎ 164202724 FAX 164203839
(From Paris (A4) take exit for Crécy-La-Chapelle, then take N34 for Coulommiers then on to La Ferté-Gaucher)
Near motorway
*Closed 24 Dec-15 Jan*
*7 en suite (bth/shr) (1 fmly) TV in all bedrooms Licensed Full central heating Open parking available Supervised Child discount available 10yrs Bicycle rental Open terrace Covered terrace V meals Last d 21.30hrs Languages spoken: English*
CARDS: 💳 ▩ Travellers cheques

### FERTÉ-SOUS-JOUARRE, LA Seine-et-Marne

**★ ★ ★ Château des Bondons**
47-49 rue des Bondons *77260*
☎ 160220098 FAX 160229701
(leave A4 exit 18)
Near river Forest area
*14 en suite (bth/shr) (8 fmly) (5 with balcony) TV in all bedrooms STV Radio in rooms Direct dial from all bedrooms Mini-bar in all bedrooms Licensed Night porter Full central heating Open parking available Supervised Boule Bicycle rental Open terrace Languages spoken: English, Italian & German*
ROOMS: (room only) d 500-550FF
CARDS: 💳 ▦ ▩ 🅓 JCB

### FLAGY Seine-et-Marne

**★ ★ ★ Au Moulin**
2 rue du Moulin *77940*
☎ 160966789 FAX 160966951
(from Fontainbleu, take N6 towards Sens and in 18km turn right towards Nemours then immediately left to Flagy)

Near river  Forest area
*Closed 21 Dec-22 Jan & 14-24 Sep*
*10 en suite (bth/shr) (3 fmly) Direct dial from all bedrooms*
*Licensed  Full central heating  Open parking available  Child*
*discount available 10yrs  Open terrace  Last d 21.30hrs*
*Languages spoken: English, German & Spanish*
CARDS: 💳 ▬ ▭ 🅾 Travellers cheques

### FONTAINEBLEAU Seine-et-Marne

★ ★ ★ **Hotel de L'Aigle Noir**
27 pl Napoléon Bonarparte *77300*
☎ 160746000 FAX 160746001
(from Paris A6 in direction Lyon, exit Fontainebleau)

Opposite the castle and gardens of Fontainbleau, the hotel has
been part of the history of France for five centuries. The
individually styled rooms and apartments offer every comfort.
There is a gastronomical restaurant where you can enjoy the
light and imaginative cuisine, a Second Empire-styled piano
bar, a spacious indoor swimming pool, a gym and sauna.
Forest area  In town centre  Near motorway
*56 en suite (bth/shr) (9 fmly) (4 with balcony) No smoking in*
*22 bedrooms  TV in all bedrooms  STV  Direct dial from all*
*bedrooms  Mini-bar in all bedrooms  Licensed  Lift  Night porter*
*Full central heating  Air conditioning in bedrooms  Open*
*parking available (charged)  Covered parking available*
*(charged)  Child discount available 12yrs  Indoor swimming*
*pool (heated)  Sauna  Solarium  Gym  Bicycle rental  Open*
*terrace  V meals  Languages spoken: English, German &*
*Spanish*
CARDS: 💳 ▬ ▭ 🅾 Travellers cheques

### FONTAINE-LA-RIVIÈRE Essonne

★ ★ ★ *Auberge de Courpain*
Courpain *91690*
☎ 164956704 FAX 160809902
(follow N20 to Étampes then onto D191 to Pithiviers 8km
further is the auberge)
Near river  Forest area  Near motorway
*Closed 15-28 Feb*
*17 en suite (bth/shr) (4 fmly) No smoking in 4 bedrooms  TV in*
*8 bedrooms  Direct dial from all bedrooms  Licensed  Night*
*porter  Air conditioning in bedrooms  Open parking available*
*Covered parking available  Supervised  Child discount available*
*Fishing  Riding  Solarium  Open terrace  V meals  Last d*
*21.15hrs  Languages spoken: English Dutch German & Spanish*
CARDS: 💳 ▬ ▭ Travellers cheques

### FONTENAILLES Seine-et-Marne

★ ★ ★ *Golf de Fontenailles*
Domaine de Bois Boudran *77370*
☎ 164605100 FAX 160675212
Near river  Forest area
*Closed Dec-Feb*
*51 en suite (bth)  TV in all bedrooms  STV  Radio in rooms*
*Direct dial from all bedrooms  Mini-bar in all bedrooms*
*Licensed  Lift  Full central heating  Open parking available*
*Child discount available  Golf Tennis  Sauna  Bicycle rental*
*Open terrace  V meals  Last d 21.15hrs  Languages spoken:*
*English & Japanese*
CARDS: 💳 ▬ ▭ 🅾 JCB

### FONTENAY-TRÉSIGNY Seine-et-Marne

★ ★ ★ *Le Manoir* (Relais et Châteaux)
rte Départementale 402 *77610*
☎ 164259117 FAX 164259549
(A4 exit 13 in direction of Provins and follow Fontenay-
Tresigny)
Forest area  Near motorway
*Closed 16 Nov-26 Mar*
*20 en suite (bth/shr) (7 fmly) (10 with balcony) TV in all*
*bedrooms  STV  Direct dial from all bedrooms  Mini-bar in all*
*bedrooms  Licensed  Full central heating  Open parking*
*available  Covered parking available  Child discount available*
*12yrs  Outdoor swimming pool (heated)  Sauna  Gym  Pool table*
*Boule  Bicycle rental  Open terrace  Covered terrace  Table*
*Tennis,Practice Golf,Library  Wkly live entertainment  V meals*
*Last d 21.00hrs  Languages spoken: English & German*
CARDS: 💳 ▬ ▭ 🅾 JCB

### GAZERAN Yvelines

★ ★ **Auberge Villa Marinette**
20 av Général-de-Gaulle *78125*
☎ 134831901 FAX 134831901
Near river  Forest area  Near motorway
*Closed Tue evening & Wed. Also seasonal*
*6 rms (3 shr) Licensed  Full central heating  Open terrace  Last*
*d 21.00hrs  Languages spoken: English*
CARDS: 💳 ▭ Travellers cheques

### GONESSE Val-D'Oise

★ ★ **Les Relais Bleus**
7 rte de l'Europe *95500*
☎ 139873666 FAX 139873470
Near motorway
*72 en suite (bth/shr) (25 fmly) TV in all bedrooms  STV  Direct*
*dial from all bedrooms  Mini-bar in all bedrooms  Licensed*
*Night porter  Open parking available  Supervised  Child*
*discount available 12yrs  Open terrace  V meals  Last d 22.00hrs*
*Languages spoken: English, German & Spanish*
ROOMS: (room only) d 285-330FF
**Reductions over 1 night  Special breaks**
MEALS: Full breakfast 37FF  Lunch 85-145FF  Dinner 85-
145FF✶
CARDS: 💳 ▭ Travellers cheques

## GRESSY Seine-et-Marne

**★ ★ ★ ★ Manoir de Gressy**
2 rue St-Denis 77410
☎ 160266800 FAX 160264546
(Approach via N2 and D212)
This manor house has been built on the site of an 17th-century farmhouse and has been faithful to the architectural style of days gone by. Attractive wood-panelling, limestone floors, and magnificent pieces of antique furniture contribute to the authentic atmosphere. All the individually styled bedrooms have views of the courtyard garden - those on the ground floor have a private terrace. The menu features classic French cuisine complemented by a choice of select wines.
Near river Near motorway
*Closed 22 Dec-3 Jan*

*86 en suite (bth/shr) (31 with balcony) No smoking in 15 bedrooms TV in all bedrooms STV Radio in rooms Direct dial from all bedrooms Licensed Lift Night porter Full central heating Open parking available Supervised Child discount available 12yrs Outdoor swimming pool (heated) Pool table Boule Bicycle rental Open terrace Covered terrace Table Tennis V meals Last d 22.00hrs Languages spoken: English,German,Italian & Spanish*
ROOMS: (room only) d 980-1290FF
MEALS: Full breakfast 95FF Lunch fr 185FF Dinner fr 185FF
CARDS: 💳 🏦 🎫 💿 Travellers cheques

## GRIGNY Essonne

**★ ★ ★ Château du Clotay**
8 rue du Port 91350
☎ 169258998 FAX 169258022
Near lake Forest area Near motorway
*25 en suite (bth/shr) 15 rooms in annexe (5 fmly) TV in all bedrooms STV Direct dial from all bedrooms Mini-bar in all bedrooms Licensed Full central heating Open parking available Supervised Child discount available 12yrs Outdoor swimming pool Boule Open terrace Covered terrace Languages spoken: English*
CARDS: 💳 🏦 🎫 💿 Travellers cheques

## HERBEVILLE Yvelines

**Le Mont au Vent** (Prop: Louise Turmel)
2 r de Maule 78580
☎ 130906522 FAX 134751254
(access via A13 and D45)
Forest area
*2 en suite (bth/shr) (2 fmly) (1 with balcony) No smoking on premises TV in all bedrooms Full central heating Open parking available Covered parking available Child discount available Tennis Fishing Boule*

## LÉSIGNY Seine-et-Marne

**★ ★ ★ Château de Grande Romaine**
Grande Romaine 77150
☎ 164431600 FAX 164431606
(from Paris follow the A4 and then the N104 take exit18 Lesigny-Romaine)
Forest area
*88 en suite (bth/shr) (16 fmly) No smoking in 8 bedrooms TV in all bedrooms STV Direct dial from all bedrooms Licensed Full central heating Open parking available Supervised Child discount available 12yrs Outdoor swimming pool (heated) Tennis Sauna Boule Bicycle rental Open terrace Covered terrace*
CARDS: 💳 🏦 🎫 💿

## LEVALLOIS-PERRET Hauts-de-Seine

**★ ★ Hotel Espace Champerret**
26 rue Louise Michel 92300
☎ 147572071 FAX 147573139
In town centre
*36 en suite (bth/shr) (3 fmly) TV in all bedrooms Direct dial from all bedrooms Mini-bar in all bedrooms Lift Night porter Full central heating Child discount available 12yrs Languages spoken: English*
CARDS: 💳 🏦 🎫 💿 JCB Travellers cheques

## LOGNES Seine-et-Marne

**★ ★ ★ Hotel Frantour**
55 bd du Mandinet 77185
☎ 164800250 FAX 164800270
(from Paris take A4 in direction of Metz/Nancy exit at Val Maulriée Sud)
Near lake Forest area Near motorway
*85 en suite (bth/shr) (28 fmly) No smoking in 5 bedrooms TV in all bedrooms STV Direct dial from all bedrooms Room-safe Licensed Lift Night porter Full central heating Open parking available Covered parking available (charged) Supervised Child discount available 12yrs Sauna Boule Open terrace Table tennis V meals Last d 22.00hrs Languages spoken: English, German & Spanish*
ROOMS: (room only) s 470-550FF; d 550-600FF
MEALS: Continental breakfast 54FF Lunch 79-150FF&alc Dinner 79-150FF&alc✱
CARDS: 💳 🏦 🎫 💿 JCB Travellers cheques

## LUZARCHES Val-D'Oise

**★ ★ ★ Hotel Blue Green Mont Griffon**
95270
☎ 134092000 FAX 134680024
(from A1 exit Survilliers follow Chantilly sign, then direction Fosses-Bellefontaine D922. Luzarches (direction Seugy)- Le Mont Griffon (D909) exit hotel after Golf de Montgriffon)
Forest area Near motorway
*54 en suite (bth/shr) (12 fmly) (16 with balcony) No smoking in 6 bedrooms TV in all bedrooms STV Direct dial from all bedrooms Licensed Lift Night porter Open parking available Supervised Child discount available 12yrs Outdoor swimming pool (heated) Golf 18 Sauna Jacuzzi/spa Bicycle rental Covered terrace Archery Table tennis Billiard table Last d 21.30hrs Languages spoken: English, Dutch, German & Italian*
CARDS: 💳 🏦 🎫 💿

**MAGNY-LE-HONGRE** Seine-et-Marne

★★ **Hotel du Moulin de Paris**
60 rue du Moulin a Vent *77700*
☎ 160437777 FAX 160437888
(A4 exit 14 Disneyland Park follow signs for Magny-Le-Hongre)
Forest area

*82 en suite (shr) (82 fmly) TV in all bedrooms STV Licensed*
*Lift Night porter Full central heating Air conditioning in*
*bedrooms Open parking available Covered parking available*
*Outdoor swimming pool (heated) Sauna Open terrace V meals*
*Last d 22.30hrs Languages spoken: English German & Spanish*
ROOMS: (room only) s 400FF; d 400FF ✱
MEALS: Full breakfast 50FF Continental breakfast 25FF
Lunch 85FF Dinner 85FF✱
CARDS: ●● ■■ ☲☲ ⑩ Travellers cheques

**MILLY-LA-FORÊT** Essonne

**Ferme de la Grange Rouge** (Prop: Jean Charles
Desforges)
*91490*
☎ 164989421 FAX 164989991
Forest area
*Closed 15-31 Dec*
*5 en suite (shr) Open parking available Supervised Child*
*discount available 6yrs*
ROOMS: s 210FF; d 250FF
CARDS: Travellers cheques

**MONTIGNY-SUR-LOING** Seine-et-Marne

**Bed & Breakfast** (Prop: J-M Gicquel)
46 rue Renée Montgermont *77690*
☎ 164458792
(at Fontainebleau, at the crossroads 'The Obelisque', take the
direction of Montigny/Loing, pass through the village of
Bourron-Jarlotte then into Montigny/Loing)
Near river Forest area In town centre Near motorway
*3 en suite (shr) (1 fmly) No smoking on premises TV in 2*
*bedrooms Full central heating Open parking available Child*
*discount available 8yrs Languages spoken: English & German*
CARDS: Travellers cheques

**MORIGNY-CHAMPIGNY** Essonne

★★★ *Hostellerie de Villemartin*
5 allée des Marronniers *91150*
☎ 164946354 FAX 164942468
(from Paris take N20 exit at Auvers Saint Georges take D148
then D17 towards Morigny. Hotel is on right)

Near river Near lake Forest area Near motorway
*14 en suite (bth/shr) Some rooms in annexe (4 fmly) (2 with*
*balcony) TV in all bedrooms Direct dial from all bedrooms*
*Licensed Night porter Full central heating Open parking*
*available Child discount available Fishing Boule Bicycle rental*
*Open terrace Covered terrace Last d 21.30hrs Languages*
*spoken: English & Spanish*
CARDS: ●● ■■ ☲☲ ⑩ Travellers cheques

**NANTERRE** Hauts-de-Seine

★★★ **Hotel et Résidence Mercure Paris la Défense**
17/20 espl Charles-de-Gaulle, rue des Trois Fontanot *92000*
☎ 146696800 FAX 147254624
(from Paris, ring west, exit La Défense/Porte Maillot, exit 7
(Valmy-Kupka) left at 2nd traffic lights)
In town centre Near motorway
*160 en suite (bth/shr) (25 fmly) No smoking in 16 bedrooms*
*TV in all bedrooms STV Radio in rooms Direct dial from all*
*bedrooms Mini-bar in all bedrooms Licensed Lift Night porter*
*Full central heating Air conditioning in bedrooms Open*
*parking available (charged) Covered parking available*
*(charged) Supervised Child discount available 16yrs Pool table*
*Last d 22.30hrs Languages spoken: English, Arabic, German &*
*Spanish*
MEALS: Full breakfast 72FF Lunch 140-185FF&alc Dinner
140-185FF&alc
CARDS: ●● ■■ ☲☲ ⑩ JCB Travellers cheques

**NEAUPHLE-LE-CHÂTEAU** Yvelines

★★★ **Domaine du Verbois**
38 av de la République *78640*
☎ 134891178 FAX 134895733
Forest area
*Closed 10-20 Aug*
*20 en suite (bth/shr) 2 rooms in annexe (6 fmly) TV in all*
*bedrooms STV Radio in rooms Direct dial from all bedrooms*
*Mini-bar in 12 bedrooms Licensed Night porter Full central*
*heating Open parking available Supervised Child discount*
*available 12yrs Tennis Solarium Boule Bicycle rental Open*
*terrace Covered terrace Table tennis V meals Last d 21.30hrs*
*Languages spoken: English & German*
ROOMS: (room only) s 490-590FF; d 590-690FF
**Reductions over 1 night Special breaks**
MEALS: Continental breakfast 68FF Lunch 155FF&alc
Dinner 155FF&alc✱
CARDS: ●● ■■ ☲☲ ⑩ Travellers cheques

**NEUFMOUTIERS-EN-BRIE** Seine-et-Marne

**Bellevue** (Prop: Isabelle & Patrick Galpin)
*77610*
☎ 164071105 FAX 164071927
(A4 exit 13 Villeneuve-le-Comte, then take direction
Neufmoutiers-en-Brie)
Isabelle and Patrick Galpin offer you refurbished guest rooms
in the wing of their ancient farmhouse which is only ten
minutes from Disneyland Paris. Five comfortable bedrooms
available which overlook the garden, also one lodge in the
garden. Evening meals are available by prior arrangement.
Forest area
*6 en suite (shr) (6 fmly) No smoking on premises TV in all*
*bedrooms Full central heating Open parking available*
*Supervised Child discount available 12yrs Fishing Bicycle*
*rental Table tennis Languages spoken: English* *contd.*

*Bellevue*

ROOMS: s 230-350FF; d 270-390FF
MEALS: Dinner 95FF

## NEUILLY-SUR-SEINE Hauts-de-Seine

**Bed & Breakfast** (Prop: Ruth Himmelfarb)
53 bd Victor-Hugo *92200*
☎ 146373728 FAX 146373728
(from place Ch-de-Gaulle take av de la Grande Armée, Porte
Maillot, av Ch-de-Gaulle; turn right after 11 red lights, then rue
du Château right after 8 red lights)
Near river  Forest area  In town centre
*1 en suite (bth/shr) (1 with balcony) Full central heating Child
discount available 12yrs Bicycle rental Languages spoken:
English, German & some Italian*

★ ★ **Hotel Charlemagne**
1 rue Charcot *92200*
☎ 146242763 FAX 146371156
*40 en suite (bth/shr) TV in all bedrooms Lift*
CARDS: ●● ■

★ ★ ★ **Hotel Neuilly Park**
23 rue Madeleine Michelis *92200*
☎ 146401115 FAX 146401478
*30 en suite (bth/shr) TV in all bedrooms STV Direct dial from
all bedrooms Lift Open parking available*

## NOGENT-SUR-MARNE Val-de-Marne

★ ★ **Climat de France**
1 rue de Nazaré *94130*
☎ 143243737 FAX 143248404
(off A4, signed Nogent s/Marne)
Near river  Forest area  Near motorway
*74 en suite (shr) TV available Direct-dial available Licensed
Lift Night porter Full central heating Open parking available
Covered parking available Last d 10pm Languages spoken:
English & German*
CARDS: ●● ▨

## NOISY-LE-GRAND Seine-St-Denis

★ ★ **Climat de France**
5 rue du Ballon *93160*
☎ 143052299 FAX 143041081
(off A4 at Champs s/Marne exit)
Forest area  Near motorway
*50 en suite (bth/shr) Some rooms in annexe (4 fmly) TV in all
bedrooms Radio in rooms Direct dial from all bedrooms*

*Licensed Full central heating Open parking available Boule
Open terrace Covered terrace V meals Last d 10pm
Languages spoken: English, German & Portuguese*
CARDS: ●● ▨

## ORGEVAL Yvelines

★ ★ ★ **Novotel Orgeval**
*78630*
☎ 139223511 FAX 139754893
(on N13)
Forest area  Near motorway
*119 en suite (bth/shr) (15 fmly) No smoking in 27 bedrooms
TV in all bedrooms STV Radio in rooms Direct dial from all
bedrooms Mini-bar in all bedrooms Licensed Lift Night porter
Full central heating Air conditioning in bedrooms Open
parking available Outdoor swimming pool Tennis Boule Open
terrace Last d 24.00hrs Languages spoken: English, German &
Spanish*
CARDS: ●● ■ ▨ ●

## ORLY (AÉROPORT D') Val-de-Marne

★ ★ ★ **Novotel Orly Rungis**
Zone du Delta, rue du Pont des Halles *94150*
☎ 145124412 FAX 145124413
Near motorway
*181 en suite (bth/shr) (53 fmly) No smoking in 70 bedrooms
TV in all bedrooms STV Radio in rooms Direct dial from all
bedrooms Mini-bar in all bedrooms Licensed Lift Night porter
Full central heating Air conditioning in bedrooms Open
parking available (charged) Supervised Child discount
available 16yrs Outdoor swimming pool Open terrace Last d
24.00hrs Languages spoken: English*
CARDS: ●● ■ ▨ ● Travellers cheques

## ORSAY Essonne

★ ★ ★ **Novotel Saclay**
rue Charles Thomassin *91410*
☎ 169356600 FAX 169410177
Forest area  Near motorway
*136 en suite (bth) (136 fmly) No smoking in 50 bedrooms TV in
all bedrooms STV Radio in rooms Direct dial from all
bedrooms Mini-bar in all bedrooms Licensed Lift Night porter
Full central heating Air conditioning in bedrooms Open
parking available Supervised Child discount available 12yrs
Outdoor swimming pool Tennis Gym Boule Mini-golf Bicycle
rental Open terrace Wkly live entertainment Last d 24.00hrs
Languages spoken: English*
ROOMS: (room only) s 580-725FF; d 630-790FF **Special
breaks: Jul-Aug discount weekend breaks**
MEALS: Continental breakfast 25FF Lunch 140-220FFalc
Dinner 140-220FFalc
CARDS: ●● ■ ▨ ● Travellers cheques

## OTHIS Seine-et-Marne

**Plaisance** (Prop: M & Mme Montrozier)
12 rue de Suisses, Beaumarchais *77280*
☎ 160033398 FAX 160035671
(from Charles-de-Gaulle airport take D401 to Dammartin-en-
Goële then D64 to Othis, then follow signs to Beaumarchais.
From Paris take A1, exit at Soissons onto N2 exit Othis then
Beaumarchais)

Forest area
*Closed Feb*
*3 en suite (bth) TV in all bedrooms Full central heating Open parking available Child discount available 8yrs Languages spoken: English*

## PARIS

### 1ST ARRONDISSEMENT

### ★ ★ *Hotel Agora*
7 rue de la Cossonerie *75001*
☎ 142334602 FAX 142338099
In town centre
*29 en suite (bth/shr) (4 fmly) (11 with balcony) TV in all bedrooms STV Direct dial from all bedrooms Lift Night porter Full central heating Languages spoken: English Arabic & Italian*
CARDS: ●● ■■ ⅠⅠ Travellers cheques

### Bed & Breakfast (Prop: Mona Pierrot)
14 rue Bertin-Poirée *75001*
☎ 142365065
(between the Louvre and Notre-Dame, the Seine and the rue Rivoli - Métro Châtelet)
Cosy accommodation in the heart of Paris, between the Louvre and Notre Dame..
Near river
*Closed School holidays*
*1 en suite (bth/shr) No smoking on premises Full central heating Languages spoken: English & Spanish*
ROOMS: s 350FF; d 420FF ✱

### ★ ★ ★ *Hotel du Continent*
30 rue du Mont Thabor *75001*
☎ 142607532 FAX 142615222
In town centre
*26 en suite (bth/shr) (6 fmly) TV in all bedrooms STV Direct dial from all bedrooms Mini-bar in all bedrooms Licensed Lift Night porter Full central heating Air conditioning in bedrooms Child discount available 12yrs Languages spoken: English & Spanish*
ROOMS: (room only) s 756-1056FF; d 962-1462FF
CARDS: ●● ■■ ⅠⅠ ⑨ JCB Travellers cheques

### ★ ★ ★ ★ *Inter-Continental*
3 rue Castiglioné *75001*
☎ 144771111 FAX 144771460
Near river In town centre
*450 en suite (bth/shr) (10 fmly) No smoking in 103 bedrooms TV in all bedrooms STV Radio in rooms Direct dial from all bedrooms Mini-bar in all bedrooms Licensed Lift Night porter Full central heating Air conditioning in bedrooms Child discount available 12yrs Open terrace V meals Languages spoken: English German Italian Japanese & Spanish*
CARDS: ●● ■■ ⅠⅠ ⑨ Travellers cheques

### ★ ★ *Hotel Louvre-Forum*
25 rue du Bouloi *75001*
☎ 142365419 FAX 142336631
Near river In town centre
*27 en suite (bth/shr) TV in all bedrooms STV Direct dial from all bedrooms Mini-bar in all bedrooms Licensed Lift Night porter Full central heating Languages spoken: German Italian & Spanish*
CARDS: ●● ■■ ⅠⅠ ⑨ Travellers cheques

### ★ ★ ★ *Hotel Louvre St-Houoie*
141 rue St-Honoré *75001*
☎ 142962323 FAX 142962161
In town centre
*40 en suite (bth/shr) (5 fmly) (1 with balcony) TV in all bedrooms STV Radio in rooms Direct dial from all bedrooms Mini-bar in 41 bedrooms Licensed Lift Night porter Full central heating Air conditioning in bedrooms Child discount available 12yrs Languages spoken: English Italian & German*
CARDS: ●● ■■ ⅠⅠ ⑨ JCB Travellers cheques

### ★ ★ ★ ★ *Madelèine Palace*
8 rue Cambon *75001*
☎ 142603782 FAX 142603821
(from Porte Maillot onto Avenue de la Grande Armée, Place Étoile, Champs Elysées, Place Concorde & Rue Royal, then turn 1st left into Rue St Honoré & at Laura Ashley shop to the right)
Near river In town centre
*82 rms (76 bth/shr) TV in all bedrooms STV Radio in rooms Direct dial from all bedrooms Mini-bar in 78 bedrooms Room-safe Licensed Lift Night porter Full central heating y Languages spoken: English Italian & Spanish*
CARDS: ●● ■■ ⅠⅠ ⑨ JCB Travellers cheques

### ★ ★ ★ *Hotel Mansart*
5 rue des Capucines *75001*
☎ 142615028 FAX 149279744
In town centre
*57 en suite (bth/shr) (3 with balcony) TV in all bedrooms STV Direct dial from all bedrooms Mini-bar in all bedrooms Room-safe Licensed Lift Night porter Full central heating Air conditioning in bedrooms Languages spoken: English, Spanish, Italian & German*
ROOMS: (room only) s 600-990FF; d 600-1600FF
CARDS: ●● ■■ ⅠⅠ ⑨ Travellers cheques

### ★ ★ ★ ★ *Meurice* (Leading Hotels)
228 rue de Rivoli *75001*
☎ 144581010 FAX 148581015
Near river In town centre
*180 en suite (bth/shr) (3 with balcony) No smoking in 24 bedrooms TV in all bedrooms STV Radio in rooms Direct dial from all bedrooms Mini-bar in all bedrooms Licensed Lift Night porter Full central heating Air conditioning in bedrooms Child discount available 14yrs V meals Languages spoken: English German Italian Portuguese Russian & Spanish*
CARDS: ●● ■■ ⅠⅠ ⑨ JCB Travellers cheques

### ★ ★ ★ ★ *Hotel Normandy*
70 rue Échelle *75001*
☎ 142603021 FAX 142604581
Near river In town centre
*115 en suite (bth/shr) (4 fmly) (18 with balcony) No smoking in 22 bedrooms TV in all bedrooms STV Radio in rooms Direct dial from all bedrooms Mini-bar in all bedrooms Licensed Lift Night porter Full central heating Child discount available 12yrs V meals Last d 22.15hrs Languages spoken: English,German,Italian,Russian & Spanish*
ROOMS: (room only) d 1400-1620FF
MEALS: Continental breakfast 75FF Lunch 160-180FF&alc Dinner 160-180FF&alc
CARDS: ●● ■■ ⅠⅠ ⑨ Travellers cheques

### ★ ★ ★ Relais du Louvre
19 rue des Pretres St Germain, l'Auxerrois *75001*
☎ 140419642 FAX 140419644
(in centre of Paris opposite the Louvre Museum)
It is unusual in a busy city to find peace and quiet, but the Relais du Louvre provides just that within its 18th-century walls. Restful colour schemes and charming period furniture, discreetly combined with modern refinements and services, provide elegant comfort - the mark of this hotel. Situated between the Louvre and Notre-Dame.
In town centre

*21 en suite (bth/shr) (5 fmly) (1 with balcony) No smoking in 10 bedrooms TV in all bedrooms STV Direct dial from all bedrooms Mini-bar in all bedrooms Room-safe Licensed Lift Night porter Full central heating Air conditioning in bedrooms Open parking available (charged) Covered parking available (charged) Supervised Child discount available 12yrs Languages spoken: English, German & Italian*
ROOMS: (room only) s 650-800FF; d 900-1000FF ✱
MEALS: Full breakfast 60FF✱
CARDS: ● ■ ■ ⬤ JCB

### ★ ★ ★ Tuileries
10 rue St-Hyacinthe *75001*
☎ 142610417 FAX 149279156
In town centre
*26 en suite (bth/shr) (14 fmly) (4 with balcony) TV in all bedrooms STV Radio in rooms Direct dial from all bedrooms Mini-bar in all bedrooms Room-safe Licensed Lift Night porter Full central heating Air conditioning in bedrooms Languages spoken: English German Italian & Spanish*
CARDS: ● ■ ■ ⬤ JCB Travellers cheques

### ★ ★ ★ Hotel Baudelaire Opéra
61 rue Sainte Anne *75002*
☎ 142975062 FAX 142868585
(Hotel is between Opéra and the Louvre. From the rue de Rivoli, turn right on toavenue de l'Opéra, then take the second right into rue Ste Anne)
Named after the poet Charles Pierre Baudelaire, the building spans an ancient passageway and is around 300 years old. It is situated within walking distance of most main attractions and shops. The owners, an English/French couple, offer a warm welcome and are very happy to correspond or converse in English or French.
Near river In town centre Near motorway
*29 en suite (bth/shr) (5 fmly) (7 with balcony) TV in all bedrooms STV Direct dial from all bedrooms Mini-bar in all*

**Hotel Baudelaire Opéra**
*bedrooms Licensed Lift Night porter Full central heating Languages spoken: English, German & Spanish*
ROOMS: (room only) s 540-570FF; d 680-740FF
MEALS: Continental breakfast 39FF
CARDS: ● ■ ■ ⬤ JCB Travellers cheques

### Boulevards (Prop: M Bonnet)
10 r de la Ville-Neuve *75002*
☎ 142360229 FAX 142361539
*18 rms (14 bth/shr) TV available Full central heating*

### ★ ★ ★ Hotel François
3 bd Montmartre *75002*
☎ 142335153 FAX 140262990
In town centre
*71 en suite (bth/shr) (9 fmly) TV in all bedrooms STV Radio in rooms Direct dial from all bedrooms Mini-bar in all bedrooms Licensed Lift Night porter Full central heating No children Child discount available 12yrs Languages spoken: English German & Spanish*
CARDS: ● ■ ■ ⬤ Travellers cheques

### ★ ★ ★ Gaillon Opéra Best Western (Best Western)
9 rue Gaillon *75002*
☎ 147424774 FAX 147420123
In town centre Near motorway
*26 en suite (bth/shr) (9 fmly) (4 with balcony) No smoking in 9 bedrooms TV in all bedrooms STV Radio in rooms Direct dial from all bedrooms Mini-bar in all bedrooms Room-safe Licensed Lift Night porter Full central heating Air conditioning in bedrooms Child discount available 12yrs Languages spoken: English Portuguese Italian & German*
ROOMS: (room only) s 690-1250FF; d 750-1250FF **Special breaks**
CARDS: ● ■ ■ ⬤ JCB Travellers cheques

### ★ ★ ★ Grand Hotel de Besançon
56 rue Montorgueil *75002*
☎ 142364108 FAX 145080879
The hotel is located in a pedestrianised street not far from all the popular tourist attractions. The renovated guest-rooms are tastefully furnished and decorated with co-ordinating fabrics, and offer a good standard of comfort.
In town centre
*26 en suite (bth/shr) No smoking in 5 bedrooms TV in all bedrooms STV Radio in rooms Direct dial from all bedrooms Mini-bar in all bedrooms Room-safe Lift Night porter Full central heating Air conditioning in bedrooms Languages spoken: English*
ROOMS: (room only) s 590-830FF; d 620-980FF
CARDS: ● ■ ■ ⬤

**★ ★ ★ ★ Hotel L'Horset Opéra**
18 rue d'Antin 75002
☎ 144718700 FAX 142665554
(200m from the Opéra Garnier & close to Place Vendôme, the Louvre, Palais Royal & Tuileries Gardens)
In town centre
*54 en suite (bth/shr) (14 with balcony) No smoking in 9 bedrooms TV in all bedrooms STV Radio in rooms Direct dial from all bedrooms Mini-bar in all bedrooms Room-safe Licensed Lift Night porter Full central heating Air conditioning in bedrooms Child discount available 3yrs Languages spoken: English,German,Spanish*
ROOMS: (room only) s fr 1340FF; d fr 1480FF
MEALS: Continental breakfast 80FF Lunch fr 90FF&alc
CARDS: ✷ ▮ ⅏ ▣ Travellers cheques

**★ ★ ★ Jardin de Paris Cusset Opéra**
95 rue de Richelieu 75002
☎ 142974890 FAX 142614820
(take direction of Opera, the street of Richelieu is at 500mtrs at the end of the boulevard de Italian starting from the Opera)
In town centre
*108 en suite (bth/shr) (18 fmly) (3 with balcony) TV in all bedrooms Direct dial from all bedrooms Mini-bar in 25 bedrooms Room-safe Licensed Lift Night porter Full central heating Child discount available 12yrs Languages spoken: English German & Italian*
CARDS: ✷ ▮ ⅏ ▣ JCB Travellers cheques

**3RD ARRONDISSEMENT**

**★ ★ ★ Pavillon de la Reine**
28 pl des Vosges 75003
☎ 142779640 FAX 142776306
Near river In town centre
*55 en suite (bth/shr) (6 fmly) (4 with balcony) TV in all bedrooms STV Radio in rooms Direct dial from all bedrooms Mini-bar in all bedrooms Licensed Lift Night porter Full central heating Air conditioning in bedrooms Covered parking available Supervised Languages spoken: German Italian & Spanish*
CARDS: ✷ ▮ ⅏ ▣ Travellers cheques

**4TH ARRONDISSEMENT**

**★ ★ ★ Beaubourg**
11 rue Simon le Franc 75004
☎ 142743424 FAX 142786811
In town centre
*28 en suite (bth/shr) 10 rooms in annexe (1 fmly) (1 with balcony) No smoking in 5 bedrooms TV in all bedrooms STV Radio in rooms Direct dial from all bedrooms Mini-bar in all bedrooms Lift Full central heating Languages spoken: English Arabic & Spanish*
ROOMS: s 490-590FF; d 590-670FF ✷
CARDS: ✷ ▮ ⅏ ▣ Travellers cheques

**Bed & Breakfast**
7 rue Niicoles Flamel 75004
☎ 148877015 FAX 148877015
*2 en suite (bth/shr) Child discount available*

**★ ★ ★ Hotel de la Bretonnerie**
22 rue Ste-Croix-Bretonnerie 75004
☎ 148877763 FAX 142772678
In town centre
*Closed Aug*

*30 en suite (bth) (5 fmly) TV in all bedrooms STV Direct dial from all bedrooms Mini-bar in all bedrooms Room-safe Lift Night porter Full central heating Languages spoken: English & German*
ROOMS: (room only) d 660-1030FF
CARDS: ✷ ⅏ Travellers cheques

**★ ★ ★ Caron de Beaumarchais**
12 rue Vielle du Temple 75004
☎ 142723412 FAX 142723463
In town centre
*19 en suite (bth/shr) (6 with balcony) TV in all bedrooms STV Direct dial from all bedrooms Mini-bar in all bedrooms Lift Night porter Full central heating Air conditioning in bedrooms Child discount available 7yrs Languages spoken: English*
ROOMS: (room only) d 630-810FF
CARDS: ✷ ▮ ⅏ ▣ Travellers cheques

**★ ★ Castex Hotel**
5 rue Castex 75004
☎ 142723152 FAX 142725791
In town centre
*27 en suite (bth/shr) 3 rooms in annexe (1 fmly) No smoking on premises Night porter Full central heating Languages spoken: English & Spanish*
CARDS: ✷ ⅏ Travellers cheques

**★ ★ ★ Deux-Iles**
59 rue St-Louis-en-l'Ile 75004
☎ 143261335 FAX 143296025
In town centre
*17 en suite (bth/shr) TV in all bedrooms Radio in rooms Direct dial from all bedrooms Room-safe Lift Night porter Full central heating Air conditioning in bedrooms Languages spoken: English*
CARDS: ✷ ▮ ⅏ Travellers cheques

**★ ★ ★ Jeu de Paumé**
54 rue St-Louis-en-l'Ile 75004
☎ 143261418 FAX 140460276
(From the highway, follow the signs for Paris Centre - exit Porte de Bercy, then follow the banks of the Seine until the island of St Louis)
In town centre
*31 en suite (bth/shr) (2 with balcony) TV in all bedrooms STV Radio in rooms Direct dial from all bedrooms Mini-bar in all bedrooms Licensed Lift Night porter Full central heating Sauna Small fitness room. Languages spoken: English German Italian & Spanish*
CARDS: ✷ ▮ ⅏ ▣ JCB Travellers cheques

**★ ★ ★ Lutèce**
65 rue St-Louis-en-l'Ile 75004
☎ 143262352 FAX 143296025
In town centre
*23 en suite (bth/shr) TV in all bedrooms STV Radio in rooms Licensed Lift Night porter Full central heating Air conditioning in bedrooms Languages spoken: English & Spanish*
CARDS: ✷ ▮ ⅏ Travellers cheques

**★ ★ Place Des Vosges**
12 rue Birague 75004
☎ 142726046 FAX 142720264
In town centre

*contd.*

*16 en suite (bth/shr) (6 fmly) TV in all bedrooms STV Lift Night porter Full central heating Child discount available 2yrs Languages spoken: English*
CARDS: ✆ ▦ ▩ ▣ Travellers cheques

### ★ ★ ★ Hotel St-Louis
75 rue St-Louis-en-l'Ile *75004*
☎ 146340480 FAX 146340213
Near river In town centre Near motorway
*Licensed Night porter Full central heating Child discount available Languages spoken: English German & Spanish*
CARDS: ✆ ▩ Travellers cheques

### ★ ★ St-Louis-Marais
1 rue Charles-V *75004*
☎ 148878704 FAX 148873326
Near river In town centre Near motorway
*Night porter Full central heating Child discount available Languages spoken: English German & Spanish*
CARDS: ▩ Travellers cheques

### ★ ★ ★ St-Merry
78 rue Verrerie *75004*
☎ 142781415 FAX 140290682
(From the Hotel de Ville on rue de Rivoli turn right into Boulevard Sebastopol, then then right again to head towards the Pompidou Centre, then another right turn into rue St Martin)
Near river In town centre
*12 rms (10 bth/shr) (3 fmly) TV in 1 bedroom Direct dial from all bedrooms Night porter Full central heating Open parking available (charged) Languages spoken: English & German*
CARDS: ✆ ▦ ▩ Travellers cheques

### ★ ★ Hotel Sansonnet
48 rue de la Verrerie *75004*
☎ 147879614 FAX 148873046
Near river In town centre
*25 rms (21 bth/shr) (3 with balcony) TV in all bedrooms STV Direct dial from all bedrooms Night porter Full central heating Languages spoken: English*
CARDS: ✆ ▩ Travellers cheques

### ★ ★ ★ ★ Sofitel Paris St-Jacques
17 bd St-Jacques *75014*
☎ 140787980 FAX 145884393
In town centre Near motorway
*782 en suite (bth/shr) No smoking in 171 bedrooms TV in all bedrooms STV Radio in rooms Direct dial from all bedrooms Mini-bar in all bedrooms Licensed Lift Night porter Full central heating Air conditioning in bedrooms Open parking available (charged) Covered parking available (charged) Supervised Child discount available 12yrs Gym V meals Last d 23.00hrs Languages spoken: English Arabic Danish German Italian Spanish*
ROOMS: (room only) d 1300-2000FF
CARDS: ✆ ▦ ▩ ▣ Travellers cheques

### ★ ★ ★ Hotel Stella
14 rue Neuve St-Pierre *75004*
☎ 144592850 FAX 144592879
In town centre
*20 rms TV in all bedrooms Direct dial from all bedrooms Mini-bar in all bedrooms Lift Night porter Full central heating Air conditioning in bedrooms Child discount available 12yrs Languages spoken: English*
CARDS: ✆ ▦ ▩ ▣ JCB Travellers cheques

### ★ ★ ★ Angleterre
44 rue Jacob *75006*
☎ 142603472 FAX 142601693
In town centre
*27 en suite (bth/shr) TV in all bedrooms STV Direct dial from all bedrooms Room-safe Licensed Lift Night porter Full central heating Languages spoken: English & Spanish*
ROOMS: (room only) d 750-1600FF
CARDS: ✆ ▦ ▩ ▣ JCB Travellers cheques

### ★ ★ ★ Hotel Le Colbert
7 rue de l'Hotel Colbert *75005*
☎ 140467950 FAX 143258019
Near river In town centre
*36 en suite (bth/shr) (2 fmly) (1 with balcony) TV in all bedrooms Radio in rooms Direct dial from all bedrooms Mini-bar in all bedrooms Room-safe Licensed Lift Night porter Full central heating Child discount available 12yrs Languages spoken: English*
CARDS: ✆ ▦ ▩ ▣ Travellers cheques

### ★ ★ Hotel de L'Espérance
15 rue Pascal *75005*
☎ 147071099 FAX 143375619
In town centre Near motorway
*38 en suite (bth/shr) TV in all bedrooms STV Direct dial from all bedrooms Licensed Lift Night porter Full central heating Child discount available Languages spoken: English & Spanish*
CARDS: ✆ ▦ ▩ ▣ Travellers cheques

### Grand Hotel de Progrés (Prop: Henri Mart)
50 r Gay Lussac *75005*
☎ 143545318 FAX 156248780
This economic hotel, situated in the heart of the Latin Quarter, is near the Luxembourg Garden and the Panthéon. All the street-side rooms overlook a small garden and some have balconies and fireplaces.
In town centre
*Closed Aug*
*35 rms (6 shr) (12 with balcony) Full central heating No children 4yrs Languages spoken: English, Italian & Portuguese*
ROOMS: s 170-330FF; d 260-350FF ✱
CARDS: Travellers cheques

### ★ ★ ★ Grands Hommes
17 pl du Panthéon *75005*
☎ 146341960 FAX 143266732
Near river Forest area In town centre
*32 en suite (bth/shr) (6 with balcony) TV in all bedrooms STV Radio in rooms Direct dial from all bedrooms Mini-bar in all bedrooms Licensed Lift Night porter Full central heating Air conditioning in bedrooms Languages spoken: English German & Spanish*
CARDS: ✆ ▦ ▩ ▣ Travellers cheques

### ★ ★ ★ Hotel de Notre-Dame
19 rue Maître-Albert *75005*
☎ 143267900 FAX 146335011
In town centre
*34 en suite (bth) TV in all bedrooms STV Direct dial from all bedrooms Mini-bar in all bedrooms Room-safe Licensed Lift Night porter Full central heating Languages spoken: English & German*
CARDS: ✆ ▦ ▩ Travellers cheques

### ★ ★ ★ Hotel Royal St-Michel
3 bd St-Michel *75005*
☎ 144070606 FAX 144073625
(close to Notre-Dame)
Near river In town centre
*39 en suite (bth) (18 with balcony) TV in all bedrooms STV Direct dial from all bedrooms Mini-bar in all bedrooms Room-safe Licensed Lift Night porter Full central heating Air conditioning in bedrooms Child discount available 12yrs Languages spoken: English Arabic Italian & Russian*
CARDS: ●● ■■ ☲☲ ⑩ Travellers cheques

### ★ ★ ★ St-Germain des Prés
36 rue Bonaparte *75005*
☎ 143260019 FAX 140468363
In town centre
*30 en suite (bth/shr) TV in all bedrooms STV Radio in rooms Direct dial from all bedrooms Mini-bar in all bedrooms Room-safe Licensed Lift Night porter Full central heating Air conditioning in bedrooms Languages spoken: English German Italian & Spanish*
ROOMS: s 700-990FF; d 940-1350FF
CARDS: ●● ■■ ☲☲

### ★ ★ Hotel des Trois Colléges
16 rue Cujas *75005*
☎ 143546730 FAX 146340299
In town centre
*44 en suite (bth/shr) (3 fmly) TV in all bedrooms STV Direct dial from all bedrooms Licensed Lift Night porter Full central heating V meals Languages spoken: Italian & Spanish*
CARDS: ●● ■■ ☲☲ ⑩ JCB Travellers cheques

#### 6TH ARRONDISSEMENT

### ★ ★ ★ Aramis St-Germain (Best Western)
124 rue de Rennes *75006*
☎ 145480375 FAX 145449929
(Peripherique (Paris ring road) exit 'Porte d'Orleans', follow directions to Montparnasse. At the Montparnasse Tower take rue De Rennes, in the direction of Saint Germain des Pres)
Near river In town centre Near motorway
*42 en suite (bth/shr) (4 with balcony) TV in all bedrooms STV Radio in rooms Direct dial from all bedrooms Mini-bar in all bedrooms Licensed Lift Night porter Full central heating Air conditioning in bedrooms Child discount available 12yrs Jacuzzi/spa Languages spoken: English*
CARDS: ●● ■■ ☲☲ ⑩ JCB Travellers cheques

### ★ ★ ★ Atelier Montparnasse
49l rue Vavin *75006*
☎ 146363000 FAX 140510421
(From the Paris Ring Road (Periferique), take the turn for Porte d'Orleans. Then travel towards Montparnasse station turn into Boulevard Montparnasse and then rue Vavin)
In town centre Near motorway
*17 en suite (bth/shr) (2 with balcony) TV in all bedrooms Radio in rooms Direct dial from all bedrooms Mini-bar in all bedrooms Lift Night porter Full central heating Supervised Child discount available 10 Languages spoken: English & Italian*
CARDS: ●● ■■ ☲☲ ⑩ JCB Travellers cheques

### ★ ★ Chaplain
11 bis rue Jules Chaplain *75006*
☎ 143264764 FAX 140517975
In town centre
*25 en suite (bth/shr) (6 fmly) (21 with balcony) TV in all bedrooms STV Direct dial from all bedrooms Lift Night porter Full central heating Supervised Child discount available 12yrs Languages spoken: English & Spanish*
CARDS: ●● ■■ ☲☲ ⑩ Travellers cheques

### ★ ★ ★ Le Clos Médicis
56 rue Monsieur-Le-Prince *75006*
☎ 143291080 FAX 143542990
In town centre
*38 en suite (bth/shr) (2 with balcony) No smoking in 4 bedrooms TV in all bedrooms STV Direct dial from all bedrooms Mini-bar in all bedrooms Licensed Lift Night porter Full central heating Air conditioning in bedrooms Child discount available 12yrs Open terrace Languages spoken: English,Italian,Spanish*
ROOMS: (room only) d 790-1200FF
CARDS: ●● ■■ ☲☲ ⑩ Travellers cheques

### ★ ★ ★ Danemark
21 r Vavin *75006*
☎ 143269378 FAX 146346606
In town centre
*15 en suite (bth/shr) TV in all bedrooms STV Direct dial from all bedrooms Mini-bar in all bedrooms Lift Night porter Full central heating Open parking available (charged) Covered parking available (charged) Supervised Languages spoken: English German & Spanish*
CARDS: ●● ■■ ☲☲ ⑩ Travellers cheques

### ★ ★ ★ ★ L'Hotel
13 rue des Beaux-Arts *75006*
☎ 144419900 FAX 143256481
Near river In town centre
*27 en suite (bth/shr) (2 with balcony) TV in all bedrooms STV Radio in rooms Direct dial from all bedrooms Mini-bar in all bedrooms Room-safe Licensed Lift Night porter Full central heating Air conditioning in bedrooms Languages spoken: English*
CARDS: ●● ■■ ☲☲ ⑩ Travellers cheques

### ★ ★ ★ Left Bank St-Germain Hotel (Best Western)
9 rue de l'Ancienne-Comédie *75006*
☎ 143540170 FAX 143261714
In town centre
*31 en suite (bth/shr) TV in all bedrooms STV Direct dial from all bedrooms Mini-bar in all bedrooms Room-safe (charged) Licensed Lift Night porter Full central heating Air conditioning in bedrooms Child discount available 12 Languages spoken: English*
CARDS: ●● ■■ ☲☲ ⑩ JCB Travellers cheques

### ★ ★ ★ Hotel Littré
9 rue Littré *75006*
☎ 145443868 FAX 145448813
The hotel is situated on the left bank between Montparnasse and Saint-Germain-des-Prés and offers traditional hospitality in classic surroundings. The bedrooms feature stylish furnishings and offer a high level of comfort. The public areas and bar have a cosy yet sophisticated atmosphere in which visitors can unwind after a busy day sightseeing.
In town centre                                                    *contd.*

**Hotel Littré**

*91 en suite (bth/shr) (7 fmly) (4 with balcony) No smoking in 13 bedrooms TV in all bedrooms STV Radio in rooms Direct dial from all bedrooms Mini-bar in all bedrooms Room-safe Licensed Lift Night porter Full central heating Air conditioning in bedrooms Covered parking available (charged) Child discount available 12 Languages spoken: English German Italian & Spanish.*

ROOMS: (room only) d 1350-1850FF

CARDS: ● ■ ■ ● JCB Travellers cheques

★ ★ ★ ★ **Lutétia**

45 bd Raspail *76006*

☎ 149544646 FAX 149544600

(Périphérique South,then Porte d'Orléans head for Place Denfert Rochereau then Boulevard Raspail)

The building has one of the most striking façades in Paris which conceals an extraordinary interior of art-déco furnishings and decorations. A popular rendezvous amongst those connected to the arts and politics, it is renowned for its traditional hospitality and impeccable service. The bedrooms - some with views of the Eiffel Tower - are furnished with meticulous attention to detail and offer modern amenities; whilst the Paris restaurant has earned many accolades for its outstanding cuisine. In addition, the hotel has a popular brasserie, a piano bar and an elegant cigar bar.

*Near river In town centre Near motorway RS Rest closed weekends & end Jul-Aug*
*250 en suite (bth/shr) (50 with balcony) TV in all bedrooms STV Radio in rooms Direct dial from all bedrooms Mini-bar in all bedrooms Room-safe Licensed Lift Night porter Full central heating Air conditioning in bedrooms Child discount available 8yrs Open terrace Jazz eve's every Tue/Thu/Fri/Sat Wkly live entertainment V meals Last d 23.00hrs Languages spoken: English German & Spanish*

ROOMS: (room only) d 1900-2500FF
MEALS: Continental breakfast 75FF Lunch 165-465FF Dinner 165-465FF
CARDS: ● ■ ■ ● JCB Travellers cheques

★ ★ ★ **Hotel des Marronniers**

21 rue Jacob *75006*

☎ 143253060 FAX 140468356

*In town centre*
*37 en suite (bth/shr) TV in all bedrooms STV Licensed Lift Night porter Full central heating Air conditioning in bedrooms Languages spoken: English*

CARDS: ● ■ Travellers cheques

★ ★ ★ **Hotel Le Montana**

28 rue St-Benoît *75006*

☎ 144397100 FAX 144397129

*In town centre*
*17 rms (1 fmly) TV in all bedrooms STV Direct dial from all bedrooms Lift Night porter Full central heating Child discount available 12yrs Languages spoken: English*

CARDS: ● ■ ■ ● JCB Travellers cheques

★ ★ ★ **Hotel Prince de Conti**

8 rue Guénégaud *75006*

☎ 144073040 FAX 144073634

*In town centre*
*26 en suite (bth/shr) 12 rooms in annexe TV in all bedrooms STV Direct dial from all bedrooms Mini-bar in all bedrooms Lift Night porter Air conditioning in bedrooms Child discount available Open terrace Covered terrace Languages spoken: English & Italian*

CARDS: ● ■ ■ ● Travellers cheques

★ ★ **Hotel Recamier**

3 bis pl St-Sulpice *75006*

☎ 143260489 FAX 146332773

*In town centre*
*30 rms Some rooms in annexe (2 fmly) (10 with balcony) No smoking on premises Licensed Lift Night porter Full central heating No children 5yrs Languages spoken: English German & Spanish*

CARDS: ● ■ Travellers cheques

★ ★ ★ **Relais Médicis**

23 rue Racine *75006*

☎ 143260060 FAX 140468339

*In town centre*
*16 en suite (bth/shr) TV in all bedrooms STV Direct dial from all bedrooms Mini-bar in all bedrooms Room-safe Lift Night porter Full central heating Air conditioning in bedrooms Child discount available Languages spoken: English*

ROOMS: d 1100-1595FF
CARDS: ● ■ ■ ● Travellers cheques

★ ★ ★ ★ **Relais St-Germain**

9 Carrefour de l'Odéon *75006*

☎ 143291205 FAX 146334530

*In town centre*
*22 en suite (bth/shr) (2 fmly) (2 with balcony) No smoking in 2 bedrooms TV in all bedrooms STV Radio in rooms Direct dial from all bedrooms Mini-bar in all bedrooms Room-safe Licensed Lift Night porter Full central heating Air conditioning in bedrooms V meals Last d 23.00hrs Languages spoken: English German Italian Portuguese & Spanish*

ROOMS: s 1290FF; d 1680-1980FF
MEALS: Full breakfast 75FF Lunch 130-220FFalc Dinner 130-220FFalc
CARDS: 💳 ■ ■ 🅓 Travellers cheques

### ★ ★ ★ Royal St-Germain
159 rue de Rennes 76006
☎ 144392626 FAX 145490923
(At Porte d'Orléans, follow Av de Gl Le Clerc until 'Place Deufert Rochereau'Then on the left Boulevard de Montparnasse until Rue de Rennes and the Hotel is just on the right, near MacDonalds)
Near river Forest area In town centre
43 en suite (bth/shr) (8 fmly) (4 with balcony) No smoking in 4 bedrooms TV in all bedrooms STV Radio in rooms Direct dial from all bedrooms Mini-bar in all bedrooms Room-safe Licensed Lift Night porter Full central heating Supervised Child discount available 12yrs Health Club(50 metres) Languages spoken: English German & Italian
ROOMS: (room only) d 400-990FF **Reductions over 1 night**
CARDS: 💳 ■ ■ 🅓 JCB

### ★ ★ ★ St-Beuve
9 rue St-Beuvé 75006
☎ 145482007 FAX 145486752
In town centre
23 en suite (bth/shr) (5 fmly) (6 with balcony) TV in all bedrooms STV Direct dial from all bedrooms Mini-bar in all bedrooms Licensed Lift Night porter Full central heating Child discount available Languages spoken: English German & Spanish
CARDS: 💳 ■ ■ Travellers cheques

### ★ ★ Hotel de St-Germain
50 rue du Four 75006
☎ 145489164 FAX 145484622
In town centre
30 en suite (bth/shr) (22 with balcony) TV in all bedrooms STV Direct dial from all bedrooms Mini-bar in all bedrooms Room-safe (charged) Licensed Lift Night porter Full central heating Languages spoken: English German Italian & Spanish
ROOMS: (room only) s 420-700FF; d 530-705FF
CARDS: 💳 ■ ■ 🅓 Travellers cheques

### ★ ★ ★ St-Gregoire
43 rue de l'Abbé Gregoire 75006
☎ 145482323 FAX 145483395
In town centre
20 en suite (bth/shr) (2 with balcony) TV in all bedrooms STV Direct dial from all bedrooms Licensed Lift Night porter Full central heating Air conditioning in bedrooms Languages spoken: English German Italian & Spanish
ROOMS: (room only) s 690-1090FF; d 890-1090FF
CARDS: 💳 ■ ■ 🅓 JCB Travellers cheques

### ★ ★ ★ Hotel des Sts-Pères
65 rue des Sts-Peres 75006
☎ 145445000 FAX 145449083
In town centre
39 en suite (bth/shr) TV in all bedrooms STV Direct dial from all bedrooms Mini-bar in all bedrooms Licensed Lift Night porter Full central heating Languages spoken: English German & Spanish
CARDS: 💳 ■ ■ Travellers cheques

### ★ ★ ★ ★ Victoria Palace
6 rue Blaise Désgoffé 75006
☎ 145443816 FAX 145492375
In town centre Near motorway
80 en suite (bth/shr) (2 fmly) (15 with balcony) TV in all bedrooms STV Radio in rooms Direct dial from all bedrooms Mini-bar in all bedrooms Licensed Lift Night porter Full central heating Air conditioning in bedrooms Covered parking available (charged) Child discount available 12yrs Languages spoken: German & Spanish
CARDS: 💳 ■ ■ 🅓 Travellers cheques

7TH ARRONDISSEMENT

### ★ ★ ★ Hotel Académie Paris
32 rue des St-Pères 75007
☎ 145498000 FAX 145498010
(located in the St-Germain-des-Prés area of Paris)
In town centre
33 en suite (bth/shr) (10 fmly) (1 with balcony) No smoking in 19 bedrooms TV in all bedrooms STV Direct dial from all bedrooms Mini-bar in all bedrooms Room-safe Lift Night porter Full central heating Air conditioning in bedrooms Open parking available (charged) Covered parking available (charged) Supervised Child discount available 12yrs Last d 22.30hrs Languages spoken: English & Spanish
CARDS: 💳 ■ ■ 🅓 JCB Travellers cheques

### ★ ★ ★ Bourdonnais
111 av de la Bourdonnais 75007
☎ 147054542 FAX 145557554
Near river In town centre
60 en suite (bth/shr) (20 fmly) (10 with balcony) TV in all bedrooms STV Radio in rooms Direct dial from all bedrooms Mini-bar in 6 bedrooms Room-safe Licensed Lift Night porter Full central heating Air conditioning in bedrooms Child discount available Open terrace Languages spoken: English, German & Spanish
CARDS: 💳 ■ ■ 🅓 JCB Travellers cheques

### ★ ★ ★ Hotel Cayre
4 bd Raspail 75007
☎ 145443888 FAX 145449873
Near river In town centre
118 en suite (bth/shr) TV in all bedrooms Direct dial from all bedrooms Mini-bar in all bedrooms Licensed Lift Night porter Child discount available 12yrs Languages spoken: English Italian & Spanish
CARDS: 💳 ■ ■ 🅓 Travellers cheques

### ★ ★ ★ Eiffel Park Hotel (Best Western)
17b rue Améilie 75007
☎ 145551001 FAX 147052868
In town centre
36 en suite (bth/shr) (4 with balcony) TV in all bedrooms STV Radio in rooms Direct dial from all bedrooms Mini-bar in all bedrooms Room-safe (charged) Licensed Lift Night porter Full central heating Air conditioning in bedrooms Child discount available 12yrs Open terrace Languages spoken: English, Spanish & German
CARDS: 💳 ■ ■ 🅓 JCB Travellers cheques

### ★ ★ ★ Elysées Maubourg
35 bd de Latour-Maubourg 75007
☎ 145561078 FAX 147056508
In town centre

contd.

*30 en suite (bth/shr) (1 with balcony) TV in all bedrooms Direct dial from all bedrooms Mini-bar in all bedrooms Licensed Lift Night porter Full central heating Child discount available 12yrs Sauna Open terrace Languages spoken: English*
CARDS: ● ■ ⚏ ⚏ Travellers cheques

### ★ ★ ★ Hotel Lénox
9 rue de l'Université *75007*
☎ 142961095 FAX 142615283
Near river In town centre Near motorway
*34 en suite (bth/shr) (4 fmly) (5 with balcony) TV in all bedrooms STV Radio in rooms Direct dial from all bedrooms Licensed Lift Night porter Full central heating No children Languages spoken: English, German & Japanese*
CARDS: ● ■ ⚏ ⚏ JCB Travellers cheques

### ★ ★ ★ ★ Hotel Montalembert
3 rue de Montalembert *75007*
☎ 145496868 FAX 145496949
(located on the left bank, just off the blvd St Germain, on the rue du Bac, not far from the Musée d'Orsay)
In town centre
*56 en suite (bth/shr) TV in all bedrooms STV Direct dial from all bedrooms Mini-bar in all bedrooms Room-safe Licensed Lift Night porter Full central heating Air conditioning in bedrooms Covered terrace Last d 22.30hrs Languages spoken: English, Spanish, German & Italian*
ROOMS: (room only) s fr 1250FF; d fr 2300FF **Reductions over 1 night**
MEALS: Continental breakfast 60FF Lunch 250-320FFalc Dinner 250-320FFalc✱
CARDS: ● ■ ⚏ ⚏ JCB Travellers cheques

### ★ ★ Hotel du Nevers
83 rue Bac *75007*
☎ 145446130 FAX 142222947
Near river In town centre Near motorway
*11 en suite (bth/shr) (2 with balcony) TV in all bedrooms Direct dial from all bedrooms Mini-bar in all bedrooms Night porter Full central heating Open terrace Languages spoken: English*
ROOMS: (room only) s fr 455FF; d 460-540FF

### ★ ★ ★ Hotel St-Romain
5 rue St-Roch *75001*
☎ 142603170 FAX 142601069
Near river In town centre
*34 en suite (bth/shr) (10 fmly) TV in all bedrooms STV Direct dial from all bedrooms Mini-bar in all bedrooms Room-safe Licensed Lift Night porter Full central heating Child discount available 12yrs Languages spoken: English, Italian & Spanish*
ROOMS: (room only) s 650-1200FF; d 750-1200FF
**Reductions over 1 night**
CARDS: ● ■ ⚏ ⚏ JCB Travellers cheques

### ★ ★ ★ Hotel de Saxe
9 Villa de Saxe *75007*
☎ 144497840 FAX 147838547
In town centre
*49 en suite (bth/shr) (7 fmly) (10 with balcony) TV in all bedrooms STV Radio in rooms Direct dial from all bedrooms Mini-bar in all bedrooms Room-safe Licensed Lift Night porter Full central heating Open parking available Child discount available 12yrs Languages spoken: English & German*
CARDS: ● ■ ⚏ ⚏ JCB Travellers cheques

### ★ ★ Solférino
91 rue de Lille *75017*
☎ 147058554 FAX 145555116
Near river In town centre
*Closed 21 Dec-3 Jan*
*33 rms (22 bth 5 shr) (1 fmly) (4 with balcony) Lift Night porter Full central heating Languages spoken: English*
CARDS: ● ⚏ Travellers cheques

### ★ ★ ★ Hotel Thoumieux
79 rue St-Dominique *75007*
☎ 147054975 FAX 147053696
Near river In town centre
*Closed 1st May*
*10 en suite (bth/shr) (3 fmly) TV in all bedrooms Radio in rooms Direct dial from all bedrooms Night porter Full central heating V meals Last d 24.00hrs Languages spoken: English German & Spanish*
CARDS: ● ■ ⚏ Eurocard

### ★ ★ ★ Tourville
16 av de Tourville *75007*
☎ 147056262 FAX 147054390
(situated on the Left Bank between the Invalides, the Rodin Museum and the Eiffel Tower)
In town centre
*30 en suite (bth/shr) (3 fmly) (3 with balcony) TV in all bedrooms STV Direct dial from all bedrooms Licensed Lift Night porter Full central heating Air conditioning in bedrooms Child discount available 12yrs Languages spoken: English, German & Spanish*
CARDS: ● ■ ⚏ ⚏ JCB Travellers cheques

### ★ ★ Hotel de Turenne
20 av de Tourville *75007*
☎ 147059992 FAX 145560604
In town centre
*34 en suite (bth/shr) (3 fmly) TV in all bedrooms STV Direct dial from all bedrooms Licensed Lift Night porter Full central heating Languages spoken: English Dutch German & Spanish*
CARDS: ● ■ ⚏ ⚏ Travellers cheques

### ★ ★ ★ Université
22 r de l'Université *75007*
☎ 142610939 FAX 142604084
Near river In town centre
*27 rms (19 bth 6 shr) No smoking on premises TV in all bedrooms STV Direct dial from all bedrooms Mini-bar in 15 bedrooms Room-safe Licensed Lift Night porter Full central heating Air conditioning in bedrooms Languages spoken: English*
CARDS: ● ■ ⚏ Travellers cheques

## 8TH ARRONDISSEMENT

### ★ ★ Hotel Amsterdam
53 rue d'Amsterdam *75008*
☎ 148747974 FAX 148783726
In town centre
*58 rms (2 fmly) TV in all bedrooms STV Radio in rooms Direct dial from all bedrooms Lift Night porter Full central heating Child discount available 12yrs Open terrace Languages spoken: English*
CARDS: ● ■ ⚏ ⚏ Travellers cheques

**★ ★ ★ ★ Beau Manoir Best Western** (Best Western)
6 rue de l'Arcade *75008*
☎ 142660307 FAX 142680300
In town centre  Near motorway
*32 en suite (bth/shr)  32 rooms in annexe  (11 fmly)  TV in all
bedrooms  STV  Radio in rooms  Direct dial from all bedrooms
Mini-bar in all bedrooms  Room-safe (charged)  Licensed  Lift
Night porter  Full central heating  Air conditioning in bedrooms
Open parking available  Child discount available 12yrs
Languages spoken: English German & Spanish*
CARDS: ●● ■■ ✘✘ Ⓓ Travellers cheques

**★ ★ ★ Hotel de Berne**
37 rue de Berne *75008*
☎ 143870892 FAX 143870893
In town centre
*38 en suite (bth)  (6 fmly)  No smoking in 15 bedrooms  TV in all
bedrooms  STV  Radio in rooms  Direct dial from all bedrooms
Licensed  Lift  Night porter  Full central heating  Air
conditioning in bedrooms  Languages spoken: English Arabic
German & Italian*
CARDS: ●● ■■ ✘✘ Ⓓ Travellers cheques

**★ ★ ★ ★ Bristol**
112 rue du faubourg St-Honoré *75008*
☎ 153434300 FAX 153434301
In town centre
*180 en suite (bth/shr)  TV in all bedrooms  STV  Radio in rooms
Direct dial from all bedrooms  Mini-bar in all bedrooms  Room-
safe  Licensed  Lift  Night porter  Full central heating  Air
conditioning in bedrooms  Open parking available  Covered
parking available  Supervised  Child discount available 12yrs
Indoor swimming pool (heated)  Sauna  Solarium  Gym
Languages spoken: English German Italian & Spanish*
ROOMS: (room only)  s 2800-3150FF;  d 3800-4200FF
CARDS: ●● ■■ ✘✘ Ⓓ Travellers cheques

**★ ★ ★ ★ Hotel Châteaubriand**
6 rue Châteaubriand *75008*
☎ 140760050 FAX 140760922
In town centre
*28 en suite (bth/shr)  No smoking in 5 bedrooms  TV in all
bedrooms  Direct dial from all bedrooms  Mini-bar in all
bedrooms  Licensed  Lift  Night porter  Air conditioning in
bedrooms  Child discount available 12yrs  Languages spoken:
English Italian & Spanish*
CARDS: ●● ■■ ✘✘ Ⓓ Travellers cheques

**★ ★ ★ Hotel Cordelia**
11 rue de Greffulhe *75008*
☎ 142654240 FAX 142651181
(Take the Peripherique, drive to Place dela Concorde, then to
the Madeleine. Behind the Madeleine take rue Tronchet, then
first street left, second right, then first right)
In town centre
*30 en suite (bth/shr)  TV available  STV  Radio in rooms  Direct
dial from all bedrooms  Mini-bar in all bedrooms  Licensed  Lift
Night porter  Full central heating  Languages spoken: English
German & Spanish*
ROOMS: (room only)  s 710-780FF;  d 780-890FF
CARDS: ●● ■■ ✘✘ Ⓓ

**★ ★ ★ ★ Hotel de Crillon**
10 pl de la Concorde *75008*
☎ 144711500 FAX 144711502
A legendary Palace in the Place de la Concorde, just a few
steps from the Champs-Elysées. A masterpiece of 18th-century

architecture this hotel always provides its guests with the
highest level of personalised service. Luxurious rooms and
suites include, the renowned Leonard Bernstein and
Presidential apartments, successfully combining the elegance
of authentic tradition and efficiency of todays business needs.
Near river  In town centre
*160 en suite (bth/shr)  (3 with balcony)  TV in all bedrooms  STV
Direct dial from all bedrooms  Mini-bar in all bedrooms  Room-
safe  Licensed  Lift  Night porter  Full central heating  Air
conditioning in bedrooms  Open parking available  Covered
parking available  Child discount available 2yrs  Gym  Open
terrace  Last d 22.30pm  Languages spoken: English German
Italian Japanese & Spanish*
ROOMS: (room only)  s 2950-3450FF;  d 3500-4300FF
MEALS: Continental breakfast 180FF  Lunch 280-650FF
Dinner 280-650FF
CARDS: ●● ■■ ✘✘ Ⓓ

**★ ★ ★ Hotel Matignon**
3 rue de Ponthieu *75008*
☎ 142257301 FAX 142560139
(between Arc de Triomphe & Concorde near the roundabout
with the Champs Elysées)
In town centre
*25 en suite (bth/shr)  (4 fmly)  (4 with balcony)  TV in all
bedrooms  STV  Direct dial from all bedrooms  Mini-bar in all
bedrooms  Room-safe  Licensed  Lift  Night porter  Full central
heating  Air conditioning in bedrooms  Languages spoken:
English Italian & Spanish*
CARDS: ●● ■■ ✘✘ Ⓓ Travellers cheques

**★ ★ ★ Hotel la Fléche d'Or**
29 rue d'Amsterdam *75008*
☎ 148740686 FAX 148740604
(in centre of Paris take direction of the Opera House then
towards St Lazare Stn and rue d'Amsterdam)
In town centre
*61 en suite (bth/shr)  (2 fmly)  (2 with balcony)  No smoking in
15 bedrooms  TV in all bedrooms  STV  Direct dial from all
bedrooms  Mini-bar in all bedrooms  Room-safe (charged)
Licensed  Lift  Night porter  Full central heating  Air
conditioning in bedrooms  Child discount available 12yrs
Languages spoken: English, German, Italian & Spanish*
CARDS: ■■ Ⓓ

**★ ★ ★ Hotel L'Horset St Augustin**
20 rue Roquépine *75008*
☎ 142681164 FAX 142681163
(200m from St Augustin Church & close to the Elysée Palace)
In town centre
*34 en suite (bth/shr)  TV in all bedrooms  STV  Direct dial from
all bedrooms  Mini-bar in all bedrooms  Licensed  Lift  Night
porter  Full central heating  Child discount available 12yrs
Languages spoken: English & Spanish*
CARDS: ●● ■■ ✘✘ Ⓓ JCB Travellers cheques

**★ ★ ★ ★ Hotel L'Horset Washington**
43 rue Washington *75008*
☎ 149539442 FAX 149539443
In town centre
*17 en suite (bth/shr)  TV in all bedrooms  Radio in rooms  Direct
dial from all bedrooms  Mini-bar in all bedrooms  Room-safe
(charged)  Licensed  Lift  Night porter  Full central heating
Child discount available 12yrs  Languages spoken: English &
German*
CARDS: ●● ■■ ✘✘ Ⓓ JCB Travellers cheques

★ ★ ★ ★ **Hotel Lancaster**
7 rue de Berri
☎ 140764076 FAX 140764000
*60 en suite (bth/shr) (4 fmly) (9 with balcony) TV in all bedrooms STV Direct dial from all bedrooms Mini-bar in all bedrooms Room-safe (charged) Lift Night porter Full central heating Air conditioning in bedrooms Open parking available (charged) Covered parking available (charged) Supervised Sauna Gym Open terrace Covered terrace V meals Languages spoken: English, German & Spanish*
CARDS: ●● ■■ ■■ ID Travellers cheques

★ ★ ★ **Hotel Lido** (Best Western)
4 passage de la Madeleine *75008*
☎ 142662737 FAX 142666123
In town centre Near motorway
*32 en suite (bth/shr) 32 rooms in annexe (11 fmly) TV in all bedrooms STV Radio in rooms Direct dial from all bedrooms Mini-bar in all bedrooms Room-safe (charged) Licensed Lift Night porter Full central heating Air conditioning in bedrooms Child discount available 12yrs Languages spoken: English German & Spanish*
CARDS: ●● ■■ ■■ ID JCB Travellers cheques

★ ★ ★ **Mayflower**
3 rue Châteaubriand *75008*
☎ 145625746 FAX 142563238
In town centre
*24 en suite (bth/shr) (4 with balcony) TV in all bedrooms STV Direct dial from all bedrooms Mini-bar in all bedrooms Licensed Lift Night porter Full central heating Child discount available 12yrs Languages spoken: English Dutch German & Italian*
CARDS: ●● ■■ ■■ Travellers cheques

★ ★ ★ **New Hotel Roblin**
6 rue Chauveau-Lagarde *75008*
☎ 144712080 FAX 142651949
In town centre
*77 en suite (bth/shr) (8 fmly) (2 with balcony) TV in all bedrooms STV Radio in rooms Direct dial from all bedrooms Mini-bar in all bedrooms Licensed Lift Night porter Full central heating Air conditioning in bedrooms Child discount available 12yrs V meals Last d 22.00hrs Languages spoken: English Arabic Italian & Spanish*
CARDS: ●● ■■ ■■ ID JCB

★ ★ ★ **L'Orangerie**
9 rue de Constantinople *75008*
☎ 142220751 FAX 145221649
In town centre
*29 en suite (bth/shr) (3 fmly) (10 with balcony) TV in all bedrooms STV Direct dial from all bedrooms Licensed Lift Night porter Full central heating Supervised Child discount available 12yrs Languages spoken: English, Arabic, German, Italian & Spanish*
CARDS: ●● ■■ ■■ ID Travellers cheques

★ ★ ★ ★ **Plaza-Athénée**
av Montaigne *75008*
☎ 153676665 FAX 153676666
Near river In town centre
*205 rms No smoking in 42 bedrooms TV in all bedrooms STV Radio in rooms Direct dial from all bedrooms Mini-bar in all bedrooms Licensed Lift Night porter Full central heating Air*

*conditioning in bedrooms Child discount available 12yrs Gym V meals Last d 22.30hrs Languages spoken: English, German, Spanish, Italian*
CARDS: ●● ■■ ■■ ID Travellers cheques

★ ★ ★ ★ **Residentiale Chambiges**
8 rue Chambiges *75008*
☎ 144318383 FAX 140709551
In town centre
*33 en suite (bth/shr) TV in all bedrooms STV Direct dial from all bedrooms Mini-bar in all bedrooms Room-safe Licensed Lift Night porter Full central heating Air conditioning in bedrooms Child discount available 12yrs Open terrace Languages spoken: English*
CARDS: ●● ■■ ■■ ID Travellers cheques

★ ★ ★ **Hotel Rochambeau**
4 rue La Boötie *75008*
☎ 142652754 FAX 142660381
In town centre
*50 en suite (bth/shr) TV in all bedrooms Direct dial from 53 bedrooms Mini-bar in 53 bedrooms Licensed Lift Child discount available 12yrs Languages spoken: English Italian & Spanish*
CARDS: ●● ■■ ■■ ID Travellers cheques

★ ★ ★ ★ **Royal**
33 av Friedland *75008*
☎ 143590814 FAX 145636992
In town centre
*58 en suite (bth/shr) (12 fmly) (12 with balcony) No smoking in 10 bedrooms TV in all bedrooms STV Radio in rooms Direct dial from all bedrooms Mini-bar in all bedrooms Licensed Lift Night porter Full central heating Air conditioning in bedrooms Open parking available (charged) Covered parking available (charged) Supervised Child discount available 12yrs Languages spoken: English German & Spanish*
CARDS: ●● ■■ ■■ ID JCB Travellers cheques

★ ★ ★ ★ **Hotel Royal Alma**
35 rue Jean Goujon *75008*
☎ 153936300 FAX 145636864
Near river In town centre
*64 en suite (bth/shr) (16 fmly) (19 with balcony) No smoking in 7 bedrooms TV in all bedrooms STV Radio in rooms Direct dial from all bedrooms Mini-bar in all bedrooms Room-safe Licensed Lift Night porter Full central heating Air conditioning in bedrooms Child discount available 12yrs Last d 23.30hrs Languages spoken: English Italian & Spanish*
CARDS: ●● ■■ ■■ ID Travellers cheques

★ ★ ★ ★ **Hotel San Regis**
12 rue Jean Goujon *75008*
☎ 144951616
In town centre
*44 en suite (bth/shr) (6 fmly) (3 with balcony) TV in all bedrooms STV Radio in rooms Direct dial from all bedrooms Mini-bar in all bedrooms Room-safe Licensed Lift Night porter Full central heating Air conditioning in bedrooms Last d 22.00hrs Languages spoken: English German Italian & Spanish*
ROOMS: (room only) s 1800-2400FF; d 2400-3200FF
MEALS: Continental breakfast 120FF Lunch fr 220FF&alc Dinner 250-380FFalc
CARDS: ●● ■■ ■■ ID JCB Travellers cheques

**★ ★ ★ ★ Sofitel Paris Arc De Triomphe**
14 rue Beaujon *75008*
☎ 153895050 FAX 153895051
In town centre
*135 en suite (bth) (21 fmly) (10 with balcony) No smoking in 80 bedrooms TV in all bedrooms STV Direct dial from all bedrooms Mini-bar in all bedrooms Licensed Lift Night porter Full central heating Air conditioning in bedrooms Bicycle rental Last d 22.30hrs Languages spoken: English, German, Italian, Portuguese & Russian*
CARDS: ●● ■■ ⅏ ⅏

**★ ★ ★ ★ Sofitel Paris Champs-Elysées**
8 rue Jean Goujon *75008*
☎ 140746464 FAX 140746499
In town centre
*40 en suite (bth) (2 with balcony) No smoking in 14 bedrooms TV in all bedrooms Direct dial from all bedrooms Mini-bar in all bedrooms Licensed Lift Night porter Full central heating Air conditioning in bedrooms Open parking available (charged) Covered parking available (charged) Child discount available 12yrs Open terrace V meals Languages spoken: English, Brazilian, German & Spanish*
CARDS: ●● ■■ ⅏ ⅏

**★ ★ ★ ★ De la Tremoille**
14 r La Tremoille *75008*
☎ 147233420 FAX 140700108
In town centre
*107 en suite (bth/shr) (36 with balcony) TV in all bedrooms STV Radio in rooms Direct dial from all bedrooms Mini-bar in all bedrooms Room-safe Licensed Lift Night porter Full central heating Air conditioning in bedrooms Child discount available 12yrs Last d 22.30hrs Languages spoken: English Italian & Spanish*
ROOMS: (room only) s 1990-2290FF; d 2450-2750FF
MEALS: Continental breakfast 120FF Lunch 220FF Dinner 220FF
CARDS: ●● ■■ ⅏ ⅏ JCB Travellers cheques

**★ ★ ★ ★ Vernet**
25 rue Vernet *75008*
☎ 144319800 FAX 144318569
In town centre Near motorway
*51 en suite (bth/shr) (12 with balcony) TV in all bedrooms STV Radio in rooms Direct dial from all bedrooms Mini-bar in all bedrooms Room-safe Licensed Lift Night porter Full central heating Air conditioning in bedrooms Open parking available (charged) Covered parking available (charged) Supervised Child discount available 12yrs Indoor swimming pool (heated) Squash Sauna Jacuzzi/spa Last d 21.00hrs Languages spoken: English German Italian & Spanish*
ROOMS: (room only) s 1950-2300FF; d 2300-2900FF
**Reductions over 1 night Special breaks**
MEALS: Continental breakfast 130FF Lunch 330-480FF&alc Dinner 530-840FF&alc
CARDS: ●● ■■ ⅏ ⅏ Travellers cheques

**★ ★ ★ ★ Hotel Waldorf-Madelèine**
12 bd Malesherbes *75008*
☎ 142657206 FAX 140071045
In town centre
*45 en suite (bth/shr) TV in all bedrooms Direct dial from all bedrooms Mini-bar in all bedrooms Licensed Lift Night porter Air conditioning in bedrooms Child discount available 12yrs Languages spoken: English Italian & Spanish*
CARDS: ●● ■■ ⅏ ⅏ Travellers cheques

**★ ★ ★ ★ Hotel le Warwick**
5 rue de Berri *75008*
☎ 145631411 FAX 143590098
In town centre
*147 en suite (bth/shr) (28 with balcony) No smoking in 26 bedrooms TV in all bedrooms STV Radio in rooms Direct dial from all bedrooms Mini-bar in all bedrooms Room-safe Licensed Lift Night porter Full central heating Air conditioning in bedrooms Open parking available (charged) Covered parking available (charged) Supervised Child discount available 12yrs Jazz Evening once a month in restaurant V meals Last d 22.30hrs Languages spoken: English Arabic German Italian & Spanish*
MEALS: Continental breakfast 135FF Lunch fr 260FF&alc Dinner fr 260FF&alc✱
CARDS: ●● ■■ ⅏ ⅏ JCB Travellers cheques

**9TH ARRONDISSEMENT**

**★ ★ ★ Anjou-Lafayette** (Best Western)
4 rue Riboutte, Square Montholon *75009*
☎ 142468344 FAX 148000897
In town centre
*39 en suite (bth/shr) (5 fmly) TV in all bedrooms STV Radio in rooms Direct dial from all bedrooms Mini-bar in all bedrooms Licensed Lift Night porter Full central heating Child discount available 12yrs Languages spoken: English Italian Portuguese & Spanish*
CARDS: ●● ■■ ⅏ ⅏ Travellers cheques

**★ ★ ★ Hotel Blanche Fontaine**
34 rue Fontaine *75009*
☎ 145267232 FAX 142810552
In town centre
*49 en suite (bth/shr) (10 fmly) (12 with balcony) No smoking in 4 bedrooms TV in all bedrooms STV Radio in rooms Direct dial from all bedrooms Licensed Lift Night porter Full central heating Covered parking available (charged) Supervised Child discount available Open terrace Languages spoken: English German Italian & Spanish*
CARDS: ●● ■■ ⅏ ⅏ Travellers cheques

**★ ★ ★ Brébant**
32 bd Poissonnière *75009*
☎ 147702555 FAX 142466570
In town centre
*122 en suite (bth/shr) (22 fmly) TV in all bedrooms STV Radio in rooms Direct dial from all bedrooms Mini-bar in all bedrooms Licensed Lift Night porter Full central heating Child discount available 12yrs Last d 22.30hrs Languages spoken: English Italian Portuguese & Spanish*
CARDS: ●● ■■ ⅏ ⅏ Travellers cheques

**★ ★ ★ Hotel du Havre**
18 rue d'Amsterdam *75009*
☎ 142857274 FAX 148742239
In town centre Near motorway
*81 en suite (bth/shr) (15 fmly) (5 with balcony) No smoking in 10 bedrooms TV in all bedrooms STV Direct dial from all bedrooms Room-safe Licensed Lift Night porter Full central heating Child discount available 12yrs Languages spoken: English, German & Spanish*
CARDS: ●● ■■ ⅏ ⅏ Travellers cheques

### ★ ★ ★ Hotel Marena
27 rue de la Tour d'Auvergne *75009*
☎ 148780133 FAX 140230711
In town centre
*36 en suite (bth/shr) TV in all bedrooms STV Direct dial from all bedrooms Lift Night porter Full central heating Languages spoken: English German Italian & Spanish*

### ★ ★ ★ Hotel de Morny
4 rue de Liège *75009*
☎ 142854792 FAX 140164484
Forest area In town centre
*41 en suite (bth/shr) (5 fmly) (2 with balcony) TV in all bedrooms Direct dial from all bedrooms Mini-bar in all bedrooms Licensed Lift Full central heating Child discount available 12yrs Languages spoken: English & Spanish*
CARDS: 💳 ■ 💳 💳 Travellers cheques

### ★ ★ Hotel Parrotel Paris Montholon
11 bis rue Pierre Sémard *75009*
☎ 148782894 FAX 142801115
In town centre
*46 en suite (bth/shr) TV in all bedrooms STV Radio in rooms Direct dial from all bedrooms Lift Night porter Full central heating Child discount available 10yrs Languages spoken: English & German*
CARDS: 💳 ■ 💳 💳 Travellers cheques

### ★ ★ Hotel Riboutte Lafayette
5 rue Riboutté *75009*
☎ 147706236 FAX 148009150
In town centre
*24 en suite (bth/shr) TV in all bedrooms STV Direct dial from all bedrooms Lift Full central heating Child discount available 8yrs Languages spoken: English Arabic Italian*
CARDS: 💳 ■ 💳 Travellers cheques

### 10TH ARRONDISSEMENT

### ★ ★ Hotel Adix
30 rue Lucien Sampaix *75010*
☎ 142081974 FAX 142082728
In town centre
*39 rms (4 fmly) TV in all bedrooms Direct dial from all bedrooms Lift Night porter Full central heating Child discount available 12yrs Open terrace Languages spoken: English German & Italian*
CARDS: 💳 ■ 💳 💳 Travellers cheques

### ★ ★ Climat de France
31 bd de Strasbourg *75010*
☎ 147702500 FAX 147703217
(City Centre near Place de la Republique)
In town centre Near motorway
*57 en suite (bth/shr) (4 fmly) No smoking in 15 bedrooms TV in all bedrooms Direct dial from all bedrooms Lift Night porter Full central heating Open terrace Languages spoken: English, Italian & Spanish*
CARDS: 💳 💳

### ★ ★ Français
13 rue du 8 Mai 1945 *75010*
☎ 140359414 FAX 140355540
(in town centre, facing East Railway Station)
This establishment is situated in a lively area, not far from all the shops. Over the years it has acquired a faithful following amongst an international clientele and features well equipped, comfortable bedrooms with extensive facilities.

**Francais**

In town centre
*71 en suite (bth/shr) (4 fmly) (20 with balcony) TV in all bedrooms STV Radio in rooms Direct dial from all bedrooms Mini-bar in all bedrooms Room-safe Licensed Lift Night porter Full central heating Child discount available 16yrs Languages spoken: English German Italian & Spanish*
ROOMS: (room only) s 405-485FF; d 450-490FF
CARDS: 💳 ■ 💳 💳 JCB Travellers cheques

### ★ ★ Hotel Frantour Château-Landon
1/3 rue Château-Landon *75010*
☎ 144653333 FAX 144653320
In town centre
*160 en suite (bth/shr) No smoking in 29 bedrooms TV in all bedrooms STV Radio in rooms Direct dial from all bedrooms Room-safe Licensed Lift Night porter Full central heating Air conditioning in bedrooms Child discount available 11yrs V meals Last d 23.00hrs Languages spoken: English German & Spanish*
CARDS: 💳 ■ 💳 💳 JCB Travellers cheques

### ★ ★ ★ Pavillon
38 rue de l'Echiquier *75010*
☎ 142469275 FAX 142470397
(100m from "Grand Boulevards" district)
In town centre
*92 en suite (bth/shr) (12 fmly) No smoking in 14 bedrooms TV in all bedrooms STV Radio in rooms Direct dial from all bedrooms Mini-bar in all bedrooms Licensed Lift Night porter Full central heating Air conditioning in bedrooms Child discount available 12yrs V meals Last d 21.30hrs Languages spoken: English German Italian & Spanish*
CARDS: 💳 ■ 💳 💳 Travellers cheques

### ★ ★ ★ Hotel de Rocroy
13 rue Rocroy *75010*
☎ 12811568 FAX 18783081
In town centre Near motorway
*55 en suite (bth/shr) No smoking in 15 bedrooms TV in all bedrooms STV Radio in rooms Direct dial from all bedrooms Licensed Lift Night porter Full central heating Child discount available 12yrs Languages spoken: English & Portugue*
CARDS: 💳 ■ 💳 💳 Travellers cheques

### 11TH ARRONDISSEMENT

### ★ ★ ★ All Suite Hotel Home Plaza
74 rue Amelot *75011*
☎ 140212223 FAX 147008240
(A1 Nord Porte de Vincennes Cours de Vincennes then rue Faubourg St-Antoine, until Place de la Bastille and then take Boulevard Beaumarchais)

In town centre
*288 en suite (bth) (8 fmly) No smoking in 18 bedrooms TV in all bedrooms STV Direct dial from all bedrooms Mini-bar in 44 bedrooms Room-safe (charged) Licensed Lift Night porter Full central heating Air conditioning in bedrooms Open parking available (charged) Covered parking available (charged) Supervised Child discount available 12yrs Open terrace V meals Last d 23.00hrs Languages spoken: English Arabic German Italian & Spanish*
ROOMS: s 415-1326FF; d 476-1939FF
MEALS: Full breakfast 78FF Lunch 80-170FF&alc Dinner 80-170FF&alc
CARDS: ● ■ ■ ● JCB, Eurocard

★ ★ ★ ★ *Holiday Inn Paris République*
10 pl de la Reépublique *75011*
☎ 143554434 FAX 147003234
In town centre
*318 en suite (bth/shr) (80 fmly) No smoking in 160 bedrooms TV in all bedrooms STV Radio in rooms Direct dial from all bedrooms Mini-bar in all bedrooms Room-safe (charged) Licensed Lift Night porter Full central heating Air conditioning in bedrooms Child discount available 12 Open terrace Last d 22.30hrs Languages spoken: English Arabic Dutch German Italian Spanish*
CARDS: ● ■ ■ ● JCB Travellers cheques

★ ★ ★ *Home Plaza St Antoine*
289 bis rue de Faubourg, St Antoine *75011*
☎ 140094000 FAX 140091155
In town centre
*89 en suite (bth) (15 fmly) No smoking in 6 bedrooms TV in all bedrooms STV Direct dial from all bedrooms Mini-bar in all bedrooms Room-safe (charged) Licensed Lift Night porter Full central heating Air conditioning in bedrooms Open parking available (charged) Covered parking available (charged) Supervised Child discount available Open terrace Languages spoken: English, German, Italian & Spanish*
CARDS: ● ■ ■ ●

★ ★ *Hotel de Méricourt*
50 rue de la Folie-Méricourt *75011*
☎ 143387363 FAX 143386613
(exit Périphérique at Porte de Vincennes)
In town centre
*28 en suite (bth) No smoking in 7 bedrooms TV in all bedrooms Radio in rooms Direct dial from all bedrooms Lift Night porter Full central heating Supervised No children Special arrangements for AA Guide users Languages spoken: English*
ROOMS: s 400-570FF; d 480-700FF **Special breaks**
CARDS: ● ■ ■ Travellers cheques

★ ★ ★ *New Hotel Candide*
3 rue Petion *75011*
☎ 143790233 FAX 143790688
In town centre
*48 en suite (bth/shr) TV in all bedrooms STV Radio in rooms Direct dial from all bedrooms Mini-bar in all bedrooms Lift Night porter Full central heating Child discount available 12yrs Languages spoken: English Arabic German Italian & Spanish*
CARDS: ● ■ ■ ●

## 12TH ARRONDISSEMENT

★ ★ ★ *Hotel Claret*
44 bd de Bercy *75012*
☎ 146284131 FAX 149280929
In town centre
*52 en suite (bth/shr) (1 fmly) No smoking in 10 bedrooms TV in all bedrooms Licensed Lift Night porter Full central heating Open parking available (charged) Covered parking available (charged) Child discount available 12yrs Open terrace Last d 23.00hrs Languages spoken: English German & Spanish*

★ ★ *Climat de France*
9 rue de Reuilly *75012*
☎ 143700404 FAX 143709653
(nr Place de la Nation)
In town centre
*43 en suite (bth/shr) (11 with balcony) TV in all bedrooms STV Direct dial from all bedrooms Lift Night porter Full central heating Open parking available (charged) Covered parking available (charged) Child discount available Open terrace Covered terrace Languages spoken: English, Spanish & Arabic*
ROOMS: (room only) s 435FF; d 440FF
CARDS: ● ■ ■ ● Travellers cheques

★ ★ *Hotel Frantour Paris-Lyon*
2 pl Louis-Armand *75012*
☎ 143448484 FAX 143474194
(From the East ring road, take the Bercy exit and follow the Gare de Lyon direction until the Frantour Paris-Lyon Hotel)
Near river Forest area In town centre Near motorway
*315 en suite (bth) (2 with balcony) TV in all bedrooms STV Radio in rooms Licensed Lift Night porter Languages spoken: German Italian & Spanish*
CARDS: ● ■ ■ ● JCB Travellers cheques

*Luxor Bastille Hotel*
22 r Moreau *75012*
☎ 143433482 FAX 144758073
(from Porte d'Italie towards place d'Italie - place de la Bastille, then rue de Charenton and rue Moreau is 1st on right)
In town centre Near motorway
*30 rms (20 bth/shr) (5 fmly) TV in all bedrooms STV Full central heating Child discount available 10yrs Languages spoken: English*
CARDS: ● ■ ■ ●

★ ★ ★ *Hotel Lyon Bastille*
3 rue Parrot *75012*
☎ 143434152 FAX 143438116
(travel east on Périphérique, leave at Porte de Vincennes & follow av de la Porte de Vincennes & cont to Place de la Nation. At rdbt turn onto Blvd Diderot, continue, then turn right at Av Daumesnil & rue Parrot just a bit further on left)
In town centre
*48 en suite (bth/shr) (5 fmly) (7 with balcony) TV in all bedrooms Radio in rooms Room-safe (charged) Licensed Lift Night porter Full central heating Child discount available 12yrs Languages spoken: English,German,Italian,Spanish*
CARDS: ● ■ ■ ● JCB Travellers cheques

★ ★ ★ *Pavillon Bastille*
65 rue de Lyon *75012*
☎ 143436565 FAX 143439652
(street is opposite the Opeéra National de Paris)
Near river In town centre Near motorway
*25 en suite (bth/shr) (7 fmly) No smoking in 3 bedrooms TV in*
contd.

*all bedrooms STV Direct dial from all bedrooms Mini-bar in all bedrooms Room-safe Licensed Lift Night porter Full central heating Air conditioning in bedrooms Covered parking available (charged) Supervised Bicycle rental Open terrace Wine tasting,Thurs/Fri/Sat Wkly live entertainment Languages spoken: English & Japanese* CARDS: 💳 🏧 💳 Travellers cheques

### ★★★ Relais Mercure Nation
61 rue de la Voûte *75012*
☎ 143454138 FAX 143430411
In town centre
*47 rms (8 fmly) TV in all bedrooms Direct dial from all bedrooms Child discount available 12yrs Languages spoken: English* CARDS: 💳 🏧 💳 JCB Travellers cheques

### 13TH ARRONDISSEMENT

### ★★★ Holiday Inn Garden Court
21 rue de Tolbiac *75013*
☎ 145846161 FAX 145844338
(From the Ring Road exit 'Quai d'Ivry' or 'Bercy')
Near river Forest area In town centre Near motorway
*71 en suite (bth/shr) (2 fmly) No smoking in 52 bedrooms TV in all bedrooms STV Direct dial from all bedrooms Mini-bar in all bedrooms Licensed Lift Night porter Full central heating Air conditioning in bedrooms Open parking available (charged) Covered parking available (charged) Child discount available 12yrs Languages spoken: English, German & Spanish* ROOMS: (room only) s 740-1200FF; d 740-1300FF CARDS: 💳 🏧 💳 JCB Travellers cheques

### 14TH ARRONDISSEMENT

### ★★ Ariane Montparnasse
35 rue de la Sablière *75014*
☎ 145456713 FAX 145453949
(between Montparnasse and Porte d'Orléans - A6. Close to the metro Pernety - Alesia.)
In town centre
*30 en suite (bth/shr) (4 fmly) TV in all bedrooms Direct dial from all bedrooms Mini-bar in all bedrooms Lift Night porter Full central heating Child discount available 14yrs Languages spoken: English German Italian & Spanish* CARDS: 💳 🏧 💳 Travellers cheques

### ★★ Climat de France
55 rue de Plaisance *75014*
☎ 145428143 FAX 145429787
(near Montparnasse (TGV Station) and 'Parc des Expositions' of Porte de Versailles)
In town centre
*40 en suite (bth/shr) TV in all bedrooms Direct dial from all bedrooms Licensed Lift Night porter Full central heating Languages spoken: English & Spanish* CARDS: 💳 🏧

### ★★★ Forum Val de Loire
20 bis rue de la Gaité *75014*
☎ 140643737 FAX 140643749
In town centre
*14 en suite (bth/shr) (4 fmly) TV in all bedrooms STV Direct dial from all bedrooms Mini-bar in all bedrooms Room-safe Licensed Lift Night porter Full central heating Air conditioning in bedrooms Open parking available (charged) Child discount available 12yrs Last d 22.30hrs Languages spoken: English, German & Spanish*

ROOMS: (room only) s 700-950FF; d 700-950FF ✱
**Reductions over 1 night Special breaks**
MEALS: Continental breakfast 65FF Lunch fr 165FF&alc Dinner fr 165FF&alc✱
CARDS: 💳 🏧 💳 JCB Travellers cheques

### ★★ Hotel Istria
29 r Campagne-Première *75014*
☎ 143209182 FAX 143224845
In town centre
*26 en suite (bth/shr) TV in all bedrooms Direct dial from all bedrooms Room-safe Lift Night porter Full central heating Languages spoken: English* CARDS: 💳 🏧 💳 Travellers cheques

### ★★ Hotel la Mascotte
22 rue Hippolyte-Maindron *75014*
☎ 140445151 FAX 140445898
In town centre
*52 rms (3 fmly) TV in all bedrooms STV Direct dial from all bedrooms Lift Night porter Full central heating Open parking available (charged) Covered parking available (charged) Supervised Child discount available 12yrs Languages spoken: English* CARDS: 💳 🏧 💳 JCB Travellers cheques

### ★★★★ Meridien Montparnasse Paris
19 rue Ct-Réné Mouchotte *75014*
☎ 144364436 FAX 144364900
(from Périphériques exit at Porte d'Orléans, follow direction of Montparnasse towards Gare Montparnasse railway station, hotel behind railway station)
Near motorway
*953 en suite (bth/shr) TV in all bedrooms STV Radio in rooms Direct dial from all bedrooms Mini-bar in all bedrooms Licensed Lift Night porter Full central heating Air conditioning in bedrooms Open parking available (charged) Covered parking available (charged) Supervised Child discount available 12yrs V meals Languages spoken: English German Italian & Spanish* CARDS: 💳 🏧 💳 JCB

### ★★ Hotel Moulin Vert
74 rue du Moulin Vert *75014*
☎ 145436538 FAX 145430886
In town centre
*28 rms TV in all bedrooms Direct dial from all bedrooms Mini-bar in all bedrooms Lift Night porter Full central heating Child discount available 15yrs Languages spoken: English & Italian* CARDS: 💳 🏧 💳 Travellers cheques

### ★★ Hotel Primavera
147 ter rue d'Alésia *75014*
☎ 145420637 FAX 145424456
In town centre
*70 rms (7 fmly) TV in all bedrooms Radio in rooms Direct dial from all bedrooms Mini-bar in all bedrooms Lift Night porter Full central heating Open parking available (charged) Covered parking available (charged) Supervised Child discount available 12yrs Languages spoken: English* CARDS: 💳 🏧 💳 Travellers cheques

## 15TH ARRONDISSEMENT

★ ★ ★ **Ares** (Relais du Silence)
7 rue du Général-de-Larminat 75015
☎ 147347404 FAX 147344856
In town centre
42 en suite (bth/shr) (12 fmly) TV in all bedrooms STV Direct
dial from all bedrooms Mini-bar in all bedrooms Room-safe
Lift Night porter Full central heating Child discount available
12yrs Languages spoken: English German Italian & Spanish
CARDS: ●● ■■ ■■ ◉ Travellers cheques

★ ★ ★ **Hotel du Bailli de Suffren**
149 av de Suffren 75015
☎ 147345861 FAX 145677582
In town centre
25 en suite (bth/shr) TV in all bedrooms STV Direct dial from
all bedrooms Mini-bar in all bedrooms Room-safe Lift Night
porter Full central heating Child discount available 12yrs
Languages spoken: English German Portuguese & Spanish
CARDS: ●● ■■ ■■ ◉ Travellers cheques

★ ★ **Hotel Délos**
7 rue du Général-Beuret 75015
☎ 148282932 FAX 148288846
In town centre
43 rms (33 shr) (4 with balcony) TV in all bedrooms Lift Night
porter Full central heating Child discount available 14yrs
Languages spoken: English & Spanish
CARDS: ●● ■■ ■■ ◉ Travellers cheques

★ ★ **Hotel Grenelle**
140-142 bd de Corenelle 75015
☎ 145752654 FAX 145777394
In town centre
56 en suite (bth/shr) TV in all bedrooms STV Mini-bar in all
bedrooms Licensed Lift Night porter Child discount available
12yrs Languages spoken: English & Italian
CARDS: ●● ■■ ■■ ◉ Travellers cheques

★ ★ **Ibis Hotel Brancion "Expo"**
105 rue Brancion
☎ 142508600 FAX 142509963
71 en suite (bth/shr) No smoking in 10 bedrooms TV in all
bedrooms STV Direct dial from all bedrooms Lift Night porter
Full central heating Covered parking available (charged)
Supervised Child discount available 12yrs Languages spoken:
English, Italian & Spanish
CARDS: ●● ■■ ■■ ◉ Travellers cheques

★ ★ **Hotel Lécourbe** (Consort)
28 rue Lécourbe 75015
☎ 147344906 FAX 147346465
Near beach In town centre
47 en suite (bth/shr) (4 fmly) TV in all bedrooms STV Radio in
rooms Direct dial from all bedrooms Mini-bar in all bedrooms
Room-safe Lift Night porter Full central heating Supervised
Child discount available 12yrs Languages spoken: English
German & Italian
CARDS: ●● ■■ ■■ ◉ Travellers cheques

★ ★ ★ **Montcalm** (Best Western)
50 av Félix Faure 75015
☎ 145549727 FAX 145541505
Near river In town centre Near motorway
41 en suite (bth/shr) (1 fmly) TV in all bedrooms STV Radio in
rooms Direct dial from all bedrooms Mini-bar in all bedrooms

Room-safe Licensed Lift Night porter Full central heating
Child discount available 12yrs Open terrace Languages
spoken: English Arabic Chinese & German
CARDS: ●● ■■ ■■ ◉ Travellers cheques

★ ★ **Hotel Tour Eiffel**
11 rue Juge 75015
☎ 145782929 FAX 145786000
(on the Périphérique, take exit Porte de Sevres, then directon
Paris center. Follow the River Seine & right at the Aerian
Metro on the boulevard de Grenelle and right on rue de
Lournel and then fist left)
In town centre
40 en suite (bth/shr) (5 fmly) (5 with balcony) No smoking in
18 bedrooms TV in all bedrooms STV Direct dial from all
bedrooms Lift Night porter Full central heating Child discount
available 12yrs Open terrace Languages spoken: English,
German, Italian & Spanish
ROOMS: (room only) d 390-950FF
CARDS: ●● ■■ ■■ ◉ JCB Travellers cheques

## 16TH ARRONDISSEMENT

★ ★ ★ **Belmont**
30 rue Bassano 75016
☎ 153577500 FAX 147230970
In town centre
79 en suite (bth/shr) (5 fmly) (12 with balcony) TV in all
bedrooms STV Radio in rooms Direct dial from all bedrooms
Mini-bar in all bedrooms Room-safe Licensed Lift Night
porter Full central heating Child discount available 12yrs
Languages spoken: English Arabic Italian Portuguese &
Spanish
CARDS: ●● ■■ ■■ ◉ Travellers cheques

★ ★ ★ **Elysées Régencia** (Best Western)
41 av Marceau 75116
☎ 147204265 FAX 149520342
In town centre
41 en suite (bth/shr) (4 fmly) No smoking in 12 bedrooms TV
in all bedrooms STV Radio in rooms Direct dial from all
bedrooms Mini-bar in all bedrooms Room-safe Licensed Lift
Night porter Full central heating Air conditioning in bedrooms
Open parking available (charged) Covered parking available
(charged) Supervised Child discount available 12yrs
Languages spoken: English & Spanish
CARDS: ●● ■■ ■■ ◉ Travellers cheques

★ ★ **Hotel Étoile Maillot**
10 rue du Bois de Boulogne 75116
☎ 145004260 FAX 145005589
28 en suite (bth/shr) (1 fmly) (10 with balcony) TV in all
bedrooms STV Direct dial from all bedrooms Mini-bar in all
bedrooms Licensed Lift Night porter Full central heating
Child discount available 12yrs Languages spoken: English &
Spanish
CARDS: ●● ■■ ■■ ◉ Travellers cheques

★ ★ ★ **Holiday Inn Garden Court**
21 rue Gudin 75016
☎ 146519922 FAX 146510724
(close to Porte St Cloud & Parc des Princes)
In town centre
47 en suite (bth/shr) (7 fmly) (10 with balcony) No smoking in
14 bedrooms TV in all bedrooms STV Direct dial from all
bedrooms Mini-bar in all bedrooms Room-safe Licensed Lift
Night porter Full central heating Air conditioning in bedrooms
contd.

Supervised Child discount available 12yrs Languages spoken: English, German, Russian & Spanish
ROOMS: (room only) s 450-820FF; d 500-820FF
**Reductions over 1 night**
CARDS: ●● ■■ ▪▪ ⬤ Travellers cheques

★ ★ ★ *Hotel Résidence Imperiale* (Best Western)
155 av Malakoff *75116*
☎ 145002345 FAX 145018882
In town centre
*37 en suite (bth/shr) (5 fmly) No smoking in 2 bedrooms TV in all bedrooms STV Radio in rooms Direct dial from all bedrooms Mini-bar in all bedrooms Licensed Lift Night porter Full central heating Air conditioning in bedrooms Child discount available 12yrs Languages spoken: English German Italian & Spanish*
CARDS: ●● ■■ ⬤ Travellers cheques

★ ★ *Hotel Keppler*
12 rue Keppler *75116*
☎ 147206505 FAX 147230229
(near pl de l'Étoile Arc de Triumph)
In town centre
*49 en suite (bth/shr) TV in all bedrooms STV Direct dial from all bedrooms Room-safe Licensed Lift Night porter Full central heating Child discount available 10yrs Languages spoken: English & Spanish*
CARDS: ●● ■■ ▪▪ Travellers cheques

★ ★ *Kléber*
7 rue de Belloy *75116*
☎ 147238022 FAX 149520720
In town centre
*22 en suite (bth/shr) 17 rooms in annexe (4 fmly) (5 with balcony) No smoking in 6 bedrooms TV in all bedrooms STV Radio in rooms Direct dial from all bedrooms Mini-bar in all bedrooms Licensed Lift Night porter Full central heating Air conditioning in bedrooms Open parking available (charged) Covered parking available (charged) Supervised Languages spoken: English Arabic Hebrew Japanese & Spanish*
CARDS: ●● ■■ ▪▪ ⬤ JCB Travellers cheques

★ ★ *Au Palais de Chaillot*
35 av Raymond Poincaré *75116*
☎ 153700909 FAX 153700908
(leave the Périphérique at Porte Maillot in direction of Trocadero Avenues Malakoff then Av Raymond Poincaré)
Near river Near lake Forest area In town centre Near motorway
*28 en suite (bth/shr) (5 fmly) TV in all bedrooms STV Direct dial from all bedrooms Lift Night porter Full central heating Child discount available 12yrs Open terrace Languages spoken: English German Italian & Spanish*
CARDS: ●● ■■ ▪▪ ⬤ JCB Travellers cheques

★ ★ ★ *Le Parc Westin Démeure Hotel*
55-57 av Raymond Poincaré *75116*
☎ 144056666 FAX 144056600
(follow direction for Périphérique Ouest at Porte Maillot exit take avenue Raymond Poincaré, after Place V-Hugo continue straight ahead until reaching Le Parc on right)
Forest area In town centre Near motorway
*116 en suite (bth/shr) (3 fmly) No smoking in 32 bedrooms TV in all bedrooms STV Radio in rooms Direct dial from all bedrooms Mini-bar in all bedrooms Room-safe Licensed Lift Night porter Full central heating Air conditioning in bedrooms Child discount available 10yrs Gym Pool table Jacuzzi/spa*

Open terrace Last d 22.30hrs Languages spoken: English German Italian Portuguese Spanish
CARDS: ●● ■■ ▪▪ ⬤ JCB Travellers cheques

★ ★ ★ *Hotel Raphaël*
17 av Kléber *75116*
☎ 153643200 FAX 1453643201
(Hotel is by the Avenue Champs Elysées, and next to the Arc de Triomphe)
In town centre
*90 en suite (bth/shr) (38 fmly) (3 with balcony) No smoking in 32 bedrooms TV in all bedrooms STV Radio in rooms Direct dial from all bedrooms Mini-bar in all bedrooms Room-safe Licensed Lift Night porter Full central heating Air conditioning in bedrooms Open terrace Last d 22.00hrs Languages spoken: English German Italian & Spanish*
MEALS: Full breakfast 175FF Continental breakfast 135FF Lunch fr 300FF&alc Dinner fr 300FF&alc✱
CARDS: ●● ■■ ▪▪ ⬤ JCB Travellers cheques

★ ★ ★ *Régina de Pasy*
6 av de la Tour *75116*
☎ 145244364 FAX 140507062
Near river In town centre
*64 en suite (bth/shr) (4 fmly) (23 with balcony) TV in all bedrooms STV Direct dial from all bedrooms Mini-bar in all bedrooms Licensed Lift Night porter Full central heating Languages spoken: English & German*
CARDS: ●● ■■ ▪▪ ⬤ Travellers cheques

★ ★ ★ *Hotel du Rond Point de Longchamp*
86 rue de Longchamp *75116*
☎ 145051363 FAX 147551280
In town centre
*57 en suite (bth/shr) Some rooms in annexe (1 fmly) (6 with balcony) No smoking in 10 bedrooms TV in all bedrooms STV Radio in rooms Direct dial from all bedrooms Mini-bar in all bedrooms Room-safe Licensed Lift Night porter Full central heating Air conditioning in bedrooms Pool table Languages spoken: English & Spanish*
CARDS: ●● ■■ ▪▪ ⬤ Travellers cheques

★ ★ ★ *Hotel St-James Paris*
43 av Bugeaud *75116*
☎ 144058181 FAX 144058182
(from the 'Périphérique' take exit 'Porte Dauphine')
Near river In town centre Near motorway
*48 en suite (bth/shr) 2 rooms in annexe (6 fmly) TV in all bedrooms STV Direct dial from all bedrooms Mini-bar in all bedrooms Room-safe Licensed Lift Night porter Full central heating Air conditioning in bedrooms Open parking available Supervised Child discount available 4yrs Sauna Solarium Gym Jacuzzi/spa Open terrace V meals Last d 22.00hrs Languages spoken: English, German, Italian & Spanish*
ROOMS: (room only) s 1800-1900FF; d 2100-4200FF
CARDS: ●● ■■ ▪▪ ⬤ JCB Travellers cheques

★ ★ ★ *Hotel de Sevigné*
6 rue de Belloy *75116*
☎ 147208890 FAX 140709873
In town centre Near motorway
*30 en suite (bth/shr) (8 fmly) (10 with balcony) TV in all bedrooms STV Radio in rooms Direct dial from all bedrooms Mini-bar in all bedrooms Licensed Lift Night porter Full central heating Open parking available (charged) Covered parking available (charged) V meals Languages spoken: English*
CARDS: ●● ■■ ▪▪ ⬤ Travellers cheques

★ ★ ★ **Hotel Résidence Trocadero** (Best Western)
3 av Raymond Poincaré *75116*
☎ 147273330 FAX 147278085
Near river In town centre Near motorway
*27 en suite (bth/shr) TV in all bedrooms STV Direct dial from all bedrooms Mini-bar in all bedrooms Room-safe Licensed Lift Night porter Full central heating Air conditioning in bedrooms Child discount available 12yrs Open terrace Languages spoken: English, Arabic & Spanish*
CARDS: ● ■ ≖ ⬤ Travellers cheques

### 17TH ARRONDISSEMENT

★ ★ ★ *Arc de Triomphe Étoile*
3 rue de l'Étoile *75017*
☎ 143803694 FAX 144404919
Forest area In town centre
*25 en suite (bth/shr) (10 fmly) TV in all bedrooms STV Radio in rooms Direct dial from all bedrooms Licensed Lift Night porter Full central heating Air conditioning in bedrooms Child discount available 12yrs Languages spoken: English Italian & Spanish*
CARDS: ● ■ ≖ ⬤ Travellers cheques

★ ★ ★ *Astor*
36 rue P-Démours *75017*
☎ 147646767 FAX 140539134
In town centre
*45 en suite (bth/shr) (6 fmly) (6 with balcony) TV in all bedrooms STV Radio in rooms Direct dial from all bedrooms Mini-bar in all bedrooms Lift Full central heating Child discount available 10yrs Indoor swimming pool (heated) Sauna Jacuzzi/spa Languages spoken: English & Spanish*
CARDS: ● ■ ≖ ⬤ Travellers cheques

★ ★ ★ *Centre Ville Étoile*
6 rue des Acacias *75017*
☎ 143805618 FAX 147549343
(take Périphérique exit Porte Maillot/La Défense in direction of Porte Maillot, at lights keep on left until roundabout of Palais de Congres, take Avenue de la Grande Armée in direction of Arc de Triomphe, Rue des Arcacias is on left)
Forest area
*20 en suite (bth/shr) (2 fmly) No smoking in 5 bedrooms TV in all bedrooms STV Direct dial from all bedrooms Mini-bar in all bedrooms Room-safe Licensed Lift Night porter Full central heating Air conditioning in bedrooms Languages spoken: English German Italian & Spanish*
CARDS: ● ■ ≖ ⬤ JCB Travellers cheques

★ ★ ★ **Hotel Champerret-Elysées**
129 av de Villiers *75017*
☎ 147644400 FAX 147631058
In town centre
*45 en suite (bth/shr) (2 fmly) No smoking in 20 bedrooms TV in all bedrooms STV Direct dial from all bedrooms Room-safe Licensed Lift Night porter Full central heating Air conditioning in bedrooms Child discount available 12yrs Languages spoken: English German & Italian*
ROOMS: (room only) s 500-700FF; d 510-710FF
**Reductions over 1 night Special breaks: wknds**
CARDS: ● ■ ≖ ⬤ Travellers cheques

★ ★ ★ ★ *Hotel Concorde la Fayette*
3 pl du Général-Koeing *75017*
☎ 140685068 FAX 140685043
Forest area In town centre Near motorway

*No smoking in 96 bedrooms TV in 970 bedrooms STV Radio in rooms Direct dial from 970 bedrooms Mini-bar in 970 bedrooms Licensed Lift Night porter Full central heating Air conditioning in bedrooms Open parking available (charged) Covered parking available (charged) V meals Languages spoken: English German Italian Japanese & Spanish*
CARDS: ● ■ ≖ ⬤ Travellers cheques

★ ★ ★ *Étoile Park Hotel*
10 av Mac Mahon *75017*
☎ 142676963 FAX 143801899
*28 en suite (bth/shr) TV in all bedrooms STV Direct dial from all bedrooms Lift Open parking available*

★ ★ ★ *Étoile Péreire* (Relais du Silence)
146 bd Péreire *75017*
☎ 142676000 FAX 142670290
In town centre
*26 en suite (bth/shr) (4 fmly) TV in all bedrooms STV Direct dial from all bedrooms Mini-bar in all bedrooms Licensed Lift Night porter Full central heating Child discount available 6yrs Languages spoken: English Italian & Spanish*
ROOMS: (room only) s 620-720FF; d 720-1120FF ✻
CARDS: ● ■ ≖ ⬤ JCB Travellers cheques

★ ★ ★ *Étoile St-Ferdinand* (Best Western)
36 rue St-Ferdinand *75017*
☎ 145726666 FAX 145741292
Near river Forest area In town centre Near motorway
*42 en suite (bth/shr) (5 fmly) TV in all bedrooms STV Direct dial from all bedrooms Mini-bar in all bedrooms Licensed Lift Night porter Full central heating Child discount available 12yrs Languages spoken: English German & Spanish*
CARDS: ● ■ ≖ ⬤ Travellers cheques

★ ★ ★ *Hotel Fertel Étoile*
4 rue des Acacias *75017*
☎ 147667775 FAX 147664790
(from the Périphérique take direction of Porte Maillot, then Avenue de la Grande Armée; drive around the Arc de Triomphe & onto Avenue Carnot, continue to end of street & Rue des Acacias on left)
In town centre
*51 en suite (bth/shr) TV in all bedrooms STV Direct dial from all bedrooms Licensed Lift Air conditioning in bedrooms Child discount available 12yrs Languages spoken: English, Arabic & Spanish*
CARDS: ● ■ ⬤ JCB

★ ★ ★ *Hotel Fertel Maillot*
269 blvd Péreire *75017*
☎ 144099292 FAX 144099494
(From the Périphérique,take exit 'Porte Maillot'. Blvd Péreire is on the left crossing Av Grande Armée)
Forest area In town centre
*35 en suite (bth/shr) (1 fmly) TV in all bedrooms STV Direct dial from all bedrooms Mini-bar in all bedrooms Lift Night porter Air conditioning in bedrooms Child discount available 12yrs Languages spoken: German & Italian*
ROOMS: (room only) s 600-720FF; d 660-780FF
CARDS: ● ■ ≖ ⬤ JCB

★ ★ *Hotel Flaubert*
19 rue Rennequin *75017*
☎ 146224435 FAX 143803234
*37 en suite (bth/shr) TV in all bedrooms Direct dial from all bedrooms Mini-bar in all bedrooms Licensed Lift Night porter*
*contd.*

Full central heating Open parking available (charged) Covered parking available (charged) Supervised Languages spoken: English, Russian & Spanish
CARDS: 👄 ▦ 🎟 ⑩ Travellers cheques

★ ★ ★ **Ibis Paris Porte de Clichy**
163 bis av de Clichy 75017
☎ 140252000 FAX 140252600
(next to the 'Périphérique' ring road)
In town centre Near motorway
700 en suite (bth/shr) (53 fmly) No smoking in 36 bedrooms TV in all bedrooms STV Direct dial from all bedrooms Room-safe (charged) Licensed Lift Night porter Full central heating Air conditioning in bedrooms Open parking available (charged) Covered parking available (charged) Supervised Child discount available 12yrs Indoor swimming pool (heated) Sauna Solarium Gym Pool table Jacuzzi/spa V meals Languages spoken: English Dutch & German
ROOMS: (room only) s 460FF; d 560FF ✱
CARDS: 👄 ▦ 🎟 ⑩

★ ★ ★ ★ **Le Meriden**
81 bd Gouvion St-Cyr 75848
☎ 140683434 FAX 140683131
Near lake Forest area In town centre Near motorway
1025 en suite (bth/shr) No smoking in 156 bedrooms TV in all bedrooms STV Radio in rooms Direct dial from all bedrooms Mini-bar in all bedrooms Licensed Lift Night porter Air conditioning in bedrooms Open parking available (charged) Covered parking available (charged) Child discount available 12yrs V meals
CARDS: 👄 ▦ 🎟 ⑩

★ ★ ★ **Eber Monceau** (Relais du Silence)
18 rue Léon Jost 75017
☎ 146226070 FAX 147630101
(From the Périphérique West take Exit 'Porte d'Asnières. Then head for Av Wagram and turn off onto Rue de Courcelles, then Rue Cardinet and first right into Rue Léon Jost)
In town centre Near motorway
18 en suite (bth/shr) (3 fmly) (1 with balcony) TV in all bedrooms STV Radio in rooms Direct dial from all bedrooms Mini-bar in all bedrooms Licensed Lift Night porter Full central heating Child discount available Open terrace Languages spoken: English & Italian
CARDS: 👄 ▦ 🎟 ⑩ Eurocard - Access Travellers cheques

★ ★ ★ **Neuville**
3 rue Verniquet 75017
☎ 143802630 FAX 143803855
Forest area In town centre Near motorway
28 en suite (bth/shr) (4 fmly) TV in all bedrooms STV Radio in rooms Direct dial from all bedrooms Licensed Lift Night porter Full central heating Open parking available (charged) Covered parking available (charged) Child discount available 12yrs Languages spoken: English German & Spanish
CARDS: 👄 ▦ 🎟 ⑩ Travellers cheques

★ ★ **L'Ouest Hotel**
165 rue de Rome 75017
☎ 142275029 FAX 142272740
48 en suite (bth/shr) TV in all bedrooms Radio in rooms Direct dial from all bedrooms Licensed Lift Night porter Full central heating Supervised Child discount available Languages spoken: English Arabic & Italian
CARDS: 👄 ▦ 🎟 ⑩ Travellers cheques

★ ★ ★ **Primotel Empire** (Best Western)
3 rue Montenotte 75017
☎ 143801455 FAX 147660433
In town centre
49 en suite (bth/shr) (6 fmly) (9 with balcony) TV in all bedrooms STV Direct dial from all bedrooms Mini-bar in all bedrooms Licensed Lift Full central heating Child discount available 12yrs Languages spoken: English Italian & Spanish
CARDS: 👄 ▦ 🎟 ⑩ Travellers cheques

★ ★ ★ **Hotel Regents Garden** (Best Western)
6 rue Pierre Demours 75017
☎ 145740730 FAX 140550142
In town centre
39 en suite (bth/shr) TV in all bedrooms Radio in rooms Direct dial from all bedrooms Mini-bar in all bedrooms Licensed Lift Night porter Full central heating Air conditioning in bedrooms Open parking available (charged) Child discount available 12yrs Languages spoken: English,German,Italian
CARDS: 👄 ▦ 🎟 ⑩ JCB Travellers cheques

★ ★ **Hotel St Cyr et des Ternes**
101 av des Ternes 75017
☎ 145748742 FAX 145725755
(in front of the Palais des Congrés)
In town centre Near motorway
34 en suite (bth/shr) (3 fmly) No smoking in 4 bedrooms TV in all bedrooms STV Direct dial from all bedrooms Mini-bar in 18 bedrooms Licensed Lift Night porter Full central heating Child discount available 10yrs Languages spoken: English & Spanish
CARDS: 👄 ▦ 🎟

★ ★ ★ **Hotel Ternes Arc de Triomphe**
97 av des Ternes 75017
☎ 153819494 FAX 153819495
In town centre Near motorway
39 en suite (bth/shr) (1 fmly) (3 with balcony) No smoking in 27 bedrooms TV in all bedrooms STV Direct dial from all bedrooms Mini-bar in all bedrooms Licensed Lift Night porter Full central heating Air conditioning in bedrooms Child discount available 16yrs Languages spoken: English German & Italian
ROOMS: (room only) d 710-1200FF
CARDS: 👄 ▦ 🎟 ⑩ JCB Travellers cheques

**18TH ARRONDISSEMENT**

**Bed & Breakfast** (Prop: Françoise Foret)
75018
☎ 144850719
1 en suite (shr) (1 fmly) (1 with balcony) No smoking on premises TV in all bedrooms Full central heating Open parking available (charged) Languages spoken: English & Italian

**Bed & Breakfast** (Prop: Eliane Letellier)
75018
☎ 142513735/142304947
(it is essential to phone for address details & directions - owner speaks good English)
2 en suite (bth/shr) No smoking on premises TV in 1 bedroom Full central heating V meals Languages spoken: English

### ★ ★ Climat de France
51 rue Letort *75018*
☎ 142576440 FAX 142576425
(from Périphérique take Porte de Clignancourt exit)
In town centre  Near motorway
*51 en suite (bth/shr) (1 fmly) TV in all bedrooms  Radio in rooms  Direct dial from all bedrooms  Lift  Night porter  Full central heating  Open terrace  Languages spoken: English, German & Spanish*
CARDS: ●● ▓▓

### ★ ★ Eden Hotel
90 rue Ordener *75018*
☎ 142646163 FAX 142641143
(Metro: Jules Joffrin /Place de la Marie du XVIIIéme)
The owners offer guests a warm welcome to their attractive, comfortable hotel in a picturesque neighbourhood at the foot of Montmartre, close to the landmark of Sacré Coeur and the famous flea market.
In town centre
*35 en suite (bth/shr) TV in all bedrooms  STV  Direct dial from all bedrooms  Lift  Night porter  Full central heating  Open parking available (charged)  Covered parking available (charged)  Child discount available 12yrs  Languages spoken: English & German*
ROOMS: (room only) s fr 395FF; d fr 440FF
CARDS: ●● ▓▓ ▓▓ ⑩ JCB Travellers cheques

### ★ ★ Hotel Ordener
131 rue Ordener *75018*
☎ 142529900 FAX 142642816
In town centre
*38 en suite (bth/shr) TV in all bedrooms  Direct dial from all bedrooms  Lift  Night porter  Full central heating  Child discount available 12yrs  Languages spoken: English & Spanish*
CARDS: ●● ▓▓ ▓▓ ⑩ JCB Travellers cheques

### ★ ★ Prima Lépic
29 rue Lépic *75018*
☎ 146064464 FAX 146066611
In town centre
*38 en suite (bth/shr) (3 fmly) (3 with balcony) TV in all bedrooms  Lift  Night porter  Full central heating  Child discount available  Languages spoken: English*
CARDS: ●● ▓▓ Travellers cheques

### ★ ★ ★ Terrass Hotel
12 rue Joseph-de-Maistre *75018*
☎ 146067285 FAX 142522911
The Hotel Terrass encapsulates the unique atmosphere of Montmartre. From the foyer to the Provencal-style restaurant, imaginative furnishings and fabrics continue to surprise. The well-appointed bedrooms offer elegant accommodation and a

high standard of comfort. The menu features a wide array of inventive dishes, and in summer meals are served on the terrace with fine views across the capital.
In town centre
*101 en suite (bth/shr) (13 fmly) (12 with balcony) No smoking in 17 bedrooms  TV in all bedrooms  STV  Direct dial from all bedrooms  Mini-bar in all bedrooms  Licensed  Lift  Night porter  Full central heating  Air conditioning in bedrooms  Child discount available 12yrs  Open terrace  Last d 22.00hrs  Languages spoken: English & German*
ROOMS: s 920-1320FF; d 1390-1540FF
MEALS: Full breakfast 75FF  Lunch 130-168FF  Dinner 130-168FF
CARDS: ●● ▓▓ ▓▓ ⑩ JCB Travellers cheques

### Titania (Prop: Mr Yahia)
70 Bis Boulevard Ornano *75010*
☎ 146064322 FAX 146065254
In town centre  Near motorway
*103 rms (4 bth 15 shr) (16 fmly) (14 with balcony) No smoking in 14 bedrooms  Full central heating  Child discount available 12yrs  Languages spoken: English, German & Russian*
CARDS: ●● ▓▓ ⑩ Travellers cheques

### ★ ★ Utrillo
7 rue Aristide Bruant *75018*
☎ 142581344 FAX 142239388
Located in a quiet street in Montmartre, and not far away from the Place du Tetre, the hotel offers contemporary accommodation and comfort. Its interior features reproductions from the famous painter Utrillo. The comfortable bedrooms have modern amenities.
In town centre

*30 en suite (bth/shr) (1 fmly) TV in all bedrooms  Direct dial from all bedrooms  Mini-bar in all bedrooms  Lift  Night porter  Full central heating  Child discount available 12yrs  Sauna  Languages spoken: English & German*
ROOMS: (room only) s fr 360FF; d fr 420FF **Reductions over 1 night**
CARDS: ●● ▓▓ ▓▓ ⑩ JCB Travellers cheques

## 19TH ARRONDISSEMENT

### ★ ★ ★ Holiday Inn Paris-La-Villette
216 av Jean Jaurès *75019*
☎ 144841818 FAX 144841820
Near river  Forest area  In town centre  Near motorway
*182 en suite (bth/shr) (56 fmly) No smoking in 28 bedrooms  TV in all bedrooms  STV  Radio in rooms  Direct dial from all bedrooms  Mini-bar in all bedrooms  Licensed  Lift  Night porter  Full central heating  Air conditioning in bedrooms  Open*
*contd.*

parking available (charged) Covered parking available (charged) Child discount available 19yrs Sauna Jacuzzi/spa Open terrace V meals Languages spoken: English,Dutch,German & Spanish
CARDS: ⬤ ▦ ▧ ⬤ Travellers cheques

## 20TH ARRONDISSEMENT

**Mary's Hotel** (Prop: Mme Chettouh)
118 r Orfila 75020
☎ 143615168 FAX 143611647
(A3 exit Bagnolet, to Gambetta then rue Orfila)
Near motorway
24 rms (18 bth/shr) (4 fmly) (4 with balcony) No smoking on premises TV available Full central heating Languages spoken: English
CARDS: ⬤ ▧ Travellers cheques

★ **Tamaris**
14 rue des Maraichers 75020
☎ 143728548 FAX 143568175
Forest area In town centre Near motorway
42 rms TV available Direct-dial available Lift Night porter Full central heating Languages spoken: English

## POMMEUSE Seine-et-Marne

**Le Moulin de Pommeuse** (Prop: Annie and Jacky Thomas)
32 Av du General Huerne 77515
☎ 164200098 FAX 164200098
(access via A4, then N34 towards Coulommiers and D15 to Pommeuse)
The Thomas family offer you a relaxing holiday in their authentic 14th century watermill, which has been completely restored to meet the traditions of the Brie region, giving very comfortable accommodation throughout. The 3 acre garden with beautiful trees and donkeys backs onto a river. Cultural and leisure pursuits are nearby in the village.
Near river Forest area
6 en suite (bth/shr) (2 fmly) (1 with balcony) No smoking on premises Radio in rooms Full central heating Open parking available Covered parking available Child discount available 12yrs Fishing Boule Bicycle rental Table tennis Last d 20.00hrs Languages spoken: English
ROOMS: s 230-320FF; d 260-350FF
MEALS: Lunch 80-120FF Dinner 90-130FF
CARDS: Travellers cheques

## PONTAULT-COMBAULT Seine-et-Marne

★ ★ ★ **Les Relais Bleus**
Parc d'Activites des Arpents 77340
☎ 360294242 Cen Res 164460616
Forest area Near motorway
60 en suite (bth/shr) TV in all bedrooms STV Direct dial from all bedrooms Licensed Lift Night porter Full central heating Open parking available Supervised Pool table Languages spoken: English German & Italian

## PROVINS Seine-et-Marne

★ ★ ★ **Hostellerie Aux Vieux Remparts**
3 rue Couverté-Ville Haute 77160
☎ 164089400 FAX 360677722
Forest area Near motorway
25 en suite (bth/shr) (2 fmly) TV in all bedrooms Radio in

rooms Licensed Lift Full central heating Open parking available Supervised Child discount available 12yrs Open terrace Last d 21.30hrs Languages spoken: English & German
CARDS: ⬤ ▦ ▧ ⬤ Travellers cheques

## PUTEAUX Hauts-de-Seine

★ ★ ★ **Hotel le Dauphin**
45 rue Jean-Jaurès 92800
☎ 147737363 FAX 146980882
(From the Périphérique take exit 'Porte Maillot' and follow signs for La Défense. After crossing the Seine, travel in the direction of Puteaux Centre and you will arrive in rue Jean-Jaurès)
Near river Near lake Forest area In town centre Near motorway
30 en suite (bth/shr) TV in all bedrooms STV Direct dial from all bedrooms Mini-bar in all bedrooms Room-safe Lift Night porter Full central heating Open parking available Covered parking available Sauna Solarium Gym Open terrace
CARDS: ⬤ ▦ ▧ ⬤

★ ★ **Hotel de Dion Bouton**
19 quai de Dion Bouton
☎ 142043554 FAX 145063951
(From the Périphérique take 'Porte Maillot' exit follow signs for Bois de Bologne and then Puteaux.Cross the Seine and the Hotel is located on the corner)
Forest area In town centre Near motorway
33 en suite (bth/shr) (3 fmly) (2 with balcony) TV in all bedrooms STV Direct dial from all bedrooms Lift Night porter Open parking available Child discount available 12 Pool table Open terrace Languages spoken: English and German
CARDS: ⬤ ▦ ▧ ⬤

★ ★ ★ **Hotel Princesse Isabelle**
72 rue Jean Jaurès 92800
☎ 147788006 FAX 147752520
(From the Périphérique take exit' Porte Maillot 'and follow the signs for La Defense. After crossing the Seine follow the directions for Puteaux Centre, you will then arrive in rue Jean Jaurès)
Near river Near lake Forest area In town centre Near motorway
36 en suite (bth/shr) 7 rooms in annexe (5 fmly) TV in all bedrooms STV Direct dial from all bedrooms Mini-bar in all bedrooms Room-safe Lift Night porter Full central heating Open parking available Covered parking available Sauna Solarium Gym
CARDS: ⬤ ▦ ▧ ⬤

★ ★ ★ **Syjac Hotel**
20 quai de Dion-Bouton 92800
☎ 142040304 FAX 145067869
(close to Porte Maillot (air terminal), take direction of La Défense & drive along the River Seine, hotel near Pont de Puteaux)
In town centre
33 en suite (bth/shr) (2 fmly) TV in all bedrooms STV Direct dial from all bedrooms Mini-bar in all bedrooms Lift Full central heating Child discount available 12yrs Sauna Solarium Open terrace Languages spoken: English German & Spanish
CARDS: ⬤ ▦ ▧ ⬤

★ ★ ★ **Hotel Victoria**
85 blvd Richard Wallace *92800*
☎ 145065551 FAX 140990597
(Arriving in Paris take the Périphérique Ouest then exit La Défense, follow signs for Puteaux Centre)
In town centre
*32 en suite (shr) (12 fmly) No smoking in 12 bedrooms TV in all bedrooms STV Direct dial from all bedrooms Mini-bar in all bedrooms Room-safe Licensed Lift Night porter Full central heating Child discount available 12yrs Gym Languages spoken: English, German & Spanish*
CARDS: ● ● ● ● Travellers cheques

RAMBOUILLET Yvelines

★ ★ **Climat de France**
Lieu dit "La Louvière" *78120*
☎ 134856262 FAX 130592357
(off N306)
Forest area  Near motorway
*67 en suite (bth/shr) 23 rooms in annexe TV available Direct-dial available Licensed Night porter Full central heating Open parking available Supervised Outdoor swimming pool (heated) Tennis V meals Last d 10pm*
CARDS: ● ●

ROISSY-CHARLES-DE-GAULLE (AÉROPORT) Val-D'Oise

★ ★ ★ **Copthorne Paris Charles de Gaulle**
allée du Verger, Zone Hotelière *95700*
☎ 134293333 FAX 134290305
(from Paris A1 or A3 towards Lille, exit Charles de Gaulle-Roissy en France. Follow Roissy en France-zone Hotelière)
Forest area  In town centre  Near motorway
*237 en suite (bth/shr) (237 fmly) No smoking in 60 bedrooms TV in all bedrooms STV Radio in rooms Direct dial from all bedrooms Mini-bar in all bedrooms Licensed Lift Night porter Full central heating Air conditioning in bedrooms Open parking available (charged) Covered parking available (charged) Supervised Child discount available 12yrs Indoor swimming pool (heated) Sauna Solarium Gym Jacuzzi/spa Open terrace Covered terrace V meals Last d 21.00hrs Languages spoken: English Dutch German Italian Spanish & Portugese*
CARDS: ● ● ● ● JCB Travellers cheques

★ ★ ★ ★ **Hotel Holiday Inn Paris Charles de Gaulle**
1 allée du Verger BP30 *95700*
☎ 134293000 FAX 134299052
Forest area  Near motorway
*243 en suite (bth) (53 fmly) No smoking in 58 bedrooms TV in all bedrooms STV Radio in rooms Direct dial from all bedrooms Licensed Lift Full central heating Air conditioning in bedrooms Open parking available (charged) Supervised Child discount available 12yrs Indoor swimming pool (heated) Sauna Gym V meals Last d 22.30hrs Languages spoken: English Dutch German& Spanish*
CARDS: ● ● ● ● Travellers cheques

★ ★ ★ **Novotel Paris Roissy Aéroport de Gaulle**
Roissypole Gare *95700*
☎ 148620053 FAX 148620011
Near motorway
*201 en suite (bth) (201 fmly) No smoking in 70 bedrooms TV in all bedrooms STV Radio in rooms Direct dial from all bedrooms Mini-bar in all bedrooms Licensed Lift Night porter Full central heating Air conditioning in bedrooms Open*

*parking available (charged) Child discount available 12yrs Pool table Languages spoken: English German & Spanish*
CARDS: ● ● ● ● Travellers cheques

★ ★ ★ ★ **Sofitel Paris Charles De Gaulle Airport**
BP 20248 Zone Centrale *95710*
☎ 149192929 FAX 149192900
Personalised, courteous service is offered at this large airport hotel. The rooms are of contemporary style, luxurious and have every modern comfort including sound-proofing. The L'Escale restaurant offers dishes for all occasions 24 hours a day. A first class service is offered for business functions covering all requirements including an interpretation service.
Forest area  Near motorway

*350 en suite (bth/shr) (8 fmly) No smoking in 88 bedrooms TV in all bedrooms STV Direct dial from all bedrooms Mini-bar in all bedrooms Licensed Lift Night porter Full central heating Air conditioning in bedrooms Open parking available (charged) Indoor swimming pool (heated) Tennis Sauna Pool table Open terrace V meals Languages spoken: English German & Spanish*
ROOMS: (room only) d 1200-2100FF
MEALS: Continental breakfast 80FF Lunch 150-250FFalc Dinner 200-350FFalc
CARDS: ● ● ● ● Travellers cheques

RUNGIS Val-de-Marne

★ ★ **Vidéotel**
4 rue Mondétour *94656*
☎ 145605252 FAX 149780625
Near motorway
*82 en suite (bth/shr) (9 fmly) No smoking in 10 bedrooms TV in all bedrooms Direct dial from all bedrooms Licensed Lift Night porter Full central heating Air conditioning in bedrooms Open parking available Supervised Child discount available 12yrs Open terrace V meals Last d 22.00hrs Languages spoken: English*
CARDS: ● ● ● ●

ST-GERMAIN-EN-LAYE Yvelines

★ ★ ★ **Cazaudéhore et la Forestière**
1 av du Prés Kennedy *78100*
☎ 139103838 FAX 139737388
Forest area
*30 en suite (bth/shr) (6 with balcony) TV in all bedrooms Radio in rooms Direct dial from all bedrooms Mini-bar in all bedrooms Room-safe Licensed Lift Night porter Full central heating Open parking available Child discount available 8yrs Last d 22.00hrs Languages spoken: English*
CARDS: ● ● ● ● JCB Travellers cheques

## ST-OUEN Seine-St-Denis

**★ ★ ★ Holiday Inn Garden Court**
9 rue la Fontaine *93400*
☎ 140125197 FAX 140126100
In town centre  Near motorway
*120 en suite (bth)  No smoking in 40 bedrooms  TV in all bedrooms  STV  Radio in rooms  Direct dial from all bedrooms  Licensed  Lift  Night porter  Full central heating  Air conditioning in bedrooms  Open parking available  Covered parking available (charged)  Supervised  Child discount available 18yrs  Open terrace  Languages spoken: English German Italian & Spanish*
CARDS: ● ■ ▓ ◑ Travellers cheques

## ST-PIERRE-LES-NEMOURS Seine-et-Marne

**★ ★ Les Roches**
av d'Ormesson *77140*
☎ 164280143 FAX 164280427
Near river  Forest area
*10 en suite (bth/shr)  5 rooms in annexe  (4 fmly)  TV in all bedrooms  Licensed  Full central heating  Open parking available  Covered parking available  Child discount available  Solarium  Open terrace  V meals  Last d 21.45hrs  Languages spoken: Spanish*
CARDS: ● ■ ▓ ◑ Travellers cheques

## SAVIGNY-SUR-ORGE Essonne

**★ ★ Hotel Albion**
9 av Garigliano *91600*
☎ 169050505 FAX 169050035
(from A6 Paris/Lyon take exit Savigny-sur-Orge turn after the traffic lights & follow signpost Hotel Albion)
*55 en suite (bth/shr)  No smoking in 10 bedrooms  TV in all bedrooms  STV  Direct dial from all bedrooms  Licensed  Night porter  Full central heating  Open parking available  Child discount available 10yrs  Outdoor swimming pool (heated)  Tennis  Riding  Pool table  Boule  Open terrace  V meals  Last d 22.00hrs  Languages spoken: English*

## SCEAUX Hauts-de-Seine

**★ ★ Colbert**
20 av Camberwell *92330*
☎ 146600221 FAX 147029578
Forest area  In town centre  Near motorway
*49 en suite (bth/shr)  TV in all bedrooms  STV  Direct dial from all bedrooms  Mini-bar in all bedrooms  Room-safe (charged)  Licensed  Lift  Night porter  Full central heating  Open parking available  Child discount available 10yrs  Last d 22.00hrs  Languages spoken: English Italian & Spanish*
ROOMS: (room only) s 340FF; d 398FF
CARDS: ● ■ ▓ ◑ Travellers cheques

## SURESNES Hauts-de-Seine

**★ ★ ★ Hotel Atrium**
68-72 blvd Henri Sellier *92150*
☎ 142046076 FAX 146977161
(Close to the Bois de Boulogne cross the Pont de Suresnes in the direction of St Cloud)
*42 en suite (bth/shr)  (1 fmly)  TV in all bedrooms  STV  Direct dial from all bedrooms  Mini-bar in all bedrooms  Licensed  Lift  Night porter  Open parking available (charged)  Covered parking available (charged)  Supervised  Child discount*

*available 12yrs  Sauna  Gym  Pool table  Languages spoken: Italian, English, Spanish, German*
CARDS: ● ■ ▓ ◑

**★ ★ ★ Royal Parc de Seine**
6 rue Chevreul *92150*
☎ 146254000 FAX 146254190
Near river  Near lake  Forest area  In town centre  Near motorway
*97 en suite (bth/shr)  (97 fmly)  (97 with balcony)  TV in all bedrooms  STV  Direct dial from all bedrooms  Room-safe (charged)  Licensed  Lift  Night porter  Full central heating  Open parking available (charged)  Covered parking available (charged)  Supervised  Child discount available 12yrs  Pool table  Jacuzzi/spa  Open terrace  V meals  Languages spoken: English German Italian & Spanish*
CARDS: ● ■ ▓ ◑ JCB,Eurocard Travellers cheques

## THOMERY Seine-et-Marne

**★ ★ ★ Vieux Logis**
5 rue Sadi Carnot *77810*
☎ 160964477 FAX 160700142
(6km south east of Fontainebleau, take N6 after Obelisque)

The hotel is situated in the town of Thomery on the banks of the River Seine. It was built in the late 18th century, and has a cheerful interior, where each bedroom is named after a flower and is equipped with modern facilities. There is an inviting bar and a restaurant with a comprehensive menu featuring a varied choice of dishes, which are complemented by an interesting wine list.
Near river  Forest area  In town centre
*14 en suite (bth/shr)  TV in all bedrooms  Direct dial from all bedrooms  Licensed  Night porter  Full central heating  Open parking available  Child discount available  Outdoor swimming pool (heated)  Tennis  Bicycle rental  Open terrace  Last d 21.30hrs  Languages spoken: English*
ROOMS: (room only) d 400FF  **Special breaks**
MEALS: Continental breakfast 55FF  Lunch 155-240FF&alc Dinner 155-240FF&alc
CARDS: ● ■ ▓ Travellers cheques

## TREUZY-LEVELAY Seine-et-Marne

**Bed & Breakfast** (Prop: M Gilles Caupin)
3 rue Creuse *77710*
☎ 164290747 & 164290111 FAX 164290521
(Motorway A6 exit Nemours, turn left at roundabout onto D403 towards Montereau. After 3km turn right onto D69 and drive through Treuzy to Levelay. In Levelay, 2nd road on right)
Set in a rural village in the Lunain Valley, 20 kilometres from

Fontainebleau, these guest rooms are situated in a recently refurbished barn, independent of the main house. Continental breakfast, using local produce, is served in the room or at the family table. A garden is available for guests' use. Restaurants, swimming pool, fishing and golf are all nearby, with climbing or walking in Fontainebleau Forest also within easy reach.
Near river Near lake Forest area In town centre
*4 rms (2 bth/shr) (2 fmly) TV in 1 bedroom Full central heating Open parking available Supervised Child discount available 4yrs Bicycle rental Languages spoken: English & Italian*
ROOMS: s fr 270FF; d fr 300FF **Reductions over 1 night**
CARDS: Travellers cheques

### VAUX-SUR-SEINE Yvelines

**La Cascade**
30 chemin des Valences *78740*
☎ 134748491 FAX 134748491
(access via A13 exit 9, then D190 towards St-Germain-en-Laye. After station & railway bridge turn right, then left into cul-de-sac)

A large house within 4000 square metres of grounds in a quiet location opposite the forest and within 30 minutes drive of Paris.
Near river Forest area
*Closed Jan-Feb*
*5 rms (4 bth/shr) (2 fmly) (2 with balcony) TV in 1 bedroom Full central heating Open parking available Child discount available 10yrs Outdoor swimming pool (heated) Languages spoken: English*
ROOMS: d 290-400FF
MEALS: Lunch fr 95FF Dinner fr 95FF

### VERSAILLES Yvelines

**★ ★ Relais Mercure**
19 rue Philippe de Dangeau, angle rue Montbauron *78800*
☎ 139504410 FAX 139506511
In town centre Near motorway
*60 en suite (bth/shr) (11 fmly) TV in all bedrooms STV Direct dial from all bedrooms Lift Night porter Full central heating Open parking available (charged) Covered parking available (charged) Supervised Child discount available 16yrs Languages spoken: English German & Spanish*
ROOMS: (room only) s 460FF; d 500FF
**Special breaks: Aug 3 night breaks**
CARDS: ●● ■■ ■■ ⑩ Travellers cheques

**★ ★ ★ ★ Sofitel Château de Versailles**
2 bis av de Paris *78000*
☎ 139533031 FAX 139538730
*152 en suite (bth/shr) (31 with balcony) No smoking in 85 bedrooms TV in all bedrooms STV Mini-bar in all bedrooms V meals*

**★ ★ ★ ★ Trianon Palace**
1 bd de la Reine *78000*
☎ 130843800 FAX 139490077
Forest area In town centre Near motorway
*192 en suite (bth/shr) (4 with balcony) TV in all bedrooms STV Radio in rooms Direct dial from all bedrooms Mini-bar in all bedrooms Room-safe Licensed Lift Night porter Full central heating Air conditioning in bedrooms Open parking available Covered parking available Supervised Child discount available 18yrs Indoor swimming pool (heated) Tennis Sauna Solarium Gym Jacuzzi/spa Bicycle rental Open terrace Covered terrace Wkly live entertainment V meals Last d 22.00hrs Languages spoken: English German Italian Japanese & Spanish*
ROOMS: (room only) d 2200-3200FF
**Special breaks: Weekend breaks**
MEALS: Full breakfast 160FF Lunch fr 155FF&alc Dinner fr 155FF&alc
CARDS: ●● ■■ ■■ ⑩ JCB

### VILLENEUVE-LA-GARENNE Hauts-de-Seine

**★ ★ Climat de France**
80 bd Charles-de-Gaulle *92390*
☎ 147995600 FAX 147998866
(Off A1 at St-Ouen, Pte de Clichy exit)
Near lake Forest area Near motorway
*60 en suite (bth) (2 fmly) TV in all bedrooms Radio in rooms Direct dial from all bedrooms Licensed Full central heating Open parking available Supervised Open terrace Last d 10pm Languages spoken: English*
CARDS: ●● ■■

### WY-DIT-JOLI-VILLAGE Val-D'Oise

**Château d'Hazéville** (Prop: M Deneck)
*95420*
☎ 134670617 & 142886700 FAX 134671782 & 145246260
Forest area Near motorway
*2 en suite (bth/shr) No smoking on premises TV in all bedrooms Full central heating Open parking available Covered parking available Supervised No children Open terrace Languages spoken: English & Spanish*
ROOMS: s 540FF; d 650FF
CARDS: Travellers cheques

# Burgundy

A wonderfully fertile land of undulating hills, forests and vineyards, with a network of peaceful waterways, Burgundy produces some of the greatest wine in the world. The region's colourful history is reflected in a legacy of fine art and architecture, with buildings ranging from ancient abbeys, through feudal fortresses to Renaissance chateaux. Through the burgeoning power of the Dukes of Burgundy in the 14th and 15th century, and a long tradition of trade, Burgundy has long been open to a variety of cultural influences and is still known today for its warm hospitality to visitors.

## ESSENTIAL FACTS

| | |
|---|---|
| DÉPARTEMENTS: | Côte-d'Or, Nièvre, Saône-et-Loire, Yonne |
| PRINCIPAL TOWNS | Autun, Auxerre, Beaune, Chalon-sur-Saône, La Charité-sur-Loire, Dijon, Fontenay, Mâcon, Nevers, Paray-le-Monial, Sens, VÉzelay |
| PLACES TO VISIT: | Abbeys: Cluny, Cîteaux, Fontenay, Vézelay; St Madeleine's Basilica. Dijon, capital of Burgundy. Beaune, centre of the wine industry. Semur-en-Auxois - ancient ramparts. Gothic Sens. Morvan Regional National Park. Le Hameau du Vin (wine museum), Musée Frédéric Blandin, Nevers (earthenware museum) |
| REGIONAL TOURIST OFFICE | Conseil Régional BP 1602 21035 Dijon Tel 03 80 50 90 00 |
| LOCAL GASTRONOMIC DELIGHTS | Boeuf bourguignon, beef casseroled in wine. Jambon persillé, ham with parsley. Escargot (snails) in their shells. Cheeses: Epoisses, Citeaux & Florentin. |
| DRINKS | Burgundy produces some of the world's greatest wines, especially around Beaune. Whites: Chablis, Mersault & Montrachet. Reds: from Chambertin to everyday Beajolais. Kir, an apéritif of white wine & Crème de Cassis (blackcurrant liqueur). |
| LOCAL CRAFTS WHAT TO BUY | Nevers: porcelain. Puisaye: pottery. Cluny: silk paintings. La Pierre-qui-Vivre, near St Leger Vaubanart: books printed by Benedictine monks. Aniseed sweets. Dijon mustard. |

256

---

### AIGNAY-LE-DUC Côte-D'Or

**Manoir de Tarperon** (Prop: M de Champsavin)
Tarperon *21510*
☎ 380938374
(30km south of Châtillon/Seine on the N71 towards Dijon, then D32 towards Aignay-le-Duc)
Near river  Forest area  Near motorway
*Closed Nov-end Mar*
*5 en suite (bth/shr)  (2 fmly)  Full central heating  Open parking available  Covered parking available  Child discount available  Fishing  Last d 20.00hrs  Languages spoken: English & German*
ROOMS: s 280FF; d 370FF  ✳ **Reductions over 1 night**
MEALS: Dinner 150FF
CARDS: Travellers cheques

### AISEY-SUR-SEINE Côte-D'Or

★ ★ **Du Roy**
*21400*
☎ 80932163 FAX 80932574
Near river  Forest area  Near motorway
*Closed Jan*
*9 rms (5 bth/shr)  TV in 5 bedrooms  Direct dial from all bedrooms  Licensed  Full central heating  Open parking available  Child discount available 2yrs  Open terrace  V meals  Last d 21.00hrs*
CARDS: ●● ■■ ⌧

### ALLUY Nièvre

**Bouteville** (Prop: M & Mme Le Jault)
*58110*
☎ 386840665 FAX 386840341
(halfway between Nevers & Château-Chinon. 1km from D978 and 5kms from Châtillon-en-Bezois)
Near lake  Forest area
*4 en suite (bth/shr)  (1 fmly)  No smoking on premises  TV in all bedrooms  Full central heating  Open parking available  Covered parking available  Supervised  Child discount available  Pool table  Boule  Bicycle rental  Languages spoken: English*
CARDS: Travellers cheques

### AMANZE Saône-et-Loire

**Bed & Breakfast** (Prop: Marie Christine Paperin)
Gaec des Collines *71800*
☎ 385706634 FAX 385706381
Forest area
*4 en suite (shr)  (1 fmly)  TV in 1 bedroom  Full central heating  Open parking available  Child discount available  Languages spoken: English*
CARDS: Eurocheques

### ANZY-LE-DUC Saône-et-Loire

**Lamy Genevieve**
Le Bourg *71110*
☎ 385251721
Near river  Forest area  In town centre  Near motorway
*Closed Nov-Etr*
*2 rms  Full central heating  Open parking available*

*contd.*

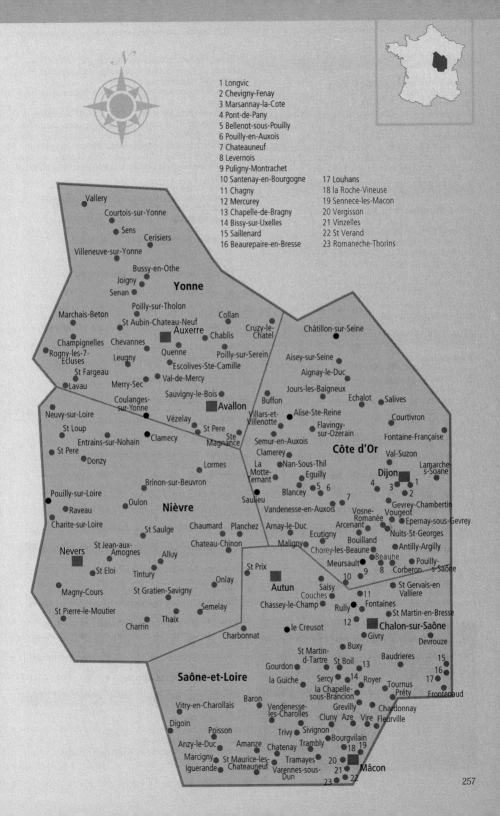

1 Longvic
2 Chevigny-Fenay
3 Marsannay-la-Cote
4 Pont-de-Pany
5 Bellenot-sous-Pouilly
6 Pouilly-en-Auxois
7 Chateauneuf
8 Levernois
9 Puligny-Montrachet
10 Santenay-en-Bourgogne
11 Chagny
12 Mercurey
13 Chapelle-de-Bragny
14 Bissy-sur-Uxelles
15 Saillenard
16 Beaurepaire-en-Bresse
17 Louhans
18 la Roche-Vineuse
19 Sennece-les-Macon
20 Vergisson
21 Vinzelles
22 St Verand
23 Romaneche-Thorins

Vallery
Courtois-sur-Yonne
Sens
Cerisiers
Villeneuve-sur-Yonne
Bussy-en-Othe
Joigny
Senan
**Yonne**
Poilly-sur-Tholon
Collan
Marchais-Beton
St Aubin-Chateau-Neuf
Cruzy-le-Chatel
Châtillon-sur-Seine
**Auxerre**
Chablis
Champignelles
Chevannes
Rogny-les-7-Ecluses
Quenne
Polly-sur-Serein
Aisey-sur-Seine
Leugny
Escolives-Ste-Camille
Aignay-le-Duc
St Fargeau
Val-de-Mercy
Jours-les-Baigneux
Lavau
Merry-Sec
Sauvigny-le-Bois
Echalot
Salives
Coulanges-sur-Yonne
**Avallon**
Buffon
Neuvy-sur-Loire
Vézelay
Villars-et-Villenotte
Alise-Ste-Reine
Courtivron
St Loup
St Pere
Flavigny-sur-Ozerain
Fontaine-Française
Entrains-sur-Nohain
Clamecy
Ste Magnance
**Côte d'Or**
Val-Suzon
St Pere
Donzy
Semur-en-Auxois
Clamerey
Lamarche-s-Soane
Lormes
La Motte-Ternant
Nan-Sous-Thil
Eguilly
**Dijon**
Pouilly-sur-Loire
Brinon-sur-Beuvron
Saulieu
Blancey
5  6
4   3   2
1
Raveau
Oulon
**Nièvre**
Vandenesse-en-Auxois
7
Gevrey-Chambertin
Charite-sur-Loire
Vosne-Romanée
Vougeot
Epernay-sous-Gevrey
Chaumard
Planchez
Arnay-le-Duc
Arcenant
Nuits-St-Georges
St Saulge
Ecutigny
Bouilland
Antilly-Argilly
Nevers
St Jean-aux-Amognes
Chateau-Chinon
Maligny
Chorey-les-Beaune
Beaune
Pouilly-
Alluy
Meursault
s-Saône
St Eloi
Tintury
St Prix
10   9   8   Corberon
Magny-Cours
Onlay
**Autun**
Saisy
11
St Gervais-en-Valliere
St Gratien-Savigny
Couches
Fontaines
St Pierre-le-Moutier
Semelay
Chassey-le-Champ
Rully
St Martin-en-Bresse
Thaix
le Creuzot
12
**Chalon-sur-Saône**
Charrin
Charbonnat
Givry
Devrouze
Buxy
St Martin-d-Tartre
Baudrieres
15
**Saône-et-Loire**
Gourdon
St Boil
13
16
la Guiche
Sercy
14
Royer
17
Vitry-en-Charollais
Baron
la Chapelle-sous-Brancion
Tournus
Préty
Frontenaud
Digoin
Vendenesse-les-Charolles
Grevilly
Chardonnay
Poisson
Cluny
Aze
Vire
Fleurville
Anzy-le-Duc
Amanze
Trivy
Sivignon
Bourgvilain
Marcigny
Chatenay
Trambly
18  19
Iguerande
St Maurice-les-Chateauneuf
Tramayes
20
**Mâcon**
Varennes-sous-Dun
21
23  22

257

### ARCENANT Côte-D'Or

**Bed & Breakfast** (Prop: Nina Campo)
r de Bruant *21700*
☎ 380612893
(leave RN 74 at Nuits-St-Georges and head in the direction of
Meuilley and Arcenant)
Forest area
*4 en suite (bth/shr) (1 fmly) (2 with balcony) Full central
heating Open parking available Child discount available 5yrs
Last d 20.00hrs Languages spoken: English*

### ANTILLY-ARGILLY Côte-D'Or

**Bed & Breakfast** (Prop: Jean François Bugnet)
*21700*
☎ 380625398 FAX 380625485
(from A31 take Nuits-St-Georges exit, then follow signs back
over the autoroute towards Seurre. After 3km turn right and
continue through Quincey and then for another 4km to house
at entrance to Antilly)
Near river  Near lake  Forest area
*4 en suite (bth/shr) (1 fmly) No smoking on premises TV
available Full central heating Open parking available*
CARDS: Travellers cheques

### ARNAY-LE-DUC Côte-D'Or

★★ **Terminus**
2 rue de l'Arquébuse *21230*
☎ 380900033 FAX 380900130
(approach via Pouilly-en-Auxois towards Autun and Arnay-le-
Duc)
Near lake  Near beach  Forest area  In town centre  Near
motorway
*8 en suite (bth/shr) TV in all bedrooms Direct dial from all
bedrooms Licensed Full central heating Open parking
available Covered parking available Open terrace V meals
Last d 21.00hrs*
ROOMS: (room only) s 180-220FF; d 180-240FF
MEALS: Continental breakfast 33FF  Lunch 63-178FF&alc
Dinner 63-178FF&alc
CARDS: ●● ■■ ■■ Travellers cheques

### AUTUN Saône-et-Loire

★★★★ **St-Louis**
6 rue de l'Arbalete *71400*
☎ 385520101 FAX 385863254
The 250-year-old Hotel Saint-Louis is located a few steps off
the main square of historic Autun in the heart of Burgundy.
Recently restored to its former charm and elegance, the new

restaurant lives up to its reputation and the chef's innovative
menu's are noted for taking advantage of local produce,
prepared with imagination and zest.
Near river  Near lake  Forest area  In town centre  Near
motorway
*38 en suite (bth/shr) (4 fmly) (4 with balcony) No smoking in
10 bedrooms TV in all bedrooms Radio in rooms Direct dial
from all bedrooms Licensed Full central heating Open parking
available (charged) Covered parking available (charged)
Supervised Child discount available 12yrs Bicycle rental Open
terrace V meals Last d 21.30hrs Languages spoken: English &
German*
ROOMS: (room only) d 450-1500FF
MEALS: Continental breakfast 50FF  Lunch 120-165FF
Dinner 165-310FF
CARDS: ●● ■■ ■■

★★ **Hotel Restaurant de la Teête Noire**
3 rue de l'Arquébuse *71400*
☎ 385865999 FAX 385863390
(A6 exit Chalon-sur-Saône/Pouilly-en-Auxois)
In town centre
*16 Jan-14 Dec*
*27 en suite (bth/shr) (6 fmly) No smoking in 18 bedrooms TV
in all bedrooms Direct dial from all bedrooms Licensed Lift
Full central heating Covered parking available (charged)
Supervised Child discount available 12yrs Bicycle rental V
meals Last d 21.45hrs Languages spoken: English*
CARDS: ●● ■■ Travellers cheques

★★★ **Hotel des Ursulines**
14 rue de Rivault *71400*
☎ 385865858 FAX 385862307
(head for the centre of the city of Autun and take the direction
of the Cathedral. Hotel is behind the Cathedral)
Near lake  Forest area  Near motorway
*43 en suite (bth/shr) (8 fmly) No smoking in 8 bedrooms TV in
all bedrooms Direct dial from all bedrooms Mini-bar in all
bedrooms Licensed Lift Night porter Full central heating
Open parking available Pool table Open terrace Covered
terrace V meals Last d 21.30hrs Languages spoken:
English,German,Portuguese & Spanish*
ROOMS: (room only) s 350-720FF; d 400-820FF
**Reductions over 1 night**
CARDS: ●● ■■ ■■ ⓓ JCB Travellers cheques

### AUXERRE Yonne

★★★ **Le Parc des Marechaux**
6 av Foch *89000*
☎ 386514377 FAX 386513172
Near river  Near lake  Near sea  Forest area  Near motorway
*25 en suite (bth/shr) (6 fmly) (2 with balcony) TV in all
bedrooms Direct dial from all bedrooms Mini-bar in all
bedrooms Licensed Lift Night porter Full central heating
Open parking available Covered parking available Child
discount available Golf Riding Bicycle rental Open terrace
Languages spoken: English & German*
CARDS: ●● ■■ Travellers cheques

### AVALLON Yonne

★★ **Les Capucins**
6 av Paul Doumer *89200*
☎ 386340652 FAX 386345847
(From motorway take exit 6 towards Paris for 5km)
*Closed Dec-Jan*

*8 rms (7 bth/shr) (1 fmly) TV in all bedrooms Direct dial from all bedrooms Licensed Full central heating Open parking available Child discount available 12yrs Open terrace V meals* CARDS: ●● ■ ☲ Travellers cheques

### ★★★★ Château de Vault-de-Lugny
11 rue du Château *89200*
☎ 386340786 FAX 386341636
(from Avallon take D957 towards Vézelay, in Pontaubert take D142)

Built in the 16th century, and situated in extensive wooded parklands, surrounded by a moat, the chateau offers a luxurious interior where bedrooms and public areas are furnished in a style befitting the origin of the building. The guest accommodation has personally styled bedrooms, with four-poster or canopy beds, and is equipped with superb modern facilities. In addition there is a private tennis court and 800 metres of river frontage for trout fishing at the guests' disposal.
*Near river Forest area*
*Closed mid Nov-mid Mar*
*12 en suite (bth/shr) (2 fmly) TV in all bedrooms STV Direct dial from all bedrooms Mini-bar in all bedrooms Room-safe Licensed Full central heating Open parking available Covered parking available Supervised Tennis Fishing Boule Bicycle rental Open terrace Hot air ballooning V meals Last d 23.00hrs Languages spoken: English & German*
ROOMS: s 850-1400FF; d 850-2500FF **Reductions over 1 night Special breaks**
MEALS: Full breakfast 50FF Dinner 290-480FF&alc
CARDS: ●● ■ ☲ ⑩ JCB Travellers cheques

### ★★★ Du Moulin des Ruats
Vallée du Cousin *89200*
☎ 386349700 FAX 386316547
(4km SW of Avallon)
This former flour mill was converted into a hotel in 1921 and

enjoys an idyllic setting tucked away in the delightful surroundings of a valley. All the bedrooms - some with terraces overlooking the river or garden - are individually furnished and are very comfortable. Guests can savour the delicacies on offer in the restaurant with a view of the slowly turning mill wheel. In summer meals are also served on the banks of the river.
*Near river Forest area Near motorway*
*Closed mid Nov-early Feb*
*25 en suite (bth/shr) (3 fmly) (8 with balcony) TV in all bedrooms STV Direct dial from all bedrooms Licensed Full central heating Open parking available Open terrace Last d 21.00hrs Languages spoken: English,German & Italian*
ROOMS: (room only) d 380-850FF
MEALS: Continental breakfast 60FF Lunch fr 155FF Dinner 155-235FF
CARDS: ●● ■ ☲ ⑩ Travellers cheques

## AZÉ Saône-et-Loire

### Bed & Breakfast (Prop: Roger Barry)
en Rizerolles *71260*
☎ 385333326 FAX 385334013
(from Mâcon take N79 towards Cluny, then D17 exit at Roche Vineuse, then onto Verze, Igé and Azé)
*Near river Forest area*
*5 en suite (shr) (2 fmly) (2 with balcony) No smoking on premises Full central heating Open parking available Covered parking available Child discount available 14yrs*
ROOMS: s 190FF; d 260FF
CARDS: Travellers cheques

## BARON Saône-et-Loire

### Bed & Breakfast (Prop: Jean Paul & Bernadette Larue)
Le Bourg *71120*
☎ 385240569
*Forest area Near motorway*
*2 en suite (bth/shr) TV available Radio in rooms Full central heating Open parking available Covered parking available Child discount available 12yrs*
CARDS: Travellers cheques

## BAUDRIÈRES Saône-et-Loire

### Bed & Breakfast (Prop: Yvonne Perrusson)
Le Bourg *71370*
☎ 385473190
*Forest area*
*2 rms (1 bth/shr) Full central heating Open parking available Covered parking available*

## BEAUNE Côte-D'Or

### ★★★ Château du Challanges
rue des Templiers-Challanges *21200*
☎ 380263262 FAX 380263252
(leave Beaune on the motorway A6, take direction of Challanges on the right, straight ahead at traffic lights and next right, in the village of Challanges take 1st right)
*Near river Forest area Near motorway*
*Closed end Nov-end Mar*
*14 en suite (bth/shr) 1 rooms in annexe (5 fmly) (1 with balcony) TV in all bedrooms Direct dial from all bedrooms Licensed Full central heating Open parking available Covered parking available Supervised Bicycle rental Open terrace Languages spoken: English, German & Spanish*
CARDS: ●● ■ ☲ ⑩ JCB Travellers cheques

★ ★ ★ **Henry II** (Best Western)
12/14 faubourg St-Nicholas *21200*
☎ 380228384 FAX 380241513
In town centre Near motorway
*50 en suite (bth/shr) (4 fmly) (2 with balcony) TV in all
bedrooms STV Direct dial from all bedrooms Mini-bar in all
bedrooms Licensed Lift Night porter Full central heating
Open parking available (charged) Covered parking available
(charged) Supervised Open terrace Languages spoken:
English & German*
CARDS: ● ■ ▆ ⑤ Travellers cheques

★ ★ ★ **Novotel**
av Charles-de-Gaulle *21200*
☎ 380245900 FAX 380245929
(from A6 take Beaune exit. Hotel on right before the Palais des
Congrès)
Near motorway
*127 en suite (bth/shr) (60 fmly) No smoking in 18 bedrooms
TV in all bedrooms STV Radio in rooms Direct dial from all
bedrooms Mini-bar in all bedrooms Licensed Lift Night porter
Full central heating Air conditioning in bedrooms Open
parking available Child discount available 16yrs Outdoor
swimming pool Open terrace Covered terrace Last d 24.00hrs
Languages spoken: English German & Spanish*
CARDS: ● ■ ▆ ⑤ Travellers cheques

★ ★ ★ **Hotel de la Poste**
5 bld Clemenceau *21200*
☎ 380220811 FAX 380241971
(follow the circle road in the direction Chalon-sur-Saône.
White house on the right corner before traffic lights)
This handsome building of significant character is situated
near the ramparts of the old town of Beaune and features
elegantly furnished bedrooms offering a high standard of
comfort. The Belle Epoque bar provides a cosy setting for a
game of bridge or billiards. A new cellar stocks Burgundian
wines and the garden is newly renovated.
In town centre Near motorway
*30 en suite (bth/shr) (9 fmly) (2 with balcony) TV in all
bedrooms STV Direct dial from all bedrooms Mini-bar in all
bedrooms Room-safe Licensed Lift Night porter Full central
heating Air conditioning in bedrooms Open parking available
(charged) Covered parking available (charged) Supervised
Child discount available 13yrs Pool table Open terrace V
meals Last d 21.30hrs Languages spoken: English, Arabic,
German, Greek, Italian & Spanish*
ROOMS: (room only) s 600-1100FF; d 700-1100FF
MEALS: Continental breakfast 80FF Lunch 99-349FF Dinner
145-349FF
CARDS: ● ■ ▆ ⑤ JCB Travellers cheques

★ ★ **Relais Motel 21**
rte de Verdun-Rocade Est *21230*
☎ 380241530 FAX 380241610
Near river Near lake Forest area Near motorway
*42 en suite (bth/shr) (2 fmly) TV in all bedrooms Direct dial
from all bedrooms Licensed Full central heating Open parking
available Supervised Outdoor swimming pool Solarium Boule
Bicycle rental Open terrace V meals Last d 22.00hrs
Languages spoken: English*
CARDS: ● ■ ▆ ⑤ Travellers cheques

★ ★ ★ **La Villa Fleurie**
19 pl Colbert *21200*
☎ 380226600 FAX 380224546
In town centre Near motorway

*Closed Dec-Feb
10 en suite (bth/shr) (2 fmly) TV in all bedrooms Direct dial
from all bedrooms Night porter Full central heating Open
parking available Supervised Languages spoken: English &
German*
ROOMS: (room only) d 395-420FF
CARDS: ● ▆

**BEAUREPAIRE-EN-BRESSE** Saône-et-Loire

★ ★ **Auberge de la Croix Blanche**
*71580*
☎ 385741322 FAX 385741325
Near river Near lake Near sea Forest area Near motorway
*15 en suite (bth/shr) (1 fmly) (13 with balcony) TV in all
bedrooms Licensed Full central heating Open parking
available Supervised Child discount available 3yrs Bicycle
rental Open terrace V meals Last d 21.30hrs Languages
spoken: English & German*
CARDS: ● ▆ Travellers cheques

**BELLENOT-SOUS-POUILLY** Côte-D'Or

**Bed & Breakfast** (Prop: Martine Denis)
*21320*
☎ 380907182
Near river Forest area Near motorway
*2 en suite (bth/shr) No smoking on premises Full central
heating Open parking available Child discount available
Languages spoken: English & German*

**BISSY-SOUS-UXELLES** Saône-et-Loire

**La Ferme** (Prop: P et D de la Bussiere)
Le Bourg *71460*
☎ 385501503 FAX 385501503
(from Tournus D14 towards Cluny, at Chapaize take D314
towards Bissy-sous-Uxelles. The house is next to church)
Forest area
*6 rms (4 bth/shr) (2 fmly) Open parking available Child
discount available 2yrs*

**BLANCEY** Côte-D'Or

**Château-de-Blancey** (Prop: Jean Yves Sevestre)
*21320*
☎ 380646680 FAX 380646680
(leave A6 motorway at Pouilly-en-Auxois exit and continue
through Chailly to Salieu and Blancey)
Forest area Near motorway
*3 en suite (bth/shr) (1 fmly) TV in all bedrooms Open parking
available Child discount available 11yrs Bicycle rental
Languages spoken: English*

**BOUILLAND** Côte-D'Or

**Bed & Breakfast** (Prop: Bernard & Christine Russo)
rue Josserand *21420*
☎ 380215956 FAX 380261303
(turn off A6 at exit 24 Beaune and drive across the industrial
estate then take D2 to Savigny and then Bouilland)
Near river Forest area
*2 en suite (shr) TV available Radio in rooms Full central
heating Open parking available Child discount available 5yrs
Tennis Languages spoken: English*
ROOMS: d fr 260FF
MEALS: Dinner 80FF

## BOURGVILAIN Saône-et-Loire

**Moulin des Arbillons** (Prop: Sylviane et Charles Dubois-Fav)
*71520*
☎ 385508283 FAX 385508632
(A6 exit Mâcon-Sud take N79 in direction of Moulin after 10km leave Cluny in the direction Tramayes and find the village of Bourgvilain)
Near river  Near lake  Forest area
*Closed Nov-14 Apr*
*5 en suite (bth/shr)  Full central heating  Open parking available  Child discount available 10yrs  Fishing  Boule*
CARDS: ■ Travellers cheques

## BRINON-SUR-BEUVRON Nièvre

**Château de Chanteloup** (Prop: Pierre Mainguet)
*Chanteloup 58420*
☎ 386290208 & 386296117 FAX 386296771
(off D5, leave N7 at Nevers/La Charité)
Near river  Near lake  Forest area
*Closed Jan*
*6 rms (2 bth/shr)  TV in 2 bedrooms  STV  Radio in rooms  Open parking available  Riding  Boule  Bicycle rental  Open terrace  Languages spoken: English & German*
CARDS: ■ Travellers cheques

## BUFFON Côte-D'Or

**Bed & Breakfast** (Prop: Sarah et Jean-Pierre Busson)
*21500*
☎ 380924600 FAX 380924600
(Buffon is 6km from Montabard to Paris route)
Near river  Forest area
*5 rms (3 shr)  (3 fmly)  TV in 3 bedrooms  Full central heating  Open parking available  Boule  Bicycle rental  Languages spoken: English & German*
CARDS: Travellers cheques

## BUSSY-EN-OTHE Yonne

**Bed & Breakfast** (Prop: Maud Dufayet)
*46/48 rue St-Julien 89400*
☎ 386919348
Near river  Near lake  Forest area
*4 en suite (bth/shr)  (1 fmly)  No smoking on premises  Full central heating  Open parking available  Child discount available 5yrs  V meals  Languages spoken: English*
CARDS: Travellers cheques

## BUXY Saône-et-Loire

**Bed & Breakfast** (Prop: Thierry Davanture)
*Davenay 71390*
☎ 385920479
(from A6 exit south of Chalon-sur-Saône and take N80 Le Creusot then left onto D977 to Buxy)
Near river  Near lake  Forest area  Near motorway
*2 en suite (shr)  No smoking on premises  Full central heating  Open parking available  Covered parking available  Billiard room  Languages spoken: Spanish*
ROOMS: s 250-300FF; d 300-360FF
MEALS: Dinner fr 160FF
CARDS: Travellers cheques

## CERISIERS Yonne

**La Montagne** (Prop: Aubert Hoogendam)
*89320*
☎ 386962258
(from Cerisiers head towards Migennes for 1km, then right and continue 1km)
Forest area
*3 en suite (shr)  (3 fmly)  Full central heating  Open parking available  Child discount available*

## CHABLIS Yonne

★ ★ ★ **Hostellerie des Clos**
rue Jules Rathier *89800*
☎ 386421063 FAX 386421711
In town centre
*Closed 23 Dec-18 Jan*
*26 en suite (bth/shr)  (1 fmly)  TV in all bedrooms  STV  Radio in rooms  Direct dial from all bedrooms  Mini-bar in all bedrooms  Licensed  Lift  Full central heating  Open parking available  Child discount available 12yrs  Open terrace  V meals  Last d 21.30hrs  Languages spoken: English & erman*
CARDS: ●● ■ ⅢⅢ Travellers cheques

★ ★ **De l'Étoile**
4 rue des Moulins *89800*
☎ 386421050 FAX 386428121
(from A6 exit 'Auxerre Sud' take N65 to Chablis)
Near river  Near lake  Forest area  In town centre  Near motorway
*Closed 15 Dec-10 Jan RS Nov-Etr*
*12 rms (7 bth/shr)  (4 fmly)  Direct dial from all bedrooms  Licensed  Full central heating  Open parking available  Covered parking available  Supervised  Bicycle rental  V meals  Last d 21.30hrs  Languages spoken: English, German & Spanish*
ROOMS: (room only) s 190-290FF; d 190-320FF
MEALS: Continental breakfast 40FF  Lunch 80-195FF&alc
Dinner 80-195FF&alc✱
CARDS: ●● ⅢⅢ ⑨ Travellers cheques

## CHAGNY Saône-et-Loire

★ ★ **Auberge La Musardière**
30 rte de Chalon *71150*
☎ 385870497 FAX 385872051
(off N6 near Tuilerie Lambert)
Near river  Forest area  Near motorway
*15 rms (8 bth 6 shr)  (1 fmly)  (1 with balcony)  TV in all bedrooms  Direct dial from all bedrooms  Licensed  Full central heating  Open parking available  Child discount available 2yrs  Open terrace  Covered terrace  Last d 21.00hrs*
ROOMS: (room only) d 230-265FF
MEALS: Continental breakfast 32FF  Lunch 70-170FF  Dinner 70-170FF
CARDS: ●● ■ ⅢⅢ JCB Travellers cheques

★ ★ ★ **Lameloise**
36 pl d'Armes *71150*
☎ 385876565 FAX 385870357
(approach via N74 from Beaune or N6 from S)
In town centre  Near motorway
*Closed mid Dec-late Jan*
*16 en suite (bth/shr)  (3 with balcony)  TV in all bedrooms  Direct dial from all bedrooms  Mini-bar in 7 bedrooms*

*contd.*

*Licensed Lift Night porter Full central heating Air conditioning in bedrooms Covered parking available Last d 21.30hrs Languages spoken: English & German*
ROOMS: (room only) d 750-1600FF
MEALS: Full breakfast 100FF Lunch 410-630FF&alc Dinner 410-630FF&alc
CARDS: ●● ■■ ☲ ◙ JCB Travellers cheques

### CHALON-SUR-SAÔNE Saône-et-Loire

★★ **Hotel Clarine**
35 pl de Beaune *71100*
☎ 385900800 FAX 385900801
Near river Near lake In town centre Near motorway
*50 en suite (bth/shr) 23 rooms in annexe (4 fmly) No smoking in 4 bedrooms TV in all bedrooms STV Radio in rooms Direct dial from all bedrooms Mini-bar in all bedrooms Licensed Full central heating Supervised Child discount available 16yrs Sauna Solarium Gym Languages spoken: English & German*
CARDS: ●● ■■ ☲ ◙ Travellers cheques

★★★ **Hotel St-Régis** (Best Western)
22 bd de la République *71100*
☎ 385480728 FAX 385489088
(From A6 exit 'Chalon Nord' follow signs 'Centre Ville'. Hotel in the same street as the Tourist Office)
Forest area In town centre Near motorway
*40 en suite (bth/shr) (4 fmly) (15 with balcony) TV in all bedrooms Radio in rooms Direct dial from all bedrooms Mini-bar in all bedrooms Licensed Lift Night porter Full central heating Air conditioning in bedrooms Open parking available (charged) Child discount available 12yrs Last d 22.00hrs Languages spoken: English*
CARDS: ●● ■■ ☲ ◙ JCB Travellers cheques

### CHAMPIGNELLES Yonne

**Les Perriaux** (Prop: M Noel Gillet)
*89350*
☎ 386451322 FAX 386451614
Near river Near lake Forest area
*Closed Jan*
*1 en suite (shr) No smoking on premises TV available Full central heating Open parking available Child discount available 10yrs Languages spoken: English*
CARDS: ●● ■■ ☲

### CHAPELLE-DE-BRAGNY Saône-et-Loire

**L'Arcane** (Prop: Jean-Pierre Jouvin)
*71240*
☎ 385922531
(from Chalon-sur-Saône on N6, take D6 at Varennes-le-Grand & continue to La Chapelle-de-Bragny. From Tournus, take D67 at Sennecey-le-Grand to Nanton, then D147 to La Chapelle-de-Bragny. B&B near church)
An old stone and oak house in the heart of Burgundy, boasting an entirely private apartment for 4/5 persons on the second floor. There is a kitchen, TV and video, a mezzanine above, and a big veranda is available, plus a large courtyard and garden. Bicycles and table-tennis on site.
Near river Near lake Forest area
*1 en suite (shr) (1 fmly) No smoking in all bedrooms TV in all bedrooms Radio in rooms Full central heating Open parking available Covered parking available Child discount available 6yrs Bicycle rental Table tennis 3 Bikes Languages spoken: English, German & Spanish*

ROOMS: s 200FF; d 250FF
MEALS: Dinner 95FF
CARDS: Travellers cheques

### CHAPELLE-SOUS-BRANCION, LA Saône-et-Loire

**Château de Nobles** (Prop: Bertrand de Cherisey)
*71700*
☎ 385510055
(14km west of Tournus on D14 exit Tournus from A6 towards Cluny and Charolles)
Near river Forest area Near motorway
*Closed 15 Nov-Mar*
*2 en suite (bth) (2 fmly) Full central heating Open parking available Bicycle rental Barbecue Languages spoken: English & Italian*
CARDS: Travellers cheques

### CHARBONNAT Saône-et-Loire

**Bed & Breakfast** (Prop: Marie Urie-Bixel)
La Montagne *71320*
☎ 385542647 FAX 385542647
(16km south of Autun, go through Étang-sur-Arroux, 9km further south turn right to St Nizier and to Charbonnat. La Montagne signposted from the church)
Near river Near lake Forest area
*Closed 16 Oct-Apr*
*2 en suite (shr) (2 fmly) Open parking available Languages spoken: English & German*
ROOMS: s fr 180FF; d fr 200FF ✱

### CHARDONNAY Saône-et-Loire

**Le Tinailler du Manoir** (Prop: J-P et R Rullière)
Manoir de Champvent *71700*
☎ 385405023 FAX 385405018
(from A6 exit Tournus onto D56 towards Lugny, 3km after Chardonnay right onto D463 & follow signs to Chambre d'hôtes/Theatre Champvent)
*Closed Jan*
*5 en suite (bth/shr) No smoking in 1 bedroom Full central heating Open parking available Child discount available Languages spoken: English German & Italian*
CARDS: ■■

### CHARITÉ-SUR-LOIRE Nièvre

★★★ **Le Grand Monarque**
33 quai Clemenceau *58400*
☎ 386702173 FAX 386696232
(exit N7 at Bourges)
Near river Forest area In town centre Near motorway
*Closed 21 Feb-19 Mar*
*15 en suite (bth/shr) (4 fmly) TV in all bedrooms STV Radio in rooms Direct dial from all bedrooms Mini-bar in all bedrooms Licensed Lift Full central heating Open parking available Covered parking available (charged) Supervised Child discount available 8yrs Last d 21.00hrs Languages spoken: English, German & Spanish*
ROOMS: (room only) s 290-310FF; d 330-620FF **Special breaks**
MEALS: Continental breakfast 50FF Lunch 108-238FF&alc Dinner 108-238FF&alc
CARDS: ●● ■■ ☲ ◙ JCB Travellers cheques

## CHARRIN Nièvre

**Bed & Breakfast** (Prop: Oliver de Brem & Broll Patrick)
Château du Vernet *58300*
☎ 386503687
(from Nevers N81 to Decize then D979 to Charrin)
Near river Forest area
*3 en suite (bth/shr) (3 fmly) Radio in rooms Full central heating Open parking available Covered parking available Supervised Child discount available 10yrs Golf 9 Boule Table tennis Last d 21.00hrs Languages spoken: English & German*
CARDS: Travellers cheques

**Bed & Breakfast** (Prop: Francoise Au Rousseau)
La Varenne *58300*
☎ 386503014 FAX 386503856
Near river Forest area
*2 en suite (shr) (1 fmly) (1 with balcony) TV in 1 bedroom Radio in rooms Full central heating Open parking available*
ROOMS: d 230FF ✱

## CHASSEY-LE-CAMP Saône-et-Loire

★ ★ ★ **Auberge du Camp Romain**
*71150*
☎ 385870991 FAX 385871151
Forest area
*Closed Jan*
*41 en suite (bth/shr) 17 rooms in annexe (7 fmly) (17 with balcony) TV in all bedrooms STV Direct dial from all bedrooms Licensed Lift Full central heating Open parking available Covered parking available Child discount available 10yrs Indoor swimming pool (heated) Outdoor swimming pool (heated) Tennis Sauna Solarium Pool table Boule Mini-golf Jacuzzi/spa Bicycle rental Open terrace V meals Last d 21.00hrs Languages spoken: English & German*
CARDS: ●● ▆▆ Travellers cheques

## CHÂTEAU-CHINON Nièvre

★ ★ **Au Vieux Morvan**
8 pl Gudin *58120*
☎ 386850501 386851011 FAX 386850278
Near river Near lake Forest area In town centre
*24 en suite (bth/shr) (8 fmly) TV in all bedrooms Direct dial from all bedrooms Licensed Night porter Full central heating Open parking available Supervised Child discount available 12yrs V meals*
CARDS: ●● ▆▆ Travellers cheques

## CHÂTEAUNEUF Côte-D'Or

★ ★ **Hostellerie du Château**
rue du Centre *21320*
☎ 380492200 FAX 380492127
(Approach via A6 exit 'Pouilly-en-Auxois')
Near lake Forest area Near motorway
*Closed Dec & Jan*
*17 en suite (bth/shr) 8 rooms in annexe (9 fmly) Direct dial from all bedrooms Licensed Full central heating Child discount available 10yrs Open terrace Last d 21.00hrs Languages spoken: English & German*
ROOMS: (room only) d 270-430FF
MEALS: Continental breakfast 50FF Lunch 140-220FF&alc Dinner 140-220FF&alc
CARDS: ●● ▆▆ ▆▆ ◫

## CHÂTENAY Saône-et-Loire

**Bed & Breakfast** (Prop: Bernadette Jolivet)
Les Bassets *71800*
☎ 385281951 FAX 385268310
Near river Forest area
*4 en suite (shr) (2 fmly) Full central heating Open parking available*

## CHAUMARD Nièvre

**Bed & Breakfast** (Prop: M Vaissettes)
Le Château *58120*
☎ 386780333 FAX 386780494
(north of Château-Chinon take D37 then D12. Establishment at entrance to village on left)
Near river Near lake Forest area
*6 rms (3 bth) (6 fmly) Full central heating Open parking available Child discount available 12yrs Fishing Boule Last d 20.00hrs Languages spoken: English*
ROOMS: d 240-260FF
MEALS: Dinner 95-130FF✱
CARDS: Travellers cheques

## CHEVANNES Yonne

**Château de Ribourdin** (Prop: Claude Brodard)
*89240*
☎ 386412316 FAX 386412316
(leave A6/N6 at exit Auxerre Nord in the direction St Georges/Baulches then Chevannes)
Five guest rooms are available in the outbuildings of this 16th-century château; one bedroom is suitable for guests with disabilities. Each room is decorated individually and furnished with antiques. Restaurants and shops close by. Well situated for visits to regional vineyards and tourist attractions.
Near river Forest area Near motorway
*5 en suite (bth/shr) (1 fmly) Full central heating Open parking available Child discount available 5yrs Outdoor swimming pool Bicycle rental Languages spoken: English*
ROOMS: s fr 300FF; d 350-400FF

## CHEVIGNY-FÉNAY Côte-D'Or

★ ★ **Relais de la Sans Fond**
rte de Seurre *21600*
☎ 380366135 FAX 380369489
Near lake Forest area Near motorway
*17 en suite (bth) (3 fmly) (1 with balcony) No smoking in 1 bedroom TV in all bedrooms Direct dial from all bedrooms Mini-bar in all bedrooms Licensed Full central heating Open parking available Supervised Child discount available 12yrs Boule Bicycle rental Open terrace V meals Last d 21.30hrs Languages spoken: English & German*
CARDS: ●● ▆▆ ▆▆ Travellers cheques

## CHOREY-LES-BEAUNE Côte-D'Or

**Le Château** (Prop: Gernain)
*21200*
☎ 380220605 FAX 380240393
(on the Autoroute Beaune take the direction of Dijon N74, 3km after Beaune 1st village on the right, Château on entry to village)
Forest area

*contd.*

*Closed Dec-Mar*
*5 en suite (bth) (4 fmly) (1 with balcony) Full central heating*
*Open parking available Languages spoken: English & German*
CARDS: ● ▨ Travellers cheques

### CLAMEREY Côte-D'Or

**La Maison du Canal**
Pont Royal *21390*
☎ 380646265 FAX 380646572
(from Paris exit A6 at Bierre-les-Semur, take D70 in the
direction of Vitteaux to just past Clamerey)
Near lake  Forest area  Near motorway
*Closed 16 Nov-14 Mar*
*6 en suite (shr) Full central heating Open parking available*
*Covered parking available (charged) Supervised Bicycle rental*
*Languages spoken: English*
CARDS: ● ▨ Travellers cheques

### CLUNY Saône-et-Loire

**★ ★ ★ Bourgogne**
pl de l'Abbaye *71250*
☎ 385590058 FAX 385590373
This establishment was constructed in 1817 on the site where
the Benedictine Abbey of Cluny originally stood. Although
simple in outlook, inside it features old stone walls and period
furnishings, spacious bedrooms and attractive apartments
with assorted 19th-century antiques and objets d'art. For
relaxation there is a bar and an interior garden. The restaurant
serves imaginative dishes complemented by an excellent
choice of wines. Many open air leisure facilities are in the
vicinity, and the town of Cluny, with its abbey and Roman
churches, is well worth a visit.
Near river  Forest area
*Closed Dec-Feb*

*15 en suite (bth/shr) (4 fmly) No smoking in 2 bedrooms TV in*
*all bedrooms Direct dial from all bedrooms Licensed Full*
*central heating Open parking available (charged) Covered*
*parking available (charged) Supervised Child discount*
*available 12yrs Bicycle rental Open terrace V meals Last d*
*21.00hrs Languages spoken: English & German*
ROOMS: s 470-570FF; d 570-1010FF
MEALS: Full breakfast 60FF Lunch 130-220FF Dinner 130-
220FF
CARDS: ● ■ ▨ Travellers cheques

**La Courtine** (Prop: Noëlle Donnadieu)
rue Pont de la Levée *71250*
☎ 385590510 FAX 385590510
(from A6 exit at Mâcon and take N79, then D980 to Cluny)

Near river  Forest area  Near motorway
*5 en suite (bth) (2 fmly) Full central heating Open parking*
*available Supervised Languages spoken: English & Italian*
CARDS: Travellers cheques

### COLLAN Yonne

**Bed & Breakfast** (Prop: M & Mme Lecolle)
2 r de l'École la Marmotte *89700*
☎ 386552644 FAX 386552644
Forest area
*3 en suite (bth/shr) No smoking on premises Full central*
*heating Open parking available Child discount available*
ROOMS: (room only) s 190FF; d 260FF
MEALS: Dinner 95FF
CARDS: ■

### CORBERON Côte-D'Or

**Bed & Breakfast** (Prop: Alain & Chantal Balmelle)
r des Ormes *21250*
☎ 380265319
Near river  Forest area
*4 en suite (bth/shr) (3 fmly) (1 with balcony) No smoking on*
*premises Full central heating Open parking available*
*Languages spoken: English*
CARDS: Travellers cheques

### COUCHES Saône-et-Loire

**★ ★ Des Trois Maures**
*71490*
☎ 385496393 FAX 385495029
Forest area
*Closed 15 Feb-15 Mar*
*16 en suite (bth/shr) (2 fmly) TV in all bedrooms Direct dial*
*from all bedrooms Full central heating Open parking available*
*Child discount available 15yrs Open terrace Covered terrace*
*Last d 21.00hrs Languages spoken: Italian*
CARDS: ● ■ ▨ Travellers cheques

### COURTIVRON Côte-D'Or

**Chalet de Genevroix** (Prop: M & Mme J Huot)
*21120*
☎ 380751255 FAX 380751562
A chalet situated on a cereal farm. Living room, library,
television, picnic area all available to guests. Restaurant in the
village.
Near river  Forest area

*2 rms No smoking on premises TV in all bedrooms Full central heating Open parking available Fishing Table tennis Languages spoken: English & German*
ROOMS: d 200-210FF **Reductions over 1 night**
CARDS: Travellers cheques

### COURTOIS-SUR-YONNE Yonne

**Bed & Breakfast** (Prop: D & H-F Lafolie)
3 rue des Champs Rouges *89100*
☎ 386970033 FAX 386970033
(from Sens take D58 through St Martin-du-Tertre and on to Courtois. In Courtois take 3rd right, establishment last house on left)
Near river Forest area Near motorway
*4 rms (3 shr) (1 fmly) Full central heating Open parking available Covered parking available Table tennis*
CARDS: Travellers cheques

### CRUZY-LE-CHÂTEL Yonne

**Bed & Breakfast** (Prop: M & Mme Batreau)
Impasse du Presbytere *89740*
☎ 386752276
Near motorway
*(1 fmly) Open parking available Supervised Child discount available Languages spoken: English*
CARDS: Travellers cheques

### DEVROUZE Saône-et-Loire

**Domaine des Druides** (Prop: A & J Hoehler)
*71330*
☎ 385724706 FAX 385724706
(from A6 exit at Tournas and take D971 to Louhans,then N78 north to crossroads at Quain.Turn right onto D24 towards St Germain-du-Bois, then right to establishment)
Near river Forest area Near motorway
Closed Jan-Feb
*4 en suite (shr) (3 fmly) No smoking on premises Full central heating Open parking available Supervised Child discount available 16yrs Fishing Riding Bicycle rental Canoeing, Donkey rides V meals Languages spoken: English,German & Italian*
CARDS: Travellers cheques

### DIGOIN Saône-et-Loire

**★ ★ Des Diligences et du Commerce**
14 rue Nationale *71160*
☎ 385530631 FAX 385889243
(From Mâcon take N79 through Charolles to Digoin)
Near river In town centre
*6 en suite (bth/shr) (3 fmly) (3 with balcony) TV in 15 bedrooms Direct dial from 15 bedrooms Mini-bar in 1 bedroom Licensed Full central heating Open parking available Covered parking available Supervised Child discount available Open terrace Covered terrace V meals Last d 21.30hrs Languages spoken: English & Spanish*
ROOMS: (room only) d 250-350FF
MEALS: Full breakfast 35FF Lunch 98-330FF&alc Dinner 98-330FF&alc
CARDS: ●● ■■ ■■ ⑩

### DIJON Côte-D'Or

**★ ★ Castel Burgond**
3 rte de Troyes, RN 71 *21121*
☎ 380565972 FAX 380576948
(From town centre take N71 towards Troyes. Hotel near last set of traffic lights on right)
Near lake Forest area Near motorway
*38 en suite (bth) (13 fmly) (2 with balcony) TV in all bedrooms Radio in rooms Direct dial from all bedrooms Mini-bar in all bedrooms Licensed Lift Night porter Full central heating Open parking available Child discount available Pool table Boule V meals Languages spoken: English, German & Spanish*
ROOMS: (room only) s 280-290FF; d 305-315FF
CARDS: ●● ■■ ■■ ⑩ Travellers cheques

**★ ★ Climat de France**
15-17 av du Maréchal-Foch *21000*
☎ 380434004 FAX 380431002
(in centre of town, near railway station)
Near lake In town centre Near motorway
*81 en suite (bth/shr) (2 fmly) TV in all bedrooms STV Radio in rooms Direct dial from all bedrooms Licensed Lift Night porter Full central heating Air conditioning in bedrooms Child discount available 12yrs V meals Last d 22.30hrs Languages spoken: English, German & Italian*
CARDS: ●● ■■ ■■ ⑩ Travellers cheques

**★ ★ ★ Hotel des Ducs**
5 rue Lamonnoye *21000*
☎ 380673131 FAX 380671951
(in the centre of Dijon , between the theatre and St Michel's church)
In town centre
*35 en suite (bth/shr) 2 rooms in annexe (13 fmly) (9 with balcony) No smoking in 4 bedrooms TV in all bedrooms STV Radio in rooms Direct dial from all bedrooms Mini-bar in 15 bedrooms Licensed Lift Night porter Full central heating Open parking available (charged) Covered parking available (charged) Supervised Child discount available 12yrs Pool table Open terrace Languages spoken: English*
CARDS: ●● ■■ ■■ Travellers cheques

### DONZY Nièvre

**★ ★ Grand Monarque**
10 rue de l'Étape *58220*
☎ 386393544 FAX 386393709
(SE of Cosne-sur-Loire on D33)
Near river Near lake Forest area In town centre Near motorway
*(4 fmly) TV in 11 bedrooms Direct dial from 11 bedrooms Licensed Full central heating Open parking available Child discount available Pool table Bicycle rental Open terrace Last d 21.00hrs Languages spoken: English*
CARDS: ●● ■■ Travellers cheques

**Jardins de Belle Rive Bagnaux** (Prop: M & Mme Juste)
Bagnaux *58220*
☎ 386394218
Near river Forest area
*3 en suite (bth/shr) (2 fmly) (1 with balcony) No smoking on premises Open parking available Supervised Child discount available Outdoor swimming pool Languages spoken: English*
CARDS: Travellers cheques

**ÉCHALOT** Côte-D'Or

**Bed & Breakfast** (Prop: Mme R Bonnefoy)
rue du Centre *21510*
☎ 380938684
Near river Forest area
*2 en suite (shr) Full central heating Open parking available
Supervised Child discount available Languages spoken:
German*

**ÉCUTIGNY** Côte-D'Or

**Château d'Ecutigny** (Prop: M & Mme P Rochet)
*21360*
☎ 380201914 FAX 380201915
(access via D970 and D33. Château on western outskirts
towards Bessey-la-Cour)
Near river Near lake Forest area
*6 en suite (bth/shr) No smoking on premises TV in 7 bedrooms
Radio in rooms Full central heating Open parking available
Covered parking available Supervised Child discount available
12yrs Tennis Boule Bicycle rental Last d am Languages
spoken: English & Spanish*
CARDS: ●● ▦ Travellers cheques

**ÉGUILLY** Côte-D'Or

**Rente d'Eguilly** (Prop: M & Mme Rance)
*21320*
☎ 380908348
Near river Near lake Forest area Near motorway
*5 rms (2 bth 1 shr) (1 fmly) No smoking on premises Full
central heating Open parking available Covered parking
available Supervised Child discount available 6yrs*

**ENTRAINS-SUR-NOHAIN** Nièvre

**Maison des Adirondacks** (Prop: Noelle Weissberg)
pl Saint-Sulpice *58410*
☎ 386292323 FAX 247202159
Forest area In town centre
*Closed 3 Nov-14 Apr
4 en suite (bth/shr) (2 fmly) STV Radio in rooms Child
discount available Languages spoken: English & Italian*

**ÉPERNAY-SOUS-GEVREY** Côte-D'Or

**La Vieille Auberge** (Prop: Jules Plimmer)
2 pl des Tilleuls *21220*
☎ 380366176 FAX 380366468
(from A6 exit at Nuits-St-Georges. Take N74 in direction of
Dijon and at large roundabout at Vougeot follow D25 for 6kms.
House next to church)
Completely renovated by the new owners, this property was
originally a farmhouse and then the village pub. Situated in a
village, with a population of only 130, between Beaune and
Dijon, the rooms look out onto the village square. All the major
Burgundy vineyards are just a short drive away. The English
hosts have two young children so their fully enclosed garden
has swings etc.
Near lake Near sea Forest area Near motorway
*Closed 16-31 Dec
6 rms (1 bth 4 shr) (2 fmly) (1 with balcony) No smoking on
premises Full central heating Open parking available
Supervised Child discount available 15yrs Languages spoken:
English*

ROOMS: s fr 250FF; d fr 330FF
MEALS: Dinner fr 100FF✱
CARDS: Travellers cheques

**ESCOLIVES-STE-CAMILLE** Yonne

**Bed & Breakfast** (Prop: M & Mme Borgnat)
1 rue de l'Église *89290*
☎ 386533528 FAX 386536500
Near river Near motorway
*5 en suite (bth/shr) (1 fmly) TV in 2 bedrooms Full central
heating Open parking available Supervised Child discount
available Outdoor swimming pool Table tennis Last d 18.00hrs
Languages spoken: English & German*
CARDS: ●● ▦

★ ★ **Le Mas des Lilas**
La Cour Barrée *89290*
☎ 386536055 FAX 386533081
(exit 20 from A6 in direction of Auxerre on N65. At roundabout
take direction of Avallon/Dijon by N6 after approx 10km from
roundabout cross village La Cour Barrée. Hotel on right just
after bridge)
Near river Near motorway
*Closed 15 days autumn & 15 days winter
17 en suite (bth/shr) (2 fmly) No smoking in 2 bedrooms TV in
6 bedrooms Direct dial from all bedrooms Licensed Full
central heating Air conditioning in bedrooms Open parking
available Child discount available 5yrs Boule Bicycle rental
Open terrace Languages spoken: English & Spanish*
CARDS: ●● ▦

**FLAVIGNY-SUR-OZERAIN** Côte-D'Or

**Couvent des Castafours** (Prop: Judith Lemoine)
*21150*
☎ 380962492
(on reaching village from 'La Porte du Bourg' proceed to the
church, and house can be seen below in courtyard)
Set in the heart of a medieval city, this house has been restored
from the remains of an old 17th-century convent. The view
over the Auxois is magnificent. Garden and parking available.
Meals served with the hosts, although reservations are
necessary. Reductions for children up to ten years.
Near river Near beach Forest area
*2 en suite (shr) No smoking on premises Full central heating
Open parking available Child discount available 10yrs Last d
17.00hrs Languages spoken: English*
ROOMS: s 200FF; d 260FF **Reductions over 1 night
Special breaks**
MEALS: Dinner fr 100FF
CARDS: Travellers cheques

**FLEURVILLE** Saône-et-Loire

★ ★ ★ **Château de Fleurville**
*71260*
☎ 385331217 FAX 385339534
Near river Near motorway
*Closed Nov-Feb
15 en suite (bth) (2 fmly) TV in all bedrooms Licensed Full
central heating Open parking available Outdoor swimming
pool (heated) Tennis Boule Open terrace Last d 21.30hrs
Languages spoken: English & German*
CARDS: ●● ▦ ⑩ Travellers cheques

## FONTAINE-FRANÇAISE Côte-D'Or

**Le Vieux Moulin** (Prop: Patrick Berger)
Le Vieux Moulin *21610*
☎ 380758216 FAX 380758216
(from A31 exit 5, take D961, then D960 to Bèze and on to
Fontaine-Française)

The old mill was constructed in the 17th century and now
offers flatlets, a living room and library for guests. Buffet
suppers on request. Garden with private swimming pool and
barbecue. Children's leisure activities available. Stores and
services within walking distance.
Near river  Near lake  Forest area  In town centre
*5 en suite (bth/shr) (2 fmly) (1 with balcony) No smoking on
premises  TV in 2 bedrooms  Full central heating  Open parking
available  Supervised  Child discount available 12yrs  Outdoor
swimming pool  Boule  Languages spoken: English*
MEALS: Dinner 95FF✱
CARDS: ● ▩ Travellers cheques

## FONTAINES Saône-et-Loire

★★ *Auberge des Fontaines*
*71150*
☎ 385914800
(north of Chalon-sur-Saône close to the N6)
Near river  Forest area  Near motorway
*Closed 21 Dec-9 Jan*
*9 rms (7 bth/shr) Direct dial from 7 bedrooms  Licensed  Full
central heating  Open parking available  Supervised  Open
terrace  V meals  Last d 21.00hrs*
CARDS: ● ▩

## FRONTENAUD Saône-et-Loire

**Bed & Breakfast** (Prop: M et Mme H Fritschi)
Le Venay *71580*
☎ 385748524 FAX 385748524
Near river  Forest area  Near motorway
*Closed Nov-Mar*
*6 en suite (shr) (2 fmly) Full central heating  Open parking
available  Child discount available 4yrs  Outdoor swimming
pool  Boule  Bicycle rental  Languages spoken: English &
German*

**Bed & Breakfast**
ROOMS: s 260FF; d 360FF  ✱ **Reductions over 1 night**
MEALS: Dinner 100FF✱

## GEVREY-CHAMBERTIN Côte-D'Or

**Bed & Breakfast** (Prop: Mme G Sylvain)
14 r de l'Église *21220*
☎ 380518639 FAX 380518639
(signposted in the village 'Mme G Sylvain')
Forest area  In town centre  Near motorway
*6 en suite (bth/shr) TV available  Full central heating*
ROOMS: s fr 230FF; d fr 280FF
CARDS: Travellers cheques

## GIVRY Saône-et-Loire

★ *Hostellerie de la Halle*
2 pl de la Halle *71640*
☎ 385443245 FAX 385444945
In town centre
*Closed 2-15 Jan*
*9 rms (1 fmly) Licensed  Full central heating  Last d 21.30hrs*
CARDS: ● ▩ Travellers cheques

## GOURDON Saône-et-Loire

**Bed & Breakfast** (Prop: Mme M Gibert)
Mont Bretange *71300*
☎ 385798078
Forest area
*2 en suite (bth) No smoking on premises  Full central heating
Open parking available  Languages spoken: Italian*
CARDS: Travellers cheques

## GREVILLY Saône-et-Loire

*Le Pre Menot* (Prop: Claude Dépreay)
*71700*
☎ 385332992 FAX 385330279
(from Tournus take D14 towards Cormatin then left onto D163
towards Gratay. 1st right onto D356 to Grevilly)
Near river  Forest area  Near motorway
*2 en suite (bth/shr) TV in all bedrooms  Radio in rooms
Licensed  Full central heating  Open parking available  Child
discount available 5yrs  Boule  Bicycle rental  Open terrace
Languages spoken: English*
CARDS: ● ▩ ◑ Travellers cheques

**IGUERANDE** Saône-et-Loire

**Bed & Breakfast** (Prop: M Martin)
Les Montées *71340*
☎ 385840969
(from D982 Roanne/Digoin turn off at Iguerande proceed to
Outre-Loire then Monteés)
Near river  Near lake  Forest area
*4 en suite (bth/shr) (3 fmly) No smoking on premises  Full
central heating  Open parking available  Supervised  Languages
spoken: English & German*

**JOIGNY** Yonne

★ ★ ★ **Hotel Rive Gauche**
Chemin du Port au Bois, BP 194 *89304*
☎ 386914666 FAX 386914693
Le Rive Gauche is situated in the town of Joigny, known for its
arts and history, on the banks of the River Yonne. The hotel
offers its clientele a charming interior with comfortable
bedrooms, equipped with well appointed, pretty bathrooms.
With its terraces, flower-filled garden and cosy cocktail bar it
meets the needs of both tourists and business travellers.

Near river  In town centre  Near motorway
*42 en suite (bth) (5 fmly) (20 with balcony)  TV in all bedrooms
Direct dial from all bedrooms  Mini-bar in all bedrooms
Licensed  Lift  Full central heating  Open parking available
Child discount available 12yrs  Tennis  Bicycle rental  Open
terrace  Last d 22.00hrs  Languages spoken: English*
ROOMS: (room only) s 260-360FF; d 360-460FF
MEALS: Continental breakfast 50FF  Lunch 168-210FF&alc
Dinner 168-210FF&alc
CARDS: ● ■ ■

**JOURS-LÈS-BAIGNEUX** Côte-D'Or

**Bed & Breakfast** (Prop: Mme Juliette Descombes)
*21450*
☎ 380965222
Forest area  Near motorway
*4 en suite (shr)  No smoking on premises  Full central heating
Open parking available*
CARDS: Travellers cheques

**LAMARCHE-SUR-SAÔNE** Côte-D'Or

★ ★ **Hostellerie Le St-Antoine**
rte de Vonges *21760*
☎ 380471133 FAX 380471356
Near river  Forest area  Near motorway
*12 en suite (bth/shr)  4 rooms in annexe (4 fmly) (4 with*

balcony)  No smoking in 4 bedrooms  TV in all bedrooms  Direct
dial from all bedrooms  Mini-bar in all bedrooms  Room-safe
(charged)  Licensed  Full central heating  Open parking
available  Supervised  Child discount available 12yrs  Outdoor
swimming pool  Fishing  Sauna  Bicycle rental  Open terrace
Covered terrace  Last d 21.30hrs  Languages spoken: English*
ROOMS: (room only) d 280-360FF
MEALS: Continental breakfast 40FF  Lunch fr 120FF&alc
Dinner fr 120FF&alc
CARDS: ● ■ ■ Travellers cheques

**LAVAU** Yonne

**La Chasseuserie** (Prop: M & Mme Marty)
*89170*
☎ 386741609
Forest area
*3 en suite (bth) (2 fmly)  Full central heating  Open parking
available  Supervised  Outdoor swimming pool  Languages
spoken: English*

**LEUGNY** Yonne

**La Borde** (Prop: M P Moreau)
*89130*
☎ 386476428 FAX 386476028
(from Toucy take D950 in the direction of Avallon)
Near river  Forest area
*4 en suite (bth/shr)  TV available  Full central heating  Open
parking available  Child discount available  Languages spoken:
English*
CARDS: ● ■

**LEVERNOIS** Côte-D'Or

★ ★ ★ ★ **Hostellerie de Levernois**
rte de Combertault *21200*
☎ 380247358 FAX 380227800
(from A6 exit at Beaune take D970 towards Verdun-sur-le-Doubs)
Near river  Near motorway
Closed 15 days in Feb, 24-28 Dec RS closed Tue/Sun nights
Nov-Mar
*16 en suite (bth/shr)  12 rooms in annexe (6 fmly)  TV in all
bedrooms  STV  Direct dial from all bedrooms  Mini-bar in all
bedrooms  Room-safe  Licensed  Full central heating  Air
conditioning in bedrooms  Open parking available  Supervised
Golf 18  Tennis  Bicycle rental  Open terrace  Last d 22.00hrs
Languages spoken: English*
ROOMS: (room only) d 950-1100FF
MEALS: Full breakfast 95FF  Lunch 150-680FF&alc  Dinner
345-680FF&alc
CARDS: ● ■ ■ ◉ Travellers cheques

**LONGVIC** Côte-D'Or

★ ★ **Climat de France**
7 rue de Beaurégard *21600*
☎ 380672222 FAX 380671511
(in direction of Airport and Lyon Par Autoroute)
Climat de France hotels feature bedrooms with modern
facilities. Restaurants serve a variety of menus often using local
produce; as well as a generous "as much as you like" buffet
menu. Many hotels are located close to major national routes
and motorways. A central reservations number is available
Monday to Friday 8.30am to 7pm and Saturdays 9am to 6pm,
by dialling 00 33 1 64460123.
Near motorway

**Climat de France**
*55 en suite (shr) (3 fmly) No smoking in 3 bedrooms TV in all bedrooms STV Direct dial from all bedrooms Licensed Full central heating Open parking available Child discount available 13yrs Open terrace Covered terrace Last d 22.00hrs Languages spoken: English*
ROOMS: (room only) s 300FF; d 320FF
MEALS: Full breakfast 38FF Continental breakfast 38FF Lunch 65-125FF&alc Dinner 78-125FF&alc
CARDS: ●● ■■ ▆▆ ⓓ Travellers cheques

### LORMES Nièvre

★★**Perreau**
8 rte d'Avallon *58140*
☎ 386225321 FAX 386228215
Near lake Forest area In town centre
*17 en suite (bth/shr) 9 rooms in annexe (2 fmly) TV in all bedrooms Direct dial from all bedrooms Licensed Full central heating Open parking available Child discount available Last d 21.00hrs Languages spoken: English*
ROOMS: (room only) s 250-270FF; d 260-280FF ✱
CARDS: ●● ▆▆

### LOUHANS Saône-et-Loire

★★*Moulin de Bourgchâteau*
rte de Chalon
☎ 385753712 FAX 385754511
(in Louhans head towards Chalon/Dijon and follow the road past the Citroën Parc Exposition)
Near river In town centre
Closed 21 Dec-19 Jan
*18 en suite (bth/shr) TV in all bedrooms STV Direct-dial available Full central heating Open parking available Supervised Fishing Jacuzzi/spa Bicycle rental Open terrace V meals Last d 21.00hrs Languages spoken: English*
CARDS: ●● ■■ ▆▆ Travellers cheques

### MÂCON Saône-et-Loire

★★★**Hotel Bellevue**
416 quai Lamartine *71000*
☎ 385210404 FAX 385210402
(centre of town)
Near river In town centre Near motorway
*25 en suite (bth/shr) (6 fmly) (1 with balcony) TV in all bedrooms STV Direct dial from all bedrooms Licensed Lift Night porter Full central heating Open parking available (charged) Covered parking available (charged) Supervised Child discount available 12yrs Last d 22.00hrs Languages spoken: English, German & Spanish*

ROOMS: (room only) d 450-750FF
MEALS: Continental breakfast 56FF Lunch 140-295FF&alc Dinner 140-295FF&alc
CARDS: ●● ■■ ▆▆ ⓓ JCB Travellers cheques

★★★*Novotel Mâcon Nord*
Sennecé-lès-Mâcon, Péage Mâcon Nord *71000*
☎ 385204000 FAX 385204033
Near motorway
*114 en suite (bth) (114 fmly) No smoking in 25 bedrooms TV in all bedrooms STV Radio in rooms Direct dial from all bedrooms Mini-bar in all bedrooms Licensed Night porter Full central heating Air conditioning in bedrooms Open parking available Child discount available 16yrs Outdoor swimming pool Pool table Boule Open terrace Volley ball Games for children V meals Last d 24.00hrs Languages spoken: English*
CARDS: ●● ■■ ▆▆ ⓓ Travellers cheques

★★**Terminus**
91 rue Victor Hugo *71000*
☎ 385391711 FAX 385380275
(A6 exit 29, in town centre)
Near river In town centre Near motorway
*48 en suite (bth/shr) (16 fmly) TV in all bedrooms STV Radio in rooms Direct dial from all bedrooms Licensed Lift Night porter Full central heating Covered parking available (charged) Supervised Child discount available Outdoor swimming pool Open terrace V meals Last d 21.30hrs Languages spoken: English, German & Spanish*
ROOMS: (room only) s 290FF; d 345-395FF **Reductions over 1 night Special breaks**
MEALS: Continental breakfast 43FF Lunch 95-175FF&alc Dinner 95-175FF&alc
CARDS: ●● ■■ ▆▆ ⓓ Eurocard Travellers cheques

### MAGNY-COURS Nièvre

★★★*Holiday Inn*
Ferme du Domaine de Bardonnay *58470*
☎ 386212223 FAX 386212203
Near motorway
*70 en suite (bth) (6 fmly) (2 with balcony) No smoking in 22 bedrooms TV in all bedrooms STV Radio in rooms Direct dial from all bedrooms Mini-bar in all bedrooms Room-safe Licensed Lift Night porter Full central heating Air conditioning in bedrooms Open parking available Supervised Child discount available 12yrs Outdoor swimming pool (heated) Tennis Sauna Gym Pool table Open terrace Table tennis Last d 22.30hrs Languages spoken: English, Spanish & german*
ROOMS: (room only) d 480-570FF **Special breaks: wknds**
MEALS: Full breakfast 60FF Lunch fr 98FF&alc Dinner fr 98FF&alc
CARDS: ●● ■■ ▆▆ ⓓ JCB Travellers cheques

★★★★**La Renaissance**
Ancienne N7 *58470*
☎ 386581040 FAX 386212260
(S of Nevers on N7 in village of Magny Cours)
Closed 3 wks Feb & Mar, 2 wks Aug
*9 en suite (bth/shr) (1 fmly) TV in all bedrooms STV Direct dial from all bedrooms Mini-bar in 5 bedrooms Room-safe Licensed Full central heating Air conditioning in bedrooms Open parking available Supervised Child discount available 10yrs Open terrace V meals Last d 21.30hrs Languages spoken: English & Italian*

*contd.*

ROOMS: (room only) s 450-500FF; d 500-600FF
MEALS: Continental breakfast 60FF Lunch 250-400FF&alc
Dinner 250-400FF&alc✱
CARDS: ●● ■■ ☲☲

### MALIGNY Côte-D'Or

**Bed & Breakfast** (Prop: Mme Veronique Paillard)
*21230*
☎ 380842650 & 380842639
Forest area
*3 en suite (bth/shr) No smoking on premises Full central heating Open parking available Covered parking available Supervised Child discount available*
CARDS: Travellers cheques

### MARCHAIS-BETON Yonne

**La Cour Alexandre** (Prop: Mme Desvignes)
*89120*
☎ 386916433 FAX 386916992
(take autoroute to Courtenay. Then go through Douchy, Charny, Chambeugle and finally Marchais-Beton on the D64)
*Near river Forest area*
*6 en suite (bth/shr) (2 fmly) (1 with balcony) TV in 2 bedrooms Full central heating Open parking available Covered parking available Supervised Child discount available Outdoor swimming pool Tennis Fishing Bicycle rental Languages spoken: English, German, Italian & Spanish*
ROOMS: s fr 300FF; d 450-500FF **Reductions over 1 night**

### MARCIGNY Saône-et-Loire

**Château de la Frédière** (Prop: J Charlier)
*71110*
☎ 385251967 FAX 385253501
*Near river*
*Closed 20 Dec-Jan RS 10 Feb-15 Mar & 15 Nov-19 Dec*
*11 en suite (bth/shr) TV in all bedrooms Full central heating Open parking available Child discount available 5yrs Outdoor swimming pool Bicycle rental Last d 21.00hrs*
CARDS: ●● ☲☲

**Les Récollets** (Prop: Josette Badin)
*71110*
☎ 385250516 FAX 385250691
*Near river*
*9 en suite (bth/shr) (3 fmly) TV in all bedrooms STV Radio in rooms Full central heating Open parking available Boule Open terrace V meals Languages spoken: English*
CARDS: ●● ■ 🔟 Travellers cheques

### MARSANNAY-LA-CÔTE Côte-D'Or

★ ★ **L'Hotellerie de la Côte**
rte de Beaune *21160*
☎ 380511000 FAX 380588297
*Forest area Near motorway*
*41 en suite (shr) (6 fmly) No smoking in 14 bedrooms TV in all bedrooms STV Mini-bar in all bedrooms Licensed Full central heating Air conditioning in bedrooms Open parking available Supervised Child discount available 12yrs Pool table Boule Bicycle rental Open terrace V meals Last d 21.00hrs Languages spoken: English,German,Italian,Spanish*
CARDS: ●● ■ ☲☲ 🔟 Travellers cheques

### MERCUREY Saône-et-Loire

★ ★ ★ **Val d'Or**
Grande Rue *71640*
☎ 385451370 FAX 385451845
In town centre
*Closed mid Dec-mid Jan*
*12 en suite (bth/shr) (2 with balcony) TV in all bedrooms Licensed Full central heating Open parking available Covered parking available Supervised Child discount available 12yrs V meals Last d 21.00hrs Languages spoken: English*
CARDS: ●● ☲☲ Travellers cheques

### MERRY-SEC Yonne

**Bed & Breakfast** (Prop: Pierre & Maryse Coevoet)
Pesteau *89560*
☎ 386416263 FAX 386416464
(leave A6 (Paris-Lyon) at Auxerre-Nord and continue towards Nevers)
*Near river Forest area Near motorway*
*7 en suite (shr) (3 fmly) (1 with balcony) No smoking in 2 bedrooms TV in 1 bedroom Full central heating Open parking available Child discount available 10yrs Riding Languages spoken: English & German*
ROOMS: s fr 200FF; d fr 220FF **Special breaks**
MEALS: Continental breakfast 25FF Dinner 65-110FF
CARDS: Travellers cheques

### MOTTE-TERNANT, LA Côte-D'Or

**Le Presbytère** (Prop: M et Mme Aylett)
*21210*
☎ 380843485 FAX 380843532
(10km east of Saulieu on the D26 at the side of the village church)
This 15th-century presbytery sits on the highest point of the village of La Motte Ternant, adjacent to the 11th-century church, offering a tranquil setting. The house has been tastefully restored to retain its original charm and guests are provided with well furnished and decorated bedrooms and an ideal base from which to tour Burgundy.
*Near river Near lake Forest area Near motorway*
*3 en suite (bth/shr) No smoking Full central heating Open parking available Covered parking available No children Fishing Bicycle rental V meals Last d 9.30am Languages spoken: English*
ROOMS: d 400FF
MEALS: Dinner 130FF
CARDS: Travellers cheques

### NAN-SOUS-THIL Côte-D'Or

**Château de Beauregard**
*21390*
☎ 380644108 FAX 380644728
(from A6 exit Bierre-les-Semur)
*Near river Near lake Forest area*
*Closed Dec-Etr*
*4 en suite (bth/shr) (1 fmly) Full central heating Open parking available Languages spoken: English*
CARDS: Travellers cheques

### NEUVY-SUR-LOIRE Nièvre

**Domaine de l'Étang** (Prop: Bernard Pasquet)
*58450*
☎ 386392006 FAX 386392006
Near river Near lake Forest area
*3 en suite (bth/shr) (4 fmly) TV available Radio in rooms Full central heating Open parking available Covered parking available Child discount available Tennis Fishing Boule Open terrace Languages spoken: English, German & Italian*

### NEVERS Nièvre

**★ ★ ★ Hotel de Diane** (Best Western)
38 rue du Midi *58000*
☎ 386572810 FAX 386594508
(from railway station take Charles-de-Gaulle Ave (in front of station gate) Hotel is in second street on the right)
In town centre
*Closed 21 Dec-10 Jan*
*30 en suite (bth/shr) (2 fmly) No smoking in 4 bedrooms TV in all bedrooms STV Radio in rooms Direct dial from all bedrooms Mini-bar in all bedrooms Licensed Lift Night porter Full central heating Open parking available (charged) Covered parking available (charged) Supervised Child discount available 12yrs Open terrace V meals Last d 22.30hrs Languages spoken: English & German*
ROOMS: (room only) s 390-540FF; d 490-590FF
**Reductions over 1 night**
MEALS: Continental breakfast 48FF Lunch 89-169FF Dinner 89-169FF
CARDS: ●● ■ ■ ⑨ Travellers cheques

### NUITS-ST-GEORGES Côte-D'Or

**Domaine Comtesse Michel de Loisy**
28 r de General de Gaulle *21700*
☎ 380610272 FAX 380613614
Family house situated in the heart of a typical Burgundian village. The Countess Michel de Loisy will give you an escorted tour of the wine cellars with tasting included. Golf and air ballooning 15 kilometres away. Swimming pool and tennis within 300 metres.

Forest area In town centre Near motorway
*Closed Dec-1 Apr*
*5 en suite (bth/shr) (2 fmly) No smoking on premises Full central heating Open parking available Child discount available 4yrs Languages spoken: English & Italian*
ROOMS: d 600-850FF
CARDS: ●● ■ ■ Travellers cheques

**★ ★ Hotel & Restaurant Iris**
1 av Chamboland *21700*
☎ 380611717 FAX 380612633
Near river Near lake Forest area Near motorway
*Closed 26 Dec-8 Jan*
*50 en suite (bth/shr) TV in all bedrooms STV Direct dial from all bedrooms Licensed Night porter Full central heating Open parking available Supervised Child discount available Indoor swimming pool (heated) Outdoor swimming pool (heated) Tennis Fishing Bicycle rental V meals Last d 21.00hrs Languages spoken: English & German*

**★ ★ Le St-Georges**
Carrefour de l'Europe *21700*
☎ 380611500 FAX 380612380
(near Nuits-St-Georges exit of A31)
This modern establishment provides an attractive base for exploring the Burgundy region with its many culinary delights and excellent wines. The cheerful bedrooms are equipped with modern facilities and the restaurant offers refined Burgundy cuisine as well as specialities such as foie gras, salmon and freshly smoked magrets de canard.
Forest area Near motorway

*47 en suite (bth/shr) 17 rooms in annexe (6 fmly) No smoking in 9 bedrooms TV in all bedrooms STV Direct dial from all bedrooms Licensed Night porter Full central heating Open parking available Covered parking available (charged) Supervised Child discount available 12yrs Outdoor swimming pool (heated) Tennis Pool table Boule Open terrace Covered terrace V meals Last d 21.30hrs Languages spoken: English, German, Italian & Spanish*
ROOMS: (room only) s 290-328FF; d 308.50-348FF
MEALS: Full breakfast 49FF Lunch 95-125FF Dinner 125-325FF
CARDS: ●● ■ ■ ⑨ Travellers cheques

### ONLAY Nièvre

**Château de Lesvault** (Prop: M Bos)
*58370*
☎ 386843291 FAX 386843578
(from Moulins-Engilbert take D18 toward Onlay and Park du Morvan, Château-Lesvault is 5.5km from Moulins-Engilbert)
Near river Near lake Forest area
*Closed Jan*
*10 rms (8 bth/shr) Full central heating Open parking available Supervised Child discount available 10yrs Fishing Open terrace V meals Last d 17.00hrs Languages spoken: English, Dutch & German*

*contd.*

**OULON** Nièvre

**Ferme Auberge du Vieux Chateau** (Prop: M & Mme Fayolle)
*58700*
☎ 386680677 FAX 386680677
Near lake Forest area
11 rms (1 bth 4 shr) (3 fmly) Open parking available Child discount available 10yrs Outdoor swimming pool Languages spoken: English
CARDS: ●● ▥

**PLANCHEZ** Nièvre

★★**Le Relais des Lacs**
*58230*
☎ 386784168 FAX 386784411
Near river Forest area In town centre
Closed mid Nov-mid Dec & early Jan-early Mar
36 en suite (bth/shr) (4 fmly) No smoking in 6 bedrooms TV in all bedrooms Mini-bar in all bedrooms Licensed Full central heating Open parking available (charged) Child discount available 12yrs Fishing Pool table Boule Bicycle rental Open terrace Last d 22.30hrs Languages spoken: English & Spanish
CARDS: ●● ■ ▥ ⑨ Travellers cheques

**POILLY-SUR-SEREIN** Yonne

**Le Moulin** (Prop: M & Mme Moreau)
*89310*
☎ 386759246 FAX 386759521
Near river Near lake Forest area Near motorway
Closed Oct-May
5 en suite (bth/shr) (2 fmly) TV available Open parking available Supervised Child discount available Languages spoken: English, German & Dutch
CARDS: Travellers cheques

**POILLY-SUR-THOLON** Yonne

**Bed & Breakfast** (Prop: Alain & Chantal Chevallier)
5 rte St Aubin Bleury *89110*
☎ 386635164 FAX 386915337
Near river Forest area
3 en suite (shr) (1 fmly) (2 with balcony) Full central heating Open parking available Covered parking available Child discount available 10yrs Languages spoken: English & German
CARDS: Travellers cheques

**POISSON** Saône-et-Loire

**Bed & Breakfast** (Prop: Maguy & Paul Mathieu)
Sermaize *71600*
☎ 385810610 FAX 385810610
(from Paray-le-Monial head for Poisson on D34. In village turn left and head for Charolle, 2km further at the crossrds, go straight on for 2.5km, the house is on right after the river bridge)
The rooms at this property are found on the first and second floor, which you access via an ancient staircase in the tower. Dinner is served by the hosts. Children's games available in the garden, swings and table-tennis. Reductions available for children under six years old, special rates for visits lasting four days or more.
Near river Forest area
Closed 15 Nov-14 Mar

4 en suite (shr) Full central heating Open parking available Child discount available 6yrs Boule Bicycle rental Table tennis Languages spoken: English
ROOMS: d 280-330FF
MEALS: Dinner fr 100FF
CARDS: ■ Travellers cheques

**Château de Martigny** (Prop: Edith Dor)
*71600*
☎ 385815321 FAX 385815940
Near river Near lake Forest area
Closed 2 Nov-Mar
4 en suite (bth/shr) Full central heating Open parking available Supervised Child discount available 7yrs Outdoor swimming pool V meals Languages spoken: Portuguese

**PONT-DE-PANY** Côte-D'Or

★★★★ **Château la Chassagne**
*21410*
☎ 380497600 FAX 380497619
Near river Forest area Near motorway
Closed 16 Nov-14 Mar
12 en suite (bth/shr) 1 rooms in annexe (1 fmly) (1 with balcony) TV in all bedrooms STV Direct dial from all bedrooms Mini-bar in all bedrooms Room-safe Licensed Lift Night porter Full central heating Open parking available Supervised Outdoor swimming pool (heated) Golf Tennis Sauna Solarium Gym Boule Bicycle rental Open terrace Covered terrace Last d 21.00hrs Languages spoken: English Dutch & German
ROOMS: (room only) s 690FF; d 780-1200FF
MEALS: Continental breakfast 80FF Lunch 185-210FF&alc Dinner 185-210FF&alc✽
CARDS: ●● ■ ▥ ⑨ Travellers cheques

**POUILLY-EN-AUXOIS** Côte-D'Or

★★★★ **Château de Chailly**
Chailly-sur-Armançon *21360*
☎ 380903030 FAX 380903000
(from the A6 exit Pouilly-en-Auxois, direction Saulieu)
Near river Near lake Forest area Near motorway
Closed 12 Dec-20 Jan
45 en suite (bth/shr) TV in all bedrooms STV Radio in rooms Direct dial from all bedrooms Mini-bar in all bedrooms Room-safe Licensed Lift Night porter Full central heating Open parking available Covered parking available Supervised Child discount available 12yrs Outdoor swimming pool (heated) Golf 18 Tennis Pool table Boule Bicycle rental Open terrace Covered terrace Hot air ballooning,wine tasting, karting Last d 21.30hrs Languages spoken: English & German
ROOMS: (room only) d 1670-2170FF
MEALS: Continental breakfast 80FF Lunch 260-450FF Dinner 260-450FF✽
CARDS: ●● ■ ▥ ⑨ Travellers cheques

**POUILLY-SUR-SAÔNE** Côte-D'Or

**Bed & Breakfast** (Prop: Mme Angélique Délorme)
rte de Dinon *21250*
☎ 380210643 & 380211876
Near river Near lake Forest area Near motorway
6 rms (5 bth) (4 fmly) (3 with balcony) No smoking on premises TV in 3 bedrooms Radio in rooms Full central heating Open parking available Supervised Child discount available Boule
ROOMS: s 200FF; d 220FF **Reductions over 1 night**

## PRÉTY Saône-et-Loire

**Le Meix Fluat**
Passage de Meix Fluat *71290*
☎ 385511061 FAX 385511061
(Leave A6 at Tournus take N6 in direction of Mâcon turn left in direction of Bourg-en-Bresse at lights take D975 across River Saône in 2km follow signs for Préty (D37 & D176))
Near river Forest area Near motorway
*6 rms (4 bth/shr) (2 fmly) (2 with balcony) No smoking in all bedrooms Full central heating Open parking available Covered parking available Child discount available 6yrs Outdoor swimming pool Boule Bicycle rental Languages spoken: English*

## PULIGNY-MONTRACHET Côte-D'Or

★ ★ ★ **Le Montracher**
pl des Marronniers *21190*
☎ 380213006 FAX 380213906
Forest area Near motorway
*Closed Dec-9 Jan*
*32 en suite (bth/shr) 10 rooms in annexe (1 with balcony) TV in all bedrooms STV Direct dial from all bedrooms Night porter Open parking available Open terrace Wine tasting,vineyard visits V meals Last d 21.30hrs Languages spoken: English & German*
ROOMS: (room only) d 550FF
MEALS: Continental breakfast 70FF Lunch 215-425FF Dinner 215-425FF
CARDS: ● ■ ▥ ▣ Travellers cheques

## QUENNE Yonne

**Les Granges** (Prop: Elaine & Christian Dapoigny)
10 rue de la Croix *89290*
☎ 386403118 FAX 386402845
(from Motorway A6 exit Auxerre Sud, head towards Auxerre, take first road on the left to Quenne. From Auxerre, take N65 and the first road on right to Quenne)
In a small village between Auxerre and Chablis, this 19th-century wine grower's house offers five cosy bedrooms all with modern comforts. A terrace, overlooking the countryside, is available for breakfast and evening picnics.
*Closed Jan*
*5 en suite (bth/shr) Full central heating Open parking available Child discount available 2yrs Covered terrace Languages spoken: English*
ROOMS: s 250-270FF; d 300-320FF ✱
CARDS: Travellers cheques

## RAVEAU Nièvre

**Bed & Breakfast** (Prop: D & J Mellet-Mandard)
Bois Dieu *58400*
☎ 386696002 FAX 386702391
(from La Charité-sur-Loire take direction of Clamecy-Auxerre N151, then D179 to Raveau and D138 for 3km Le Bois Dieu is 250m after Peteloup on the right)
Near river Forest area Near motorway
*4 en suite (bth/shr) No smoking in all bedrooms Full central heating Open parking available Fishing Last d 12.00hrs*
CARDS: Eurocheques

## ROCHE-VINEUSE, LA Saône-et-Loire

**Tinailler d'Aleane** (Prop: Eliane Heinen)
Sommere *71960*
☎ 385378068
Forest area Near motorway
*3 en suite (bth/shr) TV available Full central heating Open parking available Supervised Child discount available Languages spoken: English & German*

## ROGNY-LES-SEPT-ECLUSES Yonne

★ ★ **Auberge des 7 Ecluses**
1 rue Gaspard de Coligny *89220*
☎ 386745290 FAX 386745677
Near river Near lake Forest area Near motorway
*Closed Jan-1 Mar*
*7 en suite (bth/shr) (2 fmly) TV in all bedrooms Licensed Full central heating Open parking available Supervised Child discount available 12yrs Bicycle rental Open terrace Languages spoken: English German & Spanish*
CARDS: ● ■ ▥ ▣ Travellers cheques

**Bed & Breakfast** (Prop: Paul & Mireille Lemaistre)
Les Gonneaux *89220*
☎ 386745189 FAX 386745634
Near river Near lake Forest area
*1 en suite (bth/shr) TV available Radio in rooms Full central heating Open parking available Outdoor swimming pool Fishing Languages spoken: English*

## ROMANÈCHE-THORINS Saône-et-Loire

★ ★ ★ **Les Maritonnes**
rte de Fleurie *71570*
☎ 385355170 FAX 385355814
(on N6) From Paris exit the A6 at Mâcon Sud. From Lyon exit A6 at Belleville.
Near river Near motorway
*Closed 16 Dec-25 Jan RS closed Sun evening & Mon*
*20 en suite (bth/shr) TV in all bedrooms Direct dial from all bedrooms Mini-bar in all bedrooms Licensed Full central heating Open parking available Supervised Outdoor swimming pool (heated) Tennis Boule Open terrace Last d 21.30hrs Languages spoken: English & German*
ROOMS: (room only) s 400-430FF; d 430-590FF
MEALS: Lunch fr 200FFalc Dinner fr 250FFalc
CARDS: ● ■ ▥ ▣ Travellers cheques

## ROYER Saône-et-Loire

**Bed & Breakfast** (Prop: Thierry Meunier)
Le Bourg *71700*
☎ 385510342
Forest area
*3 en suite (shr) (3 fmly) (2 with balcony) No smoking on premises Full central heating Open parking available Languages spoken: English*

## SAILLENARD Saône-et-Loire

★ ★ **Moulin de Sauvagette**
rte de Bletterans *71580*
☎ 385741758
Near river Forest area Near motorway
*Closed 15 Jan-13 Mar*
*9 rms TV in all bedrooms Licensed Full central heating Open*
*contd.*

parking available Child discount available 7yrs Fishing Boule
Bicycle rental Open terrace V meals Languages spoken:
English & German

### ST-AUBIN-CHÂTEAU-NEUF Yonne

**La Posterie** (Prop: Daniel et Jeannette Chaumet)
2 pl Aristide Briand 89110
☎ 386736409 FAX 386736409
(approach via D955 Toucy, then Les Placeaux and right for
500mtrs to St-Aubin. House next to the church)

A completely renovated family house, formerly the village pub.
The bedrooms are individually decorated and furnished and
meals, for which reservations are needed, are taken at the
family table. A ideal base for a peaceful holiday or for touring
the surrounding area.
Near river Forest area Near motorway
4 en suite (bth/shr) (1 fmly) TV in 2 bedrooms Full central
heating Open parking available Covered parking available
Supervised Child discount available 8yrs Boule Bicycle rental
Tennis nearby Last d 18.00hrs
ROOMS: s fr 300FF; d 350-450FF ✱ **Reductions over 1
night**
MEALS: Lunch 80-120FF Dinner 80-120FF✱
CARDS: Travellers cheques

### ST-BOIL Saône-et-Loire

**Bed & Breakfast** (Prop: Mme S Perraut)
Chaumois 71390
☎ 385440796
(N 981 Buxy-Cluny road and at Saint-Boil leave village and take
left turn to Chaumois, house signposted)
Set in peaceful surroundings, comfortable guest rooms are
located in an old converted farmhouse on the famous "route
des vins" in the southern Burgundy region.
Near river Forest area
4 en suite (bth/shr) (1 fmly) (1 with balcony) No smoking on
premises Full central heating Open parking available
Supervised Languages spoken: English
ROOMS: s fr 200FF; d fr 260FF **Reductions over 1 night**
CARDS: Travellers cheques

### ST-ÉLOI Nièvre

**Domaine de Trangy**
8 rte de Trangy 58000
☎ 386371127 FAX 386371875
Near river Forest area Near motorway
3 rms (2 shr) (1 fmly) Full central heating Open parking available
Outdoor swimming pool Languages spoken: English & Spanish

### ST-FARGEAU Yonne

**Château-de-Dannery** (Prop: M. Couiteas)
89170
☎ 386740901
(from A6 exit Joigny head towards Toucy, then towards St-
Fargeau. 4km beyond Mézille turn right towards Dannery for
2km)
Near lake Forest area Near motorway
3 en suite (bth/shr) TV in 1 bedroom Open parking available
No children 5yrs Outdoor swimming pool Languages spoken:
English

**Famille Provot-Rolaz**
10 rue Porte Marlotte 89170
☎ 386740228
Near river Near lake Near beach Forest area In town centre
Near motorway
2 en suite (shr) (2 fmly) Full central heating Open parking
available Supervised Child discount available 10yrs Languages
spoken: English

### ST-GERVAIS-EN-VALLIÈRE Saône-et-Loire

**★ ★ ★ Moulin D'Hauterive**
Hameau de Chaublanc 71350
☎ 385915556 FAX 385918965
Near river Near sea Forest area Near motorway
Closed Mon & Tue noon
22 en suite (bth/shr) 3 rooms in annexe (6 fmly) No smoking
on premises TV in all bedrooms Mini-bar in all bedrooms
Licensed Full central heating Open parking available
Supervised Child discount available 12yrs Outdoor swimming
pool (heated) Tennis Fishing Sauna Solarium Gym Pool table
Boule Jacuzzi/spa Bicycle rental Open terrace Covered
terrace V meals Last d 21.00hrs Languages spoken: English
CARDS: ●● ■ ☲ ⑩

### ST-GRATIEN-SAVIGNY Nièvre

**la Marquise** (Prop: Huguette et Noel Perreau)
La Forêt 58340
☎ 386500677 FAX 386500714
Two rooms are available in this manor house, owned by the
Perreau family. There is a large living room, a swimming pool
in the garden, and riding is possible. Meals provided.
Near river Forest area
3 en suite (bth/shr) (2 fmly) No smoking in 2 bedrooms TV
available Radio in rooms Full central heating Open parking
available Fishing Riding

### ST-JEAN-AUX-AMOGNES Nièvre

**Château-de-Sury** (Prop: Hubert de Faverges)
58270
☎ 386586051 FAX 386689028
(from Nevers, follow D978 then D958 to Bona-St-Saulge. 2nd
road on right after crossing St-Jean-aux-Amognes)
Near river Forest area
3 en suite (bth/shr) TV in all bedrooms Full central heating
Open parking available Child discount available 12yrs Fishing
Riding Covered terrace Last d 18.30hrs Languages spoken:
English
ROOMS: s 250FF; d 320FF
MEALS: Dinner 100-150FF
CARDS: ●● ■ ☲ ⑩

## ST-LOUP Nièvre

**Elviré** (Prop: M & Mme Duchet)
Chauffour *58200*
☎ 386262022
(take N7 in the direction of Cours-St-Loup then D114 & after St-Loup continue for 3km towards St-Verain)
Forest area
*Closed early Nov-end Mar*
*2 en suite (shr) Open parking available Supervised Child discount available 12yrs Open terrace*
CARDS: Travellers cheques

## ST-MARTIN-DU-TARTRE Saône-et-Loire

**Bed & Breakfast** (Prop: Jacqueline Bergeret)
Maizeray *71460*
☎ 385492461
Forest area
*Closed mid Nov-mid Apr*
*2 en suite (bth/shr) (1 fmly) No smoking on premises Full central heating Open parking available Supervised Languages spoken: English*
CARDS: Travellers cheques

## ST-MARTIN-EN-BRESSE Saône-et-Loire

★ ★ **Au Puits Enchante**
*71620*
☎ 385477196 FAX 385477458
(17km E of Chalon-sur-Saône)
Forest area
*Closed 31 Dec-1 Feb*
*14 en suite (bth/shr) (1 fmly) No smoking in 8 bedrooms TV in all bedrooms Direct dial from all bedrooms Licensed Full central heating Open parking available Covered parking available Supervised Child discount available 2yrs Fishing Riding Boule Bicycle rental Open terrace V meals Last d 21.00hrs Languages spoken: English & German*
CARDS: ●● ▣ Travellers cheques

## ST-MAURICE-LES-CHATEAUNEUF Saône-et-Loire

**Bed & Breakfast** (Prop: Madeleine Chartier)
La Violetterie *71740*
☎ 385262660
Near river
*Closed 15 Nov-14 Apr*
*3 en suite (bth/shr) (1 fmly) Full central heating Open parking available Supervised Languages spoken: English*
CARDS: Travellers cheques

## ST-PÈRE Nièvre

**L'Oreé des Vignes**
Croquant *58200*
☎ 386281250 FAX 386281250
(In Cosne-sur-Loire head for Donzy, then towards St-Pére, then right towards Croquant)
Marie-Noëlle welcomes guests to her newly restored farmhouse, with comfortable bedrooms overlooking a large garden.
Near river Forest area
*5 en suite (shr) (2 fmly) No smoking in all bedrooms Full central heating Open parking available Bicycle rental V meals Languages spoken: English*

ROOMS: s fr 220FF; d fr 280FF
MEALS: Lunch fr 120FF
CARDS: Travellers cheques

## ST-PÈRE Yonne

★ ★ ★ **Espérance**
*89450*
☎ 386333910 FAX 386332615
Near river Forest area
*35 rms Some rooms in annexe (1 fmly) (1 with balcony) TV in all bedrooms STV Radio in rooms Direct dial from all bedrooms Mini-bar in all bedrooms Licensed Night porter Full central heating Open parking available Outdoor swimming pool (heated) Bicycle rental V meals Last d 22.00hrs Languages spoken: English & German*
CARDS: ●● ▦ ▥ ▣ Travellers cheques

## ST-PIERRE-LE-MOUTIER Nièvre

**Bed & Breakfast** (Prop: Roselyne Lavasseur)
La Forêt de Cougny *58240*
☎ 386581201
(from D978 take D203 in direction of St Parize le Chatel to la Foret de Cougny)
Near lake Forest area Near motorway
*3 en suite (shr) Full central heating Open parking available Languages spoken: English*

## ST-PRIX Saône-et-Loire

**L'Eau Vive** (Prop: Catherine et Rene Denis)
Le Bourg *71990*
☎ 385825934
(from Autun take road to Moulins, 4km from Autun, turn right to St-Léger-sous-Beuvray, cross La Grande Verrière, at foot of St-Léger, turn right to St-Prix, following arrows 'Le Haut Folin'-house is 200m after church)
On the edge of a village and the Morvan Parc, Catherine and René offer their guests bedrooms and a living room with open fire. Their property is in the mountains, surrounded by forests, streams and wide open spaces. The guest house has a private lake. Guests may take their evening meal with the family.
Near river Forest area
*Closed 5 Nov-Mar & 15-30 Jun*
*4 en suite (bth/shr) Full central heating Open parking available Child discount available 10yrs Fishing Boule Bicycle rental Last d 15.00hrs Languages spoken: English & Spanish*
ROOMS: s fr 230FF; d fr 270FF **Reductions over 1 night**
MEALS: Dinner fr 100FF
CARDS: Travellers cheques

## ST-SAULGE Nièvre

**Les Beauvais** (Prop: Mme M-F O'Leary)
*58330*
☎ 386582998 FAX 386582997
(in Nevers take D978 towards Autun-Dijon for 10kms, turn left on to the D958 towards St-Saulge and follow signs)
Near lake Forest area In town centre
*4 en suite (bth/shr) No smoking on premises TV in 1 bedroom Full central heating Open parking available Child discount available 10yrs Boule Bicycle rental Last d 21.00hrs Languages spoken: English*

*contd.*

275

## ST-VÉRAND Saône-et-Loire

**★ Auberge du St-Vérand**
71570
☎ 385371650 FAX 385374927
Near river Near motorway
11 rms (3 fmly) (3 with balcony) TV in all bedrooms Licensed
Full central heating Open parking available Supervised Boule
Open terrace Last d 21.30hrs Languages spoken: English
CARDS: ●● ▨▨

## STE-MAGNANCE Yonne

**Château Jacquot** (Prop: Martine Costaille)
89420
☎ 386330022
Forest area Near motorway
1 en suite (shr) Full central heating Open parking available No
children 8yrs V meals Languages spoken: English & German
CARDS: Travellers cheques

## SAISY Saône-et-Loire

**Bed & Breakfast** (Prop: Colette Comeaud)
Changey 71360
☎ 385820755
Near lake Forest area Near motorway
2 en suite (shr) No smoking on premises Radio in rooms Full
central heating Open parking available No children 4yrs

## SALIVES Côte-D'Or

**Ferme de Larcon** (Prop: Simone Ramaget)
21580
☎ 380756092 FAX 380756092
(approach via D996 towards Dijon, then D19 to Salives)
Forest area
5 en suite (shr) No smoking on premises Full central heating
Open parking available Child discount available 10yrs Boule
Bicycle rental

## SANTENAY-EN-BOURGOGNE Côte-D'Or

**Château de la Crée** (Prop: Y E & R Remy-Thévenin)
Le Hauts-de-Santenay 21590
☎ 380206266 FAX 380206650
(from A6 exit Beaune-Sud towards Chagny on N74 to
Santenay. From A6 exit Chalons-sur-Saône Nord towards
Chagny on N6 to Santenay)
This 18th-century manor, with cellars that date back even
further, has been completely renovated in the heart of the
vineyards of the Côte de Beaune. A warm welcome is extended
to guests. Bar, billiards table, library, period living room,
reception room, tennis court and private putting green.
Forest area
4 en suite (bth/shr) (4 with balcony) No smoking in all
bedrooms TV in all bedrooms Radio in rooms Full central
heating Open parking available Covered parking available
Child discount available 10yrs Tennis Boule Mini-golf Bicycle
rental Billiards Mini-golf Last d 24hrs Languages spoken:
English, German & Italian
ROOMS: s 600-900FF; d 750-950FF **Reductions over 1
night Special breaks**
MEALS: Full breakfast 55FF Lunch 200-350FF Dinner 300-
550FF&alc
CARDS: ●● ▨▨ Travellers cheques

## SAUVIGNY-LE-BOIS Yonne

**★ ★ ★ Le Relais Fleuri**
N6 89200
☎ 386340285 FAX 386340998
Near motorway
48 en suite (bth/shr) TV in all bedrooms Radio in rooms Direct
dial from all bedrooms Mini-bar in all bedrooms Licensed
Night porter Full central heating Open parking available
Outdoor swimming pool (heated) Tennis Solarium Boule
Table tennis Last d 21.45hrs Languages spoken: English &
German
CARDS: ●● ■■ ▨▨ ◉ Travellers cheques

## SÉMELAY Nièvre

**Domaine de la Chaume** (Prop: Pierre & Valerie d'Été)
58360
☎ 386309123
Near river Forest area
Closed Oct-Apr
3 en suite (shr) (1 fmly) Open parking available Child discount
available Languages spoken: English

## SEMUR-EN-AUXOIS Côte-D'Or

**Château de Flée** (Prop: Marc Francis Bach)
21140
☎ 380971707 FAX 380973432
(leave A6 at exit Bierre-lès-Semur and follow signposts
towards Lac-de-Pont)
You are offered an unforgettable stay at this château, once the
home of the Treasurer of King Louis XV. Visitors can enjoy
relaxing in the ten hectare park, horse-riding, strolls around
the château and hot air ballooning. Dinner is available at a
fixed price. Swimming pool. The ower can arrange flights over
the region.
Near river Near lake Forest area Near motorway
Closed 15 Nov-Mar
2 en suite (bth/shr) TV in all bedrooms Radio in rooms Full
central heating Open parking available No children Child
discount available 10yrs Outdoor swimming pool Fishing
Boule Bicycle rental Languages spoken: English & German
ROOMS: d fr 950FF **✱ Reductions over 1 night**

**★ ★ Hotel du Lac**
pont et Massène 21140
☎ 380971111 FAX 380972925
(from A6 exit Bierre-les-Semur, turn left, then take first right
towards Lac de Pont. After 3km go towards the Hotel du lac)
Situated in the Burgundy countryside with rolling hills and a
rich historic heritage, this magnificent residence is tucked away in
a forest on the edge of a lake. A warm and informal
atmosphere prevails throughout. The hotel offers attractive
accommodation with good amenities and a country restaurant
serving an extensive selection of tasty, regional specialities.
There is a shaded terrace and garden, and nearby is a choice of
leisure facilities.
Near river Near lake Near beach Forest area Near motorway
Feb-20 Dec
20 rms (9 bth 10 shr) (5 fmly) (4 with balcony) No smoking in 1
bedroom TV in 19 bedrooms Direct dial from all bedrooms
Mini-bar in 5 bedrooms Licensed Full central heating Open
parking available Covered parking available (charged) Child
discount available 12yrs Open terrace Covered terrace Last d
21.15hrs Languages spoken: English & German

Rooms: (room only) s 235FF; d 270-310FF **Reductions over 1 night**
Meals: Full breakfast 39FF Lunch 88-155FF&alc Dinner 88-155FF&alc
Cards: 🌑 ■ ⬜ ⬤ Travellers cheques

### SENAN Yonne

**Bed & Breakfast** (Prop: Mme Paule Defrance)
4 pl de la Liberté *89710*
☎ 386915989
(from A6 exit Joigny take D89 towards Volgré & Senan)
Near motorway
*3 en suite (bth/shr) Full central heating Open parking available Covered parking available Bicycle rental Open terrace Languages spoken: English*

### SENNECÉ-LÈS-MÂCON Saône-et-Loire

**Bed & Breakfast** (Prop: Michel & Nadine Verjat)
483 rue Vremontoise *71000*
☎ 385360392 FAX 385360392
(exit Mâcon Nord from A6 in direction of Sennecé-lès-Mâcon after the pay booth)
Accommodation is in an annexe adjacent to the main house, and one room has a kitchen. Each room, designed with rustic décor, has a TV. Meals are available in the restaurant on site and there is a barbecue in the garden for guests' use. Close to forest, with fishing available only two kilometres away, and golf and riding within five kilometres.
Forest area Near motorway
*3 en suite (shr) No smoking on premises Full central heating Open parking available Covered parking available Child discount available 3yrs*
Rooms: s 180-200FF; d 230-250FF
Cards: Travellers cheques

### SENS Yonne

★ ★ ★ **Paris Et De La Poste (S)** (Best Western)
97 rue de la République *89103*
☎ 386651743 FAX 386641575
(From Paris take N6 exit Sens/Courtenay or take A5 exit Sens)
Near river Forest area In town centre Near motorway
*25 en suite (bth/shr) (7 fmly) (1 with balcony) TV in all bedrooms STV Radio in rooms Direct dial from all bedrooms Mini-bar in all bedrooms Licensed Lift Full central heating Covered parking available (charged) Child discount available 12yrs Open terrace V meals Last d 22.00hrs Languages spoken: English Spanish & Italian*
Cards: 🌑 ■ ⬜ ⬤ Travellers cheques

### SERCY Saône-et-Loire

**Bed & Breakfast** (Prop: Pascal Biwand)
Le Bourg *71460*
☎ 385926261 FAX 385925128
(From the Motorway exit Chalon-Sud, follow signs for Buxy Cluny. House on right on entering Sercy, 100mtrs beyond the castle)
Hosts Josette and Pascal Biwand have taken care to provide all comforts for visitors to their home, a typical Burgundian building adorned with flowers and situated in a small village. There is direct access to an enclosed tree-lined garden, full of flowers and there is a library and TV room. Close to leisure facilities and shops.

**Bed & Breakfast**

Near river Forest area
*2 en suite (bth/shr) TV available Full central heating Open parking available Child discount available Languages spoken: English & German*

### SIVIGNON Saône-et-Loire

**Bed & Breakfast** (Prop: Jean Claude Geoffroy)
L'Ecousserie du Bas *71220*
☎ 385596666
(between Cluny and Charolles, in South Burgundy)
Forest area
*3 en suite (shr) Full central heating Open parking available Supervised Child discount available 6yrs Outdoor swimming pool Languages spoken: German & Italian*
Cards: Travellers cheques

### THAIX Nièvre

**L'Ombre Thaix** (Prop: Mr Moulherat)
Château de l'Ombre *58250*
☎ 386502400
Near lake Forest area
*4 en suite (bth) (1 fmly) TV available Full central heating Open parking available Supervised Child discount available*
Cards: Travellers cheques

### TINTURY Nièvre

**Fleury la Tour** (Prop: Michel Gueny)
Fleury La Tour Tintury *58110*
☎ 386841242 FAX 386841242
Near river Near lake Forest area
*4 en suite (bth/shr) (2 fmly) Full central heating Open parking available Supervised Tennis Fishing Languages spoken: German*
Cards: Travellers cheques

### TOURNUS Saône-et-Loire

★ ★ **Aux Terrasses**
18 av du 23 Janvier *71700*
☎ 385510174 FAX 385510999
Near river In town centre Near motorway
*18 en suite (bth/shr) (3 fmly) TV in all bedrooms Licensed Full central heating Air conditioning in bedrooms Open parking available Covered parking available (charged) Child discount available 12yrs Open terrace V meals Languages spoken: English*
Cards: 🌑 ⬜ Travellers cheques

**En Chazot** (Prop: Mme Lesley Cleaver)
La Croix Léonard *71700*
☎ 385511279
(from autoroute A6, take Tourus exit. Follow N6 500m, then
turn right onto D14 toward Mancey. Straight on for 1500m at
brow of hill sign La Croix Leonard take lane to left, house is
opposite)
Owned by an English family, now resident in France, who
welcome visitors to their traditional, stone-built home in a
lovely Burgundy valley. Recently restored, this bed & breakfast
establishment has its own entrance and private lounge for
guests. There is a large garden with orchard, children's swing
and deckchairs.
Near river  Near lake  Forest area  Near motorway
*1 en suite (bth/shr) (1 fmly) (1 with balcony) Full central
heating Open parking available Child discount available
swings, terrace Languages spoken: English*
ROOMS: s fr 220FF; d fr 260FF **Reductions over 1 night**
CARDS: Travellers cheques

★ ★ ★ **Le Domaine de Tremont**
rte de Plottes *71700*
☎ 385510010 FAX 385321228
Set in open countryside, surrounded by wooded hills, this
charming family establishment offers a delightful interior,
adorned with period furniture. Elegant bedrooms offer a
combination of modern comfort and traditional furnishings
and have spacious, well equipped bathrooms. The informal
restaurant serves honest, traditional cooking, whilst the
comfortable reading room with harpsichord provides
relaxation.

Forest area
*6 en suite (bth/shr) 4 rooms in annexe (1 fmly) TV in all
bedrooms STV Direct dial from all bedrooms Licensed Full
central heating Open parking available Child discount
available Boule Open terrace Last d 22.00hrs Languages
spoken: English*
ROOMS: (room only) s 420-470FF; d 550-700FF
**Reductions over 1 night**
MEALS: Full breakfast 60FF Continental breakfast 50FF
Dinner 110-150FF
CARDS: ●● ▩ Travellers cheques

★ ★ ★ **Le Sauvage** (Best Western)
pl du Champ-de-Mars *71700*
☎ 385511445 FAX 385321027
(from Paris or Lyon, on the A6 take interchange 27 (Tournus).
Then N6 direction Mâcon town centre, after about 1.7km the
hotel is on the left)

The Hotel Sauvage is an establishment with the charm of
bygone times and modern comfort. It features personalised
bedrooms, some with views of the 13th-century Saint Philibert
church, which is a fine example of Romanesque art. The
restaurant serves a choice of delicacies such as esgarcot en
coquille and poulet de Bresse, complemented by some
excellent f Burgundy wines.
Near river  In town centre  Near motorway

*Le Sauvage*
*30 en suite (bth/shr) (5 fmly) TV in all bedrooms STV Radio in
rooms Direct dial from all bedrooms Mini-bar in all bedrooms
Licensed Lift Night porter Full central heating Covered
parking available (charged) Child discount available 12yrs
Open terrace Last d 21.00hrs Languages spoken: English &
German*
ROOMS: (room only) s 290-330FF; d 390-430FF
MEALS: Full breakfast 40FF Lunch 84-200FF&alc Dinner
84-200FF&alc
CARDS: ●● ■ ▥ ⑩ Travellers cheques

★ ★ ★ *La Montagne de Brancion*
*71700*
☎ 385511240 FAX 385511864
(exit A6 at Tournus, then take D14 towards
Brancion/Cluny/Charolles. 13kms and at Col de Brancion turn
left onto small road leading to hotel)
Near sea  Forest area
*Closed 17 Nov-12 Mar*
*20 en suite (bth/shr) (1 fmly) (4 with balcony) TV in all
bedrooms Direct dial from all bedrooms Mini-bar in all
bedrooms Room-safe Licensed Full central heating Open
parking available Outdoor swimming pool (heated) Bicycle
rental Open terrace V meals Last d 21.30hrs Languages
spoken: English, German*
CARDS: ●● ▥ ⑩ Travellers cheques

★ ★ ★ **Le Rempart**
2-4 av Gambetta *71700*
☎ 385511056 FAX 385517722
(From A6/N6 follow signs for 'Centre Ville' into Tournus)
In town centre  Near motorway
*37 en suite (bth) (5 fmly) TV in all bedrooms STV Radio in
rooms Direct dial from all bedrooms Mini-bar in all bedrooms
Room-safe Licensed Lift Night porter Full central heating Air
conditioning in bedrooms Open parking available (charged)
Covered parking available (charged) Child discount available
12yrs Open terrace V meals Last d 21.30hrs Languages
spoken: English*
CARDS: ●● ■ ▥ ⑩ Travellers cheques

**TRAMAYES** Saône-et-Loire

**Bed & Breakfast** (Prop: George Moiroud)
rte de Pierreclos 71520
☎ 385505644 FAX 385505682
Near river Near lake Forest area
1 en suite (shr) (1 fmly) TV available Full central heating Open
parking available Languages spoken: English

**TRAMBLY** Saône-et-Loire

**Bed & Breakfast** (Prop: Florence Gauthier)
Les Charrières 71520
☎ 385504317
Near river Forest area
2 en suite (bth/shr) (2 fmly) (1 with balcony) Full central
heating Open parking available Supervised Child discount
available 2yrs Languages spoken: English

**TRIVY** Saône-et-Loire

**Bed & Breakfast** (Prop: M & Mme Laronze)
Le Bourg 71520
☎ 385502236
Near lake Forest area Near motorway
(2 fmly) Full central heating Open parking available
Supervised hiking Last d 19.00hrs
ROOMS: (room only) s 140-150FF; d 160-210FF ✱
MEALS: Dinner fr 80FF✱

**VAL-DE-MERCY** Yonne

**Auberge du Château**
3 rue du Pont 89580
☎ 386416000 FAX 386417328
(from Auxerre take N6 towards Avallon, at Vincelles take D38
to Val-de-Mercy)
Forest area Near motorway
Closed 15 Jan-Feb
5 en suite (bth) (1 with balcony) TV in all bedrooms Direct dial
from all bedrooms Licensed Full central heating Open parking
available Supervised Boule Open terrace V meals Last d
21.00hrs Languages spoken: English
CARDS: ● ■ ▣ Travellers cheques

**VALLERY** Yonne

**La Margottière** (Prop: M Deligand)
89150
☎ 386975797 FAX 386975380
Near river Forest area
6 en suite (bth) TV available Full central heating Open parking
available Supervised Child discount available Boule Table
tennis Last d 19.00hrs Languages spoken: English
CARDS: Travellers cheques

**VAL-SUZON** Côte-D'Or

★ ★ ★**Hostellerie du Val Suzon**
rue du Fourneau 21121
☎ 380356015 FAX 380356136
(from Dijon take N71 towards Troyes)
Near river Forest area Near motorway
Closed 16 Nov-14 Dec
17 en suite (bth/shr) 7 rooms in annexe (3 fmly) TV in all
bedrooms STV Direct dial from all bedrooms Mini-bar in all
bedrooms Room-safe Licensed Full central heating Open

parking available Covered parking available Supervised Child
discount available 12yrs Boule Open terrace Last d 21.30hrs
Languages spoken: English Portuguese & Spanish
ROOMS: (room only) s 420-550FF; d 450-650FF
MEALS: Full breakfast 60FF Lunch 130-445FF&alc Dinner
200-445FF&alc
CARDS: ● ■ ▣ ▣ JCB Travellers cheques

**VANDENESSE-EN-AUXOIS** Côte-D'Or

**Barge Lady A** (Prop: L & D Bourne)
Port du Canal
☎ 380492696 FAX 380492700
(Leave A6 at Pouilly-en-Auxois take D18 via Creancey to
Vandenesse (6km). The harbour is in the centre of the village)
Near river Near lake Near sea Forest area Near motorway
Closed Dec-Jan
3 en suite (shr) No smoking on premises Full central heating
Open parking available Fishing V meals Last d 20.00hrs
Languages spoken: English Dutch & German

**VARENNES-SOUS-DUN** Saône-et-Loire

**Bed & Breakfast** (Prop: Alain & Michele Désmurs)
La Saigne 71800
☎ 385281279 FAX 385281279
Forest area
(1 fmly) Full central heating Open parking available Last d
20.30hrs Languages spoken: English

**VENDENESSE-LÈS-CHAROLLES** Saône-et-Loire

**Bed & Breakfast** (Prop: Monique et Serge Morvan)
Virevache 71120
☎ 385247671 FAX 385247671
Near river Near lake Forest area Near motorway
2 en suite (bth) (1 with balcony) Full central heating Open
parking available Covered parking available Supervised
Outdoor swimming pool Bicycle rental
CARDS: Travellers cheques

**Bed & Breakfast** (Prop: Jean & Anne Malacher)
Plainchassagne 71120
☎ 385247022
Near river Near lake Forest area
4 en suite (bth/shr) (2 fmly) No smoking on premises Full
central heating Open parking available Supervised Child
discount available 2yrs V meals Languages spoken: English

**VERGISSON** Saône-et-Loire

**Bed & Breakfast** (Prop: Ineke & Jean-Claude Morlon)
Le Bourg 71960
☎ 385358459 FAX 385381759
(from A6 exit Mâcon Sud, direction Vinzelles, Cluny, Solutre)
Forest area Near motorway
2 en suite (shr) Radio in rooms Full central heating Open
parking available Languages spoken: English, Dutch & German
ROOMS: s 190FF; d 250FF **Reductions over 1 night**
MEALS: Dinner 80FF

**VÉZELAY** Yonne

★ ★ ★ **Residence Hotel Le Pontot**
pl du Pontot 89450
☎ 386332440 FAX 386333005
(at Veézelay, turn right up only street leading into walled city.
contd.

279

Follow one-way signs to parking lot on left. Hotel on other side of parking lot)
Near river  Near lake  Forest area  In town centre  Near motorway
*Closed 2 Nov-15 Apr*
*10 en suite (bth/shr)  Radio in rooms  Direct dial from all bedrooms  Licensed  Full central heating  Open parking available  Covered parking available (charged)  Supervised  No children 10yrs  Bicycle rental  Open terrace  Hot air ballooning  Languages spoken: English*
CARDS: ●● ☎ ▣ JCB Travellers cheques

**La Tour Gaillon** (Prop: Mme Ginisty)
rue St Pierre *89450*
☎ 386332574
(from A6 exit Avallon, go through to Vézelay. From N6 at Sermizelles, take road to Vézelay)
Situated in the centre in Vézelay, on the second floor of a 15th-century house, the two guest rooms are reached by a spiral staircase. One room looks out onto a terrace, with view of the basilica.
Forest area
*Closed 24 Dec-3 Jan*
*2 rms (1 with balcony)  No smoking on premises  Full central heating  Child discount available  Languages spoken: English*
ROOMS: d 250-290FF  ✱ **Special breaks: (10% off 3 or more nights)**

### VILLARS-ET-VILLENOTTE Côte-D'Or

**Les Langrons** (Prop: Mary & Roger Collins)
*21140*
☎ 380966511 FAX 380973228
(from Semur-en-Auxois take the D954 toward Venarey-les-Laumes for 2km to Villenotte, take 1st left in direction of Villars/Lantilly. Les Langrons is the last farm on right leaving Villars and is signposted)
Forest area
*4 rms (3 shr)  (2 fmly)  No smoking on premises  Full central heating  Open parking available  Covered parking available  Supervised  Child discount available 5 yrs  Bicycle rental  Languages spoken: English*
ROOMS: s 250FF; d 300FF  ✱
CARDS: Travellers cheques

### VILLENEUVE-SUR-YONNE Yonne

**Domaine Cochepie** (Prop: Claire Strulik)
*89500*
☎ 386873976
(leave A6 at Courtenay exit onto D15 cross railway & river & turn in the direction of Sens cross the N6 & road for establishment left off the D15)
Near river  Forest area
*2 en suite (bth/shr)  (1 fmly)  No smoking on premises  Full central heating  Open parking available  Supervised  Outdoor swimming pool  Tennis  Languages spoken: English German & Spanish*
CARDS: ●● ☎ Travellers cheques

**La Lucarne Aux Chouettes** (Prop: Leslie Caron)
Quai Bretoche *89500*
☎ 386871826 FAX 386872263
(take A6 to Lyon & exit at Courtenay/Villeneuve-sur-Yonne. After the toll, in the direction of Sens (on right). At 1st crossroads, turn right to Villeneuve, once in Villeneuve, take direction of town centre cross the bridge & turn left)

Near river  Forest area  In town centre  Near motorway
*Closed Sep-Jun Sun pm-Tue am*
*4 en suite (bth/shr)  (1 fmly)  TV in all bedrooms  Full central heating  Open parking available  Child discount available*
CARDS: ●● ■ ☎ ▣

### VINZELLES Saône-et-Loire

**Bed & Breakfast** (Prop: Dominique Mergey)
La Bruyère *71680*
☎ 385356657 FAX 385356225
Near motorway
*1 en suite (shr)  (1 fmly)  Radio in rooms  Full central heating  Open parking available  Supervised*

### VIRÉ Saône-et-Loire

**Bed & Breakfast** (Prop: Jean-Noel & Josette Chaland)
Domaine des Chazelles *71260*
☎ 385331118 FAX 385331558
(Off A6)
Near river  Forest area  Near motorway
*1 en suite (bth)  No smoking on premises  Full central heating  Open parking available  Supervised  No children 2yrs*
CARDS: Travellers cheques

### VITRY-EN-CHAROLLAIS Saône-et-Loire

**Bed & Breakfast** (Prop: Guy Merle)
Les Bruyères *71600*
☎ 385811079 FAX 385811079
(in Vitry, follow 'Chambre d'Hôte' signs)
*Closed Nov-Feb*
*6 en suite (shr)  (3 fmly)  No smoking on premises  Full central heating  Open parking available  V meals  Last d 10.00hrs  Languages spoken: English (only little)*
ROOMS: s 180-240FF; d fr 240FF  **Reductions over 1 night**
MEALS: Dinner fr 90FF

### VOSNE-ROMANÉE Côte-D'Or

**La Closerie des Ormes**
21 rue de la Grand-Velle *21700*
☎ 380623519 FAX 380623519
(leave motorway at Nuits-St-Georges in the direction of Dijon onto N74, then take the fourth turning on the left into Vosne-Romanée, property 60 metres on right)
A charming ivy covered residence situated in the heart of the Vosne-Romanée vineyard. The bedrooms are comfortable and well furnished and the establishment provides a good base for touring the surrounding area.
Near motorway
*5 en suite (bth/shr)  (2 fmly)  No smoking on premises  TV in 1 bedroom  Full central heating  Open parking available  Covered parking available  Child discount available 10yrs  Riding  Bicycle rental  Languages spoken: English & German*
ROOMS: d 450-550FF  ✱
CARDS: ☎ Travellers cheques

**VOUGEOT** Côte-D'Or

★ ★ ★ ★ *Château de Gilly*
Gilly les Citeaux *21640*
☎ 380628998 FAX 380628234
(From A31 exit Nuits-St-Georges continue towards Dijon to Vougeot, then towards Gilly-les-Citeaux)
Near river Forest area Near motorway
*Closed 26 Jan-7 Mar*

*48 en suite (bth/shr) 4 rooms in annexe (9 fmly) (2 with balcony) No smoking in 10 bedrooms TV in all bedrooms STV Radio in rooms Direct dial from all bedrooms Mini-bar in all bedrooms Licensed Lift Night porter Full central heating Open parking available Supervised Child discount available 12 years Outdoor swimming pool (heated) Tennis Fishing Boule Bicycle rental Open terrace Croquet Last d 21.30hrs Languages spoken: English & German*
CARDS: ●● ■■ ☲ ⑩ JCB Travellers cheques

## EVENTS & FESTIVALS

**Jan** Festival of St Vincent, Chablis & Irancy
**Mar** Beaune Puppet Festival; Auxonne Grand Carnival; Châtillon-sur Seine Carnival; Nuits-St-Georges Wine Sales;
**Apr** Tonnerre Wine Festival; Nolay Antiques Fair; Montbard Regional Products Fair;
**May** Feast Days: Grand Morvan & Pays de Bourgogne; Mâcon French Wine Fair; Dijon Antiques Fair;
**Jun** Auxerre Jazz Festival; Vauluisant Festival; Dijon L'Estivade Festival; French Grand Prix, Nevers Magny-Cours; Grand Pardon des Mariniers (blessing of river boats), St-Jean-de-Losne
**Jul** Burgundy Grands Crus Concerts (Noyers-sur-Serein, Meursault , Chablis); Sens Dance Festival; Tonnerre Music Festival; Chalon-sur-Saône Street Theatre Festival; Pouilly-sur-Loire Grand Crus Wine Auction; Châtillon-sur-Seine Festival; Vézelay Madeleine Pilgrimage;
**Aug** Cluny Music Concerts; Othe & Armance Festival; Arcy-sur-Festival; Halles de Nolay Antiques Fair; Pouilly-sur-Loire Wine Fair; Coulanges-sur-Yonne Nautical Jousting; Auxonne Medieval Feast Days; Grand Morvan Traditional Festival; Saulieu Charolais Festival; Dijon Folklore & Wine Festival;
**Sep** Auxerre Piano Festival; Music in the Vaults Dijon Flea Market; Chenôve Pressing Festival;
**Oct** Beaune Bread, Wine & Cheese Fair; Marsannay-la-Côte 'Grands Crus'Marathon; Nuits-St-Georges Wine Festival; Dijon Gastronomy Fair
**Nov** "Three Glories" Wine Festival: Vougeot, Beaune & Meursault; Wine Festivals:St-Bris-le-Vineux, Chablis
**Dec** Châteauneuf-en-Auxois Midnight Mass

### Burgundy Wine
Burgundy's vineyards cover some 60,000 acres, and there are 95 official appellations in four categories:-

### Regional or Generic Appellations
Wines from throughout the region, such as Bourgogne, or Bourgogne-Ordinaire.

### Communal or Village Apellations
Wines that bear the name of their home village, such as Chablis or Gevrey-Chambertin.

### Premier Cru Appellations
Wines from 'named' vineyards, known for their high standards and specific character. These names are usually included along with the village name, as in Nuits-St-Georges les Caillerets.

### Grands Crus
These are the rarest and the best wines, produced in a handful of villages, with just the vineyard's name on the label, such as Chambertin, Corton or Montrachet.

### The First Burgundians
In 422 AD, the Romans allowed a wandering tribe from an island off the Swedish coast (today the Danish island of Bornholm) to settle near Geneva. From there they expanded their kingdom across the Burgundy plateau and south to Provence and Marseille. These 'Burgundarholmers' quickly adopted Roman manners and the Christian faith and gave their name to Burgundy.

# Franche-Comté

S tretching from the Vosges to the Jura Massif on the Swiss border, Franche-Comté is as far from the sea as you can get in France, yet it is a wonderfully watery place with a thousand lakes and rivers. With its deep forests and mountain regions it is the perfect place to experience the great outdoors, winter or summer. Besançon, the fortified regional capital, set in a loop of the River Doubs, is a city of art and history, hosting prestigious international music festivals in the summer.

## ESSENTIAL FACTS

| | |
|---|---|
| DÉPARTEMENTS: | Doubs, Jura, Haute-Saône, Territoire-de-Belfort |
| PRINCIPAL TOWNS | Belfort, Besançon, Dole, Lons-le-Saunier, Luxeuil-les-Bains, Montbéliard, Pontarlier, St Claude, Vesoul |
| PLACES TO VISIT: | The Route-de-Vin from Beaford to Arbois; the Hérrison Falls at the Sout de Doubs; Haut-Jura Nature Park; the Royal Saltworks of Arc et Senans, Besançon, classified as a World Heritage Site by UNESCO; Corbusier's Chapel of Notre-Dame du Haut, Ronchamp; Coopers' Museum, Bois d'Amont |
| REGIONAL TOURIST OFFICE | 9 rue de Pontarlier F 25025 Besançon Tel 03 81 83 50 47   Fax 03 81 83 35 82 |
| LOCAL GASTRONOMIC DELIGHTS | Cheeses: Comté, Morbier, Cancoillote, Bleu de Gex, Mont d'Or, Vacherin du Haut-Doubs. Saucisse de Morteaux, smoked sausage. Ham from Luxeuil. Snails from Marnay. Tarts filled with fruit or pumpkin. Blue cheese fondue. |
| DRINKS | Wines: three main districts, Arbois, Château-Chalon & L'Etoile produce red, white or rosé. Château-Chalon: vin jaune, yellow wine, is aged in casks for 6 years; vin de paille, straw wine, where the grapes are matured on beds of straw for 3 months. Vin fou or crazy wine, is a local sparkling wine. Macvin is a liqueur wine served with melon, as an aperitif, or with dessert. |
| LOCAL CRAFTS WHAT TO BUY | Watches & clocks: Besançon. Lace: Montbéliard & Luxeuil-les-Bains. Pottery & earthenware: Mathay & Salins-les-Bain. Glassware: La Rochère. Horn products: Jeurre & Lizon. Woodcrafts: St Claude, Largillay & Mambelin. |

### ARBOIS Jura

**★ ★ Des Cepages**
rte de Villette *39600*
☎ 384662525 FAX 384374962
(A36 exit Dole)
Near motorway
*33 en suite (shr)  TV in all bedrooms  Direct dial from all bedrooms  Mini-bar in all bedrooms  Licensed  Lift  Open parking available  Child discount available 10yrs  Open terrace  Last d 21.30hrs  Languages spoken: English & German*
CARDS: ●● ■■ ▥▥ ▣ Travellers cheques

### AUBIGNEY Haute-Saône

**★ ★ Auberge du Vieux Moulin**
*70140*
☎ 384316161 FAX 384316238
(A36 exit Dole (North), 20kms follow signs for Gray)
Near river  Forest area
*7 en suite (bth/shr)  (4 fmly)  TV in all bedrooms  Direct dial from all bedrooms  Licensed  Full central heating  Open parking available  Fishing  Open terrace*
CARDS: ●● ■■ ▥▥ ▣ Travellers cheques

### BESANÇON Doubs

**★ ★ ★ Hôtel Castan**
6 Square Castan *25000*
☎ 381650200 FAX 381830102
(in the town centre. Follow signs for 'Citadelle' and Conseil Régional')
Near river  In town centre
*Closed 26 Dec-2 Jan & 3 wks Aug*
*10 en suite (bth/shr)  (1 fmly)  No smoking in 1 bedroom  TV in all bedrooms  STV  Radio in rooms  Direct dial from all bedrooms  Mini-bar in all bedrooms  Room-safe  Licensed  Night porter  Full central heating  Air conditioning in bedrooms  Open parking available  Supervised  Child discount available 13yrs  Open terrace  Languages spoken: English*
CARDS: ●● ■■ ▥▥ Travellers cheques

### BONNÉTAGE Doubs

**★ ★ Étang du Moulin**
*25210*
☎ 381689278 FAX 381689442
Near river  Forest area
*Closed 4 Jan-3 Feb*
*18 en suite (bth/shr)  Some rooms in annexe  (3 with balcony)  TV in all bedrooms  Licensed  Full central heating  Open parking available  Supervised  Child discount available 10yrs  Fishing  V meals  Last d 21.00hrs  Languages spoken: English & German*
CARDS: ●● ▥▥ Travellers cheques

### CHAMPAGNOLE Jura

**★ ★ Bois Dormant**
rte de Pontarlier *39300*
☎ 384526666 FAX 384526667
(S of town centre towards Lons-le-Saunier)
Near river  Forest area  In town centre  Near motorway

★★ **Pourchéresse**
8 av Duhamel (ex av de Châlon) *39100*
☎ 384820105 FAX 384728150
(on the main road to Lyon & Châlon)
In town centre
*18 en suite (bth/shr) (6 fmly) TV in all bedrooms Direct dial from all bedrooms Licensed Full central heating Open parking available Open terrace Languages spoken: English, German, Italian & Spanish*
ROOMS: (room only) s fr 230FF; d fr 260FF
CARDS: ● ● Travellers cheques

### ÉCOLE-VALENTIN Doubs

★★ **Climat de France**
rue des Maisonnettes *25480*
☎ 381880411 FAX 381803133
(off N83 by Esso garage)
Forest area Near motorway
*43 en suite (bth) (11 fmly) No smoking in 9 bedrooms TV in all bedrooms Radio in rooms Direct dial from all bedrooms Licensed Full central heating Open parking available Child discount available 10yrs Open terrace Languages spoken: English & German*
ROOMS: (room only) d fr 290FF ✱
CARDS: ● ● Travellers cheques

### GEVRY Jura

***Bed & Breakfast*** (Prop: M & Mme R Picard)
3 rue du Puits *39100*
☎ 384710593 FAX 384710808
(from A9 exit Dole-Choisey take N5 towards Genève-Lausanne for 1 mile to Gevry on right. Establishment is 2nd house after the church)
Near river Near beach Forest area In town centre Near motorway
*Closed Jan-Feb*
*5 en suite (bth/shr) (2 with balcony) No smoking in 2 bedrooms Full central heating Open parking available Last d 16.00hrs Languages spoken: English & German*
CARDS: Travellers cheques

### GOUMOIS Doubs

★★★ **Taillard**
*25470*
☎ 381442075 FAX 381442615
(access on A36 via Maîche)
Near river Forest area
*Closed mid Nov-end Feb*
*24 rms (17 bth/shr) 7 rooms in annexe (6 fmly) (14 with balcony) TV in all bedrooms Direct dial from all bedrooms Mini-bar in 6 bedrooms Licensed Full central heating Open parking available Covered parking available (charged) Supervised Child discount available 14yrs Outdoor swimming pool (heated) Sauna Pool table Jacuzzi/spa Bicycle rental Open terrace V meals Last d 21.00hrs Languages spoken: English & Italian*
MEALS: Full breakfast 56FF Lunch 130-360FF&alc Dinner 130-360FF&alc✱
CARDS: ● ● ■ ● ● Travellers cheques

### LEPUIX Territoire-de-Belfort

★★ **Grand Hotel du Sommet**
*90200*
☎ 384293060 FAX 384239560
Near river Near lake Forest area
*25 en suite (shr) (4 fmly) TV in all bedrooms Direct dial from all bedrooms Licensed Full central heating Open parking available Covered parking available Child discount available 14yrs Bicycle rental Open terrace Last d 21.30hrs Languages spoken: English & German*
MEALS: Full breakfast 30FF Lunch 80-150FF Dinner 80-150FF
CARDS: ● ● Travellers cheques

### LUXEUIL-LES-BAINS Haute-Saône

★★★ *Beau Site*
18 rue Georges Moulinard *70300*
☎ 384401467 FAX 384845025
Near river Near lake Forest area Near motorway
*33 en suite (bth/shr) 9 rooms in annexe (6 fmly) (5 with balcony) No smoking in 7 bedrooms TV in all bedrooms Direct dial from all bedrooms Lift Full central heating Open parking available Covered parking available (charged) Child discount available 12yrs Outdoor swimming pool (heated) Open terrace Last d 21.30hrs Languages spoken: English, German & Spanish*
CARDS: ● ● Travellers cheques

### MAÎCHE Doubs

★★ *Panorama*
36 rue St-Michel *25120*
☎ 381640478 FAX 381640895
Forest area
*Closed 7-19 Jan*
*32 en suite (bth/shr) (8 with balcony) TV in 16 bedrooms Direct dial from all bedrooms Mini-bar in 3 bedrooms Licensed Full central heating Open parking available Supervised Child discount available 10yrs Tennis Bicycle rental Open terrace V meals Last d 21.30hrs Languages spoken: English & German*
CARDS: ● ● Travellers cheques

### MONTCHAUVROT-MANTRY Jura

★★ *La Fontaine*
Montchauvrot *39230*
☎ 384855002 FAX 384855618
Near river Near lake Forest area Near motorway
*Closed 17 Dec-17 Jan*
*20 en suite (bth/shr) (3 fmly) (4 with balcony) TV in all bedrooms Licensed Full central heating Open parking available Covered parking available (charged) Child discount available 7yrs Open terrace V meals Last d 21.30hrs Languages spoken: English & German*
CARDS: ● ●

### PESMES Haute-Saône

★★ *De France*
*70140*
☎ 384312005 FAX 384312066
(from Dole enter Pesmes, cross bridge and follow road to right. Hotel 200yds on right)
Near river Near sea Near beach Forest area
*10 en suite (bth/shr) 10 rooms in annexe (2 fmly) TV in all*

285

bedrooms *Direct dial from all bedrooms* *Mini-bar in 2 bedrooms* *Licensed* *Full central heating* *Open parking available* *Supervised* *Child discount available 8yrs* *Bicycle rental* *Open terrace* *Barbeque in hotel garden* *V meals* *Last d 21.30hrs* *Languages spoken: English & Italian*
ROOMS: (room only) s 210FF; d 260FF **Reductions over 1 night** **Special breaks**
MEALS: Continental breakfast 50FF Lunch 80-170FF&alc Dinner 80-170FF&alc
CARDS: ●● ■ ☲ Travellers cheques

**La Maison Royale** (Prop: Mr Guy Hoyet)
*70140*
☎ 384312323
(from A36, take exit for 'Dole'. Join the D475 and turn right towards 'Gray')
Guests will receive a warm welcome at this 14th-century fort, which took ten years to restore and is now considered an historic monument. Unusual decorations inside, both modern and old, and art exhibitions are shown here.
Near river *Forest area* *In town centre*
*15 Mar-15 Oct*
*12 en suite (bth/shr)* *No smoking in 6 bedrooms* *Full central heating* *Open parking available* *No children 7yrs* *Fishing* *Bicycle rental* *Open terrace* *Billiards* *Languages spoken: English, German, Italian & Spanish*
ROOMS: s fr 350FF; d fr 450FF **Reductions over 1 night**
CARDS: Travellers cheques

★ ★ ★ **Domaine Vallée Heureuse**
rte de Genève *39800*
☎ 384371213 FAX 384370875
(A39 exit 7 Poligny)
Near river *Near sea* *Forest area* *Near motorway*
*9 en suite (bth/shr)* *1 rooms in annexe* *(1 fmly)* *(1 with balcony)* *No smoking in 1 bedroom* *TV in all bedrooms* *Direct dial from all bedrooms* *Mini-bar in all bedrooms* *Licensed* *Full central heating* *Open parking available* *Covered parking available (charged)* *Supervised* *Child discount available 8yrs* *Outdoor swimming pool (heated)* *Fishing* *Riding* *Sauna* *Boule* *Bicycle rental* *Open terrace* *Covered terrace* *V meals* *Last d 21.30hrs* *Languages spoken: English, German & Spanish*
ROOMS: (room only) s 400-450FF; d 500-800FF
MEALS: Continental breakfast 55FF Lunch 95-220FF&alc Dinner 205-420FF&alc
CARDS: ●● ■ ☲ 回 JCB Travellers cheques

★ ★ ★ ★ **Hostellerie des Monts de Vaux**
Monts de Vaux *39800*
☎ 384371250 FAX 384370907
(off N5 3km E of Poligny)
Forest area *Near motorway*
*Closed 31 Oct-29 Dec*
*10 en suite (bth/shr)* *TV in all bedrooms* *Direct dial from all bedrooms* *Mini-bar in 5 bedrooms* *Licensed* *Full central heating* *Open parking available* *Covered parking available* *Supervised* *Tennis* *Open terrace* *V meals* *Last d 21.30hrs* *Languages spoken: English, German & Italian*
ROOMS: (room only) s fr 600FF; d fr 800FF **Reductions over 1 night** **Special breaks**
MEALS: Full breakfast 75FF Lunch 180-400FFalc Dinner 300-450FFalc
CARDS: ●● ■ ☲ 回 Travellers cheques

★ ★ **Auberge des Moulins**
*25110*
☎ 381840999 FAX 381840444
This hotel has been entirely renovated and offers its visitors a cheerful interior, where the proprietors and their dedicated staff put a lot of effort into caring for their guests. The restaurant provides a high standard of home cooking and the bedrooms have good amenities and provide straightforward comfort.
Near river *Forest area*

*Closed 17 Dec-22 Jan*
*15 en suite (bth/shr)* *No smoking in 1 bedroom* *TV in all bedrooms* *Direct dial from all bedrooms* *Licensed* *Full central heating* *Open parking available* *Covered parking available (charged)* *Child discount available 12yrs* *Fishing* *Bicycle rental* *Open terrace* *V meals* *Last d 21.30hrs* *Languages spoken: English German & Italian*
ROOMS: (room only) s fr 230FF; d fr 290FF
MEALS: Continental breakfast 30FF Lunch 98-190FF&alc Dinner 98-190FF&alc
CARDS: ■ ☲ Travellers cheques

**Château de Salans** (Prop: M & Mme Oppelt)
*39700*
☎ 384711655 FAX 384794154
(turn off N73 (Dole to Besançon) at St-Vit and proceed to Salans)
Near river *Forest area* *Near motorway*
*4 en suite (bth/shr)* *(1 fmly)* *TV available* *Full central heating* *Open parking available* *Covered parking available* *Riding* *Languages spoken: English & German*
CARDS: Travellers cheques

★ ★ **Grand Hotel des Bains**
pl des Allies *39110*
☎ 384379050 FAX 384379680
Near river *Forest area* *In town centre* *Near motorway*
*30 en suite (bth/shr)* *(3 fmly)* *TV in all bedrooms* *Direct dial from all bedrooms* *Lift* *Open parking available* *Covered parking available (charged)* *Supervised* *Indoor swimming pool (heated)* *Sauna* *Solarium* *Gym* *Jacuzzi/spa* *Bicycle rental* *Open terrace* *Languages spoken: English & German*
CARDS: ●● ☲ Travellers cheques

## SERVANCE Haute-Saône

**Le Lodge du Monthury** (Prop: Michele Chevillat)
*70440*
☎ 384204855
(take N19, then D486 until Servance then left onto D263)
*Near river  Near lake  Forest area*
*6 en suite (shr)  (1 fmly)  TV available  Full central heating*
*Supervised  Child discount available 8yrs  Last d 21.00hrs*
*Languages spoken: English & German*
CARDS: ●● ▩ ◧ Travellers cheques

## VESOUL Haute-Saône

**Château d'Épenoux** (Prop: Mme Germaine Gauthier)
rte de St-Loup, Pusy-et-Epenoux *70000*
☎ 384751960 FAX 384764505
*Near lake  Forest area  Near motorway*
*6 en suite (bth/shr)  (2 fmly)  TV available  Full central*
*heating  Open parking available  Supervised  Child discount*
*available  V meals  Languages spoken: English*
CARDS: Travellers cheques

### VILLARD-ST-SAUVEUR Jura

**★ ★ Hostellerie 'Au Retour de la Chasse'**
*39200*
☎ 384451132 FAX 384451396
*Forest area*
*14 en suite (bth/shr)  (2 fmly)  (2 with balcony)  TV in all*
*bedrooms  Direct dial from all bedrooms  Licensed  Full central*
*heating  Open parking available  Child discount available*
*Tennis  Fishing  Gym  Boule  Open terrace  Last d 21.30hrs*
*Languages spoken: English*
CARDS: ●● ■■ ▩ ◧ Travellers cheques

### VILLERS-LE-LAC Doubs

**★ ★ ★ Hotel Restaurant Le France**
8 pl M-Cupillard *25130*
☎ 381680006 FAX 381680922
(from Bescançon, follow direction Pontarlier/Lausanne. Then
follow Valdahon, Morteau and finally Villers-le-Lac)
*Near river  Forest area  In town centre*
*Closed 3-28 Jan, 2-10 Oct & 24-28 Dec*
*14 en suite (bth/shr)  TV in all bedrooms  Direct dial from all*
*bedrooms  Mini-bar in all bedrooms  Licensed  Full central*
*heating  Museum on 1st floor  Last d 21.00hrs  Languages*
*spoken: German, English & Spanish*
ROOMS: (room only) s 300FF; d 320FF
MEALS: Full breakfast 50FF  Lunch 120-410FF&alc  Dinner
160-410FF&alc
CARDS: ●● ■■ ▩ ◧ Travellers cheques

### VILLERSEXEL Haute-Saône

**★ ★ Hotel du Commerce**
1 rue du 13 Septembre *70110*
☎ 384202050 FAX 384205957
The hotel is situated in a small, peaceful village surrounded by
unspoilt countryside and provides the setting for a relaxing
stay far away from the pressures of modern-day life. It features
bedrooms with modern facilities, a comfortable lounge and a
country-style restaurant which offers a selection of regional
dishes of high quality. Various cultural sights and leisure
opportunities are just around the corner.
In town centre

**Hotel du Commerce**
*17 en suite (bth/shr)  (3 fmly)  TV in all bedrooms  STV  Direct*
*dial from all bedrooms  Licensed  Full central heating  Open*
*parking available  Supervised  Child discount available 7yrs*
*Bicycle rental  Open terrace  Canoeing  V meals  Last d 21.30hrs*
*Languages spoken: English & German*
ROOMS: (room only) s 190-220FF; d 210-250FF
**Reductions over 1 night**
MEALS: Continental breakfast 40FF  Lunch 64-250FF&alc
Dinner 64-250FF&alc
CARDS: ●● ▩ Travellers cheques

**★ ★ De La Terrasse**
*70110*
☎ 384205211 FAX 384205690
(On D9 between Hericourt & Vesoul)
*Near river  Forest area*
*Closed 14 Dec-1 Jan*
*14 en suite (bth/shr)  (5 with balcony)  TV in all bedrooms  STV*
*Direct dial from all bedrooms  Licensed  Full central heating*
*Open parking available  Supervised  Child discount available*
*8yrs  Bicycle rental  Open terrace  Last d 21.15hrs  Languages*
*spoken: English & Spanish*
MEALS: Continental breakfast 35FF  Lunch 65-250FF alc
Dinner 85-250FF alc✱
CARDS: ●● ▩ Travellers cheques

### VILLERS-FARLAY Jura

**Château de Bel Air** (Prop: M & Mme Dromard)
*39600*
☎ 384377337 FAX 384377337
*Near river  Near sea  Forest area*
*Closed Oct-Mar*
*2 en suite (bth/shr)  (2 fmly)  Full central heating  Open parking*
*available  Supervised*

# Bed & Breakfast

in England, Scotland,
Wales & Ireland

*Choose from over 3000
places to stay, annually
assessed for quality*

**AA** Lifestyle Guides

# Poitou-Charentes

The sunniest region in the west of France with a mild climate even in the winter. Visit the old harbour at La Rochelle with its bustling quayside markets and fashionable bars, or stretch out and soak up the sun on some of the glorious beaches nearby. History-lovers should make for Chauvigny and its atmospheric remains of five castles. Royan caters for the sports-minded, offering tennis, squash, and an 18-hole golf course. Further north the villages around the Seudre rear the finest oysters, while in oak casks along the Charente Valley, the famous Cognac brandy matures.

## ESSENTIAL FACTS

| | |
|---|---|
| DÉPARTEMENTS: | Charente, Charente-Maritime, Deux Sèvres, Vienne |
| PRINCIPAL TOWNS | Angoulême, La Rochelle, Niort, Poitiers, Royan |
| PLACES TO VISIT: | La Rochelle, including the Aquarium; Cognac; the ruins of five medieval castles at Chauvigny; 'Sleeping Beauty's Castle' at La Roche-Courbon; the islands of Ré, Aix and Oléron; Mouton-Village (all about sheep) at Vasles; National Comic Strip Centre at Angoulême; the Valley des Singes at Romagne; Futuroscope Park near Poitiers; Le Moulin de Fleurac (paper mill) at Nersac; Bourg-Charente, Doll Museum; Aubeterre, Puppet Museum; Châtellerault Motor Museum. Abbey of St Savin, near Angles sur L'Anglin. |
| REGIONAL TOURIST OFFICE | BP 56, 62 rue Jean-Jaurès, F-86002 Poitiers Tel: 549 50 10 50 Fax: 549 41 37 28 |
| LOCAL GASTRONOMIC DELIGHTS | Seafood, especially mussels & oysters. Chaudrée, fish soup. Fricasée d'anguilles: eels in sauce. Lumas, snails cooked in red wine. Mojettes, haricot beans smothered in butter. Dry-cured ham. Over 50 goats' cheeses: try chabichou, served fresh or baked. If you see a small cottage loaf with a burnt, blackened crust then it is delicious Tourteau Fromager, a light domed sponge, often with raspberry sauce. |
| DRINKS | The Charente Valley, around Cognac & Jarnac, is famous for brandy |
| LOCAL CRAFTS WHAT TO BUY | Tusson: glassware. Saintes & Thouars: ceramics. Cognac: pottery |

288

## AMAILLOUX Deux-Sèvres

**Château de Tennessus** (Prop: Philippa Freeland)
*79350*
☎ 549955060 FAX 549955062
(From the A10 at Poitiers take the N149 to Parthenay (50kms). 8km N of Parthenay, still on N149 towards Bressuire, the château is signposted to the right on the D127, after 1km château is on the right)
Near lake  Forest area  Near motorway
*Closed Nov-Feb*
2 en suite (shr) (1 fmly) No smoking on premises  Full central heating  Open parking available  Outdoor swimming pool (heated)  Fishing  Boule  Badminton  croquet  Languages spoken: English German & Italian
ROOMS:  d 622.25FF
CARDS: Travellers cheques

## ANGLES-SUR-L'ANGLIN Vienne

★ ★ ★ **Le Relais du Lyon d'Or**
4 rue d'Enfer *86260*
☎ 549483253 FAX 549840228
(leave A10 at Châtellerault Nord. Take directions La Roche Posay, Vicq-sur-Gartempe, Angles-sur-l'Anglin, hotel on left as you enter village)

The hotel is situated in one of the most charming villages in France and dates back to the 14th century. It has been renovated in a style befitting the period and the individually decorated bedrooms are furnished to suit the character of the house. The menus feature fresh local produce and a range of reasonably priced local wines.
Near river  Forest area  In town centre
*Closed 3 Jan-28 Feb*
10 en suite (bth/shr) (3 fmly) TV in all bedrooms  Direct dial from all bedrooms  Licensed  Full central heating  Open parking available  Supervised  Child discount available 3yrs  Open terrace  Relaxation Centre (Steam Baths/Massage)  V meals Last d 21.00hrs  Languages spoken: English
ROOMS: (room only) d 370-450FF **Reductions over 1 night Special breaks: Painting & Health breaks**
MEALS: Continental breakfast 40FF  Lunch 110-190FF&alc Dinner 110-190FF&alc
CARDS: ●● ▄▄

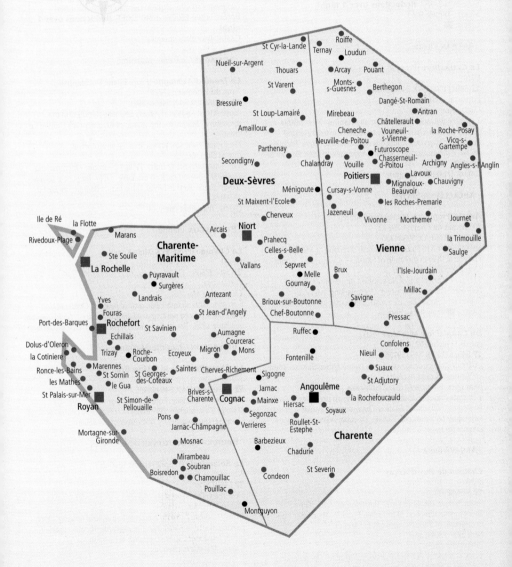

Roiffe
St Cyr-la-Lande  Ternay  Loudun
Nueil-sur-Argent
Thouars  Arcay  Pouant
St Varent  Monts-s-Guesnes  Berthegon
Bressuire
Dangé-St-Romain
St Loup-Lamairé  Mirebeau  Antran
Amailloux  Châtellerault
Cheneche  Vouneuil-s-Vienne  la Roche-Posay
Neuville-de-Poitou  Vicq-s-Gartempe
Parthenay  Futuroscope
Secondigny  Chasserneuil-d-Poitou  Archigny  Angles-s-l'Anglin
Chalandray  Vouille
**Deux-Sèvres**  Poitiers  Lavoux
Mignaloux-Beauvoir  Chauvigny
Ménigoute  Cursay-s-Vonne
St Maixent-l'Ecole  les Roches-Premarie
Cherveux  Jazeneuil
Ile de Ré  la Flotte  Arcais  Niort  Vivonne  Morthemer  Journet
Rivedoux-Plage  Marans  Prahecq  la Trimouille
Ste Soulle  **Charente-Maritime**  Celles-s-Belle  **Vienne**  Saulge
La Rochelle  Vallans  Sepvret
Puyravault  Melle  Brux  l'Isle-Jourdain
Surgères  Gournay  Millac
Yves  Landrais  Antezant  Savigne
Fouras  Brioux-sur-Boutonne  Pressac
Port-des-Barques  Rochefort  St Jean-d'Angely  Chef-Boutonne
St Savinien  Aumagne  Ruffec
Echillais  Courcerac  Confolens
Dolus-d'Oleron  Trizay  Roche-Courbon  Migron  Mons  Fontenille  Nieuil
la Cotiniere  Ecoyeux  Suaux
Ronce-les-Bains  Marennes  Saintes  Cherves-Richemont  St Adjutory
les Mathes  St Sornin  St Georges-des-Coteaux  Sigogne  la Rochefoucauld
St Palais-sur-Mer  le Gua  Brives-s-Charente  Cognac  Jarnac  **Angoulême**
Royan  St Simon-de-Pellouaille  Mainxe  Hiersac  Soyaux
Pons  Segonzac  Roullet-St-Estephe
Mortagne-sur-Gironde  Jarnac-Champagne  Verrieres  **Charente**
Mosnac  Barbezieux  Chadurie
Mirambeau
Boisredon  Soubran  Condeon  St Severin
Chamouillac
Pouillac
Montguyon

## ANTEZANT Charente-Maritime

**Le Maurençon** (Prop: P & M C Fallelour)
Les Moulins, 10 rue de Maurençon *17400*
☎ 546599452 FAX 546599452
(from St-Jean-d'Angely take D127 to Antezant)
Near river  Forest area
*Closed 25 Dec-2 Jan*
*2 rms (1 bth) (1 fmly) No smoking on premises  Radio in rooms*
*Full central heating  Open parking available  Child discount*
*available 8yrs  Bicycle rental  Billiards*
ROOMS:  d 270FF  **Reductions over 1 night**
MEALS:  Dinner 95FF
CARDS: ▆▆

## ANTRAN Vienne

**La Gatinalière** (Prop: M. B de la Touche)
*86100*
☎ 549211502 FAX 549853965
Forest area  Near motorway
*Closed Nov-end Mar*
*2 en suite (bth/shr) No smoking on premises  TV available  Full*
*central heating  Open parking available  Covered parking*
*available  Supervised  Child discount available 10yrs  Bicycle*
*rental  V meals  Last d 21.00hrs  Languages spoken: English &*
*Spanish*
CARDS: Travellers cheques

## ARÇAIS Deux-Sèvres

**Arçais** (Prop: Jean Michel Deschamps)
10 chemin du Charret *79210*
☎ 59354334 FAX 59354335
(exit Niort of A10 Paris-Bordeaux in direction of Marais
Poitevin & then in direction of Sansais-Le Vanneau & Arçais)
*Closed Xmas RS Nov-Feb*
*3 en suite (shr) (3 fmly) No smoking on premises  TV in 1*
*bedroom  Full central heating  Open parking available*
*Supervised  Boule  Bicycle rental  Languages spoken: English*
CARDS: ▆ Travellers cheques

**Du Canal** (Prop: M & Mme Plat)
rue de l'Ouché *79210*
☎ 549354259 & 549359755
(A70 exit 23 in direction of Marais Poitevin then Sansais, then
Le Vanneau & onto Arcais)
Near river  Forest area  Near motorway
*4 en suite (bth/shr) (2 fmly) No smoking on premises  TV in 2*
*bedrooms  Full central heating  Open parking available  Indoor*
*swimming pool (heated)  Fishing  By canal boating & canoes*
*Languages spoken: English*

## ARÇAY Vienne

**Château de Puy d'Arçay**
*86200*
☎ 549982911
(from Paris in the direction of Bordeaux on A10, 30km after
Tours turn in direction of Richelieu/Loudun. Then after Loudun
in direction of Thouars, turn left for Arcay)
Near lake  Forest area
*Closed Oct-Mar*
*4 rms (2 bth/shr) (4 fmly) Full central heating  Open parking*
*available  Child discount available  Languages spoken: English*
CARDS: ▆ Travellers cheques

## ARCHIGNY Vienne

**La Talbardière** (Prop: J Lonhienne)
*86210*
☎ 549853251 FAX 549856972
(south from Châtellerault take D9 towards Monthoiron. After
20kms turn left onto D3 towards La Roche-Posay. 2kms turn
left at sharp bend & continue for 1km to house)
Near river  Near lake  Forest area  Near motorway
*3 en suite (bth/shr) (2 fmly) Full central heating  Open parking*
*available  Open terrace  Table tennis  Chrildren's play area*
*Languages spoken: English, German,Italian & Russian*
ROOMS:  s 200-250FF; d 240-300FF  **Reductions over 1**
**night**
CARDS: Travellers cheques

## AUMAGNE Charente-Maritime

**Le Treuil d'Aumagne** (Prop: Eliane Dechamps)
7 rue du Pigonnier *17770*
☎ 546582380 FAX 546582391
(leave A10 at St-Jean-d'Angely and take the D939 in the
direction of Matha, for the village of Reignier turn right to Le
Treuil)
Near river  Near sea  Forest area  Near motorway
*Closed Dec-Mar*
*5 en suite (bth/shr) (2 fmly) TV in 1 bedroom  Open parking*
*available  Covered parking available  Child discount available*
*Tennis  Boule  Bicycle rental  Table tennis  Badminton  Last d*
*18.00hrs*
CARDS: Travellers cheques

## BERTHEGON Vienne

**La Chaume** (Prop: M & Mme Kosyk)
*86420*
☎ 549228669
Forest area
*Closed Nov-Mar*
*5 en suite (shr) (3 fmly) Full central heating  Open parking*
*available  Covered parking available  Supervised  Child discount*
*available 12yrs  Boule  Badminton  table tennis  Last d 20.00hrs*

## BOISREDON Charente-Maritime

**La Chapelle** (Prop: M & Mme Brunet)
*17150*
☎ 546493405 FAX 546493405
Near river  Near lake  Forest area  Near motorway
*(2 fmly) TV available  STV  Radio in rooms  Full central heating*
*Open parking available  Child discount available*

## BRIOUX-SUR-BOUTONNE Deux-Sèvres

**La Rolanderie** (Prop: Francois Riedel)
32 rue de la Gare *79170*
☎ 549072210
Near river  Forest area
*Closed Nov-Mar*
*4 rms (1 bth/shr) (2 with balcony) Full central heating  Open*
*parking available  Child discount available  Bicycle rental  V*
*meals  Languages spoken: English & German*
CARDS: Travellers cheques

**BRIVES-SUR-CHARENTE** Charente-Maritime

**Logis de Louzignac**
2 r des Verdiers *17800*
☎ 546964572 FAX 546961609
(signposted from D135 to Brives)

A beautifully restored 18th-century manor house set in a large walled garden and containing period furniture, antiques and modern art. The bedrooms are spacious and comfortably furnished and the atmosphere is pleasantly informal.
Near river Forest area
*May-Sep*
*2 en suite (shr) No smoking in all bedrooms Full central heating Open parking available Covered parking available No children 12yrs Outdoor swimming pool*
ROOMS: s fr 400FF; d fr 500FF **Reductions over 1 night**
CARDS: Travellers cheques

**BRUX** Vienne

**Bed & Breakfast** (Prop: M & Mme Grollier)
Le Bourg *86510*
☎ 549592310 FAX 549581803
(from A10 exit Poitiers Sud take N10 towards Angoulême for 40km, then D98 towards Brux. Establishment on E outskirts near war memorial)
Near motorway
*3 rms (2 shr) (1 fmly) Full central heating Open parking available Child discount available*
CARDS: Travellers cheques

**CELLES-SUR-BELLE** Deux-Sèvres

★ ★ **Hostellerie de l'Abbaye**
1 pl des Epoux Laurent *79370*
☎ 549329332 FAX 549797265
Near river Near lake Forest area In town centre Near motorway
*17 en suite (bth/shr) TV in all bedrooms STV Direct dial from all bedrooms Licensed Night porter Full central heating Open parking available Supervised Child discount available 10yrs Bicycle rental Open terrace V meals Last d 21.30hrs Languages spoken: English*
CARDS: ●● ▆ ⑩ Travellers cheques

**CHADURIE** Charente

**Le Logis du Puy Fort-Haut** (Prop: Marie Claude Bergero)
*16250*
☎ 545248074 FAX 545240826
(from Angoulême D674 then D5 Chadurie, from

Barbezieux D5 Chadurie)
Forest area
*4 en suite (shr) (3 fmly) Radio in rooms Full central heating Open parking available Child discount available Outdoor swimming pool Boule Volley ball, Table tennis*

**CHALANDRAY** Vienne

**Château de Trequel** (Prop: Laurence Sarazin)
*86190*
☎ 549601895 FAX 549601895
(from Poitiers head towards Parthenay pass Ayron to Chalandray)
Near river Near lake Forest area Near motorway
*8 en suite (bth) (2 fmly) No smoking on premises Full central heating Open parking available Boule Table tennis Pony Last d 22.00hrs Languages spoken: English*

**CHAMOUILLAC** Charente-Maritime

**La Coussaie** (Prop: Robert & Nichole Daviaud)
*17130*
☎ 546494101
(from A10 exit 37 Mirambeau in the direction of Montendre)
Near lake Forest area Near motorway
*2 en suite (bth/shr) (1 fmly) No smoking in all bedrooms TV available Full central heating Open parking available Covered parking available Languages spoken: English*
CARDS: Travellers cheques

**CHASSENEUIL-DU-POITOU** Vienne

★ ★ ★ **Château du Clos de la Ribaudière**
rue du Champ-de-Foire *86360*
☎ 549528666 FAX 549528632
(located in the centre of Chasseneuil-du-Poitou)
This gracious building dates back to the 19th century, and was once the private residence of Madame Barbot de la Motte, one of the first women to make a hot-air balloon ascent. The elegant bedrooms are equipped with modern amenities and offer a high standard of comfort. The restaurant serves skilfully executed dishes from a wide repertoire of regional specialities.
Near river Forest area Near motorway
*41 en suite (bth) (4 fmly) (2 with balcony) TV in all bedrooms STV Radio in rooms Direct dial from all bedrooms Mini-bar in all bedrooms Licensed Lift Night porter Full central heating Open parking available Supervised Child discount available 14yrs Outdoor swimming pool (heated) Fishing Open terrace V meals Last d 22.00hrs Languages spoken: English*
ROOMS: (room only) s 380-660FF; d 460-920FF ✱
MEALS: Continental breakfast 60FF Lunch 130-295FF&alc Dinner 160-295FF&alc✱
CARDS: ●● ▆ ▆ ⑩ JCB Travellers cheques

**CHÂTELLERAULT** Vienne

★ ★ ★ **Grand Hotel Moderne**
74 bd Blossac *86100*
☎ 549213011 FAX 549932519
Near river Near lake Forest area In town centre Near motorway
*26 en suite (bth/shr) (5 fmly) (6 with balcony) TV in all bedrooms Radio in rooms Mini-bar in all bedrooms Licensed Lift Night porter Full central heating Open parking available (charged) Covered parking available (charged) Open terrace Last d 21.30hrs Languages spoken: English & German*
CARDS: ●● ▆ ▆ ⑩ Travellers cheques

291

### CHAUVIGNY Vienne

**La Veaudepierre** (Prop: M et Mme Jacques de Giafferri)
8 rue du Berry *86300*
☎ 549463081 & 549414176 FAX 549476412
(in the city centre)
Near river Forest area In town centre Near motorway
*Closed Nov-Etr (ex holidays & advance bookings)*
*5 en suite (bth/shr) (2 fmly) Full central heating Open parking
available Child discount available 12yrs Table tennis
Languages spoken: English*
CARDS: Travellers cheques

### CHEF-BOUTONNE Deux-Sèvres

**La Rivière** (Prop: John Turner)
Tillou *79110*
☎ 549299662 FAX 54929662
(take D940 through Melle, continue for 4km turn right onto
D737 signed Chef-Boutonne, in 4km turn right for
Sompt/Tillou, in Tillou turn right after viallge hall, follow signs
Luche sur Brioux keep water tower on right, 2nd left signed
for La Rivère)

A restored stone house on tranquil six acre site of former
water mill. Bounded by streams and farmland, the old meal
stream flows through the grounds.
Near river Near lake Forest area Near motorway
*2 rms (1 bth/shr) (1 fmly) No smoking on premises TV in 1
bedroom Full central heating Open parking available Child
discount available 12yrs Outdoor swimming pool Fishing
Boule V meals Languages spoken: English*
ROOMS: s 180FF; d 220FF
MEALS: Dinner 65-95FF

### CHENECHÉ Vienne

**Château de Labarom** (Prop: Eric Le Gallais)
*86380*
☎ 549512422 FAX 549514738
(from A10 Futuroscope exit, take D62 towards Neuville, then
D757 to Vendeuvre. Left on D15 to Cheneché. House
signposted on right)
Near lake Forest area Near motorway
*Closed 9 Nov-Mar*
*5 rms (3 bth/shr) (3 fmly) No smoking on premises Radio in
rooms Full central heating Open parking available Child
discount available 2yrs Outdoor swimming pool Languages
spoken: English*
CARDS: Travellers cheques

### CHERVES-RICHEMONT Charente

**Logis de Boussac** (Prop: M et Mme François Mehaud)
*16730*
☎ 545831301 & 545832222 FAX 545832121
(take D731 from Cognac, in direction Niort-Poitiers, after 5km
to L'Épine, turn left towards Richemont, over 3 small bridges
house on left)

Built in 1692, this residence is now protected as a historic
monument for its architectural interest. Situated in the middle
of a vineyard in the Cognac region, five kilometres from the
town centre. You may dine with your hosts for a fixed price,
finishing off your meal with a taste of Cognac.
Near river Forest area Near motorway
*3 en suite (bth/shr) (1 fmly) Full central heating Open parking
available Covered parking available Child discount available
12yrs Outdoor swimming pool Fishing Riding Canoeing Last
d 12.00hrs Languages spoken: English*
ROOMS: d 400FF **Special breaks: Wine & food tasting
breaks**
MEALS: Dinner 180FF
CARDS: Travellers cheques

### CHERVEUX Deux-Sèvres

**Château de Cherveux** (Prop: F & M-T Redien)
*79410*
☎ 549750655 FAX 549750655
(from Niort take D743 then right onto D8 to Cherveux)

Accommodation is available in this 15th-century château,
which you can explore during your stay. The guardroom is
now used for guests. In good weather family meals are served
with the proprietors in the courtyard.
*Jan-mid Oct*

4 rms (2 bth 1 shr) (2 fmly) Open parking available Covered parking available Child discount available Fishing Riding Languages spoken: English
ROOMS: s 250-300FF; d 300-350FF ✳

### COGNAC Charente

#### ★ ★ ★ Hotellerie Les Pigeons Blancs
110 rue Jules Brisson *16100*
☎ 545821636 FAX 545822929
Near river Forest area In town centre
*7 en suite (bth/shr) TV in all bedrooms Direct dial from all bedrooms Licensed Full central heating Open parking available Child discount available 12yrs Open terrace Covered terrace Last d 21.00hrs Languages spoken: English & German*
ROOMS: (room only) d 350-600FF **Reductions over 1 night**
MEALS: Continental breakfast 50FF Lunch 138-280FF&alc Dinner 138-280FF&alc
CARDS: ●● ■■ 🗷 ⑩ Travellers cheques

#### ★ ★ ★ *Hotel le Valois*
35 rue du 14 Juillet *16100*
☎ 545827600 FAX 545827600
Near river Forest area In town centre Near motorway
*Closed 23 Dec-2 Jan*
*45 en suite (bth/shr) (1 fmly) No smoking in 3 bedrooms TV in all bedrooms STV Radio in rooms Direct dial from all bedrooms Mini-bar in all bedrooms Licensed Lift Night porter Air conditioning in bedrooms Open parking available Covered parking available Supervised Sauna Solarium Gym Languages spoken: English*
CARDS: ●● ■■ 🗷 ⑩ Travellers cheques

### CONDÉON Charente

#### *Le Bois de Mauré* (Prop: M & Mme Testard)
*16360*
☎ 545785315
Near river
*4 en suite (shr) Full central heating Open parking available Child discount available 10yrs Languages spoken: English*

### COTINIÈRE, LA Charente-Maritime

#### ★ ★ ★ *L'Écallier*
65 rue de Port *17310*
☎ 546471031 FAX 546471023
Near sea
*Closed 15 Nov-1 Feb*
*8 en suite (bth/shr) (2 fmly) TV in all bedrooms Direct dial from all bedrooms Mini-bar in all bedrooms Licensed Full central heating Air conditioning in bedrooms Open parking available (charged) Supervised Child discount available 14yrs Open terrace Last d 21.30hrs*
CARDS: ●● ■■ 🗷 ⑩ Travellers cheques

#### ★ ★ ★ *Motel Ile de Lumière*
av des Pins *17310*
☎ 546471080 FAX 546473087
Near sea
*Closed Oct-Mar*
*45 en suite (bth/shr) (13 fmly) (32 with balcony) TV in all bedrooms STV Direct dial from all bedrooms Mini-bar in all bedrooms Full central heating Open parking available Covered parking available Child discount available Outdoor swimming pool (heated) Tennis Sauna Bicycle rental Table*

Tennis,Exercise Studio Languages spoken: English, German & Spanish
CARDS: ●● 🗷 Eurocard Travellers cheques

### COURCERAC Charente-Maritime

#### *Le Bourg* (Prop: M & Mme Moreau)
8 rue de Chez Mothe *17160*
☎ 546250007
Near river Near lake Forest area
*4 en suite (bth/shr) (1 fmly) No smoking on premises Full central heating Open parking available Child discount available*

### CURZAY-SUR-VONNE Vienne

#### ★ ★ ★ ★ *Château de Curzay*
*86600*
☎ 549361700 FAX 549535769
Near river Forest area Near motorway
*22 en suite (bth) 8 rooms in annexe (3 fmly) No smoking in 6 bedrooms TV in all bedrooms STV Direct dial from all bedrooms Mini-bar in all bedrooms Licensed Night porter Full central heating Open parking available Supervised Child discount available 12yrs Outdoor swimming pool (heated) Fishing Riding Boule Bicycle rental Open terrace Last d 21.30hrs Languages spoken: English, German & Spanish*
ROOMS: (room only) d 750-1700FF
MEALS: Full breakfast 80FF Lunch 265-570FF&alc Dinner 210-410FF&alc
CARDS: ●● ■■ 🗷 ⑩ Travellers cheques

### DANGÉ-ST-ROMAIN Vienne

#### *La Grenouillère* (Prop: Noël Braguier)
17 rue de la Grenouillère *86220*
☎ 549864868 FAX 549864656
(from A10 exit at Châtellerault-Nord, take N10 to Dangé-St Romain. In town at 2nd set of lights follow signs for Chambres d'Hôtes. Over river, turn left of cross, under lime trees and into rue de Grenouillère)
Near river Forest area Near motorway
*5 en suite (bth/shr) (2 fmly) No smoking on premises TV in 2 bedrooms Full central heating Open parking available Supervised Child discount available 10yrs Fishing Boule Badminton Volleyball Table tennis Last d 20.00hrs Languages spoken: English & Spanish*
CARDS: Travellers cheques

### DOLUS-D'OLÉRON Charente-Maritime

#### ★ ★ ★ *Grande Large*
Baie de la Rémigeasse *17550*
☎ 546753789 FAX 546754915
(from Paris motorway Aquitaine exit 35 Saintes-then Marennes-Ile d'Oléron)
Near sea Forest area
*RS restaurant closed Mon-Fri (ex BHs)*
*26 en suite (bth/shr) (5 with balcony) TV in all bedrooms STV Radio in rooms Direct dial from all bedrooms Licensed Full central heating Open parking available Supervised Child discount available Indoor swimming pool (heated) Tennis Solarium Open terrace Short Tennis Last d 21.15hrs Languages spoken: English & German*
ROOMS: (incl. dinner) d 830-2010FF ✳
MEALS: Continental breakfast 95FF Dinner 190-390FF&alc
CARDS: ●● ■■ 🗷 ⑩ Eurocard Travellers cheques

### ECHILLAIS Charente-Maritime

**Bed & Breakfast** (Prop: Mme D Couraud)
5 rue du Champ Simon *17620*
☎ 546831160
Forest area
*2 rms No smoking on premises Full central heating Open
parking available No children*

### ÉCOYEUX Charente-Maritime

**Chez Quimand** (Prop: M H Forget)
*17770*
☎ 546959255 FAX 546959255
(autoroute A10 exit 35 proceeding towards Saintes)
Near sea Near beach Forest area Near motorway
*4 en suite (bth/shr) (1 fmly) No smoking on premises Night
porter Full central heating Open parking available Child
discount available 3yrs Bicycle rental V meals Last d 18.00hrs*
ROOMS: s 180-210FF; d 215-255FF **Reductions over 1
night Special breaks**
MEALS: Dinner 85FF
CARDS: Travellers cheques

### FLOTTE, LA Charente-Maritime

★ ★ ★ ★ *Le Richelieu*
44 av de la Plage *17630*
☎ 546096070 FAX 546095059
(A10 direction of Bordeaux exit 33 for La Rochelle in direction
of Île de Ré after sign for La Flotte)
Near sea Near beach
*44 en suite (bth/shr) 25 rooms in annexe TV in all bedrooms
STV Direct dial from all bedrooms Mini-bar in all bedrooms
Licensed Night porter Full central heating Open parking
available Child discount available 14yrs Outdoor swimming
pool (heated) Tennis Riding Sauna Solarium Pool table
Jacuzzi/spa Bicycle rental Open terrace Covered terrace
Centre of Thalassotherapy V meals Last d 21.30hrs Languages
spoken: English & German*
CARDS: ●● ■■ ⚹⚹ ⓘ Travellers cheques

### FOURAS Charente-Maritime

**Le Clos des Courtineurs** (Prop: Mme Lefebvre)
4 ter rue des Courtineurs, BP 47 *17450*
☎ 546840287 FAX 546840287
(24km from La Rochelle & 13km from Rochefort, leave N137
onto D937, Fouras 5km west)
In a quiet wooded area of the Fouras peninsula, with sandy
beach just 300 metres away and the shore only 150 metres.
Guest rooms are on the ground floor, in a separate wing from
the owner's home, and open onto a large garden. Enclosed
parking area.
Near sea Near beach Forest area
*15 May-15 Sep*
*5 en suite (shr) No smoking in all bedrooms Open parking
available Covered parking available Languages spoken:
English*
ROOMS: s 260FF; d 300-320FF ✱
CARDS: Travellers cheques

### GOURNAY Deux-Sèvres

★ ★ *Château des Touches*
*79110*
☎ 549299692 FAX 549299747
(NW between D948 and N740)
Forest area Near motorway
*13 en suite (bth/shr) (2 fmly) (1 with balcony) Direct dial from
all bedrooms Licensed Night porter Full central heating Open
parking available Supervised Child discount available 12yrs
Pool table Boule Bicycle rental Open terrace V meals Last d
21.00hrs Languages spoken: English*
CARDS: ●● ■■ ⚹⚹ Travellers cheques

### GUA, LE Charente-Maritime

★ ★ ★ *Moulin de Châlons*
2 rue du Bassin *17680*
☎ 546228272 FAX 546223107
(leave A10 at exit 35 towards Oléron-Marennes then Nancras
to Le Gua)
Near river Forest area Near motorway
*Closed 21 Sep-14 May*
*14 en suite (bth/shr) TV in 6 bedrooms Direct dial from all
bedrooms Licensed Full central heating Open parking
available Child discount available 8yrs Fishing Open terrace
Last d 21.30hrs Languages spoken: English & Spanish*
ROOMS: (room only) d 360-550FF
MEALS: Full breakfast 70FF Lunch 150-380FF&alc Dinner
170-380FF&alc
CARDS: ●● ■■ ⚹⚹ ⓓ

### HIERSAC Charente

★ ★ ★ *Hostellerie du Maine Brun*
RN 141 *16290*
☎ 545908300 FAX 545969114
(from Angoulême take N141 towards Cognac)
This former mill is an oasis of peace and provides a relaxed stay
amidst the vineyards of the Cognac region. All the luxurious
bedrooms, which have private balconies, are decorated with
period furniture and offer views over the garden and river. The
restaurant serves a wide selection of dishes complemented by
some great wines from the house cellar.
Near river Forest area Near motorway
*Closed 16 Oct-14 Apr*

*20 en suite (bth/shr) (20 with balcony) TV in all bedrooms STV
Direct dial from all bedrooms Mini-bar in all bedrooms
Licensed Full central heating Open parking available Outdoor
swimming pool Open terrace Last d 21.30hrs Languages
spoken: English & German*

ROOMS: (room only) s 460-510FF; d 590-750FF **Special breaks**
MEALS: Full breakfast 65FF  Lunch 105-205FF&alc  Dinner 105-205FF&alc
CARDS: ⬤⬤ ▇▇ ▇▇ ⬤ JCB Travellers cheques

### ISLE-JOURDAIN, L' Vienne

### ★ ★ ★ Hotel Val de Vienne
Port de Salles *86150*
☎ 549482727 FAX 549484747
(Off D8 towards the River Vienne)
The hotel is situated in a beautiful valley on the banks of the River Vienne. Each bedroom has a private terrace overlooking the river and is equipped with private facilities. Guests can enjoy a pleasant day by the heated swimming pool or take advantage of the various sporting and tourist activities close by, followed by a relaxing dinner in the gourmet restaurant, whilst watching the river flow by.
*Near river*

*Closed 2-30 Jan RS Restauarnt-Sun pm & Mon*
*20 en suite (bth/shr)  2 rooms in annexe  (2 fmly)  (20 with balcony)  TV in 22 bedrooms  STV  Radio in rooms  Direct dial from 22 bedrooms  Mini-bar in 22 bedrooms  Licensed  Night porter  Full central heating  Open parking available  Covered parking available (charged)  Child discount available 12yrs  Outdoor swimming pool (heated)  Fishing  Boule  Bicycle rental  Open terrace  V meals  Last d 21.30hrs  Languages spoken: English German & Spanish*
ROOMS: (room only) d 390-440FF **Reductions over 1 night**
MEALS: Full breakfast 55FF  Lunch 100-205FF  Dinner 100-205FF
CARDS: ⬤⬤ ▇▇ ▇▇ Travellers cheques

### JARNAC Charente

### Hotel Restaurant Karina
Les Metairies *16200*
☎ 545362626 FAX 545811093
(N141 onto D736 in direction of Sigogne and Les Metairies, at x-rds in Les Metairies turn right then 1st left & right again, follow sign)
*Near river*
*Closed mid Dec-mid Jan*
*10 en suite (bth/shr)  (2 fmly)  No smoking in 2 bedrooms  TV available  STV  Direct-dial available  Licensed  22828 open parking spaces  Supervised  Child discount available 10yrs  Indoor swimming pool  Solarium  Pool table  Boule  Bicycle rental  Open terrace  V meals  Last d 21.30hrs  Languages spoken: English*

ROOMS: (incl. dinner) d 640-800FF ✱
MEALS: Lunch 95-150FF&alc  Dinner 95-150FF&alc✱
CARDS: ⬤⬤

### Maison Karine (Prop: M & Mme Legon)
Bois Faucon *16200*
☎ 545362626 FAX 545811093
(from Jarnac towards Les Métairies on D376 at crossroads follow sign for Hotel Karina)
*Closed 15 Dec-15 Jan*
*10 en suite (bth/shr)  Some rooms in annexe  (2 fmly)  No smoking in 1 bedroom  TV in all bedrooms  Radio in rooms  Full central heating  Open parking available  Child discount available 10yrs  Outdoor swimming pool  Tennis  Boule  Bicycle rental  Last d 22.30hrs  Languages spoken: English*
CARDS: ⬤⬤ ▇▇

### JARNAC-CHAMPAGNE Charente-Maritime

### Domaine des Tonneaux (Prop: Mme Violette Lassalle)
*17520*
☎ 546495099 FAX 546495733
Forest area  Near motorway
*Closed Dec-Etr*
*3 en suite (bth/shr)  Radio in rooms  Full central heating  Open parking available  Supervised  Child discount available 10yrs  Boule  Table tennis  TV room*
CARDS: Travellers cheques

### JAZENEUIL Vienne

### Les Ruffinières (Prop: D Foucault)
*86600*
☎ 549535519 & 549534917
(autoroute from Paris exit Poitiers South, from south exit Lusignan)
*Near river*
*Closed 16 Sep-14 Apr RS 1-15 Nov*
*6 rms (4 bth/shr)  No smoking in 2 bedrooms  Full central heating  Open parking available  Child discount available 6yrs  Open terrace  Covered terrace  Languages spoken: English*

### JOURNET Vienne

### La Boulinière (Prop: Deborah Earls)
*86290*
☎ 549915588 FAX 549915588
(on the D727, 10kms from Montmorillon)
Near river  Near lake  Forest area
*6 en suite (bth/shr)  (1 fmly)  Full central heating  Open parking available  Covered parking available  Child discount available 10yrs  Outdoor swimming pool  Fishing  Bicycle rental  V meals  Last d 19.30hrs  Languages spoken: English & Italian*
CARDS: Travellers cheques

### LANDRAIS Charente-Maritime

### Bed & Breakfast (Prop: M Francois Caillon)
Les Granges *17290*
☎ 546277381 FAX 546278713
(at Surgères take D939 in direction of La Rochelle after 5km turn left on D117 to Landrais)
Forest area
*Closed Dec-1 Jan*
*5 en suite (shr)  (1 fmly)  No smoking on premises  Full central heating  Open parking available  Child discount available  Last d*

*contd.*

*midday* Languages spoken: English
ROOMS: s 170FF; d 200FF
MEALS: Dinner 75FF✱
CARDS: ■

### LAVOUX Vienne

**Logis du Château du Bois Dousset** (Prop: Vicomte de Villoutreys)
*86800*
☎ 549442026 FAX 549442026
(from A10, Poitiers Nord exit, N10 towards Limoges, after 7km, left to Bignoux and follow signs to Bois Dousset)
Near river Near lake Forest area
*4 rms (3 bth) (2 fmly) Full central heating Open parking available Covered parking available Child discount available 5yrs Tennis Boule* Languages spoken: English
CARDS: ■

### MAINXE Charente

**La Cour des Cloches** (Prop: Ann Thorne/John Welch)
Chez Juillier
☎ 545808686 FAX 545320438
(N10 exit onto N141 to Cognac, continue on the N141 from Cognac towards Angoulême exit onto D736 signposted

Segonzac. Take 1st left (D10) towards St-Même-les-Carrières & follow signs for La Cour des Cloches)
La Cour des Cloches eas originally a large farm complex producing grape for the major cognac houses. Built in 1812, with local stone quarried at St Meme les Carrieres, it has now been restored and renovated retaining the original external characteristics
Near river Near lake Forest area Near motorway
*9 en suite (bth/shr) (1 fmly) (4 with balcony) No smoking in all bedrooms Full central heating Open parking available Outdoor swimming pool (heated) Boule Bicycle rental V meals* Languages spoken: English
ROOMS: s 250-300FF; d 300-500FF **Special breaks**
MEALS: Lunch 50-100FF Dinner 75-150FF
CARDS: ●● ■ ▥ Travellers cheques

### MARANS Charente-Maritime

**Barbecane** (Prop: Chantal Jourdain)
rive droite de la Sevre *17230*
☎ 546017959 FAX 546017959
(off N137)
Near river

*4 en suite (bth/shr) No smoking on premises TV in all bedrooms Full central heating Open parking available Outdoor swimming pool (heated) Boule Table tennis*
ROOMS: s 230FF; d 300FF
CARDS: ●● ▥

### MARENNES Charente-Maritime

**Bed & Breakfast** (Prop: Jean & Jacqueline Ferchaud)
5 rue des Lilas, La Mesnardière *17320*
☎ 546854177
Near sea Forest area
*Closed Oct*
*4 en suite (bth/shr) No smoking on premises Full central heating Open parking available Supervised*

### MATHES, LES Charente-Maritime

★ ★ ★ **Palmyrotel**
2 allée des Passereaux, La Palmyre *17570*
☎ 546236565 FAX 546224413
(from A10 (Paris to Bordeaux) exit at Saintes, take N150 to Royan, then D25 To La Palmyre)
Near sea Near beach Forest area
*Closed 16 Nov-14 Mar RS Half board obligatory Jul-Aug 46 en suite (bth/shr) (14 fmly) (18 with balcony) TV in all bedrooms Direct dial from all bedrooms Licensed Lift Night porter Full central heating Open parking available Child discount available 12yrs Open terrace Covered terrace Wkly live entertainment* Languages spoken: English & German
CARDS: ●● ▥ ▥ Travellers cheques

### MIGNALOUX-BEAUVOIR Vienne

★ ★ ★ **Manoir de Beauvoir**
635 rte de Beauvoir *86800*
☎ 549554747 FAX 549553195
Near motorway
*Closed 19 Dec-4 Jan*
*46 en suite (bth/shr) 22 rooms in annexe (40 fmly) (10 with balcony) TV in all bedrooms STV Direct dial from all bedrooms Mini-bar in all bedrooms Licensed Lift Night porter Full central heating Open parking available Supervised Child discount available 12yrs Golf 18 Open terrace V meals Last d 22.00hrs* Languages spoken: English, Italian & Spanish
CARDS: ●● ■ Travellers cheques

### MIGRON Charente-Maritime

**Logis des Bessons** (Prop: J Philippe)
*17770*
☎ 546949116 FAX 546949822
Near river Near lake Forest area Near motorway
*5 rms (3 bth/shr) (1 fmly) Radio in rooms Open parking available Covered parking available Supervised Child discount available 3-4yrs Outdoor swimming pool Boule Bicycle rental Table tennis* Languages spoken: English

### MILLAC Vienne

**Le Peyrat Ecosse** (Prop: Alan & Hilda Jamieson)
*86150*
☎ 549845088 FAX 549845088
(from the centre of the L'Isle Jourdain - 2km on the D28 route Mouterre-sur-Blourde, large signs for Le Peyrat Ecosse)

### Le Peyrat Ecosse

Renovated 1930's farmhouse, set in thirteen acres of rural countryside, in the Vienne valley. Close to L'Isle Jourdain, the area offers many leisure activities.
Near river Near lake Forest area
5 rms (2 fmly) No smoking in all bedrooms Full central heating Open parking available Covered parking available Child discount available 3yrs V meals Languages spoken: English
ROOMS: s 150FF; d 210FF
MEALS: Lunch 50FF Dinner 90FF

### MIRAMBEAU Charente-Maritime

### ★ ★ ★ ★ Château-Hotel de Mirambeau
rte de Montendre 17150
☎ 546707177 FAX 546707110
Forest area Near motorway
TV available STV Direct-dial available Licensed Lift Night porter Full central heating Open parking available Supervised Indoor swimming pool (heated) Outdoor swimming pool (heated) Golf Tennis Sauna Gym Pool table Jacuzzi/spa Open terrace Languages spoken: English German & Spanish
CARDS: ●● ■■ ■■ Access,Eurocard Travellers cheques

### MIREBEAU Vienne

**Bed & Breakfast** (Prop: Mme Jeannin)
19 rue Jacquard 86110
☎ 549505406
Near lake Forest area In town centre Near motorway
2 en suite (bth/shr) Full central heating Open parking available Covered parking available

**Bed & Breakfast** (Prop: M et Mme Peroux)
34 rue Hoche 86110
☎ 549504214
In town centre
2 en suite (bth/shr) No smoking on premises Open parking available Tennis

### MONS Charente-Maritime

**Lambernié** (Prop: John Curtis Chamberlain)
☎ 546250857
(leave A10 junct 24 St-Jean d'Angeley, take D939 in direction of Matha, then D131 Prignac to Mons)
A classic 19th-century country house around two sides of a courtyard. In a peaceful hamlet at the heart of Charente and within easy reach of many places of interest.
Near lake

2 rms No smoking on premises Full central heating Open parking available Child discount available 5yrs Outdoor swimming pool Tennis Boule Bicycle rental Languages spoken: English
ROOMS: d 220FF
MEALS: Dinner 80FF
CARDS: Travellers cheques

### MONTS-SUR-GUESNES Vienne

**Domaine de Bourg-Ville** (Prop: Pierre Claude Fouquenet)
86420
☎ 549228158 FAX 549228989
(from Saumur, take D947 to Candes, then D147 to Loudun and D14 to Monts-sur-Guesnes. Signposted)
This traditional building, with original beams, guarantees a peaceful night's sleep. Dinner is taken on the patio, or, if the weather is bad, indoors, by candlelight. Communal living room with TV. Some reductions are available.
Near lake Forest area
5 en suite (shr) (2 fmly) No smoking in 2 bedrooms Full central heating Open parking available Supervised Child discount available 12yrs Boule Bicycle rental V meals Last d 16.00hrs Languages spoken: English
ROOMS: s 165FF; d 205FF ✱ **Reductions over 1 night**
MEALS: Lunch 110FF Dinner 110FF
CARDS: Travellers cheques

### MORTAGNE-SUR-GIRONDE Charente-Maritime

### ★ ★ Auberge de la Garenne
3 Impasse de l'Ancienne Gare 17120
☎ 546906369 FAX 546905093
Near river Near sea Near beach Forest area Near motorway
11 en suite (shr) (6 fmly) (6 with balcony) TV in all bedrooms Direct dial from all bedrooms Licensed Full central heating Open parking available Child discount available 12yrs Outdoor swimming pool Boule Bicycle rental Covered terrace Archery,badminton,table tennis,darts Last d 21.00hrs Languages spoken: English
CARDS: ●● ■■ Travellers cheques

### MORTHEMER Vienne

**Bed & Breakfast** (Prop: Mme Dupond)
Bourpeuil 86300
☎ 549564882 FAX 549564882
Near river Near lake Near beach Forest area
4 en suite (bth/shr) (2 fmly) TV available Full central heating Open parking available Languages spoken: English & German

### MOSNAC Charente-Maritime

### ★ ★ ★ Moulin de la Marcouze
17240
☎ 546704616 FAX 546704814
Near river Forest area Near motorway
Closed Feb
10 en suite (bth/shr) (5 with balcony) TV in all bedrooms STV Direct dial from all bedrooms Mini-bar in all bedrooms Licensed Full central heating Air conditioning in bedrooms Open parking available Supervised Outdoor swimming pool Fishing Bicycle rental Last d 21.30hrs Languages spoken: English
CARDS: ●● ■■ ◉

## NEUVILLE-DE-POITOU Vienne

**La Galerne** (Prop: Claude Morin)
Chemin de Couture *86170*
☎ 549511407 FAX 549544782
Near lake  Forest area
*Closed 16 Nov-14 Mar*
*5 en suite (shr)  (4 fmly)  No smoking on premises  TV available*
*Full central heating  Open parking available  Outdoor*
*swimming pool  Languages spoken: English*
CARDS: Travellers cheques

## NIEUIL Charente

★ ★ ★ ★ **Château de Nieuil**
*16270*
☎ 545713638 FAX 545714645
Near river  Near lake  Forest area
*Closed early Nov-Apr*
*14 en suite (bth/shr)  (5 fmly)  TV in all bedrooms  STV Direct*
*dial from all bedrooms  Mini-bar in all bedrooms  Room-safe*
*Licensed  Night porter  Full central heating  Open parking*
*available  Covered parking available (charged)  Outdoor*
*swimming pool  Tennis  Fishing  Boule  Mini-golf  Bicycle rental*
*Open terrace  Art gallery,antiques  V meals  Last d 21.00hrs*
*Languages spoken: English & German*
CARDS: ●● ▬ ▭ ⑨ Travellers cheques

## NIORT Deux-Sèvres

★ ★ ★ **Grand Hotel**
32-34 av de Paris *79000*
☎ 549242221 FAX 549244241
Near river  Forest area  In town centre  Near motorway
*Closed Xmas & New Year*
*37 en suite (bth/shr)  (10 fmly)  No smoking in 8 bedrooms  TV in*
*all bedrooms  Direct dial from all bedrooms  Licensed  Lift  Night*
*porter  Full central heating  Open parking available  Covered*
*parking available (charged)  Supervised  Child discount available*
*12yrs  Open terrace  Languages spoken: English*
CARDS: ●● ▬ ▭ ⑨ Travellers cheques

★ ★ **Le Paris**
12 av de Paris *79000*
☎ 549249378 FAX 549282757
(from A10 exit 32 follow signs for town centre)
Near river  In town centre  Near motorway
*Closed 23 Dec-2 Jan*
*44 en suite (bth/shr)  (4 fmly)  TV in all bedrooms  STV Direct*
*dial from all bedrooms  Licensed  Night porter  Full central*
*heating  Open parking available (charged)  Covered parking*
*available (charged)  Bicycle rental  Open terrace  Covered*
*terrace  Languages spoken: English, German & Spanish*
ROOMS: (room only)  s 260-285FF; d 285-305FF
**Reductions over 1 night**
CARDS: ●● ▭

## NUEIL-SUR-ARGENT Deux-Sèvres

**Ferme Auberge de Regueil** (Prop: Serge Ganne)
*79250*
☎ 549654256 FAX 549656987
Near river  Near beach  Forest area
*2 en suite (shr)  No smoking on premises  Full central heating*
*Open parking available  Child discount available 10yrs  Fishing*
*V meals  Last d 17.00hrs*
CARDS: ●● ▬

## PARTHENAY Deux-Sèvres

★ ★ **Renotel**
bd de l'Europe *79200*
☎ 549940644 FAX 549640194
Near motorway
*Closed Nov-Etr*
*42 rms (14 bth 25 shr)  TV in all bedrooms  STV  Direct dial*
*from all bedrooms  Licensed  Lift  Night porter  Full central*
*heating  Open parking available  Supervised  Child discount*
*available 12yrs  Open terrace  Last d 21.00hrs  Languages*
*spoken: English*
CARDS: ●● ▬ ▭ Travellers cheques

★ ★ **St-Jacques**
13 av du 114ème Régiment, d'Infanterie *79200*
☎ 549643333 FAX 549940069
In town centre  Near motorway
*46 en suite (bth/shr)  (10 fmly)  No smoking in 4 bedrooms  TV*
*in all bedrooms  STV  Direct dial from all bedrooms  Mini-bar in*
*22 bedrooms  Licensed  Lift  Night porter  Full central heating*
*Open parking available  Child discount available 10yrs*
*Languages spoken: English*
ROOMS: (room only)  d 200-350FF
CARDS: ●● ▬ ▭ Travellers cheques

## POITIERS Vienne

**Château de Vaumoret** (Prop: M et Mme Vaucamp)
rue du Breuil Mingot *86000*
☎ 549613211 FAX 549010454
(access by N10 or A10, exit 'Poitiers-Nord' No29, take eastern
ring road round Poitiers towards Limoges and take exit to
Montamise on the D3 on the left, then D18 on the right,
Vaumoret is in 2km)
M. & Mme Vaucamp welcome you to their very quiet 17th-
century château, surrounded by a 15 hectare park.
Futuroscope and Poitiers are only ten kilometres away, and
golf. tennis, horse-riding, ice-skating and swimming pools all
within 13 kilometres.
Forest area
*Closed 15 Nov-15 Jan (ex school holidays)*
*3 en suite (bth)  (1 fmly)  TV in 1 bedroom  Full central heating*
*Open parking available  Covered parking available  Supervised*
*Bicycle rental  Tennis and stables are nearby.  Languages*
*spoken: English*
ROOMS: s 300-370FF; d 350-430FF
CARDS: Travellers cheques

★ ★ **Grand Hotel de l'Europe**
39 rue Carnot
☎ 549881200 FAX 549889730
(follow directions to `centre ville' and then to `parking Carnot'
hotel just after parking on the left)
In town centre
*88 en suite (bth/shr)  Some rooms in annexe (7 fmly)  (3 with*
*balcony)  TV in all bedrooms  Direct dial from all bedrooms*
*Mini-bar in 55 bedrooms  Room-safe (charged)  Licensed  Lift*
*Night porter  Full central heating  Open parking available*
*(charged)  Covered parking available (charged)  Supervised*
*Child discount available 12yrs  Open terrace  Covered terrace*
*Languages spoken: English, German & Spanish*
ROOMS: (room only)  s 300-330FF; d 330-480FF ✱
CARDS: ●● ▬ ▭ ⑨ JCB Travellers cheques

**★ ★ ★ Le Grand Hotel**
28 rue Carnot *86000*
☎ 549609060 FAX 549628189
(follow signs to `centre ville' then `parking Carnot' just after
hotel entrance)
In town centre
*47 en suite (bth/shr) (6 fmly) TV in all bedrooms STV Radio in
rooms Mini-bar in all bedrooms Licensed Lift Night porter
Full central heating Open parking available (charged) Covered
parking available (charged) Supervised Bicycle rental Open
terrace Languages spoken: English & Spanish*
CARDS: ● ■ ▦ ◨ ◙ Travellers cheques

### PONS Charente-Maritime

**★ ★ ★ Auberge Pontoise**
23 av Gambetta *17800*
☎ 546940099 FAX 546913340
(leave A10 at exit 36, hotel in 4km)
Near river In town centre Near motorway
*Closed 15 Dec-early Feb*
*22 en suite (bth/shr) (6 fmly) TV in all bedrooms Direct dial
from all bedrooms Licensed Night porter Full central heating
Open parking available (charged) Covered parking available
(charged) Child discount available 10yrs Open terrace V meals
Last d 21.30hrs Languages spoken: English*
CARDS: ● ▦ Travellers cheques

### PORT-DES-BARQUES Charente-Maritime

**★ ★ Auberge du Labrador**
49 av de l'Ile Madame *17730*
☎ 546839260 FAX 546844318
(from A10 exit 34 head for Rochefort, cross Rive Charente and
continue to Port-des-Barques)
A small, comfortable hotel with fine views Charente estuary
and the sea.
Near river Near sea Near beach
*Closed Wed (restaurant)*

*12 en suite (bth/shr) (1 fmly) No smoking in 5 bedrooms TV in
6 bedrooms STV Direct dial from all bedrooms Full central
heating Open parking available Child discount available 12yrs
Boule Bicycle rental Open terrace Covered terrace V meals
Last d 22.00hrs Languages spoken: English, Dutch & German*
ROOMS: (room only) s 275-325FF; d 325-375FF **Special
breaks: on request**
MEALS: Lunch 125FF&alc Dinner 125FF&alc
CARDS: ● ▦

### POUANT Vienne

**Le Bois Goulu** (Prop: Jean and Marie Picard)
*86200*
☎ 549225205
*3 rms (2 shr) Full central heating Open parking available
Covered parking available Child discount available 12yrs
Languages spoken: English*
CARDS: Travellers cheques

### POUILLAC Charente-Maritime

**La Thébaide** (Prop: Denise and Piere Billat)
*17210*
☎ 564046517 FAX 546048538
Near lake Forest area Near motorway
*Closed Oct*
*4 rms (2 shr) No smoking on premises Full central heating
Open parking available Child discount available 7yrs Last d
18.00hrs*
CARDS: Travellers cheques

### PRAHECQ Deux-Sèvres

**★ ★ Hotel des Ruralies**
autoroute A10, aire des Ruralies *79230*
☎ 549756766 FAX 549758029
(The establishment is near the A10 Motorway, between exits 32
& 33)
Near motorway
*51 rms (50 bth/shr) TV in all bedrooms STV Direct dial from
all bedrooms Licensed Lift Night porter Full central heating
Air conditioning in bedrooms Open parking available
Supervised Child discount available 12yrs Last d 23.00hrs
Languages spoken: English & Spanish*
CARDS: ● ■ ▦ ◙ Travellers cheques

### PRESSAC Vienne

**L'Epine** (Prop: Mme Mary Bradshaw)
*86460*
☎ 549849777 FAX 549849777
(N147 to Fleuri, turn right onto D2 to Gençay. At Gençay onto
D741 signposted Confolens, continue on D741 through St-
Martin-l'Ars. L'Epine is just N of the village on left)
Near river Near lake Near beach Near motorway
*3 en suite (shr) (1 fmly) No smoking in all bedrooms Open
parking available Covered parking available Child discount
available Outdoor swimming pool Tennis Fishing Riding
Boule Mini-golf V meals Languages spoken: English*
ROOMS: s fr 200FF; d 250FF **Reductions over 1 night**
MEALS: Dinner fr 100FF
CARDS: Travellers cheques

### PUYRAVAULT Charente-Maritime

**Le Clos de la Garenne** (Prop: Patrick & Brigitte Francois)
9 rue de la Garenne *17700*
☎ 546354771 FAX 546354791
(A10 exit 33 in direction Surgères, at Surgères & rdbt take D115
in direction of Marans & Puyravault. Puyravault on left 5km
from Surgères)
The France you came to find: discovered at this 17th century
Manor House set in 10 acres of enclosed parkland. The rooms
are bright, spacious and very comfortable. Your hosts will
greet you as friends. An ideal place for discovering La Rochelle
and the surrounding area. *contd.*

Near river  Near lake  Forest area
*3 en suite (bth/shr) (2 fmly) No smoking on premises Full central heating Open parking available Child discount available 12yrs Tennis Boule Billiard room Last d 10.00hrs Languages spoken: English German Italian & Spanish*
ROOMS: s 320FF; d 350FF
MEALS: Dinner 120FF
CARDS: Travellers cheques

## RIVEDOUX-PLAGE Charente-Maritime

### ★ ★ ★ *Rivotel*
154 av des Dunes *17940*
☎ 546098951 FAX 546098904
Near sea  In town centre
*Closed early Oct-end Mar*
*35 en suite (bth) 26 rooms in annexe (9 with balcony) TV in all bedrooms Licensed Full central heating Open parking available Child discount available 10yrs Outdoor swimming pool (heated) Solarium Jacuzzi/spa Bicycle rental Open terrace Last d 21.45hrs Languages spoken: English & Spanish*
CARDS: ●● ■ ☲

## ROCHEFORT Charente-Maritime

### ★ ★ ★ *Hotel La Corderie Royale*
rue Audebert *17300*
☎ 546993535 FAX 546997872
Near river
*Closed 2-18Feb*
*53 en suite (bth/shr) (4 fmly) TV in all bedrooms Direct dial from all bedrooms Mini-bar in all bedrooms Licensed Lift Night porter Full central heating Open parking available Supervised Child discount available 12yrs Outdoor swimming pool Sauna Bicycle rental Open terrace Covered terrace Last d 22.00hrs Languages spoken: English*
CARDS: ●● ■ ☲ ⑨

## ROCHEFOUCAULD, LA Charente

**Château de La Rochefoucauld** (Prop: de la Rochefoucauld)
*16110*
☎ 545620742 FAX 545635494
(in centre of La Rochefoucauld)
Near river  Forest area  In town centre
*RS winter*
*3 en suite (shr) Open parking available Covered parking available Languages spoken: English, Italian & Spanish*

## ROCHELLE, LA Charente-Maritime

**Bed & Breakfast** (Prop: Mme Iribe)
33 rue Thiers *17000*
☎ 546416223 FAX 546411076
(follow signs `centre ville' to main square, turn left then 1st right to end street, right again and immediately left past market)
Near sea  Near beach  Forest area  In town centre  Near motorway
*Closed February*
*6 en suite (bth/shr) (2 fmly) (2 with balcony) No smoking on premises TV in 1 bedroom Full central heating Open parking available (charged) Supervised Child discount available 12yrs V meals Last d 21.00hrs Languages spoken: English & Spanish*
ROOMS: s 450-480FF; d 520-620FF ✱
MEALS: Dinner 180-200FF
CARDS: Travellers cheques

### ★ ★ *François-1er*
15 rue Bazoges *17000*
☎ 546412846 FAX 546413501
Forest area
*38 rms (28 bth/shr) (7 fmly) TV in all bedrooms Direct dial from all bedrooms Night porter Full central heating Open parking available (charged) Supervised Languages spoken: English*
CARDS: ●● ☲ Travellers cheques

### ★ ★ *Hotel Frantour*
13 rue Sardinerie *17000*
☎ 546417155 FAX 546417046
(exit La Rochelle from A10)
Near sea  Near beach  In town centre
*79 en suite (bth/shr) (2 fmly) TV in all bedrooms STV Direct dial from all bedrooms Licensed Lift Night porter Full central heating Open parking available (charged) Covered parking available (charged) Supervised Languages spoken: English & German*
ROOMS: (room only) s 410FF; d 440-450FF
CARDS: ●● ■ ☲ ⑨ Travellers cheques

### ★ ★ ★ *St-Jean d'Acre*
4 pl de la Chaine *17000*
☎ 546417333 FAX 546411001
Near sea  Near beach  In town centre
*69 en suite (bth/shr) (6 fmly) (4 with balcony) TV in all bedrooms STV Direct dial from all bedrooms Mini-bar in all bedrooms Licensed Lift Night porter Full central heating Last d 23.00hrs Languages spoken: English German & Spanish*
ROOMS: (room only) s 380-470FF; d 570-670FF
**Reductions over 1 night**
MEALS: Continental breakfast 52FF Lunch 86-155FF Dinner 86-155FF
CARDS: ●● ■ ☲ ⑨ Travellers cheques

### ★ ★ *Trianon et Plage*
6 rue de la Monnaie *17000*
☎ 546412135 FAX 546419578
Near sea  Near beach  In town centre
*Closed 23 Dec-Jan*
*25 en suite (bth/shr) (4 fmly) TV in all bedrooms STV Direct dial from all bedrooms Licensed Full central heating Open parking available (charged) Supervised Child discount available 12yrs Mini-golf Bicycle rental V meals Last d 21.00hrs Languages spoken: English & Spanish*
ROOMS: (room only) d 380-480FF **Special breaks**
MEALS: Continental breakfast 45FF Lunch 98-200FF&alc Dinner 98-200FF&alc
CARDS: ●● ■ ☲ ⑨ Travellers cheques

## ROCHE-POSAY, LA Vienne

### ★ ★ ★ *Hotel Saint-Roch*
4 cours Pasteur *86270*
☎ 549194900 FAX 549194940
(from A10 exit at Châtellerault-Nord/La Roche-Posay)
Near river  Forest area  In town centre
*36 en suite (bth/shr) (5 with balcony) TV in all bedrooms Direct dial from all bedrooms Room-safe Licensed Lift Night porter Full central heating Air conditioning in bedrooms Open parking available Child discount available 5yrs Outdoor swimming pool (heated) Golf 18 Tennis Riding Sauna Solarium Gym Mini-golf Jacuzzi/spa Bicycle rental Open terrace Last d 21.30hrs Languages spoken: English, Spanish and German*
CARDS: ●● ☲ Travellers cheques

### ROCHES-PRÉMARIE, LES Vienne

**Château de Prémarie** (Prop: de Boysson)
*86340*
☎ 549425001 FAX 549420763
Forest area  Near motorway
*Closed 12 Nov-Etr*
*5 en suite (bth/shr)  TV available  Full central heating  Open parking available  Child discount available 12yrs  Outdoor swimming pool (heated)  Tennis  Open terrace*
CARDS: Travellers cheques

### ROIFFÉ Vienne

**Château de la Roche Martel** (Prop: Mme Véronique de Castelbajac)
*86120*
☎ 549987754 FAX 549989830
(entrance of park is on D147, 4km S of Fontevraud Abbey, towards Loudun)
Near lake  Forest area  Near motorway
*4 en suite (bth/shr)  (1 fmly)  Open parking available  Supervised Child discount available 5yrs  Boule  Bicycle rental  Table tennis Croquet  Badminton  Languages spoken: English, German, Italian & Spanish*
CARDS: Travellers cheques

### RONCE-LES-BAINS Charente-Maritime

**Le Maumusson** (Prop: Bernard Médat)
22 av St-Martin, rte des Plages *17390*
☎ 546363690 FAX 546365691
(A10 exit 35)
Near sea  Near beach  Forest area  In town centre
*Closed Sep-mid Apr*
*24 en suite (bth/shr)  (4 fmly)  Open parking available  Child discount available 10yrs  Boule  Languages spoken: English & Spanish*
CARDS: ●● ▆ Travellers cheques

### ROULLET-ST-ESTEPHE Charente

**Logis de Romainville** (Prop: Francine Quillett)
Romainville *16440*
☎ 545663256 FAX 545663256
(from Angoulême take N10 direction Bordeaux in 12km enter village Roullet take D42 towards Mouthiers in 2km turn right for Romainville)
Near river  Forest area  Near motorway
*5 rms (1 bth 3 shr)  (1 fmly)  No smoking on premises  Full central heating  Open parking available  Child discount available 6yrs  Outdoor swimming pool  Bicycle rental  Open terrace  Last d 20.00hrs  Languages spoken: English & Italian*

**★ ★ ★ La Vieille Étable**
Les Plantes *16440*
☎ 545663175 FAX 545664745
(From Angoulême take N10 towards Bordeaux)
Near lake
*29 en suite (bth/shr)  (2 fmly)  No smoking in 1 bedroom  TV in all bedrooms  STV  Direct dial from all bedrooms  Mini-bar in all bedrooms  Licensed  Full central heating  Open parking available  Outdoor swimming pool  Tennis  Fishing  Sauna Bicycle rental  Open terrace  Covered terrace  V meals  Last d 21.30hrs  Languages spoken: English*
CARDS: ●● ▆ Travellers cheques

### ROYAN Charente-Maritime

**★ ★ ★ Hotel Miramar**
173 Conche de Pontaillac *17200*
☎ 546390364 FAX 546392375
Near sea  Near beach
*Closed Dec-Mar*
*25 en suite (bth/shr)  20 rooms in annexe  (4 fmly)  TV in all bedrooms  Direct dial from all bedrooms  Night porter  Full central heating  Open parking available  Supervised  Child discount available  Bicycle rental  Open terrace  Languages spoken: English*
CARDS: ●● ▆ ▆ ⑩ Travellers cheques

**★ ★ ★ Novotel**
bd Carnot *17200*
☎ 546394639 FAX 546394646
Near sea  Forest area
*83 en suite (bth/shr)  (83 fmly)  (83 with balcony)  No smoking in 10 bedrooms  TV in all bedrooms  STV  Licensed  Lift  Night porter  Full central heating  Air conditioning in bedrooms  Open parking available  Covered parking available (charged)  Child discount available 16yrs  Indoor swimming pool (heated)  Outdoor swimming pool  Sauna  Solarium  Gym  Jacuzzi/spa Bicycle rental  Open terrace  Last d 24.00hrs  Languages spoken: English & German*
CARDS: ●● ▆ ▆ ⑩

**★ ★ ★ Résidence de Rohan**
Parc des Fées *17640*
☎ 546390075 FAX 546382999
This charming old residence is surrounded by large pine trees and has well kept lawns leading down to the fine sandy beach. A cosy lounge, with comfortable armchairs and open fireplace, provides the setting to meet fellow guests. The peaceful bedrooms, with balcony or private terrace, provide comfortable accommodation. The hotel has no eating facilities but there are more than 20 restaurants nearby. A large heated swimming pool is also on site with a good view of the sea.

Near sea  Near beach  Forest area
*Closed 11 Nov-25 Mar*
*41 en suite (bth/shr)  19 rooms in annexe  (5 fmly)  (24 with balcony)  TV in all bedrooms  STV  Direct dial from all bedrooms  Licensed  Night porter  Full central heating  Open parking available  Supervised  Outdoor swimming pool (heated)  Tennis  Solarium  Boule  Open terrace  Languages spoken: English & German*
ROOMS: (room only)  s 350-560FF;  d 450-690FF
CARDS: ●● ▆ ▆ Travellers cheques

**St-Adjutory** Charente

**La Grénouille** (Prop: M & Mme Casper)
*16310*
☎ 545620034 FAX 545630641
Two cottages plus rooms available, in an area bordering the Dordogne. La Grenouille is an old restored farmhouse, which specialises in breeding Anglo-Arabian horses. The property is situated on the brow of a hill on the edge of a forest. Both cottages have a private garden and fully equipped kitchens. All guests have use of the private swimming pool, bikes, boules, badminton, swings and hammock.
Near river Forest area Near motorway
*2 en suite (shr) Some rooms in annexe TV in 1 bedroom Full central heating Open parking available Covered parking available Child discount available Outdoor swimming pool Fishing Boule Bicycle rental Badminton Table tennis Languages spoken: English, German & Italian*
Rooms: s fr 200FF; d fr 300FF **Reductions over 1 night**

**St-Cyr-la-Lande** Deux-Sèvres

**La Marotte**
7 r du Muguet *79100*
☎ 549677377
Near river Near lake Forest area
*Closed 16 Sep-14 Jun*
*2 en suite (bth/shr) (1 fmly) No smoking on premises Full central heating Open parking available Child discount available 12yrs Table tennis Languages spoken: English*
Cards: Travellers cheques

**Saintes** Charente-Maritime

★ ★ ★ **Le Relais du Bois St-Georges**
rue de Royan, Cours Genet *17100*
☎ 546935099 FAX 546933493
(motorway exit 35 Saintes, head for town centre, at 1st rdbt take 1st right for Saintes Centre, at next rdbt, 1st right for Relais du Bois, at 3rd rdbt, take 1st right for Relais du Bois.)
Near river Near lake Forest area Near motorway
*(18 with balcony) No smoking in 15 bedrooms TV in 30 bedrooms STV Radio in rooms Direct dial from 30 bedrooms Mini-bar in 4 bedrooms Licensed Night porter Full central heating Open parking available Covered parking available (charged) Supervised Indoor swimming pool (heated) Tennis Riding Solarium Boule Jacuzzi/spa Bicycle rental Open terrace Covered terrace Table tennis Croquet V meals Last d 21.45hrs Languages spoken: English German Russian & Spanish*
Rooms: (room only) s 490-950FF; d 700-1400FF
**Reductions over 1 night**
Meals: Full breakfast 100FF Lunch 205-590FF&alc Dinner 205-590FF&alc
Cards: ●● ■ ■ ⑨ Access Travellers cheques

★ ★ **Terminus**
Esplanade de la Gare, 2 rue Jean Moulin *17100*
☎ 546743503 FAX 546972447
(from A10 exit 35 head towards town centre, then the railway station)
Near river Forest area In town centre Near motorway
*Closed 23 Dec-4 Jan*
*28 en suite (bth/shr) (9 fmly) (5 with balcony) TV in all bedrooms STV Direct dial from all bedrooms Licensed Full central heating Languages spoken: English*
Rooms: (room only) s 210-260FF; d 260-390FF
Cards: ●● ■ ■ ⑨ Travellers cheques

**St-Georges-des-Coteaux** Charente-Maritime

**Bed & Breakfast** (Prop: M & Mme Trouve)
5 rue de l'Église *17810*
☎ 546909666 FAX 546929666
(A10 exit Saintes village of Saintonge Romane in 7km on D137)
Forest area Near motorway
*Closed 11 Nov-Mar*
*4 en suite (shr) No smoking on premises Full central heating Open parking available Child discount available Table tennis Languages spoken: English*

**St-Jean-d'Angely** Charente-Maritime

**Domaine de Rennebourg** (Prop: M & F Frappier)
St Denis-du-Pin *17400*
☎ 546321607 FAX 546597738
(from A10 exit 34 head towards St-Jean-d'Angely. In village left on N150 towards Niort. House signposted 2km beyond St-Denis-du-Pin)

Built in the 17th century, this property is situated on the edge of the Forest of Essouverts in one hectare of land. Richly furnished, with a rustic flavour. Swimming pool. Dinner is available.
Forest area
*7 rms (6 bth/shr) (1 fmly) TV in 1 bedroom Full central heating Open parking available Child discount available 5yrs Outdoor swimming pool Boule Bicycle rental Stables nearby V meals Languages spoken: English*
Rooms: (room only) d 330-400FF ✴ **Reductions over 1 night**
Meals: Continental breakfast 35FF Lunch fr 120FF✴
Cards: Travellers cheques

**St-Loup-Lamairé** Deux-Sèvres

**Château de St-Loup** (Prop: De Bartillat)
*79600*
☎ 549648173 & 54968276 FAX 549648206
(A10 taking Châtellerault-Nord exit, then D725 to Airvault. D46 to St-Loup-Lamaire. Château at entrance to village)
Set in superb gardens, this impressive château was built in the reign of Henry IV and is a jewel of France's architectural heritage. Guests' rooms, most with canopied beds, are in the keep and the house. The gardens and house are open to the public. Meals are available on request.
Near river Near lake Forest area In town centre
*14 rms (11 bth/shr) (2 fmly) Full central heating Open parking available Child discount available Fishing Languages spoken: English & German*

ROOMS: (room only) s fr 550FF; d 750-1150FF ✱
MEALS: Dinner fr 250FF
CARDS: 💳 ▨

## ST-MAIXENT-L'ÉCOLE Deux-Sèvres

★ ★ ★ **Logis St-Martin**
chemin de Pissot *79400*
☎ 549055868 FAX 549761993
(A10 exit 31/32)
Near river Forest area Near motorway
*Closed Jan*
*11 en suite (bth/shr) (1 fmly) TV in all bedrooms STV Direct*
*dial from all bedrooms Licensed Full central heating Open*
*parking available Supervised Open terrace V meals Last d*
*21.30hrs Languages spoken: English & German*
CARDS: 💳 ▨ ▨ ⑩ Travellers cheques

## ST-PALAIS-SUR-MER Charente-Maritime

★ ★ **Hotel de la Plage**
1 pl de l'Océan *17420*
☎ 546231032 FAX 546234128
Near lake Near sea Near beach Forest area In town centre
*Closed Oct-Mar*
*20 en suite (bth/shr) (6 fmly) (12 with balcony) TV in 29*
*bedrooms Radio in rooms Direct dial from 29 bedrooms*
*Licensed Full central heating Child discount available Outdoor*
*swimming pool (heated) Sauna Solarium Gym Open terrace*
*Languages spoken: English*
CARDS: 💳 ▨ Travellers cheques

★ ★ ★ **Primavera** (Relais du Silence)
12 rue du Brick *17420*
☎ 546232035 FAX 546232878
Near sea Forest area
*45 en suite (bth/shr) 2 rooms in annexe (9 fmly) (35 with*
*balcony) TV available Licensed Lift Full central heating Open*
*parking available Child discount available 10yrs Indoor*
*swimming pool (heated) Bicycle rental Last d 21.00hrs*
*Languages spoken: English Italian & Spanish*
CARDS: 💳 ▨ ▨ ⑩

## ST-SAVINIEN Charente-Maritime

**Le Moulin de la Quine** (Prop: J Elmes)
*17350*
☎ 546901931 FAX 546902837
(exit 24 from A10, go into St-Jean-d'Angely, turn right onto
D18 to St-Savinien. At traffic lights, turn right along river,
under rail bridge, left onto D124 towards Bords. After 2km at
Le Pontreau follow Chambre d'Hôte signs)
Pretty Charentais farmhouse with windmill in a quiet and
relaxing environment, three kilometres from the picturesque
town of St Savinien-sur-Charente. Charmingly decorated, both
guest rooms look out onto the superb garden, the ground floor
room having its own door onto the terrace. Dinner available at
a fixed price.
Near river
*2 en suite (bth/shr) (1 fmly) No smoking in all bedrooms Full*
*central heating Open parking available Supervised Croquet*
*lawn Languages spoken: English*
MEALS: Dinner fr 85FF✱

## ST-SEVERIN Charente

★ ★ **De La Paix**
*16390*
☎ 545985225 FAX 545989208
(In the centre of the village)
Near river In town centre
*Closed 21 Dec-3 Jan*
*15 en suite (bth/shr) (3 fmly) (1 with balcony) TV in all*
*bedrooms STV Direct dial from all bedrooms Licensed Full*
*central heating Open parking available Covered parking*
*available Child discount available 14yrs Outdoor swimming*
*pool Pool table Bicycle rental Open terrace V meals Last d*
*23.00hrs Languages spoken: English*
CARDS: 💳 ▨ ▨ Travellers cheques

## ST-SIMON-DE-PELLOUAILLE Charente-Maritime

**Château de La Tillade** (Prop: M et Mme De Salvert)
*17260*
☎ 546900020 FAX 549600223
(A10 exit 36 for Royan and Gémozac. At Gémozac take
direction Saintes la Tillade 3km on right)
Forest area Near motorway
*3 en suite (bth/shr) Full central heating Open parking available*
*Child discount available Languages spoken: English*
ROOMS: d 420-500FF
MEALS: Dinner fr 180FF✱
CARDS: 💳 ▨ Travellers cheques

## ST-SORNIN Charente-Maritime

**La Caussoliere** (Prop: A M Pinel-Peschardière)
10 rue du Petit Moulin *17600*
☎ 546854462 FAX 546854462
(take Paris-Bordeaux autoroute exit Saintes & continue in the
direction of Marennes-Oléron cross Cadeuil & St-Nadeau &
continue until St-Sornin. Rue du Petit Moulin opposite church)
Near river Near lake Forest area
*3 en suite (bth/shr) (1 fmly) No smoking on premises Full*
*central heating Open parking available Supervised No*
*children 6yrs Outdoor swimming pool Tennis Fishing Boule*
*Bicycle rental Table tennis Last d 20.00hrs Languages spoken:*
*English, Moroccan & Spanish*
CARDS: Travellers cheques

## ST-VARENT Deux-Sèvres

**Le Château de Biard** (Prop: Gilles Texier)
*79330*
☎ 549676240
(approach via D143 towards Glénay, then turn east to Biard)
Forest area Near motorway
*3 en suite (shr) (1 fmly) No smoking on premises Full central*
*heating Open parking available V meals Last d 15.00hrs*

## STE-SOULLÉ Charente-Maritime

**Bed & Breakfast** (Prop: M & Mme Gilbert)
3 bis rue de Nantes, Usseau *17220*
☎ 546375032 FAX 546375032
Near river Near sea Near beach Forest area Near motorway
*11 rms (3 shr) (1 fmly) No smoking on premises Full central*
*heating Open parking available Child discount available*
*Outdoor swimming pool Tennis Riding Bicycle rental Table*
*tennis Languages spoken: English*
CARDS: Travellers cheques

### SAULGÉ Vienne

**Les Gats** (Prop: Philippe Dudoit)
*86500*
☎ 549910610 FAX 549910610
(from N147 (Poitiers-Limoges) at Lussac-les-Châteaux head towards Montmorillan. After 4km right to Saulgé)
Near river  Forest area
*2 en suite (shr)  Full central heating  Open parking available Covered parking available  Languages spoken: English & Spanish*

### SECONDIGNY Deux-Sèvres

**Bed & Breakfast** (Prop: Pierre Julliot)
16 rue de la Vendée *79130*
☎ 549637034
(on western outskirts towards La Roche-sur-Yon 30mtrs beyond Secondigny church)
Near river  Near lake  Forest area  In town centre  Near motorway
*3 rms (1 shr)  Full central heating  Open parking available Supervised*

### SEGONZAC Charente

**Chez Bilhouet** (Prop: M & Mme Marcadier)
*16130*
☎ 545834350 FAX 545834321
The Marcadier family warmly welcome you to their home, set among the vineyards of Grande Champagne, 9 km from Cognac. Swimming pool and barbecue in the garden. Use of kitchen, games room and living room. Visitors can visit the distillery on site and find out about the production of cognac before trying the results.
Forest area
*5 rms (2 bth 1 shr)  (2 fmly)  No smoking on premises  Full central heating  Open parking available  Outdoor swimming pool*
ROOMS: d 180-260FF

### SEPVRET Deux-Sèvres

**Bed & Breakfast** (Prop: Mme Jézequel)
*79120*
☎ 549073373
Near river  Forest area
*6 en suite (bth/shr)  (1 fmly)  Full central heating  Open parking available  Supervised  Child discount available*
CARDS: ■ Travellers cheques

### SOUBRAN Charente-Maritime

**Les Simons** (Prop: E & B Louis-Joseph)
☎ 46497677 FAX 46492579
(exit Mirambeau from A10 & take D730 in direction of Montenohe until Soubran, on entering Bourg continue to La Poste then left in direction of Allas-Bocage)
Forest area
*3 rms  Radio in rooms  Full central heating  Open parking available*

### SOYAUX Charente

**Domaine de Montboulard** (Prop: M Madigout-Blanchon)
*16800*
☎ 545920735
Forest area
*5 en suite (shr)  (1 fmly)  No smoking in all bedrooms  Open parking available  Outdoor swimming pool  Languages spoken: English*

### SUAUX Charente

**L'Age** (Prop: Alain Dujoncquoy)
*16260*
☎ 545711936 FAX 545711936
(from Angoulême or Limoges in Suaux N141, follow signs "chambre d'hôte" property in 3km)
Forest area
*4 en suite (bth/shr)  (1 fmly)  No smoking on premises  Full central heating  Open parking available  Child discount available  Outdoor swimming pool  Boule  Bicycle rental  Last d 18.00hrs  Languages spoken: English & German*
ROOMS: s 220FF; d 260FF **Reductions over 1 night**
MEALS: Dinner 80FF

**Brassac** (Prop: Paule Sauzet)
*16260*
☎ 545711261
Near river  Forest area  Near motorway
*Closed mid Sep-mid Jun*
*2 en suite (bth/shr)  (1 fmly)  Radio in rooms  Full central heating  Open parking available  Supervised  Child discount available*
CARDS: Travellers cheques

### TERNAY Vienne

**Château de Ternay** (Prop: Marquis de Ternay)
*86120*
☎ 549009282 FAX 549229754
Forest area
*Closed Nov-Apr*
*3 en suite (bth/shr)  Full central heating  Open parking available Covered parking available  Outdoor swimming pool  Languages spoken: English*
CARDS: Travellers cheques

### THOUARS Deux-Sèvres

**Bed & Breakfast** (Prop: Michel & Annette Holstein)
3 ave Victor-Leclerc *79100*
☎ 549961170
Near river  Forest area  In town centre  Near motorway
*2 en suite (shr)  (1 fmly)  (1 with balcony)  No smoking on premises  Full central heating  Open parking available  Bicycle rental  Sports centre nearby  Languages spoken: English & German*

### TRIMOUILLE, LA Vienne

**Bed & Breakfast** (Prop: M & Mme Vouhé)
Toel *86290*
☎ 549916759 FAX 549915566
Near river  Forest area
*Closed end Sep & early Jan*
*6 en suite (bth/shr)  (1 fmly)  No smoking on premises  Full central heating  Open parking available  Supervised  Child discount available*
CARDS: Travellers cheques

**TRIZAY** Charente-Maritime

**Bed & Breakfast** (Prop: Roland Lopez)
Le Chize *17250*
☎ 546820956 FAX 546821667
Near lake  Near sea  Near beach  Forest area
*Apr-Oct*
*5 en suite (bth/shr) (2 fmly) No smoking on premises  Full
central heating  Open parking available  Supervised  Boule
Bicycle rental  Languages spoken: English*
ROOMS: s fr 260FF; d fr 280FF  ✱
MEALS: Dinner fr 90FF

**VALLANS** Deux-Sèvres

**Le Logis d'Antan** (Prop: M Francis Guillot)
140 rue St-Louis *79270*
☎ 549049150 FAX 549048675
(from A10 exit 33, follow signs to La Rochelle Mauzé, after 4km
turn left to Vallans)
Spacious, well-appointed, comfortable rooms with living area
on offer. Dinner available on request. Brochures and
information on the region available. Barbecue in garden. Bikes
available.
Near river  Near lake  Near sea  Forest area  Near motorway
*6 en suite (bth/shr) (2 fmly) No smoking on premises  TV in all
bedrooms  STV Full central heating  Open parking available
Covered parking available  Supervised  Child discount available
10 yrs  Open terrace  Barbecue  V meals  Last d 19.30hrs
Languages spoken: English*
ROOMS: d 350-390FF
MEALS: Dinner 129FF✱
CARDS: Travellers cheques

**VERRIÈRES** Charente

**La Chambre** (Prop: Monique & Henri Geffard)
*16130*
☎ 545830274 FAX 545860182
Near river  Near motorway
*5 en suite (shr) (1 fmly) No smoking on premises  Full central
heating  Open parking available  Child discount available 3yrs
Languages spoken: English*
CARDS: ●● ■■ ▆▆ ▣ Travellers cheques

**VICQ-SUR-GARTEMPE** Vienne

**La Serenne** (Prop: Daniel Bellande)
*86260*
☎ 549863315
Near river  Forest area
*Closed 21 Dec-28 Feb*
*3 en suite (shr) (1 fmly) No smoking on premises  Full central
heating  Open parking available  Languages spoken: English &
Italian*
CARDS: Travellers cheques

**VIVONNE** Vienne

**La Rochette** (Prop: Colette Vincent)
*86370*
☎ 549435017
Near river  Forest area  Near motorway
*4 rms (3 bth/shr) (2 fmly) Full central heating  Open parking
available  Child discount available  Languages spoken:
English*

**★ ★ Hotel Le St-Georges**
12 Grand'Rue *86370*
☎ 549890189 FAX 549890022
(Approach via N10 & D 742)
Situated in the quiet village of Vivonne in the Poitevin region,
the hotel stands on the main street leading into the centre.
More than 200 years old, it has been entirely renovated and
retains all of its original character. It features a cosy interior
where comfortable guest rooms have modern appointments,
and a homely lounge with an open fire for relaxing or reading.
Although the hotel has no restaurant facilities, a meal can be
provided on request, and there are numerous eating
establishments nearby.
Near river  In town centre  Near motorway

*26 en suite (bth/shr) 3 rooms in annexe (5 fmly) TV in all
bedrooms  STV Radio in rooms  Direct dial from all bedrooms
Licensed  Full central heating  Open parking available
Supervised  Child discount available  Open terrace  V meals
Last d 19.00hrs  Languages spoken: English*
ROOMS: (room only) s 200-230FF; d 230-280FF
**Reductions over 1 night**
MEALS: Continental breakfast 35FF  Dinner 75-90FF
CARDS: ●● ▆▆ ▣

**VOUILLÉ** Vienne

**Bed & Breakfast** (Prop: M & Mme Lecanuet)
3 rue de la Grande Maison *86190*
☎ 549519638 FAX 549544815
(from A10 exit Poitiers-Nord head towards Nantes for 10km. In
Vouille centre take 1st on right just before the post office)
Near river  Near lake  Forest area  In town centre  Near
motorway
*4 en suite (shr) (2 fmly) No smoking on premises  Full central
heating  Open parking available  River & canoe  Languages
spoken: English*

**VOUNEUIL-SUR-VIENNE** Vienne

**Les Hauts de Chabonne** (Prop: M & Mme Antoine Penot)
*86210*
☎ 549852825
(from Châtellerault take D749 to Vouneuil, then turn left by the
church and post office and continue towards Chabonne for
1km)
Rooms available in a house built at the end of the 18th-century
between a river and the nature reserve of Pinail. Three rooms
are on the ground floor, with direct access into the garden; the
other two are on the first floor and are ideal for a family.
Futuroscope, golf and many other sporting activities are all
within close proximity. Bikes and pétanque on-site.      *contd.*

Near river  Near lake  Forest area
5 en suite (bth)  (1 fmly)  No smoking on premises  Full central heating  Open parking available  Covered parking available  Child discount available  Bicycle rental  Languages spoken: English
ROOMS: d 270-290FF
MEALS: Dinner 95FF

**YVES** Charente-Maritime

**La Cabane des Fresnes** (Prop: Dominique Nadeau)
Le Marouillet 17340
☎ 546564131
Near sea
6 rms (2 shr)  (2 fmly)  Full central heating  Open parking available  Child discount available  Languages spoken: English
CARDS: Travellers cheques

## EVENTS & FESTIVALS

| | |
|---|---|
| **Jan** | Angoulême International Comic Strip Festival |
| **Apr** | Poitiers Spring Music Festival; Cognac International Police Film Festival; Royan Romanesque Festival; Cozes African Festival |
| **May** | Melle: St-Savinien Music Festival; Angoulême Multiracial Music Festival; La Rochelle International Sailing Week; Châtellerault Jazz Festival; Vivonne Song & Music Festival; |
| **Jun** | Nouaillé-Maupertius Medieval Spectacle; Creations en Val de Charente (classical music festival) at Cognac & Jarnac; Rochefort Celebrations; Poitiers Amateur Music & Dance Festival; |
| **Jul** | La Rochelle International Film Festival; Parthenay Games Festival; Saintes Folk Music & Dance Festival; Parthenay Jazz Festival; La Rochelle French Language Music Festival; Montguyon World Folk Festival; Chauvigny Summer Festival; St-Maixent International Children's Folklore Festival; Rochefort theatre, street entertainment & music; Thouars Arts Festival; Château d'Oleron Story-telling Festival; Airvault Festival of International Music & Dance; Ile de Ré Classical Music Festival; Magné Painting Festival; Montguyon Mondiofolk Festival |
| **Aug** | Montguyon Mondiofolk Festival; Chauvigny Summer Festival; Confolens International Festival of Folk Music & Dance; Parthenay-en-Gatine Traditional Music Festival; Vitrac St Vincent Music Festival; St-Palais sur Mer Folklore Festival; Royan Caribbean Festival; St-Martin-de-Ré Jazz Festival; |
| **Sep** | Cognac Street Festival; La Rochelle Boat Show; Angoulême Vintage Car Motor Racing; Fontaine-le Comte Autumn Music Festival; Regional Historic Monument Open Days (2); Rochefort Heritage Festival; |
| **Oct** | Ménigoute Ornithological Film Festival; Neuville de-Poitou European Scale Model Festival; Pamproux Wine Harvest Festival; Angoulême Piano Festival |
| **Dec** | Poitiers Short Film Festival |

## Local Markets

Most towns have local markets, which are usually held on Saturday mornings. During the summer, local markets take place every day in most of the region's coastal resorts

## Towns of Character & Charm

Angles-sur-l'Anglin, Angoulême, Aubeterre-sur-Dronne, Aulnay, Bougon, Brouage, Celles-sur-Belle, Charroux, Châtellerault, Chauvigny, Civray, Confolens, Jonzac, Loudun, Melle, Montmorillon, Nouaillé-Maupertuis, Oiron, Parthenay, Rochefort-sur-Mer, La Rochefoucauld, La Roche-Posay, St-Jean-d'Angély, St-Savin-sur Gartempe, Saintes, Talmont, Thouars, Tusson, Villebois-Lavalette .

## Beaches & Seaside Resorts

The beaches at the Port des Minimes, Aytré and Angoulins are good for swimming and windsurfing. Châtelaillon and Fouras to the south of La Rochelle offer full family and sporting holiday facilities.

## Cognac

They say serendipity played a part in the creation of the smooth liqueur pineau. An absent-minded vintner accidentally mixed unfermented grape juice with cognac, and wine drinkers have been grateful ever since. But it's brandy that the Charente Valley is famous for, produced in the 20-mile 'Golden Circle' region which includes the distillery towns of Cognac and Jarnac. One of the secrets of it's flavour is the chalky soil which nurtures a better quality grape juice. You can discover more about the production process by visiting the Cognac museum or one of the distilleries which are open throughout the year.

# Aquitaine

A quitaine is set between the Atlantic Ocean's warm Gulf Streams, and the Pyrénées bordering Spain, extending inland to the Dordogne. It is a region of huge variety, from majestic mountains to vast, surf-washed beaches and shady forests. Each of the five départements has its own traditions, foods and architectural styles, so there is much to see and enjoy. There are many historical sites, particularly in the hills of Périgord, Agen and the Basque country, which are dotted with castles, monuments and prehistoric dwellings , while the towns of Pau and Bordeaux are rich in medieval and classical heritage. The region's festivals provide an ideal introduction to local traditions and gastronomic delights.

## ESSENTIAL FACTS

| | |
|---|---|
| DÉPARTEMENTS: | Dordogne, Gironde, Landes, Lot-et-Garonne, Pyrénées-Atlantiques |
| PRINCIPAL TOWNS | Agen, Bayonne, Bergerac, Biarritz, Bordeaux, Dax, Mont-de-Basan, Pau, Périgueux, Sarlat |
| PLACES TO VISIT: | Caves at Betharram-Ste Pé, Combarelles, Font-de-Gaume, Sare, Isturiz & Oxocelhaya; prehistoric sites in the Vézère valley; the cliffs at Vatours; narrow-gauge railway at Artoiste Fabreges & La Rhune; St-Jean-Pied-de-Port, a 13th-century town with Bishops' prison; St-Jean-de-Luz including waxwork museum & Florenia floral valley; Kakouetta Gorge near Ste-Engrâce. |
| REGIONAL TOURIST OFFICE | Comité Régional de Tourisme d'Aquitaine, Cité Mondiale, 23 Parvis des Chartrons 33074, Bordeaux Tel 05 56 01 70 00   Fax 05 56 01 70 07 E-mail Tourisme@cr-aquitaine.fr |
| LOCAL GASTRONOMIC DELIGHTS | Goose or duck confit; foie gras; garbure, a rich local stew; Bayonne ham; sauce Béarnaise; poule au pot, a chicken casserole; Béarn Pastis (a cake rather than a drink); cheeses; Pyrénéen chocolates; prunes from Agen; peppers from Espelette |
| DRINKS | Bordeaux wines from Bergerac, Médoc, Sauternes, St-Emilion, Graves; brandy from Armagnac; rosé from Béarn, Izarra liqueur from Bayonne. |

## AGEN Lot-et-Garonne

★ ★ ★ ★ **Hotel Château des Jacobins**
1 ter, pl des Jacobins, 2 r Jacob *47000*
☎ 553470331 FAX 553470280
Near river  Near lake  In town centre  Near motorway
*15 en suite (bth/shr) (1 fmly) (1 with balcony) TV in all bedrooms  Direct dial from all bedrooms  Mini-bar in 13 bedrooms  Full central heating  Air conditioning in bedrooms  Open parking available  Supervised  Languages spoken: English & Spanish*
CARDS: 💳 ■ 🔳 Travellers cheques

## AGNOS Pyrénées-Atlantiques

**Château d'Agnos** (Prop: Mr & Mrs D Nears-Crouch)
*64400*
☎ 559361252 FAX 559361252
(On entering Oloron follow signs for Saragosse/Col de Somport until you see a small sign on the right for Agnos. In village turn right at church and château is behind Mairie)

An idyllic setting in twenty acres of gardens and grounds, the 16th-century Château d'Agnos is just two kilometres from the market town of Oloron Sainte Marie, in the foothills of the Pyrénées. The château offers exclusive chambre d'hôte accommodation in elegant period bedrooms.
Near river  Near lake  Near sea  Forest area  Near motorway
*Closed Feb*
*5 en suite (bth/shr) (5 fmly) Full central heating  Open parking available  Child discount available 8yrs  Fishing  Riding  Boule  Mini-golf  Bicycle rental  Satellite TV tea-making facilities  V meals  Last d 21.00hrs  Languages spoken: English*
ROOMS: d 380-650FF ✶ **Reductions over 1 night**
MEALS: Dinner 100-120FF
CARDS: 💳 🔳 Travellers cheques

## AIGUILLON Lot-et-Garonne

★ ★ *Le Jardin des Gygnes*
rte de Villeneuve *47190*
☎ 553796002 FAX 553881022
(from A62 exit6, take direction Aiguillon and avoid 'centre-ville'. Hotel on road to Villeneuve on leaving town)
Near river  Near lake  Forest area  Near motorway
*24 en suite (bth/shr) (5 fmly) (9 with balcony) TV in all bedrooms  Direct dial from all bedrooms  Full central heating  Open parking available  Child discount available 12yrs  Outdoor*

contd.

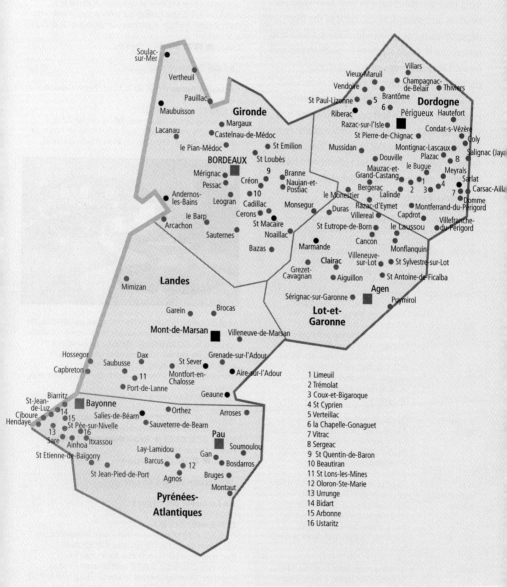

Soulac-sur-Mer

Vertheuil

Pauillac

Maubuisson

**Gironde**

Margaux

Lacanau

Castelnau-de-Médoc

le Pian-Médoc

St Emilion

**BORDEAUX**   St Loubès

Mérignac

Pessac   Créon

Andernos-les-Bains   Leogran

le Barp   Cadillac

Arcachon   Cerons

Sauternes   St Macaire

Noaillac

Bazas

Villars

Vieux-Maruil

Vendoire   Champagnac-de-Belair   Thiviers

St Paul-Lizonne   Brantôme   **Dordogne**

Riberac   6   Périgueux   Hautefort

Razac-sur-l'Isle   Condat-s-Vézère

St Pierre-de-Chignac   Coly

Mussidan   Montignac-Lascaux   Salignac (Jaya

Douville   Plazac   8

Mauzac-et-   le Bugue   Meyrals

Grand-Castang   1   Sarlat

Bergerac   2   3   4   7   Carsac-Ailla

le Monestier   Lalinde

Duras   Razac-d'Eymet   Montferrand-du-Périgord

Villereal   Capdrot   Domme

St Eutrope-de-Born   le Laussou   Villefranche-du-Périgord

Cancon

Marmande   Monflanquin

Villeneuve-   St Sylvestre-sur-Lot

Clairac   sur-Lot

Grezet-   Aiguillon   St Antoine-de-Ficalba

Cavagnan

Sérignac-sur-Garonne   **Agen**

**Lot-et-**   Puymirol

**Garonne**

**Landes**

Mimizan

Garein   Brocas

**Mont-de-Marsan**   Villeneuve-de-Marsan

Hossegor   Dax   Grenade-sur-l'Adour

Saubusse   St Sever

Capbreton   11   Aire-sur-l'Adour

Montfort-en-

Port-de-Lanne   Chalosse

Biarritz   Geaune

St-Jean-   **Bayonne**

de-Luz   14   Orthez   Arroses

Ciboure   15   Salies-de-Béarn

Hendaye   St Pée-sur-Nivelle   Sauveterre-de-Bearn

13   16   **Pau**

Sare   Itxassou   Lay-Lamidou   Soumoulou

Ainhoa   Barcus   Gan

St Etienne-de-Baïgorry   12   Bosdarros

St Jean-Pied-de-Port   Agnos   Bruges

Montaut

**Pyrénées-**

**Atlantiques**

1 Limeuil
2 Trémolat
3 Coux-et-Bigaroque
4 St Cyprien
5 Verteillac
6 la Chapelle-Gonaguet
7 Vitrac
8 Sergeac
9 St Quentin-de-Baron
10 Beautiran
11 St Lons-les-Mines
12 Oloron-Ste-Marie
13 Urrunge
14 Bidart
15 Arbonne
16 Ustaritz

swimming pool Fishing Solarium Boule Bicycle rental Open terrace Covered terrace V meals Last d 21.30hrs Languages spoken: English & Spanish
CARDS: ● ■ ⬛ Travellers cheques

### AINHOA Pyrénées-Atlantiques

### ★ ★ ★ Argi Eder
rte de la Chapelle *64250*
☎ 559937200 FAX 559937213
Forest area
Closed mid Nov-end Mar RS 15 Jun-14 Sep (half-board only) 36 en suite (bth/shr) (4 fmly) (30 with balcony) TV in all bedrooms Direct dial from all bedrooms Mini-bar in all bedrooms Licensed Full central heating Open parking available Supervised Child discount available 12yrs Outdoor swimming pool Tennis Boule Bicycle rental Open terrace V meals Last d 21.00hrs Languages spoken: English & Spanish
ROOMS: (room only) s 560-610FF; d 610-660FF
MEALS: Full breakfast 52FF Lunch 135-235FF&alc Dinner 135-245FF&alc
CARDS: ● ■ ⬛ ⬛ JCB Travellers cheques

### ★ ★ ★ Ithurria
pl du Fronton *64250*
☎ 559299211 FAX 559298128
Near river Near sea Near beach Forest area In town centre RS closed Wed (ex Jul & Aug)
27 en suite (bth/shr) (3 fmly) (13 with balcony) TV in all bedrooms STV Direct dial from all bedrooms Mini-bar in 14 bedrooms Licensed Lift Full central heating Open parking available Outdoor swimming pool Sauna Gym Boule Open terrace Last d 21.00hrs Languages spoken: English
ROOMS: (room only) s 400-550FF; d 500-650FF
**Reductions over 1 night**
MEALS: Continental breakfast 50FF Lunch 170-260FF&alc Dinner 170-260FF&alc
CARDS: ● ■ ⬛

### ★ ★ Oppoca
r Principale *64250*
☎ 559299072 FAX 559298103
This 17th-century inn is situated near the 'place du fronton' in the village of Aïnhoa in the Basque country. It features comfortable bedrooms with views of the Pyrénées, which are fitted with modern facilities, and the restaurant serves a choice of regional dishes, complemented by fine wines.
Near river Near lake Forest area Near motorway

12 en suite (bth/shr) (5 with balcony) Direct dial from all bedrooms Mini-bar in 10 bedrooms Licensed Full central

heating Open parking available Child discount available 10yrs Open terrace Last d 21.00hrs Languages spoken: English Spanish
ROOMS: (room only) s 180-280FF; d 220-320FF
MEALS: Continental breakfast 35FF Lunch 95-170FFalc Dinner 95-170FFalc
CARDS: ● ⬛ Travellers cheques

### ARBONNE Pyrénées-Atlantiques

### ★ ★ ★ Hotel Laminak
rte de St-Pée *64210*
☎ 559419540 FAX 559418765
(From A63 exit 4, follow signs Biarritz Centre and then Arbonne)
Near river Near lake Near beach Forest area Near motorway Closed mid Nov-mid Mar
10 en suite (bth/shr) TV in all bedrooms Direct dial from all bedrooms Mini-bar in all bedrooms Room-safe Licensed Full central heating Open parking available Supervised Open terrace Covered terrace Languages spoken: English & Spanish
CARDS: ● ■ ⬛ Travellers cheques

### ARCACHON Gironde

### ★ ★ Hotel de Gascogne
79 cours Héricart-de-Thury *33120*
☎ 556834252 FAX 556831555
Near sea Forest area In town centre Near motorway
33 rms (32 bth/shr) 5 rooms in annexe (4 fmly) (10 with balcony) TV available Licensed Lift Full central heating Open parking available Last d 23.00hrs Languages spoken: English & Spanish
CARDS: ● ■ ⬛ ⬛ Travellers cheques

### ★ ★ Le Nautic
20 bd de la Plage *33120*
☎ 556830148 FAX 556830467
(A10 till Bordeaux, then A63)
The hotel is ideally situated just a few steps away from the yachting harbour and the beaches. A whole range of sporting facilities such as tennis courts, three 18-hole golf courses, sailing and horse-riding can be found in the vicinity. The friendly staff will also be happy to assist you in booking offshore fishing or a cruise. The bedrooms offer a good level of comfort and have modern facilities, and there is one apartment with a kitchenette and large patio and a superb view of the harbour.

Near sea Near beach Forest area In town centre
44 en suite (bth/shr) (3 fmly) (39 with balcony) TV in all

contd.

bedrooms Direct dial from all bedrooms Licensed Lift Night porter Full central heating Open parking available Supervised Child discount available 10yrs Close by Languages spoken: English & Spanish
ROOMS: (room only) d 199-470FF
MEALS: Continental breakfast 38FF
CARDS: ●● ■■ ▣▣ ◎ Travellers cheques

**★ ★ ★ Villa Térésa-Hôtel Semiramis**
4 allée de Rebsomen *33120*
☎ 556832587 FAX 557522241
Near sea Near beach Forest area
*20 en suite (bth/shr) 8 rooms in annexe (3 fmly) (12 with balcony) TV in all bedrooms Direct dial from all bedrooms Full central heating Open parking available No children 2yrs Outdoor swimming pool Open terrace Last d 21.00hrs Languages spoken: English & Spanish*
CARDS: ■■ ▣▣ Travellers cheques

**ARROSES** Pyrénées-Atlantiques

**Sauvemea** (Prop: J Labat)
*64350*
☎ 559681601 FAX 559681608
Near lake Forest area
*6 rms (4 bth 1 shr) (1 fmly) Full central heating Open parking available Outdoor swimming pool Fishing Riding Languages spoken: English & Spanish*
CARDS: Travellers cheques

**BARCUS** Pyrénées-Atlantiques

**★ ★ Hotel Chilo**
*64130*
☎ 559289079 FAX 559289310
(From Pau take D24 towards Mauléon)
Forest area
*Closed 15 Jan-10 Feb,1 wk end Mar & Oct-15 Dec
12 rms (6 bth 4 shr) 2 rooms in annexe (1 fmly) TV in all bedrooms Direct dial from all bedrooms Licensed Full central heating Open parking available Child discount available Outdoor swimming pool Boule Open terrace V meals Last d 21.30hrs Languages spoken: English & Spanish*
CARDS: ●● ■■ ▣▣ ◎ Travellers cheques

**BARP, LE** Gironde

**★ ★ Le Resinier**
*33114*
☎ 556886007 FAX 556886737
Near river Near lake Near sea Near beach Forest area Near motorway
*TV in 9 bedrooms Mini-bar in 3 bedrooms Full central heating Open parking available Child discount available Open terrace Languages spoken: English & Spanish*

**BAYONNE** Pyrénées-Atlantiques

**★ ★ ★ Le Grand Hotel** (Best Western)
21 rue Thiers *64100*
☎ 559596200 FAX 559596201
(A64 or A63 in direction of city centre)
Near beach In town centre
*54 en suite (bth/shr) (1 fmly) No smoking in 6 bedrooms TV in all bedrooms STV Direct dial from all bedrooms Mini-bar in 25 bedrooms Licensed Lift Night porter Full central heating Open parking available (charged) Covered parking*

available (charged) Child discount available 12yrs Last d 22.30hrs
CARDS: ●● ■■ ▣▣ ◎ Travellers cheques

**★ ★ ★ Hotel Loustau**
1 pl de la République *64100*
☎ 559550808 FAX 559556936
Near river Near sea Near beach Forest area In town centre Near motorway
*44 en suite (bth/shr) (8 fmly) (2 with balcony) No smoking in 5 bedrooms TV in all bedrooms Radio in rooms Direct dial from all bedrooms Licensed Lift Night porter Full central heating Supervised Child discount available Sauna Gym Bicycle rental Open terrace Last d 21.30hrs Languages spoken: English & Spanish*
CARDS: ●● ▣▣ ◎ JCB Travellers cheques

**BAZAS** Gironde

**Château d'Arbieu**
*33430*
☎ 556251118 FAX 556259052
Forest area
*6 rms (5 bth/shr) Direct dial from all bedrooms Full central heating Open parking available Child discount available 10yrs Outdoor swimming pool Pool table Boule Bicycle rental Languages spoken: English*
CARDS: ●● ■■ ▣▣ Travellers cheques

**BEAUTIRAN** Gironde

**Château de Martignas** (Prop: Catherine Vicard-Galea)
*33640*
☎ 556675241
Near river Forest area
*2 en suite (bth) Full central heating Open parking available Child discount available Languages spoken: English, German, Japanese & Spanish*
CARDS: Travellers cheques

**BERGERAC** Dordogne

**★ ★ ★ Bordeaux**
38 pl Gambetta *24100*
☎ 553571283 FAX 553577214
(from Bordeaux direction cross the bridge and follow signs for 'Centre Ville' to the cathedral)
Near river In town centre
*Closed 21 Dec-19 Jan
40 en suite (bth/shr) (3 fmly) No smoking in 5 bedrooms TV in all bedrooms STV Direct dial from all bedrooms Licensed Lift Night porter Full central heating Open parking available (charged) Covered parking available (charged) Child discount available 12yrs Outdoor swimming pool Solarium Pool table Open terrace Last d 22.00hrs Languages spoken: English, German & Spanish*
CARDS: ●● ■■ ▣▣ ◎ JCB Travellers cheques

**★ ★ Climat de France**
*24100*
☎ 553572223 Cen Res 164460123
Near river Near motorway
*46 en suite (bth/shr) Licensed Night porter Full central heating Air conditioning in bedrooms Open parking available Covered parking available Supervised Outdoor swimming pool Mini-golf Open terrace V meals Languages spoken: English*
CARDS: ●● ▣▣

★ ★ ★ **Commerce**
36 pl Gambetta *24100*
☎ 553273050 FAX 553582382
(in town centre near the cathedral)
In town centre
*35 en suite (bth/shr) (1 fmly) (6 with balcony) TV in 33
bedrooms STV Direct dial from all bedrooms Licensed Lift
Night porter Full central heating Open parking available
(charged) V meals Last d 21.45hrs Languages spoken: English*
CARDS: 💳 ■ 🔲 ⑩ Travellers cheques

---

**BIARRITZ** Pyrénées-Atlantiques

★ ★ ★ ★ **Café de Paris**
5 pl Bellevue *64200*
☎ 559241953 FAX 559241820
(from motorway take exit Biarritz La Négresse and continue
into town centre. Hotel 50 metres from the Grande Plage)
Near sea Near beach In town centre Near motorway
*18 en suite (bth) (1 fmly) (5 with balcony) TV in all bedrooms
STV Mini-bar in all bedrooms Licensed Lift Night porter Full
central heating Open terrace Last d 22.00hrs Languages
spoken: English & Spanish*
CARDS: 💳 ■ 🔲 ⑩ Travellers cheques

★ ★ ★ **Château du Clair de Lune**
48 av Alan Séeger, rte d'Arbonne *64200*
☎ 559415320 FAX 559415329
Near sea Forest area Near motorway
*15 en suite (bth/shr) 8 rooms in annexe (4 fmly) (8 with
balcony) TV in all bedrooms STV Mini-bar in all bedrooms
Licensed Full central heating Open parking available Boule
Open terrace Languages spoken: English*
CARDS: 💳 ■ 🔲 ⑩ Travellers cheques

★ ★ **Climat de France**
RN 10 Aéroport de Parme *64200*
☎ 559234041 Cen Res 64460123 FAX 559412611
(off N10 near Airport)
Near lake Near sea In town centre Near motorway
*74 en suite (bth/shr) Some rooms in annexe TV in 60
bedrooms Radio in rooms Direct-dial available Room-safe
Licensed Night porter Full central heating Open parking
available Open terrace Covered terrace V meals Languages
spoken: English & Spanish*
CARDS: 💳 🔲

★ ★ ★ ★ **Miramar**
13 rue Louison Bobet *64200*
☎ 559413000 FAX 559247720
(halfway between the town centre and the lighthouse)
Near sea Near beach In town centre
*126 en suite (bth/shr) (126 with balcony) TV in all bedrooms
Radio in rooms Direct dial from all bedrooms Mini-bar in all
bedrooms Room-safe Lift Night porter Full central heating
Air conditioning in bedrooms Covered parking available
(charged) Supervised Child discount available 12yrs Indoor
swimming pool (heated) Outdoor swimming pool (heated)
Sauna Solarium Gym Pool table Jacuzzi/spa Open terrace
Covered terrace Wkly live entertainment Last d 22.00hrs
Languages spoken: English & Spanish*
CARDS: 💳 ■ 🔲 ⑩

★ ★ **Hotel Palacito**
1 rue Gambetta *64200*
☎ 559240489 FAX 559243343
Near sea Near beach In town centre Near motorway

*30 en suite (bth/shr) TV in all bedrooms Lift Full central
heating Child discount available 15yrs Languages spoken:
English & Spanish*
CARDS: 💳 ■ 🔲 ⑩ Travellers cheques

**Pavillon St Jean** (Prop: Gilles Pedoussaut)
17 rue Albert 1er *64200*
☎ 559245909 FAX 559223306
(leave A10 Biarritz exit follow 'centre de ville'signs. Property
100m from the Church of St Charles & close to bank)
Near river In town centre
*Closed Jul-Aug
6 rms (5 shr) (2 with balcony) No smoking on premises Full
central heating No children 7yrs Open terrace Languages
spoken: English & Japanese*

---

**BIDART** Pyrénées-Atlantiques

★ ★ ★ **Bidartéa**
rte d'Espagne - RN 10 *64210*
☎ 559549468 FAX 559548382
Near river Near sea Forest area In town centre Near
motorway
*Closed Apr-15 Oct
26 en suite (bth/shr) 6 rooms in annexe (7 fmly) (18 with
balcony) TV in all bedrooms Licensed Lift Full central heating
Open parking available Covered parking available (charged)
Supervised No children Child discount available 12yrs
Outdoor swimming pool Boule Mini-golf Open terrace
Languages spoken: English & Spanish*
CARDS: 💳 ■ 🔲 ⑩

---

**BORDEAUX** Gironde

★ ★ ★ **Bayonne Etche-Ona**
15 Cours de l'Intendance *33000*
☎ 556480088 FAX 556484160 & 556484161
(entrances: 4 rue Martignac and 11 rue Mautrec)
Near river In town centre
*Closed 23 Dec-3 Jan
63 en suite (bth/shr) (4 fmly) No smoking in 10 bedrooms TV
in all bedrooms STV Direct dial from all bedrooms Mini-bar in
all bedrooms Room-safe Licensed Lift Night porter Full
central heating Air conditioning in bedrooms Covered parking
available (charged) Supervised Child discount available 12yrs
Languages spoken: English & Spanish*
ROOMS: (room only) s 485.50-550.50FF; d 551-621FF
**Reductions over 1 night**
**Special breaks: on request**
CARDS: 💳 ■ 🔲 ⑩ JCB Travellers cheques

★ ★ ★ ★ **Burdigala**
115 rue Georges Bonnac *33000*
☎ 556901616 FAX 556931506
In town centre
*83 en suite (bth/shr) (7 fmly) TV in all bedrooms STV Direct
dial from all bedrooms Mini-bar in all bedrooms Room-safe
Licensed Lift Night porter Full central heating Air
conditioning in bedrooms Open parking available (charged)
Covered parking available (charged) Supervised Child
discount available 12yrs Jacuzzi/spa V meals Last d 22.00hrs
Languages spoken: English, Dutch, German, Japanese &
Spanish*
CARDS: 💳 ■ 🔲 ⑩ JCB Travellers cheques

★ ★ ★ **Grand Hotel Francais** (Best Western)
12 rue du Temple *33000*
☎ 556481035 FAX 556817618
This hotel is one of the great buildings in Bordeaux, reflecting the prestigious 17th-century architecture of the city. Situated near the cultural and business centres, it is the ideal setting for commercial and leisure travellers alike. Elegantly furnished throughout, it provides sophisticated surroundings for a enjoyable stay, while the attractive bedrooms offer modern amenities and provide a high level of comfort.
In town centre

*35 en suite (bth/shr) (7 with balcony) TV in all bedrooms STV Direct dial from all bedrooms Mini-bar in all bedrooms Lift Night porter Full central heating Air conditioning in bedrooms Languages spoken: English, German & Spanish*
ROOMS: (room only) s 400-590FF; d 450-680FF
**Reductions over 1 night**
CARDS: ● ■ ⅀ ● Travellers cheques

★ ★ ★ *Holiday Inn*
28-30 rue de Tauqia *33000*
☎ 556922121 FAX 556910806
*Near river In town centre Near motorway*
*89 en suite (bth) No smoking in 45 bedrooms TV in all bedrooms STV Radio in rooms Direct dial from all bedrooms Mini-bar in all bedrooms Room-safe Licensed Lift Night porter Full central heating Air conditioning in bedrooms Open parking available (charged) Covered parking available (charged) Supervised Child discount available 12yrs Gym Pool table Open terrace V meals Last d 22.00hrs Languages spoken: English, German & Spanish*
CARDS: ● ■ ⅀ ● JCB Travellers cheques

★ ★ ★ *Mercure Bordeaux Château Chartrons*
81 cours St-Louis *33300*
☎ 556431500 FAX 556691521
(From Paris A630 exit4 Bordeaux Centre & direction City Centre)
*Near river Near lake In town centre Near motorway*
*144 en suite (bth/shr) (10 fmly) No smoking in 30 bedrooms TV in all bedrooms STV Direct dial from all bedrooms Mini-bar in all bedrooms Licensed Lift Night porter Full central heating Air conditioning in bedrooms Open parking available (charged) Covered parking available (charged) Child discount available 16yrs Open terrace Covered terrace Last d 22.30hrs Languages spoken: English & Spanish*
CARDS: ● ■ ⅀ ● Travellers cheques

★ ★ ★ *Normandie*
7 crs du 30 Juillet *33000*
☎ 556521680 FAX 556516891
In town centre
*100 en suite (bth/shr) (21 with balcony) TV in all bedrooms*
*STV Radio in rooms Direct dial from all bedrooms Licensed Lift Night porter Full central heating Child discount available 12yrs Languages spoken: English & Spanish*
CARDS: ● ■ ⅀ ● JCB Travellers cheques

★ ★ ★ *Novotel Bordeaux Centre Meriadeck*
45 cours du Marechal-Juin *33000*
☎ 556514646 FAX 556982556
In town centre
*138 en suite (bth/shr) No smoking in 36 bedrooms TV in all bedrooms STV Radio in rooms Direct dial from all bedrooms Mini-bar in all bedrooms Licensed Lift Night porter Full central heating Air conditioning in bedrooms Child discount available 16yrs Open terrace Last d 24.00hrs Languages spoken: English & Spanish*
CARDS: ● ■ ⅀ ● Travellers cheques

★ ★ ★ *Hotel de Sézé*
23 allées de Tourny *33000*
☎ 556526554 FAX 556443183
*In town centre Near motorway*
*24 en suite (bth/shr) (4 fmly) (5 with balcony) TV in all bedrooms STV Direct dial from all bedrooms Mini-bar in all bedrooms Room-safe Lift Night porter Full central heating Covered parking available (charged) Supervised Child discount available 16yrs Open terrace Languages spoken: English & Spanish*
ROOMS: (room only) s 275.50-305.50FF; d 311-431FF
**Reductions over 1 night**
CARDS: ● ■ ⅀ ●

★ ★ ★ *Sofitel Aquitania*
bd J G Doumergue *33000*
☎ 556508380 FAX 556397375
*Near lake Near motorway*
*Closed 15 Dec-12 Jan*
*190 en suite (bth/shr) No smoking in 56 bedrooms TV in all bedrooms STV Radio in rooms Direct dial from all bedrooms Mini-bar in all bedrooms Licensed Lift Night porter Full central heating Air conditioning in bedrooms Open parking available Child discount available 12yrs Outdoor swimming pool Pool table Open terrace Last d 22.30hrs Languages spoken: German Italian & Portuguese*
CARDS: ● ■ ⅀ ● Travellers cheques

**BOSDARROS** Pyrénées-Atlantiques

**Bed & Breakfast** (Prop: Christianne Bordes)
Chemin de Labau, rte de Rebenacq *64290*
☎ 559217951 FAX 559216698
*Near river Forest area*
*5 en suite (bth/shr) No smoking on premises TV available STV Full central heating Open parking available No children 10yrs Child discount available Languages spoken: English & Spanish*
CARDS: Travellers cheques

**BRANNE** Gironde

★ ★ *De France*
7-9 pl du Marché *33420*
☎ 557845006 FAX 557799951
*Near river In town centre Near motorway*
*13 rms (3 bth 1 shr) TV in all bedrooms Licensed Full central heating Covered parking available (charged) Child discount available 2yrs V meals Last d 21.00hrs Languages spoken: English & Spanish*
CARDS: ● ⅀

## BRANTÔME Dordogne

### ★ ★ ★ Domaine de la Roseraie
rte d'Angoulême *24310*
☎ 553058474 FAX 553057794
(approach via D939 Angoulême-Périgueux)

This completely renovated 17th-century charterhouse is in 4 hectares of grounds at the gateway of Brantôme - the Green Venice of Périgord, and regarded as a harbour of peace and tranquillity by historians, painters, writers and nature lovers. The proprietors, Evelyne and Denis Roux, offer their visitors a pleasant, relaxing stay, with the traditional, high quality cuisine of the area. The spacious guest rooms are immaculate and furnished with antique family heirlooms. They are equipped with modern amenities and have private en suite facilities.
Near river  Forest area
*Closed 15 Nov-15 Mar*
*10 en suite (bth/shr)  (2 fmly)  (10 with balcony)  No smoking in 4 bedrooms  TV in all bedrooms  STV  Radio in rooms  Direct dial from all bedrooms  Licensed  Full central heating  Open parking available  Supervised  Outdoor swimming pool (heated)  Solarium  Boule  Open terrace  V meals  Last d 21.30hrs  Languages spoken: English & German*
ROOMS: (room only) s 540FF; d 540-830FF
**Reductions over 1 night**
MEALS: Full breakfast 65FF  Lunch 169-345FF&alc  Dinner 169-345FF&alc
CARDS: ●● ■ ■ ■ Travellers cheques

**Maison Fleurie** (Prop: Carol & Colin Robinson)
54 rue Gambetta *24310*
☎ 553351704 FAX 553051658
(On D939 between Angoulême & Périgueux. From Angoulême 3rd building on left after the bridge (parking just across bridge on left). From Périgueux over river bridge along rue Gambetta 3rd on right before next bridge. Parking just before bridge)
Guests are welcome at this family house, of Bourgeois style, with its large comfortable rooms, situated in the heart of the 'Venice of the Périgord. The house is adorned with hanging baskets and flower boxes; a pretty courtyard, a swimming pool and a pleasant 'Secret Garden'.
Near river  In town centre
*Closed 1-21 Feb*
*5 en suite (bth/shr)  No smoking on premises  Full central heating  Open parking available  Outdoor swimming pool  Languages spoken: English*
ROOMS: s 250-300FF; d 350-400FF

## BROCAS Landes

### ★ De la Gare
rte de Bélis *40420*
☎ 558514067
Near lake  Forest area
*7 en suite (shr)  (2 with balcony)  Direct dial from all bedrooms  Licensed  Full central heating  Open parking available  Child discount available  Boule  Open terrace  Last d 22.00hrs  Languages spoken: English & German*
ROOMS: (room only) d 210-220FF ★
MEALS: Continental breakfast 35FF  Lunch 100-160FF&alc  Dinner 100-160FF&alc
CARDS: ●● ■ ■

## BRUGES Pyrénées-Atlantiques

**Les Buissonets** (Prop: Mme M Bourghelle)
*64800*
☎ 559710824
Near river  Forest area
*6 en suite (shr)  (2 fmly)  No smoking on premises  Full central heating  Open parking available  Covered parking available  Supervised  Child discount available 6yrs  Languages spoken: English*
CARDS: Travellers cheques

## BUGUE, LE Dordogne

### ★ ★ ★ Domaine de la Barde
rte de Périgueux *24260*
☎ 553071654 FAX 553547619
(From Périgueux to Brive on N89 then just after Niversac turn right to Le Bugue on D710. The hotel is at the beginning of Le Bugue)
A former noble haunt in the heart of Black Perigord, the Domaine will welcome you in its Manor House, completed in the 18th-century, its walnut-oil mill and 17th-century forge recently renovated, with a high level of comfort. In the Orangery some of the leisure activities available at the hotel. All amid large meadows and century old trees in a park with a trout stream running through it.
Near river  Forest area

*Closed 16 Oct-14 Apr*
*18 en suite (bth/shr)  8 rooms in annexe  (6 fmly)  No smoking in 2 bedrooms  TV in all bedrooms  STV  Direct dial from all bedrooms  Room-safe  Licensed  Lift  Night porter  Open parking available  Child discount available 4yrs  Outdoor swimming pool (heated)  Tennis  Sauna  Gym  Boule  Open terrace  Table tennis  Last d 21.00hrs  Languages spoken: English German & Spanish* contd.

313

ROOMS: (room only) s 500-1010FF; d 590-1090FF
MEALS: Full breakfast 68FF Dinner 110-150FF&alc
CARDS: ●● ■■ ⲝ Travellers cheques

**★ ★ L'Auberge du Noyer**
Le Reclaud-de-Bouny-Bas *24260*
☎ 553071173 FAX 553545744
(5kms W of Le Bugue on the D703, direction Ste Alvère)
Near river Forest area
Closed 2 Nov-Palm Sun
10 en suite (bth) Direct dial from all bedrooms Licensed Full
central heating Open parking available Covered parking
available Child discount available 16yrs Outdoor swimming
pool Boule Bicycle rental Open terrace Last d 20.30hrs
Languages spoken: English, Arabic, German, Italian &
Spanish
CARDS: ●● ⲝ Travellers cheques

**★ ★ ★ Royal Vézère** (Best Western)
*24260*
☎ 553072001 FAX 553035180
(from Bergerac take then D29 to Sauve Boeuf. Take D703 to Le
Bugue)
Near river Forest area In town centre
Closed Oct-May
52 en suite (bth/shr) (4 fmly) (48 with balcony) TV in 39
bedrooms Direct dial from all bedrooms Mini-bar in 30
bedrooms Licensed Lift Night porter Full central heating
Open parking available Covered parking available (charged)
Child discount available 12yrs Outdoor swimming pool Open
terrace Last d 21.00hrs Languages spoken: English
CARDS: ●● ■■ ⲝ ⑩ Travellers cheques

## CADILLAC Gironde

**★ ★ ★ Château de la Tour**
10 av de la Libération *33410*
☎ 556769200 FAX 556621159
Near river Forest area In town centre
31 en suite (bth) (1 fmly) TV in all bedrooms STV Direct dial
from all bedrooms Mini-bar in all bedrooms Licensed Lift
Night porter Full central heating Air conditioning in bedrooms
Open parking available Covered parking available (charged)
Child discount available 12yrs Outdoor swimming pool Sauna
Gym Pool table Boule Jacuzzi/spa Open terrace Last d
22.00hrs Languages spoken: English
CARDS: ●● ■■ ⲝ Travellers cheques

## CANCON Lot-et-Garonne

**Chanteclair** (Prop: M & Mme Larribeau)
*47290*
☎ 553016334 FAX 553411344
(at Cancon, follow direction for Marmande on D124. After
400mtrs on left, chambres d'hôtes signed)
An elegant family mansion situated in a large wooded park.
The house dates back to the 19th century and offers large
and comfortable rooms. A swimming pool is situated in the
park.
4 en suite (shr) (1 fmly) TV available Full central heating Open
parking available Child discount available 12yrs Outdoor
swimming pool Pool table Boule Bicycle rental Open terrace
Languages spoken: English & Spanish
ROOMS: s 256-290FF; d 320-340FF
CARDS: Travellers cheques

## CAPBRETON Landes

**★ ★ ★ L'Océan**
85 av Georges Pompidou *40130*
☎ 558721022 FAX 558720843
(NW of town centre towards the marina and the lighthouse)
Near river Near sea Near beach Forest area
Closed 11 Oct-Etr
27 rms (24 bth/shr) (17 with balcony) TV in 25 bedrooms
Direct dial from all bedrooms Licensed Lift Night porter Full
central heating Open parking available Child discount
available Languages spoken: English & Spanish
CARDS: ●● ⲝ ⑩ Travellers cheques

## CAPDROT Dordogne

**★ ★ Hostellerie le St-Hubert**
*04540*
☎ 553234491 FAX 553366690
Forest area In town centre
11 en suite (bth) (1 with balcony) Direct dial from all bedrooms
Licensed Full central heating Open parking available Child
discount available Outdoor swimming pool Tennis Fishing
Riding Pool table Boule Bicycle rental Open terrace
Languages spoken: English
CARDS: ●● ■■ ⲝ ⑩ Travellers cheques

## CARSAC-AILLAC Dordogne

**★ ★ Le Relais du Touron**
*24200*
☎ 553281670 FAX 553285251
Near river Forest area
Closed mid Nov-early Apr
12 en suite (bth/shr) (1 fmly) Direct dial from all bedrooms
Licensed Full central heating Open parking available Child
discount available 12yrs Outdoor swimming pool Fishing
Open terrace Last d 21.00hrs Languages spoken: English &
Arabic
CARDS: ●● ⲝ Travellers cheques

## CASTELNAU-DE-MÉDOC Gironde

**Château de Foulon**
*33480*
☎ 556582018 FAX 556582343
Near river Near lake Near sea Forest area
5 en suite (bth) (1 fmly) Full central heating Open parking
available Bicycle rental
CARDS: Travellers cheques

## CÉRONS Gironde

**★ ★ Grillobois**
N113 *33720*
☎ 556271150 FAX 556270404
Near river Forest area Near motorway
Closed 2-28 Jan
10 en suite (shr) (5 fmly) TV in all bedrooms Direct dial from
all bedrooms Licensed Full central heating Open parking
available Child discount available 12yrs Outdoor swimming
pool Tennis Sauna Solarium Boule Bicycle rental Open
terrace Covered terrace V meals Last d 22.30hrs Languages
spoken: English & Spanish
CARDS: ●● ⲝ Travellers cheques

314

## CHAMPAGNAC-DE-BELAIR Dordogne

**Château de la Borie-Saulinier** (Prop: Claude et Michel Duseau)
*24530*
☎ 553542299 FAX 553085378
(from D939 exit at Brantôme and take rue de chez Ravilles for 3.5kms)

The owners will welcome you to this castle built during the 14th-15th centuries and located in the heart of the Périgord near Brantôme. Bedrooms offer comfort, privacy and calm.
Near river  Forest area
*Closed Jan RS Nov-15 Apr*
*5 en suite (bth/shr)  (1 fmly)  TV in 3 bedrooms  Full central heating  Open parking available  Outdoor swimming pool Languages spoken: English*

★ ★ ★ ★ **Moulin du Roc**
*24530*
☎ 553028600 FAX 553542131
(6km from Brantôme)
Nestling on the banks of the River Dronne, this hotel welcomes visitors to its lavish interior. The exquisitely appointed bedrooms offer a high degree of comfort, and throughout the delightful public areas, period furniture and delicate fabrics make this a truly exceptional residence. The menu offers a selection of tantalising dishes that may be served on the terrace with a lovely view of the river.
Near river
*Closed Jan & Feb*

*13 en suite (bth)  (3 fmly)  (2 with balcony)  TV in all bedrooms STV Radio in rooms  Direct dial from all bedrooms  Mini-bar in all bedrooms  Licensed  Full central heating  Open parking available  Covered parking available  Indoor swimming pool Outdoor swimming pool  Tennis  Fishing  Boule  Bicycle rental*

*Open terrace  Covered terrace  V meals  Last d 21.30hrs Languages spoken: English & Spanish*
ROOMS: (room only) s 570-800FF; d 570-990FF
MEALS: Full breakfast 75FF  Lunch 170-440FF
Dinner 250-440FF
CARDS: ●● ■■ ■■ ●Ⅰ JCB Travellers cheques

## CHAPELLE-GONAGUET, LA Dordogne

**Les Brunies** (Prop: M & Mme Monzies)
*24360*
☎ 553047983
(take direction of Angoulème exit Périgneux, then direction of Ribérac, Pas de l'Anglais on right look out for chambre d' hôte sign)
Near river  Near lake  Forest area  Near motorway
*2 en suite (bth/shr)  Some rooms in annexe  (2 fmly)  TV in 1 bedroom  Licensed  Full central heating  Open parking available Covered parking available  Supervised  Child discount available Outdoor swimming pool (heated)  Fishing  Languages spoken: English*

## CIBOURE Pyrénées-Atlantiques

**Villa Erresinolettean** (Prop: Henry Chardiet)
4 rue de la Tour Bordagain *64500*
☎ 559478788 FAX 559472741
(A63 (towards Spain) exit 2 for St Jean de Luz-Sud and follow signs towards Ciboure. 300mtrs after traffic lights, follow signs to Tour de Bordagain. 100mtrs before tower with weeping willow)

This Basque residence offers three rooms. There are panoramic views over the Bay of St-Jean-de-Luz, and calm and tranquillity are assured. Beach and golf in close proximity. Spain is within eleven kilometres. Private swimming pool and barbecue.
Near sea  Near beach  Near motorway
*3 en suite (bth/shr)  (2 fmly)  (1 with balcony)  TV in all bedrooms  Full central heating  Open parking available  Child discount available 2yrs  Outdoor swimming pool*
ROOMS: s 350FF; d 450FF **Reductions over 1 night**
CARDS: Travellers cheques

## CLAIRAC Lot-et-Garonne

**Caussinat** (Prop: M & Mme Massias)
*47320*
☎ 553842211 FAX 553842211
Near river
*Closed Nov-Feb*
*5 rms (1 bth 2 shr)  (1 fmly)  No smoking on premises  Open parking available  Child discount available 12yrs  Outdoor*
contd.

swimming pool Boule Bicycle rental Table tennis Last d
16.00hrs Languages spoken: Spanish
ROOMS: d 235-290FF **✽ Reductions over 1 night**
MEALS: Dinner 90FF✽

### COLY Dordogne

★ ★ ★ *Manoir d'Hautégente*
*24120*
☎ 553516803 FAX 553503852
(From Périgueux take N89 towards Brive. Take D704 towards
Montignac, then D62 to Coly)
Near river Forest area
Apr-3 Nov
14 en suite (bth) (2 fmly) (1 with balcony) TV in all bedrooms
Direct dial from all bedrooms Mini-bar in all bedrooms
Licensed Full central heating Open parking available Child
discount available 12yrs Outdoor swimming pool (heated)
Fishing Bicycle rental Open terrace V meals Last d 21.00hrs
Languages spoken: English
CARDS: ●● ■■ ☲☲ Travellers cheques

### CONDAT-SUR-VÉZÈRE Dordogne

★ ★ ★ **Château de la Fléunie**
*24570*
☎ 553513274 FAX 553505898
Near river Forest area Near motorway
Closed Jan-Mar
33 en suite (bth) 8 rooms in annexe (12 fmly) (7 with balcony)
TV in all bedrooms Direct-dial available Mini-bar in 17
bedrooms Licensed Full central heating Open parking
available Supervised Child discount available 10yrs Outdoor
swimming pool Tennis Pool table Boule Bicycle rental Open
terrace V meals Last d 21.30hrs Languages spoken: English
German & Spanish
ROOMS: (room only) s 350-450FF; d 350-800FF
MEALS: Continental breakfast 50FF Lunch 95-280FF
Dinner 135-280FF
CARDS: ●● ■■ ☲☲ ⑩ Travellers cheques

### COUX-ET-BIGAROQUE Dordogne

**Petit Chaperon Rouge**
La Faval *24220*
☎ 553293779 FAX 553294663
(from Périgueux via Le Bugue; from Sarlat via Périgueux)
Near river Near beach Forest area
11 rms (6 bth/shr) (3 fmly) Licensed Full central heating Open
parking available Child discount available 6yrs Open terrace
Last d 22.00hrs Languages spoken: English & German
ROOMS: (room only) d 150-200FF
MEALS: Continental breakfast 35FF Lunch 70-178FF&alc
Dinner 70-178FF&alc
CARDS: ●● ■■ ☲☲ Travellers cheques

### CRÉON Gironde

★ ★ ★ *Hostellerie Château Camiac*
rte de Branne D121 *33670*
☎ 556232085 FAX 556233884
Near lake Forest area
21 en suite (bth) 12 rooms in annexe (3 fmly) No smoking in 15
bedrooms TV in all bedrooms Radio in rooms Licensed Lift
Full central heating Open parking available Child discount
available Outdoor swimming pool Tennis Fishing Riding Pool
table Boule Bicycle rental Open terrace Covered terrace

Archery V meals Last d 21.45hrs Languages spoken: English
German & Spanish
CARDS: ●● ■■ ☲☲ ⑩ Travellers cheques

### DAX Landes

★ ★ *Jean le Bon*
12-14 rue Jean le Bon *40100*
☎ 558742914 FAX 558900304
Near river Forest area
27 rms (24 bth/shr) (1 fmly) (6 with balcony) TV in all
bedrooms STV Direct dial from all bedrooms Licensed Night
porter Full central heating Open parking available Covered
parking available (charged) Supervised Child discount
available 12yrs Outdoor swimming pool (heated) Solarium
Boule Bicycle rental Open terrace Last d 22.00hrs Languages
spoken: English, Italian & Spanish
CARDS: ●● ■■ ☲☲ ⑩ JCB

### DOMME Dordogne

★ ★ ★ *Esplanade*
*24250*
☎ 553283141 FAX 553284992
Near river In town centre
Closed ear Nov-mid Feb
25 en suite (bth/shr) 10 rooms in annexe (5 fmly) (1 with
balcony) TV in all bedrooms Licensed Full central heating
Child discount available 12yrs Open terrace Last d 21.15hrs
Languages spoken: English German & Spanish
CARDS: ●● ■■ ☲☲ Travellers cheques

**Le Jaonnet** (Prop: M & Mme Holleis)
Liaubou-Bas, Nabirat *24250*
☎ 553295929 FAX 553295929
(from Sarlat take D704 south. Cross Dordogne River, after
2kms turn right onto D50, after 50m turn left and follow signs
for Plan d'eau, towards Nabirat. Take 2nd turn left after Plan
d'eau)

Spacious, comfortable accommodation in the heart of
Perigord. Shady garden and sun terrace. Dinners are served in
the galleried salon or in the courtyard on fine evenings. Meals
are prepared by your host, a professional chef. Special
gourmet breaks are available. Sandy, lakeside beach
provides safe bathing. Sporting pursuits are all within a
short distance.
Near river Near lake Near beach Forest area
Closed Nov-Feb
5 en suite (bth/shr) (2 fmly) (1 with balcony) No smoking on
premises Full central heating Open parking available
Supervised No children 5yrs Tennis Fishing Riding Boule

Bicycle rental  Canoeing River swimming  V meals  Languages
spoken: English, German & Italian
ROOMS: (incl. dinner) s fr 330FF;  d 500-540FF
CARDS: Travellers cheques

### DOUVILLE Dordogne

### ★ ★ Le Tropicana
Maison Jeannette *24140*
☎ 553829831 FAX 553804550
Near lake  Forest area  Near motorway
*23 en suite (bth/shr)  (17 with balcony)  TV in all bedrooms
Direct dial from all bedrooms  Licensed  Full central heating
Open parking available  Supervised  Child discount available
10yrs  Outdoor swimming pool  Fishing  Open terrace  Last d
21.00hrs*
CARDS: ●● ▥

### DURAS Lot-et-Garonne

**Savary** (Prop: C J J Schaepman)
Baleyssagues *47120*
☎ 553837782 FAX 553837782
(from Sainte Foy-la-Grande take D708 to Duras, then D134 to
Baleyssagues. After bridge, in 2kms at crossroad follow sign
on right for Savary)
Near lake
*Closed 2 Oct-14 Apr
5 en suite (shr)  (2 fmly)  No smoking on premises  Licensed  Full
central heating  Open parking available  Outdoor swimming
pool  Open terrace  Table tennis  Languages spoken: English,
Dutch & German*

### GAN Pyrénées-Atlantiques

### ★ ★ Le Clos Gourmand
40 av Henri IV *64290*
☎ 559215043 FAX 559215663
(On left at the entrance to the town via N134)
Near river  Forest area  Near motorway
*8 en suite (bth/shr)  (2 fmly)  TV in all bedrooms  Direct dial
from all bedrooms  Licensed  Full central heating  Open parking
available  Supervised  Child discount available 10yrs  Fishing
Boule  Bicycle rental  Open terrace  Table Tennis,Volley Ball
Last d 21.00hrs  Languages spoken: English & Spanish*
CARDS: ●● ▥ ⅅ Travellers cheques

### GAREIN Landes

**Moulin Vieux** (Prop: Liliane Jehl)
*40420*
☎ 558516143 FAX 558516143
(from Bordeaux to Mont-de-Marsan onto N134 at Garein onto
D57)
A restored old country-house with attractive guest rooms, in
the heart of the Landes Forest, set among pine and oak trees.
A family run guest house with a lake and stream for fishing,
ideal for quiet relaxing holidays.
Near river  Near lake  Forest area
*7 rms (3 shr)  (2 fmly)  Full central heating  Open parking
available  Child discount available 12yrs  Tennis  Fishing
Therapy room (yoga/massage etc)  V meals  Last d 20.00hrs
Languages spoken: English & German*
ROOMS: s fr 180FF;  d 220-250FF  **Special breaks**
MEALS: Dinner 80FF

### GRENADE-SUR-L'ADOUR Landes

### ★ ★ ★ Pain Adour et Fantaisie
14-16 pl des Tilleuls *40270*
☎ 558451880 FAX 558451657
(from Bordeaux A62 exit Mont-de-Marsan and continue on
N124)
Near river  Near lake  Forest area  Near motorway
*11 en suite (bth/shr)  (8 with balcony)  TV in all bedrooms
Direct dial from all bedrooms  Mini-bar in all bedrooms  Room-
safe  Licensed  Night porter  Full central heating  Air
conditioning in bedrooms  Open parking available  Covered
parking available (charged)  Child discount available 11yrs
Bicycle rental  Open terrace  Covered terrace  Last d 22.00hrs
Languages spoken: English & Spanish*
CARDS: ●● ▥ ▦ ⅅ Travellers cheques

### GREZET-CAVAGNAN Lot-et-Garonne

**Château de Malvirade** (Prop: Cuvillier)
*47250*
☎ 553206131 FAX 553892561
(exit A62 signed Marmande)
Near lake  Forest area
*Closed 16 Oct-Mar
(1 fmly)  No smoking on premises  Full central heating  Open
parking available  Supervised  Child discount available 12yrs
Outdoor swimming pool  Bicycle rental  Languages spoken:
English & Spanish*
CARDS: Travellers cheques

**Domaine de Montfleuri** (Prop: Dominique Barron)
*47250*
☎ 553206130
(from Marmande take D933 south towards Casteljaloux. At Le
Clavier turn right for Bouglon. Montfleuri is approx 1 mile
beyond Bouglon on left)

This beautiful 18th century house is situated on a sunny
hillside, surrounded by colourful, fragrant gardens with many
trees and flowers. Enjoy the superb views over the rolling
countryside, wandering in the park and orchard, the Roman
swimming pool, bright rooms and delicious vegetarian dinners
in a restful atmosphere.
Forest area  Near motorway
*4 rms (1 shr)  (2 fmly)  No smoking on premises  Full central heat-
ing  Open parking available  Covered parking available  Child
discount available  Outdoor swimming pool  Boule  Bicycle rental
Table tennis, Badminton  V meals  Languages spoken: English*
ROOMS: s 270-320FF;  d 320-370FF  ✱
MEALS: Dinner fr 100FF✱
CARDS: Travellers cheques

## HAUTEFORT Dordogne

**L'Enclos** (Prop: D & R Ornsteen)
Pragelier Tourtoirac *24390*
☎ 553511140 FAX 553503721
(from Périgueux NE on D5 east to Tourtoirac, right onto D67 in
1 mile take left to Pragelier)
Beautifully restored 250-year-old stone cottages on historic
country estate surrounded by tranquil countryside, yet only
minutes from stores and restaurants. L'Enclos is a virtual
village in itself, including the village bakery and chapel, which
are among the seven cottages overlooking terraced gardens
filled with roses, flowers and shrubs. The Manor House and
cottages are built in typical regional style around an attractive
courtyard.
Near river  Forest area  Near motorway
*Closed early Oct-Apr*
*8 en suite (bth/shr)  (2 fmly)  No smoking in all bedrooms  Open
parking available  No children 13yrs  Outdoor swimming pool
Riding  Boule  Bicycle rental  Bicycle hire & riding nearby  Last
d 20.30hrs  Languages spoken: English, Italian & Spanish*
ROOMS: (room only)  d 400-800FF
MEALS: Lunch 40-50FF  Dinner fr 150FF

## HENDAYE Pyrénées-Atlantiques

★ ★ **Chez Antoinette**
pl Pellot *64700*
☎ 59200847 FAX 59481164
(exit autoroute à St Jean-de-Luz Sud, Plage Hendaye in
direction 'Centre Ville'. After third roundabout, second road on
left)
Near sea  Near beach  Forest area  In town centre  Near
motorway
*Closed Oct-Mar*
*16 en suite (shr)  7 rooms in annexe  (2 fmly)  (1 with balcony)
TV in all bedrooms  Direct dial from all bedrooms  Full central
heating  Open parking available  Open terrace  Languages
spoken: English German & Spanish*
CARDS: ●● ⬛ Eurocard Travellers cheques

## HOSSEGOR Landes

★ ★ **Les Helianthes**
156 av de la Côte-d'Argent *40150*
☎ 558435219 FAX 558439519
(hotel situated in City Centre. Follow signs for Casino/Plages,
cross over the bridge and turn right, then first on left)
Near lake  Near sea  Near beach  Forest area  Near motorway
*Closed mid Oct-Feb*
*18 rms (14 bth/shr)  (12 fmly)  TV in 17 bedrooms  Radio in
rooms  Direct dial from all bedrooms  Licensed  Full central
heating  Open parking available  Child discount available
Outdoor swimming pool  Bicycle rental  Open terrace  Covered
terrace  Languages spoken: English, German & Spanish*
ROOMS: (room only)  d 200-380FF
MEALS: Continental breakfast 32FF
CARDS: ●● ⬛ Travellers cheques

★ ★ **Lacotel**
av du Touring Club de France *40150*
☎ 558439350 FAX 558434949
Near lake  Near sea  Near beach  Forest area
*Closed 16 Dec-14 Jan RS Half board obligatory high season*
*42 en suite (bth)  (4 fmly)  (42 with balcony)  TV in all bedrooms
Direct dial from all bedrooms  Licensed  Lift  Full central*

*heating  Open parking available  Child discount available 15yrs
Outdoor swimming pool  Open terrace  Covered terrace  Last d
21.30hrs  Languages spoken: English & German*
CARDS: ●● ⬛ 🔵 Travellers cheques

## ITXASSOU Pyrénées-Atlantiques

★ ★ **Du Fronton**
La Place
☎ 559297510 FAX 559292350
(from Bayonne take D932 to Cambo, then D918 turn right to
Itxassou)
Forest area
*Closed Jan-15 Feb*
*25 en suite (bth/shr)  (6 fmly)  (6 with balcony)  TV in all
bedrooms  Direct dial from all bedrooms  Licensed  Lift  Full
central heating  Open parking available  Child discount
available 12yrs  Outdoor swimming pool  Open terrace  V meals
Languages spoken: English & Spanish*
CARDS: ●● ⬛ ⬛ 🔵

## LACANAU Gironde

★ ★ ★ **Vitanova**
Route du Baganais *33680*
☎ 556038000 FAX 556263555
Near lake  Near sea  Forest area
*Closed Jan*
*65 en suite (bth/shr)  (35 fmly)  (30 with balcony)  TV in all
bedrooms  STV Radio in rooms  Direct dial from all bedrooms
Licensed  Full central heating  Open parking available  Child
discount available 8yrs  Indoor swimming pool (heated)
Outdoor swimming pool  Sauna  Solarium  Gym  Boule
Jacuzzi/spa  Bicycle rental  Open terrace  Covered terrace  V
meals  Last d 21.30hrs  Languages spoken: English & German*
ROOMS: (room only)  s 310-490FF;  d 400-640FF  ✱
MEALS: Continental breakfast 45FF  Lunch 95-120FF&alc
Dinner 95-120FF&alc
CARDS: ●● ⬛ ⬛ 🔵 Travellers cheques

## LALINDE Dordogne

★ ★ ★ **Château**
1 rue de la Tour *24150*
☎ 553610182 FAX 553247460
Near river  Forest area  In town centre  Near motorway
*Closed 20 Dec-10 Feb*
*7 en suite (bth/shr)  (2 with balcony)  TV in all bedrooms  Radio
in rooms  Direct dial from all bedrooms  Full central heating
Outdoor swimming pool  Fishing  Open terrace  Covered
terrace  Last d 20.45hrs  Languages spoken: English*
CARDS: ●● ⬛ ⬛ 🔵

## LAUSSOU, LE Lot-et-Garonne

**Manoir du Soubéyrac** (Prop: Claude Rocca)
*47150*
☎ 553365134 FAX 553363520
Near river  Forest area
*5 en suite (bth/shr)  (1 fmly)  TV in all bedrooms  Radio in rooms
Full central heating  Open parking available  No children 18yrs
Outdoor swimming pool  Tennis  Fishing  Bicycle rental  Table
tennis  Last d 20.00hrs  Languages spoken: English*
CARDS: ●● ⬛

**LAY-LAMIDOU** Pyrénées-Atlantiques

**Bed & Breakfast** (Prop: Mme M-F Desbonnet)
*64190*
☎ 559660044
(exit A64 Bayonne-Toulouse for Artix and take direction for
Navarrenx. At Navarrenx take D2 then D27 to Lay-Lamidou.
Turn left then 1st right, to 2nd house on right)
Near river  Forest area  Near motorway
*2 en suite (bth/shr)  No smoking on premises  TV in 1 bedroom
Radio in rooms  Full central heating  Open parking available
Supervised  Child discount available 12yrs  Bicycle rental  V
meals  Languages spoken: English & Spanish*
ROOMS: s 240FF; d 270FF  ✱ **Special breaks**
MEALS: Dinner 90FF✱
CARDS: Travellers cheques

**LEOGNAN** Gironde

**Gravelande** (Prop: Yolande Bonnet)
*7 chemin du Bergey 33850*
☎ 556647204
(in Bordeaux on the ring road, take exit 18b towards Léognan.
On the square in Léognan, take the D214 towards Cestas, 4th
turn on right and 1st gate on left)
Near motorway
*Closed mid Oct-mid May
2 en suite (bth/shr)  No smoking on premises  TV in 1 bedroom
Radio in rooms  Full central heating  Open parking available
Supervised  Child discount available 12yrs  Outdoor swimming
pool  Languages spoken: English*
CARDS: Travellers cheques

**LIMEUIL** Dordogne

★★ **Beau Regard et Les Terrasses**
rte de Trémolat *24510*
☎ 553633085 FAX 553245355
(approach via D31 Le Bugue-Trémolat)
Near river  Near beach  Forest area
*Closed Nov-Mar
8 en suite (bth/shr)  (2 fmly)  TV in all bedrooms  STV  Direct
dial from all bedrooms  Licensed  Open parking available
Supervised  Child discount available 12yrs  Boule  Open terrace
Covered terrace  V meals  Last d 21.30hrs  Languages spoken:
English & Spanish*
ROOMS: (room only)  d 220-280FF  **Reductions over 1
night**
MEALS: Continental breakfast 40FF  Lunch 90-280FF&alc
Dinner 90-280FFalc
CARDS: ●● ▥ Travellers cheques

**MARGAUX** Gironde

★★★★ **Relais de Margaux**
chemin de l'Ile Vincent
☎ 557883830 FAX 557883173
(take D2 through Margaux then right and follow signs for hotel)
Near river  Forest area
*RS Jan
64 en suite (bth/shr)  Some rooms in annexe  TV in all
bedrooms  STV  Direct dial from all bedrooms  Mini-bar in all
bedrooms  Room-safe  Lift  Night porter  Full central heating
Open parking available  Child discount available 6yrs  Outdoor
swimming pool  Tennis  Solarium  Pool table  Boule  Bicycle
rental  Open terrace  Putting green  Last d 21.30hrs  Languages
spoken: English, German, Dutch & Spanish*

ROOMS: s 780-1090FF; d 950-1790FF
MEALS: Full breakfast 90FF  Lunch 190-450FFalc  Dinner
190-450FFalc✱
CARDS: ●● ▤ ▥ ⑩ Travellers cheques

**MAUZAC-ET-GRAND-CASTANG** Dordogne

★★★ *Métairie*
*24150*
☎ 553225047 FAX 553225293
(from Toulouse: take autoroute exit Mamande towards
Bergerac - Lalinde, look for signs. From Paris: take exit
Libourne, towards Bergerac - Lalinde.)
Near river  Forest area
*Closed Nov-Mar
10 en suite (bth)  (2 fmly)  (6 with balcony)  TV in all bedrooms
STV  Direct dial from all bedrooms  Mini-bar in all bedrooms
Licensed  Full central heating  Open parking available
Supervised  Child discount available  Outdoor swimming pool
Boule  Bicycle rental  V meals  Last d 21.30hrs  Languages
spoken: English, German & Spanish*
CARDS: ●● ▥ ⑩ JCB Travellers cheques

**MÉRIGNAC** Gironde

★★★ **Novotel Bordeaux Aéroport**
av Kennedy *33700*
☎ 556341025 FAX 556559964
In town centre  Near motorway
*137 en suite (bth/shr)  (47 fmly)  No smoking in 50 bedrooms
TV in all bedrooms  STV  Direct dial from all bedrooms  Mini-
bar in all bedrooms  Licensed  Lift  Night porter  Air
conditioning in bedrooms  Open parking available  Child
discount available 12yrs  Outdoor swimming pool  Open terrace
Last d 24.00hrs  Languages spoken: English & Spanish*
ROOMS: (room only)  s 520-525FF; d fr 550FF
MEALS: Continental breakfast 60FF  Lunch fr 98FF&alc
Dinner fr 98FF&alc
CARDS: ●● ▤ ▥ ⑩ Travellers cheques

**MEYRALS** Dordogne

★★★ **Hotel de la Ferme Lamy**
*24220*
☎ 553296246 FAX 553596141
(from Sarlat towards Périgueux/Les Eyzies on D6, then D47
after 2km. Drive 9km on D47. At cross called Benives, turn left
on the road C3 towards Meyrals and drive for 1.5km.)

The hotel is located between the medieval capital of Sarlat and
Les Eyzies with its prehistoric heritage. Individually styled
bedrooms feature high quality beds and tasteful furnishings. A
*contd.*

delicious breakfast consisting of freshly baked brioche and home-made jam is served in the lounge or outside on the shaded terrace under the lime trees.
Near river Forest area
*12 en suite (bth/shr) (7 fmly) (10 with balcony) TV in all bedrooms Direct dial from all bedrooms Mini-bar in 10 bedrooms Licensed Full central heating Open parking available Supervised Outdoor swimming pool Jacuzzi/spa Open terrace Languages spoken: English, German & Italian*
ROOMS: (room only) d 420-850FF **✳ Special breaks**
CARDS: ●● ■■ ⚏ ⚏ Travellers cheques

### MIMIZAN Landes

**★★ Hotel Club Atlantis**
19 rue de l'Abbaye
☎ 558090218 FAX 558093660
*(between the beach and the forest. Approach via A10 and N10) 12 rms (8 bth/shr) 8 rooms in annexe (4 fmly) No smoking on premises TV in all bedrooms STV Direct dial from all bedrooms Full central heating Open parking available Child discount available 12yrs Outdoor swimming pool Solarium Gym Boule Jacuzzi/spa Bicycle rental Open terrace V meals Last d 21.30hrs Languages spoken: English, German & Spanish*
ROOMS: (room only) d 260-500FF
MEALS: Continental breakfast 39FF Dinner 98-150FF
CARDS: ●● ⚏ Travellers cheques

### MONESTIER, LE Dordogne

**★★★★ Château des Vigiers**
24240
☎ 553615000 FAX 553615020
(from Bergerac take D936 then D18)
This handsome residence dates back to 1597 and was locally known as Le Petit Versailles. Entirely renovated throughout, it offers individually styled bedrooms decorated in keeping with the house. The elegant dining room serves a range of excellent dishes complemented by select vintage wines.
Near lake Forest area

*Closed 3 Jan-25 Feb*
*47 en suite (bth/shr) TV in all bedrooms STV Direct dial from all bedrooms Mini-bar in all bedrooms Room-safe Licensed Lift Night porter Full central heating Open parking available Covered parking available (charged) Child discount available 12yrs Outdoor swimming pool (heated) Golf 18 Tennis Fishing Sauna Gym Pool table Boule Jacuzzi/spa Bicycle rental Open terrace Covered terrace V meals Last d 21.30hrs Languages spoken: English Dutch German & Swedish*
ROOMS: (room only) d 890-1580FF
**Reductions over 1 night Special breaks: Golf**

MEALS: Continental breakfast 95FF Lunch fr 110FF&alc Dinner 110-425FF&alc
CARDS: ●● ■■ ⚏ ⚏ Travellers cheques

### MONFLANQUIN Lot-et-Garonne

**Domaine de Roquefère** (Prop: M Semelier)
47150
☎ 553364374
Forest area
*Closed Oct-Mar*
*5 en suite (bth) (1 fmly) Full central heating Open parking available Supervised Child discount available 12yrs Outdoor swimming pool Fishing Languages spoken: English, Italian, Portuguese & Spanish*
CARDS: Travellers cheques

### MONSÉGUR Gironde

**Grand Boucaud** (Prop: M & Mme Levy)
4 l'Aubrade, Rimons 33580
☎ 556718857 FAX 556718857
(from Libourne take D670 through Sauveterre, then left on D230 to Rimons. At Rimon sawmill on right, take 1st left. Signposted)
Near river Near lake Forest area
*2 Jan-15 Oct*
*3 en suite (bth/shr) (2 fmly) No smoking on premises Licensed Full central heating Open parking available Covered parking available Child discount available 10yrs Outdoor swimming pool Fishing Boule Bicycle rental Open terrace V meals Last d 21.00hrs Languages spoken: English & German*
ROOMS: s 270FF; d 330FF
MEALS: Dinner 120-200FF
CARDS: Travellers cheques

### MONTAUT Pyrénées-Atlantiques

**Bed & Breakfast** (Prop: Mme Toussaint)
39 rue de Lassun 64800
☎ 559719804
Near river Forest area Near motorway
*Closed Sep-Apr*
*2 en suite (bth/shr) TV available Radio in rooms Full central heating Open parking available Languages spoken: English & German*

### MONTFERRAND-DU-PÉRIGORD Dordogne

**Château de Régagnac**
Régagnac 24440
☎ 553632702 FAX 0553733908
(from Beaumont take D25 towards Cadouin, then D26 towards Bouillac. Turn left to Régagnac shortly after turning for St-Avit-Rivière)
Near river Near lake Forest area
*5 en suite (bth/shr) Open parking available Supervised No children 13yrs Tennis Fishing Open terrace Languages spoken: English & Spanish*
CARDS: Travellers cheques

### MONTFORT-EN-CHALOSSE Landes

**★★ Tauzins**
rte d'Hagetmau 40380
☎ 558986022 & 558986109 FAX 558984579
Forest area Near motorway

*Closed Jan & 1-15 Oct*
*16 en suite (bth/shr) (1 fmly) (10 with balcony) TV in all*
*bedrooms STV Direct dial from all bedrooms Licensed Full*
*central heating Open parking available Child discount*
*available 10yrs Outdoor swimming pool Golf Pool table Boule*
*Mini-golf Bicycle rental Open terrace Close to a lake and*
*riding stables V meals Last d 21.30hr Languages spoken:*
*English & Spanish*
ROOMS: s 240-260FF; d 275-295FF
MEALS: Continental breakfast 40FF Lunch fr 100FF&alc
Dinner fr 100FF&alc
CARDS: ●● ⬛ Travellers cheques

### MONTIGNAC Dordogne

★ ★ ★ ★ **Château de Puy Robert**
*24290*
☎ 553519213 FAX 553518011
Near river Forest area
*Closed 16 Oct-Apr*
*38 en suite (bth/shr) 23 rooms in annexe (4 fmly) (14 with*
*balcony) TV in all bedrooms STV Direct-dial available Mini-*
*bar in all bedrooms Licensed Lift Night porter Full central*
*heating Open parking available Supervised Child discount*
*available 12yrs Outdoor swimming pool (heated) Bicycle rental*
*Open terrace V meals Last d 21.30hrs Languages spoken:*
*English & German*
CARDS: ●● ⬛ ⬛ 🖭 Travellers cheques

### MONTIGNAC-LASCAUX Dordogne

★ ★ ★ **Hostellerie le Relais du Soleil d'Or**
16 rue du 4 Septembre *24290*
☎ 553518022 FAX 553502754
(from Motorway, A20 exit at Brive, Then go towards
Montignac - Lascaux N89. Located in town centre)
This former coaching inn is situated in a park with mature
trees and offers its visitors old fashioned hospitality combined
with modern comfort. The guest accommodation consists of
well maintained bedrooms with modern facilities. The
restaurant serves modern cuisine based on the traditional,
well-known recipes from the Périgord region.
Near river In town centre

*Closed 17 Jan-10 Feb*
*32 en suite (bth/shr) (13 fmly) TV in all bedrooms Direct dial*
*from all bedrooms Mini-bar in all bedrooms Licensed Full*
*central heating Open parking available Outdoor swimming*
*pool Boule Open terrace Last d 21.30hrs Languages spoken:*
*English, German & Spanish*

ROOMS: (room only) s 320-350FF; d 450-500FF
MEALS: Full breakfast 55FF Lunch 110-275FF
Dinner 110-275FF
CARDS: ●● ⬛ ⬛ 🖭 JCB Travellers cheques

★ ★ ★ **La Roseraie**
pl d'Armes *24290*
☎ 553505392 FAX 553510223
(Approach via N20 towards Brive, then N89 to Montignac)
Near river Forest area In town centre
*Closed 4 Nov-2 Apr*
*14 en suite (bth/shr) (4 fmly) TV in all bedrooms Direct dial*
*from all bedrooms Night porter Full central heating Open*
*parking available Child discount available 12yrs Outdoor*
*swimming pool Solarium Open terrace Last d 21.30hrs*
*Languages spoken: English*
MEALS: Full breakfast 50FF Dinner 145-215FF
CARDS: ●● ⬛

### MUSSIDAN Dordogne

**Le Bastit** (Prop: Kenneth Burt)
rue de Piqueynat, St Médard de Mussidan *24400*
☎ 553813233 FAX 553813233
(from N89 from Bourdeaux turn on the left in direction of St
Médard, just before Mussidan, the Bastit is behind the Church)
Near river Forest area
*10 en suite (bth/shr) No smoking on premises TV in 3*
*bedrooms Full central heating Open parking available*
*Outdoor swimming pool Fishing Bicycle rental Languages*
*spoken: English & French*
ROOMS: s 312FF; d 370FF ✱

### NAUJAN-ET-POSTIAC Gironde

**Les Ormeaux** (Prop: Neil & Christine Morris)
1 Chassereau *33420*
☎ 557846908 FAX 557846908
(Off the D128. 800 metres from church and 30 mtrs after La
Poste take road to right signed 'Chambre d'Hôtes 500m'.
Immediately after the stade municipal turn left, within 200 mtrs
the road bends right, then left. Les Ormeaux is tiled-roof
house)
An attractive old stone house with outbuildings, recently
modernised and renovated by the Anglo/French owners. On
the edge of a quiet village overlooking vineyards and woods,
twenty five kilometres from Bordeaux and fifteen kilometres
from St Emilion. An ideal base for walkers and cyclists
especially in spring and autumn.
Near river Near lake Near sea Near beach Forest area
*Closed 1-14 Jan & 16-31 Dec*
*3 en suite (shr) (1 fmly) Full central heating Open parking*
*available Child discount available 10yrs Last d 10.00hrs*
*Languages spoken: English & German*
ROOMS: d fr 280FF
MEALS: Dinner 95FF

### NOAILLAC Gironde

**La Tuilerie** (Prop: M & Mme Antoine Laborde)
*33190*
☎ 556710551 FAX 556710551
(from A62 take exit 4 "La Réole", after toll turn left & cross
motorway bridge. Take 1st left and follow signs for 3km. From
Bazas/La Réole take direction A62 or Bazas(D9), turn left to
Noaillac & follow signs)

*contd.*

In the heart of the famous Bordeaux wine areas, this senstively restored farmhouse provides a warm, relaxed atmosphere created by its Anglo-French owners. Guests are invited to dine with their hosts by an open log fire or on the garden terrace, with local specialities prepared by the chef-proprietor and wine enthusiast.
Forest area  Near motorway
*Closed 29 Oct-10 Nov*
*5 en suite (bth/shr) (1 fmly) Full central heating Open parking available Child discount available 12yrs Fishing Boule Bicycle rental V meals Last d noon Languages spoken: English, German & Spanish*
ROOMS: s fr 250FF; d fr 300FF
MEALS: Dinner fr 120FF
CARDS: Travellers cheques

### OLORON-STE-MARIE Pyrénées-Atlantiques

★ ★ ★ *Alysson Hotel*
bd des Pyrénées *64400*
☎ 559397070 FAX 559392447
*34 en suite (bth/shr) No smoking in 5 bedrooms TV in all bedrooms STV Direct dial from all bedrooms Licensed Lift Full central heating Open parking available Child discount available 12yrs Outdoor swimming pool Bicycle rental Open terrace Last d 21.30hrs Languages spoken: English & Spanish*
CARDS: ●● ■■ ■■ Travellers cheques

### ORTHEZ Pyrénées-Atlantiques

★ ★ *Au Temps de la Reine Jeanne*
44 rue Bourg Vieux *64300*
☎ 559670076 FAX 559690963
*(from A64 Orthez Centre Ville)*
Near river  Near lake  In town centre  Near motorway
*20 en suite (bth/shr) (2 fmly) (4 with balcony) TV in all bedrooms Direct dial from all bedrooms Full central heating Child discount available 14yrs Pool table Mini-golf Bicycle rental Open terrace Last d 22.00hrs Languages spoken: English & Spanish*
CARDS: ●● ■■ ■■ Travellers cheques

### PAU Pyrénées-Atlantiques

★ ★ ★ *Gramont*
3 pl Gramont *64000*
☎ 559278404 FAX 559276223
*(town centre)*
In town centre  Near motorway
*36 en suite (bth/shr) (5 fmly) No smoking in 1 bedroom TV in all bedrooms STV Licensed Lift Night porter Full central heating Open parking available Covered parking available Supervised Pool table Open terrace Covered terrace Languages spoken: English*
ROOMS: (room only) s 200-350FF; d 280-495FF
**Reductions over 1 night**
CARDS: ●● ■■ ■■ ⑨ Travellers cheques

### PAUILLAC Gironde

★ ★ ★ ★ *Château Cordeillan-Bages*
rte des Chareaux *33250*
☎ 556592424 FAX 556590189
*(A10 exit 7, in direction of Le Verdon then D2)*
Near river  Forest area
*Closed 16 Dec-Jan RS Restaurant closed Sat/Mon lunchtime*

*25 en suite (bth/shr) (1 fmly) (1 with balcony) TV in all bedrooms STV Radio in rooms Direct dial from all bedrooms Mini-bar in all bedrooms Room-safe Licensed Lift Night porter Full central heating Open parking available Supervised Child discount available 12yrs Boule Bicycle rental Open terrace The Ecole du Bordeaux wine lovers course Last d 21.30hrs Languages spoken: English & German*
ROOMS: (room only) d 950-1350FF
MEALS: Continental breakfast 100FF Lunch 165-260FF&alc Dinner 195-390FF&alc
CARDS: ●● ■■ ■■ ⑨ Travellers cheques

### PESSAC Gironde

★ ★ ★ *La Réserve*
74 av du Bourgailh
☎ 557265828 FAX 557265800
*(take exit 13 on the Bordeaux ring road and continue towards Merignac for 500mtrs)*
Near lake  Forest area
*22 en suite (bth/shr) (4 fmly) (12 with balcony) TV in all bedrooms Full central heating Open parking available Outdoor swimming pool Tennis Boule V meals Last d 22.00hrs Languages spoken: English & Spanish*
CARDS: ●● ■■ ■■ ⑨ Travellers cheques

### PIAN-MÉDOC, LE Gironde

★ ★ ★ *Le Pont Bernet*
rte du Verdon *33290*
☎ 556702019 FAX 556702290
Near river  Forest area  Near motorway
*18 en suite (bth/shr) TV in all bedrooms STV Direct dial from all bedrooms Mini-bar in all bedrooms Full central heating Open parking available Supervised Child discount available 8yrs Outdoor swimming pool (heated) Golf Tennis Fishing Last d 21.30hrs Languages spoken: English & Spanish*
CARDS: ●● ■■ ■■ ⑨

### PLAZAC Dordogne

*Les Tilleuls* (Prop: Donald Hamilton)
Le Bourg *24580*
☎ 553508065 FAX 553598969
*(from Périgeux take N89 towards Brive. At roundabout after level crossing at Niversac take right on D710; at Les Versannes turn left on D6 towards Rouffignac, through Rouffignac and left at roundabout to Plazac)*
Near river  Near lake  Near sea  Forest area  Near motorway
*5 rms (3 bth/shr) (1 fmly) (1 with balcony) Open parking available Child discount available Tennis Fishing Riding Boule Bicycle rental Languages spoken: English*
CARDS: Travellers cheques

### PORT-DE-LANNE Landes

*Au Masson* (Prop: M & Mme Duret)
rte du Port *40300*
☎ SENT 558891457
Near river  Forest area  Near motorway
*5 en suite (bth/shr) Open parking available Child discount available Fishing Boule Bicycle rental Open terrace*
ROOMS: d fr 260FF

## PUYMIROL Lot-et-Garonne

★ ★ ★ ★ **Les Loges de l'Aubergade** (Relais et Châteaux)
52 rue Royale *47270*
☎ 553953146 FAX 553953380
(From Toulouse take the A62 Motorway, exit Valence d'Agen
No8. Afterwards take the N113 till Lamagistère, then the D20
and D248 till Puynirol)
*Near lake Forest area Near motorway*
*Closed Feb*
*10 en suite (bth/shr) (10 fmly) (2 with balcony) TV in all*
*bedrooms STV Direct dial from all bedrooms Mini-bar in all*
*bedrooms Room-safe Licensed Full central heating Air*
*conditioning in bedrooms Open parking available Covered*
*parking available Supervised Child discount available 10*
*Outdoor swimming pool Solarium Jacuzzi/spa Open terrace V*
*meals Last d 21.30hrs Languages spoken: English*
CARDS: ●● ■ ▆ ▣ Travellers cheques

## RAZAC-D'EYMET Dordogne

★ ★ **La Petite Auberge**
*24500*
☎ 553246927 FAX 553610263
(from Bergerac D933 toward Mont de Marzan at entry to
Fonroque turn left at x-rds to Razac d'Eymet there turn right.
From A62 exit Marmande onto D933 continue to D25 in
direction of Issigeac, after 2km turn left)
A converted 17th-century farm with a warm friendly
atmosphere, in peaceful rural setting. Ideal location for visiting
the main tourist attractions of the region.
*Near motorway*
*Closed Nov-Mar*
*7 rms (3 bth 2 shr) (4 fmly) Direct dial from all bedrooms*
*Licensed Open parking available Outdoor swimming pool*
*Open terrace Various games in large garden V meals*
*Languages spoken: English*
MEALS: Continental breakfast 35FF✱
CARDS: ●● ▆ Travellers cheques

## RAZAC-SUR-L'ISLE Dordogne

★ ★ ★ **Château de Lalande**
*24430*
☎ 553545230 FAX 553074667
(On N89 W of Périgueux)
*Near river Forest area Near motorway*
*Closed 16 Nov-14 Mar*
*20 en suite (bth/shr) (5 fmly) TV in all bedrooms Direct dial*
*from all bedrooms Full central heating Open parking available*
*Child discount available 10yrs Outdoor swimming pool Boule*
*Open terrace Last d 21.30hrs Languages spoken: English*
ROOMS: (room only) d 290-500FF
MEALS: Continental breakfast 43FF Lunch fr 100FF&alc
Dinner fr 150FF&alc
CARDS: ●● ■ ▆ Travellers cheques

## ST-ANTOINE-DE-FICALBA Lot-et-Garonne

**Pechon** (Prop: M & Mme de Laneuville)
*47340*
☎ 553417159 FAX 553417159
(on N21 between Agen and Villenuve-sur-Lot)
*Near lake Forest area Near motorway*

*Closed 16 Oct-14 Mar*
*1 en suite (shr) (1 with balcony) STV Radio in rooms Full*
*central heating Open parking available Covered parking*
*available Supervised*
CARDS: Travellers cheques

## ST-CYPRIEN Dordogne

★ ★ ★ **Abbaye**
rue de l'Abbaye *24220*
☎ 553292048 FAX 553291585
*Near river*
*Closed 15 Oct-15 Apr*
*24 en suite (bth/shr) 10 rooms in annexe (4 fmly) (3 with*
*balcony) Radio in rooms Direct dial from all bedrooms*
*Licensed Full central heating Open parking available Child*
*discount available 10yrs Outdoor swimming pool Open terrace*
*V meals Last d 21.00hrs Languages spoken: English & German*
CARDS: ●● ■ ▆ Travellers cheques

★ ★ **De La Terrasse**
pl Jean Ladignac *24220*
☎ 553292169 FAX 553296088
(from Sarlat take direction of Bergerac, hotel is in village, in
direction of Les Eyzies)
*Near river Forest area In town centre*
*Closed Jan-Feb*
*19 rms (4 bth 12 shr) TV in 11 bedrooms Direct dial from all*
*bedrooms Licensed Full central heating Child discount*
*available 12yrs Boule Bicycle rental Open terrace V meals*
*Last d 21.30hrs Languages spoken: English & Spanish*
ROOMS: d 210-330FF **Reductions over 1 night**
MEALS: Continental breakfast 35FF Lunch 80-180FF&alc
Dinner 80-180FF&alc
CARDS: ●● ▆ ▣ Travellers cheques

## ST-EMILION Gironde

**Château Millaud-Montlabert**
*33330*
☎ 557247185 FAX 557246278
(D243 to Saint-Emilion then D245 towards Pomerol for 300
mtrs)
*Closed 15 Jan-15 Feb*
*5 en suite (bth/shr) No smoking on premises TV in all*
*bedrooms Full central heating Open parking available*
CARDS: ▆

## ST-ÉTIENNE-DE-BAIGORRY Pyrénées-Atlantiques

★ ★ ★ **Arce**
*64430*
☎ 559374014 FAX 559374027
(From the church head towards 'Col d'Ispéguy' and turn left
after the bridge)
*Near river Forest area*
*Closed mid Nov-mid Mar*
*23 en suite (bth/shr) 3 rooms in annexe (3 fmly) (14 with*
*balcony) TV in all bedrooms Direct dial from all bedrooms*
*Licensed Full central heating Open parking available*
*Supervised Outdoor swimming pool (heated) Tennis Pool table*
*Open terrace Last d 20.45hrs Languages spoken: English &*
*Spanish*
CARDS: ●● ▆

**ST-EUTROPE-DE-BORN** Lot-et-Garonne

**Moulin de Labique** (Prop: Helene Boulet)
47210
☎ 553016390 FAX 553017317
Near river  Near lake  Forest area
*Closed Jan-Feb & late Nov*
*5 en suite (bth/shr) (2 fmly) (2 with balcony) Full central*
*heating  Open parking available  Supervised  Child discount*
*available 9yrs  Outdoor swimming pool  V meals  Last d*
*21.30hrs  Languages spoken: English*
CARDS: ●● ⬛ Travellers cheques

**ST-JEAN-DE-LUZ** Pyrénées-Atlantiques

★ ★ ★ ★ **Parc Victoria**
5 rue Cépe *64500*
☎ 559267878 FAX 559267808
(Right at 4th traffic light after exit "St-Jean-de-Luz Nord",
direction "Quartier du Lac", hotel signposted)

This 19th-century residence is situated in Saint-Jean-de-Luz, a
colourful fishing port on the Atlantic ocean. Surrounded by a
flower garden and park with mature trees, bedrooms are
decorated in 1930s decor and equipped with marble
bathrooms. There is a delightful terrace where guests can
enjoy a generous breakfast or a drink, and the restaurant
serves a choice of enjoyable meals.
Near sea  Near beach  In town centre
*Closed 15 Nov-15 Mar*
*12 en suite (bth/shr)  2 rooms in annexe  (4 fmly) (1 with*
*balcony)  TV in all bedrooms  STV  Radio in rooms  Direct dial*
*from all bedrooms  Mini-bar in all bedrooms  Room-safe*
*Licensed  Lift  Night porter  Full central heating  Air*
*conditioning in bedrooms  Open parking available  Supervised*
*Child discount available 6yrs  Outdoor swimming pool (heated)*
*Boule  Open terrace  Covered terrace  Last d 22.00hrs*
*Languages spoken: English & Spanish*
ROOMS: (room only) s 970-1100FF; d 1100-1450FF ✳
MEALS: Continental breakfast 85FF  Lunch 230-380FF&alc
Dinner 230-380FF&alc
CARDS: ●● ⬛ ⬛ 🆔 Travellers cheques

**ST-JEAN-PIED-DE-PORT** Pyrénées-Atlantiques

★ ★ **Central**
1 pl Ch-de-Gaulle *64220*
☎ 559370022 FAX 559372779
Near river  Near lake  Forest area  In town centre
*Closed 15 Dec-15 Feb*
*13 en suite (bth/shr)  Some rooms in annexe  (8 fmly) (9 with*
*balcony)  No smoking in 2 bedrooms  TV in all bedrooms  STV*

*Licensed  Full central heating  Child discount available 10yrs*
*Open terrace  V meals  Languages spoken: English German &*
*Spanish*
CARDS: ●● ⬛ ⬛ 🆔 Travellers cheques

★ ★ ★ **Les Pyrénées**
19 pl Ch-de-Gaulle *64220*
☎ 559370101 FAX 559371897
In town centre
*Closed 5-28 Jan*
*(6 fmly) (5 with balcony)  TV available  Direct-dial available  Lift*
*Full central heating  Air conditioning in bedrooms  Covered*
*parking available (charged)  Outdoor swimming pool (heated)*
*Open terrace  Last d 21.00hrs*

**ST-LON-LES-MINES** Landes

**Château du Monbet** (Prop: M & Mme H de Lataillade)
40300
☎ 558578068 FAX 558578929
(exit St-Geours-de-Maremne off A10 & A63 or exit
Peyrehorade A64)
Forest area
*4 en suite (bth/shr)  Full central heating  Open parking available*
*Boule  Languages spoken: English*
ROOMS: (room only) s 250-450FF; d 300-500FF
**Reductions over 1 night**
**Special breaks: Group bookings**

**ST-LOUBES** Gironde

★ ★ **Au Vieux Logis**
92 av de la République *33450*
☎ 556789299 FAX 556789118
In town centre  Near motorway
*6 en suite (bth/shr) (2 fmly)  TV in all bedrooms  STV  Direct*
*dial from all bedrooms  Mini-bar in all bedrooms  Licensed  Full*
*central heating  Child discount available 9yrs  Last d 22.00hrs*
*Languages spoken: English*
ROOMS: (room only) s fr 280FF; d fr 320FF
MEALS: Full breakfast 50FF  Lunch 98-260FF&alc  Dinner
130-260FF&alc
CARDS: ●● ⬛ ⬛ 🆔 Travellers cheques

**ST-PAUL-LIZONNE** Dordogne

**La Vieille Maison** (Prop: M Marc Leclercq)
St Paul-Lizonne *24320*
☎ 553916131 FAX 553916131
(south from Angoulême towards Riberac, North of Bergerac.
The hotel is in a village on the road from Riberac to St-Severin)
Near river  Near lake  Forest area
*Closed Nov-Etr*
*12 en suite (bth/shr) (5 fmly) (4 with balcony)  No smoking on*
*premises  Full central heating  Open parking available  Child*
*discount available  Outdoor swimming pool  Tennis  Fishing*
*Riding  Boule  Bicycle rental  V meals  Last d 22.00hrs*
*Languages spoken: English & Dutch*
CARDS: ●● ⬛ ⬛ 🆔 Travellers cheques

**ST-PÉE-SUR-NIVELLE** Pyrénées-Atlantiques

**Bidachuna** (Prop: M Ormazabal)
rte Oihan Bidea *64310*
☎ 559545622 FAX 559473100
(from A63 at Bayonne take D3 to Arcangues then on to St-Pée-
sur-Nivelle, then follow D3 towards Ustaritz/Arcangues)

This 12th century converted priory welcomes visitors who will enjoy the beautiful setting, view and pool of this five-acre property. The atmosphere is informal and welcoming. A three bedroom house also available. One hour from the beach. Aromatherapy and life-enhancement programme offered.
Near river Forest area Near motorway
*4 rms (2 bth/shr) (2 fmly) (2 with balcony) No smoking on premises Full central heating Open parking available Outdoor swimming pool Boule Bicycle rental Covered terrace Aromatherapy Languages spoken: English, Portuguese & Spanish*
ROOMS: s fr 200FF; d 400-550FF
CARDS: ●● ▆

## ST-SYLVESTRE-SUR-LOT Lot-et-Garonne

★ ★ ★ ★ *Château Lalande*
*47140*
☎ 553361515 FAX 553361516
Near river Near lake Forest area In town centre
*22 en suite (bth/shr) TV in all bedrooms STV Direct dial from all bedrooms Mini-bar in all bedrooms Room-safe Licensed Lift Full central heating Open parking available Covered parking available Child discount available 13yrs Outdoor swimming pool (heated) Tennis Sauna Solarium Gym Pool table Boule Jacuzzi/spa Open terrace V meals Languages spoken: English*
CARDS: ●● ■ ▆ ⑩

## SALIGNAC (JAYAC) Dordogne

★ ★ *Coulier*
*24590*
☎ 553288646 FAX 553282633
(between Chavagnac and Salignac on the D60)
Forest area Near motorway
*Closed 15 Dec-15 Jan*
*15 rms (13 shr) (3 fmly) TV in all bedrooms Mini-bar in all bedrooms Full central heating Open parking available Child discount available 12yrs Outdoor swimming pool Open terrace V meals Last d 21.00hrs*
CARDS: ●● ■ ▆ ⑩ Travellers cheques

## SARE Pyrénées-Atlantiques

★ ★ ★ *Arraya*
*64310*
☎ 559542046 FAX 559542704
(From A63 exit at St Jean de Luz Nord, take D918 towards Ascain-Sare)
Near river Forest area In town centre
*Closed mid Nov-end Mar*
*21 en suite (bth/shr) (4 fmly) (7 with balcony) TV in all bedrooms Direct dial from all bedrooms Licensed Night porter Full central heating Air conditioning in bedrooms Open parking available Supervised Child discount available Open terrace Last d 22.00hrs Languages spoken: English German Italian & Spanish*
CARDS: ●● ■ ▆

**Errotaldekoborda** (Prop: Murielle Daux)
rte des Ventas *64310*
☎ 559542977 FAX 559513120
(Leave motorway at St Jean-de-Luz towards Ascain then Sare. Take the route des Plataus & turn right onto 1st bridge on left, continue uphill for 1km. Farmhouse on left)
Near river Forest area

**Bidachuna**
This 19th century country farm is situated at the edge of a forest just six kilometres from the village. The rooms have exposed beams and are decorated with refinement. You will enjoy exploring the Basque region from this base. Croquet available.
Near lake Forest area
*3 en suite (bth/shr) No smoking on premises TV in all bedrooms Full central heating Open parking available Croquet Languages spoken: English & Spanish*
ROOMS: s 500-600FF; d 550-700FF
**Reductions over 1 night**
CARDS: Travellers cheques

★ ★ *Bonnet* (Minotel)
Quartier Ibarron *64310*
☎ 559541026 FAX 559545315
(Exit Autoroute at 'St-Jean-de-Luz Nord'. Then 'St-Pée-sur-Nivelle/Cambo-les-Bains')
Near river Near lake Near beach
*Closed 3 Jan-15 Feb*
*75 en suite (bth/shr) 2 rooms in annexe (4 fmly) (30 with balcony) TV in all bedrooms Direct dial from all bedrooms Mini-bar in 40 bedrooms Licensed Lift Full central heating Open parking available Child discount available 10yrs Outdoor swimming pool (heated) Tennis Boule Open terrace Last d 21.00hrs Languages spoken: English & Spanish*
CARDS: ●● ■ ▆ ⑩ Travellers cheques

## ST-PIERRE-DE-CHIGNAC Dordogne

★ ★ **Le Saint Pierre**
pl de la Halle *24330*
☎ 553075504 FAX 553082647
Near river Forest area Near motorway
*Closed Feb-Mar*
*13 en suite (bth/shr) Some rooms in annexe (4 fmly) (2 with balcony) TV in all bedrooms STV Licensed Full central heating Open parking available Covered parking available (charged) Indoor swimming pool (heated) Outdoor swimming pool (heated) Open terrace Last d 21.00hrs Languages spoken: English*
CARDS: ●● ▆ Travellers cheques

## ST-QUENTIN-DE-BARON Gironde

**Le Prieure** (Prop: S de Castilho)
*33750*
☎ 557241675 FAX 557241380
(from Bordeaux take D936 towards Bergerac, through St-Quentin-de-Baron, Carre Bleu swimming pool, shell petrol station, continue for 1km yellow sign 'Le Prieuréo' right & follow on to left)

contd.

*4 en suite (shr) (1 fmly) Full central heating Open parking
available Riding Bicycle rental Trekking facilities Languages
spoken: English & Spanish*
ROOMS: s 250FF; d 300FF

## SAUBUSSE Landes

### ★★ Complexe Aubusse Thermal
*40180*
☎ 558574000 FAX 558573737
(autoroute A64 exit8, direction for Dax, complex signposted)
Near river  Forest area  Near motorway
*Closed Dec-Feb
41 en suite (bth/shr) 10 rooms in annexe (2 fmly) (5 with
balcony) TV in all bedrooms Direct dial from all bedrooms
Room-safe Licensed Night porter Full central heating Open
parking available Supervised Child discount available 12yrs
Indoor swimming pool (heated) Outdoor swimming pool
Sauna Gym Pool table Boule Jacuzzi/spa Bicycle rental Open
terrace Last d 20.00hrs Languages spoken: English & Spanish*
ROOMS: (room only) d 278-315FF
**Reductions over 1 night Special breaks**
MEALS: Continental breakfast 38FF Lunch 80-219FF Dinner
80-219FF
CARDS: ●● ▆▆ Travellers cheques

## SAUTERNES Gironde

### *Château de Commarque* (Prop: M Herfurth)
*33210*
☎ 557310186 FAX 556766430
(From Bordeaux to Toulouse motorway exit Langon at rdbt
take 1st right continue to 1st sign Sauternes 3.5km. Towards
Léogeats, then 1st right after Château Fichot)
Near river  Near sea  Near beach  Forest area  Near motorway
*7 en suite (shr) (1 fmly) No smoking in 1 bedroom Full central
heating Open parking available Covered parking available
Child discount available 10yrs Outdoor swimming pool (heated)
Bicycle rental V meals Last d 22.00hrs Languages spoken:
English Dutch German & Spanish*

## SAUVETERRE-DE-BEARN Pyrénées-Atlantiques

### ★★ *Hotel de Vieux Pont*
*64390*
☎ 559389511 FAX 559389910
Near river  Near sea  Near beach  Forest area  Near motorway
*Closed Nov-Mar
7 en suite (bth/shr) (2 fmly) (5 with balcony) TV in all
bedrooms STV Direct dial from all bedrooms Licensed Full
central heating Open terrace Last d 21.15hrs Languages
spoken: English & German*
CARDS: ●● ▆▆ Travellers cheques

## SERGEAC Dordogne

### *Auberge de Castel-Merle* (Prop: C Millinship)
*24290*
☎ 553507008 FAX 553507625
(Brive to Montignac, then D706 in direction of Les Eyzies. At
Thonac turn left over bridge, then right, to Sergeac & follow
signs)
In a delightful setting on a cliff overlooking the Vèzere river, a
warm and friendly welcome awaits you in a traditional stone
and oak-beamed auberge. The rooms are comfortable and
individually decorated. Traditional local cuisine includes wild
boar stew and truffle omelettes.

Near river  Near lake  Near sea  Forest area
*Closed 2 Nov-28 Feb & 23-30 Sep
4 en suite (shr) (1 fmly) TV in 3 bedrooms Full central heating
Open parking available Child discount available 12yrs V meals
Last d 20.30hrs Languages spoken: English*
ROOMS: s fr 350FF; d 480-520FF ✱
MEALS: Continental breakfast 30FF Lunch 69-190FF Dinner
69-190FF
CARDS: ●● ▆▆

## SÉRIGNAC-SUR-GARONNE Lot-et-Garonne

### ★★★ *Le Prince Noir*
rte de Mont-de-Marsan *47310*
☎ 553687430 FAX 553687193
(from Agen take D119 through Brax & on to Serignac-s-
Garonne, approx 12kms)
Near river  Forest area  Near motorway
*22 en suite (bth/shr) (2 fmly) TV in all bedrooms Direct dial
from all bedrooms Licensed Full central heating Open parking
available Supervised Outdoor swimming pool Tennis Boule
Bicycle rental Open terrace Last d 20.45hrs Languages
spoken: English & Spanish*
CARDS: ●● ▆▆ ▆▆ Travellers cheques

## SOUMOULOU Pyrénées-Atlantiques

### ★★ *Bearn*
14 rue de Las Bordes *64420*
☎ 559046009 FAX 559046333
Near river  Forest area  Near motorway
*14 en suite (bth/shr) (3 fmly) TV in all bedrooms Direct dial
from all bedrooms Licensed Night porter Full central heating
Open parking available Covered parking available (charged)
Child discount available Boule Open terrace Languages
spoken: English & Spanish*
CARDS: ●● ▆▆ ▆▆ ⓓ Travellers cheques

## THIVIERS Dordogne

### ★★★ *Château de Mavaleix*
*24800*
☎ 553528201 FAX 553620380
Near river  Near lake  Forest area
*Closed 8 Jan-6 Feb
15 en suite (bth/shr) 10 rooms in annexe (1 with balcony) TV
in all bedrooms Licensed Full central heating Open parking
available Child discount available Outdoor swimming pool
Fishing Boule Bicycle rental Open terrace V meals Last d
21.00hrs Languages spoken: English & Spanish*
CARDS: ●● ▆▆ Travellers cheques

## TRÉMOLAT Dordogne

### ★★★ *Le Vieux Logis et ses Logis des Champs*
*24510*
☎ 553228006 FAX 553228489
Near river  Forest area
*24 en suite (bth/shr) (6 fmly) TV in all bedrooms Direct dial
from all bedrooms Mini-bar in all bedrooms Licensed Full
central heating Open parking available Covered parking
available Child discount available 10yrs Outdoor swimming
pool Pool table Boule Open terrace Cycle hire nearby V
meals Last d 21.30hrs Languages spoken: German &
Spanish*
CARDS: ●● ▆▆ ▆▆ ⓓ Travellers cheques

**URRUGNE** Pyrénées-Atlantiques

**Château d'Urtubie**
*64122*
☎ 559543115 FAX 559546251
Near sea Near beach Forest area Near motorway
*Closed 15 Feb-23 Dec*
*6 rms (4 bth 1 shr) Licensed Full central heating Open parking available Covered parking available Child discount available Tennis Fishing Bicycle rental Open terrace Languages spoken: English & Spanish*
CARDS: ■■ ㅍ

**Château d'Urtubie** (Prop: De Coral)
*64122*
☎ 559543115 FAX 559546251
This fortified castle has been in the hands of the same family since 1341. Improvements have been carried out over time giving a residence furnished and decorated with refinement. Located in a fine Basque country location it is only a short distance from the attractive town of St-Jean-de-Luz.

Near river Near sea Near beach Forest area Near motorway
*Apr-Oct*
*6 rms (4 bth 1 shr) (1 fmly) TV in all bedrooms Full central heating Open parking available Covered parking available (charged) Child discount available Tennis Fishing Languages spoken: English & Spanish*
ROOMS: d 500-800FF
✱ **Reductions over 1 night Special breaks**
CARDS: ●● ■■ ㅍ

**USTARITZ** Pyrénées-Atlantiques

★ ★ ★ **Hotel la Patoula**
rue Principale *64480*
☎ 559930056 FAX 559931654
Near river Near sea Near beach Forest area Near motorway
*Closed 6 Dec-14 Feb*
*9 en suite (bth/shr) TV in 8 bedrooms Direct dial from all bedrooms Mini-bar in 2 bedrooms Full central heating Open parking available Fishing Open terrace V meals Last d 22.00hrs*
CARDS: ●● ㅍ Travellers cheques

**VENDOIRE** Dordogne

**Le Bouchaud** (Prop: M Andre Durieux)
*24320*
☎ 553910082
(from Angoulême D939 to Dignac, then D23 to Villebois-Lavalette and D17 Gurat. Take D102 towards Vendoise for 2km then left)

Near river Forest area
*3 en suite (bth/shr) (1 fmly) Radio in rooms Full central heating Open parking available Child discount available 7yrs Fishing Boule V meals Last d 18.00hrs*

**VERTEILLAC** Dordogne

**La Bernerie** (Prop: Tom & Patricia Carruthers)
Bouteilles St-Sebastien *24320*
☎ 553915140 FAX 553910859
(at Angoulême head for Périgueux, after 20kms turn right to Riberac. In Verteillac opp church, on sharp corner take right turn D97, in 100m left to Bouteilles. At cross roads turn left. In village, last house)
Near river Near lake Forest area
*Closed Nov-Apr*
*4 en suite (bth/shr) 1 rooms in annexe (3 with balcony) No smoking in 3 bedrooms Full central heating Open parking available Supervised No children 16yrs Outdoor swimming pool Boule Bicycle rental V meals Languages spoken: English*
CARDS: Travellers cheques

**VERTHEUIL** Gironde

**Cantemerle** (Prop: Mme Michele Tardat)
9 rue des Châtaigniers *33180*
☎ 556419624 FAX 556419624
(55km NW of Bordeaux, A630 exit7 then D1 towards Le Verdon-sur-Soulac. In Castelnau take N215 for 25km. Turn right onto D205 towards Cissac and D104 towards Vertheuil. Left at church towards Bourdin, property on left)
A beautiful house in the Spanish Moorish style in the heart of the Medoc vineyards. Guests will enjoy peace, quiet and outstanding décor. The hosts are much travelled artists and have a private vineyard on the premises, producing their own wine.
Forest area
*3 en suite (bth/shr) (1 fmly) (2 with balcony) No smoking on premises Full central heating Open parking available Child discount available 2yrs Bicycle rental Languages spoken: English & Spanish*
ROOMS: s 260-280FF; d 300-320FF
MEALS: Dinner 150FF
CARDS: Travellers cheques

**VIEUX-MARUIL** Dordogne

★ ★ ★ **Château de Vieux Mareuil**
*24340*
☎ 553607715 FAX 553564933
Near river Near lake Forest area Near motorway
*Closed 2 Jan-1 Mar*
*14 en suite (bth/shr) (4 fmly) (5 with balcony) No smoking in 7 bedrooms TV in all bedrooms STV Direct dial from all bedrooms Mini-bar in all bedrooms Licensed Night porter Full central heating Open parking available Covered parking available Supervised Child discount available 10yrs Outdoor swimming pool (heated) Fishing Riding Solarium Boule Jacuzzi/spa Bicycle rental Open terrace V meals Last d 22.00hrs Languages spoken: English German Italian & Spanish*
CARDS: ●● ■■ ㅍ ⊡ Travellers cheques

**VILLARS** Dordogne

**L'Enclos** (Prop: M & Mme Rubbens)
Lavergne *24530*
☎ 553548217 FAX 553548217
Near river Near lake Forest area *contd.*

327

*Closed Oct-end Mar*
*4 en suite (bth/shr) Open parking available Outdoor swimming pool (heated) Tennis Solarium Bicycle rental Open terrace Table tennis Languages spoken: English, German & Spanish*

### VILLEFRANCHE-DU-PÉRIGORD Dordogne

### ★ ★ Auberge la Clé des Champs
Mazeyrolles *24550*
☎ 553299594 FAX 553284296
This old inn is located in the heart of the rolling countryside of the Périgord Noir and reflects local history and traditions in its charming interior. This region is said yo have the best cuisine in France and the restaurant does this reputation justice. In addition, comfortable bedrooms offer restful accommodation, equipped with every modern facility.
*Forest area*

*Closed Nov-end Apr*
*13 en suite (bth/shr) TV in all bedrooms STV Direct dial from all bedrooms Mini-bar in all bedrooms Licensed Full central heating Open parking available Covered parking available Child discount available 12yrs Outdoor swimming pool (heated) Tennis Pool table Boule Bicycle rental Open terrace Last d 21.00hrs Languages spoken: English*
ROOMS: (room only) s 260-320FF; d 260-360FF
MEALS: Full breakfast 40FF Lunch 100-230FF&alc Dinner 100-230FF&alc
CARDS: ●● ▆

### VILLENEUVE-DE-MARSAN Landes

### ★ ★ ★ Francis Darroze
Grande-Rue *40190*
☎ 558452007 FAX 558458267
*Forest area In town centre*
*15 en suite (bth) (6 fmly) (12 with balcony) No smoking in 1 bedroom TV in all bedrooms Radio in rooms Licensed Full central heating Open parking available Covered parking available Supervised Child discount available 12yrs Outdoor swimming pool Tennis Boule Open terrace Covered terrace V meals Last d 22.00hrs Languages spoken: English German & Spanish*
CARDS: ●● ▆ ▆ ● Travellers cheques

### VILLENEUVE-SUR-LOT Lot-et-Garonne

### Domaine de Clavie Soubirous (Prop: M Marc Disgrens)
*47300*
☎ 553417430 FAX 553417750
*Near river Near lake Near sea Forest area In town centre*

*6 en suite (bth/shr) TV available Full central heating Open parking available Covered parking available Outdoor swimming pool V meals Languages spoken: English*

### Les Huguets (Prop: M & Mme Edward Poppe)
*47300*
☎ 553704934 FAX 553704934
*Near river Near lake Forest area Near motorway*
*5 en suite (bth/shr) (3 fmly) (1 with balcony) No smoking in all bedrooms TV available Full central heating Open parking available Covered parking available Child discount available 10yrs Outdoor swimming pool Tennis Riding Sauna Boule Bicycle rental Open terrace Last d 18.00hrs Languages spoken: English, Dutch & German*
CARDS: Travellers cheques

### VILLÉREAL Lot-et-Garonne

### Colombie (Prop: M Pannetier)
Dévillac *47210*
☎ 553366234 FAX 553360479
(on D272 between Monflanquin and Monpazier)
This property is located in a beautiful, peaceful area and has views of the castle of Biron. The rooms, with independant access, are situated in a stone house of great character. There is a living room for the guests' use, and picnics can be taken in the garden. There is a private swimming pool and also a sandpit for children. Fishing on the lake. Horse riding can be arranged.
*Near lake Forest area*
*3 en suite (shr) (1 fmly) TV in 1 bedroom Full central heating Open parking available Child discount available Outdoor swimming pool Fishing Languages spoken: English*
ROOMS: s 280FF; d 300FF
MEALS: Lunch 120FF Dinner 120FF✱
CARDS: Travellers cheques

### VITRAC Dordogne

### ★ ★ De Plaisance
Le Port *24200*
☎ 553283304 FAX 553281924
*Near river*
*Closed 16 Nov-6 eb*
*42 en suite (bth/shr) Some rooms in annexe TV in all bedrooms Licensed Lift Full central heating Open parking available Child discount available 12yrs Outdoor swimming pool Tennis Boule Mini-golf Open terrace Last d 20.45hrs Languages spoken: English*
CARDS: ●● ▆ ▆ ●

### ★ ★ ★ Domaine de Rochebois (S)
rte de Montfort *24200*
☎ 553315252 FAX 553293688
*Near river Forest area*
*Closed end Oct-mid Apr*
*40 en suite (bth/shr) (35 with balcony) TV in all bedrooms STV Direct dial from all bedrooms Mini-bar in all bedrooms Licensed Lift Night porter Full central heating Open parking available Supervised Child discount available 12yrs Outdoor swimming pool Golf 9 Tennis Solarium Gym Pool table Boule Bicycle rental Open terrace V meals Last d 21.30hrs Languages spoken: English & German*
CARDS: ●● ▆ ▆ ● Travellers cheques

# Limousin

Often overlooked by visitors passing through en route to the mountains and the coast, Limousin has much to offer the discerning tourist. The valleys of the Dordogne and the Creuse, Lake Vassivière, the Millevache Plain and the Monédières Mountains, are features of its varied landscape, dotted with fine châteaux and prehistoric monuments. There's plenty of scope for watersports, fishing, rambling and cycling; and for the culturally inclined there's contemporary art, exquisite porcelain and fine tapestries.

## ESSENTIAL FACTS

| | |
|---|---|
| DÉPARTEMENTS: | Limoges, Gueret, Tulle, Aubusson, Ussel, Brive-la-Gaillarde, Rochechouart |
| PRINCIPAL TOWNS | Corrèze, Creuse, Haute-Vienne |
| PLACES TO VISIT: | Limoges for porcelain; Aubusson for tapestry (see the Tapestry Museum); Vassivière for its lake; Meymac for the Contemporary Art Centre; Brive-la-Gaillarde for its distillery; Châteauponsac for the René Bauberot Museum. For more regional flavour try the Brick & Tile Factory Museum, Saint-Hilaire-Les-Places, or the Bernardaud Porcelain Factory, Limoges. |
| REGIONAL TOURIST OFFICE | 27 Boulevard de la Corderie 87 031 Limoges Tel 55 45 18 80  Fax 55 45 18 18 |
| LOCAL GASTRONOMIC DELIGHTS | Foie gras; côte de boeuf Limousin à la moelle et au vin de Cahors, a beef dish which uses deep purple Cahors wine; red cabbage with chestnuts; creamy potato pie; clafoutis (a form of cherry pie); local products (produits du terroir): mushrooms, truffles, cepes, walnuts & chestnuts. |
| DRINKS | Gentiane (a herbal aperitif), and fine fruit brandies made with cherries, plums and prunes. Good beer is produced in the area, due to the purity of the water. |
| LOCAL CRAFTS WHAT TO BUY | Tapestry from Aubusson, porcelain and enamel work from Limoges, lace from Tulle. Local produce such as Gentiane, liqueurs, sweetmeats, black pudding with chestnuts, dried mushrooms, madeleines & pâté de foie gras. |

ALBUSSAC Corrèze

★ ★ **Roche de Vic**
Les Quatre Routes *19380*
☎ 555281587 FAX 555280109
Near river  Near lake  Forest area  Near motorway
Closed Jan-1 Mar
*13 rms  TV in all bedrooms  Licensed  Full central heating  Open parking available  Covered parking available  Child discount available 12yrs  Outdoor swimming pool (heated)  Boule  Open terrace  Covered terrace  Last d 21.30hrs  Languages spoken: English*
CARDS: ●● ▦

## ARGENTAT Corrèze

**Au Pont de l'Hospital** (Prop: M & Mme Mallows)
BP 38 *19400*
☎ 555289035 FAX 555282070
(from A20 (Vierzon-Toulouse) exit at Uzerche. On N120, follow blue sign posts to establishment)
Near river  Near lake  Forest area  Near motorway
RS Dec-Mar
*11 rms (4 bth/shr) (4 fmly) Full central heating  Open parking available  Child discount available 12yrs  Outdoor swimming pool (heated)  Tennis  Fishing  Riding  Boule  Bicycle rental  Open terrace  Covered terrace  Languages spoken: English & Spanish*

## BEAULIEU-SUR-DORDOGNE Corrèze

**Château d'Arnac** (Prop: Joe Webb)
Nonards *19120*
☎ 555915413 FAX 555915262
English owned turretted 12th-century chateau, lovingly restored and retaining all its charm and character. Set beside a trout stream and lake in 20 acres of parkland. In spring and autumn, log fires are lit in all the rooms adding to the romantic atmosphere of the chateau.
Near river  Near lake  Forest area  Near motorway
*4 en suite (bth/shr)  Full central heating  Open parking available  No children 14yrs  Outdoor swimming pool  Tennis  Fishing  Boule  Open terrace  V meals  Last d 19.30hrs  Languages spoken: English*
ROOMS: (room only) s 490FF; d 540FF
**Reductions over 1 night**
MEALS: Continental breakfast 40FF  Dinner 200FF✱
CARDS: N Travellers cheques

## BERSAC Haute-Vienne

**Château de Chambon** (Prop: M & Mme Bersac)
*87370*
☎ 555714704 FAX 555715141
Near river  Near lake  Near sea  Forest area  Near motorway
Closed Nov-Mar
*4 en suite (bth/shr) (4 fmly)  Full central heating  Open parking available  Covered parking available  Child discount available  Last d 20.00hrs*
contd.

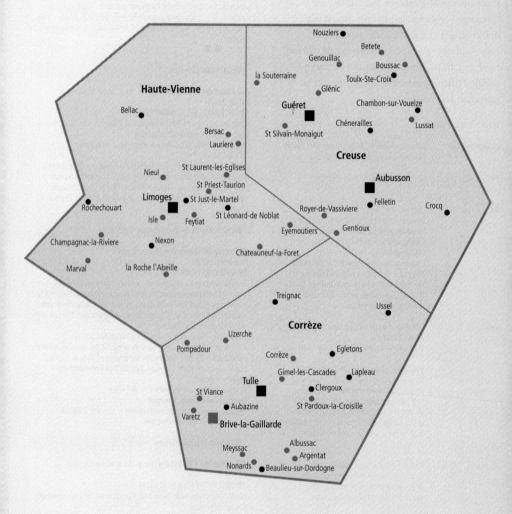

**Haute-Vienne**

Bellac

Bersac
Lauriere

Nieul
St Laurent-les-Eglises
St Priest-Taurion
**Limoges** St Just-le-Martel
Rochechouart St Léonard de Noblat
Isle Feytiat
Champagnac-la-Riviere Nexon
Marval la Roche l'Abeille

Nouziers
Betete
Genouillac
Boussac
la Souterraine Toulx-Ste-Croix
Glénic
**Guéret** Chambon-sur-Voueize
Chénerailles Lussat
St Silvain-Monaigut

**Creuse**

**Aubusson**
Felletin
Royer-de-Vassiviere Crocq
Eymoutiers Gentioux

Chateauneuf-la-Foret

Treignac
Ussel
**Corrèze**
Uzerche
Pompadour
Corrèze Egletons
Gimel-les-Cascades Lapleau
**Tulle**
St Viance Clergoux
Aubazine St Pardoux-la-Croisille
Varetz
**Brive-la-Gaillarde**
Albussac
Meyssac Argentat
Nonards Beaulieu-sur-Dordogne

## BÉTÊTE Creuse

**Château de Moisse** (Prop: M & Mme Deboutte)
*23270*
☎ 555808425 FAX 555808425
(take D940 to Guéret, towards Genouillac and take local road to Bétête and Boussac. The castle is 3.5km on left)
Near river  Forest area
*Closed Oct-May*
*4 en suite (bth/shr) (1 fmly) (2 with balcony) No smoking on premises Open parking available Child discount available Languages spoken: English & Dutch*
CARDS: Travellers cheques

## BOUSSAC Creuse

**Bed & Breakfast** (Prop: Françoise & Daniel Gros)
3 rue des Loges *23600*
☎ 555658009
(at junct off D916/D917)
Near river  Forest area
*RS Oct & Jan*
*4 rms (3 bth/shr) (1 fmly) Full central heating Child discount available 12yrs Open terrace Boules Table tennis*

## BRIVE-LA-GAILLARDE Corrèze

★ ★ **La Cremaillère**
53 av de Paris *19100*
☎ 555743247 FAX 555179183
In town centre
*9 en suite (bth/shr) TV in all bedrooms Licensed Full central heating Last d 21.30hrs Languages spoken: English & Spanish*
CARDS: ●● ☲ Travellers cheques

## CHAMPAGNAC-LA-RIVIÈRE Haute-Vienne

**Château de Brie**
*87150*
☎ 555781752 FAX 555781402
Near lake  Forest area
*Closed Jan-Mar*
*4 en suite (bth/shr) Full central heating Open parking available Child discount available 5yrs Languages spoken: English*

## CHÂTEAUNEUF-LA-FORÊT Haute-Vienne

**La Croix du Reh** (Prop: M & Mme McLaughlin)
*87130*
☎ 555697537 FAX 555697538
(from Limoges take A20 (Toulouse) exit, 24kms to town. From Brive take A20 (Paris) exit 42, 20kms to town)
This beautiful 17th-century residence, set in a three acre landscaped park, has been tastefully restored and is now owned by a Scottish family, from whom a warm welcome and delicious food are guaranteed. There is a lake with a beach, fishing and tennis. Mountain bike hire at 500 metres.
Near river  Near lake  Near beach  Forest area  Near motorway
*5 en suite (bth/shr) (1 fmly) No smoking on premises Full central heating Open parking available Child discount available 12yrs Boule Basketball Table tennis V meals Last d 12.00hrs Languages spoken: English*
ROOMS: s 200-260FF; d 300-350FF
MEALS: Dinner fr 120FF✱
CARDS: ●● ☲ Carte Bleu Travellers cheques

## CORRÈZE Corrèze

★ ★ ★ **Hotel la Séniorie de Corrèze**
Le Bourg *19800*
☎ 555212288 FAX 555212400
(from Tulle N89 towards Clermont-Ferrand, at Corrèze station turn left to village centre and continue up hill)
Built in the 19th century, this magnificent mansion towers over the medieval village of Corrèze. There are 29 quiet comfortable bedrooms of great charm. The convivial restaurant offers regional and typical French cuisine.
Forest area  In town centre
*Closed Feb*
*29 en suite (bth/shr) (4 fmly) (8 with balcony) TV in all bedrooms STV Direct dial from all bedrooms Mini-bar in all bedrooms Licensed Lift Full central heating Open parking available Covered parking available Child discount available 12yrs Outdoor swimming pool (heated) Tennis Sauna Solarium Pool table Boule Open terrace Last d 12.00hrs Languages spoken: English, German & Spanish*
ROOMS: (room only) s 535FF; d 600FF
**Reductions over 1 night**
MEALS: Continental breakfast 40FF  Lunch 98-120FF&alc  Dinner 98-120FF&alc
CARDS: ●● ■■ ☲ ◙ Travellers cheques

## EYMOUTIERS Haute-Vienne

**Bed & Breakfast** (Prop: Josette et Michel Jaubert)
La Roche *87120*
☎ 555696188
(from Eymoutiers take D30 & follow direction of Domps (Chamberet-La Croisille), drive to village of La Roche house 1st on the left)
Near river  Near lake  Near beach  Forest area
*Closed Dec-Jan*
*2 en suite (shr) No smoking on premises Open parking available Languages spoken: English*

## FEYTIAT Haute-Vienne

★ ★ **Climat de France**
ZI Le Ponteix-Secteur Laugerie *87220*
☎ 555061460 FAX 555063893
(near A20, junction 36)
Near river  Forest area  Near motorway
*50 en suite (bth) (1 fmly) No smoking in 10 bedrooms TV in all bedrooms STV Radio in rooms Direct dial from all bedrooms Licensed Full central heating Open parking available Supervised Open terrace Last d 10pm Languages spoken: English*
CARDS: ●● ☲

## GENOUILLAC Creuse

★ ★ **Le Relais d'Oc**
N 940 *23350*
☎ 555807245
Near river  Forest area  In town centre
*Closed 15 Nov-Palm Sunday*
*7 rms (5 shr) No smoking in 4 bedrooms Licensed Full central heating Open parking available Child discount available 8yrs Last d 20.00hrs Languages spoken: German*
CARDS: Travellers cheques

## GENTIOUX Creuse

**La Commanderie** (Prop: M Y Gomichon)
Pallier 23340
☎ 555679173 FAX 555679173
(from Clermont-Ferrand take D941 to Aubussion. Then take D982 to Felletin, then D992 to Gentioux. D8 to Pallier)
Near river Forest area
Closed Jan-Mar RS Apr-May & Oct-Dec
4 en suite (bth/shr) No smoking on premises Full central heating Open parking available Supervised Child discount available 8yrs Fishing Last d 20.00hrs
CARDS: Travellers cheques

## GIMEL LES CASCADES Corrèze

★ ★ **L'Hostellerie de la Vallée**
19800
☎ 555214060 FAX 555213874
(W of Egletons, N89 exit 'The Cascades")
Near river Near lake Forest area Near motorway
Closed Oct-Mar
9 en suite (bth/shr) (1 fmly) TV in all bedrooms Direct dial from all bedrooms Licensed Night porter Full central heating Air conditioning in bedrooms Child discount available 12yrs Boule Open terrace V meals Last d 22.00hrs Languages spoken: English
CARDS: ●● ▨

## GLÈNIC Creuse

★ ★ **Moulin Noyé**
23380
☎ 55528144 FAX 55528194
(N of Guéret on the D940)
Near river Near lake Near beach Forest area Near motorway
16 en suite (bth/shr) 6 rooms in annexe (3 fmly) (10 with balcony) No smoking in 4 bedrooms TV in all bedrooms STV Direct dial from all bedrooms Mini-bar in 6 bedrooms Licensed Full central heating Open parking available Supervised Child discount available Outdoor swimming pool (heated) Fishing Boule Bicycle rental Open terrace V meals Last d 21.15hrs Languages spoken: English
ROOMS: (room only) d 290FF ✱ **Reductions over 1 night**
MEALS: Continental breakfast 25FF Lunch 110-200FF&alc Dinner 110-200FF&alc✱
CARDS: ●● ▨ Travellers cheques

## ISLE Haute-Vienne

**Bed & Breakfast** (Prop: Edith Brunier)
Verthamont, Pic de l'Aiguille 87170
☎ 555361289
(from Limoges take N21 towards Périgueux. After 9kms at 'Bas Verthamont' follow road sign on right 'Chambres d'Hôtes 600m' and take small road on right)
This is a modern house which enjoys a magnificent view of the Vienne Valley. Each room has its own terrace and independent entrance. Close to the centre of Limoges. All meals are prepared with organic produce. Guests have full use of the swimming pool.
Near river Forest area Near motorway
3 en suite (shr) (1 fmly) (2 with balcony) No smoking on premises TV in 2 bedrooms Full central heating Open parking available Child discount available Outdoor swimming pool Languages spoken: English & German
ROOMS: s 180FF; d 230FF
MEALS: Dinner 80FF

## LAURIÈRE Haute-Vienne

**La Bezassade** (Prop: M & Mme Chanudet)
87370
☎ 555717807
Near river Near lake Forest area
Closed mid Sep-Jun
2 rms (1 shr) TV available Open parking available Supervised Child discount available 4yrs Languages spoken: English & Spanish

## LUSSAT Creuse

**Puy-Haut** (Prop: M & Mme Ribbe)
23170
☎ 555821307
Closed Nov-Mar
3 en suite (bth) Full central heating Open parking available
CARDS: Travellers cheques

## MARVAL Haute-Vienne

**Le Val du Goth** (Prop: M et Mme F Pez)
Le Vansanaud 87440
☎ 555787665 FAX 555782379
(from St-Mathieu towards Marval for 1 mile after Nilhagnet. Then left to Cussac and right after 500mtrs to Le Vansanaud)
Near lake Forest area
2 en suite (bth/shr) No smoking on premises TV in all bedrooms Full central heating Open parking available Child discount available 12yrs Outdoor swimming pool Fishing Bicycle rental Table tennis Languages spoken: English
ROOMS: (room only) s 200FF; d 300FF
MEALS: Dinner 110FF
CARDS: Travellers cheques

## MEYSSAC Corrèze

**Manoir de Bellerade** (Prop: Mme Jeanne Foussac-Lassalle)
19500
☎ 555254142 FAX 558840751
(on the D38 between Collonges-la-Rouge and Meyssac. Entrance 60mtrs beyond Meyssac sign via a long driveway)
Forest area
Closed Nov-Mar
4 en suite (bth/shr) (3 fmly) No smoking on premises TV in 2 bedrooms Full central heating Open parking available Covered parking available Supervised Child discount available 6yrs Languages spoken: English
CARDS: Travellers cheques

★ ★ **Relais du Quercy**
19500
☎ 555254031 FAX 555253622
Forest area In town centre
12 rms (9 bth/shr) 1 rooms in annexe (2 fmly) TV in all bedrooms Licensed Full central heating Open parking available Covered parking available Child discount available 12yrs Outdoor swimming pool Open terrace Last d 23.00hrs Languages spoken: English & Spanish
CARDS: ●● ■ ▨ ▨ Travellers cheques

## NIEUL Haute-Vienne

### ★ ★ ★ ★ La Chapelle St-Martin
*87510*
☎ 555758017 FAX 555758950
Near lake Forest area
*13 en suite (bth/shr) (2 fmly) (5 with balcony) TV in all bedrooms STV Direct dial from all bedrooms Room-safe Licensed Night porter Full central heating Open parking available Covered parking available Supervised Child discount available Outdoor swimming pool (heated) Tennis Fishing Sauna Pool table Bicycle rental Open terrace Covered terrace V meals Last d 22.00hrs Languages spoken: English & Spanish*
ROOMS: (room only) d 590-980FF
MEALS: Continental breakfast 75FF Lunch 170-300FF&alc Dinner 170-300FF&alc
CARDS: ●● ■ ☎ Travellers cheques

## NONARDS Corrèze

### Le Marchoux (Prop: M & Mme Greenwood)
*19120*
☎ 555915273 FAX 555915273
(from Beaulieu-sur-Dordogne take D940 towards Tulle. After 5km turn left at garage, Le Marchoux is 400m on the right)
The Greenwoods offer two bedrooms in their lovingly restored 150-year-old farmhouse, nestling in the foothills of the Massif Central surrounded by beautiful countryside and historic tourist sites. Continental breakfast is served, and dinner is available on request. Wine and coffee is included in the price. Meals are served in the family living/dining room.
Forest area
*2 rms No smoking in all bedrooms Full central heating Open parking available Languages spoken: English*
ROOMS: s 130FF; d 180FF
MEALS: Dinner 80FF

## POMPADOUR Corrèze

### ★ ★ Auberge de la Mandrie
rte de Périgueux *19230*
☎ 555733714 FAX 555736713
The inn is peacefully located in leafy surroundings and features chalet-style guest accommodation situated in large grounds with views over the open countryside. The restaurant has large windows which create a spacious, bright setting, where a choice of regional dishes is served. There are numerous leisure opportunities nearby, and the medieval market town of Ségur le Château is well worth a visit.

*24 rms (14 bth 8 shr) TV in all bedrooms Direct dial from all bedrooms Licensed Open parking available Child discount*

*available 10yrs Indoor swimming pool (heated) Outdoor swimming pool (heated) Boule Bicycle rental Open terrace Covered terrace Last d 21.15hrs Languages spoken: English*
ROOMS: (room only) d 245FF
MEALS: Full breakfast 38FF Lunch 72-180FF&alc Dinner 72-180FF&alc
CARDS: ●● ☎ ◎ Travellers cheques

## ROCHE-L'ABEILLE, LA Haute-Vienne

### ★ ★ ★ Moulin de la Gorce
*87800*
☎ 555007066 FAX 555007657
Near river Near lake Forest area
*Closed Oct-1 Apr*
*10 en suite (bth/shr) (3 fmly) TV in all bedrooms Licensed Full central heating Open parking available Supervised Child discount available Fishing Boule Open terrace V meals Languages spoken: English*
CARDS: ●● ■ ☎ ◎ Travellers cheques

## ROYÈRE-DE-VASSIVIÈRE Creuse

### La Borderie (Prop: M Marc Deschamps)
St-Pierre Bellevue *23460*
☎ 555649651
(from Royère-de-Vassivière, D8 towards Bourganeuf. Turn right just before reaching Le Compeix. Signposted)
Set in the heart of the forest, in a wild and unspoilt part of France, this old stone building offers accommodation for up to fifteen people, including 2 separate cottages. Quiet is guaranteed. Evening meals available at a fixed price. Swings and barbecue in the garden.
Near river Forest area

*5 rms (2 shr) (2 fmly) No smoking on premises Full central heating Open parking available Child discount available 7yrs V meals Last d 20.00hrs Languages spoken: English*
ROOMS: s 170-190FF; d 190-250FF
MEALS: Dinner fr 90FF
CARDS: Travellers cheques

## ST-LAURENT-LES-ÉGLISES Haute-Vienne

### ★ ★ Domaine de la Fontaine
*87240*
☎ 555565611 FAX 555565067
Near river Near lake Forest area
*10 en suite (bth/shr) (10 with balcony) TV in all bedrooms Direct-dial available Licensed Lift Full central heating Open parking available Child discount available 10yrs Fishing Boule Open terrace Languages spoken: English*
CARDS: ●● ☎ Travellers cheques

### ST-PARDOUX-LA-CROISILLE Corrèze

**★ ★ ★ Beau Site**
*19320*
☎ 552277944 FAX 555276952
Near river  Near lake  Forest area
*Closed Oct-Apr*
*28 en suite (bth/shr) (6 fmly) (2 with balcony) Direct dial from*
*all bedrooms Licensed Full central heating Open parking*
*available Supervised Child discount available 14yrs Outdoor*
*swimming pool (heated) Tennis Fishing Boule Mini-golf*
*Bicycle rental Open terrace Last d 21.00hrs Languages*
*spoken: English*
CARDS: ●● ☰ Travellers cheques

### ST-PRIEST-TAURION Haute-Vienne

**★ ★ Relais du Taurion**
2 chemin des Contamines *87480*
☎ 555397014 FAX 555396763
(12km NE of Limoges)
Near river  Forest area  In town centre
*Closed mid Dec-mid Jan Mon RS Sun*
*8 en suite (bth/shr) (1 fmly) No smoking on premises TV in all*
*bedrooms Direct dial from all bedrooms Licensed Full central*
*heating Open parking available Supervised Child discount*
*available 12yrs Bicycle rental V meals Last d 21.00hrs*
*Languages spoken: English*
ROOMS: (room only) d 260-300FF
MEALS: Continental breakfast 40FF  Lunch 100-200FF&alc
Dinner 100-200FF&alc
CARDS: ●● ☰

### ST-SILVAIN-MONTAIGUT Creuse

**Bed & Breakfast** (Prop: M et Mme Lécaille)
Le Pont du Cher *23320*
☎ 555819517 FAX 555819517
(Off D914 between Guéret and Bénévent l'Abbaye)
An old restored farm, situated in a green wooded area with a
pond and brook. There is a big lounge for the use of guests, a
private car park and evening meals available to order.
Near river  Near lake  Forest area
*4 rms (3 shr) No smoking on premises Full central heating*
*Open parking available Child discount available 7yrs Fishing*
*Last d noon*
ROOMS: s fr 240FF; d 260FF **Reductions over 1 night**
**Special breaks**
MEALS: Dinner 90FF

### ST-VIANCE Corrèze

**★ ★ Auberge des Prés de la Vezère**
*19240*
☎ 555850050 FAX 555842536
(At approximately 10 km from Brive, follow signs for Objat and
Varetz. Shortly before Varetz turn right and follow directions
for Saint-Viance. Before entering Saint-Viance, drive down a
small road on the left hand side)
Near river  Forest area  Near motorway
*Closed mid Oct-end Apr*
*11 en suite (bth) (2 fmly) TV in all bedrooms Direct dial from*
*all bedrooms Licensed Full central heating Open parking*
*available Child discount available 12yrs Bicycle rental Open*
*terrace Last d 21.30hrs Languages spoken: English*

ROOMS: (room only) s 280-380FF; d 380FF
MEALS: Full breakfast 40FF  Lunch 105-185FF
Dinner 105-185FF
CARDS: ●● ■■ ☰ Travellers cheques

### SOUTERRAINE, LA Creuse

**★ ★ De La Porte St-Jean**
2 rue des Bains *23300*
☎ 555639000 FAX 555637727
(From N145 follow signs for town centre)
In town centre  Near motorway
*32 rms (7 bth 21 shr) 16 rooms in annexe (2 fmly) (2 with*
*balcony) TV in all bedrooms STV Direct dial from all*
*bedrooms Licensed Full central heating Covered parking*
*available (charged) Supervised Child discount available 12yrs*
*Jacuzzi/spa Open terrace V meals Last d 21.00hrs Languages*
*spoken: English & German*
CARDS: ●● ■■ ☰ ⓓ Travellers cheques

### UZERCHE Corrèze

**★ ★ Teyssier**
rue du Pont Turgot *19140*
☎ 555731005 FAX 555984331
(A20 exit44/45)

Standing on the banks of the River Vézère, the Hotel Teyssier
has been in the same family for three generations, and
provides good food and comfortable accommodation in a
warm and friendly atmosphere. Guests are met upon arrival by
the owners Annie and Jean-Michel Teyssier, who both share a
passion for refined cuisine. Annie will explain and describe
your dishes, whilst her husband creates them with great talent,
using market produce and rare ingredients. Most of the
bedrooms offer the normal range of amenities, although some
are more basic.
Near river  Forest area  In town centre  Near motorway
*Closed 4 Nov-14 Apr*
*14 en suite (bth/shr) (3 fmly) No smoking in 1 bedroom TV in*
*all bedrooms Direct dial from all bedrooms Licensed Full*
*central heating Open parking available Covered parking*
*available (charged) Open terrace Last d 21.00hrs Languages*
*spoken: English & Spanish*
MEALS: Continental breakfast 42FF  Lunch 90-250FF&alc
Dinner 90-250FF&alc
CARDS: ●● ■■ ☰ ⓓ JCB Travellers cheques

**VARETZ** Corrèze

★ ★ ★ ★ **Castel Novel**
19240
☎ 555850001 FAX 555850903
(from A20 exit at Brive Nord. Follow signs for Objat on D901 to Varetz (approx 8kms).On entering village turn immediately left. Castle is on the hill)
Near river  Forest area  Near motorway
Closed end Oct-beg May
37 en suite (bth/shr)  10 rooms in annexe  (2 fmly)  (7 with balcony)  TV in all bedrooms  STV  Direct dial from all

bedrooms  Mini-bar in all bedrooms  Room-safe  Licensed  Lift  Night porter  Full central heating  Air conditioning in bedrooms  Open parking available  Covered parking available  Child discount available 12yrs  Outdoor swimming pool  Golf 3  Tennis  Bicycle rental  Open terrace  Last d 21.30hrs  Languages spoken: English German & Spanish
ROOMS: s 680FF;  d 1360FF
MEALS: Full breakfast 90FF  Lunch 230-450FF&alc  Dinner 230-450FF&alc
CARDS: 🔴 ■ 🔳 🔵 JCB Travellers cheques

## EVENTS & FESTIVALS

**May**  Chénerailles Horse Market; Beaulieu-sur Dordogne Strawberry Fair; Aubazine Holy Music & Heritage (concerts, readings, light shows)
**Jun**  Glénic Craft Fair; Tours de Merle Sound & Light Show; Bellac Festival
**Jul**  Chénerailles Son et Lumière; La Souterraine Arts Festival; Felletin Ewe-Lamb Fair; Egletons Medieval Pageant
**Jul/Aug**  Le Dorat Sound & Light Show; Rilhac Images, Torches & Lights; Clergoux Music Festival, Château de Sédières; St-Léonard de Noblat Classical Music Summer Festival; Nexon Art running to Circus; St-Robert Summer Classical Music Festival; Chambon sur Voueize Son et Lumière, Robeyie Lake; Tulle International Lace Festival (with folk entertainment)
**Jul/Sep**  Annual Limoges Porcelain Festival
**Aug**  Toulx-Ste-Croix Theatre Festival; Pays de Trois Lacs Three Lakes Music Festival; Plateau de Millevaches Summer Music Festival; Treignac Traditional Music Festival; Lapleau Festival de la Luzége (theatre); Felletin International Folklore Festival; Brive-la Gaillarde Youth Orchestra Festival; Crocq Horse Festival; Collognes-la Rouge Traditional Market; Nouziers Cider Festival; Pompadour National Stud Presentation of Arab Horses
**Sep**  Tulle 'Les Nuits de Nacre' Accordion Festival
**Sep/Oct**  Limoges French Language Festival (theatre, wor shops, exhibitions, music); St-Just-le-Martel International Cartoon Show
**Oct**  Guéret Piano Festival; Limoges Butcher Guild Festival; Limoges Traditional & Gastronomic Festival
**Nov**  Limoges Jazz Festival
**Dec**  Brive-la-Gaillarde Foie Gras Fair

### Local markets

Beaulieu-sur-Dordogne: Strawberry Market in May (sells local merchandise, the highlight is the feasting on an 8 metre wide strawberry tart. Exhibitions & street theatre.) Brive-la-Gaillarde: Market Hall in Georges Brassens sells: local produce, Tue, Thu & Sat 8am-12 noon, also Foie Gras Market on selected days in Dec, Jan & Feb. Limoges: antiques/ flea market, 2nd Sun in month; Brousseau Market, last Sun in month; Food Markets: Place des Bancs, daily exc Sun; Place des Carmes, Sat am; market halls - every morning, Place de la Motte & Place Carnot. St-Yrieix-la-Perche: livestock Fri am; Books 2nd & 4th Fri in month. Tulle: Wed & Sat am

### Dordogne River by Gabare Boat

The Valley of the Dordogne from Argentat to Liourdes is officially classified for its exceptional landscapes, architectural heritage and scenic areas. The valley covers an area of 12,500 hectares including 16 towns and villages, and is the largest protected site in Limousin and one of five outstanding national sites. The gabare boat provides the ideal means of exploring the Dordogne River. It is a flat-bottomed boat, of the sort used to transport the chestnut wood used for the Bordeaux cooperage industry. For further information on La Dordogne en Gabares, tel 00 33 555 93 90 32.

Limousin Porcelain was first manufactured in France when deposits of kaolin were discovered at Saint-Yrieix, near Limoges, in 1768. By the beginning of the 19th-century the porcelain industry was flourishing, and the artists associated with the product include Jouve, Dufy, Lalique and Van Dongen. Limoges porcelain is known for its extreme whiteness and its brilliance when fired.

Limoges has a 1,000-year-old tradition of producing enamel work. Since the 12th century, religious artefacts, including crosses and offertory plates, have been exported across Europe from the region. The art of enamelling was developed during the Renaissance, notably by Léonard Limosin, and revived once again by the likes of Léon Jouhaud with the art deco movement.

# Auvergne

Auvergne, in the Massif Central highlands which has long extinct volcanoes, offers some of the most wild and breathtaking scenery in France. Two regional parks, with signposted walks designed for the whole family, present excellent vantage points from which to view the winding rivers, cascading waterfalls and mountainous slopes. In the Haut-Allier, the spectacular gorges are rich in wildlife, including peregrine falcons, red kites, owls and otters. There are plenty of opportunities for water sports, horse-riding, cycling, hang-gliding or even hot air ballooning. While the region's châteaux, Romanesque churches, village inns and spa towns will inform and refresh those who prefer a gentler pace.

## ESSENTIAL FACTS

| | |
|---|---|
| DÉPARTEMENTS: | Allier, Cantal, Haute-Loire, Puy-de-Dôme |
| PRINCIPAL TOWNS | Moulins, Clermont-Ferrand, Aurillac, Vichy, Le Puy-en-Velay, Thiers, Montluçon, Issoire, Riom |
| PLACES TO VISIT: | Parc Régional des Volcans d'Auvergne with its array of old volcanic cones; Le Puy-en-Velay for its outstanding religious art and architecture; Tronçais Forest, rich in wildlife, especially deer; the valley of the Dordogne |
| REGIONAL TOURIST OFFICE | 43 Avenue Julien BP 395 - 63011 Clermont-Ferrand Tel 04 73 29 49 49  Fax 04 73 34 11 11 |
| LOCAL GASTRONOMIC DELIGHTS | Potée Auvergnate, stew of cabbage, potato, bacon, pork, sausage. Cassoulet, haricot beans, smoked & fresh pork stew. Hams & sausages. Cheeses: Cantal, St-Nectaire, Salers, Bleu d'Auvergne, Fourme d'Ambert, & many local cheeses. |
| DRINKS | Mineral waters: Vichy, Saint-Yourre & Volvic. Wines: Chanturgue, Châteaugay, Corent, Boudes; white wines & light fruity reds of St-Pourçain |
| LOCAL CRAFTS WHAT TO BUY | Pastilles from Vichy, paper from Ambert, lace from Haute-Loire, Côte d'Auvergne wine and local products such as liqueurs, honey, jams & cheeses. |

## ABREST Allier

**La Colombière**
rte de Thiers *03200*
☎ 470986915 FAX 470315089
Near river  Near motorway
*Closed 1st wk Oct & mid Jan-mid Feb*
*4 en suite (bth/shr)  TV in all bedrooms  Direct dial from all bedrooms  Licensed  Full central heating  Open parking available  Last d 21.00hrs  Languages spoken: English*
CARDS: ●● ■ ■ ▣

## AGONGES Allier

**Les Locateries** (Prop: M & Mme Schwartz)
*03210*
☎ 470439363 & 685651101
(take N7 from Nevers to Moulins, turn right at Villeneuve-sur-Allier, through Bagneux to Agonges, follow sign "Chambre d'hôte")

Chantal and Philippe Schwartz welcome you to their 18th-century home. Situated in a medieval village which boasts many châteaux, this property is very close to the medieval Bourbon city of Souvigny. The spa town of Bourbon l'Archambault is just seven minutes away, as is the famous arboretum of Balaine.
Near river  Forest area  Near motorway
*2 en suite (bth/shr)  Full central heating  Open parking available  Child discount available 4yrs  Bicycle rental  Open terrace  V meals  Last d 19.30hrs  Languages spoken: English German Italian & Spanish*
ROOMS: s fr 250FF; d fr 280FF  ✱ **Reductions over 1 night**
MEALS: Dinner fr 75FF

## AIGUEPERSE Puy-de-Dôme

★ ★ ★ **Château de la Roche-Aigueperse**
La Roche-Chaptuzat *63260*
☎ 473636581 FAX 473637679
(A10 S of Paris onto A71 towards Clermont Ferrand. From A71 exit Gannat towards Riom, Clermont Ferrand via N9. On N9 in Aigueperse (10km S of Gannat) turn right to Chaptuzat D7)
Near motorway
*3 en suite (bth/shr)  Full central heating  Open parking available  Covered parking available  Supervised  Child discount available*
*contd.*

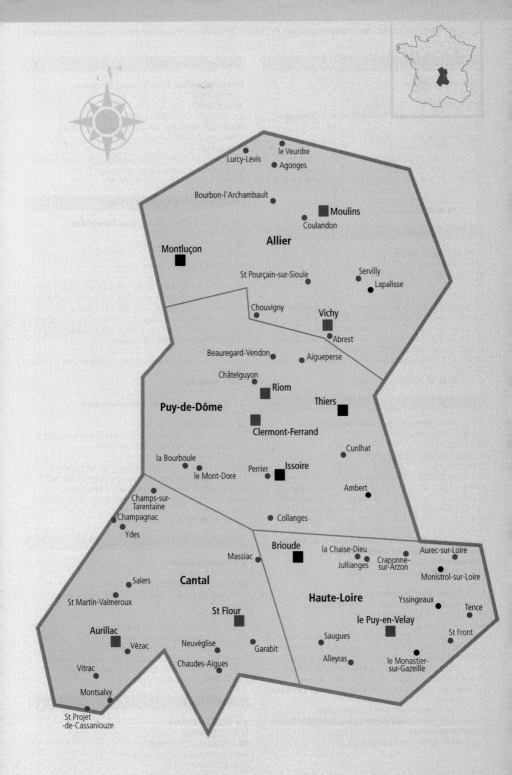

le Veurdre
Lurcy-Levis
Agonges
Bourbon-l'Archambault

Moulins
Coulandon

**Allier**

Montluçon

St Pourçain-sur-Sioule
Servilly
Lapalisse

Chouvigny
**Vichy**
Abrest

Beauregard-Vendon
Aigueperse

Châtelguyon
Riom

**Puy-de-Dôme**
**Thiers**

Clermont-Ferrand

Cunlhat

la Bourboule
Perrier    Issoire
le Mont-Dore

Ambert

Champs-sur-Tarentaine
Champagnac
Collanges

Ydes

Brioude
la Chaise-Dieu
Aurec-sur-Loire

Massiac
Jullianges
Craponne-sur-Arzon

Monistrol-sur-Loire

Salers
**Cantal**
**Haute-Loire**
Yssingeaux

St Martin-Valmeroux
Tence

St Flour
le Puy-en-Velay
St Front

Aurillac
Vézac
Neuvéglise
Garabit
Saugues

Vitrac
Chaudes-Aigues
Alleyras
le Monastier-sur-Gazeille

Montsalvy

St Projet
-de-Cassaniouze

## ALLEYRAS Haute-Loire

**★ ★ Du Haut Allier**
*43580*
☎ 471575763 FAX 471575799
(from Lyon direction on N88 take D33 towards Cayres and Alleyras)
Near river  Near lake  Forest area
*Closed mid Nov-early Mar*
*14 en suite (bth/shr) (7 with balcony)  TV in all bedrooms Direct dial from all bedrooms  Mini-bar in 4 bedrooms Licensed  Lift  Full central heating  Child discount available 7yrs Boule  Bicycle rental  Open terrace  Covered terrace  V meals Last d 21.00hrs  Languages spoken: English & Spanish*
CARDS: ●● ■■ ☲☲ Travellers cheques

## AUREC-SUR-LOIRE Haute-Loire

**★ ★ Les Cèdres Bleus**
23 rue la Rivière *43110*
☎ 477354848 FAX 477353704
(NE towards Bas-en-Basset)
Near river  Near motorway
*15 en suite (bth/shr)  TV in all bedrooms  Direct dial from all bedrooms  Licensed  Full central heating  Open parking available  Supervised  Child discount available 10yrs  Open terrace  V meals  Last d 21.00hrs  Languages spoken: English*
ROOMS: (room only) s 250FF; d 320-340FF
MEALS: Continental breakfast 40FF  Lunch 98-355FF  Dinner 98-355FF
CARDS: ●● ■■ ☲☲ Travellers cheques

## AURILLAC Cantal

**★ ★ ★ Grand Hotel de Bordeaux** (Best Western)
2 av de la République *15000*
☎ 471480184
(A71 exit Massiac Nord/Saint Flour)
In town centre
*33 en suite (bth/shr) (8 fmly)  No smoking in 12 bedrooms  TV in all bedrooms  STV  Direct dial from all bedrooms  Mini-bar in all bedrooms  Licensed  Lift  Night porter  Full central heating  Open parking available (charged)  Covered parking available (charged)  Supervised  Child discount available 12yrs  Bicycle rental  Languages spoken: English & Spanish*
ROOMS: (room only) s 340FF **Reductions over 1 night Special breaks: special weekends for walking,riding,cycling & golf**
CARDS: ●● ■■ ☲☲ ☺ Travellers cheques

**★ ★ ★ Grand Hotel St-Pierre**
16 crs Monthyon, Promenade du Gravier *15000*
☎ 471480024 FAX 471648183
Near river  In town centre
*35 en suite (bth/shr) (4 fmly) (2 with balcony)  No smoking in 2 bedrooms  TV in all bedrooms  Direct dial from all bedrooms  Mini-bar in all bedrooms  Licensed  Lift  Night porter  Full central heating  Open parking available (charged)  Covered parking available (charged)  Supervised  Child discount available 10yrs  Golf  Covered terrace  V meals  Last d 21.30hrs  Languages spoken: English & Spanish*
ROOMS: (room only) s 300-480FF; d 360-680FF
MEALS: Continental breakfast 42FF  Lunch 88-280FF&alc Dinner 88-280FF&alc
CARDS: ●● ■■ ☲☲ ☺ Travellers cheques

## BEAUREGARD-VENDON Puy-de-Dôme

**Bed & Breakfast** (Prop: Elizabeth Beaujeard)
Chaptes *63460*
☎ 473633562
(by motorway A71, exit Riom then take N144 towards Montluçon. .5kms after Davayat turn right onto D122)
Forest area  Near motorway
*RS Nov-Mar*
*3 en suite (shr)  No smoking on premises  Full central heating Open parking available  Languages spoken: English*
ROOMS: s 250-270FF; d 300-350FF ✱

## BOURBON-L'ARCHAMBAULT Allier

**★ ★ ★ Grand Hotel Montespan-Talleyrand**
1-3 pl des Thermes *03160*
☎ 470670024 FAX 470671200
(Near the Parc Thermes)
Near lake  Forest area  Near motorway
*Closed 26 Oct-3 Apr*
*59 rms (2 fmly) (10 with balcony)  TV in all bedrooms  Direct dial from all bedrooms  Licensed  Lift  Full central heating Covered parking available  Child discount available 10yrs Outdoor swimming pool (heated)  Solarium  Gym  Jacuzzi/spa Bicycle rental  Open terrace  V meals  Last d 20.30hrs Languages spoken: English & German*
ROOMS: d 300-800FF
MEALS: Continental breakfast 35FF  Lunch 95-190FF  Dinner 95-190FF
CARDS: ●● ■■ ☲☲

**★ ★ Hotel du Parc et de L'Etablissement**
*03160*
☎ 470670255 FAX 470671395
(next to health spa & leisure centre, hotel is well signposted)
Forest area  In town centre  Near motorway
*Closed Nov-4 Apr*
*52 rms (44 bth/shr)  14 rooms in annexe (6 fmly) (24 with balcony)  Direct dial from all bedrooms  Licensed  Lift  Full central heating  Open parking available  Child discount available 10yrs  Boule  Jacuzzi/spa  Bicycle rental  Open terrace Last d 20.30hrs*
CARDS: ●● ■■ ☲☲ ☺ Travellers cheques

## BOURBOULE, LA Puy-de-Dôme

**★ ★ Aviation Hotel**
rue de Metz *63150*
☎ 473813232 FAX 473810285
Near river  Near lake  Forest area  In town centre  Near motorway
*Closed Oct-19 Dec*
*50 rms  8 rooms in annexe (14 fmly) (11 with balcony)  TV in 43 bedrooms  Direct dial from all bedrooms  Licensed  Lift  Full central heating  Covered parking available  Child discount available 8yrs  Indoor swimming pool (heated)  Pool table  Open terrace  Last d 20.45hrs*
CARDS: ●● ☲☲ Travellers cheques

## CHAISE-DIEU, LA Haute-Loire

**★ ★ Echo et Abbaye**
pl de l'Echo *43160*
☎ 471000045 FAX 471000022
Near lake  Forest area  In town centre
*Closed 12 Nov-Etr*

*19 rms (6 bth 5 shr) TV in all bedrooms Direct dial from 11 bedrooms Licensed Full central heating Open parking available Child discount available 10yrs Fishing Riding Boule Open terrace V meals Last d 21.15hrs Languages spoken: English & Spanish*
CARDS: ●● ■■ ⅢⅢ Travellers cheques

## CHAMPAGNAC Cantal

### ★ ★ ★ Château de Lavendes
rte de Neuvic *15350*
☎ 471696279 FAX 471696533
(Access via D15 from Bort-les-Orgues)
Built on the site of an ancient manor house, this 18th-century residence occupies a secluded location surrounded by three hectares of private grounds. Converted into a hotel-restaurant in 1986, it now features an inviting foyer with an imposing fireplace where visitors can enjoy afternoon tea. There are two dining rooms, individually furnished with period pieces, which serve a delicious range of house specialities.
Near river Near lake Forest area

*Mar-Sep*
*8 en suite (bth/shr) (1 fmly) TV in all bedrooms Direct dial from all bedrooms Licensed Full central heating Open parking available Outdoor swimming pool (heated) Open terrace Last d 21.00hrs Languages spoken: English*
ROOMS: (room only) d 460-625FF **Reductions over 1 night**
MEALS: Full breakfast 55FF Lunch 130-195FF&alc Dinner 130-195FF&alc
CARDS: ●● ■■ ⅢⅢ Travellers cheques

## CHAMPS-SUR-TARENTAINE Cantal

### ★ ★ *Auberge du Vieux Chêne*
34 rte des Lacs *15270*
☎ 471787164 FAX 471787088
Near river Forest area
*Closed Nov-Mar*
*15 en suite (bth/shr) TV in 5 bedrooms Direct dial from all bedrooms Licensed Full central heating Open parking available Fishing Riding Boule Open terrace V meals Last d 21.00hrs Languages spoken: English*
CARDS: ●● ⅢⅢ 🔘 Travellers cheques

## CHÂTELGUYON Puy-de-Dôme

### ★ ★ Régence
31 av des Étas-Unis *63140*
☎ 473860260 FAX 473861249
(from A70/A71 take exit 'Riom Nord' for Châtelguyon, then follow Thermal drive for 200mtrs)

**Regence Hotel**
This turn-of-the century building is situated in Châtel-Guyon, a well-known spa town in the Auvergne region. Fully renovated, it features spacious day rooms adorned with period furniture and assorted antiques, which create the atmosphere of bygone times. All the bedrooms are equipped with modern amenities and offer comfortable accommodation. Guests can enjoy the sunshine in the garden or on the terrace, before sampling the fine cuisine, carefully prepared by the chef-proprietor.
Near river Forest area In town centre Near motorway
*Closed 21 Oct-14 Apr*
*27 en suite (bth/shr) (3 fmly) (10 with balcony) TV in 12 bedrooms Direct dial from all bedrooms Licensed Lift Full central heating Open parking available Supervised Child discount available 8yrs Open terrace Covered terrace Last d 21.00hrs Languages spoken: English & Spanish*
ROOMS: (room only) s 200FF; d 235FF
MEALS: Continental breakfast 40FF Lunch 90-125FF Dinner 80-110FF✱
CARDS: ●● ⅢⅢ Travellers cheques

## CHAUDES-AIGUES Cantal

### ★ ★ Beauséjour
9 av Président Pompidou *15110*
☎ 471235237 FAX 471235689
(access from St-Flour via D921)
Near river Near lake Forest area
*Closed Dec-Mar*
*40 rms (39 bth/shr) (5 fmly) (3 with balcony) TV in all bedrooms Direct dial from all bedrooms Licensed Lift Full central heating Open parking available Covered parking available (charged) Child discount available Outdoor swimming pool (heated) Open terrace V meals Last d 21.00hrs Languages spoken: English & Spanish*
MEALS: Continental breakfast 38FF Lunch 73-165FF Dinner 73-165FF✱
CARDS: ●● ⅢⅢ Travellers cheques

### ★ ★ Thermal du Ban
*15110*
☎ 471235106 FAX 471235846
Located at the southern end of the village this hotel offers guest rooms with modern facilities and a choice of thermal treatments and fitness facilities. There are no restaurant facilities, but guests may like to seek out the various eating establishments nearby.
In town centre
*Closed Oct-Apr*
*46 rms (46 with balcony) TV in all bedrooms Direct dial from all bedrooms Lift Night porter Full central heating Open parking available Supervised Solarium Jacuzzi/spa Languages spoken: English* contd.

***Thermal du Ban***
ROOMS: s 203-213FF; d 231-276FF
**Reductions over 1 night Special breaks**
CARDS: ● ▆ Travellers cheques

### CHOUVIGNY Allier

**★ ★ Des Gorges de Chouvigny**
*03450*
☎ 470904211
Near river Forest area Near motorway
*Closed Nov-Mar*
*8 en suite (shr) (2 fmly) Direct dial from all bedrooms Full central heating Open parking available Child discount available 12yrs Open terrace Covered terrace Canoeing,fishing & horseriding nearby Last d 21.00hrs Languages spoken: English*
CARDS: ● ▆

### CLERMONT-FERRAND Puy-de-Dôme

**★ ★ ★ Hotel Frantour Arverne**
16 pl Delille *63000*
☎ 473919206 FAX 473916025
In town centre Near motorway
*57 en suite (bth/shr) (8 fmly) (21 with balcony) TV in all bedrooms STV Radio in rooms Direct dial from all bedrooms Licensed Lift Night porter Full central heating Air conditioning in bedrooms Open parking available (charged) Covered parking available (charged) Supervised Pool table Open terrace Covered terrace V meals Last d 22.30hrs Languages spoken: English & German*
CARDS: ● ■ ▆ ⑩ Travellers cheques

**★ ★ ★ Novotel**
32-34 rue G-Besse-ZI, Le Brezet Est *63100*
☎ 473411414 FAX 473411400
(from Paris/Orléans/Bourges: direction A75 Montpellier, exit 16 Brezet Alnat. From city center: direction Aulnat Airport-1km)
Novotel offer their clients comfortable accommodation in modern, well equipped bedrooms and have refined restaurants serving good quality cuisine They have excellent business meeting and conference facilities and some have food and beverages available 24 hours a day. All their hotels have at least one bedroom for disabled guests.
Near lake Near motorway
*96 en suite (bth/shr) (56 fmly) No smoking in 32 bedrooms TV in all bedrooms STV Radio in rooms Direct dial from all bedrooms Mini-bar in all bedrooms Licensed Lift Night porter Full central heating Air conditioning in bedrooms Open parking available Child discount available 16yrs Outdoor swimming pool (heated) Open terrace Covered terrace Last d 24.00hrs Languages spoken: English, German, Italian & Spanish*

***Novotel***
ROOMS: (room only) s 540-590FF; d 590FF
MEALS: Continental breakfast 28FF Lunch 100-140FF&alc Dinner 100-140FF&alc
CARDS: ● ■ ▆ ⑩ Travellers cheques

### COLLANGES Puy-de-Dôme

**Château de Collanges** (Prop: M & Mme Huillet)
*63340*
☎ 473964730 FAX 473965872
(exit 17 from A75 to St-Germain-Lembron and on to Collanges)
A 15th century château in a wooded park. Evening meals by reservation. Games area, French billiards and boules on site.
Forest area Near motorway
*6 en suite (bth/shr) (1 fmly) Full central heating Open parking available Child discount available 3yrs Boule French billiards Last d 20.30hrs Languages spoken: English*
ROOMS: s 380-450FF; d 380-600FF
MEALS: Dinner 200FF
CARDS: Travellers cheques

### COULANDON Allier

**★ ★ ★ Le Chalet**
*03000*
☎ 470445008 FAX 470440709
(on D945)
Near river Near lake Forest area
*Closed mid Dec-end Jan*
*28 en suite (bth/shr) Some rooms in annexe (8 fmly) (3 with balcony) TV in all bedrooms STV Licensed Full central heating Open parking available Supervised Child discount available 10yrs Outdoor swimming pool (heated) Fishing Boule Open terrace Last d 21.30hrs Languages spoken: English & German*
CARDS: ● ■ ▆ ⑩ Travellers cheques

### CRAPONNE-SUR-ARZON Haute-Loire

**★ ★ ★ Mistou**
Pontempeyrat *43500*
☎ 477506246 FAX 477506670
Near river Forest area
*Closed Nov-Etr*
*14 en suite (bth/shr) (2 fmly) (4 with balcony) No smoking in 1 bedroom TV in all bedrooms STV Direct dial from all bedrooms Mini-bar in 13 bedrooms Full central heating Open parking available Outdoor swimming pool (heated) Sauna Solarium Bicycle rental Open terrace Covered terrace Last d 21.00hrs Languages spoken: English*

ROOMS: (room only) d 480-660FF
**Reductions over 1 night**
MEALS: Full breakfast 55FF Dinner 175-315FF
CARDS: 💳 ■ 🔲 JCB Travellers cheques

### CUNLHAT Puy-de-Dôme

**Bed & Breakfast** (Prop: Mme B Laroye)
7 rue du 8 Mai *63590*
☎ 473722087
(A72 exit at Thiers & take D906 towards Ambert. After
Courpière right to Cunlhat, D225. At church establishment is
signposted)
Near lake Near beach Forest area
*9 rms (7 bth/shr) (1 fmly) (2 with balcony) TV available Full
central heating Open parking available Supervised Child
discount available 3yrs Languages spoken: English*
ROOMS: s fr 230FF; d 280-330FF
✱ **Reductions over 1 night**
MEALS: Dinner 100FF
CARDS: Travellers cheques

### GARABIT Cantal

★ ★ **Garabit-Hotel**
*15320*
☎ 471234275 FAX 471234960
(from A75 exit 30/31 through Le Viaduct de Garabit to hotel)
Near river Near lake Forest area Near motorway
RS Nov-Mar
*47 en suite (bth/shr) (8 fmly) (16 with balcony) TV in all
bedrooms Direct dial from all bedrooms Mini-bar in all
bedrooms Licensed Lift Full central heating Open parking
available Covered parking available Child discount available
12yrs Indoor swimming pool (heated) Fishing Boule Open
terrace Covered terrace V meals Last d 21.30hrs Languages
spoken: English, Dutch, German & Spanish*
CARDS: 💳 🔲

### JULLIANGES Haute-Loire

**Domaine de la Valette** (Prop: Michele Mejean)
*43500*
☎ 471032335 FAX 471032335
This charming 18th century manor house is beautifully
decorated with antique furniture and surrounded by garden.
At the crossroads of the forests of Auvergne and Velay. A
kitchen is available for guests', or a local grocer is happy to
deliver meals.
Near river Near lake Forest area Near motorway
*5 en suite (bth/shr) (2 fmly) (1 with balcony) No smoking on
premises TV in 4 bedrooms Radio in rooms Full central
heating Open parking available Covered parking available
Supervised Child discount available 5yrs Table tennis Croquet
Languages spoken: English, Italain & Spanish*
ROOMS: s 350FF; d 400-550FF **Reductions over 1 night**

### LURCY-LÉVIS Allier

**Domaine le Plaix** (Prop: Claire Rauaz)
Pouzy Mesangy *03320*
☎ 470662406 FAX 470662582
(35km S of Nevers, take N7 for Moulins, exit at St-Pierre-le-
Moutier. SW on D978a to Le Veurdre, left 1.5km on D13, right
on D234, house signposted 3km on left)
Hidden between gentle hills and fields in the peace and
tranquillity of the countryside, this 16th-century building is a

place to get back to nature. Fishing on site, River Bieudre
borders the property. Bike rides, walks and pony rides all
nearby.
Near river Forest area
*5 en suite (bth/shr) (3 fmly) No smoking in all bedrooms TV
available Full central heating Open parking available Covered
parking available Supervised Child discount available 10yrs
Fishing Boule Open terrace Last d noon Languages spoken:
English*
ROOMS: s 200FF; d 220-250FF **Reductions over 1 night**
MEALS: Dinner 100FF
CARDS: Travellers cheques

### MASSIAC Cantal

★ ★ **Grand Hotel de la Poste**
26 av Général-de-Gaulle *15500*
☎ 471230201 FAX 471230923
(A75 to Clermont-Ferrand Paris exit23 or A75 to Montpellier
exit 24)
Near motorway
*32 en suite (bth/shr) (2 fmly) TV in all bedrooms Direct dial
from all bedrooms Licensed Lift Full central heating Open
parking available Supervised Child discount available 10yrs
Indoor swimming pool (heated) Outdoor swimming pool
(heated) Squash Pool table Mini-golf Jacuzzi/spa Open
terrace Covered terrace V meals Last d 21.00hrs Languages
spoken: English*
MEALS: Continental breakfast 36FF Lunch 80-200FF&alc
Dinner 80-200FF&alc
CARDS: 💳 ■ 🔲 🔘 Travellers cheques

### MONT-DORE, LE Puy-de-Dôme

★ ★ ★ **Panorama**
av de la Libération *63240*
☎ 473651112 FAX 473652080
Near river Near lake Forest area
Closed 14 Oct-24 Dec & 21 Mar-14 May
*39 en suite (bth/shr) (2 fmly) TV in all bedrooms Direct dial
from all bedrooms Licensed Lift Full central heating Open
parking available Child discount available 12yrs Indoor
swimming pool (heated) Sauna Pool table Open terrace
Covered terrace Languages spoken: English & German*
CARDS: 💳 🔲 Travellers cheques

### MONTSALVY Cantal

★ ★ **Inter Hotel du Nord**
pl du Barry *15120*
☎ 471492003 FAX 471492900
Forest area
Closed Jan-Mar
*20 en suite (bth/shr) TV in all bedrooms STV Direct dial from
all bedrooms Mini-bar in all bedrooms Licensed Full central
heating Open parking available Child discount available 12yrs
Boule Covered terrace V meals Last d 21.30hrs Languages
spoken: English*
CARDS: 💳 ■ 🔲 🔘 JCB Travellers cheques

### MOULINS Allier

★ ★ **Le Parc**
31 av Général Leclerc *03000*
☎ 470441225 FAX 470467935
(signposted from railway station)
In town centre
*contd.*

*Closed 10-25 Jul, 2-10 Oct & 22 Dec-3 Jan RS Restaurant closed Sat*
28 en suite (bth/shr) Some rooms in annexe (8 fmly) (5 with balcony) TV in all bedrooms Direct dial from all bedrooms Licensed Night porter Full central heating Open parking available Supervised Open terrace Last d 21.15hrs Languages spoken: English & German
ROOMS: (room only) d 210-350FF
MEALS: Full breakfast 38FF Lunch 98-220FF&alc Dinner 98-220FF&alc
CARDS: ●● ☲☲ Travellers cheques

### ★ ★ ★ Hotel de Paris-Jacquemart
21 rue de Paris *03000*
☎ 470440058 FAX 470340539
In town centre  Near motorway
*Closed 2-12 Feb & 2-18 Aug*
27 en suite (bth/shr) (4 fmly) TV in all bedrooms STV Direct dial from all bedrooms Mini-bar in all bedrooms Licensed Lift Night porter Full central heating Open parking available Supervised Outdoor swimming pool (heated) Open terrace Last d 21.30hrs Languages spoken: English, German & Spanish
CARDS: ●● ■■ ☲☲ ⑩

### NEUVÉGLISE Cantal

### ★ ★ Auberge du Pont de Lanau
Lanau *15260*
☎ 471235776 FAX 471235384
Near river  Near lake  Forest area  Near motorway
*Closed Jan & Feb*
8 en suite (bth/shr) Some rooms in annexe TV in all bedrooms Licensed Full central heating Open parking available Covered parking available (charged) Supervised Last d 21.30hrs Languages spoken: English
ROOMS: d 270-360FF
MEALS: Full breakfast 37FF Lunch 125-280FF Dinner 125-280FF
CARDS: ●● ■■ ☲☲

### PERRIER Puy-de-Dôme

### Chemin de Siorac (Prop: M Paul Gebrillat)
*63500*
☎ 473891502 FAX 473550885
(A75 take exit 11 or 14 (Issoire Centre) towards Champeix)
Near river  Forest area  Near motorway
2 en suite (bth) (1 fmly) Full central heating Open parking available Supervised Child discount available Open terrace Languages spoken: English

### PUY-EN-VELAY, LE Haute-Loire

### ★ ★ Bristol
7 av Foch *43000*
☎ 471091338 FAX 471095170
In town centre
*Closed 26 Oct-1 Nov*
40 en suite (bth/shr) 20 rooms in annexe (2 fmly) TV in all bedrooms Direct dial from all bedrooms Licensed Lift Night porter Full central heating Open parking available (charged) Covered parking available (charged) Supervised Open terrace Last d 21.30hrs Languages spoken: English & German
CARDS: ●● ■■ ☲☲ ⑩ Travellers cheques

### RIOM Puy-de-Dôme

### ★ ★ Anemotel
Les Portes de Riom *63200*
☎ 473337100 FAX 473640060
Near river  Near lake  Forest area  Near motorway
43 en suite (bth/shr) (7 fmly) TV in all bedrooms STV Direct dial from all bedrooms Licensed Lift Night porter Full central heating Air conditioning in bedrooms Open parking available Supervised Child discount available 9yrs Boule Open terrace V meals Last d 22.00hrs Languages spoken: English
CARDS: ●● ■■ ☲☲ Travellers cheques

### ST-FLOUR Cantal

### ★ ★ Des Messageries
23 av Charles-de-Gaulle *15100*
☎ 471601136 FAX 471604679
Near river  In town centre  Near motorway
*Closed Oct-Mar*
18 en suite (bth/shr) (3 fmly) (6 with balcony) TV in all bedrooms STV Direct dial from all bedrooms Mini-bar in all bedrooms Licensed Full central heating Open parking available Covered parking available (charged) Child discount available 12yrs Outdoor swimming pool (heated) Sauna Pool table Boule Open terrace Last d 21.30hrs Languages spoken: English
ROOMS: (room only) d 200-600FF
**Reductions over 1 night**
MEALS: Continental breakfast 50FF Lunch 80-99FF&alc Dinner 80-99FF&alc
CARDS: ●● ☲☲ ⑩ Travellers cheques

### ★ ★ St-Jacques
8 pl de la Liberté *15100*
☎ 471600920 FAX 471603381
Near river  Near lake  Forest area  In town centre  Near motorway
28 en suite (bth/shr) (5 fmly) TV in all bedrooms STV Direct dial from 280 bedrooms Licensed Lift Full central heating Open parking available Covered parking available (charged) Outdoor swimming pool (heated) Bicycle rental Open terrace V meals Last d 21.00hrs Languages spoken: English
CARDS: ●● ☲☲ ⑩

### ST-FRONT Haute-Loire

### Les Bastides du Mézenc (Prop: Paul Coffy)
*43550*
☎ 471595157 FAX 471595157
(At Le Puy take direction of Valence (D15). In Les Pandraux take D29 then D36 & D500 towards Fay, follow signs)
Near river  Near lake  Forest area
6 en suite (shr) (2 fmly) (1 with balcony) Full central heating Open parking available No children 8yrs Child discount available 12yrs

### ST-MARTIN-VALMEROUX Cantal

### ★ ★ ★ Hostellerie de la Maronne
Le Theil *15140*
☎ 471692033 FAX 471682822
(D922 Aurillac-Mauriac, at St-Martin-Valmeroux take D37 in direction of Fontanges for 3.5km)
Near river  Forest area
*Apr-4 Nov*

21 en suite (bth) (7 fmly) (9 with balcony) TV in 17 bedrooms
STV Direct dial from all bedrooms Mini-bar in all bedrooms
Licensed Lift Full central heating Open parking available
Supervised Child discount available 12yrs Outdoor swimming
pool (heated) Tennis Riding Boule Bicycle rental Open terrace
V meals Last d 21.30hrs Languages spoken: English
CARDS: ●● ■■ ▆▆ ◑ Travellers cheques

### ST-POURÇAIN-SUR-SIOUL Allier

★★ Le Chêne Vert
35 bd Ledru-Rollin 03500
☎ 470454065 FAX 470456850
(From A71 take exit Montmarault)
Near river In town centre Near motorway
31 rms (20 bth 8 shr) 14 rooms in annexe (1 fmly) TV in all
bedrooms Direct dial from all bedrooms Licensed Full central
heating Open parking available (charged) Supervised Child
terrace Last d 21.00hrs Languages spoken: English & Spanish
ROOMS: (room only) s 230-280FF; d 280-340FF
MEALS: Full breakfast 45FF Lunch 95-220FF&alc Dinner
95-220FF&alc
CARDS: ●● ■■ ▆▆ ◑ Travellers cheques

### ST-PROJECT-DE-CASSANIOUZE Cantal

★ Du Pont
15340
☎ 471499421 FAX 471499610
Near river Forest area
Closed Dec-12 Mar
12 rms (1 bth 7 shr) (1 fmly) (1 with balcony) TV in 1 bedroom
Direct dial from all bedrooms Mini-bar in 1 bedroom Licensed
Full central heating Open parking available Supervised Child
discount available 12yrs Boule Bicycle rental Open terrace
Childrens games V meals Last d 21.30hrs Languages spoken:
English & Spanish
CARDS: ●● ▆▆ Travellers cheques

### SALERS Cantal

★★ Bailliage
15140
☎ 471407195 FAX 471407490
Near river Forest area
Closed 15 Nov-1 Feb
30 rms 4 rooms in annexe (4 fmly) (4 with balcony) TV in all
bedrooms Licensed Full central heating Open parking
available Covered parking available (charged) Child discount
available 10yrs Outdoor swimming pool (heated) Boule Open
terrace Last d 21.00hrs Languages spoken: English
ROOMS: (room only) d 250-380FF
Reductions over 1 night
MEALS: Full breakfast 39FF Lunch 75-170FF&alc Dinner
75-170FF
CARDS: ●● ■■ ▆▆ ◑ Travellers cheques

★★★ Le Gerfaut
rte du Puy-Mary 15140
☎ 471407575 FAX 471407345
(A75 exit Massiac towards Murat then Puy Mary, then Salers)
Near river
Closed 31 Oct-Etr
25 en suite (bth/shr) 3 rooms in annexe (3 fmly) (10 with
balcony) TV in all bedrooms Direct dial from all bedrooms
Licensed Lift Full central heating Open parking available
Child discount available 10yrs Outdoor swimming pool (heated)

Boule Open terrace Table tennis Childs play area Last d
20.30hrs Languages spoken: English & Spanish
ROOMS: (room only) s 220-390FF; d 310-430FF
MEALS: Lunch 69-170FF&alc Dinner 69-170FF&alc
CARDS: ●● ■■ ▆▆ ◑ Travellers cheques

★★ Remparts
Esplanade de Barrouzé 15140
☎ 471407033 FAX 471407532
Near river Forest area In town centre
18 rms (16 shr) 6 rooms in annexe (8 fmly) (11 with balcony)
TV in all bedrooms Direct dial from all bedrooms Licensed
Full central heating Open parking available Child discount
available 12yrs Open terrace Last d 20.45hrs Languages
spoken: English
ROOMS: (room only) s 220-265FF; d 260-295FF
Reductions over 1 night
MEALS: Continental breakfast 37FF Lunch 68-165FF&alc
Dinner 68-165FF&alc
CARDS: ●● ▆▆ Travellers cheques

### SAUGUES Haute-Loire

Le Rouve
43170
☎ 471776415 FAX 471778384
(4km W of Saugues on the D589 in direction of Malzieu)
Forest area
3 rms
ROOMS: d 220FF ✷
MEALS: Dinner 70FF✷

### SERVILLY Allier

Les Vieux Chênes (Prop: M & Mme Cotton)
03120
☎ 470990753 FAX 470993471
Near river Forest area Near motorway
6 en suite (bth/shr) (1 fmly) No smoking on premises Full
central heating Child discount available 10yrs Languages
spoken: English

### TENCE Haute-Loire

★★★ Hostellerie Placide
rte d'Annonay 43190
☎ 471598276 FAX 471654446
Near river Near lake Forest area
Closed mid Nov-mid Mar
17 en suite (bth/shr) (6 fmly) (1 with balcony) TV in all
bedrooms Direct dial from all bedrooms Licensed Full central
heating Open parking available Child discount available 12yrs
Boule Bicycle rental Open terrace V meals Last d 21.30hrs
Languages spoken: English & Spanish
ROOMS: (room only) s fr 320FF; d 430-450FF
MEALS: Continental breakfast 55FF Lunch fr 85FF&alc
Dinner 160-300FF&alc
CARDS: ●● ■■ ▆▆ ◑ Travellers cheques

### VEURDRE, LE Allier

★★ Pont Neuf
rte de Lurcy Levis 03320
☎ 470664012 FAX 470664415
(from Nevers take N7 to St Pierre-le-Moutier, then take D978 to
le Veurdre. From Moulins take N7 to Chantenay St Imbert,
then D22) contd.

**Pont Neuf**

The hotel offers a large garden and pleasant public areas where guests can relax or read. The restaurant serves excellent cuisine, incorporating dishes with a regional touch and using local produce. Guests enjoy a special blend of hospitality, provided by attentive staff which offer personal attention and service at all times.

Near river Near lake Near sea Forest area Near motorway
*Closed late Oct & 15 Dec-15 Jan RS Sun eve late Oct-Etr - rest closed*
*36 en suite (bth/shr) 11 rooms in annexe (4 fmly) No smoking in 4 bedrooms TV in all bedrooms STV Direct dial from all bedrooms Licensed Full central heating Open parking available Covered parking available (charged) Supervised Child discount available 12yrs Outdoor swimming pool Tennis Fishing Sauna Gym Boule Bicycle rental Open terrace V meals Last d 21.30hrs Languages spoken: English & Spanish*
ROOMS: (room only) s 235-450FF; d 245-450FF
MEALS: Full breakfast 42FF Continental breakfast 42FF Lunch 90-235FF Dinner 90-235FF
CARDS: ●● ■■ ☲ �ⓓ JCB Travellers cheques

### VÉZAC Cantal

**Château de Salles Hostellerie**
Château de Salles *15130*
☎ 471624141 FAX 471624414
Near river Forest area
*18 en suite (bth/shr) 6 rooms in annexe (6 fmly) TV in all bedrooms STV Licensed Lift Night porter Open parking available Child discount available Outdoor swimming pool Tennis Sauna Gym Pool table Jacuzzi/spa Open terrace Languages spoken: English & German*
CARDS: ●● ■■ ☲

### VICHY Allier

**★ ★ Hotel Arcade**
11-13 Av Pierre Coulon *03200*
☎ 470981848 FAX 470977263
Near river Near lake Near beach In town centre
*48 en suite (shr) TV in all bedrooms Direct dial from all bedrooms Lift Full central heating Open parking available Child discount available 12yrs Indoor swimming pool Sauna Solarium Open terrace Covered terrace Languages spoken: English*
CARDS: ●● ■■ ☲ Travellers cheques

### VITRAC Cantal

**★ ★ La Tomette**
Centre du Bourg *15220*
☎ 471647094 FAX 471647711
(Access via A75 exit Massiac, then N122 through Aurillac and St-Mamet)

Surrounded by hills and 25 kilometres south of Aurillac, the hotel is situated in the charming village of Vitrac, and provides the peaceful setting for a relaxing stay. The bedrooms offer a good level of comfort. Breakfast is served in the garden, and at dinner there is a choice of enjoyable dishes, with an Auvergne touch, served in the restaurant. Nearby there are a range of leisure facilities and guests may like to explore the Cantal mountains nearby.

Forest area
*Closed 16 Dec-1 Apr*
*15 en suite (bth/shr) 15 rooms in annexe (6 fmly) TV in all bedrooms STV Direct dial from all bedrooms Licensed Full central heating Open parking available Supervised Child discount available 12yrs Outdoor swimming pool (heated) Sauna Pool table Boule Bicycle rental Open terrace Covered terrace Last d 20.30hrs Languages spoken: English*
ROOMS: (room only) d 295-340FF
**Reductions over 1 night**
MEALS: Continental breakfast 45FF Lunch 98-200FF&alc Dinner 98-200FF&alc
CARDS: ●● ■■ ☲ Travellers cheques

### YDES Cantal

**★ ★ ★ Château de Trancis**
Trancis *15210*
☎ 471406040 FAX 471406213
(From Bort-les-Orgues take D922 towards Mauriac for 6km then left onto D15 towards Saignes. Hotel 500mtrs on right)
Near river Near lake Near beach Forest area Near motorway
*7 en suite (bth/shr) TV in all bedrooms STV Direct dial from all bedrooms Mini-bar in all bedrooms Licensed Full central heating Open parking available Supervised Outdoor swimming pool Open terrace V meals Last d 22.00hrs Languages spoken: English*
CARDS: ●● ■■ ☲ ⓓ JCB, Carte Bleue Travellers cheques

# Rhône Alpes

Superbly situated to the west of Italy and Switzerland, the Rhône Alpes offers some of the most spectacular scenery in France. Towering, snow-covered peaks, vast glaciers, wooded hillslopes and lush pastures make a natural haven for outdoor leisure activities. To the east lies the Savoie, the largest ski playground in the world, while to the south-west are the Ardèches. Upstream from Lyon, the Dombes stretch eastwards, and to the west the Beaujolais vineyards reach out towards the Monts du Lyonnais. Follow the Rhône Valley and Mont Blanc can be seen soaring majestically above the Alps. In sharp contrast are the lavender fields and olive groves of the Drôme, or the sun-baked hills of the Ardèche.

## ESSENTIAL FACTS

| | |
|---|---|
| DÉPARTEMENTS: | Ain, Ardèche, Drôme, Isère, Loire, Rhône, Haute-Savoie, Savoie |
| PRINCIPAL TOWNS | Lyon, St Etiénne, Roanne, Bourg-en-Bresse, Villefrance-sur-Saône, Vienne, St-Chamond, Romans-sur-Isère, Valence, Montélimar, Grenoble, Chamonix-Mont Blanc, Annecy, Chambery, Aix-le-Bains |
| PLACES TO VISIT: | Grenoble: cable car up to the Alps; the gorges of the Ardèche, one of 28 nature reserves; Samoens, beautiful alpine gardens; the vineyards of the Côtes du Rhône & the Savoy Wine Route. |
| REGIONAL TOURIST OFFICE | 104, Route de Paris, 69260 Charbonnières-les-Bains. Tel: 72 59 21 59 |
| LOCAL GASTRONOMIC DELIGHTS | Lyon: andouilette, chitterling sausage in mustard sauce, truffled saveloy sausage, pigs' trotters (tablier de sapeur). The Dombes: carp, pike, chicken in cream sauce, game birds, fattened pullets. Loire: Charolais beef. Grenoble: walnut pie. |
| DRINKS | Yellow or green Chartreuse liqueur, once produced by monks. Wines: a vast choice of Beaujolais, Côtes du Rhône & Savoy wines produced in small local vineyards. |
| LOCAL CRAFTS WHAT TO BUY | Lyon: silk, linen & woollen ornaments. Grenoble: watches, leather goods & bookbinding. Meilonas, Ain: stone carvings & earthenware. Dieulefit: pottery & porcelain. |

### AIGUEBELETTE-LE-LAC Savoie

★★ De La Comné
73610
☎ 479360502 FAX 479441193
Near lake  Near sea  Forest area  Near motorway
9 rms (2 bth 3 shr) (4 with balcony)  TV in all bedrooms  STV  Direct dial from all bedrooms  Licensed  Full central heating  Open terrace  V meals  Last d 21.30hrs  Languages spoken: English
CARDS: ●● ▬▬ Travellers cheques

### AIX-LES-BAINS Savoie

★★★ Agora
rue de Chambéry 73100
☎ 479342020 FAX 479342030
(from Geneva on motorway exit Aix-Nord; from Lyon exit Aix-Sud follow directions to town centre)
Near lake  Near beach  Forest area  In town centre  Near motorway
64 en suite (bth/shr) (8 fmly)  TV in all bedrooms  STV  Direct dial from all bedrooms  Mini-bar in all bedrooms  Licensed  Lift  Night porter  Full central heating  Covered parking available (charged)  Supervised  Child discount available 12yrs  Indoor swimming pool (heated)  Sauna  Solarium  Body Building  V meals  Last d 21.30hrs  Languages spoken: English, German & Spanish
CARDS: ●● ■■ ▬▬ ◑ Travellers cheques

★★ Dauphinois et Nyvolet
14 av de Trésserve 73100
☎ 479612256 FAX 479340462
Near lake  Forest area  In town centre  Near motorway
Closed mid Dec-mid Feb
83 rms (48 bth/shr)  75 rooms in annexe  (14 with balcony)  Licensed  Lift  Night porter  Full central heating  Open parking available  Supervised  Child discount available 10yrs  Open terrace  Last d 21.30hrs  Languages spoken: German
CARDS: ●● ■■ ▬▬ ◑ Travellers cheques

★★★ Le Manoir (Relais du Silence)
37 rue Georges ler, BP512 73100
☎ 479614400 FAX 479356767
(from motorway exit Aix-Nord from Geneva, Aix-Sud from Lyon, follow direction Les Thermes Naturoux, 300 meters above Les Thermes)
Near lake  Near beach  Forest area  Near motorway
73 en suite (bth/shr)  10 rooms in annexe  (5 fmly) (30 with balcony)  TV in all bedrooms  STV  Direct dial from all bedrooms  Room-safe  Licensed  Lift  Night porter  Full central heating  Open parking available  Covered parking available (charged)  Supervised  Child discount available 12yrs  Indoor swimming pool (heated)  Sauna  Solarium  Pool table  Jacuzzi/spa  Open terrace  Covered terrace  Body Building, gymnastics room  V meals  Last d 21.30hrs  Languages spoken: English, German, Italian & Spanish
CARDS: ●● ■■ ▬▬ ◑ Travellers cheques

★★★ La Pastorale
221 av Grand Port 73100
☎ 479634060 FAX 479634426
Near lake  Near beach  Forest area  Near motorway

contd.

1 Confrancon
2 Revonnas
3 St Andre-s-Vieux-Jonc
4 Lancie
5 Chiroubles
6 Villie-Morgan
7 Lantignie
8 St Verand
9 Trevignin
10 St Felix
11 Doussard
12 Flumet
13 St Clair-du-Rhone
14 St Hilaire-du-Touvet

15 Lans-en-Vercors
16 Villard-de-Lans
17 St Lattier
18 Chanos-Curson
19 St Marcel-les-Valence
20 St Pierreville
21 St Julien-du-Gua
22 Pourcheres
23 Vals-les-Bains
24 St Julien-du-Serre
25 Montboucher-sur-Jabron
26 Reauville

**Haute-Savoie**
Thonan-les-Bains
Evian-les-Bains
St Paul-en-Chablais
Mijoux
Divonne-les-Bains
Echenevex
Fernay-Voltaire
Habère-Poche
Morzine
Annemasse
St Genis-Pouilly
Bonne
Farges
Ambilly
Samoëns
Bellegarde-sur-Valserine
Châtillon-sur-Cluses
les Carroz-d'Arâches
la Roche-sur-Foron
Avriernoz
le Grand-Bornand
les Praz-de-Chamonix
Col-du-Mont-Sion
Seyssel
Annecy-le-Vieux
**Annecy**
Veyrier-du-Lac
la Clusaz
les Houches
Sevrier
Megève
Chamonix-Mont-Blanc
Talissieu
Alby-sur-Chéran
Talloires
N.D-de-Bellecombe
Crest-Voland
Bellay
Féverges

Pont-de-Vaux
St Benigne
Replonges
Attignat
**Bourg-en-Bresse**
**Nantua**
Juliénas
Vonnas
Châtillon-sur-Chalaronne
Pont-d'Ain
Taponas
St Jean-d'Ardières
St Pierre-la-Noaille
Charlieu
Noailly
Cours-la-Ville
Quincie-en-Beaujolias
Monthieux
**Ain**
**Roanne**
Lentigny
le Coteau
Jarnioux
Villefranche-sur-Saône
les Echets
St Marcel-d'Urfe
Anse
Bagnols
Violay
**Rhône**
Dardilly
**Loire**
Tassin-la-Demi-Lune
Meyzieu
Crimieu
les Halles
**Lyon**
Chazelles-sur-Lyon
Sérézin-du-Rhône
Chasse-sur-Rhône
les Abrets
Andrezieux-Bouthéon
Torchefelon
Bonson
St Chamond
Reventin-Vaugris
Champier
Che025reilles
**St Etienne**
St Prim
Bossieu
Gillonnay
Charavines
Arzay
Chapareillan
Beaurepaire
St Pierre-de-Chartreuse

**Savoie**
Aix-les-Bains
Montailleur
**Chambéry**
Coise
Celliers
Champagny-en-Vanoise
Aiguebelette-le-Lac
Valmorel
Brides-les-Bains
Méribel-les-Allues
Courchevel
St Martin-de-Belleville
les Menuires
Lanslebourg
Allevard-les-Bains
Val-Thorens
Sollières-Sardière
Aussois
St Sorlin-d'Arves

**Vienne**
Ste Foy-Tarentaise
Peisey-Nancroix

Fontanil-Cornillon
Sappey-en-Chartreuse
Marges
**Grenoble**
Meylan
Satillieu
St Donat-sur-l'Herbasse
Autrans
Eybens
Villard-Reculas
Mercurol
Méaudre
Seyssins
Bourg-d'Oisans
**Tournon**
Bouvante
Varces-Allières-et-Risset
Lamastre
Romans-sur-Isere
les Deux-Alpes
Désaignes
St Agnan-en-Vercors
Gresse-en-Vercors
Villard-St-Christophe
**Valence**
la Salle-en-Beaumont
Vernoux-en-Vivarais
Beaumont-les-Valence
**Die**
Clelles
St Georges-les-Bains
Corps
Ste Eulalie
Mirmande
Mens
St Cirgues-en-Montagne
**Privas**
Crest
Lanarce
Thueyts
**Drôme**
Pont-de-Barret
Aubenas
Montélimar
le Poët-Laval
Malataverne
Beaumont
Mirabel
Montbrison-sur-Lez
Grignan
**Nyons**
**Ardèche**
Solerieux
la Baume-de-Transit
Bourg-St-Andéol
Suze-la-Rousse
Buis-les-Baronnies

346

20 Mar-2 Nov
30 en suite (bth/shr) (6 fmly) TV in all bedrooms STV Direct
dial from all bedrooms Licensed Lift Full central heating Open
parking available Child discount available 10yrs Boule Open
terrace Last d 21.30hrs Languages spoken: English, German &
Italian
ROOMS: s 295-330FF; d 350-430FF ✱
MEALS: Continental breakfast 45FF Lunch 100-205FF&alc
Dinner 100-205FF&alc
CARDS: ✹ ▦ ▥ ⑩ Travellers cheques

★★ **Thermal**
2 rue Davat 73100
☎ 479352000 FAX 479881648
Near lake Forest area In town centre Near motorway
80 en suite (bth/shr) (50 fmly) (45 with balcony) TV in all
bedrooms Direct dial from all bedrooms Licensed Lift Night
porter Full central heating Open parking available Covered
parking available (charged) Supervised Child discount
available Open terrace Last d 21.00hrs Languages spoken:
English & German
CARDS: ✹ ▦ ▥ ⑩ Travellers cheques

### ABRETS, LES Isère

**La Bruyère** (Prop: M & Mme Chavalle)
38490
☎ 476320166 FAX 476320666
(from Lyon A43 Chimilin/Les Abrets exit towards Les Abrets
and follow signs)
Near river Near lake Forest area Near motorway
Closed 1st 2 wks Nov
6 en suite (bth) TV available Full central heating Open parking
available Child discount available 12yrs Outdoor swimming
pool Boule Open terrace Last d 20.00hrs Languages spoken:
English
CARDS: ✹ ▥

### ALBY-SUR-CHÉRAN Haute-Savoie

★★ **Alb'Hotel**
Sur N201 74540
☎ 450682493 FAX 450681301
Near river Near lake Forest area Near motorway
37 en suite (bth/shr) (1 fmly) STV Direct dial from all
bedrooms Mini-bar in all bedrooms Licensed Night porter
Full central heating Open parking available Child discount
available 12yrs Outdoor swimming pool Boule Open terrace
Covered terrace Last d 22.00hrs Languages spoken: English
Arabic German & Spanish
CARDS: ✹ ▦ ▥ ⑩ Travellers cheques

### ALLEVARD-LES-BAINS Isère

★★ **Pervenches** (Relais du Silence)
rte de Grenoble 38580
☎ 476975073 FAX 476450952
(equi-distant between Grenoble and Chambery)
Forest area Near motorway
Closed 16 Oct-Jan
25 en suite (bth/shr) 16 rooms in annexe (6 fmly) (1 with
balcony) TV in all bedrooms Direct dial from all bedrooms
Licensed Full central heating Open parking available Child
discount available 10yrs Outdoor swimming pool (heated)
Tennis Pool table Boule V meals Last d 21.00hrs
CARDS: ✹ ▦ ▥ ⑩ Travellers cheques

★★ **Speranza**
rte du Moutaret 38580
☎ 476975056
(A41 Chambery exit Pontchana. A41 Grenoble exit le Touvet)
Near lake Forest area
Closed Oct-mid May
18 rms (11 bth 6 shr) (6 fmly) (5 with balcony) Direct dial from
all bedrooms Licensed Full central heating Open parking
available Supervised Child discount available 12yrs Boule
Open terrace Last d 22.00hrs
CARDS: Travellers cheques

### AMBILLY Haute-Savoie

★★★ **New Hotel Genève**
38 rte de Genève 74100
☎ 450387066 FAX 450387223
Near river Near lake Forest area In town centre Near
motorway
93 en suite (bth) (3 fmly) TV in all bedrooms STV Mini-bar in
all bedrooms Licensed Lift Night porter Full central heating
Air conditioning in bedrooms Open parking available Covered
parking available (charged) Supervised Languages spoken:
English German & Spanish
CARDS: ✹ ▦ ▥ ⑩ Travellers cheques

### ANDRÉZIEUX-BOUTHÉON Loire

★★★ **Les Iris**
32 av Jean Martouret 42160
☎ 477360909 FAX 477360900
Near river Forest area In town centre Near motorway
Closed 1-5 Jan & 11-25 Aug
10 en suite (bth) No smoking in 2 bedrooms TV in all
bedrooms STV Direct dial from all bedrooms Mini-bar in all
bedrooms Licensed Open parking available Outdoor
swimming pool Solarium Boule Bicycle rental Open terrace
Table Tennis Children's playground V meals Last d 21.30hrs
Languages spoken: English German & Spanish
CARDS: ✹ ▦ ▥ JCB Travellers cheques

### ANNECY Haute-Savoie

★★★ **Atria Novotel Annecy Centre**
1 av Berthollet 74000
☎ 450335454 FAX 450455068
(exit Annecy South and follow signs for Annecy centre)
Near lake Near beach In town centre Near motorway
95 en suite (bth/shr) (35 fmly) No smoking in 29 bedrooms TV
in all bedrooms STV Radio in rooms Direct dial from all
bedrooms Mini-bar in all bedrooms Licensed Lift Night porter
Full central heating Air conditioning in bedrooms Open
parking available (charged) Covered parking available
(charged) Supervised Child discount available 16yrs Open
terrace V meals Languages spoken: English,German,Italian &
Spanish
CARDS: ✹ ▦ ▥ ⑩ Travellers cheques

★★★ **Hotel Carlton** (Best Western)
5 rue des Glieres 74000
☎ 450100909 FAX 450100960
Near river Near lake Forest area In town centre Near
motorway
55 en suite (bth/shr) (4 fmly) (23 with balcony) TV in all
bedrooms STV Direct dial from all bedrooms Licensed Lift
Night porter Full central heating Child discount available 12yrs
*contd.*

Open terrace Covered terrace Languages spoken: English
German Italian & Spanish
ROOMS: (room only) s 480-530FF; d 525-605FF
CARDS: ● ■ ■ ⑨ Travellers cheques

### ★★★ Au Faisan Doré
34 av d'Albigny 74000
☎ 450230246 FAX 450231110
(exit Annecy South A41 in the direction Thones then Imperial)
Near lake Near beach Forest area In town centre
Closed 20 Dec-1 Feb
40 en suite (bth/shr) (2 fmly) (2 with balcony) TV in all
bedrooms STV Direct dial from all bedrooms Licensed Lift
Full central heating Open parking available (charged) Open
terrace Last d 20.45hrs Languages spoken: English & German
ROOMS: (room only) s 320-500FF; d 350-550FF
**Reductions over 1 night**
MEALS: Continental breakfast 48FF Lunch 100-180FF&alc
Dinner 100-180FF&alc
CARDS: ● ■ ■ ⑨ JCB Travellers cheques

### ANNECY-LE-VIEUX Haute-Savoie

### ★★★★ Abbaye
15 chemin de l'Abbaye 74940
☎ 450236108 FAX 450277765
Near lake In town centre
18 en suite (bth/shr) (3 fmly) (1 with balcony) No smoking in 4
bedrooms TV in all bedrooms STV Radio in rooms Direct dial
from all bedrooms Mini-bar in all bedrooms Licensed Night
porter Full central heating Open parking available Supervised
Child discount available V meals Last d 23.00hrs Languages
spoken: English & Spanish
CARDS: ● ■ ■ ⑨ Travellers cheques

### ANNEMASSE Haute-Savoie

### ★★ Maison Blanche
41 rte de St-Julien 74100
☎ 450920101 FAX 450376050
(A40 exit14 from Paris signed Annemasse, turn right after
50mtrs and left through a small bridge. From Annemasse
1.5km towards St Julien)
Near river Forest area Near motorway
12 en suite (bth/shr) TV in all bedrooms Direct dial from all
bedrooms Full central heating Child discount available Open
terrace Last d 21.30hrs Languages spoken: English & Italian
CARDS: ● ■ ■ ⑨ Travellers cheques

### ANSE Rhône

### ★★ St-Romain
rte de Graves 69480
☎ 474602446 FAX 474671285
Near river Forest area Near motorway
Closed Dec
24 en suite (bth/shr) (2 fmly) TV in all bedrooms Radio in
rooms Licensed Full central heating Open parking available
Supervised Child discount available Tennis Boule Mini-golf
Bicycle rental Open terrace V meals Last d 21.30hrs
Languages spoken: English & German

### ARZAY Isère

**Bed & Breakfast** (Prop: M & Mme Virenque)
38260
☎ 474542155 FAX 474542474
Forest area

Closed Nov-Mar
3 rms (1 bth 1 shr) (1 fmly) Full central heating Open parking
available Child discount available 12yrs Languages spoken:
English

### ATTIGNAT Ain

### ★★ Dominique Marcepoil
481 Grande Rue 01340
☎ 474309224 FAX 474259348
Near river Near lake Near beach Forest area Near motorway
10 en suite (bth/shr) (3 fmly) TV in all bedrooms Direct dial
from all bedrooms Licensed Air conditioning in bedrooms
Open parking available Supervised No children Child discount
available 12yrs Open terrace Covered terrace V meals
Languages spoken: English
CARDS: ● ■ ■

### AUSSOIS Savoie

### ★★ Le Choucas
15 Le Plan Champ 73500
☎ 479203277 FAX 479203987
(from Chambéry take A43 (direction Albertville) then take N6
to Modane. D215 to Aussois)
Forest area
Closed May & Oct-Nov
28 en suite (bth) (4 fmly) TV in all bedrooms STV Direct dial
from all bedrooms Licensed Full central heating Open parking
available Child discount available 10yrs Solarium Gym Pool
table Open terrace Table tennis V meals Last d 21.00hrs
Languages spoken: English & Italian
ROOMS: (room only) s 200-230FF; d 300-340FF
**Reductions over 1 night**
MEALS: Continental breakfast 40FF Lunch 90-120FF&alc
Dinner 90-120FF&alc
CARDS: ● ■ ⑨ Travellers cheques

### AUTRANS Isère

### ★★ De La Buffe
38880
☎ 476947070 FAX 476957248
Near river Near beach Forest area
23 en suite (bth) (2 fmly) (16 with balcony) TV in all bedrooms
STV Direct dial from all bedrooms Mini-bar in all bedrooms
Licensed Full central heating Open parking available Child
discount available 12yrs Sauna Solarium Pool table
Jacuzzi/spa Bicycle rental Open terrace Covered terrace V
meals Last d 21.00hrs Languages spoken: English
CARDS: ● ■ ■ Travellers cheques

### ★★★ De La Poste
"Le Village" 38880
☎ 476953103 FAX 476953017
Forest area Near motorway
Closed Nov
29 en suite (bth/shr) (1 with balcony) TV in all bedrooms STV
Direct dial from all bedrooms Licensed Lift Full central
heating Child discount available 8yrs Indoor swimming pool
(heated) Sauna Solarium Gym Pool table Jacuzzi/spa Open
terrace Table tennis V meals Last d 21.00hrs Languages
spoken: English Italian & Spanish
CARDS: ● ■ Travellers cheques

## AVIERNOZ Haute-Savoie

**★★ Auberge Camelia**
*74570*
☎ 450224424 FAX 450224325
(from Annecy take N203 towards Chamonix take D175 towards
Villaz, then left onto D5 to Aviernoz. Hotel on left)
Near river Near lake Near beach Forest area Near
motorway
*12 en suite (bth/shr) (3 fmly) (3 with balcony) TV in all
bedrooms Direct dial from all bedrooms Licensed Full central
heating Open parking available Supervised Child discount
available 12yrs Open terrace V meals Last d 20.30hrs
Languages spoken: English*
CARDS: 💳 💳 Travellers cheques

## BAGNOLS Rhône

**★★★★ Château de Bagnols**
Le Bourg *69620*
☎ 474714000 FAX 474714049
(A6 in direction of Lyon exit Villefranche-sur-Saône and then
take D38)
Forest area
*20 en suite (bth) TV in all bedrooms STV Direct dial from all
bedrooms Room-safe Licensed Lift Night porter Full central
heating Open parking available Covered parking available
Child discount available 10yrs Outdoor swimming pool Bicycle
rental Open terrace Last d 21.00hrs Languages spoken:
English German Italian & Spanish*
CARDS: 💳 💳 💳 💳 Travellers cheques

## BAUME-DE-TRANSIT, LA Drôme

**Domaine de Saint-Luc** (Prop: L & E Cornillon)
*26970*
☎ 475981151 FAX 475981922
(from A7 exit at Bollène & take D994 towards Nyons. At Suze-
la-Rousse Take D59 then D117 to la Baume-de-Transit)
Near river Forest area
*6 rms (5 bth/shr) (1 fmly) (1 with balcony) Full central heating
Open parking available Outdoor swimming pool Bicycle rental
V meals Last d 8pm Languages spoken: English*
CARDS: Travellers cheques

## BEAUMONT Ardèche

**★★ Le Sentier des Arches** (Prop: Pascal Romanet)
Le Gua, rte de Valgorge *07110*
☎ 475394409
(From A7 take exit Loriol/Montelimar, then go to Aubenas. In
Aubenas take the road to Alès, then in Joyeuse take the road to
Valgorge. In Le Gua follow signs to Hotel)
Near river Forest area
*Closed Nov-Mar*
*12 en suite (bth) (3 fmly) (12 with balcony) Full central heating
Open parking available Child discount available 10yrs Bicycle
rental Last d 20.30hrs Languages spoken: English*

## BEAUMONT-LÈS-VALENCE Drôme

**Bed & Breakfast** (Prop: L de Chivré-Dumond)
Chambedeau *26760*
☎ 475597170 FAX 475597524
(from A7 exit at Valence Sud onto A49 towards Grenoble. Exit
at no 33 towards Beaumont, right onto D538A. Approx 2.6kms
after roundabout follow sign on right)

**Bed & Breakfast**
Situated in a former shepherd's hut built in the 19th-century
from the distinctive local round stones. There is a sitting room
with indoor games, and a large breakfast is served. Your
hostess has an extremely good knowledge of the region.
Near river Forest area Near motorway
*3 en suite (shr) (1 with balcony) No smoking in all bedrooms
Open parking available Child discount available 5yrs
Languages spoken: English*
ROOMS: s 185-235FF; d 255-275FF **Reductions over 1
night Special breaks: weekends or 2/3 days**
CARDS: Travellers cheques

## BEAUREPAIRE Isère

**★★ Fiard-Zorelle**
av des Terreaux *38270*
☎ 474846202 FAX 474847113
Near river Forest area In town centre Near motorway
*Closed 15 Jan-15 Feb*
*15 en suite (bth/shr) (4 fmly) TV in all bedrooms Direct dial
from all bedrooms Licensed Full central heating Covered
parking available (charged) Supervised Child discount
available 10yrs V meals Last d 21.00hrs Languages spoken:
English German & Spanish*
CARDS: 💳 💳 💳 💳 Travellers cheques

## BELLEGARDE-SUR-VALSERINE Ain

**★★★ Belle Époque**
10 pl Gambetta *01200*
☎ 450481446 FAX 450560171
(Approach via A40 exit 10 or 11)
Near river Forest area In town centre Near motorway
*Closed 2-18 Jul & 17 Dec-9 Jan*
*20 en suite (bth/shr) TV in all bedrooms Direct dial from all
bedrooms Licensed Full central heating Air conditioning in
bedrooms Open parking available Covered parking available
(charged) Supervised Child discount available V meals Last d
21.00hrs Languages spoken: English & German*
ROOMS: (room only) s 300-350FF; d 350-400FF
MEALS: Full breakfast 50FF Lunch 130-270FF
Dinner 130-270FF
CARDS: 💳 💳 Travellers cheques

## BONNE Haute-Savoie

**★★ Baud**
*74380*
☎ 450392015 FAX 450362896
Near river Near lake Forest area Near motorway
*8 rms (7 bth/shr) (1 fmly) (1 with balcony) TV in all bedrooms
Licensed Full central heating Open parking available Covered
contd.*

parking available (charged) Supervised Child discount available 10yrs Fishing Boule Open terrace V meals Last d 22.00hrs Languages spoken: English, German & Italian
CARDS: ●● ■■ ☲ Travellers cheques

### BONSON Loire

### ★ ★ Des Voyageurs
4 av de St-Rambert 42160
☎ 477551615 FAX 477555850
In town centre Near motorway
Closed Aug
7 rms (6 bth/shr) TV in all bedrooms Direct dial from all bedrooms Licensed Full central heating Open terrace Covered terrace Last d 21.00hrs Languages spoken: English & German
CARDS: ●● ■■ ☲ ⓪ Travellers cheques

### BOSSIEU Isère

### Le Cellier (Prop: J L Chaboud)
38260
☎ 474543285 FAX 474542904
(From Lyon A43 direction Grenoble exit La Verpillière, then follow Vienne, Diemoz, St-Jean-de-Bournay, Semons to Bossieu. From the south A7 exit Chanas, then Beaurepaire, Pommier-de-Beaurepaire to Bossieu)
Near river Near lake Forest area Near motorway
20 Dec-10 Dec
3 en suite (bth/shr) (1 fmly) (1 with balcony) Full central heating Open parking available Child discount available 12yrs Riding Bicycle rental Languages spoken: English German & Italian

### BOURG-D'OISANS Isère

### Les Petites Sources (Prop: Pauline Durdan)
Le Vert 38520
☎ 476801392
Near river Near lake Forest area
Closed Oct-20 Dec & 17 May-5 Jun
6 en suite (bth/shr) (3 fmly) (4 with balcony) No smoking on premises Full central heating Open parking available Child discount available 13yrs Last d 21.00hrs Languages spoken: English
CARDS: Travellers cheques

### BOURG-EN-BRESSE Ain

### ★ ★ ★ Le Mail
46 av du Mail 01000
☎ 474210026 FAX 474212955
(leave town centre via the tunnel under the railway line towards Villefranche. Hotel on right)
Closed 15 Jul, 4 Aug & 24 Dec-7 Jan
9 en suite (bth/shr) (1 fmly) (1 with balcony) TV in all bedrooms Direct dial from all bedrooms Licensed Full central heating Open parking available Open terrace V meals Last d 21.30hrs Languages spoken: English
ROOMS: (room only) s 200-220FF; d 220-300FF
MEALS: Continental breakfast 35FF Lunch 110-320FF&alc Dinner 110-320FF&alc
CARDS: ●● ■■ ☲ ⓪ Travellers cheques

### BOURG-ST-ANDÉOL Ardèche

### ★ ★ Le Prieuré
Quai Fabry 63760
☎ 475546299 FAX 475546373
Near river Forest area In town centre Near motorway
16 en suite (bth/shr) (7 fmly) (3 with balcony) TV in all bedrooms Licensed Full central heating Child discount available 4yrs Boule Open terrace Covered terrace Last d 21.30hrs Languages spoken: English & Italian
CARDS: ●● ■■ ☲

### BOUVANTE Drôme

### ★ Auberge du Pionnier
26190
☎ 475485712 FAX 475485826
(A7 exit Tain L'Hermitage in direction Romans/St Nazaire/St Jean en Royans/Bouvante, also access via D131 or D331)
Near lake Forest area
Closed 20 Oct-20 Dec
9 rms (7 shr) (4 fmly) Direct dial from all bedrooms Licensed Full central heating Open parking available Covered parking available Child discount available 10yrs Boule Open terrace Private park Last d 20.00hrs Languages spoken: English & Italian
ROOMS: (room only) d 160-260FF
MEALS: Continental breakfast 35FF Lunch 52-170FF Dinner 52-170FF
CARDS: Travellers cheques

### BRIDES-LES-BAINS Savoie

### ★ ★ ★ Grand Hotel Des Thermes
73570
☎ 479552977 FAX 479552829
Near river Forest area In town centre
102 en suite (bth/shr) (8 fmly) (78 with balcony) TV in all bedrooms STV Radio in rooms Licensed Lift Night porter Full central heating Open parking available Covered parking available (charged) Supervised Child discount available 12yrs Outdoor swimming pool Tennis Sauna Gym Pool table Boule Jacuzzi/spa Bicycle rental Open terrace Covered terrace Wkly live entertainment Casino V meals Languages spoken: English
CARDS: ●● ■■ ☲ Travellers cheques

### ★ ★ Sources
av des Marronniers, BP34 73571
☎ 479552922 FAX 479552706
(Motorway from Abbeville in direction of Moûtiers, from here take direction of Tarentaise Valley, Méribel, Courchevel. Follow signs to Brides-les-Bains, here cross the main road & follow the road on the left at bakery, after bridge hotel on right)
Forest area In town centre Near motorway
Closed Nov-25 Dec
70 rms (45 bth 17 shr) (20 fmly) (41 with balcony) TV in all bedrooms Direct dial from all bedrooms Licensed Lift Full central heating Open parking available Covered parking available Child discount available 7yrs Indoor swimming pool (heated) Sauna Solarium Pool table Jacuzzi/spa Open terrace Last d 20.30hrs Languages spoken: English & German
ROOMS: (room only) s 215-385FF; d 245-480FF
MEALS: Continental breakfast 40FF Lunch 100FF Dinner 100FF
CARDS: ●● ☲

### CARROZ-D'ARÂCHES, LES Haute-Savoie

★ ★ *Les Belles Pistes*
56 rte du Pernand *74300*
☎ 450900017 FAX 450903070
(from A40 exit at junction Cluses Central and take N205. Take
turn for Les Carroz/Flaine for 10km)
Near lake  Forest area  In town centre  Near motorway
*Closed Apr-Jun & Sep-Dec*
*18 en suite (bth/shr)  (7 fmly)  (2 with balcony)  No smoking in*
*all bedrooms  Radio in rooms  Direct dial from all bedrooms*
*Licensed  Full central heating  Open parking available*
*Supervised  Child discount available 11yrs  Open terrace*
*Last d 21.00hrs  Languages spoken: English*
CARDS: ●● ⚏ Access Travellers cheques

### CELLIERS Savoie

★ ★ *Le Grand Pic*
*73260*
☎ 479240372 FAX 479243878
Forest area
*Closed 26 Sep-25 Dec & 16 Apr-24 May*
*15 rms (4 shr)  6 rooms in annexe  (5 fmly)  (13 with balcony)*
*Licensed  Full central heating  Open parking available*
*Supervised  Child discount available 7yrs  Open terrace  Library*
*V meals  Last d 21.00hrs  Languages spoken: English &*
*German*
CARDS: ●● ⚏ Travellers cheques

### CHAMBÉRY Savoie

★ ★ **Arcantis City Hotel**
9 rue Denfert Rochereau *73000*
☎ 479857679 FAX 479858611
(take direction of Chambéry then Centre-Ville then Carré
Curial & Espace Malraux where the hotel is nearby)
In town centre
*40 en suite (bth/shr)  (7 fmly)  (2 with balcony)  No smoking in 4*
*bedrooms  TV in all bedrooms  STV  Direct dial from all*
*bedrooms  Lift  Night porter  Full central heating  Covered*
*parking available (charged)  Bicycle rental  Languages spoken:*
*English German & Italian*
ROOMS: (room only) s fr 265FF; d fr 300FF
**Reductions over 1 night**
CARDS: ●● ⚏ Travellers cheques

★ ★ *Aux Pervences*
600 Chemin des Charmettes *73000*
☎ 479333426 FAX 479600252
(take the direction of Chambéry centre, then Carre Curial and
the Jean Jacques Rousseau's Museum to Charmettes)
Near lake  Forest area
*11 rms (2 bth)  (1 fmly)  TV in 8 bedrooms  Direct dial from all*
*bedrooms  Licensed  Full central heating  Open parking*
*available  Covered parking available  Boule  Open terrace  Last*
*d 22.00hrs  Languages spoken: English, German, Italian &*
*Spanish*
CARDS: ●● ■■ ⚏ Travellers cheques

★ ★ ★ ★ *Château de Candie*
rue du Bois de Candie *73000*
☎ 479966300 FAX 479966310
Forest area  Near motorway
*19 en suite (bth/shr)  3 rooms in annexe  (5 fmly)  (4 with*
*balcony)  TV in all bedrooms  Direct dial from all bedrooms*
*Licensed  Lift  Full central heating  Open parking available*

*Supervised  Child discount available 12yrs  Open terrace  V*
*meals  Last d 21.30hrs  Languages spoken: English German*
*Italian & Spanish*
CARDS: ●● ■■ ⚏ Travellers cheques

★ ★ ★ *France*
22 fbg Réclus *73000*
☎ 479335118 FAX 479850630
In town centre  Near motorway
*48 en suite (bth/shr)  (42 with balcony)  No smoking in 16*
*bedrooms  TV in all bedrooms  STV  Radio in rooms  Direct dial*
*from all bedrooms  Licensed  Lift  Night porter  Full central*
*heating  Air conditioning in bedrooms  Open parking available*
*(charged)  Covered parking available (charged)  Supervised*
*Languages spoken: English & German*
CARDS: ●● ■■ ⚏ ⓓ Travellers cheques

★ ★ ★ **Hotel des Princes**
4 rue de Boigne *73000*
☎ 479334536 FAX 479703147
(follow directions for city centre then Hotel-de-Ville, Hotel de
Princes is close by)
Near lake  In town centre  Near motorway
*45 en suite (bth/shr)  (3 fmly)  (6 with balcony)  TV in all*
*bedrooms  STV  Direct dial from all bedrooms  Lift  Night porter*
*Full central heating  Supervised  Languages spoken: English*
ROOMS: (room only) s 340FF; d 390FF
CARDS: ●● ■■ ⚏ ⓓ

★ ★ *Savoyard*
35 pl Monge *73000*
☎ 479333655 FAX 479852570
Near river  Near lake  Forest area  In town centre  Near
motorway
*10 en suite (shr)  (3 fmly)  (3 with balcony)  TV in all bedrooms*
*STV  Licensed  Full central heating  Air conditioning in*
*bedrooms  Open parking available  Supervised  Child discount*
*available 12yrs  Open terrace  V meals  Last d 22.30hrs*
*Languages spoken: English, Italian & Spanish*
CARDS: ●● ■■ ⚏ Travellers cheques

### CHAMONIX-MONT-BLANC Haute-Savoie

★ ★ *De l'Arve*
60 Impasse des Anémones *74400*
☎ 450530231 FAX 450535692
Near river  Forest area  In town centre
*Closed Nov-19 Dec*
*39 rms (26 bth 9 shr)  (5 fmly)  (29 with balcony)  TV in all*
*bedrooms  STV  Direct dial from all bedrooms  Licensed  Lift*
*Night porter  Full central heating  Open parking available  Child*
*discount available 10yrs  Pool table  Open terrace  Last d*
*20.30hrs  Languages spoken: English & German*
ROOMS: (room only) s 174-237FF; d 218-476FF
MEALS: Full breakfast 47FF  Lunch fr 99FF&alc
Dinner fr 99FF&alc
CARDS: ●● ■■ ⚏ ⓓ Travellers cheques

**Chalet Beauregard** (Prop: Manuel & Laurence Dos
Santos)
182 rue de la Mollard *74400*
☎ 450558630 FAX 450558630
(from 'route Blanche', exit at Chamonix Sud, at 3rd rdbt take
left uphill to 'rue de la Mollard' in direction of Brévent left to
3rd house on right after Gendarmerie)
Near river  Forest area  In town centre
*Closed mid Oct-mid Dec*                              *contd.*

351

*7 rms (1 bth 4 shr) (2 fmly) (4 with balcony) TV in 2 bedrooms Full central heating Open parking available Child discount available 4yrs Languages spoken:* English Portuguese & Spanish
ROOMS: s 219-369FF; d 369-499FF **✱ Special breaks**
CARDS: Travellers cheques

### ★ ★ Hotel Frantour
39 rue des Allobroges *74400*
☎ 450530756 FAX 450535479
*Near river Near lake Forest area In town centre Near motorway*
*Closed mid Oct-mid Dec*
*133 en suite (bth) 45 rooms in annexe (66 fmly) (133 with balcony) TV in all bedrooms STV Direct dial from all bedrooms Licensed Lift Night porter Full central heating Open parking available Covered parking available (charged) Supervised Child discount available 11yrs Sauna Solarium Pool table Jacuzzi/spa Open terrace Covered terrace Last d 21.30hrs Languages spoken:* English Dutch German Italian & Spanish,
CARDS: ■ ▨ ▣ Travellers cheques

### ★ ★ ★ Hotel Le Labrador
rte du Golf *74400*
☎ 450559009 FAX 450531585
*(at 100km of Geneva Airport by motorway directly to Chamonix. At entrance of Chamonix take right direction Argentiere, hotel at 3km in village of Les Praz on golf course)*
*Near river Forest area*
*Closed early Nov-early Dec*
*31 en suite (bth/shr) (5 fmly) (27 with balcony) TV in all bedrooms STV Direct dial from all bedrooms Mini-bar in all bedrooms Licensed Lift Night porter Full central heating Open parking available Covered parking available (charged) Child discount available 10yrs Golf 18 Sauna Gym Pool table Jacuzzi/spa Open terrace Covered terrace Last d 21.30hrs Languages spoken:* English Italian & Portuguese
ROOMS: s 440-640FF; d 440-1100FF **Special breaks**
MEALS: Continental breakfast 55FF Lunch 159FF Dinner 159FF✱
CARDS: ●● ▦ ▨ ▣

### ★ ★ Au Relais des Gaillands
964 rte des Gaillands *74400*
☎ 450531358 FAX 450558506
*Near lake Forest area*
*Closed Oct-20 Dec & 12-29 Apr*
*21 en suite (shr) (6 fmly) (8 with balcony) TV in all bedrooms STV Direct dial from all bedrooms Licensed Full central heating Open parking available Child discount available 10yrs Pool table Open terrace Last d 22.00hrs Languages spoken:* English & Italian
CARDS: ●● ▨ Travellers cheques

**CHAMPAGNY-EN-VANOISE** Savoie

### ★ ★ L'Ancolie
Les Hauts du Crey *73350*
☎ 479550500 FAX 479550442
*(from Albertville travel to Moutiers then to Bozel and Champagny-en-Vanoise)*
*Forest area*
*Closed 20 Apr-10 Jun & 10 Sep-20 Dec*
*31 en suite (bth/shr) (7 fmly) (24 with balcony) TV in all bedrooms STV Direct dial from all bedrooms Licensed Lift Full central heating Open parking available Covered parking*

*available (charged) Child discount available Outdoor swimming pool (heated) Sauna Solarium Pool table Jacuzzi/spa Open terrace Covered terrace V meals Last d 21.30hrs Languages spoken:* English & German
CARDS: ●● ▨ Travellers cheques

**CHAMPIER** Isère

### ★ ★ Auberge de la Source
*36260*
☎ 474544044 FAX 474545036
*(15km from Bourgoin-Jallieu on N85)*
*Forest area*
*10 rms (2 bth 7 shr) (3 fmly) TV in all bedrooms Radio in rooms Direct dial from all bedrooms Licensed Full central heating Open parking available Child discount available 12yrs Outdoor swimming pool Open terrace Covered terrace V meals Last d 21.00hrs Languages spoken:* English
CARDS: ●● ▨

### Côteau des Bruyères (Prop: M & Mme Crepin)
*38260*
☎ 474544218
*Near river Near lake Forest area Near motorway*
*4 en suite (bth/shr) (2 fmly) No smoking on premises Full central heating Open parking available Child discount available 10yrs Boule Open terrace Table tennis V meals Languages spoken:* English & Dutch
CARDS: Travellers cheques

**CHANOS-CURSON** Drôme

### Les Pichères
*26600*
☎ 475073272 FAX 475073065
*Near motorway*
*Closed Oct-Etr*
*2 en suite (bth/shr) (2 fmly) No smoking on premises Full central heating Open parking available Languages spoken:* English
CARDS: Travellers cheques

**CHAPAREILLAN** Isère

### ★ De l'Avenue
*38530*
☎ 476452335 FAX 476455650
*(5km from N90 exit Pontcharra towards Chambéry)*
*Near river Near lake Forest area Near motorway*
*Closed 8 days in Apr, 15 in Sep*
*(5 fmly) Direct dial from 8 bedrooms Licensed Full central heating Open parking available Covered parking available Child discount available 7yrs Boule Open terrace Languages spoken:* English
ROOMS: (room only) s 150-210FF; d 170-280FF
CARDS: ●●

**CHARAVINES** Isère

### ★ ★ Hostellerie du Lac Bleu
Lac de Paladru *38850*
☎ 476066048 FAX 476066681
*(Access from A43/A48)*
Situated in leafy surroundings on the shores of Lac de Paladru, with shady, flower-decked terraces, a restaurant and veranda with views of the lake. The guest rooms, with every modern convenience, create the pleasant setting for an enjoyable stay.

The restaurant serves an array of specialities including fresh fish from the lake, and a beach bar serves ice cream and snacks near the shoreline. The hotel has a range of leisure facilities on offer.
Near lake  Near beach  Forest area  Near motorway
*Closed 16 Oct-14 Mar*
*11 en suite (bth/shr) (1 fmly) TV in all bedrooms  Direct dial from all bedrooms  Licensed  Full central heating  Open parking available  Child discount available 10yrs  Solarium  Boule  Open terrace  Covered terrace  Last d 21.00hrs  Languages spoken: English & German*
ROOMS: (room only) s fr 200FF; d 260-290FF
MEALS: Continental breakfast 40FF  Lunch 80-160FF&alc
Dinner 80-160FF&alc
CARDS: ●● ▆▆ Travellers cheques

**★ ★ De la Poste**
965 rue Principale *38850*
☎ 476066041 FAX 476556242
(A48 exit Rives or A43 exit Les Abrets-Chimilin, hotel in the village near the church 500metres from the lake)
Near lake  Near beach  Forest area  In town centre  Near motorway
*Closed 15-28 Feb*
*15 en suite (bth/shr) (2 fmly) TV in all bedrooms  STV  Direct dial from all bedrooms  Licensed  Full central heating  Child discount available 5yrs  Pool table  Boule  Open terrace  Last d 21.30hrs  Languages spoken: English & Spanish*
CARDS: ●● ▆▆ ▆▆ Travellers cheques

**★ ★ Relais de l'Abbaye**
*42190*
☎ 477600088 FAX 477601460
Near river
*27 en suite (bth/shr) (8 fmly) TV in all bedrooms  Direct dial from all bedrooms  Licensed  Full central heating  Open parking available  Boule  Bicycle rental  Open terrace  V meals  Last d 21.15hrs  Languages spoken: English & German*
CARDS: ●● ▆▆ ▆▆ Travellers cheques

**Domaine de Gorneton** (Prop: J et J Fleitou)
Hameau de Trembas *38670*
☎ 476407940 FAX 472241915
(at the intersection of A7/A46/A47 towards St Etienne exit Chasse to 'Centre Commercial' under railway bridge, then left & right towards Trembas, 2km on right)
Forest area
*3 en suite (bth/shr) (1 fmly) Full central heating  Open parking available  Covered parking available  Child discount available 14yrs  Outdoor swimming pool  Tennis  Fishing  Boule  Table tennis  Last d 18.00hrs  Languages spoken: English & Spanish*
CARDS: Travellers cheques

**★ ★ De la Tour**
*01400*
☎ 474550512 FAX 474550919
Near river
*20 en suite (bth/shr) (6 fmly) No smoking in 1 bedroom  TV in all bedrooms  Direct dial from all bedrooms  Licensed  Lift  Full central heating  Air conditioning in bedrooms  Open parking available  Child discount available  Open terrace  V meals  Last*

*d 21.30hrs  Languages spoken: English*
ROOMS: (room only) d 285-370FF
MEALS: Continental breakfast 49FF  Lunch 115-355FF&alc
Dinner 115-355FF&alc
CARDS: ●● ▆▆ Travellers cheques

**★ ★ Le Bois du Seigneur**
Col de Châtillon *74300*
☎ 450342740 FAX 450348020
Near river  Near lake  Forest area
*10 en suite (bth/shr) (2 fmly) No smoking in 5 bedrooms  TV in all bedrooms  Direct dial from all bedrooms  Licensed  Full central heating  Open parking available  Supervised  Child discount available 12yrs  Open terrace  V meals  Last d 22.00hrs  Languages spoken: English & German*
CARDS: ●● ▆▆ ▆▆ ▆▆ Travellers cheques

**★ ★ Château Blanchard**
36 rte de St-Galmier *42140*
☎ 477542888 FAX 477543603
(approach via A72 or A6 and D11)
Near river  Near lake  Forest area  In town centre  Near motorway
*12 en suite (bth/shr) (2 fmly) No smoking in 1 bedroom  TV in all bedrooms  Direct dial from all bedrooms  Licensed  Full central heating  Open parking available  Supervised  Child discount available  Boule  Mini-golf  Bicycle rental  Open terrace  Children's play area  V meals  Last d 21.15hrs  Languages spoken: English*
CARDS: ●● ▆▆ ▆▆ ▆▆ Travellers cheques

**Les Vikings** (Prop: M & Mme Roux)
*42560*
☎ 477757418
Near river  Forest area  In town centre  Near motorway
*Closed Oct-Mar*
*2 en suite (shr) Radio in rooms  Open parking available  Child discount available  Outdoor swimming pool (heated)  Sauna  Solarium  Boule  Open terrace  Covered terrace*
CARDS: Travellers cheques

**La Grosse Pierre** (Prop: V & A Passot)
*69115*
☎ 474691217 FAX 474691352
(enter Fleurie/Villie Morgan D68 in direction of Chiroubles D119 and follow signs to La Grosse Pierre)
Forest area
*5 en suite (shr) No smoking on premises  Full central heating  Open parking available  Covered parking available  Supervised  Child discount available  Outdoor swimming pool  Boule  Languages spoken: English*
CARDS: ●● ▆▆ Travellers cheques

**★ ★ Ferrat**
*38930*
☎ 476344270 FAX 476344747
Forest area  Near motorway                                  *contd.*

Closed Dec-14 Feb
23 en suite (bth/shr) 7 rooms in annexe (2 fmly) (7 with
balcony) TV in all bedrooms Licensed Full central heating
Open parking available Covered parking available (charged)
Supervised Child discount available Outdoor swimming pool
Boule Bicycle rental Open terrace Table tennis, volley ball
Last d 21.00hrs Languages spoken: English & Italian
CARDS: ●● ▦ ⑩ Travellers cheques

### CLUSAZ, LA Haute-Savoie

★ ★ **Le Bellachat**
74220
☎ 450326666 FAX 450326584
Near lake Forest area
Closed 21 Apr-May & 21 Oct-14 Dec
30 en suite (bth/shr) (8 fmly) (13 with balcony) TV in all
bedrooms STV Licensed Full central heating Air conditioning
in bedrooms Open parking available Supervised Child
discount available 7yrs Open terrace Table tennis,playroom
Last d 21.00hrs Languages spoken: English
CARDS: ●● ■ ▦

### COISE Savoie

★ ★ ★ **Château de la Tour du Puits**
Le Puits 73800
☎ 479288800 FAX 479888801
(from Chambéry or Grenoble take motorway towards
Albertville then exit 23, from Albertville take motorway
towards Chambéry and exit 23)
Forest area Near motorway
Closed Jan RS Sun evening & Mon
7 en suite (bth/shr) No smoking in 4 bedrooms TV in all
bedrooms STV Radio in rooms Direct dial from all bedrooms
Licensed Full central heating Open parking available
Supervised Child discount available 12yrs Outdoor swimming
pool (heated) Solarium Gym Bicycle rental Open terrace
Covered terrace Wkly live entertainment Last d 21.30hrs
Languages spoken: English
CARDS: ●● ■ ▦ ⑩ Travellers cheques

### COL DU MONT-SION Haute-Savoie

★ ★ **La Clef des Champs et Hotel Rey**
St-Blaise 74350
☎ 450441329 FAX 450440548
Near lake Forest area Near motorway
Closed 6-26 Jan & 25 Oct-15 Nov
30 en suite (bth/shr) (3 fmly) TV in all bedrooms STV Direct
dial from all bedrooms Mini-bar in 20 bedrooms Room-safe
Licensed Lift Full central heating Open parking available
Child discount available Outdoor swimming pool Tennis Boule
Open terrace Last d 21.00hrs Languages spoken: English &
German
CARDS: ●● ▦ Travellers cheques

### CONFRANÇON Ain

★ ★ ★ **Auberge La Sarrasine**
01310
☎ 474302565 FAX 474252423
(From A40 exit3/4 for Bourg-en-Bresse on to N79. From A6 exit
Mâcon-Sud onto N6 then N79)
This charming, ancient Bresse farmhouse has been converted
to offer its guests an enjoyable stay in delightful flower-filled
surroundings. The bedrooms are furnished to provide the

**Auberge La Sarrasine**

maximum comfort and the restaurant offers an innovative
selection of freshly prepared local specialities. The hotel is
ideally situated for excursions to various tourist attractions in
the area and six different golf resorts.
Forest area Near motorway
Closed 2 Jan-14 Feb
10 en suite (bth) (2 fmly) TV in all bedrooms STV Radio in
rooms Direct dial from all bedrooms Mini-bar in all bedrooms
Licensed Night porter Full central heating Open parking
available Supervised Outdoor swimming pool (heated) Open
terrace Covered terrace Table tennis V meals Last d 21.30hrs
Languages spoken: English
ROOMS: (room only) s 398-580FF; d 490-680FF
**Reductions over 1 night**
MEALS: Full breakfast 65FF Dinner 99-230FF
CARDS: ●● ■ ▦ ⑩ Travellers cheques

### CORPS Isère

★ ★ **Hotel Restaurant de la Poste**
rte Napoléon 38970
☎ 476300003 FAX 476300273
(on the Route Napoléon)
Near lake Forest area In town centre Near motorway
Closed Dec-mid Jan
29 en suite (bth/shr) 9 rooms in annexe (4 fmly) (2 with
balcony) TV in all bedrooms Direct dial from all bedrooms
Licensed Full central heating Air conditioning in bedrooms
Open parking available Covered parking available Supervised
Child discount available 10yrs Tennis Fishing Sauna Boule
Mini-golf Bicycle rental Open terrace Covered terrace Wkly
live entertainment V meals Last d 22.00hrs Languages spoken:
English
CARDS: ●● ■ ▦ Travellers cheques

### COTEAU, LE Loire

★ ★ ★ **Artaud**
133 av de la Libération 42120
☎ 477684644 FAX 477722350
In town centre Near motorway
Closed 1-20 Aug
25 en suite (bth/shr) (3 fmly) (2 with balcony) No smoking in 4
bedrooms TV in all bedrooms STV Direct dial from all
bedrooms Licensed Full central heating Covered parking
available (charged) Supervised Child discount available 8yrs V
meals Last d 21.00hrs Languages spoken: English
ROOMS: (room only) s 310-480FF; d 310-490FF
**Reductions over 1 night**
MEALS: Full breakfast 50FF Lunch 100-240FF&alc Dinner
100-240FF&alc
CARDS: ●● ■ ▦ ⑩ JCB Travellers cheques

## COURCHEVEL Savoie

### ★ Les Allobroges
St-Bon le Haut *73120*
☎ 479081015 FAX 479081015
Near lake Forest area
*9 en suite (bth/shr) (6 fmly) (8 with balcony) TV in all
bedrooms Direct dial from all bedrooms Licensed Full central
heating Open parking available Covered parking available
Child discount available 10yrs Boule Open terrace V meals
Last d 22.30hrs Languages spoken: English*
CARDS: ●● ■■ ☎ ⑩ Travellers cheques

### ★ ★ ★ Les Ancolies
rue des Gravelles *73120*
☎ 479082766 FAX 479080564
Near sea Forest area
*31 en suite (bth/shr) (3 fmly) (30 with balcony) No smoking in
10 bedrooms TV in 30 bedrooms STV Direct dial from 30
bedrooms Licensed Lift Night porter Full central heating
Open parking available Covered parking available (charged)
Sauna Solarium Open terrace Languages spoken: English,
German, Italian & Spanish*
MEALS: Full breakfast 65FF Lunch 95-105FFalc✱
CARDS: ●● ■■ ☎ ⑩ Travellers cheques

### ★ ★ ★ ★ Hotel Bellecote
*73120*
☎ 479081019 FAX 479081716
(motorway A43 to Albertville then Moutiers and Courchevel)
Forest area
*Closed mid Dec-mid Apr*
*56 en suite (bth/shr) TV in all bedrooms STV Radio in rooms
Mini-bar in all bedrooms Licensed Lift Night porter Full
central heating Open parking available Covered parking
available (charged) Child discount available Indoor swimming
pool (heated) Golf Sauna Solarium Gym Pool table
Jacuzzi/spa Open terrace Covered terrace Gym Languages
spoken: English, German, Italian & Spanish*
CARDS: ●● ■■ ☎ ⑩

### ★ ★ ★ ★ Hotel Carlina
*73120*
☎ 479080030 FAX 479080403
(motorway A43 to Albertville, then Moutiers, then Courchevel)
Forest area In town centre
*63 en suite (bth/shr) TV in all bedrooms STV Radio in rooms
Direct dial from all bedrooms Licensed Lift Night porter Full
central heating Open parking available Covered parking
available (charged) Indoor swimming pool (heated) Sauna
Solarium Gym Jacuzzi/spa Open terrace Covered terrace
Languages spoken: English, German, Italian & Spanish*
CARDS: ●● ■■ ☎ ⑩

### ★ ★ ★ Hotel Les Ducs de Savoie
Le Jardin Alpin *73120*
☎ 479080300 FAX 479081630
(take motorway Albertville to Moutiers then in direction
Courchevel and Le Jardin Alpin area)
Forest area
*Closed mid Dec-mid Apr*
*70 en suite (bth/shr) TV in all bedrooms STV Radio in rooms
Direct dial from all bedrooms Licensed Lift Night porter Full
central heating Open parking available Covered parking
available (charged) Indoor swimming pool (heated) Sauna
Solarium Gym Pool table Jacuzzi/spa Open terrace Covered
terrace Languages spoken: English, German, Italian & Spanish*
CARDS: ●● ■■ ☎ ⑩

### ★ ★ ★ ★ Nèiges
*73121*
☎ 479080377 FAX 479081870
Forest area
*Closed mid Dec-mid Apr*
*42 en suite (bth/shr) (5 fmly) (30 with balcony) TV in all
bedrooms STV Radio in rooms Licensed Lift Night porter
Full central heating Open parking available Covered parking
available (charged) Child discount available Sauna Pool table
Jacuzzi/spa Open terrace Last d 21.30hrs Languages spoken:
English, Italian & Spanish*
CARDS: ●● ■■ ☎ ⑩ Travellers cheques

### ★ ★ ★ Peupliers
Le Praz - St-Bon *73120*
☎ 479084147 FAX 479084505
Near lake Forest area
*30 en suite (bth/shr) (3 fmly) (20 with balcony) TV in all
bedrooms STV Radio in rooms Direct dial from all bedrooms
Licensed Lift Full central heating Open parking available
Child discount available 13yrs Fishing Sauna Gym Pool table
Boule Bicycle rental Open terrace Last d 21.00hrs Languages
spoken: English & Spanish*
CARDS: ●● ■■ ☎ ⑩ Travellers cheques

### ★ ★ ★ ★ Pralong 2000
rte de l'Altiport, BP13 *73120*
☎ 479082482 FAX 479083641
(from Albertville to Moutiers then Courchevel)
Forest area
*Closed mid Dec-mid Apr*
*65 en suite (bth/shr) (37 with balcony) TV in all bedrooms STV
Radio in rooms Direct dial from all bedrooms Mini-bar in all
bedrooms Room-safe Licensed Lift Night porter Full central
heating Air conditioning in bedrooms Open parking available
Covered parking available (charged) Indoor swimming pool
(heated) Sauna Solarium Pool table Covered terrace Last d
21.30hrs Languages spoken: English, German, Italian & Spanish*
ROOMS: (incl. dinner) s 1495-2470FF; d 2300-3600FF
MEALS: Lunch 410-410FF&alc Dinner 410-600FF&alc
CARDS: ●● ■■ ☎ ⑩ JCB Travellers cheques

### ★ ★ ★ La Sivolière
*73120*
☎ 479080833 FAX 479081573
(from Paris A6 - Bourg en Bresse, A7 - Lyon, A47 Albertville-
Moutiers-Courchevel)
Forest area
*Closed 29 Nov-3 May*
*33 en suite (bth/shr) (6 fmly) (18 with balcony) TV in 30
bedrooms STV Direct dial from all bedrooms Room-safe
Licensed Night porter Full central heating Open parking
available (charged) Covered parking available (charged)
Child discount available Sauna Solarium Pool table Open
terrace Covered terrace Languages spoken: English &
Spanish*
CARDS: ●● ■■ ☎

## COURS-LA-VILLE Rhône

### ★ ★ Le Pavillon
Col du Pavillon *69470*
☎ 474898355 FAX 474647026
The completely renovated hotel has a bright green façade
which blends in with the surrounding countryside. The
unusual architecture conceals a modern interior with two bars
and lounges as well as a top class restaurant, which serves
*contd.*

***Le Pavilion***
traditional, generously portioned cuisine. The surrounding
park provides a peaceful haven, containing pigs, goats and
sheep.
*Near lake Near beach Forest area Near motorway*
*21 en suite (bth/shr) (2 fmly) (2 with balcony) TV in all*
*bedrooms Direct dial from all bedrooms Licensed Night*
*porter Full central heating Open parking available Child*
*discount available Boule Open terrace V meals Last d*
*21.00hrs Languages spoken: English, German & Italian*
ROOMS: (room only) s 270-290FF; d 330-350FF
**Reductions over 1 night**
MEALS: Full breakfast 39FF Lunch fr 78FF&alc Dinner fr
99FF&alc
CARDS: ▆ Travellers cheques

**Les Heures Claires** (Prop: Annie Huguet)
Chemin de Montradis *38460*
☎ 474907549
(from eastern Lyon take D517 to Crémieu)
*Near lake Forest area*
*Jun-15 Oct*
*2 en suite (shr) No smoking on premises Full central heating*
*Open parking available Supervised No children Languages*
*spoken: English & Spanish*
ROOMS: d 320FF
✳ **Reductions over 1 night Special breaks**

★ ★ **Grand Hotel**
60 rue de l'Hôtel-de-Ville *26400*
☎ 475250817 FAX 475254642
(from motorway coming from S exit Loriol, from N exit Valence
Sud and follow arrows Crest/Gap)
*Near river In town centre Near motorway*
*Closed 21 Dec-20 Jan*
*20 rms (3 bth 6 shr) (2 fmly) TV in 15 bedrooms Direct dial*
*from all bedrooms Full central heating Covered parking*
*available (charged) Last d 21.00hrs Languages spoken: English*
ROOMS: (room only) s fr 150FF; d 150-330FF
**Reductions over 1 night**
MEALS: Full breakfast 35FF Lunch 92-200FF&alc Dinner
92-200FF&alc
CARDS: ● ▆ Travellers cheques

**Bed & Breakfast** (Prop: Mme Pascale Le Puil)
Le Saphir, Paravy *73590*
☎ 479316958 FAX 479316958
(from Annecy take N508, then N212 towards Megêve. Then
right onto D71 to Crest-Voland. From Office du Tourisme take
road to Saisies. Before 'Mission 1940 cross', entrance at the
top)
Set in a mountain chalet at an altitude of 1250 metres, with a
superb view over the Aravis Mountain. Skiing in the winter
with a ski-lift just 50 metres from the chalet. Evening meals
available, served in the living room with your hosts and other
guests. You will be welcomed with a bouquet of flowers.
*Near lake Forest area*
*3 en suite (shr) (2 fmly) No smoking on premises Full central*
*heating Open parking available Child discount available 8yrs*
*Languages spoken: English*
ROOMS: s 185-205FF; d 255-295FF
MEALS: Lunch 90FF Dinner 90FF
CARDS: Travellers cheques

★ ★ **Hotel du Mont Charvin**
*73590*
☎ 479316121 FAX 479318210
*Near river Forest area In town centre*
*23 rms (6 fmly) (6 with balcony) Direct dial from all bedrooms*
*Licensed Night porter Full central heating Open parking*
*available Covered parking available (charged) Supervised*
*Child discount available 7yrs Boule Open terrace V meals Last*
*d 20.30hrs Languages spoken: English*
CARDS: ● ▆

★ ★ **Ibis Hotel**
Porte de Lyon - A6 *69570*
☎ 478660220 FAX 478474793
(A6 exit Limonest/Dardilly from the N after Villefranche/Toll,
from S take Feyzin Lyon Centre in direction of Paris)
*Forest area Near motorway*
*68 en suite (bth/shr) (12 fmly) No smoking in 11 bedrooms TV*
*in all bedrooms STV Direct dial from all bedrooms Licensed*
*Night porter Full central heating Open parking available*
*Supervised Child discount available 12yrs Outdoor swimming*
*pool Pool table Boule Open terrace French billards Table*
*tennis V meals Last d 22.30hrs Languages spoken: English,*
*Danish, Norwegian,Italian, Spanish & german*
ROOMS: (room only)
MEALS: Full breakfast 40FF Lunch 95-110FF&alc Dinner
95-110FF&alc✳
CARDS: ● ▆ ▆ ▣ Travellers cheques

★ ★ ★ **Novotel Lyon Nord**
Porte de Lyon-Autoroute A6 *69570*
☎ 472172929 FAX 478350845
*Near motorway*
*107 rms TV in all bedrooms Direct dial from all bedrooms*
*Mini-bar in all bedrooms Lift Air conditioning in bedrooms*
*Open parking available Outdoor swimming pool Pool table*
*Boule Open terrace Languages spoken: English, German &*
*Spanish*

**DÉSAIGNES** Ardèche

### ★ ★ Hotel des Voyageurs
07570
☎ 475066148 FAX 475066443
Near river  Forest area
*Closed end Sep-Etr*
*40 rms (18 bth/shr)  TV in all bedrooms  Licensed  Full central heating  Open parking available  Covered parking available  Child discount available  Outdoor swimming pool  Tennis  Boule  Open terrace  Covered terrace  V meals  Last d 21.00hrs*
CARDS: ●● ▆▆ Travellers cheques

**DEUX-ALPES, LES** Isère

### ★ ★ ★ ★ La Berangère
11 rte de Champamé 38860
☎ 476792411 FAX 476795508
Near lake  Forest area
*Closed 24 Apr-19 Jun & Sep-Nov*
*49 en suite (bth/shr)  (6 fmly)  (59 with balcony)  TV in all bedrooms  STV  Radio in rooms  Direct dial from all bedrooms  Room-safe  Licensed  Lift  Night porter  Full central heating  Open parking available  Covered parking available (charged)  Child discount available 9yrs  Indoor swimming pool (heated)  Outdoor swimming pool (heated)  Sauna  Solarium  Pool table  Boule  Jacuzzi/spa  Bicycle rental  Open terrace  V meals  Last d 21.00hrs  Languages spoken: English, German, Italian & Spanish*
MEALS: Full breakfast 70FF  Lunch 180-420FF&alc  Dinner 180-420FF&alc
CARDS: ●● ▆▆

### ★ ★ ★ La Mariande
38860
☎ 476805060 FAX 476790499
*26 en suite (bth/shr)  (4 fmly)  (14 with balcony)  TV in all bedrooms  Licensed  Full central heating  Open parking available  Child discount available  Outdoor swimming pool (heated)  Tennis  Sauna  Solarium  Pool table  Jacuzzi/spa  Open terrace  Last d 21.00hrs  Languages spoken: English & German*
CARDS: ●● ▆▆ Travellers cheques

**DIE** Drôme

### ★ ★ Des Alpes
87 rue C Buffardel 26150
☎ 475221583 FAX 475220939
Near river  Forest area  In town centre  Near motorway
*24 en suite (bth/shr)  (5 fmly)  TV in 10 bedrooms  STV  Direct dial from all bedrooms  Full central heating  Covered parking available (charged)  Languages spoken: English & German*
CARDS: ●● ▆▆ ▆▆ Travellers cheques

### ★ ★ St-Dominque
44 rue C Buffardel 26150
☎ 475220308 FAX 475222448
Forest area  In town centre
*26 en suite (bth/shr)  Direct dial from all bedrooms  Licensed  Full central heating  Covered parking available (charged)  Child discount available  Outdoor swimming pool  V meals  Last d 22.00hrs  Languages spoken: English & Spanish*
CARDS: ●● ▆▆ ▆▆ Travellers cheques

**DIVONNE-LES-BAINS** Ain

### ★ ★ Bellevue Marquis
av du Mont-Mussy 01220
☎ 450200216 FAX 450202655
Near lake  Forest area
*Closed Nov-early Mar*
*15 en suite (bth/shr)  (6 with balcony)  TV in all bedrooms  Licensed  Full central heating  Open parking available  Child discount available  Open terrace  V meals  Last d 21.30hrs*
CARDS: ●● ▆▆ ▆▆ ⑩

### ★ ★ ★ ★ Château de Divonne
115 rue des Bains 01220
☎ 450200032 FAX 450200373
(motorway N1 Geneva-Lausanne, exit Coppet)
This beautiful white 19th-century residence is situated in a park and offers panoramic views over the surrounding countryside. The spacious bedrooms with en suite facilities are furnished in a style befitting the house, and feature personal touches including fresh flower arrangements. The elegant lounges and dining room are complemented by the superb cuisine which is widely acknowledged for its comprehensive choice of dishes and fabulous desserts.
Near lake  Forest area  Near motorway

*28 en suite (bth/shr)  TV in all bedrooms  STV  Direct dial from all bedrooms  Mini-bar in all bedrooms  Licensed  Lift  Night porter  Full central heating  Open parking available  Covered parking available  Child discount available 12yrs  Outdoor swimming pool (heated)  Tennis  Boule  Bicycle rental  Open terrace  Last d 22.00hrs  Languages spoken: English & German*
ROOMS: (room only) s 650FF; d 1050-1950FF
MEALS: Continental breakfast 95FF  Lunch 290-580FF  Dinner 290-580FF
CARDS: ●● ▆▆ ▆▆ ⑩ JCB Travellers cheques

**DOUSSARD** Haute-Savoie

### ★ ★ Arcalod Grand Parc
74210
☎ 450443022 FAX 450448503
(from Duingt take N508 to Doussard)
Near river  Near lake  Forest area
*Closed Nov-Mar*
*33 en suite (bth/shr)  (10 fmly)  (18 with balcony)  No smoking in 10 bedrooms  TV in all bedrooms  STV  Direct dial from all bedrooms  Licensed  Lift  Full central heating  Air conditioning in bedrooms  Open parking available  Covered parking available  Supervised  Child discount available 12yrs  Outdoor swimming pool (heated)  Gym  Pool table  Boule  Mini-golf*

*contd.*

Bicycle rental  Open terrace  Covered terrace  V meals  Last d
20.30hrs  Languages spoken: English & Italian
CARDS: ●● ■■ ⊒⊒ ⑩ Travellers cheques

### ★ ★ ★ Marceau-Hotel
115 ch de la Chapellière 74210
☎ 450443011 FAX 450443944
(N508 in direction of Albertville)
Near lake  Forest area
16 en suite (bth/shr)  (6 fmly)  (6 with balcony)  TV in all
bedrooms  Radio in rooms  Direct dial from all bedrooms
Licensed  Full central heating  Open parking available  Covered
parking available (charged)  Tennis  Boule  Open terrace  Table
tennis  Childrens play area  Languages spoken: English
CARDS: ●● ■■ ⊒⊒ ⑩ Travellers cheques

### ÉCHENEVEX Ain

### ★ ★ ★ Auberge des Chasseurs
Naz-Dessus 01170
☎ 450415407 FAX 450419061
(leave Ferney Voltaire in the direction of Gex, 2km before Gex
turn left)
Near river  Forest area  In town centre
Closed 11 Nov-Feb
15 en suite (bth/shr)  (1 fmly)  (4 with balcony)  TV in all
bedrooms  STV  Direct dial from all bedrooms  Room-safe
Licensed  Night porter  Full central heating  Open parking
available  Outdoor swimming pool (heated)  Tennis  Open
terrace  V meals  Languages spoken: English, Italian & Spanish
CARDS: ●● ■■ ⊒⊒ Travellers cheques

### ÉCHETS, LES Ain

### ★ ★ Marguin
916 rte de Strasbourg 01700
☎ 478918004 FAX 478910683
Near lake  Near motorway
8 rms (7 bth/shr)  (2 fmly)  (4 with balcony)  TV in 19 bedrooms
Licensed  Full central heating  Open parking available  Boule
Open terrace  V meals  Last d 21.00hrs  Languages spoken:
English & German
CARDS: ●● ■■ ⊒⊒

### ÉVIAN-LES-BAINS Haute-Savoie

### ★ ★ Panorama
Grande Rive 74500
☎ 450751450 FAX 450755912
Near lake  Near motorway
Closed early Oct-end Apr
29 en suite (bth/shr)  (5 fmly)  (26 with balcony)  TV in all
bedrooms  Licensed  Full central heating  Child discount
available  Open terrace  V meals  Last d 21.30hrs  Languages
spoken: English
CARDS: ●● ■■ ⊒⊒ Travellers cheques

### ★ ★ ★ Verniaz
rte d'Abondance 74500
☎ 450750490 FAX 450707892
Near lake  Forest area  Near motorway
Closed mid Nov-mid Feb
34 en suite (bth)  (28 with balcony)  TV in all bedrooms  Direct
dial from all bedrooms  Licensed  Lift  Night porter  Full central
heating  Open parking available  Outdoor swimming pool
(heated)  Golf  Tennis  Riding  Solarium  Pool table  Open terrace
Last d 21.00hrs  Languages spoken: English & German
CARDS: ●● ■■ ⊒⊒ ⑩ Travellers cheques

### EYBENS Isère

### ★ ★ ★ Château de la Commanderie
17 av d'Echirolles 38320
☎ 476253458 FAX 476240731
(arriving in the suburbs of Grenoble, follow Rocade Sud, take
exit 5, then follow signs)
Forest area  Near motorway
25 en suite (bth/shr)  (6 fmly)  (3 with balcony)  TV in all
bedrooms  STV  Radio in rooms  Direct dial from all bedrooms
Mini-bar in all bedrooms  Licensed  Night porter  Full central
heating  Open parking available  Outdoor swimming pool
Boule  Open terrace  Covered terrace  Last d 21.15hrs
Languages spoken: English & Spanish
CARDS: ●● ■■ ⊒⊒ ⑩ Travellers cheques

### FARGES Ain

### ★ ★ Château de Farges
01550
☎ 450567171 FAX 450567127
(from Paris leave motorway at Bellegarde in direction
Gex/Geneva. from Zurich Geneva, leave at Ferney-Voltaire in
direction Bellegarde)
Near river  Forest area  Near motorway
34 rms (10 bth 16 shr)  Some rooms in annexe  TV in all
bedrooms  Direct dial from all bedrooms  Licensed  Full central
heating  Open parking available  Covered parking available
Child discount available  12yrs  Open terrace  V meals  Last d
21.15hrs  Languages spoken: English & German
CARDS: ●● ■■ ⊒⊒

### FAVERGES Haute-Savoie

### ★ ★ Hotel de Genève
34 rue de la République 74210
☎ 450324690 FAX 450444809
(in town centre)

This renovated coaching inn dates back to the 19th century.
The bedrooms are spacious with good quality beds and offer
all modern conveniences. There is a peaceful lounge, cosy bar
and attractive garden. Enjoyable meals are served in the
informal restaurant and the staff provide a friendly and
attentive service. Many outdoor leisure activities can be
arranged.
Near lake  Forest area  In town centre
30 en suite (bth/shr)  (4 fmly)  (7 with balcony)  TV in all
bedrooms  STV  Direct dial from all bedrooms  Licensed  Lift
Full central heating  Open parking available  Supervised Child
discount available  12yrs  Open terrace  Last d 21.00hrs
Languages spoken: English, German & Spanish

ROOMS: (room only) s 195-230FF; d 270-350FF
**Reductions over 1 night Special breaks**
MEALS: Full breakfast 35FF Lunch 65-120FF&alc Dinner
85-120FF&alc
CARDS: ●● ■■ ▆▆ Travellers cheques

### FERNEY-VOLTAIRE Ain

**★ ★ Hotel de France**
1 rue de Genève 01210
☎ 450406387 FAX 450404727
Near lake Forest area In town centre Near motorway
14 en suite (shr) TV in all bedrooms STV Radio in rooms
Direct dial from all bedrooms Licensed Full central heating
Open parking available Child discount available 11yrs Fishing
Squash Riding Pool table Boule Bicycle rental Open terrace
Covered terrace V meals Last d 22.00hrs Languages spoken:
English & German
CARDS: ●● ■■ ▆▆ Travellers cheques

**★ ★ ★ Novotel Genève Aéroport**
rte de Meyrin 01210
☎ 450408523 FAX 450407633
Near lake Forest area Near motorway
80 en suite (bth/shr) (40 fmly) No smoking in 2 bedrooms TV
in all bedrooms STV Radio in rooms Direct dial from all
bedrooms Mini-bar in all bedrooms Licensed Night porter
Full central heating Air conditioning in bedrooms Open
parking available Outdoor swimming pool Tennis Open
terrace Covered terrace Last d 24.00hrs Languages spoken:
English, German, Portuguese & Spanish
CARDS: ●● ■■ ▆▆ ⑩ Travellers cheques

### FLUMET Savoie

**La Cour** (Prop: Beatrice Burnet-Merlin)
Les Seigneurs 73590
☎ 479317215
Near river Near lake Forest area
2 en suite (shr) Full central heating Open parking available
Supervised Child discount available 10yrs

### FONTANIL-CORNILLON Isère

**★ ★ Clarine**
8 av de Louisiane 38120
☎ 476752738 FAX 476756779
Forest area Near motorway
50 en suite (bth) No smoking in 25 bedrooms TV in all
bedrooms STV Direct dial from all bedrooms Licensed Lift
Full central heating Open parking available Child discount
available 12yrs Outdoor swimming pool Open terrace V meals
Last d 22.00hrs Languages spoken: English & Spanish
CARDS: ●● ■■ ▆▆ ⑩ Travellers cheques

### GILLONNAY Isère

**La Ferme des Collines** (Prop: M Meyer)
Hameau Notre Dame 38260
☎ 474202793 FAX 474202793
(access via A43 exit Ruy 'Le Rivet' or A48 exit Rives.
Signposted at the entrance to the village)
Near lake Forest area

4 en suite (shr) Full central heating Open parking available
Covered parking available Supervised Child discount available
11yrs Bicycle rental Last d 17.00hrs Languages spoken:
English & Italian
CARDS: Travellers cheques

### GRAND-BORNAND, LE Haute-Savoie

**★ ★ Le Cortina**
74450
☎ 450270022 FAX 450270631
(from Annecy take D909 to St Jean-de-Sixtthen take D4 to Le
Chinaillon)
Near river Near lake Forest area
Closed 16 Apr-19 Jun & 15 Sep-19 Dec
30 en suite (bth/shr) (24 with balcony) TV in all bedrooms
Direct dial from all bedrooms Licensed Lift Full central
heating Child discount available Outdoor swimming pool
(heated) Pool table Open terrace Table tennis(summer only)
Last d 21.00hrs Languages spoken: English & Italian
CARDS: ●● ▆▆ Eurocard Travellers cheques

### GRENOBLE Isère

**★ ★ ★ Angleterrie**
pl Victor-Hugo 38000
☎ 476873721 FAX 476509410
In town centre
66 en suite (bth/shr) (2 fmly) (30 with balcony) No smoking in
5 bedrooms TV in all bedrooms STV Direct dial from all
bedrooms Mini-bar in all bedrooms Room-safe Licensed Lift
Night porter Full central heating Air conditioning in bedrooms
Child discount available 12yrs Languages spoken: English,
German, Italian & Spanish
ROOMS: (room only) d 420-720FF
**Special breaks: weekends**
CARDS: ●● ■■ ▆▆ ⑩ JCB Travellers cheques

**★ ★ ★ Grand Hotel**
5 rue de la République 38000
☎ 476444936 FAX 476631406
In town centre
51 en suite (bth/shr) (6 fmly) (18 with balcony) No smoking in
5 bedrooms TV in all bedrooms STV Direct dial from all
bedrooms Mini-bar in all bedrooms Licensed Lift Night porter
Full central heating Air conditioning in bedrooms Child
discount available 12yrs Languages spoken: English & Italian
ROOMS: (room only) s 380-580FF; d 450-600FF
**Special breaks**
CARDS: ●● ■■ ▆▆ ⑩ JCB Travellers cheques

### GRESSE-EN-VERCORS Isère

**★ ★ ★ Le Chalet**
38650
☎ 476343208 FAX 476343106
Near river Near lake Forest area
Closed Apr-7 May & 20 Oct-20 Dec
25 en suite (bth/shr) 14 rooms in annexe (6 fmly) (14 with
balcony) TV in all bedrooms Mini-bar in all bedrooms
Licensed Full central heating Open parking available Covered
parking available (charged) Supervised Child discount
available 10yrs Outdoor swimming pool (heated) Tennis Boule
Open terrace Last d 21.00hrs Languages spoken: English
CARDS: ●● ▆▆ Travellers cheques

## GRIGNAN Drôme

**★ ★ ★ ★ Manoir de la Roseraie**
rte de Valréas 26230
☎ 475465815 FAX 475469155
(exit Montélimar Sud A7, follow the N7 direction Avignon for
2km. Then take D541 to Grignan, the hotel is on the other side
of the village)
The residence is set in extensive grounds amidst rose gardens
and immaculate lawns. It features elegant bedrooms with
individual furnishings, and in the restaurant guests can enjoy
delicious dishes prepared with home-grown produce, and
complemented by fine wines personally selected by the
sommelier.
Near river Near beach Forest area

*Closed 4 Jan-13 Feb & 4-10 Dec*
*17 en suite (bth/shr) 4 rooms in annexe (1 fmly) No smoking in*
*1 bedroom TV in all bedrooms STV Radio in rooms Direct dial*
*from all bedrooms Licensed Full central heating Air*
*conditioning in bedrooms Open parking available Child*
*discount available 12yrs Outdoor swimming pool (heated)*
*Tennis Boule Bicycle rental Open terrace V meals Last d*
*21.15hrs Languages spoken: English, German & Dutch*
ROOMS: (room only) s 865-1150FF; d 865-1850FF
MEALS: Full breakfast 95FF Lunch 200-265FF&alc
Dinner 200-265FF&alc
CARDS: ●● ■ ⬛ ⓓ Travellers cheques

## HABÈRE-POCHE Haute-Savoie

**★ ★ ★ Hotel le Chardet**
Reuble 74420
☎ 450395146 FAX 450395718
(from Geneva take direction of Annemasse and exit 15 to Vallée
Verte then follow directions to Boége and Habére-Poche)
Near river Near lake Forest area Near motorway
*Closed Oct-Nov*
*32 en suite (bth/shr) (6 fmly) (7 with balcony) No smoking in 4*
*bedrooms TV in all bedrooms Direct dial from all bedrooms*
*Licensed Lift Full central heating Air conditioning in*
*bedrooms Open parking available Covered parking available*
*(charged) Child discount available 12yrs Indoor swimming*
*pool (heated) Outdoor swimming pool (heated) Tennis Sauna*
*Pool table Boule Jacuzzi/spa Bicycle rental Open terrace*
*Covered terrace V meals Last d 20.00hrs Languages spoken:*
*English*
ROOMS: (room only) d 640-790FF
MEALS: Full breakfast 50FF Lunch fr 120FF&alc
Dinner fr 120FF&alc
CARDS: ●● ⬛ Travellers cheques

## HALLES, LES Rhône

**Château de la Bonnetière** (Prop: Denise Roches)
69610
☎ 474266278 FAX 472720225
Nineteenth-century house set in five hectares of parkland has a
splendid romantic setting and much of the furniture is antique.
Receptions, parties and weddings can all be catered for. Living
room and library available. Tennis on site.
Forest area

*Closed Nov-Apr*
*10 rms (4 shr) Open parking available Outdoor swimming pool*
*Riding Boule Bicycle rental Open terrace Languages spoken:*
*English & Italian*
ROOMS: s 300FF; d 400FF ✱

## HOUCHES, LES Haute-Savoie

**★ ★ ★ Le Mont Alba**
475 av des Alpages 74310
☎ 450545035 FAX 450555087
Near lake Forest area Near motorway
*Closed Nov-15 Dec*
*43 en suite (bth/shr) (1 fmly) (39 with balcony) TV in all*
*bedrooms STV Radio in rooms Direct dial from all bedrooms*
*Mini-bar in all bedrooms Licensed Lift Full central heating*
*Open parking available Covered parking available (charged)*
*Child discount available 12yrs Indoor swimming pool (heated)*
*Sauna Open terrace Last d 21.30hrs Languages spoken: English*
CARDS: ●● ■ ⬛ Travellers cheques

## JARNIOUX Rhône

**Château de Bois Franc** (Prop: Robert Doat)
69640
☎ 474582091 FAX 474651003
(from A6 exit Villeneuve-sur-Saône, head towards Roanne,
Chervignes (D31) and Jarnioux)
Near motorway
*2 en suite (bth/shr) Open parking available Child discount*
*available Languages spoken: English & German*

## JULIÉNAS Rhône

**★ ★ Chez la Rose**
69840
☎ 474044120 FAX 474044929
Forest area Near motorway
*Closed 7-20 Dec & 10-28 Feb*
*10 en suite (bth/shr) 5 rooms in annexe (4 fmly) (1 with*
*balcony) TV in all bedrooms STV Direct dial from all*

bedrooms Licensed Full central heating Open parking
available Child discount available 12yrs Open terrace V meals
Last d 21.30hrs Languages spoken: English
ROOMS: (room only) d 200-570FF
MEALS: Continental breakfast 45FF Lunch 98-340FF&alc
Dinner 98-340FF&alc
CARDS: ●● ■■ ■■ ⫶D⫶ JCB Travellers cheques

### LAMASTRE Ardèche

**Maison d'Hôtes de Mounens**
Mounens 07270
☎ 475064759
(From Lamastre in direction of Les Nonières le Cheylaud,
continue through village of Lapras. Approx 700 metres after
Lapras left onto small road signed Mounens)
Near river Forest area
Closed mid Nov-Etr
4 en suite (bth/shr) (3 fmly) Open parking available Child
discount available 14yrs Outdoor swimming pool Boule Last d
20.00hrs Languages spoken: English
MEALS: Dinner 120FF✱
CARDS: Travellers cheques

### LANARCE Ardèche

★ ★ *Le Provence*
07660
☎ 466694606 FAX 466694156
(between Aubenas and Le Puy)
Near river Forest area Near motorway
Closed 16 Nov-Mar
15 en suite (bth/shr) (3 fmly) TV in all bedrooms Direct dial
from all bedrooms Licensed Full central heating Open parking
available Covered parking available Child discount available
14yrs Fishing Boule Open terrace Last d 21.00hrs Languages
spoken: English
CARDS: ●● ■■ Travellers cheques

### LANCIE Rhône

**Les Pasquiers** (Prop: Jacques Gandilhon)
69220
☎ 474698633 FAX 474698657
(from A6 exit Mâcon-Sud, or Belleville on N6 to Romanèche,
3km to Lancie. In village take road into Les Pasquiers, house is
on square)
Set in a hamlet surrounded by vineyards, Les Pasquiers is ideal
for a family holiday with a suite available. Delicious evening
meals are served on a covered terrace near the swimming pool,
if weather permits. A warm and friendly welcome awaits you.
Near river Forest area Near motorway
4 en suite (bth/shr) (1 fmly) No smoking on premises TV
available Full central heating Open parking available Child
discount available Outdoor swimming pool Tennis Boule Last
d 20.00hrs Languages spoken: English & German
ROOMS: s 400FF; d 400FF
MEALS: Dinner 120FF

### LANS-EN-VERCORS Isère

*Le Renardière* (Prop: M Rabot)
Les Blancs 38250
☎ 476951376
Forest area
2 en suite (bth/shr) (1 fmly) (2 with balcony) No smoking on
premises Full central heating Open parking available

Supervised Child discount available 12yrs Languages spoken:
English German & Spanish
CARDS: Travellers cheques

### LANSLEBOURG Savoie

★ ★ ★ *Alpazur*
73480
☎ 479059369 FAX 479058655
Near river Forest area Near motorway
Closed 20 Apr-30 May & 21 Sep-19 Dec
24 en suite (bth/shr) (2 fmly) (14 with balcony) No smoking in
10 bedrooms TV in all bedrooms Direct dial from all bedrooms
Licensed Full central heating Open parking available Covered
parking available Child discount available 12yrs Bicycle rental
Open terrace V meals Last d 21.00hrs Languages spoken:
English & Italian
CARDS: ●● ■■ ■■ ⫶D⫶ Travellers cheques

### LANTIGNIE Rhône

**Domaine des Quarante Écus** (Prop: Bernard Nesme)
Les Vergers 69430
☎ 474048580 FAX 474692779
(exit Belleville from A6 in direction of Beaujeu, then D37 Pins &
onto D26 in direction of Julienas in 2km turn right)
Forest area
5 en suite (shr) (1 fmly) TV in 1 bedroom Full central heating
Open parking available Supervised Child discount available
12yrs Outdoor swimming pool Languages spoken: English
ROOMS: s fr 200FF; d fr 260FF

### LENTIGNY Loire

**Domaine de Champfleury** (Prop: Maurice Gaume)
42155
☎ 477633143 FAX 477633143
(from Roanne take D53 in the direction Thiers/Clermont for
8km then take D18 to Lentigny approx 1km)
Near lake Forest area
Closed 16 Nov-16 Mar
3 en suite (bth/shr) (1 fmly) No smoking on premises Full
central heating Open parking available Tennis Boule Bicycle
rental Badminton Table tennis Languages spoken: German
ROOMS: s 300FF; d 350FF
✱ Reductions over 1 night Special breaks

### LYON Rhône

★ ★ ★ *Hotel Bristol Frantour*
28 Cours Verdun 69002
☎ 478375655 FAX 478370258
In town centre Near motorway
113 en suite (bth/shr) No smoking in 24 bedrooms TV in all
bedrooms STV Radio in rooms Direct dial from all bedrooms
Licensed Lift Night porter Full central heating Air
conditioning in bedrooms Child discount available 12yrs Pool
table Languages spoken: English, German, Italian & Spanish
CARDS: ●● ■■ ■■ ⫶D⫶ Travellers cheques

★ ★ ★ *Hotel Carlton*
4 rue Jussieu 69002
☎ 478425651 FAX 478421071
In town centre Near motorway
83 en suite (bth/shr) (83 fmly) (62 with balcony) TV in all
bedrooms STV Radio in rooms Direct dial from all bedrooms
Mini-bar in all bedrooms Licensed Lift Night porter Full
*contd.*

central heating Air conditioning in bedrooms Child discount available 12yrs Languages spoken: English, German & Spanish
CARDS: ✸ ▦ ▥ ▣ JCB Travellers cheques

★ ★ ★ **Grand Hotel des Beaux-Arts** (Best Western)
73-75 rue du Prés E Herriot *69002*
☎ 478380950 FAX 478421919
In town centre
*75 en suite (bth/shr) (20 with balcony) No smoking in 11 bedrooms TV in all bedrooms STV Radio in rooms Direct dial from all bedrooms Mini-bar in all bedrooms Room-safe (charged) Licensed Lift Night porter Full central heating Air conditioning in bedrooms Child discount available 12yrs Languages spoken: English, German, Italian & Spanish*
ROOMS: (room only) s 535-660FF; d 590-700FF
CARDS: ✸ ▦ ▥ ▣ JCB Travellers cheques

★ ★ ★ ★ **Grand Hotel Mercure Château-Perrache**
12 cours de Verdun-Rambaud, et espl de la Gare
☎ 472771500 FAX 478370656
(close to the Gare de Perrache)

An elegant, comfortable hotel, dating originally from 1906 and tastefully restored. In a convenient position for all forms of public transport including a shuttle service to and from Satolas Airport.
In town centre Near motorway
*111 en suite (bth/shr) No smoking in 12 bedrooms TV in all bedrooms STV Direct dial from all bedrooms Licensed Lift Night porter Full central heating Air conditioning in bedrooms Open parking available (charged) Covered parking available (charged) Supervised Child discount available 16yrs Wkly live entertainment Last d 22.30hrs Languages spoken: English, German & Spanish*
ROOMS: (room only) s 740-840FF; d 840-940FF
**Reductions over 1 night Special breaks: wkends**
MEALS: Full breakfast 75FF Lunch 140-185FFalc Dinner 140-185FFalc
CARDS: ✸ ▦ ▥ ▣ Travellers cheques

★ ★ ★ ★ **Hotel Royal**
20 pl Bellecour *69002*
☎ 478375731 FAX 478370136
Near river In town centre Near motorway
*80 en suite (bth/shr) (7 fmly) (44 with balcony) No smoking in 13 bedrooms TV in all bedrooms STV Radio in rooms Direct dial from all bedrooms Mini-bar in all bedrooms Room-safe Licensed Lift Night porter Full central heating Air conditioning in bedrooms Covered parking available (charged) Supervised Child discount available 12yrs V meals Languages spoken: English, Arabic, German, Italian, Russian & Spanish*

ROOMS: (room only) s 720-785FF; d 820-2000FF
**Special breaks: Weekend breaks**
MEALS: Full breakfast 80FF
CARDS: ✸ ▦ ▥ ▣

*St Columban Lodge* (Prop: Annick & Michael Altuna)
7 rue du Hétre Pourpré *69130*
☎ 478330557 FAX 472189080
(from A6 exit Ecully, continue 1.7km to Ecully centre. After church straight ahead towards Tassin then 2nd left (fire station))
Near motorway
*6 en suite (bth/shr) No smoking in all bedrooms TV in all bedrooms Full central heating Open parking available Supervised No children 2yrs Child discount available Open terrace Languages spoken: English & Spanish*
CARDS: ✸ ▥

★ ★ ★ ★ *Sofitel Lyon Bellecour*
20 quai Gailleton *69002*
☎ 472412020 FAX 472400550
Near river In town centre Near motorway
*167 en suite (bth/shr) No smoking in 48 bedrooms TV in all bedrooms STV Radio in rooms Direct dial from all bedrooms Mini-bar in all bedrooms Licensed Lift Night porter Full central heating Air conditioning in bedrooms Open parking available (charged) Covered parking available (charged) Supervised Child discount available Last d 22.00hrs Languages spoken: English, German & Italian*
CARDS: ✸ ▦ ▥ ▣

★ ★ ★ ★ *La Tour Rose* (Small Luxury Hotels)
22 rue du Boeuf *69005*
☎ 478372590 FAX 478422602
In town centre Near motorway
*12 en suite (bth/shr) 5 rooms in annexe (5 fmly) (2 with balcony) TV in all bedrooms Direct dial from all bedrooms Mini-bar in all bedrooms Licensed Lift Full central heating Air conditioning in bedrooms Open parking available (charged) Covered parking available (charged) Supervised Child discount available 15yrs Open terrace Covered terrace Wkly live entertainment V meals Last d 22.30hrs Languages spoken: English, Italian & Spanish*
CARDS: ✸ ▦ ▥ ▣ JCB Travellers cheques

**MALATAVERNE** Drôme

★ ★ ★ *Domaine du Colombier*
rte de Donzère *26780*
☎ 475908686 FAX 475907940
(exit A7 at Montélimar Sud in the direction Malataverne, pass through village and take direction of Donzère for 4km)
Forest area
*25 en suite (bth/shr) (8 fmly) (6 with balcony) TV in all bedrooms Direct dial from all bedrooms Licensed Full central heating Open parking available Covered parking available (charged) Outdoor swimming pool Boule Bicycle rental Open terrace Covered terrace 4ha park V meals Last d 21.30hrs Languages spoken: English, German & Italian*
CARDS: ✸ ▦ ▥ ▣ Travellers cheques

**MARGES** Drôme

★ ★ *Auberge Le Pont du Chalon*
*26260*
☎ 475426213 FAX 475456019
Near river Near lake Forest area Near motorway

*RS Mon*
*23 rms (3 bth 5 shr) 4 rooms in annexe (4 fmly) (3 with balcony)*
*TV in 5 bedrooms Direct dial from 9 bedrooms Lift Night porter*
*Open parking available Covered parking available Open terrace*
*Covered terrace V meals Last d 21.30hrs*
CARDS: ●● ■■

### MÉAUDRE Isère

★ ★ *Auberge du Furon*
*38112*
☎ 476952471 FAX 476952471
Forest area
*Closed mid Nov-mid Dec*
*9 en suite (bth) (1 fmly) (3 with balcony) TV in all bedrooms*
*STV Direct dial from all bedrooms Licensed Full central*
*heating Open parking available Child discount available 12yrs*
*Boule Open terrace Covered terrace Last d 21.00hrs*
*Languages spoken: English*
CARDS: ●● ■■ Travellers cheques

### MEGÈVE Haute-Savoie

★ ★ ★ **Les Fermes de Marie**
chemin de Riante Colline *74120*
☎ 450930310 FAX 450930984
(approach via A40 exit Sallanches)
Forest area Near motorway
*Closed mid Sep-mid Dec & mid Apr-mid Jun*
*69 en suite (bth/shr) (62 fmly) (62 with balcony) TV in all*
*bedrooms STV Direct dial from all bedrooms Mini-bar in all*
*bedrooms Licensed Lift Night porter Full central heating*
*Open parking available Covered parking available Supervised*
*Child discount available Indoor swimming pool (heated) Sauna*
*Solarium Pool table Jacuzzi/spa Bicycle rental Open terrace*
*Covered terrace Wkly live entertainment Casino Last d*
*22.00hrs Languages spoken: English & Italian*
ROOMS: (incl. dinner) s 1290-2020FF; d 890-1630FF
MEALS: Continental breakfast 80FF Lunch 350-630FFalc
Dinner 350-630FFalc
CARDS: ●● ■ ■■ Travellers cheques

★ ★ ★ ★ **Le Mont Blanc**
pl de l'Église, rue Ambroise Martin
☎ 450212002 FAX 450214528
(approach via A40 exit Sallanches)
Forest area
*40 en suite (bth/shr) (16 fmly) (37 with balcony) TV in all*
*bedrooms STV Direct dial from all bedrooms Mini-bar in all*
*bedrooms Room-safe Lift Night porter Full central heating*
*Outdoor swimming pool (heated) Sauna Jacuzzi/spa Open*
*terrace Covered terrace Languages spoken: English, Italian &*
*Spanish*
ROOMS: (room only) s 1310-1570FF; d 2290-3010FF
CARDS: ●● ■■ ▣

★ **Les Pommiers**
2370 rte de Praz *74120*
☎ 450210167 FAX 450215688
(A40 Sallanches exit 20 take direction of Albertville, cross
Megève the hotel is situated at exit on N212)
Forest area In town centre
*18 rms (15 shr) 2 rooms in annexe TV in 7 bedrooms Licensed*
*Full central heating Open parking available Supervised Child*
*discount available 12yrs Open terrace Last d 21.30hrs*
*Languages spoken: English*
CARDS: ●● ■ ■■ ▣ Travellers cheques

### MENS Isère

**Chez Pierrette**
rue du Bourg *38710*
☎ 476346014 476348404
Near lake Forest area
*Closed Jan-Feb*
*5 en suite (bth/shr) (1 fmly) No smoking on premises TV*
*available Full central heating Child discount available 12yrs V*
*meals Languages spoken: English*
CARDS: Travellers cheques

**L'Engrangeou** (Prop: Janic Grinberg)
pl de la Halle *38710*
☎ 476349448 & 476348563
(from Grenoble take N75 to Monestier then D34 to Mens, or
from Grenoble take N85 (rte Napoléon) to La Mure then D526
to Mens)
Near river Near lake Forest area In town centre Near
motorway
*3 en suite (shr) No smoking on premises TV in all bedrooms*
*STV Full central heating Open parking available Child*
*discount available Riding Boule Bicycle rental Languages*
*spoken: English*

### MENUIRES, LES Savoie

★ ★ **Hotel de l'Oisans**
☎ 479006296 FAX 479002646
(on D117 towards Moûtiers)
*15 en suite (bth) (4 fmly) TV in all bedrooms STV Direct dial*
*from all bedrooms Night porter Full central heating Air*
*conditioning in bedrooms Open parking available (charged)*
*Child discount available 11yrs V meals Last d 23.00hrs*
*Languages spoken: English, Dutch & German*
CARDS: ●● ■■

### MERCUROL Drôme

★ ★ **De La Tour**
Le Village, 11 rue de la République *26600*
☎ 475074007 FAX 475074620
(exit A7 at Tain L'Hermitage-Romans and follow signs
Mercurol-Romans, then take 1st left to village of Mercurol)
Forest area Near motorway
*20 rms (5 bth 12 shr) (8 fmly) TV in 13 bedrooms Direct dial*
*from all bedrooms Licensed Night porter Full central heating*
*Covered parking available (charged) Child discount available*
*12yrs Boule V meals Last d 22.00hrs Languages spoken:*
*English*
CARDS: ●● ■■

### MÉRIBEL-LES-ALLUES Savoie

★ ★ **Orée du Bois**
rte du Belvédère *73550*
☎ 479005030 FAX 479085752
Forest area
*Closed Etr,Jul,Aug & Xmas*
*35 rms (26 bth 6 shr) (2 fmly) (35 with balcony) TV in all*
*bedrooms STV Radio in rooms Direct dial from all bedrooms*
*Licensed Lift Full central heating Open parking available*
*Covered parking available (charged) Child discount available*
*Outdoor swimming pool Golf Solarium Bicycle rental Open*
*terrace Last d 21.00hrs Languages spoken: English*
CARDS: ●● ■ ■■ Travellers cheques

**MEYLAN** Isère

★ ★ ★ **Hotel Alpha**
34 av de Verdun *38240*
☎ 476906309 FAX 476902827
Near river Forest area In town centre Near motorway
*83 en suite (bth/shr) (23 with balcony) No smoking in 24
bedrooms TV in all bedrooms STV Radio in rooms Direct dial
from all bedrooms Mini-bar in 64 bedrooms Licensed Lift
Night porter Full central heating Open parking available
Covered parking available (charged) Child discount available
12yrs Outdoor swimming pool Pool table Open terrace
Covered terrace Last d 22.30hrs Languages spoken: English,
German, Italian & Spanish*
ROOMS: (room only) s 450-500FF; d 550-670FF
MEALS: Continental breakfast 55FF Lunch fr 115FF&alc
Dinner fr 115FF&alc
CARDS: ●● ■■ ▆▆ 🄰 Travellers cheques

**MEYZIEU** Rhône

★ ★ ★ **Mont Joyeux**
av Victor Hugo-Le Carreau *69330*
☎ 478042132 FAX 472028572
(off A46)
Located just a few minutes outside Lyon, the hotel offers its
clientele a complete change of scenery and a peaceful stay.
Situated opposite a large lake it attractive bedrooms with
balconies, a restaurant with fine views over the water and a
terrace for relaxation. The cuisine consists of a wide range of
dishes including light pastries, fresh fish and regional specialities
skilfully executed by the chef-proprietor Jean-Bernard Mollard.
Near lake Near sea Forest area Near motorway

*20 en suite (bth) (2 fmly) (20 with balcony) TV in all bedrooms
STV Radio in rooms Direct dial from all bedrooms Mini-bar in
all bedrooms Licensed Full central heating Open parking
available Child discount available 6yrs Outdoor swimming
pool Fishing Boule Open terrace V meals Last d 21.30hrs
Languages spoken: English, German & Spanish*
ROOMS: (room only) s 430-500FF; d 470-530FF
MEALS: Continental breakfast 58FF Lunch 130-280FF&alc
Dinner 130-280FF&alc
CARDS: ●● ■■ ▆▆ 🄰 Travellers cheques

**MIJOUX** Ain

**Le Boulu** (Prop: B et C Grosfilley)
*01410*
☎ 450413147
(from A40 exit at Germain-de-Joux & take N84 towards
Bellegarde. Take left onto D14/D991 to Mijoux/Col de la Faucille)

Near river Near lake Near sea Forest area Near motorway
*RS Winter except Xmas contact for details
5 en suite (bth/shr) No smoking on premises Full central
heating Open parking available Child discount available
Tennis Last d 19.00hrs Languages spoken: English &
Spanish*
MEALS: Dinner 110FF✱

**MIRABEL** Ardèche

**Le Mas des Vignes** (Prop: M & Mme Meerloo)
La Prade *07170*
☎ 475942854 FAX 475942854
(off A7 at Montélimar N direction Le Teil-Aubenas. At
Lavilledieu turn right to Lussas, follow direction Mirabel, after
1km, immediately after bridge, take sharp right)
Near river Forest area Near motorway
*June-Sep*
*4 en suite (bth/shr) (1 with balcony) Full central heating Open
parking available Child discount available Languages spoken:
English, Dutch & German*
ROOMS: s 250-300FF; d 250-370FF
CARDS: Travellers cheques

**MIRMANDE** Drôme

★ ★ *Capitelle*
rue du Rémpart *26270*
☎ 475630272 FAX 475630250
Forest area Near motorway
*Closed Tuesday and Wednesday noon
11 en suite (bth/shr) (2 fmly) (3 with balcony) Full central
heating 22828 covered parking spaces (charged) Supervised
Child discount available 10yrs Open terrace Last d 21.30hrs
Languages spoken: English*
CARDS: ●● ■■ ▆▆ 🄰 Travellers cheques

**MONTAILLEUR** Savoie

★ ★ *Tour de Pacoret*
*73460*
☎ 479379159 FAX 479379384
Near river Near lake Forest area
*Closed end of Oct-Etr
9 en suite (bth/shr) TV in all bedrooms Direct dial from all
bedrooms Licensed Full central heating Open parking
available Covered parking available (charged) Boule Open
terrace Last d 21.30hrs Languages spoken: English*
CARDS: ●● ▆▆ Travellers cheques

**MONTBOUCHER-SUR-JABRON** Drôme

★ ★ ★ *Castel*
Le Castel *26740*
☎ 475460816 FAX 475014409
Near river Forest area Near motorway
*12 en suite (bth/shr) (1 fmly) (2 with balcony) TV in all
bedrooms STV Mini-bar in all bedrooms Licensed Full central
heating Open parking available Supervised Child discount
available 12yrs Outdoor swimming pool Tennis Boule Open
terrace V meals Last d 21.00hrs Languages spoken: English &
Hungarian*
CARDS: ●● ■■ ▆▆ Travellers cheques

## MONTBRISON-SUR-LEZ Drôme

**Bed & Breakfast** (Prop: M & Mme R Barjavel)
*26770*
☎ 475535404
(approach via D538)
Forest area
*3 en suite (bth/shr) (2 fmly) (2 with balcony) Full central heating Open parking available Supervised Outdoor swimming pool*

## MONTÉLIMAR Drôme

★ ★ **Le Printemps**
8 ch de la Manche *26200*
☎ 475013263 FAX 475460314
*Closed 1-15 Dec*
*25 rms (2 fmly) (2 with balcony) TV in all bedrooms STV Direct dial from all bedrooms Mini-bar in all bedrooms Licensed Full central heating Open parking available Supervised No children 14yrs Outdoor swimming pool Open terrace Last d 21.00hrs*
CARDS: ●● ■ ■■

## MONTHIEUX Ain

★ ★ ★ ★ **Gouverneur**
Lieu-dit Le Breuil *01390*
☎ 472264200 FAX 472264220
(on D82)
Near river Near lake Forest area
*Closed 15-30 Dec*
*53 en suite (bth/shr) (8 fmly) TV in all bedrooms STV Radio in rooms Direct dial from all bedrooms Mini-bar in all bedrooms Licensed Lift Night porter Full central heating Air conditioning in bedrooms Open parking available Supervised Child discount available 12yrs Outdoor swimming pool Golf 45 Tennis Fishing Pool table Boule Bicycle rental Open terrace V meals Last d 21.30hrs Languages spoken: English & German*
ROOMS: (room only) s 460-540FF d 540-590FF
**Reductions over 1 night Special breaks**
MEALS: Full breakfast 65FF Lunch 185-350FF&alc Dinner 185-350FF&alc
CARDS: ●● ■ ■■ ◉ Travellers cheques

## MORESTEL Isère

**Domaine de la Garenne**
558 rte de Sermerieu *38510*
☎ 474505915 FAX 474503169
(from Morestel, towards Lyon, then take the right towards Semerieu, in 800 metres on right is entrance to property)
Forest area
*Closed 5-31 Jan*
*6 rms (5 bth) (1 fmly) TV in 2 bedrooms Full central heating Open parking available Child discount available 10yrs Outdoor swimming pool Tennis Bicycle rental V meals Languages spoken: English & German*
CARDS: ●● ■■

## MORZINE Haute-Savoie

★ ★ **Des Bruyères**
Im des Champs de la Plagne *74110*
☎ 450791576 FAX 450747009
Near river Near lake Forest area In town centre Near motorway

*Closed 21 Apr-19 Jun & 11 Sep-19 Dec*
*24 en suite (bth/shr) 4 rooms in annexe (12 fmly) (24 with balcony) TV in all bedrooms Direct dial from all bedrooms Full central heating Open parking available Child discount available 12yrs Outdoor swimming pool (heated) Sauna Pool table Bicycle rental Open terrace Last d 20.30hrs Languages spoken: English*
CARDS: ●● ■■ Travellers cheques

**L'Equipe Hotel**
☎ 450791143 FAX 450792607
(on southern outskirts, near the ski station)
Near river Near lake
*Closed 16 Sep-14 Dec & 16 Apr-15 Jun*
*35 en suite (bth/shr) (9 fmly) (33 with balcony) No smoking in 2 bedrooms TV in 30 bedrooms STV Direct dial from all bedrooms Lift Full central heating Open parking available Child discount available 8yrs Indoor swimming pool (heated) Solarium Gym Pool table Boule Jacuzzi/spa Open terrace Covered terrace V meals Languages spoken: English & Spanish*
CARDS: ●● ■ ■■ ◉ Travellers cheques

## NOAILLY Loire

★ ★ ★ **Château de la Motte**
rte D4- La Motte *42640*
☎ 477666460 FAX 477666438
Near river Forest area Near motorway
*Closed Rest. only Sun eve & Mon (ex Jul-Aug)*
*12 en suite (bth/shr) (1 with balcony) TV in all bedrooms Direct dial from all bedrooms Licensed Full central heating Open parking available Supervised Child discount available 12yrs Outdoor swimming pool Fishing Riding Boule Bicycle rental Open terrace Covered terrace Table tennis, Canal cruise arranged V meals Last d 21.30hrs Languages spoken: English, Italian, Russian & Spanish*
CARDS: ●● ■■ Travellers cheques

## NOTRE-DAME-DE-BELLECOMBE Savoie

★ ★ **Bellevue**
*73590*
☎ 479316056 FAX 479316984
Forest area In town centre Near motorway
*Closed 20 Apr-20 Jun & 10 Sep-20 Dec*
*18 rms (15 bth/shr) (9 with balcony) TV in all bedrooms Direct dial from all bedrooms Licensed Full central heating Open parking available Child discount available 10yrs Solarium Boule Open terrace Last d 21.00hrs Languages spoken: English*
CARDS: ●● ■■

## NYONS Drôme

★ ★ ★ **Auberge du Vieux Village d'Aubres**
Aubres *26110*
☎ 475261289 FAX 475263810
(3km NE of Nyons on D94)
This traditional inn has been built on the site of a medieval castle and thanks to the mild local climate guests can enjoy breakfast on the terrace all year round. It features very comfortable bedrooms - most with terrace - which are equipped with modern amenities, while the restaurant offers a cuisine which includes classic dishes. Special diets catered for.
Near river Forest area
*Closed Jan*

*contd.*

**Auberge du Vieux Village d'Aubres**
23 en suite (bth/shr) (6 fmly) (20 with balcony) TV in all
bedrooms STV Radio in rooms Direct dial from all bedrooms
Mini-bar in all bedrooms Room-safe Licensed Night porter
Full central heating Open parking available Child discount
available Indoor swimming pool (heated) Outdoor swimming
pool (heated) Sauna Solarium Gym Boule Jacuzzi/spa Bicycle
rental Open terrace Covered terrace Table tennis, Library,
Table Football V meals Last d 20.30hrs Languages spoken:
English & German
ROOMS: (room only) s 300-420FF; d 420-780FF
**Reductions over 1 night**
MEALS: Continental breakfast 67FF Lunch 80-178FF&alc
Dinner 80-178FF&alc
CARDS: ●● ■■ ▆▆ ⓪ Travellers cheques

**PEISEY-NANCROIX** Savoie

★ ★ **La Vanoise**
Plan Peisey 73210
☎ 479079219 FAX 479079748
Closed early Sep-late Dec
34 en suite (bth/shr) (5 fmly) (20 with balcony) TV in all
bedrooms Licensed Full central heating Open parking
available Child discount available Outdoor swimming pool
(heated) Pool table Boule Bicycle rental Open terrace V meals
Last d 20.30hrs
CARDS: ●● ▆▆ Travellers cheques

**POËT-LAVAL, LE** Drôme

★ ★ ★ **Hospitaliers**
Vieux Village 26160
☎ 475462232 FAX 475464999
Near river Forest area In town centre Near motorway
Closed 16 Nov-14 Mar
22 en suite (bth/shr) 12 rooms in annexe (4 fmly) (1 with
balcony) TV in 15 bedrooms Direct dial from all bedrooms
Licensed Full central heating Open parking available Outdoor
swimming pool Open terrace Last d 21.15hrs Languages
spoken: English
ROOMS: (room only) d 380-1100FF
MEALS: Continental breakfast 50FF Lunch 160-340FF&alc
Dinner 160-340FF&alc
CARDS: ●● ■■ ▆▆ ⓪ Travellers cheques

**PONT-D'AIN** Ain

★ ★ **Des Allies**
01160
☎ 474390009 FAX 474391366
Near river Near lake Forest area In town centre Near
motorway

Closed 31 Oct-Jan
18 rms (14 bth/shr) (4 fmly) TV in all bedrooms Radio in rooms
Direct dial from all bedrooms Licensed Full central heating
Covered parking available (charged) Supervised Languages
spoken: English
CARDS: ●● ▆▆ ⓪ Travellers cheques

**PONT-DE-BARRET** Drôme

**Les Tuillieres** (Prop: S & H Jenny)
26160
☎ 475904391
(from A7 exit Montélimar Nord take N7 to La Coucourde then
D74 to Sauzet, D6 to Cléon-d'Andran, D9 to Charols then D128
towards Pont-de-Barret. Les Tuillières on right)
Near river Forest area Near motorway
Closed 17 Oct-Etr
6 en suite (bth/shr) (3 fmly) No smoking on premises Full
central heating Open parking available Covered parking
available No children 12yrs Outdoor swimming pool (heated)
Boule V meals Last d 20.00hrs Languages spoken: English,
German & Italian
CARDS: Travellers cheques

**PONT-DE-CHERUY** Isère

★ **Bergeron**
3 rue Giffard 38230
☎ 478321008 FAX 478321170
Near river Near lake Near sea Forest area In town centre
Near motorway
16 rms 8 rooms in annexe (2 fmly) (1 with balcony) Full
central heating Open parking available Covered parking
available (charged) Open terrace
CARDS: ●● ▆▆

**PONT-DE-VAUX** Ain

★ ★ **Le Raisin**
2 pl Michel Poosat 01190
☎ 385303097 FAX 385306789
(leave A6 at Tournus onto N6 in direction of Mâcon)
Near river Forest area
Closed 5 Jan-5 Feb
18 en suite (bth/shr) (3 fmly) TV in all bedrooms Direct dial
from all bedrooms Licensed Full central heating Open parking
available Supervised Child discount available 12yrs Boule
Open terrace V meals Languages spoken: English & Spanish
CARDS: ●● ■■ ▆▆ ⓪ Travellers cheques

**POURCHÈRES** Ardèche

**Bed & Breakfast** (Prop: Marcelle & Jean-Nicholas Goetz)
07000
☎ 475668199 FAX 475668199
(from Aubenas via N104 after Col de L'Escrinet turn left on
D122, then right for Pourchères after 2km)
Forest area
5 en suite (bth/shr) No smoking on premises Full central
heating Open parking available Supervised Child discount
available 5yrs V meals Last d 20.00hrs Languages spoken:
English & German
ROOMS: (incl. dinner) s 200-350FF; d 250-530FF ✱
MEALS: Dinner 110FF

### PRAZ-DE-CHAMONIX, LES Haute-Savoie

**★★ Eden**
35 rte des Gaudenays *74400*
☎ 450531843 FAX 450535150
Forest area Near motorway
*20 rms (3 with balcony) TV in all bedrooms STV Direct dial
from all bedrooms Mini-bar in all bedrooms Licensed Open
parking available Supervised Child discount available 10yrs
Languages spoken: English & Italian*
CARDS: ●● ■■ ☲ ⑩ Travellers cheques

### QUINCIÉ-EN-BEAUJOLAIS Rhône

**Domaine de Romarand** (Prop: Annie & Jean Berthelot)
*69430*
☎ 474043449 FAX 474043449
(from A6 exit Belleville-sur-Saône in the direction Beaujeu D37,
before Beaujeu turn left to Quincié-en-Beaujolais D9 through
village, before Grand Château right to Romarand)
Near lake Forest area Near motorway
*3 en suite (shr) No smoking on premises Full central heating
Open parking available Child discount available Outdoor
swimming pool Languages spoken: English*
ROOMS: d 295-320FF
MEALS: Dinner 100-120FF
CARDS: Travellers cheques

**★★ Le Mont Brouilly**
*69430*
☎ 474043373 FAX 474043010
(leave A6 at Bellville/Saône in direction of Beaujeu D37
approx 8km)
Near river Forest area Near motorway
*29 en suite (bth/shr) (1 fmly) TV in 27 bedrooms Direct dial
from all bedrooms Licensed Full central heating Open parking
available Covered parking available (charged) Supervised
Child discount available 10yrs Outdoor swimming pool Boule
Open terrace Last d 21.00hrs Languages spoken: English*
MEALS: Continental breakfast 36FF Lunch 90-230FF&alc
Dinner 90-230FF&alc
CARDS: ●● ■■ ☲ Travellers cheques

### REAUVILLE Drôme

**Mas de Pantai** (Prop: Sergio Chiorino)
☎ 475985110 FAX 475985859
(Exit Montélimar Sud go left in direction of Avignon in 2km left
again in direction of Grignan after 10km left in direction of
Reauville)
Near river Forest area
*Closed mid Nov-Mar
6 rms (5 bth/shr) TV in 1 bedroom Full central heating Open
parking available No children 7yrs Child discount available
12yrs Outdoor swimming pool Boule*

### REPLONGES Ain

**★★★ Hostellerie Sarrasine**
533 rte de Madeleine *01750*
☎ 385310241 FAX 385311174
(From Paris A40 exit2, Feillens. From Lyon A6 exit Mâcon-Sud)
Amid fountains and flowers a former "Bressanne Farm",
peaceful and delightful base to visit Burgundy. Fine traditional
cuisine using the best local produce, served with excellent
wines of the region. Very comfortable and spacious rooms with

***Hostellerie Sarrasine***
air-conditioning. A friendly English speaking staff will take
care of you during your stay.
Near river Near motorway
*Closed 16 Nov-12 Dec & 7 Jan-2 Feb
7 en suite (bth) (2 fmly) TV in all bedrooms STV Radio in
rooms Direct dial from all bedrooms Mini-bar in all bedrooms
Room-safe Licensed Night porter Full central heating Air
conditioning in bedrooms Open parking available Covered
parking available Supervised Outdoor swimming pool (heated)
Open terrace Covered terrace V meals Last d 21.00hrs
Languages spoken: English German & Italian*
ROOMS: (room only) s fr 398FF; d 590-870FF
**Reductions over 1 night**
MEALS: Dinner 99-350FF✱
CARDS: ●● ■■ ☲ ⑩ JCB Travellers cheques

### REVENTIN-VAUGRIS Isère

**★★ Le Reventel**
*38121*
☎ 4474788350 FAX 4474852788
(Access via N7 towards Valence)
Near motorway
*Closed 23 Aug-5 Sep & Xmas
16 rms (8 bth 11 shr) (2 fmly) TV in all bedrooms Direct dial
from all bedrooms Licensed Full central heating Open parking
available Covered parking available Open terrace V meals
Languages spoken: English*
ROOMS: (room only) d 240-350FF
CARDS: ●● ■■ ☲ ⑩ Travellers cheques

### REVONNAS Ain

**Grillerin** (Prop: M et Mme de Pompignan)
*01250*
☎ 474300268
(A40 exit Bourg-Sud in direction of Pont-d'Ain then towards
Tossiat & finally Revonnas)
*2 en suite (shr) Open parking available Last d 20.00hrs*

### ROANNE Loire

**★★★ Grand Hotel (S)**
18 cours de la République *42300*
☎ 477714882 FAX 477704240
(situated close by the railway station)
In town centre
*Closed 1-18 Aug & Xmas
33 en suite (bth/shr) TV in all bedrooms STV Direct dial from
all bedrooms Mini-bar in all bedrooms Licensed Lift Night
porter Full central heating Open parking available (charged)*
contd.

Supervised Child discount available 12yrs Languages spoken: English
ROOMS: s 280-350FF; d 330-430FF
CARDS: 😊 ■ 😊 😊 Travellers cheques

### ★ ★ ★ ★ Troisgros
pl de la Gare 42300
☎ 477716697 FAX 477703977
(Autoroute A6-exit 'Chalon-sur-Saône-sud' then 'Montceau-les-Mines/Paray-le-Monial/Roanne'. Or autoroute A6-exit 'Belleville-sur-Saône'. Then 'Beaujeu/Charlieu'- Tourist Route)
In town centre
Closed 2 wks Feb & 2 wks Aug
19 en suite (bth/shr) (2 fmly) (1 with balcony) TV in all bedrooms Direct dial from all bedrooms Mini-bar in all bedrooms Licensed Lift Night porter Full central heating Air conditioning in bedrooms Open parking available Covered parking available Supervised Child discount available Bicycle rental Open terrace Boutique Troisgros Last d 21.30hrs
Languages spoken: English, German & Spanish
CARDS: 😊 ■ 😊 😊 JCB Travellers cheques

### ROCHE-SUR-FORON, LA Haute-Savoie

### ★ ★ Foron
50 Imp de l'Étang 74800
☎ 450258276 FAX 450258154
Forest area Near motorway
Closed 20 Dec-5 Jan
26 en suite (bth/shr) (1 with balcony) TV in all bedrooms Direct dial from all bedrooms Full central heating Open parking available Covered parking available (charged) Child discount available 12yrs Languages spoken: English & Italian
CARDS: 😊 ■ 😊 😊 Travellers cheques

### ST-AGNAN-EN-VERCORS Drôme

### ★ ★ Veymont
26420
☎ 475482019 FAX 475481034
(A49 to Baume-d'Horsun, D531 St-Nazaire-en-Royans, La Chapelle-en-Vercors)
Forest area
Closed Nov-Dec
17 en suite (bth/shr) (2 fmly) Direct dial from all bedrooms Licensed Full central heating Open parking available Child discount available 15yrs Sauna Jacuzzi/spa Open terrace V meals Last d 20.30hrs Languages spoken: English
CARDS: 😊 😊 Travellers cheques

### ST-ANDRÉ-SUR-VIEUX-JONC Ain

### Château-de-Marmont (Prop: Genevieve Guido-Alheritiere)
01960
☎ 474527974
(turn off Lyon-Bourg-en-Bresse road and continue for 5km towards Condeissiat)
Near lake Forest area
3 en suite (bth/shr) Full central heating Open parking available Covered parking available Supervised Child discount available Languages spoken: English Italian & Spanish

### ST-BÉNIGNE Ain

### Petites Varennes (Prop: Christine A Treal)
01190
☎ 385303198
Near river Forest area
5 rms (2 bth 1 shr) No smoking in all bedrooms Licensed Full central heating Open parking available Indoor swimming pool (heated) Open terrace Covered terrace Languages spoken: English

### ST-CIRGUES-EN-MONTAGNE Ardèche

### ★ ★ ★ Domaine du Lac Ferrand
07510
☎ 475389557 FAX 475389558
Near lake Forest area
Closed 16 Nov-30 Dec
18 en suite (bth/shr) TV in all bedrooms STV Direct dial from all bedrooms Licensed Full central heating Open parking available Supervised Child discount available 10yrs Fishing Sauna Gym Boule Jacuzzi/spa Open terrace Languages spoken: English, Portuguese & Spanish
CARDS: 😊 ■ 😊 😊

### ST-CLAIR-DU-RHÔNE Isère

### Les Prailles (Prop: Raymond Pasquarelli)
6 chemin de Prailles 38370
☎ 474872915 & 686526121
(take N86 to Condrieu and cross bridge to Les Roches-de-Condrieu, follow signs as far as St Clair-du-Rhône, exit 3km after the village)
Near river Forest area
5 en suite (bth/shr) (4 fmly) (1 with balcony) No smoking on premises TV in 1 bedroom Full central heating Open parking available Child discount available 10yrs Outdoor swimming pool Table tennis V meals Last d 17.00hrs Languages spoken: English
ROOMS: d 250-300FF ✳
MEALS: Dinner fr 100FF
CARDS: Travellers cheques

### ST-DONAT-SUR-L'HERBASSE Drôme

### ★ ★ ★ Chartron
1 av Gambetta 26260
☎ 475451182 FAX 475450136
(take Tain-l'Hermitage exit from A7 in the direction of Romans, continue towards Chanos Curson then turn right & follow road to St Donat-sur-l'Herbasse)
Near river Near lake In town centre
7 en suite (bth/shr) TV in all bedrooms Mini-bar in all bedrooms Licensed Full central heating Air conditioning in bedrooms Open parking available Covered parking available (charged) Child discount available Open terrace Last d 21.45hrs Languages spoken: English
ROOMS: (room only) s 340FF; d 360FF
MEALS: Continental breakfast 45FF Lunch 150FF&alc Dinner 160FF
CARDS: 😊 ■ 😊 😊 Travellers cheques

### ST-FÉLIX Haute-Savoie

**Les Bruyères** (Prop: B L Betts)
Mercy *74540*
☎ 450609653 FAX 450609465
(leave N201 at St-Félix. In village take road in front of church
then left after the cemetery signposted 'Mercy'. Up hill, right at
statue, then sharp left through farm and left through double
iron gates)
Situated at the foot of the Alps, this restored 19th-century
Savoy farm offers luxurious accommodation surrounded by a
landscaped park ablaze with flowers. Regional breakfasts are
served and afternoon tea is offered on the terrace. On site
facilities include tennis and croquet. Two beautiful lakes are
situated nearby: Lake du Bourget and Lake d'Annecy. English
spoken. A maisonette is available for weekly rental.
Near river Near lake Near sea Near beach Forest area Near
motorway
*3 en suite (bth/shr) No smoking on premises TV in all
bedrooms STV Full central heating Open parking available
Covered parking available Supervised Child discount available
14yrs Tennis Croquet V meals Last d 20.30hrs Languages
spoken: English*
ROOMS: d 650FF
CARDS: 💳 🚊 Travellers cheques

### ST-GENIS-POUILLY Ain

★ ★ **Climat de France**
85 rte de la Faucille *06130*
☎ 450420520 Cen Res 164460123 FAX 450420814
(on D984 off N1)
Near river Forest area Near motorway
*42 en suite (bth) TV in all bedrooms STV Radio in rooms
Direct dial from all bedrooms Full central heating Open
parking available Child discount available 12 yrs Open terrace
Covered terrace Last d 22.00hrs Languages spoken: English*
ROOMS: (room only) d 295-310FF
**Reductions over 1 night**
CARDS: 💳 ■ 🚊 💳 Travellers cheques

### ST-GEORGES-LES-BAINS Ardèche

*St-Marcel-de-Crussol* (Prop: Madame Biosse Duplan)
*07800*
☎ 475608177 FAX 475608632
Near river Near lake Forest area Near motorway
*2 en suite (bth) (1 fmly) TV available Full central heating Open
parking available Child discount available Languages spoken:
Spanish*

### ST-HILAIRE-DU-TOUVET Isère

**Les Hauts Granets** (Prop: Nicole Raibon)
*38660*
☎ 476083056 FAX 476083056
(from autoroute towards Chambéry, exit 25 St-Ismier take N90
to Les Eymes, then D30 to St-Hilaire-du-Touvet. In St-Hilaire
pass football ground then 1st left)
Near lake Forest area
*2 en suite (shr) TV in all bedrooms Full central heating Open
parking available No children 12yrs Table Tennis Languages
spoken: English*

### ST-JEAN-D'ARDIÈRES Rhône

★ ★ ★ ★ **Château de Pizay**
rte de Villier Morgon *69220*
☎ 474665141 FAX 474696563
(from A6 exit 'Belleville' take N6 towards Mâcon to hotel on
left)
Forest area Near motorway
*Closed 24 Dec-2 Jan*
*62 en suite (bth/shr) (8 fmly) TV in all bedrooms STV Radio in
rooms Direct dial from all bedrooms Mini-bar in all bedrooms
Room-safe Licensed Night porter Full central heating Air
conditioning in bedrooms Open parking available Supervised
Child discount available 12yrs Outdoor swimming pool Tennis
Pool table Boule Bicycle rental Open terrace Basketball, ping
pong Last d 21.30hrs Languages spoken: English & Italian*
MEALS: Continental breakfast 75FF Lunch 220-395FF&alc
Dinner 220-395FF&alc
CARDS: 💳 ■ 🚊 💳 JCB Travellers cheques

### ST-JULIEN-DU-GUA Ardèche

*Le Folastère* (Prop: Jean-Pierre Lambert)
Hameau de Intres *07190*
☎ 475668504
(N104 in direction of Aubenas 1km after Col de l'Arènies take
D122 right in direction of Mezillac-Gerbier continue for 9km,
stop at Col de la Fayolle. Look for "Chambre d'hôte" sign - do
not go into village)
Near river Forest area
*Closed mid Sep-Apr*
*1 en suite (shr) No smoking on premises Open parking
available Outdoor swimming pool (heated) Fishing Boule*

### ST-JULIEN-DU-SERRE Ardèche

*Le Moulinage* (Prop: V Vandamme-Lefevre)
Le Chambon *07200*
☎ 475930509
(from Aubenas take N104 to St-Privat, turn left opposite the
post office and take small road to St-Julien-du-Serre. After
approx 1.5km cross small village of Le Chambon and then take
last road on right)
Near river Forest area Near motorway
*1 en suite (shr) (1 fmly) No smoking on premises Full central
heating Open parking available Child discount available 2yrs
Riding Languages spoken: English*

### ST-LATTIER Isère

**Lièvre Amoureux** (Prop: M Breda)
La Gare *38840*
☎ 476645067 FAX 476643121
Forest area Near motorway
*Closed Oct-24 Mar*
*12 rms (10 bth/shr) TV in 5 bedrooms Full central heating
Open parking available Outdoor swimming pool Open terrace*

### ST-MARCEL-D'URFÉ Loire

**Il Fut un Temps** (Prop: Anne-Marie Hauck)
Lieu-dit Les Gouttes *42430*
☎ 477625219 FAX 477625219
(D24 St-Marcel-d'Urfé and D20 in direction of St-Martin-la-
Sauveté 1.7km after St-Marcel take next right "Les Foultes" at
Montée turn right and right again at sign)
Near river Forest area Near motorway *contd.*

*5 en suite (shr) (2 fmly) No smoking on premises Full central heating Open parking available Boule Bicycle rental V meals Last d 18.00hrs Languages spoken: English & German*
ROOMS: s 200-300FF; d 250-350FF
MEALS: Dinner fr 85FF

## ST-MARCEL-LES-VALENCE Drôme

**La Pineraie** (Prop: Marie Jeanne Katchikian)
Chemin Bel Air *26320*
☎ 475587225
(exit Valence Nord or Sud A7 then take A49/N532 & exit at St Marcel-Les Valence)
*Near river Near lake Near beach Forest area Near motorway 3 rms (2 bth/shr) (2 with balcony) No smoking on premises Full central heating Open parking available Supervised Child discount available 12yrs Languages spoken: English, Italian & Spanish*
ROOMS: s 250FF; d 300FF **Reductions over 1 night**
CARDS: Travellers cheques

## ST-MARTIN-DE-BELLEVILLE Savoie

★ ★ ★ **Novotel**
pl de la Lombarde-Val Thorens *73440*
☎ 479000404 FAX 479000593
In town centre
*Closed Dec-Apr*
*104 rms (104 fmly) No smoking in 52 bedrooms TV in all bedrooms STV Radio in rooms Direct dial from all bedrooms Licensed Lift Night porter Full central heating Open parking available (charged) Covered parking available (charged) Supervised Child discount available 16yrs Solarium Pool table Open terrace yoga,snow scoot V meals Last d 22.00hrs Languages spoken: English, German & Japanese*
CARDS: 💳 🪪 🔲 🌐

## ST-PAUL-EN-CHABLAIS Haute-Savoie

★ ★ **Bois Joli**
*74500*
☎ 450736011 FAX 450736528
(From Thonon or Evian head towards St Paul and Bernex)
*Near lake Near sea Forest area*
*Closed mid Mar-mid Apr & 21 Oct-19 Dec*
*24 rms (20 bth/shr) 4 rooms in annexe (2 fmly) (24 with balcony) TV in all bedrooms Direct dial from all bedrooms Full central heating Open parking available Child discount available Outdoor swimming pool (heated) Tennis Sauna Solarium Pool table Boule Bicycle rental Open terrace Last d 20.30hrs Languages spoken: English*
CARDS: 💳 🪪 🔲 🌐 Travellers cheques

## ST-PIERRE-DE-CHARTREUSE Isère

**L'Arbi** (Prop: M Baffert)
Les Egaux *38380*
☎ 476886086 FAX 476886922
Forest area
*3 rms (2 bth/shr) (3 fmly) No smoking on premises TV in 2 bedrooms Full central heating Open parking available Child discount available 12yrs*
CARDS: Travellers cheques

★ ★ **L'Atre Fleuri**
*38380*
☎ 4768868021 FAX 476886497
Near river Forest area
*Closed mid Oct-end Dec*
*7 en suite (bth/shr) Licensed Full central heating Open parking available Supervised Child discount available Open terrace Last d 21.00hrs Languages spoken: English & Spanish*
CARDS: 💳 🔲 Travellers cheques

## ST-PIERRE-LA-NOAILLE Loire

**Domaine Château de Marchangy** (Prop: Marie Colette Rufener)
*42190*
☎ 477699676 FAX 477607037
Near river Forest area
*3 en suite (bth) (2 fmly) (1 with balcony) TV in all bedrooms Full central heating Open parking available Covered parking available Child discount available 10yrs Outdoor swimming pool Bicycle rental Languages spoken: English*
CARDS: Travellers cheques

## ST-PIERREVILLE Ardèche

**Le Moulinage Chabriol** (Prop: E de Lang)
Chabriol Bas *07190*
☎ 475666208 FAX 475666599
(leave A7 at Loriol-exit (S of Valence), cross the Rhone continue to La Voulte and St-Laurent-du-Pape, then take D120 direction St-Sauveur-de-Montagut,then take D102 direction Albon stay on D102 approx 15km until blue sign Chabriol)
*Near river Near lake Forest area Near motorway 6 en suite (shr) No smoking on premises Full central heating Open parking available Fishing Boule Languages spoken: English, Dutch & German*
ROOMS: d 300-350FF

## ST-PRIM Isère

**Bed & Breakfast** (Prop: M & Mme Briot)
Chemin de Pré Margot *38370*
☎ 474564427 FAX 474563093
Near lake Forest area
*6 en suite (shr) No smoking on premises TV available Open parking available Child discount available 10yrs Languages spoken: English & German*

## ST-SORLIN-D'ARVES Savoie

★ ★ **Beausoleil**
*73530*
☎ 479577142 FAX 479597525
Near river Near lake Forest area
*Closed May-late Jun & mid Sep-mid Dec*
*23 rms (21 bth/shr) (6 fmly) (15 with balcony) TV in all bedrooms STV Direct dial from all bedrooms Licensed Full central heating Open parking available Supervised Child discount available 10yrs Boule Bicycle rental Open terrace Last d 21.00hrs Languages spoken: English & Italian*
CARDS: 💳 🔲

## ST-VERAND Rhône

**Fondvielle** (Prop: M & Mme Anning)
Lieu dit Taponas *69620*
☎ 474716264
(head south on A6 exit Villefranche-sur-Saône, follow D38 &
cross D485 onto D13. In the village Fondvielle is signposted)
Near lake  Forest area  Near motorway
*6 rms (4 bth/shr) (2 fmly) Open parking available  Child
discount available  Boule  Bicycle rental  V meals  Last d
20.00hrs  Languages spoken: English & Spanish*
CARDS: Travellers cheques

## STE-EULALIE Ardèche

**★ ★ Hotel de la Poste**
*07510*
☎ 475388109 FAX 475388664
Near river  Near sea  Forest area
*Closed 1 Oct-30 Dec*
*10 rms (6 shr) (2 fmly) (1 with balcony) Direct dial from all
bedrooms  Licensed  Full central heating  Open parking
available  Supervised  Child discount available 9yrs  Boule
Open terrace  Last d 20.30hrs  Languages spoken: English*

## STE-FOY-TARENTAISE Savoie

**Yellow Stone Chalet** (Prop: Nancy Tabardel)
Bonconseil *73640*
☎ 479069606 FAX 479069605
(off D902, follow signs for Ste-Foy winter sports station where
chalet is signposted)
This property can offer either guest rooms or an independent
chalet. Set high up in the Alps (1550 metres above sea level), it
has access to the ski-lifts of the Bonconseil Station. The snow
in this area is amongst the best in France. Ski-safaris are
available thanks to the 600 kilometres of piste in this area, and
a guide can be provided. Summer stays offer fabulous walks.
Near river  Near lake  Forest area

*Closed 16 Sep-19 Dec & 22 Apr-14 Jun*
*5 en suite (bth/shr) (2 fmly) (2 with balcony) No smoking on
premises  TV in all bedrooms  Full central heating  Open
parking available  Covered parking available (charged)
Supervised  Child discount available 12yrs  Sauna  Gym
Jacuzzi/spa  Fitness centre  Jacuzzi  Sauna  Last d 20.00hrs
Languages spoken: English*
ROOMS: s 450-750FF; d 550-850FF
MEALS: Dinner 185FF
CARDS: ●● ▅▅ Travellers cheques

## SALLE-EN-BEAUMONT, LA Isère

**Villa a la Mitemps** (Prop: Martine Grand)
*38350*
☎ 476304204 FAX 476304454
(on the N85 rte Napoléon between Grenoble and Gap)
Forest area  Near motorway
*4 en suite (shr) (2 fmly) (1 with balcony) Full central heating
Open parking available  Covered parking available  Child
discount available  Boule*
CARDS: Travellers cheques

## SAMOËNS Haute-Savoie

**★ ★ ★ Les Sept Monts**
pl des 7 Monts *74340*
☎ 450344058 FAX 450341389
Near river  Near lake  Forest area  In town centre  Near
motorway
*Closed 15 Sep-20 Dec & 15 Apr-1 Jun*
*31 rms (28 bth/shr) 6 rooms in annexe (22 with balcony) TV in
15 bedrooms  STV  Direct dial from 15 bedrooms  Licensed  Lift
Full central heating  Open parking available  Covered parking
available (charged) Supervised  Child discount available 12yrs
Indoor swimming pool (heated) Outdoor swimming pool
(heated) Riding  Sauna  Solarium  Gym  Pool table  Boule  Mini-
golf  Bicycle rental  Open terrace  Covered terrace  V meals
Last d 21.00hrs  Languages spoken: English & Italian*
ROOMS: (room only) d 280-450FF
MEALS: Full breakfast 40FF  Lunch 85-130FF
Dinner 85-130FF
CARDS: ●● ■■ ▅▅ Travellers cheques

## SAPPEY-EN-CHARTREUSE, LE Isère

**Chant de l'Eau** (Prop: Colette & Bruno Charles)
Mollard Giraud *38700*
☎ 476888316 FAX 476888316
(In Grenoble take D512 to Le Col de Porte & St-Pierre-de-
Chartreuse, Le Sappey in 8 miles. 50 metres before village
church turn right again & in 150 metres is the property)
Near river  Forest area
*5 en suite (bth/shr) (1 fmly) (10 with balcony) TV in 1 bedroom
Full central heating  Open parking available  Languages spoken:
English*
CARDS: ●● ▅▅

## SATILLIEU Ardèche

**★ ★ ★ Gentilhommière** (Best Western)
*07290*
☎ 475692323 FAX 475349192
(outside the village on the road to Lalouvesc)
Near river  Forest area
*49 en suite (bth/shr) 35 rooms in annexe  TV in all bedrooms
STV  Direct dial from all bedrooms  Licensed  Lift  Full central
heating  Open parking available  Supervised  Child discount
available  Indoor swimming pool (heated) Outdoor swimming
pool (heated) Tennis  Riding  Sauna  Solarium  Gym  Pool table
Boule  Mini-golf  Jacuzzi/spa  Bicycle rental  Open terrace
Covered terrace  V meals  Last d 20.30hrs  Languages spoken:
English*
CARDS: ●● ▅▅ ◑ Travellers cheques

## SÉRÉZIN-DU-RHÔNE Rhône

### ★ ★ La Bourbonnaise
69360
☎ 478028058 FAX 478021739
Near river Near motorway
39 rms (34 bth/shr) 13 rooms in annexe (1 fmly) No smoking in 2 bedrooms TV in all bedrooms Radio in rooms Direct dial from all bedrooms Licensed Full central heating Open parking available Supervised Child discount available 12yrs Solarium Boule Bicycle rental Open terrace Covered terrace V meals Last d 21.45hrs Languages spoken: English & German
CARDS: ●● ■■ ⅢⅢ ⑩ CB Travellers cheques

## SEVRIER Haute-Savoie

### ★ ★ La Fauconnière
Lieu-dit Letraz-Chuguet 74320
☎ 450524118 FAX 450526333
Near lake Near sea Near beach Forest area Near motorway
29 rms (4 bth 21 shr) (4 fmly) (8 with balcony) TV in all bedrooms Direct dial from all bedrooms Licensed Full central heating Open parking available Covered parking available Child discount available 10yrs Boule Open terrace V meals Last d 21.00hrs Languages spoken: English
CARDS: ●● ■■ ⅢⅢ ⑩ Travellers cheques

### ★ ★ Inter Hotel Beaurégard
rte d'Albertville 74320
☎ 450524059 FAX 450524471
(from Annecy in direction of Albertville on N508)
Near lake Near sea Near beach Forest area Near motorway
Closed 15 Dec-15 Jan
46 rms (29 bth 16 shr) (12 fmly) (20 with balcony) TV in all bedrooms STV Direct dial from all bedrooms Lift Full central heating Open parking available Covered parking available (charged) Child discount available Boule Bicycle rental Open terrace Table tennis,water ski-ing Last d 21.25hrs Languages spoken: English
CARDS: ●● ⅢⅢ ⑩ Travellers cheques

### ★ ★ Les Tonnelles
rte d'Albertville 74320
☎ 550524158 FAX 550526005
Near lake Forest area Near motorway
26 rms (9 bth 1 shr) 7 rooms in annexe (5 fmly) (2 with balcony) TV in all bedrooms STV Direct dial from all bedrooms Licensed Full central heating Open parking available Child discount available 10yrs Open terrace Last d 21.45hrs Languages spoken: English
CARDS: ●● ■■ ⅢⅢ Travellers cheques

## SEYSSEL Ain

### ★ ★ Rhône
10 quai Charles-de-Gaulle 01420
☎ 450592030
Near river Forest area In town centre Near motorway
10 rms (5 bth/shr) (1 fmly) TV in all bedrooms STV Licensed Full central heating Outdoor swimming pool (heated) Fishing Boule Open terrace Languages spoken: English & Spanish
CARDS: ●● ⅢⅢ Eurocard Travellers cheques

## SEYSSINS Isère

### ★ ★ Climat de France
15 rue Docteur Schweitzer 38180
☎ 476217612 FAX 476217880
(off A480 junction 5B)
Near river Near sea Forest area Near motorway
45 en suite (bth/shr) (1 fmly) TV in all rooms STV Radio in rooms Direct dial from all bedrooms Licensed Night porter Full central heating Open parking available Supervised Golf Tennis Sauna Pool table Mini-golf Open terrace Covered terrace Last d 22.00hrs Languages spoken: English & German
CARDS: ●● ⅢⅢ

## SOLERIEUX Drôme

### ★ ★ Ferme St-Michel
26130
☎ 475981066 FAX 475981909
Forest area
14 rms (13 bth) (1 fmly) TV in all bedrooms Direct dial from all bedrooms Full central heating Open parking available Child discount available Outdoor swimming pool Boule Open terrace Last d 21.15hrs
CARDS: ●● ⅢⅢ Travellers cheques

## SOLLIÈRES-SARDIÈRES Savoie

### ★ ★ Hotel du Parc
73500
☎ 479205173 FAX 479205173
(from Modane take N6 east towards Lanslebourg. Left to Sollières-Sardières)
Near river Forest area
Closed Sep-22 Dec & 31 Mar-29 Jun
26 rms (14 bth 8 shr) (24 fmly) (10 with balcony) Direct dial from all bedrooms Licensed Full central heating Open parking available Supervised Child discount available 12yrs Solarium Pool table Boule Open terrace V meals Last d 21.00hrs Languages spoken: English & Italian
ROOMS: (room only) s 230-250FF; d 260-280FF
**Special breaks**
MEALS: Full breakfast 42FF Lunch 110-150FF&alc Dinner 110-150FF&alc
CARDS: ●● ⅢⅢ Travellers cheques

## SUZE-LA-ROUSSE Drôme

### ★ ★ Relais du Château
26790
☎ 475048707 FAX 475982600
(leave A7 at Bollène, towards Nyons)
Near river Forest area
Mar 15-Oct 31
39 en suite (bth/shr) (4 fmly) (8 with balcony) TV in 38 bedrooms Direct dial from 38 bedrooms Licensed Lift Full central heating Open parking available Supervised Outdoor swimming pool Tennis Boule Bicycle rental Open terrace V meals Last d 22.00hrs Languages spoken: English & Italian
CARDS: ●● ■■ ⅢⅢ ⑩ Travellers cheques

## TALISSIEU Ain

### Domaine de Château Froid (Prop: M Gilbert Pesenti)
01510
☎ 479873999 FAX 479874569
(leave A43 at Aix les Bains, follow D991 towards Seyssel

turning left onto D904. Talissieu is 5km past Culoz. Leave A42 at Amberieu, follow N504 turning left into D904, 13kms to Talissiu)
Near river  Near lake  Forest area
*Apr-Dec*
*10 en suite (bth/shr) (2 fmly) TV available  STV  Full central heating  Open parking available  Supervised  Child discount available 10yrs  Outdoor swimming pool (heated)  Tennis Fishing  Boule  Bicycle rental  Billiards  Library  Last d morning  Languages spoken: English*
ROOMS: s fr 620FF; d fr 720FF  **Special breaks**
MEALS: Dinner 150FF✱
CARDS: ●● ▆▆ Travellers cheques

### TALLOIRES Haute-Savoie

★ ★ ★ ★ *Auberge du Père Bise*
rte du Port *74290*
☎ 450607201 FAX 450607305
Near lake  Near sea  Near beach  Forest area
*Closed 2 Nov-8 Feb*
*34 en suite (bth/shr)  24 rooms in annexe  (6 fmly)  (20 with balcony)  TV in all bedrooms  STV  Direct dial from all bedrooms  Mini-bar in all bedrooms  Licensed  Lift  Full central heating  Open parking available  Supervised  Child discount available  Boule  Open terrace  V meals  Last d 21.00hrs  Languages spoken: English, German, Italian & Japanese*
CARDS: ●● ■■ ▆▆ ◨ Travellers cheques

★ ★ ★ ★ *Le Cottage*
Au Bord du Lac *74290*
☎ 450607110 FAX 450607751
Near lake  Near sea  Near beach  Forest area
*Closed approx Oct-Apr*
*35 rms (31 shr)  14 rooms in annexe  (21 with balcony)  TV in all bedrooms  STV  Direct dial from all bedrooms  Licensed  Lift Night porter  Full central heating  Open parking available Covered parking available (charged)  Supervised  Child discount available 12yrs  Outdoor swimming pool (heated) Tennis  Boule  Mini-golf  Bicycle rental  Open terrace  V meals Last d 21.00hrs  Languages spoken: English, German & Italian*
ROOMS: (room only) d 500-1300FF
**Reductions over 1 night  Special breaks**
MEALS: Full breakfast 80FF  Lunch 180-270FF&alc  Dinner 180-270FF&alc
CARDS: ●● ■■ ▆▆ ◨ JCB Travellers cheques

★ ★ ★ ★ *Prés du Lac*
Marie-Paule Conan *74290*
☎ 450607611 FAX 450607342
(from Annecy follow road to 'Casino Imperial' Veyrier, Menthon and Talloires)
Near lake  Forest area  In town centre  Near motorway
*Closed Nov-1 Mar*
*16 en suite (bth/shr)  7 rooms in annexe  (3 fmly)  (15 with balcony)  TV in all bedrooms  STV  Radio in rooms  Direct dial from all bedrooms  Mini-bar in all bedrooms  Room-safe Licensed  Night porter  Full central heating  Air conditioning in bedrooms  Open parking available  Covered parking available (charged)  Supervised  Child discount available  Tennis Solarium  Open terrace  Languages spoken: English, German & Italian*
CARDS: ●● ■■ ▆▆ ◨ Travellers cheques

★ ★ ★ **Villa des Fleurs**
rte du Port *74290*
☎ 450607114 FAX 450607406
Near lake  Near sea  Near beach  Forest area  In town centre
*Closed 15 Nov-15 Dec*
*8 en suite (bth/shr)  TV in all bedrooms  Direct dial from all bedrooms  Mini-bar in all bedrooms  Licensed  Full central heating  Open parking available  Child discount available 10yrs Golf 18  Bicycle rental  Covered terrace  Last d 21.30hrs Languages spoken: English & German*
CARDS: ●● ■■ ▆▆ Travellers cheques

### TAPONAS Rhône

★ ★ *Auberge des Sablons*
*69220*
☎ 474663480 FAX 474663522
Near river  Near lake  Near beach  Forest area  Near motorway
*15 en suite (bth/shr)  TV in all bedrooms  Direct dial from all bedrooms  Licensed  Night porter  Full central heating  Open parking available  Supervised  Child discount available  Fishing Open terrace  V meals  Last d 21.30hrs  Languages spoken: English*
CARDS: ●● ▆▆ Travellers cheques

### TASSIN-LA-DEMI-LUNE Rhône

★ ★ ★ *Novotel Lyon Tassin Vaise*
av Victor Hugo *69160*
☎ 478646869 FAX 478646111
Near motorway
*104 en suite (bth)  (39 fmly)  No smoking in 26 bedrooms  TV in all bedrooms  STV  Radio in rooms  Direct dial from all bedrooms  Mini-bar in all bedrooms  Licensed  Lift  Night porter Full central heating  Air conditioning in bedrooms  Open parking available  Covered parking available (charged)  Child discount available 16yrs  Outdoor swimming pool  Open terrace Last d 24.00hrs  Languages spoken: English, German, Italian & Spanish*
CARDS: ●● ■■ ▆▆ ◨ Travellers cheques

### THUEYTS Ardèche

★ ★ *Des Marronniers*
*07330*
☎ 475364016 FAX 475364802
Near river  Forest area  In town centre  Near motorway
*Closed 21 Dec-6 Mar*
*19 rms  TV in all bedrooms  Direct dial from all bedrooms Licensed  Full central heating  Open parking available  Child discount available 10yrs  Outdoor swimming pool  Boule  Open terrace  Last d 21.00hrs  Languages spoken: English & German*
CARDS: ▆▆

### TORCHEFELON Isère

*Le Colombier* (Prop: Nicole Pignoly)
La Taillat *38690*
☎ 474922928 FAX 474922733
Near lake  Near sea  Forest area
*5 en suite (bth/shr)  No smoking in all bedrooms  Radio in rooms  Full central heating  Open parking available  Child discount available 7yrs  Riding  Open terrace  V meals Languages spoken: English*
CARDS: ▆▆ ◨

373

## TOURNON Ardèche

**★ ★ ★ Hotel du Château**
Quai Marc-Seguin *07300*
☎ 475086022 FAX 475070295
(from Tain take A7. In Tournon cross over bridge, turn right,
hotel 100mtrs)
Near river In town centre Near motorway
*14 en suite (bth/shr) TV in all bedrooms STV Direct dial from
all bedrooms Mini-bar in all bedrooms Licensed Full central
heating Covered parking available (charged) Supervised Pool
table Open terrace Covered terrace V meals Last d 21.00hrs
Languages spoken: English*
Rooms: (room only) s fr 290FF; d 340-370FF
Meals: Full breakfast 40FF Lunch 110-225FF&alc Dinner
110-225FF&alc
Cards: ●● ■■ ⬛⬛ ⬛ JCB Travellers cheques

## TOURNON-SUR-RHÔNE Ardèche

**Château Chavagnac** (Prop: C Reale & C Mocquet)
*07300*
☎ 475083308 FAX 475083308
(leave A7 at exit for Tain l'Hermitage in direction of Tournon
then Lamastre for D532 in 3.5km go right to St Victor for Pont-
Roman-sur-Le-Doux in 4.5km, just 0.5km after Lubac, turn
right for château)
Near river Near lake Forest area
*RS reservation in winter*
*3 en suite (bth/shr) (2 fmly) No smoking on premises Full
central heating Open parking available Covered parking
available Languages spoken: English*
Rooms: s 300-400FF; d 350-450FF
**✻ Reductions over 1 night**

## TRÉVIGNIN Savoie

**La Jument Verte** (Prop: Chappaz)
pl de l'Église *73100*
☎ 479614752 FAX 479354080
(from Aix-les-Bains D913 to Trévignin, then follow signs.)
Near lake Near sea Forest area
*7 en suite (shr) Full central heating Open parking available
Child discount available 10yrs Outdoor swimming pool Tennis
Pool table Boule Mini-golf Bicycle rental Open terrace
Languages spoken: English*

## VALMOREL Savoie

**★ ★ ★ Planchamp**
Hameau Planchamp *73260*
☎ 479098391 FAX 479098393
(from Albertville follow signs for Moutiers (N90). Then exit at
junction 37 for Valmorel)
Near river Forest area Near motorway
*Closed 15 Apr-1 Jul, 30 Aug-15 Dec*
*37 en suite (bth/shr) 15 rooms in annexe (11 fmly) (11 with
balcony) TV in all bedrooms STV Direct dial from all
bedrooms Mini-bar in 25 bedrooms Licensed Full central
heating Air conditioning in bedrooms Open parking available
Covered parking available (charged) Child discount available
Tennis Fishing Riding Solarium Pool table Boule Bicycle
rental Open terrace V meals Last d 22.00hrs Languages
spoken: English, German & Spanish*
Rooms: (room only) d 300-600FF
Meals: Continental breakfast 55FF Lunch 180-250FF&alc
Dinner 180-250FF&alc
Cards: ●● ⬛⬛ ⬛ JCB Travellers cheques

## VALS-LES-BAINS Ardèche

**Domaine-de-Combelle** (Prop: Caroline Mocquet)
Asperjoc *07600*
☎ 475376277
(leave Vals-les-Bains, head for Awtraigues D578, after 1.5km,
take the private bridge on left which is 0.2km after public
bridge)
Near river Forest area
*4 en suite (bth/shr) Full central heating Open parking available
Covered parking available Supervised Languages spoken:
English*

## VAL-THORENS Savoie

**★ ★ ★ ★ Fitz Roy Hotel**
*73440*
☎ 479000478 FAX 479000611
*Closed Dec-5 May*
*36 en suite (bth) (3 fmly) (36 with balcony) TV in all bedrooms
STV Radio in rooms Direct dial from all bedrooms Mini-bar in
all bedrooms Licensed Lift Night porter Full central heating
Child discount available Indoor swimming pool (heated) Sauna
Solarium Gym Jacuzzi/spa Open terrace Beauty salon Last d
22.00hrs Languages spoken: English, German & Spanish*
Cards: ●● ■■ ⬛⬛ ⬛

## VARCES-ALLIÈRES-ET-RISSET Isère

**★ ★ ★ Relais l'Escale**
pl de la République *38760*
☎ 476728019 FAX 476729258
Forest area In town centre Near motorway
*Closed Early Nov, Sun evening & Mon RS Half board
obligatory at high season*
*7 en suite (bth) (7 with balcony) TV in all bedrooms Radio in
rooms Direct dial from all bedrooms Mini-bar in all bedrooms
Licensed Air conditioning in bedrooms Open parking available
Supervised Outdoor swimming pool Solarium Open terrace
Last d 21.00hrs Languages spoken: English, German & Italian*
Cards: ●● ■■ ⬛⬛ Travellers cheques

## VERNOUX-EN-VIVARAIS Ardèche

**Roiseland** (Prop: R Esposito-Maschio)
rue Boissy d'Anglace *07420*
☎ 475581932
(off D2)
Near river Near lake Near beach Forest area In town centre
*Closed mid Nov-Mar*
*5 en suite (bth/shr) (2 fmly) No smoking on premises Full
central heating Outdoor swimming pool*
Rooms: s 270FF; d 310FF

## VEYRIER-DU-LAC Haute-Savoie

**★ ★ ★ ★ Auberge de l'Eridan**
13 Vieille rte de Pensières *74290*
☎ 450602400 FAX 450602363
Near lake
*11 en suite (bth/shr) TV in all bedrooms STV Radio in rooms
Mini-bar in all bedrooms Licensed Lift Night porter Full
central heating Air conditioning in bedrooms Open parking
available Covered parking available Supervised Open terrace
Last d 22.00hrs Languages spoken: English, German, Italian &
Spanish*
Cards: ●● ■■ ⬛⬛ ⬛ Travellers cheques

★ ★ ★ ★ **Demeure de Chavoire**
71 rte d'Annecy - Chavoire *74290*
☎ 450600438 FAX 450600536
Near lake  Near sea  Near beach  Forest area  Near motorway
*13 en suite (bth/shr) (3 fmly) (2 with balcony) TV in all
bedrooms  Radio in rooms  Direct dial from all bedrooms  Mini-
bar in all bedrooms  Licensed  Night porter  Full central heating
Open parking available  Supervised  Open terrace  Languages
spoken: English*
CARDS: ●● ■ ■ ①

### VIENNE Isère

★ ★ ★ **Château des 7 Fontaines**
Les 7 Fontaines *38200*
☎ 474852570 FAX 474317447
(A46 toward Marseille, exit 16, 3km to Vienne)
The château is set on the Vienne Hills in the Rhône Valley and,
surrounded by a lush green park, it provides a peaceful setting
for a relaxing stay. It features spacious bedrooms, decorated in
a discreet fashion and equipped with modern appointments,
complemented by indoor and outdoor leisure facilities.
Near motorway
*Closed Nov-Mar
14 en suite (bth/shr) (2 fmly) TV in 11 bedrooms  Direct dial
from all bedrooms  Licensed  Full central heating  Open parking
available  Covered parking available  Supervised  Tennis  Boule
Open terrace  Languages spoken: English, German &
Spanish*
ROOMS: (room only) s 325-380FF; d 325-380FF ✳
MEALS: Continental breakfast 35FF✳
CARDS: ●● ■ ■ ①

### VILLARD-DE-LANS Isère

**La Musardière** (Prop: Odette & Marcel Haubert)
rte des Vieres *38250*
☎ 476959777
Near river  Forest area
*2 en suite (bth/shr) (1 with balcony) No smoking on premises
Full central heating  Open parking available*

**Les 4 Vents** (Prop: Jean Paul Uzel)
Bois Barbu *38250*
☎ 476951068
Near river  Forest area
*Closed 16 Sep-20 Dec & 16 Apr-14 Jun
5 en suite (shr) (4 fmly) (3 with balcony) No smoking on
premises  Full central heating  Open parking available  Covered
parking available  Child discount available 16yrs  Last d
17.00hrs  Languages spoken: English*
CARDS: Travellers cheques

**Le Val Sainte Marie** (Prop: Agnes Bon)
Bois Barbu *38250*
☎ 476959280 FAX 476955679
(from Sassenage, take D531 to Villard-de-Lans. Turn right
towards Bois-Barbo for 4km to the cross-country ski centre
and then turn left)
Near river  Forest area
*3 en suite (shr) (1 fmly) No smoking on premises  Open
parking available  Supervised  Child discount available 5yrs
Boule  Table tennis  Last d 16.00hrs  Languages spoken:
English*
CARDS: ■

### VILLARD-RECULAS Isère

**La Source** (Prop: M Baldwin)
*38114*
☎ 476803032 FAX 476803032
(from Grenoble take road toward Briançon. 6km before Bourg
d'Oisans turn left for Villard-Reculas. At village go down hill
and leave car in parking on right, take first small lane right,
then left)
This is an old stone barn, facing south, with spectacular views
and is owned by Mike Baldwin, a mountaineer, hotelier and ski
enthusiast. The house has been renovated to an extremely high
standard keeping the charm and character of the building
whilst creating modern facilities. Situated at 1480 metres, the
village links up with the skiing area of Alpe d'Huez.
Forest area  Near motorway
*5 rms (3 shr) (1 with balcony) No smoking on premises  Full
central heating  Open parking available  Child discount
available 14yrs  Boule  Languages spoken: English*
ROOMS: s 300-400FF; wkly bb fr 2760FF
**Reductions over 1 night**
CARDS: Travellers cheques

### VILLARD-ST-CHRISTOPHE Isère

**Bed & Breakfast** (Prop: Mme M Audinos)
*38119*
☎ 476830739
Near river  Near lake  Forest area
*3 rms (1 shr) (1 fmly) No smoking on premises  Full central
heating  Open parking available (charged)  Child discount
available 3yrs*

### VILLIÉ-MORGON Rhône

★ ★ **Villon**
Le Bourg *69910*
☎ 474691616 FAX 474691681
Forest area  In town centre
*45 en suite (bth/shr) (2 fmly) (15 with balcony) TV in all
bedrooms  Direct dial from all bedrooms  Licensed  Night
porter  Full central heating  Open parking available  Child
discount available 11yrs  Outdoor swimming pool  Tennis  Boule
Open terrace  Last d 21.00hrs  Languages spoken: English &
German*
CARDS: ●● ■ Travellers cheques

### VIOLAY Loire

★ ★ **Perrier**
pl de l'Église *42780*
☎ 474639101 FAX 474639177
(take Autoroute (Clermont Ferrand), exit Balbiguy, take
direction Tarare then Violay)
Near lake  Forest area  In town centre  Near motorway
*10 rms (8 bth) TV in 3 bedrooms  Direct dial from all bedrooms
Licensed  Full central heating  Covered parking available  Child
discount available 12yrs  Open terrace  Last d 22.00hrs
Languages spoken: English & Spanish*
ROOMS: (room only) s 150-190FF; d 150-220FF
MEALS: Full breakfast 40FF  Lunch 85-185FF&alc  Dinner
85-185FF&alc
CARDS: ●● ■

## VONNAS Ain

**★ ★ ★ ★ Georges Blanc**
pl du Marché 01540
☎ 474509090 FAX 474500880
Near river
Closed 2 Jan–10 Feb
48 en suite (bth/shr) (15 fmly) (12 with balcony) TV in all bedrooms STV Direct dial from all bedrooms Mini-bar in all bedrooms Room-safe Licensed Lift Night porter Full central heating Air conditioning in bedrooms Open parking available Supervised Outdoor swimming pool (heated) Golf Tennis Fishing Mini-golf Jacuzzi/spa Bicycle rental Open terrace Last d 21.30hrs Languages spoken: English, German & Spanish
CARDS: ●● ■■ ■■ ⬤ Travellers cheques

## EVENTS & FESTIVALS

| | |
|---|---|
| Feb | Chamonix 24-hour Ice Race; Lyon Art Fair |
| Mar | St-Gervais-les-Bains Comedy & Theatre Festival; Grenoble Jazz Festival; Isère Story-telling Festival; Chamrousse Husky Sleigh Race; Flaine Snow Jazz Festival |
| Apr | Bourg-d'Oisans International Mineral & Crystal Market ; Valloire Chess Festival; Lyons International Fair |
| May | Condrieu Wine Festival; St-Etienne Music Festival |
| Jun | Bell Festivals: Annecy, Lyon, Miribel, St Genis Laval, St Nicholas, Aussois, Farnay, Taninges; Gex Festival (fairground, music, comic parade); Annonay Street Art Festival |
| Jul | St-Gervais Alpine Festival; Montélimar Miniature Art Festival; Albertville Military Music Festival; Buis-les Baronnies Lime Blossom Fair; Olive Festivals at Nyons & Les Vans; Saoû Picodon Cheese Festival; Les Aillons Bread Oven Festival; Tournon-sur-Rhône Musical Nights; Grignan Nocturnal Festival at the Château; Folklore Festivals:Bourg-St Maurice, Chambery & Voiron; Megève Jazz Contest; La Plagne Kite Festival; St Antoine l'Abbaye Medieval Nights |
| Aug | Tarentaise Baroque Music & Art Festival; Crest Acoustic Art Festival; Aix-les-Bains Steam Festival; Les Saises Lumberjack Competition; Coligny Traditional Fair; Ruoms Ardèche Vintners' Festival; Aix-les-Bains Flower Festival; La Rosière Shepherds' Festival, Col de Petit St Bernard; Châtel Alpine Festival |
| Sep | Romans Brioche Festival; Charlieu Weaver Festival; Tain l'Hermitage Vintage Wine Festival; |
| Oct | Montbrison Cheese Fair; Montbrison Folklore & Gastronomic Event; Lyons Pottery Festival "Foire aux Tupiniers" |
| Nov | Grenoble Contemporary Music Festival; Villefranche sur-Saône Beaujolais Nouveau Lauch; Bourg-en Bresse Flower Festival |
| Dec | Autrans Snow, Ice & Adventure Film Festival; Lans en-Vercors Festival of Children's Films; Val Thorens Motor Race on snow & ice |

## St-Etienne

The town of St-Etiénne begs to be explored, inviting you to leave the well-trodden paths and discover for yourself its many surprises. One of the best tours of St-Etiénne is to the echo of the tramway bell, trundling along bustling streets to green spaces, searching out historical sites and sunny squares. Once you have climbed aboard, marvel at the examples of industrial prosperity, succumb to the charm of the St Jacques quarter, and inhale the sweet perfume of the chocolate factories, wafting out between the buildings. Plunge into the mysterious depths of the mine and then, above ground once more, head for the Place du Peuple and the 18th-century quarters.

Another of St-Etiénne's attractions is a gentle stroll in the fascinating antiques quarter, through the old weaving factories of Giron Park. You can also admire the two 'stairless' houses designed by the architect Bossu and built in a pure Art Deco style with traditional steps replaced by gently sloping ramps. Equally fascinating are the 600 peashooter 'marksmen' which help to maintain a popular 18th-century French tradition. To see them in action, aiming their peashooters at targets more than eight metres away, is certainly a memorable experience! For the art lover, there is the Modern Art Museum, opened in 1987 and containing one of the finest collections of Modern Art in France. Ranging from Buren to Lichtenstein and from Zadkine to Dubuffet, it offers a unique insight into the evolution of art since the 1940s. Once you have seen the sights and soaked up the atmosphere of this lively town, why not relax on the banks of the Loire and then take a cruise on this loveliest of French rivers.

## White Wilderness

The internationally renowned Olympic site of Rhône -Alpes is the world's largest snow playground where skiing of all kinds and categories can be enjoyed. Here there are 6,000 kilometres of safe ski runs - all superbly equipped and expertly marked out. But there is much more to this spectacular part of France than skiing and its mountain summits brilliant while wine. Most of the stations in Rhône-Alpes provide an extensive choice of recreational activities and leisure entertainment - in fact, everything from skating rinks, swimming pools and paragliding to trekking, nightclubs and cinemas. There are a staggering 220 resorts in Rhône-Alpes, including Les Deux Alpes, Les Arcs and Chamonix Mont-Blanc, where the ski-passes provide access to miles of snow-covered open spaces. The great Nordic snowfields of Haute-Savoie include Aravis, Chablais, Bauges and Mont-Blanc, and Savoie has 860 kilometres of marked trails in the Beaufortain, Revard, Maurienne and Tarentaise.

# Midi-Pyrénées

The Midi-Pyrénées is the largest region of France, but the least populated. It is an area of enormous geographical diversity, through which some of country's most beautiful rivers flow: the Ariège, Aveyron, Garonne, Gers, Lot and Tarn, naming most of the region's départements as they do so. This is a land of bustling street markets and traditional festivals, some involving whole départements and others just a town or village. Standing on the banks of the River Garonne, Toulouse is a lively city where art and technology live side by side amid the characteristic squares and streets.

## ESSENTIAL FACTS

| | |
|---|---|
| DÉPARTEMENTS: | Ariège, Aveyron, Gers, Haute-Garonne, Haute-Pyrénées, Lot, Tarn, Tarn-et-Garonne |
| PRINCIPAL TOWNS | Albi, Castres, Foix, Lourdes, Millau, Montauban, Tarbes, Toulouse |
| PLACES TO VISIT: | Archeological sites: La Graufenesque & Montmaurin. Beaulieu-en-Rouergue Abbey; Castles: Assier, Gramont, Castelnau-Bretenoux. Carmelite Chapel, Toulouse. Tarbes- home of Marchal Foch & National Anglo-Arab Stud. Bagnères-de-Bigorre - spa town since Roman era. Lourdes.- a pilgrimage town. |
| REGIONAL TOURIST OFFICE | 54 Boulevard de l'Embouchure BP 2166 31022 Toulouse Tel 05 61 13 55 55  Fax 05 61 47 17 16 E-mail crt.midi-pyrenees@wanadoo.fr |
| LOCAL GASTRONOMIC DELIGHTS | Cassoulet, a casserole of haricot beans (70%) & meat (30%). Foie gras (goose or duck liver pâté). Cheeses:  Roquefort, Bleu des Causses, Lagioule, Cabécou de Rocamadour (goats' cheese). Black truffles; Toulouse sausage. Pastis gascon (light pastry with Armagnac). Prunes in Armagnac. Toulouse crystallised violets |
| DRINKS | Armagnac brandy.  Wines :Cahors, Gaillac, Madiran, Buzet, Pacherenc, Fronton & Villaudric. |
| LOCAL CRAFTS WHAT TO BUY | Aubrac, Aveyron: Laguiole knives. Durfort: brass & copperware. Millau: gloves. Bethmale: clogs. The Ariège: horn combs. Martres-Tolosane: earthenware, terracotta urns & pots. |

## ALBAS Lot

**La Meline** (Prop: N & E Vos)
rte de Sauzet D37 *46140*
☎ 565369725 FAX 565369725
(take D911 (Cahors-Villeneuve-sur-Lot). In Castlefranc take D45, then D8 towards Albas, then take D37 towards Sauzet for 4km)
Situated on a hillside in the Lot Valley, with beautiful views over forests and the Cahors vineyards, La Meline offers its guests a peaceful and relaxing stay. Cycling and walking tours, and visits to farms and the vineyards are added attractions.
Near river  Forest area
*Closed Oct-Mar*
*3 en suite (bth/shr)  TV in all bedrooms  STV  Full central heating  Open parking available  Child discount available  Boule  Bicycle rental  Last d 19.00hrs  Languages spoken: English, Dutch & German*
ROOMS: s 190FF; d 275FF **Reductions over 1 night**
MEALS: Dinner 110FF
CARDS: Travellers cheques

## ALBI Tarn

**Hotel Chiffre-Le Bateau Ivre**
50 r Séré de Riviéres *81000*
☎ 563485848 FAX 563472061
In town centre  Near motorway
*40 en suite (bth/shr) (1 fmly) (1 with balcony)  No smoking in 2 bedrooms  TV in all bedrooms  STV  Direct dial from all bedrooms  Licensed  Lift  Night porter  Full central heating  Air conditioning in bedrooms  Open parking available (charged)  Covered parking available (charged)  Supervised Child discount available 8yrs  Bicycle rental  Open terrace  Covered terrace  Last d 22.00hrs  Languages spoken: English, Italian, German & Spanish*
ROOMS: (room only) s 330-380FF; d 380-490FF
**Special breaks**
MEALS: Full breakfast 55FF  Lunch 130-380FF&alc  Dinner 130-380FF&alc
CARDS: 💳 💳 💳 💳 Travellers cheques

★ ★ **Lapérouse**
21 pl Laperouse *81000*
☎ 563346922 FAX 563380369
Set in the very heart of the town, and a stone's throw from all the sights, this establishment provides comfortable bedrooms, each with their own personal touch. There is a delightful terrace, with pot plants situated around the swimming pool.
In town centre
*24 rms (9 bth 13 shr) (1 with balcony)  TV in all bedrooms  STV  Direct dial from all bedrooms  Licensed  Full central heating  Outdoor swimming pool  Languages spoken: English & Portuguese*
ROOMS: (room only) s 210-280FF; d 250-350FF
CARDS: 💳 💳 💳 💳 Travellers cheques

★ ★ ★ ★ **La Réserve** (Relais et Châteaux)
rte de Cordes *81000*
☎ 563608080 FAX 563476360
(on the Cordes road just outside Albi)
On the way to Cordes, just outside Albi and situated on the

*contd.*

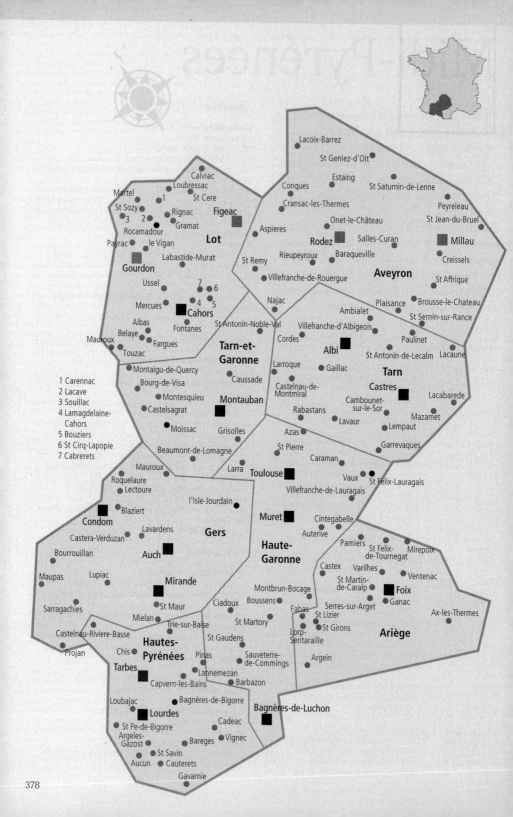

Midi-Pyrénées

**Lacoix-Barrez**

St Geniez-d'Olt

Calviac
Loubressac
St Cere
Martel
St Sozy
1
Rignac
**Figeac**
3  2  Gramat
Rocamadour
Payrac  le Vigan
**Lot**

Labastide-Murat

**Gourdon**

Ussel
7   6
Mercues
4  5
Albas   **Cahors**
Belaye   Fontanes
Mauroux   Fargues
Touzac

1 Carennac
2 Lacave
3 Souillac
4 Lamagdelaine-
   Cahors
5 Bouziers
6 St Cirq-Lapopie
7 Cabrerets

Montaigu-de-Quercy
Bourg-de-Visa
Montesquieu
Castelsagrat
Moissac

**Tarn-et-
Garonne**
Caussade
**Montauban**
Grisolles

Beaumont-de-Lomagne
Mauroux
Larra
Roquelaure
Lectoure
Blaziert
l'Isle-Jourdain
**Condom**
Lavardens
Castera-Verduzan   **Gers**
Bourrouillan
**Auch**
Maupas   Lupiac
**Mirande**
Sarragachies
St Maur
Mielan
Castelnau-Riviere-Basse   Trie-sur-Baise
Projan   Chis
**Hautes-
Pyrénées**
Pinas
Tarbes
Lannemezan
Capvern-les-Bains   Barbazon
Loubajac   Bagnères-de-Bigorre
**Lourdes**
St Pe-de-Bigorre   Cadeac
Argeles-   Bareges   Vignec
Gazost
St Savin
Aucun   Cauterets
Gavarnie

Conques
Estaing   St Saturnin-de-Lenne
Cransac-les-Thermes   Peyreleau
Onet-le-Château   St Jean-du-Bruel
Aspieres   Salles-Curan
**Rodez**   **Millau**
Rieupeyroux   Baraqueville   Creissels
St Remy
Villefranche-de-Rouergue   St Affrique
**Aveyron**
Najac   Plaisance   Brousse-le-Chateau
Ambialet   St Sernin-sur-Rance
St Antonin-Noble-Val   Villefranche-d'Albigeois   Paulinet
Cordes   **Albi**   Lacaune
St Antonin-de-Lecalm
Larroque   Gaillac   **Tarn**
Castelnau-de-   **Castres**   Lacabarede
Montmiral   Cambounet-
Rabastans   sur-le-Sor   Mazamet
Lavaur   Lempaut
Azas
St Pierre   Garrevaques
Caraman
**Toulouse**   Vaux
Villefranche-de-Lauragais   St Felix-Lauragais
**Muret**   Cintegabelle
Auterive
Pamiers   Mirepoix
St Felix-
de-Tournegat
Castex   Varilhes   Ventenac
Montbrun-Bocage   St Martin-
Boussens   de-Caralp   **Foix**
Fabas   Serres-sur-Arget   Ganac
St Martory   St Lizier   Ax-les-Thermes
Lorp-   St Girons
Sentaraille   **Ariège**
St Gaudens
Sauveterre-
de-Comminges   Argein
Bagnères-de-Luchon

**Haute-
Garonne**

378

bank of the River Tarn, La Réserve provides an oasis of **_La Reserve_** tranquillity and enjoyment. Privately owned by a family who over five generations have perfected the art of hospitality, it offers bedrooms with private facilities, TV and direct-dial telephones. It also has an outdoor swimming pool, and clay tennis-courts. Albi, with its magnificent cathedral dating back to the 13th century and its famous Toulouse-Lautrec museum, offers many places of historic interest.
Near river
*Closed early Nov-late Apr*
*24 en suite (bth/shr) 4 rooms in annexe (4 fmly) (12 with balcony) No smoking in 10 bedrooms TV in all bedrooms STV Direct dial from all bedrooms Mini-bar in all bedrooms Roomsafe Licensed Lift Night porter Full central heating Air conditioning in bedrooms Open parking available Supervised Child discount available 12yrs Outdoor swimming pool (heated) Tennis Fishing Solarium Pool table Boule Bicycle rental Open terrace V meals Last d 21.00hrs Languages spoken: English, German & Spanish*
ROOMS: (room only) s 550-1000FF; d 780-1450FF
MEALS: Full breakfast 85FF Lunch 125-300FF&alc Dinner 125-300FF&alc
CARDS: ●● ■■ ■■ ⓪ JCB Travellers cheques

### ★ ★ ★ ★ St-Antoine
17 rue St-Antoine *81000*
☎ 563540404 FAX 563471047
The Hostellerie Saint-Antoine is one of the most peaceful and comfortable of its kind in the region, and amongst the oldest in the whole of France. Founded in 1734 and renovated in both 1964 and 1998, it has been in the capable hands of the same family for five generations. The bedrooms are equipped with private facilities, TV and direct-dial telephones. The restaurant is renowned for its extensive range of regional specialities. Guests can use the swimming pool and tennis courts of the Hotel La Réserve, which is owned by the same family.

In town centre
*44 en suite (bth/shr) (4 fmly) No smoking in 10 bedrooms TV in all bedrooms STV Direct dial from all bedrooms Mini-bar in all bedrooms Licensed Lift Night porter Full central heating Air conditioning in bedrooms Open parking available (charged) Supervised Child discount available 12yrs Bicycle rental Open terrace V meals Last d 21.00hrs Languages spoken: English, German & Spanish*
ROOMS: (room only) s 420-650FF; d 650-950FF
**Reductions over 1 night**
MEALS: Full breakfast 60FF Lunch 95-197FF&alc Dinner 95-197FF&alc
CARDS: ●● ■■ ■■ ⓪ JCB Travellers cheques

### AMBIALET Tarn

### ★ ★ Du Pont
*81430*
☎ 563553207 FAX 563533721
Near river Forest area
*Closed 4 Jan-Feb*
*20 en suite (bth/shr) 6 rooms in annexe (6 fmly) (6 with balcony) TV in all bedrooms STV Direct dial from all bedrooms Licensed Full central heating Open parking available Child discount available 12yrs Outdoor swimming pool (heated) Tennis Bicycle rental Open terrace V meals Languages spoken: English*
ROOMS: (room only) s 283-293FF; d 320-335FF
CARDS: ●● ■■ ■■ ⓪ Travellers cheques

### ARGEIN Ariège

### ★ ★ La Terrasse
*09140*
☎ 561967011
Near river Near beach In town centre
*Closed mid Nov-end Jan*
*10 rms (5 bth 3 shr) (1 fmly) (1 with balcony) Licensed Night porter Child discount available 12yrs Open terrace Last d 21.00hrs*

### ARGELÈS-GAZOST Hautes-Pyrénées

### ★ ★ Beau Site
10 rue Capitaine Digoy *65400*
☎ 562970863 FAX 562970601
(in the town centre near the Office de Tourisme)
Near river Near lake Forest area In town centre Near motorway
*Closed 5 Nov-5 Dec*
*16 en suite (bth/shr) 5 rooms in annexe (6 with balcony) No smoking on premises TV in all bedrooms STV Direct dial from all bedrooms Licensed Full central heating Child discount available 10yrs Open terrace V meals Last d 20.00hrs Languages spoken: English & Italian*
ROOMS: (room only) d 235-245FF
**Reductions over 1 night**
MEALS: Continental breakfast 32FF Lunch 80-85FF Dinner 80-85FF
CARDS: ●● ■■ Travellers cheques

### ★ ★ Bon Répos
av du Stade *65400*
☎ 562970149 FAX 562970397
Near river Forest area
*Closed Oct-mid May*
*18 en suite (bth/shr) (10 fmly) (7 with balcony) TV in all*
*contd.*

bedrooms Direct dial from all bedrooms Licensed Full central heating Open parking available Covered parking available (charged) Outdoor swimming pool Boule Open terrace Languages spoken: English & Spanish
CARDS: ●● ▆▆ Travellers cheques

**★ ★ Hostellerie Le Relais**
25 rue Maréchal Foch 65400
☎ 562970127 FAX 562979000
In town centre Near motorway
Closed Nov-Jan
23 en suite (bth/shr) TV in all bedrooms STV Direct dial from all bedrooms Licensed Full central heating Open parking available Supervised Child discount available Open terrace Last d 21.00hrs Languages spoken: English & Spanish
CARDS: ●● ▆▆ Travellers cheques

### ASPRIÈRES Aveyron

**Le Mas de Clamouze** (Prop: Serge Maurel)
12700
☎ 565638989
Near river Forest area Near motorway
Closed Oct-Apr
5 en suite (shr) (3 fmly) Full central heating Open parking available Covered parking available Supervised No children 3yrs Child discount available 6yrs Languages spoken: English German & Italian
CARDS: Travellers cheques

### AUCH Gers

**★ ★ ★ ★ Hotel de France** (Relais et Châteaux)
2 pl de la Libération 32003
☎ 562617171 FAX 562617181
Near river Near lake In town centre Near motorway
29 en suite (bth/shr) (3 fmly) TV in all bedrooms STV Radio in rooms Mini-bar in all bedrooms Licensed Lift Night porter Full central heating Open parking available (charged) Covered parking available (charged) Supervised Child discount available 12yrs Open terrace Boutique Wkly live entertainment Languages spoken: English,German & Spanish
CARDS: ●● ▆▆ ▆▆ ⑩ Travellers cheques

### AUCUN Hautes-Pyrénées

**★ ★ Le Pocors**
rte de l'Aubisque 65400
☎ 562974090 FAX 562974156
Near river Near lake Forest area
48 en suite (bth) (8 fmly) TV in all bedrooms Direct dial from all bedrooms Licensed Lift Full central heating Open parking available Child discount available 10yrs Indoor swimming pool (heated) Tennis Sauna Pool table Boule Open terrace Covered terrace V meals Last d 21.30hrs Languages spoken: English
CARDS: ●● ▆▆ ▆▆ Travellers cheques

### AUTERIVE Haute-Garonne

**Les Murailles** (Prop: M & Mme Tourniant)
rte de Grazac 31190
☎ 561507698
Near river Near lake Forest area Near motorway
5 en suite (shr) No smoking on premises Full central heating Open parking available Covered parking available Supervised Child discount available 7yrs Boule Bicycle rental Table tennis Languages spoken: English

CARDS: ●● ▆▆ ▆▆ ⑩ Travellers cheques

### AX-LES-THERMES Ariège

**★ ★ Lauzéraie**
prom du Couloubret 09110
☎ 561642070 FAX 561643850
Near river Forest area In town centre Near motorway
Closed mid Nov-mid Dec
33 en suite (bth/shr) (1 fmly) (15 with balcony) TV in all bedrooms STV Direct dial from all bedrooms Licensed Lift Full central heating Open parking available Child discount available 11yrs Open terrace V meals Last d 21.00hrs Languages spoken: English & Spanish
CARDS: ●● ▆▆ ▆▆ Travellers cheques

### AZAS Haute-Garonne

**En Tristan** (Prop: Gerard & Chantal Zabé)
31380
☎ 561849488 FAX 561849488
(from Toulouse on the A68 exit 3 Montastruc, after Montastruc on N88 turn right towards Lavaur D30 in 4m turn left to Azas and follow signs)
This renovated farmhouse is set among fields approximately two kilometress from the village, and on fine days you may have views of the Pyrénées. There are four large bedrooms all with private bathroom and wc, two double rooms, and two triple and a sitting area is available on the landing with books and stereo.
Near river Near lake Forest area Near motorway
4 en suite (bth/shr) (2 fmly) No smoking on premises Full central heating Open parking available Covered parking available Child discount available 14yrs Boule Bicycle rental Table tennis Languages spoken: English
ROOMS: s 200-230FF; d 230-260FF
MEALS: Dinner fr 80FF
CARDS: Travellers cheques

### BARAQUEVILLE Aveyron

**★ De l'Agriculture**
449 av du Centre 12160
☎ 565690979 FAX 565690979
(A75 in direction of Severac-le-Château.From Rodez take N88 to Baraqueville)
Near lake Forest area In town centre Near motorway
10 rms (3 bth) Direct dial from all bedrooms Licensed Full central heating Open parking available Covered parking available Child discount available 10yrs Open terrace Last d 21.30hrs
CARDS: ●● ▆▆ ⑩

### BARBAZAN Haute-Garonne

**★ ★ Bella Vista**
(Hameau de Burs) 31510
☎ 561883523 FAX 561890602
(A64 Toulouse-Tarbes exit Montrejeau in direction of Luchen & Spain)
Near river Near lake Forest area Near motorway
20 en suite (bth/shr) (2 fmly) (7 with balcony) Direct dial from all bedrooms Licensed Full central heating Open parking available Supervised Child discount available 18yrs Sauna Boule Open terrace Covered terrace Table tennis Last d 21.30hrs Languages spoken: English & Spanish
CARDS: ●● ▆▆ Travellers cheques

## BARÈGES Hautes-Pyrénées

**★ ★ *Richelieu***
rue Ramond *65120*
☎ 562926811 FAX 562926600
(from Lourdes head S through Argèles-Gazost then to Luz-St-Sauveur, turn left to Barèges)
Near river  Forest area  In town centre  Near motorway  Closed 11 Apr-May & Oct-19 Dec RS Winter half board only  35 en suite (bth/shr)  (4 fmly)  (14 with balcony)  Direct dial from all bedrooms  Licensed  Lift  Full central heating  Child discount available 10yrs  Sauna  Pool table  Open terrace  Last d 21.00hrs  Languages spoken: English & Spanish
CARDS: ● ▇ ▆ ⑨ Travellers cheques

## BEAUMONT-DE-LOMAGNE Tarn-et-Garonne

**L'Arbre d'Or** (Prop: Tony and Peggy Ellard)
16 rue Déspéyrous *82500*
☎ 563653234 FAX 563652985
(A62 Bordeaux/Toulouse, exit Castelsarrasin, Beaumont de Lomagne is on the D928 between Montauban/Auch. A20 Paris/Toulouse exit Montauban in direction of Arch)

Nestling in the beautiful Gascon countryside, lies the ancient Bastide town of Beaumont de Lomagne, with a population of just 3,800. Elegant rooms are waiting for you at this superb 17th century house. Relax in the tree-shaded garden, and sample the excellent Gascon cuisine at the family table. Confirm in advance if you wish to dine. Weekends catered for at special rates. English hosts.
Near river  Near lake  Forest area  In town centre  Near motorway  6 rms (5 bth/shr)  (1 fmly)  Radio in rooms  Full central heating  Open parking available  Covered parking available (charged)  Child discount available 10yrs  Bicycle rental  V meals  Last d 20.00hrs  Languages spoken: English
ROOMS: s 190FF;  d 260-290FF
**Reductions over 1 night  Special breaks**
MEALS: Dinner 100-120FF
CARDS: Travellers cheques

## BELAYE Lot

**Marliac** (Prop: Veronique Stroobant)
*46140*
☎ 565369550
Near river  Near lake  Forest area
6 en suite (bth/shr)  (2 fmly)  No smoking in 1 bedroom  Open parking available  Child discount available 12yrs  Outdoor swimming pool  Table tennis  Languages spoken: English, Dutch & Italian
CARDS: Travellers cheques

## BLAZIERT Gers

**La Bajonne** (Prop: Mme Ingrid D'Aloia)
*32100*
☎ 562682709
Forest area
4 en suite (bth/shr)  Full central heating  Open parking available  Child discount available 12yrs  Outdoor swimming pool  Languages spoken: English, German & Italian

## BOURG-DE-VISA Tarn-et-Garonne

**Le Marquise** (Prop: M & Mme Doi)
Brassac *82190*
☎ 563942516
Near river  Forest area
4 en suite (shr)  Full central heating  Open parking available  Child discount available 10yrs
CARDS: Travellers cheques

## BOURROUILLAN Gers

**★ ★ Moulin du Comté**
*32370*
☎ 562090672 FAX 562091049
(NW off N124)
Near river  Near lake  Forest area
10 en suite (bth/shr)  (6 fmly)  (6 with balcony)  TV in all bedrooms  Direct dial from all bedrooms  Licensed  Full central heating  Open parking available  Supervised  Child discount available 12yrs  Outdoor swimming pool  Fishing  Boule  Open terrace  Covered terrace  V meals  Last d 22.00hrs  Languages spoken: English & Spanish
ROOMS: (room only) s 250-300FF;  d 250-450FF
**✳ Reductions over 1 night**
MEALS: Continental breakfast 30FF  Lunch 140FF&alc  Dinner 140FF&alc
CARDS: ● ▇ ⑨

## BOUSSENS Haute-Garonne

**Hotel du Lac**
7 promenade du Lac *31360*
☎ 561900185 FAX 561971557
Near river  Near lake  Forest area  Near motorway  Closed 1-15 Feb
12 rms (2 fmly)  (6 with balcony)  TV in all bedrooms  Mini-bar in all bedrooms  Licensed  Night porter  Full central heating  Open parking available  Supervised  No children  Child discount available 10yrs  Boule  Open terrace  Last d 21.30hrs  Languages spoken: Portuguese & Spanish
CARDS: ● ▇ ▆

## BOUZIÈS Lot

**★ ★ Les Falaises**
*46330*
☎ 565312683 FAX 565302387
(from Cahors, follow signs for Figeac/Vallée du Lot et du Cele, take D653. Once in Vers follow signs for St-Cirq-La-Popie on the D662. The Hotel is situated past the Bouzies Bridge)
Situated amidst green surroundings in a tiny village of only 68 inhabitants on the banks of the River Lot, the hotel is the ideal venue for an active holiday. Organised excursions and a multitude of leisure facilities are available to guests. The bedrooms are comfortable and equipped with modern amenities, complemented by a cosy bar, crêperie and restaurant.
*contd.*

**Les Falaises**

Near river  Forest area
*Closed 4 Nov-24 Mar*
*39 en suite (bth/shr) (11 fmly) (1 with balcony) TV in all bedrooms  Direct dial from all bedrooms  Licensed  Full central heating  Open parking available  Child discount available 12yrs  Outdoor swimming pool (heated)  Tennis  Fishing  Pool table  Boule  Bicycle rental  Open terrace  Table tennis,canoeing  V meals  Last d 21.00hrs  Languages spoken: English, German & Spanish*
ROOMS: (room only) d 365FF
MEALS:  Full breakfast 43FF  Lunch 80-230FF
Dinner 80-230FF
CARDS: ●● ■■ ▨▨ Travellers cheques

---

**BROUSSE-LE-CHÂTEAU** Aveyron

★ ★ **Le Relays du Chasteau**
*12480*
☎ 565994015 FAX 565994015
(Take A75 to Millau, then take the direction St-Affrique on the D902. Follow signs for Brousse-le-Château)
Near river  Forest area
*12 en suite (bth/shr) (1 fmly)  Direct dial from all bedrooms  Licensed  Full central heating  Open parking available  Child discount available 8yrs  Boule  Open terrace  Languages spoken: English & Spanish*
ROOMS: (room only) d 215-275FF ✱
MEALS:  Full breakfast 35FF
CARDS: ●● ▨▨ Travellers cheques

---

**CABRERETS** Lot

★ ★ **Auberge de la Sagne**
rte de Pech Merle *46300*
☎ 565312662 FAX 565302743
(From Cahors take east direction on D653 until Vers then D662 towards St Cirq Lapopie (in the Lot valley) then D41 to Cabrerets (5km along River Célé). Then follow signs towards Pech Merle)
Nestling in a pretty country setting. A quiet family-run hotel between St Cirq Lapopie, said to be one of the most beautiful villages in France, and Pech Merle. A charming residence, with a warm welcome, whether for just one night or for a longer stay,. In the heart of the main beauty spots of Quercyland.
Near river  Forest area
*Closed 16 Sep-14 May*
*10 en suite (bth/shr)  Direct dial from all bedrooms  Licensed  Full central heating  Open parking available  Outdoor swimming pool  Boule  Open terrace  Last d 20.30hrs  Languages spoken: German*

**Auberge de la Sagne**

ROOMS: (room only) d 310FF
MEALS:  Full breakfast 35FF  Dinner 85-135FF&alc
CARDS: ●● ▨▨ Travellers cheques

---

**CADÉAC** Hautes-Pyrénées

★ ★ **Val d'Auré**
rte de St-Lary *65240*
☎ 562986063 FAX 562986899
(motorway Bayonne to Toulouse, exit at Lannemezan. Proceed in direction of Spain until village of Arreau, hotel in next village)
Near river  Near lake  Forest area
*Closed Oct-19 Dec RS half board only in season*
*23 en suite (bth/shr)  4 rooms in annexe (7 fmly) (9 with balcony) TV in all bedrooms  Radio in rooms  Direct dial from all bedrooms  Licensed  Air conditioning in bedrooms  Open parking available  Covered parking available  Supervised Child discount available  Outdoor swimming pool (heated)  Golf  Tennis  Fishing  Pool table  Boule  Bicycle rental  Open terrace  Covered terrace  Last d 21.00hrs  Languages spoken: English & Spanish*
CARDS: ●● ▨▨ Travellers cheques

---

**CAHORS** Lot

★ ★ **Climat de France**
Rond Point de Régourd *46000*
☎ 565300000 FAX 565225619
(at junction with D911 and D662)
In town centre  Near motorway
*100 en suite (bth/shr)  59 rooms in annexe (12 fmly)  No smoking in 2 bedrooms  TV in all bedrooms  Radio in rooms  Direct dial from all bedrooms  Licensed  Lift  Night porter  Full central heating  Open parking available  Outdoor swimming pool  Sauna  Pool table  Boule  Open terrace  Last d 22.00hrs  Languages spoken: English*
CARDS: ●● ■■ ▨▨ Travellers cheques

---

**CALVIAC** Lot

★ ★ **Le Ranfort**
Lieu-dit Pont de Rhodes *46190*
☎ 565330106 FAX 565330132
Near river  Forest area
*Closed 25 Sep-15 Oct*
*11 en suite (bth/shr) (4 fmly)  No smoking in all bedrooms  TV in all bedrooms  Direct dial from all bedrooms  Licensed  Full central heating  Open parking available  Child discount available 10yrs  Outdoor swimming pool (heated)  Boule  Open terrace  V meals  Last d 21.00hrs*

ROOMS: (room only) d 240-310FF **Reductions over 1 night**
MEALS: Full breakfast 35FF Lunch 65-200FFalc
Dinner 65-200FFalc
CARDS: ●● Ⅲ Eurocard Travellers cheques

### CAMBOUNET-SUR-LE-SOR Tarn

**Château de la Serre**
*81580*
☎ 563717573 FAX 563717606
(situated 15km west of Castres via N126 & D4)
*Near river Near lake Forest area*
*3 en suite (bth) (2 fmly) Full central heating Open parking*
*available Child discount available 12yrs Outdoor swimming*
*pool Boule Languages spoken: English & Spanish*
ROOMS: d 550-700FF
MEALS: Dinner 120-180FF

### CAPVERN-LES-BAINS Hautes-Pyrénées

★ ★ **Bellevue**
rte de Mauvezin *65130*
☎ 562390029
*Near river Forest area*
*Closed early Oct-early May*
*33 rms (22 shr) 15 rooms in annexe (3 fmly) Full central*
*heating Open parking available Covered parking available*
*Solarium Boule Open terrace Covered terrace Last d 20.30hrs*
*Languages spoken: English & Spanish*
CARDS: ●● Ⅲ Travellers cheques

### CARAMAN Haute-Garonne

**Le Croisillat** (Prop: Guerin)
Château du Croisillat *31460*
☎ 561831009 FAX 561833011
*Near river Near lake Near sea Forest area In town centre*
*Closed Nov-Mar*
*6 rms (3 bth 2 shr) (1 fmly) Open parking available Indoor*
*swimming pool Languages spoken: English*
CARDS: Travellers cheques

### CARENNAC Lot

★ ★ **Hostellerie Fenelon**
*46110*
☎ 565109646 FAX 565109486
*Near river Forest area*
*Closed 4 Jan-14 Mar RS Fri & Sat low season*
*15 en suite (bth/shr) (2 fmly) TV in all bedrooms STV Direct*
*dial from all bedrooms Licensed Full central heating Open*
*parking available Child discount available 12yrs Outdoor*
*swimming pool (heated) Riding V meals Last d 21.00hrs*
*Languages spoken: English*
ROOMS: (room only) s 240-290FF; d 290-350FF
✱ **Reductions over 1 night**
MEALS: Full breakfast 45FF Lunch 100-290FF&alc Dinner
100-290FF&alc
CARDS: ●● Ⅲ Travellers cheques

### CASTELNAU-DE-MONTMIRAL Tarn

**La Croix du Sud** (Prop: Catherine Sordoillet)
*81140*
☎ 563331846 FAX 563331846
(From Toulouse or Albi take motorway to Gaillac. From Gaillac
take D964 to Castelnau de Montmiral, don't go into village take

road to right (after petrol station) to Vieux-le-Verdière. After
200m turn right to Mazars, La Coix-du-Sud on left)
*Near river Near lake Near sea Forest area*
*3 en suite (bth/shr) (1 fmly) No smoking on premises TV in all*
*bedrooms Full central heating Open parking available Covered*
*parking available Child discount available 10yrs Outdoor*
*swimming pool Boule Languages spoken: English & Spanish*
ROOMS: s 230FF; d 300FF **Special breaks**
MEALS: Dinner 100FF

### CASTELNAU-RIVIÈRE-BASSE Hautes-Pyrénées

**Châateau du Tail** (Prop: Claudie Bolac)
*65700*
☎ 562319375 FAX 562319326
(on the D935 Tarbes/Bordeaux.Village centre uphill, then
towards Goux)
*Near river Near lake Forest area Near motorway*
*5 en suite (bth/shr) (1 fmly) No smoking on premises Full*
*central heating Open parking available Covered parking*
*available Child discount available 10yrs Outdoor swimming*
*pool Boule Bicycle rental Table tennis Last d 20.00hrs*
*Languages spoken: English, German & Spanish*
MEALS: Dinner 100-130FF✱

**Flanerie** (Prop: J L Guyot)
Hameau du Mazères *65700*
☎ 562319056 FAX 562319288
(from Maubourguet take D935 north. Turn right to Mazères.
Flânerie is behind the church)
*Near river Near lake Forest area*
*3 en suite (bth/shr) (2 fmly) TV in 1 bedroom Full central*
*heating Open parking available Child discount available 12yrs*
*Boule Bicycle rental Boules Table tennis V meals Languages*
*spoken: English & German*

### CASTELSAGRAT Tarn-et-Garonne

**Le Castel** (Prop: Danielle Jonqua-Clement)
*82400*
☎ 563942055 FAX 563942055
(from Agen towards Puymirol and Bourg-de-Visa then
Moissac; from Castelsarrasin-Moissac towards Bourg-de-Visa;
from Valence d'Argen towards Cahors and after Lalande turn
left onto D46)
*3 en suite (bth/shr) (1 fmly) TV in 1 bedroom STV Open*
*parking available Covered parking available Child discount*
*available 13yrs Indoor swimming pool Boule Bicycle rental V*
*meals Last d 18.00hrs Languages spoken: English*

### CASTERA-VERDUZAN Gers

**Sonnard** (Prop: M Guiraud)
*32410*
☎ 562681539 FAX 562681047
*Near river Near lake Near sea*
*6 en suite (bth/shr) (3 fmly) Full central heating Open parking*
*available Child discount available Last d 19hrs Languages*
*spoken: English & Italian*
CARDS: Travellers cheques

### CASTEX Ariège

**Manzac d'En Bas** (Prop: Hopkins)
*09350*
☎ 561698525 FAX 561698525
(leave Daumazan in the direction of Foix & take D19 to Castex
*contd.*

and Lézat, after 2km turn right,after 600m turn left, Manzac d'en Bas is 200m up the hill on the left)
Near lake  Forest area  Near motorway
*3 rms (1 shr)  (2 fmly)  Full central heating  Open parking available  Child discount available  Outdoor swimming pool*
*Languages spoken: English*
CARDS: Travellers cheques

## CAUSSADE Tarn-et-Garonne

### ★ ★ *Dupont*
25 rue des Récollets *82300*
☎ 563650500 FAX 563651262
Forest area  In town centre  Near motorway
*Closed Nov-Mar*
*30 en suite (bth/shr)  8 rooms in annexe  (8 with balcony)  TV in all bedrooms  Direct dial from all bedrooms  Licensed  Full central heating  Open parking available  Covered parking available  Supervised  Child discount available 10yrs  V meals*
*Languages spoken: English & Spanish*
CARDS: ●● ☲ Travellers cheques

### ★ ★ *Larroque*
av de la Gare *82300*
☎ 563651177 FAX 563651204
(opposite the railway station)
Near river  Near lake  Forest area  In town centre  Near motorway
*Closed 21 Dec-15 Jan*
*18 en suite (bth)  5 rooms in annexe  (4 fmly)  (2 with balcony)  TV in all bedrooms  Direct dial from all bedrooms  Mini-bar in 8 bedrooms  Licensed  Full central heating  Open parking available  Covered parking available  Supervised  Child discount available 12yrs  Outdoor swimming pool  Bicycle rental  Open terrace  Table tennis  V meals  Last d 21.30hrs  Languages spoken: English & Spanish*
ROOMS: (room only) s 215-245FF; d 245-300FF
**Reductions over 1 night**
MEALS: Continental breakfast 30FF  Lunch 80-200FF&alc  Dinner 80-200FF&alc
CARDS: ●● ■■ ☲ ⑩ Travellers cheques

## CAUTERETS Hautes-Pyrénées

### ★ ★ ★ Hotel Asterides
9 bd Latapie Flurin *65110*
☎ 562925043 FAX 562926489
(head towards Lourdes then to Pierrefitte-Nestalas at traffic lights turn right to Cauterets, 8km)
Near river  Near lake  Forest area  In town centre
*Closed 20 Oct-15 Dec RS Sun rest closed*
*12 en suite (bth)  (4 fmly)  (7 with balcony)  TV in all bedrooms  Direct dial from all bedrooms  Licensed  Lift  Full central heating  Child discount available  Open terrace  Last d 20.30hrs  Languages spoken: English*
ROOMS: (room only) s 270-350FF; d 320-380FF
MEALS: Full breakfast 35FF  Lunch 75-89FF&alc  Dinner 75-89FF&alc
CARDS: ●● ☲ ⑩

### ★ ★ ★ Club Aladin
av du Gen Leclerc *65112*
☎ 562926000 FAX 562926330
Near river  Forest area  In town centre
*Closed 29 Apr-3 Jun & 30 Sep-18 Dec*
*(40 fmly)  (90 with balcony)  TV in 126 bedrooms  STV  Direct dial from 126 bedrooms  Licensed  Lift  Night porter  Full*

central heating  Open parking available (charged)  Covered parking available (charged)  Child discount available 12yrs  Indoor swimming pool (heated)  Sauna  Solarium  Gym  Last d 20.30hrs  Languages spoken: English, Italian & Spanish
ROOMS: s fr 482FF; d fr 714FF
MEALS: Full breakfast 52FF  Dinner 150FF✱
CARDS: ●● ☲ Travellers cheques

### ★ ★ *Etche Ona*
20 rue de Richelieu *65110*
☎ 562925143 FAX 562925499
(S of Lourdes via N21 and D920)
Near river  Forest area
*Closed 21 Apr-May & Oct-Nov*
*30 rms (28 bth/shr)  (7 fmly)  (4 with balcony)  TV in all bedrooms  Direct dial from all bedrooms  Licensed  Lift  Full central heating  Child discount available 6yrs  Sauna  Open terrace  Last d 20.45hrs  Languages spoken: English & Spanish*
CARDS: ●● ■■ ☲ Travellers cheques

### ★ *Le Pas de l'Ours*
21 rue de la Raillère *65110*
☎ 562925807 FAX 562920649
(S of Lourdes via N21 and D920)
Near river  Near lake  Forest area  In town centre
*Closed 15 Apr-1 May & 30 Sep-1 Dec*
*13 en suite (bth/shr)  (6 fmly)  (5 with balcony)  No smoking on premises  Direct dial from all bedrooms  Licensed  Full central heating  Child discount available 12yrs  Sauna  Open terrace  Last d 22.00hrs  Languages spoken: English*
CARDS: ●● ☲

## CHIS Hautes-Pyrénées

### ★ ★ Hotel de la Tour
*65800*
☎ 562362114 FAX 562366810
Near river  Near lake  Forest area  Near motorway
*10 en suite (bth/shr)  (1 fmly)  (1 with balcony)  TV in all bedrooms  Direct dial from all bedrooms  Licensed  Full central heating  Open parking available  Supervised  Outdoor swimming pool  Boule  Bicycle rental  Open terrace  Last d 22.00hrs  Languages spoken: English & Spanish*
ROOMS: (room only) d fr 280FF
MEALS: Continental breakfast 30FF  Lunch fr 48FF&alc  Dinner fr 78FFalc
CARDS: ●● ■■ ☲ Travellers cheques

## CIADOUX Haute-Garonne

### *Le Manoir de la Rivière* (Prop: Inge Roehrig)
*31350*
☎ 561881088 FAX 561881088
Near river  Near lake  Forest area  Near motorway
*4 rms (3 bth/shr)  (1 with balcony)  TV available  STV  Full central heating  Open parking available  Covered parking available  Child discount available 12yrs  Riding  V meals*
*Languages spoken: English & German*

## CINTEGABELLE Haute-Garonne

### *Serres d'en Bas* (Prop: P & M J Deschamps-Chevrel)
rte de Nailloux *31550*
☎ 561084111 FAX 561084111
(Toulouse take direction of Foix on the N20)
Forest area

5 en suite (bth/shr) No smoking on premises Full central heating Open parking available Child discount available Outdoor swimming pool Tennis Boule Table tennis V meals Last d 20.00hrs Languages spoken: Spanish

## CONDOM Gers

### ★ ★ ★ Hotel des Trois Lys
38 rue Gambetta 32100
☎ 562283333 FAX 562284185
In town centre
Closed Feb
10 rms (9 bth/shr) (3 fmly) TV in all bedrooms Direct dial from all bedrooms Licensed Full central heating Open parking available Supervised Outdoor swimming pool Solarium Open terrace Last d 21.30hrs
CARDS: ●● ■■ ■■ ◎ Travellers cheques

### ★ ★ Logis des Cordeliers
rue de la Paix 32100
☎ 562280368 FAX 562682903
Near river Near lake Forest area In town centre Near motorway
(11 with balcony) TV in 21 bedrooms Direct dial from 21 bedrooms Licensed Full central heating Open parking available Covered parking available (charged) Outdoor swimming pool Bicycle rental Open terrace Languages spoken: English
ROOMS: d 270-420FF
CARDS: ●● ■■ ◎

## CONQUES Aveyron

### ★ ★ Auberge St-Jacques
12320
☎ 565728636 FAX 565728247
Forest area
13 en suite (bth/shr) No smoking in 1 bedroom Licensed Full central heating Air conditioning in bedrooms Open parking available Open terrace V meals Last d 21.30hrs Languages spoken: English
CARDS: ●● ■■ ■■ ◎

### ★ ★ ★ Grand Hotel Ste-Foy
12320
☎ 565698403 FAX 565728104
Near river Forest area
Closed Nov-Etr
17 en suite (bth/shr) (6 fmly) TV in 7 bedrooms Direct dial from all bedrooms Licensed Lift Full central heating Air conditioning in bedrooms Open parking available (charged) Covered parking available (charged) Child discount available 12yrs Open terrace Covered terrace V meals Last d 21.30hrs Languages spoken: Italian, German & Spanish
ROOMS: (room only) s 590-790FF; d 650-1200FF
**Reductions over 1 night**
MEALS: Full breakfast 80FF Lunch 100-300FF&alc Dinner 165-300FF&alc
CARDS: ●● ■■ ■■ ◎ Travellers cheques

## CORDES Tarn

### ★ ★ ★ ★ Le Grand Ecuyer
Haut de Lacite 81170
☎ 563537950 FAX 563537951
(from Toulouse take direction of Albi exit at Gaillac exit 9 in direction Cordes)
Near river

Closed 16 Nov-Etr
13 en suite (bth/shr) (3 with balcony) No smoking in all bedrooms TV in all bedrooms Mini-bar in 12 bedrooms Licensed Night porter Full central heating Air conditioning in bedrooms Languages spoken: English
CARDS: ●● ■■ ■■

### Les Tuileries (Prop: Christian Rondel)
81170
☎ 563560593 FAX 563560593
(from Toulouse take N88 towards Albi. At Gaillac take D922 to Cordes. In Cordes follow directions for parking(P1 & P2). Approx 700m from car park)
This 200-year-old property is situated in the heart of the countryside at Cordes, with an exceptional view of the walled town of Cathares. Rooms are quiet, comfortable and spacious. Farm produce available at the dinner table, together with other specialities of the house. Gastronomic menu on request. Meals served in the garden in fine weather, in the shade of the chestnut trees. Many leisure pursuits are available nearby.
Near river Forest area
5 en suite (shr) (2 fmly) Full central heating Open parking available Covered parking available Supervised Child discount available 12yrs Outdoor swimming pool Boule Table tennis Last d midday Languages spoken: English
ROOMS: d 290FF
MEALS: Dinner 105FF✱
CARDS: Travellers cheques

### ★ ★ ★ Hostellerie du Vieux Cordes
rue St-Michel 81170
☎ 563560012 FAX 563560247
Forest area In town centre
Closed Jan
21 en suite (bth/shr) 8 rooms in annexe (5 fmly) TV available Licensed Night porter Full central heating Open terrace V meals Last d 21.30hrs Languages spoken: English & Spanish
CARDS: ●● ■■ ■■ ◎

## CRANSAC-LES-THERMES Aveyron

### ★ ★ Hotel du Parc
rue Général Louis Artous 12110
☎ 565630178 FAX 565632036
Near lake Forest area In town centre
Closed Nov-Mar
25 rms 15 rooms in annexe (4 fmly) TV in all bedrooms Direct dial from all bedrooms Licensed Full central heating Open parking available Covered parking available Supervised Child discount available 10yrs Outdoor swimming pool Fishing Riding Solarium Boule Mini-golf Bicycle rental Open terrace Covered terrace Last d 21.00hrs
CARDS: ●● ■■ ■■ Travellers cheques

## CREISSELS Aveyron

### ★ ★ Château de Creissels
rte de St-Affrique 12100
☎ 565601659 FAX 565612463
Near river Forest area
Closed Jan
31 en suite (bth/shr) (4 fmly) (5 with balcony) TV available STV Direct-dial available Licensed Full central heating Open parking available Child discount available 10yrs Fishing Pool table Boule Open terrace Covered terrace V meals Last d 21.30hrs Languages spoken: English & Spanish
CARDS: ●● ■■ ■■ ◎ Travellers cheques

## ESTAING Aveyron

**Bed & Breakfast** (Prop: M A Alazard)
Cervel, rte de Vinnac *12190*
☎ 565650989 FAX 565650989
(from Rodez take D988 to Bozouls then D920 to Espalion. From here continue on D920 to Estaing)
Near river
*Closed 15 Nov-1 Apr*
*4 en suite (shr) (2 fmly) No smoking on premises TV in all bedrooms Full central heating Open parking available Child discount available 10yrs Last d 19.30hrs*
CARDS: Travellers cheques

## FABAS Ariège

**Estivades de Peyre** (Prop: Rosina de Peira)
Peyre *09230*
☎ 561964016 FAX 561964236
(from Toulouse towards Tarbes, leave A64 for Cazère D6 into Ste Croix-Volvestre. Onto D35 Fabas in approx 4km)
Near river Forest area
*6 en suite (shr) No smoking on premises Full central heating Open parking available Child discount available 6yrs Outdoor swimming pool*

## FARGUES Lot

**Mondounet** (Prop: Peter James Scott)
*46800*
☎ 565369632 FAX 565318489
(D656 towards Tournon, passing Villesèque, Sauzet and Bovila take 3rd turning left to Mondounet - signposted)
Near river Near lake Near beach Forest area
*11 rms (9 bth/shr) Full central heating Open parking available Child discount available 10yrs Outdoor swimming pool (heated) Fishing Boule Open terrace Table tennis Badminton Languages spoken: English*
ROOMS: s 180-200FF; d 250-300FF *
CARDS: Travellers cheques

## FIGEAC Lot

**Château du Viguier du Roy**
rue Droite (Emile Zola) *46100*
☎ 565500505 FAX 565500606
Near river Forest area In town centre
*Closed 16 Nov-25 Mar*
*21 en suite (bth/shr) (2 fmly) (4 with balcony) No smoking in 12 bedrooms TV in all bedrooms Direct dial from 6 bedrooms Mini-bar in all bedrooms Licensed Lift Full central heating Air conditioning in bedrooms Open parking available (charged) Covered parking available (charged) Supervised Outdoor swimming pool (heated) Solarium Jacuzzi/spa Open terrace Last d 21.30hrs Languages spoken: English, German & Spanish*
CARDS: ● ■ ▨ ▨ Travellers cheques

**Liffernet Grange** (Prop: M & Mme Nielson de Lamothe)
*46100*
☎ 565346976 FAX 565500624
(from Figeac centre take N140 towards Rodez & Decazeville. After 3kms turn left onto D2 to Montredon and right on to D210 towards Lunan. Signposted from main road)
Five miles from the pretty medieval town of Figeac is the country home of Anthony and Dominique Nielson. They have tastefully restored their large 19th-century barn to provide six spacious en suite guest bedrooms. Antique furniture and oak floorboards provide the setting for candlelit regional dinners, accompanied by music. This is an ideal base for visiting the famous sites of Lot.
Near river Near lake Forest area Near motorway
*Closed Oct-Apr*
*6 en suite (bth/shr) (2 fmly) (1 with balcony) TV in all bedrooms Radio in rooms Open parking available Supervised No children 10yrs Outdoor swimming pool Tennis Fishing Riding Boule Bicycle rental Canoeing Kayaking Last d 20.30hrs Languages spoken: English, German & Spanish*
CARDS: ▨▨

## FONTANES Lot

**Lamourio**
*46230*
☎ 565243004 FAX 565247267
(From Cahors follow signs to Montauban for approx 18km then follow directions for Fontanes. From autoroute take Monatauban direction then follow signs for Fontanes)
*6 en suite (shr) (2 fmly) No smoking on premises Full central heating Open parking available Child discount available 10yrs Outdoor swimming pool (heated)*
ROOMS: s 210-250FF; d 240-300FF **Special breaks**
MEALS: Dinner 80-150FF

## GAILLAC Tarn

**Bed & Breakfast** (Prop: Mme Lucile Pinon)
8 pl St-Michel *81600*
☎ 563576148 FAX 563410656
(from centre of Gaillac follow directions for Lavaur. House by River Tarn as you leave the village)
Near river Forest area In town centre Near motorway
*6 en suite (bth/shr) Full central heating Open parking available Child discount available 10yrs Languages spoken: English*
CARDS: Travellers cheques

**Mas de Sudre** (Prop: Richmond Brown)
*81600*
☎ 563410132 FAX 563410132
(from Gaillac take D999 towards Montauban for 2kms to Ste-Cécile-d'Aves and turn right onto D18 towards Castelnau-de-Montmiral. Straight ahead for 2kms and left onto D4 towards Téoulet, straight ahead for 1.5kms and first left to house)
Near river Near lake Forest area Near motorway
*4 en suite (shr) 2 rooms in annexe Licensed Full central heating Open parking available Child discount available Outdoor swimming pool Tennis Boule Bicycle rental Open terrace Last d 20.00hrs Languages spoken: English*

## GANAC Ariège

**Le Carcis** (Prop: Mme Piednoel)
rte de Micou *09000*
☎ 561029654
Near river Forest area
*1 en suite (bth/shr) TV in all bedrooms Full central heating Open parking available Fishing*

## GARREVAQUES Tarn

**Château de Garrevaques** (Prop: Marie-Christine Combes)
*81700*
☎ 563750454 FAX 563702644
(from Revel city on D1 to Caraman, opposite police station

onto D79 to Garrevaques. Cross the village, château at the end on the right)
The château was built in the 15th century and refurbished in the 19th century. Guests are welcomed by the 15th generation living in this castle. Attractive bedrooms with furniture of the period and today's modern comforts.
Near river  Near lake  Forest area  Near motorway
*10 rms (8 bth) Full central heating Open parking available Covered parking available Child discount available 12yrs Outdoor swimming pool Tennis Pool table Boule Bicycle rental Open terrace Billiard room V meals Languages spoken: English & Spanish*
ROOMS: s 450-500FF; d 650-700FF
**Reductions over 1 night**
MEALS: Dinner 150-170FF
CARDS: ●● ■■ ▆▆ ▆ Travellers cheques

### GAVARNIE Hautes-Pyrénées

### ★ ★ ★ Hotel Club Vignemale
BP 2 *65120*
☎ 562924000 FAX 562924008
Near river  Forest area
*RS 15 Apr-May & mid Sep-mid Oct*
*25 en suite (bth/shr) (2 fmly) (7 with balcony) No smoking in 13 bedrooms TV in all bedrooms STV Direct dial from all bedrooms Licensed Lift Full central heating Open parking available Supervised Child discount available 5yrs Fishing Riding Solarium Bicycle rental Open terrace Languages spoken: English & Spanish*
CARDS: ●● ■■ ▆▆

### ★ ★ Le Marbore
*65120*
☎ 562924040 FAX 562924030
Near river  Forest area
*25 en suite (shr) (6 with balcony) TV in all bedrooms STV Licensed Full central heating Open parking available Child discount available 10yrs Sauna Gym Pool table Open terrace Covered terrace Wkly live entertainment V meals Last d 21.30hrs Languages spoken: English, German, Italian & Spanish*
CARDS: ●● ■■ ▆▆ ▆ Travellers cheques

### GOURDON Lot

### ★ ★ ★ Hostellerie de la Bouriane
pl du Foirail *46300*
☎ 565411637 FAX 565410492
(From Cathedral take first on right and continue for 100yds)
Near lake  Near sea  Forest area
*Closed mid Jan-early Mar*
*20 en suite (bth/shr) (5 fmly) TV in all bedrooms STV Radio in rooms Direct dial from all bedrooms Licensed Lift Full central heating Open parking available Supervised Open terrace V meals Last d 21.00hrs Languages spoken: English*
CARDS: ●● ■■ ▆▆ ▆ Travellers cheques

### ★ ★ ★ Hostellerie Domaine du Berthiol
Rte Dep 704 *46300*
☎ 565413333 FAX 565411452
(SE of Gourdon on D704)
This is a residence full of character situated amidst green scenery and that offers peaceful bedrooms equipped with modern conveniences. The restaurant serves a wide choice of regional dishes which are complemented by the excellent wines of the Cahors.

Forest area
*Closed Nov-Mar*
*29 en suite (bth/shr) (4 fmly) (2 with balcony) TV in all bedrooms Direct dial from all bedrooms Licensed Lift Night porter Full central heating Open parking available Child discount available 8yrs Outdoor swimming pool Tennis Solarium Boule Open terrace Last d 21.00hrs Languages spoken: English & German*
ROOMS: (room only) s 210-230FF; d 370-450FF
MEALS: Full breakfast 58FF  Lunch 100-275FFalc  Dinner 100-275FFalc
CARDS: ●● ■■ ▆▆ ▆ Travellers cheques

### GRAMAT Lot

### ★ ★ Hotel du Centre
pl de la République *46500*
☎ 565387337 FAX 565387366
(centre of village)
In town centre  Near motorway
*14 en suite (bth/shr) (4 fmly) TV in all bedrooms STV Direct dial from all bedrooms Licensed Full central heating Open parking available Covered parking available (charged) Child discount available 10yrs Open terrace Last d 21.00hrs Languages spoken: English*
ROOMS: (room only) s 240FF; d 320FF ✱
MEALS: Continental breakfast 40FF  Lunch fr 85FF&alc  Dinner fr 85FF&alc
CARDS: ●● ■■ ▆▆ ▆ Travellers cheques

### Ferme du Gravier (Prop: Lydia & Patrice Ravet)
*46500*
☎ 565334188 FAX 565337375
(at Gramat to Figéac, Fina petrol station turn at 1st road just before passing behind petrol station. House in 800m, signposted)
*5 en suite (shr) (2 fmly) No smoking on premises Full central heating Open parking available Child discount available Boule Last d 16.00hrs Languages spoken: English & Italian*
ROOMS: s 200FF; d 240-260FF
MEALS: Dinner fr 90FF
CARDS: Travellers cheques

### ★ ★ ★ Le Lion d'Or
8 pl de la République *46500*
☎ 565387318 FAX 565388450
(approach via N140 from Figeac or Bretenoux)
Near river  Forest area  In town centre  Near motorway
*Closed mid Dec-mid Jan*
*15 en suite (bth/shr) TV in all bedrooms STV Radio in rooms Direct dial from all bedrooms Licensed Lift Full central heating Air conditioning in bedrooms Open parking available Child discount available 10yrs Tennis Riding Sauna Gym Boule Bicycle rental Open terrace Covered terrace Last d 21.15hrs Languages spoken: English*
MEALS: Continental breakfast 52FF  Lunch 110-320FF&alc  Dinner 110-320FF&alc
CARDS: ●● ■■ ▆▆ ▆ Travellers cheques

### Moulin de Fresquet (Prop: M & Mme Ramelot)
*46500*
☎ 565387060 FAX 565387060
(at Gramat take N140 towards Figéac, then after 500 metres turn left into a small lane that leads to Mill)
Near river  Forest area
*Closed Nov-Mar*

contd.

5 en suite (shr) No smoking in all bedrooms Open parking available No children 8yrs Fishing Boule Open terrace Covered terrace Languages spoken: English
CARDS: Travellers cheques

### ★★ Relais des Gourmands
2 av de la Gare 46500
☎ 565388392 FAX 565387099
16 en suite (bth) (4 fmly) No smoking in 1 bedroom TV in all bedrooms STV Direct dial from all bedrooms Licensed Full central heating Child discount available 12yrs Outdoor swimming pool Open terrace V meals Last d 21.00hrs Languages spoken: English & German
CARDS: ●● � Travellers cheques

## GRISOLLES Tarn-et-Garonne

### ★★ Relais des Garrigues
rte de Fronton 82170
☎ 563673759 & 563673159 FAX 563641376
(W, off N20 towards Fronton)
Situated en route to the Pyrénées and Spain, the hotel stands just a few steps away from the Canal du Midi. Located on the garden side, the functional bedrooms have private facilities, whilst the restaurant serves regional cooking of good flavour.
Near river Forest area Near motorway

Closed 23 Dec-mid Jan
15 en suite (bth/shr) (1 fmly) (5 with balcony) TV in 14 bedrooms Direct dial from 14 bedrooms Licensed Full central heating Open parking available Covered parking available (charged) Supervised Child discount available 12yrs Boule Open terrace Covered terrace V meals Last d 22.00hrs Languages spoken: English & Spanish
ROOMS: (room only) s 200-230FF; d 215-250FF
**✱ Reductions over 1 night**
MEALS: Continental breakfast 30FF Lunch 62-140FF&alc Dinner 62-140FF&alc✱
CARDS: ●● ▆ Travellers cheques

## LABASTIDE-MURAT Lot

### ★★ Climat de France
pl de la Mairie 46240
☎ 565211880 FAX 565211097
(off A20 onto D677, hotel in village centre)
Climat de France hotels feature bedrooms with modern facilities. Restaurants serve a variety of menus often using local produce as well as a generous as-much-as-you-like buffet menu. Many hotels are located close to major national routes and motorways. A central reservations number is available

### Climat de France
Monday to Friday 8.30am to 7pm and Saturdays 9am to 6pm, by dialling 00 33 1 64460123.
Forest area In town centre
Closed 15 Dec-15 Jan
20 rms (19 bth/shr) (2 fmly) No smoking in 3 bedrooms TV in 19 bedrooms Radio in rooms Direct dial from 19 bedrooms Licensed Full central heating Child discount available 13yrs Open terrace V meals Last d 22.00hrs Languages spoken: English & Spanish
ROOMS: (room only) s 290-325FF; d 310-345FF
**Special breaks**
MEALS: Continental breakfast 35FF Lunch 65-140FF&alc Dinner 80-140FF&alc
CARDS: ●● ▆ ▆ ▆ Travellers cheques

## LACABARÈDE Tarn

### ★★★ Demeure de Flore
106 Grande Rue 81240
☎ 563983232 FAX 563984756
(on N112 opposite the FINA service station in Lacabarède village)
The house is set in landscaped gardens with mature trees, and offers its clientele an oasis of peace combined with modern day comfort. Its delightful interior is adorned with assorted antiques, whilst the bedrooms are furnished with flair and well co-ordinated colours and fabrics. Meals are served in the intimate restaurant or, in summer, guests can enjoy lunch by the side of the swimming pool or on the terrace overlooking the mountains of the Haut-Languedoc.
Near river Near lake Forest area Near motorway

RS Mondays From 1 Oct-31 Mar
11 en suite (bth/shr) 3 rooms in annexe (3 fmly) (7 with balcony) TV in all bedrooms Direct dial from all bedrooms Licensed Full central heating Open parking available Child discount available 6yrs Outdoor swimming pool Open terrace

Covered terrace V meals Last d 21.30hrs Languages spoken: English, Italian, German
ROOMS: (room only) s 390-450FF; d 500FF
MEALS: Continental breakfast 60FF Lunch fr 130FF&alc Dinner fr 175FF&alc
CARDS: ●● ▆▆ Travellers cheques

### LACAUNE Tarn

★ ★ ★ **Central Hotel Fusies**
2 rue de la République 81230
☎ 563370203 FAX 563371098
Near river Near lake Forest area In town centre
120 rms (104 bth/shr) (10 fmly) (10 with balcony) TV in all bedrooms Direct dial from all bedrooms Licensed Lift Night porter Full central heating Open parking available Covered parking available Supervised Child discount available Outdoor swimming pool (heated) Tennis Boule Bicycle rental Open terrace Covered terrace V meals Last d 21.00hrs Languages spoken: English & Spanish
ROOMS: (room only) s 250-260FF; d 320-380FF
**Reductions over 1 night Special breaks**
MEALS: Full breakfast 45FF Lunch 110FF&alc Dinner 110FF&alc✱
CARDS: ●● ▆▆ ▆▆ ◉ Travellers cheques

### LACAVE Lot

★ ★ ★ ★ **Château de la Tréyne** (Relais et Châteaux)
46200
☎ 565276060 FAX 565276070
Near river Forest area Near motorway
Closed mid Nov-Etr
14 en suite (bth) (4 fmly) TV in all bedrooms STV Direct dial from all bedrooms Licensed Lift Open parking available Supervised Child discount available 10yrs Outdoor swimming pool (heated) Tennis Fishing Riding Pool table Open terrace Last d 21.30hrs Languages spoken: English & Italian
CARDS: ●● ▆▆ ▆▆ ◉ Travellers cheques

### LACROIX-BARREZ Aveyron

**Vilherols** (Prop: Laurens)
12600
☎ 565660824 FAX 565661998
Near river Near lake Forest area Near motorway
4 en suite (shr) (1 fmly) (1 with balcony) TV in 1 bedroom Open parking available Child discount available Languages spoken: English
CARDS: Travellers cheques

### LAMAGDELAINE-CAHORS Lot

**Claude Marco**
Lamagdelaine 46090
☎ 565353064 FAX 565303140
(from N20 take D653 take left turn for Lamagdelaine)
Near river Forest area Near motorway
Closed 5 Jan-5 Mar
4 en suite (bth/shr) TV in all bedrooms STV Radio in rooms Direct dial from all bedrooms Mini-bar in all bedrooms Room-safe Licensed Full central heating Open parking available Supervised Child discount available 10yrs Outdoor swimming pool Open terrace V meals Last d 21.30hrs Languages spoken: English & Spanish
CARDS: ●● ▆▆ ▆▆

### LANNEMEZAN Hautes-Pyrénées

★ ★ **Pyrénées** (Minotel)
33 rue Didérot-pl des Pyrénées 65300
☎ 562980153 FAX 562981185
In town centre Near motorway
30 en suite (bth/shr) (1 fmly) (6 with balcony) TV in all bedrooms Direct dial from all bedrooms Licensed Lift Full central heating Open parking available Covered parking available Covered parking available Supervised Child discount available Open terrace V meals Last d 21.00hrs Languages spoken: English & Spanish
CARDS: ●● ▆▆ ▆▆ ◉ Travellers cheques

### LARRA Haute-Garonne

**Château de Larra** (Prop: Baronne de Carrière)
31330
☎ 561826251
(access via D17 or D87, then D64b for 1km)
Forest area
Closed 16 Nov-14 Apr
6 rms (5 bth/shr) (3 fmly) Open parking available Supervised Child discount available 7yrs Boule Languages spoken: English
ROOMS: d fr 350FF ✱
MEALS: Dinner 120FF✱
CARDS: Travellers cheques

### LARROQUE Tarn

**Meilhouret** (Prop: Christian Jouard)
81140
☎ 563331118 FAX 563331118
(from Gaillac on D964 for 22km then left onto D1 towards Monclar. After 3km turn right and follow signs)
Near river Near lake Forest area
Apr-1 Oct
2 en suite (bth/shr) No smoking on premises Full central heating Covered parking available Supervised Outdoor swimming pool Languages spoken: English
ROOMS: d 290FF

### LAVARDENS Gers

**Mascara** (Prop: Roger Hugon)
32360
☎ 562645217 FAX 562645833
4 en suite (bth/shr) (1 with balcony) Full central heating Open parking available Covered parking available Supervised Child discount available 9yrs Outdoor swimming pool Languages spoken: English, German & Italian

### LAVAUR Tarn

**Le Cottage** (Prop: Mme Y Ronjat-Valero)
Castex-Giroussens 81500
☎ 563416372
Forest area
3 en suite (bth/shr) (1 fmly) No smoking on premises Radio in rooms Full central heating Open parking available Supervised Child discount available 7yrs Outdoor swimming pool V meals Last d 19.00hrs Languages spoken: English & Spain

*contd.*

## LECTOURE Gers

**★ ★ Hotel de Bastard**
rue la Grange *32700*
☎ 562688244 FAX 562687681
(take A62 Agen/Auch road, Lectoure is on the N21 35kms from Agen)
Near lake Forest area
*Closed 21 Dec-Jan*
*29 en suite (bth/shr) 5 rooms in annexe (3 fmly) TV in all bedrooms Direct dial from all bedrooms Licensed Full central heating Covered parking available Outdoor swimming pool (heated) Bicycle rental Open terrace Last d 21.30hrs Languages spoken: English*
ROOMS: (room only) d 270-780FF **Special breaks**
MEALS: Full breakfast 50FF Lunch 88-300FF&alc Dinner 88-300FF&alc
CARDS: 💳 💳 💳 💳 Travellers cheques

## LEMPAUT Tarn

**Villa "Les Pins"** (Prop: Mme Delbreil)
*81700*
☎ 563755101
(on the D12, leave N126 between Puylaurens/Soual or leave D622 between Revel/Soual)
Near river Near lake Near sea Forest area
*Closed 16 Oct-Apr*
*7 en suite (bth/shr) (1 fmly) (1 with balcony) Full central heating Open parking available Child discount available 12yrs Fishing Boule Table tennis V meals Languages spoken: English*

## LORP-SENTARAILLE Ariège

**★ ★ Horizon 117**
rte de Toulouse *09190*
☎ 561662680 FAX 561662608
*20 en suite (bth/shr) (2 fmly) (10 with balcony) TV in all bedrooms STV Direct dial from all bedrooms Licensed Full central heating Open parking available Child discount available 12yrs Outdoor swimming pool Tennis Sauna Solarium Boule Open terrace Covered terrace Last d 21.15hrs Languages spoken: English*
ROOMS: (room only) s 230-280FF; d 270-320FF
**Reductions over 1 night**
MEALS: Continental breakfast 35FF Lunch 65-200FF Dinner 65-200FF
CARDS: 💳 💳 💳 💳 Travellers cheques

## LOUBAJAC Hautes-Pyrénées

**Bed & Breakfast** (Prop: Vives)
28 rte de Bartres *65100*
☎ 562944417 FAX 562423858
(from Loubajac take D3 towards Bartres)
Near river Near lake Forest area Near motorway
*6 en suite (bth/shr) (4 fmly) (2 with balcony) No smoking on premises Full central heating Open parking available Child discount available 3yrs Last d 20.00hrs*
CARDS: Travellers cheques

## LOUBRESSAC Lot

**Château de Gamot** (Prop: M & Mme Belieres)
Gamot *46130*
☎ 565109203 FAX 565385850
(from Loubressac take D30 towards St-Cére then right on D14 to Gamot to château 500mtrs from crossroads)
Near river Forest area
*Closed Oct-14 Apr*
*4 en suite (bth/shr) No smoking on premises Full central heating Open parking available Outdoor swimming pool*
ROOMS: s 180-280FF; d 280-370FF

**★ ★ Relais de Castelnau**
rte de Padirac, Rocamadour *46130*
☎ 565108090 FAX 565382202
(access on D20 via Bretenoux)
Near river Forest area Near motorway
*Apr-Nov*
*40 en suite (bth) (4 fmly) (9 with balcony) TV in all bedrooms Direct dial from all bedrooms Mini-bar in all bedrooms Licensed Full central heating Open parking available Child discount available 12yrs Outdoor swimming pool Tennis Boule Open terrace Last d 21.00hrs Languages spoken: English & Spanish*
ROOMS: (room only) d fr 500FF
CARDS: 💳 💳 💳

## LOURDES Hautes-Pyrénées

**★ ★ America Hotel**
6 rue de la Rine Astrid *65100*
☎ 562422525 FAX 562947169
*127 en suite (bth/shr) (12 fmly) TV in all bedrooms STV Radio in rooms Direct dial from all bedrooms Licensed Lift Night porter Full central heating Air conditioning in bedrooms Open parking available Supervised Child discount available Languages spoken: English, German & Italian*
CARDS: 💳 Travellers cheques

## LUPIAC Gers

**Domaine de Hongrie** (Prop: Jacqueline Gillet)
*32290*
☎ 562065958 FAX 562644193
(access via N124 & D31)
Near lake Forest area
*Closed Nov-Jan*
*3 en suite (bth/shr) TV in 1 bedroom Full central heating Open parking available Child discount available 6yrs Boule Last d 20.00hrs Languages spoken: English*
CARDS: 💳 💳

## MARTEL Lot

**★ ★ Les Falaises**
a Gluges *46600*
☎ 565373359 FAX 565373419
Near river Near sea Forest area
*Closed 31 Oct-Feb*
*16 en suite (bth/shr) Some rooms in annexe (4 fmly) (2 with balcony) Direct dial from all bedrooms Licensed Full central heating Open parking available Covered parking available (charged) Supervised Child discount available Boule Open terrace Canoeing V meals Last d 21.30hrs Languages spoken: English, German, Italian & Spanish*
CARDS: 💳 💳 Travellers cheques

## MAUPAS Gers

**Le Pouy** (Prop: M & Mme Ducasse)
*32240*
☎ 562090807 562096068
Near river Forest area
*Closed 2 Nov-Mar*
*4 en suite (bth/shr) No smoking on premises Full central heating Open parking available Covered parking available Supervised Child discount available 10yrs Outdoor swimming pool Play area Last d 21.00hrs Languages spoken: English, German & Spanish*

## MAUROUX Lot

**La Ferme d'Encarion** (Prop: Lidy Van Wijk-Bentum)
*32380*
☎ 562663441 FAX 562663441
(Follow signs for camping 'Les Roches' between St Clar and Goudonville, from 'Les Roches' there are signposts for Encarion)
Forest area
*3 en suite (bth/shr) Open parking available No children 4yrs Child discount available 6yrs Outdoor swimming pool Boule Languages spoken: English & German*
CARDS: ◉ ▥

**La Ferme des Étoiles** (Prop: M & Mme Monflier)
Le Cormeillon *32380*
☎ 562664683 FAX 562663296
(from A62, exit 8, direction St-Clar)
Forest area Near motorway
*Closed Dec-Mar*
*6 rms (5 bth/shr) (2 fmly) Full central heating Open parking available Child discount available 12yrs Outdoor swimming pool Library Languages spoken: English, German, Italian, Portuguese & Spanish*

**★ ★ Hostellerie le Vert**
Le Vert *46700*
☎ 565365136 FAX 565365684
Near river Forest area
*Closed 12 Nov-15 Feb*
*7 en suite (bth/shr) 2 rooms in annexe TV in all bedrooms Direct dial from all bedrooms Licensed Full central heating Open parking available Child discount available 10yrs Outdoor swimming pool Bicycle rental Open terrace V meals Last d 20.30hrs Languages spoken: English & German*
CARDS: ◉ ▤ ▥ Travellers cheques

## MAZAMET Tarn

**Les Pierres Bleues** (Prop: Erika & Jean Tricon)
3 bis rue de la République *81200*
☎ 563988863 FAX 563988862
(in the centre of Mazamet close to the Office of Tourisme)
This 19th-century residence is in the centre of pretty Mazamet, at the foot of the Montagne Noire. There are three luxurious private guest rooms and a hearty breakfast is served.
Near river Near lake Forest area In town centre Near motorway
*3 en suite (bth/shr) TV in all bedrooms Full central heating Open parking available Covered parking available Child discount available 7yrs Languages spoken: German*

*Les Pierres Bleues*

ROOMS: s fr 295FF; d fr 340FF
MEALS: Dinner fr 100FF

## MERCUÈS Lot

**Le Mas Azemar** (Prop: Claude Patrolin)
*46090*
☎ 565309685 FAX 565305382
(Mercues is on the D911)
An attractive 18th-century manor house restored and furnished to a high standard. Professional owners make every effort to ensure a comfortable stay. Meals can be taken with your hosts, who use only local produce. The house is pleasantly located at one end of the Cahors vineyard. While you're in the area, why not sample the local Cahors 'vin noir'.
Near river Forest area
*6 en suite (bth/shr) Full central heating Open parking available Supervised No children 8yrs Outdoor swimming pool (heated) Languages spoken: English*
ROOMS: d 390-450FF **Reductions over 1 night**
MEALS: Dinner 150-195FF
CARDS: Travellers cheques

## MIÉLAN Gers

**La Tannerie** (Prop: B & C Bryson)
*32170*
☎ 562676262 FAX 562676262
(40km SW of Auch on N21, in Miélan turn right after church)
Near lake Forest area Near motorway
*Closed Nov-Feb*
*4 en suite (bth) (1 fmly) Full central heating Open parking available No children 5yrs Languages spoken: English & Spanish*

## MILLAU Aveyron

**Bed & Breakfast** (Prop: M & Mme Decroix)
8 ave J-Cambetorte-Creissels *12100*
☎ 565612515
Near river Forest area In town centre
*Closed Oct-May*
*2 rms (1 shr) Open parking available Covered parking available No children 2yrs Open terrace Covered terrace*

## MIREPOIX Ariège

**★ ★ ★ La Maison des Consuls**
*09500*
☎ 561688181 FAX 561688115
(from Toulouse or Narbonne A61 exit Bram Mirepoix)

*contd.*

Near river  Near lake  Forest area  In town centre  Near motorway
*8 en suite (bth/shr)  No smoking in 1 bedroom  TV in all bedrooms  Direct dial from all bedrooms  Mini-bar in all bedrooms  Licensed  Full central heating  Child discount available 8yrs  Languages spoken: English & Spanish*
ROOMS: (room only)  s 420-480FF;  d 430-500FF
CARDS: ●● ■■ ■■ Travellers cheques

## MONTAIGU-DE-QUERCY Tarn-et-Garonne

**Les Chênes de Ste-Croix** (Prop: M & Mme Hunt)
*82150*
☎ 563953078 FAX 563953078
(5kms SE of Montaigu-de-Quercy on D2)
Your English hosts offer bed and breakfast in six rooms in a 250-year-old stone farmhouse with shaded lawns, woodland and a swimming pool. The house is set well back from the road in a quiet country area, yet within easy reach of a small town with a market, restaurants and shops. Dinner available on request.
Near lake
*6 en suite (shr)  1 rooms in annexe  (2 fmly)  Open parking available  Covered parking available  Child discount available 10yrs  Outdoor swimming pool  Boule  Open terrace  Last d 10.00hrs  Languages spoken: English*
ROOMS: s 175FF;  d 240FF
MEALS: Dinner 70FF

## MONTBRUN-BOCAGE Haute-Garonne

**Hameau de Pavé** (Prop: Mme Josette Parinaud)
*31310*
☎ 561981125
(from Toulouse towards St Gaudens on N117 as far as Carbonne, then left as far as Daumazan via Montesquieu-Volvestre (D627 & D628), Turn right until Montbrun-Bocage and farm further 5kms on right)
Near river  Near lake  Forest area
*4 en suite (shr)  (2 fmly)  Full central heating  Open parking available  Child discount available 10yrs*
CARDS: Travellers cheques

## MONTESQUIEU Tarn-et-Garonne

**La Bayssé** (Prop: M & Mme Delente)
*82200*
☎ 563045400
(at Moissac, take D957 for Cahors - at Laujol crossroads, take D16 for Dufort-Lacapelette and follow signs)
Near river  Forest area  Near motorway
*4 en suite (bth/shr)  No smoking in all bedrooms  Full central heating  Open parking available  Supervised  Child discount available 12yrs  Outdoor swimming pool  Bicycle rental  Table tennis  V meals  Languages spoken: English*
CARDS: Travellers cheques

## NAJAC Aveyron

★ ★ **Hotel Oustal Del Barry**
pl du Bourg *12270*
☎ 565297432 FAX 565297532
(20km from Villefranche-de-Rouergue. Najac is signposted from Villefranche.)
Near river  Forest area  In town centre  Near motorway
*Closed Dec-Mar*

*21 rms (7 bth 10 shr)  (1 fmly)  (2 with balcony)  TV in all bedrooms  Direct dial from all bedrooms  Licensed  Lift  Full central heating  Open parking available  Covered parking available  Supervised  Child discount available 12yrs  Boule  Bicycle rental  Open terrace  Covered terrace  Last d 21.30hrs  Languages spoken: English*
ROOMS: (room only)  s fr 270FF;  d 320-390FF
MEALS: Continental breakfast 50FF  Lunch 135-250FF  Dinner 135-250FF✱
CARDS: ●● ■■ ■■ ●● Travellers cheques

## ONET-LE-CHÂTEAU Aveyron

**Domaine de Vialatelle** (Prop: Patrick & Anne David)
*12850*
☎ 565427656 FAX 565427656
(from Rodez D988 towards Aurillac in 2km right for St-Mayme (D224) Vialatelle on left)
Near river  Forest area  Near motorway
*11 en suite (bth/shr)  (4 fmly)  TV in 6 bedrooms  Full central heating  Open parking available  Child discount available 10yrs  Outdoor swimming pool  Riding  Boule  Bicycle rental  V meals  Last d 21.30hrs  Languages spoken: English, Italian & Spanish*
CARDS: ●● ■■ Travellers cheques

## PAMIERS Ariège

★ ★ **Hotel de France**
5 rue Dr Rambaud, 13 rue Hospice *09100*
☎ 561602088 FAX 561672948
Near river  Forest area  In town centre  Near motorway
*30 en suite (bth/shr)  (4 fmly)  (10 with balcony)  No smoking in 2 bedrooms  TV in all bedrooms  Direct dial from all bedrooms  Night porter  Full central heating  Open parking available  Covered parking available (charged)  Supervised  Child discount available 10yrs  Solarium  Boule  Bicycle rental  Open terrace  V meals  Last d 21.30hrs  Languages spoken: English & Spanish*
CARDS: ●● ■■ ■■ ●● Travellers cheques

★ ★ **Hotel de la Paix**
4 pl Albert Tournier *09100*
☎ 561671271 FAX 561606102
Near river  Near sea  Forest area  In town centre  Near motorway
*16 en suite (bth/shr)  (7 fmly)  TV in all bedrooms  STV  Direct dial from all bedrooms  Licensed  Night porter  Full central heating  Air conditioning in bedrooms  Open parking available  Covered parking available  Supervised  Child discount available 4yrs  Boule  Bicycle rental  Open terrace  V meals  Last d 22.30hrs  Languages spoken: English & Spanish*
CARDS: ●● ■■ ■■ ●● Travellers cheques

## PAULINET Tarn

**Domaine des Juliannes** (Prop: M et MMe Nick Hudswell)
*81250*
☎ 563559438 FAX 563559438
(37km SW of Albi via D999 towards Millau, before Alban go right onto D86 towards Realmont, then 3rd road on left, turning after Paulinet road)
*3 en suite (bth/shr)  (2 fmly)  Full central heating  Open parking available  Child discount available 11yrs  Outdoor swimming pool  Riding  Bicycle rental  Last d 20.00hrs  Languages spoken: English*
CARDS: ●● ■■

## PAYRAC Lot

**★★ Petit Relais**
Calès *46350*
☎ 565379609 FAX 565379593
(N20 to Payrac and take direction for Rocamadour)
Near river  Near motorway
*15 en suite (bth/shr)  (2 fmly)  TV in all bedrooms  Direct dial from all bedrooms  Licensed  Full central heating  Open parking available  Supervised  Child discount available 10yrs  Outdoor swimming pool  Boule  Open terrace  Covered terrace  Last d 21.30hrs  Languages spoken: English & Spanish*
CARDS: ●● 💳 Travellers cheques

## PEYRELEAU Aveyron

**★★★ Grand Hotel de la Muse et du Rozier**
*12720*
☎ 565626001 FAX 565626388
(take D907 along river Tarn, at Rozier roundabout head in direction of Sainte Enimie. Hotel further 500 metres)
Near river  Near beach  Forest area
*Closed 3 Nov-20 Mar*
*38 en suite (bth/shr)  (3 fmly)  (14 with balcony)  TV in all bedrooms  STV  Direct dial from all bedrooms  Licensed  Lift  Full central heating  Open parking available  Covered parking available (charged)  Child discount available 8yrs  Outdoor swimming pool (heated)  Tennis  Fishing  Open terrace  Canoeing  V meals  Last d 21.30hrs  Languages spoken: English, German & Italian*
ROOMS: (room only) s 360-440FF; d 510-610FF
**Reductions over 1 night**
MEALS: Full breakfast 65FF  Lunch 95-220FF&alc  Dinner 160-220FF&alc
CARDS: ●● ■■ 💳 ◎

## PINAS Hautes-Pyrénées

**Domaine de Jean Pierre** (Prop: Mme Marie Colombier)
20 route de Villeneuve *65300*
☎ 562981508 FAX 562981508
(5km E of Lannemezan on N117. At Pinas church, take D158 for Villeneuve. 800m on right-follow signs)
Near river  Forest area  Near motorway
*3 en suite (bth)  (2 fmly)  No smoking on premises  Full central heating  Open parking available  Supervised  Child discount available 2yrs  Languages spoken: English & Spanish*
CARDS: ◎

## PLAISANCE Aveyron

**★★ Les Magnolias**
rue des Magnolias *12550*
☎ 565997734 FAX 565997057
Near river  Forest area
*Closed Jan-Mar*
*6 en suite (bth/shr)  1 rooms in annexe  TV in all bedrooms  Direct dial from all bedrooms  Full central heating  Open parking available  Child discount available 9yrs  Boule  Bicycle rental  Open terrace  Last d 22.00hrs  Languages spoken: English & Spanish*
CARDS: ●● ■■ 💳 ◎ Travellers cheques

## PROJAN Gers

**Château de Projan**
*32400*
☎ 562094621 FAX 562094408
(located 3km from road between Aire-sur-Adour and Pau. In Aire-sur-Adour follow direction of Pau, drive through village of St Agnet then turn left to Riscle and follow signs to Projan)
Near river  Forest area  Near motorway
*Closed Dec-Jan*
*9 rms (3 bth 1 shr)  (1 fmly)  No smoking in 2 bedrooms  Direct dial from 8 bedrooms  Licensed  Full central heating  Open parking available  Covered parking available  Child discount available 12yrs  Fishing  Boule  Bicycle rental  Open terrace  Table tennis  Last d 21.00hrs  Languages spoken: English & German*
ROOMS: (room only) d 320-650FF  **Special breaks**
MEALS: Continental breakfast 45FF  Dinner 110-250FF
CARDS: ●● 💳

## RABASTENS Tarn

**★★ Hotel du Pré Vert**
54 promenade des Lices *81800*
☎ 563337051 FAX 563338258
(on outskirts towards Toulouse)
Near river  Near lake  In town centre  Near motorway
*Closed Jan*
*27 rms (4 bth 8 shr)  (2 fmly)  TV in 9 bedrooms  Direct dial from 14 bedrooms  Licensed  Full central heating  Open parking available  Child discount available 10yrs  Mini-golf  Open terrace  V meals  Last d 21.30hrs  Languages spoken: English*
ROOMS: (room only) s 220-260FF; d 240-350FF
MEALS: Continental breakfast 43FF  Lunch 69-150FF&alc  Dinner 90-150FF&alc
CARDS: ●● ■■ 💳 ◎ Travellers cheques

## RIEUPEYROUX Aveyron

**★★ Hotel du Commerce**
*12240*
☎ 565655306 FAX 565655658
Near lake  Forest area
*Closed end Dec-mid Jan*
*(3 fmly)  (3 with balcony)  TV available  Licensed  Lift  Full central heating  Open parking available  Covered parking available  Child discount available 6yrs  Outdoor swimming pool  Boule  Open terrace  V meals  Last d 21.00hrs  Languages spoken: English*
CARDS: ●● ■■ 💳 Travellers cheques

## RIGNAC Lot

**Chambres d'Hôte à Darnis** (Prop: Lillian Bell)
*46500*
☎ 565336684 FAX 565337131
(at Alvignac, take the D673 to Padirac. Just before the 'Grill de Berger' turn right and follow the 'Chambre d'hôte' signs to Pouch.)
Restored farmhouse set in a tiny hamlet only seven kilometres from Rocamadour, one of the most famous pilgrimage destinations in Christendom. Evening meals are served. South African hosts.
Near river  Near lake  Forest area  Near motorway

*contd.*

3 en suite (bth/shr) (1 fmly) Open parking available Child discount available 10yrs Outdoor swimming pool Bicycle rental Tennis and boules nearby V meals Languages spoken: English
ROOMS: s 200FF; d 240FF
MEALS: Dinner 90FF

**★ ★ ★ ★ Château de Roumegouse**
☎ 565336381 FAX 565337118
Forest area
Closed 25 Oct-Mar
15 en suite (bth/shr) (2 fmly) (1 with balcony) TV in all bedrooms Mini-bar in all bedrooms Licensed Full central heating Open parking available Child discount available 12yrs Outdoor swimming pool Bicycle rental Open terrace V meals Last d 22.00hrs Languages spoken: English & Spanish
CARDS: ●● ■■ ☲☲ ⑩ Travellers cheques

### ROCAMADOUR Lot

**★ ★ ★ Beau Site** (Best Western)
Cité Medievale 46500
☎ 565336308 FAX 565336523
(from Brive follow the A20 until Cressensac and take the N140 for 20km and you will arrive 3 miles from the village and see signposts. The Hotel is situated inside the Medieval City, do not hesitate to pass through the gate into the Hotel carpark)
Forest area
43 en suite (bth/shr) (5 fmly) TV in all bedrooms STV Direct dial from all bedrooms Licensed Lift Full central heating Open parking available Covered parking available (charged) Supervised Child discount available 12yrs Bicycle rental Open terrace Last d 21.00hrs Languages spoken: English
ROOMS: (room only) s 315-495FF; d 385-695FF
MEALS: Full breakfast 55FF Lunch 120-350FF&alc Dinner 120-350FF&alc
CARDS: ●● ■■ ☲☲ ⑩ JCB Travellers cheques

**★ ★ ★ Hotel Domaine de la Rhue**
La Rhue 46500
☎ 565337150 FAX 565337248
(from Rocamadour take D673 in direction of Brive, then N140 for 1km & take small road on left)
Closed mid Oct-Etr
14 en suite (bth/shr) 2 rooms in annexe (2 fmly) TV in 2 bedrooms Direct dial from all bedrooms Mini-bar in 2 bedrooms Full central heating Open parking available Supervised Child discount available 3yrs Outdoor swimming pool Bicycle rental Open terrace Languages spoken: English & German
ROOMS: (room only) s 380-580FF
CARDS: ●● ☲☲ ⑩ Travellers cheques

**★ ★ Terminus Hotel et Des Pelerins**
pl Carretta-Cité Medievale 46500
☎ 565335214 FAX 565337210
(from Brive to Rocamadour the city at the first gate, cross the street, the hotel is situated between 2nd and 3rd gates)
A small family hotel in the heart of this historic town, noted for its fine regional cuisine and the warm welcome afforded to its guests.
Near river
Closed Nov-14 Apr
12 en suite (bth/shr) (1 fmly) (3 with balcony) TV in all bedrooms Direct dial from all bedrooms Licensed Full central heating Open parking available Child discount available 10yrs Open terrace V meals Last d 21.30hrs Languages spoken: English

*Terminus Hotel et Des Pelerins*
ROOMS: (room only) s 220-280FF; d 260-340FF
MEALS: Continental breakfast 37FF Lunch 70-245FF&alc Dinner 70-245FF&alc
CARDS: ●● ■■ ☲☲ ⑩ JCB Travellers cheques

**★ ★ Troubadour**
Le Belvéyré 46500
☎ 565337027 FAX 565337199
Head towards Cave of Padirac
Near river Forest area
Closed 15 Nov-15 Feb
10 en suite (bth/shr) (2 fmly) (10 with balcony) TV in all bedrooms STV Direct dial from all bedrooms Licensed Air conditioning in bedrooms Open parking available Supervised Child discount available 10yrs Outdoor swimming pool Boule Bicycle rental Open terrace V meals Last d 21.00hrs Languages spoken: English
CARDS: ●● ☲☲ ⑩ Travellers cheques

**★ ★ Les Vielles Tours**
Lafage 46500
☎ 565336801 FAX 565336859
(Take the D673 in the direction of Gourdon/Payrac, Rocamadour is 3km from the exit)
Near river Forest area
Closed Mid Nov-27 Mar
18 en suite (bth/shr) (7 fmly) TV in all bedrooms Direct dial from all bedrooms Full central heating Open parking available Child discount available 12yrs Outdoor swimming pool Bicycle rental Open terrace Badminton, Volleyball, Boules Last d 21.00hrs
CARDS: ●● ■■ ☲☲ Travellers cheques

### RODEZ Aveyron

**★ ★ ★ Tour Maje**
bd Gally 12000
☎ 565683468 FAX 565682756
In town centre
41 en suite (bth/shr) (3 fmly) TV in 44 bedrooms STV Direct dial from 44 bedrooms Mini-bar in 44 bedrooms Licensed Lift Night porter Full central heating Covered parking available (charged) Pool table Open terrace Languages spoken: English
ROOMS: (room only) s 310-360FF; d 340-390FF
**Reductions over 1 night**
CARDS: ●● ■■ ☲☲ ⑩ Travellers cheques

## ROQUELAURE Gers

**En Boutan** (Prop: Jeanne and Jean Dauzere)
*32810*
☎ 562655466 FAX 562655122
Forest area
*Closed Nov-Etr*
*3 en suite (shr) (1 fmly) TV available Full central heating Open parking available Covered parking available Supervised Child discount available 10yrs Languages spoken: English & Spanish*

## ST-AFFRIQUE Aveyron

★ ★ **Moderne**
54 av A Pezet *12400*
☎ 565492044 FAX 565493655
(A75, Exit Millau, toward Albi for 30km)
Near river Forest area
*Closed 1-28 Jan*
*35 en suite (bth/shr) 7 rooms in annexe (4 fmly) (8 with balcony) No smoking in 1 bedroom TV in all bedrooms Direct dial from all bedrooms Licensed Full central heating Covered parking available (charged) Supervised Child discount available 7yrs Pool table Open terrace library V meals Last d 21.30hrs Languages spoken: English,Spanish*
ROOMS: (room only) s 200-250FF; d 250-390FF
**Reductions over 1 night Special breaks: wknds**
CARDS: ●● ▆▆ ▣ Travellers cheques

## ST-ANTONIN-DE-LACALM Tarn

**La Ginestarie** (Prop: C H Teotski)
*81120*
☎ 563455346
(at Albi take direction for Réalmont-Castres and at Réalmont direction for "Lac de La Bancalie", house signposted)
Near river Near lake Near sea Near beach Forest area
*3 en suite (bth/shr) (3 fmly) No smoking on premises Full central heating Open parking available Supervised Child discount available 8yrs V meals Last d 18.00hrs*
CARDS: Travellers cheques

## ST-ANTONIN-NOBLE-VAL Tarn-et-Garonne

**La Residence** (Prop: Sean O'Shea)
rue Droite *82140*
☎ 563682160 FAX 563682160
(via A20 or N20 exit at Caussade take D929 towards Septfonds, just before Septfonds take D5 towards St-Antonin-Noble-Val, La Résidence is in the centre of town signposted)
Situated in the beautiful Aveyron Gorge in the centre of the 12th-century market town of St Antonin Noble Val. The property has been lovingly restored by its owners to create an atmosphere of luxury, style and relaxation, making it an ideal location from which the whole family can enjoy this fascinating area of south-west France. All rooms have en suite bathrooms and one boasts its own sun terrace.
Near river Near lake Forest area In town centre Near motorway
*5 en suite (bth) (5 fmly) (1 with balcony) No smoking on premises Full central heating Open parking available Last d 9pm Languages spoken: English*
ROOMS: s 350-400FF; d 400-450FF
**Special breaks: fishing/painting/sport**
MEALS: Dinner 110FF
CARDS: ●● ▆▆ Travellers cheques

## ST-CÉRÉ Lot

★ ★ ★ **Hotel de France**
181 av François de Maynard *46400*
☎ 565380216 FAX 565380298
Forest area In town centre
*Closed Nov-15 Mar*
*23 en suite (bth/shr) (2 fmly) (12 with balcony) TV in all bedrooms STV Direct dial from all bedrooms Licensed Full central heating Open parking available Covered parking available (charged) Supervised Child discount available 10yrs Outdoor swimming pool (heated) Open terrace Last d 21.15hrs*
CARDS: ●● ▆▆ Travellers cheques

★ ★ ★ **Ric**
rte de Leyne *46400*
☎ 565380408 FAX 565380014
Forest area
*Closed Dec-Mar*
*5 en suite (bth/shr) TV in all bedrooms Licensed Full central heating Open parking available Child discount available Outdoor swimming pool Boule Bicycle rental Open terrace Last d 21.30hrs Languages spoken: English*
CARDS: ●● ▆▆

★ ★ **Le Victor Hugo**
7 av des Marquis *46400*
☎ 565381615 FAX 565383991
Near river Near lake Forest area In town centre
*13 en suite (bth/shr) (3 fmly) TV in all bedrooms Direct dial from all bedrooms Licensed Night porter Full central heating Open parking available Covered parking available (charged) Open terrace V meals Last d 21.00hrs Languages spoken: English & Spanish*
ROOMS: (room only) s fr 250FF; d 250-300FF
MEALS: Continental breakfast 35FF Lunch 90-220FF&alc Dinner 90-220FF&alc
CARDS: ●● ▆▆ ▆▆ ▣ Travellers cheques

## ST-CIRQ-LAPOPIE Lot

★ ★ ★ **Pelissaria**
Le Bourg *46330*
☎ 565312514 FAX 565302552
Near river
*Closed 16 Nov-Mar*
*10 en suite (bth) 3 rooms in annexe (3 fmly) (4 with balcony) TV in all bedrooms Full central heating Outdoor swimming pool (heated) Open terrace Languages spoken: English & German*
CARDS: ●● ▆▆ Travellers cheques

## ST-FÉLIX-DE-TOURNEGAT Ariège

**Domaine de Montagnac** (Prop: M & Mme Bertolino)
*09500*
☎ 561687275 FAX 561674484
(N20 to Pamiers, then to Mirepoix. 5km from Pamiers, at Les Pujols, left to St-Amadou. 1km further turn right to St-Félix and continue through village to farm approx 200mtrs away)
Forest area
*16 rms (2 bth 4 shr) Full central heating Open parking available Child discount available 14yrs Outdoor swimming pool Riding Boule Open terrace Table tennis Library Languages spoken: English, German & Italian*
CARDS: Travellers cheques

### ST-GAUDENS Haute-Garonne

**★★ Pedussaut**
9 av de Boulogne *31800*
☎ 561891570 FAX 561891126
In town centre Near motorway
*25 rms (5 bth 15 shr) (5 fmly) (1 with balcony) TV in all bedrooms STV Direct dial from all bedrooms Licensed Full central heating Open parking available Covered parking available Child discount available 12yrs Open terrace Last d 21.30hrs Languages spoken: English & Spanish*
CARDS: ●● ☲ Travellers cheques

**★★ Tuilère**
Sur RN 117 *31800*
☎ 561890851 FAX 561892164
Near river Forest area Near motorway
*20 en suite (shr) (13 fmly) TV in all bedrooms Direct dial from all bedrooms Mini-bar in all bedrooms Licensed Night porter Full central heating Open parking available Child discount available 8yrs Outdoor swimming pool Open terrace Languages spoken: Italian & Spanish*
CARDS: ●● ■ ☲ Travellers cheques

### ST-GENIEZ-D'OLT Aveyron

**★★ Hotel du Lion d'Or**
*12130*
☎ 565474332 FAX 565474980
Near river Forest area In town centre
*Closed Jan-1 Mar*
*12 en suite (bth/shr) (1 with balcony) TV in all bedrooms Licensed Night porter Full central heating Open parking available Child discount available 10yrs Boule Bicycle rental Open terrace Last d 22.00hrs Languages spoken: English*
CARDS: ●● ☲ ⑩ Travellers cheques

### ST-GIRONS Ariège

**★★★ Château de Seignan**
rte de Foix *09200*
☎ 561960880 FAX 561960820
(on D117)
Near river Forest area
*Closed 31 Oct-1 Apr*
*9 en suite (bth/shr) (3 fmly) TV in all bedrooms Direct dial from all bedrooms Mini-bar in all bedrooms Licensed Full central heating Open parking available Child discount available 12yrs Outdoor swimming pool Tennis Open terrace V meals Last d 22.00hrs Languages spoken: English & Spanish*
CARDS: ●● ■ ☲ ⑩

**★★★ Eychenne**
8 av Paul Laffont *09200*
☎ 561040450 FAX 561960720
(A64 exit Saint Girons)
Near river
*42 en suite (bth/shr) (7 fmly) (2 with balcony) TV in all bedrooms STV Direct dial from all bedrooms Mini-bar in 15 bedrooms Room-safe Licensed Night porter Full central heating Open parking available (charged) Covered parking available (charged) Supervised Child discount available 12yrs Outdoor swimming pool (heated) Open terrace V meals Last d 21.30hrs Languages spoken: English*
MEALS: Continental breakfast 49FF Lunch 140-325FF&alc Dinner 140-325FF&alc
CARDS: ●● ■ ☲ Travellers cheques

**Le Relais d'Encaussé** (Prop: H Kawczynski)
*09200*
☎ 561660580
(1km from St-Girons, on the hill to Saudech. )
Forest area
*5 rms (2 bth 2 shr) (1 fmly) Full central heating Open parking available Child discount available 10yrs Table tennis Billiards Last d 20.00hrs Languages spoken: English*

### ST-JEAN-DU-BRUEL Aveyron

**★★ Midi-Papillon**
pl Albin Lémasson *12230*
☎ 565622604 FAX 565621297
Near river
*Closed 11 Nov-Palm Sunday*
*19 en suite (bth/shr) (4 fmly) (11 with balcony) Direct dial from all bedrooms Licensed Full central heating Open parking available Covered parking available (charged) Child discount available 7yrs Outdoor swimming pool (heated) Jacuzzi/spa Open terrace Last d 21.30hrs Languages spoken: English & Spanish*
CARDS: ●● ☲ Travellers cheques

### ST-LIZIER Ariège

**Le Maison Blanche** (Prop: Agnes and Alain Roques)
Prat du Ritou *09190*
☎ 612523600 FAX 561663671
(3km from St Girons on D117. In Lorp turn right signed "chambres d'hôte". Le Maison Blanche is 0.6km from D117)
Near river
*3 en suite (bth/shr) No smoking on premises Full central heating Open parking available Covered parking available Child discount available 12yrs Fishing Riding Boule Bicycle rental V meals Last d 20.00hrs Languages spoken: English & Spanish*
ROOMS: s 200FF; d 250FF **Reductions over 1 night**
MEALS: Dinner 80FF

### ST-MARTIN-DE-CARALP Ariège

**★★ Le Grandgousier**
*09000*
☎ 561029002
Near river Forest area Near motorway
*8 en suite (bth/shr) Licensed Full central heating Open parking available Child discount available Open terrace Last d 21.30hrs Languages spoken: English & Spanish*
CARDS: ●● ☲ Travellers cheques

### ST-MARTORY Haute-Garonne

**Domaine de Menaut** (Prop: Mme Gabrielle Jander)
Auzas *31360*
☎ 561902151
(leave N117 or motorway at Boussens for Mancioux, take D33 Auzas-Aurignac for 5km to end. Before D52 St Marjory-Aurignac turn right and follow fence)
Near river Near lake Near sea Near beach Forest area Near motorway
*3 en suite (bth/shr) (1 fmly) Full central heating Open parking available Covered parking available Supervised Fishing Boule Languages spoken: English & German*
ROOMS: s 250-300FF; d 350FF
**✱ Reductions over 1 night**
CARDS: Travellers cheques

## ST-MAUR Gers

**Noailles** (Prop: Louis et Marthe Sabathier)
*32300*
☎ 562675798
Near river Near lake Near sea Near beach Forest area Near motorway
*Closed Jan-Apr*
*4 en suite (shr) (3 fmly) (2 with balcony) Open parking available Child discount available 12yrs Fishing Boule*
CARDS: ● ▬

## ST-PÉ-DE-BIGORRE Hautes-Pyrénées

**Le Grand Cèdre** (Prop: M Christian Peters)
6 rue de Barry *65270*
☎ 562418204 FAX 562418585
Near river Near lake Forest area In town centre Near motorway
*4 en suite (bth/shr) (1 fmly) (4 with balcony) No smoking on premises TV in all bedrooms Full central heating Open parking available Child discount available Last d 19.00hrs Languages spoken: English, German, Italian & Spanish*

## ST-PIERRE Haute-Garonne

**Château de St-Martin** (Prop: M Georges Maury)
*31590*
☎ 561357157 FAX 561747113
Forest area
*Closed Nov-Apr*
*Full central heating Open parking available No children 14yrs Child discount available 18yrs Languages spoken: English & Spanish*
CARDS: Travellers cheques

## ST-RÉMY Aveyron

**Mas de Jouas** (Prop: Pierre Salvage)
Villefranche-de-Rouergue *12200*
☎ 565816472 FAX 565815070
Near river Forest area Near motorway
*Closed Oct-Apr*
*6 en suite (bth) (1 fmly) (3 with balcony) TV available STV Full central heating Open parking available Child discount available Languages spoken: English & Spanish*

## ST-SATURNIN-DE-LENNE Aveyron

**Château St-Saturnin** (Prop: Cliff & Victoria Lenton)
*12560*
☎ 565703600 FAX 565703619
Forest area
*Closed 5 Jan-1 Apr*
*12 en suite (bth/shr) (2 with balcony) TV in all bedrooms Licensed Full central heating Open parking available Supervised Child discount available Outdoor swimming pool (heated) Tennis Boule Bicycle rental Open terrace Covered terrace Last d 20.30hrs Languages spoken: English*
CARDS: ● ▬ ▬

## ST-SAVIN Hautes-Pyrénées

★ ★ ★ **Le Viscos**
*65400*
☎ 562970228 FAX 562970594
In town centre

16 en suite (bth/shr) TV in all bedrooms Licensed Open parking available Child discount available 3yrs Open terrace V meals Last d 21.30hrs Languages spoken: English & Spanish
CARDS: ●● ▬ ▬ Travellers cheques

## ST-SERNIN-SUR-RANCE Aveyron

★ ★ **Carayon**
pl du Fort *12380*
☎ 565981919 FAX 565996926
(between Albi and Millau on the D999)
Near river Forest area In town centre
*60 en suite (bth/shr) 6 rooms in annexe TV in all bedrooms STV Direct dial from all bedrooms Mini-bar in all bedrooms Room-safe Licensed Lift Full central heating Open parking available Covered parking available (charged) Supervised Child discount available Outdoor swimming pool Tennis Fishing Sauna Solarium Gym Boule Mini-golf Jacuzzi/spa Bicycle rental Open terrace Covered terrace V meals Last d 21.00hrs Languages spoken: English & Spanish*
ROOMS: (room only) d 199-399FF
**Reductions over 1 night Special breaks**
MEALS: Full breakfast 46FF Lunch 85-350FF&alc Dinner 85-350FF&alc
CARDS: ●● ▬ ▬ ◑ Travellers cheques

## ST-SOZY Lot

★ ★ **Grangjier**
*46200*
☎ 565322014 FAX 565322797
Near river Forest area
*Closed Feb*
*13 rms (1 bth 9 shr) 7 rooms in annexe (2 fmly) TV in all bedrooms Licensed Full central heating Open parking available Child discount available 12yrs Boule Open terrace V meals Last d 20.45hrs Languages spoken: English*
CARDS: ●● ▬ Travellers cheques

## SALLES-CURAN Aveyron

★ ★ **Hostellerie du Levézou**
*12410*
☎ 565463416 FAX 565460119
Near lake Near beach Forest area
*Closed Nov-Etr*
*20 rms 4 rooms in annexe TV in all bedrooms Direct dial from all bedrooms Licensed Full central heating Open parking available Child discount available 12yrs Bicycle rental Open terrace V meals Languages spoken: English*
CARDS: ▬ ◑ CB

## SARRAGACHIES Gers

**La Buscasse** (Prop: M & Mme Abadie)
*32400*
☎ 562697607 FAX 562697917
(between Sarragachies and Termes-d'Armagnac on top of the hill)
Forest area
*3 en suite (bth/shr) TV in all bedrooms Radio in rooms Full central heating Open parking available Covered parking available Child discount available Outdoor swimming pool Fishing Boule Bicycle rental Archery Badminton Croquet V meals Languages spoken: English*
ROOMS: s 250FF; d 280FF
MEALS: Dinner 90FF
CARDS: Travellers cheques

### SAUVETERRE-DE-COMMINGES Haute-Garonne

### ★★★ Hostellerie des 7 Molles (Relais et Châteaux)
31510
☎ 561883087 FAX 561883642
Near river  Forest area
*Closed Jan-mid Mar*
*19 en suite (bth/shr)  (2 fmly)  (19 with balcony)  TV in all bedrooms  STV  Direct dial from all bedrooms  Mini-bar in all bedrooms  Licensed  Lift  Full central heating  Open parking available  Child discount available  Outdoor swimming pool (heated)  Tennis  Pool table  Boule  Open terrace  Covered terrace  V meals  Last d 21.30hrs  Languages spoken: English & Spanish*
CARDS: ●● ■■ ☲ 🔟 Travellers cheques

### SERRES-SUR-ARGET Ariège

### Le Poulsieu (Prop: Jenny et Bob Brogneaux)
09000
☎ 561027772 FAX 561027772
(from Foix take D17 in the direction of Col de Marrous after 10km at La Mouline to the left then follow signs for Chambre d'hôte)

This property is situated in open countryside surrounded by woods with a superb view over the mountains. Continental breakfast served and meals available in the evening by reservation. Swimming pool, trout river, horses and mountain walks on site. Tennis within five kilometres. Medieval festivals at nearby Foix during July and August.
Near river  Forest area
*Closed Oct-1 Apr*
*5 en suite (shr)  (1 fmly)  No smoking in 4 bedrooms  Full central heating  Open parking available  Supervised  Outdoor swimming pool  Table tennis  V meals  Last d 10.00hrs  Languages spoken: English Dutch German & Spanish*
ROOMS: s 180-200FF; d 230-250FF **Special breaks**
MEALS: Dinner 70FF✱

### SOUILLAC Lot

### ★★★ Hotel Renaissance (Minotel)
2 rue Jean-Jaurès 46200
☎ 565327804 FAX 565370759
Near river  In town centre  Near motorway
*Closed Jan-Feb*
*27 en suite (bth/shr)  6 rooms in annexe  (4 fmly)  TV in all bedrooms  Direct dial from all bedrooms  Licensed  Lift  Full central heating  Open parking available  Covered parking available  Child discount available  Indoor swimming pool (heated)  Outdoor swimming pool (heated)  Open terrace  V meals  Last d 21.00hrs  Languages spoken: English*
CARDS: ●● ☲

### ★★ Inter Hotel Le Quercy
rue de la Recégé 46200
☎ 565378356 FAX 566370722
All the hotels in the Inter Hotel group offer guest accommodation which is designed with the individual needs of its clients in mind. Whether situated in the capital or in a seaside resort, they offer old-fashioned hospitality and up-to-date amenities. Staff are friendly and helpful throughout.
Near river  Forest area  In town centre  Near motorway
*Closed early Dec-mid Mar*

*25 en suite (bth/shr)  (3 fmly)  (20 with balcony)  TV in all bedrooms  STV  Direct dial from all bedrooms  Licensed  Night porter  Full central heating  Covered parking available (charged)  Supervised  Outdoor swimming pool (heated)  Bicycle rental  Open terrace  Languages spoken: English*
ROOMS: (room only)  s 260-300FF;  d 300-350FF
CARDS: ●● ■■ ☲ 🔟 Travellers cheques

### ★★★ La Vieille Auberge
46200
☎ 565327943 FAX 565326519
Situated in a quiet part of this little town that offers a peaceful setting for a relaxing holiday. The gastronomic restaurant offers numerous regional specialities, complemented by an extensive wine list. The pretty, comfortable bedrooms are equipped with modern amenities. The hotel has a good range of leisure facilities, and there is no shortage of outdoor activities in the surrounding area.
Near river  Forest area  In town centre  Near motorway

*Closed 15 Nov-20 Dec RS 3 Jan-Mar,Sun eve & Mon - rest closed*
*19 en suite (bth/shr)  12 rooms in annexe  (8 fmly)  (2 with balcony)  TV in all bedrooms  STV  Direct dial from all bedrooms  Mini-bar in all bedrooms  Licensed  Full central heating  Open parking available  Covered parking available*

*(charged)* Child discount available 12yrs Indoor swimming pool *(heated)* Outdoor swimming pool *(heated)* Sauna Solarium Gym Jacuzzi/spa Bicycle rental V meals Last d 21.30hrs Languages spoken: English
ROOMS: (room only) s 240-280FF; d 280-360FF
MEALS: Continental breakfast 40FF Lunch 120-350FF Dinner 120-350FF
CARDS: ●● ■■ ⚏ ⅅ Travellers cheques

### TOULOUSE Haute-Garonne

### ★ ★ ★ Hotel des Beaux-Arts
1 pl du Pont Neuf *31000*
☎ 534454242 FAX 534454243
*(follow signs centre ville hotel is situated on the banks of river Garonne next to the Pont Neuf bridge)*
Near river In town centre
*19 en suite (bth/shr) No smoking in 6 bedrooms TV in all bedrooms STV Direct dial from all bedrooms Mini-bar in all bedrooms Room-safe Licensed Lift Night porter Full central heating Air conditioning in bedrooms Open parking available Supervised Child discount available Languages spoken: English, German & Spanish*
ROOMS: (room only) s 600-980FF; d 600-1000FF
CARDS: ●● ■■ ⚏ ⅅ JCB Travellers cheques

### ★ ★ ★ Hotel Frantour
76 rue Bayard *31000*
☎ 561625090 FAX 561992102
*(A61 Carcassonne to Nice exit Centre Ville or Gare Matabiau)*
In town centre
*Closed Xmas & New Year*
*71 en suite (bth/shr) (5 fmly) (32 with balcony) TV in all bedrooms STV Direct dial from all bedrooms Licensed Night porter Full central heating Air conditioning in bedrooms Open parking available (charged) Covered parking available (charged) Languages spoken: English, German & Spanish*
CARDS: ●● ■■ ⚏ ⅅ Travellers cheques

### ★ ★ ★ Grand Hotel Capoul *(Best Western)*
13 pl Wilson *31000*
☎ 561107070 FAX 561219670
Near river Near lake Near sea Forest area Near motorway
*140 rms Some rooms in annexe No smoking on premises Radio in rooms Night porter Open parking available Covered parking available No children Indoor swimming pool (heated) Outdoor swimming pool (heated) Golf Tennis Fishing Squash Riding Sauna Solarium Gym Pool table Boule Mini-golf Jacuzzi/spa Bicycle rental Last d 23.30hrs Languages spoken: English, German, Italian & Spanish*

### ★ ★ ★ ★ Grand Hotel de l'Opera
1 pl du Capitole *31000*
☎ 561218266 FAX 561234104
*(from motorway 61 or 62 follow exit 15 then follow signs to Capitole)*
In town centre
*50 en suite (bth/shr) (1 fmly) (5 with balcony) No smoking in 5 bedrooms TV in all bedrooms Direct dial from all bedrooms Mini-bar in all bedrooms Licensed Lift Night porter Full central heating Air conditioning in bedrooms Indoor swimming pool (heated) Sauna Solarium Gym Jacuzzi/spa Open terrace Covered terrace V meals Last d 0.30hrs Languages spoken: English & Spanish*
CARDS: ●● ■■ ⚏ ⅅ Travellers cheques

### ★ ★ ★ ★ Holiday Inn-Crowne Plaza
7 pl du Capitole *31000*
☎ 561611919 FAX 561237996
In town centre Near motorway
*162 en suite (bth) TV in all bedrooms STV Direct dial from all bedrooms Mini-bar in all bedrooms Licensed Lift Night porter Full central heating Air conditioning in bedrooms Covered parking available (charged) Supervised Child discount available 12yrs Sauna Solarium Jacuzzi/spa Open terrace V meals Last d 23.00hrs Languages spoken: English, Dutch, German, Italian & Spanish*
CARDS: ●● ■■ ⚏ ⅅ

### ★ ★ ★ Jean Mermoz
50 rue Matabiau *31100*
☎ 561630404 FAX 561631564
In town centre
*52 en suite (bth) (6 fmly) (1 with balcony) TV in all bedrooms STV Direct-dial available Mini-bar in all bedrooms Licensed Lift Night porter Full central heating Air conditioning in bedrooms Covered parking available (charged) Child discount available 12yrs Open terrace Languages spoken: English, Italian & Spanish*
CARDS: ●● ■■ ⚏ ⅅ Travellers cheques

### ★ ★ ★ Novotel Toulouse Aeroport
23 Impasse de Maubec *31000*
☎ 561150000 FAX 561158844
*(from city centre take exit 1 towards Auch)*
Near motorway
*123 en suite (bth/shr) (40 fmly) No smoking on premises TV in all bedrooms STV Radio in rooms Direct dial from all bedrooms Mini-bar in all bedrooms Licensed Lift Night porter Full central heating Air conditioning in bedrooms Open parking available Child discount available 16yrs Outdoor swimming pool Tennis Open terrace Last d 24.00hrs Languages spoken: English, German & Spanish*
ROOMS: (room only) s fr 530FF; d fr 550FF
MEALS: Full breakfast 60FF Lunch fr 85FF&alc Dinner fr 850FF&alc
CARDS: ●● ■■ ⚏ ⅅ JCB Travellers cheques

### ★ ★ ★ ★ Sofitel Toulouse Centre
84 allée Jean-Jaurès *31000*
☎ 561102310 FAX 561102320
In town centre Near motorway
*119 en suite (bth/shr) (2 fmly) No smoking in 51 bedrooms TV in all bedrooms STV Radio in rooms Direct dial from all bedrooms Mini-bar in all bedrooms Licensed Lift Night porter Full central heating Air conditioning in bedrooms Open parking available (charged) Covered parking available (charged) Child discount available V meals Last d 23.00hrs Languages spoken: English & Spanish*
CARDS: ●● ■■ ⚏ ⅅ Travellers cheques

### ★ ★ Videotel
77 bd de Liembouchure *31200*
☎ 5561573477 FAX 5561235474
Near river In town centre Near motorway
*90 en suite (bth/shr) (2 fmly) No smoking in 10 bedrooms TV in all bedrooms Direct dial from all bedrooms Mini-bar in all bedrooms Licensed Lift Night porter Full central heating Air conditioning in bedrooms Open parking available Covered parking available (charged) Supervised Child discount available 12yrs Pool table Open terrace V meals Last d 22.00hrs Languages spoken: English*
CARDS: ●● ■■ ⚏ ⅅ

## TOUZAC Lot

**★★★ Source Bleue**
Moulin de Léygues *46700*
☎ 565365201 FAX 565246569
(on D911, 6km W of Puy-l'Évêque on the left bank of the River Lot)
Near river Near lake Forest area
*Closed Jan-25 Mar*
*15 en suite (bth/shr) (3 fmly) No smoking in 2 bedrooms TV in all bedrooms Direct dial from all bedrooms Mini-bar in 2 bedrooms Licensed Night porter Full central heating Open parking available Supervised Child discount available 10yrs Outdoor swimming pool Fishing Sauna Solarium Gym Boule Jacuzzi/spa Bicycle rental Open terrace V meals Last d 21.30hrs Languages spoken: English & Spanish*
MEALS: Continental breakfast 37FF Lunch fr 100FF&alc Dinner fr 148FF&alc
CARDS: ●● ■■ ▨▨ ▣ Travellers cheques

## TRIE-SUR-BAÏSE Hautes-Pyrénées

**Jouandassou** (Prop: M & Mme Collinson)
Fontrailles *65220*
☎ 562356443 FAX 562356613
(from Trie-sur-Baise take D939 towards Auch/Mirande for 1km then left at 'Chambre d'Hôtes' sign. 1st house on left)
Near river Near lake Forest area Near motorway
*4 en suite (shr) No smoking on premises TV available Full central heating Open parking available Supervised Child discount available 12yrs Outdoor swimming pool Tennis Boule Bicycle rental Table tennis Languages spoken: English, German, Italian & Spanish*
CARDS: Travellers cheques

## USSEL Lot

**★ Le Belle Vue**
RN20 Le Pouzat *46240*
☎ 565368654 FAX 565368472
Near lake Forest area Near motorway
*14 en suite (bth/shr) (2 fmly) (4 with balcony) TV in all bedrooms Direct dial from all bedrooms Mini-bar in 10 bedrooms Licensed Full central heating Open parking available Child discount available 10yrs Open terrace Last d 22.00hrs*
MEALS: Full breakfast 35FF Lunch 85-150FFalc Dinner 85-150FFalc✱
CARDS: ●● ▨▨ ▣ Travellers cheques

## VARILHES Ariège

**Las Rives** (Prop: M & Mme Baudeigne)
*09120*
☎ 561607342 FAX 561607876
Near river Forest area
*4 rms (3 shr) (1 fmly) No smoking on premises Open parking available Supervised Child discount available 2 yrs Outdoor swimming pool Tennis table tennis, park for children Languages spoken: English & Spanish*
CARDS: Travellers cheques

## VAUX Haute-Garonne

**Mazière de Sers** (Prop: M & Mme de Kermel)
*31540*
☎ 561838777
(approach via D2, then D59 for 2km)
Near river Near lake Forest area
*2 en suite (bth/shr) TV available Radio in rooms Covered parking available Child discount available 10yrs Outdoor swimming pool Open terrace*

## VENTENAC Ariège

**★★★ Domaine de Guinot**
*09120*
☎ 561607001 FAX 561670081
Near lake Near beach Forest area
*Closed 30 Sep-1 Apr*
*8 rms (7 shr) (1 fmly) (1 with balcony) Full central heating Open parking available Supervised Child discount available 8yrs Outdoor swimming pool Tennis Boule Bicycle rental Open terrace Last d 21.00hrs Languages spoken: English, Italian & Spanish*
CARDS: ●● ▨▨

## VIGAN, LE Lot

**Manoir La Barrière** (Prop: Michel Auffret)
*46300*
☎ 565414073 FAX 565414020
Your hosts welcome you to this 13th-century manor house which offers external access to each of the rooms, which are decorated and furnished with taste. Tennis, swimming, fishing, riding and golf nearby. Dinners available on request. Situated in parkland, in the heart of the Périgord-Quercy region.
Near river Near lake Forest area
*Closed Nov-Etr*
*5 en suite (bth/shr) (1 fmly) Open parking available Child discount available 10yrs Outdoor swimming pool Fishing Last d 24hrs*
ROOMS: d 350-500FF
MEALS: Dinner 150FF✱

## VIGNEC Hautes-Pyrénées

**★★ Hotel de la Neste**
Vignec *65170*
☎ 562394279 FAX 562395877
Near river Near lake Forest area
*Closed May & Oct-14 Dec*
*22 en suite (bth/shr) (4 fmly) (6 with balcony) No smoking in 15 bedrooms TV in all bedrooms STV Radio in rooms Direct dial from all bedrooms Mini-bar in all bedrooms Licensed Night porter Full central heating Air conditioning in bedrooms Open parking available Supervised Child discount available 10yrs Outdoor swimming pool (heated) Fishing Solarium Jacuzzi/spa Open terrace Covered terrace V meals Last d 21.00hrs Languages spoken: English & Spanish*
CARDS: ●● ▨▨ Travellers cheques

### VILLEFRANCHE-D'ALBIGEOIS Tarn

*La Barthe* (Prop: Michele Wise)
*81430*
☎ 563559621 FAX 563559621
(from Albi take D999 to Millau. Through Villefranche-
d'Albigeois to La Croix Blanche. Turn left on D163, follow signs
for Chambres-d'Hôtes.)
Forest area
*3 rms (2 bth/shr) No smoking on premises Full central heating
Open parking available Covered parking available Child
discount available 7yrs Outdoor swimming pool Boule Bicycle
rental V meals Last d 15.00hrs Languages spoken: English*
CARDS: Travellers cheques

### VILLEFRANCHE-DE-LAURAGAIS Haute-Garonne

*Château du Mauremont* (Prop: M & Mme de Rigaud)
*31290*
☎ 561816438 FAX 561816438
Near lake  Forest area  Near motorway
*4 en suite (bth) (4 fmly) No smoking on premises Full central
heating Open parking available Child discount available 6yrs
Outdoor swimming pool Tennis Languages spoken: English &
Spanish*

### VILLEFRANCHE-DE-ROUERGUE Aveyron

★ ★ ★ **Le Relais de Farrou**
rte de Figeac *12200*
☎ 565451811 FAX 565453259
This pleasant establishment offers its visitors a fully up-to-date
setting which combines ancient wood-panelling and original
stone walls with 20th-century facilities. It has well equipped
bedrooms, a comfortable lounge with an open fireplace and a
charming restaurant. In addition, it has unsurpassed fitness
and leisure facilities.
Near river  Forest area  Near motorway

**Le Relais de Farrou**

*26 en suite (bth/shr) (4 fmly) (15 with balcony) No smoking in 8
bedrooms TV in all bedrooms STV Radio in rooms Direct dial
from all bedrooms Room-safe Licensed Night porter Full
central heating Air conditioning in bedrooms Open parking
available Covered parking available (charged) Supervised Child
discount available 12yrs Outdoor swimming pool Tennis Sauna
Solarium Boule Mini-golf Jacuzzi/spa Bicycle rental Open
terrace V meals Last d 21.30hrs Languages spoken: English*
ROOMS: (room only) s 260-380FF; d 315-470FF
**Reductions over 1 night**
MEALS: Continental breakfast 45FF  Lunch 128-228FF&alc
Dinner 128-228FF&alc
CARDS: ●● ▆▆ Travellers cheques

*Le Mas de Comte* (Prop: Agnes Jayr)
Les Pesquies *12200*
☎ 565811648 FAX 565811648
(leave Villefranche by D922 (Najac-Albi) then right and follow
signs for 1km)
Near river  Forest area
*3 en suite (bth/shr) (1 fmly) Full central heating Open parking
available Child discount available 5yrs Barbecue Languages
spoken: English & German*
CARDS: Travellers cheques

## EVENTS & FESTIVALS

**Mar** Lourdes Sacred Music Festival; Toulouse
International Fair; St-Félix Traditional Fair;
Montauban 'Carambole' Festival

**Apr** Albi Jazz Festival; Tarbes French Song Festival;
Auterive Medieval Festival

**May** Toulouse International Children's Theatre
Festival; Montauban French Song Festival;
Festival at Condom; Bourg St Bernard
Traditional Celebration

**June** Cahors Spring Festival; Vic-Fezensac Whit
Sunday Feria; Toulouse Grand Férétra Festival

**Jul** Foix Medieval Pageant; Puylaurens Summer
Festival; St-Girons Folklore & Dance Festival;
Germ-Louron Jazz Festival; St-Félix Lauragais
Classical & Traditional Music Festival; Toulouse
Summer Festival; Mirande Country Music
Festival; Jazz Festivals at Luz-St-Sauveur,
Souillac & Montauban; Sylvanès Sacred Music
Festival; Galvarnie Theatre Festival; Tarbres
Equestria; Montréal-du-Gers Festival; St-Lizier
Classical Music Festival; Cordes Great Falconer

Medieval Festival; Lisle sur Tarn Wine Festival;
Mirepoix Medieval Festival; St Girons Festival;
Ax-les-Thermes Street Festival

**Aug** Ax-les-Thermes Street Festival; St Félix Lauragais
Classical & Traditional Music Festival; Toulouse
Summer Festival; Sylvanès Sacred Music Festival
(music, dance, theatre); Gourdon Summer
Festival; Mirepoix International Puppet Festival;
Assier Festival; Aveyron Département Folklore
Festival; Vaour Comedy Festival; Fleurance
Festival of the Heavens; Marciac Jazz Festival; St-
Paul Cap de Joux Historical Festival; Wine
Festivals: Gaillac, Madiran; Trie sur- Baïse
Pourcailhade (pork) Festival; Sauveterre-du-
Rouergue Festival of Light; Peyrusse-le-Roc
Medieval Festival

**Sep** Toulouse Jacobin Piano Festival; Cordes
Gastronomic Festival; Moissac Chasselas
Grape Festival;

**Oct** Auch Festival of Contemporary Music &
Dance; Toulouse Jazz Festival

# Languedoc-Roussillon

From the Camargue to the eastern boundary of the Pyrénées, and from the wild and lonely Causses to the sun-drenched Mediterranean coast, Languedoc-Roussillon has a wealth of diverse scenery, a fascinating past and a superb architectural heritage. One of France's most popular coastal and romantic destinations, with more than 20,000 moorings between the Camargue and the coast of Catalonia, the Languedoc coastline has 25 ports, 125 miles of sandy beaches and is a perfect sporting playground for sailing, water skiing, big game fishing and scuba diving - among other leisure pursuits. The juxtaposition of French, Catalan and Spanish cultures creates a unique blend of traditions.

## ESSENTIAL FACTS

| | |
|---|---|
| DÉPARTEMENTS: | Aude, Gard, Hérault, Lozère, Pyrénées-Roussillon |
| PRINCIPAL TOWNS | Perpignan, Béziers, Âles, Nîmes, Carcassonne, Narbonne, Mende, Montpellier |
| PLACES TO VISIT: | The Cevennes Park, the largest of the 7 National Parks; the Canal du Midi; the fortified town of Marvejols; St Jean du Gard for swimming, local walks, horse-riding & mountain bike circuits. |
| REGIONAL TOURIST OFFICE | 20 rue de la République, 34000 Montpellier Tel: 04 67 22 81 00. |
| LOCAL GASTRONOMIC DELIGHTS | Fresh and salt water fish, oysters, wild game, and a huge variety of local cheeses |
| DRINKS | From the Pyrénées to the Rhône, the Languedoc-Roussillon vineyards form a vast mosaic of wine-growing areas, each with its own special soil and climate. A wide range of wines, including Vin du Pays d'Oc and Vin du Pays. |
| LOCAL CRAFTS WHAT TO BUY | Glass-making, silk products, basket weaving, pottery & ceramics |

## AIGUES-MORTES Gard

**★ ★ ★ Hotel les Templiers**
23 rue de la République 30220
☎ 466536656 FAX 466536961
(leave A9 at Gallargues (between Nîmes and Montpellier) and follow signs)
Near sea  Near beach  In town centre
*Closed Nov-Feb*
*10 en suite (bth/shr)  (3 fmly)  (1 with balcony)  TV in all bedrooms  STV  Direct dial from all bedrooms  Licensed  Full central heating  Air conditioning in bedrooms  Open parking available  Languages spoken: English*
CARDS: ● ■ ▒ Travellers cheques

## ALÉNYA Pyrénées-Orientales

**Domaine du Mas Bazan** (Prop: M & Mme Favier)
*66200*
☎ 468229826 FAX 468229737
(from N114 exit 3 to Saleilles, then D22 towards Alénya. Just before entering Alénya turn left in to vineyard)
The guest rooms are situated in a renovated 18th-century Catalan country house in a peaceful setting amidst peach trees and vines, surrounded by palm trees and bamboo. Delicious home-made meals are available, with seafood a speciality. Taste the wines prepared from grapes from the owners' own vineyards. The property offers a games room, library and large private heated swimming pool. Children may ride the two ponies belonging to the owners. Golf is within three kilometres. The sea is also just three kilometres away.
Near river  Near lake  Near sea  Near beach  Forest area
*10 rms (6 bth/shr)  (1 fmly)  (4 with balcony)  TV in 2 bedrooms  Full central heating  Open parking available  Covered parking available  Child discount available  Indoor swimming pool (heated)  Boule  Languages spoken: English & Spanish*
ROOMS: s 260FF; d 310FF  ✱ **Reductions over 1 night**
MEALS: Dinner 120FF✱
CARDS: Travellers cheques

## ALET-LES-BAINS Aude

**★ ★ L'Évêché**
*11580*
☎ 468699025 FAX 468699194
(Leave Autoroute to Carcassonne and head in the direction of Perpignan Bis. After 9km turn left into Alet-les-Bains. The Hotel is situated after the bridge).
Near river  Near lake  Forest area  In town centre  Near motorway
*Closed Nov-Mar*
*30 en suite (bth/shr)  10 rooms in annexe  (6 fmly)  Direct dial from all bedrooms  Licensed  Full central heating  Open parking available  Child discount available 7yrs  Bicycle rental  Open terrace  V meals  Last d 21.00hrs  Languages spoken: English & Spanish*
ROOMS: (room only) s fr 210FF; d 250-290FF
MEALS: Full breakfast 40FF  Lunch 110-220FF&alc  Dinner 110-220FF&alc
CARDS: ● ▒ ▨ Travellers cheques

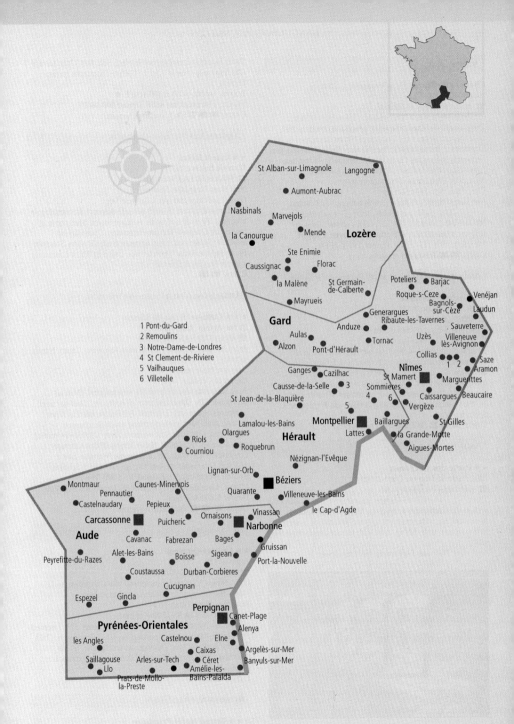

Lozère

St Alban-sur-Limagnole
Langogne
Aumont-Aubrac
Nasbinals
Marvejols
la Canourgue
Mende
Ste Enimie
Caussignac
Florac
la Malène
St Germain-
de-Calberte
Mayrueis

Gard

Poteliers
Barjac
Roque-s-Ceze
Bagnols-
sur-Cèze
Venéjan
Laudun
Generargues
Ribaute-les-Tavernes
Sauveterre
Anduze
Uzès
Villeneuve
lès-Avignon
Aulas
Tornac
Alzon
Pont-d'Hérault
Collias
1  2
Saze
Aramon
Ganges
Cazilhac
Nîmes
St Mamert
Marguerittes
Causse-de-la-Selle
3
Sommières
St Jean-de-la-Blaquière
4    6
Caissargues
Beaucaire
5
Vergèze
Montpellier
Baillargues
St Gilles
Lamalou-les-Bains
Lattes
la Grande-Motte
Olargues
Hérault
Aigues-Mortes
Riols
Roquebrun
Courniou
Nézignan-l'Evêque
Lignan-sur-Orb
Montmaur
Caunes-Minervois
Béziers
Pennautier
Quarante
Villeneuve-les-Bains
Castelnaudary
Pepieux
Vinassan
le Cap-d'Agde
Carcassonne
Puicheric
Ornaisons
Aude
Narbonne
Cavanac
Fabrezan
Bages
Alet-les-Bains
Boisse
Sigean
Gruissan
Peyrefitte-du-Razes
Coustaussa
Durban-Corbieres
Port-la-Nouvelle
Cucugnan
Espezel
Gincla
Perpignan
Pyrénées-Orientales
Canet-Plage
Alenya
les Angles
Castelnou
Elne
Saillagouse
Caixas
Argelès-sur-Mer
Arles-sur-Tech
Céret
Banyuls-sur-Mer
Llo
Amélie-les-
Prats-de-Mollo-
Bains-Palalda
la-Preste

1 Pont-du-Gard
2 Remoulins
3 Notre-Dame-de-Londres
4 St Clement-de-Riviere
5 Vailhauques
6 Villetelle

403

## ALZON Gard

**Château du Mazel** (Prop: Françoise Galliot)
rte du Villaret *30770*
☎ 467820633 FAX 467820637
(on the D999 between Nîmes/Millau, 15km from le Vigan)
The Château du Mazel,a haven of peace and greenery and once the residence of the Bishops of Nîmes, is situated in the Cevennes at the gateway to the Averyon. Each of the spacious bedrooms is decorated in its own individual style and boasts a harmonious blend of period and modern furniture.
Near river  Forest area  Near motorway
*Closed mid Nov-Palm Sunday*
*6 en suite (bth/shr) (1 fmly) (3 with balcony) Full central heating Open parking available Boule TV room,(tennis courts 500 metres) Last d 21.00hr Languages spoken: English*
ROOMS: d 650-890FF **✴ Reductions over 1 night**
MEALS: Lunch 115-165FF Dinner 115-165FF✴
CARDS: ●● ▦ Travellers cheques

## AMÉLIE-LES-BAINS-PALALDA Pyrénées-Orientales

★ ★ *Castel Emeraude*
rte de la Corniche *66112*
☎ 468390283 FAX 468390217
Near river  Near sea  Forest area
*Closed early Dec-end Jan*
*59 en suite (bth/shr) (6 fmly) (34 with balcony) TV in all bedrooms Direct dial from all bedrooms Mini-bar in all bedrooms Licensed Lift Full central heating Open parking available Supervised Child discount available Solarium Boule Jacuzzi/spa Bicycle rental Covered terrace V meals Last d 21.00hrs Languages spoken: English German Portuguese & Spanish*
CARDS: ●● ■ ▦ ▣ Travellers cheques

## ANDUZE Gard

★ ★ **Porte des Cévennes**
2300 rte de St-Jean-du-Gard *30140*
☎ 466619944 FAX 466617365
This newly opened hotel features peacefully situated bedrooms with modern amenities and private loggias. A high standard of home cooking, complemented by good local wines, is served in the country-style dining-room with terrace overlooking the valley.
Near river  Near sea  Forest area  Near motorway

*Apr-Oct*
*37 en suite (bth/shr) (3 fmly) (34 with balcony) TV in 34 bedrooms STV Direct dial from all bedrooms Night porter Open parking available Supervised Child discount available*

*10yrs Indoor swimming pool (heated) Solarium Open terrace Children's playground Last d 21.00hrs Languages spoken: English*
ROOMS: (room only) d 300-400FF ✴
MEALS: Full breakfast 48FF Dinner 100-160FF
CARDS: ●● ■ ▦ ▣ Travellers cheques

## ANGLES, LES Pyrénées-Orientales

★ ★ *Llaret Hotel*
12 av de Balcere *66210*
☎ 468309090 FAX 468309166
Near river  Near lake  Near beach
*Closed mid May-mid Jun & Oct-mid Dec*
*26 en suite (bth/shr) (8 fmly) (20 with balcony) No smoking on premises TV in all bedrooms Radio in rooms Mini-bar in all bedrooms Licensed Full central heating Open parking available Supervised Child discount available 12yrs Solarium Boule Bicycle rental Open terrace Last d 21.30hrs Languages spoken: English & Spanish*
CARDS: ●● ▦

## ARGELÈS-SUR-MER Pyrénées-Orientales

★ ★ ★ **Cottage** (Relais du Silence)
21 rue Arthur Rimbaud *66700*
☎ 468810733 FAX 468815969
(from A9 exit 'Le Boulou' circle town following 'Centre Plage' signs)
Near sea  Near beach
*Closed 16 Oct-Mar*
*34 en suite (bth/shr) (8 fmly) (21 with balcony) TV in all bedrooms STV Direct dial from all bedrooms Mini-bar in all bedrooms Room-safe Licensed Full central heating Open parking available Covered parking available (charged) Supervised Child discount available 11yrs Outdoor swimming pool Solarium Pool table Boule Mini-golf Open terrace Covered terrace Mini golf Table tennis Petanque Last d 21.30hrs Languages spoken: English, German & Spanish*
ROOMS: (room only) s 350-450FF; d 380-560FF
MEALS: Continental breakfast 60FF Lunch 100-200FFalc Dinner 170-200FF&alc
CARDS: ●● ■ ▦ Eurocard Travellers cheques

## AULAS Gard

★ ★ *Le Mas Quayrol*
Aulas *30120*
☎ 467811238 FAX 467812384
(from Nîmes-Montpellier motorway take Ganges exit to Le Vigan, then through Le Mont Aigoual to Aulas)
Near river  Forest area
*Closed Jan-20 Mar RS 15 Nov-15 Dec*
*16 en suite (bth/shr) (4 fmly) TV in all bedrooms STV Licensed Full central heating Open parking available Supervised Child discount available 5yrs Outdoor swimming pool Tennis Solarium Open terrace Last d 22.00hrs Languages spoken: English & Spanish*
CARDS: ●● ▦

## AUMONT-AUBRAC Lozère

★ ★ ★ *Grand Hotel Prouhéze*
2 rte du Languedoc *48130*
☎ 466428007 FAX 466428778
(From A75, exit 35)
Forest area  Near motorway

Closed 31 Oct-Mar
27 en suite (bth/shr) (4 fmly) TV in all bedrooms Radio in
rooms Licensed Full central heating Open parking available
Child discount available 10yrs Open terrace Last d 21.00hrs
Languages spoken: English
CARDS: ●● ■ ￭

## AVIGNON Gard

**Le Rocher Pointu** (Prop: M & Mme Malek)
Plan de Dève 30390
☎ 466574187 FAX 466570177
(from Avignon follow D2 S along W bank of Rhône. Turn right in
direction of Saze at D126. After approx 2.5kms, signed, turn left)
An old farmhouse situated near Provence and Avignon. Guests
will relax in this oasis of calm where a comfortable sitting
room with TV and music system , a large swimming pool and
patio/barbecue area are available. Four rooms are on offer.
Reductions for children up to two years old.
Forest area
Closed Nov-Mar
4 en suite (bth/shr) No smoking on premises Open parking
available Child discount available 2yrs Outdoor swimming
pool Boule Languages spoken: English
ROOMS: d 390-445FF
CARDS: Travellers cheques

## BAGES Aude

**Domaine de L'Estarac** (Prop: Alexandre Van der Elst)
Prat de Cest 11100
☎ 468415731
(from Narbonne take the N9 in the direction of Perpignan, after
8km arrive in Prat-de-Cest, after last house on your left turn
left to chambre d'hôte in 1km)
This Catalonian style house is situated in a protected maritime
area. Rooms are large, sleeping 1-4 persons, and breakfast is
served in the room or in the garden.
Near lake Near sea Near beach Forest area Near motorway
5 en suite (shr) Full central heating Open parking available Child
discount available 4yrs Languages spoken: English & Dutch
ROOMS: s 200FF; d 240FF
CARDS: Travellers cheques

## BAGNOLS-SUR-CÈZE Gard

★ ★ ★ ★ **Château de Montcaud**
Hameau de Combe-Sabran 30200
☎ 466896060 FAX 466894504
(on entering Bagnols, turn towards Alès on D6, then right at
first crossing after 4km)
Near river Forest area Near motorway
1 Dec-2 Jan & 14 Apr-29 Oct
29 en suite (bth/shr) (2 fmly) (2 with balcony) TV in all
bedrooms STV Radio in rooms Direct dial from all bedrooms
Mini-bar in all bedrooms Licensed Lift Full central heating Air
conditioning in bedrooms Open parking available Covered
parking available (charged) Supervised Child discount
available 12yrs Outdoor swimming pool (heated) Tennis Sauna
Gym Boule Jacuzzi/spa Bicycle rental Open terrace V meals
Last d 21.30hrs Languages spoken: English, Spanish, Italian,
Dutch & German
ROOMS: s 1220-2440FF; d 1330-3330FF
**Reductions over 1 night Special breaks**
MEALS: Full breakfast 110FF Lunch 175-360FF&alc Dinner
290-450FF&alc
CARDS: ●● ■ ￭ ● JCB

## BAILLARGUES Hérault

★ ★ ★ **Golf Hotel de Montpellier Massané**
Domaine de Massane 34670
☎ 467878787 FAX 467878790
(from Montpellier A9 exit number 28 in the direction of Nîmes
or N113 in the direction of Nîmes)
Near sea Near beach
32 en suite (bth/shr) (16 fmly) No smoking in 2 bedrooms TV
in all bedrooms STV Radio in rooms Direct dial from all
bedrooms Mini-bar in all bedrooms Room-safe Licensed
Night porter Full central heating Air conditioning in bedrooms
Open parking available Supervised Indoor swimming pool
(heated) Outdoor swimming pool Golf 18 Tennis Sauna
Solarium Gym Pool table Boule Jacuzzi/spa Bicycle rental
Open terrace Covered terrace Jaccuzzi Last d 21.45hrs
Languages spoken: English,German & Spanish
CARDS: ●● ■ ￭ ●

## BANYULS-SUR-MER Pyrénées-Orientales

★ ★ **Les Elmes**
Plage des Elmes 66650
☎ 468880312 FAX 468885303
(on N114 between Collioure and Cerbère)
Near sea Near beach Near motorway
Closed 6-20 Jan & 4-19 Dec
31 en suite (bth/shr) (14 fmly) (7 with balcony) TV in all
bedrooms STV Direct dial from all bedrooms Licensed Night
porter Full central heating Air conditioning in bedrooms Open
parking available (charged) Covered parking available
(charged) Supervised Child discount available 12yrs Boule
Bicycle rental Open terrace Boating V meals Languages
spoken: English, German & Spanish
CARDS: ●● ■ ￭ ● Travellers cheques

## BARJAC Gard

**Mas Escombelle** (Prop: Isabelle Agapitos)
La Villette 30430
☎ 466245477 FAX 466245477
(from Barjac in the direction of Vallon-Pont d'Arc)
Forest area
4 en suite (bth/shr) (2 fmly) Full central heating Open parking
available Child discount available Outdoor swimming pool
Languages spoken: English
CARDS: Travellers cheques

## BEAUCAIRE Gard

★ ★ ★ **Robinson**
rte de Remoulin 30300
☎ 466592132 FAX 466590003
(approach via A9 and D986)
This large house is surrounded by lush scenery and features an
attractive interior carefully decorated, with well matching
fabrics and furnishings. The foyer-lounge with open fire opens
into the gardens, where in the summer meals are served on the
terrace. The bedrooms offer good amenities and the restaurant
serves a range of dishes to suit all tastes. Run by the same
family for four generations it provides a pleasant setting for a
relaxing holiday in Provence.
Near river Forest area
Closed Febuary
30 en suite (bth/shr) (12 fmly) TV in all bedrooms Direct dial
from all bedrooms Licensed Full central heating Open parking
contd.

*available* Covered parking available (charged) Child discount available Outdoor swimming pool (heated) Tennis Solarium Boule Open terrace Covered terrace V meals Last d 21.30hrs Languages spoken: English, German & Italian
ROOMS: (room only) d 380-440FF
MEALS: Continental breakfast 48FF Lunch 110-200FF Dinner 110-200FF
CARDS: ●● ■■ ▆▆ ◉ Travellers cheques

## BOUISSE Aude

**Domaine des Goudis** (Prop: Michèle & Michel Delattre)
*11190*
☎ 468700276 FAX 468700074
(from D54 at Arques take D54 then D70)
Renovated 18th-century stone house situated on a hill which is the start of the 200 kilometre stretch of the Pyrénées. Swimming, rambling and table-tennis are on site but if you wish you can help out on the farm. Simple regional cuisine available, made with local farm produce. There is something for everyone with châteaux visits, boat rides up the Midi canal and visits to historical sites.
Near river Near lake Forest area
*Closed 15 Nov-28 Mar*
6 en suite (bth/shr) (2 fmly) No smoking on premises Full central heating Open parking available Covered parking available No children Outdoor swimming pool (heated) Table tennis V meals Languages spoken: English & German
ROOMS: s 400FF; d 450FF
MEALS: Dinner 129FF
CARDS: ●● ▆▆ ◉ Travellers cheques

## CAISSARGUES Gard

★ ★ ★ **Les Aubuns** (Best Western)
*30132*
☎ 466701044 FAX 466701497
(on D442, 2km from the airport)
Forest area Near motorway
26 en suite (bth/shr) (4 fmly) (26 with balcony) TV in all bedrooms STV Radio in rooms Direct dial from all bedrooms Licensed Night porter Full central heating Open parking available Child discount available 10yrs Outdoor swimming pool Golf 18 Tennis Riding Solarium Boule Open terrace Last d 21.30hrs Languages spoken: English & Spanish
ROOMS: (room only) s 440FF; d 500FF
MEALS: Full breakfast 55FF Dinner 115-155FF
CARDS: ●● ■■ ▆▆ ◉ Travellers cheques

## CAIXAS Pyrénées-Orientales

**Auberge des Comédiens** (Prop: J Vissenaeken & A Vaes)
*66300*
☎ 468388227 FAX 468388367
(from A9 exit at Perpignan Sud and take D612 through Thuir to Llupia. Take D615 to Fourques, then D2 to Caixas. Continue on this road until sign for house)
Near river Forest area
*Closed Jan & Dec*
6 en suite (shr) Full central heating Open parking available Child discount available 8yrs Outdoor swimming pool Open terrace V meals Last d 21.00hrs Languages spoken: English, German & Dutch
CARDS: ●● ▆▆ Travellers cheques

**Mas St-Jacques** (Prop: Jane Richards & Ian Mayes)
*66300*
☎ 468388783 FAX 468388783
(A9 exit Perpignan-Sud towards Thuir. At entrance to Thuir follow direction Elne for approx 2km turn right in direction of Céret, driving for a further 5.5km to Fourques. In Fourques turn right onto D2 to Caixas, 11km then follow signs Mairie-Église)
Forest area
5 en suite (bth/shr) (1 fmly) (4 with balcony) Child discount available 8yrs Outdoor swimming pool Boule Languages spoken: English & German
CARDS: Travellers cheques

## CANET-PLAGE Pyrénées-Orientales

★ ★ ★ **Galion**
20 bis av du Grand Large *66140*
☎ 468802046 FAX 468732441
Near lake Near sea Near beach In town centre
*Closed Oct-Apr*
28 en suite (bth/shr) (10 fmly) (28 with balcony) TV in all bedrooms Direct dial from all bedrooms Licensed Lift Night porter Full central heating Open parking available Child discount available 10yrs Outdoor swimming pool Bicycle rental Open terrace pedalos Last d 21.00hrs Languages spoken: English
ROOMS: (room only) s 250-400FF; d 290-445FF
**Special breaks**
MEALS: Full breakfast 45FF Lunch 80-150FF&alc Dinner 120-200FFalc
CARDS: ●● ▆▆ Travellers cheques

★ ★ **St-Georges**
45 prom Côte Vermeille *66140*
☎ 468803377 FAX 468806504
Near sea Near beach In town centre
*Closed Oct-Apr*
18 en suite (bth/shr) (10 fmly) (8 with balcony) TV in all bedrooms STV Direct dial from all bedrooms Room-safe (charged) Licensed Night porter Full central heating Open parking available Covered parking available (charged) Supervised Child discount available 12yrs Outdoor swimming pool Boule Open terrace Last d 2.45hrs Languages spoken: English, German, Spanish & Swedish
ROOMS: (room only) s 180-300FF; d 200-320FF
MEALS: Full breakfast 38FF Lunch 80-100FF Dinner 80-100FF
CARDS: ●● ■■ ▆▆ ◉ Travellers cheques

## LE CAP-D'AGDE Hérault

★ ★ ★ *Hotel du Golf*
Ile des Loisirs *34300*
☎ 467268703 FAX 467262689
Near sea
*Closed early Nov-late Mar*
50 en suite (bth/shr) 20 rooms in annexe (4 fmly) (20 with balcony) TV in all bedrooms Mini-bar in all bedrooms Licensed Night porter Full central heating Air conditioning in bedrooms Open parking available Covered parking available (charged) Supervised Child discount available Outdoor swimming pool (heated) Solarium Pool table Boule Bicycle rental Open terrace Covered terrace Last d 23.00hrs Languages spoken: English, German & Spanish
CARDS: ●● ■■ ▆▆ ◉ Travellers cheques

## CARCASSONNE Aude

### ★ ★ ★ Bristol
7 av Foch M Sartore 11000
☎ 468250724 FAX 468257189
Near river In town centre Near motorway
Closed Dec-Feb
58 rms (55 bth/shr) (4 fmly) TV in 55 bedrooms STV Direct
dial from all bedrooms Licensed Lift Night porter Full central
heating Covered parking available (charged) Last d 21.30hrs
Languages spoken: English, Italian & German
CARDS: ●● ══ Travellers cheques

### ★ ★ ★ ★ Hotel de la Cité
place de l'Église 11000
☎ 468719871 FAX 468715015
(from A61 exit Carcassonne-Est, hotel close to Basilique St-
Nazaire)
As befits a hotel of such unique character, bedrooms and
suites are individually furnished and decorated with more than
a dash of aristocartic style. The very finest fabrics are
complemented by superb furnishings crafted by local
workshops. Traditional style is of course matched by modern
comfort and all rooms feature the most up-to-date facilities.
The gastronomic reputation of the hotel rests on La Barbacane
Restaurant, its Gothic rooms feature magnificent fireplaces,
high ceilings and cathedral chairs. Regularly recommended by
gastronomic guides. The restaurant offers a menu which
combines the freshest local ingredients with innovative recipes
and exquisite attention to details.
Near river In town centre
Closed 1-4 Jan & Dec RS % Jan-5 Mar & Nov
61 en suite (bth/shr) (5 fmly) (12 with balcony) TV in all
bedrooms STV Direct dial from all bedrooms Mini-bar in

all bedrooms Room-safe Licensed Lift Night porter Full
central heating Air conditioning in bedrooms Open parking
available (charged) Covered parking available (charged)
Supervised Child discount available 12yrs Outdoor swimming
pool (heated) Open terrace Covered terrace V meals
Languages spoken: English, Dutch, German, Italian, Japanese
& Spanish
ROOMS: (room only) s 1200-1750FF; d 1750-3200FF
Reductions over 1 night
MEALS: Full breakfast 130FF
CARDS: ●● ■■ ══ ⑩ JCB & CB Travellers cheques

### ★ ★ ★ ★ Domaine d'Auriac
rte de St-Hilaire, BP 554 11000
☎ 468257222 FAX 468473554
(from the motorway take the exit `Carcassonne Guest` and
follow signs for` Contre hospitalier`, hotel adjacent in a park)

Near river Near lake Forest area Near motorway
24 en suite (bth/shr) 4 rooms in annexe (11 fmly) (4 with
balcony) TV in all bedrooms STV Direct dial from all
bedrooms Mini-bar in all bedrooms Room-safe Licensed Lift
Night porter Full central heating Air conditioning in bedrooms
Open parking available Covered parking available Supervised
Child discount available 12yrs Outdoor swimming pool
Golf 18 Tennis Pool table Boule Open terrace Covered
terrace Last d 21.15hrs Languages spoken: English,
German & Spanish
CARDS: ●● ■■ ══ ⑩ Travellers cheques

### ★ ★ ★ Hotel Le Donjon (Best Western)
2 rue Comte Roger 11000
☎ 468231100 FAX 468250660
(whether coming from A61 motorway exit Carcassonne Est
(junct 24) or the RN 113 follow signs for `La Cité`. La Cité is a
protected monument and traffic is controlled within its walls)
The traditional hotel Le Donjon is situated in the medieval
heart of the city and dates back to the 16th century. With its
half-timbered façade, mullioned windows, exposed beams and
ornate French-style ceilings, it reflects the atmosphere of times
past. Most of the comfortable bedrooms are decorated in Louis
XIII style.
In town centre Near motorway
56 rms (26 bth 11 shr) 19 rooms in annexe (2 fmly) TV in all
bedrooms STV Radio in rooms Direct dial from all bedrooms
Mini-bar in all bedrooms Licensed Lift Night porter Full
central heating Air conditioning in bedrooms Open parking
available (charged) Supervised Child discount available 12yrs
Open terrace V meals Last d 23.00hrs Languages spoken:
English & Spanish
ROOMS: (room only) s 330-660FF; d 400-800FF
Reductions over 1 night
MEALS: Lunch 76-130FF&alc Dinner 76-130FF&alc✱
CARDS: ●● ■■ ══ ⑩ JCB Travellers cheques

### ★ ★ ★ Trois Couronnes
2 r des Trois Couronnes 11000
☎ 468253610 FAX 468259292
Near river In town centre
68 en suite (bth) (5 fmly) (44 with balcony) No smoking in 20
bedrooms TV in all bedrooms STV Mini-bar in all bedrooms
Licensed Lift Night porter Full central heating Air
conditioning in bedrooms Open parking available (charged)
Covered parking available (charged) Supervised Child
discount available Indoor swimming pool (heated) Tennis
Sauna Solarium Gym Jacuzzi/spa Bicycle rental V meals
Last d 22.30hrs Languages spoken: English, German &
Spanish
CARDS: ●● ■■ ══ ⑩ Travellers cheques

## CASTELNAUDARY Aude

### ★ ★ Grand Hotel Fourcade
14 rue des Carnes 11400
☎ 468230208 FAX 468941067
Near river Near lake In town centre Near motorway
12 rms (8 bth/shr) (4 fmly) (3 with balcony) TV in 29 bedrooms
Mini-bar in 29 bedrooms Licensed Full central heating Open
parking available Covered parking available (charged)
Supervised Child discount available Last d 21.30hrs
Languages spoken: English & Italian
CARDS: ●● ■■ ══ ⑩ Travellers cheques

## CASTELNOU Pyrénées-Orientales

**Domaine de Querubi** (Prop: Francoise Nabet)
*66300*
☎ 468531908 FAX 468531896
(leave A9 at Perpignan-Sud exit and drive towards Thuir. Pass through village of Castelnou and continue for 3km)
Near river Near lake Forest area
*6 en suite (bth/shr) (2 fmly) (1 with balcony) TV in all bedrooms STV Full central heating Open parking available Child discount available Outdoor swimming pool (heated) Boule Last d 20.30hrs Languages spoken: English & Spanish*

## CAUNES-MINERVOIS Aude

★ ★ **Hotel d'Alibert**
pl de la Marie *11160*
☎ 468780054
Forest area In town centre
*Closed Dec-Feb*
*7 rms (2 bth 3 shr) (3 fmly) Licensed Full central heating Open parking available Covered parking available Bicycle rental Open terrace V meals Languages spoken: English*
CARDS: ●● ▄▄

**L'Ancienne Boulangerie** (Prop: Terry & Lois Link)
rue St Genes *11160*
☎ 468780132
(leave A61 at Carcassonne west exit, follow signs in direction Mazamet from first 4 rdbts at 5th rdbt follow D620 to Caunes-Minervois. In Caunes follow signs to chambre d'hôte)
Near river Forest area
*5 rms (3 shr) (2 fmly) Bicycle rental Riding, petanque & tennis in the village Languages spoken: English*
CARDS: Travellers cheques

## CAUSSE-DE-LA-SELLE Hérault

★ ★ **Hostellerie le Vieux Chêne**
*34380*
☎ 467731100 FAX 467731054
Near river Forest area
*Closed 12 Nov-12 Feb RS 20 Dec-2 Jan*
*3 en suite (bth/shr) 2 rooms in annexe (1 fmly) (1 with balcony) TV in 5 bedrooms STV Radio in rooms Direct dial from all bedrooms Mini-bar in all bedrooms Licensed Full central heating Open parking available Supervised Outdoor swimming pool Solarium Boule Open terrace Covered terrace V meals Last d 21.30hrs*
ROOMS: (room only) s 350FF; d 350-390FF ✱
MEALS: Continental breakfast 50FF Lunch 130-170FF&alc Dinner 130-170FF&alc
CARDS: ●● ▄▄ ▄▄ Travellers cheques

## CAUSSIGNAC Lozère

★ ★ **Les Aires de la Carline**
rte de l'Aven Armand *48210*
☎ 466485479 FAX 466485759
Near river Forest area
*Closed Oct-Mar*
*12 en suite (bth/shr) (2 fmly) TV in all bedrooms Direct dial from all bedrooms Full central heating Air conditioning in bedrooms Open parking available Child discount available 10yrs Boule Open terrace Last d 22.00hrs Languages spoken: English*
CARDS: ●● ▄▄ ▄▄ ▣

## CAVANAC Aude

★ ★ ★ **Château de Cavanac**
*11570*
☎ 468796104 FAX 468797967
(5km from Carcassonne via D104 to St-Hilaire)
Forest area
*Closed mid Jan-mid Feb*
*14 en suite (bth/shr) (3 fmly) No smoking in 1 bedroom TV in all bedrooms STV Direct dial from all bedrooms Room-safe Licensed Lift Full central heating Air conditioning in bedrooms Open parking available Outdoor swimming pool Tennis Sauna Pool table Boule Open terrace Covered terrace Languages spoken: English*
ROOMS: (room only) d 395-695FF
MEALS:
CARDS: ●● ▄▄

## CAZILHAC Hérault

★ ★ ★ **Auberge les Norias**
254 av des Deux Ponts *34190*
☎ 467735590 FAX 467736208
Near river
*11 en suite (bth) 1 rooms in annexe (1 with balcony) TV in all bedrooms Licensed Full central heating Open parking available Covered parking available (charged) Child discount available 10yrs Open terrace Covered terrace Wkly live entertainment Last d 21.30hrs Languages spoken: English & German*
CARDS: ●● ▄▄ ▄▄ Travellers cheques

## CÉRET Pyrénées-Orientales

★ ★ ★ **Mas Trilles**
Pont de Reynes *66400*
☎ 468873837 FAX 468874262
(from A9 take D115, then 2km after Céret in direction of Amélie-les-Bains)
Near river Forest area Near motorway
*Closed mid Oct-mid April*
*10 en suite (bth) (7 fmly) (8 with balcony) TV in all bedrooms Direct dial from all bedrooms Licensed Night porter Full central heating Open parking available Supervised Child discount available Outdoor swimming pool (heated) Fishing Boule Bicycle rental Open terrace Last d 20.30hrs Languages spoken: English & Italian*
CARDS: ●● ▄▄

★ ★ ★ ★ **Terrasse au Soleil**
rte de Fontfrède *66400*
☎ 468870194 FAX 468873924
(from A9, take D115 to Céret. Hotel signposted from town centre)
Forest area
*Closed 15 Oct-14 Mar*
*27 en suite (bth/shr) 14 rooms in annexe (8 fmly) (20 with balcony) No smoking in 1 bedroom TV in all bedrooms Direct dial from all bedrooms Mini-bar in all bedrooms Room-safe Licensed Night porter Full central heating Air conditioning in bedrooms Open parking available Child discount available Outdoor swimming pool (heated) Golf Tennis Boule Open terrace Covered terrace Last d 21.30hrs Languages spoken: English & Spanish*
CARDS: ●● ▄▄ ▄▄ ▣ JCB

### COLLIAS Gard

**★ ★ ★ Hostellerie du Castellas**
Grand'rue 30210
☎ 466228888 FAX 466228428
(A9 exit Remoulins. Take D981 direction Uzes, then left turn for Collias)
Near river
Closed Jan-early Mar
17 en suite (bth/shr) (3 fmly) (5 with balcony) TV in all bedrooms Direct dial from all bedrooms Mini-bar in all bedrooms Licensed Full central heating Air conditioning in bedrooms Open parking available Supervised Child discount available 5yrs Outdoor swimming pool Open terrace V meals Last d 21.30hrs Languages spoken: English & German
ROOMS: (room only) s 550-800FF; d 600-800FF
MEALS: Full breakfast 90FF Lunch fr 140FF&alc Dinner 190-360FF&alc
CARDS: ●● ■■ ■■ ⑩

### COURNIOU Hérault

**Bed & Breakfast** (Prop: M & Mme J L Lunes)
Hameau de Prouilhe 34220
☎ 467972159 FAX 467972159
(from Beziers in direction of St Paul on N112)
Forest area
Closed Oct-Mar
2 en suite (bth) Open parking available Boule Open terrace
CARDS: Travellers cheques

### COUSTAUSSA Aude

**★ ★ Peyré Picade**
87500
☎ 468741111 FAX 468740037
Forest area
10 en suite (bth/shr) (1 fmly) (3 with balcony) Open parking available Covered parking available Supervised Child discount available 12yrs Outdoor swimming pool Riding Solarium Pool table Boule Open terrace V meals Last d 21.00hrs Languages spoken: English & Spanish
CARDS: ●● ■■ ■■ ⑩

### CUCUGNAN Aude

**★ ★ Auberge du Vigneron**
2 rue A Mir 11350
☎ 468450300 FAX 468450308
(from Perpignan North take direction of Foix and turn off for Maury then direction of Cucugnan)
Near river Near lake Forest area
Closed 16 Dec-14 Feb, Sun eve & Mon
6 en suite (shr) TV in all bedrooms Direct dial from all bedrooms Licensed Full central heating Open parking available Boule Open terrace V meals
ROOMS: (room only) d 220-270FF
CARDS: ●● ■■ Travellers cheques

### DURBAN-CORBIÈRES Aude

**Château Haut-Gléon**
Villeseque-des-Corbières 11360
☎ 468488595 FAX 468484620
(exit from motorway in direction of Portel-des-Corbières. 6.5km from Portel cross small bridge on left & climb 300m to Château)

Near river Forest area
6 rms (1 bth 4 shr) No smoking on premises Open parking available Boule Caves & Wine cellars Languages spoken: English & Spanish
CARDS: ●● ■■ Travellers cheques

### ELNE Pyrénées-Orientales

**★ ★ Week-End**
29 av Paul Reig 66200
☎ 468220668 FAX 468221716
Near river Near lake Near sea Near beach Forest area Near motorway
Closed Dec-Mar
8 rms (7 bth/shr) (1 fmly) (4 with balcony) TV in all bedrooms Direct dial from all bedrooms Full central heating Air conditioning in bedrooms Covered parking available (charged) Supervised Child discount available 12yrs Bicycle rental Open terrace Last d 22.00hrs Languages spoken: English, Dutch, German, Italian & Spanish
CARDS: ●● ■■ ■■ ⑩ Travellers cheques

### ESPEZEL Aude

**★ Grau**
11340
☎ 468203014 FAX 468203362
(from Quillan take the road towards Foix, at the top of hill turn left to follow the road signed `Ax-les-Thermes` by the Plateau de Sault, Espezel is 25km from Quillan)
Near river Near lake Forest area In town centre
8 en suite (bth/shr) (2 fmly) No smoking in 2 bedrooms Direct dial from all bedrooms Licensed Full central heating Open parking available Child discount available 12yrs Fishing Boule V meals Last d 20.55hrs Languages spoken: English & Spanish
CARDS: ●● ■■ Travellers cheques

### FABREZAN Aude

**★ ★ Le Clos des Souquets**
av de Lagrasse 11200
☎ 468435261 FAX 468435676
Near river Forest area
Closed early Nov-Apr
5 en suite (bth) TV in all bedrooms Licensed Full central heating Open parking available Supervised Outdoor swimming pool Pool table Boule Bicycle rental Open terrace Covered terrace V meals Last d 21.45hrs Languages spoken: English & Spanish
CARDS: ●● ■■ ⑩

### FLORAC Lozère

**★ ★ ★ Grand Hotel du Parc**
47 av Jean Honestier 48400
☎ 466450305 FAX 466451181
Near river Forest area In town centre
Closed Dec-14 Mar
60 rms (36 bth 18 shr) 26 rooms in annexe (10 fmly) (4 with balcony) TV in 54 bedrooms Direct dial from all bedrooms Licensed Full central heating Open parking available Covered parking available Outdoor swimming pool (heated) Boule Open terrace Covered terrace Last d 20.45hrs Languages spoken: English, German & Spanish
CARDS: ●● ■■ ■■ ⑩ JCB Travellers cheques

**★ ★ Le Rochefort**
RN 106, rte des Gorges du Tarn *48400*
☎ 466450257 FAX 466452585
(2km N)
Near river Forest area Near motorway
*Closed Nov-Mar*
*24 en suite (bth/shr) (6 fmly) (8 with balcony) TV in all*
*bedrooms Direct dial from all bedrooms Licensed Full central*
*heating Open parking available Child discount available 12yrs*
*Boule Open terrace V meals Last d 21.30hrs Languages*
*spoken: English*
CARDS: ●● ⚏ Travellers cheques

### GANGES Hérault

**★ ★ ★ ★ Château de Madières Hostellerie**
Madièères *34190*
☎ 467738403 FAX 467735571
Near river Forest area Near motorway
*Closed Nov-Mar*
*12 en suite (bth/shr) (4 fmly) TV in all bedrooms STV Direct*
*dial from all bedrooms Mini-bar in all bedrooms Licensed Full*
*central heating Open parking available Child discount*
*available 10yrs Outdoor swimming pool (heated) Fishing Gym*
*Boule Bicycle rental Open terrace Covered terrace V meals*
*Last d 21.30hrs Languages spoken: English, German & Spanish*
CARDS: ●● ⚏ ⚏ ⚏ Travellers cheques

### GÉNÉRARGUES Gard

**Le Gamaos** (Prop: Victor & Johanne Vivian)
Cammaou et Roucan *30140*
☎ 466619379 FAX 466619379
(from Anduze take D129 to Générargues. In Générargues turn
left onto D50 in direction of Mialet for 2km. Pass Le Roucan on
right and then Les Trois Barbus Hotel on left. After approx
150mtrs on right is entrance to Le Gamaos)
Set in a clearing amongst Spanish chestnut trees, intermingled
with acacia and wild cherry, a comfortable home offering good
accommodation. Breakfast can be taken by the pool in good
weather and the evening meals are extremely good value.
Near river Near sea Forest area Near motorway
*3 en suite (shr) (3 with balcony) Full central heating Outdoor*
*swimming pool Last d 21.00hrs Languages spoken: English &*
*Norwegian*
ROOMS: s 280FF; d 300FF
MEALS: Dinner 100FF✱
CARDS: Travellers cheques

### GINCLA Aude

**★ ★ Hostellerie du Grand Duc**
2 rte de Boucheville *11140*
☎ 468205502 FAX 468206122
(take direction towards Foix on N117 at Lapradelle Puylaurens
turn left onto D22 & continue for 7km)
Near river Forest area
*Closed mid Nov-mid Mar*
*10 en suite (bth/shr) TV in all bedrooms Direct dial from all*
*bedrooms Room-safe Licensed Full central heating Open*
*parking available Child discount available 10yrs Open terrace*
*V meals Last d 21.00hrs Languages spoken: English &*
*German*
CARDS: ●● ⚏ Travellers cheques

### GRANDE-MOTTE, LA Hérault

**★ ★ ★ Hotel Frantour**
1641 av du Golf *34280*
☎ 467298888 FAX 467291701
(from Nîmes leave A9 at exit Gallargues and follow 'Golf' signs.
From Narbonne leave A9 at exit 'Montpellier Est' direction La
Grande Motte-once in town follow Golf Signs)
Near lake Near sea Near motorway
*Closed Nov-Mar*
*81 en suite (bth) (42 fmly) (81 with balcony) No smoking in 5*
*bedrooms TV in all bedrooms STV Radio in rooms Direct dial*
*from all bedrooms Mini-bar in all bedrooms Room-safe*
*Licensed Lift Night porter Full central heating Air*
*conditioning in bedrooms Child discount available Supervised*
*Child discount available 12yrs Outdoor swimming pool Golf*
*Sauna Solarium Pool table Boule Bicycle rental Open terrace*
*Covered terrace V meals Languages spoken: English &*
*German*
CARDS: ●● ⚏ ⚏ ⚏ Travellers cheques

### LAMALOU-LES-BAINS Hérault

**★ ★ ★ Hotel de la Paix**
rue Alphonse Daudet *34240*
☎ 467956311 FAX 467956778
(from A9 exit Béziers Est, take D909 towards Bédarieux)
Near river Forest area In town centre
*31 en suite (bth/shr) (4 fmly) TV in all bedrooms Direct dial*
*from all bedrooms Licensed Lift Full central heating Open*
*parking available Covered parking available (charged) Child*
*discount available 12yrs Open terrace Covered terrace V*
*meals Last d 21.30hrs Languages spoken: English & German*
ROOMS: (room only) s 215-220FF; d 290-320FF
**Reductions over 1 night**
MEALS: Continental breakfast 40FF Lunch 90-250FF&alc
Dinner 90-250FF&alc
CARDS: ●● ⚏ ⚏ ⚏ Travellers cheques

### LANGOGNE Lozère

**★ ★ ★ Domaine de Barres**
rte de Mende *48300*
☎ 466697100 FAX 466697129
Near river Near lake Forest area Near motorway
*Closed 16 Nov-14 Mar*
*20 en suite (bth) TV in all bedrooms Direct dial from all*
*bedrooms Mini-bar in all bedrooms Licensed Lift Full central*
*heating Open parking available Supervised Indoor swimming*
*pool (heated) Golf 9 Sauna Open terrace Last d 21.30hrs*
*Languages spoken: English, German & Spanish*
CARDS: ●● ⚏ ⚏ ⚏ Travellers cheques

### LATTES Hérault

**★ ★ Mas de Couran**
rte de Fréjorgues *34970*
☎ 467655757 FAX 467653756
(off D172)
Near sea
*18 en suite (bth/shr) (2 fmly) (1 with balcony) TV in all*
*bedrooms Direct dial from all bedrooms Mini-bar in all*
*bedrooms Licensed Night porter Open parking available*
*Supervised Child discount available 12yrs Outdoor swimming*
*pool Bicycle rental Open terrace Covered terrace V meals*
*Last d 21.30hrs Languages spoken: English & Spanish*
CARDS: ●● ⚏ ⚏ ⚏ Travellers cheques

## LAUDUN Gard

**Château de Lascours** (Prop: Jean Louis Bastouil)
*30290*
☎ 466503961 FAX 466503008
(exit A9 at Roquemaure/Tavel)
Near river Near lake Forest area Near motorway
*6 en suite (bth/shr) (2 fmly) (1 with balcony) TV in 1 bedroom*
*Full central heating Open parking available Supervised Child*
*discount available Outdoor swimming pool Fishing Sauna*
*Solarium Boule Bicycle rental Open terrace Languages*
*spoken: English & Italian*
ROOMS: s fr 450FF; d 500FF
CARDS: Travellers cheques

## LIGNAN-SUR-ORB Hérault

★ ★ ★ *Château de Lignan*
*34490*
☎ 467379147 FAX 467379925
(from A9 exit at Béziers Est, follow signs for Béziers centre
then take D19)
Near river Forest area In town centre Near motorway
*49 en suite (bth/shr) (1 fmly) TV in all bedrooms STV Direct*
*dial from all bedrooms Mini-bar in all bedrooms Licensed Lift*
*Night porter Full central heating Air conditioning in bedrooms*
*Open parking available Supervised Outdoor swimming pool*
*Sauna Solarium Boule Bicycle rental Open terrace Last d*
*22.00hrs Languages spoken: English, German & Spanish*
CARDS: ●● ■ ▆ ▣ Travellers cheques

## LLO Pyrénées-Orientales

★ ★ ★ *L'Atalaya*
*66800*
☎ 468047004 FAX 468040129
(from N116 at Saillagouse take D33 to Llo)
Forest area
*Closed 11 Jan-Mar & 6 Nov-19 Dec RS Mon & Tue lunchtine*
*13 en suite (bth/shr) 3 rooms in annexe (2 fmly) (4 with*
*balcony) TV in all bedrooms STV Direct dial from all*
*bedrooms Mini-bar in all bedrooms Room-safe (charged)*
*Licensed Night porter Full central heating Open parking*
*available Covered parking available Child discount available*
*5yrs Outdoor swimming pool Open terrace Last d 21.30hrs*
*Languages spoken: English & Spanish*
CARDS: ●● ▆ ▣ Eurocard Travellers cheques

## MALÈNE, LA Lozère

★ ★ ★ **Manoir de Montesquiou**
*48210*
☎ 466485112 FAX 466485047
Near river
*Closed 31 Oct-Mar*
*12 en suite (bth/shr) TV in all bedrooms Direct dial from all*
*bedrooms Full central heating Open parking available Solarium*
*Open terrace Last d 21.00hrs Languages spoken: English*
ROOMS: (room only) d 420-800FF
MEALS: Full breakfast 65FF Lunch 135-255FF Dinner 135-
255FF
CARDS: ●● ▆ ▣ Travellers cheques

## MARGUERITTES Gard

★ ★ *Climat de France*
La Panché Sud-RN 86 *30320*
☎ 466263050 FAX 466264466
Near sea Forest area Near motorway
*46 en suite (shr) (1 fmly) TV available Radio in rooms Direct-*
*dial available Licensed Lift Night porter Open parking*
*available Supervised Outdoor swimming pool Solarium Open*
*terrace Last d 10pm*
CARDS: ●● ▆

★ ★ ★ *L'Hacienda*
Mas de Brignon
☎ 466750225 FAX 466754558
(from A9 exit Nîmes Est follow Avignon signs. After 3km trun
right for Marguerittes at 3rd roundabout. In Marguerittes
follow red arrows for L'Hacienda on other side of village, 2km
away)
*10 en suite (bth/shr) 1 rooms in annexe No smoking in 1*
*bedroom TV in all bedrooms Direct dial from all bedrooms*
*Mini-bar in all bedrooms Full central heating Open parking*
*available Covered parking available Supervised Child discount*
*available Outdoor swimming pool Sauna Solarium Boule*
*Bicycle rental Open terrace Covered terrace Table tennis Last*
*d 21.15hrs Languages spoken: English & German*
CARDS: ●● ▆ Travellers cheques

## MARVEJOLS Lozère

★ ★ *Hotel de la Gare et des Rochers*
pl de la Gare *48100*
☎ 466321058 FAX 466323063
(A75 exit 37/38/39, exit S of town direction La Gare)
Near river Forest area Near motorway
*Closed 2 Dec-9 Mar*
*30 rms (18 bth 10 shr) (4 fmly) (12 with balcony) TV in all*
*bedrooms Direct dial from all bedrooms Licensed Lift Full*
*central heating Open parking available Covered parking*
*available Open terrace V meals Last d 21.00hrs Languages*
*spoken: English & Spanish*
CARDS: ●● ▆ Travellers cheques

## MENDE Lozère

**La Boulène**
Aspres *48000*
☎ 466492337 FAX 466493443
Near river Near lake Forest area Near motorway
*Closed 6 Nov-Mar*
*8 en suite (shr) 2 rooms in annexe (1 fmly) Direct dial from 7*
*bedrooms Licensed Full central heating Open parking available*
*Child discount available Riding Boule Bicycle rental Open*
*terrace V meals Last d 21.15hrs Languages spoken: English*
ROOMS: d 220FF **Reductions over 1 night Special
breaks**
MEALS: Lunch 98-125FF Dinner 98-125FF✱
CARDS: ●● ■ ▆ ▣ Travellers cheques

★ ★ ★ *Hotel du Pont Roupt*
2 av du 11 November
☎ 66650143 FAX 66652296
(at south entrance of Mende by N88, towards 'Zone
Antisanale')
Near river Forest area
*26 en suite (bth/shr) TV in all bedrooms Direct dial from all*
*bedrooms Mini-bar in all bedrooms Lift Full central heating*
*contd.*
411

Open parking available  Covered parking available  Supervised
Child discount available 12yrs  Indoor swimming pool (heated)
Sauna Solarium  Bicycle rental  V meals  Last d 21.30hrs
Languages spoken: English & German
CARDS: ●● ▩▩ ▥▥ ⑩ Travellers cheques

## MEYRUEIS Lozère

### ★ ★ ★ Château d'Ayres
*48150*
☎ 466456010 FAX 466456226
Near river  Forest area
Closed 22 Nov-26 Mar RS Half board obligatory 10 Jul-26 Aug
27 en suite (bth/shr)  (7 fmly)  (3 with balcony)  TV in all
bedrooms  STV  Direct dial from all bedrooms  Mini-bar in 24
bedrooms  Licensed  Full central heating  Open parking
available  Supervised  Child discount available 7yrs  Outdoor
swimming pool (heated)  Tennis  Riding  Boule  Open terrace  V
meals  Last d 22.00hrs  Languages spoken: English
ROOMS: (room only) s 420-530FF; d 420-785FF
MEALS: Continental breakfast 67FF  Lunch 110-265FF&alc
Dinner 159-265FF&alc
CARDS: ●● ▩▩ ▥▥ ⑩ Travellers cheques

### ★ ★ *Le Renaissance*
rue de la Ville *48150*
☎ 466456019 FAX 466456594
In town centre
Closed mid Nov-late Mar
18 en suite (bth/shr)  (2 fmly)  TV in 12 bedrooms  Direct dial
from all bedrooms  Licensed  Child discount available 7yrs
Open terrace  Last d 22.00hrs  Languages spoken: English
CARDS: ●● ▥▥ Travellers cheques

## MONTMAUR Aude

### La Castagne (Prop: Gerda & Zip Vanderzeypen)
*11320*
☎ 468600040 FAX 468600040
(from the N113 between Villefranche-du-Lauragais and
Avignonet take the D43 towards Revel 6km and follow signs)
Near river  Near lake  Forest area  Near motorway
2 en suite (shr)  (1 fmly)  No smoking on premises  Full central
heating  Open parking available  Covered parking available
Child discount available 7yrs  Outdoor swimming pool  Boule
Bicycle rental  Billiards  Table tennis  Languages spoken:
English, Dutch & German

## MONTPELLIER Hérault

### ★ ★ ★ Hotel Le Guilhem (Best Western)
18 rue Jean-Jacques Rousseau *34000*
☎ 467529090 FAX 467606767
(from A9 exit 'Montpellier Est' follow signs for 'Centre
Historique')
In town centre  Near motorway
33 en suite (bth/shr)  9 rooms in annexe  TV in all bedrooms
STV  Direct dial from all bedrooms  Mini-bar in all bedrooms
Licensed  Lift  Night porter  Full central heating  Air
conditioning in bedrooms  Open terrace  Languages spoken:
English & German
CARDS: ●● ▩▩ ▥▥ ⑩ JCB Travellers cheques

### ★ ★ ★ Holiday Inn Métropole
3 rue Clos Réné *34000*
☎ 467581122 FAX 467921302

(from A9 exit 'Montpellier Sud' follow signs for city
centre/railway station)
In town centre
81 en suite (bth/shr)  (4 fmly)  No smoking in 20 bedrooms  TV
in all bedrooms  STV  Direct dial from all bedrooms  Mini-bar in
all bedrooms  Room-safe  Licensed  Lift  Night porter  Full
central heating  Air conditioning in bedrooms  Open parking
available (charged)  Covered parking available (charged)
Supervised  Child discount available 14yrs  Pool table  Last d
22.00hrs  Languages spoken: English, Arabic, German &
Spanish
CARDS: ●● ▩▩ ▥▥ ⑩ JCB Travellers cheques

### ★ ★ ★ New Hotel du Midi
22 bd Victor Hugo *34000*
☎ 467926961 FAX 467927363
In town centre
47 en suite (bth/shr)  (6 fmly)  (10 with balcony)  TV in all
bedrooms  STV  Direct dial from all bedrooms  Mini-bar in all
bedrooms  Licensed  Lift  Night porter  Full central heating  Air
conditioning in bedrooms  Languages spoken: English,
German, Italian & Spanish

### ★ ★ ★ Novotel
125 bis av de Palavas *34000*
☎ 499523434 FAX 499523433
(from A9 take exit 'Montpellier Sud' to the city centre, then
follow signs for 'Palavas' and 'Prés d'Arenes')
Near sea  Near motorway
162 en suite (bth)  (60 fmly)  No smoking in 24 bedrooms  TV in
all bedrooms  STV  Radio in rooms  Direct dial from all
bedrooms  Mini-bar in 140 bedrooms  Licensed  Lift  Night
porter  Full central heating  Air conditioning in bedrooms  Open
parking available  Supervised  Child discount available 16yrs
Outdoor swimming pool  Pool table  Open terrace  Last d
24.00hrs  Languages spoken: English, German, Italian &
Spanish
CARDS: ●● ▩▩ ▥▥ ⑩ Travellers cheques

## NARBONNE Aude

### ★ ★ Climat de France
chemin des Hoteliers, Z I Plaisance *11100*
☎ 468410490 FAX 468413413
(from A9 take N113 Narbonne exit then at 2nd rbt take 3rd exit
and next right)
Near motorway
40 en suite (bth)  TV in all bedrooms  Radio in rooms  Direct dial
from all bedrooms  Licensed  Open parking available (charged)
Covered parking available (charged)  Supervised  Last d 10pm
Languages spoken: English, German & Spanish
CARDS: ●● ▥▥

### ★ ★ ★ Novotel
Quartier Plaisance, rte de Perpignan *11100*
☎ 468427200 FAX 468427210
Near motorway
96 en suite (bth/shr)  (40 fmly)  No smoking in 20 bedrooms  TV
in all bedrooms  STV  Radio in rooms  Direct dial from all
bedrooms  Mini-bar in all bedrooms  Licensed  Lift  Night porter
Full central heating  Air conditioning in bedrooms  Open
parking available  Child discount available 16yrs  Outdoor
swimming pool  Pool table  Open terrace  Covered terrace  V
meals  Last d 24.00hrs  Languages spoken: English, German,
Italian & Spanish
CARDS: ●● ▩▩ ▥▥ ⑩ JCB Travellers cheques

### NASBINALS Lozère

**★ ★ La Maison de Rosalie**
Montgros *48260*
☎ 466325514 FAX 466325646
(A75 exit Aumont-Aubrac direction Nasbinals)
Near river Near lake Forest area
*Closed 4 Nov-24 Apr*
*9 rms (4 bth 3 shr) Some rooms in annexe (8 fmly) Direct dial from all bedrooms Licensed Full central heating Open parking available Child discount available 10yrs Sauna Gym Boule Open terrace V meals Last d 21.00hrs Languages spoken: English, Italian & Spanish*
CARDS: Travellers cheques

### NÉZIGNAN-L'ÉVÊQUE Hérault

**★ ★ ★ Hostellerie de St-Alban**
31 rte d'Agde *34120*
☎ 467981138 FAX 467989163
(from A9 exit 34 take D13 towards Pézenas for 4km)
This charming establishment is housed in a refined 19th-century residence situated in a peaceful village surrounded by vineyards. It is an ideal base from which to tour the Languedoc-Roussillon region or to use as a stop-over on the way to Spain.
Near river Near lake Near sea Near beach Near motorway
*Closed Dec-Jan*

*14 en suite (bth/shr) (4 fmly) (9 with balcony) TV in all bedrooms STV Direct dial from all bedrooms Licensed Full central heating Open parking available Child discount available 7yrs Outdoor swimming pool Tennis Jacuzzi/spa Open terrace V meals Last d 21.00hrs Languages spoken: English & German*
ROOMS: (room only) s 350-530FF; d 390-530FF
MEALS: Continental breakfast 60FF Lunch 110-300FFalc Dinner 110-300FFalc✱
CARDS: ●● ▆▆ ▆▆ ▆ Travellers cheques

### NÎMES Gard

**★ ★ ★ ★ Hôtel Imperator Concorde**
quai de la Fontaine *30900*
☎ 466219030 FAX 466677025
In town centre Near motorway
*63 en suite (bth/shr) (6 fmly) (5 with balcony) No smoking in 3 bedrooms TV in all bedrooms Direct dial from all bedrooms Mini-bar in all bedrooms Licensed Lift Night porter Full central heating Air conditioning in bedrooms Open parking available (charged) Covered parking available (charged)*

*Supervised Child discount available 12yrs Covered terrace V meals Last d 22.00hrs Languages spoken: English, German, Italian & Spanish*
CARDS: ●● ▆▆ ▆▆ ▆ Travellers cheques

**★ ★ ★ New Hotel la Baume**
21 rue Nationale *30000*
☎ 466732842 FAX 466762845
(follow signs 'Centre Ville')
In town centre Near motorway
*33 en suite (bth/shr) (2 fmly) (2 with balcony) TV in all bedrooms Radio in rooms Direct dial from all bedrooms Mini-bar in all bedrooms Licensed Lift Night porter Full central heating Air conditioning in bedrooms Child discount available 12yrs Open terrace Last d 22.00hrs Languages spoken: English, German & Spanish*
CARDS: ●● ▆▆ ▆▆ ▆ JCB Travellers cheques

**★ ★ ★ Hotel L'Orangerie**
755 rue Tour de l'Évêque *30000*
☎ 466845057 FAX 466294455
Forest area In town centre Near motorway
*31 en suite (bth/shr) (5 fmly) (16 with balcony) TV in all bedrooms STV Direct dial from all bedrooms Mini-bar in all bedrooms Licensed Night porter Full central heating Air conditioning in bedrooms Open parking available Supervised Child discount available 10yrs Outdoor swimming pool Boule Jacuzzi/spa Open terrace ping pong Last d 22.00hrs Languages spoken: English*
CARDS: ●● ▆▆ ▆▆ ▆ Travellers cheques

### NOTRE-DAME-DE-LONDRES Hérault

**Domaine du Pous** (Prop: Elizabeth Noualhac)
Le Pous *34380*
☎ 467550136
(Exit A9 at Montpellier Sud or Est for Notre Dame de Londres & Le Pous)
Forest area
*6 en suite (bth/shr) Full central heating Open parking available*

### OLARGUES Hérault

**★ ★ ★ Domaine de Rieumége**
rte de St-Pons *34390*
☎ 467977399 FAX 467977852
(from A9 exit at Beziers Est,follow directions for Bedarieu/Herepian/Olargues)
This 17th-century establishment, standing at the foot of the Cévennes, is surrounded by 35 acres of private grounds and provides a charming setting for visitors who love unspoilt countryside. It features a warm, informal interior incorporating pleasant bedrooms with modern facilities, a cosy lounge with open fireplace and a restaurant with exposed brickwork and beams.
Near river Forest area
*Closed 2 Jan-15 Mar*
*14 en suite (bth/shr) 5 rooms in annexe (4 fmly) TV in 10 bedrooms Direct dial from all bedrooms Mini-bar in 10 bedrooms Licensed Full central heating Open parking available Covered parking available Supervised Child discount available 16yrs Outdoor swimming pool Tennis Fishing Boule Bicycle rental Open terrace V meals Last d 21.30hrs Languages spoken: English*
ROOMS: (room only) s 396-1140FF; d 430-1140FF

**Reductions over 1 night  Special breaks**
MEALS: Continental breakfast 65FF  Lunch fr 120FFalc
Dinner fr 190FFalc
CARDS: 💳 ▬ ▬ 💳 Carte Bleue Travellers cheques

## ORNAISONS Aude

### ★ ★ ★ Relais du Val d'Orbieu
*11200*
☎ 468271027 FAX 468275244
(from A9 exit Narbone Sud, take N113 towards Lézignan-
Corbières, then D24)
Situated in the heart of the rolling countryside of the Corbières
region, the inn occupies a peaceful location. It features
tastefully decorated guest rooms with en suite facilities
offering good levels of comfort. There is a summer restaurant,
shaded by a pergola, and another indoors. Both serve a high
standard of cooking. Open all year round, this charming
residence provides the ideal place for an overnight stop or a
longer break.
Near river  Forest area

*Closed 20 Dec-31 Jan RS Nov-Mar*
*20 en suite (bth/shr) (5 fmly) (8 with balcony) TV in all*
*bedrooms STV Direct dial from all bedrooms Mini-bar in all*
*bedrooms Licensed Full central heating Open parking*
*available Supervised Outdoor swimming pool Tennis Boule*
*Bicycle rental Open terrace Covered terrace Practice golf V*
*meals Last d 21.00hrs Languages spoken: English & Spanish*
ROOMS: (room only) s 390-590FF; d 490-750FF
**Special breaks**
MEALS: Continental breakfast 75FF  Lunch 145-295FF&alc
Dinner 145-295FF&alc
CARDS: 💳 ▬ ▬ 💳 JCB Travellers cheques

## PENNAUTIER Aude

### Château de Liet (Prop: M. Meynier)
*11610*
☎ 468111919 FAX 468470522
(from N113 towards Toulouse take Pennautier turn and
continue through village towards Aragon-Brousse to house
in 2km)
19th-century château set in 15 hectares of parkland with good-
sized swimming pool. Table-tennis, walks, riding, fishing,
tennis, sailing and rafting all on site or nearby.
Near river  Forest area  Near motorway
*Closed 15 Dec-15 Jan*
*6 en suite (bth/shr) (3 fmly) (2 with balcony) Full central*
*heating Open parking available Outdoor swimming pool*

*Chateau de Liet*
*Bicycle rental Badminton Table tennis Last d 21.00hrs*
*Languages spoken: English & Spanish*
ROOMS: d 300-400FF
CARDS: 💳 ▬

## PÉPIEUX Aude

### Carrefour (Prop: Sally Worthington)
1 rue de l'Étang *11700*
☎ 468916929 FAX 468916929
(from A61 take Léxignan-Corbières exit to Olonzac then on to
Pépieux)
A rambling house dating from the 17th century, originally a
halt for coaches, furnished in a comfortable mixture of antique
and contemporary.

Near lake  Near sea  Near beach  Forest area  In town centre
Near motorway
*4 rms (3 bth/shr) (2 fmly) No smoking on premises Full central*
*heating Open parking available Covered parking available No*
*children 12yrs Boule Bicycle rental Last d 8pm Languages*
*spoken: English*
ROOMS: d 350FF
MEALS: Dinner 150FF
CARDS: 💳 ▬

## PERPIGNAN Pyrénées-Orientales

### ★ ★ De La Poste et de la Perdrix
6 rue Fabriques Nabot *66000*
☎ 468344253 FAX 468345820
Near sea  In town centre  Near motorway
*38 rms (10 bth 20 shr) (35 with balcony) TV in 25 bedrooms*
*Direct dial from all bedrooms Lift Night porter Full central*
*heating Child discount available 10yrs V meals Last d 21.15hrs*
*Languages spoken: English, German & Spanish*
CARDS: 💳 ▬ ▬ 💳 Travellers cheques

### PEYREFITTE-DU-RAZÈS Aude

**Domaine de Couchet** (Prop: Jean-Pierre Ropers)
*11230*
☎ 468695506 FAX 468695506
(from Carcassonne take D118 towards Limoux, then D620 towards Chalabre for 7km. Fork right on D626 to Peyrefitte. Signposted from village)
Near river Near lake Forest area
*4 rms (3 shr) TV in 3 bedrooms Radio in rooms Full central heating Open parking available Child discount available 7yrs Outdoor swimming pool Boule Last d 20.00hrs*
ROOMS: d fr 350FF
MEALS: Dinner fr 130FF✱

### PONT-D'HÉRAULT Gard

★ ★ *Château de Rey*
Le Rey *30570*
☎ 467824006 FAX 467824779
Near river Forest area
*Closed Jan*
*13 en suite (bth/shr) (2 fmly) TV in all bedrooms STV Direct dial from all bedrooms Full central heating Open parking available Covered parking available Supervised Child discount available Fishing Open terrace V meals Last d 22.00hrs Languages spoken: English*
CARDS: ●● ▬

### PONT-DU-GARD Gard

★ ★ ★ *Vieux Moulin*
Pont-du-Gard *30210*
☎ 466371435 FAX 466372648
Near river Near sea Near beach Forest area Near motorway
*Closed 16 Oct-15 Mar*
*17 rms (7 bth 3 shr) (5 fmly) (5 with balcony) Direct dial from all bedrooms Licensed Full central heating Open parking available Child discount available 10yrs Boule Open terrace V meals Last d 22.00hrs Languages spoken: English & German*
CARDS: ●● ▬ Travellers cheques

### PORT-LA-NOUVELLE Aude

★ ★ ★ *Méditerranée*
Front de Mer *11210*
☎ 468480308 FAX 468485381
(from Narbonne travel S on A9 and exit Sigean and take Port la Nouvelle N9)

The hotel offers fine views over the beach and the sea and contains pleasant bedrooms with balconies. The menu provides a choice of tasty dishes and fresh fish specialities take pride of place. A good venue for a seaside holiday.
Near sea Near beach Near motorway
*31 en suite (bth/shr) (10 fmly) (17 with balcony) No smoking in 1 bedroom TV in all bedrooms Direct dial from all bedrooms Mini-bar in 6 bedrooms Licensed Lift Night porter Full central heating Air conditioning in bedrooms Covered parking available (charged) Supervised Child discount available 14yrs Open terrace V meals Last d 21.30hrs Languages spoken: English, German & Spanish*
ROOMS: (room only) s 260-390FF; d 260-490FF
**Special breaks: Fishing breaks**
MEALS: Continental breakfast 35FF Lunch 70-240FF&alc Dinner 70-240FF&alc
CARDS: ●● ▬ ▭ ⑩ Travellers cheques

### POTELIÈRES Gard

. *Le Château* (Prop: J & F De Tcherepakhine)
*30500*
☎ 466248092 FAX 466248243
Near river Near lake Forest area Near motorway
*8 en suite (bth/shr) TV in 2 bedrooms Radio in rooms Full central heating Open parking available Covered parking available Supervised Child discount available 12yrs Outdoor swimming pool Languages spoken: English*
CARDS: Travellers cheques

### PRATS-DE-MOLLO-LA-PRESTE Pyrénées-Orientales

★ ★ *Bellevue*
Le Foiral *66230*
☎ 468397248 FAX 468397804
Forest area In town centre
*Closed 3 Nov-Mar(except school hols)*
*18 rms (11 bth 5 shr) (3 fmly) (5 with balcony) TV available Direct dial from all bedrooms Licensed Full central heating Open parking available Supervised Child discount available 12yrs Boule Open terrace Last d 20.45hrs Languages spoken: English & Spanish*
CARDS: ●● ▬ Travellers cheques

### PUICHÉRIC Aude

*Château de St-Aunay* (Prop: M C Berge)
*11700*
☎ 468437220 FAX 468437672
(from Carcassonne take N113 to Trèbes and D610 to entrance to town then Rieux-Minervois road)
Near river Near lake Near motorway
*Closed 5 Oct-Mar*
*10 rms (9 shr) (4 fmly) (2 with balcony) Full central heating Open parking available Child discount available Outdoor swimming pool Pool table Bicycle rental Last d 18.30hrs Languages spoken: English*
CARDS: Travellers cheques

### QUARANTE Hérault

*Château de Quarante* (Prop: M & Mme N Neukirch)
24 av du Château de Quarante *34310*
☎ 467894041 FAX 467894041
(W of Béziers, take D11 which becomes the D5, drive 2 km and turn right onto D184. Cross Canal du Midi drive 4km, château at village entrance. N of Narbonne take D13 onto D36 for 20km, cross village to reach château on D184)
Near river Near sea Near beach Forest area Near motorway
*contd.*

*Closed Jan-Mar*
*5 en suite (bth/shr) (3 with balcony) No smoking on premises*
*Open parking available Child discount available Bicycle rental*
*Languages spoken: English & German*

### REMOULINS Gard

**★ ★ ★ ★ Le Vieux Castillon**
Castillon-du-Gard *30210*
☎ 466376161 FAX 466372817
(from A9 take N86 towards Montélimar, then D19A towards Alès)
*Closed Jan-early Mar*
*35 en suite (bth/shr) 12 rooms in annexe TV in all bedrooms*
*STV Direct dial from all bedrooms Mini-bar in all bedrooms*
*Room-safe Licensed Lift Night porter Full central heating Air*
*conditioning in bedrooms Outdoor swimming pool Sauna Pool table Open terrace Last*
*d 21.00hrs Languages spoken: English & German*
CARDS: ●● ■ ▆ ⑤ JCB Travellers cheques

### RIBAUTE-LES-TAVERNES Gard

**Château de Ribaute** (Prop: Chamski-Mandajors)
*30720*
☎ 466830166 FAX 466838693
Near river
*6 en suite (bth/shr) Open parking available Supervised Child*
*discount available 12yrs Outdoor swimming pool Golf Tennis*
*Riding Boule Open terrace V meals Languages spoken:*
*English*
CARDS: ●● ▆

### RIOLS Hérault

**La Cerisaie** (Prop: M R Weggelaar)
1 av de Bédarieux *34220*
☎ 467970387 FAX 467970388
(leave A9 at Béziers Ouest, head for Castures, Mazamet, St
Pons on the N112. Approx 1km before St Pons, turn right
towards Bédarieux, Riols La Cerisaie is on left hand side, just
after passing the church)
Near river Forest area
*6 en suite (bth/shr) Licensed Open parking available*
*Supervised Child discount available Outdoor swimming pool*
*Boule Bicycle rental Open terrace Tennis nearby Languages*
*spoken: English, Dutch & German*
CARDS: ●● ▆

### ROQUEBRUN Hérault

**Les Mimosas** (Prop: Sarah & Denis La Touche)
av des Orangers *34460*
☎ 467896136 FAX 467896136
(A9 to Béziers then D14 to Roquebrun)
Situated in the beautiful village of Roquebrun, on the banks of
the river Orb, in the regional park of the Haut-Languedoc.
Charming, renovated 19th-century manor house. The rooms
are spacious, with excellent showers. Delicious evening meals
are served. A sumptuous breakfast are served. Cooking courses in
French country cooking are held spring and summer.
Near river Near lake Near sea Near beach Forest area Near
motorway
*5 en suite (shr) (1 fmly) (1 with balcony) No smoking on*
*premises Open parking available Covered parking available*
*Child discount available 5yrs Tennis Fishing Riding Boule*
*Mini-golf Bicycle rental Open terrace wine tasting, cooking*

*classes Last d noon Languages spoken: English*
ROOMS: s 350-430FF; d 365-445FF
MEALS: Dinner 150-175FF
CARDS: ●● ▆ Travellers cheques

### ROQUE-SUR-CÈZE Gard

**La Tonnelle** (Prop: Rigaud)
*30200*
☎ 466827937
Near river Forest area In town centre
*6 en suite (shr) (3 fmly) Outdoor swimming pool Boule Open*
*terrace*

### SAILLAGOUSE Pyrénées-Orientales

**★ ★ Planes "La Vieille Maison Cerdane"**
pl de Cerdagne *66800*
☎ 468047208 FAX 468047593
Forest area Near motorway
*Closed 16 Oct-19 Dec RS 17 Oct-1 Nov*
*19 en suite (bth/shr) 19 rooms in annexe (16 with balcony) TV*
*in all bedrooms Direct dial from all bedrooms Licensed Lift*
*Full central heating Open parking available Child discount*
*available 12yrs Indoor swimming pool (heated) Outdoor*
*swimming pool (heated) Sauna Solarium Open terrace Last d*
*21.00hrs Languages spoken: English & Spanish*
CARDS: ●● ■ ▆ ⑤ Travellers cheques

### ST-ALBAN-SUR-LIMAGNOLE Lozère

**★ ★ ★ Relais St-Roch**
Château de la Chastre *48120*
☎ 466315548 FAX 466315326
(A75 exit 34 in direction of St-Alban)
This beautiful, pink-granite residence stands in the heart of
this town in the Margeride region and is the ideal place for
those who are looking for a peaceful stay, fresh air, attentive
service and good food. The guest rooms are very comfortable
and the restaurant La Petite Maison, with its charming interior,
offers an extensive choice of specialities, more than 150
different whiskies and an extensive wine selection. Nearby are
first-class fishing waters, paths for hiking, and nature parks,
that are home to wolves and European bison.
Near river Near beach Forest area

*Closed Nov-Mar*
*9 en suite (bth/shr) (2 fmly) (1 with balcony) TV in all*
*bedrooms STV Radio in rooms Direct dial from all bedrooms*
*Mini-bar in all bedrooms Licensed Night porter Full central*
*heating Open parking available Child discount available 12yrs*
*Outdoor swimming pool (heated) Fishing Boule Bicycle rental*

*Open terrace V meals Last d 21.30hrs Languages spoken:*
*English German & Spanish*
ROOMS: (room only) d 590-790FF
**✷ Reductions over 1 night**
MEALS: Continental breakfast 64FF Lunch 98-298FF&alc
Dinner 148-298FF&alc
CARDS: ● ■ ☰ ◉ JCB Travellers cheques

### ST-CLÉMENT-DE-RIVIÈRE Hérault

**Domaine de St-Clément** (Prop: M & Mme H Bernabé)
*34980*
☎ 467667089 FAX 467840796
(approach via D112 (Route de St-Gély). After passing town hall
head for Commercial Centre. After roundabout with sculpture,
left at stop sign into entrance)
Near river Near lake Near sea Near beach Forest area
*5 en suite (bth/shr) (2 fmly) Full central heating Open parking*
*available Supervised Outdoor swimming pool Languages*
*spoken: English*
CARDS: Travellers cheques

### ST-GERMAIN-DE-CALBERTE Lozère

**Le Pradel** (Prop: M Jean Nicole Bechard)
*48370*
☎ 466459246 FAX 466459246
(from Florac take N106 (direction of Alès) at Col de Jalcreste
take D984 to La Croix de Bourel then D54 and D13 to Le
Pradel)
Forest area
*3 en suite (shr) (2 fmly) No smoking on premises Full central*
*heating Open parking available Child discount available 6yrs*
*Bicycle rental Languages spoken: English & German*
CARDS: Travellers cheques

### ST-GILLES Gard

**★ ★ Le Cours**
10 av François Griffeuille *30800*
☎ 466873193 FAX 466873183
Situated close to the centre of Saint-Gilles-du Gard, on the
edge of the Camargue, the hotel offers its visitors the
opportunity to experience the charming ambience of a
southern French village. The comfortable bedrooms have
modern facilities, and guests can enjoy regional specialities in
the attractive dining room, or on the terrace under the plane
trees.
In town centre

*Closed 15 Dec-1 Mar*
*33 en suite (bth/shr) (5 fmly) TV in all bedrooms STV Radio in*

rooms Direct dial from all bedrooms Licensed Lift Full central
heating Open parking available Child discount available 2yrs
Open terrace V meals Last d 22.00hrs Languages spoken:
English & Italian
ROOMS: (room only) s 215-325FF; d 250-360FF
**Reductions over 1 night**
MEALS: Continental breakfast 35FF Lunch 60-160FF&alc
Dinner 60-160FF&alc
CARDS: ● ■ ☰ ◉ JCB Travellers cheques

### ST-JEAN-DE-LA-BLAQUIÈRE Hérault

**★ ★ ★ Le Sanglier**
Domaine de Cambourras *34700*
☎ 467447051 FAX 467447233
(from A75 exit 54/56 to St-Jean-de-Blaquière)
Forest area
*Closed 25 Oct-23 Mar*
*10 en suite (bth) (3 fmly) (8 with balcony) TV in all bedrooms*
*Direct dial from all bedrooms Licensed Full central heating*
*Open parking available Covered parking available Supervised*
*Child discount available Outdoor swimming pool Tennis*
*Solarium Boule Open terrace V meals Last d 21.00hrs*
*Languages spoken: English & Spanish*
ROOMS: (room only) d 380-440FF **Reductions over 1 night**
CARDS: ● ☰ Travellers cheques

### ST-MAMERT Gard

**La Mazade** (Prop: Eliette Couston)
12 rue de la Mazade *30730*
☎ 466811756 FAX 466296260
(exit Nîmes Ouest in direction Le Vigau continue 10km turn
right, St Mamert in 4km)
*5 rms (1 bth 3 shr) (2 fmly) No smoking in 2 bedrooms Full*
*central heating Open parking available Supervised Child*
*discount available*
CARDS: Travellers cheques

### STE-ENIMIE Lozère

**★ ★ ★ ★ Hotel Château de la Caze**
La Malène *48210*
☎ 466485101 FAX 466485575
(5km from La Malène towards Ste-Enimie)
Near river Forest area Near motorway
*Closed 15 Nov-1 Apr*
*19 en suite (bth) 6 rooms in annexe (7 fmly) (5 with balcony)*
*TV in all bedrooms STV Direct dial from all bedrooms Mini-*
*bar in 6 bedrooms Licensed Open parking available Covered*
*parking available Supervised Child discount available 12yrs*
*Outdoor swimming pool (heated) Fishing Open terrace Table*
*tennis Canoeing Last d 21.30hrs Languages spoken: English &*
*Dutch*
CARDS: ● ■ ☰ Travellers cheques

### SAUVETERRE Gard

**★ ★ ★ Hostellerie de Varenne**
pl St-Jean *30150*
☎ 466825945 FAX 466828483
Near river Forest area Near motorway
*14 en suite (bth/shr) (3 fmly) (2 with balcony) TV in all*
*bedrooms Radio in rooms Mini-bar in all bedrooms Licensed*
*Full central heating Open parking available Boule Open*
*terrace V meals*
CARDS: ☰ ◉

### SAZE Gard

**★ ★ Auberge la Gelinotte**
N100 *30650*
☎ 490317213 FAX 490269583
(from Avignon towards Nîmes for 12km. From A9 Remoulins towards Avignon for 7km.)
Forest area  Near motorway
*Closed 15 Nov-1 Mar*
*10 en suite (bth/shr)  5 rooms in annexe  (4 fmly)  Direct dial from all bedrooms  Licensed  Full central heating  Open parking available  Child discount available 12yrs  Outdoor swimming pool  Boule  Open terrace  Covered terrace  Volleyball  Table tennis  V meals  Last d 21.00hrs  Languages spoken: English*
CARDS: ● ▆ Travellers cheques

### SIGEAN Aude

**★ ★ ★ Château de Villefalse**
Le Lac *11130*
☎ 468485429 FAX 468483437
(from A9 exit at Sigean, through Péage, then left to Portel des Corbières, then on to Gué - Villefalse on left)
Near river  Near lake  Near sea  Near beach  Forest area  Near motorway
*25 en suite (bth)  10 rooms in annexe  TV in all bedrooms  STV  Direct dial from all bedrooms  Mini-bar in 15 bedrooms  Licensed  Lift  Full central heating  Air conditioning in bedrooms  Open parking available  Child discount available  Indoor swimming pool (heated)  Outdoor swimming pool  Tennis  Fishing  Sauna  Solarium  Gym  Pool table  Jacuzzi/spa  Open terrace  Covered terrace  V meals  Languages spoken: English & Spanish*
CARDS: ● ▆ ▆ ▣ Travellers cheques

### SOMMIÈRES Gard

**★ ★ ★ Auberge du Pont Romain**
2 rue Emile Jamais *30250*
☎ 466800058 FAX 466803152
(access via A9 exit Lunel)
Near river  Forest area  Near motorway
*Closed 15 Jan-15 Mar & Nov*
*19 rms (14 bth 4 shr)  3 rooms in annexe  (2 fmly)  (1 with balcony)  Direct dial from all bedrooms  Licensed  Lift  Full central heating  Open parking available  Child discount available  Outdoor swimming pool (heated)  Bicycle rental  Open terrace  Covered terrace  V meals  Last d 21.30hrs  Languages spoken: English & Spanish*
CARDS: ● ▆ ▆ ▣ Travellers cheques

**Hotel de l'Orange** (Prop: Phillippe de Frémont)
7 rue des Beaumes, chemin du Château Fort *30250*
☎ 466777994 FAX 466804487
17th-century house in local style at the heart of Sommiers. Enjoy the view from the terraces and gardens, the warm hospitable owners provide a friendly welcome.
Near river  Near sea  Near beach
*6 en suite (bth/shr)  (1 with balcony)  TV in all bedrooms  Full central heating  Open parking available  Outdoor swimming pool  Bicycle rental  Languages spoken: English*
ROOMS: s 340-400FF; d 380-500FF
**✱ Reductions over 1 night**
MEALS: Dinner 120FF✱
CARDS: ▆

*Hotel de l'Orange*

### TORNAC Gard

**★ ★ ★ Démeures du Ranquet**
rte de St-Hippolyte du Fort *30140*
☎ 466775163 FAX 466775562
(access via D982)
Forest area
*Closed Nov-14 Mar*
*10 en suite (bth/shr)  (10 with balcony)  No smoking in 2 bedrooms  TV in all bedrooms  STV  Radio in rooms  Direct dial from all bedrooms  Mini-bar in all bedrooms  Room-safe  Licensed  Air conditioning in bedrooms  Open parking available  Supervised  Child discount available 10yrs  Outdoor swimming pool  Boule  Bicycle rental  Open terrace  Golf practice hole  V meals  Last d 21.30hrs  Languages spoken: English & Spanish*
ROOMS: (room only) s 560-720FF; d 850-950FF
MEALS: Continental breakfast 80FF  Lunch 200-380FF&alc  Dinner 200-380FF&alc
CARDS: ● ▆ ▣ JCB Travellers cheques

### UZÈS Gard

**★ ★ Hotel D'Entraigues**
8 rue de la Colodé *30700*
☎ 466223268 FAX 466225701
Near river  Forest area  In town centre  Near motorway
*35 en suite (bth)  (9 fmly)  TV in all bedrooms  Direct dial from all bedrooms  Licensed  Lift  Full central heating  Air conditioning in bedrooms  Open parking available  Covered parking available (charged)  Supervised  Child discount available 12yrs  Outdoor swimming pool  Solarium  Open terrace  V meals  Last d 22.00hrs  Languages spoken: English & German*
CARDS: ● ▆ ▆ ▣

**★ ★ ★ Hotel Marie D'Agoult**
Château d'Arpaillargues *30700*
☎ 466221448 FAX 466225610
(4km from Uzès towards Anduze)
Far from the crowded beaches of the south, this hotel provides a peaceful stopping place three miles from the town of Uzès. Once the private residence of Marie d'Agoult - a talented writer who eloped with the composer Franz Liszt - it conceals behind its massive walls the charming atmosphere of a Provençale mansion. Bedrooms, decorated with flair and a good eye for detail, have excellent en suite facilities. The dining-rooms, with exposed brickwork and vaulted ceilings, serve outstanding cuisine.
*Closed early Nov-end Mar*

**Hotel Marie d'Agoult**

28 en suite (bth) (4 fmly) (8 with balcony) TV in all bedrooms
Direct dial from all bedrooms Mini-bar in 26 bedrooms Room-
safe Full central heating Air conditioning in bedrooms Open
parking available Outdoor swimming pool Tennis Open
terrace table tennis Last d 21.30hrs Languages spoken:
English & Spanish
ROOMS: (room only) d 500-1200FF
MEALS: Full breakfast 65FF Lunch fr 160FF&alc Dinner fr
230FF&alc
CARDS: ●● ■■ ⚍ ⓓ Travellers cheques

### VAILHAUQUES Hérault

**Mas de la Coste** (Prop: M & Mme Bottinelli-Faidherbe)
114 Chemin de la Fontaine 34570
☎ 467844126
Near river Near sea Forest area Near motorway
4 en suite (shr) (3 fmly) (2 with balcony) No smoking in 2
bedrooms TV available Full central heating Open parking
available Supervised Child discount available 10yrs
CARDS: Travellers cheques

### VERGÈZE Gard

**★ ★ La Passiflore**
1 rue Neuve 30310
☎ 466350000 FAX 466350921
(exit A9 at Gallargues, then take N113 towards Nîmes. At first
traffic lights in Codognan turn left and follow signs to Vergèze
centre ville.)
Forest area In town centre Near motorway
RS Restaurant closed Dec-Jan
11 rms (2 bth 8 shr) (1 fmly) (1 with balcony) Direct dial from
all bedrooms Licensed Full central heating Air conditioning in
bedrooms Open parking available Supervised Child discount
available 7yrs Open terrace Last d 21.30hrs Languages
spoken: English
CARDS: ●● ■■ ⚍ Travellers cheques

### VILLENEUVE-LÈS-AVIGNON Gard

**★ ★ Hotel de L'Atelier**
5 rue de la Foire 30400
☎ 490250184 FAX 490258006
(2km W of Avignon)
Near river In town centre Near motorway
Closed beg Nov-beg Dec
19 en suite (bth/shr) (3 fmly) TV in 17 bedrooms Direct dial
from all bedrooms Licensed Night porter Full central heating

Covered parking available (charged) Supervised Solarium
Open terrace Languages spoken: English
CARDS: ●● ■■ ⚍ ⓓ JCB Travellers cheques

**★ ★ Résidence les Cédres**
39 av Pasteur Bellevue 30400
☎ 490254392 FAX 490251466
(from Avignon town centre follow directions for Bellevue-les-
Angles after le Pont Dalladier)
Closed 16 Nov-15 Mar
21 en suite (bth/shr) (5 fmly) TV in all bedrooms STV Direct
dial from all bedrooms Mini-bar in all bedrooms Licensed Full
central heating Open parking available Supervised Child
discount available 2yrs Outdoor swimming pool Boule Open
terrace Last d 21.30hrs Languages spoken: English & German
CARDS: ●● ⚍ Travellers cheques

### VILLENEUVE-LÈS-BÉZIERS Hérault

**Bed & Breakfast** (Prop: Andrew & Jennifer-Jane Viner)
7 rue de la Fontaine 34420
☎ 467398715 FAX 467398715
(from A6 take exit Béziers Est. At toll booth keep left, then left
at traffic lights. Continue to roundabout, then 1st exit signed
Villeneuve. Follow signs to village centre and house opposite
town hall)

Along a quiet road in Villeneuve, near the Canal du Midi,
guests will find this 15th-century building which has been
lovingly restored by the Viner family, with the spacious rooms
having many authentic details. A staircase in the tower dates
back to the Middle Ages. Dinner available.
Near river In town centre Near motorway
4 en suite (bth/shr) (4 fmly) (2 with balcony) Full central
heating V meals Languages spoken: English
ROOMS: d 270FF **Reductions over 1 night**
MEALS: Dinner 90FF
CARDS: ●● ⚍

### VILLETELLE Hérault

**Bed & Breakfast** (Prop: Daniel & Simone Barlaguet)
343 Chemin des Combes Noires 34400
☎ 467868700 FAX 467868700
Near river Near sea
6 en suite (bth/shr) (6 with balcony) TV available Full central
heating Open parking available Covered parking available
Child discount available Outdoor swimming pool Tennis Boule
Table tennis Last d 20.00hrs Languages spoken: English
CARDS: Travellers cheques

## VINASSAN Aude

**★ ★ Aude Hotel**
Aire Narbonne Vimmattan Nord *11110*
☎ 468452500 FAX 468452520
Located in a peaceful poplar grove near the rest area of the Narbonne-Vinassan motorway(A9), the hotel is not far away from the beaches. The sound-proofed bedrooms have modern amenities and provide a peaceful night's sleep. From an early hour a delicious breakfast is served in a spacious day room, whilst dinner consists of regional specialities accompanied by a selection of the finest vintages.

Near motorway
*59 en suite (bth/shr) (9 fmly) TV in 30 bedrooms STV Direct dial from 30 bedrooms Licensed Lift Night porter Full central heating Air conditioning in bedrooms Open parking available Covered parking available (charged) Supervised Open terrace Last d 22.00hrs Languages spoken: English, German & Spanish*
ROOMS: (room only) s 270-290FF; d 295-360FF
MEALS: Full breakfast 39FF Dinner 75-130FF&alc
CARDS: 💳 🏧 💳 💳 Travellers cheques

## EVENTS AND FESTIVALS:

**Jan-Mar**    Limoux Traditional Carnival (every weekend)

**Feb**    Arles-sur-Tech Bear Festival; Nîmes Feria
**Mar**    Cap d'Agde Cerfvolantissimo;
**Apr**    Gruissan Easter Monday Pilgrimage to Seamens'Cemetery; La Canourgue Bachelors' Festival; Nîmes Jazz Festival;
**Jun**    Nîmes Whit Monday Feria; Uzès Garlic Fair; Amélie-les-Bains Mule Driver Festival; Montpellier Dance Festival;
**July**    Céret Feria; St Ambroix Traditional Volo Biou Festival (parade, theatre); Beaucaire Ste Madeleine's Fair(medieval procession); Cap d'Agde Sea Festival; Carcassonne Festival; Le Grau-du-Roi/Port-Camargue Jazz Festival; Ouveillan Fontcalvy Festival (music, street theatre); Béziers Classical Music Festival; Nîmes Summer Concerts
**Aug**    Béziers Feria; Aigues-Mortes St Louis Festival (historical parade, street entertainment); Amélie-les-Bains Folklore Festival; Nîmes Summer Concerts
**Sep**    Cap d'Agde Catamaran Sailing Trophy; Arles sur-Tech Medieval Festival; Mialet Protestant gathering at Mas Soubeyran (1st Sun); Nîmes Grape Harvest Feria (5 days of celebration)
**Nov**    Garons Salon des Santons (Christmas ornament fair)

### Beaches & Seaside Resorts
The Languedoc-Roussillon coast is a place of contrast with over 125 miles of sandy beaches, interspersed with rocky outcrops. The lack of tides or currents and the largest concentration of Blue Flag beaches in France makes this an ideal holiday destination and also a firm favourite amongst the yachting fraternity, with over 20,000 moorings offered in the 25 marinas along the coast. Watersports and game fishing add to the universal appeal of this delightful area.

### Blue Flag Beaches
Twenty-one beaches conform to the European Directive on the purity of the seawater and the cleanliness of the beaches: Port Camargue, Le Grau du Roi, La Grande Motte, Carnon, Sete, Meze, Le Cap d'Agde, Vias, Portiragnes, Valras-Plage, Serignan, Vendres, Les Cabanes de Fleury, Narbonne Plage, Gruissan, Port la Nouvelle, Port Leucate, Le Barcares, Torreilles, Ste Marie la Mer, Canet en Roussillon, St Cyprien, Argeles sur Mer, Collioure, Port Vendres, Banyuls sur Mer, Cerbere.

### Watersports & Game Fishing
Sailing, windsurfing, water-skiing and diving opportunities abound, with numerous schools in the lively coastal resorts offering to teach beginners the basics or help to improve the skills of the more experienced. You can try your hand at game fishing all the year round, with tuna, swordfish, blue and fox shark as the most prized catches. Recent records include a 807lbs tuna fish and a 937lbs fox shark.

### Seaside Markets
Le Grau du Roi: daily quayside fish market; Carnon: local produce - Tue, Thu, Sat ams, Flea market - Wed (Summer)

### The home of Denim
Everyone knows that jeans are made of denim but few are aware that the word comes from 'de Nîmes', meaning 'from Nîmes'. It was a Mr Levi, a Bavarian emigré tailor living in San Francisco, who was the first to use this ultra-strong fabric when he made trousers for gold prospectors, strengthening the pockets with rivets to stop them splitting under the weight of the gold.

### Historic Sites
Littered with fascinating heritage sites, France bears the seal of the medieval Crusades. At the crest of a slope or on the bend of a path, the 'vertiginous citadels' suddenly loom up in front of you - great abbeys and collegiates nestling in the heart of the hills. Carcassonne, the largest medieval city in Europe, looks as if it belongs on a Hollywood film set. Many of these magnificent sites are brought to life each year with sound and light shows, colourful festivals and traditional carnivals.

### Coastal Conservation
Sandy beaches, dunes, cliffs, and garrigues (moorland) are all protected under various planning regulations. The land, controlled by the Conservation Board, is open to the public and access points are indicated by signs bearing the Board's logo - the thistle of the dunes, but to preserve the quality of these areas, camping, caravanning, cars, and motorcross are prohibited.

# Côte d'Azur

The towns of Cannes and Nice have long been associated with all things chic and exclusive, wonderful for shopping (or at least having a look) and experiencing the rich heritage of 19th and 20th-century art. The region has wall-to-wall arts festivals, trade fairs and sports events, many of international repute. The pace of life is rather more gentle in the villages of the Alpes-Maritimes. Here you can take a leisurely drive through hills and forests, past Roman churches and Gothic palaces, with the scent of lavender, rosemary and wild thyme in the air.

## ESSENTIAL FACTS

| | |
|---|---|
| DÉPARTEMENTS: | Alpes-Maritimes |
| PRINCIPAL TOWNS | Antibes, Cannes, Grasse, Nice |
| PLACES TO VISIT: | Antibes: old town and ramparts, Le Cap d'Antibes, Picasso Museum. Cannes: shopping, Boulevard la Croisette, Palais des Festivals, Suquet Quarter. Grasse: perfume museum & tours at Molinard, Fragonard or Galimard Perfumeries. Nice:old town, Promenade des Anglais, Matisse Musuem. |
| REGIONAL TOURIST OFFICE | 55 Promenade des Anglais BP 1602 06011 Nice Tel 04 93 37 78 78  Fax 04 93 86 01 06 Web site: http://www.crt-riviera.fr E-mail: crt06@nicematin.fr |
| LOCAL GASTRONOMIC DELIGHTS | Bouillabaisse, a fish stew. Aïoli, garlic-flavoured mayonnaise. Calissons, small diamond-shaped almond-paste biscuits. Rascasse, a spiny fish. Salade Niçoise, tuna fish salad. Pissaladière, onion tart; Tapénade, olive paste. Pistou, thick vegetable soup with basil & garlic. Bourride, fish soup. Anchoïade, an anchovy mixture. Socca, a hot, crusty dish of chick-peas & olive oil. |
| DRINKS | Pastis, aniseed-flavoured aperitif often diluted with water. Aperitif wines: Muscat des Beaume de Venise, Rasteau. Local spirits: Vieux Marc, Elixir du Révérend Père Gaucher, Eau de vie de Poire, Genepy des Alpes. |
| LOCAL CRAFTS WHAT TO BUY | Grasse: soaps & perfume. Vallauris: pottery. Biot: glassware. Local produce: honey, jams, lavender, herbs, olive oil, spiced & flavoured oils, candied fruits. |

## D'ANGERS (NEAR CANNES) Alpes-Maritimes

### ★ ★ ★ ★ Hotel Cristal
13 Rond Point Duboys d'Angers *06400*
☎ 493394545 FAX 493386466
(from A8, follow signs for town centre, then for 'Croisette' and 'Rond Point Duboys d'Angres)
Near sea  Near beach  In town centre
*Closed 20 Nov-28 Dec*
*51 en suite (bth)  No smoking in 12 bedrooms  TV in all bedrooms  Direct dial from all bedrooms  Mini-bar in all bedrooms  Room-safe  Licensed  Lift  Night porter  Full central heating  Air conditioning in bedrooms  Covered parking available (charged)  Child discount available 12yrs  Solarium Open terrace  Last d 22.00hrs  Languages spoken: English, German, Italian & Spanish*
ROOMS: (room only) s 830-1925FF;  d 990-2145FF
**Reductions over 1 night**
MEALS:  Continental breakfast 72FF  Lunch 150FF&alc Dinner 150FF&alc
CARDS: ● ■ ▭ ▣ JCB Travellers cheques

## ANTIBES Alpes-Maritimes

### *La Bastide du Bosquet* (Prop: C & S Aussel)
14 chemin des Sables *06160*
☎ 493673229 FAX 493673229
(from town centre follow signs for Le Cap; at L'Ilet crossroads follow signs for Juan-Les-Pins Direct. No 14 is at top of chemin des Sables)
Near sea  Near beach  Forest area  Near motorway
*Closed Nov*
*3 en suite (bth/shr)  (1 fmly)  Full central heating  Open parking available  Child discount available 3yrs  Languages spoken: English & Finnish*
CARDS: Travellers cheques

### ★ ★ Climat de France
2317 chemin de St-Claude *06600*
☎ 493748001 Cen Res 164460123 FAX 493952248
(800m from de Antibes Juan-les-Pins motorway exit in the new activity area of Nova Antipolis)
Near sea  Near beach  In town centre  Near motorway
*46 en suite (bth/shr)  TV in all bedrooms  STV  Direct dial from all bedrooms  Licensed  Lift  Full central heating  Air conditioning in bedrooms  Open parking available  Child discount available 13yrs  Outdoor swimming pool  Solarium Open terrace  Covered terrace  Last d 22.00hrs  Languages spoken: English & Greek*
CARDS: ● ■ ▭ ▣ Travellers cheques

### ★ ★ Le Ponteil
11 Impasse Jean Mensier *06600*
☎ 493346792 FAX 493344947
Near sea  Near beach  In town centre
*Closed mid Nov-late Dec & mid Jan-early Feb RS Jun-Sep (half board only)*
*15 rms (3 bth 7 shr)  (1 fmly)  (1 with balcony)  TV in 10 bedrooms  Direct dial from all bedrooms  Room-safe  Licensed Full central heating  Open parking available  Supervised Child discount available 2-7yrs  Open terrace  Languages spoken: English, German & Italian*
CARDS: ● ■ ▭ Travellers cheques

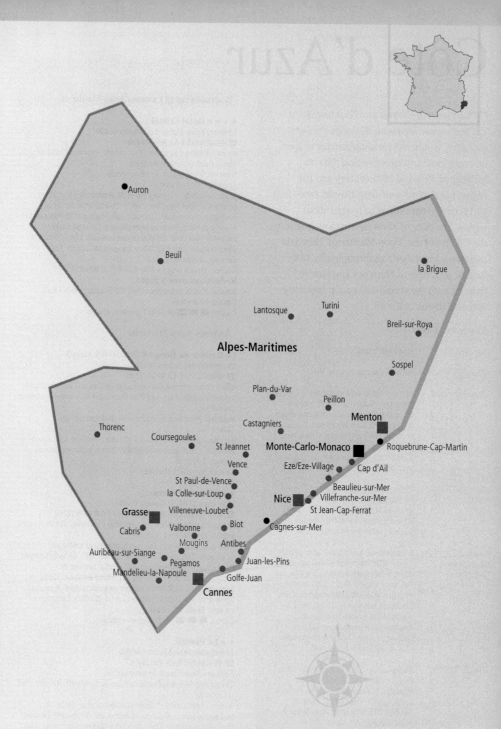

Auron

Beuil

la Brigue

Lantosque

Turini

Breil-sur-Roya

**Alpes-Maritimes**

Sospel

Plan-du-Var

Peillon

Thorenc

Castagniers

Menton

Coursegoules

Roquebrune-Cap-Martin

St Jeannet

Monte-Carlo-Monaco

Vence

Eze/Eze-Village

Cap d'Ail

St Paul-de-Vence

Beaulieu-sur-Mer

la Colle-sur-Loup

Villefranche-sur-Mer

Nice

Grasse

Villeneuve-Loubet

St Jean-Cap-Ferrat

Cabris

Valbonne

Biot

Cagnes-sur-Mer

Auribeau-sur-Siange

Mougins

Antibes

Pegamos

Juan-les-Pins

Mandelieu-la-Napoule

Golfe-Juan

Cannes

★ ★ ★ ★ **Auberge de la Vignette Haute**
370 rte du Village *06810*
☎ 493422001 FAX 493423116
(off D109)
Situated just ten minutes from Cannes and Grasse, and an hour from St Tropez and Monaco, this establishemnt can be found on a rocky peak amidst peaceful and verdant countryside. It offers luxurious, individually appointed bedrooms where refined comfort is complemented by numerous pieces of antique furniture, reminiscent of by-gone days. There is a private museum, Le Curiosa, and the gastronomic restaurant is lit only by oil lamps and has a view of the Bergerie and its animals. There are lots of golf courses in the area.
Near river Near beach Forest area

*15 en suite (bth/shr) (2 fmly) (13 with balcony) TV in all bedrooms STV Direct dial from all bedrooms Mini-bar in all bedrooms Room-safe Licensed Full central heating Air conditioning in bedrooms Open parking available Covered parking available (charged) Child discount available 12yrs Outdoor swimming pool Fishing Boule Jacuzzi/spa Bicycle rental Open terrace V meals Last d 23.00hrs Languages spoken: English & Italian*
ROOMS: (room only) d 1300-1830FF
MEALS: Continental breakfast 90FF Lunch 190-330FFalc Dinner 390-520FFalc
CARDS: 💳 ■ 💳 Travellers cheques

★ ★ ★ ★ **Le Metropole** (Relais et Châteaux)
15 bd Maréchal Leclerc *06130*
☎ 493010008 FAX 493011851
(From A8 exit 50 or 58 follow signs for 'Basse Corniche')
This Italian palatial-style hotel, with a delightful flower garden and terrace, occupies a splendid beach-front position with breathtaking views over the Mediterranean. The smart bedrooms, with good quality furniture and matching fabrics, offer maximum comfort. The restaurant has earned a good reputation for its outstanding cuisine, where meat specialities and fresh seafood, combined with seasonal ingredients, feature strongly on the menu.
Near sea Near beach In town centre
*Closed 20 Dec-20 Oct*
*35 en suite (bth/shr) (20 with balcony) TV in all bedrooms STV Direct dial from all bedrooms Mini-bar in all bedrooms Room-safe Licensed Lift Night porter Full central heating Air conditioning in bedrooms Open parking available Supervised*

*Le Metropole*
*Child discount available 15yrs Outdoor swimming pool (heated) Solarium Open terrace Covered terrace Last d 21.30hrs Languages spoken: English German & Italian*
ROOMS: (room only) s 1000-2900FF; d 1300-3200FF
**Special breaks**
MEALS: Continental breakfast 130FF Lunch 320-530FF&alc Dinner 430-530FF&alc
CARDS: 💳 ■ 💳 💳 JCB Travellers cheques

★ ★ **L'Escapade**
*06470*
☎ 493023127
Forest area
*Closed 15 Nov-19 Dec*
*11 rms (9 bth/shr) (2 fmly) (6 with balcony) TV in all bedrooms STV Direct dial from all bedrooms Mini-bar in all bedrooms Licensed Full central heating Child discount available 10yrs Boule Bicycle rental Open terrace Last d 21.30hrs Languages spoken: English & Italian*
CARDS: Travellers cheques

★ ★ ★ **Hotel le Domaine du Jas**
625 rte de la Mer *06410*
☎ 493655050 FAX 296650201
Near sea Forest area Near motorway
*Closed Jan-Feb*
*17 en suite (bth/shr) (3 fmly) (17 with balcony) TV in all bedrooms Direct dial from all bedrooms Night porter Full central heating Open parking available Covered parking available Supervised Outdoor swimming pool Solarium Open terrace Covered terrace Languages spoken: English, Italian & Spanish*
CARDS: 💳 ■ 💳 Travellers cheques

★ ★ **Castel du Roy**
rte de Tende *06540*
☎ 493044366 FAX 493049183
(approach via A8 and D2204 through Sospel)
Near river Near lake Forest area
*Closed 31 Oct-1 Mar*
*19 en suite (bth/shr) (1 fmly) TV in all bedrooms Direct dial from all bedrooms Mini-bar in all bedrooms Licensed Full central heating Open parking available Supervised Child discount available 3yrs Outdoor swimming pool (heated)*
*contd.*

Fishing Boule Bicycle rental Open terrace Badminton Last d 21.00hrs Languages spoken: English
ROOMS: (room only) s 260-325FF; d 320-440FF
MEALS: Continental breakfast 40FF Lunch 125-225FF&alc Dinner 125-225FF&alc
CARDS: ●● ■■ ⅓ Travellers cheques

### ★★ Le Roya
pl Biancheri 06540
☎ 493044810 FAX 493049270
Near river Near lake Forest area In town centre
18 en suite (bth/shr) (5 fmly) (3 with balcony) TV in 10 bedrooms STV Radio in rooms Direct dial from 10 bedrooms Mini-bar in 10 bedrooms Licensed Full central heating Open parking available Covered parking available (charged) Supervised Child discount available Open terrace V meals Last d 22.30hrs Languages spoken: Italian
ROOMS: (room only) s 250-300FF; d 300FF ✱
MEALS: Continental breakfast 35FF Lunch 98FF&alc Dinner 98FF&alc
CARDS: ●● ⅓ Travellers cheques

**BRIGUE, LA** Alpes-Maritimes

### ★★ Le Mirval
06430
☎ 493046371 FAX 493047981
Near river Forest area
Closed 3 Nov-Mar
18 en suite (bth/shr) (6 fmly) (4 with balcony) TV in all bedrooms Direct dial from all bedrooms Licensed Full central heating Open parking available Child discount available 12yrs Solarium Boule Open terrace Last d 20.30hrs Languages spoken: Italian
CARDS: ●● ■■ ⅓ Travellers cheques

**CABRIS** Alpes-Maritimes

**Bed & Breakfast** (Prop: Mme Jocelyne Faraut)
14 rue de l'Agachon 06530
☎ 493605236
(Exit Les Adrêts from the motorway in the direction of Peymeinade/Cabris)
Near river Near lake Near sea Near beach Forest area Near motorway
Closed Nov-Mar
5 en suite (bth/shr) (2 fmly) No smoking on premises Child discount available Languages spoken: English & Spanish

**CANNES** Alpes-Maritimes

### ★★★★ Cannes Palace Hotel (Best Western)
14 av de Madrid 06400
☎ 493434445 FAX 493434130
Near sea Near beach In town centre Near motorway
Closed 21 Nov-19 Dec
101 en suite (bth/shr) 60 rooms in annexe (6 fmly) (41 with balcony) No smoking in 5 bedrooms TV in all bedrooms STV Radio in rooms Direct dial from all bedrooms Mini-bar in all bedrooms Room-safe Licensed Full central heating Air conditioning in bedrooms Open parking available (charged) Covered parking available (charged) Supervised Child discount available 12yrs Outdoor swimming pool (heated) Tennis Sauna Gym Bicycle rental Open terrace Fitness Studio V meals Last d 21.45hrs Languages spoken: English, Arabic, Dutch, German & Spanish

ROOMS: (room only) s 760-940FF; d 860-1150FF
**Reductions over 1 night**
MEALS: Continental breakfast 75FF Lunch 145FF&alc Dinner 145FF&alc
CARDS: ●● ■■ ⅓ ⓓ Travellers cheques

### Hotel Cezanne
40 bd d'Alsace 06400
☎ 493385070 FAX 493382044
((From motorway follow Cannes centre, straight onto Boulevard Carnot & at final X-rds, go left)
Near sea Near beach In town centre Near motorway
29 en suite (bth) (6 with balcony) TV in all bedrooms STV Direct dial from all bedrooms Licensed Lift Night porter Full central heating Air conditioning in bedrooms Open parking available Covered parking available Child discount available 12yrs Open terrace Covered terrace Languages spoken: Englsih Italian Russian & Spanish
CARDS: ●● ■■ ⅓ ⓓ Travellers cheques

### ★★★★ Croisette Beach Hotel
13 rue du Canada 06400
☎ 492188800 FAX 493683538
(A8 exit Cannes centre, take direction city centre/centre croisette, behind the Carlton hotel)
Near beach In town centre
Closed 21 Nov-25 Dec
94 en suite (bth/shr) (10 fmly) (55 with balcony) No smoking in 13 bedrooms TV in all bedrooms STV Direct dial from all bedrooms Mini-bar in all bedrooms Room-safe Licensed Lift Night porter Full central heating Air conditioning in bedrooms Covered parking available (charged) Supervised Child discount available 16yrs Outdoor swimming pool (heated) Sauna Solarium Covered terrace Languages spoken: English, German, Italian & Spanish
CARDS: ●● ■■ ⅓ ⓓ Travellers cheques

### Hotel Embassy
6 rue de Bone 06400
☎ 493387902 FAX 493990798
(between the Voie Rapide and rue d'Antibes)
Near sea Near beach In town centre Near motorway
60 en suite (bth/shr) (3 fmly) TV in all bedrooms STV Radio in rooms Direct dial from all bedrooms Mini-bar in all bedrooms Room-safe Licensed Lift Night porter Full central heating Air conditioning in bedrooms Open parking available (charged) Covered parking available (charged) Supervised Child discount available Solarium Pool table Jacuzzi/spa Open terrace Wkly live entertainment Last d 22.00hrs Languages spoken: English, Dutch, German & Italian
CARDS: ●● ■■ ⅓ ⓓ Travellers cheques

### ★★★ Hotel de l'Olivier
5 rue des Tambourinaires 06400
☎ 493395328 FAX 493395585
(NE of junction of Voie Rapide with avenue Dr-Picaud)
Near sea In town centre Near motorway
24 en suite (bth/shr) (6 with balcony) TV in all bedrooms Direct dial from all bedrooms Licensed Night porter Full central heating Air conditioning in bedrooms Open parking available (charged) Outdoor swimming pool Languages spoken: English & German
ROOMS: (room only) s 430-550FF; d 490-740FF
CARDS: ●● ■■ ⅓ ⓓ JCB Travellers cheques

★ ★ ★ **Hotel de Paris**
34 bd d'Alsace *06400*
☎ 493383089 FAX 493390461
Near sea In town centre
*Closed 15 Nov-26 Dec*
*50 en suite (bth/shr) (2 fmly) (15 with balcony) TV in all*
*bedrooms STV Radio in rooms Direct dial from all bedrooms*
*Room-safe Licensed Lift Night porter Full central heating Air*
*conditioning in bedrooms Open parking available (charged)*
*Covered parking available (charged) Supervised Child*
*discount available 12yrs Outdoor swimming pool Golf*
*Solarium Jacuzzi/spa Open terrace Languages spoken:*
*English, German & Italian*
ROOMS: (room only) s 360-670FF; d 470-750FF
CARDS: ●● ■■ ■■ 🔟 JCB Travellers cheques

★ ★ ★ **Primotel Canberra**
120 rue d'Antibes *06400*
☎ 493382070 FAX 492980347
Near sea Near beach In town centre Near motorway
*44 en suite (bth/shr) (6 fmly) (6 with balcony) TV in all*
*bedrooms STV Direct dial from all bedrooms Mini-bar in all*
*bedrooms Room-safe Licensed Lift Night porter Full central*
*heating Air conditioning in bedrooms Open parking available*
*(charged) No children Child discount available 12yrs*
*Languages spoken: English, German & Italian*
CARDS: ●● ■■ ■■ 🔟 Travellers cheques

**CAP-D'AIL** Alpes-Maritimes

★ ★ **La Cigogne**
rte de la Plage Mala *06320*
☎ 493782960 FAX 493418662
(approach from town centre via N98)
Near sea Near beach Near motorway
*Closed 15 Jan-15 Mar*
*15 rms (7 bth 7 shr) (3 fmly) TV in 10 bedrooms STV Direct*
*dial from all bedrooms Licensed Full central heating Open*
*parking available No children 4yrs Child discount available*
*10yrs V meals Last d 21.00hrs Languages spoken: English,*
*German & Italian*
ROOMS: s 300-350FF; d 400-450FF
MEALS: Continental breakfast 40FF Lunch 100-150FF
Dinner 100-150FF
CARDS: ●● ■■

**CASTAGNIERS** Alpes-Maritimes

★ ★ **Servotel**
1976 rte de Grenoble *06670*
☎ 493082200 FAX 493290366
(from A8 exit 'Nice St-Isidore' follow N202 towards Digne for
8km)
Near river Near motorway
*44 rms (38 bth/shr) 31 rooms in annexe (2 fmly) (44 with*
*balcony) No smoking in 5 bedrooms TV in all bedrooms STV*
*Direct dial from all bedrooms Licensed Lift Full central*
*heating Open parking available Covered parking available*
*Supervised Child discount available Outdoor swimming pool*
*Tennis Riding Sauna Solarium Gym Boule Jacuzzi/spa Open*
*terrace Covered terrace Beauty Salon V meals Last d 21.30hrs*
*Languages spoken: English, Germna & Italian*
CARDS: ●● ■■ ■■ Travellers cheques

**COURSECOULES** Alpes-Maritimes

★ ★ **L'Escaou**
*06140*
☎ 493591128 FAX 493591370
(take A48, exit 48 direction Cagnes-sur-Mer/Vence/Col-de-
Vence, then Coursegoules)
Near river Forest area
*12 en suite (bth) (2 fmly) TV in all bedrooms Direct dial from*
*all bedrooms Licensed Lift Full central heating Child discount*
*available 10yrs Boule Open terrace V meals Last d 20.30hrs*
*Languages spoken: English & Italian*
ROOMS: s 245FF; d 390FF
MEALS: Full breakfast 40FF Lunch 99-165FF&alc Dinner
99-165FF&alc
CARDS: ●● ■■ Travellers cheques

**EZE** Alpes-Maritimes

★ ★ ★ ★ **Château Eza**
rue de la Pise *06360*
☎ 493411224 FAX 493411664
(look sign A8 Monaco/Italy, leave A8 at exit 57 La Turbie (after
Nice & Monaco), arriving in Turbie keep right Eze-Le Col, 1km
further take left in direction Eze village)

An attractive building, once the private residence of European
royalty throughout this century, that commands stunning
views over the Côte d'Azur and the Mediterranean from the
restaurant and terrace. All the guest rooms are individually
appointed and offer elegant accommodation combined with
modern amenities. The cuisine encompasses an outstanding
repertoire of dishes carefully prepared with regional
ingredients, herbs and spices.
Near sea Near beach Forest area Near motorway
*Closed 2 Nov-Mar*
*10 en suite (bth/shr) (2 fmly) (7 with balcony) TV in all*
*bedrooms STV Radio in rooms Direct dial from all bedrooms*
*Room-safe Licensed Night porter Full central heating Air*
*conditioning in bedrooms Open parking available Supervised*
*Open terrace Covered terrace V meals Last d 22.30hrs*
*Languages spoken: English, German & Italian*
ROOMS: s 2000-4000FF; d 2000-4000FF
MEALS: Full breakfast 120FF Continental breakfast 80FF
Lunch fr 250FF&alc Dinner 390-550FF&alc
CARDS: ●● ■■ ■■ 🔟 JCB Travellers cheques

## EZE-VILLAGE Alpes-Maritimes

### ★★ L'Hermitage du Col d'Eze
*06360*
☎ 493410068 FAX 493412405
*Forest area*

*Closed Dec-Jan*
*14 en suite (bth/shr) (3 fmly) (2 with balcony) TV in all bedrooms STV Direct dial from all bedrooms Licensed Full central heating Open parking available Outdoor swimming pool Solarium Boule Open terrace Last d 21.00hrs Languages spoken: English & Italian*
ROOMS: (room only) s 220-350FF; d 220-350FF **✱**
CARDS: 💳 💳 💳 Travellers cheques

## GOLFE-JUAN Alpes-Maritimes

### ★★★ *Beau Soleil*
Impasse Beau Soleil *06220*
☎ 493636363 FAX 493630289
*Near sea In town centre Near motorway*
*Closed 15 Oct-24 Mar*
*30 en suite (bth/shr) (2 fmly) (10 with balcony) TV in all bedrooms STV Direct dial from all bedrooms Room-safe Licensed Lift Night porter Full central heating Air conditioning in bedrooms Open parking available Covered parking available Child discount available 12yrs Outdoor swimming pool Tennis Boule Open terrace Covered terrace Last d 21.00hrs Languages spoken: English*
CARDS: 💳 💳 💳 Travellers cheques

### ★★ *Hotel de Crijansy*
av Juliette Adam *06220*
☎ 493638444 FAX 493634204
*Near sea Near motorway*
*20 en suite (bth/shr) (13 with balcony) TV available Child discount available Boule Open terrace Last d 21.00hrs Languages spoken: English*
CARDS: 💳 Travellers cheques

## GRASSE Alpes-Maritimes

### ★★★ *Hotel des Parfums*
bd Eugene Charabot *06130*
☎ 493361010 FAX 493363548
*In town centre*
*71 en suite (bth/shr) (9 fmly) (60 with balcony) TV in all bedrooms STV Direct dial from all bedrooms Mini-bar in all bedrooms Licensed Lift Night porter Full central heating Air conditioning in bedrooms Open parking available Supervised*

*Child discount available 12yrs Outdoor swimming pool Sauna Jacuzzi/spa Open terrace Last d 22.00hrs Languages spoken: English, German & Italian*

### La Rivolte (Prop: Mr P Usborne)
chemin des Lierres *06130*
☎ 493368158 FAX 493368729
(Take N85 at bus station go towards Nice via Ave Thiers. After 300m take 1st left, then immediately right, entrance gate is 150m up the hill, follow private road for further 100m)

Charming 19th-century mansion set in two acres of gardens in the heart of the perfume country. All rooms have stunning views of the old town of Grasse, as well as the coast through the huge palm trees which adorn the sunny terrace.
*In town centre Near motorway*
*7 rms (6 bth/shr) (1 fmly) (2 with balcony) Room-safe Full central heating 22828 open parking spaces Outdoor swimming pool Boule Bicycle rental Table tennis Languages spoken: English & Spanish*
ROOMS: d 350-700FF **✱ Special breaks**
CARDS: 💳 💳 💳 Travellers cheques

## JUAN-LES-PINS Alpes-Maritimes

### Bed & Breakfast (Prop: Mme Christine Camia)
7 chemin du Parc Saramartel, Villa "Lou Mazet" *06160*
☎ 493613884 FAX 493613884
(A8, exit 44 Antibes, follow city centre, then follow the sign "Cap d'Antibes Direct" BD Ducap, Chem Ducrouton on the right, then first cul-de-sac on the left = Ch du Parc Saramartel No.7)
*Near sea Near beach Near motorway*
*Closed Nov-Mar*
*1 en suite (bth) TV in all bedrooms Full central heating Open parking available Child discount available 2yrs Table tennis*
ROOMS: s fr 320FF; d 350FF

## LA COLLE-SUR-LOUP Alpes-Maritimes

### Le Clos de St Paul (Prop: Beatrice Ronin Pillet)
71 ch de la Rouguière *06480*
☎ 493325681 FAX 493325681
(on A8 exit 47 Villeneuve-Loubet, then towards St-Paul-de-Vence. In la Colle/Loup turn right at lights. Towards la Rouguière. House on right in 2nd valley after old houses)
*Near sea Forest area Near motorway*
*3 en suite (bth/shr) (1 fmly) (2 with balcony) No smoking on premises Outdoor swimming pool Boule Table tennis Languages spoken: English & German*
ROOMS: s 260-280FF; d 300-320FF
**✱ Reductions over 1 night**
CARDS: Travellers cheques

## LANTOSQUE Alpes-Maritimes

### ★ ★ ★ Hostellerie de l'Ancienne Gendarmerie
*06450*
☎ 493030065 FAX 493030631
Near river Forest area
*Closed early Nov-mid Dec*
*8 en suite (bth/shr) (1 with balcony) TV in all bedrooms Direct*
*dial from all bedrooms Mini-bar in all bedrooms Licensed*
*Night porter Full central heating Open parking available*
*Supervised Outdoor swimming pool Fishing Jacuzzi/spa Open*
*terrace Covered terrace Last d 21.30hrs Languages spoken:*
*English & German*
CARDS: ✹ ■■ ☲ ⑩ Travellers cheques

## MANDELIEU-LA-NAPOULE Alpes-Maritimes

### ★ ★ ★ ★ Ermitage du Riou
av Henri Clens *06210*
☎ 493499556 FAX 492976905
Near river Near sea Forest area In town centre Near
motorway
*41 en suite (bth/shr) 5 rooms in annexe (4 fmly) (29 with*
*balcony) No smoking in 8 bedrooms TV in all bedrooms STV*
*Radio in rooms Direct dial from all bedrooms Mini-bar in all*
*bedrooms Licensed Lift Night porter Full central heating Air*
*conditioning in bedrooms Open parking available Covered*
*parking available (charged) Supervised Child discount*
*available Outdoor swimming pool Solarium Gym Boule Open*
*terrace Last d 22.00hrs Languages spoken: English, German &*
*Italian*
CARDS: ✹ ■■ ☲ ⑩ Travellers cheques

### ★ ★ ★ ★ Royal Hôtel Casino
605 av du Général de Gaulle *06212*
☎ 492977000 FAX 493495150
(situated just off A8 (Marseille-Nice) exit 40 and follow red and
white sign posts)
Near river Near sea Near beach
*213 en suite (bth/shr) (213 fmly) (213 with balcony) No*
*smoking in 5 bedrooms TV in all bedrooms STV Direct dial*
*from all bedrooms Mini-bar in all bedrooms Licensed Lift*
*Night porter Full central heating Air conditioning in bedrooms*
*Open parking available (charged) Supervised Child discount*
*available 10yrs Indoor swimming pool Outdoor swimming*
*pool Tennis Sauna Solarium Open terrace Casino Last d*
*22.30hrs Languages spoken: English, German, Italian &*
*Spanish*
CARDS: ✹ ■■ ☲ ⑩ JCB

## MENTON Alpes-Maritimes

### ★ ★ ★ Hotel Prince de Galles (Best Western)
4 av Général-de-Gaulle *06500*
☎ 493282121 FAX 493359591
Near sea In town centre
*68 en suite (bth/shr) (4 fmly) (40 with balcony) TV in all*
*bedrooms STV Direct dial from all bedrooms Licensed Lift*
*Night porter Full central heating Open parking available*
*Supervised Child discount available 12yrs Open terrace Last d*
*21.00hrs Languages spoken: English, German & Italian*
CARDS: ✹ ■■ ☲ ⑩ Travellers cheques

## MOUGINS Alpes-Maritimes

### ★ ★ ★ ★ Mas Candille
Clement-Rebuffel *06250*
☎ 493900085 FAX 492928556
(A8 exit Cannes Mougins, follow signs to village)
Forest area Near motorway
*Closed Nov-Apr*
*23 en suite (bth/shr) (4 fmly) TV in all bedrooms STV Radio in*
*rooms Direct dial from all bedrooms Mini-bar in all bedrooms*
*Room-safe Licensed Night porter Full central heating Air*
*conditioning in bedrooms Open parking available Supervised*
*Child discount available 12yrs Outdoor swimming pool (heated)*
*Golf 18 Tennis Open terrace Last d 22.00hrs Languages*
*spoken: English, German & Italian*
CARDS: ✹ ■■ ☲ ⑩ Travellers cheques

### ★ ★ ★ ★ Moulin de Mougins
Quartier Notre Dame de Vie *06250*
☎ 493757824 FAX 493901855
(A8 exit Cannes/Mougins, at 1st rdbt take Grasse/Mougins
express way then exit Mougins village and turn right)
Near sea Near beach Forest area Near motorway
*Closed 28 Jan-8 Mar RS Closed Mon*
*7 en suite (bth/shr) (2 fmly) (2 with balcony) TV in all*
*bedrooms STV Direct dial from all bedrooms Mini-bar in 3*
*bedrooms Room-safe Licensed Night porter Full central*
*heating Air conditioning in bedrooms Open parking available*
*Supervised Open terrace V meals Last d 22.30hrs Languages*
*spoken: English, German & Italian*
ROOMS: (room only) d 850-950FF
MEALS: Continental breakfast 90FF Lunch 270-740FF&alc
Dinner 550-740FF&alc
CARDS: ✹ ■■ ☲ ⑩ Travellers cheques

## NICE Alpes-Maritimes

### ★ ★ ★ ★ Acropolé-Nice-Hôte
25 bd Dubouchage *06000*
☎ 493805733 FAX 493626911
Near sea Near beach In town centre
*130 en suite (bth/shr) (5 fmly) (12 with balcony) No smoking in*
*10 bedrooms TV in all bedrooms STV Direct dial from all*
*bedrooms Mini-bar in all bedrooms Licensed Lift Night porter*
*Full central heating Air conditioning in bedrooms Open*
*parking available (charged) Covered parking available*
*(charged) Child discount available 6yrs Bicycle rental Open*
*terrace Languages spoken: English, German, Italian & Spanish*
CARDS: ✹ ■■ ☲ ⑩ Travellers cheques

### ★ ★ ★ Hotel Albert 1er
4 av des Phocéens *06000*
☎ 493857401 FAX 493803609
Near sea Near beach In town centre
*79 en suite (bth/shr) (10 with balcony) TV in all bedrooms Lift*
*Night porter Full central heating Air conditioning in bedrooms*
*Child discount available 6yrs Bicycle rental Languages spoken:*
*English, German & Italian*
CARDS: ✹ ■■ ☲ ⑩ Travellers cheques

### ★ ★ ★ Boréal (Minotel)
9 rue Paul Dérouléde *06000*
☎ 493823636 FAX 493823494
Near sea Near beach Forest area In town centre Near
motorway
*45 en suite (bth/shr) (5 fmly) No smoking in 5 bedrooms TV in*
*all bedrooms STV Radio in rooms Direct dial from all* contd.

427

bedrooms Room-safe (charged) Licensed Lift Night porter
Full central heating Air conditioning in bedrooms Child
discount available 12yrs Open terrace V meals Last d 22.30hrs
Languages spoken: English & Spanish
CARDS: ● ■ ■ Travellers cheques

### ★ ★ Campanile
58 bd Risso 06300
☎ 493262060 FAX 493260034
Near sea In town centre
70 en suite (bth/shr) (1 fmly) TV in all bedrooms STV Lift
Night porter Full central heating Air conditioning in bedrooms
Open terrace Languages spoken: English, Italian & Spanish
CARDS: ● ■ ■ ● Travellers cheques

### ★ ★ Climat de France
6 rue E Philibert 06300
☎ 493558000 FAX 493558030
(from A8 take exit 50, signed Nice Centre and follow signs to
The Port)
Near sea Forest area In town centre
110 en suite (shr) (11 fmly) TV in all bedrooms Direct dial from
all bedrooms Licensed Lift Night porter Full central heating
Air conditioning in bedrooms Open parking available (charged)
Covered parking available (charged) Supervised Open terrace
Covered terrace V meals Last d 10pm Languages spoken:
English, German, Italian & Spanish
CARDS: ● ■

### ★ ★ ★ Négresco
37 Promenade des Anglais 06000
☎ 493166400 FAX 493883568
(exit Autoroute A8 Nice West and take direction Town
Centre/Promenade des Anglais)
Near sea Near beach In town centre Near motorway
141 en suite (bth/shr) (5 with balcony) TV in all bedrooms STV
Direct dial from all bedrooms Mini-bar in all bedrooms
Licensed Lift Night porter Full central heating Air
conditioning in bedrooms Gym Open terrace Private beach
Wkly live entertainment Last d 23.30hrs Languages spoken:
English, Arabic, Italian, Russian & Spanish
ROOMS: (room only) d 1350-2750FF **Special breaks**
MEALS: Full breakfast 190FF Lunch 135-620FF&alc Dinner
135-620FF&alc
CARDS: ● ■ ■ ● JCB Travellers cheques

### ★ ★ ★ La Pérouse (Best Western)
11 quai Rauba Capeu 06000
☎ 493623463 FAX 493625941
Near sea Near beach Forest area In town centre Near
motorway
64 en suite (bth/shr) (60 with balcony) TV in all bedrooms STV
Radio in rooms Direct dial from all bedrooms Mini-bar in all
bedrooms Room-safe Licensed Lift Night porter Full central
heating Air conditioning in bedrooms Child discount available
16yrs Outdoor swimming pool Sauna Solarium Jacuzzi/spa
Open terrace Covered terrace Last d 22.00hrs Languages
spoken: English, German, Italian & Spanish
CARDS: ● ■ ■ ● Travellers cheques

### ★ ★ Petit Palais
10 av E Bickert 06000
☎ 493621911 FAX 493625360
Near sea Near beach In town centre Near motorway
25 en suite (bth/shr) (1 fmly) (10 with balcony) TV in all
bedrooms STV Direct dial from all bedrooms Licensed Lift
Full central heating Open parking available (charged) Child

discount available 12yrs Solarium Open terrace Languages
spoken: English, German & Spanish
CARDS: ● ■ ■ ● Travellers cheques

### ★ ★ ★ Primotel Suisse
15 quai Rauba Capeu 06300
☎ 493623300 FAX 493853070
Near sea In town centre Near motorway
42 en suite (bth/shr) (30 with balcony) TV in all bedrooms
Radio in rooms Direct dial from all bedrooms Mini-bar in all
bedrooms Licensed Lift Full central heating Air conditioning
in bedrooms Child discount available 12yrs Languages spoken:
English, German & Italian
CARDS: ● ■ ■ ● Travellers cheques

### ★ ★ Hotel St-Gothard
20 rue Paganini 06000
☎ 493881341 FAX 493822755
Near sea Near beach In town centre
64 en suite (bth/shr) (12 fmly) (10 with balcony) TV in all
bedrooms STV Radio in rooms Direct dial from all bedrooms
Lift Night porter Full central heating Child discount available
12yrs Special rates for AA Guide users Last d 21.00hrs
Languages spoken: English, Italian & Spanish
CARDS: ● ■ ■ ● Travellers cheques

### ★ ★ ★ Splendid Hotel
50 bd Victor-Hugo 06000
☎ 493164100 FAX 493164270
(from A8, exit to airport/Promenade des Anglais, follow
seaside road into town (about 5 miles). After Negresco Hotel,
turn left into rue Meyerbeer)
Near sea Near beach
128 en suite (bth/shr) (10 fmly) (100 with balcony) No smoking
on premises TV in all bedrooms STV Radio in rooms Direct
dial from all bedrooms Mini-bar in all bedrooms Licensed Lift
Night porter Full central heating Air conditioning in bedrooms
Covered parking available (charged) Supervised Child
discount available 12yrs Outdoor swimming pool Jacuzzi/spa
Open terrace V meals Last d 22.00hrs Languages spoken:
English, German, Italian & Spanish
CARDS: ● ■ ■ ● JCB Travellers cheques

---

**PÉGOMAS** Alpes-Maritimes

**Les Bosquet** (Prop: M & Mme Cattet)
74 Chemiq du Perissols 06580
☎ 492602120 FAX 492602149
(exit Mandelieu-la-Napoule and take direction of Pégomas and
follow signs to hotel)
Near river Near lake Forest area
Closed 15 Feb-2 Mar
16 en suite (bth/shr) (7 with balcony) TV in all bedrooms Radio
in rooms Full central heating Open parking available Covered
parking available Outdoor swimming pool Tennis Boule
Bicycle rental Open terrace Table tennis Languages spoken:
English & Italian
ROOMS: (room only) s 250-280FF; d 300-320FF
CARDS: ● ■ ■ Travellers cheques

---

**PEILLON** Alpes-Maritimes

### ★ ★ ★ Auberge de la Madone
pl du Village 06440
☎ 493799117 FAX 493799936
(A8 exit Nice-Est towards Sospel, take D121 then D21 into
Peillon)

*Closed 20 Oct-20 Dec & 7-24 Jan*
*20 en suite (bth/shr) 6 rooms in annexe (2 fmly) Direct dial from all bedrooms Full central heating Open parking available Child discount available Outdoor swimming pool Tennis Riding Solarium Boule Open terrace V meals Languages spoken: English & Italian*
CARDS: ●● ⅢⅡ Travellers cheques

## PLAN-DU-VAR Alpes-Maritimes

### ★ ★ Cassini
231 av de la Porte des Alpes, (N 202) *06670*
☎ 493089103 FAX 493084548
*(from Nice airport, take the 202 to Digne and stay on this road until you reach Plan-du-Var. The Hotel is situated in the middle of the village on the right)*
Located between the sea and the mountains this pleasant family hotel is ideally situated for visiting Nice and the neighbouring ski slopes.
Near river Forest area Near motorway
*12 rms (3 bth 8 shr) (1 with balcony) TV in all bedrooms Direct dial from all bedrooms Licensed Full central heating Covered parking available (charged) Child discount available 10yrs Open terrace Last d 22.00hrs Languages spoken: English, German & Italian*
ROOMS: (room only) d 180-250FF ✱
MEALS: Continental breakfast 30FF Lunch 85-230FF&alc Dinner 85-230FF&alc
CARDS: ●● ■■ ⅢⅡ Travellers cheques

## ST-JEAN-CAP-FERRAT Alpes-Maritimes

### ★ ★ ★ ★ Grand Hotel du Cap Ferrat
1 bd Général-de-Gaulle *06230*
☎ 493765050 FAX 493760452
*(in a private park at the southernmost end of the Cap Ferrat peninsula)*
Near sea Near motorway
*Closed Jan 3-Mar 3*
*57 en suite (bth/shr) 6 rooms in annexe (11 fmly) (7 with balcony) TV in all bedrooms STV Radio in rooms Mini-bar in all bedrooms Room-safe Licensed Lift Night porter Full central heating Air conditioning in bedrooms Open parking available Covered parking available (charged) Supervised Child discount available 12yrs Outdoor swimming pool (heated) Tennis Solarium Bicycle rental Open terrace Last d 21.45hrs Languages spoken: English, German, Italian & Spanish*
CARDS: ●● ■■ ⅢⅡ ⑩

## ST-JEANNET Alpes-Maritimes

### Bed & Breakfast (Prop: M et Mme Benoit)
136 rue St-Claude *06640*
☎ 493247630 FAX 493247877
*(exit the A8 at St-Laurent-du-Var in the direction of St-Jeannet)*
Comfortable, quiet and self-contained rooms, in a private house looking out onto a south-facing garden, with a view over the bay of Nice and Antibes. Set at an altitude of 450 metres in a village perched at the foot of St Jeannet. Swimming pool with sun-loungers. The sea is 20 minutes away.
Near sea Forest area

**Bed & Breakfast**
*3 en suite (bth/shr) TV in 1 bedroom Full central heating Open parking available Supervised Child discount available 15yrs Outdoor swimming pool Languages spoken: English*
ROOMS: s 400FF; d 500FF

## ST-PAUL-DE-VENCE Alpes-Maritimes

### ★ ★ ★ Hameau
528 rte de la Colle *06570*
☎ 493328024 FAX 493325575
*(From the A8 exit 'Cagnes-sur-Mer',D7 from la Colle. Establishment is 1km before St Paul on the rte de la Colle)*
Forest area
*Closed 16 Nov-14 Feb*
*17 rms (5 fmly) (3 with balcony) TV in 6 bedrooms STV Direct dial from all bedrooms Mini-bar in all bedrooms Room-safe Licensed Full central heating Air conditioning in bedrooms Open parking available Outdoor swimming pool Boule Open terrace Languages spoken: Italian-English-Spanish*
CARDS: ●● ⅢⅡ Maestro-Eurocard-Access Travellers cheques

### ★ ★ ★ ★ Mas d'Artigny
rte de la Colle *06570*
☎ 493328454 FAX 493329536
*(from A8 or N7 exit Cagnes-sur-Mer towards St-Paul and Vence. After La Colle-sur-Loup turn left and follow signs)*
Near beach Forest area
*85 en suite (bth/shr) (40 with balcony) TV in all bedrooms STV Direct dial from all bedrooms Mini-bar in all bedrooms Licensed Lift Night porter Full central heating Air conditioning in bedrooms Open parking available Covered parking available (charged) Supervised Child discount available 10yrs Outdoor swimming pool (heated) Tennis Pool table Boule Bicycle rental Open terrace table tennis, hair and beauty salons V meals Last d 22.00hrs Languages spoken: English, Dutch, German, Italian & Spanish*
CARDS: ●● ■■ ⅢⅡ ⑩ JCB Travellers cheques

### ★ ★ ★ ★ St-Paul Relais et Châteaux (Relais et Châteaux)
86 rue Grande *06570*
☎ 493326525 FAX 493325294
*(from the A8 towards Vence take exit Cagnes-sur-Mer. Then head for La Colle-sur-Loup/ St-Paul. Hotel is in the heart of the village)*
*Closed 18 Dec-14 Jan*
*18 en suite (bth/shr) (1 with balcony) No smoking in 1 bedroom TV in all bedrooms STV Direct dial from all bedrooms Mini-bar in all bedrooms Room-safe Licensed Lift Night porter Full central heating Air conditioning in bedrooms Open terrace V meals Last d 21.30hrs Languages spoken: English, Italian*
ROOMS: (room only) s 950-1300FF; d 1250-1700FF

MEALS: Continental breakfast 95FF  Lunch 250-560FF&alc
Dinner 290-560FF&alc
CARDS: ●● ■■ ☲☲ ⮂ Travellers cheques

## SOSPEL Alpes-Maritimes

### ★ ★ L'Auberge Provencale
rte du Col de Castillon 06380
☎ 493040031
Near river  Forest area
Closed 11 Nov-11 Dec
9 rms (2 fmly) (6 with balcony) Licensed  Full central heating
Open parking available  Supervised  Child discount available
Boule  Open terrace  Languages spoken: English & Italian
CARDS: Travellers cheques

### Domaine du Parais (Prop: Marie Mayer)
Chemin du Paradis, La Vasta 06380
☎ 493041578
(exit Menton from A8 onto D2566 in direction of Sospel,
continue until La Mairie (townhall) then turn left towards
Moulinet, continue for nearly 2km then left to La Vasta. For
1300m, Domaine be on right after 2 camp sites and a ranch)
An imposing 19th century Italian-style manor house, carefully
renovated to retain its authentic appearance. In a peaceful
location surrounded by 10 acres of woodland it is an ideal spot
for those wishing to explore the Mercantour National Park
with its many hiking trails and bird life.
Forest area
4 en suite (shr) (1 fmly) Open parking available  Languages
spoken: English & German
ROOMS: s 250-350FF; d 280-450FF
CARDS: Travellers cheques

## THORENC Alpes-Maritimes

### ★ ★ Auberge les Merisiers
24 av de Belvédère 06750
☎ 493600023 FAX 493600217
(leave motorway at Cannes and follow directiopns to Grasse.
Then follow the N85 to St-Vallier. Turn right on leaving St-
Vallier and follow the signs to Thorenc- approx 25km)
Near lake  Forest area  Near motorway
Closed 31 May-11 June
12 rms (9 shr) (1 fmly) (4 with balcony) TV in all bedrooms
Direct dial from all bedrooms  Licensed  Full central heating
Covered parking available (charged)  Supervised  Child
discount available 10yrs  Open terrace  Last d 21.00hrs
Languages spoken: English & Italian
CARDS: ●● ■■ ☲☲ Travellers cheques

### ★ ★ Hotel des Voyageurs
av de Belvédère 06750
☎ 493600018 FAX 493600351
Near river  Near lake  Forest area  Near motorway
Closed 15 Nov-Jan
12 en suite (bth/shr) (3 fmly) TV in all bedrooms  Licensed  Full
central heating  Open parking available  Covered parking
available  Supervised  Child discount available 12yrs  Solarium
Boule  Open terrace  V meals  Last d 20.30hrs  Languages
spoken: English, Italian & Spanish
CARDS: ●● ☲☲ Travellers cheques

## TURINI Alpes-Maritimes

### ★ ★ Trois Vallees
Col de Turini 06440
☎ 493915721 FAX 493795362
(A8 exit Nice (east) in direction of Sospel)
Forest area
30 en suite (bth/shr) 11 rooms in annexe (3 fmly) (21 with
balcony) TV in all bedrooms  STV  Direct dial from all
bedrooms  Room-safe (charged)  Licensed  Full central heating
Open parking available  Supervised  Child discount available
12yrs  Boule  Bicycle rental  Open terrace  Last d 22.00hrs
Languages spoken: English, Dutch, German & Spanish
CARDS: ●● ■■ ☲☲ ⮂ Travellers cheques

## VALBONNE Alpes-Maritimes

### Le Cheneau (Prop: Christiane & Alain Ringenbach)
205 rte d'Antibes 06560
☎ 493121394 FAX 493129185
(from A8 exit Antibes towards Antibes,Grasse & Mougins, then
Valbonne/at Boullides rndbt follow signs for Valbonne on
Route du Parc & 100mts after Bois Dore restaurant take right at
nb.205 into private lane that leads to Le Cheneau top on left)

Large Provence-style house in a shaded private park, and
located near the old village of Valbonne. Bedrooms are well
kept and sunny. Beaches, harbours and Nice International
Airport are only a 20 minute drive away. An ideal location from
which to discover the Côte d'Azur.
Near sea  Forest area
3 en suite (bth/shr) (2 fmly) No smoking on premises  Full
central heating  Open parking available  Covered parking
available  Child discount available 2yrs  Boule  Languages
spoken: English
ROOMS: s 320-400FF; d 350-430FF
CARDS: Travellers cheques

## VENCE Alpes-Maritimes

### ★ ★ ★ ★ Château St-Martin
av des Templiers, BP102 06140
☎ 493580202 FAX 493240891
(leave A8 & follow signs for Cagnes-sur-Mer and Vence. In
Vence take directions for Coursegoules/Col de Vence/D2.
Château is 2kms outside Vence)
Closed Oct-Apr
40 en suite (bth/shr) 8 rooms in annexe (36 with balcony) TV
in all bedrooms  STV  Radio in rooms  Direct dial from all
bedrooms  Mini-bar in 5 bedrooms  Room-safe  Licensed  Lift
Night porter  Full central heating  Air conditioning in bedrooms
Open parking available  Covered parking available  Supervised

*Outdoor swimming pool (heated) Tennis Boule Open terrace Last d 22.00hrs Languages spoken: English, German, Italian & Spanish*
ROOMS: (room only) d 3000-4500FF
MEALS: Continental breakfast 125FF Lunch 320-550FF&alc Dinner 400-550FF&alc
CARDS: 💳 💳 💳 💳 JCB Travellers cheques

★ ★ ★ **La Roseraie**
av Henri Giraud *06140*
☎ 493580220 FAX 493589931
This beautiful old Mediterranean-style villa dates back to the turn of the century and is surrounded by the lush vegetation of palm trees, yuccas, magnolias and roses. With spectacular views over the medieval village of Vence and Bayou Hill, it provides the charming setting for a peaceful stay. The bedrooms are decorated in the pretty Provençale style and have fine views over the surrounding countryside. A generous breakfast of home-baked croissants and traditional preserves is served on the terrace in the delightful garden by the swimming pool.
*Forest area*

*14 en suite (bth/shr) (2 fmly) (7 with balcony) TV in all bedrooms Direct dial from all bedrooms Mini-bar in all bedrooms Full central heating Open parking available Outdoor swimming pool Solarium Boule Bicycle rental Open terrace Covered terrace Childrens Play area Languages spoken: English, German & Italian*
ROOMS: (room only) s 395FF; d 490-750FF
**Reductions over 1 night**
CARDS: 💳 💳 💳 Travellers cheques

★ ★ *Mas de Vence*
539 av Emile Hugues *06140*
☎ 493580616 FAX 493240421
*41 en suite (bth/shr) 3 rooms in annexe (5 fmly) (35 with balcony) TV in all bedrooms Direct dial from all bedrooms Licensed Lift Night porter Full central heating Open parking available Covered parking available Supervised Child discount available 10yrs Outdoor swimming pool Solarium Boule Open terrace V meals Last d 21.30hrs Languages spoken: English, German, Italian & Spanish*
CARDS: 💳 💳 💳 💳 Travellers cheques

VILLEFRANCHE-SUR-MER Alpes-Maritimes

★ ★ ★ *La Flore*
bd Princesse Grace de Monaco *06230*
☎ 493763030 FAX 493769999
*Near sea Near beach Near motorway*

*31 en suite (bth/shr) 8 rooms in annexe (6 fmly) (20 with balcony) TV in all bedrooms STV Direct dial from all bedrooms Mini-bar in all bedrooms Room-safe Licensed Lift Night porter Full central heating Air conditioning in bedrooms Open parking available Covered parking available (charged) Supervised Child discount available 2yrs Outdoor swimming pool Solarium Open terrace Last d 22.00hrs Languages spoken: English, German & Italian*
CARDS: 💳 💳 💳 💳 Travellers cheques

★ ★ ★ **Welcome**
1 quai Amiral Courbet *06230*
☎ 493762762 FAX 493762766
(A8 exit 50, through Nice along Promenade des Anglais; then to Villefranche-sur-Mer, follow 'centre ville, plage' down to

sea.)
Ideally situated on one of the most beautiful stretches of the Côte d'Azur, and just a few minutes away from Nice and Monaco, the hotel offers a tastefully decorated interior with fully equipped bedrooms and a renowned restaurant, where a choice of superb dishes is served by competent, attentive staff.
*Near sea Near beach*
*Closed 15 Nov-20 Dec*
*32 en suite (bth/shr) (3 fmly) (27 with balcony) TV in all bedrooms STV Direct dial from all bedrooms Mini-bar in all bedrooms Room-safe (charged) Licensed Lift Night porter Full central heating Air conditioning in bedrooms Covered parking available (charged) Supervised Open terrace Last d 22.00hrs Languages spoken: English, German, Italian & Spanish*
ROOMS: s 500FF; d 690-950FF
**Reductions over 1 night Special breaks**
MEALS: Lunch 160-300FF&alc Dinner 160-300FF&alc✶
CARDS: 💳 💳 💳 💳 JCB Travellers cheques

VILLENEUVE-LOUBET Alpes-Maritimes

★ ★ ★ **Inter Hotel Hamotel**
Les Hameaux du Soleil, rte de la Colle *06270*
☎ 493208660 FAX 493733394
*Near river*
*30 en suite (bth) (30 with balcony) TV in all bedrooms STV Radio in rooms Mini-bar in all bedrooms Licensed Lift Night porter Full central heating Open parking available Covered parking available Child discount available 12yrs Languages spoken: English & Portuguese*
ROOMS: (room only) s 400-450FF; d 450-500FF
**Reductions over 1 night**
CARDS: 💳 💳 💳 💳 Travellers cheques

# Provence

Provence, a land of romantic landscapes, ancient history and passionate people has long been an inspiration for writers and artists and a favourite destination for visitors from the world over. This is a sun-drenched land, bounded by the Mediterranean, the great Rhone river and the towering Alps with its sleepy, medieval hilltop villages and hillsides scented with pine and wild herbs. The rolling slopes are covered with fragrant lavender, ancient olive groves and laden vines. Discover the wild untamed expanse of the Camargue, and the dramatic coastline with its lively ports, chic resorts and peaceful coves.

## ESSENTIAL FACTS

| | |
|---|---|
| DÉPARTEMENTS: | Alpes-de-Haute-Provence, Bouches-du-Rhone, Hautes Alpes, Var, Vaucluse |
| PRINCIPAL TOWNS | Arles, Avignon, Carpentras, Gap, Sisteron, Digne les Bains, Aix-en-Provence, Marseille, Toulon. |
| PLACES TO VISIT: | The Camargue- white horses, black bulls & wild birds; Roman remains at Arles & Orange; Popes' Palace at Avignon; Cezanne's studio at Aix-en-Provence; Les Ecrins; the National Nature Park in Hautes-Alpes; Luberon hill villages |
| REGIONAL TOURIST OFFICE | 13 rue Roux de Brignoles 13006 Marseille Tel: 91 13 84 13 |
| LOCAL GASTRONOMIC DELIGHTS | Bouillabaisse, fish stew. Calissons, small diamond-shaped almond-paste biscuits. Rascasse, spiny fish. Salade Nicoise, tuna fish salad. Daube, casserole. Poutargue, roe paste. Pissaladière, onion tart. Tapenade, olive paste. Cheeses: Brousse du Rove, Le Ventoux & Arles Tome, Champsaur, Genepy des Alpes. |
| DRINKS | Red wines: Chateauneuf-du-Pape & Gigondas. Herbal aperitif from Forcalquier. Pastis, aniseed-flavoured aperitif usually diluted with water. Local brandies: Vieux Marc de Provence, Elixir du Révérend Père Gaucher, Eau de Vie de Poire, and Genepy des Alpes. |
| LOCAL CRAFTS WHAT TO BUY | Provencal fabrics, honey perfumed with lavender & rosemary, pottery & earthenware, olive oil, lavender products, ornamental santons (regional dolls), crystallised fruits. |

## AGAY Var

### ★ ★ Le Lido
bd de la Plage 83530
☎ 494820159 FAX 494820975
Near river  Near lake  Near sea  Near beach  Forest area  Near motorway
*Closed 16 Oct-Feb*
*25 en suite (shr) (1 fmly) (8 with balcony) TV in all bedrooms STV Direct dial from all bedrooms  Licensed  Full central heating  Open parking available  Supervised  Boule  Covered terrace  Private beach  V meals  Languages spoken: English & Italian*

## AIGUINES Var

### ★ ★ Hotel du Grande Canyon du Verdon (Minotel)
Falaise des Cavaliers 83630
☎ 494769131 FAX 494769229
Near river  Forest area
*22 Apr-15 Oct*
*16 en suite (bth/shr) (6 fmly) (10 with balcony) TV in all bedrooms STV Direct dial from all bedrooms  Licensed  Full central heating  Open parking available  Child discount available 12yrs  Solarium  Pool table  Boule  Open terrace  Table tennis  Languages spoken: English & Italian*
ROOMS: (room only) s 300-400FF; d 380-460FF
**✳ Reductions over 1 night  Special breaks**
MEALS: Continental breakfast 40FF  Lunch 95-180FF&alc
CARDS: ● ■ ■ ⬚ JCB Travellers cheques

## AIX-EN-PROVENCE Bouches-du-Rhône

### ★ ★ ★ ★ Le Pigonnet
5 av du Pigonnet 13090
☎ 442590290 FAX 442594777
(from Autoroute A7 or A8 exit Aix Pont-de-l'Arc, head for 'Centre Ville'. Then turn right at the 3rd traffic light onto Av du Pigonnet)
Set in an attractive garden, half a mile from the town centre, this hotel has connections with the painter Cézanne and provides fine accommodation and excellent regional cuisine.
Forest area  In town centre
*52 en suite (bth/shr) (1 fmly) (11 with balcony) TV in all bedrooms STV Direct dial from all bedrooms  Mini-bar in all bedrooms  Lift  Night porter  Full central heating  Air conditioning in bedrooms  Open parking available (charged) Covered parking available  Supervised  Child discount available 15yrs  Outdoor swimming pool (heated)  Boule  Open terrace Last d 21.30  Languages spoken: English/German/Spanish*
ROOMS: (room only) s 800-1300FF; d 900-1600FF
MEALS: Continental breakfast 80FF  Lunch 270-340FF&alc Dinner 270-340FF&alc
CARDS: ● ■ ■ ⬚ JCB Travellers cheques

### ★ ★ ★ Hotel Bleu Marine
42 rte de Galice 13090
☎ 442950441 FAX 442594729
(From motorways A8 & A51 (Marseille-Sisteron) exit Aix West, Jas de Bouffan)
In town centre  Near motorway
*84 en suite (bth/shr) TV in all bedrooms STV Direct dial from all bedrooms  Mini-bar in all bedrooms  Licensed  Lift  Night porter  Full central heating  Air conditioning in bedrooms  Open*

contd.

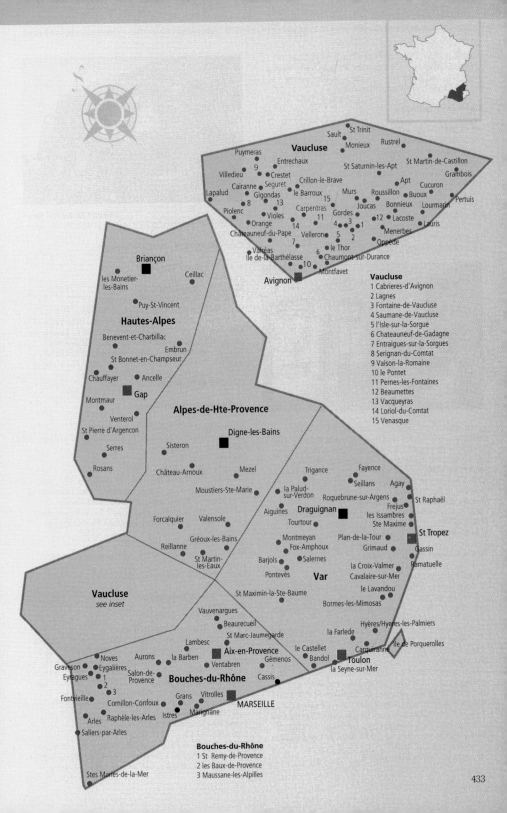

**Vaucluse**

St Trinit
Sault
Monieux
Rustrel
Puymeras
Entrechaux
St Saturnin-les-Apt
St Martin-de-Castillon
Villedieu
9
Crestet
Crillon-le-Brave
Apt
Grambois
Cairanne
Seguret
Cucuron
Lapalud
Gigondas
le Barroux
Murs
Roussillon
Buoux
Pertuis
8
13
15
Joucas
Bonnieux
Lourmarin
Piolenc
Violes
Carpentras
Gordes
Menerbes
Orange
11
4
3
1
12
Lacoste
Lauris
14
Velleron
5
2
Chateauneuf-du-Pape
7
Menerbes
Valréas
6
le Thor
Oppède
Ile-de-la-Barthélasse
10
Chaumont-sur-Durance
**Avignon**
Montfavet

**Vaucluse**

1 Cabrieres-d'Avignon
2 Lagnes
3 Fontaine-de-Vaucluse
4 Saumane-de-Vaucluse
5 l'Isle-sur-la-Sorgue
6 Chateauneuf-de-Gadagne
7 Entraigues-sur-la-Sorgues
8 Serignan-du-Comtat
9 Vaison-la-Romaine
10 le Pontet
11 Pernes-les-Fontaines
12 Beaumettes
13 Vacqueyras
14 Loriol-du-Comtat
15 Venasque

**Briançon**

les Monetier-
les-Bains
Ceillac

Puy-St-Vincent

**Hautes-Alpes**

Benevent-et-Charbillac
Embrun
St Bonnet-en-Champsaur
Chauffayer
Ancelle
**Gap**
Montmaur
Venterol
St Pierre d'Argencon
Serres
Rosans

**Alpes-de-Hte-Provence**

Digne-les-Bains
Sisteron
Château-Arnoux
Mezel
Trigance
Fayence
Seillans
Agay
Moustiers-Ste-Marie
la Palud-
sur-Verdon
Roquebrune-sur-Argens
St Raphaël
Aiguines
**Draguignan**
Frejus
les Issambres
Forcalquier
Valensole
Tourtour
Ste Maxime
**St Tropez**
Gréoux-les-Bains
Montmeyan
Plan-de-la-Tour
Reillanne
Fox-Amphoux
Grimaud
Gassin
St Martin-
les-Eaux
Barjols
Salernes
la Croix-Valmer
Ramatuelle
Pontevès
Cavalaire-sur-Mer
**Var**
le Lavandou
**Vaucluse**
*see inset*
St Maximin-la-Ste-Baume
Bormes-les-Mimosas
Vauvenargues
Beaurecueil
Hyères/Hyeres-les-Palmiers
St Marc-Jaumegarde
la Farlede
Ile de Porquerolles
Lambesc
le Castellet
Carquiranne
Noves
Aurons
la Barben
**Aix-en-Provence**
Bandol
**Toulon**
Graveson
Eygalières
Ventabren
Gémenos
la Seyne-sur-mer
Eyragues
1
Salon-de-
Provence
Cassis
**Bouches-du-Rhône**
Fontvieille
2
3
Grans
Vitrolles
Cornillon-Confoux
Istres
**MARSEILLE**
Arles
Raphèle-les-Arles
Marignane
Saliers-par-Arles

Stes Maries-de-la-Mer

**Bouches-du-Rhône**
1 St Remy-de-Provence
2 les Baux-de-Provence
3 Maussane-les-Alpilles

parking available (charged) Covered parking available (charged) Supervised Child discount available 12yrs Outdoor swimming pool Sauna Solarium Open terrace Covered terrace Fitness room V meals Last d 22.30hrs

### Château de la Pioliné
13546
☎ 442200781 FAX 442599612
This magnificent residence is situated in splendid parkland, exudes an atmosphere of elegance and sophistication and is furnished throughout with meticulous attention to detail. It provides a haven of charm and tranquillity for those who are on holiday or attending a conference, and yet is just 20 minutes away from the Marseille-Provence airport. The menu offers an extensive range of imaginatively cooked dishes made from fresh local produce. A unique place, where the owners offer warm hospitality and attentive service to satisfy the every need of their guests.
Near river Forest area Near motorway

33 en suite (bth) 12 rooms in annexe (2 fmly) TV in all bedrooms STV Direct dial from all bedrooms Mini-bar in all bedrooms Room-safe Lift Night porter Full central heating Air conditioning in bedrooms Open parking available Supervised Child discount available 12yrs Outdoor swimming pool Open terrace Last d 22.00hrs Languages spoken: English, Spanish, Italian & German
ROOMS: (room only) d 850-1150FF
MEALS: Full breakfast 90FF Lunch 190-250FF&alc Dinner 250-390FF&alc
CARDS: ●● ▆▆ ▆▆ ▆ JCB Travellers cheques

### ★ ★ ★ ★ Grand Hotel Roi René
24 bd du Roi René 13100
☎ 442376100 FAX 442376111
(From Marseille (A51) to Aix-en-Provence exit Aix Centre Ville in direction of Gare SNCF. From Toulon (A50) to Aubagne onto A520 then A52 Aix-en-Provence to A8 exit Aix. From Avignon A7 exit Aix Centre Ville)
On arriving at the Grand Hotel Roi René, guests discover the city devoted to art. Pleasant gardens, flowery terrace and patio, this is a hotel of high tradition.
In town centre
134 en suite (bth/shr) No smoking in 40 bedrooms TV in all bedrooms STV Direct dial from all bedrooms Mini-bar in all bedrooms Room-safe Licensed Lift Night porter Full central heating Air conditioning in bedrooms Open parking available (charged) Covered parking available (charged) Child discount available 16yrs Outdoor swimming pool Sauna Solarium Boule Open terrace Covered terrace V meals Last d 22.30hrs Languages spoken: English
ROOMS: (room only) d 865-1600FF

**Grand Hotel Roi René**
MEALS: Full breakfast 100FF Lunch fr 195FF&alc Dinner fr 250FF&alc
CARDS: ●● ▆▆ ▆▆ ▆ Travellers cheques

### ★ ★ ★ ★ Hotel Mascotte
av de la Cible 13100
☎ 442375858 FAX 442375859
Forest area In town centre Near motorway
93 en suite (bth/shr) No smoking in 20 bedrooms TV in all bedrooms STV Direct dial from all bedrooms Mini-bar in all bedrooms Licensed Lift Night porter Full central heating Air conditioning in bedrooms Open parking available Child discount available 12yrs Outdoor swimming pool (heated) Solarium Pool table Mini-golf Open terrace V meals Last d 22.30hrs Languages spoken: English & Spanish
CARDS: ●● ▆▆ ▆▆ ▆ Travellers cheques

### ★ ★ ★ Mas de la Bertrande
Beaurecueil 13100
☎ 442667575 FAX 442668201
(leave the road from Nice at Canet and take the N7 and turn right for Beaurecueil)
Near sea Forest area
Closed School Holidays
10 en suite (bth/shr) (5 fmly) TV in all bedrooms STV Direct dial from all bedrooms Mini-bar in all bedrooms Licensed Full central heating Open parking available Child discount available 12yrs Outdoor swimming pool Boule Bicycle rental Open terrace Covered terrace Last d 20.30hrs Languages spoken: English
ROOMS: (room only) d 380-550FF
MEALS: Continental breakfast 50FF Lunch 150FF&alc Dinner 150FF&alc
CARDS: ●● ▆▆ ▆▆ Travellers cheques

### ★ ★ ★ ★ Mas d'Entremont
RN7 13090
☎ 442174242 FAX 442211583
(follow N7 Avignon-Sisteron-Celony)
Set in extensive parkland, three kilomotres from the centre of Aix-en-Provence, this hotel offers bedrooms that overlook the beautiful garden with its earthenware pots, abundant with flowers. Weather permitting, meals are served on the terrace and guests can enjoy the view of old stone fountains and the pond with waterlillies. Combined with the hosts' warm hospitality and the authentic local cuisine, guests will find this a place to remember.
Forest area Near motorway
Closed Nov-14 Mar
17 en suite (bth) 12 rooms in annexe (2 fmly) (17 with balcony) TV in all bedrooms STV Direct dial from all bedrooms Mini-bar in all bedrooms Room-safe Licensed Lift Full central

heating *Air conditioning in bedrooms Open parking available
Supervised Child discount available 15yrs Outdoor swimming
pool Tennis Solarium Gym Boule Bicycle rental Open terrace
Covered terrace Last d 21.30hrs Languages spoken: English &
Italian*
ROOMS: (room only) s 680FF; d 780-880FF
MEALS: Full breakfast 80FF Lunch 210-250FF&alc Dinner
210-250FF&alc
CARDS: ●● ▆▆ JCB Travellers cheques

★ ★ ★ **Mas des Ecureuils**
chemin de Castel Blanc, petite rte des Milles *13090*
☎ 442244048 FAX 442392457
*Forest area*
*23 en suite (bth/shr) (6 fmly) (15 with balcony) TV in all
bedrooms Direct dial from all bedrooms Mini-bar in all
bedrooms Room-safe Licensed Night porter Full central
heating Open parking available Supervised Child discount
available Outdoor swimming pool (heated) Sauna Boule
Bicycle rental Open terrace V meals Last d 22.00hrs
Languages spoken: English German & Spanish*
CARDS: ●● ▆▆ ▆▆ ▆ Travellers cheques

★ ★ **Hotel des 4 Dauphins**
54 rue Roux-Alphéran *13100*
☎ 442381639 FAX 442386019
(from motorway A8 or A51 direction Aix-centre. From Pl
General de Gaulle to Cours Mirabeau then 3rd street on the
right (rue du 4 Septembre) then straight ahead)
*In town centre*
*12 en suite (bth/shr) TV in all bedrooms Direct dial from all
bedrooms Mini-bar in 2 bedrooms Night porter Full central
heating Languages spoken: English*
ROOMS: (room only) s 299-339FF; d 303-403FF
CARDS: ●● ▆▆ Travellers cheques

★ ★ ★ **Villa Gallici** (Relais et Châteaux)
av de la Violette *13100*
☎ 442232923 FAX 442963045
(follow yellow panel signs for Hotel Villa Gallici)
*In town centre*
*22 rms (19 bth/shr) 2 rooms in annexe (3 with balcony) TV in
all bedrooms STV Radio in rooms Direct dial from all
bedrooms Mini-bar in all bedrooms Room-safe Licensed
Night porter Full central heating Air conditioning in bedrooms
Open parking available Supervised Outdoor swimming pool
Boule Open terrace Languages spoken: English, German &
Italian*
CARDS: ●● ▆▆ ▆▆ ▆ Travellers cheques

**ANCELLE** Hautes-Alpes

**L'Edelweiss** (Prop: Mme Josiane Meizel)
Les Auches *05260*
☎ 492508239 & 86189152
(leave N85 for D944 continue to Ancelle)
Guests have their own entrance at this recently built property.
The bedrooms have modern facilities and guests have use of
the dining room, sitting area, conservatory and an outdoor
bowling alley. Nearby there are walking trails and a ski resort.
*Near river Forest area*
*4 en suite (bth/shr) (1 fmly) (2 with balcony) Open parking
available Child discount available 8yrs Boule
Last d 20.00hrs*

*L'Edelweiss*

ROOMS: s 200-220FF; d 270-295FF
**Reductions over 1 night**
MEALS: Dinner fr 80FF

**APT** Vaucluse

★ ★ ★ **Auberge du Luberon**
8 pl du Faubourg du Ballet *84400*
☎ 490741250 FAX 490047949
*Near river Forest area In town centre Near motorway*
*14 en suite (bth/shr) 6 rooms in annexe (5 with balcony) TV in
all bedrooms STV Direct dial from all bedrooms Mini-bar in 8
bedrooms Licensed Night porter Full central heating Covered
parking available (charged) Supervised Child discount
available 12yrs Open terrace V meals Last d 21.30hrs
Languages spoken: English & Spanish*
ROOMS: (room only) s fr 295FF; d 315-445FF
MEALS: Full breakfast 45FF Lunch 155-420FF&alc Dinner
155-420FF
CARDS: ●● ▆▆ ▆▆ ▆ Eurocard Travellers cheques

**Moulin du Lavon** (Prop: Yves Nief)
*84400*
☎ 490743454 FAX 490742013
*Near river Near lake Forest area*
*10 rms (4 bth) (3 fmly) Full central heating Open parking
available Child discount available 13yrs Outdoor swimming
pool Boule Table tennis,Piano Last d 20.00hrs*
CARDS: ▆▆ Travellers cheques

★ ★ ★ **Auberge du Presbytère**
pl de la Fontaine *84400*
☎ 490741150 FAX 490046851
(highway to Avignon, N100 to Apt, 3.5km from Saignon, on the
Luberon mountain) *contd.*

A family hotel renowned for its hospitality with a truly international clientele. Guests from many different countries including Australia, New Zealand, Japan and America stay at this charming auberge.
Forest area  In town centre  Near motorway
*10 en suite (bth/shr) (2 fmly) (2 with balcony) TV available Direct dial from all bedrooms Licensed Full central heating Child discount available 12yrs Last d 21.00hrs Languages spoken: English, Italian & Spanish*
ROOMS: d 290-580FF
MEALS: Continental breakfast 50FF Lunch 180FF&alc Dinner 180FF&alc
CARDS: ●● ■ ☰ Travellers cheques

### ARLES Bouches-du-Rhône

★ ★ ★ **Arlatan**
26 rue du Sauvage *13200*
☎ 490935666 FAX 490496845
Near river  Near sea  In town centre  Near motorway
*41 en suite (bth/shr) (6 fmly) TV in 40 bedrooms STV Direct dial from all bedrooms Mini-bar in all bedrooms Room-safe Lift Night porter Full central heating Air conditioning in bedrooms Covered parking available (charged) Supervised Languages spoken: English & German*
CARDS: ●● ■ ☰ ⑩ Travellers cheques

★ ★ ★ **Atrium**
1 rue Emile Fassin *13200*
☎ 490499292 FAX 490933859
(opposite the Office du Tourisme)
In town centre
*91 en suite (bth) (6 fmly) (10 with balcony) TV in all bedrooms STV Direct dial from all bedrooms Mini-bar in all bedrooms Licensed Lift Night porter Full central heating Air conditioning in bedrooms Open parking available (charged) Covered parking available (charged) Supervised Child discount available 12yrs Outdoor swimming pool Solarium Open terrace Last d 21.30hrs Languages spoken: English,Italian & Spanish*
CARDS: ●● ■ ☰ ⑩ Travellers cheques

★ ★ **Hotel Calendal**
22 pl du Dr Pomme *13200*
☎ 490961189 FAX 490960584
(from town centre follow signs for 'Amphitheatre')
In town centre
*27 en suite (bth/shr) (10 fmly) (3 with balcony) TV in all bedrooms STV Direct dial from all bedrooms Licensed Night porter Full central heating Child discount available 10yrs Open terrace Last d 21.00hrs Languages spoken: English & Italian*
CARDS: ●● ■ ☰ ⑩ JCB Travellers cheques

★ ★ ★ **Grand Hotel du Nord Pinus**
14 pl du Forum *13200*
☎ 490934444 FAX 490933400
(from Arles centre take direction Place de la République then Place du Forum)
Near river  Near sea  Near beach  Forest area  In town centre  Near motorway
*23 en suite (bth/shr) TV in all bedrooms STV Direct dial from all bedrooms Mini-bar in all bedrooms Licensed Lift Night porter Full central heating Air conditioning in bedrooms Open parking available (charged) Covered parking available (charged) Bicycle rental Last d 21.15hrs Languages spoken: English, Dutch & German*

ROOMS: (room only) s fr 770FF; d 840-1700FF
MEALS: Continental breakfast 75FF Lunch fr 98FF&alc Dinner fr 180FF&alc
CARDS: ●● ■ ☰ Travellers cheques

★ ★ ★ ★ **Jules César** (Relais et Châteaux)
9 bd des Lices *13631*
☎ 490934320 FAX 490933347
(on autoroute A54 exit 5)
In town centre  Near motorway
*Closed 12 Nov-23 Dec*
*56 en suite (bth/shr) TV in all bedrooms STV Radio in rooms Direct dial from all bedrooms Mini-bar in all bedrooms Room-safe Licensed Night porter Full central heating Air conditioning in bedrooms Open parking available (charged) Covered parking available (charged) Supervised Child discount available 10yrs Outdoor swimming pool (heated) Solarium Open terrace Covered terrace Last d 21.30hrs Languages spoken: English, German, Italian & Spanish*
ROOMS: (room only) s 750-1100FF; d 850-1250FF
MEALS: Full breakfast 85FF Lunch 150-380FF&alc Dinner 210-380FF&alc
CARDS: ●● ■ ☰ ⑩ JCB Travellers cheques

★ ★ ★ ★ **Le Mas de Peint**
Le Sambuc *13200*
☎ 490972062 FAX 490972220
(from A55 or N113 at Arles follow the road to Stes Maries D570, then D36 direction Salin de Giraud after 20kms, cross the village of le Sambug and in 2kms turn left)
Near beach
*Closed 10 Jan-10 Mar*
*11 en suite (bth/shr) (1 fmly) (3 with balcony) TV in all bedrooms STV Direct dial from all bedrooms Mini-bar in all bedrooms Room-safe (charged) Licensed Full central heating Air conditioning in bedrooms Open parking available Covered parking available Supervised Child discount available 10yrs Outdoor swimming pool Riding Bicycle rental Open terrace V meals Last d 21.00hrs Languages spoken: English & German*
ROOMS: (room only) d 1195-2180FF **Special breaks**
MEALS: Full breakfast 100FF Lunch fr 190FF Dinner fr 245FF
CARDS: ●● ■ ☰ ⑩ Travellers cheques

★ ★ ★ **Mireille**
2 pl St-Pierre *13200*
☎ 490937074 FAX 490938728
(cross River Rhône via rue Gambetta (heading north). Hotel on right)
*Closed Nov-Mar*
*34 en suite (bth/shr) 4 rooms in annexe (1 fmly) No smoking in 4 bedrooms TV in all bedrooms STV Radio in rooms Direct dial from all bedrooms Mini-bar in 29 bedrooms Room-safe Licensed Night porter Full central heating Air conditioning in bedrooms Open parking available Covered parking available (charged) Outdoor swimming pool (heated) Boule Mini-golf Bicycle rental Open terrace Table tennis V meals Last d 21.30hrs Languages spoken: English & Italian*
ROOMS: (room only) s 350-650FF; d 390-650FF
MEALS: Full breakfast 59FF Lunch 110-170FF&alc Dinner 110-170FF&alc
CARDS: ●● ■ ☰ ⑩ JCB Travellers cheques

★ ★ ★ **New Hotel Arles Camargue**
45 av Sadi-Carnot *13200*
☎ 490994040 FAX 490933250
In town centre  Near motorway

67 en suite (bth/shr) (7 fmly) (1 with balcony) TV in all
bedrooms STV Radio in rooms Direct dial from all bedrooms
Mini-bar in all bedrooms Licensed Lift Night porter Full
central heating Air conditioning in bedrooms Open parking
available Covered parking available (charged) Supervised
Child discount available 16yrs Indoor swimming pool (heated)
Outdoor swimming pool (heated) Pool table Open terrace
Covered terrace V meals Last d 22.30hrs Languages spoken:
English,German,Italian & Spanish
CARDS: ●● ■■ ⚡ JCB Travellers cheques

### ★★★ Primotel Camargue
Face au Palais des Congrés 13200
☎ 490939880 FAX 490499276
Near river In town centre Near motorway
144 en suite (bth/shr) TV in all bedrooms Direct dial from all
bedrooms Licensed Lift Night porter Full central heating Air
conditioning in bedrooms Open parking available Child
discount available 12yrs Outdoor swimming pool Tennis Pool
table Open terrace Last d 22.00hrs Languages spoken:
English, German, Italian & Spanish
CARDS: ●● ■■ ⚡ Travellers cheques

## AURONS Bouches-du-Rhône

### ★★ Domaine de la Reynaude
Les Sonnaillets 13121
☎ 490593024 FAX 490593606
(from Marseille take A7 and follow signs for Avignon/Lyon and
then Salon/Montpellier. Take exit for Salon centre and follow
signs to Pelissanne and then Aurons. Hotel approx 4km after
Aurons)

Relax in the magnificent setting of the heart of Provence. The
charming 18th-century coaching inn provides well appointed
rooms, all with bay windows opening onto surrounding
countryside. Many leisure activities are offered within the
grounds.
Forest area
Closed 25 Dec
32 en suite (bth/shr) 2 rooms in annexe (6 with balcony) TV in
all bedrooms STV Direct dial from all bedrooms Licensed Full
central heating Open parking available Supervised Child
discount available 11yrs Outdoor swimming pool (heated)
Tennis Pool table Boule Covered terrace Volley ball Last d
21.00hrs Languages spoken: English
ROOMS: (room only) s 320FF; d 370-690FF
MEALS: Full breakfast 45FF Lunch 115-210FF&alc Dinner
115-210FF&alc
CARDS: ●● ■■ ⚡ Travellers cheques

## AVIGNON Vaucluse

### ★★★ Hotel Bristol (Best Western)
44 cours Jean Jaurès 84009
☎ 490822121 FAX 490862272
(in town centre near the railway station)
In town centre Near motorway
67 en suite (bth/shr) (3 fmly) (6 with balcony) No smoking in 5
bedrooms TV in all bedrooms STV Direct dial from all
bedrooms Mini-bar in all bedrooms Room-safe Licensed Lift
Night porter Full central heating Air conditioning in bedrooms
Covered parking available (charged) Supervised Sauna Bicycle
rental Languages spoken: English, German, Italian & Spanish
CARDS: ●● ■■ ⚡ Travellers cheques

### ★★★ Mirande
4 pl de l'Amirande 84000
☎ 490859393 FAX 490862685
(from Marseille or Lyon on A8/A7 take the Avignon Nord exit
and drive towards city centre until you reach the gate 'Porte de
la Ligne', hotel is signposted)
Near river In town centre Near motorway
20 en suite (bth/shr) (2 fmly) (3 with balcony) TV in all
bedrooms Direct dial from all bedrooms Mini-bar in all
bedrooms Room-safe Licensed Lift Night porter Full central
heating Air conditioning in bedrooms Open parking available
(charged) Covered parking available (charged) Child discount
available Open terrace Last d 22.15hrs Languages spoken:
English, German, Italian, Spanish & Swedish
CARDS: ●● ■■ ⚡ Travellers cheques

### ★★★ Primotel Horloge
1 rue Felicien David 84000
☎ 490868861 FAX 490821732
(approach on A9 exit Remoulins or A7 exit Avignon Nord)
In town centre
70 en suite (bth/shr) 13 rooms in annexe (1 fmly) (5 with
balcony) TV in all bedrooms STV Radio in rooms Direct dial
from all bedrooms Mini-bar in all bedrooms Licensed Lift
Night porter Full central heating Air conditioning in bedrooms
Child discount available 12yrs Languages spoken: English,
German, Italian & Spanish
CARDS: ●● ■■ ⚡ JCB Travellers cheques

## BANDOL Var

### ★★★ Le Provencal
rue des Escoles 83150
☎ 494295211 FAX 494296757
Near sea Near beach
22 rms (20 bth/shr) Licensed Full central heating Open
parking available Covered parking available Child discount
available 5yrs Open terrace V meals Last d 22.00hrs
Languages spoken: English & Spanish
CARDS: ●● ■■ ⚡ Travellers cheques

## BARBEN, LA Bouches-du-Rhone

### ★★ La Touloubre
☎ 90551685 FAX 90551799
(from Salon-de-Provence take the direction of Aix-en-Provence
on the D572 then D22 to La Barben)
Near river
Closed 15 days Oct/15 days Feb

contd.

7 en suite (bth/shr) (3 fmly) Direct dial from all bedrooms Licensed Full central heating Open parking available Child discount available 10yrs Boule Open terrace V meals Last d 21.30hrs Languages spoken: English, Italian & Spanish
CARDS: ● ▦ Travellers cheques

### BARJOLS Var

**Séjours Decouverte et Nature** (Prop: Michel Passebois)
St-Jaume 83670
☎ 494771801 FAX 494771801
(from Barjols take D560 towards St Maxmin. After approx 1.7km take turning to right and follow signs 'Saint-Jaume'. After 500m,there is a red gate on left & farm entrance)
Near river Forest area
Closed Nov-Feb
6 en suite (shr) (2 fmly) No smoking on premises Full central heating Open parking available Child discount available 10yrs Outdoor swimming pool Boule Open terrace Table tennis Languages spoken: English
ROOMS: s 310FF; d 415FF
MEALS: Dinner 125FF
CARDS: Travellers cheques

### BARROUX, LE Vaucluse

**★ ★ ★ Hostellerie François Joseph**
chemin des Rabassières 84330
☎ 490625278 FAX 490623354
(Leave A7 onto D950 to Carpentras.Then take D938 to Barroux)

The Hostellerie François Joseph is situated at the foot of Mont-Ventoux in parklands filled with the flowers, trees and heady fragrances which are so typical of Provence. It consists of three country houses, painted in pink and ochre, featuring spacious guest rooms with private balconies overlooking the delightful grounds, a shaded terrace and an attractive swimming pool.
Forest area
Closed 16 Nov-14 Mar
18 en suite (bth/shr) (4 fmly) (4 with balcony) TV in all bedrooms Direct dial from all bedrooms Mini-bar in 5 bedrooms Room-safe Night porter Full central heating Open parking available Supervised Outdoor swimming pool Solarium Boule Bicycle rental Open terrace Wkly live entertainment Languages spoken: English & French
ROOMS: s fr 300FF; d 330-800FF
**✳ Reductions over 1 night**
CARDS: ● ▮ ▦ Travellers cheques

### ★ ★ Geraniums
pl de la Croix 84330
☎ 490624108 FAX 490625648
Near lake Forest area
Closed 15 Nov-15 Mar
22 en suite (bth/shr) 9 rooms in annexe (2 fmly) (4 with balcony) Direct dial from all bedrooms Licensed Full central heating Open parking available Supervised Child discount available 12yrs Solarium Boule Open terrace V meals Last d 21.00hrs Languages spoken: English & Spanish
ROOMS: (room only) d 260-290FF
MEALS: Full breakfast 40FF Lunch 90-180FF&alc Dinner 90-180FF&alc
CARDS: ● ▮ ▦ Travellers cheques

### BAUX-DE-PROVENCE, LES Bouches-du-Rhône

### ★ ★ ★ La Benvengudo
Vallon de l'Arcoulé 13520
☎ 490543254 FAX 490544258
Forest area
Closed end Oct-early Feb
20 en suite (bth/shr) (4 fmly) (3 with balcony) TV in all bedrooms Licensed Night porter Full central heating Air conditioning in bedrooms Open parking available Covered parking available Supervised Outdoor swimming pool Tennis Boule Open terrace V meals Last d 21.45hrs Languages spoken: English, German,Italian & Spanish
CARDS: ● ▮ ▦ Travellers cheques

### ★ ★ ★ ★ La Cabro d'Or (Relais et Châteaux)
13520
☎ 490543321 FAX 490544598
Forest area Near motorway
Closed 11 Nov-15 Dec RS restaurant close Tue lunch/Mon (Oct-Mar)
31 en suite (bth/shr) TV in all bedrooms STV Radio in rooms Direct dial from all bedrooms Mini-bar in all bedrooms Room-safe Full central heating Air conditioning in bedrooms Open parking available Covered parking available Supervised Outdoor swimming pool Tennis Riding Open terrace V meals Last d 21.30hrs Languages spoken: English & German
ROOMS: (room only) d 700-1870FF
MEALS: Full breakfast 85FF Lunch 200-280FF&alc Dinner 280-440FF&alc
CARDS: ● ▮ ▦ ▣ Travellers cheques

### ★ ★ ★ Oustau de Baumanière
Vallon de la Fontaine 13520
☎ 490543307 FAX 490544046
Forest area
Closed 4 Jan-6 Mar
22 en suite (bth) 14 rooms in annexe (14 fmly) TV in all bedrooms STV Radio in rooms Direct dial from all bedrooms Mini-bar in all bedrooms Room-safe Night porter Full central heating Air conditioning in bedrooms Open parking available Outdoor swimming pool Riding Open terrace Covered terrace V meals Last d 21.30hrs Languages spoken: English, German, Italian & Spanish
ROOMS: (room only) d 1350-2300FF
MEALS: Full breakfast 120FF Lunch 650-900FF&alc Dinner 500-750FF&alc
CARDS: ● ▮ ▦ ▣ Travellers cheques

## BEAUMETTES Vaucluse

**Le Ralenti du Lierre** (Prop: Thierry Dulieu)
Le Village *84220*
☎ 490723922 FAX 490724312
(on N100 between Apt/Coustellet)
Near river  Forest area
*5 en suite (bth/shr) (1 fmly) (1 with balcony) No smoking on premises Full central heating Open parking available No children Outdoor swimming pool*
ROOMS: d 380-550FF
MEALS: Dinner 150FF
CARDS: Travellers cheques

## BEAURECUEIL Bouches-du-Rhône

**★ ★ ★ Relais Sainte Victoire**
*13100*
☎ 442669498 FAX 442669649
(10km from Aix en Provence)
Just a few minutes from Aix-en-Provence, at the foot of the St Victoire mountains, surrounded by landscapes made familiar by the paintings of Cézanne, sits Le Relais Sainte Victoire. The rooms overlook the gardens, with swimming pool and mini tennis, and are equipped with every comfort including air conditioning and jacuzzi. In the restaurant the Jugy-Bergès family offer an imaginative and refined menu of authentic Provence dishes.
Forest area  Near motorway
*Closed 1st wk Nov & Jan also 1-15 Mar*
*12 en suite (bth) (1 fmly) (2 with balcony) TV in all bedrooms Direct dial from all bedrooms Mini-bar in 10 bedrooms Licensed Full central heating Air conditioning in bedrooms Open parking available Child discount available 12yrs Outdoor swimming pool Riding Solarium Boule Jacuzzi/spa Mini tennis Last d 21.30hrs Languages spoken: English*
ROOMS: (room only) s 400FF; d 500-800FF
MEALS: Full breakfast 75FF  Lunch 150-400FFalc  Dinner 150-400FFalc
CARDS: ▆ ▆

## BÉNÉVENT-ET-CHARBILLAC Hautes-Alpes

**Bed & Breakfast** (Prop: M & Mme Gourdou-Pedrosa)
Le Cairn, Charbillac *05500*
☎ 492505487 FAX 492505487
(from St-Bonnet take D23 to La Motte for 4km then right for 1.2km to Charbillac. Signposted from St-Bonnet)
Enjoy the beauty of the Alps in this restored house in the heart of the Champsaur Valley. Bring your skis in the winter or enjoy lovely walks in the summer. Climbing and other alpine sports are available. Tennis, water-sports, horse-riding, golf and bungee-jumping are all within minutes of the property.
Near river  Near lake  Forest area
*4 en suite (shr) (3 fmly) No smoking on premises Open parking available Child discount available 12yrs Languages spoken: English, Italian & Spanish*
ROOMS: d fr 240FF **Reductions over 1 night**

## BESSE-SUR-ISSOLE Var

**Bastide de L'Avellanne**
quartier l'Avellanne *83890*
☎ 494698991 FAX 494688954
(A8 in direction of Nice exit at Brignoles onto N7 in direction of Draguignan)

Near river  Near lake  Near sea  Near beach  Forest area  Near motorway
*Closed Dec & Jan*
*12 en suite (bth/shr) (6 fmly) TV available  Full central heating Open parking available Child discount available Outdoor swimming pool (heated) Tennis Boule Bicycle rental Languages spoken: English Dutch & German*
ROOMS: d 422-736FF **Special breaks**
CARDS: ●● ▆

## BONNIEUX Vaucluse

**La Bouquière** (Prop: Angel Escobar)
*84480*
☎ 490758717 FAX 490758356
(take D3 in direction of Apt in 2km signposted left)

Situated three and a half kilometres from the village of Bonnieux, lost in a profusion of greenery in the heart of the regional park, this old, restored house has a magnificent view over the valley of Luberon. Four comfortable rooms are available, each with its own independent entrance, looking out onto the garden. Guests also have the use of a fully equipped kitchenette and a communal living area with a large fireplace.
Forest area
*4 en suite (bth/shr) Full central heating Open parking available Outdoor swimming pool Languages spoken: English & Spanish*
ROOMS: s 350-420FF; d 385-450FF ✱
CARDS: Travellers cheques

## BORMES-LES-MIMOSAS Var

**★ ★ ★ Hostellerie de la Reine Jeanne**
Forêt du Dom *83230*
☎ 494150083 FAX 494647789
(mid way between Toulon and St Tropez on N98)
Near sea  Near beach  Forest area  Near motorway
*Closed 16 Oct-14 Mar*
*8 en suite (bth/shr) (3 fmly) (8 with balcony) No smoking in 2 bedrooms TV in all bedrooms STV Direct dial from all bedrooms Mini-bar in all bedrooms Room-safe (charged) Licensed Full central heating Open parking available Supervised Child discount available 12yrs Outdoor swimming pool Solarium Boule Bicycle rental Open terrace Covered terrace V meals Last d 22.00hrs Languages spoken: English, German & Italian*
ROOMS: (room only) d 700-800FF
**Reductions over 1 night**
MEALS: Continental breakfast 70FF  Lunch fr 160FF&alc  Dinner 250-320FF&alc
CARDS: ●● ▆ Travellers cheques

## BUOUX Vaucluse

**Domaine de la Grande Bastide** (Prop: Jean-Alain Cayla)
*84480*
☎ 490742910
(from A7 exit at Avignon Sud and take N100 to Apt. From Apt take D113 south to Buoux.)
A 17th-century farm set in 70 hectares of beautiful countryside, and in the middle of lavender fields. Five spacious and comfortable rooms available.
Near river  Forest area
*5 rms (4 shr)  Full central heating  Open parking available Covered parking available  Supervised  Child discount available 12yrs  Boule  Languages spoken: English & Spanish*
ROOMS: d 300-350FF
CARDS: Travellers cheques

## CABRIÈRES-D'AVIGNON Vaucluse

**Bed & Breakfast** (Prop: Jacquy Truc)
*84220*
☎ 490769703 FAX 490767467
(situated equidistance between Gordes/Fontaine de Vaucluse)
Forest area
*5 en suite (shr)  (1 with balcony)  No smoking on premises  TV available  Full central heating  Open parking available  Child discount available  Outdoor swimming pool*

## CAIRANNE Vaucluse

**Le Moulin Agapé** (Prop: Denise Molla)
*84290*
☎ 490307704
(from N7 take D8 from Bollène or D13 from Orange, to Cairanne)
Near river  Forest area  Near motorway
*6 en suite (bth/shr)  (3 fmly)  No smoking on premises  Full central heating  Open parking available  Child discount available 10yrs  Outdoor swimming pool  Boule  Table tennis Languages spoken: English*

## CARPENTRAS Vaucluse

★ ★ ★ **Les 3 Colomes**
148 av des Garrigues *84200*
☎ 490660701 FAX 490661154
Forest area
*Closed Jan-Feb*
*30 en suite (bth/shr)  (6 fmly)  (9 with balcony)  No smoking in 6 bedrooms  TV in all bedrooms  STV  Direct dial from all bedrooms  Licensed  Full central heating  Open parking available  Supervised  Child discount available 12yrs  Outdoor swimming pool  Tennis  Gym  Pool table  Boule  Bicycle rental Open terrace  V meals  Last d 21.30hrs  Languages spoken: English & Italian*
ROOMS: (room only) d 350-510FF
**Reductions over 1 night**
MEALS: Full breakfast 55FF  Lunch 120-230FF  Dinner 120-230FF
CARDS: ●● ■■ ☲ Travellers cheques

**Bastide Ste-Agnes** (Prop: Jacques Apotheloz)
route de Caromb, Chemin de le Fourtrose *84200*
☎ 490600301 FAX 490600253
(from Carpentras take D974 towards Orange/Mont-Ventoux then along the aqueduct towards Bédoin. After about 500m, take the D13 towards Caromb, after 300m go left into the

Chemin de la Fourtrouse, house is 200m on right)
Near river  Near lake  Forest area
*Closed 16 Nov-14 Mar*
*6 en suite (bth/shr)  (32 fmly)  (2 with balcony)  TV in 2 bedrooms  Full central heating  Open parking available  Child discount available 4yrs  Outdoor swimming pool  Boule Languages spoken: English & German*
CARDS: ●● ☲ Travellers cheques

★ ★ ★ **Hostellerie du Blason de Provence**
rte de Capentras a Montreux *84200*
☎ 490663134 FAX 490668305
Near river  Forest area  Near motorway
*Closed mid Dec-mid Jan*
*20 en suite (bth/shr)  (4 fmly)  (2 with balcony)  TV in all bedrooms  Mini-bar in all bedrooms  Licensed  Full central heating  Open parking available  Supervised  Child discount available 12yrs  Outdoor swimming pool  Tennis  Boule  Open terrace  Last d 21.30hrs  Languages spoken: English, Dutch, German & Spanish*
CARDS: ●● ■■ ☲ ⑩ Travellers cheques

★ ★ ★ **Safari**
1 av J H Fabre *84200*
☎ 490633535 FAX 490604999
(from town centre take Avignon road and hotel is on the right just before the large rdbt)
*Closed Jan-Feb*
*42 en suite (bth/shr)  14 rooms in annexe  (3 fmly)  (21 with balcony)  TV in all bedrooms  STV  Radio in rooms  Direct dial from all bedrooms  Licensed  Lift  Night porter  Full central heating  Open parking available  Supervised  Child discount available 10yrs  Outdoor swimming pool  Boule  Open terrace Last d 22.00hrs  Languages spoken: English & German*
CARDS: ●● ■■ ☲ ⑩ Travellers cheques

## CARQUEIRANNE Var

**L'Aumonerie** (Prop: P et D Menard)
620 av de Fontbrun *83320*
☎ 494585356
(from exit 2 on Toulon-Hyères motorway to Carqueiranne. In town after 3rd roundabout take 2nd on right)
Near sea  Near beach  Forest area
*3 en suite (bth/shr)  Full central heating  Open parking available Child discount available 2yrs  Boule  Open terrace*
CARDS: Travellers cheques

## CASTELLET, LE Var

★ ★ ★ **Castel Lumière**
1 rue Portail *83330*
☎ 494326220 FAX 494327033
Near motorway
*Closed Jan*
*6 rms  TV in all bedrooms  Licensed  Full central heating  Air conditioning in bedrooms  Child discount available 6yrs  Boule Open terrace  Last d 22.00hrs  Languages spoken: English, Italian & Spanish*

## CAUMONT-SUR-DURANCE Vaucluse

**Bed & Breakfast** (Prop: Michelle & Bernard Lefebvre)
12 chemin des Terres de Magues *84510*
☎ 490230749 FAX 490231427
(exit A7 at Avignon Sud follow signs Cavaillon. Over 2 bridges & take D973 on left towards Caumont/Le Thor. Through

Caumont, at lights turn left, then right after 150m towards Le Thor. Gite 0.5 mile on left)
Forest area
*8 rms (3 shr) No smoking in 2 bedrooms TV in 3 bedrooms Full central heating Open parking available Child discount available 10yrs Bicycle rental Last d 22.00hrs*

### CAVALAIRE-SUR-MER Var

### ★ ★ Raymond
av des Allies *83240*
☎ 494640732 FAX 494640273
(approach from A8 via Le Muy & Ste-Maxime)
Near sea  Near beach  Forest area
*Closed Oct-Mar*
*36 en suite (bth/shr) (5 fmly) (24 with balcony) No smoking in 4 bedrooms TV in all bedrooms STV Direct dial from all bedrooms Licensed Full central heating Open parking available Covered parking available Supervised Child discount available 12yrs Outdoor swimming pool Pool table Boule Bicycle rental Open terrace Last d 21.30hrs Languages spoken: English, German & Italian*
CARDS: ●● ■■ ⬚⬚ Travellers cheques

### CEILLAC Hautes-Alpes

### ★ ★ La Cascade
*05600*
☎ 492450592 FAX 492452209
Near river  Forest area
*Closed 11 Apr-end May & 11 Sep-19 Dec*
*23 rms (15 bth 6 shr) (5 fmly) (11 with balcony) TV in all bedrooms Direct dial from all bedrooms Licensed Full central heating Open parking available Child discount available 12yrs Last d 21.00hrs Languages spoken: English*

### CHÂTEAU-ARNOUX Alpes-de-Haute-Provence

### ★ ★ ★ ★ Bonne Étape
chemin du Lac *04160*
☎ 492640009 FAX 492643736
(in front of the castle)
Near river  Near lake  Forest area  Near motorway
*Closed early Jan-mid Feb & 10 days late Nov RS Nov-Mar*
*18 en suite (bth/shr) (2 fmly) (2 with balcony) TV in all bedrooms STV Radio in rooms Direct dial from all bedrooms Mini-bar in all bedrooms Licensed Full central heating Air conditioning in bedrooms Open parking available Covered parking available Supervised Outdoor swimming pool (heated) Open terrace Covered terrace V meals Last d 21.30hrs Languages spoken: English, German, Italian & Spanish*
CARDS: ●● ■■ ⬚⬚ ⓪ JCB Travellers cheques

### CHÂTEAUNEUF-DE-GADAGNE Vaucluse

### Bed & Breakfast (Prop: Colette Pabst)
211 Chemin de Bompas *84470*
☎ 490225302
Forest area
*3 rms No smoking on premises Full central heating Open parking available Covered parking available Child discount available 3yrs Languages spoken: English*

### CHÂTEAUNEUF-DU-PAPE Vaucluse

### ★ ★ ★ La Sommellerie
rte de Roquemaure *84230*
☎ 490835000 FAX 490835185
(exit A7 Orange centre to Châteauneuf-du-Pape, in the village follow directions to Roquemaure for 3km you will find La Sommellerie on the D17)

Set amid famous vineyards, La Sommellerie, once an ancient sheep-fold of the 17th century, is now a charming and comfortable country house, where Annie Paumel will receive you as a friend. Pierre Paumel, Master Chef of France creates Provençal specialities served with the matching wines. In summer, meals can be enjoyed in the arbour or at the pool side, where barbecue specialities are available from the charcoal grill. In winter a warm fire awaits you in the dining room.
Near river  Forest area
*Closed 1 week Feb*
*14 en suite (bth/shr) (3 fmly) TV in all bedrooms Direct dial from all bedrooms Licensed Full central heating Open parking available Supervised Outdoor swimming pool Solarium Boule Open terrace V meals Last d 21.30hrs Languages spoken: English, German & Italian*
ROOMS: (room only) d 450-550FF
MEALS: Continental breakfast 60FF  Lunch 170-420FF&alc  Dinner 240-420FF&alc
CARDS: ●● ■■ ⬚⬚

### CHAUFFAYER Hautes-Alpes

### ★ ★ Le Bercail
*05800*
☎ 492552221 FAX 492553155
Near river  Forest area  Near motorway
*11 en suite (bth) (2 fmly) TV in all bedrooms Radio in rooms Direct dial from all bedrooms Licensed Night porter Full central heating Open parking available Supervised Child discount available Boule Bicycle rental Open terrace Covered terrace V meals Last d 22.00hrs Languages spoken: English & German*
CARDS: ●● ■■ ⬚⬚ ⓪ Travellers cheques

### CORNILLON-CONFOUX Bouches-du-Rhône

### ★ ★ ★ Le Devem de Mirapier
rte de Grans-D19 *13250*
☎ 490559922 FAX 490558614
Forest area
*Closed 16 Dec-19 Jan*

*contd.*

15 en suite (bth/shr) No smoking in 5 bedrooms TV in all bedrooms STV Direct dial from all bedrooms Licensed Full central heating Air conditioning in bedrooms Open parking available Child discount available 12yrs Outdoor swimming pool Tennis Solarium Pool table Boule Open terrace Covered terrace V meals Last d 21.00hrs Languages spoken: English & Italian
ROOMS: (room only) s 520-620FF; d 650-780FF
CARDS: ●● ■■ ■■

---

### CRESTET Vaucluse

★ ★ **Mas de Magali**
quartier Chante Coucou 84110
☎ 490363991 FAX 490287340
(leave A7 at exit Bollèe, follow direction Vaison-la-Romaine, continue direction of Malaucene-Cardentras, then follow hotel signs)
Near river Near lake Near sea Forest area Near motorway
Closed 19 Oct-14 Mar
9 en suite (bth/shr) (2 fmly) (4 with balcony) No smoking in 2 bedrooms TV in all bedrooms STV Direct dial from all bedrooms Licensed Full central heating Open parking available Child discount available 10yrs Outdoor swimming pool Sauna Boule Bicycle rental Open terrace V meals Last d 20.30hrs Languages spoken: English, Dutch, German & Spanish
CARDS: ●● ■■ ■■ Travellers cheques

---

### CRILLON-LE-BRAVE Vaucluse

**Bed & Breakfast** (Prop: Alaine Moine)
Chemin de la Sidoiné 84410
☎ 490128096
(exit A7 at Orange in direction of Carpentras, at Carpentras take direction for Bedoin)
Forest area
5 en suite (shr) (3 fmly) Full central heating Open parking available Child discount available 8yrs Table tennis Petanque

**Domaine la Condamine** (Prop: Mme M J Eydoux)
84410
☎ 490624728 FAX 490624728
(exit A7 for Orange, take D950 for Carpentras, then D974 for Bedoin. Take right turn onto D224)
Forest area
4 en suite (shr) (1 fmly) No smoking on premises TV in all bedrooms STV Full central heating Open parking available Covered parking available Supervised Outdoor swimming pool Languages spoken: English, Italian & Spanish
CARDS: Travellers cheques

**Moulin d'Antelon** (Prop: M & Mme Ricquart)
84410
☎ 490627789 FAX 490624490
Near river Forest area
5 en suite (bth/shr) Full central heating Open parking available Covered parking available Child discount available 8yrs
CARDS: Travellers cheques

---

### CROIX-VALMER, LA Var

★ ★ ★ **Les Moulins de Paillas**
plage de Gigaro 83420
☎ 494797111 FAX 494543705
(take direction of Gigaro from the centre of La Croix-Valmer)
Near sea Near beach Forest area

---

Closed Oct-mid May
30 en suite (bth) 38 rooms in annexe (15 with balcony) TV in all bedrooms Radio in rooms Direct dial from all bedrooms Mini-bar in all bedrooms Licensed Full central heating Air conditioning in bedrooms Open parking available Child discount available 7yrs Outdoor swimming pool Solarium Open terrace Private beach Last d 22.30hrs Languages spoken: English, German, Italian & Spanish
CARDS: ●● ■■ ■■ Travellers cheques

---

### CUCURON Vaucluse

★ ★ **L'Arbre de Mai**
rue de l'Église 84160
☎ 490772510 FAX 490772510
(from Cavaillon (A7) take turning for Pertuis, after Cadenet turn left signed Cucuron)
Near river Near lake Forest area In town centre Near motorway
Closed Nov-Feb
6 en suite (shr) (3 fmly) (1 with balcony) Licensed Full central heating Child discount available 5yrs Open terrace Last d 21.30hrs Languages spoken: English, Spanish & Italian
ROOMS: (room only) d 380FF
MEALS: Lunch fr 90FF&alc Dinner fr 145FF&alc
CARDS: ●● ■■ Travellers cheques

---

### EMBRUN Hautes-Alpes

★ ★ **De la Mairie**
pl Barthélon 05200
☎ 492432065 FAX 492434702
Near lake In town centre
Closed Oct, Nov & 15 days in Mar
24 en suite (bth/shr) (5 fmly) TV in all bedrooms STV Direct dial from all bedrooms Licensed Lift Full central heating Child discount available Open terrace Casino V meals Last d 21.30hrs Languages spoken: English & German
CARDS: ●● ■■ ■■ ● Travellers cheques

---

### ENTRAIGUES-SUR-LA-SORGUES Vaucluse

**Domaine du Grand Causeran** (Prop: M Papapietro)
allée du Grand Causeran 84320
☎ 490232909 FAX 490232907
Near river Near motorway
5 rms (4 bth/shr) TV available Full central heating Open parking available Supervised No children 7yrs Outdoor swimming pool Boule Table tennis Croquet Languages spoken: English
CARDS: Travellers cheques

**Mas de 4 Chemins** (Prop: M & Mme Martin)
19 Chemin des Tempines 84320
☎ 490621439
Near river
Closed Nov-Etr
3 en suite (shr) No smoking on premises Full central heating Open parking available Child discount available

---

### ENTRECHAUX Vaucluse

**L'Éscleriade** (Prop: Vincent Gallo)
rte de St-Marcellin 84340
☎ 490460132 FAX 490460371
Near river Near lake Forest area
Closed Nov-Feb

6 en suite (bth/shr) (1 fmly) (5 with balcony) TV available
Direct-dial available Full central heating Open parking
available Supervised Last d 19.30hrs Languages spoken:
English & Italian
CARDS: ● ■ Carte Bleue,Eurocard

## EYGALIÈRES Bouches-du-Rhône

### ★ ★ Auberge Crin Blanc
rte d'Orgon 13810
☎ 490959317 FAX 490906062
Forest area
Closed 16 Nov-14 Mar
10 en suite (bth/shr) (10 fmly) Direct dial from all bedrooms
Licensed Open parking available Supervised Child discount
available 11yrs Outdoor swimming pool Tennis Boule Last d
21.30hrs Languages spoken: English

## EYRAGUES Bouches-du-Rhône

### Le Mas des Chats Qui Dorment (Prop: Robert &
Christiane Poli)
Chemin des Prés 13630
☎ 490941971 FAX 490941971
(from Avignon take D571 to Châteaurenard and on to
Eyragues. In Eyragues from 'La Place' take the road with the
pharmacy on your right, past 2 stops and after 1.5kms follow
sign on left)
Forest area
Closed 16 Sep-Mar
3 rms (1 shr) (2 fmly) No smoking on premises Open parking
available Child discount available 3yrs Bicycle rental Open
terrace Languages spoken: English Italian
ROOMS: d 250-280FF
CARDS: Travellers cheques

## FARLÈDE, LA Var

### Bed & Breakfast (Prop: Maryse Lallier)
1417 rue de la Gare 83210
☎ 494330179 FAX 494330179
Forest area
5 en suite (bth/shr) (1 fmly) (3 with balcony) No smoking on
premises Full central heating Open parking available Child
discount available Outdoor swimming pool Boule Table tennis
Library TV room

## FAYENCE Var

### ★ ★ ★ Moulin de la Camandoule
chemin Notre Dame des Cyprès 83400
☎ 494760084 FAX 494761040
This authentic mill is situated in the village of Fayence, which
reputedly has more hours of sun in a year than anywhere else
in France, and the purest air to breath in. Located in the
hinterland of the Côte d'Azur, it features an exceptional
interior where the old millstones and presses have been
preserved and can be found in the lounge and restaurant.
Bedrooms vary in style and size, but are all equipped with
modern appointments. The menu offers classic dishes based
on regional recipes and ingredients,augmented by a selection
of fine wines.
Near river Near lake Forest area Near motorway
11 en suite (bth/shr) (1 fmly) (2 with balcony) TV in all
bedrooms STV Direct dial from all bedrooms Licensed Full
central heating Open parking available Child discount
available 9yrs Outdoor swimming pool Boule Open terrace

Covered terrace V meals Last d 21.30hrs Languages spoken:
English, German & Italian
ROOMS: (room only) s 335-515FF; d 515-980FF
MEALS: Full breakfast 75FF Lunch 165-320FF&alc Dinner
165-320FF&alc
CARDS: ● ■ Carte Bleu,Eurocard Travellers cheques

## FONTAINE-DE-VAUCLUSE Vaucluse

### ★ ★ Hotel du Parc
Les Bourgades 84800
☎ 490203157 FAX 490202703
(off N100 Apt/Avignon)
Near river
Closed 2 Jan-15 Feb
12 en suite (bth/shr) (2 fmly) (6 with balcony) Direct dial from
all bedrooms Licensed Full central heating Open parking
available Child discount available 8yrs Fishing Open terrace V
meals Last d 21.30hrs Languages spoken: Italian & Spanish
CARDS: ● ■ ■ ■ Travellers cheques

## FONTVIEILLE Bouches-du-Rhône

### Bed & Breakfast (Prop: E & J Ricard-Damidot)
107 av Frederic Mistral 13990
☎ 490547267 FAX 490546443
Forest area In town centre
Closed Nov-Etr
2 en suite (bth/shr) No smoking on premises Full central
heating Covered parking available Supervised Child discount
available Languages spoken: English
CARDS: Travellers cheques

### ★ ★ ★ ★ La Régalido (Relais et Châteaux)
rue Frederic Mistral 13990
☎ 490546022 FAX 490546429
(approach via D17 from Arles)
Forest area In town centre
Closed 3 Jan-11 Feb
15 en suite (bth/shr) (3 fmly) (3 with balcony) TV in all
bedrooms STV Direct dial from all bedrooms Mini-bar in all
bedrooms Licensed Night porter Full central heating Air
conditioning in bedrooms Open parking available Supervised
Open terrace V meals Last d 21.15hrs Languages spoken:
German & Spanish
CARDS: ● ■ ■ ■ JCB Travellers cheques

### ★ ★ La Ripaille
rte des Baux 13990
☎ 490547315 FAX 490546069
Near river Near lake Near sea Forest area In town centre
Near motorway
Closed mid Oct-mid Mar
20 en suite (bth/shr) (2 fmly) (9 with balcony) TV in all
bedrooms Direct-dial available Licensed Full central heating
Open parking available Supervised Child discount available
9yrs Outdoor swimming pool (heated) Riding Solarium Boule
Open terrace Last d 21.00hrs Languages spoken: English &
Spanish
CARDS: ● ■ Travellers cheques

### ★ ★ Hostellerie de la Tour
3 rue des Plumelets 13990
☎ 490547221
(just before entering Fontvieille from the direction of Arles
turn left towards Tarascon. Hotel in 800mtrs)
Forest area Near motorway
*contd.*

*Closed 31 Oct-1 Mar*
*10 en suite (shr) (1 fmly) Direct dial from all bedrooms*
*Licensed Night porter Full central heating Open parking*
*available Child discount available 2yrs Outdoor swimming*
*pool Open terrace V meals Languages spoken: English &*
*German*
ROOMS: (room only) s fr 220FF; d fr 275FF
MEALS: Continental breakfast 45FF Lunch 85FF
Dinner 95FF
CARDS: 🔵 ⬛ Travellers cheques

## FORCALQUIER Alpes-de-Haute-Provence

### ★ ★ ★ Hostellerie des 2 Lions
11 pl du Bourguet *04300*
☎ 492752530 FAX 492750641
In town centre Near motorway
*Closed Jan-Mar*
*16 en suite (bth/shr) (2 fmly) No smoking on premises TV in*
*all bedrooms STV Mini-bar in all bedrooms Licensed Full*
*central heating Open parking available (charged) Child*
*discount available 10yrs Last d 21.15hrs Languages spoken:*
*Italian*
CARDS: 🔵 ⬛ ⬛ Travellers cheques

## FOX-AMPHOUX Var

### ★ ★ ★ Auberge du Vieux Fox
pl de l'Église *83670*
☎ 494807169 FAX 494807838
Near lake Forest area
*8 en suite (bth/shr) (1 fmly) TV in all bedrooms Licensed Full*
*central heating Child discount available Pool table Open*
*terrace V meals Last d 21.30hrs Languages spoken: English &*
*German*
CARDS: 🔵 ⬛ ⬛ ⬛ Travellers cheques

## GAP Hautes-Alpes

### ★ ★ Carina-Pavillon
Chabanas rte de Veynes *05000*
☎ 492520273 FAX 492533472
((at 2km from town centre in direction of Valence-Orange)
Forest area
*Closed Xmas-early Jan*
*82 en suite (bth/shr) 50 rooms in annexe (30 fmly) (50 with*
*balcony) TV in all bedrooms STV Direct dial from all*
*bedrooms Mini-bar in 8 bedrooms Licensed Full central*
*heating Open parking available Covered parking available*
*Child discount available Indoor swimming pool (heated)*
*Tennis Boule Mini-golf Bicycle rental Open terrace Covered*
*terrace Last d 21.00hrs Languages spoken: English &*
*German*
CARDS: 🔵 ⬛ ⬛ ⬛ Travellers cheques

### ★ ★ Fons-Regina
13 av de Fontreyne *05000*
☎ 492539899 FAX 492515451
(off the main road to Marseille)
Forest area
*25 en suite (bth/shr) (1 with balcony) TV in all bedrooms STV*
*Direct dial from all bedrooms Licensed Full central heating*
*Open parking available Child discount available 10yrs Outdoor*
*swimming pool (heated) Boule Open terrace V meals*
*Languages spoken: English & Italian*
CARDS: 🔵 ⬛ ⬛ ⬛ Travellers cheques

## GASSIN Var

### ★ ★ ★ ★ Domaine de l'Astragale
chemin de la Gassine *83580*
☎ 494974898 FAX 494971601
(50m before the entrance of St Tropez, before the Garage
Ferrari on the right)
Near sea Near beach Near motorway
*Closed mid Oct-mid May*
*34 en suite (bth/shr) (16 fmly) (18 with balcony) TV in all*
*bedrooms STV Radio in rooms Direct dial from all bedrooms*
*Mini-bar in all bedrooms Room-safe Licensed Night porter*
*Full central heating Air conditioning in bedrooms Open*
*parking available Covered parking available Child discount*
*available 7yrs Outdoor swimming pool (heated) Tennis*
*Solarium Boule Jacuzzi/spa Open terrace Table tennis, private*
*beach Last d 22.00hrs Languages spoken: English, German,*
*Italian & Spanish*
CARDS: 🔵 ⬛ ⬛ ⬛ Travellers cheques

### ★ ★ ★ ★ Le Mas de Chastelas
quartier Bertaud *83580*
☎ 494567171 FAX 494567156
(leave A8 exit Le Muy in direction of Ste-Maxime, follow signs
to St Tropez, pass Port Grimaud, on arrival at lights crossing at
La Foux continue on D98, main St Tropez road, turn right at
big sign "Domaine Bertaud Relieu")
Near sea Near beach Forest area Near motorway
*30 rms (28 bth/shr) 6 rooms in annexe (4 fmly) (6 with*
*balcony) TV in all bedrooms STV Direct dial from all*
*bedrooms Mini-bar in 18 bedrooms Room-safe Licensed Lift*
*Night porter Air conditioning in bedrooms Open parking*
*available Supervised Child discount available Outdoor*
*swimming pool Boule Open terrace Last d 21.30hrs*
*Languages spoken: English, German, Italian & Sapnish*
CARDS: 🔵 ⬛ ⬛ ⬛

### ★ ★ Relais Bon Accueil
Presqu'île de Giens *83400*
☎ 494582048 FAX 494589046
Near sea Near beach
*10 en suite (bth/shr) 1 rooms in annexe TV in all bedrooms*
*Direct dial from all bedrooms Licensed Full central heating*
*Open parking available Child discount available 12yrs*
*Languages spoken: English, German & Italian*
CARDS: 🔵 ⬛ ⬛ Travellers cheques

## GÉMENOS Bouches-du-Rhône

### ★ ★ ★ ★ Relais de la Magdeleine
rte d'Aix-en-Provence *13420*
☎ 442322016 FAX 442320226
(access via A50 exit Toulon)
Set in a park, this residence offers its visitors a friendly
reception in informal surroundings. The pleasant bedrooms
have good amenities and in summer meals are served on the
terrace in the shade of the plane trees.
Near river Forest area Near motorway
*Closed Dec-15 Mar*
*24 en suite (bth/shr) (3 fmly) TV in all bedrooms STV Direct*
*dial from all bedrooms Licensed Lift Full central heating Open*
*parking available Supervised Child discount available 7yrs*
*Outdoor swimming pool Boule Open terrace Covered terrace*
*V meals Last d 21.30hrs Languages spoken: English & German*

**Relais de la Magdeleine**
ROOMS: (room only) s 440-550FF; d 560-900FF
**Reductions over 1 night**
MEALS: Full breakfast 75FF Lunch 160-260FF&alc Dinner
260-320FF&alc
CARDS: ●● ☲☲ Travellers cheques

### GIGONDAS Vaucluse

★ ★ **Florets**
rte des Dentelles *84190*
☎ 490658501 FAX 490658380
(from N by motorway exit Bollène, then follow directions of
Carpentras, 28km from Bollène)
Forest area
*Closed 2 Jan-Feb*
*14 en suite (bth/shr) 5 rooms in annexe (1 fmly) (5 with*
*balcony) TV in all bedrooms Direct dial from all bedrooms Full*
*central heating Open parking available Supervised Child*
*discount available Boule Open terrace Covered terrace V*
*meals Last d 21.00hrs Languages spoken: English & Spanish*
CARDS: ●● ■■ ☲☲ ⑩ Travellers cheques

### GORDES Vaucluse

★ ★ ★ **Les Bories**
rte de l'Abbaye de Senanque *84220*
☎ 490720051 FAX 490720122
(Motorway to Avignon-Sud in direction of Apt. Before Gordes
centre turn left rte de l'Abbaye de Sénanque)
Forest area In town centre Near motorway
*Closed mid Nov-mid Feb*
*18 en suite (bth/shr) 8 rooms in annexe (1 fmly) (10 with*
*balcony) TV in all bedrooms STV Direct dial from all*
*bedrooms Mini-bar in all bedrooms Licensed Lift Full central*
*heating Air conditioning in bedrooms Open parking available*
*Indoor swimming pool (heated) Outdoor swimming pool*
*Tennis Solarium Boule Open terrace Last d 21.00hrs*
*Languages spoken: English & German*
CARDS: ●● ■■ ☲☲ ⑩ Travellers cheques

**Villa La Lèbre** (Prop: P Lawrence)
St-Pantaléon *84220*
☎ 490722074 FAX 490722074
(from Avignon take N100 towards Apt. At Coustellet take D2
for Gordes. After Les Imberts take D207 & D148 to St
Pantaléon. Pass church & stay on D104 for 50metres, take left
onto small uphill road. 3rd drive on right)
*1 en suite (bth/shr) Full central heating Open parking available*
*Supervised Open terrace Languages spoken: English, German,*
*Italian & Arabic*
ROOMS: s 220FF; d 270FF ✱ **Reductions over 1 night**

### GRAMBOIS Vaucluse

★ ★ ★ *Le Clos des Sources*
Quartier Le Brusquet *84240*
☎ 490779355 FAX 490779296
Near river Forest area Near motorway
*Closed mid Nov-end Feb*
*(3 fmly) (12 with balcony) No smoking in 4 bedrooms TV in 12*
*bedrooms Licensed Night porter Full central heating Open*
*parking available Supervised Child discount available Outdoor*
*swimming pool Golf Solarium Boule Open terrace Last d*
*22.00hrs Languages spoken: English & Italian*
CARDS: ●● ■■ Travellers cheques

★ ★ ★ *Clos des Sources*
quartier le Breusquet *84240*
☎ 490779738 FAX 490779296
(Leave A7 at Cavaillon/Aix-en-Provence take direction of
Pertuis on D973 continue to La Tour d'Aigues and onto
Grambois)
Forest area
*Closed Jan*
*12 en suite (bth/shr) (3 fmly) (12 with balcony) No smoking in*
*2 bedrooms TV in all bedrooms STV Direct dial from all*
*bedrooms Licensed Night porter Full central heating Open*
*parking available Supervised Child discount available 10yrs*
*Outdoor swimming pool Solarium Boule Open terrace Wkly*
*live entertainment Last d 21.15hrs Languages spoken: English*
*& Italian*
CARDS: ●● ■■ ☲☲ Travellers cheques

### GRANS Bouches-du-Rhône

**Domaine de Bois Vert** (Prop: J-P & V Richard)
Quartier Montauban *13450*
☎ 490558298 FAX 490558298
(from A7 exit at Salon Sud follow signs for Marseille. At
Lancon-de-Provence turn right onto D19 for Grans. After 5kms
follow signs for establishment & turn right)
Near river Forest area
*Closed 5 Jan-Feb*
*3 en suite (bth/shr) (2 fmly) No smoking on premises Full*
*central heating Open parking available Covered parking*
*available Supervised Child discount available 12yrs Outdoor*
*swimming pool Table tennis Languages spoken: English*
ROOMS: s fr 280FF; d 310-360FF
CARDS: Travellers cheques

### GRAVESON Bouches-du-Rhône

★ ★ *Mas des Amandiers*
rte d'Avignon *13690*
☎ 490958176 FAX 490958518
Near motorway
*Closed mid Oct-mid Mar*
*25 en suite (bth) (3 fmly) (1 with balcony) TV in all bedrooms*
*Direct dial from all bedrooms Licensed Full central heating*
*Open parking available Supervised Outdoor swimming pool*
*(heated) Tennis Fishing Boule Bicycle rental Open terrace*
*Languages spoken: English & Spanish*
CARDS: ●● ■■ ☲☲ ⑩ Travellers cheques

## GRÉOUX-LES-BAINS Alpes-de-Haute-Provence

### ★ ★ ★ Hotel Villa Borghése
av des Thermes 04800
☎ 492780091 FAX 492780755
(access via A51 exit 'Manosque')
Near river  Near lake  Forest area  In town centre  Near motorway
Closed 26 Nov-24 Mar
67 en suite (bth/shr) (4 fmly) (36 with balcony) TV in all bedrooms  STV  Radio in rooms  Direct dial from all bedrooms  Mini-bar in all bedrooms  Licensed  Lift  Night porter  Full central heating  Air conditioning in bedrooms  Open parking available  Covered parking available (charged)  Child discount available 12yrs  Outdoor swimming pool (heated)  Tennis  Sauna  Solarium  Boule  Jacuzzi/spa  Open terrace  Covered terrace  Last d 21.30hrs  Languages spoken: English, German & Italian
CARDS: ●● ■■ ■■ ⑨ Travellers cheques

## GRIMAUD Var

### ★ ★ ★ Hotel de La Boulangerie
rte de Collobrières 83310
☎ 494432316 FAX 494433827
Forest area
Closed 11 Oct-Mar
10 en suite (bth/shr) (1 fmly) (1 with balcony) TV in 4 bedrooms  STV  Direct dial from all bedrooms  Mini-bar in 1 bedroom  Licensed  Full central heating  Open parking available  Outdoor swimming pool  Tennis  Open terrace

## HYÈRES Var

### ★ ★ Inter Hotel Centrotel
45 av Edith Cavell 83400
☎ 494383810 FAX 494383773
Near sea  In town centre  Near motorway
24 en suite (bth/shr) (5 fmly) (2 with balcony) TV in all bedrooms  Direct dial from 23 bedrooms  Mini-bar in 4 bedrooms  Full central heating  Air conditioning in bedrooms  Covered parking available (charged)  Supervised Child discount available 12yrs  Languages spoken: English & German
CARDS: ●● ■■ ■■ ⑨ Travellers cheques

### ★ ★ ★ Le Manoir
Ile de Port-Cros 83400
☎ 494059052 FAX 494059089
Near sea  Near beach  Forest area
Closed Oct-Apr
22 en suite (bth/shr) 2 rooms in annexe (5 fmly) (8 with balcony) Mini-bar in all bedrooms  Room-safe  Licensed  Full central heating  Child discount available 10yrs  Solarium  Boule  Open terrace  Covered terrace  Last d 21.00hrs  Languages spoken: English & Italian
CARDS: ●● ■■ Travellers cheques

### ★ ★ Du Parc
7 bd Pasteur 83400
☎ 494650665 FAX 494659328
(motorway arrives in Hyères from Toulon/Nice A570, 600m further turn left at Hotel Mecure, 600m further turn right at Casino de Jeux, hotel is 100m on left)
In town centre  Near motorway
41 en suite (bth/shr) (13 fmly) TV in all bedrooms  STV  Direct dial from all bedrooms  Licensed  Night porter  Full central

heating  Open parking available  Child discount available 12yrs  Bicycle rental  Last d 20.30hrs  Languages spoken: English, Italian, German, Russian & Spanish
CARDS: ●● ■■ Travellers cheques

## HYÈRES-LES-PALMIERS Var

### Villa Li Rouvre (Prop: Jacqueline & Pierre Brunet)
Chemin de Beauvallon Haut 83400
☎ 494354344
(A57 towards Hyères/Nice. Then A570 towards Hyères, at rdbt (where rail station is indicated) take 4th exit/2nd exit at next rdbt/ left at t-junc/1st right(Av.Victor)/2nd left(Ch Maurettes)/2nd right/1stleft)
Near sea  Forest area  In town centre  Near motorway
2 rms (1 bth/shr) (2 with balcony) Full central heating  Open parking available  Child discount available 10yrs  Outdoor swimming pool  Open terrace

## ILE-DE-LA-BARTHÉLASSE Vaucluse

### ★ ★ La Ferme
chemin des Bois, Ile de la Barthelasse 84000
☎ 490825753 FAX 490271547
(from A7 exit at Avignon Nord, towards Avignon, take N100 over bridge turn right onto D228, hotel is 5kms)
Near river  Forest area
Closed Nov-Feb
20 en suite (bth/shr)  No smoking in 3 bedrooms  TV in all bedrooms  Direct dial from all bedrooms  Licensed  Full central heating  Air conditioning in bedrooms  Open parking available  Outdoor swimming pool  Open terrace  Last d 21.30hrs  Languages spoken: Italian
ROOMS: (room only) s 340-370FF;  d 420-460FF
MEALS: Continental breakfast 53FF  Lunch 115-220FF  Dinner 115-220FF
CARDS: ●● ■■ ■■ JCB Travellers cheques

## ILE DE PORQUEROLLES Var

### ★ ★ ★ ★ Le Mas de Langoustier
chemin du Langoustier 83400
☎ 494583009 FAX 494583602
(by boat from La Tour-Fondue and by shuttle from Porquerolles port to the hotel)
Near sea  Near beach  Forest area
Closed 16 Oct-Mar
51 en suite (bth/shr) (6 fmly) TV in all bedrooms  Direct dial from all bedrooms  Mini-bar in all bedrooms  Room-safe  Licensed  Lift  Night porter  Full central heating  Child discount available 6yrs  Tennis  Boule  Bicycle rental  Open terrace  V meals  Last d 21.00hrs  Languages spoken: English & Italian
CARDS: ●● ■■ ■■ ⑨

## ISLE-SUR-LA-SORGUE, L' Vaucluse

### Domaine de la Fontaine (Prop: M & Mme Sundheimer)
920 chemin du Bosquet 84800
☎ 490380144 FAX 490385342
(from A7 exit at Avignon Sud. Take D25 to L'Isle-sur-la-Sorgue. Take N100 towards Apt, on outskirts of village after Citroen Station take 1st right then 1st left)
Situated in the Luberon Valley, near Avignon, is the Isle sur Sorgue, a typical Provence village. This property is an old Provençal house, where Irmi and Dominique Sundheimer welcome guests.Five charming rooms available, and a private swimming pool. The house is set in four hectares of lush

garden. Dine on the terrace in the romantic atmosphere, under the shadow of the plane tree.
Near river Forest area
*Closed 16 Jan-28 Feb*
*5 en suite (shr) (2 fmly) (1 with balcony) TV in all bedrooms Full central heating Open parking available Outdoor swimming pool Boule Last d 20.00hrs Languages spoken: English & German*
ROOMS: d 490-580FF
MEALS: Dinner 140FF

**Domaines des Costières** (Prop: Mme Josette Pecchi) *84800*
☎ 490383919
(16 kms east of Avignon via N100)
Near river Forest area Near motorway
*6 en suite (bth/shr) (2 fmly) No smoking on premises Full central heating Open parking available Supervised Child discount available 15yrs Open terrace Last d 17.30hrs Languages spoken: English & Italian*
CARDS: Travellers cheques

★ ★ ★ **Mas de Cure Bourse**
rte de Caumont *84800*
☎ 490381658 FAX 490385231
(travel in direction Caumont, establiment has large sign)
Near river Forest area
*13 en suite (bth/shr) (3 fmly) (3 with balcony) TV in all bedrooms Direct dial from all bedrooms Licensed Full central heating Open parking available Supervised Outdoor swimming pool Boule Open terrace Last d 21.30hrs Languages spoken: English, German & Spanish*
CARDS: ●● ▆▆

**La Meridienne** (Prop: M & Mme G Tarayre)
Chemin de la Lone *84800*
☎ 490384026 FAX 490385846
(enter L'Isle-sur-Sorgue and continue across town towards Apt on N100. House 3km on left)
Near river Forest area Near motorway
*5 en suite (shr) (1 fmly) Open parking available Covered parking available Supervised Outdoor swimming pool Languages spoken: English & Spanish*
CARDS: Travellers cheques

**ISSAMBRES, LES** Var

★ ★ **La Quiétude**
N98 *83380*
☎ 494969434 FAX 494496782
Near sea Near beach Near motorway
*Closed 15 Oct-20 Feb*
*19 en suite (bth/shr) (6 fmly) (17 with balcony) TV in all bedrooms Direct dial from all bedrooms Room-safe Licensed Full central heating Open parking available Supervised Child discount available 12yrs Outdoor swimming pool Open terrace Covered terrace Last d 21.30hrs Languages spoken: English & Spanish*
CARDS: ●● ▆▆ Travellers cheques

**JOUCAS** Vaucluse

★ ★ **Hostellerie des Commandeurs**
Le Village *84220*
☎ 490057801 FAX 490057447
Forest area
*13 en suite (shr) TV in all bedrooms Radio in rooms Direct dial*

*from all bedrooms Licensed Full central heating Open parking available Supervised Child discount available 10yrs Outdoor swimming pool Boule Open terrace V meals Last d 21.00hrs Languages spoken: English & German*
CARDS: ●● ▆▆ Travellers cheques

★ ★ ★ ★ **Mas des Herbes Blanches**
rte de Murs *84220*
☎ 490057979 FAX 490057196
(A7 exit Cavaillon, direction Apt (D2) at Coustellet direction Gordes then Joucas)
*Closed 3 Jan-11 Mar*
*19 en suite (bth/shr) (2 fmly) (9 with balcony) TV in all bedrooms STV Direct dial from all bedrooms Mini-bar in all bedrooms Licensed Full central heating Air conditioning in bedrooms Open parking available Covered parking available Supervised Outdoor swimming pool (heated) Tennis Boule Bicycle rental Open terrace Last d 21.30hrs Languages spoken: English & Italian*
CARDS: ●● ▆▆ ▆▆ ⓪

**LACOSTE** Vaucluse

**Bonne Terre** (Prop: Roland Lamy)
rte de St Veran *84480*
☎ 490758553 FAX 490758553
(In Apt, take N100 towards Avignon, Lacoste is on the left, the house is close to the post office)
Forest area
*6 en suite (bth/shr) (5 with balcony) No smoking on premises TV in 3 bedrooms Full central heating Open parking available Outdoor swimming pool Bicycle rental*
ROOMS: s 540FF; d 570FF
CARDS: ▆▆ Travellers cheques

**Domaine de Layaude-Basse** (Prop: Oivier Mazel)
*84710*
☎ 490759006 FAX 490759903
(Cavaillon to N100 in direction of Apt turn right at traffic lights in direction of Lacoste)
Near sea Forest area
*6 en suite (shr) (2 fmly) Full central heating Open parking available Child discount available 10yrs Outdoor swimming pool*
ROOMS: d 400-500FF
MEALS: Dinner 120FF*

**Relais du Procureur** (Prop: Antoine de Gebelin)
rue Basse *84480*
☎ 490758228 FAX 490758694
(from Avignon take N100 toward Apt, turn right at the village of Lumieres following signs for Lacoste, once in the village Relais du Procureur is well signed although the narrow streets can be difficult to navigate in a large car)
Forest area Near motorway
*RS Jan & Feb*
*7 en suite (bth/shr) TV in 6 bedrooms Full central heating No children 7yrs Outdoor swimming pool Last d 9pm Languages spoken: English*
ROOMS: (incl. dinner) s 500FF; d 500-650FF
**✱ Reductions over 1 night**
CARDS: ●● ▆▆

## LAGNES Vaucluse

**L'Hacienda** (Prop: Elayne Murphy)
Chemin des Ballardes *84800*
☎ 490382464
(from Isle sur la Sorgue, take Route d'Apt for approx 4km, at
sign on left 'Mas de Curebourg-Antiquaires, take the opposite
right turn, at crossrds turn left for approx 50m, at first electric
pole on right, turn left, house on right at end of lane)
Near river  Forest area
*7 rms (5 shr) (2 fmly) Open parking available  Child discount
available  Outdoor swimming pool  Boule  Open terrace
Languages spoken: English & Spanish*
CARDS: Travellers cheques

**Le Mas du Grand Jonquier** (Prop: M & Mme Greck)
*84800*
☎ 490209013 FAX 490209118
(exit autoroute Avignon Sud in the direction of Apt-Sisteron-
Digne)
Forest area
*6 en suite (shr) (1 fmly) (3 with balcony) TV in all bedrooms
Full central heating  Open parking available  Child discount
available 8yrs  Outdoor swimming pool  Boule  Bicycle rental
Last d 8pm  Languages spoken: English, German, Italian &
Spanish*
MEALS: Dinner 130FF✱
CARDS: ●● ▆▆ Travellers cheques

**La Pastorale** (Prop: Elizabeth Negrel)
Les Gardiolles, rte de Fontaine de Vaucluse *84800*
☎ 490202518 FAX 490202186
(from Avignon Sud/L'Isle-sur-la-Orgue motorway junction
head towards Apt for 13km, through Petit Palais then towards
Fontaine de Vaucluse. Cross N100 onto D24 and La Pastorale in
7th house on left)
Near river  Forest area  Near motorway
*4 en suite (bth/shr) (3 fmly) Full central heating  Open parking
available  Covered parking available  Child discount available
Boule  Languages spoken: English & German*
CARDS: Travellers cheques

## LAMBESC Bouches-du-Rhône

**Bed & Breakfast** (Prop: Mme Jeanne Meunier)
Mas de Rabarin, Chemin des Fédons *13410*
☎ 442571489 FAX 442570367
Near river  Forest area
*1 en suite (shr) Radio in rooms  Full central heating  Open
parking available  Child discount available 10yrs  Open terrace
Covered terrace  Languages spoken: English & Spanish*
CARDS: Travellers cheques

## LAPALUD Vaucluse

**Le Bergerie les Iles** (Prop: Simone et Gabriel Guet)
*84840*
☎ 490403082 FAX 490402429
(leave A7 at Bollène, follow signs to Lapalud. At rdbt, go N
towards Montélimar, turning is about 500yds along road)
Near lake  Forest area
*2 rms (1 shr) No smoking on premises  Full central heating
Open parking available  Child discount available 10yrs  Fishing
Last d 17.00hrs  Languages spoken: English, Spanish &
Italian*

## LAURIS Vaucluse

**Le Maison des Sources** (Prop: Martin Collart)
Chemin des Fraysses *84360*
☎ 490082219 & 608330640 FAX 490082219
(A7 exit Cavaillon towards Pertuis or D973 Cavaillon-Pertuis)
Near river  Near lake  Forest area  Near motorway
*4 en suite (bth/shr) (2 fmly) (1 with balcony) Full central
heating  Open parking available  Table tennis*
ROOMS: s 370-380FF; d 430-450FF
MEALS: Dinner fr 140FF✱

## LAVANDOU, LE Var

★ ★ **Auberge de la Falaise**
34 bd de la Balèine, St-Clair *83980*
☎ 494710135 FAX 494717948
Near sea  Near beach
*Closed 26 Oct-24 Mar*
*14 rms (5 bth 8 shr) 1 rooms in annexe  (2 fmly) (7 with
balcony) TV in all bedrooms  STV  Direct dial from all
bedrooms  Room-safe  Licensed  Night porter  Full central
heating  Open parking available  Supervised  Open terrace  Last
d 21.00hrs  Languages spoken: English, German & Italian*
CARDS: ●● ▆▆ Travellers cheques

★ ★ ★ **Belle Vue**
St-Clair *83980*
☎ 494710106 FAX 494716472
Near sea  Near beach
*Closed Nov-Mar*
*19 en suite (bth/shr) (7 with balcony) TV in all bedrooms  STV
Radio in rooms  Direct dial from all bedrooms  Mini-bar in all
bedrooms  Full central heating  Open parking available
Covered parking available (charged) Languages spoken:
English & German*
CARDS: ●● ■■ ▆▆ ⑩ Travellers cheques

★ ★ ★ **Hotel Les Roches**
1 av des 3 Dauphins-Aiguebelle *83980*
☎ 494710507 FAX 494710840
(from Toulon A57 towards Hyères-Le Lavandou. D559 until
Aiguebelle)
Near sea  Near beach  Forest area  Near motorway
*7 Apr-8 Oct*
*40 en suite (bth/shr) (8 fmly) (40 with balcony) TV in all
bedrooms  STV  Direct dial from all bedrooms  Mini-bar in all
bedrooms  Room-safe  Licensed  Night porter  Full central
heating  Air conditioning in bedrooms  Open parking available
Outdoor swimming pool  Solarium  Open terrace  Last d
22.00hrs  Languages spoken: English, German, Italian &
Spanish*
ROOMS: s 1600-2700FF; d 1700-2700FF
MEALS: Continental breakfast 110FF
Dinner 350-450FF&alc
CARDS: ●● ■■ ▆▆ ⑩ Travellers cheques

## LORGUES Var

**La Matabone** (Prop: M et Mme Discacciati)
1614 rte de Vidauban *83510*
☎ 494676206 FAX 494676206
(A8 exit Le Luc N7 Vidauban)
Near river  Near sea  Forest area  Near motorway
*6 en suite (shr) (2 fmly) No smoking in 1 bedroom  TV in all
bedrooms  Full central heating  Open parking available  Child*

discount available 10 yrs  Outdoor swimming pool  Boule
Bicycle rental  Open terrace  Last d 17.00hrs  Languages
spoken: Italian & Spanish
ROOMS: d 375-675FF

### LORIOL-DU-COMTAT Vaucluse

**Château Talaud** (Prop: M et Mme H Deiters-Kommer)
*84870*
☎ 490657100 FAX 490657793
(A7 exit 23 Avignon North, after toll booth left D942 direction
of Carpentras for 10km, exit D107 Loriol-du-Comtat/Monteux
Est, after 1.8km château on left at end long entrance)
A small, fully restored castle dated 1732, located in its own
vineyard just 15 minutes from the cathedral city of Avignon.
The atmosphere is one of calm and tranquillity, the rooms
luxuriously decorated and the Dutch owners give their guests
every consideration.
Near river  Forest area  Near motorway
*Closed Feb*
*6 en suite (bth/shr)  (2 fmly)  No smoking on premises  TV in all
bedrooms  STV  Direct-dial available  Full central heating  Open
parking available  Covered parking available  Child discount
available 12yrs  Outdoor swimming pool  Boule  Bicycle rental
Languages spoken: English, Dutch, German & Russian*
ROOMS: s fr 700FF; d 750-1000FF
**Reductions over 1 night**
MEALS: Dinner fr 250FF
CARDS: ●● ☲ Travellers cheques

**Famille Guillermin** (Prop: Claude & Josette Guillermin)
Le Deves *84870*
☎ 490657062
(on the D950 3km from Carpentras in the direction of Orange)
Near river  Near lake  Forest area  Near motorway
*6 en suite (bth/shr)  Full central heating  Open parking available
Outdoor swimming pool  Boule  Languages spoken: English*
CARDS: Travellers cheques

### LOURMARIN Vaucluse

★ ★ ★ **Guilles**
rte de Vaugines *84160*
☎ 490683055 FAX 490683741
(from A7 exit at Senas follow signs for Mallemort (D23), then
take D973 to Lauris, then D27 to Lourmarin)
Forest area
*Closed 6 Nov-end Feb*
*28 en suite (bth)  (1 fmly)  (8 with balcony)  TV in all bedrooms
Mini-bar in all bedrooms  Licensed  Night porter  Full central
heating  Open parking available  Supervised  Child discount
available 12yrs  Outdoor swimming pool  Tennis  Boule  Open
terrace  Covered terrace  Last d 21.15hrs  Languages spoken:
English & Italian*

### MARIGNANE Bouches-du-Rhône

★ ★ ★ **Sofitel Marseille Aéroport**
Aéroport de Marseille Provence *13700*
☎ 442784278 FAX 442784270
Near sea  Near motorway
*179 en suite (bth)  No smoking in 22 bedrooms  TV in all
bedrooms  STV  Radio in rooms  Mini-bar in all bedrooms
Licensed  Lift  Night porter  Full central heating  Air
conditioning in bedrooms  Open parking available  Supervised
Child discount available  Outdoor swimming pool  Tennis
Sauna  Solarium  Gym  Boule  Jacuzzi/spa  Open terrace*

Covered terrace  ping pong  Last d 24.00hrs  Languages
spoken: English, Arabic, German, Italian & Spanish
CARDS: ●● ■■ ☲ ⑩ Travellers cheques

### MARSEILLE Bouches-du-Rhône

★ ★ **Climat de France**
6 rue Beauvau *13001*
☎ 491330233 FAX 491332134
(adjacent to the port area)
Near sea  Near beach  In town centre  Near motorway
*49 en suite (bth)  No smoking in 25 bedrooms  TV in all
bedrooms  Direct dial from all bedrooms  Licensed  Lift  Night
porter  Air conditioning in bedrooms  Child discount available
13yrs  Bicycle rental  Languages spoken: English & Spanish*
CARDS: ●● ■■ ☲ ⑩ JCB Travellers cheques

★ ★ **Climat de France**
13 rue Lafon *13006*
☎ 491333434 FAX 491541059
(from highway take direction of "Préfecture" until boulevard
"d'Athène" continue to green bridge then 1st street on the
right (rue Dreudré), then 1st on left (rue Longate, then 1st
street on right)
Near sea  In town centre
*83 en suite (bth)  (17 fmly)  No smoking in 4 bedrooms  TV in all
bedrooms  Direct dial from all bedrooms  Licensed  Lift  Night
porter  Full central heating  Open parking available  Covered
parking available  Supervised  Child discount available 12yrs
Open terrace  Covered terrace  Last d 22.00hrs  Languages
spoken: English & German*
CARDS: ●● ■■ ☲ ⑩ Travellers cheques

★ ★ ★ **Holiday Inn Marseille**
103 av du Prado *13008*
☎ 491831010 FAX 491798412
Near sea  Near beach  In town centre  Near motorway
*119 en suite (bth/shr)  (4 fmly)  (8 with balcony)  No smoking in
22 bedrooms  TV in all bedrooms  STV  Radio in rooms  Direct
dial from all bedrooms  Mini-bar in all bedrooms  Room-safe
Licensed  Lift  Night porter  Full central heating  Air
conditioning in bedrooms  Open parking available (charged)
Covered parking available (charged)  Supervised  Child
discount available 12yrs  Open terrace  V meals  Last d 22.30hrs
Languages spoken: English & Spanish*
ROOMS: (room only) d 690-750FF
MEALS: Continental breakfast 60FF  Lunch 90-150FF&alc
Dinner 90-150FF&alc
CARDS: ●● ■■ ☲ ⑩ JCB Travellers cheques

★ ★ ★ **New Hotel Bompard**
2 rue des Flots Bleus *13007*
☎ 491521093 FAX 491310214
(from the downtown (Vieux-Port), direction Corniche Kennedy
and rue des Flots Bleus)
Set in the leafy surroundings of a park, this beautiful building
provides an oasis of peace. Situated near the bustling town
centre and not far from the sea, it features a large salon-bar,
comfortable bedrooms, decorated in pastel shades, and a
shaded terrace with views of the park.
Near sea  Near beach  Forest area  Near motorway
*46 en suite (bth/shr)  (4 fmly)  (9 with balcony)  TV in all
bedrooms  STV  Radio in rooms  Direct dial from all bedrooms
Mini-bar in all bedrooms  Licensed  Lift  Night porter  Full
central heating  Air conditioning in bedrooms  Open parking
available  Supervised  Child discount available 14yrs  Outdoor
swimming pool  Solarium  Boule  Open terrace  Covered terrace*
*contd.*

**New Hotel Bompard**
*Last d 22.00hrs Languages spoken: English & German*
ROOMS: (room only) s 460-480FF; d 490-500FF
**Reductions over 1 night**
MEALS: Continental breakfast 55FF Lunch 76-188FFalc
Dinner 76-188FFalc
CARDS: ● ■ ▬ ▣ Travellers cheques

★ ★ ★ **Novotel Marseille Est-La Valentine**
St-Menet *13011*
☎ 491439060 FAX 491270674
(A50 in direction Toulon to Marseille exit la Penne sur
Huveaune)
*Near motorway*
*131 en suite (bth/shr) (25 fmly) No smoking on premises TV in
all bedrooms STV Radio in rooms Direct dial from all
bedrooms Mini-bar in all bedrooms Licensed Lift Night porter
Full central heating Air conditioning in bedrooms Open
parking available Supervised Child discount available 16yrs
Outdoor swimming pool Tennis Solarium Boule Open terrace
Covered terrace Table tennis Last d 24.00hrs Languages
spoken: English, German & Italian*
CARDS: ● ■ ▬ ▣ Travellers cheques

★ ★ ★ **St-Ferréol's Hotel**
19 rue Pisançon *13001*
☎ 491331221 FAX 491542997
*Near sea Near beach In town centre Near motorway*
*20 en suite (bth/shr) TV in all bedrooms STV Radio in rooms
Direct dial from all bedrooms Lift Night porter Full central
heating Air conditioning in bedrooms Child discount available
4yrs Jacuzzi/spa Languages spoken: English, Arabic, German
& Spanish*
CARDS: ● ■ ▬ ▣ JCB Travellers cheques

★ ★ **Hostellerie Les Magnanarelles**
104 av Vallée des Baux *13520*
☎ 490543025 FAX 490545004
(exit A7 Avignon Sud and proceed to St-Rémy-de-Provence
and then onwards in southerly direction to Maussane-les-
Alpilles)
*Forest area In town centre Near motorway*
*Closed 3 Jan-28 Feb*
*18 en suite (bth/shr) 6 rooms in annexe (2 fmly) (1 with
balcony) TV in 1 bedroom Direct dial from all bedrooms
Licensed Full central heating Open parking available (charged)
Supervised Child discount available 7yrs Outdoor swimming
pool Tennis Boule Bicycle rental Open terrace Covered
terrace Last d 21.00hrs Languages spoken: English & Spanish*
CARDS: ● ▬

★ ★ ★ **Hotel Val Baussenc**
122 av de la Vallée-de-Baux *13520*
☎ 490543890 FAX 490543336
(A7 exit Cavaillon direction St-Rémy, Maussane. A54 exit St-
Martin-de-Crau direction Les Baux, Maussane)
*Forest area*
*Closed Jan-end Feb*
*21 en suite (bth/shr) (18 with balcony) TV in all bedrooms
Direct dial from all bedrooms Mini-bar in all bedrooms
Licensed Open parking available Supervised Child discount
available 12yrs Outdoor swimming pool Open terrace
Covered terrace Last d 21.00hrs Languages spoken: English,
German & Spanish*
ROOMS: (room only) s 380-540FF; d 530-680FF
✱ **Reductions over 1 night**
MEALS: Full breakfast 65FF Dinner 190FF&alc
CARDS: ●● ■■ ▬ ▣ Travellers cheques

**Mas du Magnolia** (Prop: Monika Hauschild)
Quartier le Fort *84560*
☎ 490724800 FAX 490724800
(from the north: A7 exit Avignon in direction Apt-Digne on
D22 then N100, after village of Coustellet and before Les
Beaumettes turn right direction of Ménerbes on D103 Mas du
Magnolia 2km on left)
*Near river Near sea Forest area In town centre Near
motorway*
*Closed Jan & Feb*
*4 en suite (bth/shr) No smoking on premises Radio in rooms
Full central heating Open parking available Supervised
Outdoor swimming pool Sauna Boule Pool house Barbecue
Languages spoken: English, German, Greek, Italian & Spanish*
CARDS: Eurocheques, FF Travellers cheques

★ ★ **Domaine de Préfaissal** (Prop: Georges Giraud)
*04270*
☎ 492355209 FAX 492355209
*Near river Near lake Forest area Near motorway*
*3 en suite (shr) (1 with balcony) No smoking on premises Full
central heating Open parking available Covered parking
available Supervised Child discount available Outdoor
swimming pool Boule Table tennis Languages spoken: English
& Spanish*
ROOMS: s fr 187FF; d fr 229FF
MEALS: Dinner fr 85FF
CARDS: Travellers cheques

★ ★ ★ **Auberge du Choucas**
17 rue de la Fruitière *05220*
☎ 492244273 FAX 492245160
*Near river Near lake Forest area Near motorway*
*Closed 2-11 Dec & 4-29 May*
*12 en suite (bth/shr) 4 rooms in annexe (4 fmly) (8 with
balcony) No smoking in 2 bedrooms TV in all bedrooms Radio
in rooms Direct dial from all bedrooms Mini-bar in all
bedrooms Room-safe Licensed Full central heating Air
conditioning in bedrooms Child discount available Open
terrace Last d 21.30hrs Languages spoken: English, Italian,
Spanish & German*

ROOMS: (room only) d 570-1070FF ✳
MEALS: Continental breakfast 70FF Lunch 95-380FF&alc
Dinner 95-380FF&alc
CARDS: ●● ▆▆ Travellers cheques

## MONIEUX Vaucluse

**Le Moulin** (Prop: M & Mme Picca)
*84390*
☎ 490640464
Near river Forest area
*5 rms Full central heating Open parking available Supervised
Child discount available Outdoor swimming pool Tennis
Languages spoken: English*
CARDS: Travellers cheques

## MONTFAVET Vaucluse

**★ ★ Auberge de Bonpas**
rte de Cavaillon *84140*
☎ 490230764 FAX 490230700
Near river Near motorway
*11 rms (7 bth 3 shr) (3 fmly) TV in all bedrooms STV Direct
dial from all bedrooms Mini-bar in 3 bedrooms Licensed Full
central heating Open parking available Supervised Child
discount available Outdoor swimming pool Riding Solarium
Bicycle rental Open terrace Table tennis Last d 22.00hrs
Languages spoken: English & Spanish*
CARDS: ●● ▆▆ ▆▆ ▣ Travellers cheques

**★ ★ ★ ★ Frènes**
av des Vertes Rives, Montfavet *84140*
☎ 490311793 FAX 490239503
Forest area
*Closed Dec-Mar*
*20 en suite (bth/shr) (4 fmly) (5 with balcony) TV in all
bedrooms STV Radio in rooms Direct dial from all bedrooms
Mini-bar in all bedrooms Room-safe Licensed Lift Night
porter Full central heating Air conditioning in bedrooms Open
parking available Covered parking available Supervised Child
discount available 15yrs Outdoor swimming pool (heated)
Sauna Solarium Pool table Jacuzzi/spa Open terrace Covered
terrace V meals Last d 21.30hrs Languages spoken: English,
Italian & Spanish*
ROOMS: (room only) s 1250FF; d 2190FF ✳
MEALS: Full breakfast 100FF Lunch 200-500FF&alc
Dinner 320-500FF&alc
CARDS: ●● ▆▆ ▆▆ ▣ Travellers cheques

## MONTMAUR Hautes-Alpes

**Château-de-Montmaur** (Prop: M & Mme Laurens)
*05400*
☎ 492581142
(take D994 from Gap to Veynes and 4 kms before Veynes take
D320 towards Devoluy. Château on edge of village after 2kms,
visible from the road)
Near river Forest area
*Closed Nov-Mar*
*3 en suite (shr) Full central heating Open parking available
Covered parking available Supervised*
ROOMS: d fr 450FF

## MONTMEYAN Var

**Bed & Breakfast** (Prop: M & Mme Gonfond)
rte de Quinson *83670*
☎ 494807803
Forest area
*3 en suite (shr) TV available Full central heating Open parking
available Supervised Child discount available 10yrs*

## MOUSTIERS-STE-MARIE Alpes-de-Haute-Provence

**★ ★ ★ ★ Bastide de Moustiers**
Chemin de Quinson *04360*
☎ 492704747 FAX 492704748
(from A8 towards Marseille take exit 36 to Draguignan, then
follow signs for Flauosc, Salelnes, Aups and Moustiers)
Near river Near lake Forest area
*RS 4 Jan-1 Mar Restaurant only*
*12 en suite (bth/shr) 7 rooms in annexe (1 fmly) TV in all
bedrooms STV Direct dial from all bedrooms Mini-bar in all
bedrooms Room-safe Licensed Night porter Full central
heating Air conditioning in bedrooms Open parking available
Covered parking available Supervised Outdoor swimming pool
(heated) Boule Jacuzzi/spa Bicycle rental Open terrace V
meals Last d 21.45hrs Languages spoken: English & Italian*
ROOMS: (room only) s 800-1650FF; d 900-1750FF
MEALS: Full breakfast 80FF Lunch 225-295FF
Dinner 225-295FF
CARDS: ●● ▆▆ ▆▆ ▣ Travellers cheques

## MURS Vaucluse

**Les Hauts de Veroncle** (Prop: Didier Del Corso)
*84220*
☎ 490726091 FAX 490726207
(from Gordes, travel in direction of Murs. After 6km follow
sign for 'Chambre d'hôtes')
Near river Forest area
*Closed 16 Nov-Feb*
*3 en suite (shr) (2 fmly) No smoking in 2 bedrooms TV in 1
bedroom Full central heating Open parking available Child
discount available 14yrs Bicycle rental V meals Last d 19.30hrs
Languages spoken: English & Italian*
ROOMS: s fr 250FF; d 280-290FF
MEALS: Dinner fr 120FF
CARDS: Travellers cheques

## NOVES Bouches-du-Rhône

**★ ★ ★ ★ Auberge de Noves**
Domaine de Deves *13550*
☎ 490941921 FAX 490944776
(by A7 exit Avignon Sth, then towards Châteaurenard)
Near river Forest area Near motorway
*23 en suite (bth/shr) (3 fmly) (16 with balcony) TV in all
bedrooms STV Direct dial from all bedrooms Mini-bar in all
bedrooms Room-safe Licensed Lift Night porter Full central
heating Air conditioning in bedrooms Open parking available
Covered parking available (charged) Supervised Child
discount available 8yrs Outdoor swimming pool (heated)
Tennis Fishing Boule Bicycle rental Open terrace V meals
Last d 22.00hrs Languages spoken: English, German & Italian*
CARDS: ●● ▆▆ ▆▆ ▣ Travellers cheques

### ★ ★ ★ Mas des Capélans
Le Plan des Capelans N100 *84580*
☎ 490769904 FAX 490769029
(from A7 exit Avignon Sud, follow directions for Apt on N100.
After Coustellet follow signs for Oppède)
*Near river Forest area*
*RS 16 Nov-14 Feb*
*10 en suite (bth/shr) (2 fmly) (1 with balcony) No smoking on*
*premises TV in all bedrooms Radio in rooms Direct dial from*
*all bedrooms Licensed Full central heating Open parking*
*available Supervised Outdoor swimming pool (heated)*
*Solarium Pool table Boule Open terrace Last d 20.30hrs*
*Languages spoken: English & German*
ROOMS: (room only) d fr 900FF **Reductions over 1 night**
MEALS: Full breakfast 60FF Dinner fr 160FF
CARDS: ●● ■■ ▓▓ Travellers cheques

### Le Petit Creuil (Prop: M Edmund Goudin)
*84580*
☎ 490768089 FAX 490769286
(west of Oppède-le-Vieux via D176)
*Forest area*
*May-15 Nov*
*6 en suite (bth/shr) (2 fmly) TV in all bedrooms Full central*
*heating Open parking available Outdoor swimming pool*
*Boule Bicycle rental Table tennis*

### Le Village (Prop: Dominique Bal)
Le Vieux Village *84580*
☎ 490768908 & 490769352
(leave motorway at Cavaillon and drive towards Apt. After
village of Robion, turn right)
*Forest area Near motorway*
*5 en suite (bth/shr) Full central heating Open parking available*
*Tennis Boule Bicycle rental*
ROOMS: s fr 245FF; d fr 300FF ✱
CARDS: Travellers cheques

### ★ ★ ★ Arène
pl de Langes *84100*
☎ 490114040 FAX 490114045
(from A7 exit Orange in the direction of the town centre)
*In town centre Near motorway*
*Closed 9-31 Nov*
*30 en suite (bth/shr) (6 fmly) (12 with balcony) TV in all*
*bedrooms STV Direct dial from all bedrooms Mini-bar in all*
*bedrooms Room-safe Licensed Night porter Full central*
*heating Air conditioning in bedrooms Open parking available*
*(charged) Covered parking available (charged) Supervised*
*Child discount available Open terrace V meals Last d 21.30hrs*
*Languages spoken: English German & Spanish*
ROOMS: (room only) s 440-500FF; d 440-600FF
MEALS: Lunch fr 120FF&alc Dinner 120-300FF&alc
CARDS: ●● ■■ ▓▓ ⑩ Travellers cheques

### ★ ★ Le Panaoramic
rte de Moustiers *04120*
☎ 492773507 FAX 492773017
(on the D952 west of La Palud-sur-Verdon)

*Near river Near lake Forest area*
*Closed 12 Nov-31 Mar*
*20 en suite (bth/shr) (3 fmly) (8 with balcony) TV in all*
*bedrooms STV Direct dial from all bedrooms Licensed Full*
*central heating Open parking available Supervised Child*
*discount available Outdoor swimming pool (heated) Boule*
*Open terrace Covered terrace V meals Last d 21.30hrs*
*Languages spoken: English*
CARDS: ●● ▓▓ Travellers cheques

### ★ ★ Hotel Restaurant Belvedere
Saint Antoine
☎ 492233699 FAX 492234520
(from north take motorway to Grenoble, then in dircetion of
Briançon, towards Gap, at L'Argentière La Bessé take right in
direction of Vallée de Vallouse to Pelvoux, in village pass the
church hotel approx 300 metres on right)
This chalet style hotel is situated in the village of Pelvoux in the
heart of the National Park of Ecrins. The hotel has been
renovated and provides comfort in a charmimg and warm
atmosphere. The restaurant serves a combination of flavoured
French dishes and traditional mountain specialities.
*Near river Forest area*

*Closed mid Nov-mid Dec*
*27 en suite (bth/shr) (5 fmly) (27 with balcony) TV in all*
*bedrooms Direct dial from all bedrooms Licensed Full central*
*heating Open parking available Child discount available*
*Bicycle rental Open terrace V meals Last d 22.30hrs*
*Languages spoken: English*
ROOMS: s 350FF; d 540FF **Special breaks**
MEALS: Continental breakfast 35FF Lunch 75-145FF&alc
Dinner 90-145FF&alc
CARDS: ●● ▓▓

### Domaine de la Petite Cheylude (Prop: M J Hak)
518 route de la Gasqui *84210*
☎ 490613724 FAX 490616700
(from A7, Avignon Nord/le Pantet, head towards Carpentras,
follow 'Monteux Centre', at 3rd set lights turn right (D31),
towards Velleron/Pernes-les-Fontaines. After 5km turn left
towards Carpentras-D49, after 1km, 'Domaine' on left hand
side)
*Near river Near lake Forest area Near motorway*
*5 en suite (shr) (1 fmly) Full central heating Open parking*
*available Outdoor swimming pool Boule Bicycle rental Table*
*tennis Languages spoken: English & German*
CARDS: Travellers cheques

### ★ ★ L'Hermitage
rte de Carpentras *84210*
☎ 490665141 FAX 490613641
(exit N7 Cavaillon and take direction of Pernes-les-Fontaines then Carpentras, or exit A9 Avignon North then direction Carpentras and Pernes-les-Fontaines)
*20 en suite (bth) (5 fmly) (2 with balcony) TV in all bedrooms Direct dial from all bedrooms Licensed Open parking available Supervised Child discount available 6yrs Outdoor swimming pool Boule Open terrace Languages spoken: English*
CARDS: 💳 💳 💳 💳 Travellers cheques

### Mas La Bonoty
chemin de la Bonioty
☎ 490616109 FAX 490613514
(from Avignon follow signs for Carpentras/Pernes-les-Fontaines. Hotel is signposted in Pernes)

A restored 17th-century farmhouse set in 2 acres of private, landscaped grounds. The bedrooms are well equipped and fine Provençal cusine is available in the restaurant. There is a cherry orchard, a lavender field and the terrace has views over Mount Ventoux.
Forest area
*Closed mid Nov-early Dec & mid Jan-early Feb RS Oct-Mar rest closed Sun eve & Mon*
*8 en suite (bth/shr) (2 fmly) TV in 4 bedrooms Direct dial from all bedrooms Full central heating Open parking available No children 6yrs Outdoor swimming pool Boule Open terrace Covered terrace V meals Last d 21.30hrs Languages spoken: English & German*
ROOMS: (room only) d 300-350FF
MEALS: Continental breakfast 50FF Lunch 170-230FF&alc Dinner 170-230FF&alc
CARDS: 💳 💳 💳 Travellers cheques

### St-Barthélemy (Prop: Jacqueline Mangeard)
*84210*
☎ 490664779 FAX 490664779
(from Pernes-les-Fontaines tourist office take D1 Mazan road for 2km, then right into chemin de la Roque for 100mtrs)
Near river Forest area
*5 en suite (bth/shr) Full central heating Open parking available Covered parking available Outdoor swimming pool Tennis Fishing Boule Bicycle rental Badminton Table tennis Languages spoken: English*
ROOMS: s 220FF; d 300FF

### PERTUIS Vaucluse

### Bed & Breakfast (Prop: Gerard Bidault)
Campagne St-Loup, Quartier de Crozé *84120*
☎ 490790365
Near river Forest area
*4 en suite (bth/shr) (2 fmly) Radio in rooms Full central heating Open parking available Child discount available 12yrs*
CARDS: Travellers cheques

### ★ ★ ★ Sévan (Best Western)
rte de Manosque *84120*
☎ 490791930 FAX 490793577
(A7 to Cavaillon D973 to Pertuis or A51 to Pertuis)
Forest area
*Closed 2-14 Jan*
*46 en suite (bth/shr) (4 fmly) (25 with balcony) TV in all bedrooms STV Direct dial from all bedrooms Mini-bar in all bedrooms Licensed Lift Night porter Open parking available Supervised Child discount available 12yrs Outdoor swimming pool Tennis Sauna Pool table Boule Mini-golf Bicycle rental Open terrace Table tennis,night club,volley ball Last d 22.00hrs Languages spoken: English, German & Spanish*
CARDS: 💳 💳 💳 💳 Travellers cheques

### PIOLENC Vaucluse

### ★ ★ ★ Auberge de l'Orangerie
4 rue de l'Ormeau *84420*
☎ 490295988 FAX 490296774
(from north follow A7 south from Lyon and exit at South Montélimar, following N7 south. After 40km -in Piolenc, turn left after post office and hotel is in park)
Near river Forest area In town centre Near motorway
*6 rms (5 bth/shr) 6 rooms in annexe (2 fmly) (1 with balcony) TV in 5 bedrooms Direct dial from 4 bedrooms Licensed Full central heating Open parking available Supervised Solarium Boule Bicycle rental Open terrace V meals Last d 21.00hrs Languages spoken: English, German & Spanish*
ROOMS: (room only) d 350-480FF
MEALS: Full breakfast 50FF Lunch 90-200FF Dinner 140-200FF✱
CARDS: 💳 💳 Eurocard Travellers cheques

### PLAN-DE-LA-TOUR Var

### Bed & Breakfast (Prop: Mme Chantal Vandame)
rte du Muy *83120*
☎ 494437169
(main road to le Muy, then head towards Ste-Maxime, at crossroads turn towards Plan-de-la-Tour, go through village, turn right. At the sign 'Chêne al Pierre' right again and follow path)
Near sea Forest area
*Closed 15 days in Aug*
*2 rms (1 bth/shr) No smoking on premises Open parking available Child discount available 10yrs Outdoor swimming pool Languages spoken: English & Spanish*

### PONTET, LE Vaucluse

### ★ ★ ★ ★ Auberge de Cassagne
450 allée de Cassagne *84130*
☎ 490310418 FAX 490322509
(from A7 exit Avignon-Nord take road immediately on left after the toll booths and follow red arrows)
This hotel, within easy reach of the centre of Avignon, offers
*contd.*

453

**Auberge de Cassagne**
comfortable accommodation decorated in typical Provençal style and a fine restaurant.
Near river Near lake Forest area
*30 en suite (bth/shr) (17 fmly) (2 with balcony) TV in all bedrooms STV Direct dial from all bedrooms Mini-bar in all bedrooms Room-safe Lift Full central heating Air conditioning in bedrooms Open parking available (charged) Supervised Child discount available 5yrs Outdoor swimming pool Tennis Squash Boule Open terrace Covered terrace V meals Last d 21.30hrs Languages spoken: English, German & Dutch*
MEALS: Full breakfast 105FF Lunch 195-380FF Dinner 290-3800FF✱
CARDS: 💳 💳 💳 💳 Travellers cheques

**★ ★ ★ Hostellerie des Agassins**
Lieu-dit Le Pigeonnier *84130*
☎ 490324291 FAX 490320829
Near river Near lake Forest area Near motorway
*Closed Jan-Feb*
*30 en suite (bth) 4 rooms in annexe (26 with balcony) No smoking in 5 bedrooms TV in all bedrooms STV Radio in rooms Direct dial from all bedrooms Mini-bar in all bedrooms Room-safe Licensed Lift Night porter Full central heating Air conditioning in bedrooms Open parking available Supervised Child discount available 6yrs Outdoor swimming pool (heated) Tennis Solarium Boule Bicycle rental Open terrace Covered terrace Last d 22.00hrs Languages spoken: English, German, Italian & Spanish*
CARDS: 💳 💳 💳 💳 JCB Travellers cheques

**★ ★ ★ Le Rouge Gorge**
*83670*
☎ 494770397
Near river Forest area
*10 en suite (bth/shr) (2 fmly) No smoking on premises TV in all bedrooms Direct dial from all bedrooms Full central heating Open parking available Supervised Child discount available Outdoor swimming pool Boule Bicycle rental Open terrace Covered terrace Last d 21.00hrs Languages spoken: English*
CARDS: 💳 💳 Travellers cheques

**Bed & Breakfast** (Prop: Marie Françoise Rouston)
L'Oustaou des Oliviers *84110*
☎ 490464589 FAX 490464093
Forest area
*Closed 8 Jan-Feb*

*4 en suite (shr) No smoking on premises Full central heating Open parking available Boule*
CARDS: Travellers cheques

**Domaine le Puy du Maupas** (Prop: M & Mme Sauvayre)
rte de Nyons *84110*
☎ 490464743 FAX 490464851
Near lake Forest area
*5 en suite (bth/shr) No smoking in all bedrooms Full central heating Open parking available Child discount available Outdoor swimming pool Boule Table tennis Last d 19.30hrs*
CARDS: Travellers cheques

**Le Saumalier** (Prop: M Sauvayre)
*84110*
☎ 490464961 FAX 490464961
Forest area
*2 en suite (bth/shr) (1 fmly) No smoking on premises TV available Open parking available Covered parking available Child discount available 5yrs*

**★ ★ La Pendine**
*05290*
☎ 492233262 FAX 492234663
Forest area
*Closed 11 Apr-19 Jun & 11 Sep-15 Dec*
*28 rms (23 bth) 6 rooms in annexe (2 fmly) TV in all bedrooms Direct dial from all bedrooms Licensed Full central heating Open parking available Child discount available 10yrs Pool table Boule Open terrace Last d 21.15hrs Languages spoken: Italian*
ROOMS: (room only) s 215-320FF; d 330-428FF
**Reductions over 1 night**
**Special breaks: Weekend breaks**
MEALS: Full breakfast 45FF Lunch 80-180FF&alc Dinner 105-180FF&alc✱
CARDS: 💳 💳 Travellers cheques

**★ ★ ★ Hotel les Bouis**
rte de Pampelonne *83350*
☎ 494798761 FAX 494798520
(3km NE of Ramatuell, off D93)
Near sea Near beach Near motorway
*Closed mid Oct-mid Mar*
*17 en suite (bth/shr) (17 with balcony) TV in all bedrooms STV Direct dial from all bedrooms Mini-bar in all bedrooms Room-safe Licensed Night porter Full central heating Air conditioning in bedrooms Open parking available Supervised Outdoor swimming pool Solarium Bicycle rental Open terrace Languages spoken: English & German*
CARDS: 💳 💳 💳 Travellers cheques

**★ ★ ★ Ferme d'Augustin**
Plage de Tahiti *83350*
☎ 494559700 FAX 494974030
(close to the Tahiti Beach)
Near sea Near beach Forest area
*Closed Oct-Mar*
*46 en suite (bth/shr) (16 fmly) (6 with balcony) TV in all bedrooms STV Radio in rooms Direct dial from all bedrooms Mini-bar in all bedrooms Room-safe Licensed Lift Night porter Full central heating Air conditioning in bedrooms Open parking available Supervised Child discount available None*

**Ferme d'Augustin**
*Outdoor swimming pool (heated) Sauna Solarium Jacuzzi/spa*
*Bicycle rental Open terrace Languages spoken: English,*
*German, Italian & Spanish*
ROOMS: (room only) s 580-1600FF; d 680-1600FF *∗*
CARDS: ●● ■■ ▥ Travellers cheques

### RAPHÈLE-LES-ARLES Bouches-du-Rhône

**★ ★ ★ Auberge La Feniere**
N453 *13280*
☎ 490984744 FAX 490984839
Near river Near lake Near sea Forest area Near motorway
*25 en suite (bth/shr) (2 fmly) (3 with balcony) TV in all*
*bedrooms Licensed Full central heating Open parking*
*available Covered parking available (charged) Supervised*
*Child discount available 6yrs Boule Open terrace Covered*
*terrace Last d 21.30hrs Languages spoken: English*
CARDS: ●● ■■ ▥ ▣ Travellers cheques

### REILLANNE Alpes-de-Haute-Provence

**Auberge De Reillanne**
*04110*
☎ 492764595
Near motorway
RS Wed
*7 en suite (bth/shr) (2 fmly) Direct dial from all bedrooms*
*Mini-bar in all bedrooms Licensed Night porter Full central*
*heating Open parking available Child discount available 10yrs*
*Last d 21.00hrs Languages spoken: English & German*
CARDS: ●● ▥

### ROQUEBRUNE-SUR-ARGENS Var

**La Maurette** (Prop: Daniel & Katrin Rapin)
*83520*
☎ 494454681 FAX 494454681
(leave N7 between Le Muy and Puget, take D7 towards
Roquebrune-sur-Argens)
Near river Near lake Forest area Near motorway
*Closed 21 Oct-14 Mar*
*11 en suite (bth/shr) (11 with balcony) TV in all bedrooms Full*
*central heating Open parking available No children 8yrs*
*Outdoor swimming pool Languages spoken: English & German*
CARDS: ●● ▥ Travellers cheques

### ROSANS Hautes-Alpes

**L'Ensoleillée** (Prop: M & Mme D Pacaud)
*05150*
☎ 492666272 FAX 492666287
(between Nyons and Serres on D994)

Near river Near lake Forest area
*6 en suite (bth/shr) (3 fmly) (5 with balcony) TV in all*
*bedrooms Full central heating Open parking available*
*Covered parking available Child discount available 12yrs*
*Outdoor swimming pool Languages spoken: English*
CARDS: Travellers cheques

### ROUSSILLON Vaucluse

**Mamaison** (Prop: Marine Guillemot)
quartier les Devens *84220*
☎ 490057417 FAX 490057463
An 18th-century farm, set in the heart of Luberon, restored
and decorated by regional artists. Situated in the middle of
three hectares of luxurious garden, with a large swimming
pool. All food is cooked using produce grown in the garden or
bought from local markets. Fish a speciality. Mamaison has its
own internet site http://www.mamaison-provence.com
Forest area

*20 Mar-Oct*
*5 en suite (bth/shr) (2 fmly) Full central heating Open parking*
*available Child discount available Outdoor swimming pool*
*Languages spoken: English & Italian*
ROOMS: d fr 450FF
CARDS: ●● ▥

### RUSTREL Vaucluse

**La Forge** (Prop: D & C Berger-Ceccaldi)
Notre Dame des Anges *84400*
☎ 490049222 FAX 490049522
(from Apt D22 in the direction of Rustrel, in 7.5km (2.5km
before Rustrel) turn right for La Forge)
Near river Near lake Forest area
*Closed 16 Nov-14 Jan*
*3 en suite (bth/shr) (1 fmly) Full central heating Open parking*
*available Covered parking available Outdoor swimming pool*
*Boule Languages spoken: English*
CARDS: Travellers cheques

### ST-BONNET-EN-CHAMPSEUR Hautes-Alpes

**★ ★ La Cremaillère**
*05500*
☎ 492500060 FAX 492500157
This hotel benefits from a tranquil, leafy setting on the edge of
the village of Saint Bonnet with its healthy dry and sunny
climate. It has guest rooms with modern appointments and a
shaded park and a terrace with magnificent views towards the
Dévoluy mountain range.
Near river Near lake Forest area Near motorway

*contd.*

**La Cremaillere**
*Closed Nov-Mar*
*21 en suite (bth/shr) TV in all bedrooms Direct dial from all bedrooms Licensed Full central heating Open parking available Covered parking available (charged) Supervised Child discount available 12 yrs Boule Open terrace Covered terrace Last d 21.00hrs Languages spoken: English & German*
ROOMS: (room only) s 220-250FF; d 270-300FF
MEALS: Continental breakfast 40FF Lunch 100-195FF&alc Dinner 100-195FF&alc
CARDS: ●● ☎ Travellers cheques

### STES-MARIES-DE-LA-MER Bouches-du-Rhône

⋆⋆⋆ **Hotel Clamador**
route d'Aigues-Mortes *13460*
☎ 490978426 FAX 490979338
(from Arles head towards Stes-Maries-de-la-Mer and take D38 just before the port)

The hotel Clamador is a large, white farmhouse peacefully situated one kilometre from the beach, between the Rhône and the lakes. The bedrooms with modern facilities offer a good level of comfort, and are complemented by a congenial bar and a quiet reading room.
Near river Near sea Near beach
*Closed 31 Oct-1 April*
*20 en suite (bth/shr) (7 with balcony) TV in all bedrooms STV Direct dial from all bedrooms Licensed Night porter Full central heating Open parking available Covered parking available Child discount available 12yrs Outdoor swimming pool (heated) Riding Solarium Boule Mini-golf Bicycle rental Open terrace Languages spoken: English & Italian*
ROOMS: (incl. full-board) s 280-330FF; d 385-435FF
**Reductions over 1 night**
CARDS: ●● ■■ ☎ ⑩ Travellers cheques

⋆⋆⋆⋆ **Mas de la Fouques**
Stes-Maries *13640*
☎ 490978102 FAX 490478102
Near river Near lake Near sea Near beach
*Closed 2 Nov-24 Mar*
*14 en suite (bth/shr) (1 fmly) (14 with balcony) TV in all bedrooms Direct dial from all bedrooms Mini-bar in all bedrooms Licensed Full central heating Air conditioning in bedrooms Open parking available Supervised Child discount available 7yrs Outdoor swimming pool (heated) Tennis Fishing Riding Solarium Boule Bicycle rental Open terrace Covered terrace V meals Last d 21.30hrs Languages spoken: English & Italian*
CARDS: ●● ■■ ☎ ⑩ Eurocard Travellers cheques

⋆⋆⋆ **Le Mithra**
rte d'Aigues Mortes *13460*
☎ 490979940 FAX 490979773
(4kms from village, on D38)
Near beach
*20 en suite (bth/shr) TV in all bedrooms Direct dial from all bedrooms Licensed Full central heating Open parking available Supervised Child discount available 10yrs Outdoor swimming pool Boule Bicycle rental Covered terrace*
CARDS: ●● ☎ ⑩ Travellers cheques

⋆⋆ **Hostellerie du Pont de Gau**
rte d'Arles *13460*
☎ 490978153 FAX 490979854
Near motorway
*Closed 5 Jan-20 Feb*
*9 en suite (bth) TV in all bedrooms STV Direct dial from all bedrooms Licensed Full central heating Open parking available Child discount available 10yrs Last d 21.30hrs Languages spoken: English*
CARDS: ●● ■■ ☎ Travellers cheques

### ST-MARC-JAUMEGARDE Bouches-du-Rhône

**Mas des Bartavelles** (Prop: Marie Françoise Mattei)
chemin des Savoyards *13100*
☎ 442249298 FAX 442249299
(from Aix-en-Provence take D10 for St Marc-Jaumegarde)
Near lake Forest area
*RS 15 Nov-15 Feb*
*3 en suite (shr) (1 fmly) No smoking on premises TV in 1 bedroom Full central heating Open parking available Outdoor swimming pool Tennis Boule*

### ST-MARTIN-DE-CASTILLON Vaucluse

⋆⋆ **Lou Caleu**
*84750*
☎ 490752888 FAX 490752549
Near river Forest area Near motorway
*16 en suite (bth/shr) (8 fmly) (11 with balcony) TV in all bedrooms STV Mini-bar in all bedrooms Licensed Full central heating Open parking available Covered parking available Supervised Child discount available 10yrs Outdoor swimming pool Tennis Riding Boule Bicycle rental Open terrace Covered terrace V meals Last d 22.00hrs Languages spoken: English & German*
CARDS: ●● ■■ ☎ ⑩ Travellers cheques

### ST-MARTIN-LES-EAUX Alpes-de-Haute-Provence

**Domaine d'Aurouze** (Prop: J & V Noel-Schriber)
*04300*
☎ 492876651 FAX 492875635
(halfway between Manosque and Forcalquier, 3km from
Dauphin and 2.5km from village of St-Martin-les-Eaux - 800m
from the chapel of Notre-Dame-d'Ubage)
Near river Near lake Forest area
*Etr-mid Oct*
*5 en suite (bth/shr) (2 fmly) TV in all bedrooms STV Full
central heating Open parking available Child discount
available 6yrs Outdoor swimming pool (heated) Tennis Fishing
Riding Boule Bicycle rental Languages spoken: English
German Spanish & Dutch*

### ST-MAXIMIN-LA-SAINTE-BAUME Var

★ ★ ★ **France**
1-3 av Albert *83470*
☎ 494780014 FAX 494598380
(off A8)
In town centre Near motorway
*26 en suite (bth/shr) (2 fmly) TV in all bedrooms STV Direct
dial from all bedrooms Night porter Full central heating Open
parking available (charged) Covered parking available
(charged) Supervised Child discount available 6yrs Outdoor
swimming pool Open terrace Last d 22.00hrs Languages
spoken: English & Italian*
CARDS: ● ■ ▦ Ⅾ Travellers cheques

### ST-PIERRE-D'ARGENÇON Hautes-Alpes

**La Source** (Prop: M et Mme Rene Leautier)
*05140*
☎ 492586781
(from Aspres-les-Buëch take D994 towards Valence. Continue
through St-Pierre-d'Argençon to house on right)
Near river Forest area Near motorway
*Closed Oct-Apr*
*5 rms (3 shr) Full central heating Open parking available
Boule V meals Languages spoken: English & Italian*

### ST-RAPHAËL Var

**Le Clocher** (Prop: Riccardo & Sonia Ferrigno)
50 rue de la République *83700*
☎ 494190696 FAX 668128348
(A8 exit 38 Fréjus to St Raphaël, follow signs for "Centre Ville",
Le Clocher next to town hall "'Mairie")
Situated in the medieval quarter of the town this property has
been tastefully renovated in traditional Provençal style. The
buffet breakfast offers a wide range of dishes.
Near sea Near beach In town centre
*3 rms (1 shr) Full central heating Open parking available
(charged) Covered parking available (charged) Child discount
available 12 yrs Tennis Fishing Riding Boule Mini-golf
Bicycle rental Languages spoken: English Italian & Spanish*
ROOMS: s 200-240FF; d 290-330FF

★ ★ ★ **Excelsior**
193 bd Felix Martin *83700*
☎ 494950242 FAX 494953382
(on the Sea Front adjacent to the Casino)
Near sea Near beach In town centre Near motorway
*36 rms (34 bth/shr) (3 fmly) (3 with balcony) TV in all
bedrooms STV Direct dial from all bedrooms Mini-bar in all*

*bedrooms Licensed Lift Night porter Full central heating Air
conditioning in bedrooms Supervised Child discount available
8yrs Open terrace Last d 22.00hrs Languages spoken: English,
German & Italian*
ROOMS: (room only) s 300-400FF; d 720-900FF
**Reductions over 1 night**
MEALS: Continental breakfast 35FF Lunch 140-218FF&alc
Dinner 160-218FF&alc✳
CARDS: ● ■ ▦ Ⅾ Travellers cheques

★ ★ ★ **Golf de Valescure**
av Paul l'Hermité *83700*
☎ 494528500 FAX 494824188
(From Nice: exit A8 No.38 (Fréjus-St Raphaël), after 3km take a
left at the roundabout in the direction of St Raphaël. Then
Valescure-Agay Valescure-Agay par Valescure-Golf de
Valescure)
Forest area
*Closed 7-31 Jan & 14 Nov-22 Dec*
*40 en suite (bth/shr) (40 with balcony) TV in all bedrooms STV
Direct dial from all bedrooms Mini-bar in all bedrooms Room-
safe Licensed Lift Night porter Full central heating Air
conditioning in bedrooms Open parking available Supervised
Child discount available 12yrs Outdoor swimming pool Golf 18
Tennis Pool table Boule Mini-golf Bicycle rental Open terrace
Covered terrace Last d 21/21.30 Languages spoken: English,
Dutch, German & Italian*
ROOMS: s 625-750FF; d 830-960FF
**Special breaks: Golf**
MEALS: Full breakfast 55FF Lunch 105-135FF&alc Dinner
175-205FF&alc
CARDS: ● ■ ▦ Ⅾ Travellers cheques

★ ★ ★ **La Potinière** (Relais du Silence)
169 av de Boulouris, BP 5 *83700*
☎ 494198172 FAX 494198172
(exit No.38 (Fréjus-St-Raphaël), and take the coast road N98 in
the direction of Cannes. 4km after St-Raphaël turn left at the
traffic lights and follow the arrows)
Near sea Near beach Forest area
*29 en suite (bth/shr) (11 fmly) (26 with balcony) No smoking in
1 bedroom TV in all bedrooms STV Radio in rooms Direct dial
from all bedrooms Mini-bar in all bedrooms Room-safe
(charged) Night porter Full central heating Open parking
available Covered parking available (charged) Supervised
Child discount available 11yrs Indoor swimming pool (heated)
Outdoor swimming pool Sauna Solarium Boule Bicycle rental
Open terrace Wkly live entertainment Last d 21.00hrs
Languages spoken: English, Dutch, German & Italian*
CARDS: ● ■ ▦ Ⅾ Travellers cheques

### ST-RÉMY-DE-PROVENCE Bouches-du-Rhône

**Château de Roussan**
rte de Tarascon *13210*
☎ 490921163 FAX 490925059
(the château is 2.5km from the centre of St-Rémy on the left
hand side of the D99 towards Tarascon)
Near motorway
*21 en suite (bth/shr) Direct dial from all bedrooms Night
porter Full central heating Open parking available Supervised
Child discount available 14yrs Boule Bicycle rental Open
terrace Television room, Table tennis, Pool(tabl V meals
Last d 21.30hrs Languages spoken: English, German &
Spanish*
CARDS: ● ■ ▦ Eurocard Travellers cheques

### ★ ★ ★ ★ Domaine de Valmouriane
Petite rte des Baux *13210*
☎ 490924462 FAX 490923732
(exit A7 motorway at Cavaillon and follow signs to St-Rémy
(D99), near St-Rémy take direction Beaucaire/Tarascon still on
D99, in approx 2kms turn left direction Les Baux D27, hotel in
2kms on the right)
Discover the true Provence in this 18th century house halfway
between St Remy-de Provence and Les Baux. In the wooded
foothills of the protected Alpilles the hotel offers restful days
by the pool, or activity playing tennis or pentanque before a
fine meal on the flowered terrace or restaurant. At night the
only sound likely to wake you is the hoot of the eagle owl.
Forest area

*14 en suite (bth/shr) (2 fmly) (5 with balcony) TV in all
bedrooms STV Direct dial from all bedrooms Mini-bar in all
bedrooms Room-safe Licensed Lift Night porter Full central
heating Air conditioning in bedrooms Open parking available
Supervised Child discount available 12yrs Outdoor swimming
pool (heated) Tennis Sauna Solarium Pool table Boule
Jacuzzi/spa Open terrace Covered terrace Last d 21.30hrs
Languages spoken: English, German, Portuguese & Spanish*
ROOMS: (room only) s 890-1350FF; d 890-1350FF
**Reductions over 1 night**
MEALS: Full breakfast 75FF Lunch 175-290FF&alc Dinner
230-290FF&alc
CARDS: 🏧 💳 💳 💳 JCB Travellers cheques

### ★ ★ ★ ★ Hostellerie du Vallon de Valrugues
Chemin Canto Cigalo *13210*
☎ 490920440 FAX 490924401
(from A7 exit Cavaillon head towards St-Rémy. At entrance to
the town turn left and follow signs)

A Provençal Roman-style villa with elegant bedrooms, a fine
restaurant specialising in local cuisine, and a variety of leisure

facilities. An ideal centre for touring the Arles, Nîmes and
Avignon areas.
Near lake  Forest area
*Closed Feb*
*53 en suite (bth) (15 fmly) (24 with balcony) TV in all bedrooms
STV  Direct dial from all bedrooms  Mini-bar in all bedrooms
Room-safe  Licensed  Lift  Night porter  Full central heating  Air
conditioning in bedrooms  Open parking available  Supervised
Child discount available 14yrs  Outdoor swimming pool  Tennis
Sauna  Gym  Pool table  Boule  Mini-golf  Jacuzzi/spa  Open
terrace  Wkly live entertainment  Last d 21.30hrs  Languages
spoken: English, German, Italian & Spanish*
ROOMS: (room only) s 780FF; d 990-1650FF
MEALS: Continental breakfast 110FF  Lunch 195-480FF&alc
Dinner 290-480FF&alc
CARDS: 🏧 💳 💳 💳 JCB Travellers cheques

### Mas de Gros (Prop: Schneider Reboul)
rte du Lac *13210*
☎ 490924685 FAX 490924778
Near lake  Forest area
*Closed Nov-Mar*
*7 en suite (bth/shr)  4 rooms in annexe (2 fmly) TV in 4
bedrooms  Full central heating  Open parking available
Outdoor swimming pool  Riding  Boule  Bicycle rental
Languages spoken: English*
ROOMS: s 500FF; d 1100-1800FF
CARDS: Travellers cheques

### Mas de la Tour (Prop: Christian Blaser)
Chemin de Bigau *13210*
☎ 490926100 FAX 490926100
(exit A7 at Cavaillon and take D99 west to St-Rémy, before
entering town turn left on first street after the 'Centre Ville'
sign, Mas de la Tour is signposted)
Forest area  In town centre  Near motorway
*Closed Nov-Mar*
*4 en suite (shr) TV available  Full central heating  Open parking
available  Covered parking available  Outdoor swimming pool
Languages spoken: English, German, Italian & Spanish*
CARDS: Travellers cheques

### ★ ★ ★ Le Mas des Carassins
1 chemin Gaulois *13210*
☎ 490921548 FAX 490926347
(located near the Roman ruins, 10mins by foot from the town
centre, by the D5)

An old house, typical of the south of France, located in the
tranquillity of the Provençal countryside. At the foot of the
Alpilles hills, and ten minutes by foot from the village centre,
this establishment has a large garden and two guest lounges.

Near lake Forest area
*Closed Nov-Mar*
*10 en suite (bth/shr) (2 fmly) (1 with balcony) Direct dial from all bedrooms Licensed Night porter Full central heating Open parking available Supervised Covered terrace Languages spoken: English & Italian*
ROOMS: (room only) s 380-480FF; d 400-600FF
CARDS: ⊛ ⅏ Electron, Maestro, EDC Travellers cheques

**Mas Shamrock**
chemin de Velleren et du Prud', Homme, Les Jardins *13210*
☎ 490925579 FAX 490925580
(A6 exit Avignon Sud follow signs to St-Rémy (18km on D99) on reaching St-Rémy take direction of Avignon (D571); on D571 after 2 rdbts & 2nd bus stop on left called "Lagoy" turn left, Mas Shamrock is 5th house on the right)
Near lake Forest area

*5 en suite (shr) (1 fmly) (3 with balcony) No smoking on premises Full central heating Outdoor swimming pool Languages spoken: English & German*
ROOMS: s 475FF; d 500FF

**ST-SATURNIN-LÈS-APT** Vaucluse

★★ **Des Voyageurs**
*84490*
☎ 490754208
Near lake Forest area In town centre
*14 rms (5 fmly) (3 with balcony) Licensed Full central heating Open terrace V meals Languages spoken: English & German*
CARDS: ⊛ ⅏

**ST-TRINIT** Vaucluse

**Ferme Auberge Les Bayles** (Prop: Mr Gerard Sanchez)
*84390*
☎ 490750091
Forest area
*Closed Dec-Jan*
*5 en suite (shr) Full central heating Open parking available Child discount available 10yrs Outdoor swimming pool Languages spoken: Spanish*

**ST-TROPEZ** Var

★★★★ **La Mandarine**
rte de Tahiti *83990*
☎ 494790666 FAX 494973367
(from St-Tropez town centre, take the direction of Tahiti Beach)
Near sea Near beach Forest area
*Closed mid Oct-mid May*

*43 en suite (bth) (12 fmly) (34 with balcony) TV in all bedrooms STV Direct dial from all bedrooms Mini-bar in all bedrooms Licensed Night porter Full central heating Air conditioning in bedrooms Open parking available Covered parking available (charged) Child discount available 7yrs Outdoor swimming pool (heated) Solarium Open terrace Private beach Last d 22.30hrs Languages spoken: English, German, Italian & Spanish*
CARDS: ⊛ ⅏ Travellers cheques

★★★★ **Ponche**
pl du Révelin, Port des Pecheurs *83990*
☎ 494970253 FAX 494977861
(from the Motorway: exit Le Muy- In the town, follow the signs for the City centre and Citadelle)
Near sea Near beach Forest area In town centre
*Closed 13 Nov-30 Mar*
*18 en suite (bth/shr) 2 rooms in annexe (2 fmly) (4 with balcony) TV in all bedrooms STV Direct dial from all bedrooms Mini-bar in all bedrooms Room-safe Licensed Lift Night porter Full central heating Air conditioning in bedrooms Open parking available (charged) Covered parking available (charged) Child discount available Open terrace V meals Last d 24.00hrs Languages spoken: English, German & Italian*
ROOMS: (room only) s 800-1000FF; d 1650-1900FF
**Reductions over 1 night**
MEALS: Continental breakfast 90FF Lunch 130-190FF&alc Dinner 190-250FF&alc
CARDS: ⊛ ⅏ Travellers cheques

★★★★ *Residence de la Pinède*
Plage de la Bouillabaisse *83991*
☎ 494970421 FAX 494977364
Near sea
*Closed Nov-Apr*
*50 rms (4 fmly) (46 with balcony) TV available STV Radio in rooms Mini-bar in all bedrooms Licensed Lift Night porter Full central heating Air conditioning in bedrooms Open parking available Supervised Outdoor swimming pool (heated) Fishing Open terrace V meals Last d 22.30hrs Languages spoken: English, German, Italian & Spanish*
CARDS: ⊛ ⅏ Travellers cheques

★★★ *Hotel Sube*
quai Suffren *83990*
☎ 494973004 FAX 494548908
(A8 exit Le Muy take direction Sainte Maxime)
Near sea Near beach Forest area In town centre
*30 en suite (bth/shr) (4 fmly) (9 with balcony) TV in all bedrooms STV Direct dial from all bedrooms Licensed Night porter Full central heating Air conditioning in bedrooms Open terrace Languages spoken: English & Italian*
CARDS: ⊛ ⅏ Travellers cheques

**Le Yaca**
1 bd d'Aumale *83990*
☎ 494558100 FAX 494975850
(motorway A8 to Nice exit Le Muy and follow direction Ste Maxime and St Tropez)
Near sea Near beach In town centre
*27 en suite (bth/shr) (8 fmly) (8 with balcony) TV in 26 bedrooms STV Direct dial from 26 bedrooms Mini-bar in 26 bedrooms Room-safe Licensed Night porter Full central heating Air conditioning in bedrooms Open parking available Covered parking available (charged) Supervised Outdoor swimming pool (heated) Open terrace Last d 23.00hrs*
ROOMS: (room only) d 1250-2500FF
CARDS: ⊛ ⅏ Travellers cheques

## STE-MAXIME Var

**★ ★ ★ ★ Golf Plaza - Hotel & Country Club**
BP 29 *83120*
☎ 494566666 FAX 494566600
Near sea Near beach Forest area
*106 en suite (bth/shr) (106 with balcony) TV in all bedrooms
STV Direct dial from all bedrooms Mini-bar in all bedrooms
Room-safe Licensed Lift Night porter Full central heating Air
conditioning in bedrooms Open parking available Covered
parking available Supervised Indoor swimming pool (heated)
Outdoor swimming pool Golf 18 Tennis Sauna Solarium
Jacuzzi/spa Open terrace Covered terrace Last d 22.00hrs
Languages spoken: English German & Italian*
ROOMS: (room only) s 690-1300FF; d 800-1420FF
**Reductions over 1 night Special breaks**
MEALS: Full breakfast 90FF Lunch fr 115FF&alc Dinner fr
205FF&alc
CARDS: ●● ■■ ⬛ ⑩

**Mas des Brugassières** (Prop: Annick Engrand)
Plan-de-la-Tour *83120*
☎ 494555055 FAX 494555051
Near sea Forest area Near motorway
*Closed 10 Oct-20 Mar*
*10 en suite (bth/shr) (3 with balcony) No smoking in 4
bedrooms Full central heating Open parking available Child
discount available Outdoor swimming pool Tennis Boule
Open terrace Table tennis Languages spoken: English German
& Italian*
ROOMS: (room only) s 500FF; d 560FF
CARDS: ●● ⬛

## SALERNES Var

**La Bastide Rose** (Prop: Karel & Caroline Henny)
Quartier Haut-Gaudran *83690*
☎ 494706330 FAX 494707734
(approach Salernes on D31 and turn left just before entering
town. Cross bridge and continue for 2.5km and follow signs)
This pink farmhouse dates back to the 18th century. In addition
to the 12 acres of vines, there are fruit trees, olive trees,
rabbits, goats and poultry on the property. You are invited to
dine at your hosts' table at a fixed price. Separate building
available which can house family groups. It has a large lounge,
dining room with television and children's games. Markets
held in the local village on Wednesday and Sunday.
Near river Near lake Forest area
*RS Nov-30 Mar*
*4 en suite (bth/shr) (3 fmly) (4 with balcony) No smoking on
premises Open parking available Child discount available
12yrs Outdoor swimming pool Riding Boule Basketball Table
tennis Volleyball Languages spoken: English*
ROOMS: d 350-450FF
MEALS: Dinner 110-120FF
CARDS: Travellers cheques

## SALIERS-PAR-ARLES Bouches-du-Rhône

**★ ★ ★ Les Cabanettes**
N572 *13200*
☎ 466873153 FAX 466873539
(off the N572 between Arles and St-Gilles)
Near motorway
*Closed 25 Jan-28 Feb*
*29 en suite (bth) (1 fmly) (29 with balcony) TV in all bedrooms
Radio in rooms Direct dial from all bedrooms Mini-bar in all*

*bedrooms Licensed Full central heating Air conditioning in
bedrooms Open parking available Covered parking available
(charged) Child discount available 12yrs Outdoor swimming
pool Open terrace Covered terrace Last d 21.00hrs
Languages spoken: English, German & Italian*
CARDS: ●● ■■ ⬛ ⑩ Travellers cheques

## SALON-DE-PROVENCE Bouches-du-Rhône

**★ ★ ★ Abbaye de Sainte-Croix**
rte du Val de Cuech *13300*
☎ 490562455 FAX 490563112
Forest area
*Closed early Nov-mid Mar RS half board obligatory at certain
times*
*24 en suite (bth/shr) (1 fmly) (9 with balcony) TV in all
bedrooms STV Direct dial from all bedrooms Mini-bar in all
bedrooms Room-safe Licensed Full central heating Air
conditioning in bedrooms Open parking available Supervised
Child discount available 12yrs Outdoor swimming pool Boule
Bicycle rental Open terrace Covered terrace Park Table tennis
Last d 21.30hrs Languages spoken: English, Italian &
Spanish*
ROOMS: (room only) d 840-1560FF
MEALS: Continental breakfast 120FF Lunch 345-430FF&alc
Dinner 430-595FF&alc
CARDS: ●● ■■ ⬛ ⑩ Travellers cheques

**★ ★ Domaine de Roquerousse**
rte d'Avignon *13300*
☎ 490595011 FAX 490595375
*30 en suite (bth/shr) (8 with balcony) TV in all bedrooms
Direct dial from all bedrooms Licensed Full central heating
Open parking available Supervised Outdoor swimming pool
Tennis Gym Pool table Boule Bicycle rental Covered terrace
riding stables near by Last d 21.15hrs Languages spoken:
English & Spanish*
CARDS: ●● ■■ ⬛ ⑩ Travellers cheques

**★ ★ ★ Le Mas du Soleil**
38 chemin Saint-Come *13300*
☎ 490560653 FAX 490562152
Forest area
*10 en suite (bth) TV in all bedrooms Direct dial from all
bedrooms Mini-bar in all bedrooms Room-safe Licensed Full
central heating Air conditioning in bedrooms Open parking
available Supervised Outdoor swimming pool Jacuzzi/spa
Open terrace Covered terrace Last d 21.30hrs Languages
spoken: English*
ROOMS: (room only) s 550-630FF; d 780-820FF
MEALS: Continental breakfast 70FF Lunch 230-650FF&alc
Dinner 230-650FF&alc
CARDS: ●● ■■ ⬛ ⑩ JCB Travellers cheques

## SAULT Vaucluse

**★ ★ ★ Hostellerie du Val de Sault**
Route de St Trinit, Ancien chemin d'Aurel *84390*
☎ 490640141 FAX 490641274
(A7 exit Avignon Nord, toward Carpentras, Mazan, Sault)
Forest area
*Closed Nov-28 Mar*
*16 en suite (bth/shr) (16 fmly) (16 with balcony) TV in all
bedrooms STV Direct dial from all bedrooms Mini-bar in all
bedrooms Full central heating Open parking available
Supervised Child discount available 10 yrs Outdoor swimming
pool (heated) Tennis Solarium Gym Boule Bicycle rental*

Open terrace V meals Last d 22.00hrs Languages spoken:
English & Italian
CARDS: ●● ■■ ⚏ Eurocard Travellers cheques

## SAUMANE-DE-VAUCLUSE Vaucluse

**Bed & Breakfast** (Prop: Robert Beaumet)
chemin de la Tapy 84800
☎ 490203297
Near river  Forest area
3 en suite (shr)  (1 fmly)  Full central heating  Boule
ROOMS: s fr 230FF; d fr 250FF

## SÉGURET Vaucluse

**St-Jean** (Prop: Gisele Augier)
84110
☎ 490469176
(exit A7 at Orange and head in the direction of Vaison-la-
Romaine N977 until you reach Séguret then take D88 to
establishment)
Near river  Forest area
3 en suite (shr)  (2 fmly)  (1 with balcony)  TV available  Full
central heating  Open parking available  Outdoor swimming
pool  Languages spoken: English & Spanish

## SEILLANS Var

**★ ★ ★ Deux Rocs**
pl Font d'Amont 83440
☎ 494768732 FAX 494768868
In town centre
Closed Nov-Mar
14 en suite (bth/shr)  Direct dial from all bedrooms  Licensed
Full central heating  Child discount available 12yrs  Open
terrace V meals Last d 21.00hrs  Languages spoken: English,
Dutch & German
ROOMS: (room only)  d 300-580FF
MEALS: Full breakfast 50FF  Dinner 160-225FF
CARDS: ●● ⚏ Travellers cheques

## SÉRIGNAN-DU-COMTAT Vaucluse

**★ ★ ★ Hostellerie du Vieux Chateau**
rte de St-Cécile 84830
☎ 490700558 FAX 490700562
Near river  Forest area  In town centre
Closed 20-30 Dec
7 en suite (bth/shr)  TV in all bedrooms  Licensed  Full central
heating  Open parking available  Supervised  Child discount
available  Outdoor swimming pool  Solarium  Jacuzzi/spa  Open
terrace V meals Last d 21.30hrs  Languages spoken:
English
CARDS: ●● ■■ ⚏ JCB Travellers cheques

## SERRES Hautes-Alpes

**Bed & Breakfast** (Prop: M & Mme Emile Moynier)
L'Alpillonne, Sigottier 05700
☎ 492670898
Near river  Near sea  Near beach  Forest area
Closed mid Sep-mid Jan
3 en suite (bth/shr)  (1 with balcony)  Full central heating  Child
discount available 10yrs  Languages spoken: English
CARDS: ⚏

## SEYNE-SUR-MER, LA Var

**★ ★ ★ Novotel Toulon la Seyne**
La Camp Laurent 83500
☎ 494630950 FAX 494630376
Near motorway
86 en suite (bth/shr)  (20 fmly)  No smoking in 17 bedrooms  TV
in all bedrooms  STV  Radio in rooms  Direct dial from all
bedrooms  Mini-bar in all bedrooms  Licensed  Lift  Night porter
Full central heating  Air conditioning in bedrooms  Open
parking available  Supervised  Child discount available 16yrs
Outdoor swimming pool  Pool table  Open terrace  Last d
24.00hrs  Languages spoken: English
CARDS: ●● ■■ ⚏ ⓪ Travellers cheques

## SISTERON Alpes-de-Haute-Provence

**★ ★ Touring Napoléon**
04200
☎ 492610006 FAX 492610119
Near river  Forest area  In town centre  Near motorway
28 en suite (bth/shr)  (6 fmly)  (14 with balcony)  TV in all
bedrooms  STV  Direct dial from all bedrooms  Licensed  Full
central heating  Open parking available (charged)  Covered
parking available (charged)  Supervised  Child discount
available 2yrs  Bicycle rental  Open terrace  Last d 21.30hrs
Languages spoken: English, German & Italian
CARDS: ●● ■■ ⚏ ⓪ Travellers cheques

## TARASCON Bouches-du-Rhône

**★ ★ ★ Mazets des Roches**
rte de Fontvieille, St Gabriel
☎ 490913489 FAX 490435329
(A9 exit at Avignon Nord in direction of Arles. A2 exit at
Cavaillon in direction of St-Rémy-de-Provence)
Charming hotel located at the beginning of the western
Alpilles in a densely wooded domain abounding with wildlife.
Tastefully decorated rooms and air conditioning throughout
add to the relaxing ambiance. The cuisine offered features
regional specialities.
Forest area

Closed Dec-Mar
38 en suite (bth/shr)  14 rooms in annexe  (19 with balcony)  TV
in all bedrooms  STV  Direct dial from all bedrooms  Mini-bar in
15 bedrooms  Licensed  Full central heating  Air conditioning in
bedrooms  Open parking available  Supervised  Child discount
available 8yrs  Outdoor swimming pool  Tennis  Solarium  Boule
Bicycle rental  Covered terrace  Last d 21.30hrs  Languages
spoken: English German Spanish

contd.

461

Rooms: (room only) s 350-600FF; d 380-900FF
Meals: Continental breakfast 50FF  Lunch 100-210FF&alc
Dinner 100-210FF&alc
Cards: ●● ■■ ▄▄ ⑩ Travellers cheques

### THOR, LE Vaucluse

**Mas des Gerbauts** (Prop: Mme Doribi)
Qaurtier le Trentin *84250*
☎ 490338885
Near river  Forest area
*Closed Oct-mid Apr*
*2 en suite (bth/shr)  No smoking on premises  Full central
heating  Open parking available*
Cards: Travellers cheques

### TOULON Var

★ ★ ★ **Holiday Inn Garden Court**
1 av Ragéotdé la Touché *83000*
☎ 494920021 FAX 494620815
Near sea  In town centre  Near motorway
*81 en suite (bth/shr)  No smoking in 40 bedrooms  TV in all
bedrooms  STV  Radio in rooms  Direct dial from 18 bedrooms
Mini-bar in all bedrooms  Licensed  Lift  Night porter  Full
central heating  Air conditioning in bedrooms  Open parking
available  Covered parking available  Child discount available
12yrs  Outdoor swimming pool  Pool table  Open terrace  Last d
22.30hrs  Languages spoken: English & Italian*
Cards: ●● ■■ ▄▄ ⑩ Travellers cheques

★ ★ ★ **New Hotel Amirauté**
4 rue A Guiol *83000*
☎ 494221967 FAX 494093672
Near sea  Near beach  In town centre  Near motorway
*58 en suite (bth/shr)  TV in all bedrooms  STV  Radio in rooms
Direct dial from all bedrooms  Mini-bar in all bedrooms  Room-
safe  Licensed  Lift  Night porter  Full central heating  Air
conditioning in bedrooms  Child discount available 5yrs
Languages spoken: English, Dutch, German, Italian & Spanish*
Rooms: (room only) s fr 400FF; d fr 440FF
Cards: ●● ■■ ▄▄ ⑩ JCB Travellers cheques

★ ★ ★ **New Hotel Tour Blanche**
*83200*
☎ 494244157 FAX 494224225
(follow Mont Faron cable-car, hotel situated below Mont Faron)
Near sea  Forest area  Near motorway
*91 en suite (bth/shr)  (6 fmly)  (42 with balcony)  TV in all
bedrooms  STV  Radio in rooms  Direct dial from all bedrooms
Mini-bar in all bedrooms  Licensed  Lift  Night porter  Full
central heating  Air conditioning in bedrooms  Open parking
available  Supervised  Child discount available 5yrs  Outdoor
swimming pool  Solarium  Pool table  Boule  Open terrace  V
meals  Last d 22.30hrs  Languages spoken: English, Dutch,
German, Italian & Spanish*
Rooms: (room only) s fr 470FF; d fr 510FF
Meals: Continental breakfast 60FF  Lunch fr 180FF&alc
Dinner fr 180FF&alc✱
Cards: ●● ■■ ▄▄ ⑩ JCB Travellers cheques

### TOURTOUR Var

★ ★ ★ **Auberge de Saint-Pierre**
*83690*
☎ 494705717 FAX 494705904
Near river  Forest area

*Closed Nov-Mar*
*16 en suite (bth/shr)  (4 fmly)  (9 with balcony)  TV in 5
bedrooms  Direct dial from all bedrooms  Licensed  Full central
heating  Open parking available  Outdoor swimming pool
(heated)  Tennis  Fishing  Sauna  Boule  Bicycle rental  Open
terrace  archery  V meals  Last d 21.00hrs*
Cards: ▄▄ Travellers cheques

★ ★ ★ **Bastide de Tourtour**
*83690*
☎ 494705730 FAX 494705490
(from Le Muy take N555 towards Draguignan. Follow sign
'Zone Industrielle de Salamandrier' on left. Then signs for
Flayosc. Through Flayosc, 7kms, then right towards Tourtour.
Hotel on left before village)

At an altitude of 650 metres, close to the medieval village of
Tourtour, the establishment provides the peaceful setting for a
restful holiday. Because of its geographical position it is a good
base for touring the surrounding region or visiting St-Tropez
and Cannes on the coast. The bedrooms are tastefully
furnished and have panoramic views, whilst the cosy
restaurant serves a gastronomic cuisine in informal
surroundings.
Forest area
*25 en suite (bth/shr)  (13 fmly)  (12 with balcony)  TV in all
bedrooms  STV  Direct dial from all bedrooms  Mini-bar in all
bedrooms  Room-safe  Licensed  Lift  Full central heating  Open
parking available  Supervised  Child discount available 12yrs
Outdoor swimming pool (heated)  Tennis  Pool table  Boule
Jacuzzi/spa  Bicycle rental  Open terrace  V meals  Last d
21.00hrs  Languages spoken: English & German*
Rooms: (room only) s 380-590FF; d 720-1400FF
**Reductions over 1 night**
Meals: Full breakfast 75FF  Lunch 160-320FF
Dinner 160-320FF
Cards: ●● ■■ ▄▄ ⑩ Travellers cheques

### TRIGANCE Var

★ ★ ★ **Château de Trigance**
*83840*
☎ 494769118 FAX 494856899
(A8 exit Le Muy/Draguignan onto D955 in direction of
Castellane after Jabron 4km on left)
Near river  Forest area
*Closed Nov-24 Mar*
*10 en suite (bth)  (2 fmly)  (1 with balcony)  TV in all bedrooms
STV  Direct dial from all bedrooms  Licensed  Night porter  Full
central heating  Open parking available  Supervised  Tennis
Solarium  Boule  Bicycle rental  Open terrace  Last d 21.30hrs
Languages spoken: English, German, Italian*

ROOMS: (room only) d 650-750FF
**Reductions over 1 night**
MEALS: Continental breakfast 75FF Lunch 210-320FF&alc
Dinner 210-320FF&alc
CARDS: ●● ■■ ✖✖ ⑩ JCB Travellers cheques

**★ ★ Le Viel Amandier**
Montée de St-Roch *83840*
☎ 494769292 FAX 494856865
(exit Gorges du Verdon to A8 toward Comps on the D955)
Near river Forest area
*Closed 11 Nov-15 Apr*
*12 en suite (bth/shr) TV in all bedrooms STV Direct dial from*
*all bedrooms Open parking available Child discount available*
*14yrs Outdoor swimming pool Solarium Open terrace*
*Covered terrace V meals Last d 21.00hrs Languages spoken:*
*English & Italian*
MEALS: Full breakfast 40FF Lunch 120-360FF&alc Dinner
120-360FF&alc✱
CARDS: ●● ■■ ✖✖ ⑩ JCB Travellers cheques

**VACQUEYRAS** Vaucluse

**Les Ramières** (Prop: M & Mme Bruel)
*84190*
☎ 490658961
Forest area
*Closed 16 Sep-Apr*
*5 en suite (shr) (1 fmly) Open parking available Covered*
*parking available Supervised Outdoor swimming pool*

**VAISON-LA-ROMAINE** Vaucluse

**Château de Taulignan** (Prop: M Rémy Daillet)
St-Marcellin Les Vaison *84110*
☎ 490287116 FAX 490288763
(from Vaison-la-Romaine, head towards Carpentras, Mont
Ventoux. Leave town and turn left at crossed sign for Vaison-la-
Romaine, towards 'Chemin de Planchette', castle is signposted)
Near river Near lake Near sea Forest area Near motorway
*6 en suite (bth/shr) No smoking on premises Full central heating*
*Open parking available Supervised Child discount available 4yrs*
*Outdoor swimming pool Riding Boule Bicycle rental Last d*
*14.00hrs Languages spoken: English, Spanish & Japanese*
ROOMS: d 550FF
MEALS: Dinner 160FF
CARDS: ●● ■■ ✖✖ ⑩ Travellers cheques

**Les Cigales** (Prop: Mme Claudette Horte)
Chemin des Abeilles *84110*
☎ 490360225
Near river Forest area Near motorway
*Closed Oct-Mar*
*4 en suite (bth/shr) (2 fmly) Full central heating Open parking*
*available Covered parking available Outdoor swimming pool*
*Languages spoken: English*
CARDS: ■ Travellers cheques

**Délesse**
Quartier le Brusquet *84110*
☎ 490363838
Near lake Forest area Near motorway
*2 rms (1 bth/shr) (2 fmly) (1 with balcony) No smoking on*
*premises Full central heating Open parking available Child*
*discount available 10yrs Outdoor swimming pool Languages*
*spoken: English & German*
CARDS: Travellers cheques

**L'Évêché** (Prop: M A Verdier)
Ville Medievale *84110*
☎ 490361346 FAX 490363243
(in Vaison-la-Romaine follow signs 'Ville Mediévale')
This former Bishop's Palace, in the medieval part of Vaison-la-
Romaine, was built in the 17th century. Four rooms are on
offer. Breakfast is served on the terrace, which offers a
stunning view of Vaison-la-Romaine. Your hosts love having
visitors and certainly enjoy sharing a glass or two of wine.
Near river Forest area Near motorway
*5 rms (1 bth 3 shr) Full central heating Child discount available*
*4yrs Bicycle rental Covered terrace Languages spoken:*
*English*
ROOMS: s 350-400FF; d 400-440FF
CARDS: Travellers cheques

**★ ★ Le Logis du Château**
*84110*
☎ 490360998 490362424 FAX 490361095
Forest area
*Closed end Oct-early Apr*
*45 en suite (bth/shr) (1 fmly) (6 with balcony) TV in all*
*bedrooms STV Direct dial from all bedrooms Licensed Lift*
*Full central heating Open parking available Covered parking*
*available Supervised Child discount available 10yrs Outdoor*
*swimming pool Tennis Open terrace Covered terrace Area for*
*children to play games V meals Languages spoken: English*
CARDS: ●● ✖✖

**VALENSOLE** Alpes-de-Haute-Provence

**★ ★ ★ Hostellerie la Fuste**
Lieu dit La Fuste *04210*
☎ 492720595 FAX 492729293
(from A51 exit at Manosque, at 1st rndbt turn right. At 2nd
rndbt straight ahead. Cross River la Durance bridge. At
junction follow signs for Oraison. Hotel 800m on left)
Near river Near lake Forest area Near motorway
*Closed 15 Jan -15 Feb*
*14 en suite (bth/shr) (8 with balcony) No smoking in 4*
*bedrooms TV in all bedrooms Direct dial from all bedrooms*
*Mini-bar in all bedrooms Full central heating Air conditioning*
*in bedrooms Open parking available Covered parking*
*available Indoor swimming pool (heated) Outdoor swimming*
*pool (heated) Solarium Boule Jacuzzi/spa Open terrace V*
*meals Last d 22.00hrs Languages spoken: English, Italian &*
*Spanish*
CARDS: ●● ■■ ✖✖ ⑩ Travellers cheques

**★ ★ Pies**
*04210*
☎ 392748313
Forest area
*Closed Dec-Mar*
*16 rms (3 fmly) (12 with balcony) TV in all bedrooms Direct*
*dial from all bedrooms Mini-bar in all bedrooms Full central*
*heating Open parking available Child discount available 10yrs*
*Boule Bicycle rental Open terrace*
CARDS: ●● ✖✖ Travellers cheques

**VALRÉAS** Vaucluse

**★ ★ Grand Hotel**
28 av General de Gaulle *84600*
☎ 490350026 FAX 490356093
Forest area In town centre
*RS 21 Dec-28 Jan*

contd.

15 en suite (bth/shr) No smoking in 2 bedrooms TV in all bedrooms STV Direct dial from all bedrooms Licensed Full central heating Open parking available (charged) Covered parking available (charged) Child discount available 12yrs Outdoor swimming pool Boule Open terrace Covered terrace Last d 21.00hrs Languages spoken: English, German & Italian
CARDS: ● ▣

### VAUVENARGUES Bouches-du-Rhône

**★ Au Moulin de Provence**
33 av des Maquisards 13126
☎ 442660222 FAX 442660121
(take D10 from Aix-en-Provence to Vauvenargues or travelling west on N7 towards Aix. Take right for Pourières then D23/D223/D10 to Vauvenargues)
Near river  Forest area
Closed 2 Nov-Feb RS Nov-31 Dec
12 rms (9 bth/shr) (5 with balcony) Direct dial from all bedrooms Licensed Full central heating Open parking available Open terrace V meals Last d 21.00hrs Languages spoken: English,German, Italian, Spanish
CARDS: ● ▣ Travellers cheques

### VELLERON Vaucluse

**Villa Velleron** (Prop: Wim Visser et Simone Sanders)
rue Roquette 84740
☎ 490201231 FAX 490201034
(from A7 exit 'Avignon Nord/Centre' then follow direction Carpentras until Monteux. Follow Monteux Centre. At lights follow signs for Velleron, in Velleron find post office, the house is opposite.)
Near river  Forest area
Closed Nov-Etr weekend
6 en suite (bth/shr) (1 fmly) (2 with balcony) Full central heating Covered parking available (charged) Supervised No children 8yrs Outdoor swimming pool Boule Bicycle rental Last d 20.00hrs Languages spoken: English, Dutch & German
CARDS: Travellers cheques

### VENASQUE Vaucluse

**Les Basses Garrigues** (Prop: Celine Borel)
84210
☎ 490661420 FAX 490661420
Forest area
Apr-Oct
5 en suite (bth/shr) (2 fmly) Open parking available Boule
ROOMS: s 140-210FF; d 180-260FF

**Auberge La Fontaine**
pl la Fontaine 84210
☎ 490660296 FAX 490661314
(from Avignon take D942 to Carpentras then D4 to Venasque)
RS (restaurant closed mid Nov-mid Dec)
5 en suite (bth/shr) (5 fmly) (4 with balcony) TV in all bedrooms Direct dial from all bedrooms Mini-bar in all bedrooms Licensed Air conditioning in bedrooms Open parking available Child discount available Boule Bicycle rental Last d 22.00hrs Languages spoken: English, German & Spanish
CARDS: ● ▣ EC Travellers cheques

**La Maison aux Volets Bleus** (Prop: Martine Maret)
pl des Bouviers-Le Village 84210
☎ 490660304 FAX 490661614
(near Carpentras by the D4)

Forest area  In town centre  Near motorway
Closed Nov-14 Mar
5 en suite (bth/shr)  TV available  Full central heating  Last d 19.30hrs Languages spoken: English
CARDS: Travellers cheques

**Maison Provencale** (Prop: M Gerard Ruel)
Le Village 84210
☎ 490660284 FAX 490666132
Forest area  In town centre
5 en suite (bth/shr) (1 fmly) Full central heating Open parking available Open terrace

### VENTABREN Bouches-du-Rhône

**Val Lourdes** (Prop: Murielle Lesage)
rte de Berre 13122
☎ 442287515 FAX 442289291
Near river  Forest area  Near motorway
Closed Nov-Mar
2 en suite (shr) No smoking on premises TV in all bedrooms Radio in rooms Full central heating Open parking available Supervised Languages spoken: English & Spanish
CARDS: ■ Travellers cheques

### VENTEROL Hautes-Alpes

**La Meridienne** (Prop: M Claude Boyer)
Le Blanchet 05130
☎ 492541851 FAX 492541851
Near lake  Forest area
6 en suite (bth/shr) (6 fmly) TV in 5 bedrooms Full central heating Open parking available Supervised Child discount available 12yrs Tennis Riding Gym Boule Bicycle rental Open terrace Last d 21.00hrs Languages spoken: English
CARDS: ● ■ ▣ 🔳

### VILLEDIEU Vaucluse

**Château la Baude** (Prop: Gerard Monin)
84110
☎ 490289518 FAX 490289105
Near river  Forest area
Closed Dec-Feb
6 en suite (bth/shr) (2 fmly) No smoking on premises TV in all bedrooms Full central heating Open parking available Supervised Child discount available 12yrs Outdoor swimming pool Tennis Boule Table tennis Languages spoken: English & Italian
CARDS: Travellers cheques

### VIOLES Vaucluse

**La Farigoulé** (Prop: Augustine Cornaz)
Le Plan de Dieu 84150
☎ 490709178
Near river  Forest area  Near motorway
Closed Nov-Mar
5 en suite (shr) Full central heating Open parking available Supervised Boule Bicycle rental Open terrace Table tennis Languages spoken: German & Spanish
CARDS: ● ▣ 🔳 Travellers cheques

## VITROLLES Bouches-du-Rhône

### ★ ★ Hotel Loiisiana
Aéroport de Marseille Provence, Imp Pythagoré - La
Couperigné 13127
☎ 442108500 FAX 442108501
Near lake Forest area Near motorway
*100 en suite (bth/shr) 20 rooms in annexe No smoking in 10
bedrooms TV in all bedrooms STV Direct dial from all
bedrooms Licensed Night porter Open parking available
Supervised Child discount available Outdoor swimming pool
Sauna Boule Open terrace Covered terrace Last d 22.00hrs
Languages spoken: English, German, Italian & Spanish*
CARDS: ● ▆ Travellers cheques

### ★ ★ ★ Primotel Aéroport Marseille Provence
13127
☎ 442797919 FAX 442896918
Near motorway
*120 en suite (bth/shr) TV in all bedrooms STV Radio in rooms
Direct dial from all bedrooms Licensed Lift Night porter Full
central heating Air conditioning in bedrooms Open parking
available Child discount available 12yrs Outdoor swimming
pool Tennis Open terrace V meals Last d 23.00hrs Languages
spoken: English*
CARDS: ● ▆ ▆ ◐ Travellers cheques

## CORSICA

## BRANDO Haute-Corse

### Hotel Castel-Brando
Bp 20 - Erbalunga
☎ 495301030 FAX 495339818

## EVENTS & FESTIVALS

| | |
|---|---|
| **Jan** | Coudoux Wine Festival |
| **Mar** | Les Orres Comic Book Festival; Digne les Bain Film Festival, Aix Wine Fair |
| **Apr** | Brignoles Agricultural Wine-Growing Fair & Exhibition; Aix-en-Provence Timbrel Festival; Chateauneuf-du-Pape Easter Festival |
| **May** | Les Mées Olive Tree Festival; Flower Shows at Tarascon & Sanary-sur-Mer; Stes-Maries-de-la-Mer Gypsy Pilgrimage of Ste      Sarah to the |
| Sea; | Rognes Wine Fair; Barbentane Horse Fair; |
| **Jun** | Cassis Fishermans Festival; Marseille Garlic Festival; Stes-Maries-de-la-Mer ' Jornadido Biou' (the day of the bull); Manosque Medieval Fair; Valréas Petit St Jean Night (since 1504); Le Val Holy Art Festival; Gréoux-les-Bains Craft Fairs; Trets Wine Festival; Wine Fairs at Gemenos & La Destrousse; Arles Guardian's Feast; Port-Saint-Louis-du-Rhone Mussel Fair; Tarascon Tarasque Festival |
| **Jul** | Ferrassieres Lavender Festival; JazzFestivals at Toulon, Chateau-Arnoux, St Raphael, Salon-de Provence, Forcalquier, Ramatuelle; Martiques Venetian celebrations; Visan Wine & Harvest Festival; Stes-Maries-de-la-Mer Festival of the Virgin Mary; Chateauvallon Contemporary Dance Festival; Folklore Festival at Cavaillon; Marseille (Chateau Gombert); Arles International Photo Workshop & Exhibitions; Festivals at Avignon, Vaison-la-Romaine, Colmars-les-Alpes, Marseille, Carpentras; St |
| | Etienne-les-Orgues Herb & Craft Fair; Aix-en Provence International Ballet Festival; Arles Festival & Costume Fair; St-Remy-de-Provence ine & Craft Fair |
| **Aug** | Frejus Grape Festival; Chateauneuf-du-Pain Medieval Festival of La Veraison; Montfort Wine Festival; Chateauneuf-du-Pape Medieval Celebration of Fruit Harvest; Draguignan ' Draguifollies' (jazz, rock, blues, street artists); Pont de Cervières ' Bacchu-ber' ancient sword dance parade; Castellane Craft Fair; Salon de Provence Chamber Music Festival; Sault Notre Dame Fair & Lavender Festival; Forcalquier Provence Products Fair; Aix-en-Provence Jazz Festival; Chateaurenard Fete de la Madeleine |
| **Sep** | Peyruis Apple & Fruit Festival; Le Val Sausage Fair; Marseille International Fair; Allemagne en-Provence Old Crafts Festival; Riez Honey & Lavender Fair; Plan-de-la-Tour Fortified Wine (Vin Cuit) Festival; Cassis Wine Fair; Arles Rice Harvest Festival |
| **Oct** | Apt Wine Harvest Festival; Draguignan Jazz Festival; Stes-Maries-de-la-Mer Gypsy Festival & Pilgrimage; Marseille Folklore Fair |
| **Nov** | Marseille ' Santons' Fair; Aups Truffle Market; Avignon Naming of Cote du Rhone Wine; Marseille Christmas Ornaments Fair; Wine Fairs at Istres & Martiques |
| **Dec** | Istres Shepherds Festivals; Bandol Wine Festival; Seguret Yule Evening |

465

# Index

## A

Abbeville, Somme 111
Abreschviller, Moselle 144
Abrest, Allier 336
Abrets, Les, Isère 347
Acqueville, Manche 63
Acquigny, Eure 63
Agay, Var 432
Agen, Lot-et-Garonne 307
Agnetz, Oise 111, 113
Agnos, Pyrénées-Atlantiques 307
Agonges, Allier 336
Aigle, l', Orne 63
Aignay-le-Duc, Côte-D'Or 256
Aiguebelette-le-Lac, Savoie 345
Aigueperse, Puy-de-Dôme 336
Aigues-Mortes, Gard 402
Aiguillon, Lot-et-Garonne 307, 309
Aiguines, Var 432
Ainhoa, Pyrénées-Atlantiques 309
Aire-sur-la-Lys, Pas-de-Calais 130
Aisey-sur-Seine, Côte-D'Or 256
Aix-d'Angillon, Les, Cher 165
Aix-les-Bains, Savoie 345, 347
Aix-en-Othe, Aube 122
Aix-en-Provence, Bouches-du-
    Rhône 432, 434-5
Albas, Lot 377
Albert, Somme 113
Albi, Tarn 377, 379
Albussac, Corrèze 329
Alby-sur-Chéran, Haute-Savoie 347
Alençon, Orne 63, 66
Alénya, Pyrénées-Orientales 402
Alet-les-Bains, Aude 402
Allevard-les-Bains, Isère 347
Alleyras, Haute-Loire 338
Allonnes, Maine-et-Loire 204
Alluy, Nièvre 256
Alzon, Gard 404
Amailloux, Deux-Sèvres 288
Amanze, Saône-et-Loire 256
Ambialet, Tarn 379
Ambilly, Haute-Savoie 347
Amblie, Calvados 66
Amboise, Indre-et-Loire 165, 167-8
Amélie-les-Bains-Palalda, Pyrénées-
    Orientales 404
Amettes, Pas-de-Calais 130
Amiens, Somme 113
Ammerschwihr, Haut-Rhin 154
Ancelle, Hautes-Alpes 435

Ancemont, Meuse 144
Ancteville, Manche 66
Andard, Maine-et-Loire 204
Andolsheim, Haut-Rhin 154
Andrézieux-Bouthéon, Loire 347
Anduze, Gard 404
D'Angers, Alpes-Maritimes 421
Angers, Maine-et-Loire 204, 206
Angerville, Essonne 224
Angles, Les, Pyrénées-Orientales
    404
Angles-sur-L'Anglin, Vienne 288
Angoville-au-Plain, Manche 66
Annebault, Calvados 66
Annecy, Haute-Savoie 347-8
Annecy-le-Vieux, Haute-Savoie 348
Annemasse, Haute-Savoie 348
Anse, Rhône 348
Antezant, Charente-Maritime 290
Antibes, Alpes-Maritimes 421
Antilly-Argilly, Côte-D'Or 258
Antran, Vienne 290
Anzy-le-Duc, Saône-et-Loire 256
Appeville-Annebault, Eure 66
Apt, Vaucluse 435-6
Arbadon, Morbihan 32
Arbois, Jura 282
Arbonne, Pyrénées-Atlantiques 309
Arcachon, Gironde 309-10
Arçais, Deux-Sèvres 290
Arçay, Vienne 290
Arcenant, Côte-D'Or 258
Archigny, Vienne 290
Ardenais, Cher 168
Ardres, Pas-de-Calais 130
Argein, Ariège 379
Argelès-Gazost, Hautes-Pyrénées
    379-80
Argelès-sur-Mer, Pyrénées-
    Orientales 404
Argences, Calvados 66
Argentat, Corrèze 329
Argenton-sur-Creuse, Indre 168
Argoules, Somme 113
Argueil, Seine-Maritime 66
Arles, Bouches-du-Rhône 436-7
Armentières-en-Brie, Seine-et-
    Marne 224
Arnay-le-Duc, Côte-D'Or 258
Arques-la-Bataille, Seine-Maritime
    67
Arras, Pas-de-Calais 132
Arromanches-les-Bains, Calvados
    67
Arroses, Pyrénées-Atlantiques 310
Arry, Moselle 144
Arsonval, Aube 122
Arzano, Finistère 32
Arzay, Isère 348
Asnières-sur-Vegre, Sarthe 206

Asprières, Aveyron 380
Athée-sur-Cher, Indre-et-Loire 168
Attignat, Ain 348
Aubigney, Haute-Saône 282
Aubigny-sur-Nère, Cher 168
Aucey-la-Plaine, Manche 67
Auch, Gers 380
Auchy-au-Bois, Pas-de-Calais 132
Aucun, Hautes-Pyrénées 380
Audierne, Finistère 32
Aulas, Gard 405
Aulnay-sous-Bois, Seine-St-Denis
    224
Aumagne, Charente-Maritime 290
Aumont-Aubrac, Lozère 405
Aunay-sur-Odon, Calvados 67
Auray, Morbihan 34
Aurec-sur-Loire, Haute-Loire 338
Auribeau-sur-Siagne, Alpes-
    Maritimes 423
Aurillac, Cantal 338
Aurons, Bouches-du-Rhône 437
Aussois, Savoie 348
Auterive, Haute-Garonne 380
Authieux-sur-Calonne, Les,
    Calvados 67
Autrans, Isère 348
Autreville, Vosges 144, 146
Autun, Seine-et-Loire 258
Auxerre, Yonne 258
Auzouville-sur-Ry, Seine-Maritime
    67
Avallon, Yonne 258-9
Avaray, Loir-et-Cher 168
Aviernoz, Haute-Savoie 349
Avignon, Vaucluse 437
Avranches, Manche 67-8
Avrillé, Maine-et-Loire 206
Ax-Les-Thermes, Ariège 380
Azannes, Meuse 146
Azas, Haute-Garonne 380
Azay-sur-Cher, Indre-et-Loire 169
Azay-sur-Indre, Indre-et-Loire 169
Azay-le-Rideau, Indre-et-Loire
    168-9
Azé, Loir-et-Cher 169
Azé, Saône-et-Loire 259
Azincourt, Pas-de-Calais 132

## B

Bacilly, Manche 68
Bages, Aude 405
Bagnoles-de-l'Orne, Orne 68-9
Bagnols, Rhône 349
Bagnols-sur-Cèze, Gard 405
Baillargues, Hérault 405
Bailleul, Nord 132
Baldersheim, Haut-Rhin 154, 156
Bandol, Var 437
Bangor, Morbihan 224

Bannalec, Finistère 34
Bannay, Marne 122, 124
Bannegon, Cher 169
Banteux, Nord 132
Bantzenheim, Haut-Rhin 156
Banville, Calvados 69
Banyuls-sur-Mer, Pyrénées-
  Orientales 405
Baraqueville, Aveyron 380
Barbazan, Haute-Garonne 380
Barben, La, Bouches-du-Rhône
  437-8
Barbery, Aube 124
Barbizon, Seine-et-Marne 226
Barcus, Pyrénées-Atlantique 310
Barèges, Hautes-Pyrénées 381
Barembach, Bas-Rhin 156
Barjac, Gard 405
Barjols, Var 438
Barneville-Carteret, Manche 69
Baron, Saône-et-Loire 259
Barp, Le, Gironde 310
Barr, Bas-Rhin 156
Barroux, Le, Vaucluse 438
Basly, Calvados 69
Baudrières, Saône-et-Loire 259
Baule, La, Loire-Atlantique 206
Baulne-en-Brie, Aisne 113-14
Baume-de-Transit, La, Drôme 349
Baux-de-Breteuil, Les, Eure 69
Baux-de-Provence, Les, Bouches-
  du-Rhône 438
Bayeux, Calvados 69-70
Bayon, Meurthe-et-Moselle 146
Bayonne, Pyrénées-Atlantiques 310
Bayonville, Ardennes 124
Bazas, Gironde 310
Bazouges-la-Pérouse, Ille-et-Vilaine
  34
Beaucaire, Gard 405-6
Beaugency, Loiret 169-70
Beaulieu-sur-Dordogne, Corrèze
  329
Beaulieu-sur-Layon, Maine-et-Loire
  207
Beaulieu-lès-Loches, Indre-et-Loire
  170
Beaulieu-sur-Mer, Alpes-Maritimes
  423
Beaumettes, Vaucluse 439
Beaumont, Ardèche 349
Beaumont-Hague, Manche 70
Beaumont-de-Lomagne, Tarn-et-
  Garonne 381
Beaumont-lès-Valence, Drôme 349
Beaumont-en-Véron, Indre-et-Loire
  170
Beaune, Côte-D'Or 259-60
Beaurecueil, Bouches-du-Rhône
  439

Beauregard-Vendon, Puy-de-Dôme
  338
Beaurepaire, Isère 349
Beaurepaire-en-Bresse, Saône-et-
  Loire 260
Beautiran, Gironde 310
Beauvais, Oise 114
Bec-Hellouin, Le, Eure 70-1
Behen, Somme 114
Belaye, Lot 381
Bellegarde-sur-Valserine, Ain 349
Belle-Ile-en-Mer, Morbihan 34
Bellenot-sous-Pouilly, Côte-D'Or
  260
Belval, Manche 71
Belz, Morbihan 34
Bémécourt, Eure 71
Bénévent-et-Charbillac, Hautes-
  Alpes 439
Bénodet, Finistère 34-5
Bénouville, Calvados 71
Berck-sur-Mer, Pas-de-Calais 132
Bergerac, Dordogne 310-11
Bernay, Eure 71
Berné, Morbihan 35
Bernières-sur-Mer, Calvados 71
Berry-Buoy, Cher 170
Bersac, Haute-Vienne 329
Berthegon, Vienne 290
Berthenay, Indre-et-Loire 170-1
Berzy-le-Sec, Aisne 114
Besançon, Doubs 282
Besné, Loire-Atlantique 207
Besneville, Manche 72
Bessé-sur-Braye, Sarthe 207
Besse-sur-Issole, Var 439
Bétête, Creuse 331
Beuil, Alpes-Maritimes 423
Beuzeville, Eure 72
Biarritz, Pyrénées-Atlantiques 311
Bidart, Pyrénées-Atlantiques 311
Bieuzy-les-Eaux, Morbihan 35
Biéville-Beuville, Calvados 72
Bigne, La, Calvados 72
Billé, Ille-et-Vilaine 35
Billiers, Morbihan 35
Bionville, Meurthe-et-Moselle 146
Biot, Alpes-Maritimes 423
Bissy-sous-Uxelles, Saône-et-Loire
  260
Bitche, Moselle 146
Blainville-sur-Mer, Manche 72-3
Blancey, Côte-D'Or 260
Blanc, Le, Indre 171
Blaziert, Gers 381
Bléré, Indre-et-Loire 171
Blet, Cher 171
Blévy, Eure-et-Loir 171
Blois, Loir-et-Cher 171
Blonville-sur-Mer, Calvados 73

Boëcé, Orne 73
Bois-de-la-Chaize, Vendée 207
Boisredon, Charente-Maritime 290
Bollezeele, Nord 132
Boncourt, Eure 73
Bonne, Haute-Savoie 349-50
Bonnemain, Ille-et-Vilaine 35
Bonnétage, Doubs 282
Bonneval, Eure-et-Loir 171
Bonneville-La-Louvet, Calvados 73
Bonnieux, Vaucluse 439
Bonson, Loire 350
Bony, Aisne 114
Bordeaux, Gironde 311-12
Bormes-les-Mimosas, Var 439
Bosc-Roger-en-Roumois, Le, Eure
  73
Bosdarros, Pyrénées-Atlantiques
  312
Bossieu, Isère 350
Botmeur, Finistère 35
Bouguenais, Loire-Atlantique 207
Bougy-lez-Neuville, Loiret 172
Bouilland, Côte-D'Or 260
Bouisse, Aude 406
Boulogne-Billancourt, Hauts-de-
  Seine 226
Boulogne-sur-Mer, Pas-de-Calais
  132
Boulon, Calvados 73
Bourbon-l'Archambault, Allier 338
Bourbonne-les-Bains, Haute-Marne
  124
Bourboule, La, Puy-de-Dôme 338
Bourg-en-Bresse, Ain 350
Bourg-de-Visa, Tarn-et-Garonne
  381
Bourg-d'Oisans, Isère 350
Bourg-Dun, Seine-Maritime 73
Bourgeauville, Calvados 73
Bourges, Cher 172
Bourget, Le, Seine-St-Denis 226
Bourg-St-Andéol, Ardèche 350
Bourgtheroulde, Eure 74
Bourgueil, Indre-et-Loire 172
Bourgvilain, Saône-et-Loire 261
Bourneville, Eure 74
Bourré, Loir-et-Cher 172
Bourrouillan, Gers 381
Boursay, Loir-et-Cher 172
Bourth, Eure 74
Boussac, Creuse 331
Boussac, La, Ille-et-Vilaine 35
Boussens, Haute-Garonne 381
Boutigny-sur-Opton, Eure-et-Loir
  172
Bouvante, Drôme 350
Bouziès, Lot 381-2
Brando, Haute-Corse 465
Branne, Gironde 312

Index

**Index**

Brantôme, Dordogne 313
Brasparts, Finistère 36
Breau, Seine-et-Marne 226
Bréhal, Manche 74
Bréhémont, Indre-et-Loire 172
Breil-sur-Roya, Alpes-Maritimes 423-4
Brélidy, Côtes-D'Armor 36
Brémoy, Calvados 74
Brest, Finistère 36
Breteuil-sur-Iton, Eure 74
Bretteville-sur-Dives, Calvados 74
Bretteville-sur-Laize, Calvados 74
Brévands, Manche 74
Bréviandes, Aube 124
Brézolles, Eure-et-Loir 172
Briare, Loiret 172-3
Briarres-sur-Essonne, Loiret 173
Bricquebec, Manche 74
Bricqueville-sur-Mer, Manche 74-5
Brides-les-Bains, Savoie 350
Brigue, La, Alpes-Maritimes 424
Brimeux, Pas-de-Calais 133
Brinon-sur-Beuvron, Nièvre 261
Brinon-sur-Sauldre, Cher 173
Brionne, Eure 75
Brioux-sur-Boutonne, Deux-Sèvres 290
Briouze, Orne 75
Brissac-Quincé, Maine-et-Loire 207
Brive-la-Gaillarde, Corrèze 331
Brives-sur-Charente, Charente-Maritime 291
Brix, Manche 75
Brocas, Landes 313
Brouckerque, Nord 133
Brousse-le-Château, Aveyron 382
Bruges, Pyrénées-Atlantiques 313
Brumath, Bas-Rhin 156
Brux, Vienne 291
Bu, Eure-et-Loir 173
Bubry, Morbihan 36
Buc, Yvelines 226
Buffon, Côte-D'Or 261
Bugue, Le, Dordogne 313-14
Buicourt, Oise 114
Bulgnéville, Vosges 146
Buoux, Vaucluse 440
Burnhaupt-le-Haut, Haut-Rhin 156
Burtoncourt, Moselle 146
Bussang, Vosges 146-7
Bussy-en-Othe, Yonne 261
Buxy, Saône-et-Loire 261
Buzançais, Indre 173

**C**

Cabrerets, Lot 382
Cabrières-d'Avignon, Vaucluse 440

Cabris, Alpes-Maritimes 424
Cadéac, Hautes-Pyrénées 382
Cadillac, Gironde 314
Caen, Calvados 75-6
Cahagnes, Calvados 76
Cahors, Lot 382
Cairanne, Vaucluse 440
Caissargues, Gard 406
Caixas, Pyrénées-Orientales 406
Calais, Pas-de-Calais 133
Calviac, Lot 382-3
Cambounet-sur-le-Sor, Tarn 383
Cambrai, Nord 133-4
Cambremer, Calvados 76
Cambronne-les-Ribecourt, Oise 114
Camiers, Pas-de-Calais 134
Campeaux, Calvados 76
Campigny, Eure 76
Cancale, Ille-et-Vilaine 36
Cancon, Lot-et-Garonne 314
Canehan, Seine-Maritime 76
Canet-Plage, Pyrénées-Orientales 406
Cannes, Alpes-Maritimes 424-5
Canville-la-Rocque, Manche 76
Caours, Somme 114-15
Le Cap-d'Agde, Hérault 406-7
Cap-d'Ail, Alpes-Maritimes 425
Capbreton, Landes 314
Cap-Coz, Finistère 36
Capdrot, Dordogne 314
Capelle-les-Grands, Eure 76-7
Capvern-les-Bains, Hautes-Pyrénées 383
Caraman, Haute-Garonne 383
Carcassonne, Aude 407
Carennac, Lot 383
Carhaix-Plouguer, Finistère 36
Carnac, Morbihan 36-7
Carnac-Plage, Morbihan 37
Carpentras, Vaucluse 440
Carqueiranne, Var 440
Carroz-d'Arâches, Les, Haute-Savoie 383
Carsac-Aillac, Dordogne 314
Castagniers, Alpes-Maritimes 425
Castellet, Le, Var 440
Castelnaudary, Aude 407
Castelnau-de-Médoc, Gironde 314
Castelnau-de-Montmiral, Tarn 383
Castelnau-Rivière-Basse, Hautes-Pyrénées 383
Castelnou, Pyrénées-Orientales 407
Castelsagrat, Tarn-et-Garonne 383
Castera-Verduzan, Gers 383
Castex, Ariège 383-4
Catteville, Manche 77
Caudebec-en-Caux, Seine-Maritime 77

Caumont-sur-Durance, Vaucluse 440-1
Caumont-l'Éventé, Calvados 77
Caunes-Minervois, Aude 408
Caurel, Côtes-D'Armor 37
Caussade, Tarn-et-Garonne 384
Causse-de-la-Selle, Hérault 408
Caussignac, Lozère 408
Cauterets, Hautes-Pyrénées 384
Cavalaire-sur-Mer, Var 441
Cavanac, Aude 408
Cazilhac, Hérault 408
Ceaux, Manche 77
Ceillac, Hautes-Alpes 441
Celle-Guenand, La, Indre-et-Loire 173
Celles-sur-Belle, Deux-Sèvres 291
Celliers, Savoie 351
Céré-la-Ronde, Indre-et-Loire 173-4
Céret, Pyrénées-Orientales 408
Cergy-Pontoise, Val-D'Oise 226
Cerisiers, Yonne 261
Cérons, Gironde 314
Cesson-Sevigne, Ille-et-Vilaine 37
Chablis, Yonne 261
Chabris, Indre 174
Chadurie, Charente 291
Chagny, Saône-et-Loire 261-2
Chaise-Dieu, La, Haute-Loire 338-9
Chalais, Indre 174
Chalandray, Vienne 291
Challans, Vendée 207-8
Chalon-sur-Saône, Saône-et-Loire 262
Châlons-en-Champagne, Marne 124-5
Chambéry, Savoie 351
Chambois, Orne 77-8
Chambourg-sur-Indre, Indre-et-Loire 174
Chambray-les-Tours, Indre-et-Loire 174
Chamonix-Mont-Blanc, Haute-Savoie 351-2
Chamouillac, Charente-Maritime 291
Champagnac, Cantal 339
Champagnac-de-Belair, Dordogne 315
Champagnac-la-Rivière, Haute-Vienne 331
Champagnole, Jura 282, 284
Champagny-en-Vanoise, Savoie 352
Champfleur, Sarthe 208
Champier, Isère 352
Champignelles, Yonne 262
Champigné, Maine-et-Loire 208
Champillon, Marne 125

Champs-sur-Tarentaine, Cantal 339
Champtoceaux, Maine-et-Loire 208
Chançay, Indre-et-Loire 174
Chanceaux-sur-Choisille, Indre-et-
Loire 174
Chanos-Curson, Drôme 352
Chantilly, Oise 115
Chantonnay, Vendée 208-9
Chapareillan, Isère 352
Chapelle-sous-Brancion, La, Saône-
et-Loire 262
Chapelle-de-Bragny, Saône-et-Loire
262
Chapelle-Gonaguet, La, Dordogne
315
Chapelle-Monthodon, La, Aisne
115
Chapelles-Bourbon, Les, Seine-et-
Marne 226-7
Charavines, Isère 352-3
Charbonnat, Saône-et-Loire 262
Chardonnay, Saône-et-Loire 262
Charency-Vezin, Meurthe-et-
Moselle 147
Charenton-du-Cher, Cher 174-5
Charezier, Jura 284
Charité-sur-Loire, Nièvre 262
Charlieu, Loire 353
Charmel, Le, Aisne 115
Charmes, Vosges 147
Charrin, Nièvre 263
Chartres, Eure-et-Loir 175
Chartre-sur-le-Loir, Sarthe 209
Chasseneuil-du-Poitou, Vienne 291
Chasse-sur-Rhône, Isère 353
Chassey-le-Camp, Saône-et-Loire
263
Château-Arnoux, Alpes-de-Haute-
Provence 441
Châteaubourg, Ille-et-Vilaine 37
Châteaubriant, Loire-Atlantique
209
Château-Chinon, Nièvre 263
Château-du-Loir, Sarthe 209
Châteaudun, Eure-et-Loir 175
Château-Gontier, Mayenne 209-10
Château-la-Vallière, Indre-et-Loire
175
Châteaulin, Finistère 37
Châteauneuf, Côte-D'Or 263
Châteauneuf-du-Faou, Finistère 37
Châteauneuf-la-Forêt, Haute-
Vienne 331
Châteauneuf-de-Gadagne, Vaucluse
441
Châteauneuf-sur-Loire, Loiret 175
Châteauneuf-du-Pape, Vaucluse
441
Châteauneuf-sur-Sarthe, Maine-et-
Loire 210

Châteauroux, Indre 175
Châtelblanc, Doubs 284
Châtelet-en-Berry, Le, Cher 176
Châtelguyon, Puy-de-Dôme 339
Châtellerault, Vienne 291
Châtenay, La, Saône-et-Loire 263
Châtillon-la-Borde, Seine-et-Marne
227
Châtillon-sur-Chalaronne, Ain 353
Châtillon-sur-Cluses, Savoie 353
Châtillon-sur-Indre, Indre 176
Chatres, Seine-Maritime 78
Châtres-sur-Cher, Loir-et-Cher 176
Chaudes-Aigues, Cantal 339-40
Chauffayer, Hautes-Alpes 441
Chaumard, Nièvre 263
Chaumont-en-Vexin, Oise 115
Chaumont-sur-Tharonne, Loir-et-
Cher 176
Chauny, Aisne 115
Chauvigny, Vienne 292
Chaux-des-Crotenay, Jura 284
Chaveignes, Indre-et-Loire 176
Chazelles-sur-Lyon, Loire 353
Chaze-sur-Argos, Maine-et-Loire
210
Chécy, Loiret 176
Chef-Boutonne, Deux-Sèvres 292
Chemellier, Maine-et-Loire 210
Chémery, Loir-et-Cher 176
Cheneché, Vienne 292
Chênehutte-Trèves-Cunault,
Maine-et-Loire 210-11
Chenereilles, Loire 353
Chenonceaux, Indre-et-Loire
176-7
Chepy, Somme 115
Cherbourg, Manche 78
Chérêt, Aisne 115
Cherisy, Eure-et-Loir 177
Cherrueix, Ille-et-Vilaine 37-8
Cherves-Richemont, Charente 292
Cherveux, Deux-Sèvres 292-3
Chevannes, Loiret 177
Chevannes, Yonne 263
Cheverny, Loir-et-Cher 177
Chevigny-Fénay, Côte-D'Or 263
Chevillon-sur-Huillard, Loiret 177
Chigny, Aisne 115-16
Chille, Jura 284
Chinon, Indre-et-Loire 177-8
Chiroubles, Rhône 353
Chis, Hautes-Pyrénées 384
Chissay-en-Touraine, Loir-et-Cher
178
Choisy-le-Roi, Val-de-Marne 227
Cholet, Maine-et-Loire 211
Chorey-les-Beaune, Côte-D'Or
263-4
Chouvigny, Allier 340

Chouze-sur-Loire, Indre-et-Loire
178
Ciadoux, Haute-Garonne 384
Ciboure, Pyrénées-Atlantiques 315
Cinq-Mars-la-Pile, Indre-et-Loire
178
Cintegabelle, Haute-Garonne
384-5
Cirey-sur-Vezouze, Meurthe-et-
Moselle 147
Civray-de-Touraine, Indre-et-Loire
178-9
Clairac, Lot-et-Garonne 315-16
Clamerey, Côte-D'Or 264
Clécy, Calvados 78
Cléguérec, Morbihan 38
Clelles, Isère 353-4
Clermont-Ferrand, Puy-de-Dôme
340
Clichy, Hauts-de-Seine 227
Cliponville, Seine-Maritime 78
Cluny, Saône-et-Loire 264
Clusaz, La, Haute-Savoie 354
Cognac, Charente 293
Coiffy-le-Haut, Haute-Marne 125
Coigny, Manche 78
Coise, Savoie 354
Col du Mont-Sion, Haute-Savoie
354
Collanges, Puy-de-Dôme 340
Collan, Yonne 264
La Colle-sur-Loup, Alpes-
Maritimes 426
Colleville-sur-Mer, Calvados 79
Collias, Gard 408-9
Colmar, Haut-Rhin 156-7
Colombes, Hauts-de-Seine 227
Colombiers-sur-Seulles, Calvados
79
Coly, Dordogne 316
Combourg, Ille-et-Vilaine 38
Combreux, Loiret 179
Commes, Calvados 79
Concarneau, Finistère 38
Condat-sur-Vézère, Dordogne 316
Condeau, Orne 79
Condéon, Charente 293
Condé-sur-Noireau, Calvados 79
Condé-sur-Sarthe, Orne 79
Condom, Gers 385
Confrançon, Ain 354
Connelles, Eure 79
Conques, Aveyron 385
Conteville, Eure 79
Continvoir, Indre-et-Loire 179
Contres, Loir-et-Cher 179
Coquelles, Pas-de-Calais 134
Corbehem, Pas-de-Calais 134
Corbeil-Essones, Essonne 227
Corberon, Côte-D'Or 264

Index

Cordes, Tarn 385
Cornillon-Confoux, Bouches-du-
    Rhône 441-2
Corps, Isère 354
Corrèze, Corrèze 331
Coteau, Le, Loire 354
Cotinière, La, Charente-Maritime
    293
Couches, Saône-et-Loire 264
Coulandon, Allier 340
Couptrain, Mayenne 211
Courbevoie, Hauts-de-Seine 227
Courcay, Indre-et-Loire 179
Courcelles-de-Touraine, Indre-et-
    Loire 179-80
Courcelles-sur-Vesles, Aisne 116
Courcerac, Charente-Maritime 293
Courchevel, Savoie 355
Cour-Cheverny, Loir-et-Cher 180
Courneuve, La, Seine-St-Denis 227
Courniou, Hérault 409
Coursecoules, Alpes-Maritimes 415
Cours-la-Ville, Rhône 355-6
Courson, Calvados 80
Courtils, Manche 80
Courtivron, Côte-D'Or 264-5
Courtois-sur-Yonne, Yonne 265
Coustaussa, Aude 409
Coust, Cher 180
Coutances, Manche 80
Couture-sur-Loir, Loir-et-Cher 180
Coux-et-Bigaroque, Dordogne 316
Cransac-les-Thermes, Aveyron 385
Craponne-sur-Arzon, Haute-Loire
    340-1
Crécy-la-Chapelle, Seine-et-Marne
    227
Creissels, Aveyron 385
Crémieu, Isère 356
Créon, Gironde 316
Crépon, Calvados 80
Crest, Drôme 356
Crestet, Vaucluse 442
Crest-Voland, Savoie 356
Créteil, Val-de-Marne 227-8
Creully, Calvados 80
Criel-sur-Mer, Seine-Maritime 80
Crillon-le-Brave, Vaucluse 442
Criquebeuf-en-Caux, Seine-
    Maritime 80
Criquetot-l'Esneval, Seine-Maritime
    80-1
Crisenoy, Seine-et-Marne 228
Croissy-Beaubourg, Seine-et-Marne
    228
Croix-Valmer, La, Var 442
Crotoy, Le, Somme 116
Cruzy-le-Châtel, Yonne 265
Cubry, Doubs 284
Cucugnan, Aude 409

Cucuron, Vaucluse 442
Culey-le-Patry, Calvados 81
Cunlhat, Puy-de-Dôme 341
Curzay-sur-Vonne, Vosges 293

## D

Dangé-St-Romain, Vienne 293
Danne-et-Quatre-Vents, Moselle
    147
Danzé, Loir-et-Cher 180
Dardilly, Rhône 356
Dax, Landes 316
Deauville, Calvados 81
Défense, La, Hauts-de-Seine 228
Désaignes, Ardèche 357
Descartes, Indre-et-Loire 180
Deux-Alpes, Les, Isère 357
Devrouze, Saône-et-Loire 265
Die, Drôme 357
Dieffenbach-au-Val, Bas-Rhin 158
Digoin, Saône-et-Loire 265
Dijon, Côte-D'Or 265
Dinan, Côtes-D'Armor 38
Dinard, Ille-et-Vilaine 38-9
Dinéault, Finistère 39
Diors, Indre 180
Dissay-sous-Courcillon, Sarthe 211
Divonne-les-Bains, Ain 357
Dol-de-Bretagne, Ille-et-Vilaine 39
Dole, Jura 284-5
Dolus-D'Oléron, Charenet-
    Maritime 293
Domalain, Ille-et-Vilaine 39
Domfront, Orne 81
Domme, Dordogne 316-17
Donnery, Loiret 180-1
Donzy, Nièvre 265
Douai, Nord 134
Douains, Eure 81
Douarnenez, Finistère 40
Doullens, Somme 116
Doussard, Haute-Savoie 357-8
Douville, Dordogne 317
Douville-en-Auge, Calvados 81
Dragey, Manche 81
Dreux, Eure-et-Loir 181
Ducey, Manche 82
Duclair, Seine-Maritime 82
Duisans, Pas-de-Calais 134
Dunkerque, Nord 135
Duras, Lot-et-Garonne 317
Durban-Corbières, Aude 409
Durtal, Maine-et-Loire 211

## E

Échalot, Côte-D'Or 266
Échenevex, Ain 358
Échets, Les, Ain 358
Echillais, Charente-Maritime 294
Échilleuses, Loiret 181

Echinghen, Pas-de-Calais 135
Eclaron, Marne 125
École-Valentin, Doubs 285
Écoyeux, Charente-Maritime 294
Ecrammeville, Calvados 82
Écrosnes, Eure-et-Loir 181
Écutigny, Côte-D'Or 266
Éguilly, Côte-D'Or 266
Eguisheim, Haut-Rhin 158
Élincourt-Ste-Marguerite, Oise 116
Elliant, Finistère 40
Elne, Pyrénées-Orientales 409
Émalleville, Eure 82
Embrun, Hautes-Alpes 442
Emmerin, Nord 135
Englos, Nord 135
Ennordres, Cher 181
Entraigues-sur-la-Sorgues, Vaucluse
    442
Entrains-sur-Nohain, Nièvre 266
Entrechaux, Vaucluse 442-3
Éperlecques, Pas-de-Calais 135
Épernay, Marne 125
Épernay-sous-Gevrey, Côte-D'Or
    266
Épinal, Vosges 147
Épine-aux-Bois, L', Aisne 116
Épine, L', Marne 125
Epping, Moselle 147
Equeurdreville, Manche 82
Erdeven, Morbihan 40
Ermenonville, Oise 116-17
Ermenouville, Seine-Maritime 82
Erquy, Côtes-D'Armor 40
Escalles, Pas-de-Calais 135-6
Escolives-Ste-Camille, Yonne 266
Espezel, Aude 409
Estaing, Aveyron 386
Estissac, Aube 125-6
Étampes, Essonne 228
Étoges, Marne 126
Étréaupont, Aisne 117
Étrechet, Indre 181
Étretat, Seine-Maritime 82
Eu, Seine-Maritime 83
Évian-les-Bains, Haute-Savoie 358
Évreux, Eure 83
Évry, Essonne 228
Eybens, Isère 358
Eygalières, Bouches-du-Rhône 443
Eymoutiers, Haute-Vienne 331
Eyragues, Bouches-du-Rhône 443
Eze, Alpes-Maritimes 425
Eze-Village, Alpes-Maritimes 426

## F

Fabas, Ariège 386
Fabrezan, Aude 409
Farges, Ain 358
Fargues, Lot 386

Farlède, La, Var 443
Faverges, Haute-Savoie 358-9
Faverolles, Orne 83
Fayence, Var 443
Feings, Loir-et-Cher 181
Fére-en-Tardenois, Aisne 117
Ferney-Voltaire, Ain 359
Férolles, Loiret 181
Ferrette, Haut-Rhin 158
Ferrières-St-Hilaire, Eure 83
Ferté-Bernard, La, Sarthe 211
Ferté-Frênel, La, Orne 83
Ferté-Gaucher, La, Seine-et-Marne 228
Ferté-St-Aubin, La, Loiret 181
Ferté-sous-Jouarre, La, Seine-et-Marne 228
Ferté-Vidame, La, Eure-et-Loir 182
Féy, Moselle 147
Feytiat, Haute-Vienne 331
Figeac, Lot 386
Fiquefleur-Équainville, Eure 83
Flagy, Seine-et-Marne 228-9
Flamanville, Manche 83
Flavigny-sur-Ozerain, Côte-D'Or 266
Flèche, La, Sarthe 211
Fleurville, Saône-et-Loire 266
Fleury-La-Forêt, Eure 83
Flocellière, La, Vendée 212
Florac, Lozère 409
Flotte, La, Charente-Maritime 294
Flumet, Savoie 359
Foëcy, Cher 182
Fontainebleau, Seine-et-Marne 229
Fontaine-Chaalis, Oise 117
Fontaine-de-Vaucluse, Vaucluse 443
Fontaine-Française, Côte-D'Or 267
Fontaine-la-Rivière, Essonne 229
Fontaine-le-Pin, Calvados 83
Fontaines, Saône-et-Loire 267
Fontanes, Lot 386
Fontanil-Cornillon, Isère 359
Fontenailles, Seine-et-Marne 229
Fontenai-sur-Orne, Orne 84
Fontenay-le-Comte, Vendée 212
Fontenay-sur-Loing, Loiret 182
Fontenay-Trésigny, Seine-et-Marne 229
Fontevraud-l'Abbaye, Maine-et-Loire 212
Fontvieille, Bouches-du-Rhône 443-4
Forcalquier, Alpes-de-Haute-Provence 444
Forêt-Fouesnant, La, Finistère 40-1
Forges-les-Eaux, Seine-Maritime 84
Fouesnant, Finistère 41
Fougères, Ille-et-Vilaine 41
Fouras, Charente-Maritime 294

Fourges, Eure 84
Fourmetot, Eure 84
Fox-Amphoux, Var 444
Francueil, Indre-et-Loire 182
Fréhel, Côtes-D'Armor 41
Fresné-la-Mère, Calvados 84
Fresville, Manche 84
Fréteval, Loir-et-Cher 182
Frontenaud, Saône-et-Loire 267
Futeau, Meuse 147

**G**

Gacé, Orne 84-5
Gahard, Ille-et-Vilaine 41
Gaillac, Tarn 386
Gan, Pyrénées-Atlantique 317
Ganac, Ariège 386
Ganges, Hérault 410
Gap, Hautes-Alpes 444
Garabit, Cantal 341
Garein, Landes 317
Garrevaques, Tarn 386-7
Gassin, Var 444
Gauchin-Verloingt, Pas-de-Calais 136
Gavarnie, Hautes-Pyrénées 387
Gavrelle, Pas-de-Calais 136
Gazeran, Yvelines 229
Géfosse-Fontenay, Calvados 85
Gehée, Indre 182
Geispolsheim, Bas-Rhin 158
Gémenos, Bouches-du-Rhône 444-5
Générargues, Gard 410
Genêts, Manche 85
Genillé, Indre-et-Loire 182
Genneville, Calvados 85
Genouillac, Creuse 331
Gentioux, Creuse 332
Gérardmer, Vosges 148
Gerbepal, Vosges 148
Germigny-des-Prés, Loiret 183
Gevrey-Chambertin, Côte-D'Or 267
Gevry, Jura 285
Gien, Loiret 183
Giffaumont-Champaubert, Marne 126
Gigondas, Vaucluse 445
Gillonnay, Isère 359
Gimel-les-Cascades, Corrèze 332
Ginchy, Somme 117
Gincla, Aude 410
Givry, Saône-et-Loire 267
Glatigny, Manche 85
Glènic, Creuse 332
Glos, Calvados 85
Glos-la-Ferrière, Orne 85
Golfe-Juan, Alpes-Maritimes 426
Gonesse, Val-D'Oise 229

Gonneville-sur-Honfleur, Calvados 85
Gordes, Vaucluse 445
Gosnay, Pas-de-Calais 136
Goumois, Doubs 285
Gourdon, Lot 387
Gourdon, Saône-et-Loire 267
Gournay, Deux-Sèvres 294
Gouvieux, Oise 117
Grainville, Eure 85
Gramat, Lot 387-8
Grambois, Vaucluse 445
Grand-Ballon, Haut-Rhin 158
Grand-Bornand, Le, Haute-Savoie 359
Grandcamp-Maisy, Calvados 85-6
Grande-Motte, La, Hérault 410
Grandpré, Ardennes 126
Grandvillers, Vosges 148
Grans, Bouches-du-Rhône 445
Grasse, Alpes-Maritimes 426
Graveson, Bouches-du-Rhône 445
Grenade-sur-l'Adour, Landes 317
Grenoble, Isère 359
Gréoux-les-Bains, Alpes-de-Haute-Provence 446
Gresse-en-Vercors, Isère 359
Gressy, Seine-et-Marne 230
Grevilly, Saône-et-Loire 267
Grezet-Cavagnan, Lot-et-Garonne 317
Grez-Neuville, Maine-et-Loire 212
Grignan, Drôme 360
Grigny, Essonne 230
Grimaud, Var 446
Grisolles, Tarn-et-Garonne 388
Gua, Le, Charente-Maritime 294
Guerville, Seine-Maritime 86
Guiclan-St-Thegonnec, Finistère 41
Guimiliau, Finistère 42
Guînes, Pas-de-Calais 136
Guipavas, Finistère 42
Guisseny, Finistère 42

**H**

Habére-Poche, Haute-Savoie 360
Hagenthal-le-Bas, Haut-Rhin 158
Halles, Les, Rhône 360
Hambye, Manche 86
Hardelot-Plage, Pas-de-Calais 136
Hatrize, Meurthe-et-Moselle 148
Hautefort, Dordogne 318
Haye-Aubrée, La, Eure 86
Haye-du-Theil, La, Eure 86
Hazebrouck, Nord 136-7
Hendaye, Pyrénées-Atlantiques 318
Hennebont, Morbihan 42
Herbeviller, Meurthe-et-Moselle 148
Herbeville, Yvelines 230

Index

Herbignac, Loire-Atlantique 212
Herry, Cher 183
Hesdin, Pas-de-Calais 137
Hesdin l'Abbé, Calvados 137
Hibel, Ille-et-Vilaine 42
Hiersac, Charente 294-5
Hommes, Indre-et-Loire 183
Honfleur, Calvados 86
Hossegor, Landes 318
Hottot-les-Bagues, Calvados 86
Houches, Les, Haute-Savoie 360
Houdetot, Seine-Maritime 86
Houlbec-Cocherel, Eure 86-7
Huismes, Indre-et-Loire 183
Husseren-les-Châteaux, Haut-Rhin 158
Hyères, Var 446
Hyères-les-Palmiers, Var 446

I

Iffs, Les, Ille-et-Vilaine 42
Iguerande, Saône-et-Loire 268
Ile-de-la-Barthelasse, Vaucluse 446
Ile-de-Groix, Morbigan 43
Ile-aux-Moines, Morbihan 42-3
Ile de Porquerolles, Var 446
Illhaeusern-Guémar, Haut-Rhin 158
Ingouville-sur-Mer, Seine-Maritime 87
Ingrandes-de-Touraine, Indre-et-Loire 183
Ingrandes-sur-Loire, Maine-et-Loire 212
Inxent, Pas-de-Calais 137
Inzinzac-Lochrist, Morbihan 43
Isdes, Loiret 183-4
Isigny-sur-Mer, Calvados 87
Isle, Haute-Vienne 332
Isle-Jourdain, L', Vienne 295
Isle-sur-la-Sorgue, L', Vaucluse 446-7
Issambres, Les, Var 447
Issoudun, Indre 184
Itxassou, Pyrénées-Atlantiques 318

J

Jaille-Yvon, La, Maine-et-Loire 212
Jard-sur-Mer, Vendée 212
Jarnac, Charente 295
Jarnac-Champagne, Charente-Maritime 295
Jarnioux, Rhône 360
Jars, Cher 184
Jaux, Oise 117
Jazeneuil, Vienne 295
Jenlain, Nord 137
Joigny, Yonne 268
Joinville, Haute-Marne 126
Josselin, Morbihan 43

Joucas, Vaucluse 447
Joué-les-Tours, Indre-et-Loire 184
Journet, Vienne 295
Jours-lès-Baigneux, Côte-D'Or 268
Jouy-le-Potier, Loiret 184-5
Juan-les-Pins, Alpes-Maritimes 426
Juignettes, Eure 87
Juliénas, Rhône 360-1
Jullianges, Haute-Loire 341
Jumièges, Seine-Maritime 87
Juvigny-le-Tertre, Manche 87-8

K

Katzenthal, Haut-Rhin 158-9
Kaysersberg, Haut-Rhin 159
Kerlaz, Finistère 43
Kientzheim, Haut-Rhin 159

L

Labastide-Murat, Lot 388
Lacabarède, Tarn 388-9
Lacanau, Gironde 318
Lacaune, Tarn 389
Lacave, Lot 389
Lacoste, Vaucluse 447
Lacroix-Barrez, Aveyron 389
Lagnes, Vaucluse 448
Lalinde, Dordogne 318
Lamagdelaine-Cahors, Lot 389
Lamalou-les-Bains, Hérault 410
Lamarche-sur-Saône, Côte-D'Or 268
Lamastre, Ardèche 361
Lamballe, Côtes-D'Armor 43
Lamberville, Manche 88
Lambesc, Bouches-du-Rhône 448
Lampaul-Guimiliau, Finistère 43-4
Lanarce, Ardèche 361
Lancie, Rhône 361
Lancieux, Côtes-D'Armor 44
Landaul, Morbihan 44
Landébia, Côtes-D'Armor 44
Landes-sur-Ajon, Calvados 88
Landes-Vieilles-et-Neuves, Les, Seine-Maritime 88
Landouzy-la-Ville, Aisne 118
Landrais, Charente-Maritime 295-6
Landudec, Finistère 44
Landujan, Ille-et-Vilaine 44
Langeais, Indre-et-Loire 185
Langoat, Côtes-D'Armor 44
Langogne, Lozère 410
Langres, Haute-Marne 126
Langrune-sur-Mer, Calvados 88
Lannemezan, Hautes-Pyrénées 389
Lans-en-Vercors, Isère 361
Lanslebourg, Savoie 361
Lantignie, Rhône 361
Lantosque, Alpes-Maritimes 427
Laon, Aisne 118

Lapalud, Vaucluse 448
Larmor-Plage, Morbihan 44
Larra, Haute-Garonne 389
Larroque, Tarn 389
Lattes, Hérault 410
Laudun, Gard 410
Laurière, Haute-Vienne 332
Lauris, Vaucluse 448
Laussou, Le, Lot-et-Garonne 318
Laval, Mayenne 213
Lavandou, Le, Var 448
Lavardens, Gers 389
Lavaur, Tarn 389
Lavau, Yonne 268
Lavenay, Sarthe 213
Lavoux, Vienne 296
Lay-Lamidou, Pyrénées-Atlantiques 319
Le Bourg-Dun, Seine-Maritime 88
Lectoure, Gers 390
Lempaut, Tarn 390
Lentigny, Loire 361
Leognan, Gironde 319
Lepuix, Territoire-de-Belfort 285
Lesconil, Finistère 44
Lesigny, Seine-et-Marne 230
Lessay, Manche 88
Leugny, Yonne 268
Levallois-Perret, Hauts-de-Seine 230
Levernois, Côte-D'Or 268
Lignan-sur-Orb, Hérault 411
Ligré, Indre-et-Loire 185
Ligueil, Indre-et-Loire 185
Lille, Nord 137-8
Limeray, Indre-et-Loire 185
Limeuil, Dordogne 319
Lingreville, Manche 88
Lion-d'Angers, Le, Maine-et-Loir 213
Lisieux, Calvados 89
Livry, Calvados 89
Llo, Pyrénées-Orientales 411
Loc-Eguiner-St-Thégonnec, Finistère 45
Loches, Indre-et-Loire 185-6
Locminé, Morbihan 45
Locoal-Mendon, Morbihan 45
Locquirec, Finistère 45
Locunolé, Finistère 45
Loges, Les, Seine-Maritime 89
Lognes, Seine-et-Marne 230
Lomme, Nord 138
Longchamps, Eure 89
Longues-sur-Mer, Calvados 89
Longuyon, Meurthe-et-Moselle 149
Longvic, Côte-D'Or 268-9
Longvillers, Calvados 89
Lorgues, Var 448-9
Loriol-du-Comtat, Vaucluse 449

Lormes, Nièvre 269
Lorp-Sentaraille, Ariège 390
Louargat, Côtes-D'Or 45
Loubajac, Hautes-Pyrénées 390
Loubressac, Lot 390
Loudéac, Côtes-D'Armor 45
Louhans, Saône-et-Loire 269
Lourdes, Hautes-Pyrénées 390
Lourmarin, Vaucluse 449
Louroux, Le, Indre-et-Loire 186
Louviers, Eure 90
Louvigné-du-Désert, Ille-et-Vilaine 45
Luc-sur-Mer, Calvados 90
Lunay, Loir-et-Cher 186
Lunéville, Meurthe-et-Moselle 149
Lupiac, Gers 390
Lurcy-Lévis, Allier 341
Lussat, Creuse 332
Lutzelbourg, Moselle 149
Luxeuil-les-Bains, Haute-Saône 285
Luynes, Indre-et-Loire 186
Luzarches, Val-D'Oise 230
Lyon, Rhône 361-2
Lyons-La-Forêt, Eure 90

**M**

Macé, Orne 90
Mâcon, Saône-et-Loire 269
Magny-Cours, Nièvre 269-70
Magny-le-Hongre, Seine-et-Marne 231
Maîche, Doubs 285
Mailly-Maillet, Somme 118
Mainneville, Eure 91
Mainxe, Charente 296
Maisons, Calvados 91
Malataverne, Drôme 362
Malène, La, Lozère 411
Maligny, Côte-D'Or 270
Mancelière-Montmureau, La, Eure-et-Loir 186-7
Mandelieu-la-Napoule, Alpes-Maritimes 427
Mans, Le, Sarthe 213
Marans, Charente-Maritime 296
Marçay, Indre-et-Loire 187
Marchais-Beton, Yonne 270
Marcigny, Saône-et-Loire 270
Mareil-sur-Loir, Sarthe 213
Marennes, Charente-Maritime 296
Margaux, Gironde 319
Marges, Drôme 362-3
Marguerittes, Gard 411
Marignane, Bouches-du-Rhône 449
Marlenheim, Bas-Rhin 159
Marles-sur-Canche, Pas-de-Calais 138
Marsannay-la-Côte, Côte-D'Or 270

Marseille, Bouches-du-Rhône 449-50
Martagny, Eure 91
Martainville, Eure 91
Martel, Lot 390
Martin-Église, Seine-Maritime 91
Martragny, Calvados 91
Marval, Haute-Vienne 332
Marvejols, Lozère 411
Massiac, Cantal 341
Massigny, Vendée 213
Mathes, Les, Charente-Maritime 296
Matougues, Marne 126-7
Maubeuge, Nord 139
Maulevrier, Maine-et-Loire 213-14
Maupas, Gers 391
Mauroux, Lot 391
Maussane-les-Alpilles, Bouches-du-Rhône 450
Mauzac-et-Grand-Castang, Dordogne 319
Maxey-sur-Vaise, Meuse 149
Mayenne, Mayenne 214
Mazamet, Tarn 391
Mazis, Le, Somme 118
Méaudre, Isère 363
Megève, Haute-Savoie 363
Meillac, Ille-et-Vilaine 46
Melleville, Seine-Maritime 91
Melrand, Morbihan 46
Mende, Lozère 411
Ménerbes, Vaucluse 450
Ménestreau-en-Villette, Loiret 187
Menetou-Salon, Cher 187
Mens, Isère 363
Menton, Alpes-Maritimes 427
Menuires, Les, Savoie 363
Méobecq, Indre 187
Mer, Loir-et-Cher 187
Mercuès, Lot 391
Mercurey, Saône-et-Loire 270
Mercurol, Drôme 363
Merdrignac, Côtes-D'Armor 46
Mereville, Meurthe-et-Moselle 149
Méribel-les-Allues, Savoie 363
Mérignac, Gironde 319
Merry-Sec, Yonne 270
Meslan, Morbihan 46
Mesnil-Aubert, Le, Manche 91
Mesnil-Gilbert, Le, Manche 91-2
Mesnil-Rogues, Le, Manche 92
Metz, Moselle 149-50
Meung-sur-Loire, Loiret 187
Meurdraquière, La, Manche 92
Meylan, Isère 364
Meyrals, Dordogne 319-20
Meyrueis, Lozère 411-12
Meyssac, Corrèze 332
Meyzieu, Rhône 364

Mézangers, Mayenne 214
Mézel, Alpes-de-Haute-Provence 450
Mézières-en-Vexin, Eure 92
Miélan, Gers 391
Mignaloux-Beauvoir, Vienne 296
Migron, Charente-Maritime 296
Mijoux, Ain 364
Millac, Vienne 296-7
Millau, Aveyron 391
Milly-la-Forêt, Essonne 231
Mimizan, Landes 320
Mirabel, Ardèche 364
Mirambeau, Charente-Maritime 297
Mirebeau, Vienne 297
Mirecourt, Vosges 150
Mirepoix, Ariège 391-2
Mirmande, Drôme 364
Missillac, Loire-Atlantique 214
Mittois, Calvados 92
Moëlan-sur-Mer, Finistère 46
Mollkirch, Bas-Rhin 159
Monestier, Le, Dordogne 320
Monetier-les-Bains, Les, Hautes-Alpes 450-1
Monflanquin, Lot-et-Garonne 320
Monhoudou, Sarthe 214
Monieux, Vaucluse 451
Mons, Charente-Maritime 297
Monségur, Gironde 320
Montaigu-de-Quercy, Tarn-et-Garonne 392
Montailleur, Savoie 364
Montargis, Loiret 187
Montaut, Pyrénées-Atlantiques 320
Montbazon, Indre-et-Loire 187-8
Montboucher-sur-Jabron, Drôme 364
Montbrison-sur-Lez, Drôme 365
Montbrun-Bocage, Haute-Garonne 392
Montchaton, Manche 92
Montchauvrot-Mantry, Jura 285
Mont-Doré, Le, Puy-de-Dôme 341
Montélimar, Drôme 365
Montereau-en-Gatinais, Loiret 188
Montesquieu, Tarn-et-Garonne 392
Montfarville, Manche 92
Montfavet, Vaucluse 451
Montferrand-du-Périgord, Dordogne 320
Montfort-en-Chalosse, Landes 320-1
Montgardon, Manche 92
Monthieux, Ain 365
Monthodon, Indre-et-Loire 188
Montignac, Dordogne 321
Montignac-Lascaux, Dordogne 321

Montigny-sur-Avre, Eure-et-Loir 188
Montigny-sur-Loing, Seine-et-Marne 231
Montilouis-sur-Loire, Indre-et-Loire 188
Montlandon, Eure-et-Loir 189
Montmaur, Aude 412
Montmaur, Hautes-Alpes 451
Montmeyan, Var 451
Montpellier, Hérault 412
Montrésor, Indre-et-Loire 189
Montreuil-Bellay, Maine-et-Loire 215
Montreuil-Poulay, Mayenne 215
Montreuil-sur-Loir, Maine-et-Loire 215
Montreuil-sur-Mer, Pas-de-Calais 139
Mont-St-Michel, Le, Manche 92-3
Mont-St-Père, Aisne 118
Montsalvy, Cantal 341
Monts-en-Bessin, Calvados 93
Monts-sur-Guesnes, Vienne 297
Montviette, Calvados 93
Montviron, Manche 93
Moréac, Morbihan 46
Moreilles, Vendée 215
Morestel, Isère 365
Morhange, Moselle 150
Morigny-Champigny, Essonne 231
Morsbronn-les-Bains, Bas-Rhin 159
Mortagne-au-Perche, Orne 93
Mortagne-sur-Gironde, Charente-Maritime 297
Mortagne-sur-Sèvre, Vendée 215
Morthemer, Vienne 297
Morzine, Haute-Savoie 365
Mosles, Calvados 93
Mosnac, Charente-Maritime 297
Motte-Ternant, La, Côte-D'Or 270
Mougins, Alpes-Maritimes 417
Moulicent, Orne 94
Moulins, Allier 341-2
Moustiers-Ste-Marie, Alpes-de-Haute-Provence 451
Munster, Haut-Rhin 159
Murs, Vaucluse 451
Mussidan, Dordogne 321

**N**

Najac, Aveyron 392
Nancy, Meurthe-et-Moselle 150
Nan-sous-Thil, Côte-D'Or 270
Nanterre, Hauts-de-Seine 231
Nantes, Loire-Atlantique 215
Narbonne, Aude 412
Nasbinals, Lozère 412
Naujan-et-Postiac, Gironde 321
Neauphle-le-Château, Yvelines 231

Négreville, Manche 94
Neufmoutiers-en-Brie, Seine-et-Marne 231-2
Neuil, Indre-et-Loire 189
Neuilly-en-Thelle, Oise 118
Neuilly-sur-Seine, Hauts-de-Seine 232
Neuvéglise, Cantal 342
Neuville-de-Poitou, Vienne 298
Neuville-en-Ferrain, Nord 139
Neuvy-le-Roi, Indre-et-Loire 189
Neuvy-sur-Barangeon, Cher 189
Neuvy-sur-Loire, Nièvre 271
Nevers, Nièvre 271
Nevoy, Loiret 189
Nézignan-l'Évêque 413
Nice, Alpes-Maritimes 417-8
Niedersteinbach, Bas-Rhin 159
Nieuil, Charente 298
Nieul, Haute-Vienne 333
Nîmes, Gard 413
Niort, Deux-Sèvres 298
Noaillac, Gironde 321-2
Noailly, Loire 365
Nogent-sur-Marne, Val-de-Marne 232
Nogent-sur-Seine, Aube 127
Noirmoutier-en-l'Ille, Vendée 215-16
Noisy-le-Grand, Seine-St-Denis 232
Noizay, Indre-et-Loire 189
Nonards, Corrèze 333
Notre-Dame-de-Bellecombe, Savoie 365
Notre-Dame-de-Livaye, Calvados 94
Notre-Dame-de-Londres, Hérault 413
Notre-Dame-d'Estrées, Calvados 94
Noves, Bouches-du-Rhône 451
Noyal Pontivy, Morbihan 46
Noyant-de-Touraine, Indre-et-Loire 189-90
Noyers-sur-Cher, Loir-et-Cher 190
Noyon, Oise 118
Nuaillé, Maine-et-Loire 216
Nueil-sur-Argent, Deux-Sèvres 298
Nuits-St-Georges, Côte-D'Or 271
Nyons, Drôme 365-6

**O**

Obernai, Bas-Rhin 160
Obersteigen, Bas-Rhin 160
Obersteinbach, Bas-Rhin 160
Oie, L', Vendée 216
Oizé, Sarthe 216
Oizon, Cher 190
Olargues, Hérault 413
Olivet, Loiret 190

Oloron-Ste-Marie, Pyrénées-Atlantique 322
Onet-le-Château, Aveyron 392
Onlay, Nièvre 271
Onzain, Loir-et-Cher 190
Oppède, Vaucluse 452
Oppède-le-Vieux, Vaucluse 452
Orange, Vaucluse 452
Orbec, Calvados 94
Orbey, Haut-Rhin 160
Orchies, Nord 139
Orgeval, Yvelines 232
Orléans, Loiret 190
Orly (Aéroport d'), Val-de-Marne 232
Ornaisons, Aude 413-14
Orsay, Essonne 232
Orthez, Pyrénées-Atlantiques 322
Orval, Cher 190-1
Osmanville, Calvados 94
Ostheim, Haut-Rhin 160
Ostwald, Bas-Rhin 161
Othis, Seine-et-Marne 232-3
Ottrott, Bas-Rhin 161
Ouchamps, Loir-et-Cher 191
Oucques, Loir-et-Cher 191
Oudon, Loire-Atlantique 216
Oulon, Nièvre 272

**P**

Pacé, Ille-et-Vilaine 46
Paimpol, Côtes-D'Armor 46-7
Paimpont, Ille-et-Vilaine 47
Palud-sur-Verdon, La, Alpes-de-Haute-Provence 452
Pamiers, Ariège 392
Panzoult, Indre-et-Loire 191
Paris 233-52
1st arrondissement 233-4
2nd arrondissement 234-5
3rd arrondissement 235
4th arrondissement 235-6
5th arrondissement 236-7
6th arrondissement 237-9
7th arrondissement 239-40
8th arrondissement 240-3
9th arrondissement 243-4
10th arrondissement 244
11th arrondissement 244-5
12th arrondissement 245-6
13th arrondissement 246
14th arrondissement 246
15th arrondissement 247
16th arrondissement 247-9
17th arrondissement 249-50
18th arrondissement 250-1
19th arrondissement 251-2
20th arrondissement 252
Parthenay, Deux-Sèvres 298
Passy-Grigny, Marne 127

Pau, Pyrénées-Atlantiques 322
Paudy, Indre 191
Pauillac, Gironde 322
Paulinet, Tarn 392
Payrac, Lot 393
Pégomas, Alpes-Maritimes 428
Peillon, Alpes-Maritimes 428-9
Peisey-Nancroix, Savoie 366
Pelvoux, Hautes-Alpes 452
Pennautier, Aude 414
Pennedepie, Calvados 94
Pépieux, Aude 414
Perbusson, Indre-et-Loire 191
Percy, Manche 94-5
Périers-sur-le-Dan, Calvados 95
Pernes-les-Fontaines, Vaucluse
    452-3
Péronne, Somme 118-19
Perpignan, Pyrénées-Orientales
    414
Perrier, Puy-de-Dôme 342
Perros-Guirec, Cotes-D'Armor 47
Pertuis, Vaucluse 453
Pesmes, Haute-Saône 285-6
Pessac, Gironde 322
Petite-Pierre, La, Bas-Rhin 161
Peyrefitte-du-Razès, Aude 414
Peyreleau, Aveyron 393
Pian-Médoc, Le, Gironde 322
Picauville, Manche 95
Pierrefonds, Oise 119
Pinas, Hautes-Pyrénées 393
Piney, Aube 127
Pin-la-Garenne, Orne 95
Piolenc, Vaucluse 453
Piré-sur-Seiche, Ille-et-Vilaine 47
Piriac-sur-Mer, Loire-Atlantique
    216
Placy-Montaigu, Manche 95
Plailly, Oise 119
Plaisance, Aveyron 393
Planchez, Nièvre 272
Plancoët, Côtes-D'Armor 47
Plan-de-la-Tour, Var 453
Plan-du-Var, Alpes-Maritimes 429
Planguenoual, Côtes-D'Armor 47
Plazac, Dordogne 322
Pléneuf-Val-André, Côtes-D'Armor
    47
Plérin, Côtes-D'Armor 47
Pleudihen-sur-Rance, Côtes-
    D'Armor 48
Pleugueneuc-Plesder, Ille-et-Vilaine
    48
Pleurtuit, Ille-et-Vilaine 48
Pléven, Côtes-D'Armor 48
Ploemeur, Morbihan 48
Ploërmel, Morbihan 48
Ploëzal, Côtes-D'Armor 48
Plogastel-St-Germain, Finistère 49

Plogoff, Finistère 49
Plomeur, Finistère 49
Plonéour-Lavern, Finistère 49
Plonévez-Porzay, Finistère 49
Plouaret, Côtes-D'Armor 49
Plouër-sur-Rance, Côtes-D'Armor
    49-50
Plouescat, Finistère 50
Plouguenast, Côtes-D'Armor 50
Plouharnel, Morbihan 50
Plouhinec, Morbihan 50-1
Plouigneau, Finistère 51
Plozevet, Finistère 51
Pluvigner, Morbihan 51
Poët-Laval, Le, Drôme 366
Poilley-sur-le-Holme, Manche 95
Poilly-sur-Serein, Yonne 272
Poilly-sur-Tholon, Yonne 272
Poire-sur-Vie, Vendée 216
Poislay, Le, Loir-et-Cher 191
Poisson, Saône-et-Loire 272
Poitiers, Vienne 298-9
Poligné, Ille-et-Vilaine 51
Poligny, Jura 286
Pommerit-Jaudy, Côtes-D'Armor
    51-2
Pommeuse, Seine-et-Marne 252
Pompadour, Corrèze 333
Poncé-sur-le-Loir, Sarthe 217
Pons, Charente-Maritime 299
Pont-Audemer, Eure 95-6
Pontault-Combault, Seine-et-Marne
    252
Pont-Aven, Finistère 52
Pont-D'Ain, Ain 366
Pont-de-Barret, Drôme 366
Pont-de-Briques, Pas-de-Calais 139
Pont-de-Cheruy, Isère 366
Pont-de-l'Arche, Eure 96
Pont-de-Pany, Côte-D'Or 272
Pont-de-Vaux, Ain 366
Pont-d'Hérault, Gard 415
Pont-du-Gard, Gard 415
Pontet, Le, Vaucluse 453-4
Ponteves, Var 454
Pontivy-Neuillac, Morbihan 52
Pont-L'Abbé, Finistère 52
Pont-les-Moulins, Doubs 286
Pont-l'Évêque, Calvados 96
Pontlevoy, Loir-et-Cher 191
Pont-St-Martin, Loire-Atlantique
    217
Pont-St-Pierre, Eure 96
Pornichet, Loire-Atlantique 217
Port Blanc, Côtes-D'Armor 52
Port-de-Lanne, Landes 322
Port-des-Barques, Charente-
    Maritime 299
Port-la-Nouvelle, Aude 415
Port-Louis, Morbihan 52-3

Possonnière, La, Maine-et-Loire
    217
Potelières, Gard 415
Pouant, Vienne 299
Pouillac, Charente-Maritime 299
Pouilly-en-Auxois, Côte-D'Or 272
Pouilly-sur-Saône, Côte-D'Or 272
Pouldergat, Finistère 53
Pouldreuzic, Finistère 53
Pouldu, Le, Finistère 53
Pourchères, Ardèche 366
Prahecq, Deux-Sèvres 299
Prats-de-Mollo-la-Preste, Pyrénées-
    Orientales 415
Praz-de-Chamonix, Les, Haute-
    Savoie 367
Préaux-Bocage, Calvados 97
Précorbin, Manche 97
Prefailles, Loire-Atlantique 217
Pré-St-Martin, Eure-et-Loir 191
Pressac, Vienne 299
Préty, Saône-et-Loire 273
Projan, Gers 393
Provins, Seine-et-Marne 252
Puchay, Eure 97
Puichéric, Aude 415
Puligny-Montrachet, Côte-D'Or
    273
Puteaux, Hauts-de-Seine 252-3
Puy-en-Velay, Haute-Loire 342
Puyméras, Vaucluse 454
Puymirol, Lot-et-Garonne 323
Puy-Notre-Dame, Le, Maine-et-
    Loire 217
Puyravault, Charente-Maritime
    299-300
Puy-St-Vincent, Hautes-Alpes 454

**Q**

Quantilly, Cher 191
Quarante, Hérault 415
Quelles, Les, Bas-Rhin 161
Quemper-Guézennec, Côtes-
    D'Armor 53
Quenne, Yonne 273
Querrien, Finistère 53
Querrieu, Somme 119
Questembert, Morbihan 53
Quettreville-sur-Sienne, Manche 97
Quévert, Côtes-D'Armor 53
Quimper, Finistère 53
Quincié-en-Beaujolais, Rhône 367
Quincy, Cher 192

**R**

Rabastens, Tarn 393
Rahling, Moselle 150-1
Ramatuelle, Var 454-5
Rambouillet, Yvelines 253
Ramecourt, Pas-de-Calais 139

Index

Rancourt, Somme 119
Ranes, Orne 97
Raphèle-les-Arles, Bouches-du-Rhône 455
Raveau, Nièvre 273
Razac-D'Eymet, Dordogne 323
Razac-sur-l'Isle, Dordogne 323
Reauville, Drône 367
Reboursin, Indre 192
Rehainviller, Meurthe-et-Moselle 151
Reillanne, Alpes-de-Haute-Provence 455
Reims, Marne 127-8
Relanges, Vosges 151
Rembercourt-aux-Pots, Meuse 151
Remoulins, Gard 415-16
Remungol, Morbihan 53
Renazé, Mayenne 217
Rennes, Ille-et-Vilaine 53-4
Replonges, Ain 367
Restigné, Indre-et-Loire 192
Reuilly, Eure 97
Reventin-Vaugris, Isère 367
Reviers, Calvados 97
Réville, Manche 97
Revonnas, Ain 367
Rheu, Le, Ille-et-Vilaine 54
Ribaute-les-Tavernes, Gard 416
Ribeauvillé, Haut-Rhin 161
Richelieu, Indre-et-Loire 192
Rieupeyroux, Aveyron 393
Rignac, Lot 393-4
Rigny-Ussé, Indre-et-Loire 192
Riols, Hérault 416
Riom, Puy-de-Dôme 342
Riquewihr, Haut-Rhin 161
Rivarennes, Indre 192
Rivedoux-Plage, Charente-Maritime 300
Roanne, Loire 367-8
Rocamadour, Lot 394
Rocé, Loir-et-Cher 192
Roche-Bernard, La, Morbihan 54
Rochecorbon, Indre-et-Loire 193
Rochefort, Charente-Maritime 300
Rochefort-en-Terre, Morbihan 54
Rochefoucauld, La, Charente 300
Roche-l'Abeille, La, Haute-Vienne 333
Rochelle, La, Charente-Maritime 300
Rochelle-Normande, La, Manche 97
Roche-Posay, La, Vienne 300
Roches-Prémarie, Les, Vienne 301
Roche-sur-Foron, La, Haute-Savoie 368
Roche-Vineuse, La, Saône-et-Loire 273

Rodalbe, Moselle 151
Rodez, Aveyron 394
Roe, La, Mayenne 217
Rogny-les-Sept-Écluses, Yonne 273
Rohrbach-lès-Bitche, Moselle 151
Roiffé, Vienne 301
Roissy-Charles-de-Gaulle (Aéroport), Val-D'Oise 253
Romaneche-Thorins, Saône-et-Loire 273
Romorantin-Lanthenay, Loir-et-Cher 193
Ronce-les-Bains, Charente-Maritime 301
Ronvaux, Meuse 151
Roquebrun, Hérault 416
Roquebrune-sur-Argens, Var 455
Roquelaure, Gers 395
Roque-sur-Ceze, Gard 416
Rosans, Hautes-Alpes 455
Roscoff, Finistère 54
Rosiers-sur-Loire, Les, Maine-et-Loire 217-18
Rosnoën, Finistère 54
Rosporden, Finistère 54
Rouen, Seine-Maritime 97-8
Rouffach, Haut-Rhin 161-2
Rougemontiers, Eure 98
Roullet-St-Estephe, Charente 301
Roussillon, Vaucluse 455
Rouville, Seine-Maritime 98
Royan, Charente-Maritime 301
Royère-de-Vassivière, Creuse 333
Royer, Saône-et-Loire 273
Roz-Landrieux, Ille-et-Vilaine 54
Roz-sur-Couesnon, Ille-et-Vilaine 54-5
Ruffiac, Morbihan 55
Rungis, Val-de-Marne 253
Rustrel, Vaucluse 455

S

Saäne-St-Just, Seine-Maritime 98
Sables-d'Olonne, Les, Vendée 218
Saché, Indre-et-Loire 193
Saillagouse, Pyrénées-Orientales 416
Saillenard, Saône-et-Loire 273-4
Sains-lès-Fressin, Pas-de-Calais 139-40
St-Adjutory, Charente 302
St-Affrique, Aveyron 395
St-Agnan-en-Vercors, Drôme 368
St-Aignan, Loir-et-Cher 193
St-Alban, Côtes-D'Armor 55
St-Alban-sur-Limagnole, Lozère 416
St-Amand-Montrond, Cher 193
St-André-sur-Vieux-Jonc, Ain 368

St-Antoine-de-Ficalba, Lot-et-Garonne 323
St-Antonin-de-Lacalm, Tarn 395
St-Antonin-Noble-Val, Tarn-et-Garonne 395
St-Arnoult, Seine-Maritime 98
St-Aubin-d'Appenai, Orne 98-9
St-Aubin-Château-Neuf, Yonne 274
St-Aubin-sur-Mer, Seine-Maritime 99
St-Aubin-de-Terregatte, Manche 99
St-Avold, Moselle 151
St-Bauld, Indre-et-Loire 193-4
St-Bénigne, Ain 368
St-Benoît-sur-Loire, Loiret 194
St-Benoît-du-Sault, Indre 194
St-Blaise-la-Roche, Bas-Rhin 162
St-Boil, Saône-et-Loire 274
St-Bonnet-en-Champseur, Hautes-Alpes 455-6
St-Branchs, Indre-et-Loire 194
St-Briac-sur-Mer, Ille-et-Vilaine 55
St-Calais, Sarthe 218
St-Caradec, Côtes-D'Armor 55
St-Cast-le-Guildo, Côtes-D'Armor 55
St-Ceré, Lot 395
St-Chartier, Indre 194
St-Christophe-sur-le-Nais, Indre-et-Loire 194
St-Cirgues-en-Montagne, Ardèche 368
St-Cirq-Lapopie, Lot 395
St-Clair-d'Arcey, Eure 99
St-Clair-du-Rhône, Isère 368
St-Clément-de-Rivière, Hérault 416
St-Côme-de-Fresné, Calvados 99
St-Coulomb, Ille-et-Vilaine 56
St-Cyprien, Dordogne 323
St-Cyr-la-Campagne, Eure 99
St-Cyr-la-Lande, Deux-Sèvres 302
St-Denis-d'Anjou, Mayenne 218
St-Denis-le-Ferment, Eure 99
St-Denis-Maisoncelles, Calvados 99
St-Désir, Calvados 99
St-Didier-des-Bois, Eure 99
St-Donat-sur-l'Herbasse, Drôme 368
St-Dyé-sur-Loire, Loir-et-Cher 194
St-Éloi, Nièvre 274
St-Éloi-de-Fourques, Eure 99-100
St-Éloy-Hanvec, Finistère 56
St-Emilion, Gironde 323
St-Épain, Indre-et-Loire 194-5
St-Étienne-de-Baigorry, Pyrénées-Atlantiques 323
St-Étienne-la-Thillaye, Calvados 100
St-Eutrope-de-Born, Lot-et-Garonne 324

St-Fargeau, Yonne 274
St-Félix, Haute-Savoie 369
St-Félix-de-Tournegat, Ariège 395
St-Flour, Cantal 342
St-Front, Haute-Loire 342
St-Gaudens, Haute-Garonne 396
St-Geniez-d'Olt, Aveyron 396
St-Genis-Pouilly, Ain 369
St-Georges-les-Bains, Ardèche 369
St-Georges-des-Coteaux, Charente-Maritime 302
St-Georges-d'Elle, Manche 100
St-Georges-sur-Eure, Eure-et-Loir 195
St-Georges-sur-Loire, Maine-et-Loire 218
St-Georges-de-la-Rivière, Manche 100
St-Germain-sur-Ay, Manche 101
St-Germain-des-Bois, Cher 195
St-Germain-de-Calberte, Lozère 417
St-Germain-du-Crioult, Calvados 100
St-Germain-en-Laye, Yvelines 253
St-Germain-de-Montgomery, Calvados 100
St-Germain-de-Tournbut, Manche 100
St-Germain-le-Vasson, Calvados 100-1
St-Gervais-en-Vallière, Saône-et-Loire 274
St-Gilles, Gard 417
St-Gilles-Croix-de-Vie, Vendée 218
St-Girons, Ariège 396
St-Gratien-Savigny, Nièvre 274
St-Hilaire-de-Court, Cher 195
St-Hilaire-Petitville, Manche 101
St-Hilaire-du-Touvet, Isère 369
St-Hippolyte, Haut-Rhin 162
St-Hymer, Calvados 101
St-James, Manche 101
St-Jean-d'Angely, Charente-Maritime 302
St-Jean-d'Ardières, Rhône 369
St-Jean-aux-Amognes, Nièvre 274
St-Jean-de-la-Blaquière, Hérault 417
St-Jean-aux-Bois, Oise 119
St-Jean-du-Bruel, Aveyron 396
St-Jean-Cap-Ferrat, Alpes-Maritimes 429
St-Jean-de-Liversay, Charente-Maritime
St-Jean-de-Luz, Pyrénées-Atlantiques 324
St-Jean-de-Monts, Vendée 218-19
St-Jean-le-Thomas, Manche 101
St-Jeannet, Alpes-Maritimes 429

St-Jean-Pied-de-Port, Pyrénées-Atlantiques 324
St-Jouan-des-Guérets, Ille-et-Vilaine 56
St-Julien-du-Gua, Ardèche 369
St-Julien-du-Serre, Ardèche 369
St-Lambert-des-Levees, Maine-et-Loire 219
St-Lattier, Isère 369
St-Laurent-en-Caux, Seine-Maritime 101
St-Laurent-les-Églises, Haute-Vienne 333
St-Laurent-du-Mont, Calvados 101
St-Laurent-Nouan, Loir-et-Cher 195
St-Laurent-sur-Oust, Morbihan 56
St-Laurent-sur-Sèvre, Vendée 219
St-Léger, Manche 102
St-Léger-en-Bray, Oise 119
St-Lizier, Ariège 396
St-Lon-les-Mines, Landes 324
St-Loubes, Gironde 324
St-Loup, Nièvre 275
St-Loup-Hors, Calvados 102
St-Loup-Lamairé, Deux-Sèvres 302-3
St-Lumine-de-Clisson, Loire-Atlantique 219
St-Lyphard, Loire-Atlantique 219
St-Maclou, Eure 102
St-Maixent-l'École, Deux-Sèvres 303
St-Malo-de-Guersac, Loire-Atlantique 219
St-Malo, Ille-et-Vilaine 56-7
St-Mamert, Gard 417
St-Marcel, Eure 102
St-Marcel-d'Urfé, Loire 369-70
St-Marcel-les-Valence, Drôme 370
St-Marc-Jaumegarde, Bouches-du-Rhône 456
St-Martin-d'Abbat, Loiret 195
St-Martin-le-Beau, Indre-et-Loire 195
St-Martin-des-Bois, Loir-et-Cher 195
St-Martin-en-Bresse, Saône-et-Loire 275
St-Martin-des-Champs, Finistère 57
St-Martin-de-Belleville, Savoie 370
St-Martin-de-Blagny, Calvados 102
St-Martin-de-Caralp, Ariège 396
St-Martin-de-Castillon, Vaucluse 456
St-Martin-les-Eaux, Alpes-de-Haute-Provence 457
St-Martin-des-Fontaines, Vendée 220
St-Martin-sur-Oust, Morbihan 57

St-Martin-de-la-Place, Maine-et-Loire 219
St-Martin-du-Tartre, Saône-et-Loire 275
St-Martin-Valmeroux, Cantal 342-3
St-Martin-de-Varreville, Manche 102
St-Martin-du-Vivier, Seine-Maritime 102
St-Martory, Haute-Garonne 396
St-Mathurin, Vendée 220
St-Mathurin-sur-Loire, Maine-et-Loire 220
St-Maur, Gers 397
St-Maurice-les-Chateauneuf, Saône-et-Loire 275
St-Maurice-St-Germain, Eure-et-Loir 195-6
St-Maximin-la-Sainte-Baume, Var 457
St-Méloir-des-Ondes, Ille-et-Vilaine 57-8
St-Meslin-du-Bosc, Eure 102
St-Michel-sur-Loire, Indre-et-Loire 196
St-Mihiel, Meuse 151
St-Molf, Loire-Atlantique 220
St-Nazaire, Loire-Atlantique 220
St-Nicolas-de-Bourgueil, Indre-et-Loire 196
St-Omer, Pas-de-Calais 140
St-Ouen, Seine-St-Denis 254

St-Ouen-la-Rouërie, Ille-et-Vilaine 58
St-Pair-sur-Mer, Manche 102
St-Palais-sur-Mer, Charente-Maritime 303
St-Pardoux-la-Croisille, Corrèze 334
St-Paterne, Sarthe 220
St-Paul-en-Chablais, Haute-Savoie 370
St-Paul-Lizonne, Dordogne 324
St-Paul-de-Vence, Alpes-Maritimes 429-30
St-Pé-de-Bigorre, Hautes-Pyrénées 397
St-Pée-sur-Nivelle, Pyrénées-Atlantiques 324-5
St-Père, Nièvre 275
St-Père, Yonne 275
St-Père-Marc-en-Poulet, Ille-et-Vilaine 58
St-Philibert-sur-Mer, Morbihan 58
St-Pierre, Haute-Garonne 397
St-Pierre, Hautes-Pyrénées 397
St-Pierre-d'Argençon, Hautes-Alpes 457
St-Pierre-de-Chartreuse, Isère 370

Index

St-Pierre-de-Chignac, Dordogne 325
St-Pierre-sur-Dives, Calvados 103
St-Pierre-des-Fleurs, Eure 103
St-Pierre-de-Manneville, Seine-Maritime 102
St-Pierre-le-Moutier, Nièvre 275
St-Pierre-les-Nemours, Seine-et-Marne 254
St-Pierre-des-Nids, Mayenne 220
St-Pierre-la-Noaille, Loire 370
St-Pierre-de-Plesguen, Ille-et-Vilaine 58
St-Pierre-Quiberon, Morbihan 58
St-Pierreville, Ardèche 370
St-Pourçain-sur-Sioul, Allier 343
St-Prest, Eure-et-Loir 196
St-Priest-Taurion, Haute-Vienne 334
St-Prim, Isère 370
St-Prix, Saône-et-Loire 275
St-Project-de-Cassaniouze, Cantal 343
St-Quentin, Aisne 119-20
St-Quentin-de-Baron, Gironde 325
St-Quentin-sur-le-Homme, Manche 103
St-Raphaël, Var 457
St-Rémy, Aveyron 397
St-Rémy-de-Provence, Bouches-du-Rhône 457-9
St-Riquier, Somme 120
St-Romphaire, Manche 103
St-Satur, Cher 196
St-Saturnin, Sarthe 220
St-Saturnin-les-Apt, Vaucluse 459
St-Saturnin-de-Lenne, Aveyron 397
St-Saulge, Nièvre 275
St-Sauveur-de-Landemont, Maine-et-Loire 220-1
St-Savin, Hautes-Pyrénées 397
St-Savinien, Charente-Maritime 303
St-Senier-sous-Avranches, Manche 103
St-Sernin-sur-Rance, Aveyron 397
St-Severin, Charente 303
St-Silvain-Montaigut, Creuse 334
St-Simon-de-Pellouaille, Charente-Maritime 303
St-Sorlin-d'Arves, Savoie 370
St-Sornin, Charente-Maritime 303
St-Sozy, Lot 397
St-Suliac, Ille-et-Vilaine 59
St-Sylvestre-sur-Lot, Lot-et-Garonne 325
St-Symphorien-des-Bruyères, Orne 103
St-Symphorien-le-Château, Eure-et-Loir 196

St-Thégonnec, Finistère 59
St-Thonan, Finistère 59
St-Trinit, Vaucluse 459
St-Tropez, Var 459
St-Vaast-la-Hougue, Manche 103
St-Vaast-du-Val, Seine-Maritime 103
St-Varent, Deux-Sèvres 303
St-Verand, Haute-Savoie 276
St-Verand, Rhône 371
St-Viance, Corrèze 334
St-Victor-d'Épine, Eure 103
St-Wandrille-Rançon, Seine-Maritime 103
Ste-Croix, Aisne 120
Ste-Enimie, Lozère 417
Ste-Eulalie, Ardèche 371
Ste-Foy-Tarentaise, Savoie 371
Ste-Gauburge, Orne 103
Ste-Geneviève, Manche 103-4
Ste-Geneviève, Meurthe-et-Moselle 152
Ste-Magnance, Yonne 276
Ste-Marie-Laumont, Calvados 104
Ste-Marie-du-Mont, Manche 104
Ste-Maure-de-Touraine, Indre-et-Loire 196-7
Ste-Maxime, Var 460
Ste-Menehould, Marne 128
Ste-Mère-Église, Manche 104
Ste-Opportune-la-Mare, Eure 104
Ste-Pience, Manche 104

Stes-Maries-de-la-Mer, Bouches-du-Rhône 456
Ste-Soullé, Charente-Maritime 303
Saintes, Charente-Maritime 302
Saisy, Saône-et-Loire 276
Salans, Jura 286
Salbris, Loir-et-Cher 197
Salernes, Var 460
Salers, Cantal 343
Saliers-par-Arles, Bouches-du-Rhône 460
Salignac (Jayac), Dordogne 325
Salins les Bains, Jura 286
Salives, Côte-D'Or 276
Salle-en-Beaumont, Isère 371
Salles-Curan, Aveyron 397
Salon-de-Provence, Bouches-du-Rhône 460
Samoëns, Haute-Savoie 371
Sancerre, Cher 197
Santenay-en-Bourgogne, Côte-D'Or 276
Sappey-en-Chartreuse, Le, Isère 371
Saran, Loiret 197
Sare, Pyrénées-Atlantiques 325-6
Sarragachies, Gers 397
Sarrebourg, Moselle 152

Sarreguemines, Moselle 152
Sassetot-le-Mauconduit, Seine-Maritime 104-5
Satillieu, Ardèche 371
Saubusse, Landes 326
Saugues, Haute-Loire 343
Saulges, Mayenne 221
Saulgé, Vienne 304
Saulnay, Indre 197
Sault, Vaucluse 460-1
Saulty, Pas-de-Calais 140
Saumane-de-Vaucluse, Vaucluse 461
Saumont-la-Poterie, Seine-Maritime 105
Saumur, Maine-et-Loire 221
Saussaye, La, Eure 105
Sauternes, Gironde 326
Sauveterre, Gard 417
Sauveterre-de-Bearn, Pyrénees-Atlantiques 326
Sauveterre-de-Comminges, Haute-Garonne 398
Sauvigny-le-Bois, Yonne 276
Saverne, Bas-Rhin 162
Savigny-sur-Orge, Essonne 254
Savonnières, Indre-et-Loire 197
Saxon-Sion, Meurthe-et-Moselle 152
Saze, Gard 417-18
Scaer, Finistère 59
Sceaux, Hauts-de-Seine 254
Seclin, Nord 141
Secondigny, Deux-Sèvres 304
Segonzac, Charente 304
Séguret, Vaucluse 461
Seillac, Loir-et-Cher 197-8
Seillans, Var 461
Selles-sur-Cher, Loir-et-Cher 198
Semblancay, Indre-et-Loire 198
Sémelay, Nièvre 276
Semur-en-Auxois, Côte-D'Or 276-7
Senan, Yonne 277
Sennecé-lès-Mâcon, Saône-et-Loire 277
Senneville-sur-Fécamp, Seine-Maritime 105
Senonches, Eure-et-Loir 198
Senones, Vosges 152
Sens, Yonne 277
Sepmes, Indre-et-Loire 198
Sept-Saulx, Marne 128
Sepvret, Deux-Sèvres 304
Sercy, Saône-et-Loire 277
Sérézin-du-Rhône, Rhône 372
Sergeac, Dordogne 326
Sérignac-sur-Garonne, Lot-et-Garonne 326
Sérignan-du-Comtat, Vaucluse 461

Séris, Loir-et-Cher 198
Serres, Hautes-Alpes 461
Serres-sur-Arget, Ariège 398
Servance, Haute-Saône 287
Servilly, Allier 343
Servon, Manche 105
Seur, Loir-et-Cher 198-9
Sevrier, Haute-Savoie 372
Sewen, Haut-Rhin 162
Seyne-sur-Mer, La, Var 461
Seyssel, Ain 372
Seyssins, Isère 372
Sigean, Aude 418
Silly-en-Gouffern, Orne 105
Sisteron, Alpes-de-Haute-Provence 461
Sivignon, Saône-et-Loire 277
Soings-en-Sologne, Loir-et-Cher 199
Solerieux, Drôme 372
Solesmes, Sarthe 222
Sollières-Sardières, Savoie 372
Solre-le-Château, Nord 141
Sommery, Seine-Maritime 105
Sommières, Gard 418
Sospel, Alpes-Maritimes 430
Sottevast, Manche 105
Sotteville-sur-Mer, Seine-Maritime 106
Soubran, Charente-Maritime 304
Souillac, Lot 398-9
Soultzmatt, Haut-Rhin 162
Soumoulou, Pyrénées-Atlantiques 326
Sourdeval, Manche 106
Souterraine, La, Creuse 334
Souvigny-en-Sologne, Loir-et-Cher 199
Soyaux, Charente 304
Strasbourg, Bas-Rhin 162-4
Suaux, Charente 304
Suèvres, Loir-et-Cher 199
Sully-sur-Loire, Loiret 199
Suresnes, Hauts-de-Seine 254
Survie, Orne 106
Surville, Calvados 106
Sury-aux-Bois, Loiret 199
Suze-la-Rousse, Drôme 372

**T**

Talissieu, Ain 372-3
Talloires, Haute-Savoie 373
Tamerville, Manche 106
Tancarville, Seine-Maritime 106
Taponas, Rhône 373
Tarascon, Bouches-du-Rhône 461-2
Tassin-la-Demi-Lune, Rhône 373
Tavers, Loiret 199-200
Tence, Haute-Loire 343
Tendu, Indre 200

Ternay, Vienne 304
Tessé-la-Madeleine, Orne 106
Thaix, Nièvre 277
Thannenkirch, Haut-Rhin 164
Thann, Haut-Rhin 164
Thaumiers, Cher 200
Thillombois, Meuse 152
Thiviers, Dordogne 326
Thomery, Seine-et-Marne 254
Thorenc, Alpes-Maritimes 430
Thorigné-sur-Due, Sarthe 222
Thor, Le, Vaucluse 462
Thouars, Deux-Sèvres 304
Thueyts, Ardèche 373
Tigny-Noyelle, Pas-de-Calais 141
Tilleul, Le, Seine-Maritime 107
Tilly, Eure 107
Tilly-sur-Seulles, Calvados 107
Tilques, Pas-de-Calais 141
Tinqueux, Marne 128
Tintury, Nièvre 277
Tocqueville-les-Murs, Seine-Maritime 107
Torchefelon, Isère 373
Tornac, Gard 418
Tortisambert, Calvados 107
Touffréville, Eure 107
Toulon, Var 462
Toulouse, Haute-Garonne 399
Touquet-Paris-Plage, Le, Pas-de-Calais 141-2
Tour-en-Bessin, Calvados 107
Tournehem-sur-la-Hem, Pas-de-Calais 142
Tournières, Calvados 107
Tournon, Ardèche 374
Tournon-St-Martin, Indre 200
Tournon-sur-Rhône, Ardèche 374
Tournus, Saône-et-Loire 277-8
Tours, Indre-et-Loire 200-1
Tourtour, Var 462
Tourville-la-Campagne, Eure 107
Touzac, Lot 400
Tracy-sur-Mer, Calvados 107-8
Tramayes, Saône-et-Loire 279
Trambly, Saône-et-Loire 279
Tranche-sur-Mer, La, Vendée 222
Trébeurden, Côtes-D'Armor 59
Tréflez, Finistère 59
Trégastel, Côtes-D'Armor 59
Tréglonou, Finistère 60
Tréhorenteuc, Morbihan 60
Trémolat, Dordogne 326
Tréogat, Finistère 60
Tressaint, Côtes-D'Armor 60
Treuzy-Levelay, Seine-et-Marne 254-5
Trévé, Côtes-D'Armor 60
Tréviérés, Calvados 108
Trévignin, Savoie 374

Trie-sur-Baïse, Hautes-Pyrénées 400
Trigance, Var 462-3
Trimouille, La, Vienne 304
Trinité-sur-Mer, La, Morbihan 60
Triqueville, Eure 108
Trivy, Saône-et-Loire 279
Trizay, Charente-Maritime 305
Troarn, Calvados 108
Trois-Épis, Haut-Rhin 164
Tronquay, Le, Eure 108
Troo, Loir-et-Cher 201
Troyes, Aube 128
Turballe, La, Loire-Atlantique 222
Turini, Alpes-Maritimes 430

**U**

Uffholtz, Haut-Rhin 164
Urrugne, Pyrénées-Atlantiques 327
Urville-Nacqueville, Manche 108
Ussel, Lot 400
Ustaritz, Pyrénées-Atlantiques 327
Uzel, Côtes-D'Armor 60
Uzerche, Corrèze 334
Uzès, Gard 418-19

**V**

Vacqueyras, Vaucluse 463
Vailhauques, Hérault 419
Vaison-la-Romaine, Vaucluse 463
Valbonne, Alpes-Maritimes 430
Val-d'Ajol, Vosges 152
Val-de-Mercy, Yonne 279
Valenciennes, Nord 142
Valensole, Alpes-de-Haute-Provence 463
Valframbert, Orne 108
Vallans, Deux-Sèvres 305
Vallery, Yonne 279
Vallières-les-Grandes, Loir-et-Cher 201
Valmont, Seine-Maritime 108
Valmorel, Savoie 374
Valréas, Vaucluse 463-4
Vals-les-Bains, Ardèche 374
Val-Suzon, Côte-D'Or 279
Val-Thorens, Savoie 374
Vandenesse-en-Auxois, Côte-D'Or 279
Vannes, Morbihan 60-1
Vannes-sur-Cosson, Loiret 201
Varades, Loire-Atlantique 222
Varces-Allières-et-Risset, Isère 374
Varennes, Indre-et-Loire 201
Varennes-sous-Dun, Saône-et-Loire 279
Varetz, Corrèze 335
Varilhes, Ariège 400
Varnéville-Bretteville, Seine-Maritime 108-9
Vassy, Calvados 109

Index

Vasteville, Manche 109
Vast, Le, Manche 109
Vaudrimesnil, Manche 109
Vauvenargues, Bouches-du-Rhône 464
Vaux, Haute-Garonne 400
Vaux-sur-Aure, Calvados 109
Vaux-sur-Seine, Yvelines 255
Vaux-sur-Seulles, Calvados 109
Veigne, Indre-et-Loire 201
Velleron, Vaucluse 464
Velles, Indre 201
Velluire, Vendée 222
Venasque, Vaucluse 464
Vence, Alpes-Maritimes 430-1
Vendenesse-lès-Charolles, Saône-et-Loire 279
Vendoire, Dordogne 327
Vendôme, Loir-et-Cher 201
Vengeons, Manche 109
Ventabren, Bouches-du-Rhône 464
Ventenac, Ariège 400
Venterol, Hautes-Alpes 464
Verdun, Meuse 152
Vergèze, Gard 419
Vergisson, Saône-et-Loire 279
Verneuil-sur-Avre, Eure 109-10
Verneuil-sur-Indre, Indre-et-Loire 201-2
Vernou-sur-Brenne, Indre-et-Loire 202
Vernoux-en-Vivarais, Ardèche 374
Verrières, Charente 305
Versailles, Yvelines 255
Verteillac, Dordogne 327
Vertheuil, Gironde 327
Vertus, Marne 129
Vervins, Aisne 120
Vesoul, Haute-Saône 287
Veurdre, Le, Allier 343-4
Veyrier-du-Lac, Haute-Savoie 374-5
Vezac, Cantal 344
Vézelay, Yonne 279-80
Vézilly, Aisne 121
Vichy, Allier 344
Vicq-sur-Gartempe, Vienne 305
Vic-sur-Aisne, Aisne 121
Vieil-Baugé, Le, Maine-et-Loire 222-3
Vienne, Isère 375

Vieux-Maruil, Dordogne 327
Vieux-Viel, Ille-et-Vilaine 61
Vigan, Le, Lot 400
Vignats, Calvados 110
Vignec, Hautes-Pyrénées 400
Vigoulant, Indre 202
Villandry, Indre-et-Loire 202
Villard-de-Lans, Isère 375
Villard-Reculas, Isère 375
Villard-St-Christophe, Isère 375
Villard-St-Sauveur, Jura 287
Villars, Dordogne 327-8
Villars-et-Villenotte, Côte-D'Or 280
Villebarou, Loir-et-Cher 202
Ville, Bas-Rhin 164
Villedieu, Vaucluse 464
Villedieu-les-Poêles, Manche 110
Villedieu-sur-Indre, Indre 202
Villedômer, Indre-et-Loire 202-3
Villefranche-d'Albigeois, Tarn 401
Villefranche-de-Lauragais, Haute-Garonne 401
Villefranche-de-Rouergue, Aveyron 401
Villefranche-du-Périgord, Dordogne 328
Villefranche-sur-Mer, Alpes-Maritimes 431
Villeneuve-lès-Béziers, Hérault 419
Villeneuve-de-Marsan, Landes 328
Villeneuve-Frouville, Loir-et-Cher 203
Villeneuve-la-Garenne, Hauts-de-Seine 255
Villeneuve-lès-Avignon, Gard 419
Villeneuve-Louret, Alpes-Maritimes 431
Villeneuve-sur-Lot, Lot-et-Garonne 328
Villeneuve-sur-Yonne, Yonne 280
Villéreal, Lot-et-Garonne 328
Villers-Agron, Aisne 121
Villers-sur-Authie, Somme 121
Villersexel, Haute-Saône 287
Villers-Farlay, Jura 287
Villers-le-Lac, Doubs 287
Villetelle, Hérault 419
Villié-Morgon, Rhône 375
Vilosnes, Meuse 152
Vimoutiers, Orne 110

Vinassan, Aude 419-20
Vineuil-St-Firmin, Oise 121
Vingt-Hanaps, Orne 110
Vinzelles, Saône-et-Loire 280
Violay, Loire 375
Violes, Vaucluse 464
Vire, Calvados 110
Virecourt, Meurthe-et-Moselle 152-3
Viré, Saône-et-Loire 280
Vitrac, Cantal 344
Vitrac, Dordogne 328
Vitre, Ille-et-Vilaine 61
Vitrolles, Bouches-du-Rhône 465
Vitry-en-Charollais, Saône-et-Loire 280
Vittel, Vosges 153
Vivier-sur-Mer, Le, Ille-et-Vilaine 61
Vivoin, Sarthe 223
Vivonne, Vienne 305
Vonnas, Ain 376
Vosne-Romanée, Côte-D'Or 280
Voué, Aube 129
Vougeot, Côte-D'Or 281
Vouillé, Vienne 305
Vouneuil-sur-Vienne, Vienne 305-6
Vouthon-Bas, Meuse 153
Vouvant, Vendée 223
Vouvray, Indre-et-Loire 203
Vouziers, Ardennes 129
Voves, Eure-et-Loir 203

**W**

Warmeriville, Marne 129
Wattignies, Nord 142
Westhalten, Haut-Rhin 164
Wimereux, Pas-de-Calais 142
Wy-Dit-Joli-Village, Val-D'Oise 255

**Y**

Ydes, Cantal 344
Yffiniac, Côtes-D'Armor 61
Yves, Charente-Maritime 306
Yvetot, Seine-Maritime 110

**Z**

Zellenberg, Haut-Rhin 164
Zouafques, Pas-de-Calais 142-3